54TH EDITION

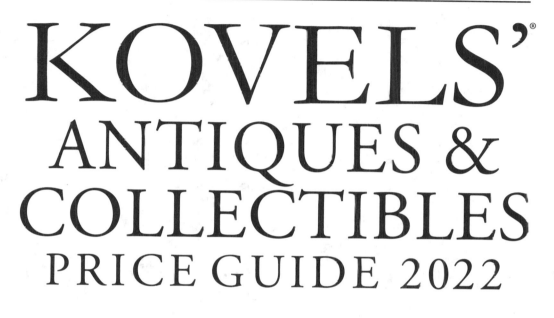

KOVELS'
ANTIQUES &
COLLECTIBLES
PRICE GUIDE 2022

BLACK DOG
& LEVENTHAL
PUBLISHERS
NEW YORK

BOOKS BY RALPH AND TERRY KOVEL

American Country Furniture, 1780–1875

A Directory of American Silver, Pewter, and Silver Plate

Kovels' Advertising Collectibles Price List

Kovels' American Antiques 1750–1900

Kovels' American Art Pottery

Kovels' American Collectibles 1900–2000

Kovels' American Silver Marks, 1650 to the Present

Kovels' Antiques & Collectibles Fix-It Source Book

Kovels' Antiques & Collectibles Price Guide (1968–2009)

Kovels' Bid, Buy, and Sell Online

Kovels' Book of Antique Labels

Kovels' Bottles Price List (1971–2006)

Kovels' Collector's Guide to American Art Pottery

Kovels' Collector's Guide to Limited Editions

Kovels' Collectors' Source Book

Kovels' Depression Glass & Dinnerware Price List (1980–2004)

Kovels' Dictionary of Marks— Pottery and Porcelain, 1650 to 1850

Kovels' Guide to Selling, Buying, and Fixing Your Antiques and Collectibles

Kovels' Guide to Selling Your Antiques & Collectibles

Kovels' Illustrated Price Guide to Royal Doulton (1980, 1984)

Kovels' Know Your Antiques

Kovels' Know Your Collectibles

Kovels' New Dictionary of Marks— Pottery and Porcelain, 1850 to the Present

Kovels' Organizer for Collectors

Kovels' Price Guide for Collector Plates, Figurines, Paperweights, and Other Limited Edition Items

Kovels' Quick Tips: 799 Helpful Hints on How to Care for Your Collectibles

Kovels' Yellow Pages: A Resource Guide for Collectors

The Label Made Me Buy It: From Aunt Jemima to Zonkers— The Best-Dressed Boxes, Bottles, and Cans from the Past

BOOKS BY TERRY KOVEL AND KIM KOVEL

Kovels' Antiques & Collectibles Price Guide (2010–2022)

INTRODUCTION

Kovels' Antiques & Collectibles Price Guide 2022 has current, reliable price information and makers' marks. The book has 12,500 prices, 3,000 new color photographs, more than 720 categories, hundreds of dated marks, plus an all-new center section on "Collecting Trends: Twentieth-Century American Studio Jewelry."

We are frequently asked questions like "How old is my grandmother's dish?" Each of the 720 categories includes an introductory paragraph with history, locations, explanations, and other important information to help identify unknown pieces, and some include information about reproductions. We update these introductory paragraphs every year to indicate new owners, new distributors, or new information about production dates. This year we made updates to more than 14 paragraphs, many that tell of the sale or closing of a company. This guide includes more than 500 marks. Even more dated marks can be found online at Kovels.com. You will also find more than 200 added facts of interest and tips about care and repair. Each collectible's photograph is shown with a caption that includes the item's description, price, and source. Information about the seller of the item, including address, is listed at the end of the book. The book has color tabs and color-coded categories that make it easy to find listings, and it uses a modern, readable typestyle. All antiques and collectibles priced here were offered for sale during the past year, most of them in the United States, from June 2020 to June 2021. Prices also came from virtual sales that accepted bids from all over the world. Almost all auction prices given include the buyer's premium since that is part of what the buyer paid. Very few include local sales tax or extra charges for things such as phone bids, online bids, credit card usage, storage, or shipping.

Most items in our original 1968 price book were made before 1860, so they were more than a century old. Today in *Kovels' Antiques & Collectibles Price Guide*, we list pieces made as recently as 2020. There is great interest in furniture, glass, ceramics, and design made since 1950 in the midcentury modern style and pieces made after the 1980s. The word "design" has taken on a more contemporary meaning. Design isn't only about the way things look or function, but about incorporating new elements in new ways to make things better.

The 2022 edition is 632 pages long and crammed full of prices and photographs. We try to include a balance of prices and do not include too many items that sell for more than $5,000. By listing only a few very expensive pieces, you can realize that a great paperweight may cost $10,000, but an average one is only $25. Nearly all prices are from the American market for the American market. Only a few European sales are reported. These are for items that may be of interest to American collectors. We don't include prices we think result from "auction fever," but we do list verified bargains or amazingly high prices.

There is an index with cross-references. Use it often. It includes categories and much more. For example, there is a category for Celluloid. Most celluloid will be there, but a toy made of celluloid may be listed under Toy as well as indexed under Celluloid. There are also cross-references in the listings and in the category introductions. But some searching must be done. For example, Barbie dolls are in the Doll category; there is no Barbie category. And when you look at "doll, Barbie," you find a note that "Barbie" is under "doll, Mattel, Barbie" because Mattel makes Barbie dolls and most dolls are listed by maker.

Wherever we had extra space on a page, we filled it with tips about the care of collections and other useful information. Don't discard this book. Old Kovels' price guides can be used in the coming years as a reference source for identifying pictures and price changes and for tax, estate, and appraisal information.

The prices in this book are reports from the general antiques market. As we said, every price in the book is new. We do not estimate or "update" prices. Prices are either realized prices from auctions or completed sales in stores or at shows. We have also included a few that are asking prices, knowing that a buyer may have negotiated a lower price. We do not pay dealers, collectors, or experts to estimate prices. If a price range is given, at least two identical items were offered for sale at different prices. Price ranges are found only in categories such as Pressed Glass, where identical items can be identified. Some prices in *Kovels' Antiques & Collectibles Price Guide* may seem high and some low because of regional variations, but each price is what you could have paid for the object somewhere in the United States. Internet prices from individual sellers' ads or listings are avoided. Because so many noncollectors sell online but know little about the objects they are describing, there can be inaccuracies in descriptions. Sales from well-known Internet sites, shops, and sales, carefully edited, are included.

If you are selling your collection, do not expect to get retail value unless you are a dealer. Wholesale prices for antiques are 30 to 40 percent of retail prices. The antiques dealer must make a profit or go out of business. Internet auction prices are less predictable; because of an international audience or "auction fever," prices can be higher or lower than retail. The estimated price listed in an auction shows the expected retail price range.

Time has changed what people collect, the prices they pay, what is "best," and what has dropped in price. There are also laws about endangered species, not a concern when we started, and many changes in tax laws, estate problems, and even more and better reproductions and fakes that make buying more difficult. But there are many more ways to buy and sell. When we started, it was house sales, flea markets, and a few formal antiques shows and auctions. Now, computers and the Internet have made it possible for anyone to buy and sell any day of the week, in every price range. This year many shows were canceled because of the coronavirus, a number of auction houses merged, and many more people bid at virtual auctions. Almost every auction is online as well as available by phone to buyers around the world. And there are frequently live bidders at the more expensive sales. But many auctions end up with unsold pieces, some offered for sale at a set price after the auction. Even eBay is selling only some of the offered antiques. There are thousands of places for us to look for prices!

READ THIS FIRST

This is a book for the buyer and the seller. It is an organized, illustrated list of average pieces, not million dollar paintings and rare Chinese porcelains. Everything listed in this book was sold between June 2020 and June 2021. We check prices, visit shops, shows, and flea markets, read hundreds of publications and catalogs, check Internet sales, auctions, and other online services, and decide which antiques and collectibles are of most interest to most collectors in the United States. We concentrate on average pieces in any category. Prices of some items were very high because a major collection of top-quality pieces owned by a well-known collector, expert, or celebrity was auctioned. Fame adds to the value. Many catalogs now feature the name, picture, and biography of the collector and advertise the auction with the collector's name in all the ads. This year there were major sales such as Paul Muchinsky's collection of pinback buttons, Aaron and Abby Schroeder's collection of antique toys and banks, Bud and Judy Newman's collection of board games and folk art, and Pat Cole's collection of trains and early tin and pressed steel toys. The sales were well advertised and prices were high. Some of these high prices are reported. The most important bottle auctions are run by major bottle auction companies that feature only bottles, including American flasks. Some of these high prices are also reported, along with less expensive inkwells, bitters bottles, and more. Recently there have been many sales of beer cans, including recent brands.

The largest item listed this year is a Flemish-style tapestry from the early 1900s picturing the Battle Of Pavia. It is 111 inches by 206 inches and sold for $4,720. The smallest is a set of 18-karat gold cuff links with gemstones, made by Trianon, ½ inch, that sold for $610. Five ½-inch agate and Dzi bead buttons, c.1800, sold for $1,088. A pair of 18-karat gold earrings with prong-set citrine stones that sold for $480 and a pair of Victorian goldtone buttons with an eagle that sold for $3 were also only ½ inch. The most expensive is a stoneware water cooler with cobalt blue Broadway street scene, made in 1846, seven gallon, that sold for $480,000. The least expensive entry was a plastic figural Spider-Man bookmark made in the 1980s by Nasta Co. It sold for $2. A Royal China Country Charm saucer also sold for $2.

There are always some strange and even weird things listed in our price books. We have listed artificial legs several times, usually the plain wooden stump that is pictured in stories of pirates of earlier days. This year the weirdest item was an iron child's coffin with decoration and a glass window. It was 55 inches long and sold for $11,250.

RECORD-SETTING PRICES

COMICS, COMIC BOOKS & ORIGINAL COMIC ART

Comic book, Action Comics No. 1 (image 1): $3,250,000 for Action Comics No. 1, published in 1938, the issue that introduced Superman to the world, graded 8.5 by CGC. Sold April 6, 2021, in an online auction by ComicConnect.com.

Comic, Gottfredson original artwork (image 2): $61,729 for original artwork by Floyd Gottfredson and inks by Earl Duval for daily comic strip "Mickey Mouse vs Kat Nipp," February 4, 1931, 7 x 29 ⅛ in. artboard. Sold February 25, 2021, by Hake's Auctions, York, Pennsylvania.

Comic, Peanuts daily comic strip (image 3): $192,000 for Charles Schulz Peanuts comic strip featuring Snoopy, dated November 17, 1950, United Feature Syndicate, 4 panels, signed in the last panel, ink over graphite on Bristol board, image size 26 ½ x 5 in. Sold November 22, 2020, by Heritage Auctions, Dallas, Texas.

1.   *2.*

3.

Comic, Peanuts original artwork (image 4): $288,000 for a group of 8 portraits by Charles Schultz of his classic Peanuts characters, Lucy, Linus, Snoopy, Schroeder, Patty, Violet, Shermy, *4.* and Charlie Brown, pen and ink and gray wash on illustration paper, drawn in 1953 for a promotional giveaway, frame, 33 x 24 in. Sold December 13, 2020, by Heritage Auctions, Dallas, Texas.

Comic book, first printing of Zap Comix (image 5): $27,000 for the underground comic book by R. Crumb, his personally owned first-edition copy of Zap Comix #1 (Nov. 1967). Sold December 10, 2020, by PBA Galleries, Berkeley, California.

Comic book, most expensive (image 6): $2.22 million for Batman No. 1 (Spring 1940), graded 9.4 by CGC. Sold January 17, 2021, by Heritage Auctions, Dallas, Texas. **Previous record:** Detective Comics No. 27, 1939, sold for $1,500,000, graded 7.0 by CGC. Sold November 22, 2020, at Heritage Auctions, Dallas, Texas.

5.

6.

Comic book, work by Hergé & original cover art: $3.8 million for the original Blue Lotus cover artwork for the fifth album of Tintin, by Hergé (Georges Remi), done in India ink, watercolor, and gouache on lined Japanese paper, 1936, 13⅜ x 13⅜ in. Sold January 14, 2021, by Artcurial, Paris, France.

7.

8.

9.

10.

FURNITURE

Carlo Mollino (image 7): $6,181,350 for a Carlo Mollino (1905-1973) dining table, molded plywood, maple, brass, and glass with metal label, designed in 1949, executed in 1950 by Appelli & Varesio, Turin, Italy, 30⅜ x 98½ x 31½ in. Sold October 28, 2020, by Sotheby's, New York.

Shaker sewing table (image 8): $98,400 for a butternut, cherry, and pine Shaker sewing table, dropleaf, drawers consisting of long drawer under top, central square drawer with 2 drawers on either side, and larger bottom drawer, dovetail construction, and cherry wood pulls, c.1840, 28 x 35 x 17 in. Sold July 15, 2020, by Morphy Auctions, Denver, Pennsylvania.

Vladimir Kagan (image 9): $132,300 for Vladimir Kagan's "Contour" rocking chair, model no. 175F, walnut and embroidered fabric upholstery. Sold December 9, 2020, by Phillips, New York.

Works by Charles Rohlfs (image 10): $412,500 for a rare mahogany desk chair by Charles Rohlfs, carved decoration on upper backrest and front seat apron, 3-leg triangular base, maker's "sign of the saw" cipher, 1900-1910, 54 x 17¼ x 16 in. Sold July 30, 2020, by Sotheby's, New York.

GLASS

Andrew Clemens sand art bottle: $275,000 for the presentation sand art bottle by Andrew Clemens with patriotic and geometric designs, heart, hand, and mortar and pestle, "From Two Friends to Dr. Prosper Harvey Ellsworth of Hot Springs, Arkansas," 1885-90, 7¼ in. Sold November 13, 2020, by Skinner, Inc., Marlborough, Massachusetts.

Cut glass bowl (image 11): $75,000 for a two-color cut glass bowl with sterling silver mounts, marked Gorham, last quarter 19th century, 6 x 11⅞ in. Sold October 2, 2020, at Cowan's Auctions, Cincinnati, Ohio.

11.

LAMPS & LIGHTING

Any railroad lantern (image 12): $49,560 for Union Pacific tall cast blue globe lantern, with UNION PACIFIC lettering embossed around the globe, wire frame with flat verticals, and embossed maker's mark "The Buck" M.M. BUCK & CO ST. LOUIS on the cap, and original twist-off font. Sold March 20, 2021, by Soulis Auctions, Kansas City, Missouri.

12.

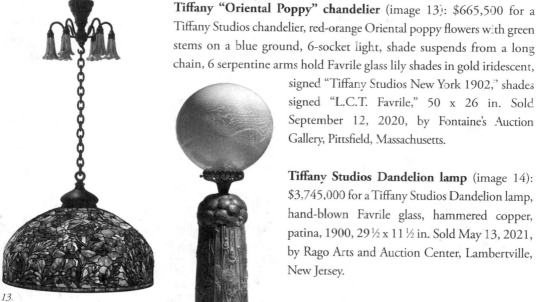

Tiffany "Oriental Poppy" chandelier (image 13): $665,500 for a Tiffany Studios chandelier, red-orange Oriental poppy flowers with green stems on a blue ground, 6-socket light, shade suspends from a long chain, 6 serpentine arms hold Favrile glass lily shades in gold iridescent, signed "Tiffany Studios New York 1902," shades signed "L.C.T. Favrile," 50 x 26 in. Sold September 12, 2020, by Fontaine's Auction Gallery, Pittsfield, Massachusetts.

Tiffany Studios Dandelion lamp (image 14): $3,745,000 for a Tiffany Studios Dandelion lamp, hand-blown Favrile glass, hammered copper, patina, 1900, 29½ x 11½ in. Sold May 13, 2021, by Rago Arts and Auction Center, Lambertville, New Jersey.

13.

14.

MISCELLANEOUS

Any Nantucket decoy (image 15): $108,000 for a Nantucket curlew decoy by Charles Coffin, carved, three-piece construction with intricate stippled paint, c.1870, 15 ½ in. Sold July 23, 2020, by Copley Fine Art Auctions, Hingham, Massachusetts.

15.

Archaic Jade (image 16): $6,927,856 for a rare zitan-mounted imperial inscribed archaic jade bi, inscription and stand dated to the Qianlong period (corresponding to 1770), disc 9 ⅜ in., overall 12 ⅛ in. h. Sold April 22, 2021, by Sotheby's, Hong Kong.

16.

Bird tree by Schtockschnitzler Simmons (image 17): $103,700 for a carved and painted bird tree with 8 painted birds by Schtockschnitzler Simmons, (active 1865-1910), Berks County, Pennsylvania, 20 ½ in. h. Sold July 10, 2020, by Pook & Pook, Downingtown, Pennsylvania.

Chinese Beijing wine ewer (image 18): $497,723 for an 18th-century Chinese Beijing wine ewer, enamel on copper, yellow with pink and blue peonies, green leaves, squared handle and spout, lid with finial of raised flower petals, and metal edge finished in gilt, carries the mark of China's Qianlong Emperor, 6 in. Sold September 24, 2020, by Hansons Auctioneers and Valuers, Ltd., Derbyshire, England.

Dinosaur skeleton: $31,847,500 for a male Tyrannosaurus Rex skeleton, a T-Rex nicknamed "Stan" after Stan Sacrison who first discovered the bones in the spring of 1987 in Hell Creek Formation, South Dakota, 188 original bones mounted on a custom frame with additional cast elements, c.67 million years old, 13 ft. h. x 37 ft. l. Sold October 5, 2020, by Christie's, New York.

18.

17.

Fabric smoothing iron (image 19): $55,350 for a fabric smoothing iron in the form of a fist holding a roller, detachable hand, made by J.G.F. Libby, wing nut for adjusting, brass cufflink holds parts of iron together, ring on right finger, 5 in. Sold May 2, 2020, by Hartzell's Auction Gallery, Inc., Bangor, Pennsylvania.

19.

Hiram Powers carved bust of Diana (image 20): $88,500 for the carved marble bust "Diana," by Hiram Powers, signed, 30 ½ x 21 x 13 ½ in. Sold January 17, 2021, by Amero Auctions, Sarasota, Florida.

20.

Most expensive pair of sneakers (image 21): $1.8 million for Kanye West's Grammy-worn Nike Air Yeezy 1 prototype sneakers, worn at the 2008 Grammy awards, black leather with classic Nike Swoosh, Yeezy forefoot strap, and pink "Y" medallion lace lock, designed by Ye and Mark Smith, size 12. Sold April 16, 2021, by Sotheby's, Hong Kong.

21.

Most valuable coin (image 22): $9,360,000 for a 1787 U.S. New York-style Brasher Doubloon gold coin with "EB" on the wing, W-570 graded NGC MS65. Sold January 24, 2021, by Heritage Auctions, Dallas, Texas, photo by NGC Photo Vision.

Slide-lid box decorated by Drissel (image 23): $134,200 for a painted pine slide-lid box by John Drissel of Bucks County, Pennsylvania, inscribed "Zum gruck / Anne von Red / John Drissel his hand 1796," decorated with stylized flowers and ivory wavy bands on a salmon ground, 2¾ x 4⅜ x 7⅝ in. Sold July 10, 2020, by Pook & Pook, Downingtown, Pennsylvania.

22.

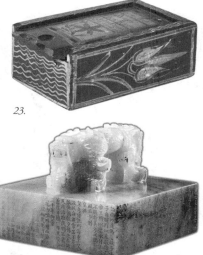

23.

White Jade and Imperial Jade seal (image 24): $18,770,828 for an imperial white jade "Ji'entang" seal, a pair of intertwining dragons, sides incised with a poem entitled "Ji'entangji" ("The Memoirs of the Hall of Grace Remembrance"), dated to the bingxu year (corresponding to 1766), 4 x 4 x 3 in. Sold April 22, 2021, by Sotheby's, Hong Kong.

PAINTINGS & PRINTS

Alexander Calder lithograph (image 25): $14,760 for the lithograph "Pyramids at Night" in colors (red, white, blue, and yellow), by Alexander Calder, 1970. Sold December 19, 2020, by Michaan's Auctions, Alameda, California.

24.

Ansel Adams print (image 26): $988,000 for the mural-size gelatin silver print titled, "The Grand Tetons and The Snake River, Grand Teton National Park, Wyoming," frame, 1942, image size 38⅞ x 51⅞ in. Sold December 14, 2020, by Sotheby's, New York.

26.

25.

27.

Banksy painting: $23,695,812 for the oil on canvas painting Game Changer by Banksy, a young boy in overalls playing with a nurse doll wearing a face mask in a Red Cross uniform, 2020, 35 ⅞ x 35 ⅞ in. Sold March 23, 2021, by Christie's, London.

J.C. Leyendecker art (image 27): $4.12 million for the cover illustration for The Saturday Evening Post, November 21, 1914, "Beat-up Boy, Football Hero," by Joseph Christian Leyendecker, oil on canvas, signed, 30 x 21 in. Sold May 7, 2021, by Heritage Auctions, Dallas, Texas.

John James Trumbull Arnold painting (image 28): $81,900 for folk artist John James Trumbull Arnold (1812-1865), oil on canvas folk art, double portrait of the Parsons children, matching oval reserves, she in white gown, he in yellow dress, signed, frame, 1856, overall size 32 x 41 in. Sold November 14, 2020, by Jeffrey S. Evans & Associates, Mt. Crawford, Virginia.

28.

PAPER

Concert poster, most expensive (image 29): $150,000 for the Hank Williams 1953 concert poster for his performance scheduled for January 1, 1953, Canton Memorial Auditorium, Canton, Ohio, yellow cardboard, red and black lettering, 21 ⅞ x 28 ⅛ in. This was the "concert that never was." Hank Williams died of a heart attack in the back seat of the car en route to the concert. Sold by Heritage Auctions, Dallas, Texas.

29.

30.

Martin Luther King signed item (image 30): $130,909 for logbook pages from the Birmingham jailhouse signed 12 times by Dr. Martin Luther King Jr., during his incarceration with entries dated between 3/4/1963 to 11/27/1963, where he also wrote his manifesto known as "Letter from A Birmingham Jailhouse." Sold February 24, 2021, by Hake's Auctions, York, Pennsylvania.

POLITICAL

Kennedy sweater (image 31): $85,266 for John F. Kennedy's crimson wool Harvard cardigan sweater with "H" in large black block letter, shawl collar with label embroidered "Kennedy," 8 mother-of-pearl buttons and 2 front pockets. Sold February 18, 2021, by RR Auction, Boston, Massachusetts.

31.

32.

Political button, James M. Cox and Franklin D. Roosevelt (image 32): $35,695 for a 1920 jugate, celluloid, pinback, portraits of Cox and Roosevelt, flag, eagle, and rays, back paper with St. Louis Button Co., ⅞ in. Sold September 23, 2020, by Hake's Auctions, York, Pennsylvania.

POTTERY & PORCELAIN

American art pottery, Grueby (image 33): $431,250 for a vase with butterscotch glaze and incised leaves, impressed "Grueby Pottery Boston, U.S.A." in a circle, incised artist's monogram CH-39, and original paper label, early 20th century, 6¾ in. Sold July 30, 2020, by Sotheby's, New York.

33.

34.

Porcelain, Chinese bowl (image 34): $721,800 for a white Chinese porcelain bowl, blue floral designs, lotus bud shape on a narrow foot, Ming dynasty (1400s), 6¼ in. Sold March 17, 2021, by Sotheby's, New York.
Originally purchased at a yard sale in Connecticut for $35.

Pottery, toby jug (image 35): $113,813 for a toby jug and cover of British naval officer "Lord Rodney," seated, holding jug on one hand and rifle in the other, 11½ in. Sold December 15, 2020, by Bonhams, London.

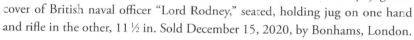

Stoneware, Peter Voulkos (image 36): $1,264,200 for the Peter Voulkos stoneware sculpture "Black Bulerias," constructed from paddled, wheel-thrown and slab elements, brushed slip and clear glaze, 1958, 63 x 44 x 41 in. Sold December 9, 2020, by Phillips, New York.

Stoneware, ginger beer, crown-seal soft drink bottle (image 37): $17,500 for a stoneware crown-seal soft drink bottle, "Doneley & Butler / Ginger Beer / Warwick," white with green lip, 1930s. Sold June 15, 2020, by Graham Lancaster Auctions, Toowoomba, Australia.

35.

36.

37.

Stoneware, Massachusetts (image 38): $180,000 for the Boston stoneware jar incised "Mrs Elesebeth Tarbell 1806," highlighted in cobalt blue, produced in Charlestown, Massachusetts, incised with a bird perched on a branch and the reverse side with a flowering plant and 2 fan-shaped blossoms all highlighted in cobalt blue, 2 handles, 10 in. Sold April 9, 2021, by Crocker Farm, Inc., Sparks, Maryland.

38.

39.

Stoneware, New Jersey (image 39): $252,000 for a stoneware cooler deeply incised with a 3-masted sailing ship, double open handles, with date "1839" and the name "John B. Wilson," reverse side with tulip and leaves in the form of a wreath, 4 gal., 16 ½ in. Sold December 4, 2020, by Crocker Farm, Inc., Sparks, Maryland.

40.

41.

SPORTS

Mickey Mantle Fan Club button (image 40): $23,250 for a 1952 postwar, celluloid, pinback button with photo of Mantle, originally mailed exclusively to the small number of fan club members, 1 ½ in. Sold September 23, 2020, by Hake's Auctions, York, Pennsylvania.

Red Sox champion baseball button (image 41): $62,980 for a Boston Red Sox American League and World's Champions 1916, center circle with ad "Drink Alpen Brau Detroit's Champion Beer," 24 portraits of Red Sox players, including Babe Ruth, and baseball graphics, round, 6 in. Sold September 23, 2020, by Hake's Auctions, York, Pennsylvania.

Mickey Mantle baseball card (image 42): $5.2 million for a 1952 Topps Mickey Mantle trading card graded PSA 9, the highest price in a private sale. Sold January 14, 2021, by PWCC Marketplace, Tigard, Oregon.

Surpassing the previous auction record of $3.93 million for a Topps 2009 Bowman Chrome Superfractor Mike Trout rookie card, Beckett grade of 9.5. Sold August 2020, by Goldin Auctions, Runnemede, New Jersey.

Honus Wagner baseball card (image 43): $3.25 million for a Honus Wagner 1909-11 T206 baseball card, graded PSA 3. Sold October 8, 2020, by Mile High Card Company, Castle Rock, Colorado.

42.

43. 44.

Kobe Bryant rookie basketball card (image 44): $1.795 million for the 1996-97 Topps Chrome Refractors #138 Kobe Bryant rookie card, BGS Pristine/Black Label 10. Sold March 7, 2021, by Goldin Auctions, Runnemede, New Jersey.

LeBron James rookie basketball card, most expensive (image 45): $5.2 million for a 2003-04 Lebron James autographed rookie card, Upper Deck Exquisite Collection RPA (rookie patch autograph), Beckett graded 9. Sold in a private sale, April 27, 2021, by PWCC Marketplace, Tigard, Oregon.

46.

45.

Michael Jordan basketball card (image 46): $1,440,000 for a Michael Jordan 1997-98 Upper Deck Game Jersey autographed card, with a jersey swatch inside the card from a jersey Jordan wore during the 1992 NBA All-Star Game. Sold February 4, 2021 at Heritage Auctions, Dallas, Texas.

Tiger Woods rookie golf card (image 47): $369,000 for a Tiger Woods 2001 rookie golf card, SP Authentic Golf, PSA graded Gem Mint 10. Sold April 4, 2021, by Goldin Auctions, Runnemede, New Jersey.

Wayne Gretzky rookie hockey card (image 48): $1.29 million for a 1979 O-Pee-Chee Wayne Gretzky Edmonton Oilers rookie card, graded PSA Gem Mint 10. Sold December 13, 2020, by Heritage Auctions, Dallas, Texas.

47. 48.

Michael Jordan Nike sneakers, most expensive pair: $615,000 for a pair of Michael Jordan Nike "Air Jordan 1" sneakers, game-worn, signed, leather, rubber, and nylon, size 13 ½, 1985. Sold August 13, 2020, by Christie's Online Auctions in partnership with Stadium Goods.

Tom Brady 2000 rookie football ticket Tom Brady rookie autograph (image 49): $2,252,854 for a Championship Playoff Contenders Rookie Ticket #144, Tom Brady autographed rookie card graded 8.5 with an autograph grade of 9. Sold April 2, 2021, by Lelands, Matawan, New Jersey.

49.

TOYS, DOLLS & GAMES

Pokémon, booster box (image 50): $360,000 for a 1st edition base set sealed booster box of Pokémon cards. Sold November 22, 2020, at Heritage Auctions, Dallas, Texas.

50.

This sale broke the previous world record, which was set at Heritage Auctions in September 2020, when a similar Pokémon set sold for $198,000.

Pokémon card, most expensive (image 51): $233,578 for a rare Pokémon card of the character Pikachu that features the original art by Pikachu illustrator Atsuko Nishida, PSA-graded mint-9.

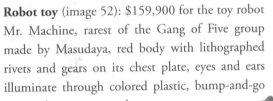

Originally given out as a promotion to winners of a comic contest held in Japan in 1997-98. Sold July 22, 2020, by ZenPlus, Japan.

51.

Robot toy (image 52): $159,900 for the toy robot Mr. Machine, rarest of the Gang of Five group made by Masudaya, red body with lithographed rivets and gears on its chest plate, eyes and ears illuminate through colored plastic, bump-and-go action, battery operated, and in original box, 1960, 15 in. tall. Sold

52.

September 24, 2020, by Morphy Auctions, Denver, Pennsylvania. (NL Jan. 2021)

Rudolph the Red-Nosed Reindeer & Santa Claus Puppets (image 53): $368,000 for the Rudolph the Red-Nosed Reindeer and Santa Claus puppets from the 1964 animated children's Christmas TV special, Rudolph the Red-Nosed Reindeer, a Rankin/Bass Production, figures created by puppet maker Ichiro Komuro, constructed of wood, wire, cloth, and leather, Santa's beard is made from yak hair, Santa is 11 in. h., Rudolph is 6 in. h. Sold November 13, 2020, Profiles in History, Calabasas, California.

53.

54.

55.

Super Mario Bros. video game, most expensive (image 54): $660,000 for a sealed hangtab copy of the NES classic Super Mario Bros., 1985, graded Wata 9.6 A+. Sold April 5, 2021, by Heritage Auctions, Dallas, Texas.

Super Mario Bros. 3 video game (image 55): $156,000 for a sealed copy of the 1990's Super Mario Bros. 3, NES Nintendo, graded Wata 9.2 A+ with Bros. formatted to the left on the front of the box is a first production and considered rare. Sold November 22, 2020, by Heritage Auctions, Dallas, Texas.

Previous record was set in July 2020 at $114,000 for Super Mario Bros. 1985 sealed box, also sold at Heritage Auctions.

Triple Centaur Jackpot slot machine (image 56): $240,000 for a Caille Bros. Triple Centaur Jackpot musical upright slot machine, 3 separately operated sections in a single oak cabinet, accepts 5 cents/25 cents/5 cents denominations, tin lithograph wheels, original music box, with keys, 1898-1905, 62 ½ x 70 x 19 in. Sold October 29, 2020, by Morphy Auctions, Denver, Pennsylvania.

56.

HOW TO USE THIS BOOK

There are a few rules for using this book. Each listing is arranged in the following manner: CATEGORY (such as silver), OBJECT (such as vase), DESCRIPTION (as much information as possible about size, age, color, and pattern). Some types of glass, pottery, and silver are exceptions to this rule. These are listed CATEGORY, PATTERN, OBJECT, DESCRIPTION, PRICE. All items are presumed to be in good condition and undamaged, unless otherwise noted. In most sections, if a maker's name is easily recognized, such as Gustav Stickley, we include it near the beginning of the entry. If the maker is obscure, the name may be near the end.

- To save space, dollar amounts do not include dollar signs, commas, or cents at the end so $1,234.00 is written 1234.
- You will find silver flatware in either Silver Flatware Plated or Silver Flatware Sterling. There is also a section for Silver Plate, which includes coffeepots, trays, and other plated hollowware. Most solid or sterling silver is listed by country, so look for Silver-American, Silver-Danish, Silver-English, etc. Silver jewelry is listed under Jewelry. Most pottery and porcelain is listed by factory name, such as Weller or Wedgwood; by item, such as Calendar Plate; in sections like Dinnerware or Kitchen; or in a special section, such as Pottery-Art, Pottery-Contemporary,

Pottery-Midcentury, etc.

- Sometimes we make arbitrary decisions. "Fishing" has its own category, but "Hunting" is part of the larger category called "Sports." We have listed historic guns in "Weapons" and toy guns in the Toy category. It is not legal to sell weapons without a special license, so guns are not part of the general antiques market. Air guns, BB guns, rocket guns, and others are listed in the Toy section. Everything is listed according to the computer alphabetizing system.

- We made several editorial decisions. A butter dish is listed as a "butter." A salt dish is called a "salt" to differentiate it from a saltshaker. It is always "sugar and creamer," never "creamer and sugar." Where one dimension is given, it is the height; if the object is round, it's the diameter. The height of a picture is listed before width. Glass is clear unless a color is indicated. We never call glass "crystal." A crystal is a natural shape of a mineral.

- Some antiques terms, such as "Sheffield" or "Pratt," have two meanings. Read the paragraph headings to know the definition being used. All category headings are based on the vocabulary of the average person, and we use terms like "mud figures" even if not technically correct. Some categories are known by several names. Pressed glass is also called pattern glass or EAPG (Early American Pattern Glass). We use the name "pressed glass" because much of the information found in old books and articles uses that name.

- This book does not include price listings for fine art paintings, antiquities, stamps, coins, or most types of books. Comic books are listed only in special categories like Batman, but original comic art is listed in Comic Art, and cels are listed in Animation Art.

- Prices for items pictured can be found in the appropriate categories. Look for the matching entry with the abbreviation "illus." The color photograph will be nearby.

- Thanks to computers, the book is produced quickly. The last entries are added in June; the book is available in September. But humans find prices and check accuracy. We read everything at least five times, sometimes more. We edit more than 20,000 entries down to the 12,500 entries found here. We correct spelling, remove incorrect data, write category paragraphs, and decide on new categories. We proofread copy and prices many times, but there may be some misspelled words and other errors. Information in the paragraphs is updated each year, and this year more than 14 updates and additions were made.

- Prices are reported from all parts of the United States, Canada, Europe, and Asia, and converted to U.S. dollars at the time of the sale. The average rate of exchange on June 1, 2021, was $1.00 to about $1.21 Canadian, €0.82 (euro), and £0.71 (British pound). Meltdown price for silver was $27.75 per ounce in June. Prices are from auctions, shops, Internet sales, shows, and even some flea markets. Every price is checked for accuracy, but we are not responsible for errors. We cannot always answer your letters asking for price information, or where to sell, but please write if you have any requests for categories to be included or any corrections to the paragraphs or prices. You may find the answers to your other questions at Kovels.com or in our newsletter, *Kovels On Antiques & Collectibles*.

- When you see us at shows, auctions, house sales, flea markets, or even the grocery store, please stop and say hello. Don't be surprised if we ask for your suggestions. You can write to us at P.O. Box 22192, Beachwood, OH 44122, or visit us at our website, Kovels.com.

TERRY KOVEL AND KIM KOVEL
July 2021

ACKNOWLEDGMENTS

The world of antiques and collectibles is filled with people who share knowledge and help, tell stories of record prices, amazing sales, online activities, and news, and make books like this possible. Dealers, auction galleries, antiques shops, serious collectors, clubs, publications, and even museum experts have given advice and opinions, sent pictures and prices, and made suggestions for changes. Thank you to all of them! Each picture is labeled with the name of the source. We list a phone number, postal address, and Web address at the end of the book, so you can learn more about any pictured piece. We also include the names of many of the people or places that reported some prices. Anyone who sells collectibles and antiques must also buy them, so you may want to contact a source listed here.

And we want to give special thanks to the staff at Kovels'. They deserve the most credit. They helped gather the 12,500 prices, 3,000 pictures, marks, tips on care of collections, and hotlines (bits of information too important to ignore), put it all together, and made it work. This year it was completed during the days we were all following the pandemic rules and we had to invent new ways to share responsibilities.

Special thanks to Hachette Book Group, our publisher. Our thanks to the Hachette staff:

- Lisa Tenaglia, our editor who has worked with us for 10 years, who makes sure the book gets finished on time. She is also our advocate and problem solver.
- Joe Davidson, who stepped in while Lisa was on maternity leave. He kept us on track and was always helpful resolving any issues that arose.
- Lillian Sun, senior production manager, Melanie Gold, senior production editor, and the others at Hachette who do all the things we never see that create the quality of the finished product.
- Kara Thornton, publicity manager, who worries about getting stories in newspapers, magazines, book reviews, social media, TV talk shows, and the many online sites that are interested in collecting.
- Betsy Hulsebosch, director of marketing, who creates the modern online advertising and explanations.
- Katie Benezra, associate art director, who knows how to be sure the art is at its best.
- Mary Flower, Robin Perlow, and Cynthia Schuster Eakin, copyeditors, who seem to find every typo, mislabeled picture, and misspelled name. They make sure the names and dates of every royal family, period of furniture, historic event, the spelling of the Chinese dynasties, and the most misspelled name of them all—Wedgwood—are correct.
- Sheila Hart, who has worked on many editions of the book—redesigning the pages to look great, and adapting the layout each time we change the content, adding things such as pages of marks, number of prices, and more color pictures. She also does the layout and design of the special features such as the record prices and the yearly fact-filled insert. Somehow she has solved the problem of getting all 12,500 prices and all 3,000 pictures in position in alphabetical order near one another so readers can see them nearby.

And to those on the Kovels' staff who work on both the digital and print versions of this book:

- Janet Dodrill, our art director, who somehow can keep track of all of the pictures and permissions for the items shown in this book as well as extra pictures used for our columns and other publications. She then uses her superior photo-editing skills to improve the look and the quality of the pictures by outlining the objects, checking the color, and even working magic with close-ups of details.
- Our in-house price staff, Elizabeth Burroughs-Heineman and Renee McRitchie, who know the vocabulary needed to get prices from all parts of the country and turn them into the proper form to sort into the book.
- Cherrie Smrekar, who takes time from her job running our newsletter to help with prices, tips, hotlines, record prices, and other special features of the book.

- Liz Lillis, the Kovels' staff copyeditor, writer, and researcher, who not only knows all the dates and names but tells us where the commas and periods go and solves other grammar problems. She also writes online publicity for the book and our webpage.
- Gay Hunter, who is the official boss of the price book production, tracks the prices and pictures in and out, suggests sources for prices at sales and shows, records where and when it was sold, and what the seller said about it. But most of all, she keeps us meeting the book deadlines by reminding us all year that we are way behind.
- And Alberto Eiber, the expert who makes sure we are accurate with articles and reports of the recent things we include that are now called "Design" by art and auction gallery dealers. He also writes about the twentieth-century and contemporary designers.
- Special thanks to Bill and Jill Meier of billandjillinsulators.com, who gave their expert opinion for our Insulator category.

CONTRIBUTORS

The world of antiques and collectibles is filled with people who have answered our every request for help. Dealers, auction houses, and shops have given advice and opinions, supplied photographs and prices, and made suggestions for changes. Many thanks to all of them.

Photographs and information were furnished by: 21st Century Auctions, A.B. Levy's Palm Beach Auctions, Abington Auction Gallery, Ahlers & Ogletree Auction Gallery, Alderfer Auction Company, Alex Cooper Auctioneers, Amazon.com, Amero Auctions, Andrew Jones Auctions, AntiqueAdvertising.com, Apple Tree Auction Center, Artcurial, Auctions at Showplace, Austin Auction Gallery, Bertoia Auctions, Bill and Jill Insulators, Blackwell Auctions, Bonhams, Bruneau & Co. Auctioneers, Brunk Auctions, Bunch Auctions, California Historical Design, Charleston Estate Auctions, Charlton Hall Auctions, Christie's, Chupp Auctions & Real Estate, LLC, Clars Auction Gallery, ComicConnect.com, Conestoga Auction Company (a division of Hess Auction Group), Copake Auction, Copley Fine Art Auctions, Cordier Auctions, Cottone Auctions, Cowan's Auctions, Crescent City Auction Gallery, CRN Auctions, Crocker Farm, Inc., Donley Auctions, DuMouchelles, Early American History Auctions, eBay, Eldred's, Fairfield Auction, Fontaine's Auction Gallery, Forsythes' Auctions, Fox Auctions, Freeman's, Garth's Auctioneers & Appraisers, Glass Works Auctions, Goldin Auctions, Graham Lancaster Auctions, Gray's Auctioneers, Inc., Greenwich Auction, Grey Flannel Auctions, Grogan & Company, Hake's Auction, Hampton Estate Auction, Hansons Auctioneers and Valuers Ltd., Hartzell's Auction Gallery Inc., Heritage Auctions, Hindman, Homestead Auctions, Humler & Nolan, Jaremos, Jeffrey S. Evans & Associates, John McInnis Auctioneers, John Moran Auctioneers, Julien's Auctions, Kamelot Auctions, Kaminski Auctions, Keystone Auctions LLC, Kodner Galleries, Inc., Leland Little Auctions, Lelands, Lion and Unicorn, Locati Auctions, Main Auction Galleries, Inc., Martin Auction Co., Matthew Bullock Auctioneers, Merrill's Auctions, Michaan's Auctions, Mid-Hudson Auction Galleries, Mile High Card Company, Milestone Auctions, Morphy Auctions, Nadeau's Auction Gallery, Neal Auction Company, Neue Auctions, New Haven Auctions, New Orleans Auction Galleries, North American Auction Co., Nye & Company, Palm Beach Modern Auctions, PBA Galleries, Perfume Bottles Auction, Phillips, Pook & Pook, Potter & Potter Auctions, Profiles in History, PWCC Marketplace, Rachel Davis Fine Arts, Rafael Osona Nantucket Auctions, Rago Arts and Auction Center, Richard D. Hatch & Associates, Richard Opfer Auctioneering, Inc., Rich Penn Auctions, Ripley Auctions, Roland Auctioneers & Valuers, Ron Rhoads Auctioneers, RR Auction, Ruby Lane, Santa Fe Art Auction, Seeck Auctions, Selkirk Auctioneers & Appraisers, Skinner, Inc., Sotheby's, Soulis Auctions, Stair Galleries, Stephenson's Auction, Stevens Auction Co.,

Stony Ridge Auction, Strawser Auction Group, Susanin's Auctioneers & Appraisers, Swann Auction Galleries, Theriault's, Thomaston Place Auction Galleries, Toomey & Co. Auctioneers, Treadway, Treasureseeker Auctions, Turner Auctions + Appraisals, Weiss Auctions, White's Auctions, Wiederseim Associates, Woody Auction, Wright, and ZenPlus.

To the others who knowingly or unknowingly contributed to this book, we say thank you: A-1 Auction, AAA Auction Service Inc., Abell Auction, Absolute Auction Gallery, Aether Auctions, Affiliated Auctions, Akiba Antiques, Albion Auctions, All American Auction, Amazing Collectible Galleries, American Glass Gallery, Antique Kingdom, Antique Arena Inc., Antiques Online Auctions, Anzardo's Fine Arts, Appraisal & Estate Sale Specialists Inc., Artemis Gallery, Asselmeier May Auctions, Atlas Auction House, Auctions at Showplace, Auctions by Jennifer, Barry S. Slosberg Inc., Beachwood Auctions LLC, Berner's Auction Gallery, Bill Hood & Sons Art & Antique Auctions, Blanchard's Auction Service, Boston Sportscard Exchange, Boyd Auctions, Briggs Auction Inc., Brimfield Antique Shows & Auctions, Broken Arch Auction Gallery, Broward Auction Gallery, Bunte Auction Services, C. Biddle Auction Gallery Inc., Capsule Auctions, Casco Bay Auctions, Clark's Auction Company, Collectible Auctions LLC, Connoisseur Auctions, Converse Auctions, Coral Gables Auction, Cosas Auction, Cowboy Joe's Antiques, Creighton McCreary Auctions LLC, Crown Company Inc., D.G.W. Auctioneers, Dennis Auction Service Inc., Denotter Auctions LLC, Devin Moisan Auctioneers Inc., Diefenderfer Auction Company, District Auction, Donny Malone Auctions, Dutch Auction Sales, Early American History Auctions, EJ's Auction & Appraisal, Elite Auctioneers LLC, Elstob & Elstob, Emanon Auctions and Estate Sales, Embassy Auctions International, EstateOfMind Auctions, Etsy, Fidelity Estate Services, Flying Pig Auctions, Fox & Crane Online Auctions, Franckearth, Frasher's Doll Auction, Freedom Auction Company, French Broad River Auctions, Frost & Nicklaus, Gallery 63, Grant Zahajko Auctions, GWS Auctions Inc., Heroes & Legends, Hess Auction Group, Hill Auction Gallery, Holabird Western Americana Collections, Horst Auctioneers, Hyde Park Country Auctions, International Auction Gallery, Jackson's International Auctioneers and Appraisers, Jaybird Auctions, John Atzbach Antiques, Keno Auctions, Kleinfelter's Auction Inc., Kotler Galleries & Auctioneers, Kraft Auction Service, Lakelands Auction Services, Langston Auction Gallery, Ledbetter Folk Art & Americana Auction, Leonard Auction, Lettieri Auction & Appraisals, Link Auction Galleries, Litchfield Auctions, Lodestar Auctions, Louvre Antiques, M.J. Stasak Auctions, Marion Antique Auctions, Mebane Antique Auction Gallery, Millea Bros. Ltd., Morean Auctions, Morford's Antique Advertising Auctions, Mroczek Brothers Auctioneers & Associates, Noble House Collection Gallery, Oakridge Auction Gallery, Old Barn Auction, Old Toy Soldier Auctions, Ole Hound Auction House, Omnia Auctioneers & Appraisers, One Source Auctions, Pasarel, Phoebus Auction Gallery, Piece of the Past Inc., PosterConnection Inc., Premier Auction Galleries, PremiumSold Auctioneers, Preston Hall Gallery, Preston Opportunities Auction, Quinn's Auction Galleries, Rapid Estate Liquidators & Auction Gallery, Rbfinearts LLC, Redlands Antique Auction, Replacements Ltd., Revere Auctions, Reverie, Roberson's Auctions, Rock Legends Ltd., Rockabilly Auction Co., RR Auction, Sabertooth Auctions, Saco River Auction Co., Sarasota Estate Auction, Scheerer McCulloch Auctioneers Inc., Schmidt's Antiques Inc., Schmitt Horan & Co., Schultz Auctioneers, Scott Daniel's Auction, Showtime Auction Services, Sloans & Kenyon, St. Louis Estate Buyers, Stallion Hill Gallery, Stanton's Auctioneers & Realtors, Taurus Auctions, Taylor & Harris, The Antique Collective LLC, The Benefit Shop Foundation Inc., The Lodge Auction House Inc., The Saucon Valley Auction Company, Tom Hall Auctions, Toys Trains and Other Old Stuff, Tremont Auctions, Turkey Creek Auctions, Uniques and Antiques Auction Sales, Valley Auctions LLC, Vallot Auctioneers, Van Eaton Galleries, Vero Beach Auction, Vidi Vici Gallery, Vintage Accents Auctions, Vogt Auction, Westport Auction, William A. Smith Inc., Witherell's, Wooten & Wooten, World Auction Gallery, Wright Collectibles, Wright's Estate Liquidators, and Younger Auction Company.

A. WALTER

A. Walter made pate-de-verre glass under contract at the Daum
glassworks from 1908 to 1914. He decorated pottery during his early
years in his studio in Sevres, where he also developed his formula for pale, translucent
pate-de-verre. He started his own firm in Nancy, France, in 1919. Pieces made before
1914 are signed *Daum, Nancy* with a cross. After 1919 the signature is *A. Walter Nancy.*

Inkstand, Stag Beetle, Blue & Green, 2 Inkwells, Lids, Signed, Henri Berge, 1920s, 2 1/2 x 6 1/2 In. ... 2375
Vase, Landscape, Trees, Water, Shades Of Blue, Earthenware, Glazed, Footed, 7 In. .... *illus* 693

ABC PLATES

ABC plates, or children's alphabet plates, were most popular from 1780 to 1860 but
are still being made. The letters on the plate were meant as teaching aids for children
learning to read. The plates were made of pottery, porcelain, metal, or glass. Mugs and
other items were also made with alphabet decorations. Many companies made ABC
plates. Shown here are marks used by three English makers.

Charles Allerton & Sons c.1890–1912 | Enoch Wood & Sons 1818–1846 | William E. Oulsnam & Sons c.1880–1892

Plate, Peter Rabbit, School Scene, Tin Lithograph, Harrison Cady, Thornton W. Burgess, 7 3/4 In. ... 123
Plate, There Was A Crooked Man, Multicolor Transfer, Brownhills Pottery, c.1880, 6 1/2 In. ... 139
Plate, Wild Animals, Leopard, Transfer, Brownhills Pottery, Staffordshire, c.1880, 7 1/2 In. ... 200

ABINGDON POTTERY

Abingdon Pottery was established in 1908 by Raymond E. Bidwell as
the Abingdon Sanitary Manufacturing Company. The company started
making art pottery in 1934. The factory ceased production of art pottery
in 1950.

Vase, Garniture, Pansies, Scrolled Handles, Gilt Trim, Artist Signed, 6 7/8 In., Pair ... 38
Vase, Light Blue, 2 Handles, Horizontal Band, Relief Leaves, Footed, 8 In. ... 25

ADAMS

Adams china was made by William Adams and Sons of Staffordshire, England. The
firm was founded in 1769 and became part of the Wedgwood Group in 1966. The name
Adams appeared on various items through 1998. All types of tablewares and useful
wares were made. Other pieces of Adams may be found listed under Flow Blue and
Tea Leaf Ironstone.

William Adams & Co. 1905–1917 | William Adams & Sons 1917–1965 | Adams under Wedgwood 1966–1975

Plate, Adams' Rose, Red, Green Rainbow, Spatter, 7 1/2 In. ... 549
Platter, Navarino, Blue & White, Octagonal, Ironstone, Marked, 15 1/2 x 11 3/4 In. ... 50

A. Walter, Vase, Landscape, Trees,
Water, Shades Of Blue, Earthenware,
Glazed, Footed. 7 In.
$693

Fontaine's Auction Gallery

Advertising, Bin, Jersey Coffee, Slant
Top, Red, Black Stencil, Softwood Case,
31 x 22 x 17 In.
$678

Souns Auctions

Advertising, Box, A & P Tea Co., Cream
Cheese, Bentwood, Round, Stenciled,
1800s, 5 x 15 In.
$188

Cowan's Auctions

This is an edited listing of current
prices. Visit Kovels.com to check thousands of prices from previous years and
sign up for free information on trends,
tips, reproductions, marks, and more.

Snap! Crackle! Pop!

The phrase *"Snap! Crackle! Pop!,"* without characters, first appeared on the Kellogg's Rice Crispies box in 1932.

Advertising, Cabinet, Dr. Lesure's Famous Remedies, Veterinary, Horse, Display, c.1900, 23 x 18 In.
$1,920

Cowan's Auctions

Advertising, Cabinet, Dy-O-La Dyes, Poplar, Hinged Door, Painted, Base, 2-Sided, 17 x 14 x 9 In.
$148

Leland Little Auctions

Advertising, Cabinet, Franklin Tea & Spice Co., Oak, Drawers, Dove Brand Spices, c.1900, 13 x 25 In.
$215

Rich Penn Auctions

ADVERTISING

Advertising containers and products sold in the old country store are now all collectibles. These stores, with crackers in a barrel and a potbellied stove, are a symbol of an earlier, less hectic time. Listed here are many advertising items. Other similar pieces may be found under the product name, such as Planters Peanuts. We have tried to list items in logical places, so enameled tin dishes will be found under Graniteware, auto-related items in the Auto category, paper items in the Paper category, etc. Store fixtures, cases, signs, and other items that have no advertising as part of the decoration are listed in the Store category. The early Dr Pepper logo included a period after "Dr," but it was dropped in 1950. We list all Dr Pepper items without a period so they alphabetize together. Some collectors call enameled iron or steel signs "porcelain signs." For more prices, go to kovels.com.

Banner, 101 Ranch Cantina, Booth, Red Edge, Holes, 25 x 27 In.	443
Banner, Circus, Master Of The Swords, 3 At One Time, Ernie Winn, Late 1900s, 33 x 23 In.	576
Bin, Coffee, Hinged Lid, Van Patten & Marks Wholesale Grocers, Late 1800s, 28 In.	295
Bin, Jersey Coffee, Slant Top, Red, Black Stencil, Softwood Case, 31 x 22 x 17 In. .... *illus*	678
Books may be included in the Paper category.	
Bottles are list in the Bottle category.	
Bottle Openers are listed in the Bottle Opener category.	
Bowl, Bernheimer Brothers, Millersburg, Blue Carnival Glass, Stars, 10 x 10 x 3 In.	1353
Box, see also Box category.	
Box, A & P Tea Co., Cream Cheese, Bentwood, Round, Stenciled, 1800s, 5 x 15 In. .... *illus*	188
Box, Biscuit, Lu Petit Beurre Nantes, Biscuit Shape, Bisque, France, 3 1/4 x 2 1/4 In.	74
Box, Cigar, Alejandro Villar Y Villar, Reyna Fina, Bronze, Silver, 4 x 5 x 10 In.	569
Box, Display, Colburn's Mustard, Lithograph, Dovetail, Philadelphia, c.1890, 2 1/2 x 19 x 12 In.	158
Box, Lift Lid, Side Handle, Easton Sanitary Milk Co., Easton, Pa., 13 1/4 x 15 1/4 In.	31
Box, Malt Nutrine, Wood, Duck, Anheuser-Busch, Early 1900s, 6 x 10 1/2 In.	235
Box, Milk, Willard Dairy, Wood, Metal Sides, Carved, Ohio, 11 In.	31
Box, Phillips Seeds, Choice Seeds, Display, Painted, c.1875, 4 3/4 x 25 1/2 x 11 In.	452
Cabinet, Clark's Spool Cotton, Maple, Pine, 2 Drawer, Rectangular, 6 x 30 x 21 In.	104
Cabinet, Diamond Dyes, Children With Balloon, Tin Lithograph, 1908, 24 x 8 x 15 In.	1243
Cabinet, Dr. Lesure's Famous Remedies, Veterinary, Horse, Display, c.1900, 23 x 18 In. *illus*	1920
Cabinet, Dy-O-La Dyes, Poplar, Hinged Door, Painted, Base, 2-Sided, 17 x 14 x 9 In. ... *illus*	148
Cabinet, Franklin Tea & Spice Co., Oak, Drawers, Dove Brand Spices, c.1900, 13 x 25 In. *illus*	215
Cabinet, Humphrey's Remedies, 2-Sided, Metal Door Panels, 20 x 18 x 7 In.	469
Cabinet, Humphrey's Veterinary Specifics, Medicines, Door, 34 Drawers, Tin, 28 x 22 In.	900
Cabinet, Spool, Brainerd & Armstrong Co., Fruitwood, 3 Drawers, 11 x 18 1/2 x 16 In.	225
Cabinet, Spool, Clark's O.N.T., 2 Drawers, Brass Pulls, c.1900, 7 1/2 x 22 In. .... *illus*	200
Cabinet, Spool, Willimantic, Six Cord, 4 Drawers, Late 1800s, 15 x 24 x 16 In. .... *illus*	2223
Calendars are listed in the Calendar category.	
Can, Pure Milk, Engraved, Embossed, Handle, Zelienople Pure Milk Co., Follansbee, 13 3/8 In.	192
Canisters, see introductory paragraph to Tins in this category.	
Cards are listed in the Card category.	
Case, Display, Crispo Biscuits, Sawyer Biscuit Co., Tin, 11 1/2 In.	102
Catalog, Park & Carnival Equipment, H.C. Evans, c.1932, 9 x 6 In.	124
Catalog, Shreve & Company, H.S. Crocker, San Francisco, Hardbound, Embossed Front, 1911 .	150
Change Receiver, see also Tip Tray in this category.	
Cheese Cutter, The Dunn, Cast Iron, Wood Cutting Board, c.1900, 15 3/4 In.	188
Chest, Hinged Lid, New Crop Seeds, Crosman Bros. Co., Pine, 14 x 35 In.	275
Cigar Cutter, Artie, Best Cigar Of The Year, Figural, Iron, Mechanical, 10 x 5 x 6 In.	1476
Cigar Cutter, J.G. Blaine, Cigar, 5 Cent, Handle, Dish Base, Brunhoff Mfg., Cincinnati, 5 x 6 In.	354
Clocks are listed in the Clock category.	
Cup, Trinidad & Tobago Cocoa, Tree, Royal Doulton, 1900s, 3 1/4 x 2 3/4 In.	17
Cutout, Ferry's Seeds, Cardboard, Frog, Seated, Holding Book, Spring Song, 1900s, 16 x 12 In. *illus*	344
Dispenser, Armour's Veribest Root Beer, Milk Glass, Barrel Shape, Red Letters, c.1910, 15 In. .	819
Dispenser, Cherry Smash Syrup, Spherical, Flared Base, Porcelain, Early 1900s, 14 x 9 In.	1750
Dispenser, Fowler's Cherry Smash Syrup, Red Glass Insert, Metal Clamp, Spigot, 16 x 7 In.	150

Advertising, Cabinet, Spool, Clark's O.N.T., 2 Drawers, Brass Pulls, c.1900, 7 ½ x 22 In.
$200

Pook & Pook

Advertising, Cabinet, Spool, Willimantic, Six Cord, 4 Drawers, Late 1800s, 15 x 24 x 16 In.
$2,223

Jeffrey S. Evans & Associates

Advertising, Cutout, Ferry's Seeds, Cardboard, Frog, Seated, Holding Book, Spring Song, 1900s, 16 x 12 In.
$344

Cowan's Auctions

Advertising, Dispenser, Ward's Orange Crush, Stainless Siphon Pump, Milk Glass Cabochon, 13 x 8 In.
$904

Souls Auctions

Advertising, Display, Craftsmen Jeweler's, Tara, Bust, Female, c.1940, 15 x 12 In.
$215

Rich Penn Auctions

Advertising, Display, Girson's, Glad Hand Dress Gloves, White & Black, c.1920, 21 x 26 In.
$154

Rich Penn Auctions

Advertising, Display, Pabst Blue Ribbon Beer, Boxer, Metal, Countertop, c.1960, 15 x 12 In.
$152

Jeffrey S. Evans & Associates

Advertising, Display, Wayne Knit Hosiery, Wire Leg Shape, Iron, Bronze Base, 42 In.
$277

Rich Penn Auctions

Advertising, Door, Screen, Country Store Colonial Bread, Painted, Pine Frame, 47 x 28 In.
$185

Advertising, Figure, RCA Radiotron Man, Figural, Wood, Jointed, Maxfield Parrish, 15 In.
$900

Advertising, Ironing Board, EZ Life Starch Ad, Woman, Man, Make A Husband Happy, c.1930, 61 In.
$531

Hires History

Charles E. Hires, a Philadelphia druggist, became "The Father of Root Beer" in the early 1870s when he concocted a drink made of roots and herbs. He sold the syrup at his drugstore, at soda fountains, and at grocery stores for home use. He promoted the syrup through advertising pieces, such as mugs, signs, bottles, trays, and trade cards. Some of the most desirable early pieces feature the Hires boy, who was illustrated wearing a dress from 1891 to 1906, a bathrobe from 1907 to 1914, and a dinner jacket from 1915 to 1926.

Advertising, Mirror, Eagle Rare Bourbon, Kentucky Straight Bourbon Whiskey, White, Frame, 1900s, 49 In.
$219

Advertising, Pie Safe, Rushton's Famous Pies, Door, Shelves, Screen, Countertop, 1910s, 21 x 11 In.
$1,872

Dispenser, Prize, Golden Eggs, Red Goose Shoes, Goose, Biting Tag, Painted, c.1950, 16 In. .	704
Dispenser, Raspberry Scrub, Red Lettering, Silver Lid, 14 In.	420
Dispenser, Ward's Lemon Crush, Embossed Black Lettering, 1920s, 14 In.	1075
Dispenser, Ward's Orange Crush, Stainless Siphon Pump, Milk Glass Cabochon, 13 x 8 In. *illus*	904
Display, Craftsmen Jeweler's, Tara, Bust, Female, c.1940, 15 x 12 In. *illus*	215
Display, Formfit Corsets, Woman, Standing, Wearing Lingerie, Limed Oak Stand, 31 In.	923
Display, Girson's, Glad Hand Dress Gloves, White & Black, c.1920, 21 x 26 In. *illus*	154
Display, Ideal Goggles, Figural Bust, Drive, Clothing, Chalkware, 15 x 13 In.	1770
Display, Pabst Blue Ribbon Beer, Boxer, Metal, Countertop, c.1960, 15 x 12 In. *illus*	152
Display, Swatch, Acrylic, Plastic, Chrome Plated Steel, Keith Haring, Switzerland, 1984, 11 In.	3000
Display, Sweetser & Arnold, Duxbury, Mass., Cart Shape, Wood, c.1870, 25 x 68 In.	213
Display, Wayne Knit Hosiery, Wire Leg Shape, Iron, Bronze Base, 42 In. *illus*	277
Dolls are listed in the Doll category.	
Door, Screen, Country Store Colonial Bread, Painted, Pine Frame, 47 x 28 In. *illus*	185
Doorstop, Frog, I Croak For The Webster Wagon, Cast Iron, 5 ½ In.	221
Fans are listed in the Fan category.	
Figure, Case, Eagle, Standing On Ball, Painted, c.1915, 8 x 5 x 3 In.	1469
Figure, Kellergeist, Man, Wine Barrel Body, Funnel Hat, Carved Wood, 20 ½ In.	819
Figure, Rainer Beer, Stein Man, Plaster, Painted, 10 In.	300
Figure, RCA Radiotron Man, Figural, Wood, Jointed, Maxfield Parrish, 15 In. *illus*	900
Figure, RCA, Victor, Dog, Nipper, Molded, Polypropylene, 39 x 40 In.	738
Figure, Shenango China, Indian, Seated, Holding Jar, Gilt, Porcelain, Mid 1900s, 12 In.	188
Figure, White Eagle Gas Company, Eagle, Standing, Painted, Iron, c.1920, 33 x 19 x 12 In.	3616
Gum Ball Machine, Bub-O-Gum, Glass Globe, Decal, Pure, Good, Cast Iron, 1900s, 13 In.	175
Hatchet, Gold, Molded, Plastic, Estwing Unbreakable Tools, 37 In.	49
Ironing Board, EZ Life Starch Ad, Woman, Man, Make A Husband Happy, c.1930, 61 In. *illus*	531
Jar, Ball, Ideal, Clear, Lid, Engraved, Metal Handle, 20 In.	37
Jar, Bowey's Hot Chocolate, Served Exclusively, Engraved, Stoneware, 1900s, 8 ½ In.	256
Jar, Chew Beeman's Pepsin Gum, Lid, Reverse Label Under Glass, 12 x 5 In.	950
Jar, Eat Tom's Toasted Peanuts, Black Script Letters, Red Knob, Tom's, 11 x 9 In.	148
Jar, Seyfert's Butter Pretzels, Clear, 5 Cent Price Label, Ball Finial, Lid, 13 In.	58
Jar, Taylor's Saponaceous Compound, Shaving Soap, Pa., 1 ⅞ x 3 ⅝ In.	288
Jug, Whiskey, Cobalt Blue Stamp, John Widderburn Co., Late 1800s, 14 In.	177
Lamps are listed in the Lamp category.	
Lunch Boxes are also listed in the Lunch Box category.	
Menu Board, Dad's Root Beer, Embossed, Tin Litho, Chalkboard, c.1950, 27 x 19 In.	308

Advertising mirrors of all sizes are listed here. Pocket mirrors range in size from 1 ½ to 5 inches in diameter. Most of these mirrors were given away as advertising promotions and include the name of the company in the design.

Mirror, Eagle Rare Bourbon, Kentucky Straight Bourbon Whiskey, White, Frame, 1900s, 49 In. *illus*	219
Mirror, Kellogg's Corn Flakes, Celluloid, Woman, Cornstalks, Pocket, 3 x 2 In.	1355
Pails are also listed in the Lunch Box category.	
Pail, Mosemann's Brand Peanut Butter, Animals, Tin Lithograph, Bail Handles, 16 Oz.	175
Pie Safe, Rushton's Famous Pies, Door, Shelves, Screen, Countertop, 1910s, 21 x 11 In. *illus*	1872
Pin, Drink Alpen Brau, Boston Red Sox Portraits, 1916, Celluloid, 6 In. *illus*	62980
Pin, Strawbridge & Clothier Toy Store, Gold Text, Santa Claus, WW I Troops, 1918, 1 ¼ In.	235
Plate, Clark's Pure Rye, Bottled By The Government, c.1870, 10 ¾ In.	20
Puzzle, Cremo Cigars, Twin Girls, Holding Open Box, Frame, c.1925, 34 ½ x 28 ½ In. *illus*	152
Puzzle, Jigsaw, Anheuser-Busch, Budweiser, Custer's Last Fight, c.1936, Box *illus*	50
Rolling Pin, Davy & Company, Big Busy Grocery, Stoneware, Blue, White, Wood Handles, 14 In.	150
Rolling Pin, Wm. Stieren, General Merchandise, West Point, Nebr., Rust Bands, Stoneware, Wood	375
Salt & Pepper Shakers are listed in the Salt & Pepper category.	
Scales are listed in the Scale category.	
Sign, 15 MPH, School Zone, Safety Sal, Girl, Painted, Salesman's Sample, c.1950, 8 x 4 In. *illus*	2712
Sign, Angel Blowing Horn, Gilt Wing, Painted, Sheet Metal, 47 x 29 In.	236
Sign, B.S. Kingman, Pocket Watch Shape, Iron Ring Hanger, 2-Sided, Late 1800s, 28 In.	2500
Sign, Best Drugs, Gilt Lettering, Painted, Black Ground, Wood, 13 ½ x 42 In. *illus*	882
Sign, Billiards, Blue Ground, White Text, Enamel, 2-Sided, 6 x 15 In.	1380

Advertising, Pin, Drink Alpen Brau, Boston Red Sox Portraits, 1916, Celluloid, 6 In.
$62,980

Hake's Auctions

Advertising, Puzzle, Cremo Cigars, Twin Girls, Holding Open Box, Frame, c.1925, 34 ½ x 28 ½ In.
$152

Jeffrey S. Evans & Associates

ADVERTISING

Advertising, Puzzle, Jigsaw, Anheuser-Busch, Budweiser, Custer's Last Fight, c.1936, Box
$50

Amazon.com/Lantern Press

Advertising, Sign, 15 MPH, School Zone, Safety Sal, Girl, Painted, Salesman's Sample, c.1950, 8 x 4 In.
$2,712

Soulis Auctions

Advertising, Sign, Best Drugs, Gilt Lettering, Painted, Black Ground, Wood, 13 ½ x 42 In.
$882

Fontaine's Auction Gallery

Advertising, Sign, Certainly We Do First Class Pressing, Wood Frame, c.1920, 19 x 47 ½ In.
$497

Jeffrey S. Evans & Associates

Advertising, Sign, Coffeepot Shape, Fresh Ground Coffee, Blue & White, Brown Base, 1900s, 43 In.
$875

Eldred's

> **TIP**
> *If you live in a damp climate, keep a small lightbulb lit in each closet to retard mildew.*

> **TIP**
> *Install large windows in your house—burglars avoid shattering them because of noise.*

Advertising, Sign, Cushman Motor Scooters, Yellow Scooter, White, Red, Black, 24 In.
$62

Apple Tree Auction Center

Advertising, Sign, Cutty Sark Scotch Whisky, Hot Air Balloons, Boats, Buildings, N. Gifford, 41 In.
$2,016

Fontaine's Auction Gallery

Advertising, Sign, Elsie The Cow Logo, Borden's, Porcelain, 7 Colors Of Neon, Round, 42 In.
$3,200

Morphy Auctions

A

Advertising, Sign, For Rent, Elizabeth M. Hussey, So. Yarmouth, Wood, 1910s, 11 ½ x 22 In.
$138

Advertising, Sign, Garfield Tea, Constipation, Sick Headache, Tin Lithograph, Senttenne & Green, 30 x 22 In.
$660

Advertising, Sign, Jeweler's, Stookey, 2-Sided Pocket Watch Shape, Iron Frame, Late 1800s, 50 x 38 In.
$492

Advertising, Sign, Kayo Chocolate Drink, Kayo Carrying Big Bottle, Embossed, Tin Litho, 27 x 14 In.
$483

Advertising, Sign, Mail Pouch Tobacco, 2 Frontier Men, 1900s, 20 x 16 In.
$192

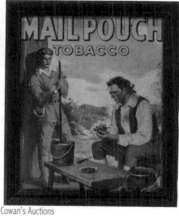

Advertising, Sign, Miller High Life, Stag, Neon, White, Yellow, Red, Black Ground, Box, 26 x 36 x 6 In.
$338

Advertising, Sign, Optician, Eyeglasses, J. Gumbinger, 131 West Bay St., Wood, c.1890, 11 x 36 In.
$1,000

Advertising, Sign, Point Special Beer, Porcelain, Die Cut, 2-Sided, Red & Blue Neon, 39 x 44 In.
$7,380

Advertising, Sign, Pub, Dog & Bacon, Painted, Metal Panel, 2-Sided, Wood Frame, 1900s, 53 x 45 In.
$1,534

TIP
Don't assume that the antique you are admiring today will be available tomorrow. Good pieces sell quickly.

Advertising, Sign, Time For Beverwyck, Man, Drinking, Dog, Beverwyck Breweries, Frame, N.Y., 15 x 12 In.
$83

Copake Auction

Store Signs

Some old store signs were lithographed directly on tin and made to look like a picture with a wooden frame. The Grape-Nuts sign picturing a girl and her St. Bernard is one of the best known examples.

Advertising, Sign, Warren's Featherbone Corsets, Townsend, Hostetter & Co., Chicago, c.1890, 21 x 15 In.
$4,305

Rich Penn Auctions

Advertising, Sign, Whistle, Soda Fountain, Bottle, Lithograph, Frame, 1930, 37 x 13 In.
$185

Rich Penn Auctions

Advertising, Tin, Biscuit, Clock Shape, Brass, Roman Numerals, Handle, Confiteria A. Maron, c.1920, 5 In.
$369

Hartzell's Auction Gallery Inc.

Advertising, Tin, Biscuit, Cottage, Hinged Lid, Haeberlein Metzger, Germany, 6 x 7 In.
$102

Hartzell's Auction Gallery Inc.

Advertising, Tin, Biscuit, Girl Mailing Letter, Gray, Dunn & Co., Glasgow, c.1909, 5 ¼ In.
$254

Hartzell's Auction Gallery Inc.

Advertising, Tin, Biscuit, Grandfather Clock Shape, Peek Frean & Co., c.1900, 7 In.
$492

Hartzell's Auction Gallery Inc.

Sign, Breyers Ice Cream, Embossed Logo & Lettering, White Ground, Metal, 20 x 92 In. 375
Sign, Bud Man, Multicolor Neon, Glass, Actown Electrocoil Inc., Illinois, 1900s, 18 In. 250
Sign, Budweiser, Eagle, Neon Logo, Beer In 5 Languages, 3 Colors, 24 x 48 In. 201
Sign, Case, American Eagle, On Globe, Flange Base, Keystone Co., c.1920, 59 x 34 x 21 In. 5265
Sign, Catham Airlines, Black & Red Font, Black Border, Wood, Morristown, N.J., 7 x 36 In. ... 221
Sign, Certainly We Do First Class Pressing, Wood Frame, c.1920, 19 x 47 ½ In. .... *illus* 497
Sign, Coffee House, Wood Panel, Black, Gold Shadow, White Ground, Frame, 10 x 59 In. 1170
Sign, Coffeepot Shape, Fresh Ground Coffee, Blue & White, Brown Base, 1900s, 43 In. . *illus* 875
Sign, Cognac Monnet, Woman, Holding Glass, Lithograph, Leonetto Cappiello, 1927, 51 x 79 In. 3795
Sign, Cowboy, Reithosen, Breeches, Frame, Germany, c.1904, 43 x 31 ½ In. 207
Sign, Cushman Motor Scooters, Yellow Scooter, White, Red, Black, 24 In. .... *illus* 62
Sign, Cutty Sark Scotch Whisky, Hot Air Balloons, Boats, Buildings, N. Gifford, 41 In. .. *illus* 2016
Sign, D.M. Ferry & Co's Seeds, Painted, Multicolor, Wood, Late 1800s. 10 ¼ x 40 ¾ In. 2925
Sign, Drink Blatz Beer, Porcelain, Die Cut, Neon, Artcraft, Milwaukee, 32 x 72 In. 6000
Sign, Edison Mazda, Venetian Lamplighter, By M. Parrish, 8 ½ x 7 In. 73
Sign, Elsie The Cow Logo, Borden's, Porcelain, 7 Colors Of Neon, Round, 42 In. .... *illus* 3200
Sign, Fairfax Cigar 5 Cent, Union Made, Paper Litho, McLoughlin Bros., 1898, 26 In. 1090
Sign, For Rent, Elizabeth M. Hussey, So. Yarmouth, Wood, 1910s, 11 ½ x 22 In. .... *illus* 138
Sign, Frontier Gun Club, Man Standing, Painted, 25 x 36 In. 354
Sign, Garfield Tea, Constipation, Sick Headache, Tin Lithograph, Senttenne & Green, 30 x 22 In. .*illus* 560
Sign, Geo Little, Boot Shape, Red Ground, 2-Sided, Projecting Frame, 1800s, 41 x 31 In. 813
Sign, Hoffman Quality Beverages, Rectangular, Enamel, c.1950, 8 x 22 ½ In. 129
Sign, Ice Cold, Watermelon Image, Frosty Letters, Tin, Painted, 20 x 28 In. 702
Sign, IGA Shield Shape, Sky Blue Ground, Porcelain, 12 ½ x 13 In., Pair.................... 369
Sign, Jeweler's, Stookey, 2-Sided Pocket Watch Shape, Iron Frame, Late 1800s, 50 x 38 In. .*illus* 492
Sign, Joshua Hutton & Son, Pig, Wood, Carved, Multicolor, 1800s, 26 ½ x 43 In. 448
Sign, Kayo Chocolate Drink, Kayo Carrying Big Bottle, Embossed, Tin Litho, 27 x 14 In. *illus* 483
Sign, Knightsbridge, Billiards Saloon, Smoking Club, Pub, Wood, Painted, 48 x 25 ¾ In. 443
Sign, L'Alsacienne, Verft En Verfrisscht, Girl, Yellow Dress, Red Bow, Frame, 70 x 52 In......... 384
Sign, Life Savers, Bathing Beauty, Package Images, Cardboard, Frame, 1920s, 21 In. 2200
Sign, Macy's Shop, White Letters & Border, Black Ground, Leaf Ends, c.1850, 6 x 62 In. 1375
Sign, Mail Pouch Tobacco, 2 Frontier Men, 1900s, 20 x 16 In. .... *illus* 192
Sign, Miller High Life, Stag, Neon, White, Yellow, Red, Black Ground, Box, 26 x 36 x 6 In. *illus* 338
Sign, Moon River, World's Best Pickerel Fishing, Boats, Room, Bait, Oak, 1900s, 22 x 44 In... 563
Sign, Nantucket, Whale Shape, Pine, Painted, White, 35 In. 750
Sign, Navajo Trail, White Lettering, Brown Ground, Orange Border, Tin, 20 x 15 In. 461
Sign, North Side Meat Market, Pigs, Walking, Painted, Emil Herziger, Early 1900s, 15 ½ In. . 94
Sign, O'Brien Fine Cutlery, Jackknife Shape, Gilt, Painted, 2-Sided, Late 1800s, 12 x 118 In. . 1750
Sign, Optician, Eyeglasses, J. Gumbinger, 131 West Bay St., Wood, c.1890, 11 x 36 In. ... *illus* 1000
Sign, Optometrist, Molded, Sheet Tin Eyes, Chain Hanger, Yellow, Early 1900s, 34 ¼ In. 2900
Sign, P.H. Nevill Optometrist, Glasses, Cast Iron, Hanging Hook, Early 1900s, 11 x 23 In. 1695
Sign, Pepsi, Customer Parking, Arrow, Sheet Metal, Rectangle, Painted, 34 x 67 ½ In. 148
Sign, Pickett Slide Rule, Movable Wood. Plastic Sliding, Yellow, Black, 1900s, 12 ½ x 84 In... 185
Sign, Point Special Beer, Porcelain, Die Cut, 2-Sided, Red & Blue Neon, 39 x 44 In. ...... *illus* 7380
Sign, Popsicles, 5 Cents, Cardboard, Girl Wearing Sailor Suit, 1920-30s, 15 x 12 In............. . 175
Sign, Pub, Dog & Bacon, Painted, Metal Panel, 2-Sided, Wood Frame, 1900s, 53 x 45 In. *illus* 1534
Sign, Pub, The Windmill Tavern, Painted, Fiberglass, Late 1900s, 44 ½ x 32 In. 236
Sign, Radio, Reverse Painted, Steel Frame, Electric, Illuminated, 9 x 35 x 6 In. 221
Sign, Rat Killer, Rat-Tox, Village, Dead Rats, Cardboard, Die Cut, Frame, 19 x 24 In. 1050
Sign, Red Man, Indian, Cigar Leaf, Cutout, Frame, 1900s, 21 x 15 ¾ In. 438
Sign, Sierra National Forest, Muir Trail, U.S. Forest Service Logo, Metal, 4 x 12 In. 1170
Sign, Sleigh Rides 25 Cents, Wood, Painted, Black & White, Iron Trim, 14 x 42 In. 135
Sign, Street, Barnstable 12 Ms, Pointing Hand, Tin & Iron, 36 ½ In. 2375
Sign, Superior Havana Cigars, 3 Cigars, Mahogany Frame, 1892, 32 x 10 ½ In................... 1755
Sign, Texas Lone Star 1836, Red Ground, Painted, Metal, 18 x 30 x 2 In...................... 384
Sign, Thames Fire Insurance Co., Scenes, Norwich, Connecticut, c.1870, 19 x 24 In. 1190
Sign, The First White Lead Factory, Carved Walnut, Riband, Scrollwork, c.1875, 18 x 64 In... 585
Sign, Tiger Chewing Tobacco, Paper Lithograph, Early 1900s, 32 x 26 In.................... 3900
Sign, Time For Beverwyck, Man, Drinking, Dog, Beverwyck Breweries, Frame, N.Y., 15 x 12 In. ..*illus* 83

Advertising, Tin, Biscuit, Huntley &
Palmer, Money Box Shape, Children,
Snowman, Dog, 5 ¼ In.
$98

Hartzell's Auction Gallery Inc.

Advertising, Tin, Biscuit, Time Is
Money, Clock, Children, Painted,
W. Dumore & Son, c.1930, 5 ¼ In.
$234

Hartzell's Auction Gallery Inc.

A

Advertising, Tin, Biscuit, Windmill, 8-Sided, John Gray & Co. Ltd., England, 1920s, 10 In.
$509

Hartzell's Auction Gallery Inc.

Advertising, Tin, Bus, Double-Decker, Victory V, Gums & Lozenges, c.1930, 6 x 13 In.
$2,938

Hartzell's Auction Gallery Inc.

Advertising, Tin, Comfort Antiseptic Powder, Medicated, Nurse Image, 4 x 2½ In.
$118

AntiqueAdvertising.com

Sign, Toys Of All Kinds, For Children Old & Young, Toy Soldier, Wood, Paint, 36 x 24 In.	244
Sign, Twin Drive-In Theater, Turn Right, Arrow, Metal, Green Paint, Yellow Letters, 24 In.	750
Sign, Unverdorben's Market, Produce, Oil On Pressboard, 18 x 74 In.	113
Sign, Walk-Over Shoes, Carved & Painted, Rosettes, c.1920, 20 x 44 In.	266
Sign, Warren's Featherbone Corsets, Townsend, Hostetter & Co., Chicago, c.1890, 21 x 15 In. *illus*	4305
Sign, Whistle, Soda Fountain, Bottle, Lithograph, Frame, 1930, 37 x 13 In. *illus*	185
Sign, William Holsum Bread, Orange, Blue Striped Ground, Frame, c.1920, 40½ x 30½ In.	152
Thermometers are listed in the Thermometer category.	

Advertising tin cans or canisters were first used commercially in the United States in 1819 and were called tins. Today the word *tin* is used by most collectors to describe many types of containers, including food tins, biscuit boxes, roly poly tobacco containers, gunpowder cans, talcum powder sprinkle-top cans, cigarette flat-fifty tins, and more. Beer Cans are listed in their own category. Things made of undecorated tin are listed under Tinware.

Tin, Biscuit, Clock Shape, Brass, Roman Numerals, Handle, Confiteria A. Maron, c.1920, 5 In. *illus*	369
Tin, Biscuit, Clock Shape, Calendar, Faux Crocodile Skin, Handle, MacFarlane Lang & Co., 6 In.	86
Tin, Biscuit, Cottage, Hinged Lid, Haeberlein Metzger, Germany, 6 x 7 In. *illus*	102
Tin, Biscuit, Girl Mailing Letter, Gray, Dunn & Co., Glasgow, c.1909, 5¼ In. *illus*	254
Tin, Biscuit, Grandfather Clock Shape, Peek Frean & Co., c.1900, 7 In. *illus*	492
Tin, Biscuit, Huntley & Palmer, Money Box Shape, Children, Snowman, Dog, 5¼ In. *illus*	98
Tin, Biscuit, Merry Christmas, Ship, Thor Dahl, Greenery, Flag, c.1935, 5 x 7 In.	57
Tin, Biscuit, Round, Children, Waiting For Christmas, Painted, C.W.S., c.1925, 5¾ In.	523
Tin, Biscuit, Time Is Money, Clock, Children, Painted, W. Dumore & Son, c.1930, 5¼ In. *illus*	234
Tin, Biscuit, Windmill, 8-Sided, John Gray & Co. Ltd., England, 1920s, 10 In. *illus*	509
Tin, Bus, Double-Decker, Victory V, Gums & Lozenges, c.1930, 6 x 13 In. *illus*	2938
Tin, Candy Bucket, Lid, Beach Scene, Litho, Bail Handle, Blanke-Wenneker, 1910s, 12 x 12 In.	50
Tin, Comfort Antiseptic Powder, Medicated, Nurse Image, 4 x 2½ In. *illus*	118
Tin, Continental Cubes, Tobacco, One Match, One Puff, Hinged Lid, 5¼ x 5¼ In.	6150
Tin, Drako Coffee, Duck, Cylindrical Shape, 1900s, 6 In.	320
Tin, Hartz Mountain Song Food, Yellow Bird, 35 Cents, Made In U.S.A., 3½ x 2 In.	40
Tin, Monarch Teenie Weenie Toffees, Brownie-Like Figures, Reid, Murdoch, 14 x 12 In.	2125
Tin, Mrs. Dinsmore's Cough Drops, Lithograph, Portrait, Somers Bros., 8 x 5 In. *illus*	295
Tin, Our High Test Baking Powder, Label, Bentley & Settle Grocers, Sealed, 4¼ x 2⅝ In. *illus*	118
Tin, Sure Shot, Chewing Tobacco, It Touches The Spot, 1900s, 8 x 15¼ x 10¼ In.	416
Tin, Toffee, Mackintosh's, Pram, Cardboard Figures Fold Out, Litho, Sample, 7 x 4 In. *illus*	1130

Advertising tip trays are decorated metal trays less than 5 inches in diameter. They were placed on the table or counter to hold either the bill or the coins that were left as a tip. Change receivers could be made of glass, plastic, or metal. They were kept on the counter near the cash register and held the money passed back and forth by the cashier. Related items may be listed in the Advertising category under Change Receiver.

Toilet, Blue, White, Lions, Victoria Ware Ironstone, Salesman's Sample, 7 In. *illus*	614
Tray, Fehr's Ambrosia, Nectar Of The Gods, Frank Fehr Brewing Co. Inc., 1917, 13 In. *illus*	615
Tray, Lu Petit Beurre Nantes, Biscuit Shape, Porcelain, France, 8 x 10 In.	31
Tray, Senior & Senatore Whiskies, Wheeling, West Virginia, Tin, Girl, Horse, 17 x 14 In.	660
Tray, Tip, see Tip Trays in this category.	

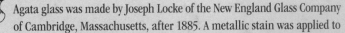

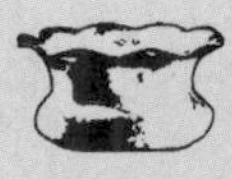

AGATA

Agata glass was made by Joseph Locke of the New England Glass Company of Cambridge, Massachusetts, after 1885. A metallic stain was applied to New England Peachblow, which the company called Wild Rose, and the mottled design characteristic of agata appeared. There are a few known items made of opaque green with the mottled finish.

Toothpick Holder, Pink, Glossy, Square Inverted Top, Art Glass, New England, 2½ In.	58

Advertising, Tin, Mrs. Dinsmore's Cough Drops, Lithograph, Portrait, Somers Bros., 8 x 5 In.
$295

AntiqueAdvertising.com

Advertising, Tin, Our High Test Baking Powder, Label, Bentley & Settle Grocers, Sealed, 4½ x 2⅝ In.
$118

AntiqueAdvertising.com

Advertising, Tin, Toffee, Mackintosh's, Pram, Cardboard Figures Fold Out, Litho, Sample, 7 x 4 In.
$1,130

Hartzell's Auction Gallery Inc.

Advertising, Toilet, Blue, White, Lions, Victoria Ware Ironstone, Salesman's Sample, 7 In.
$614

AntiqueAdvertising.com

Advertising, Tray, Fehr's Ambrosia, Nectar Of The Gods, Frank Fehr Brewing Co. Inc., 1917, 13 In.
$615

Rich Penn Auctions

Alabaster, Bust, Woman, Flowers, Yellow Dress, Plinth Base, Signed, P. Sarchy, Italy, 7½ In.
$252

Fontaine's Auction Gallery

Alabaster, Sculpture, Man, Woman, Walking, Carved, Square Base, Italy, Late 1800s, 28 x 12 In.
$640

Hindman

Alabaster, Sculpture, Woman, Nude, Pillow, Stella By Starlight, Signed, John Coleman, Arizona, 10 In.
$2,125

Eldred's

Aluminum, Ashtray, Anodized, Waterloo, Ali Tayar, Metalteks, 1¼ × 4 In.
$188

Wright

11

Aluminum, Bowl, Stafford, Glass Stem, Lurelle Guild, c.1934, 13¾ In.
$625

Wright

Amber Glass, Pitcher, Knight, Coat Of Arms, Flowers, Pinched Spout, Enamel, c.1980, 8 In.
$125

Woody Auction

Amberina, Celery Vase, Cylindrical, Scalloped Rim, Spot Optic, Bluerina, 1880s, 6⅞ In.
$152

Jeffrey S. Evans & Associates

Amberina, Pitcher, Water, Pink, Swirled Optic Ribs, Frosted, Clear, Reeded Handle, c.1887, 7 In.
$222

Jeffrey S. Evans & Associates

Amberina, Vase, Stork, Capturing Snake, Rocky Ground, Pressed, New England Glassworks, 1884, 4 x 2 In.
$702

Jeffrey S. Evans & Associates

Amethyst Glass, Compote, Hanging Cherries, Ruffled Rim, Engraved, Millersburg, 6¾ In.
$960

Morphy Auctions

Amethyst Glass, Vase, Cut To Clear, Engraved Flower Panels, 8½ x 5¼ In.
$275

Woody Auction

Vase, Pink To White, Fluted Rim, Mottled, New England, 7¾ x 3¼ In.   900
Vase, Pink To White, Glossy, Tulip Top, Tapered Base, Art Glass, New England, 7¼ In.   69

AKRO AGATE

Akro Agate glass was founded in Akron, Ohio, in 1911 and moved to Clarksburg, West Virginia, in 1914. The company made marbles and toys. In the 1930s it began making other products, including vases, lamps, flowerpots, candlesticks, and children's dishes. Most of the glass is marked with a crow flying through the letter *A*. The company was sold to Clarksburg Glass Co. in 1951. Akro Agate marbles are listed in this book in the Marble category.

Cup, Octagonal, Green, Closed Handle, Child's, 1½ In.   26
Urn, White, Gilt, Bronze Mounted, France, 1800s, 23½ x 12½ In., Pair   5625

ALABASTER

Alabaster is a very soft form of gypsum, a stone that resembles marble. It was often carved into vases or statues in Victorian times. There are alabaster carvings being made even today.

Bowl, Rolled Rim, Pedestal, 6½ x 10 In.   384
Bust, Child, Crossed Arms, Holding Roses, Butterfly, Waisted Circular Socle, 1800s, 17 In.   344
Bust, Laurel Wreath Hair, Stand, Prof. Giuseppe Bessi, Frilli, Late 1800s, 15¼ In.   330
Bust, Woman, Flowers, Yellow Dress, Plinth Base, Signed, P. Sarchy, Italy, 7½ In. .... *illus*   252
Bust, Young Woman, Carved, Green Marble Pedestal, Octagonal Base, 19 In.   1534
Bust, Young Woman, Flower In Hair, Art Nouveau, Carved, Italy, c.1920, 8½ x 9 x 4½ In.   125
Bust, Young Woman, Wearing Crown, Eyes Closed, Carved, Plinth Base, 1800s, 22 In.   1080
Chandelier, 6-Light, Gilt Bronze, Center Bowl, Shades, France, 17½ x 26 In.   375
Figure, Dying Gaul Model, Warrior, Oval Base, 1800s, 11½ x 20¾ In.   563
Figure, Infant, Lying On Pillow, Inscribed, 1900s, 15 x 13 In.   531
Group, 2 Young Children, Carved, Circular Stepped Base, Italy, c.1900, 24 In.   277
Group, Dante & Beatrice, Busts, Facing, Laurel Wreath, Italy, Early 1900s, 14 x 8 x 17 In.   431
Lamp, 3 Curious Polar Bears, Stepped Arctic Landscape, Black Shade, 1930, 29½ In.   384
Lamp, Beethoven, Playing The Piano, Metal, J.B. Hirsch, 12 In.   71
Lamp, Dancer, Female, Red Slag Glass, Art Deco, Continental, Early 1900s, 31 In.   480
Lamp, Figural, 2 Female Dancers, Marble Base, B. Errico, Italy, Early 1900s, 33 In.   960
Lamp, Figural, Carved, Man Strumming Guitar, Light Post, Early 1900s, 29 In.   320
Lamp, Figural, Smiling Woman, Scantily Clad, Art Deco, Early 1900s, 29 x 11 x 10¼ In.   632
Panel, Relief Of Christ, White Ground, 16 x 14 In.   540
Pedestal, Carved, Plaster Bust, Octagonal Base, Fluted Column, 62 x 13 x 10 In.   854
Pedestal, Circular Top, Swirl & Straight Stem, Octagonal Base, 1800s, 33 In.   420
Pedestal, Cream Ground, Octagonal Top & Base, 48 In.   106
Pedestal, Fluted Column, Allover Gray Veining, Reeded Stem, 46 x 9½ In.   438
Pedestal, Neoclassical Style, Knopped Stem, Round Top, Octagonal Base, Italy, 30 x 11½ In. ..   125
Sculpture, Man, Woman, Walking, Carved, Square Base, Italy, Late 1800s, 28 x 12 In. *illus*   640
Sculpture, Woman, Nude, Pillow, Stella By Starlight, Signed, John Coleman, Arizona, 10 In. .*illus*   2125
Sculpture, Woman, Standing, Seminude, Carved, 22¼ In.   756
Urn, Brown Ground, 2 Handles, Gilt, Brushed Gold, Cream Shade, Mounted As Lamp, 30 In., Pair.   59

ALUMINUM

Aluminum was more expensive than gold or silver until the 1850s. Chemists learned how to refine bauxite to get aluminum. Jewelry and other small objects were made of the valuable metal until 1914, when an inexpensive smelting process was invented. The aluminum collected today dates from the 1930s through the 1950s. Hand-hammered pieces are the most popular.

Ashtray, Anodized, Waterloo, Ali Tayar, Metalteks, 1¼ × 4 In. .... *illus*   188
Bowl, Stafford, Glass Stem, Lurelle Guild, c.1934, 13¾ In. .... *illus*   625

Animal Trophy, Blackbuck Head, Shoulder Mount, Wood Plaque, 37 x 19 x 16 In.
$295

Austin Auction Gallery

Animal Trophy, Brown Bear, Full Body Mount, Standing, Stone, Octagonal, Wood Base, 70 In.
$1,475

Apple Tree Auction Center

Animal Trophy, Fallow Deer, Antlers, Wall Mount, Weissenhauser, Germany, 1890, 15½ x 21 x 4 In.
$115

Blackwell Auctions

ALUMINUM

Animation Art, Cel, Fauna, Waving Wand, Pouring Tea, Sleeping Beauty, Walt Disney, Frame, 13¾ x 17 In. $375

Selkirk Auctioneers & Appraisers

TIP
Never bend or roll an animation cell—it might crack.

Animation Art, Print, Three For Justice, Batman, Robin, Batgirl, Warner Brothers, Frame, 36 x 26 In. $148

Austin Auction Gallery

Animation Art, Sericel, Batman, Lithograph Background, Warner Brothers, Frame, 18 x 21½ In. $236

Austin Auction Gallery

Owl, Fencepost Decoy, Cast, Glass Eyes, Swisher Soules, Early 1900s, 12½ In.	375
Plaque, Wall, Eagle, Open Wings, Perched, On 2 Arrows, Gilt, Sexton, 1900s, 9 x 27 In.	108
Plate, Oval, Engraved, Parker Amuse Co., C.W. Parker, Leavenworth, 7¾ x 23 In.	1243
Sculpture, Abstract, Square Base, Signed, Menashe Kadishman, 15½ x 9 In.	1150
Sculpture, Free-Form, Lucite Base, Signed, Dan Murphy, Dated, 2001, 13 x 33 x 14½ In.	275
Sculpture, Gazelle Skull, Triangular Base, Arthur Court, 61 In.	313
Suitcase, 2 Wheels, Carry On, Silver, Hard Shell Luggage, Halliburton, 22 x 13 x 9 In.	460
Tray, Fruits & Flowers, Hammered, Folding Handle, Marked, 9¾ x 7½ In.	18

AMBER, *see Jewelry category.*

AMBER GLASS

Amber glass is the name of any glassware with the proper yellow-brown shading. It was a popular color just after the Civil War and many pressed glass pieces were made of amber glass. Depression glass of the 1930s–1950s was also made in shades of amber glass. Other pieces may be found in the Depression Glass, Pressed Glass, and other glass categories. All types are being reproduced.

Pitcher, Knight, Coat Of Arms, Flowers, Pinched Spout, Enamel, c.1980, 8 In.	*illus*	125
Vase, Applied Pink Rigoree, Flowers, Blue Leaf & Stem, Round Base, 11 In.		150

AMBERINA

Amberina, a two-toned glassware, was originally made from 1883 to about 1900. It was patented by Joseph Locke of the New England Glass Company but was also made by other companies and is still being made. The glass shades from red to amber. Similar pieces of glass may be found in the Baccarat, Libbey, Plated Amberina, and other categories. Glass shaded from blue to amber is called *Blue Amberina* or *Bluerina*.

Celery Vase, Cylindrical, Scalloped Rim, Spot Optic, Bluerina, 1880s, 6⅞ In.	*illus*	152
Pitcher, Water, Pink, Swirled Optic Ribs, Frosted, Clear, Reeded Handle, c.1887, 7 In.	*illus*	222
Vase, Lily-Of-The-Valley, Optic Paneled, Multicolor, New England Glassworks, 1880s, 7 In.		527
Vase, Stork, Capturing Snake, Rocky Ground, Pressed, New England Glassworks, 1884, 4 x 2 In.	*illus*	702

AMERICAN DINNERWARE, *see Dinnerware.*

AMETHYST GLASS

Amethyst glass is any of the many glasswares made in the dark purple color of the gemstone amethyst. Included in this category are many pieces made in the nineteenth and twentieth centuries. Very dark pieces are called *black amethyst.*

Compote, Hanging Cherries, Ruffled Rim, Engraved, Millersburg, 6¾ In.	*illus*	960
Finger Bowl, 15 Ribs, Black Interior, Polished Pontil, American, 1830s, 3½ x 4½ In.		132
Vase, Cut To Clear, Engraved Flower Panels, 8½ x 5¼ In.	*illus*	275

AMPHORA *pieces are listed in the Teplitz category.*

ANDIRONS *and related fireplace items are included in the Fireplace category.*

ANIMAL TROPHY

Animal trophies, such as stuffed animals (taxidermy), rugs made of animal skins, and other similar collectibles made from animal, fish, or bird parts, are listed in this category. Collectors should be aware of the endangered species laws that make it illegal to buy and sell some of these items. Any eagle feathers, many types of pelts or rugs (such as leopard), ivory, rhinoceros horn, and many forms of tortoiseshell can be confiscated by the government. Related trophies may be found in the Fishing category. Ivory items may be found in the Scrimshaw or Ivory categories.

African Giant Eland, Head, Shoulder Mount, 53 x 60 In.	438
Antelope Head, Pronghorn, Antler Rack, Glass Eyes, Wall Mount, 1900s, 31 x 12 In.	115
Antelope, Pronghorn, Wood, Shield Mount, 1900s, 33 x 16 In.	344
Axis Deer, Antlers, Shield Mount, Wood, 35 x 28 ½ x 16 ½ In.	207
Bird, Hawk, Brown, Perched, Square Base, 20 In.	130
Black Bear, Head, Open Mouth, Mounted	181
Blackbuck Head, Shoulder Mount, Wood Plaque, 37 x 19 x 16 In. .... illus	295
Brown Bear, Full Body Mount, Standing, Stone, Octagonal, Wood Base, 70 In. .... illus	1475
Caribou, Head, Antler Rack, Glass Eyes, Wall Mount, Early 1900s, 55 x 33 In.	805
Caribou, Head, Mounted, Pointed Antlers, 41 In.	295
Cow Skull, Horns, On Wood Mount, 5 ½ In.	94
Deer Antler, Black Forest Style, Carved, Leafy Plaque, Taxidermy, 26 ½ x 17 ½ x 11 ½ In.	236
Deer, Head, 7-Point Antlers, Shield Shape Mount, 47 In.	148
Elk, Head, Mounted, Pointed Horns, 56 In.	354
Fallow Deer, Antlers, Wall Mount, Weissenhauser, Germany, 1890, 15 ½ x 21 x 4 In. ... illus	115
Mountain Sheep Head, Ram, Glass Eyes, Big Horns, Wall Mount, 34 x 29 In.	403
Steer Horns, Skull, Longhorn, Black Wood Mount, 40 In.	295
Steer, Longhorn, Wrapped At Center, Wood Mount, 35 ½ In.	177
Turkey, Perched, Tree Branch, Mounted, Frank Julian, Claysville, Pa., 37 In.	106

ANIMATION ART

Animation art collectibles include cels that are painted drawings on celluloid needed to make animated cartoons shown in movie theaters or on TV. Hundreds of cels were made, then photographed in sequence to make a cartoon showing moving figures. Early examples made by the Walt Disney Studios are popular with collectors today. Original sketches used by the artists are also listed here. Modern animated cartoons are made using computer-generated pictures. Some of these are being produced as cels to be sold to collectors. Other cartoon art is listed in Comic Art and Disneyana.

Cel, Fauna, Waving Wand, Pouring Tea, Sleeping Beauty, Walt Disney, Frame, 13 ¾ x 17 In. ....illus	375
Cel, Joker, Ceramic Tile, Signed, Warner Brothers, Paul Vought, Frame, 15 ¼ x 15 ¼ In.	590
Drawing, Harley & Ivy, Warner Brothers, Black Frame, 16 ¼ x 9 ½ In.	207
Print, Three For Justice, Batman, Robin, Batgirl, Warner Brothers, Frame, 36 x 26 In. illus	148
Senigraph, Batman The Animated Series, Signed, Warner Brothers, Frame, 23 ½ x 22 ½ In.	354
Sericel, Batman, Lithograph Background, Warner Brothers, Frame, 18 x 21 ½ In. ...... illus	236
Sericel, Little Mermaid, He Loves Me, Lithograph, Disney, Frame, 23 x 22 In. .... illus	148
Sericel, Singing Frog, Michigan J. Frog, Warner Brothers, Mat, Frame, 1998, 17 ½ x 15 In. ...	148
Storyboard, Batman & Joker, Warner Brothers, Lithograph, Shadowbox, 1994, 28 x 27 In. ....illus	236

ANNA POTTERY

Anna Pottery

Anna Pottery was started in Anna, Illinois, in 1859 by Cornwall and Wallace Kirkpatrick. They made many types of utilitarian wares, bricks, drain tiles, and giftware. The most collectible pieces made by the pottery are the pig-shaped bottles and jugs with special inscriptions, applied animals, and figures. The pottery closed in 1894.

Flask, Pig, Brown, Inscribed, Fine Old Bourbon In, Lard Oil Drill, 3 x 6 ⅝ In.	3250
Flask, Pig, Sow, Dark Brown Glaze, Good Old Rye, In A Hogs, Late 1800s, 7 ½ In. .... illus	2560

APPLE PEELERS *are listed in the Kitchen category under Peeler, Apple.*

Animation Art, Sericel, Little Mermaid, He Loves Me, Lithograph, Disney, Frame, 23 x 22 In.
$148

Austin Auction Gallery

Animation Art, Storyboard, Batman & Joker, Warner Brothers, Lithograph, Shadowbox, 1994, 28 x 27 In.
$236

Leland Little Auctions

Anna Pottery, Flask, Pig, Sow, Dark Brown Glaze, Good Old Rye, In A Hogs, Late 1800s, 7 ½ In.
$2,560

Cowan's Auctions

Arabia, Dish, Origami Style, Black, Glazed, Kaj Franck, c.1965, 9¾ In.
$313

Wright

Architectural, Bracket, Shelf, Cast Iron, Geometric Style, Victorian, 10 x 7½ In., Pair
$98

Hartzell's Auction Gallery Inc.

Architectural, Column, Rouge Marble, Brass, Plinth Base, Early 1900s, 42¾ x 11 x 11 In.
$649

Leland Little Auctions

TIP

If you clean brass plated hardware too well and remove some of the plating, try this first-aid suggestion. Get a gold or brass wax at a craft shop. Rub a little on the bad spot. Then seal with clear lacquer. Don't use brass-colored spray paint.

Architectural, Door Lock, Wood, Dogon, Seated, Carved, Steel Stand, West Africa, 15 x 12 In.
$148

Austin Auction Gallery

Architectural, Doorknocker, Brass, Kissing Couple, Romantic, 1900s, 5¼ In., Pair
$94

Bruneau & Co. Auctioneers

Architectural, Doorknocker, Bronze, Seahorse, Edward T. Hurley, Signed, 5½ x ¾ x 3¾ In.
$3,000

Toomey & Co. Auctioneers

Architectural, Element, Bronze, Eagle, Spread Wings, Mirror, 1800s, 29 x 20½ In., Pair
$2,091

Brunk Auctions

Architectural, Finial, Wood, Flame Shape, Carved, Painted, Faux Marble Plinth, 1900s, 21 x 18 x 9 In.
$944

Leland Little Auctions

ARABIA

Arabia began producing ceramics in 1874. The pottery was established in Helsinki, Finland, by Rörstrand, a Swedish pottery that wanted to export porcelain, earthenware, and other pottery from Finland to Russia. Most of the early workers at Arabia were Swedish. Arabia started producing its own models of tiled stoves, vases, and tableware about 1900. Rörstrand sold its interest in Arabia in 1916. By the late 1930s, Arabia was the largest producer of porcelain in Europe. Most of its products were exported. A line of stoneware was introduced in the 1960s. Arabia worked in cooperation with Rörstrand from 1975 to 1977. Arabia was bought by Hackman Group in 1990 and Hackman was bought by Iittala Group in 2004. Fiskars Corporation bought Iittala in 2007 and Arabia is now a brand owned by Fiskars.

ARABIA
FINLAND

Dish, Origami Style, Black, Glazed, Kaj Franck, c.1965, 9¾ In. .... *illus*	313
Plate, Elegance 5, Stylized Vines, Blue, Black, Tan, White, Birger Kaipiainen, c.1965. 9¾ x 9 In.	1250

ARCHITECTURAL

Architectural antiques include a variety of collectibles, usually very large, that have been removed from buildings. Hardware, backbars, doors, paneling, and even old bathtubs are now wanted by collectors. Pieces of the Victorian, Art Nouveau, and Art Deco styles are in greatest demand.

Bracket, Hanging, Openwork, Scrolled Design Wrought Iron, Early 1900s, 45 x 63 In.	384
Bracket, Shelf, Cast Iron, Geometric Style, Victorian, 10 x 7½ In., Pair .... *illus*	98
Canopy, Wood, Carved, Gilt, France, 1800s, 5½ x 37 In.	1063
Column, Mahogany, Classical, Acanthus Leaf, Carved, Fluted, Pine Base, c.1900s, 63 x 15 In..	266
Column, Marble, Gilt, Spiral, Round Socle, Octagonal Base, Late 1900s, 78¾ x 18 In., Pair..	767
Column, Morish Wood, Carved, Spiral, Ionic Capital, Multicolor. 66 In.................................	403
Column, Parcel Gilt, Black, Fluted, Circular Top, Square Pedestal, 1900s, 48¼ x 12 In.........	767
Column, Rouge Marble, Brass, Plinth Base, Early 1900s, 42¾ x 11 x 11 In. .... *illus*	649
Corbel, Parcel Gilt, Canted Ledge, Leaves, Winged, Cherubim Masks, Late 1800s, 26 In........	354
Corbel, Wood, Foo Dog, Carved, Multicolor, Painted, Chinese, 30½ x 8½ In., Pair...............	826
Crest, Linden Wood, Gilt, Carved, Leaves, Flowers, Treetop, Birds, c.1872, 16 x 35 In.	420
Door Lock, Wood, Dogon, Seated, Carved, Steel Stand, West Africa, 15 x 12 In. .... *illus*	148
Door, Barn, Oak & Steel, Stenciled, Salesman's Sample, c.1900, 14½ x 29 In.	390
Door, Hardwood, Iron Hardware, Mounted On Stand, 84 x 29½ x 12 In., Pair.....................	1875
Door, Quartersawn Oak, Coat Of Arms, Linen Fold, Iron Hardware, 1800s, 58 x 27 In., Pair .	1560
Door, Rustic, Carved Balusters, Lower Chamfered Panel, Iron Hardware, 1900s, 82 x 30 In., Pair.	708
Door, Sliding, Cast Iron, Mahogany Frame, 2 Panels, 10 Ft. 9½ In. x 34½ In., Pair	863
Door, Wood, Brown Paint, 9 Glass Panes, Dutch, 81 x 36 In.	123
Doorknocker, Brass, Circular, Symmetrical Flowers, Leaves, Lion's Head, Mid 1900s, 9 x 8 In....	590
Doorknocker, Brass, Kissing Couple, Romantic, 1900s, 5¼ In., Pair .... *illus*	94
Doorknocker, Brass, Lion's Head, Flowers, Engraved, Embossed, 6 In......................... ..	52
Doorknocker, Bronze, Lion's Head, Flowers, Knocking Ring, Late 1800s, 9 x 8½ In.	768
Doorknocker, Bronze, Seahorse, Edward T. Hurley, Signed, 5½ x ¾ x 3¾ In. .... *illus*	3000
Element, Bronze, Eagle, Spread Wings, Mirror, 1800s, 29 x 20½ In., Pair .... *illus*	2091
Element, Cast Iron, Lion Shape, 7½ In., Pair	59
Element, Foo Dog, Patterned Ball, Cub, Carved, Wood, Chinese, 30 In., Pair.....................	885
Element, Wood, Carved, Crown, Insignia, Leaf & Ribbon Design, 1800s, 15 x 27½ In.	625
Element, Wood, Phoenix, Pierced Flowers, Multicolor, 14 ft. 5 In.0............................	688
Fan, Wood, Molded Top Edge, Ribbed, White, 1800s, 16 x 70¾ In.	813
Finial, Wood, Flame Shape, Carved, Painted, Faux Marble Plinth, 1900s, 21 x 18 x 9 In. *illus*	944
Finial, Wood, Flame Shape, Gadrooning, Gilt, Silver Base, 1900s, 17 In.	536
Finial, Wood, Urn, Carved & Painted, Stepped Base, Early 1800s, 20¼ In., Pair	563
Fireboard, Oil On Wood, Seaside Village, Hope R. Angier, Grain Painted Frame, 1900s, 30 x 34 In.	288
Fireplace Surround, Rouge Marble, Scalloped Shape Top, 40 x 43 In.	896
Fountain, Enamel, Iron Bowl, Tripod Base, Haws Drinking Faucet Co., Berkeley, c.1920, 37 In. .. *illus*	615
Fragment, Iron, Garden Fence, Berries, Early 1900s, 21 x 73 In.	188

Architectural, Fountain, Enamel, Iron Bowl, Tripod Base, Haws Drinking Faucet Co., Berkeley, c.1920, 37 In.
$615

Rich Penn Auctions

Architectural, Gate, Wrought Iron, Scrolled Heart Shape, France, 1900s, 66 x 15¾ In.
$767

Austin Auction Gallery

Architectural, Gate, Wrought Iron, Scrollwork, Urn, Flowers, Serpent Handles, 75 x 48 In.
$1,250

Charlton Hall Auctions

Architectural, Grate, Floor, Cast Iron, Square, Victorian, 18 x 22 In.
$55

Hartzell's Auction Gallery Inc.

Architectural, Mailbox, Cast Iron, Blue, Red, White Lettering, U.S. Mail, c.1908, 25 x 17 x 10 In.
$351

Jeffrey S. Evans & Associates

Architectural, Mantel, Fireplace, Bronze, 3 Parts, Fluted Columns, 1900, 47 ¾ x 65 In.
$2,500

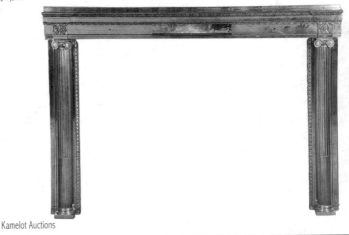

Kamelot Auctions

Architectural, Mantel, Pine, Gray & Black, Smoke Style, Painted, Dovetailed Foot Trim, 1910s, 63 x 64 In.
$531

Leland Little Auctions

> **TIP**
> *Old glass in a mirror reflects with an off-white tone. Hold the edge of a white card against the glass. If it has a white reflection that matches the color of the card, it is probably late Victorian or newer. The card reflection will be more yellow or gray if the glass was made before 1850.*

Architectural, Overmantel Mirror, Giltwood, Empire, Acorns, Rope, Pilasters, 2 Parts, 1830s, 36 x 23 In.
$330

Garth's Auctioneers & Appraisers

Architectural, Overmantel Mirror, Giltwood, Sheraton, 3 Parts, c.1830, 26 x 60 In.
$575

Pook & Pook

Architectural, Overmantel Mirror, Rococo Revival Style, Giltwood, Scrollwork, c.1950, 48 In.
$384

Leland Little Auctions

Architectural, Panel, Plaster, Madonna & Child, Angels, 3 Panels, Painted, Giltwood Frame, 15 x 11 In.
$1,230

Alderfer Auction Company

Architectural, Panel, Wood, Dragon, Sailing Ship, Carved, Painted, Japan, 1900s, 31 x 7 x 4 In.
$406

Bruneau & Co. Auctioneers

Architectural, Pedestal, Wood, Mahogany, Bronze Mounted, Continental, 1800s, 41 x 16 ½ In., Pair
$5,625

Abington Auction Gallery

Architectural, Shutters, 2 Hinged Panel Doors, Painted, Geometric Decor, Morocco, 1910s, 49 x 32 ½ In.
$1,003

Leland Little Auctions

A

Architectural, Urn, Cast Iron, Campana Form, Leafy Rim, Palmettes, Pedestal Base, 32 x 35 In., Pair
$590

Austin Auction Gallery

Architectural, Valance, Parcel Gilt, Louis XV Style, Painted, Red, Carved, Rocaille, Floral Crest, 13 x 66 In.
$236

Austin Auction Gallery

Architectural, Wall Bracket, Eagle, Gold Gilded, Leaves, Floral, 12½ x 9½ x 7½ In., Pair
$173

Stevens Auction Co.

Architectural, Wall Bracket, Giltwood, Eagle, Shaped Shelf, Acorn Pendant, Early 1900s, 12 In., Pair
$1,750

Charlton Hall Auctions

Fretwork, Oak, Stick & Ball, Carved, Filigree, c.1900, 31 x 72 In.	221
Fretwork, Wood, Shou Symbols, Late 1800s, 27½ x 14½ In., 4 Piece	154
Frieze, Plaster, Painted, Gray, Mounted, Custom Pine, Early 1900s, 14½ x 68 In., Pair	649
Frieze, Terra-Cotta, Semicircular, Shield, Stylized Dragons, Acanthus, 10 Sections	480
Gate, Wood, Curved Top, Pointed Slats, Brown, Late 1800s, 66½ In., Pair	250
Gate, Wrought Iron, Scrolled Heart Shape, France, 1900s, 66 x 15¾ In. *illus*	767
Gate, Wrought Iron, Scrolled Top, 28 x 21¾ In., Pair	236
Gate, Wrought Iron, Scrollwork, Urn, Flowers, Serpent Handles, 75 x 48 In. *illus*	1250
Grate, Cast Iron, Scrolled Flowers, 22 x 30 In.	148
Grate, Floor, Cast Iron, Square, Victorian, 18 x 22 In. *illus*	55
Grate, Window, Ornate, Scrolled, Acanthus Design, Bronze, 1800s, 22 x 35½ In.	221
Grill, Window, Wrought Iron, Fan Shape, Spherule, Boss Accents, 21 x 41½ In.	976
Hook, Cast Iron, Buck, Antlers, Leaf Background, Painted, 9 x 10 In.	135
Lintel, Carved Walnut Crest, Rococo Style, 2 Cherubs, 14 x 29 x 4½ In.	1112
Mailbox, Cast Iron, Blue, Red, White Lettering, U.S. Mail, c.1908, 25 x 17 x 10 In. *illus*	351
Mantel, Fireplace, Bronze, 3 Parts, Fluted Columns, 1900, 47¾ x 65 In. *illus*	2500
Mantel, Oak, Quartersawn, Mirror Top, Carved, Filigree, Squared Legs, 94 x 60 In.	1890
Mantel, Pine, Applied Molded Diamonds, Green, New England, Early 1800s, 51 x 45 x 6 In.	375
Mantel, Pine, Federal, Stepped, Pilasters, Carved Rosettes, c.1815, 64 x 87 x 10 In.	1750
Mantel, Pine, Gray & Black, Smoke Style, Painted, Dovetailed Foot Trim, 1910s, 63 x 64 In. *illus*	531
Mantel, Wood, Scrollwork, Hand Carved, Victorian, 49½ x 65 In.	369
Newel Post, Light, Wood, Gilt, Patina, Metal Shade, Whimsical, 28 In.	567
Obelisk, Marble, Pointed Top, Stone Accent, Square Pedestal Base, Late 1900s, 72½ In., Pair	1770
Ornament, Gilt Brass, Eagle, Spread Wings, Arrows, Talons, Olive Branch, Late 1800s, 12 In.	156
Ornament, Tole, Cattails, Painted, Brass, Rococo Style Base, France, c.1950, 10¼ In., Pair	944
Overmantel Mirror, Giltwood, Empire, Acorns, Rope, Pilasters, 2 Parts, 1830s, 36 x 23 In. *illus*	330
Overmantel Mirror, Giltwood, Sheraton, 3 Parts, c.1830, 26 x 60 In. *illus*	575
Overmantel Mirror, Louis XV Style, Giltwood, Carved, 1800s, 92 x 42 In.	6300
Overmantel Mirror, Rococo Revival Style, Giltwood, Scrollwork, c.1950, 48 In. *illus*	384
Overmantel Mirror, Urn Shape, Giltwood, Pediment, 32 x 53 In.	150
Overmantel Mirror, Walnut, Carved, Bronze Sconces, Provincial Style, France, 58 x 52 In.	472
Panel, Cast Iron, Knight's Helm, Plumes, Shield, Eagle Claws, Lions Rampant, 1800s, 31x 34 In.	531
Panel, Plaster, Madonna & Child, Angels, 3 Panels, Painted, Giltwood Frame, 15 x 11 In. *illus*	1230
Panel, Wood, Dragon, Sailing Ship, Carved, Painted, Japan, 1900s, 31 x 7 x 4 In. *illus*	406
Panel, Wood, Rectangular, Green Ground, Painted & Carved, 1800s, 24 x 42 In., Pair	480
Pedestal, Concrete, Spiraling Shape, White, 27 In.	141
Pedestal, Marble, Green, Rectangular Top, Circular Base, Doric Style, 42 x 19 In.	492
Pedestal, Oak, Square Top, Arts & Crafts, c.1920, 36 x 12 In.	55
Pedestal, Parcel Gilt, French Style, Circular Top, Platform Base, Late 1900s, 57¾ x 21 In.	148
Pedestal, Wood, Chelsea House, French Empire, Cream & Gold, 43 x 12 x 12 In.	625
Pedestal, Wood, Grape Press Screw, Round Base, France, 30¼ x 13¾ In.	266
Pedestal, Wood, Mahogany, Bronze Mounted, Continental, 1800s, 41 x 16½ In., Pair . *illus*	5625
Peg Rail, Pine, 5 Iron Hooks, Multicolor, Painted, Flowers, Continental, Late 1800s, 8 x 66 In.	439
Plaque, Plaster, Figure, Head Of Pan, Lower Body Of Lion, Late 1900s, 16 x 23 In.	177
Post Office, Box Holder, Wood, 33½ x 34 In.	124
Post Office Box, Wood Frame, 8 Doors, Combination Locks, McLane Mfg., Early 1900s, 47 In.	308
Post, Wrought Iron, Leaves Finial, Painted, Black, Scrollwork Panels, 1900s, 71 In., Pair	1062
Railing, Wrought Iron, Scrolls, Leaves & Flowers, 11 Sections, Early 1900s, 112 In.	2772
Railing, Wrought Iron, Scrollwork, White, 35¾ x 110 x 1 In.	406
Sconce, Bronze, Hexagonal, Glass Sides, Finial, Domed Base, Electric, 12 In., Pair	649
Sconce, Bronze, Pierced, Vertical, Cone Shape Candlelight, Jeweled, 83 x 8 x 5 In., Pair	2337
Screens are also listed in the Fireplace and Furniture categories.	
Shutters, 2 Hinged Panel Doors, Painted, Geometric Decor, Morocco, 1910s, 49 x 32½ In. *illus*	1003
Urn, Cast Iron, Campana Form, Leafy Rim, Palmettes, Pedestal Base, 32 x 35 In., Pair *illus*	590
Valance, Parcel Gilt, Louis XV Style, Painted, Red, Carved, Rocaille, Floral Crest, 13 x 66 In. *illus*	236
Valence, Mother-Of-Pearl, Fretwork Design, Inlay, Syria, c.1920, 22 x 60½ In.	281
Wall Bracket, Cast Iron, Eagle, On Branch, Swivel Mount, 1950s, 15 In., Pair	720

Wall Bracket, Eagle, Gold Gilded, Leaves, Floral, 12 ½ x 9 ½ x 7 ½ In., Pair .... *illus*	173
Wall Bracket, Giltwood, Eagle, Scroll Branch, Openwork Shelf, 1900s, 13 In., Pair	4613
Wall Bracket, Giltwood, Eagle, Shaped Shelf, Acorn Pendant, Early 1900s, 12 In., Pair *illus*	1750
Wall Bracket, Giltwood, Rococo, Mottled Pink, Gray Marble Top, 1730s, 19 x 30 x 16 In.	1134
Wall Bracket, Mahogany, Giltwood, Molded Top, Rope Twist, Leaves Pendant, c.1820, 11 In. .	384
Wall Bracket, Ram's Head, Carved, Plaster, Painted, 20 x 11 ½ In., Pair .... *illus*	125
Wall Bracket, Wrought Iron, Ornate, Flowers, Swirl, Slide-In Mounting Extension, 43 ½ x 36 In.	644

AREQUIPA POTTERY

Arequipa Pottery was produced from 1911 to 1918 by the patients of the Arequipa Sanatorium in Marin County, north of San Francisco. The patients were trained by Frederick Hurten Rhead, who had worked at Roseville Pottery.

Bowl, Strawberry Matte Glaze, Leaves Around Rim, Round Shoulders, c.1915, 3 ¼ x 6 ¼ In. *illus*	625
Tile, Landscape, Trees, Mountains, Cloud, Squeezebag, Earthenware, F.H. Rhead, 1912, 6 x 6 In. *illus*	9375
Vase, Mirror Black Glaze, Hand Carved, Dated, 1912, 4 ⅞ x 3 ½ In.	1680

ARGY-ROUSSEAU, *see G. Argy-Rousseau category.*

ARITA

Arita is a port in Japan. Porcelain was made there from about 1616. Many types of decorations were used, including the popular Imari designs, which are listed under Imari in this book.

Bowl, Landscape Scene, Flower Border, Blue, White, Signed, Aoki, c.1900, 9 ¾ In...................	62
Charger Center Flowers, Vine & Fern Border, Blue, White, c.1675, 22 In. Diam. ... . *illus*	2304
Charger, Reticulated Rim, Interlaced Circles, Peacock Center, Blue, White, c.1900, 13 In......	36
Charger, Veranda, House Interior, Crackle Ground, Blue, White, Edo Period, Japan, 12 In....	148
Dish, Delft Style, Blue, White, Rococo Shape, Cut Rim, 3-Footed, 18th Century, 1 ½ x 5 In....	219
Dish, Octagonal, Center Flowers, Birds, Bamboo, Geometric Border, Marked, c.1900, 11 ½ x 13 ⅛ In..	26
Ewer, Wine, Flowers, Blue, White, Silver Fitting On Spout, 17th Century, 7 ¼ x 5 ½ In.............	313
Jardiniere, Cranes, Flowers, Branches, Blue, White, Flared Lip, Wood Stand, c.1900, 14 In. ..	127
Statue, Bodhisattva, Lotus Headdress, Robe, Scroll, Blue, White, Late 1800s, 28 x 8 In............	1024
Tureen, Lid, Bowl Shape, Blue, White, Dragons, Flaming Pearls, 18th Century, 7 x 9 ½ In....	75

ART DECO

Art Deco, or Art Moderne, a style started at the Paris Exposition of 1925, is characterized by linear, geometric designs. All types of furniture and decorative arts, jewelry, book bindings, and even games were designed in this style. Additional items may be found in the Furniture category or in various glass and pottery categories, etc.

Ashtray, Clay, Nude Woman, Cast Metal Body, Albergo Continentale, c.1910, 11 In. ...... *illus*	144
Centerpiece, Spelter Figural Nymphs, Vase, Blue Glass, Rectangular, 9 ½ x 8 In. .... *illus*	288
Drawer Pull, Bakelite, Red, Rectangular, c.1940, 5 x ½ In., 8 Piece	39
Dresser Jar, Frosted Glass, Perfume Atomizer Base, Green Stain, Embossed, 5 ¼ x 1 ½ In....	50
Figurine, Dog, Scottie, Sitting, Bronze, Marble Base, 3 ¼ In..........	69
Figurine, Elephant, Standing, Whimsical Design, Painted, King Amusement Co., 17 ½ x 20 In.	1921
Figurine, Nude Woman, Running, Leaping Dolphins Base, Paul Manship, 23 In.	250
Figurine, Pheasant, Glass Beads, Wirework Frame, Lozenge Shape Base, 13 In., Pair .. *illus*	250
Garniture, Nude Women, Pagoda Center, 2 Chinese Scholar Lamps, c.1920, 15 x 8 x 6 In., 3 Piece	250
Jar, Lid, Serapis Wahliss, White Earthenware, Flowers, 9 ½ x 6 In. .... *illus*	1180
Sculpture, Nude Woman, Balancing On Ball, Metal, Rectangle Base, 7 ¼ x 6 In. .... *illus*	144
Sculpture, Sea Gull, Cast Metal, Black Metal Base, Painted, Signed, H. Lechesne, 18 x 26 In. .	156
Tray, Jazz, Painted Glass, Chrome-Plated Steel Border, Wood, 1 ⅜ x 12 x 19 In.	750

ART GLASS, *see Glass-Art category.*

Architectural, Wall Bracket, Ram's Head, Carved, Plaster, Painted, 20 x 11 ½ In., Pair
$125

Charlton Hall Auctions

Arequipa, Bowl, Strawberry Matte Glaze, Leaves Around Rim, Round Shoulders, c.1915, 3 ¼ x 6 ¼ In.
$625

California Historical Design

Arequipa, Tile, Landscape, Trees, Mountains, Cloud, Squeezebag, Earthenware, F.H. Rhead, 1912, 6 x 6 In.
$9,375

Rago Arts and Auction Center

Arita, Charger Center Flowers, Vine & Fern Border, Blue, White, c.1675, 22 In. Diam.
$2,304

Alex Cooper Auctioneers

Art Deco, Ashtray, Clay, Nude Woman, Cast Metal Body, Albergo Continentale, c.1910, 11 In.
$144

Blackwell Auctions

Art Deco, Centerpiece, Spelter Figural Nymphs, Vase, Blue Glass, Rectangular, 9 ½ x 8 In.
$288

Blackwell Auctions

Art Deco, Figurine, Pheasant, Glass Beads, Wirework Frame, Lozenge Shape Base, 13 In., Pair
$250

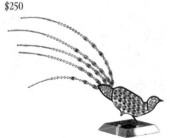

Charlton Hall Auctions

TIP
If you travel when it might snow at your house, have a neighbor run a car up the driveway and make footprints to the door. Untouched drifts in the drive show the house is empty.

ART NOUVEAU

Art Nouveau is a style of design that was at its most popular from 1895 to 1905. Famous designers, including Rene Lalique and Emile Galle, produced furniture, glass, silver, metalwork, and buildings in the new style. Ladies with long flowing hair and elongated bodies were among the more easily recognized design elements. Copies of this style are being made today. Many modern pieces of jewelry can be found. Additional Art Nouveau pieces may be found in Furniture or in various glass and porcelain categories.

Incense Burner, Nude, Frog Legs, Iron, Copper Bowl, Round Hammered Base, Vienna, 4 In. *illus*	185
Jardiniere, Peacock, Blue Bordered Rim, Painted, Marked, Galileo Chini, Firenze, 11 ¼ In. *illus*	1770
Jardiniere, Pottery, Multicolor, Glaze, Lion's Head Lug Handles, c.1900, 33 In.	469
Lamp, Figural, 2 Women, Standing, Green Shade, Rectangular Base, 9 In. *illus*	203
Lamp, Woman, Standing, Turning Vines, Spelter, Bronze, Signed, Moreau, 25 In.	369
Pitcher, Flowers, Leaves, Cut Glass, Silver Mount, Handle, Marked, Germany, 12 ½ In.	224
Sculpture, Woman, Standing, Floral Base, Patina White Metal, 15 In. *illus*	163
Vase, Figural, Pair Of Women, Flowing Gowns, Glass Insert, Metal, Patina, 1910s, 11 ¾ In. *illus*	439
Vase, Flowers, Woman, Marked, EW, Turn Wein, Austria, 17 ½ x 13 In.	200
Vase, Mixed Earth, Multicolor, Cream Ground, Pichon, c.1880, 14 ¼ In., Pair	256

ART POTTERY, *see Pottery-Art category.*

ARTS & CRAFTS

Arts & Crafts was a design style popular in American decorative arts from 1894 to 1923. In the 1970s collectors began to rediscover Mission furniture, art pottery, metalwork, linens, and light fixtures from this period. The interest has continued. Today everything from this era is collectible, including jewelry, graphics, and silverware. Additional items may be found in the Furniture category and other categories.

Humidor, Hinged Lid, Green Jade Plaque, Brass, Potter Studio, Early 1900s, 6 ¾ In.	1625
Lamp, Lantern Style, Hammered Brass, Slag Glass Insert, 8 ½ x 21 In., Pair	608

AURENE *pieces are listed in the Steuben category.*

AUSTRIA *is a collecting term that covers pieces made by a wide variety of factories. They are listed in this book in categories such as Royal Dux or Porcelain.*

AUTO

Auto parts and accessories are collectors' items today. Gas pump globes and license plates are part of this specialty. Prices are determined by age, rarity, and condition. Collectors say "porcelain sign" for enameled iron or steel signs. Packaging related to automobiles may also be found in the Advertising category. Lalique hood ornaments are listed in the Lalique category.

Can, Camel Motor Oil, 100 Percent Pure Pennsylvania, Endurance, Long Life, Camel, 5 Qt.	1845
Clock, Ford Sales & Service, Octagonal, Painted, Glass, Spinning Bezel, Neon Motion, 18 In. *illus*	861
Dispenser, Towel, Texaco, Fire Chief Gasoline, White Ground, Circular Base, 52 In.	384
Gas Pump Globe, Husky Gasoline, Dog, Sun Rays, White Ground, Gillco Body, 1940s, 13 ½ In.	5535
Gas Pump Globe, Red Crown Gasoline, White & Blue, 16 In.	86
Gas Pump, Texaco, Sky Chief, Red, Black Hose, 1940s, 79 In.	885
Hood Ornament, Rolls-Royce, Spirit Of Ecstasy, Gilt, Marble Plinth, Mid 1900s, 4 ½ In. *illus*	443
License Plate, 370-868, Pennsylvania, Orange, Metal, 1924 *illus*	28
License Plate Topper, Buckeye Beer, Picks You Up, Waiter, Tin Litho, 7 x 5 In. *illus*	543
Oil Can, Diamond, Tin, Brown, Embossed, Spout, Bail Handle, 1900s, 11 ¼ In.	128

Art Deco, Jar, Lid, Serapis Wahliss, White Earthenware, Flowers, 9 ½ x 6 In.
$1,180

Leland Little Auctions

Art Deco, Sculpture, Nude Woman, Balancing On Ball, Metal, Rectangle Base, 7 ¼ x 6 In.
$144

Blackwell Auctions

Art Nouveau, Incense Burner, Nude, Frog Legs, Iron, Copper Bowl, Round Hammered Base, Vienna, 4 In.
$185

Locati Auctions

Art Nouveau, Jardiniere, Peacock, Blue Bordered Rim, Painted, Marked, Galileo Chini, Firenze, 11 ¼ In.
$1,770

Bunch Auctions

Art Nouveau, Lamp, Figural, 2 Women, Standing, Green Shade, Rectangular Base, 9 In.
$203

Strawser Auction Group

Art Nouveau, Sculpture, Woman, Standing, Floral Base, Patina White Metal, 15 In.
$163

Pook & Pook

Art Nouveau, Vase, Figural, Pair Of Women, Flowing Gowns, Glass Insert, Metal, Patina, 1910s, 11 ¾ In.
$439

Jeffrey S. Evans & Associates

Auto, Clock, Ford Sales & Service. Octagonal, Painted, Glass, Spinning Bezel, Neon Motion, 18 In.
$861

Rich Penn Auctions

Auto, Hood Ornament, Rolls-Royce, Spirit Of Ecstasy, Gilt, Marble Plinth, Mid 1900s, 4 ½ In.
$443

Leland Little Auctions

23

Auto, License Plate, 370-868, Pennsylvania, Orange, Metal, 1924
$28

Auto, License Plate Topper, Buckeye Beer, Picks You Up, Waiter, Tin Litho, 7 x 5 In.
$543

AntiqueAdvertising.com

Auto, Sign, Atlantic Motor Oil, Logo, Red, Blue, White, Metal, 52 x 36 In.
$695

Auto, Sign, Esso, Happy Motoring, Yellow, White, Red, Porcelain, 7 x 12 In.
$106

Copake Auction

Auto, Sign, Ford Tractor, Porcelain, Red, Green & White Neon, 40 x 72 In.
$4,305

Morphy Auctions

Auto, Sign, Goodyear Tire & Battery Service, Die Cut, Embossed Tin, Marked, 1954, 30 x 30 In.
$995

Jeffrey S. Evans & Associates

Auto, Sign, Shell, Porcelain, Neon Lighting Around Edge, 2-Sided, 61 x 54 In.
$17,220

Morphy Auctions

Parking Meter, Red, Round Top, Coin-Operated. Circular Pedestal Base, 61 In.	324
Rack, Gulfpride Motor Oil, Porcelain, Metal Sign. 46 ½ x 21 ½ In.	500
Sign, Amoco, American Gas, Rectangular, Porcelain, 2-Sided, c.1950, 16 x 24 In.	819
Sign, Atlantic Motor Oil, Logo, Red, Blue, White, Metal, 52 x 36 In. *illus*	695
Sign, Authorized Studebaker Service, Round, Brown, Yellow, White, Walker & Co., Porcelain, 42 In.	5700
Sign, Auto, Phillips 66 Motor Oil, Orange Ground, Porcelain, 12 ½ x 16 In.	192
Sign, Bear Wheel & Alignment Balancing Service, Figural Bear, Neon Lighting, 19 x 26 In.	840
Sign, Bus Stop, Harmony, Painted, Black, White, Cast Iron, Pittsburgh, Pa., c.1912, 56 ¾ In.	1125
Sign, Esso, Happy Motoring, Yellow, White, Red, Porcelain, 7 x 12 In. *illus*	106
Sign, Ford Tractor, Porcelain, Red, Green & White Neon, 40 x 72 In. *illus*	4305
Sign, Ford, Genuine Parts, On Steel, Dark Blue Ground, White Text, Late 1900s, 18 x 24 In.	338
Sign, Goodyear Tire & Battery Service, Die Cut, Embossed Tin, Marked, 1954, 30 x 30 In. *illus*	995
Sign, Mobil, Red Pegasus Logo, Red, White, Blue, Marked SPS, Porcelain, 2-Sided, 1959, 30 x 59 In.	1476
Sign, Packard, Ask The Man Who Owns One, White, Blue, Walker & Co., Detroit, Porcelain, 24 x 55 In.	6765
Sign, Shell Gasoline, Enamel, Die Cut, Black, Orange, 1930, 25 x 24 In.	2770
Sign, Shell, Porcelain, Neon Lighting Around Edge, 2-Sided, 61 x 54 In. *illus*	17220
Sign, Texaco, Metal, White Ground, Red Star, Round, Porcelain, 2-Sided, 72 In.	1250
Sign, We Use Genuine Chevrolet Auto Parts, Bow Tie Logo, Flange, Tin, 19 x 18 In.	2160
Stop Sign, Pressed Metal, Green Ground, Reflectors, Yellow Border, Octagonal, 24 x 24 In. *illus*	523
Traffic Light, Yellow, 3 Lights, Control Box, 48 In.	584

AUTUMN LEAF

Autumn Leaf pattern china was made for the Jewel Tea Company beginning in 1933. Hall China Company of East Liverpool, Ohio, Crooksville China Company of Crooksville, Ohio, Harker Potteries of Chester, West Virginia, and Paden City Pottery, Paden City, West Virginia, made dishes with this design. Autumn Leaf has remained popular and was made by Hall China Company until 1978. Some other pieces in the Autumn Leaf pattern are still being made. For more prices, go to kovels.com.

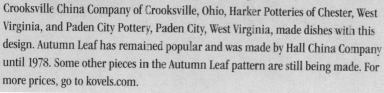

Casserole, Baker, Rayed, Round, No. 505, Hall's Superior Quality, 3 Pt., 2 ¾ x 7 ¾ In.	16
Coffeepot, Ribbed, 8 Cup, 9 In.	45
Mixing Bowl, Nesting, Set Of 3	75
Pitcher, Ball, Ice Lip, 7 x 8 ½ In.	32
Pitcher, Rayed, Gilt Trim, Marked, Hall's Superior Quality, 6 x 7 x 5 In.	25
Sugar & Creamer	22

AVON *bottles are listed in the Bottle category under Avon.*

AZALEA

Azalea dinnerware was made for Larkin Company customers from about 1915 to 1941. Larkin, the soap company, was in Buffalo, New York. The dishes were made by Noritake China Company of Japan. Each piece of the white china was decorated with pink azaleas.

Bowl, Grapefruit, Footed, 3 ⅝ x 4 ⅝ In.	180
Compote, Glass, Clear, Round, Painted Rim, Footed, Larkin Co., c.1930, 3 ½ x 10 In.	37
Cup & Saucer, Gold Trim, 2 x 3 ½ In.	12
Dish, Mayonnaise, Ladle, Underplate, Scalloped Rim, Red Flower Mark	153
Plate, Dinner, 9 ⅞ In.	25
Plate, Dinner, Green Mark, 1920s, 9 ¾ In , Pair	22
Plate, Luncheon, Square, Scalloped Edges, 7 ¾ In.	600
Platter, 8 ¾ x 11 ¾ In.	55
Serving Bowl, Cutout Side Handles, Gilt Trim, c.1920, 10 In.	15
Sugar & Creamer, Green Backstamp, c.1920	47
Sugar Shaker, Red Mark, 7 In.	30

Auto, Stop Sign, Pressed Metal, Green Ground, Reflectors, Yellow Border, Octagonal, 24 x 24 In.
$523

Hartzell's Auction Gallery Inc.

Baccarat, Bowl, Porcelain, Fruit, Flower, Leaves, Dolphin Fish Feet, Marked, c.1890, 7 x 16 In.
$469

Crescent City Auction Gallery

Baccarat, Bucket, Champagne, Maxim, Cut Glass, 2 Gilt Handles, Ribbed Shape, 9 ¼ In.
$531

Austin Auction Gallery

This is an edited listing of current prices. Visit **Kovels.com** to check thousands of prices from previous years and sign up for free information on trends, tips, reproductions, marks, and more.

Baccarat, Decanter, Ball Shape Lid, Clear
Bottom, Amberina Top, 9 In.
$106

Apple Tree Auction Center

Baccarat, Figurine, Poisson, Carp, Frosted,
Polished Accents, Marked, Late 1900s, 6¾ In.
$207

Leland Little Auctions

Baccarat, Lampshade, Gilt Stork, Frosted
Cranberry, Gilt Metal Top Ring, 6¾ x 7½ In.
$1,800

Woody Auction

Baccarat, Paperweight, Church Weight,
Millefiori, 12 Zodiac Canes, Date Cane, 1968,
3¼ In.
$960

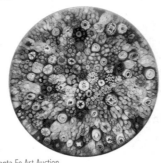

Santa Fe Art Auction

Baccarat, Paperweight, Concentric
Millefiori, Stardust Cane Outer Band, Green
Center, 1800s, 1⅞ In.
$234

Jeffrey S. Evans & Associates

Baccarat, Paperweight, Dog, Racing, Lying
Down, Glass, Rectangular Base, Signed,
1⅜ x 7¼ In.
$92

Blackwell Auctions

Baccarat, Paperweight, Millefiori, Spaced,
Central Butterfly Cane, Silhouette, Muslin
Ground, 1848, 2 In.
$1,287

Jeffrey S. Evans & Associates

Baccarat, Vase, Cranberry Overlay, Acid Cut,
Branch & Blossom, Gold Highlights,
9¾ x 4 In.
$250

Woody Auction

Baccarat, Vase, Gilt Bronze Mounted,
Pineapple Finials, Maiden Heads, Round
Base, 33 x 13 In., Pair
$1,750

Abington Auction Gallery

BACCARAT

Baccarat glass was made in France by La Compagnie des Cristalleries de Baccarat, located 150 miles from Paris. The factory was started in 1765. The firm went bankrupt and began operating again about 1822. Cane and millefiori paperweights were made during the 1845 to 1880 period. The firm is still working near Paris making paperweights and glasswares.

Bowl, Corail, Lobed, Cut Glass, Acid Etched, Marked, 7⅞ In.	105
Bowl, Porcelain, Fruit, Flower, Leaves, Dolphin Fish Feet, Marked, c.1890, 7 x 16 In. .... *illus*	469
Box, Piano Shape, Gilt Bronze Mount, Hinged Lid, Egg & Dart Trim, Tapered Feet, 4 x 6 In...	640
Bucket, Champagne, Maxim, Cut Glass, 2 Gilt Handles, Ribbed Shape, 9¼ In. ...... *illus*	531
Candlestick, Massena, Cut Glass, Curved Stem, Domed Base, 6¼ In., 5 Piece	384
Candlestick, Spiral Twist, Thick Polished Glass, Late 1900s, 6¼ In., Pair	118
Centerpiece, Empire Style Bronze Base, Paw Feet, Cut Glass, 18½ x 10 In.	461
Champagne Cooler, 8-Sided Body, Gilt Metal Handles, 9½ x 11¾ In.	275
Cocktail Shaker, Cut Glass, Silver Plate Cap, c.1945, 9¾ In.	1500
Cologne Bottle, Rose Teinte, Swirl Body, Stopper, 7 In.	50
Decanter, Ball Shape Lid, Clear Bottom, Amberina Top, 9 In. .... *illus*	106
Decanter, Louis XIII, Embossed, Fleur-De-Lis Stopper, Ruffled Sides, 11 In.	295
Decanter, Merillon, Etched Leafy Scrolls, Bulbous, Fan Stopper, 1946-61, 10 In., Pair	344
Decanter, Perfection, Clear Glass, Stopper, Ribbed, 9½ In., Pair	313
Decanter, Stopper, Acid Etched, Clear, Bulbous Rib, Round Base, Marked, 10½ In., Pair	153
Figurine, Cat, Lying Down, Molded, Crystal, Marked, Box, Late 1900s, France, 3 x 4½ In.	236
Figurine, Dog, Labrador Retriever, Standing, Black Crystal, Red Box, 5½ In.	153
Figurine, Falcon, Circular Logo, Signed, 10 In.	115
Figurine, Poisson, Carp, Frosted, Polished Accents, Marked, Late 1900s, 6¾ In. .... *illus*	207
Goblet, Massena, Cut Glass, Domed Base, 7⅜ In., 7 Piece	1298
Ice Bucket, Brass Handles, Signed, 7½ x 7½ In.	209
Lampshade, Gilt Stork, Frosted Cranberry, Gilt Metal Top Ring, 6¾ x 7½ In. .... *illus*	1800
Mustard, Lid, Underplate, Harcourt, Mid 1900s, 4½ In., Pair	266
Paperweight, Church Weight, Millefiori, 12 Zodiac Canes, Date Cane, 1968, 3¼ In. ... *illus*	960
Paperweight, Concentric Millefiori, Stardust Cane Outer Band, Green Center, 1800s, 1⅞ In. *illus*	234
Paperweight, Dog, Racing, Lying Down, Glass, Rectangular Base, Signed, 1⅜ x 7¼ In. *illus*	92
Paperweight, Millefiori, Ruffled Cane, Bands Of Multicolor Canes, Marked, 3¼ In.	5566
Paperweight, Millefiori, Spaced, Central Butterfly Cane, Silhouette, Muslin Ground, 1848, 2 In. *illus*	1287
Vase, Cranberry Overlay, Acid Cut, Branch & Blossom, Gold Highlights, 9¾ x 4 In. ...... *illus*	250
Vase, Edith Pattern, Cut Glass, Clear, Octagonal Shape, 7⅛ In.	313
Vase, Gilt Bronze Mounted, Pineapple Finials, Maiden Heads, Round Base, 33 x 13 In., Pair. *illus*	1750
Wine, Harcourt Empire, Cut Glass, Rhine Stems, Orange, Hexagonal Foot, 7½ In., 8 Piece ..	2006
Wine, Montaigne Optic, Red, Clear, Disc Foot, 7 In., 9 Piece	885

BADGES

Badges have been used since before the Civil War. Collectors search for examples of all types, including law enforcement and company identification badges. Well-known prison or law enforcement badges are most desirable. Most are made of nickel or brass. Many recent reproductions have been made.

Children Of American Revolution, Blue Ring, Eagle Holding Flag, Silver, Enamel, c.1910, 1 x ¾ In.	64
City Planning Department, Los Angeles, Goldtone, Blue Enamel, c.1930, 3 x 2 In.	204
GAR, Brass, Shield, 7th Infantry, Engraved, George H. Davis, Mounted, Frame, 6 x 7 In.	544
National Air Races, Cleveland, Silk Ribbon Attached, Committee & Executive, 1935, 2 x 4½ In., Pair	63
Police, Inauguration, Franklin D. Roosevelt, Silvered Metal Shield, 1937, 2¼ x 3 In.	4063
Rank, Embroidered, Dragon, Clouds, Peaches, Bats, Buddhist Crosses, Chinese, Frame, 1800s, 10 In.	1512
Security Officer, Walt Disney World, Logo In Center, 1970s, 3 x 2 In.	269
US Naval Academy, Class Of 1961, Rocket, Orbits, 14K Gold, ¾ x ¾ In.	160

Bank, Bear, Begging, Standing, Cast Iron, A.C. Williams, c.1910, 5⅜ In.
$69

Blackwell Auctions

Bank, Elephant, McKinley, Roosevelt, Cast Iron, Traces Of Gold Paint, 1900
$507

AntiqueAdvertising.com

Bank, Mechanical, Beehive, Registering, Nickel Finish, Embossed, 1890s
$270

Bertoia Auctions

Bank, Mechanical, Cowboy, Holding Tray, Please One Penny, Tin Litho, Keim Co., Germany, 1920s
$1,080

Bertoia Auctions

Bank, Mechanical, Elephant, Howdah, Jumbo, Man Pops Out, Enterprise Mfg., c.1880, 6 x 7 In.
$2,700

Morphy Auctions

Bank, Mechanical, Lion & 2 Monkeys, Cast Iron, Glass Eyes, Kyser & Rex, c.1883, 9½ x 9 In.
$702

Jeffrey S. Evans & Associates

Bank, Mechanical, Magician, Cast Iron, Paint, J. & E. Stevens, 1901, Base 7 x 4 In.
$1,534

Donley Auctions

Bank, Mechanical, Mary Roebling, Trenton Trust, 75th Anniversary, Cast Iron, Painted
$540

Bertoia Auctions

Bank, Mechanical, Mason, Cast Iron, Paint, Shepard Hardware, 1887, 7½ x 4 In.
$1,652

Donley Auctions

Bank, Mechanical, Organ Grinder & Bear, Cast Iron, Kyser & Rex, 5½ In.
$1,512

Fontaine's Auction Gallery

Bank, Mechanical, Owl, Turns Head, Glass Eyes, Cast Iron, J. & E. Stevens, c.1880, 7½ In.
$615

Rich Penn Auctions

Bank, Mechanical, Speaking Dog, Cast Iron, Paint, Shepard Hardware, 1885, Base 7¼ x 3 In.
$590

Donley Auctions

BANKS

Banks of metal have been made since 1868. There are still banks, mechanical banks, and registering banks (those that show the total money deposited on the face of the bank). Many old iron or tin banks have been reproduced since the 1950s in iron or plastic. Some old reproductions marked *Book of Knowledge, John Wright,* or *Capron* may be listed. Pottery, glass, and plastic banks are also listed here. Mickey Mouse and other Disneyana banks are listed in Disneyana.

Apple, Cast Iron, Green, Red, Leaves, Beetle, Marked, Kern, c.1885, 3 ¼ In.	572
Barrel, White City Puzzle Savings, Cart, Cast Iron, Late 1800s, 4 In.	192
Bear, Begging, Standing, Cast Iron, A.C. Williams, c.1910, 5 ⅜ In. *illus*	69
Building, Bank, Flat Iron Bank, Cast Iron, Triangular Form, Kenton Hardware, c.1920, 5 ¾ In.	270
Building, Bank, Home Savings, Arched Dormers, Cast Iron, Nickel Plate, 11 x 6 x 7 In.	431
Building, House, Chimney, Windows, Door, Cast Iron, 3 ¼ In.	25
Building, Independence Hall Tower, Cast Iron, Old Paint, Red, Brown, Late 1800s, 9 In.	516
Bulldog, Seated, Piggy, Brown, Black Collar, Rectangular Base, Cast Iron, 8 In.	81
Cash Register, Easy Saver, Buddy L, Nickels, Dimes, Quarters, Metal	20
Church, Gold, Painted, Steeple, 5 ¼ x 4 ¾ In.	148
Devil With 2 Faces, Cast Iron, Black Paint, A.C. Williams, c.1906, 4 ½ x 3 ¼ In.	313
Dog, Seated, Red Paint, Aluminum, 5 In.	37
Dog, Standing, Cast Iron, Black & White Paint, 9 ½ In.	81
Eagle, Perched, Open Wings, Nest, 2 Babies, Cast Iron, Marked, 1883, 6 x 8 x 4 In.	158
Elephant, McKinley, Roosevelt, Cast Iron, Traces Of Gold Paint, 1900 *illus*	507
Hall's Excelsior, Cashier, Painted, J. & E. Stevens, c.1869, 5 ¼ x 4 In.	720

Mechanical banks were first made about 1870. Any bank with moving parts is considered mechanical. The metal banks made before World War I are the most desirable. Copies and new designs of mechanical banks have been made in metal or plastic since the 1920s. The condition of the paint on the old banks is important. Worn paint can lower a price by 90 percent.

Mechanical, Beehive, Registering, Nickel Finish, Embossed, 1890s *illus*	270
Mechanical, Boy On Trapeze, Cast Iron, Painted, Red Pants, Blue Shirt, J. Barton Smith	4200
Mechanical, Boy Stealing Watermelon, Cast Iron, Kyser & Rex, c.1885, 5 x 6 ½ In.	3600
Mechanical, Butting Buffalo, Boy Climbs Up Tree Trunk, Cast Iron, Kyser & Rex, 8 x 3 In.	2460
Mechanical, Cash Register, 4 Keys, Bell, Coin Slots, Cast Iron, J. & E. Stevens, 6 x 4 In.	246
Mechanical, Cowboy, Holding Tray, Please One Penny, Tin Litho, Keim Co., Germany, 1920s *illus*	1080
Mechanical, Elephant, Howdah, Jumbo, Man Pops Out, Enterprise Mfg., c.1880, 6 x 7 In. *illus*	2700
Mechanical, Elephant, Walking, Cast Iron, Gold Paint, 4 ¾ In.	81
Mechanical, Frog, On Lattice Base, Pierced, Cast Iron, Painted, J. & E. Stevens, 4 In.	780
Mechanical, Lion & 2 Monkeys, Cast Iron, Glass Eyes, Kyser & Rex, c.1883, 9 ½ x 9 In. *illus*	702
Mechanical, Magician, Cast Iron, Paint, J. & E. Stevens, 1901, Base 7 x 4 In. *illus*	1534
Mechanical, Mary Roebling, Trenton Trust, 75th Anniversary, Cast Iron, Painted *illus*	540
Mechanical, Mason, Cast Iron, Paint, Shepard Hardware, 1887, 7 ½ x 4 In. *illus*	1652
Mechanical, Monkey & Parrot, Tin, Saalheimer & Strauss, 4 ½ x 2 x 6 In.	461
Mechanical, Organ Grinder & Bear, Cast Iron, Kyser & Rex, 5 ½ In. *illus*	1512
Mechanical, Owl, Turns Head, Glass Eyes, Cast Iron, J. & E. Stevens, c.1880, 7 ½ In. *illus*	615
Mechanical, Speaking Dog, Cast Iron, Paint, Shepard Hardware, 1885, Base 7 ¼ x 3 In. *illus*	590
Mechanical, Tammany, Brown Jacket, Gray Pants, Cast Iron, J. & E. Stevens, c.1873, 5 ¾ In.	188
Mechanical, Tiger, Sticks Out Tongue, Red Box Back, Tin, Saalheimer & Strauss, 5 ¼ In.	7200
Mechanical, Trick Dog, Cast Iron, Painted, Hubley, c.1925, Base 3 x 8 ¾ In. *illus*	384
Mechanical, Trick Dog, Clown, Dog Jumps Through Hoop, Cast Iron, Paint, Hubley, 1930s	500
Mechanical, Trick Dog, Dog Jumps Through Hoop, Cast Iron, Shepard Hardware, 3 x 8 ¾ In.	338
Mechanical, Trick Pony, Cast Iron, Shepard Hardware Co., c.1880, 7 ¾ In. *illus*	920
Mechanical, Uncle Sam, Coin Falls Into Bag, Shepard Hardware Co., c.1886, 11 ½ In.	527
Mechanical, Vending, Victoria, Spar-Automat, Tin Lithograph, Stollwerck, Germany, 11 In. *illus*	175
Safe, Globe, Tripod Base, Cast Iron, Kenton, c.1915, 5 In.	180
Safe, Shimer Toy Co., Cast Iron, Black, Gold, Old Homestead, 4 ¼ In.	388
Watch Me Grow Tall With Coins, Cylinder, Tin Lithograph, Man In Suit, Apex Novelty, 6 In.	23

Bank, Mechanical, Trick Dog, Cast Iron, Painted, Hubley, c.1925, Base 3 x 8 ¾ In. $384

Donley Auctions

Bank, Mechanical, Trick Pony, Cast Iron, Shepard Hardware Co., c.1880, 7 ¾ In. $920

Blackwell Auctions

Bank, Mechanical, Vending, Victoria, Spar-Automat, Tin Lithograph, Stollwerck, Germany, 11 In. $175

Pook & Pook

Barber, Cabinet, Shaving Mug, Oak, 2 Tiers, 49 Slots, Paneled Base, c.1915, 92 x 42 x 15 In.

$984

Rich Penn Auctions

Barber, Chair, Horse's Head, Wood, Carved, Painted, 1850s, 18 x 18 In.

$492

Rich Penn Auctions

Barber, Chair, Oak, Black Vinyl Upholstery, Adjustable, Iron Footrest, Archer Mfg. Co., 45 x 26 In.

$615

Rich Penn Auctions

Yellow Cab, Cast Iron, Black Trim, Nickel Driver, White Rubber Tires, Hubley, 8 x 3 x 3 In.... 832

BARBER

Barber collectibles range from the popular red and white striped pole that used to be found in front of every shop to the small scissors and tools of the trade. Barber chairs are wanted, especially the older models with elaborate iron trim.

Cabinet, Shaving Mug, Oak, 2 Tiers, 49 Slots, Paneled Base, c.1915, 92 x 42 x 15 In. ...... *illus* 984
Chair, Horse's Head, Brown, Light Green, Leather Seat, Emil J. Paidar, Chicago, c.1910, Child's 1375
Chair, Horse's Head, Wood, Carved, Painted, 1850s, 18 x 18 In. .... *illus* 492
Chair, Oak, Black Vinyl Upholstery, Adjustable, Iron Footrest, Archer Mfg. Co., 45 x 26 In. *illus* 615
Coat Rack, Aluminum, Walnut, White Enamel Iron, Brass Label, Koken, Early 1900s, 75 In. .. 384
Pole, 4 Sections, Red & White, Stripes, Globe Finial, Squared Base, Early 1800s, 91 In. *illus* 1599
Pole, Pine, Red, Blue, White, Cannonball Finial, Early 1900s, 60 ½ In.......................... 388
Pole, Silver Painted Ball Finials, Turned Red, White, Blue, Late 1800s, 29 ½ In. 1375
Pole, Swollen Midsection, Crisp Turnings, Gold Acorns, White, Red, Blue, 1800s, 36 In. 3616
Pole, Tapered Square Shape, Diamond Finial, Red, Blue Stripes, Cream, Late 1800s, 87 In. .. 1722
Pole, Turned Wood, Ball Finial, Red & White Stripes, Multicolor, Late 1800s, 70 In. 322
Pole, Turned Wood, Red Layers, White Paint, American, Late 1800s, 45 ½ In.......................... 330
Rack, Shaving Mug, 18 Slots, Pine, Scalloped Top, Spindled Front, Hooks, 20 x 35 In............ 338
Shaving Stand, Victorian, Copper, Cast Iron, Oak Mug Storage, Beveled Mirror, 38 x 13 ½ In. 584
Sign, Barber Shop, William Marvy Co., Porcelain, Flange, 2-Sided, c.1940, 12 x 24 In. . *illus* 369
Sterilizer, Nickel Plated, Copper & Brass, Globe, 4-Legged, 59 x 19 In. .... *illus* 1169

BAROMETER

Barometers are used to forecast the weather. Antique barometers with elaborate wooden cases and brass trim are the most desirable. Mercury column barometers are also popular with collectors. It is difficult to find someone to repair a broken one, so be sure your barometer is in working condition.

Aneroid, Thermometer, Clock, Roman Numerals, Wood, Carved, 26 In. 135
Angle, Charles Howorth, Mahogany, Pendulum, Paper Scales, Signed, Victorian, 39 x 27 In. 3625
Banjo, Hygrometer, Thermometer, F. Amadio, George III, Mahogany, Inlay, 1800s, 42 In...... 610
Banjo, Hygrometer, Thermometer, Mahogany, Convex Mirror, London, c.1850, 38 In. .. *illus* 118
Broken Pediment, P. Ortelli, Mahogany, George III, Eagle Finial, Inlaid, Signed, 1800s, 38 In. .*illus* 531
English, Glass Tubes, Printed Papers, Walnut Case, Late 1900s, 38 In............................. 236
Gimbal, J. Hicks, Brass & Steel, Wooden Case, London, 1800s, 35 ½ In......................... 767
Nautical, Brass, Stick Style, Ring Hanger, R.N. Desterrro, Lisbon, 37 In............................. 460
Stick, Dollond, William IV, Bird's-Eye Maple, Bowed Glass, c.1837, 38 In.......................... 4270
Stick, Gimbaled, Brass, Mahogany, Glass Tube, 1800s, 37 In. 1250
Stick, Oak, Bone Panels, Engraved, Wood Backboard, Marked, London, 1800s, 37 In...................... 688
Stick, Storm King, E.C. Spooner, Ebonized, Walnut, Boston, 41 In. 344
Thermometer, Mahogany, Airguide, 1900s, 30 In. 71
Thermometer, Oak Case, String Inlay, Dial, Mother-Of-Pearl Medallions, Arts & Crafts, 19 In.. 284
Thermometer, Sheraton, Mahogany, Beveled Glass, Inlay, 38 ½ x 10 In. 63
Wheel, Brass Frame & Dial, Wood Panel, Louis XV Style, Germany, 1900s, 33 In. 96
Wheel, J.D. Caris, Gateshead, Banjo Shape, Rosewood Case, Brass Bezel, c.1870, 39 x 12 In... 293
Wheel, P. Caminada, Mahogany, Inlaid Conch Shells, Silvered Dial, England, c.1810, 39 In... 315
Wheel, Thermometer, A. Ortolli, Mahogany, Convex Mirror, Marked, Oxford, 1810, 37 x 10 In. .... *illus* 322
Wheel, Thermometer, Mahogany, Marquetry, 1810s, 38 ½ In................................. 192
Wood, W. Hunold, Eilbeck, Carved, Horse Head Design, 19 In. .... *illus* 86

BASALT

Basalt is a special type of ceramic invented by Josiah Wedgwood in the eighteenth century. It is a fine-grained, unglazed stoneware. The most common type is black, but many other colors were made. It was made by many factories. Some pieces may be listed in the Wedgwood section.

Jar, Lid, Inverted Baluster Shape, Medallion, Gilt, Mounted As Lamp, 23 In., Pair.................. 1024

Barber, Pole, 4 Sections, Red & White, Stripes, Globe Finial, Squared Base, Early 1800s, 91 In.
$1,599

Rich Penn Auctions

Barber, Sign, Barber Shop, William Marvy Co., Porcelain, Flange, 2-Sided, c.1940, 12 x 24 In.
$369

Rich Penn Auctions

Barber, Sterilizer, Nickel Plated, Copper & Brass, Globe, 4-Legged, 59 x 19 In.
$1,169

Rich Penn Auctions

Barometer, Banjo, Hygrometer, Thermometer, Mahogany, Convex Mirror, London, c.1850, 38 In.
$118

Bunch Auctions

Barometer, Broken Pediment, P. Ortelli, Mahogany, George III, Eagle Finial, Inlaid, Signed, 1800s, 38 In.
$531

Charlton Hall Auctions

Barometer, Wheel, Thermometer, A. Ortolli, Mahogany, Convex Mirror, Marked, Oxford, 1810, 37 x 10 In.
$322

Jeffrey S. Evans & Associates

Barometer, Wood, W. Hunold, Eilbeck, Carved, Horse Head Design, 19 In.
$86

Apple Tree Auction Center

Basalt, Vase, Porphyry, Gilt Garland, Creamware, Black, Wedgwood & Bentley, 1700s, 9¼ In.
$688

Neal Auction Company

Basket, Armadillo Shell, Irregular Shape, Handle, 10½ In. $200

Pook & Pook

Basket, Bee Skep, Coil, Rye Straw, White Oak Splints, 1850s, 20 In. $468

Jeffrey S. Evans & Associates

Basket, Gathering, Splint, 2 Handles, New England, 1800s, 22 In. $238

Eldred's

Jug, Hinged Lid, Pewter, Enamel Flowers, Multicolor, England, 9 x 5 x 4 In., Pair	256
Rose Bowl, Victorian Pattern, Flowering Branches, Birds, Devonware Fieldings, 6½ In.	48
Teapot, Lid, Finial, Seated Figure, Oval, Straight-Sided, Draped Swags, England, 1800s, 11 In.	102
Vase, Neoclassical, Handles, Molded Leaves, Scrolls, Square Base, F. Gerbing, 1800s, 11 In., Pair	132
Vase, Porphyry, Gilt Garland, Creamware, Black, Wedgwood & Bentley, 1700s, 9¼ In. . *illus*	688
Vase, Spill, Flared, Raised Putto & Dolphin, Gilt Trim At Base, Unmarked, c.1800, 4 x 3½ In., Pair	45

BASEBALL *collectibles are in the Sports category. Baseball cards are listed under Baseball in the Card category.*

BASKET

Baskets of all types are popular with collectors. American Indian, Japanese, African, Nantucket, Shaker, and many other kinds of baskets may be found in other sections. Of course, baskets are still being made, so a collector must learn to judge the age and style of a basket to determine its value. Also see Purse.

Apple, Vertical Slats, Metal Bands, Old Blue Paint, 2 Bentwood Handles, New England, 19 In. .	395
Armadillo Shell, Irregular Shape, Handle, 10½ In. *illus*	200
Ash, Splint, Rectangular, 2 Bentwood Handles, Late 1800s, 8 x 22½ x 12½ In.	469
Bee Skep, Coil, Rye Straw, White Oak Splints, 1850s, 20 In. *illus*	468
Bee Skep, Cone Shape, Vine & Vertical Bentwood Stiles, Mud Packed Straw, Early 1900s, 24 In.	448
Bentwood, Graduated Hoops, Iron Straps, Turned Wood Handles, Hickory Base, c.1900, 16 x 26 In. .	138
Buttocks, Handle, Red Paint, Eye Of God, 1800s, 3½ x 4 x 3¾ In.	565
Buttocks, Hanging, Bent Hickory Handle, Blue Ground, Early 1900s, 12 x 7 x 12½ In.	161
Buttocks, Splint, Cane, Handle, 19 In.	37
Cheese, Splint, Hexagonal Weave, Late 19th Century, 6½ x 26 In.	469
Coiled, Rye Straw, Bulbous, Round Flattened Lid, Mid 1800s, 30 In.	178
Egg, Splint, White Oak, Kidney Shape, Handle, Shelton Sisters, Late 1800s, 6½ In.	1755
Feed, Split, Elongated Handle, Interior Bell, Late 1800s, 11 In.	125
Food, Bamboo, Lacquered, 2 Tiers, Brass Fittings, Meander Bands, Chinese, 17 x 14 x 9 In. .	125
Gathering, Flower, Split Cane, Green, Bentwood Handle, 16 x 19 x 38½ In.	115
Gathering, Splint, 2 Handles, New England, 1800s, 22 In. *illus*	238
Gathering, Splint, Wrapped Rim, Green, Brown Interior, 1800s, 15½ x 17 In.	138
Hops, Fold-Open Lid, Split Oak, c.1920, 21 x 44 In.	531
Ilala Palm & Wild Banana, Lid, Zulu, Phuzile Sibiya, South Africa, 25 In.	295
Key, Leather, Oval, Arched Handle, Wood Base, Mid 1800s, 5½ x 6½ x 4½ In.	472
Market, Stave Style, Splint, Swing Bentwood Handle, Wrapped Rim, 1850s, 15½ In.	234
Nantucket, Lid, Handle, Fruit & Leaves, Gilt, Marked, Harry A. Hilbert, 1998, 6½ In.	750
Nantucket, Lightship, Bentwood Swing Handle, John Boyer, Late 1900s, 3 x 6½ In.	563
Nantucket, Lightship, Circular Stave Style, Wrapped Rim, Davis Hall, c.1880, 11¼ In.	2574
Nantucket, Lightship, Oval, Carved Porpoise Plaque, Horn Peg, S. Gibbs, 10 x 7 In.	826
Nantucket, Lightship, Oval, Stave, Wrapped Rim, Swing Handle, Late 1800s, 9 x 4 x 9 In. *illus*	1521
Nantucket, Mitchell Ray, Round, Single Wrapped Rim, Label, 1910s, 12 x 13 In.	1134
Nantucket, Oval, Bentwood, Swing Handle, Davis Hall, 12 In.	1188
Nantucket, Oval, Swing Handle, Green, Fabric Lined Interior, Late 1800s, 11 In.	3250
Nantucket, Round, 2 Carved Handles, Turned Wood Base, Early 1900s, 4½ x 11 In.	688
Nantucket, Round, Heart Shape Handles, Signed, A.D.R., Massachusetts, 1900s, 5¼ In. *illus*	500
Nantucket, Round, Swing Handle, Brass Ears, 1900s, 6 x 6½ In.	531
Nantucket, Round, Whalebone Discs, Handle, Inlay, Signed, Herbert Sandsbury, 1954, 15½ In. *.illus*	875
Nantucket, Scrimshaw Design, Whaling Ship, Mike Kane, 1973, 8¼ In.	1638
Nantucket, Shallow, Bentwood Swing Handle, Early 1900s, 3 x 6½ In.	594
Nantucket, Swing Handle, Shaped Bentwood, Turned Mahogany Base, Early 1900s, 7 x 7½ In.	344
Rye Straw, Coil Feather, Lid, 2 Handles, Pa., 1800s, 30 x 20 In.	154
Splint, Bentwood, Swing Handle, Late 1800s, 3½ x 5 In.	360
Splint, Flared Oval Shape, Fixed Handle, White, Blue Rim, 1800s, 13 x 16 In.	875
Splint, Herb, Circular, Scalloped Rim, White Oak, Arched Handle, c.1915, 13½ In. *illus*	129
Splint, Hickory, Buttocks Shape, Bentwood Handle, Patina, Late 1800s, 14 x 16 x 19 In.	92
Splint, Stave, Circular, Arched Handle, Painted, Page Co., Late 1800s, 11½ In. *illus*	263

Basket, Nantucket, Lightship, Oval, Stave, Wrapped Rim, Swing Handle, Late 1800s, 9 x 4 x 9 In.
$1,521

Jeffrey S. Evans & Associates

Basket, Splint, Herb, Circular, Scalloped Rim, White Oak, Arched Handle, c.1915, 13½ In.
$129

Jeffrey S. Evans & Associates

Basket, Splint, White Oak, Wrapped Rim, Arched Handle, Shelton Sisters, Late 1800s, 6¾ In.
$878

Jeffrey S. Evans & Associates

Basket, Nantucket, Round, Heart Shape Handles, Signed, A.D.R., Massachusetts, 1900s, 5¼ In.
$500

Eldred's

Basket, Nantucket, Round, Whalebone Discs, Handle, Inlay, Signed, Herbert Sandsbury, 1954, 15½ In.
$875

Eldred's

Basket, Splint, Stave, Circular, Arched Handle, Painted, Page Co., Late 1800s, 11½ In.
$263

Jeffrey S. Evans & Associates

Basket, Splint, Stave, Wrapped Rim, Arched Handle, 1850s, 5¾ x 5½ In.
$410

Jeffrey S. Evans & Associates

Basket, Wood, Wire Mesh, Arching Handle, Red Paint, c.1800, 16½ x 16½ In.
$424

Soulis Auctions

Batchelder, Tile, Los Angeles Scenic, Tree, Road, House, Blue Sky, c.1915, 8 x 8 In., Pair
$1,625

California Historical Design

BASKET

Batman, Clock, Batman & Robin, Alarm, Talking, Janex Corp., 1974, 6¾ In.
$50

Selkirk Auctioneers & Appraisers

Batman, Comic Book, DC Comics Giant Batman Annual, First Collection Ever Published, 1961
$146

Matthew Bullock Auctioneers

Batman, Figure, Batman & Robin, Stone Base, Ron Lee, Warner Brothers, 8 x 4½ In.
$207

Austin Auction Gallery

Splint, Stave, Wrapped Rim, Arched Handle, 1850s, 5¾ x 5½ In. .... *illus*	410
Splint, White Oak, Wrapped Rim, Arched Handle, Shelton Sisters, Late 1800s, 6¾ In. .... *illus*	878
Split, Red Paint, Round, Upright Handle, Flat Base, New England, Late 19th Century, 16 x 13 In.	500
Wedding, Parcel Gilt, Applied, Dragon Handle, Red Lacquer, Wood, Chinese, 15 In., Pair......	177
Wedding, Wood, Handle, Red Lacquer, Parcel Gilt, Dragon, 15½ In., Pair..............................	354
Wicker, Round Woven, Bail Handle, Carved Wood Frame, 1900s, 9 In.	92
Wood, Wire Mesh, Arching Handle, Red Paint, c.1800, 16½ x 16½ In. .... *illus*	424

BATCHELDER

BATCHELDER LOS ANGELES

Batchelder products are made from California clay. Ernest Batchelder established a tile studio in Pasadena, California, in 1909. He went into partnership with Frederick Brown in 1912 and the company became Batchelder and Brown. In 1920 he built a larger factory with a new partner. The Batchelder-Wilson Company made all types of architectural tiles, garden pots, and bookends. The plant closed in 1932. In 1936 Batchelder opened Batchelder Ceramics, also in Pasadena, and made bowls, vases, and earthenware pots. He retired in 1951 and died in 1957. Pieces are marked *Batchelder Pasadena* or *Batchelder Los Angeles*.

Bookends, Sleepy Reader, Brown Glaze, Unsigned, c.1915, 4¼ x 4½ In.....................................	450
Tile, Hexagonal, 3 Raised Trefoils, Blue Ground, Terra Cotta, Stamped, 1920s, 3½ In., 3 Piece...	148
Tile, Los Angeles Scenic, Tree, Road, House, Blue Sky, c.1915, 8 x 8 In., Pair .... *illus*	1625
Tile, Rooster, Blue Ground, Signed, c.1920, 2⅞ In.	180
Wall Pocket, 3-Sided, Red Exterior, Incised Triangle, Turquoise Interior, 1920s, 4 x 3½ In.	225

BATMAN

Batman and Robin are characters from a comic book created by Bob Kane. Batman first appeared in a 1939 issue of *Detective Comics*. The first Batman comic book was published in 1940. In 1966, the characters became part of a popular television series. There have been radio and movie serials that featured the pair. The first full-length movie was made in 1989.

Clock, Batman & Robin, Alarm, Talking, Janex Corp., 1974, 6¾ In. .... *illus*	50
Comic Book, DC Comics Giant Batman Annual, First Collection Ever Published, 1961 *illus*	146
Figure Molds, Batman, Batgirl, Robin, Resin, c.1970, 5¾ x 3 x 1¾ In., 3 Piece	288
Figure, Batman & Robin, Stone Base, Ron Lee, Warner Brothers, 8 x 4½ In. .... *illus*	207
Hat, Attached Eye Mask, Black, Yellow Batman Patch, Arlington, 1966, 9 In............................	77
Illustration, Dark Knight, Pen & Marker, Signed, Dated, Frame, 1989, 12 x 9 In....................	120
Poster, Adam West, Dobritch International Circus, Red, Yellow, Blue, 1967, 32½ x 47 In.	2500
Toy, Batzooka Pop Gun, Plastic, Scope Sight, 4 Targets, Box, Lone Star, 1966, 16 In..............	390

BAUER

Bauer pottery is a California-made ware. J.A. Bauer bought Paducah Pottery in Paducah, Kentucky, in 1885. He moved the pottery to Los Angeles, California, in 1910. The company made art pottery after 1912 and introduced dinnerware marked *Bauer* in 1930. The factory went out of business in 1962 and the molds were destroyed. Since 1998, a new company, Bauer Pottery Company of Los Angeles, has been making Bauer pottery using molds made from original Bauer pieces. The pottery is now made in Highland, California. Pieces are marked *Bauer Pottery Company of Los Angeles*. Original pieces of Bauer pottery are listed here. See also the Russel Wright category.

Oil Jar, Blue, Rolled Rim, 23 x 16 In., Pair .... *illus*	4375
Oil Jar, White, Rolled Rim, 16 x 12 In..	1000
Vase, Orange, Twisted Side Handles, Flared Rim, 3 Horizontal Rings, Matt Carlton, c.1930, 7½ x 6 In.	50

BAVARIA

Bavaria is a region in Europe where many types of porcelain were made.
In the nineteenth century, the mark often included the word *Bavaria*. After 1871,
the words *Bavaria, Germany*, were used. Listed here are pieces that include the
name *Bavaria* in some form, but major porcelain makers, such as Rosenthal, are
listed in their own categories.

Cup & Saucer, Black, Gold, Flowers, Tripod Feet, Marked, Mitterteich .... *illus*	80
Figurine, Boy Playing Flute, 2 Goats, Blue, White, Oval Base, Gerold, 20th Century, 6¾ In. .	13
Figurine, Woman, Seated, 18th Century Dress, Blue, Fan, Gilt Trim, Alka Kunst Kronach, 1900s, 4½ In.	25
Plate, Fairies, Medallion, Leaves, Painted, Gilt Rim, Marked, JKW Carlsbad, 11 In.	81
Platter, Medallions & Corners, Woman, Flowers, Green Ground, Rectangular, Mitterteich, 14 In.	37
Serving Plate, Round, Brown To White, Pink Roses, Cutout Handles, Marked, Z.S. & Co., 1910s, 10 In.	10

BEADED BAGS *are included in the Purse category.*

BEATLES

Beatles collectors search for any items picturing the four members of the
famous music group or any of their recordings. The condition is very important and top prices are paid for items in mint condition. The Beatles first
appeared on American network television in 1964. The group disbanded in 1971.
Ringo Starr and Paul McCartney are still performing. John Lennon died in 1980.
George Harrison died in 2001.

Album, Help!, Soundtrack From The Movie, Vinyl LP, 33⅓, c.1965	50
Phonograph, 4 Speeds, Tan Case, Portraits, Portadyne UK, 1964, 11 x 14 In.	2125
Poster, Concert, Candlestick Park, 1966, Psychedelic, Yin Yang, W. Wilson, 24 x 17 In.	7188
Poster, Concert, London Palladium, Royal Command Performance, 1963, 40 x 25 In............	3125
Puzzle, Beatles Lyrics Illustrated Puzzle, Poster, 800 Pieces, UK, 1970, 12 x 22 In. ...... *illus*	134
Tin, Talcum Powder, Images Of All 4 Beatles, Lithograph, Contents, 1960s, 7 x 4 x 2 In. *illus*	307
Toy, Drum Set, Ringo Starr, Snare With Ringo's Face, Tripod, Drumsticks, Box, Selcol UK, 1964	3250
Toy, Yellow Submarine, Metal, Painted, Hatches Open, 4 Beatles Inside, Corgi, c.1968, 5 In.....	90

BEEHIVE

Beehive, Austria, or Beehive, Vienna, are terms used in English-speaking countries to
refer to the many types of decorated porcelain bearing a mark that looks like a beehive.
The mark is actually a shield, viewed upside down. It was first used in 1744 by the Royal
Porcelain Manufactory of Vienna. The firm made what collectors call Royal Vienna
porcelains until it closed in 1864. Many other German, Austrian, and Japanese factories
have reproduced Royal Vienna wares, complete with the original shield or beehive mark.
This listing includes the expensive, original Royal Vienna porcelains and many other
types of beehive porcelain. The Royal Vienna pieces include that name in the description.

Imperial and Royal Porcelain Manufactory Vienna, Austria 1749–1827	Bourdois & Bloch Paris, France c.1900	Waechtersbach Earthenware Factory Schlierbach, Hesse, Germany 1921–1928

Charger, Prussian Queen Louise, Standing, White Dress, Pastel Blue, Pink Panels, 14 In. *illus*	1230
Cup & Saucer, Yellow, Orange, Classic Medallion Scene, Gold Stencil, Marked, Boucher.......	80
Jar, Lid, Classical Figural Scene, Geometric Field, Royal Vienna, Late 1800s, 14 In., Pair	59
Plaque, Women At Fountain, Filling Jugs, Hand Painted, Royal Vienna, 5 x 7 In. .... *illus*	156

Bauer, Oil Jar, Blue, Rolled Rim,
23 x 16 In., Pair
$4,375

Crescent City Auction Gallery

Bavaria, Cup & Saucer, Black, Gold,
Flowers, Tripod Feet, Marked, Mitterteich
$80

Woody Auction

Beatles, Puzzle, Beatles Lyrics
Illustrated Puzzle, Poster, 800 Pieces,
UK, 1970, 12 x 22 In.
$134

Heritage Auctions

TIP

*To make a reproduc-
tion box for a jigsaw
puzzle, assemble the
puzzle, scan it into
a computer or copy
it on a color copier,
then paste it on a
suitable box.*

Beatles, Tin, Talcum Powder, Images Of All 4 Beatles, Lithograph, Contents, 1960s, 7 x 4 x 2 In.
$307

AntiqueAdvertising.com

Beehive, Charger, Prussian Queen Louise, Standing, White Dress, Pastel Blue, Pink Panels, 14 In.
$1,230

Alderfer Auction Company

Beehive, Plaque, Women At Fountain, Filling Jugs, Hand Painted, Royal Vienna, 5 x 7 In.
$156

Fox Auctions

Beehive, Plate, Painted, Nude Women, Gold Enamel Highlights, Royal Vienna, Frame, 9 ½ In.
$567

Fontaine's Auction Gallery

Beehive, Plate, Portrait Of Young Woman, Maroon Border, Gold Stencil, 9 ¼ In.
$50

Woody Auction

> **TIP**
> Billy Beer cans are not worth hundreds of dollars even though this myth appears in newspapers.

Beehive, Plate, Woman, Long Hair, Garden Scene, Hand Painted, Royal Vienna, 9 ½ In.
$660

Fox Auctions

Beehive, Vase, Iridescent Lavender Ground, Oval Medallion, Woman, Handles, Signed, Wagner, 16 x 5 In.
$1,400

Woody Auction

Beer Can, Gilt Edge Premium Beer, Pull Top, Yellow & Black Ground, 1967, 12 Oz.
$55

meatstout on eBay

Beer Can, Oertels '92 Lager Beer, Cone Top, Red, Blue, 12 Oz.
$81

ballchip on eBay

Plate, 6 Fish, Gilt Rim, Green Ground, Royal Vienna, 9 1/2 In.	51
Plate, Fruhling, Spring, Woman, Cherub, Maroon Border, Gilt, Signed, Heer, 9 1/2 In.	200
Plate, Garden Scene, Acanthus & Scrollwork Frame, Royal Vienna, 17 1/2 In., Pair	189
Plate, Mythological, Gilt, Raspberry Border, Painted, Signed, 1800s, 8 In., Pair	313
Plate, Painted, Nude Women, Gold Enamel Highlights, Royal Vienna, Frame, 9 1/2 In. .. illus	567
Plate, Portrait Of Young Woman, Maroon Border, Gold Stencil, 9 1/4 In. .... illus	50
Plate, Smoker, Man, Lighting Pipe, Mounted, Giltwood Frame, Royal Vienna, 17 x 14 In.	311
Plate, Woman, Cupid Sitting On Her Lap, Gilt, Maroon Border, Royal Vienna, 9 1/2 In.	189
Plate, Woman, Long Hair, Garden Scene, Hand Painted, Royal Vienna, 9 1/2 In. .... illus	660
Plate, Woman, Standing, Holding Sheaf Of Wheat, Gilt, Signed, Wagner, 9 1/2 In.	523
Vase, Iridescent Lavender Ground, Oval Medallion, Woman, Handles, Signed, Wagner, 16 x 5 In. .illus	1400
Vase, Portrait, Woman, Basket, Flowers, Gilt, Enamel, Red Ground, Royal Vienna, 10 1/4 In. ..	1764
Vase, Ruth, Woman, Standing, Maroon Ground, Gilt, Wagner, Royal Vienna, 15 3/4 In.	1197
Vase, Women, Animals, Cherubs, Urn, Pedestal, Royal Vienna, 7 x 3 1/2 x 3 1/2 In.	81

BEER CAN

Beer cans are a twentieth-century idea. Beer was sold in kegs or returnable bottles until 1934. The first patent for a can was issued to the American Can Company in September of that year, and Gotfried Kruger Brewing Company, Newark, New Jersey, was the first to use the can. The cone-top can was first made in 1935, the aluminum pop-top in 1962. Collectors should look for cans in good condition, with no dents or rust. Serious collectors prefer cans that have been opened from the bottom.

Bob's Special Beer, Pull Top, August Schell, Minn., c.1980, 12 Oz.	3
Budweiser Lager Beer, Flat Top, Opening Instructions, Anheuser-Busch, 12 Oz.	92
Burkhardt's Diamond Jubilee Beer, Flat Top, Akron, Oh., 1955, 12 Oz.	40
Fitzgerald's Garryowen Ale, Cone Top, 12 Oz.	1225
Gilt Edge Premium Beer, Pull Top, Yellow & Black Ground, 1967, 12 Oz. .... illus	55
Oertels '92 Lager Beer, Cone Top, Red, Blue, 12 Oz. .... illus	81
Pabst Blue Ribbon, Cone Top, Snap-Cap, Milwaukee, Wis., Qt.	200
Reserve Beer, Flat Top, Birdwatcher, Peter Hand Brewing Co., Chicago, c.1950, 12 Oz.	244
Stroh's Bohemian Style Beer, Pull Tab, Detroit, Mich., 16 Oz.	6
Stroh's Bohemian Style Beer, Flat Top, Keglined, Detroit, Mich., 1960s, 12 Oz. .... illus	32
Topper Genuine Draught, Mini Keg, Standard Rochester Brewing Co., 1960s, Gal.	32

BELL

Bell collectors collect all types of bells. Favorites include glass bells, figural bells, school bells, and cowbells. Bells have been made of porcelain, china, or metal through the centuries.

Brass, Wrought Iron, Hanging Arm, Late 1800s, 16 x 10 In. .... illus	308
Bronze, Horizontal Mounting Bar, Looped Pull Rod, Patina, Early 1800s, 11 x 10 3/4 x 13 In. ..illus	610
Church, Cast Iron, Mounted On Church Pew, 1900, 41 x 29 x 26 In.	250
Figure, Baka, Brass Mask, Wire Wrapped Neck, Wood Mallet, Stand, Cameroon, 27 1/2 x 8 In. ..	354
Gong, Brass, Circular, Mallet, Wood Stand, Asian, 18 1/4 x 17 3/4 In. .... illus	37
Gong, Dinner, Arts & Crafts, Cane Handle Mallet, Brass Stand, Copper, 11 x 16 In. .... illus	781
Gong, Dinner, Tabletop, Brass, Striking Mallet, Oak Frame, Bun Feet, Early 1900s, 17 x 11 In.	325
Gong, Temple, Metal, Deities, Demons, Gilt, Lacquer, Thailand, 16 1/2 In.	384
Hand, Free-Blown, Marbrie Loop, Cranberry Bowl, Clear Handle, Late 1800s, 15 x 6 In. illus	59
Ringer, Doorbell, Iron, Figure In Ecclesiastical Dress, Arm Rings Bell, Pull Chain, c.1915, 30 In.	590
School, Brass, Ebony Wood Handle, Ball Finial, 10 x 4 1/2 In.	30
Sleigh, 25 Graduated Bells, Brass, Black Leather Strap .... illus	172
Sleigh, 30 Graduated Metal Bells, Leather Strap, 80 In.	138
Temple, Bronze, Wood, Metal Stand, Chinese, 15 1/2 x 10 1/2 x 5 1/2 In.	250

Beer Can, Stroh's Bohemian Style Beer, Flat Top, Keglined, Detroit, Mich., 1960s, 12 Oz.
$32

quickbuild1914 on eBay

Bell, Brass, Wrought Iron, Hanging Arm, Late 1800s, 16 x 10 In.
$308

Locati Auctions

Bell, Bronze, Horizontal Mounting Bar, Looped Pull Rod, Patina, Early 1800s, 11 x 10 3/4 x 13 In.
$610

Neal Auction Company

B

Bell, Gong, Brass, Circular, Mallet, Wood Stand, Asian, 18 1/4 x 17 3/4 In. $37

Hartzell's Auction Gallery Inc.

Bell, Gong, Dinner, Arts & Crafts, Cane Handle Mallet, Brass Stand, Copper, 11 x 16 In. $781

Treadway

Bell, Hand, Free-Blown, Marbrie Loop, Cranberry Bowl, Clear Handle, Late 1800s, 15 x 6 In. $59

Jeffrey S. Evans & Associates

BELLEEK

Belleek china was made in Ireland, other European countries, and the United States. The glaze is creamy yellow and appears wet. The first Belleek was made in 1857 in the village of Belleek, County Fermanagh, in what is now Northern Ireland. In 1884 the name of the company became the Belleek Pottery Works Company Ltd. The mark changed through the years. The first mark, black, dates from 1863 to 1891. The second mark, black, dates from 1891 to 1926 and includes the words *Co. Fermanagh, Ireland*. The third mark, black, dates from 1926 to 1946 and has the words *Deanta in Eireann*. The fourth mark, same as the third mark but green, dates from 1946 to 1955. The fifth mark (second green mark) dates from 1955 to 1965 and has an *R* in a circle added in the upper right. The sixth mark (third green mark) dates from 1965 to 1981 and the words *Co. Fermanagh* have been omitted. The seventh mark, gold, was used from 1981 to 1992 and omits the words *Deanta in Eireann*. The eighth mark, used from 1993 to 1996, is similar to the second mark but is printed in blue. The ninth mark, blue, includes the words *Est. 1857*, and the words *Co. Fermanagh Ireland* are omitted. The tenth mark, black, is similar to the ninth mark but includes the words *Millennium 2000* and *Ireland*. It was used only in 2000. The eleventh mark, similar to the millennium mark but green, was introduced in 2001. The twelfth mark, black, is similar to the eleventh mark but has a banner above the mark with the words *Celebrating 150 Years*. It was used in 2007. The thirteenth trademark, used from 2008 to 2010, is similar to the twelfth but is brown and has no banner. The fourteenth mark, the Classic Belleek trademark, is similar to the twelfth but includes Belleek's website address. The Belleek Living trademark was introduced in 2010 and is used on items from that giftware line. All pieces listed here are Irish Belleek. The word *Belleek* is now used only on pieces made in Ireland even though earlier pieces from other countries were sometimes marked *Belleek*. These early pieces are listed in this book by manufacturer, such as Ceramic Art Co., Lenox, Ott & Brewer, and Willets.

Belleek Pottery Co. 1863–1891	Ceramic Art Co. 1894–1906	Willets Manufacturing Co. 1879–1912+

Basket, Lid, 4 Strand, Multicolor, Flowers, Openwork, 2 Pad, Marked, 5 1/4 x 7 x 9 In. ... *illus*	259
Cup & Saucer, Nautilus, 13th Brown Mark..	40
Ice Pail, Lid, Prince Of Wales, Gold Brown, Marked, Ireland, 1900s, 19 In. .... *illus*	750
Pitcher, Mask, Garland Low Relief, White, Stylized Handle, Footed, 1800s, 6 x 5 x 6 In.........	123
Vase, Water Lily, Painted, Green Ground, Gilt, Ruffled Rim, 14 In..	283

BENNINGTON

Bennington ware was the product of two factories working in Bennington, Vermont. Both the Norton Company and Lyman Fenton & Company were out of business by 1896. The wares include brown and yellow mottled pottery, Parian, scroddled ware, stoneware, graniteware, yellowware, and Staffordshire-type vases. The name is also a generic term for mottled brownware of the type made in Bennington.

Bottle, Coachman, Brown & Cream Glaze, Flint Enamel, Fenton & Co., 1849, 10 3/4 In. *illus*	354
Creamer, Rockingham Glaze, Flint, Banded Neck, Scalloped Rim, Octagonal, 1849, 6 1/4 In.	1053
Crock, Cobalt Blue Design, Black Shade, Wood Base, Stoneware, Converted To Lamp, 24 In..	177
Doorstop, Dog, Spaniel, Brown Glaze, Rockingham, 11 In..	107
Pitcher, Scroddled Ware, Marbled Brown & Cream, Octagonal, 1853, 12 1/2 In. .... *illus*	1638

Bell, Sleigh, 25 Graduated Bells, Brass, Black Leather Strap
$172

Belleek, Basket, Lid, 4 Strand, Multicolor, Flowers, Openwork, 2 Pad, Marked, 5 ¼ x 7 x 9 In.
$259

Belleek, Ice Pail, Lid, Prince Of Wales, Gold Brown, Marked, Ireland, 1900s, 19 In.
$750

Bennington, Bottle, Coachman, Brown & Cream Glaze, Flint Enamel, Fenton & Co., 1849, 10 ¾ In.
$354

Bennington, Pitcher, Scroddled Ware, Marbled Brown & Cream, Octagonal, 1853, 12 ½ In.
$1,638

Berlin, Vase, Lid, Pastoral Scenes, Ram's Head Handles, Footed, c.1820, 14 In., Pair
$2,400

Beswick, Figurine, Beatrix Potter, Old Mr. Brown, Owl, Squirrel, Hand Painted, 20th Century, 3 ¼ In.
$75

Bicycle, Schwinn, Tandem, Red Frame, Black Leather Seats, Chromed Steel Fenders, 1950s, 39 x 90 In.
$443

Bicycle, Tricycle, Auto Wheel, Spring Seat, Red & Cream, Coaster Co., c.1935, 19 x 26 In.
$82

Jeffrey S. Evans & Associates

Bicycle, Tricycle, Velocipede, John Bull Grips, Klaxon Horn & Fender, c.1939, 36 x 19 x 40 In.
$554

Rich Penn Auctions

Bicycle, Whizzer, Motorbike, Schwinn Frame, Painted, 1948, 26 In.
$2,950

Apple Tree Auction Center

TIP

When you see or buy a new treasure, take a picture with your phone; write down when and where you got it and the price and any marks or history.

Sugar, Lid, Mottled Brown Glaze, 8-Sided, Lyman, Fenton & Co., Vt., c.1850, 9 In. 1750

BERLIN

Berlin, a German porcelain factory, was started in 1751 by Wilhelm Kaspar Wegely. In 1763, the factory was taken over by Frederick the Great and became the Royal Berlin Porcelain Manufactory. It is still in operation today. Pieces have been marked in a variety of ways.

Tureen, Lid, Kneeling Woman Finial, Flowers, Handles, Blue Scepter Mark, 11 ½ x 15 In...... 640
Vase, Lid, Pastoral Scenes, Ram's Head Handles, Footed, c.1820, 14 In., Pair .... *illus* 2400

BESWICK

Beswick started making pottery in Staffordshire, England, in 1894. The pottery became John Beswick Ltd. in 1936. The company became part of Royal Doulton Tableware, Ltd. in 1969. Production ceased in 2002 and the John Beswick brand was bought by Dartington Crystal in 2004. Figurines, vases, and other items are being made and use the name Beswick. Beatrix Potter figures were made from 1948 until 2002. They shouldn't be confused with Bunnykins, which were made by Royal Doulton.

Figurine, Beatrix Potter, Old Mr. Brown, Owl, Squirrel, Hand Painted, 20th Century, 3 ¼ In.....*illus* 75
Plaque, Christmas In Mexico, Multicolor Scene, Square, Box, 1970s, 8 ¼ In. 6
Teapot, Figural, Cat, Persian, Gray, Front Paw Raised, Removable Head.................................. 50

BETTY BOOP

Betty Boop, the cartoon figure, first appeared on the screen in 1930. Her face was modeled after the famous singer Helen Kane and her body after Mae West. In 1935, a comic strip was started. Her dog was named Pudgy. Although the Betty Boop cartoons ended by 1938, there was a revival of interest in the Betty Boop image in the 1980s and new pieces are being made.

Doll Quilt, Geometric Border, Jaymar Specialty Co., 1930s, 12 x 15 In.................................... 58
Doll, Ceramic, Jointed, Black Dress, Painted, 9 In. 100
Doll, Devil Betty, Cotton Stuffed, 1999, 20 In. 29
Nodder, Celluloid, Pink Dress, Rubber Band Drive, Tin Base, Japan, 1930s, 7 In. 210
Toy, Acrobat, Celluloid, Metal Frame, Windup, Fleischer Studios, Box, Japan, 1930s, 9 In....... 425

BICYCLE

Bicycles were invented in 1839. The first manufactured bicycle was made in 1861. Special ladies' bicycles were made after 1874. The modern safety bicycle was not produced until 1885. Collectors search for all types of bicycles and tricycles. Bicycle-related items are also listed here. Many posters have been reproduced.

Model, Velocipede, Tricycle, Wood, Cast Iron, 17 ½ In. 31
Schwinn, Motorbike, Whizzer, Spring Leather Seat, Kick Stand, Red, 37 x 72 x 27 In. 2000
Schwinn, Tandem, Red Frame, Black Leather Seats, Chromed Steel Fenders, 1950s, 39 x 90 In. ...*illus* 443
Tricycle, Auto Wheel, Spring Seat, Red & Cream, Coaster Co., c.1935, 19 x 26 In. .... *illus* 82
Tricycle, Boneshaker, Wood Spokes, Hub, Iron Frame, Rim, Saddle Seat, 1876, 32 x 18 x 45 In.. 565
Tricycle, Velocipede, John Bull Grips, Klaxon Horn & Fender, c.1939, 36 x 19 x 40 In. .. *illus* 554
Tricycle, Wheels, Banana Grip, Painted, Child's, c.1930 118
Velocipede, Figural Horse, Running, Leather Saddle, 1980s, 32 x 30 In. 105
Whizzer, Motorbike, Schwinn Frame, Painted, 1948, 26 In. .... *illus* 2950

BING & GRONDAHL

Bing & Grondahl is a famous Danish factory making fine porcelains from 1853 to the present. Underglaze blue decoration was started in 1886. The annual Christmas plate series was introduced in 1895. Dinnerware, stoneware, and other ceramics are still being made today. The figurines remain popular. The firm has used the initials *B & G* and a stylized castle as part of the mark since 1898. The company became part of Royal Copenhagen in 1987.

B. & G.	B&G	B&G
Bing & Grondahl 1895+	Bing & Grondahl 1915+	Bing & Grondahl 1983+

Cake Plate, Butterflies, Blue & White, Pedestal, 9 x 5 In.	125
Figurine, Boy Playing With Blocks, 4 In.	50
Group, Shepherdess, Sheep, Blue Dress, c.1950s, 10 In.	175
Plate, Christmas In Greenland, 1972, 7 1/4 In.	15

BINOCULARS

Binoculars of all types are wanted by collectors. Those made in the eighteenth and nineteenth centuries are favored by serious collectors. The small, attractive binoculars called opera glasses are listed in their own category.

Carl Zeiss, 7x50 B, Rubber Coated, SN 151970, Lens Caps, Strap, Germany	480
Carl Zeiss, Jena, Deltrintem, 8x30, Brown Leather Strap & Case	54
Evans, Butterfly, Folding, Aluminum, Black Leather Case, c.1940, 2 1/2 x 4 In.	62
J. Bauce, Brass, Stamped, Early 20th Century, 7 1/2 In. *illus*	88
Josef Schneider & Co., Chrome Plated Steel, Brass, Bakelite, Wood, German Navy, 27 In.	8125
Universal Camera Corp., U.S. Navy Bureau Of Ships, Model MK-XXX1M, Leather Strap, WW II	31

BIRDCAGE

Birdcages are collected for use as homes for pet birds and as decorative objects of folk art. Elaborate wooden cages of the past centuries can still be found. The brass or wicker cages of the 1930s are popular with bird owners.

Brass, Gold, Painted, Scrolled Top & Base, Hook, 76 x 30 In.	234
Brass, Pierced, Platform Top, Hanging Loop, Footed, Early 1900s, 20 x 10 In. *illus*	126
Iron, Brown, Painted, Scrolled Stand, Hinged Door, Removable Tray, 1950s, 72 x 24 x 17 In. *illus*	177
Iron Wire, Gold Paint, 2 Feeds, Hanging Perch, Mounted Parrot, Porcelain, c.1900, 25 x 15 In.	123
Mahogany, 2 Parts, Architectural, Carved, Wire, Hinged Door, Pierced Stand, Late 1900s, 75 In. *illus*	826
Wicker, Circular, Hanging, Stand, Straight Columnar, Conical Base, c.1950, 73 In.	16
Wood, Wire Bars, Orientalist, 34 x 28 In.	438
Wrought Iron, Hanging, 2 Rosettes, Scrolled Feet, Mexico, c.1950, 31 x 15 In.	62

BISQUE

Bisque is an unglazed baked porcelain. Finished bisque has a slightly sandy texture with a dull finish. Some of it may be decorated with various colors. Bisque gained favor during the late Victorian era when thousands of bisque figurines were made. It is still being made. Additional bisque items may be listed under the factory name.

Bowl, Bacchus Shape Handles, Winged Putti, Draping Swags, Mounted, Gilt Base, 1800s, 9 In.	150
Bust, Diana, Goddess Of The Hunt, Pedestal Base, Continental, 1900s, 20 In. *illus*	100
Centerpiece, Family, Sitting, Talking, Gilt Bronze Base, 13 1/4 x 9 1/2 In. *illus*	615
Figurine, 2 Dolphins, Leaping, Kaiser, West Germany, 7 x 11 1/2 In.	118
Figurine, 3 Pandas, Bamboo Tree, Rock Base, Signed, 8 1/2 x 7 1/2 In.	59
Figurine, Man, Seated, Woman, Standing, Vase, Classical Scene, Continental, 15 1/2 In.	75
Figurine, Nude Woman, Standing, Circular Base, Early 1900s, 19 1/4 In.	125
Lamp, Porcelain, Woman, White, Standing, Electrified, Square Base, 32 In.	344

Binoculars, J. Bauce, Brass, Stamped, Early 20th Century, 7 1/2 In. $88

Garth's Auctioneers & Appraisers

TIP
Remove small rust spots from old metal with an ink-removing eraser or an old typewriter eraser.

Birdcage, Brass, Pierced, Platform Top, Hanging Loop, Footed, Early 1900s, 20 x 10 In. $126

Fontaine's Auction Gallery

This is an edited listing of current prices. Visit **Kovels.com** to check thousands of prices from previous years and sign up for free information on trends, tips, reproductions, marks, and more.

Birdcage, Iron, Brown, Painted, Scrolled Stand, Hinged Door, Removable Tray, 1950s, 72 x 24 x 17 In.
$177

Leland Little Auctions

Birdcage, Mahogany, 2 Parts, Architectural, Carved, Wire, Hinged Door, Pierced Stand, Late 1900s, 75 In.
$826

Leland Little Auctions

BLACK AMERICANA

Black Americana has become an important area of collecting since the 1970s. The best material dates from past centuries, but many recent items are also of interest. F & F is the mark used on plastic made by Fiedler & Fiedler Mold & Die Works, Inc. in the 1930s and 1940s. Objects that picture a black person may also be listed in this book under Advertising, Sign; Bank; Bottle Opener; Cookie Jar; Doll; Salt & Pepper; Sheet Music; Toy; etc.

Chair, Metal Frame, Plywood Back & Seat, Painted Mother, Father & Child, 33 In..............	229
Cigar Store Figure, Share Cropper, Wood, Painted, Checked Shirt, Suspenders, Straw Hat, 67 In..	740
Clock, Figural, Joe Louis World Champion, Leaves, Bronze, 13 In. .... *illus*	431
Cookie Jars are listed in the Cookie Jar category.	
Figurine, Uncle Tom, Little Eva On Knee, Staffordshire, 1800s, 10 ¼ In................................	88
Humidor, Tobacco, Head, Wearing Hat, Marked, J. Maresch, 5 ½ In...............................	369
Quilt, Crib, Pieced, 12 Squares, Black Uncle Sam Figures, Red Border, c.1945, 28 x 21 In......	229
Sculpture, 3 Young Boys, Seated, On Wall, Plaster, Painted, 23 x 13 In.	2646
Stand, Smoking, Bellboy, Elongated Legs, Red Jacket & Cap, Holds Tray, c.1920, 41 In.	366
Toys are listed in the Toy category.	

BLENKO GLASS COMPANY

Blenko Glass Company is the 1930s successor to several glassworks founded by William John Blenko in Milton, West Virginia. In 1933, his son, William H. Blenko Sr., took charge. The company made tablewares and vases in classical shapes. In the late 1940s it hired talented designers and made innovative pieces. The company made a line of reproductions for Colonial Williamsburg. It is still in business and is best known today for its decorative wares and stained glass.

Bowl, Black, Asymmetrical, Cutout Handle, Marked, c.1960, 5 ¼ x 6 ½ In.	150
Bowl, Blue, Hat Shape, Wide Rim, 13 In.	75
Bowl, Wide Rim, Amberina, Red To Gold, John Nickerson, 1970s, 5 x 16 In..........................	270
Pitcher, Red, Lobed Body, Applied Handle, Downturned Spout, Joel Myers, 13 ½ In................	225
Tumbler, Highballs, Blown Clear Glass, Applied, Yellow Bands, 7 In., 6 Piece.........................	384
Vase, Blue Glass, Applied Decor, Original Label, 14 ¼ In. .... *illus*	47
Vase, Fan, Yellow, Cobalt Blue Foot, Hand Blown, 11 ¾ In.	68
Vase, Tulip, Red, Footed, Handmade, Sandblasted Mark, c.1960, 7 x 4 ½ In.	150
Wine Bucket, Top Hat Shape, Black, Handblown, Label, Don Shepherd, 7 ¾ x 6 In................	120

BLOWN GLASS, *see Glass-Blown category.*

BLUE GLASS, *see Cobalt Blue category.*

BLUE ONION, *see Onion category.*

BLUE WILLOW, *see Willow category.*

BOCH FRERES

Boch Freres factory was founded in 1841 in La Louviere in eastern Belgium. The pottery wares resemble the work of Villeroy & Boch. The factory closed in 1985. M.R.L. Boch took over the production of tableware but went bankrupt in 1988. Le Hodey took over Boch Freres in 1989, using the name Royal Boch Manufacture S.A. It went bankrupt in 2009.

Vase, Art Deco, Black Ground, Blue & Yellow, Charles Catteau, Belgium, c.1935, 9 In...... *illus*	854
Vase, Art Deco, Blue & White Flowers, Charles Catteau, Signed, Keramis, 10 ¾ x 7 In.	1265
Vase, Deer, Blue, Green, Black, Enamel, Earthenware, Charles Catteau, 12 ½ In....................	1188
Vase, Oval, Deer, Antelope, Craquelure Ground, Molded, Charles Catteau, c.1925, 9 x 7 In. .. *illus*	1112

B

Bisque, Bust, Diana, Goddess Of The Hunt, Pedestal Base, Continental, 1900s, 20 In.
$100

Selkirk Auctioneers & Appraisers

Bisque, Centerpiece, Family, Sitting, Talking, Gilt Bronze Base, 13¼ x 9½ In.
$615

Alderfer Auction Company

Black, Clock, Figural, Joe Louis World Champion, Leaves, Bronze, 13 In.
$431

Rich Penn Auctions

Blenko, Vase, Blue Glass, Applied Decor, Original Label, 14¼ In.
$47

Bunch Auctions

Boch Freres, Vase, Art Deco, Black Ground, Blue & Yellow, Charles Catteau, Belgium, c.1935, 9 In.
$854

Neal Auction Company

Boch Freres, Vase, Oval, Deer, Antelope, Craquelure Ground, Molded, Charles Catteau, c.1925, 9 x 7 In.
$1,112

Thomaston Place Auction Galleries

Boehm, Mask, Treasures Of King Tutankhamun, Gilt, c.1976, 13 x 9½ In.
$554

Rich Penn Auctions

Boehm, Snow Leopard, On Rock, Black Base, 1978, 11½ In.
$492

Rich Penn Auctions

Boehm, Stallion, Rocky & Grassy Base, Black Spotted Coat, Appaloosa, c.1981, 13 x 10 In.
$410

Jeffrey S. Evans & Associates

B

Bone, Pie Crimper, Bearded Sailor, Wearing Hat, Black Square Stand, Early 1900s, 6¾ In.
$250

Eldred's

Bookends, Book Slide, Gilt Metal, Mounted, Jasperware Plaque, Stamped, Betjemann & Sons, 1800s, 20 In.
$594

Hindman

Bookends, Figure, Young Woman, Dancing, Copper, Square Base, Art Deco, 6½ x 3½ x 4 In.
$156

Charlton Hall Auctions

BOEHM

Boehm is the collector's name for the porcelains of Edward Marshall Boehm. In 1953 the Osso China Company was reorganized as Edward Marshall Boehm Inc. In the early days of the factory, dishes were made, but the elaborate and lifelike bird figurines are the best-known ware. Edward Marshall Boehm, the founder, died in 1969, but the firm continued to design and produce porcelain. The Museum of American Porcelain Art bought the assets, including the molds and trademarks, in 2015. The museum is located in South Euclid, Ohio, a suburb of Cleveland. The Boehm Showroom in Trenton, New Jersey, has exclusive use of the molds and trademarks. It also does restoration work and has some retired figures for sale.

Boehm Porcelain, LLC 1952–1954	Boehm Porcelain, LLC 1959–1970	Boehm Porcelain, LLC 1971+

Blue Jay, Perched, On Old Stump, Entwined, Morning Glory Vines, 10 In.		443
Duck, Perched On Wood, Bisque, Hand Painted, 1981, 6 x 4 x 4 In.		403
Fox, Orange, Alert Position, Rocky Base, 5 x 5 In.		236
Horse, Adios, Brown & Black, Bisque, Oval Base, Wood Stand, Marked, 14⅜ In.		424
Mask, Treasures Of King Tutankhamun, Gilt, c.1976, 13 x 9½ In.	*illus*	554
Roadrunner, Stamped, 13¾ x 13 In.		153
Snow Leopard, On Rock, Black Base, 1978, 11½ In.	*illus*	492
Stallion, Rocky & Grassy Base, Black Spotted Coat, Appaloosa, c.1981, 13 x 10 In.	*illus*	410

BOHEMIAN GLASS, *see Glass-Bohemian*

BONE

Bone includes those articles made of bone not listed elsewhere in this book.

Figurine, Elephants, Reclining Pose, Blue, Enameled Flowers, Chinese, 7 x 13½ In., Pair		177
Pie Crimper, Bearded Sailor, Wearing Hat, Black Square Stand, Early 1900s, 6¾ In.	*illus*	250

BONE DISH

 Bone dishes were considered a necessary part of a table setting for the Victorian table. The crescent-shaped dish was kept at the edge of the dinner plate so the bones removed from the fish could be stored away from the uneaten food. Some bone dishes were made in more fanciful shapes and many resemble fish.

Flow Blue, Flowers, Gilt Scalloped Rim, Marked, Balmoral Royal Blue, B&C, 5 Piece		25
Flowers, Rust, Blue, Gilt Rim, 1906, 7¾ In., Royal Crown Derby, 6 Piece		277
Flowers, Vines, Multicolor, White Ground, Fluted Edges, Hand Painted, 3 x 6⅝ In., 8 Piece		13
Glass, Clear, Flattened Corners, Marked, Val St. Lambert, 12 Piece		32
Onion & Flower, Blue, Gilt Trim, 3 Lobes, Meissen, 7 Piece		30

BOOKENDS

Bookends have probably been used since books became inexpensive. Early libraries kept books in cupboards, not on open shelves. By the 1870s bookends appeared, especially homemade fret-carved wooden examples. Most bookends listed in this book date from the twentieth century. Bookends are also listed in other categories by manufacturer or material. All bookends listed here are pairs.

Book Slide, Gilt Metal, Mounted, Jasperware Plaque, Stamped, Betjemann & Sons, 1800s, 20 In. *illus*		594

Bookends, Foo Dog, Seated, White Marble, Carved, Pedestal Base, Chinese, 7 ½ In.
$207

Austin Auction Gallery

Bookends, Horn, Black, Brass, Enameled Steel, Carl Aubock III, Austria, c.1958, 6 ¾ x 5 ½ In.
$625

Toomey & Co. Auctioneers

Bookends, Horse Head, Shield, Quiver, Bronze, Signed, Pummill, 10 ½ x 6 ½ In.
$1,416

Austin Auction Gallery

Bookends, Lions, Lying Down, Brass, Rectangular Base, Early 1900s, 4 ½ x 8 In.
$502

Leland Little Auctions

Bookends, Native American Chief, Scalloped Headdress, Cast Iron, Gilt, c.1920, 6 x 4 ¼ In.
$106

Copake Auction

> **TIP**
> Wash your hands before and after shopping. It keeps you healthy and helps the condition of the antiques.

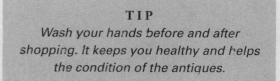

Bookends, Ring, Nickel Plated, Oxidized, Brass, Walter Von Nessen, Chase Brass & Copper Co., 1933, 5 In.
$1,500

Wright

Bookends, Whale, Sperm, Tail Raised, Brass, Rocky Base, 1900s, 7 ½ In.
$213

Eldred's

Bottle, Barber, Rubina, Crosscut Diamond, Honeycomb Neck, Silver Twist Cap, Webb, 8 In., Pair
$300

Woody Auction

Bottle, Barber, Vegederma Hair Tonic, Purple, Mary Gregory Style, Enameled Letters, Open Pontil, 8 In.
$366

AntiqueAdvertising.com

Bull's Head, Brass, Brown Patina, Black Base, Maitland-Smith, Late 1900s, 14 ½ x 8 ½ In...	266
Canada Goose Head, Glass Eyes, Carved, Painted Pine Base, Byron Bruffee, 1900s, 7 x 8 In..	125
Cornucopia, Glass, White, Yellow, Circular Base, Barovier & Toso, 9 ¾ x 11 x 6 In.	1188
Curled Pattern, Copper, Brass, Chase, Walter Von Nessen, Early 1900s, 5 x 4 x 2 ¾ In.	110
Figure, Young Woman, Dancing, Copper, Square Base, Art Deco, 6 ½ x 3 ½ x 4 In. ...... *illus*	156
Foo Dog, Seated, White Marble, Carved, Pedestal Base, Chinese, 7 ½ In. .... *illus*	207
Horn, Black, Brass, Enameled Steel, Carl Aubock III, Austria, c.1958, 6 ¾ x 5 ½ In. ...... *illus*	625
Horse Head, Shield, Quiver, Bronze, Signed, Pummill, 10 ½ x 6 ½ In. .... *illus*	1416
Liberty & Justice, Brass, Embossed, Portrait, Quotes, On Back, Virginia Metalcrafters, 7 In...	83
Lion, Sitting, Sheet Bronze, Art Deco, 7 ½ In.	138
Lions, Lying Down, Brass, Rectangular Base, Early 1900s, 4 ½ x 8 In. .... *illus*	502
Monk, Holding Glass Of Wine, Standing, Bronze, c.1900, 6 ½ x 4 ½ In..........................	150
Native American Chief, Scalloped Headdress, Cast Iron, Gilt, c.1920, 6 x 4 ¼ In. .... *illus*	106
Old Salt, Fisherman, Yellow Slicker, Rain Hat, Cast Iron, Painted, 7 In...........................	95
Ring, Nickel Plated, Oxidized, Brass, Walter Von Nessen, Chase Brass & Copper Co., 1933, 5 In. *illus*	1500
Skull, Steer & Mouse, Bronze, Shallow Relief, 1800s, 6 ½ x 7 ¼ In................................	861
Whale, Sperm, Tail Raised, Brass, Rocky Base, 1900s, 7 ½ In. ....*illus*	213

BOOKMARK

Bookmarks were originally made of parchment, cloth, or leather. Soon woven silk ribbon, thin cardboard, celluloid, wood, silver, tortoiseshell, and metals were used. Examples made before 1850 are scarce, but there are many to be found dating before 1920.

Advertising, Zavelle's Philadelphia Greeting Cards, Dog, Terrier, Cardboard, 6 ½ In.	8
Brass, Cloisonne Medallion, Multicolor, Engraved, Paris, 19th Century, 3 ½ x ¾ In.	75
Chain, Sterling Silver, Pendant At Ends, Marked, Bali 96, John Hardy, Box, 13 ½ In..............	62
Gold Plate, Clip, Double G Emblem, Embossed Red Leather Case, Gucci, 6 In......................	74
Golfer, Reverse Painted, Intaglio Glass, Silver Clip, White Tassel, Hallmarked, 4 In.	100
Spider-Man, Figural, Red, Blue, Plastic, Nasta Co., 1980s, 3 ¾ In..................................	2
Sterling Silver, Acanthus Leaf, Clip, Brodrene Mylius, Norway, c.1940, 2 ⁵⁄₁₆ x 1 In.	48
Sterling Silver, Navajo, Stamped, Wavy Line, Stylized Animals, Signed, J. Wright, 3 ½ x ½ In.	27
Sterling Silver, Openwork Bow, Clip, Marked, Gucci, 20th Century, 3 x 2 ½ In......................	100
Sterling Silver, Teddy Bear, Clip, Hallmarks, 2 ⅛ In.	31

BOSSONS

Bossons character wall masks (heads), plaques, figurines, and other decorative pieces of chalkware were made by W.H. Bossons, Limited, of Congleton, England. The company was founded in 1946 and closed in 1996. Dates shown are the date the item was introduced.

Plaque, Dog, Cocker Spaniel Head, Black & White, 1980, 4 ¾ In.	18
Plaque, Irish Cottages, Sunny Scene, Rectangular, Back Loop, Marked, c.1950, 5 x 8 In........	50
Wall Figure, Osprey & Fish, Hand Painted, 1970, 17 x 13 ½ In....................................	23
Wall Mask, Aviator & USAF Fighter Pilot, Signed, 1991, 7 x 6 ½ In., Pair	63
Wall Mask, Dog, Basset Hound, Brown & White, Mouth Open, 1960s, 5 ½ x 4 In.	18
Wall Mask, Dog, Cocker Spaniel, Black & White, Dogs Of Distinction, 1980-96, 4 ¾ In.........	16
Wall Mask, Sea Captain, Black Cap, Gray Hair, Norman Rockwell Design, Fred Wright, 1972-96, 5 In..	49
Wall Mask, Sherlock Holmes, Dr. Watson, 1984, Pair	48

BOSTON & SANDWICH CO. *pieces may be found in the Sandwich Glass category.*

BOTTLE

Bottle collecting has become a major American hobby. There are several general categories of bottles, such as historic flasks, bitters, household, and figural. ABM means the bottle was made by an automatic bottle machine after 1903. Pyro is the shortened form of the word *pyroglaze,* an enameled lettering used on bottles after the mid-1930s.

This form of decoration is also called ACL or applied color label. Shapes of bottles often indicate the age of the bottle. For more prices, go to kovels.com.

Case gin bottle
1650–1920

Teakettle ink
1830–1885

Calabash flask
1840–1870

Avon started in 1886 as the California Perfume Company. It was not until 1929 that the name Avon was used. In 1939, it became Avon Products, Inc. Avon has made many figural bottles filled with cosmetic products. Ceramic, plastic, and glass bottles were made in limited editions from 1965 to 1980. There was a limited-edition bottle collecting frenzy and prices rose. By 2018 the bottle prices were back to a very low level.

Avon, After Shave, Wild Country, Figural, Car, Bugatti '27, Black & White, Box, 3 x 9 In.	13
Avon, Decanter, Perfume, Bird Of Paradise, Peacock, Clear, Goldtone Plastic Head, 1970s, 8 x 4 In.	15
Barber, Panel Optic, Flowers, Ceramic Spout, Blue, Late 1800s, 10 x 9 In.	176
Barber, Rubina, Crosscut Diamond, Honeycomb Neck, Silver Twist Cap, Webb, 8 In., Pair *illus*	300
Barber, Vegederma Hair Tonic, Purple, Mary Gregory Style, Enameled Letters, Open Pontil, 8 In. *illus*	366
Bininger, A.M. & Co., Old Dominion Wheat Tonic, Honey Amber, Applied Collar, c.1862, 9⅞ In.	920
Bininger, A.M. & Co., No. 19 Broad St., N.Y., Amber, Cannon, Sheared Mouth, 12⅜ In.	1131
Bininger, A.M. & Co., No. 19 Broad St., N.Y., Old Kentucky Bourbon, 1849, Green, 9¾ In.	774
Bininger, A.M. & Co., No. 19 Broad St., New York, Amber, Jug, Double Collar, Handle, 8 In.	249
Bininger, A.M. & Co., No. 19 Broad St., New York, Amber, Urn, Funnel Mouth, Handle, 8¾ In.	2618
Bininger, A.M. & Co., No. 19 Broad St., Olive Green, Applied Handle, Double Collar, 8 In.	3163
Bitters, Barrel, Cobalt Blue, Applied Lip, 1860-70, 9⅞ In.	1785
Bitters, Berkshire, Amann & Co., Cincinnati, O., Pig, Red Amber, Tapered Collar, 1870-75, 9¾ In. *illus*	1560
Bitters, Brown's Celebrated Indian Herb, Indian Princess, Amber, Gold Trim, c.1868, 12¼ In.	1320
Bitters, Brown's Celebrated Indian Herb, Indian Princess, Dark Chocolate Amber, 12¼ In.	893
Bitters, Brown's Celebrated Indian Herb, Indian Queen, Amber, Patented 1868, 12½ In.	350
Bitters, Cabin, Embossed Cannons, Cannonballs, Tent, Crossed Swords, Amber, c.1865, 10 In.	2618
Bitters, Dr. Birmingham's Anti-Bilious, Blood Purifying, Green, 12 Panels, 9 In.	4463
Bitters, Dr. C.W. Roback's Stomach, Cincinnati, O., Barrel, Amber, Sloping Collar, 9⅜ In.	214
Bitters, Dr. C.W. Roback's Stomach, Cincinnati, O., Barrel, Yellow Green, 9⅛ In.	5355
Bitters, Fish, W.H. Ware, Patented 1866, Amber, Applied Lip, 11½ In.	330
Bitters, Great Stomach, Calisaya, Tobacco Amber, 12 Shoulder Panels, Tapered, 11 In.	1785
Bitters, Greeley's Bourbon, Barrel, Smoky Olive Topaz, 1860-70, 9¼ In.	1190
Bitters, H.P. Herb Wild Cherry, Cherry Tree, Cabin, 7-Up Green, Double Collar, 9 In.	8925
Bitters, H.P. Herb Wild Cherry, Reading, Pa., Cherry Tree, Cabin, Amber, c.1800, 10⅛ In.	655
Bitters, Holtzermanns Patent Stomach, Cabin, Orange Amber, Sloping Collar, 9⅝ In.	1785
Bitters, J. Hostetter's Stomach, Deep Olive, Case, Sloping Collar, 1860-70, 9½ In.	714
Bitters, John Moffat, New York, Phoenix, Price 1 Dollar, Yellow Amber, Rolled Lip, 5⅝ In.	1547
Bitters, John W. Steele's Niagara Star, Semi-Cabin, 5-Point Stars, Bird, Amber, 9⅞ In.	952
Bitters, Kimball Jaundice, Brown, Rectangular, Troy, N.H., 6¾ x 2¾ In.	1107
Bitters, Langley's Root Herb Bitters, Light Blue, Pontil, 7 In.	74
Bitters, Lediard's Morning Call, Emerald Green, Cylindrical, Sloping Collar, 10 In.	327
Bitters, M.G. Landsberg, Chicago, 1776, 1876, Semi-Cabin, Amber, 11 In. *illus*	1680
Bitters, McKeever's Army, Red Amber, Cannonballs & Civil War Drum On Shoulder, 10⅜ In.	3570
Bitters, National, Ear Of Corn, 1867, Figural, Red Amber, Sheared Mouth, 12⅜ In.	774
Bitters, National, Ear Of Corn, Patent 1867, Yellow, Olive Tone, Double Collar, 12½ In.	1547
Bitters, Old Sachem & Wigwam Tonic, Barrel, Shaded Peach Topaz, Applied Lip, c.1865, 9⅜ In.	833
Bitters, Old Sachem & Wigwam Tonic, Barrel, Topaz, Applied Lip, 1860-70, 9⅜ In.	3900
Bitters, Rexford's, Olive Green, Twisted Gold Bands, Decanter, Double Collar, 7½ In.	1428
Bitters, Smith's Green Mountain Renovator, Brown, 8-Sided, East Georgia, Vt., 7 x 3 In.	1968
Bitters, Yerba Buena, Brown, Sloped Shoulders, Partial Paper Label, c.1890, Qt.	50
Bitters, Yerba Buena, S.F., Cal., Aqua, Strapside Flask, Double Collar, 1875-90, 8 In.	595

Bottle, Bitters, Berkshire, Amann & Co., Cincinnati, O., Pig, Red Amber, Tapered Collar, 1870-75, 9¾ In.
$1,560

Glass Works Auctions

Bottle, Bitters, M.G. Landsberg, Chicago, 1776, 1876, Semi-Cabin, Amber, Sloping Collar, 11 In.
$1,680

Glass Works Auctions

Bottle, Cologne, Ruby Stain, Pressed Hob & Lace, Cylindrical, Gilt, 1800s, 6 x 4 In., Pair
$140

Jeffrey S. Evans & Associates

Bottle, Decanter, Cut Neck, Thumbprint Chain, Applied Bar Lip, Blown Glass, Stopper, Teal, 1860s, 11 x 9 In. $527

Jeffrey S. Evans & Associates

Bottle, Decanter, Pusser's Rum, British Navy, Stone Flagon, Sealed, 1¾ Liter $115

Blackwell Auctions

Bottle, Decanter, Starburst Cut, Silver Overlay, Flowers, Openwork, Blown Glass, William Conyas, 1895, 8 In. $144

Garth's Auctioneers & Appraisers

Blown, Jar, Red Amber, Wide Mouth, Flared-Out Lip, Ellenville, N.Y., 9⅝ In.	595
Coca-Cola Bottles are listed in the Coca-Cola category.	
Cologne, Ruby Stain, Pressed Hob & Lace, Cylindrical, Gilt, 1800s, 6 x 4 In., Pair .... *illus*	140
Cordial, Charles London, Emerald Green, Case, Sloping Collar, 1845-60, 9¾ In.	536
Cosmetic, Haywood's Balm Of Savannah, Aqua, Oval, Sloping Collar, Pontil, c.1850, 8 In.	450
Decanter, Bar, Aqua, 8 Ribs, Swirled Neck, Applied Lip, 1830s, 10½ In.	570
Decanter, Cut Neck, Thumbprint Chain, Applied Bar Lip, Blown, Stopper, Teal, 1860s, 11 x 9 In. ..*illus*	527
Decanter, Mezza Filigrana, Blue, White, Fratelli Toso, Italy, 1950s, 18 In.	500
Decanter, Olive Green, Geometric Panels, Mold Blown, Tooled Lip, Keene, c.1835, 7¾ In.	655
Decanter, Purple, Ring Neck, Clear Faceted Stopper, c.1830, 11¾ x 4½ In.	104
Decanter, Pusser's Rum, British Navy, Stone Flagon, Sealed, 1¾ Liter .... *illus*	115
Decanter, Ruby Flash Panels, Floral, Embossed Silver Collar, Figural Stopper, Bohemian Glass, 13 In.	70
Decanter, Starburst Cut, Silver Overlay, Flowers, Openwork, Blown, William Conyas, 1895, 8 In...*illus*	144
Decanter, Twist Flame Stopper, Turquoise, Ribbed, Alfredo Barbini, Murano, 25⅜ x 5¾ In.	406
Decanter, Yellow Cut To Clear, Oblong Stopper, Duck, Cattails, Bohemian Glass, c.1950, 16 In., Pair.	177
Demijohn, Blown Glass, Honey Amber, Ribbed Bottle, Applied Lip, Bulbous Base, 1900s, 17 x 10 In.	330
Flask, 21 Ribs, Vertical, Amethyst, Teardrop, Sheared Mouth, 1810-24, 6⅝ In.	536
Flask, Benjamin Franklin, T.W. Dyott On Reverse, Amber, Kensington Glass Works, 6¾ In. ..*illus*	15680
Flask, Book Shape, Glazed, Marked Ladie's Companion, Rockingham, Early 1800s, 5⅝ In.	344
Flask, Book Shape, Man On Horse Metal Stopper, Rockingham, 1800s, 2 Qt., 10 In.	255
Flask, Chestnut, 24 Ribs, Swirled To Left, Red Amber, Sheared & Crimped Rim, 4¾ In.	357
Flask, Chestnut, Grass Green, Outward Rolled Lip, Pontil, 1750-80, 9⅜ In.	600
Flask, Clear, Oval, Metal Casing, Shipwreck Salvage, c.1900, 5½ x 3½ x 1 In. .... *illus*	563
Flask, Cornucopia & Urn, Blue Green, Inward Rolled Lip, Pontil, Lancaster, ½ Pt.	774
Flask, Double Eagle, 10 Stars, Ribbed Sides, 1850s, 6¾ In.	313
Flask, Double Eagle, Ice Blue, Sheared Mouth, Pontil, Louisville Glass Works, 1835-45, Qt.	480
Flask, Flag, Eagle, Flag, Coffin & Hay, Green, Sheared Mouth, Hammonton, 8 In.	6100
Flask, Flora Temple & Horse, Smoky Gray, Olive Tone, Ring Mouth, Handle, 8½ In.	1190
Flask, Gimmel, Clear, Copper Wheel Engraved Oak Leaves, Acorns, Farmer's Arms, Blown, 1838, 7 In.	72
Flask, Hunter & Fisherman, Calabash, Strawberry Puce, Sloping Collar, Iron Pontil	535
Flask, Jenny Lind, Calabash, Cobalt Blue, Rolled Lip, Iron Pontil, Ravenna, 1855-60	3868
Flask, Lafayette & Liberty, Liberty Cap, Old Amber, Tooled Lip, Pontil, Pt.	1309
Flask, Lafayette & Liberty, Yellow Amber, Olive Tone, Sheared Mouth, Pontil, ½ Pt.	960
Flask, Pitkin Type, 30 Broken Ribs, Swirled To Right, Sheared Mouth, 5½ In.	357
Flask, Pitkin Type, 36 Broken Ribs, Swirled Left, Amber, Sheared Mouth, Pontil, c.1850, 6 In.	600
Flask, Pitkin Type, 36 Broken Ribs, Swirled To Left, Popcorn Pattern, Half Post, 6 In.	4463
Flask, Pitkin Type, 36 Broken Ribs, Swirled To Left, Tobacco Amber, Yellow Tint, Tooled, 6⅝ In.	565
Flask, Scroll, Amber, Pontil, ½ Pt.	1428
Flask, Scroll, Aqua, Sheared Mouth, Pontil, 1840-50, 2 Qt.	1020
Flask, Scroll, Shaded Cobalt Blue, Iron Pontil, Tooled Mouth, 1840-50, Pt.	5355
Flask, Sheaf Of Grain & Tree, Calabash, Deep Claret, Applied Double Collar, c.1860	774
Flask, Silver Plate Cap, Swirl, Blown Glass, c.1900, 5¾ In.	94
Flask, Stiegel Type, Amethyst, Diamond Diaper, Flattened Globular Shape, 6¾ In.	1200
Flask, Success To The Railroad, Gray Blue, Lancaster Glass, 1840-60, 6¼ x 3 In. .... *illus*	450
Flask, Success To The Railroad, Smoky Moss Green, Sheared Mouth, Open Pontil, 1835-45, Pt....	5100
Flask, Sunburst, Old Amber, Yellow Tone, Tooled Top, Keene Glass Works, 1815-35, Pt.	833
Flask, Sunburst, Strawberry Puce, Sheared, Baltimore Glass Works, 1825-35, ½ Pt.	1904
Flask, Traveler's Companion & Lockport, Starburst, Teal Blue, Pt.	2261
Flask, Union, Clasped Hands & Eagle, Red Amber Shaded To Yellow, Ring Mouth, ½ Pt.	226
Flask, Union, Clasped Hands, Shaded Cornflower Blue, Applied Ring Mouth, 1860-70, Qt.	7200
Flask, Washington & Eagle, Apple Green, Tooled Lip, 1825-40, Pt.	388
Flask, Washington & Taylor, Never Surrenders, Light Green, Sheared Mouth, Pontil, 1848-55, Pt. *illus*	510
Flask, Washington & Taylor, A Little More Grape, Cobalt Blue, Tooled Mouth, Pontil, Qt.	2499
Flask, Washington & Taylor, Yellow Green, Sloping Double Collar, 1850-55, Qt.	1310
Flask, Whiskey, U.S., Eagle, Label Under Glass, Canteen Shape, G.A.R. Souvenir, 5 x 4½ In. ..*illus*	215
Food, Dorlon & Shaffer Pickled Oysters, Fulton Market, Aqua, Glass Lid, Wire, c.1880, 1½ Pt.	192
Food, John M. Boyer, Baltimore Star Oysters, Yellow, Glass Lid, Wire, Label, Cohansey, Qt. .*illus*	960
Food, Storage, Packed By M.H. Davis & Son, Milford, Aqua, Glass Lid, Wire, Cohansey, c.1880, Qt. *illus*	1800
Globular, 24 Ribs, Swirled To Left, Amber, Elongated Neck, Outward Rolled Lip, 7½ In.	298

B

Globular, 24 Ribs, Swirled To Left, Yellow Olive, Elongated Neck, Outward Rolled Lip, 8 In.	8925
Ink, 24 Vertical Ribs, Amber, Tooled Funnel Mouth, Zanesville, 1¾ In.	2261
Ink, Aqua, B-U-T-L-E-R, 8-Sided, Letters On Panels, Squat, Rolled Lip, Ohio, c.1850, 2¼ In.	274
Ink, Cabin, Colorless, Sheared & Ground Mouth, 1875-90, 3⅛ In. .... *illus*	1680
Ink, Carter's Permanent Ink, Cobalt Blue, Cathedral, Paper Label, Stopper, 11 In.	132
Ink, Cut Glass, Clear, Swirls, Squat Ball Form, Gorham Silver Neck Ring & Cap, c.1900, 4 In.	345
Ink, E. Waters, Troy, N.Y., Light Blue Green, Applied Lip, Master, 1840-60, 5½ In.	952
Ink, Estes, N.Y., Aqua, 8 Curved Tapered Panels, Pontil, Rolled Lip, 1840-60, 4 In.	655
Ink, Harrison's Columbian, 12-Sided, Apple Green, Flattened Lip, 7⅜ In.	446
Ink, Stoneware, Mottled Brown Glaze, Cylindrical, 5 In.	12
Ink, Teakettle, 6-Sided, Bull's-Eye Pattern On Each, Fluted Dish Top, c.1885, 2⅝ In.	2261
Ink, Teakettle, 6-Sided, Porcelain, Green Splashed Glaze, France, 1875-1900, 2¼ In.	95
Ink, Teakettle, 8-Sided, Cobalt Blue, Cylindrical Spout, Brass Ring & Cap, c.1880, 2⅔ In.	1670
Ink, Teakettle, 8-Sided, Milk Glass, Mother-Of-Pearl Panels, 2 Fonts, Brass Caps, 2¼ In.	3273
Ink, Teakettle, 8-Sided, Pink Amethyst, Sheared Lip, 1875-90, 2 In.	655
Ink, Teakettle, 8-Sided, Pottery, Painted, White, Blue Flowers & Birds, 2⅛ In.	387
Ink, Teakettle, 10-Sided, Fiery Opalescent Milk Glass, Flowers, Brass Cap, Sandwich, 2½ In.	475
Ink, Teakettle, 16 Vertical Rounded Ribs, Clear, Double Pen Rest Top, 2¼ In.	226
Ink, Teakettle, Vertical Ribs, Black Topaz Puce, Beaded Edge, Sheared Lip, 2⅛ In.	1023
Ink, Teakettle, Vertical Ribs, Double Gourd, Green, Hinged Cap, c.1885, 2⅝ In.	714
Ink, Teakettle, Vertical Ribs, Emerald Green, 2 Pen Rests On Top, Sheared Lip, 1875-90, 2 In.	1020
Ink, Umbrella, 8-Sided, Deep Cobalt Blue, Applied Flattened Lip, 2⅝ In.	655
Ink, Umbrella, 8-Sided, Deep Red, Pontil, Rolled Lip, Stoddard Glass Works, c.1855, 2⅔ In.	417
Ink, Umbrella, 8-Sided, Emerald Green, Baltimore Glass Works, c.1850, 2¼ In.	3868
Ink, Underwood's, Red Ink, Paper Label, Cap, 10½ In.	75
Ink, Waters, Troy, N.Y., Aqua, 6 Curved Tapered Panels, Squat, Rolled Rim, c.1850, 2¾ In.	774
Jar, Blown Glass, Green, Wide Mouth, Viresa, 9¼ In., Pair	35
Jar, Blown Glass, Medicine, Apothecary, Short Lid, Cylindrical, Flared Foot, 1800s, 12¼ In., Pair	625
Medicine, Apothecary, Cobalt Blue, Blown Glass, Cannabis, Cocaine, Opium, 7 In., 3 Piece	1512
Medicine, Apothecary, Lid, Urn Shape, Gold Trim, Footed, Acorn Finial, 38 In., Pair ... *illus*	671
Medicine, Apothecary, Mascotte, Cylindrical, Ground Stopper, 1910s, 23¾ x 4½ In.	263
Medicine, Apothecary, Stopper, Counter Display, Clear, 4 Sections, 27 x 6 In.	69
Medicine, Apothecary, Wedding Ring Panel, Stopper, Circular Base, 1860s, 6 x 5 In.	293
Medicine, Follansbee's Elixir, Blue, Applied Sloping Collar, Iron Pontil, c.1850, 8¾ In.	1755
Medicine, Griswold's Malarian Antidote, Aqua, Indented Panels, Sloping Collar, Iron Pontil, 7 In.	1904
Medicine, New England Cough Syrup, Yellow Amber, Sloping Collar, Label, c.1850, 7 In. .... *illus*	900
Mineral Water, Alburgh, A, Springs, Vt., Olive Yellow, Rounded Shoulder, Double Collar, Qt.	833
Mineral Water, Buffum & Co., Sarsaparilla, Tenpin Shape, Blue, Sloping Collar, c.1860, 8 In.	780
Mineral Water, Gleason & Cole, Pittsbg., Cobalt Blue, 10-Sided, Sloping Collar, 7½ In.	833
Mineral Water, J. & A. Dearborn, New York, Cobalt Blue, 8-Sided, Union Glass, c.1850, 7⅜ In.	714
Mineral Water, J. Steel, Premium, Slug Plate, Emerald Green, 8-Sided, Blob Top, 7½ In.	655
Mineral Water, John Diehls, D, Philada, Cobalt Blue, 8-Sided, Sloping Collar, 7⅜ In.	893
Mineral Water, Keys, Burlington, N.J., Blue Green, Blob Top, Iron Pontil, Pony, 1840-60, 7 In. .. *illus*	228
Mineral Water, Taylor's Best, Cobalt Blue, 8-Sided Cucumber Form, Blob Top, 8¼ In.	1785
Mineral Water, Vermont Spring, Saxe & Co., Sheldon, Vt., Yellow Olive, Qt.	833
Perfume bottles are listed in the Perfume Bottle category.	
Pickle, Aqua, Clear, Embossed, Gothic Arch Cathedral, c.1870, 13½ x 5½ In., Pair	254
Pickle, Cathedral, 4-Sided, Arched Panels, Blue Green, Outward Collar, Iron Pontil, c.1855, 12 In. *illus*	1320
Pickle, Cathedral, Draped Shoulder, Emerald Green, Outward Rolled Lip, 13 In.	2023
Pickle, Cathedral, Indented Panels, Cornflower Blue, Outward Rolled Lip, 10¾ In.	1121
Pickle, Cathedral, Indented Side Panels, Shaded Emerald Green, Rolled Lip, 11⅝ In.	952
Pickle, Cylindrical, 12-Panel Shoulder & Neck, Shaded Green, Outward Rolled Lip, 12 In.	2499
Pickle, Gothic Cathedral, Aquamarine, Embossed, Concave Base, c.1870, 13 x 5½ In. . *illus*	94
Pickle, Shaker Brand, E.D. Pettengill Co., Portland, Me., c.1910, 11½ In.	1375
Scent, Black, Scattered Millefiori, Portrait Canes, Aventurine, Murano, 1880s, 3 In. .... *illus*	234
Scent, Cameo Glass, Teardrop Shape, Opaque White, Citron, Monogram, AW, c.1886, 3⅜ In. *illus*	468
Seal, Neal's Ambrosia Whiskey, Philada., Cobalt Blue, Sloping Double Collar, 1865-75, 9¼ In.	1800
Snuff, Amber, Carved, Birds, Rich Honey, Chinese, 3½ x 3¼ In.	531
Snuff, Famille Rose, Immortal Design, Oval Foot, Wood Base, 3½ x 2 In., Pair	375

Bottle, Flask, Benjamin Franklin, T.W. Dyott On Reverse, Amber, Kensington Glass Works, 6¾ In.
$15,680

Pook & Pook

Bottle, Flask, Clear, Oval, Metal Casing, Shipwreck Salvage, c.1900, 5½ x 3½ x 1 In.
$563

Ahlers & Ogletree Auction Gallery

Bottle, Flask, Success To The Railroad, Gray Blue, Lancaster Glass, 1840-60, 6¼ x 3 In.
$450

Bruneau & Co. Auctioneers

Bottle, Flask, Washington & Taylor Never Surrenders, Light Green, Sheared Mouth, Pontil, 1848-55, Pt.
$510

Glass Works Auctions

Bottle, Flask, Whiskey, U.S., Eagle, Label Under Glass, Canteen Shape, G.A.R. Souvenir, 5 x 4 ½ In.
$215

Rich Penn Auctions

Bottle, Food, John M. Boyer, Baltimore Star Oysters, Yellow, Glass Lid, Wire, Label, Cohansey, Qt.
$960

Glass Works Auctions

Bottle, Food, Storage, Packed By M.H. Davis & Son, Milford, Aqua, Glass Lid, Wire, Cohansey, 1874-90, Qt.
$1,800

Glass Works Auctions

Bottle, Ink, Cabin, Colorless, Sheared & Ground Mouth, 1875-90, 3 ⅛ In.
$1,680

Glass Works Auctions

Bottle, Medicine, Apothecary, Lid, Urn Shape, Gold Trim, Footed, Acorn Finial, 38 In., Pair
$671

Neal Auction Company

Bottle, Medicine, New England Cough Syrup, Yellow Amber, Sloping Collar, Label, c.1850, 7 In.
$900

Glass Works Auctions

Bottle, Mineral Water, Keys, Burlington, N.J., Blue Green, Blob Top, Iron Pontil, Pony, 1840-60, 7 In.
$228

Glass Works Auctions

Wooden Molds Are Hot
Early glass was made from wooden molds. The mold was soaked in water, then hot glass was blown into it. Each was used 100 to 1,000 times; after that, it would be burned and useless. The hot glass and water created steam that polished the glass.

Bottle, Pickle, Cathedral, 4-Sided, Arched
Panels, Blue Green, Outward Rolled Collar,
Iron Pontil, c.1855, 12 In.
$1,320

Glass Works Auctions

Bottle, Pickle, Gothic Cathedral,
Aquamarine, Embossed, Concave Base,
c.1870, 13 x 5 ½ In.
$94

Bruneau & Co. Auctioneers

Bottle, Scent, Black, Scattered Millefiori,
Portrait Canes, Aventurine, Murano, 1880s,
3 In.
$234

Jeffrey S. Evans & Associates

Bottle, Scent, Cameo Glass, Teardrop Shape,
Opaque White, Citron, Monogram, AW,
c.1886, 3 ⅜ In.
$468

Jeffrey S. Evans & Associates

Bottle, Snuff, Glass, Reverse Painted,
Festive Village, Dragon Dancers, Drummers,
Chinese, 3 x 2 In.
$144

Blackwell Auctions

Bottle, Snuff, Peking Glass, Bubbled Pink,
Green Spots, Jade Stopper, Chinese,
Mid 1900s, 2 ½ In.
$96

Garth's Auctioneers & Appraisers

Bottle, Soda, Grape Smash, Enameled Label,
Lid, c.1910-15, 12 ½ In.
$677

Morphy Auctions

Bottle, Whiskey, D.E. Becker's, Pure Old Rye,
Easton Pa., Amber, 1880s, 12 In.
$322

Jeffrey S. Evans & Associates

Bottle, Whiskey, Golden Wedding, Carnival Glass, Marigold, Paper Label, 4 x 7 ½ In.
$15

Woody Auction

Bottle Cap, Crown, Joe Louis Punch, Red Ground, White Letters, Cork Lined
$26

btlcapman on eBay

Bottle Cap, Crown, Reseal, Cork N Seal, Bottled Carbonated Beverages, Good & Good For You, Blue, Yellow
$8

bz105 on eBay

Snuff, Glass, Deep Olive Amber, Cylindrical, Dip Mold, Applied Ring Lip, c.1790, 6 In.	714
Snuff, Glass, Reverse Painted, Festive Village, Dragon Dancers, Drummers, Chinese, 3 x 2 In. *illus*	144
Snuff, Ivory, Bas Relief Carving, Engraved Lake Scene, Domed Nipple Lid, 1800s, 5 ⅝ In.	585
Snuff, Jade, White Milky Color, Carved, Crosshatch, Squares, 1800s, 2 ⅜ x 1 ½ In.	1875
Snuff, Peking Glass, Bubbled Pink, Green Spots, Jade Stopper, Chinese, Mid 1900s, 2 ½ In. *illus*	96
Snuff, Porcelain, Clipper Ship, American Flag, Chinese Export, 2 ¾ In.	71
Soda, Carpenter & Cobb, Knickerbocker, Saratoga, Sapphire Blue, 10-Sided, Blob Top, 7 ½ In.	655
Soda, Grape Smash, Enameled Label, Lid, c.1910-15, 12 ½ In. *illus*	677
Soda, J.C. Hubinger & Bros., New Haven, Conn., Aqua, Embossed Flat Iron, 6 ½ In.	86
Soda, Smile, Orange, Metal Cap, July 11, 1922, Gal., 18 x 6 In.	1353
Soda, Smith & Fotheringham, St. Louis, Cobalt Blue, 10-Sided, Sloping Collar, 7 ⅜ In.	774
Storage, Deep Olive Green, Chestnut, Long Neck, Outward Rolled Lip, c.1800, 10 ½ In.	417
Storage, Pale Green, Chestnut, Free-Blown, Sheared Mouth, Ring Lip, c.1800, 8 ¾ In.	238
Whiskey, D.E. Becker's, Pure Old Rye, Easton Pa., Amber, 1880s, 12 In. *illus*	322
Whiskey, Dr. Girard's, London, Ginger Brandy, Seal, Yellow Amber, Cone, Double Collar, 9 ⅜ In.	274
Whiskey, Golden Wedding, Carnival Glass, Marigold, Paper Label, 4 x 7 ½ In. *illus*	15
Whiskey, Griffith Hyatt & Co., Baltimore, Yellow Copper, Jug, Applied Lip, 7 ⅛ In.	298
Whiskey, J.F.T. & Co., Vertical Ribs, Yellow Amber, Tapered Jug, Double Collar, 7 In.	536
Whiskey, Pure Cognac, Yellow Amber, Seal, Ring Mouth, Handle, c.1860, 8 ⅞ In.	655
Whiskey, T.J. Dunbar & Co., Schnapps, Schiedam, Teal Blue, Sloping Double Collar, 8 ¼ In.	1071
Whiskey, Wharton's, 1850, Chestnut Grove, Amber, Flask, Crimped Spout, Handle, 10 In.	833
Wine, Carboy, Clear, Marked MCAG STD, 1948, 25 ¼ In.	148
Wine, Shaft & Globe, Deep Green, Sheared String Lip, Pontil, England, c.1675, 7 ⅛ In.	7735

BOTTLE CAP

Bottle caps for milk bottles are the printed cardboard caps used since the 1920s. Crown caps, used after 1892 on soda bottles, are also popular collectibles. Unusual mottoes, graphics, and caps from bottlers that are out of business bring the highest prices.

Borden's, Elsie The Cow, Your California Friends, Red, White, Blue, 1 ⅝ In.	30
Christmas Greetings, Let's Not Forget, Help Fight Tuberculosis, Red, White, Blue, 1940	16
Crown, Fleckenstein Choc Malt, Brown, White Lettering	30
Crown, Howel's Grapefruit Drink, Yellow, Green Lettering, Cork Lined	3
Crown, Joe Louis Punch, Red Ground, White Letters, Cork Lined *illus*	26
Crown, Kreuger, Beer, K Logo, Red Ground, White Letters, Cork Lined	28
Crown, Moxie, New, The Moxie Co., Boston, Mass., Red, White Letters, Cork Lined	19
Crown, RC Cola, Red & White, Cork Lined	3
Crown, Reseal, Cork N Seal, Bottled Carbonated Beverages, Good & Good For You, Blue, Yellow *illus*	8
Crown, S'More, Grade A Milk, Blue Ground, White Letters, Red Trim, Cork Lined	16
Gracefield Dairy, Jersey Milk, Pasteurized, Yellow, Red, White, Box-Board, 1 ⅜ In.	5
Presidential, Disc Seal, John Adams, Red, White, Blue, c.1964, 1 ¼ In.	4
Sunrise View Farm, Raw Milk, R.F. & M.S. Hinkley, Blue Letters, Sun, Rangely, Maine, 2 In. *illus*	5

BOTTLE OPENER

Bottle openers are needed to open many bottles. As soon as the commercial bottle was invented, the opener to be used with the new types of closures became a necessity. Many types of bottle openers can be found, most dating from the twentieth century. Collectors prize advertising and comic openers.

C&C Drink Super, Brass, Cone Top Can On End, 6 In.	150
Dolphin, Brass, Opener On Tail, Sand Cast, Penco, 1980s, 6 ½ x 2 ½ In.	25
Elephant, Curled Trunk, Brass, Marked, Hagenauer Wein, Austria, 3 ⅛ In. *illus*	74
Enamel, Stainless Steel Opener, Blue, Renato Salimbeni, Italy, Late 20th Century, 5 ¼ In.	113
Fish, Articulated, Abalone, Open Mouth, Attributed To Los Castillos, Mexico, 7 In. *illus*	30
Mermaid, Arching Tail, Cast Iron, Bronze, Patina, 6 In. *illus*	36
Park Inn, Nude Woman, Silhouette, Engraved, For Fun, Livingston Montana, 1900s, 3 In. *illus*	62
Parrot, On Perch, Mouth Open, Cast Iron, Painted, Multicolor, Hubley, 6 In.	56
Sea Gull, Perched On Stump, Painted, Cast Iron, Paper Label, Souvenir Of Maine, 3 x 2 ½ In.	63

Shark, Pewter, Open Mouth, 20th Century, 7 x 1 In. ... 100
Silver, Modernist, Ring Handle, Marked, Hermes, 1970s, 5 x 2 In. ... 371
Whalebone, Sperm Whale Shape Grip, Bronze Fluke, Patina, 19th Century, 6 In. *illus* ... 313
Whistle, Wood, Brass Ends, Italy, 6¾ In. ... 25

BOTTLE STOPPER

Bottle stoppers are made of glass, metal, plastic, and wood. Decorative and figural stoppers are used to replace the original cork stoppers and are collected today.

14K Gold, Cut Corners, Embossed, Monogram, Glass Bottom, Perfume, 1865-1915, 2 x 1¾ In. *illus* ... 325
Plastic, Seagram's Extra Dry Gin, Pourer, Blue & White, 1950s, 3½ x 2 x 1 In. ... 10
Porcelain, Figural, Man With Cap, 1930s, 2 In. ... 38
Wood, Cloth, Figural, Man, Beard, Plaid Tam O'Shanter, 2⅝ In. ... 19
Wood, Figural, Man Wearing Hat, Woman Wearing Scarf, Anri, 5 In. ... 40
Wood, Man, Sitting, Chin In Hand, Long Arms & Neck, Carved, Nigeria, 8 In. *illus* ... 88

BOX

Boxes of all kinds are collected. They were made of wood, metal, tortoiseshell, embroidery, or other material. Additional boxes may be listed in other sections, such as Advertising, Battersea, Ivory, Shaker, Tinware, and various Porcelain categories. Tea Caddies are listed in their own category.

Artist's, Hinged Lid, Walnut, Carved, Eagle, 1800s, 8¾ x 13¾ In. ... 188
Artist's, Walnut, Dog, Star, Palette Inlays, 1800s, 6½ x 20½ x 13½ In. *illus* ... 793
Baguette, Hinged Lid, Walnut, Copper Panel, Fruit Gatherers, Flat Feet, Late 1900s, 34 In. ... 148
Ballot, Blue Green Paint, 2 Drawers, Wood Knobs, 1800s, 7¼ x 6¾ x 5¾ In. *illus* ... 1017
Ballot, Hinged Top, Cutout Slot, White Oak, Brass Pull, Painted, c.1880, 14 x 16 In. ... 211
Bandbox, Lid, Wallpaper, Cardboard, Block Printed, Tan, White, Green Accent, c.1850, 6¾ x 9½ In. ... 180
Bandbox, Oval, Flowers & Leaves, Ewer Design, Hannah Davis, New Hampshire, 1810s, 13 In. *illus* ... 688
Bandbox, Round, Black Band, Teddy With Honey, 16 In. Diameter ... 25
Bandbox, Wallpaper, Hot Air Balloon, Rope Handle, Richard Clayton, 1800s, 10 x 15 x 12 In. *illus* ... 1586
Bandbox, Wallpaper, Labeled, Hannah Davis Jaffrey, 1800s, 16½ x 12½ In. ... 1220
Bandbox, Wallpaper, Red Squirrel, Flowers, Hand Sewn Lid, Susan DeCurtins, 12 x 15 x 19 In. ... 219
Barber, Woman, Black Hair, Blue Dress, Carved, Folk Art, c.1920s, 10½ x 12½ x 5¾ In. ... 1130
Bentwood, Round, Forged Rosehead Nails, Finger Lap, Wood Pegs, Signed, Beulah, 1800s, 3 x 6 In. ... 791
Betel Nut, Peacock Shape, Hinged Lid, Latch, Dhokra, India, 9½ x 9½ In. *illus* ... 236
Bible, Lid, Stand, English Oak, Dovetailed, Chip Carved Ends, Inside Branded 1765, 17 x 27 In. ... 190
Bible, Pine, Slant Lid, Wrought Iron Butterfly Hinges, 12 x 13 x 17¾ In. ... 259
Bone, Hinged Lid, Metal Inset, Faux Shell Decoration, Painted, Aztec Style, 4 x 10¼ In. ... 125
Bride's, Bentwood, Oval, Laced Seams, Multicolor, Flowers, Woman, Mid 1800s, 7 x 16 In. ... 570
Bride's, Lid, Bentwood, Flowers, Oval, Moyer, 1800s, 6¾ x 16½ In. *illus* ... 732
Bride's, Oval, Carved Handles, Multicolor, Flowers, Leaves, Scandinavia, 1800s, 13 In. ... 375
Burl, Carved, Tortoiseshell Lining, Continental, 1800s, 3½ In. ... 406
Button, Rosewood, Screw-On Lid, Wedgwood, Blue Jasperware Insert, 1½ In. ... 73
Candle, Carved, 4-Tier Slide Lid, Green, Bittersweet, Mustard, Dovetail Case, 1852, 8 x 12 In. *illus* ... 1074
Candle, Hanging, Curly Maple, Lollipop Cutout Crest, Spoon Rack, David Smith, 25 x 6 x 12 In. ... 58
Candle, Lid, Pine, Green Paint, Bird, Folk Art, 1800s, 6 x 2¾ x 1½ In. ... 1074
Candle, Pine, Red, Slanted Lift Lid, 2 Drawers, Bench, John Glenn, Late 1900s, 18 x 10 In. ... 59
Candle, Slide Lid, Cherry, Dovetail, Red, J.C. Cutter, Early 1800s, 4¾ x 10 x 5 In. ... 688
Candle, Slide Lid, Pine, White Compasswork, Red Dot, Dark Blue Ground, 1850s, 3 x 5 x 7 In. ... 2000
Candle, Sliding Panel Lid, Mahogany, Dovetailed Case, Lower Drawer, 1800s, 5 x 11 In. ... 354
Card, Bridge, Hammered Copper, Enamel, Wood, Hinged Lock, Patina, Arts & Crafts, 2 x 7 In. ... 691
Card, Hinged Lid, Sterling Silver, Mahogany, Burl Laminate, c.1945, 4 x 11 In. *illus* ... 2500
Casket, Dome Lid, Satinwood, Decoupage, Velvet Lined, Bun Feet, Early 1800s, 9 x 12 In. ... 826
Casket, Jewelry, Floral Pietra Dura Lid Panel, Bronze Mount, Late 1800s, 4 x 9 x 5 In. ... 351
Casket, Jewelry, Hinged, Silver Plate, High Relief Panels, Late 1800s, 5 x 7 x 5 In. *illus* ... 640
Casket, Jewelry, Roundel Scenes Of Neptune, Venus, Amphitrite, Gilt Metal, Copper, c.1860, 11 In. ... 2394
Casket, Lid, Sevres Style, Octagonal, Painted Scene, Gilt, 1800s, 3½ x ⅞ x 7¾ In. ... 640

BOX

Bottle Cap, Sunrise View Farm, Raw Milk, R.F. & M.S. Hinkley, Blue Letters, Sun, Rangely, Maine, 2 In.
$5

capman2 on eBay

Bottle Opener, Elephant, Curled Trunk, Brass, Marked, Hagenauer Wein, Austria, 3⅛ In.
$74

Merrill's Auctions

Bottle Opener, Fish, Articulated, Abalone, Open Mouth, Attributed To Los Castillos, Mexico, 7 In.
$30

Auctions at Showplace, NYC

Bottles

After 1860, cast-iron molds were used to made inexpensive bottles and wooden molds were discontinued. But iron molds were made with the help of a wooden pattern.

53

B

Bottle Opener, Mermaid, Arching Tail, Cast Iron, Bronze, Patina, 6 In.
$36

21st Century Auctions

Bottle Opener, Park Inn, Nude Woman, Silhouette, Engraved, For Fun, Livingston Montana, 1900s, 3 In.
$62

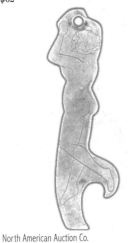

North American Auction Co.

Bottle Opener, Whalebone, Sperm Whale Shape Grip, Bronze Fluke, Patina, 19th Century, 6 In.
$313

Rafael Osona Nantucket Auctions

> **TIP**
> *Loud dogs and nosy neighbors are good security.*

Chestnut, Grain Painted, Drawer, Scalloped Rim, Divider, Canted, Late 1800s, 9 x 7 x 12 In. .	350
Cigar, Book Shape, Hinged Lid, Flowers, Sliding Divider, c.1880, 5 ¼ x 8 x 2 ½ In.	58
Cigarette, Die Shape, White Ground, Silver & Gold Plate, Hermes, France, c.1945, 3 ¾ In. .. *illus*	2750
Cigarette, Etched Brass, Cedar Lined Interior, Rockwell Kent, 1930, 2 x 7 x 5 ½ In.	438
Cigarette, Hinged Lid, Silver, Chase Repousse, Birds, Flowers, 1910s, 1 ¼ x 5 ¾ In.	84
Circular, Lid, Painted, Star Design, Black Band, Red Ground, 1800s, 6 ¾ In.	200
Clock & Barometer Lid, Burl, Silver Plate, Art Deco, Ch. Bertin Deauville, c.1935, 2 x 10 In.	4063
Coin, Ancient Roman, Cedar, Sterling Silver, Bulgari, Italy, c.1975, 1 ¾ x 7 In.	9375
Container, Spool, 2 Tiers, Teardrop Finials, Feeder Holes, Folk Art, 1800s, 6 x 7 x 5 In. *illus*	94
Cricket, Tortoiseshell, Reticulated, Pierced, Landscape, Carved, Chinese, 1700s, 5 x 7 In. ... *illus*	1625
Cutlery, Bird's-Eye Maple, Canted, Pierced Divider, Turned Handle, 1800s, 5 x 13 x 8 ¾ In.	300
Cutlery, Oak, Marquetry, Inlay, 16 x 8 In. .... *illus*	64
Desk, Oak, Carved, Lift Top, Iron Strap Hinges, 2 Drawers Interior, Floral, 11 x 22 x 17 In.	750
Ditty, Lid, Knob, Whalebone, Wood, Diamond Shape, c.1850, 5 ½ In. .... *illus*	5625
Document, Dome Lid, Brown, Leather Cover, Brass Tacks, 1800s, 5 ½ x 9 In.	281
Document, Dome Lid, Burlwood Veneer, Mounted, Brass, Marked, P. Moore, 1800s, 4 ½ x 6 ½ In.	384
Document, Dome Lid, Cotter Pin Hinges, Iron Lock & Hasp, Multicolor, Painted, 1800s, 6 x 10 In.	322
Document, Dome Lid, Pine, Painted, Brass Bail Handle, New England, Early 1800s, 7 x 12 In. . *illus*	1250
Document, Dome Lid, White Pine, Hearts, Branching Flowers, Vining Plants, 8 x 17 x 10 In. .	1150
Document, Hinged Dome Lid, Coromandel, Gilt, Leaves, Brass, c.1850, 6 x 9 In.	325
Document, Hinged Lid, Parquetry, Anglo-Colonial, 1800s, 5 ¾ x 12 x 9 In. .... *illus*	384
Document, Hinged Lid, Pine, Reddish Brown, Applied Base Molding, 1850s, 6 ¼ x 14 x 8 In.	187
Document, Hinged Lid, Poplar, Oval, Multicolor Federal Shield, 1850s, 3 ¾ x 8 ¾ x 12 ¾ In.	187
Document, Lift Lid, Bail Handle, Painted, Green, Brown, Yellow, 1800s, 7 x 14 In.	225
Dome Lid, Drawer, Flowers, Yellow Ground, Hinged, Dominoes Inside, 1800s, 6 ¼ x 8 In. ..*illus*	2684
Dome Lid, Pinwheel, Black, White Hearts, Dot, Tin Hasp, Red, c.1820, 8 ⅞ x 17 x 10 ¾ In.	5625
Dresser, Anglo-Indian, Mahogany, Shaped Cornice, Secretary Drawer, Bun Feet, 1800s, 14 In.	200
Dresser, Casket, Rectangular, Flowers, Ornate, Gilt, Art Deco, Chain, 5 x 6 ½ In. .... *illus*	354
Dresser, Dome Lid, Poplar, Wallpaper, Hinged, 1800s, 2 ¾ x 4 ¼ In.	915
Dresser, Hinged Dome Lid, Pine, Knob Handle, Red, c.1800, 7 x 8 In.	580
Dresser, Hinged Lid, Blue Opaline, Metal Band, Early 1900s, 2 x 4 ⅛ In. .... *illus*	384
Dresser, Hinged Lid, Cobalt Blue, Brass, Mounted, Ring Handle, Ball Feet, c.1900, 5 x 6 In.	1342
Dresser, Hinged Lid, Diamond Cut, Ormolu Mounts, Crystal Taille & M. Lubliner, c.1950, 4 In.	207
Dresser, Hinged Lid, Painted, Schoolgirl, Rectangular, New England, 4 x 10 In. .... *illus*	732
Dresser, Hinged Lid, Poplar, Flowers, Black Ground, 1800s, 6 ¼ x 18 In.	275
Dresser, Lid, Northern Hemisphere, Powder Blue, Round, Tiffany & Co., 2000, 5 ½ In.	31
Dresser, Mahogany, Ivory Escutcheon, Bird, Landscape, Inlay, 1810s, 4 x 10 In. .... *illus*	1188
Dresser, Maple, Walnut, Carved Bone Feet, 1800s, 6 ¾ x 9 ½ x 6 In.	313
Dresser, Poplar, Yellow Ground, Flowers, Black Pinstripes, c.1830, 4 ¾ x 11 x 5 In.	688
Earthenware, Lid, Bamboo Borders, Leaves, Acorn, Treacle Glaze, 1800s, 13 ½ In. ...... *illus*	468
Glove, Dome Lid, Staghorn, Carved, Bun Feet, 1850s, 5 ⅝ x 11 ¼ x 4 ¾ In.	832
Honor, Tobacco, Mechanical, Red, Painted, Brass & Metal, 1825, 5 x 7 In. .... *illus*	300
Humidor, Bronze, Engraved, Patina, Cedar Wood, Oscar Bach, 2 ¼ x 7 x 4 ½ In. .... *illus*	115
Iron, Inlaid Gold, Hinged Lid, Bird, Waves, Fish, Dragonfly Seal, Komei, 1 ⅛ x 2 x 2 In.	1143
Ironwood, Sculpted Desert, Inlaid Turquoise, Larry Favorite, 6 ¼ x 9 ¾ In. .... *illus*	148
Jewelry, Art Nouveau, Copper, Brass, Pottery Insert, McVitie & Price, 3 ¾ x 7 In. .... *illus*	756
Jewelry, Casket, Ormolu Frame, Cherubs, Nude, 3 Compartments, 6 x 6 ½ x 11 In.	316
Jewelry, Casket, Parquetry Inlay, Hardwood, Gilt Feet, Bronze Handles, 1900s, 7 x 12 x 15 In..	115
Jewelry, Casket, Trapezoidal, Hinged Lid, Brass Mount, Early 1900s, 5 x 6 ½ x 7 In.	431
Jewelry, Dome Lid, Gilt, Mixed Metal, Bracket Feet, Japan, c.1900, 3 x 4 ½ In. .... *illus*	480
Jewelry, Hinged Lid, Gilt, Bronze, Painted, Enamel, Acanthus Feet, c.1900, 2 ¾ x 4 In., Pair .	384
Jewelry, Hinged Lid, Mahogany, Carved, Tiger Motifs, 12 x 8 In. .... *illus*	885
Jewelry, Hinged Lid, Silver Plate, Classical Figure Heads, L. Oudry Pre Editeur, 5 ¾ In.	441
Kindling, Brass, Griffin Decor, Metal Liner, 1900s, 24 In., Pair	215
Knife, Flame Mahogany Veneers, Ebony Line Inlay, Divided Interior, Early 1800s, 14 ½ In. ..*illus*	502
Knife, Georgian Style, Mahogany, Fitted Interior, Late 1900s, 14 x 9 In., Pair .... *illus*	813
Knife, Hinged Lid, Mahogany, Serpentine Front, 6-Point Star, 1880s, 11 x 8 In., Pair ... *illus*	1872
Knife, Mahogany, Hinged Lid, Serpentine Front, 1800s, 13 ½ In.	207

Bottle Stopper, 14K Gold, Cut Corners, Embossed, Monogram, Glass Bottom, Perfume, 1865-1915, 2 x 1 ¾ In.
$325

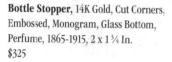

Apple Tree Auction Center

Bottle Stopper, Wood, Man, Sitting, Chin In Hand, Long Arms & Neck, Carved, Nigeria, 8 In.
$88

Mid-Hudson Auction Galleries

Box, Artist's, Walnut, Dog, Star, Palette Inlays, 1800s, 6 ½ x 20 ½ x 13 ½ In.
$793

Pook & Pook

Box, Ballot, Blue Green Paint, 2 Drawers, Wood Knobs, 1800s, 7 ¼ x 6 ¾ x 5 ¾ In.
$1,017

Soulis Auctions

Box, Bandbox, Oval, Flowers & Leaves, Ewer Design, Hannah Davis, New Hampshire, 1810s, 13 In.
$688

Eldred's

Box, Bandbox, Wallpaper, Hot Air Balloon, Rope Handle, Richard Clayton, 1800s, 10 x 15 x 12 In.
$1,586

Pook & Pook

Box, Betel Nut, Peacock Shape, Hinged Lid, Latch, Dhokra, India, 9 ½ x 9 ½ In.
$236

Austin Auction Gallery

Box, Bride's, Lid, Bentwood, Flowers, Oval, Moyer, 1800s, 6 ¾ x 16 ½ In.
$732

Pook & Pook

Box, Candle, Carved, 4-Tier Slide Lid, Green, Bittersweet, Mustard, Dovetail Case, 1852, 8 x 12 In.
$1,074

Soulis Auctions

Box, Card, Hinged Lid, Sterling Silver, Mahogany, Burl Laminate, c.1945, 4 x 11 In.
$2,500

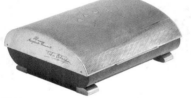

Wright

Box, Casket, Jewelry, Hinged, Silver Plate, High Relief Panels, Late 1800s, 5 x 7 x 5 In.
$640

Brunk Auctions

Box, Cigarette, Die Shape, White Ground, Silver & Gold Plate, Hermes, France, c.1945, 3¾ In.
$2,750

Wright

Box, Container, Spool, 2 Tiers, Teardrop Finials, Feeder Holes, Folk Art, 1800s, 6 x 7 x 5 In.
$94

Bruneau & Co. Auctioneers

Box, Cricket, Tortoiseshell, Reticulated, Pierced, Landscape, Carved, Chinese, 1700s, 5 x 7 In.
$1,625

Charlton Hall Auctions

Box, Cutlery, Oak, Marquetry, Inlay, 16 x 8 In.
$64

Hindman

Box, Ditty, Lid, Knob, Whalebone, Wood, Diamond Shape, c.1850, 5½ In.
$5,625

Eldred's

Box, Document, Dome Lid, Pine, Painted, Brass Bail Handle, New England, Early 1800s, 7 x 12 In.
$1,250

Eldred's

Box, Document, Hinged Lid, Parquetry, Anglo-Colonial, 1800s, 5¾ x 12 x 9 In.
$384

Hindman

Box, Dome Lid, Drawer, Flowers, Yellow Ground, Hinged, Dominoes Inside, 1800s, 6¼ x 8 In.
$2,684

Pook & Pook

Box, Dresser, Casket, Rectangular, Flowers, Ornate, Gilt, Art Deco, Chain, 5 x 6½ In.
$354

Bunch Auctions

Box, Dresser, Hinged Lid, Blue Opaline, Metal Band, Early 1900s, 2 x 4⅛ In.
$384

Leland Little Auctions

Box, Dresser, Hinged Lid, Painted, School Girl, Rectangular, New England, 4 x 10 In.
$732

Pook & Pook

Box, Dresser, Mahogany, Ivory Escutcheon, Bird, Landscape, Inlay, 1810s, 4 x 10 In.
$1,188

Eldred's

Box, Earthenware, Lid, Bamboo Borders, Leaves, Acorn, Treacle Glaze, 1800s, 13½ In.
$468

Jeffrey S. Evans & Associates

Box, Honor, Tobacco, Mechanical, Red, Painted, Brass & Metal, 1825, 5 x 7 In.
$300

Cottone Auctions

B

Box, Humidor, Bronze, Engraved, Patina, Cedar Wood, Oscar Bach, 2¼ x 7 x 4½ In.
$115

Blackwell Auctions

Box, Ironwood, Sculpted Desert, Inlaid Turquoise, Larry Favorite, 6¼ x 9¾ In.
$148

Leland Little Auctions

TIP
Dust frequently if you live near the seashore. Salt air causes problems.

Box, Jewelry, Art Nouveau, Copper, Brass, Pottery Insert, McVitie & Price, 3¾ x 7 In.
$756

Fontaine's Auction Gallery

Box, Jewelry, Dome Lid, Gilt, Mixed Metal, Bracket Feet, Japan, c.1900, 3 x 4½ In.
$480

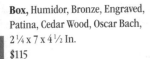

Cottone Auctions

Knife, Mahogany, Inlay, 1800s, 4¼ x 9 In. .... *illus*	188
Knife, Mahogany, Silver Escutcheons, Pulls, George III, England, Late 1700s, 14 x 9 In., Pair .*illus*	1375
Knife, Mahogany, Slant & Hinged Lid, George III, c.1790, 15 x 9 In.	443
Knife, Satinwood, Urn Shape, Fitted Interior, Leafy Border, Festoons, 1800s, 25 In., Pair.......	4688
Knife, Urn Shape, Inlay, Finial, Square Base, Ogee Bracket Feet, 25 x 7½ In., Pair ...... *illus*	677
Lapis Lazuli, Hinged Lid, Silvertone Metal Laurel Wreath, Blue Ground, 1950s, 1 x 5 x 3 In. ..*illus*	413
Letter, Hinged Lid, Chinoiserie, Black Lacquer, Divided Interior, Early 1900s, 8 x 7 In.	531
Letter, Hinged Lid, Painted, Gilt, Hanging Handles, John Little & Co., Late 1800s, 7 x 16½ x 11½ In..	177
Letter, Oak, Brass, 2 Hinged Doors, Pull-Out Drawer, Fitted Interior, 1880s, 12 x 12 x 9 In. *illus*	527
Letter, Stone, Painted, Red, Leaves, Lion Mask & Ribbon, Gadrooned Finial, 2 Doors, 1900s, 44 In.....	708
Liqueur, Black Forest Style, Walnut, Carved, Leaves, Scalloped Ornamentation, 9 x 9½ In...	148
Malachite, Lift Lid, Ormolu Mounted, Cupid, Green Ground, 1900s, 1½ x 3 x 2¼ In...........	266
Memento Mori, Human Skull Shape, Carved, Quartz Crystal, 1900s, 2 In.	266
Oak, Chamfered Lid, Brass Escutcheon, Divided Compartment, Turned Legs, 1700s, 5 x 9 x 6 In..	406
Opaline, Egg Shape, Blue, Glass, Brass Feet, France, 7 x 8 In. .... *illus*	688
Pantry, Bentwood, Painted, Black, Dovetailed, 1800s, 6¼ In.	300
Pantry, Lid, Bentwood, Painted, Oval, Pine & Oak, Mid 1800s, 12¾ In.	293
Pencil, Slide Lid, Painted Shield, Flower Scrolls, Black Ground, 1800s, 2 x 7 x 2¾ In.	200
Pill, Micro Mosaic, Flower Lid, Gilt Metal, 1¼ x 2¼ In.	60
Pine, Hinged Dome Lid, Painted, Bird, Red Ground, Stand, Continental, 1800s, 16 x 23 In. ..	322
Pine, Hinged Lid, Gray Ground, Central Tree, Sawtooth Border, 1850s, 7 x 9 x 11 In.	4000
Pine, Hinged Lid, Rectangular, Brass Bail Handle, Sponge, 1800s, 7 x 18 In.	263
Pine, Lift Lid, Cutout Open Handle, Slanted Lid, Canted Front, 1850s, 36 x 8½ x 8½ In.	202
Pine, Lift Lid, Grained Tiger Maple Veneer, Panels & Sides, Mahogany Top, c.1850, 5 x 10 In...*illus*	469
Pine, Lift Lid, Grapevine, Rectangular, Line Border, 1850s, 2½ x 8¼ x 5¼ In.	138
Pine, Slant Lid, Shaped Hanger, Yellow, Gray Pinstripes, H.M., Early 1800s, 14 x 11 In.	750
Pine, Slide Lid, Drawer, Wall, Gray, Pennsylvania, 1800s, 10 x 9 x 5½ In.	488
Pine, Slide Lid, Lollipop Handle, Green, Grandmother Levia's Box, 1830, 6¾ In.	1037
Pine, Slide Lid, White & Blue Tulip, Salmon Ground, 1800s, 14 x 11 x 7 In........................	1098
Poplar, Flower Decals, Cherubs, Base Molding, Joseph Long Lehn, Late 1800s, 7 x 10 x 6 In..	750
Poplar, Slide Lid, Salmon Swirl, Reeded, Painted, Pa., Early 1800s, 8 x 6½ x 16 In.	458
Receipt, Hinged Lid, Yellow Lettering, Katie, Black Pinstripes, Late 1800s, 5 x 10 x 6 In.......	531
Salt, Slant Lift Lid, Pine, Arched Back, Yellow, Dovetailed, c.1850, 10 x 8½ x 5½ In. ... *illus*	1053
Sandalwood, Dome Lid, Carved, Figures, Animals, Leafy, Anglo-Indian, 1800s, 4 x 4 x 11 In..	369
Scent, Bronze, Gilt Mounted, 3 Gilt & Enamel Bottles, France, 1900, 3½ x 7 x 3¾ In. . *illus*	250
Schoolgirl's, Landscape, Bird's-Eye Maple, Brass Ball Feet, Painted, Mass., 1800s, 5 x 13 In.	3750
Stationary, Slant Lid, Copper Tacks, Shell, Elizabeth Eaton Burton, 8¾ x 5½ x 11 In..........	4688
Storage, Dome Lid, Bentwood Handle, Red, Carved Initials, Oval, 11 x 12 x 23 In. .... *illus*	460
Storage, Dome Top, Leafy, Flower Border, Lattice Drapery, c.1820, 11 x 24 x 11 In.................	1125
Storage, Hinged Convex Lid, Parquetry Inlay, Mixed Wood, Bun Feet, c.1900, 9 x 15 In.	413
Storage, Hinged Lid, Raised Panel, Removable Tray, Scroll Foot Base, 1900s, 25 x 17 x 13 In..	207
Strong, Hinged Lid, Black Lacquer, Brass, Lock Plate & Corners, Early 1900s, 6 x 15 In.	94
Tabernacle, Repousse Copper, Brass Over Iron, Arched Top, Hinged Barrels, 1600s, 15 x 9 In.	1287
Table, Cofre Sol, Sun Chest, Talavera Style, Blue & White, Jesus Guerrero Santos, c.1990, 9 x 11 In. *illus*	325
Table, Mahogany, Circular, Concentric Rings, Gilt, Ball Handle, 4 Alligators, 4 x 8 In...........	106
Table, Mahogany, Hinged Lid, Brass Top Handle, Batwing Escutcheon, Bracket Feet, c.1750, 5 x 9 In..	325
Tantalus, 3 Decanters, Presentation, To Brigadier General Albert Ordway, 1890, 14 x 18 In..	288
Teak, Lift Lid, Bail Handles, Engraved, Swatow Pewter, Chinese, Early 1900s, 3 x 7¼ In.	138
Tobacco, Lid, Cannon Lift, Painted, Black, Cast Iron, Horatio Nelson, 5 x 4½ x 4½ In. *illus*	160
Tobacco, Lid, Kneeling Slave, Humanity, Rectangular, Cast Iron, 1800s, 3 x 5½ x 3⅝ In. ...	960
Tobacco, Oval, Brass, Copper, Animals, Carved, Dutch, 1700s, 1¼ x 1¾ In. .... *illus*	88
Travel, Mother-Of-Pearl Inlay, Flowers, Doors, Drawers, Fold-Out Desk, Gilt, Black, 15½ In. ..*illus*	315
Trinket, Gold Theme, Brass, Rectangular, Round Finial, Footed, Marked, JB, 6½ x 4 x 4 In.	177
Trinket, Walnut Lid, Woven Curlicue, Carved, Porcupine Weave, 1800s, 3 x 8 x 4 In.	1098
Turtle Shape, Lid, Brass, Copper, Wood, Arthur Court, 33 x 21 x 10 In. .... *illus*	313
Valuables, Hinged Lid, Mahogany Veneer, Ribbon Molded Edge, 1800s, 4 x 12 In.	148
Vanity, Coromandel, Glass Jars, Silver Plate Lids, Marked, S. Mordan, London, 1800s, 7 x 12 In. .*illus*	281
Wall, Hinged Lid, Walnut, Shaped Backboard, c.1815, 14 x 8½ In...............................	322

Box, Jewelry, Hinged Lid, Mahogany, Carved, Tiger Motifs, 12 x 8 In.
$885

Copake Auction

Box, Knife, Flame Mahogany Veneers, Ebony Line Inlay, Divided Interior, Early 1800s, 14 1/2 In.
$502

Leland Little Auctions

Box, Knife, Georgian Style, Mahogany, Fitted Interior, Late 1900s, 14 x 9 In., Pair
$813

Charlton Hall Auctions

Box, Knife, Hinged Lid, Mahogany, Serpentine Front, 6-Point Star, 1880s, 11 x 8 In., Pair
$1,872

Jeffrey S. Evans & Associates

Box, Knife, Mahogany, Inlay, 1800s, 4 1/4 x 9 In.
$188

Charlton Hall Auctions

Box, Knife, Mahogany, Silver Escutcheons, Pulls, George III, England, Late 1700s, 14 x 9 In., Pair
$1,375

Eldred's

Box, Knife, Urn Shape, Inlay, Finial, Square Base, Ogee Bracket Feet, 25 x 7 1/2 In., Pair
$677

Alderfer Auction Company

Box, Lapis Lazuli, Hinged Lid, Silvertone
Metal Laurel Wreath, Blue Ground, 1950s,
1 x 5 x 3 In.
$413

Austin Auction Gallery

Box, Letter, Oak, Brass, 2 Hinged Doors,
Pull-Out Drawer, Fitted Interior, 1880s,
12 x 12 x 9 In.
$527

Jeffrey S. Evans & Associates

Box, Opaline, Egg Shape, Blue, Glass,
Brass Feet, France, 7 x 8 In.
$688

Abington Auction Gallery

Box, Pine, Lift Lid, Grained Tiger Maple
Veneer, Panels & Sides, Mahogany Top,
c.1850, 5 x 10 In.
$469

Eldred's

Box, Salt, Slant Lift Lid, Pine, Arched Back,
Yellow, Dovetailed, c.1850, 10 x 8 ½ x 5 ½ In.
$1,053

Jeffrey S. Evans & Associates

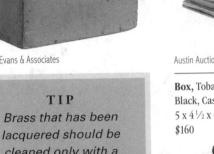

TIP

*Brass that has been
lacquered should be
cleaned only with a
solution of liquid dish-
washing detergent and
warm sudsy water, then
rinsed in warm water
and dried. Polish will
harm the lacquer.*

Box, Scent, Bronze, Gilt Mounted, 3 Gilt &
Enamel Bottles, France, 1900,
3 ½ x 7 x 3 ¾ In.
$250

Kamelot Auctions

Box, Storage, Dome Lid, Bentwood Handle,
Red, Carved Initials, Oval, 11 x 12 x 23 In.
$460

Forsythes' Auctions

Box, Table, Cofre Sol, Sun Chest, Talavera
Style, Blue & White, Jesus Guerrero Santos,
c.1990, 9 x 11 In.
$325

Austin Auction Gallery

Box, Tobacco, Lid, Cannon Lift, Painted,
Black, Cast Iron, Horatio Nelson,
5 x 4 ½ x 4 ½ In.
$160

Hartzell's Auction Gallery Inc.

Box, Tobacco, Oval, Brass, Copper, Animals,
Carved, Dutch, 1700s, 1 ¼ x 1 ¾ In.
$88

Charlton Hall Auctions

Box, Travel, Mother-Of-Pearl Inlay, Flowers,
Doors, Drawers, Fold-Out Desk, Gilt, Black,
15 ½ In.
$315

Fontaine's Auction Gallery

Wall, Oak, Scrolled & Incised Backboard, 2 Shelves, Shaped Sides, Late 1800s, 12 x 9 x 3 In.	275
Wall, Slant Lift Lid, Maple, Dovetail, Cutout Tombstone Crest, c.1840, 10 x 7 x 12 In.	161
Wallpaper, Lozenge Shape, Flowers, German Language Interior, c.1847, 3¾ x 12 x 6½ In. ...	750
Walnut, Faire, Saus, Dire, Flowers, Shields, Carved, Gothic Revival, 1923, 11½ In.	150
Wood, Geometrics, Pinwheel, Checkerboard, Inlay, Sailor Made, 1800s, 6 x 12 x 7½ In.	156
Wood, Hinged Lid, Black, Carved, Eagle, Crossed Swords, Ohio, 5¼ x 7½ In.	875
Wood, Slide Lid, Red Ground, Black Interior, Flowers, 4¾ x 12¼ x 12¼ In.	125
Writing, Lift Lid, Cross, 5 Tiger's-Eye Agate Cabochons, Silk Lining, 1800s, 3 x 8 x 8 In.........	281
Writing, Mahogany, Leather, Slant Front, George III, 1700s, 7½ x 28¼ In.	141

BOY SCOUT

Boy Scout collectibles include any material related to scouting, including patches, manuals, and uniforms. The Boy Scout movement in the United States started in 1910. The first Jamboree was held in 1937. Girl Scout items are listed under their own heading.

Blanket, 285 Council Patch, Red Velvet, Late 1900s, 81 x 63 In. .... *illus*	113
Book, The Boy Scouts At The Canadian Border, Howard Payson, Hurst & Co., 1918, 7½ x 5 In.	12
Calendar, 1942, Boy Scouts Of America, Cardboard Frame, Norman Rockwell, 46 x 22½ In..	277
Hat, Scout Master, Olive Green, Wool Felt, Stetson, 1930s, 8¼ In.................................	59
Panel, Boy Scouts, Be Prepared, Scout, Flag, Applique, Frame, c.1950, 23 x 15 In. .... *illus*	532
Patch, Junior Life Saving Scout, Diamond Shape, Center Cross, 1930s, 5 x 3 In.	18
Pin, 5 Year Service Star, Yellow & Green, Enameled, Gilt, Bronze, 1900s, ¾ In..................*illus*	74
Shirt, Red, Patches On 2 Pockets, Wolf Head On Back, Wool, c.1960, Size 42	22
Toy, 3 Scouts, Campfire With Hanging Pot, Aluminum, Wend-Al, c.1950, 4 Piece..........	77
Toy, Figure, American Boy Scout, Metal Arts Miniatures, Jones, 1931, 3 In.	480
Toy, Figurine, Group, Scout Cutting Tree Branch, Britains, Prewar, 27 Piece	320

BRADLEY & HUBBARD

Bradley & Hubbard is a name found on many metal objects. Walter Hubbard and his brother-in-law, Nathaniel Lyman Bradley, started making cast iron clocks, tables, frames, andirons, bookends, doorstops, lamps, chandeliers, sconces, and sewing birds in 1854 in Meriden, Connecticut. The company became Bradley & Hubbard Manufacturing Company in 1875. Charles Parker Company bought the firm in 1940. There is no mention of Bradley & Hubbard after the 1950s. Bradley & Hubbard items may be found in other sections that include metal.

Lamp, Asian Style Brass Frame, Reticulated, Gilt Base, Slag Glass Shade, c.1910, 28 x 19 In..	531
Lamp, Brass, Domed Glass Shade, 8 Panels, Flowers, Victorian, 24 x 20 In. .... *illus*	540
Lamp, Bronze, Frogskin Finish, Slag Glass, Octagonal Cherry Shade, 22 x 18 x 19 In.............	1125
Lamp, Electric, Bronze, Slag Glass, Landscape Scene, Engraved, Early 1900s, 13 x 11 In. *illus*	448
Lamp, Piano, Gilt, Brass, Dragons, Reticulated Font, Ornate, Tripod Base, c.1880, 60 In. *illus*	2337
Sconce, French Empire Style, Brass, Green, Slag Glass Leaf Shade, Early 1900s, 14 In., Pair .*illus*	236
Stand, Lamp, Gilt, Iron, Cast Tray, Cherub Heads, Tripod Feet, 1800s, 32 In.	215

BRASS

Brass has been used for decorative pieces and useful tablewares since ancient times. It is an alloy of copper, zinc, and other metals. Additional brass items may be found under Bell, Candlestick, Tool, or Trivet.

Alms Dish, Nuremburg, Adam & Eve, Punchwork Leaves, Central Figural Cartouche, 1700s, 14 In.	1500
Ashtray, Dorade Vent, Mounted, Red Leather Base, Paul Dupre Lafon, Hermes, c.1945, 6½ In.	2250
Bar Cart, Glass, Faux Bamboo, 2 Tiers, Handle, Italy, 26 x 20 x 31 In.	750
Bar Cart, Wood Shelves, Turned Handle, Egyptianesque Mount, Wheels, 30 x 20 x 29 In. *illus*	1152
Bed Warmer, Embossed, Rampant Lion, Turned Handle, Pierced Pan, 1700s, 44 In..............	580
Bed Warmer, Hinged Lid, Tooled Flowers, Turned Handle, Black Paint, Early 1800s, 41 In...	225

Box, Turtle Shape, Lid, Brass, Copper, Wood, Arthur Court, 33 x 21 x 10 In. $313

Abington Auction Gallery

> **Storage Lockers**
> Storage lockers available for rent were first built in the 1960s. The units store unneeded household furniture and belongings. Are we acquiring too many things? Moving more often? Or are houses smaller?

Box, Vanity, Coromandel, Glass Jars, Silver Plate Lids, Marked, S. Mordan, London, 1800s, 7 x 12 In. $281

Kamelot Auctions

Boy Scout, Blanket, 285 Council Patch, Red Velvet, Late 1900s, 81 x 63 In. $113

Selkirk Auctioneers & Appraisers

B

Boy Scout, Panel, Boy Scouts, Be Prepared, Scout, Flag, Applique, Frame, c.1950, 23 x 15 In.
$532

Garth's Auctioneers & Appraisers

Boy Scout, Pin, 5 Year Service Star, Yellow & Green, Enameled, Gilt, Bronze, 1900s, ¾ In.
$74

Rich Penn Auctions

Bradley & Hubbard, Lamp, Brass, Domed Glass Shade, 8 Panels, Flowers, Victorian, 24 x 20 In.
$540

Nadeau's Auction Gallery

Bed Warmer, Pierced Pan, Engraved, Flowers, Metal Handle, Continental, 1700, 40 In.	125
Bed Warmer, Punched Decor, Wood Handle, N. Newell, 1800s, 49 In. .... *illus*	225
Bowl, Lotus Leaf, Metalcraft, Harvin Co., 1948, 7 x 15 x 13 In.	767
Box, Dome Lid, Marquetry, Stationary, Key, Marked, Andre Charles Boulle, London, 7¾ x 6 x 10¾ In.	1750
Box, Octagonal, Castle, Sayings, Engraved, Dutch, 1786, 2¼ x 6 x 1½ In.	58
Bucket, Apple, Iron Swing Bail Handle, Copper Rivets, Late 1800s, 15 x 20 In. .... *illus*	295
Charger, Flower Blossom Design, Bands Of Lettering, Hand Tooled, Germany, c.1650, 16 In. ..*illus*	1000
Charger, Wall, Islamic, Mixed Metal Inlay, Arabesque & Calligraphic Design, 26¼ In.	177
Coal Scuttle, Repousse, English Heraldic Motifs, 2 Hinged Lids, Early 1900s, 21 x 13 In.	148
Coat Rack, 4 Hooks, Splayed Legs, Circle Stretcher, 66 In.	37
Compote, 3 Lucite & Brass Pillars, Midcentury, Triangular Top & Base, 19¾ In., Pair	375
Desk Stand, 2 Inkwells, Winged Beast Center, Leaves, Cartouche, Late 1800s, 5 x 11 In.	384
Dish, Cross, Turned Baluster Center, Footed, India, 1900s, 19¾ In.	148
Figurine, Buddha, Seated, Draped Robe, Phoenix Design, Wood Base, 9½ x 10 In.	59
Gong, Hammered, Stacked Leather, Rawhide Washer Hammer, Tibet, 1800s, 8 x 5 x 24 In.	316
Humidor, Cockatoo Shape, Hinged Lid, Gilt, Glass, Cork, Mark Cross, c.1975, 17¼ In. . . *illus*	1430
Jardiniere, Rococo Style, Scrolls, Flowers, Handles, Removable Metal Liner, c.1950, 6 x 17 In.	207
Jardiniere, Undertray, Figural Scenes, Koi Handles, Chinese, c.1950, 5¾ In.	720
Kettle, Lid, Gooseneck Spout, Molded Stand, Massachusetts, 1800s, 13½ In.	315
Kettle, Swing Bail Handle, Wrought Iron Stand, Stamped, W. Minar, 1800s, 30 x 25 In.	413
Mailbox, Raised Lion's Head, Envelope Style Hinged Lid, Wire Paper Holder, England, 14 In.	71
Model, Cannon, Signal, Wooden Carriage, Cord, Marked, Strong Fire Arms Co., 1900s, 18 In. *illus*	3250
Model, Cannon, Touch Hole, Wheels, 15 In., Pair	154
Model, Cannon, Wood Carriage, Mounted On Square Base, 1900s, 7 x 9½ In. .... *illus*	250
Pail, Swing Handle, Oval Mouth, Marked, 12 In. .... *illus*	62
Planter, 3 Tiers, Camel Saddle Shape, Dromedary, Wood, Splayed Legs, 52½ In.	443
Receptacle, Tapered Shape, Repousse, Leaves Decor, Iron Support Hooks, 1800s, 33 In.	236
Sculpture, Antelope Head, Removable Glass Horn, Hexagonal Base, 1970s, 31½ x 8 In.	400
Sculpture, Biomorphic Kinetic Fish, Circular, Oval, Signed, MEL, c.1950-60, 37 x 28 In. *illus*	219
Sculpture, Female Torso, Modernist, Brass, France, 1960s, 26 x 20 x 12 In. .... *illus*	875
Stand, Kettle, Serpentine Front, Faux Drawer, Cabriole Legs, Early 1800s, 13½ x 17 In.	192
Sundial, Roman Numerals, Engraved, Star Design, On Slate Base, Van Cort, 1900s, 11 x 11 In.	344
Teapot, Ribbed Teardrop Shape, Dragon Scroll Handle, Tapered Spout, 1700s, 10 x 12 x 5 In.	439
Torchere, Cast Decorative Band, Circular Base, Late 1900s, 55 In., Pair	84
Tub, Molded Rim, Side Handles, Paw Feet, 24½ In.	165
Urn, 2 Shaped Handles, Rounded Rim, Waist Design, Beldray, 1900s, 12½ In., Pair	177
Urn, Onyx, Egyptian Style, Black, Brown Stone Base, 13 In., Pair	225
Vase, Bulbous, Flared Mouth, Engraved, Rope Shape, 12 In., Pair	156
Wall Hanging, Lion's Head Shape, Tapered Scepter, Late 1900s, 40 In., Pair	885
Wax Jack, Box Shape, Round, Lid, Finial, Loop Handle, Stamped A.G.F., c.1800, 3½ In.	280

BRASTOFF, *see Sascha Brastoff category.*

BREAD PLATE, *see various silver categories, porcelain factories, and pressed glass patterns.*

BRIDE'S BOWL OR BASKET

Bride's bowls or baskets were usually one-of-a-kind novelties made in American and European glass factories. They were especially popular about 1880 when the decorated basket was often given as a wedding gift. Cut glass baskets were popular after 1890. All bride's bowls lost favor about 1905. Bride's bowls and baskets may also be found in other glass sections. Check the index at the back of the book.

Blue Cased, Bowl, Ruffled Edge, Silver Plate Frame, Cast Acorns, 11 x 10 In.	57
Cased Glass, White, Pink, Ruffled Edge, Silver Plate Frame, Late 1800s, 11 x 5 x 11 In.	164
Glass, Blue, Ruffled Crimped Edge, Silver Plate Frame, 8 In.	230
Green, Iridescent, Cranberry Ruffled Edge, Silver Plate Frame, 1½ In.	184
Green, Satin Glass, Pink Interior, Flowers, Gold Plate Frame, Cherub, 17 x 10 In.	1700
Pink & White Cased, Peg Bowl, Leaf & Acorn, Silver Plate Frame, 16 x 11 In. .... *illus*	150

Bradley & Hubbard, Lamp, Electric, Bronze, Slag Glass, Landscape Scene, Engraved, Early 1900s, 13 x 11 In.
$448

Hindman

Bradley & Hubbard, Lamp, Piano, Gilt, Brass, Dragons, Reticulated Font, Ornate, Tripod Base, c.1880, 60 In.
$2,337

Rich Penn Auctions

Bradley & Hubbard, Sconce, French Empire Style, Brass, Green, Slag Glass Leaf Shade, Early 1900s, 14 In., Pair
$236

Leland Little Auctions

Brass, Bed Warmer, Punched Decor, Wood Handle, N. Newell, 1800s, 49 In.
$225

Pook & Pook

Brass, Bucket, Apple, Iron Swing Bail Handle, Copper Rivets, Late 1800s, 15 x 20 In.
$295

Leland Little Auctions

TIP

Lemon oil is a good polish for brass inside the house. After polishing brass kept outdoors, use a thin coat of paste wax to protect the shine.

Brass, Bar Cart, Wood Shelves, Turned Handle, Egyptianesque Mount, Wheels, 30 x 20 x 29 In.
$1,152

Neal Auction Company

Brass, Charger, Flower Blossom Design, Bands Of Lettering, Hand Tooled, Germany, c.1650, 16 In.
$1,000

Eldred's

B

Brass, Humidor, Cockatoo Shape, Hinged Lid, Gilt, Glass, Cork, Mark Cross, c.1975, 17¼ In.
$1,430

Wright

Brass, Model, Cannon, Signal, Wooden Carriage, Cord, Marked, Strong Fire Arms Co., 1900s, 18 In.
$3,250

Eldred's

Brass, Model, Cannon, Wood Carriage, Mounted On Square Base, 1900s, 7 x 9½ In.
$250

Eldred's

Brass, Pail, Swing Handle, Oval Mouth, Marked, 12 In.
$62

Hartzell's Auction Gallery Inc.

Brass, Sculpture, Biomorphic Kinetic Fish, Circular, Oval, Signed, MEL, c.1950-60, 37 x 28 In.
$219

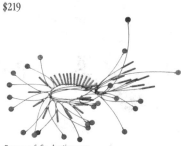

Bruneau & Co. Auctioneers

Brass, Sculpture, Female Torso, Modernist, Brass, France, 1960s, 26 x 20 x 12 In.
$875

Abington Auction Gallery

Bride's Basket, Pink & White Cased, Peg Bowl, Leaf & Acorn, Silver Plate Frame, 16 x 11 In.
$150

Woody Auction

Bride's Basket, Pink & White Opalescent, Ruffled Rim, Meriden, Silver Plate Frame, 7 x 14 In.
$125

Woody Auction

Bristol, Vase, Trumpet, Transfer, Painted, Child, Cream Ground, Footed, 1800s, 11½ In.
$74

Locati Auctions

TIP

To remove an unwanted gummed price sticker, try heating it with a hair dryer. The glue will melt a bit, and it will be easier to peel off the sticker.

B

Pink & White Opalescent, Ruffled Edge, Meriden, Silver Plate Frame, 7 x 14 In. .... *illus* 125
Satin Glass, Yellow Cased Rose, Mother-Of-Pearl, Herringbone, 1880s, 12 ½ x 7 ⅞ In............ 1404

BRISTOL

Bristol glass was made in Bristol, England, after the 1700s. The Bristol glass most often seen today is a Victorian, lightweight opaque glass that is often blue. Some of the glass was decorated with enamels.

Charger, Tin Glaze, Oriental Panels, Blue, White, Ginsburg & Levy, New York, 13 ½ In., Pair . 427
Plate, Liberta Populi, Blue & White, Justice Figure, Lambrequin Border, c.1734, 8 ¾ In. 3780
Vase, Trumpet, Transfer, Painted, Child, Cream Ground, Footed, 1800s, 11 ½ In. .... *illus* 74

BRITANNIA, *see Pewter category.*

BRONZE

Bronze is an alloy of copper, tin, and other metals. It is used to make figurines, lamps, and other decorative objects. Bronze lamps are listed in the Lamp category. Pieces listed here date from the eighteenth, nineteenth, and twentieth centuries. Shown here are marks used by three well-known makers of bronzes.

Armor Bronze Corp.
c.1919–c.1926, 1934–1948

Bradley and Hubbard Mfg. Co.
1875–c.1940

POMPEIAN BRONZE COMPANY

Pompeian Bronze Co.
1920s

Basin, Bouval, Maurice, Art Nouveau, Female Nude, Reclining On Blossom, Footed, 6 x 13 x 7 In. 1404
Bowl, Gilt, Leafy Band, Footed, Signed, Chinese, 4 ½ x 12 ½ In...................... 360
Box, Hurley, E.T., Lid, Seahorse, Seaweed, Patina, 1 ⅜ x 2 ⅞ x 4 ¾ In......................... 938
Bust, Aizelin, Eugene, Woman, Wearing Tiara, Verdigris Patina, 1821, 14 In........................... 215
Bust, Andersen, Roy, Indian, Many Coups, Walnut Base, Signed, 11 x 6 ¼ In. 765
Bust, Bakerman, Edwin, Brutalist, Man With Beard, Black Marble Base, Marked, 1945, 4 ½ In.. 94
Bust, Bernini, Gian Lorenzo, Ajax, Facing Right, Greek Warrior, Square Base, 16 In. ... *illus* 960
Bust, Colombo, R., Napoleon, Eagle, Signed, France, 1885, 22 x 16 In. 1750
Bust, Cottrill, Alan, Nathan Bedford Forrest, Stepped Base, Signed, 1996, 20 In. 960
Bust, De Groot, Guillaume, King Leopold II, Gentleman, Signed, 1900, 22 ¾ x 22 In........ 625
Bust, George Washington, Carved, Turned Head, Circular Base, 1800s, 14 x 10 In.............. 2768
Bust, Homer, Patina, Engraved, Stand, Signed, Socle, 1900s, 27 In............................ 2286
Bust, La Monaca, Francesco, Napoleon, Military Garb, Eagle, Stepped, Marble Base, 17 ¼ In.. 360
Bust, Napoleon Bonaparte, Eagle, Marble, Foundry Stamp, France, Late 1800s, 12 ¾ In....... 322
Bust, Richard, Felix Pierre, Woman, Esperance, Hope, Patina, Signed, 1880s, 17 ¾ In.. 322
Bust, Whitney, Gertrude, Head Of Spanish Peasant, Scarf On Head, Marble Base, Signed, 14 x 7 ½ In. 7188
Bust, Winston S. Churchill, Cigar, Mount, Circular Marble Base, 1900s, 13 ½ x 7 In. 748
Bust, Woman, Braided Hair, Floral Wreath, Neoclassical Style, 1800s, 26 ½ In................ 1280
Candleholder, Ram's Heads, Hoof Feet, Mounted On Ram's Horns, 8 ½ x 9 ½ In., Pair........ 688
Cannon, Royal Navy, Half Scale, Oak Carriage, 1800s, 15 x 13 x 30 In. 1404
Cassolette, Neoclassical Style, Gilt, Patina, Head Handle, 1900s, 16 ½ In., Pair.................... 960
Censer, Artichoke Shape Bowl, Dome Lid, Guanyin Finial, Legs, Claw Feet, Chinese, 25 In.... 2091
Censer, Elephant Head Feet, Mythical Beast Handles, Archaic Seal, Chinese, 1800s, 7 x 5 In. 644
Censer, Houston, James, Unicorn Head, Glass, 18K Gold Horn, Signed, c.1965, 17 In. 325
Censer, Lid, Square Shape, Curved Mask Head Legs, Gilt Phoenix, Chinese, Late 1800s, 7 In.. 1121
Censer, Qilin, Dragon, Standing, Incense Burner, Wood Stand, Chinese, 16 x 14 In. ....*illus* 3163
Censer, Quatrefoil Shape, Dragon, Footed, Japan, Late 19th Century, 11 ¼ In. 300
Centerpiece, 2 Winged Putti, Hippogriff, Glass Rimmed Dish, Gilt, France, 1800s, 14 x 10 In. 625
Centerpiece, Circular Top, Beaded, Relief, Cherubs, Garland, Tripod Base, 1800s, 8 ½ In ... 120
Cigarette Box, Square, Hammer, Compass, Cog, Wheat Design, Embossed, Russia, 4 x 3 ¼ In. 118

Bronze, Bust, Bernini, Gian Lorenzo, Ajax, Facing Right, Greek Warrior, Square Base, 16 In.
$960

Hindman

Bronze, Censer, Qilin, Dragon, Standing, Incense Burner, Wood Stand, Chinese, 16 x 14 In.
$3,163

Blackwell Auctions

TIP
Be careful when cleaning bronze figurines, lamp bases, bowls, etc. Never use steel wool, stiff brushes, or chemicals. Never wash a bronze. Never use metal polish on a bronze. Dust frequently.

Bronze, Ewer, Mythological, Renaissance Design, Symbol Of Hope, Sphinxes, Grand Tour, 1800s, 11 ½ In. **$443**

Leland Little Auctions

Bronze, Holy Water Font, Marble, Putti, Mold Edge, Shallow Shell Design, Late 1800s, 20 x 10 In. **$472**

Austin Auction Gallery

Clock, Hebert, E., Woman, Child, Roman Numerals, Signed, 24 ½ x 12 ½ In.	1216
Column, Renaissance Style, Spiral, Leafy Shaft, 4 Bands, Gilt, Rounded Base, 1900s, 75 In.	1750
Compote, Empire Style, Scrolled Handles, Flowers, Leafy Socle, Footed, 1800s, 6 x 10 In.	200
Container, Lid, Foo Dog Finial, Tripod Feet, Circular Base, Asia, 11 In.	106
Crucifix, Jesus On Cross, Mary & Joseph, Below, Platform Base, 16 In.	1638
Dish, Marsden, Robert, 4 Nude Women, Round Cup, Patina, 8 In.	188
Dish, Vautrin, Line, Talosel, Resin, France, c.1960, 8 In.	6250
Ewer, Giroux, Maison Alphonse, Figural, Putti, Drapery Swags, Stepped Base, 1800s, 13 In., Pair.	469
Ewer, Mythological, Renaissance Design, Symbol Of Hope, Sphinxes, Grand Tour, 1800s, 11 ½ In. *illus*	443
Ewer, Nautical Theme Relief, Mythological, Classical Imp Handle, 1800s, 19 In., Pair	625
Ewer, Neoclassical Style, Cast Figures, Forest Landscape, 24 x 15 ½ x 14 ½ In., Pair	900
Frame, Gilt, Inset Jewels, Pierced Filigree, Early 1900s, 19 ½ x 14 In.	347
Garniture, Wong Lee, Cherub, Playing Musical Instrument, On Black Ball, 1900s, 9 In., Pair	325
Girandole, Cut Glass, Rock Crystal, Gilt, Regence Style, 1800s, 32 ½ In., Pair	882
Head, Bateman, Robert, Red Tail Hawk, Onyx Base, Signed, Canada, 10 ½ x 5 ½ In.	1625
Head, Mitoraj, Igor, Visage Bande, Wrap Face, Hinged Doors, Signed, Poland, 4 ½ x 3 In.	6563
Holy Water Font, Marble, Putti, Mold Edge, Shallow Shell Design, Late 1800s, 20 x 10 In. *illus*	472
Incense Burner, Lid, Dolphin Tails Central Support Stem, Triangular Base, 1800s, 6 In.	2125
Medal, Gasparo, Frank, Engraved, Albert Gallatin, Secretary Of The Treasury, 1801-04, 3 In.	69
Pin Tray, Bergman, Franz, Arabic, Snake Charmer, Standing, Green Onyx, 2 ¾ x 3 In. *illus*	81
Planter, Woman, Holding Circular Planter, Circular Base, 1900s, 61 ½ x 17 In.	2176
Plaque, Brenner, Victor, Abraham Lincoln, Signed, 1907, 9 ½ x 7 In. *illus*	945
Plaque, Cullar, Clifford Warren, Rock & Roll, Wall, Maroon Ground, Signed, 11 x 12 In.	177
Plaque, Cullar, Warren, Horse Power, Signed, Frame, 15 ¼ x 18 In.	767
Plaque, Dropsy, Henri, Pan Playing His Pipes, Signed, 3 x 1 ¼ In.	313
Plaque, Galdini, R., Saint Barbara, Castoro II, Round, Hollow, Signed, 15 ½ In.	236
Plaque, Luini, Costanzo, Relief Profile, Abraham Lincoln, Signed, Italy, 1880s, 10 x 7 In. *illus*	300
Plaque, Merit Co., Nude Woman, Walking, 2 Greyhounds, Chicago, Early 1900s, 12 x 8 In.	450
Plaque, Meyer, Seymour, Flame, Polished, Black, Rectangular Base, 27 ½ x 12 x 8 In.	732
Sconce, 3-Light, Louis XV Style, Gilt, Flower Shape Holder, Stem Arms, 14 In.	576
Sconce, Cherubs, Holding Scrolled Branches, 1800s, 22 ¼ x 12, Pair	1500
Sconce, Single Arm, Putti, Cartouche, Wall Mount, France, Late 1800s, 19 x 5 x 7 In., Pair	750
Sculpture, 2 Figures, Black Boat, Rectangular, Marble Base, Art Deco, 1900s, 8 ½ x 15 In. *illus*	126
Sculpture, Arman, Statue Of Liberty, Granite Base, Signed, Numbered 117/150, 29 x 9 x 4 In.	5000
Sculpture, Bargas, Henri, Man, Turning Ship's Capstan, Black Marble Base, 1900s, 13 x 17 x 7 In.	546
Sculpture, Barye, Tiger, Striding, Mounted, Marble Base, Signed, 1833, 13 x 24 In.	246
Sculpture, Basso, A., Daphne, Multicolor Figure, Marble Base, Numbered, Signed, 26 x 6 x 7 In.	1000
Sculpture, Bateman, Swanton, Lofty Perch, Mountain Goat, Patina, 10 In.	158
Sculpture, Bergman, Franz, Tiger Hunt, Riding Elephant, Geschutz, Vienna, c.1910, 11 ¾ In.	3276
Sculpture, Bergman, Shoemaker's Cottage, Glass Window, Austria, 12 In.	1560
Sculpture, Black, Judy, Bucking Donkey, Jumping, Signed, Texas, 1900s, 11 ¾ In. *illus*	594
Sculpture, Blackamoor, Holding Torch, Plumed Headdress, 55 x 17 In.	863
Sculpture, Botero, Fernando, Mujer Fumando, Signed, 10 ½ x 21 x 10 ¼ In. *illus*	640
Sculpture, Bousquet, Robert, Tiger & Serpent, Fighting, Gilt, Marble Base, France, 13 x 10 x 19 In.	1500
Sculpture, Buddha, Great Kamakura, Blue Hair, Lotus Flower Base, Japan, 1900s, 13 x 12 In. *illus*	1250
Sculpture, Buddha, Thephanom, Kneeling, Anjali Mudra Gesture, Gilt, Thailand, 39 x 17 In.	826
Sculpture, Buhot, Louis Charles Hippolyte, Woman, Seated, On Eagle, Patina, 17 In. . *illus*	576
Sculpture, Carbonell, Manuel, Mother & Child, Rectangle Base, Signed, Cuba, 6 x 3 In.	1375
Sculpture, Carlier, Emile Joseph Nestor, Woman, Pin Dish Base, Art Nouveau, Signed, 8 ½ In.	207
Sculpture, Carlier, Woman, Holding Jar, Fountain, Signed, 23 In.	230
Sculpture, Carrier-Belleuse, Albert-Ernest, Leda & The Swan, Marble Base, 13 x 20 x 11 In.	1298
Sculpture, Chariot, Man, 4 Horses, Marble Base, Roman Style, 1800s, 16 x 17 ½ In.	1152
Sculpture, Clara, Flapper, Draped Dress, Headpiece, Patina, 1900s, 14 In.	138
Sculpture, Coleman, Millennium Dawn, Stepped Base, Arizona, 1989, 34 In.	1000
Sculpture, Cotterill, Tim, Leap Frog, Jump, Multicolor, Frogman, Mark, Signed, 10 x 9 x 3 In.	469
Sculpture, Cullar, Warren, Always A Winner, Scissors, Paper, Rock Shape Base, 12 ¾ In.	413
Sculpture, Dancing Woman, After Preiss, Marble Base, Cold Paint, France, 12 ½ x 14 ½ In. *illus*	633
Sculpture, Davidson, Jim, Signed, No. 7 Jersey, Riddell Helmet, Marble Base, 42 In.	313
Sculpture, De La Vega, Alberto, Mother & Child, Patina, Marble Base, Signed, 1900s, 11 ¾ In. *illus*	1062

Bronze, Pin Tray, Bergman, Franz, Arabic, Snake Charmer, Standing, Green Onyx, 2¾ x 3 In.
$81

Blackwell Auctions

Bronze, Plaque, Brenner, Victor, Abraham Lincoln, Signed, 1907, 9½ x 7 In.
$945

Fontaine's Auction Gallery

Bronze, Plaque, Luini, Costanzo, Relief Profile, Abraham Lincoln, Signed, Italy, 1880s, 10 x 7 In.
$300

Garth's Auctioneers & Appraisers

Bronze, Sculpture, 2 Figures, Black Boat, Rectangular, Marble Base, Art Deco, 1900s, 8½ x 15 In.
$126

Fontaine's Auction Gallery

Bronze, Sculpture, Black, Judy, Bucking Donkey, Jumping, Signed, Texas, 1900s, 11¾ In.
$594

Eldred's

Bronze, Sculpture, Botero, Fernando, Mujer Fumando, Signed, 10½ x 21 x 10¼ In.
$640

Neal Auction Company

Bronze, Sculpture, Buddha, Great Kamakura, Blue Hair, Lotus Flower Base, Japan, 1900s, 13 x 12 In.
$1,250

Bruneau & Co. Auctioneers

Bronze, Sculpture, Buhot, Louis Charles Hippolyte, Woman, Seated, On Eagle, Patina, 17 In.
$576

Neal Auction Company

Bronze, Sculpture, Dancing Woman, After Preiss, Marble Base, Cold Paint, France, 12½ x 14½ In.
$633

Blackwell Auctions

Bronze, Sculpture, De La Vega, Alberto, Mother & Child, Patina, Marble Base, Signed, 1900s, 11¾ In.
$1,062

Austin Auction Gallery

Bronze, Sculpture, Delabrierre, Edouard-Paul, Setter, Duck, Oval Stepped Base, Signed, 8 x 4 x 13 In.
$1,169

Brunk Auctions

Bronze, Sculpture, Deluca, Ferdinando, Woman, Nude, Seated, Chair, Art Deco Style, Signed, 28½ In.
$563

Charlton Hall Auctions

Bronze, Sculpture, Dwight, Ed, Presentation Plaque, United Negro College Fund, 1900s, 15 x 23 In.
$702

Jeffrey S. Evans & Associates

Sculpture, Degrois, Feliz Benneteau, Pavlova & Mordkin, Marble, Signed, France, 13 x 29 x 5 In.	2125
Sculpture, Deity, Lord Vishnu Narayana, Lotus Base, Patina, 32½ x 18 x 11 In.	7605
Sculpture, Delabrierre, Edouard-Paul, Setter, Duck, Oval Stepped Base, Signed, 8 x 4 x 13 In. *illus*	1169
Sculpture, Deluca, Ferdinando, Woman, Nude, Seated, Chair, Art Deco Style, Signed, 28½ In. *illus*	563
Sculpture, Demartino, Louis, Herself, Seated Woman, Legs Crossed, 1975, 19 In.	500
Sculpture, Dog, Biting The Bird, Marble Base, 17 In.	518
Sculpture, Dog, Male & Female Hound, Marble Base, Early 1900s, 7½ In.	295
Sculpture, Dubucand, Alfred, Stag, Gilded, Brown Patina, Stepped Oval Base, Signed, 8 In.	750
Sculpture, Dwight, Ed, Presentation Plaque, United Negro College Fund, 1900s, 15 x 23 In. *illus*	702
Sculpture, Eagle, Wings Raised, Preparing To Fly, Round Marble Base, 35½ x 20¾ In.	502
Sculpture, Echo, Draped Female Figure, Mounted, Marble Base, Late 1800s, 13 In.	225
Sculpture, Escobedo, Augusto Ortega, Mother & Child, Modernist, Rectangular Base, 1976, 63 In. *illus*	9440
Sculpture, Franklin, Gilbert, Night Figure, Woman, Standing, Square Base, 1998, 15 x 4½ In.	1250
Sculpture, Fritchie, Charles, Female, Nude, Seated, Holding Handkerchief, Patina, 1993, 12 In. *illus*	500
Sculpture, Garreau, Georges, Indian Chief Head, Marble Base, France, 18 x 10 x 9 In.	1599
Sculpture, God Of War, Stands, Guan Yu, Marked, Early 1900s, 15 In.	180
Sculpture, Gornik, Friedrich, Sleigh, 3 Horses, 2 Men, Silvered, 8½ x 17 x 10 In.	531
Sculpture, Gregoire, Jean Louis, Perseus & Andromeda, Swords, Monster Head, Signed, 16 In.	938
Sculpture, Greidiaga Bueno, Keiff Antonio, Totem, Wood Base, c.1980, 14 In.	500
Sculpture, Harvey, Andre, Flying Frog, Green Patina, Wood Stand, 1900s, 3½ x 6 x 2¼ In.	944
Sculpture, Hopkins, Mark, Man, Gun, Horse, Good Trade, Signed, Georgia, 1900s, 21 x 16 In.	561
Sculpture, Horse, Flowers, Saddle Blanket, Tassels, Waving Tail, 1900s, 12 x 17 In.	384
Sculpture, Kalish, Max, Young Boy, Inscribed, Gorham Co. Founders, Obic, Signed, 14½ In.	1464
Sculpture, Kauba, Carl, Chief, Standing, Holding Pistol, Tomahawk, Signed, 8⅛ In.	384
Sculpture, Lambeaux, Jef, Dancing Nude Couple, Neoclassical, Loony Song, c.1900, 24 x 15 In.	9200
Sculpture, Laplanche, Pierre, Sheep, Brebis Des Vosges, Oval Base, France, 1800s, 8 x 10 In.	450
Sculpture, Laporte, Emile, Vercingetorix, Brownish Green Patina, Signed, 23 In.	3360
Sculpture, Lehmann, Owl Standing, Open Book, Green Marble Base, Signed, 9 x 5 In.	275
Sculpture, Lieberich, N., Hunting Party, Hounds, Marble Base, Early 1900s, 12 x 21 x 14½ In.	1250
Sculpture, Lindner, Doris, Rolling Dachshund, Patina, Cast, Signed, 4 x 20¾ x 5½ In.	266
Sculpture, Lion & Snake, Mounted, Slate Base, 4¼ x 4¾ In.	123
Sculpture, Lopez, Miguel Fernando, Harem Dancer, Egyptian Revival Style, 20 x 9 x 6 In.	295
Sculpture, Madrassi, Luca, Diane Aux Bois, Woman, Seated, Red Sienna, Marble Base, 27 In. *illus*	431
Sculpture, Man, Classical, Seated, Marble Base, 17¼ In.	416
Sculpture, Man, Riding Horse, Wood, Round Base, Signed, U.G., 18¼ x 19½ In.	2950
Sculpture, Martin, F., Horse, Galloping, Brown Patina, Marble Base, Art Deco, 1930, 16 x 20 In. *illus*	1062
Sculpture, Mason, Jimilu, Ying & Yang, Carrara Marble Base, Signed, 1970, 12 x 20 In. *illus*	410
Sculpture, Meyer, Seymour, 2 Figures, Black, Rectangular Base, 20 x 12 x 6 In.	732
Sculpture, Moigniez, Jules, Lion, Oblong Base, Signed, Italy, 4½ In.	473
Sculpture, Moigniez, Jules, Mother Bird, Perched, Nest, Signed, 1800s, 14½ In. *illus*	756
Sculpture, Moreau, Diana The Huntress, Marble Pedestal Base, Signed, 9¼ x 3 In.	150
Sculpture, Moreau, Hippolyte, Young Woman, Seated On Tree Stump, Swivel Base, 1910s, 31 In. *illus*	1440
Sculpture, Nude Woman, Lying Down, Eating Grapes, Gilt, Mounted, Marble Base, 1800s, 11 x 14 In.	420
Sculpture, Okimono, Standing, Short Robe, Straw Hat, Japan, Late 1900s, 8½ In.	295
Sculpture, Okimono, Tiger, Crouching, Head Raised, Open Mouth, Japan, 1910s, 7 x 13 In.	502
Sculpture, Parker, Daniel Bear, Wood Base, Buried Treasure, 10 x 8 In.	172
Sculpture, Parsons, E.B., 2 Children, Peering, Standing, Octagon Base, Signed, 15 x 11 In.	3075
Sculpture, Parzinger, Hanz, Nude, Cubist Style, Patina, Signed, 20 In.	863
Sculpture, Picault, Emile, Roman Style Soldier, Shield, Spear, Signed, Le Devoir, 1910s, 17 In.	780
Sculpture, Pietrasanta, Femme En Flamme, Engraved, Square Base, Signed, 1980, 33 In.	4370
Sculpture, Pigalle, Jean-Baptiste, Mercury Affixing His Sandals, Marble Base, 1745, 19 In.	1625
Sculpture, Portrait, Woman, Classic Greek Costume, Bare Breast, Grand Tour, 1800s, 24 x 7 In.	644
Sculpture, Rysback, Michael, Allegorical Figure Of Flora, Wood Base, 18¾ x 6 x 5 In.	450
Sculpture, Saint, Winged Man, Walking Stick, Vessel On His Back, 12 In.	94
Sculpture, Smith, Helene E., Nude Female Figure, Suzanne, 1900s, 8½ In.	225
Sculpture, Soldier, Seated, Holding Sword, Octagonal Base, 16 In.	98
Sculpture, Strindberg, Tore, Nude Male Bather, Inscribed, A. Pettersson Fud., 19½ In.	4375
Sculpture, Tanara, Art Deco, Seated, Stepped, Black, Marble Base, 15 In.	420
Sculpture, Tibetan, Woman, Lying Down, Wood Base, Tibet, 1800s, 25½ In.	510
Sculpture, Tiot, A., Owl In Flight, Spread Wings, Patina, Signed, 25 x 12½ In.	354

Sculpture, Titze, A., Mephistopheles, Painted, Rectangular Base, Signed, 15 ½ In.	2646
Sculpture, Torso, Green Finish, Rectangular Stand, 26 x 25 ½ In.	1625
Sculpture, Trudel, Hans, Arabesque, Nudes, Man Lifting Woman, Marked, Roma, 1925, 10 x 3 In.	527
Sculpture, Truffot, Emile Louis, Fox & Pheasant, Patina, Signed, 14 ½ In.	826
Sculpture, Turner, David H., Eagle Bust, American Flag, Patina, 17 In.	413
Sculpture, U.S. Marine Corps Insignia, Globe, Eagle, Anchor, Marble Base, 8 x 6 x 3 ½ In. illus	510
Sculpture, Van De Voorde, Georges, Woman, 2 Greyhounds, Agate Base, 17 In. illus	420
Sculpture, Van Der Straeten, Georges, Woman, Hat, Marble Base, Marked, 7 ¾ In.	177
Sculpture, Vuchetich, Evgeniy, Man, Nude, Cut The Swords, Signed, 7 ½ x 3 ½ x 10 In.	201
Sculpture, Weinart, A., Stevens T. Mason Standing, Stamped, Roman Bronze Works, N.Y. 19 In.	1445
Sculpture, Weiner, Egon, Man, Woman, Sitting On Bench, Kissing, Signed, 11 ½ x 7 x 5 In.	219
Sculpture, Woman, Native American, Standing, Leaves, Cast Iron, Square Base, 1800s, 66 In.	6780
Sculpture, Zegut, Tusey, Woman Carrying Sheaf Of Wheat, Marble Base, 1900s, 16 x 5 In. illus	200
Tazza, Figures Of Atlas, Standing, Shallow Bowl, Circular Base, 15 In. illus	472
Tazza, Gilt, Agate Cabochons, 2 Rope Design, Insects, Europe, c.1870, 4 x 14 In.	369
Tazza, Gothic, Bronze & Cut Glass, c.1900, 10 In., Pair	188
Tazza, Neoclassical, Black Stone, Lion Mask, Paw Feet, 1800s, 6 ½ x 19 In.	354
Tazza, Portrait Medallion, Palmette Handle, Baluster Stem, Marble Base, Silvered, 8 In.	86
Tazza, Renaissance, Shallow, Putti, Bird Shape Supports, Late 1800s, 8 ¼ x 8 In.	177
Teapot, Lid, Peaches, Bird, Deer, Bats, 4 Character Mark, 1900s, 3 ¾ In.	63
Urn, Campana, Satyr Family, Loop Handles, Cast Foot, Embossed, Early 1800s, 6 ½ In.	71
Urn, Charles X, Bracket Handle, Rouge Griotte, Sienna Marble Base, 1810s, 22 x 9 x 9 In.	885
Urn, Globular, Archaic Style, Taotie Mask, Elephant Head Handles, Chinese, 17 ½ In.	443
Urn, Lid, Marble, Pedestal Foot, Square Base, Louis XVI Style, 21 ½ x 8 ¾ In., Pair	266
Urn, Marble, Green, Gilt, Handles, Square Base, 4 Ball Feet, France, 1900s, 13 x 14 In., Pair	750
Urn, Neoclassical Style, Campana, Beaded Rim, Gilt, Square Base, 1800s, 12 In., Pair	832
Urn, Neoclassical, Greek, Mother, Children, Dog, Engraved, Handles, Circular Base, 1900s, 19 In.	138
Urn, Parker, Dan, Dolphins, Swimming, Reef, Gilt, Signed, 10 ¼ In.	156
Urn, Porcelain, Bowls, Mythological Faces, 25 ½ In., Pair	1495
Urn, Repousse, 2 Scrolled Handles, 1800s, 14 ½ In., Pair illus	236
Vase, 2 Handles, Engraved, Turtle, Lily Pad, Bird, Embossed, Leafy Foot, Japan, 5 In.	35
Vase, Asymmetrical Offset Handles, Flared, Scalloped Rim, Japan, Late 1800s, 10 x 4 In., Pair	293
Vase, Beaker, Square Base, Flared Rim, Archaic, Chinese, 19 In., Pair	1524
Vase, Butterflies, Birds, Peonies, Japan, Early 1900s, 11 ¾ In.	266
Vase, Cloisonne, Floral, Leaves, Molded Rim, Brown Patina, Chinese, 12 In.	177
Vase, Gothic, Hexagonal Shape, Swivel Handles, Engraved, 11 x 7 In., Pair	250
Vase, Gu, Foo Dogs, Archaistic Designs, Chinese, 9 ¾ In. illus	173
Vase, Kauba, Carl, Figures, Carved, Onyx Base, Art Nouveau, Marked, Signed, Geschutzt, 8 ¾ In.	156
Vase, Usubata, Ikebana, Flower, Mask Handles, Figural Panels, Japan, c.1900, 10 In., Pair illus	250
Vase, Woman Handle, Nude, Green, Flowers, Engraved, Marble Base, 12 ½ In.	74

BROWNIES

Brownies were first drawn in 1883 by Palmer Cox (1840–1924). They are characterized by large round eyes, downturned mouths, and skinny legs. Toys, books, dinnerware, and other objects were made with the Brownies as part of the design.

Stein, Lid, Figural Policeman Finial, 12 Brownies Encircling, Gerzit, Early 1900s, 7 In. illus	187
Tobacco Jar, Brownie Head, Red & Yellow Hat, Looking Down, Ceramic, Painted, Germany, 6 In.	160

BRUSH-MCCOY, *see Brush category and related pieces in McCoy category.*

BRUSH POTTERY

Brush Pottery was started in 1925. George Brush first worked in 1901 in Zanesville, Ohio. He started his own pottery in 1907, but it burned to the ground soon after. In 1909 he became manager of the J.W. McCoy Pottery. In 1911, Brush and J.W. McCoy formed the Brush-McCoy Pottery Co. After a series of name changes, the company became The Brush Pottery in 1925. It closed in 1982. Old Brush was marked with impressed letters or a palette-shaped mark. Reproduction pieces are being

Bronze, Sculpture, Escobedo, Augusto Ortega, Mother & Child, Modernist, Rectangular Base, 1976, 63 In.
$9,440

Austin Auction Gallery

Bronze, Sculpture, Fritchie, Charles, Female, Nude, Seated, Holding Handkerchief, Patina, 1993, 12 In.
$500

Neal Auction Company

Bronze, Sculpture, Madrassi, Luca, Diane Aux Bois, Woman, Seated, Red Sienna, Marble Base, 27 In.
$431

Brunk Auctions

Bronze, Sculpture, Martin, F., Horse, Galloping, Brown Patina, Marble Base, Art Deco, 1930, 16 x 20 In.
$1,062

Leland Little Auctions

Bronze, Sculpture, Mason, Jimilu, Ying & Yang, Carrara Marble Base, Signed, 1970, 12 x 20 In.
$410

Jeffrey S. Evans & Associates

Bronze, Sculpture, Moigniez, Jules, Mother Bird, Perched, Nest, Signed, 1800s, 14½ In.
$756

Fontaine's Auction Gallery

made. They are marked in raised letters or with a raised mark. Collectors favor the figural cookie jars made by this company. Because there was a company named Brush-McCoy, there is great confusion between Brush and Nelson McCoy pieces. Most collectors today refer to Brush pottery as Brush-McCoy. See McCoy category for more information.

Umbrella Stand, Art Nouveau, Yellow to Brown Glaze, Cameo, Majolica, c.1917, 22 x 11 In.	128
Umbrella Stand, Woodland, Green, Relief Forest, Geese Top Band, Rabbits Lower Band, c.1913, 20 In.	281
Vase, Blue Matte Glaze, Closed Handles, Unmarked, 5 In.	23
Vase, King Tut, Scenic, Squeezebag, Small Craft Sailing, Bottom Drill Hole, 12 In. ...... *illus*	3872
Wall Pocket, Raised Bird On Leafy Branch, Green Glaze, Unmarked, 10 In.	161

BUCK ROGERS

Buck Rogers was the first American science fiction comic strip. It started in 1929 and continued until 1967. Buck has also appeared in comic books, movies, and, in the 1980s, a television series. Any memorabilia connected with the character Buck Rogers is collectible.

Binoculars, Super Sonic Glasses, Plastic, Neck Band, Box, 7 In.	108
Box, 25th Century Rocket Ship, Yellow, Box Only, Louis Marx, 12½ In.	400
Toy, Rocket Police Patrol, Lithograph Pilot, Tail Fin, Tin, Marx, 4¾ x 12½ x 4½ In.	1024
Toy, Water Pistol, Liquid Helium, Tin Litho, Red, Yellow, Spark, Daisy Mfg., 1930s, 7½ In.	150

BUFFALO POTTERY

Buffalo Pottery was made in Buffalo, New York, beginning in 1901. The company was established by the Larkin Company, famous manufacturers of soap. The wares are marked with a picture of a buffalo and the date of manufacture. Deldare ware is the most famous pottery made at the factory. It has either a khaki-colored or green background with hand-painted transfer designs. The company reorganized in 1956 and was renamed Buffalo China before being bought by Oneida Silver Company in 1983. Oneida sold the company to Niagara Ceramics in 2004 but Oneida still sells a few lines of Buffalo China dinnerware.

Buffalo Pottery 1907   Deldare Ware 1909 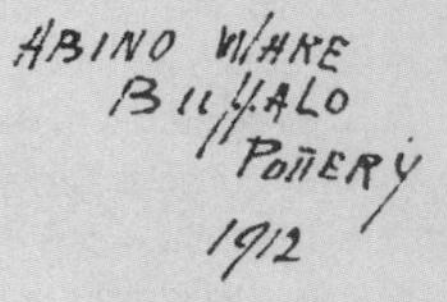   Emerald Deldare 1912

BUFFALO POTTERY

Charger, Monks, Fishing, Mustard Color, Thursday, 1917, 13 In.	390
Pitcher, George Washington, Horseback, Mt. Vernon, Blue Glaze, Gilt, c.1900, 7½ In.	37
Pitcher, Roosevelt Bears, Bear Riding Giraffe, Vignettes, 8 In.	1484
Salt & Pepper, White, Green Band & Letters, Red Squares, Roycroft, 1920s, 3 x 2¼ In.	438

BUFFALO POTTER DELDARE

Bowl, Dr. Syntax Reading His Tour, Green Rim, Marked, 1911, 4 x 8 In.	68
Bowl, Ye Village Tavern, 3 Men At Table, Drinking, 9 x 3 In.	400
Cup, Buildings, Clouds, 3¼ In.	60
Garden Seat, The Great Controversy, Hexagonal, Marked, 1908, 13½ x 14 In. .... *illus*	1430
Mug, Fallowfield Hunt, c.1908, 4½ In.	40
Mug, Ye Lion Inn, Marked, 1901, 4¼ x 5¼ In.	84
Pitcher, This Amazed Me, 8-Sided, Pinched Handle, Marked, 1908, 9 In.	68
Plate, Dinner, Ye Village Gossips, Men, Buildings, 10 In.	185
Plate, Fallowfield Hunt, The Start, Marked, 1908, 9½ In.	54
Plate, Ye Town Crier, Marked, 1925, 8⅜ In.	30

Bronze, Sculpture, Moreau, Hippolyte, Young Woman, Seated On Tree Stump, Swivel Base, 1910s, 31 In.
$1,440

Bronze, Sculpture, Van De Voorde, Georges, Woman, 2 Greyhounds, Agate Base, 17 In.
$420

Bronze, Tazza, Figures Of Atlas, Standing, Shallow Bowl, Circular Base, 15 In.
$472

B

Austin Auction Gallery

Garth's Auctioneers & Appraisers

Michaan's Auctions

Bronze, Sculpture, Zegut, Tusey, Woman Carrying Sheaf Of Wheat, Marble Base, 1900s, 16 x 5 In.
$200

Bronze, Urn, Repousse, 2 Scrolled Handles, 1800s, 14 1/2 In., Pair
$236

Leland Little Auctions

Bronze, Sculpture, U.S. Marine Corps Insignia, Globe, Eagle, Anchor, Marble Base, 8 x 6 x 3 1/2 In.
$510

Michaan's Auctions

Bronze, Vase, Gu, Foo Dogs, Archaistic Designs, Chinese, 9 3/4 In.
$173

Blackwell Auctions

Woody Auction

Bronze, Vase, Usubata, Ikebana, Flower, Mask Handles, Figural Panels, Japan, c.1900, 10 In., Pair
$250

Charlton Hall Auctions

Brownies, Stein, Lid, Figural Policeman Finial, 12 Brownies Encircling, Gerzit, Early 1900s, 7 In.
$187

Jeffrey S. Evans & Associates

Brush, Vase, King Tut, Scenic, Squeezebag, Small Craft Sailing, Bottom Drill Hole, 12 In.
$3,872

Humler & Nolan

BURMESE GLASS

Burmese glass was developed by Frederick Shirley at the Mt. Washington Glass Works in New Bedford, Massachusetts, in 1885. It is a two-toned glass, shading from peach to yellow. Some pieces have a pattern mold design. A few Burmese pieces were decorated with pictures or applied glass flowers of colored Burmese glass. Other factories made similar glass also called Burmese. Burmese glass was made by Mt. Washington until about 1895, by Gundersen until the 1950s, and by Webb until about 1900. Fenton made Burmese glass after 1970. Related items may be listed in the Fenton category and under Webb Burmese.

Biscuit Jar, Cream Ground, Purple, Yellow, Floral, Silver Plate Lid & Bail, Finial, 6 x 5 In. ...	125
Bowl, Centerpiece, Plush, Ruffled Rim, Polished Pontil Mark, Mt. Washington, c.1885, 3 x 9 In..	263
Cruet, Opaque Handle, Plush, Pattern Stopper, Mt. Washington, c.1885, 6 x 4 In. ...	263
Dish, Jelly, Hinged Lid, Enamel Flowers, Applied Handle, Mt. Washington, 4 In. ...	79
Fairy Lamp, Epergne Type, 3 Scroll Arms, Metal Frame, Scalloped Rim Base, 1880s, 12 x 8 In. .	1287
Toothpick Holder, Tricorner Top, Enamel, Flowers, Mt. Washington, 2 x 2¼ In. ... *illus*	225
Vase, Bud, Matte, Pairpoint, Silver Plate, Figural Stepped Base, 7½ In. ...	125
Vase, Jack-In-The-Pulpit, Ruffled Rim, Round Base, Mt. Washington, 12¾ x 5½ In. ...	200
Vase, Long Tapered Neck, Oval Base, Flowers, Mt. Washington, 17 In. ...	144 to 173
Vase, Plush, Pinched Rim, Oval Body, 3 Reeded Feet, Mt. Washington, c.1885, 7 x 4 In. ...	211

BUSTER BROWN

Buster Brown, the comic strip, first appeared in color in 1902. Buster and his dog, Tige, remained a popular comic and soon became even more famous as the emblem for a shoe company, a textile firm, and other companies. The strip was discontinued in 1920. Buster Brown sponsored a radio show from 1943 to 1955 and a TV show from 1950 to 1956. The Buster Brown characters are still used by Brown Shoe Company, Buster Brown Apparel, Inc., and Gateway Hosiery.

Match Holder, Mary Jane & Tige, Holding Bouquet & Purse, Germany, 1900s, 2 x 4 In. ...	75
Mirror, Buster Brown Shoes, Celluloid, Multicolor Graphics, Pocket, 2¼ In. ... *illus*	212
Rattle, Mother-Of-Pearl Ring, Buster Brown Charm, Sterling Silver, c.1900, 2½ In. ...	347
Sign, Buster Brown Bread, Golden Sheaf Bakery, Buster, Tige, Wheat, Tin, 22 x 30 In. ...	1534
Sign, Figural, Froggy The Gremlin, 31 In. ... *illus*	660
Tobacco Jar, Barrel Shape, Buster Lid, Terra-Cotta, R.F. Outcault, c.1900, 7½ x 5 In. ...	179

BUTTER CHIP

Butter chips, or butter pats, were small individual dishes for butter. They were the height of fashion from 1880 to 1910. Earlier as well as later examples are known. Many sell for under $15.

Flow Blue, Touraine, Center Flower Spray, Fluted Edge, 9 Piece ...	87
Glass, Ray Cut Center, Diamond & Miter Border, Gorham Silver Rim, Square, 3½ In., 8 Piece	300
Majolica, Morning Glory, Napkin, Red Flowers, White Ground, Blue Border, 5 Piece ...	24
Porcelain, Flora Danica, Pink Inner Border, Gilt Beaded Rim, Royal Copenhagen, 3 In., Pair	266
Sterling Silver, Scalloped Border, Scrolls, Flowers, Center Monogram, 3¼ In., 6 Piece ...	84

BUTTER MOLDS *are listed in the Kitchen category under Mold, Butter.*

BUTTON

Button collecting has been popular since the nineteenth century. Buttons have been used on clothing throughout the centuries, and there are millions of styles. Gold, silver, or precious stones were used for the best buttons, but most were made of natural materials, like bone or shell, or from inexpensive metals. Only a few types favored by collectors are listed for comparison. Political buttons may also be listed in Political.

Agate, Banded, Black & White, Dzi Bead, Chinese, c.1800, ½ In., 5 Piece	1088
Bakelite, Figural, Snowman, Butterscotch, Black Paint, Red Paste Buttons, 1940s, 1½ In.	375
Bakelite, Perfume Bottle Shape, Painted, Brown Ground, Pink Lattice, Yellow Spots, 1½ In.	625
Bakelite, School Set, Red, Engraved, White Paint, 1 In., 6 Piece	63
Basalt, Oval, Intaglio Cut, Human Figure, Silvered Brass Mounting, 2 Shanks, 19th Century, 1½ In.	138
Brass, Silvered Copper, George Washington Portrait, Yellow Bakelite Back, c.1920, 2 In.	150
Garnet, Cabochon, Applied Diamond Star, Ruby Center, 18K Gold Setting, France, ½ x ⅝ In., Pair	210
Glass, Poured, Green, Center Faux Amethyst, Rhinestones, Brass Setting, Shank, c.1900, 1⁵⁄₁₆ In.	185
Goldtone, Eagle, Outstretched Wings, Round Frame, Victorian, ½ In., Pair	3
Goldtone, Repousse, 97th French Regiment, Revolutionary War, Wood Back, Catgut, c.1780, ⅝ In.	275
Gutta-Percha, Circular, Molded, Man With Walking Stick, Sign, Shank Back, 1800s, 1½ In.	282
Porcelain, Pink & Orange Flowers, Satsuma, Japan, ⅝ In., 6 Piece	26
Porcelain, Teddy Bear, Reticulated Arms & Legs, White Matte Finish, Self Shank	375
Silvertone, Repousse Dog's Head, Shank Back, 19th Century, 1 In., Pair	26

BYBEE POTTERY

Bybee Pottery of Bybee, Kentucky, was started by Webster Cornelison. The company claims it started in 1809, although sales records were not kept until 1845. The pottery was operated by members of the Cornelison family until January 2021. Various marks were used, including the name *Bybee*, the name *Cornelison*, or the initials *BB*. Not all pieces are marked. A mark shaped like the state of Kentucky with the words *Genuine Bybee* and similar marks were also used by a different company, Bybee Pottery Company of Lexington, Kentucky. It was a distributor of various pottery lines from 1922 to 1929.

Bank, Pig, Pink Spongeware, 5 x 3 In.	29
Bank, Potbelly Pig, Blue & Tan Spongeware, 14 In.	95
Bowl, Blue Spongeware, Fluted, Crimped, 8 In.	30
Casserole, Blue Spongeware, Tab Handles, 13 In.	20
Cuspidor, Blue On Green Spongeware, 6¾ In.	24
Figurine, Frog, Blue Speckled, 3¾ In.	50
Flower Frog Vase, Globular, Ruffled Rim, Red, 5¼ x 5¼ In.	42
Pitcher, Blue, Embossed Grapes, 6¾ In.	25
Vase, Globular, 2 Handles, Blue Glaze, Flared Rim, 9 In.	95
Vase, Green Over Brown Glaze, 2 Applied Scrolled Handles, Marked, Selden, 1927, 10 x 9 In.	480

CALENDAR

Calendars made to hang on the wall or to be displayed on a desk top have been popular since the last quarter of the nineteenth century. Many were printed with advertising as part of the artwork and were given away as premiums. Calendars illustrated by famous artists or with guns, gunpowder, or Coca-Cola advertising are most prized.

1904, Butterfly Girls, Chromolithograph, Christian Herald, Frame, 33½ x 14¾ In.	71
1906, Pabst Extract Indian, Black Frame, Victorian, 38 x 8½ In. .... *illus*	615
1909, Mother, Daughter Feeding Bird, Grocer, S. Van Bruggen, Muskegon, Frame, 19 x 13 In.	47
1913, Winchester, Old Man, Holding Gun, December, 1913, Repeating Arms Co., 42 x 28 In.	224
1919-20, Anchor White Lead, Dutch Boy Painter, Chromolitho, Canvas, Frame, 40 x 16 In.	252
1932, Edison Mazda, G.E., Solitude, Maxfield Parrish, Color Print, Feiling & Ingram, 19 x 8½ In.	246
1969, Treasure Chests, Nude Woman, Ward Hard Chrome & Engineering Inc., California	37

CALENDAR PLATE

Calendar plates were popular in the United States as advertising giveaways from 1906 to 1929. Since then, a few plates have been made every year. A calendar and the name of a store, a picture of flowers, a girl, or a scene were featured on the plate.

1909, Stanton, Nebraska, Water Lilies, 22K Gold Trim, Person & Dewitt, 9 In.	58
1912, Hugo, Colorado, Owl, Book, Gold Trim, E.J. Blades & Co., 7 In.	18

Buffalo Pottery Deldare, Garden Seat, The Great Controversy, Hexagonal, Marked, 1908, 13½ x 14 In.
$1,430

Toomey & Co. Auctioneers

Burmese, Toothpick Holder, Tricorner Top, Enamel, Flowers, Mt. Washington, 2 x 2¼ In.
$225

Woody Auction

Buster Brown, Mirror, Buster Brown Shoes, Celluloid, Multicolor Graphics, Pocket, 2¼ In.
$212

AntiqueAdvertising.com

TIP
Don't put celluloid in the sun. It is highly flammable and may burn.

Buster Brown, Sign, Figural, Froggy
The Gremlin, 31 In.
$660

Bertoia Auctions

Calendar, 1906, Pabst Extract Indian,
Black Frame, Victorian,
38 x 8 ½ In.
$615

Rich Penn Auctions

1975, Blue, Currier & Ives, Royal China, 10 In. 16
1978, Samurai Warriors, Wedgwood, 10 In. 24

CAMARK POTTERY

Camark Pottery started out as Camden Art Tile and Pottery Company in Camden, Arkansas. Jack Carnes founded the firm in 1926 in association with John Lessell, Stephen Sebaugh, and the Camden Chamber of Commerce. Many types of glazes and wares were made. The company was bought by Mary Daniel in 1965 and it became Camark Pottery Incorporated. Production ended in 1982.

Pitcher, Ball Shape, Orange, Green Drip Matte Glaze, Lid, 1930s 135
Plaque, Horse Head, Brown, Black, c.1930, 7 ½ In. 145
Vase, Blue & Gray Drip, Blue Interior, 5 x 4 In. 33
Wall Pocket, Globe Shape, Yellow, 5 x 5 ¾ In. 65

CAMBRIDGE GLASS COMPANY

Cambridge Glass Company was founded in 1901 in Cambridge, Ohio. The company closed in 1954, reopened briefly, and closed again in 1958. The firm made all types of glass. Its early wares included heavy pressed glass with the mark *Near Cut*. Later wares included Crown Tuscan, etched stemware, and clear and colored glass. The firm used a *C* in a triangle mark after 1920.

NEAR – CUT

Cambridge Glass Co.
c.1906–c.1920

Cambridge Glass Co.
c.1937

TUSCAN

Cambridge Glass Co.
1936–1954

Caprice, Candy Dish, Lid, Ritz Blue, Opaque, Footed, 10 In. 18
Carmen, Compote, Red, Footed, 7 In. 49
Crown Tuscan, Compote, Gilt, Scalloped Rim, Nude Woman Stem, Flower Center, 5 ½ In. .. 49
Crown Tuscan, Vase, Cornucopia, Ruffled Rim, Scrolled Tail, Shell & Pearl Foot, 10 In. 48
Everglade, Platter, Cheese & Crackers, Tulips, Leaves, Clear, 16 In. 24
Everglade, Platter, Swan, 16 In. 12
Keyhole, Vase, Carmen Red, Flared, Clear Stem & Foot, 12 In. 42
Nautilus, Crown Tuscan, Vase, Footed, Rose Point Etch, 12 In. 31

CAMBRIDGE POTTERY

Cambridge Pottery was made in Cambridge, Ohio, from about 1895 until World War I. The factory made brown-glazed decorated artwares with a variety of marks, including an acorn, the name *Cambridge,* the name *Oakwood,* and the name *Terrhea.*

Vase, Cone Shape, Molded Ribs, Bronze Green Matte Glaze, Early 1900s, 11 In. 406
Vase, Sweet Pea, Leaves, Reticulated, Green Matte Glaze, 8 ¾ In. .... *illus* 1694

CAMEO GLASS

Cameo glass was made in much the same manner as a cameo in jewelry. Parts of the top layer of glass were cut away to reveal a different colored glass beneath. The most famous cameo glass was made during the nineteenth century. Signed cameo glass pieces by famous makers are listed under the glasswork's name, such as Daum, Galle, Legras, Mt. Joye, Webb, and more. Others, signed or unsigned, are listed here. These marks were used by three lesser-known cameo glass manufacturers.

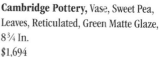

Albert Dammouse	Ernest–Baptiste Lèveillé	François–Eugène Rousseau
1892+	c.1869–c.1900	1855–1885

Biscuit Jar, Flowers, Silver Plate Mount, Marked, R. Favell, Elliot & Co., 1880s, 8 x 5 In.	380
Bowl, Clear & Cranberry, Carved Relief, Signed, Cristallerie De Pantin, c.1900, 2 x 7 In. *illus*	300
Fairy Lamp, Pilgrim, Rose, Maroon, Cranberry, White, Carved, Kelsey Murphy, 5 In....	380
Jar, Lid, Pilgrim, Cobalt Blue, Amber, Peacock Feather, Sand Carved, Kelsey Murphy, c.2000, 5 In..	380
Plate, White Ground, Blue, Flowers, Leaves, Stem & Border, Early 1900s, 9 In.	63
Tray, Serving, 2 Tiers, Flower Overlay, Cranberry, Gilt Metal Fittings, 12 ½ x 7 In...........	300
Vase, Figure & Deer, Fairy, Tree, Waterfall Design, Bertil Vallien, 7 ½ In............	413
Vase, Flowers, Opaque, Amethyst, Carved, Burgun & Schverer, 9 ¼ In.	6930
Vase, Gourd Shape, Marine, Seashells, Seaweed, Carved Bands, Opaque White, Blue, 1880s, 6 In *illus*	1872
Vase, Pilgrim, Desert, Oasis, Sand-Carved, Multicolor, Kelsey Murphy, c.1992, 14 ⅜ In.	819
Vase, Pink To Green Shading, Carved Bird, Branch, Signed, Sovanka, 10 x 4 In. .... *illus*	1900

CAMPAIGN *memorabilia are listed in the Political category.*

CAMPBELL KIDS

Campbell Kids were first used as part of an advertisement for the Campbell Soup Company in 1904. The kids were created by Grace Drayton, a popular illustrator of the day. The kids were used in magazine and newspaper ads until about 1951. They were presented again in 1966; and in 1983, they were redesigned with a slimmer, more contemporary appearance.

Display, Tin Litho Sign, Ready In A Jiffy, Chrome Rack, Electric Heater, 2 Cups, 28 x 18 x 11 In..	185
Doll, American Character Petite, Molded Hair, Painted Face, Purple Playsuit, 13 In.	336
Doll, Girl, Composition, Molded Hair, Painted Face & Shoes, Original Dress, Horsman, 1948, 12 In.	70
Tin, Soup Can Shape, 3 Kids On Front, Red Lid, 5 In...............	3

CANDELABRUM

Candelabrum refers to a candleholder with more than one arm to hold many candles; a candlestick is designed to hold one candle. The eccentricity of the English language makes the plural of *candelabrum* into *candelabra*.

2-Light, Brass, Hanging, Glass Prisms, Footed, 12 In., Pair .... *illus*	504
2-Light, Bronze, French Empire, Figural, Young Classical, Marble Base, 1800s, 26 In., Pair..	2250
2-Light, Bronze, Louis XV Style, Gilt, Scrolls, Shaped Standard, c.1885, 13 In., Pair..............	190
2-Light, Bronze, Woman, Circular Base, Art Nouveau, Signed, Moigniez, 1902, 13 x 9 In. *illus*	344
2-Light, Cast Metal, Dolphin Shape, Entwined Tails, Footed, Early 1900s, 10 In., Pair .. *illus*	413
2-Light, Cut Glass, Prism Finials, Garland Strands, 1900s, 23 ½ x 17 In., Pair......................	101
2-Light, Ebonized, Winged Woman, Flame Shape Finial, Gilt, Metal Base, 1900s, 26 In...... ...	219
2-Light, Gilt Bronze, Egyptian Revival Style, Ushabti Figures, Marble Base, 12 In., Pair *illus*	315
2-Light, Gilt Bronze, Louis XV Style, Acanthus Scrolls, 1800s, 7 ¾ In., Pair	325
2-Light, Glass, Gilt Bronze, Regency, Teardrop Prisms, Knopped Stem, c.1810, 16 x 11 In., Pair	10800
2-Light, Silver Plate, Parrot, Malachite Veneer, Emilia Castillo, 16 x 10 ½ In.	375
2-Light, Silver, Acorn Finial, Hand Chased Design, Theodore B. Starr, 14 In., Pair	1320
2-Light, Silver, Finials, Marked, Donaver Dabbene, Italy, c.1775, 15 In., Pair......................	4410
2-Light, Wrought Iron, Adjustable, Urn Finial, Medial Knop, Tripod Legs, 1700s, 59 In.........	1188
3-Light, Bronze, Baby Birds In Nest, Snails, Auguste Nicolas Cain, c.1885, 20 In., Pair . *illus*	1000
3-Light, Bronze, Flame Finial, Bobeches, Gadroon Rims, Napoleon III, 1800s, 19 x 6 In., Pair	527
3-Light, Bronze, Neoclassical Style, Vines, Woman, Marble Base, Late 1800s, 35 In., Pair.....	502
3-Light, Empire, Figural, Gilt, Flame Shape Finial, Tripartite Base, 19 In., Pair	4480
3-Light, Empire, Gilt & Patina, Bronze, Turned Stem, 3 Claw Feet, 20 ¾ In., Pair	378

C

Cambridge Pottery, Vase, Sweet Pea, Leaves, Reticulated, Green Matte Glaze, 8 ¾ In.
$1,694

Humler & Nolan

Cameo Glass, Bowl, Clear & Cranberry, Carved Relief, Signed, Cristallerie De Pantin, c.1900, 2 x 7 In.
$300

Woody Auction

Cameo Glass, Vase, Gourd Shape, Marine, Seashells, Seaweed, Carved Bands, Opaque White, Blue, 1880s, 6 In.
$1,872

Jeffrey S. Evans & Associates

CANDELABRUM

Cameo Glass, Vase, Pink To Green Shading, Carved Bird, Branch, Signed, Sovanka, 10 x 4 In.
$1,900

Woody Auction

Candelabrum, 2-Light, Brass, Hanging, Glass Prisms, Footed, 12 In., Pair
$504

Fontaine's Auction Gallery

Candelabrum, 2-Light, Bronze, Woman, Circular Base, Art Nouveau, Signed, Moigniez, 1902, 13 x 9 In.
$344

Bruneau & Co. Auctioneers

Candelabrum, 2-Light, Cast Metal, Dolphin Shape, Entwined Tails, Footed, Early 1900s, 10 In., Pair
$413

Leland Little Auctions

Candelabrum, 2-Light, Gilt Bronze, Egyptian Revival Style, Ushabti Figures, Marble Base, 12 In., Pair
$315

Fontaine's Auction Gallery

Candelabrum, 3-Light, Bronze, Baby Birds In Nest, Snails, Auguste Nicolas Cain, c.1885, 20 In., Pair
$1,000

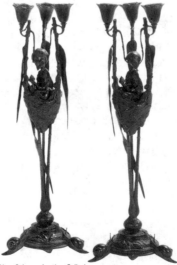

New Orleans Auction Galleries

Candelabrum, 3-Light, Silver, Scroll Arms, Fisher, 15¾ x 14 In., Pair
$295

Bunch Auctions

Candelabrum, 4-Light, Bronze, Empire, Leafy Castings, Tapered Column Stem, Trefoil Base, 1810s, 22 In.
$300

Garth's Auctioneers & Appraisers

Candelabrum, 4-Light, Silver Plate, Scroll Arms, Stag, Palm Tree, Thomas Bradbury, c.1865, 26 In.
$2,750

New Orleans Auction Galleries

3-Light, Firenze, Glass & Bronze, Diamond Point Prisms, 1920, 17 ½ x 12 x 5 In.		1375
3-Light, Gilt Bronze, Empire, Black Warrior, Base, 22 x 8 ½ In., Pair		2520
3-Light, Metal, Round Base, Antkoviak, 26 ¼ x 18 x 9 In.		75
3-Light, Porcelain, Cherub, Flowers, Leaves, Painted, Continental, 17 In., Pair		115
3-Light, Sheffield Plate, Banquet, Ornate, Thomas & James Creswick, Early 1800s, 21 x 17 x 6 In		644
3-Light, Sheffield Silver Plate, Acanthus, Shell & Scroll Borders, Creswick, 1820, 20 x 16 In., Pair		375
3-Light, Silver Plate, Beaded Borders, Domed Base, 9 ¾ In., Pair		118
3-Light, Silver Plate, Gadroon, Flame Finial, Ellis Barker, Early 1900s, 14 In., Pair		246
3-Light, Silver Plate, Renaissance Pattern, Reed & Barton, 16 x 16 In., Pair		413
3-Light, Silver Plate, Tapered Stem, Waisted Sconces, 1800s, 22 In., Pair		95
3-Light, Silver Urn Socket, 2-Spool Support, Twist Arm, Bobeche, Mexico, 12 x 10 ¼ In.		1250
3-Light, Silver, Biomorphic, Georg Jensen, c.1970, 3 ½ In., Pair		7500
3-Light, Silver, Convertible, Pedestal Base, Gorham, 11 ½ x 11 ½ In., Pair		209
3-Light, Silver, Gadroon Domed Base, Weighted, Gorham, 14 ½ In., Pair		225
3-Light, Silver, George III, Chased Acanthus Leaves, Paul Storr, 1827, 14 ¼ In.		3000
3-Light, Silver, Melrose, Gorham, Rhode Island, 1938, 14 In., Pair		250
3-Light, Silver, No. 8901, Weighted Base, Wallace, 7 ¼ In., Pair		325
3-Light, Silver, Rope Twist Border, Bobeches, Stepped Round Base, 13 ½ x 13 In.		489
3-Light, Silver, Rosebud Holder, Stem Arms, Georg Jensen, 4 5/16 x 5 x 9 ¾ In., Pair		875
3-Light, Silver, Scroll Arms, Fisher, 15 ¾ x 14 In., Pair *illus*		295
3-Light, Silver, Scroll, Acanthus Capped Stem, Milan, c.1940, 7 ¼ In., Pair		938
3-Light, Silver, Weighted Base, Marked, Towle, 10 ½ In., Pair		165
3-Light, Silver, Weighted, Curved Arms, Marked, Duchin, 4 In., Pair		767
3-Light, Silver, Weighted, Gorham, 11 ¼ In., Pair		153
4-Light, Bronze, Empire, Leafy Castings, Tapered Column Stem, Trefoil Base, 1810s, 22 In. *illus*		300
4-Light, Bronze, Gilt, Louis XIV Style, Curved Stem, 1800s, 17 x 16 ½ In., Pair		1008
4-Light, Bronze, Patina & Gilt, Charles X Style, Tapered Column, Pedestal Base, 22 In., Pair		1188
4-Light, Bronze, Scroll Leafy Arms, Tripod Stand, Onyx Plinth, France, 1800s, 18 In., Pair		281
4-Light, Cut Glass, Harvard, Skirted Base, Silver Plate Arms, American Brilliant, 22 x 19 In.		125
4-Light, Epergne, Silver, Filigree Bowls, Williams Birmingham Ltd., England, 1910, 1 x 27 x 19 In.		1750
4-Light, Gilt, Birds & Flowers, Arms Swivel, Marked, DG 108, France, 16 In., Pair		144
4-Light, Gilt, Bronze, Blued Steel, Louis XVI Style, 19 ½ In., Pair		756
4-Light, Iron, Running Deer, Parcel Gilt Rectangular Base, Late 1900s, 16 x 28 x 5 ½ In.		207
4-Light, Silver Plate, Scroll Arms, Stag, Palm Tree, Thomas Bradbury, c.1865, 26 In. *illus*		2750
4-Light, Silver Plate, Taper Holder, U-Shape Shafts, Denmark, c.1960, 7 ½ In.		50
4-Light, Silver, Curved Arms, Round Base, Ball Finial, Marked, 1900s, 9 ¼ In., Pair		750
5-Light, Brass, Ecclesiastical, Flowers, Grapes, Leaves, 22 ½ In., Pair		125
5-Light, Bronze & Marble, Winged Cherub, Standing, Square Base, 1800s, 35 In., Pair		590
5-Light, Bronze, Cast, Claw Feet, Black Marble Base, Mounted As Lamp, Fr., 1800s, 26 In., Pair		250
5-Light, Bronze, Cast, Leaves, Torch Finial, Candle Cup, Trifoil, 1850s, 21 ½ x 13 In.		120
5-Light, Gilt Bronze, Scrollwork, Filigree, 3-Legged Base, Mythical Faces, 33 In., Pair *illus*		504
5-Light, Metal, Baluster Center, Painted, Hurricane Shades, Pedestal Base, 45 In., Pair		236
5-Light, Silver Plate, Openwork Shell, Bun Feet, Reed & Barton, 1900s, 16 x 16 x 7 In., Pair		492
5-Light, Silver Plate, Removable Bobeches, Marked, c.1950, 18 In., Pair		266
5-Light, Silver Plate, Scrolled & Reeded, Central Snuffer, E.G Webster & Son, 13 In., Pair		207
5-Light, Silver, Acanthus, Urns, Drip Pans, Marked, Buccellati, Italy, c.1950, 14 In., Pair		6300
5-Light, Silver, Curved Arm, Bobeches, Stepped Base, Empire Silver Co., 16 x 14 In., Pair		700
5-Light, Silver, Neoclassical Style, Reeded Stem, Round Base, Italy, 1900s, 17 ¼ In., Pair		563
5-Light, Silver, Tulip, Art Nouveau, Alabaster Shades, Electrified, 21 x 10 x 10 In., Pair		3780
5-Light, Tin, Petal Edges, Cone Shape Holder, Wire, Leaf Branches, 14 ¼ x 17 ½ In.		1500
5-Light, Wrought Iron, Torchiere, Leaves, Scroll Tripod Base, 1950s, 69 x 17 x 16 In., Pair		767
6-Light, Bronze, Empire Style, Winged Victory, Gilt, Marble Base, 1900s, 33 In., Pair *illus*		1920
6-Light, Bronze, Flower Bobeches, Curved Arms, Grecian Figural Base, 31 x 12 In., Pair		805
6-Light, Bronze, Leafy Arms, Stepped Base, Cornelius & Co., 1850s, 28 x 18 In., Pair		500
6-Light, Gilt Bronze, Neoclassical, Paw Feet, Late 1800s, 28 ¾ In.		192
6-Light, Silver, Removable Glass Bobeche, Georg Jensen, 1969, 6 x 13 In. *illus*		6250
6-Light, White Metal, Renaissance Revival, Leaves, Brass Bobeches, Tripod Base, 1800s, 26 In., Pair		295
6-Light, Zinc, Curved Arms, Pointed Finial, Square Base, 41 ½ x 27 In.		127
7-Light, Gilt Bronze, Leafy Scroll Arms, Removable Bobeches, Late 1800s, 28 x 14 In., Pair		832

Candelabrum, 5-Light, Gilt Bronze, Scrollwork, Filigree, 3-Legged Base, Mythical Faces, 33 In., Pair
$504

Fontaine's Auction Gallery

TIP
The best time to buy an antique is when you see it.

Candelabrum, 6-Light, Bronze, Empire Style, Winged Victory, Gilt, Marble Base, 1900s, 33 In., Pair
$1,920

Neal Auction Company

Candelabrum, 6-Light, Silver, Removable Glass Bobeche, Georg Jensen, 1969, 6 x 13 In.
$6,250

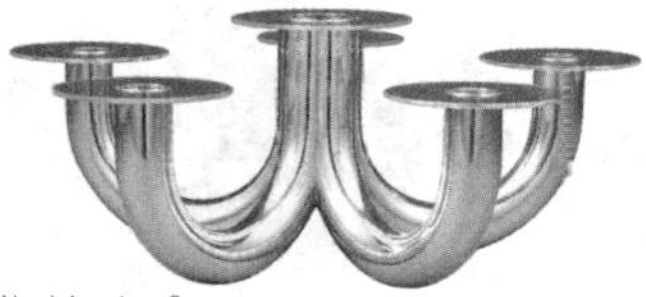

Neal Auction Company

CANDELABRUM

Candelabrum, 8-Light, Brass, Marked, Svend Aage Holm Sorensen, Denmark, c.1955, 11 In.
$500

Wright

Candelabrum, Bronze, Black Marble Base, Gilt, France, Early 1900s, 12 x 9 In., Pair
$238

Eldred's

Candelabrum, Girandole, 5-Light, Bronze, Flowers, Dove, Glass Drops, Isaac F. Baker, 1800s, 21 In., Pair
$704

Brunk Auctions

Candlestick, Brass, Pricket, Fluted, 3-Part Base, Paw Feet, Continental, Late 1800s, 28½ In., Pair
$207

Austin Auction Gallery

Candlestick, Chamber, Silver, Engraved, 2 Armorials, Bobeche, Emma Dear, Victorian, 1845, 5½ In.
$281

Eldred's

Candlestick, Glass, Holder, Signed, Tapio Wirkkala, Finland, 1954, 5¾ In., Pair
$1,188

Wright

Candlestick, Patinated Metal, Fluted, Pricket Top, Marked, Obaso Bronze, Oscar Bach, c.1920, 15 In., Pair
$438

Rago Arts and Auction Center

Candlestick, Silver, Louis XV, 6 Flowers, Detachable Nozzle, Pierre-Nicolas Somme, 1762, 10 In., Pair
$6,048

Sotheby's

Candlestick, Silver, Repousse Castle Pattern, Marked, Loring Andrews, Early 1900s, 12 x 5¼ In., Pair
$2,944

Cowan's Auctions

78

7-Light, Gilt Bronze, Patina, Louis Phillippe, Ribbed Shade, Scroll Arms, 1830s, 42 x 13 In.	3024
7-Light, Gilt Bronze, Rococo Style, White, Scroll Arm, 32 In.	38
7-Light, Louis XVI Style, Brass, Urn, Garland, Putti, Circular Foot, 37 ½ In.	531
7-Light, White Glass, Bronze Flowers, Leaves, Leafy Socle, Scroll Base, 1800s, 33 In.	438
8-Light, Brass, Marked, Svend Aage Holm Sorensen, Denmark, c.1955, 11 In. .... *illus*	500
8-Light, Gilt Bronze, Louis XVI Style, Leaves, Hexagonal Base, Late 1800s, 32 In., Pair	767
9-Light, Silver Plate, Frosted Center Bowl, Reeded Arms, Registry Hallmarks, 23 x 23 In.	1243
14-Light, Silver Plate, Gadroon Cup, Bobeches, Scroll, Leafy, Footed Base, 21 x 19 In.	502
16-Light, Gothic Style, Wrought Iron, Tripod Feet, Floor, Late 1900s, 71 In.	531
Bronze, 5 Leafy Cups, Ornate, Gilt, Marble, Paw Feet, Sienna, 24 x 10 In., Pair	688
Bronze, Black Marble Base, Gilt, France, Early 1900s, 12 x 9 In., Pair .... *illus*	238
Girandole, 3-Light, Embossed Scene, Man In Jungle, Hanging Prisms, Marble Base, 15 x 17 In.	90
Girandole, 5-Light, Bronze, Flowers, Dove, Glass Drops, Isaac F. Baker, 1800s, 21 In., Pair ..*illus*	704

CANDLESTICK

Candlesticks were made of brass, pewter, glass, sterling silver, plated silver, and all types of pottery and porcelain. The earliest candlesticks, dating from the sixteenth century, held the candle on a pricket (sharp pointed spike). These lost favor because in times of strife the large church candlesticks with prickets became formidable weapons, so the socket was mandated. Candlesticks changed in style through the centuries, and designs range from Classical to Rococo to Art Nouveau to Art Deco.

Altar, Iron Pricket, Carved, Scrolled, Leafy, Paw Feet, Italy, 1800s, 23 x 7 x 7 In., Pair	590
Bilston Enamel, Tapered, Flowers, Lobed Base, England, 1760s, 6 ½ In.	163
Brass, Chased, Flowers, Domed, Scalloped Rim Base, Late 1800s, 9 ½ In., Pair	189
Brass, Chrome Plated, Oxidized, Disc Shape Top, c.1950, 6 In.	313
Brass, Cylindrical Sockets, Faceted Rings, Square Bases, Spain, c.1650, 6 In., Pair	1440
Brass, Disc Foot, Jessie Preston, c.1905, 12 ¾ In.	910
Brass, Dome Lid, Cross Finial, Gilt, Cranberry Glass Insert, 18 In., Pair	106
Brass, Female Bust Stoppers, Round Base, 12 ¾ In., Pair	115
Brass, Flemish Capstan, Spun, Socket Stub Gouge Port, Petite, 1700s, 3 ¼ x 3 ¼ In.	468
Brass, Hog Scraper, Wedding Bands, Lip Hanger, Push-Up, 1800s, 6 In., Pair	432
Brass, Neoclassical, Flowers, Paneled, Tapered Stems, Paw Foot Base, c.1800, 10 ½ In., Pair	192
Brass, Polished & Matte Bands, Midway Drip Catcher, Trumpet Base, England, c.1690, 7 In.	3500
Brass, Pricket, Baluster Shape, Wide Drip Pan, Domed Base, 1750s, 14 ½ In., Pair	468
Brass, Pricket, Fluted, 3-Part Base, Paw Feet, Continental, Late 1800s, 28 ½ In., Pair .. *illus*	207
Brass, Pricket, Glass Hurricane Shade, Wood Base, 1970, 20 In.	89
Brass, Prisms, Glass Shade, Marble Base, 27 In., Pair	144
Brass, Queen Anne, Knob Stem, Scalloped Rim & Base, 1700s, 8 ¼ In., Pair	469
Brass, Queen Anne, Petal Shape Bobeche, Lobed Base, 1700s, 8 In., Pair	625
Brass, Queen Anne, Petal, Shell Base, Petal Shape Bobeche, 7 ½ In., Pair	461
Brass, Ring Turned Stem, Medial Concave Drip, Circular Base, Ottoman, 1700s, 12 x 7 In.	2250
Brass, Shaped Stem, Circular Domed Base, Molded Foot, 1700s, 9 In., Pair	527
Brass, Spiral Stem, Stepped, Octagonal Base, 14 In., Pair	360
Brass, Spun, Ejectors, Circular Base, 1800s, 12 In., Pair	100
Brass, Tiered Octagonal Base, 1800s, 10 ¼ In., Pair	62
Brass, Tree Of Life, Nozzle Below Branches, Animals, Round Base, 1900s, 16 x 5 x 15 In.	185
Bronze, Crane, Seashell Body, On Turtle, Japonisme, Late 1800s, 11 x 5 In., Pair	250
Bronze, Delta, Bobeche, Robert Riddle Jarvie, Signed, 14 x 5 ¾ In., Pair	2000
Bronze, Empire Style, Prisms, Marble Base, 12 In., Pair	173
Bronze, Empire, Figural, Woman, Gilt, Patinated, 1800s, 19 ½ x 4 x 4 In., Pair	813
Bronze, Flared Socket, Slender Shaft, Queen Anne's Lace Flower Base, 1910s, 19 ½ x 8 In., Pair	344
Bronze, Gothic Revival, Column Shape, Gilt Dragon, c.1900s, 13 ¾ In.	325
Bronze, Low Bell Shape, Drip Pan, Hexagonal Base, Dutch, 1700s, 8 ⅞ In.	1063
Bronze, Man, Woman, Standing, Holding Column, Flame Finials, Hexagonal Base, 17 ½ In., Pair	369
Bronze, Neoclassical, Reeded Stem, Flower Bobeche, Marble Base, 1800s, 13 ½ In., Pair	384
Bronze, Patina, Petal Shape Base, Knopped Stem, 1700s, 6 In.	125

Candlestick, Silver, Repousse, Grapevine Design, Mauser, 1800s, 9⅜ In., Pair
$160

Neal Auction Company

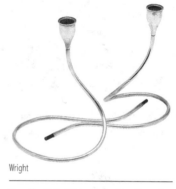

Candlestick, Silver, Spiral Stem, Plastic, Marion Anderson Ncyes, Towle Silversmiths, c.1950, 8 ¼ In., Pair
$750

Wright

Candlestick, Silver, Victorian, Figural, Rococo Base, Charles & George Fox, 1846, 7 In.
$1,250

Charlton Hall Auctions

Candy Container, Airplane, Tin Wings, Fuselage, Propeller, Wheels, Lithograph, Liberty Motor, c.1920, 3 x 5 In. $1,521

Jeffrey S. Evans & Associates

> **TIP**
> Most glass candy container reproductions do not have original-looking closures or paint or old candy.

Candy Container, George Washington, On White Horse, Blue Coat, Red Trim, Composition, Germany, 8½ In. $513

Pook & Pook

Candy Container, Greyhound Bus, Snap-On Closure, Stamped Tin Wheels, Victoria Glass Co., c.1930, 1 x 5 In. $263

Jeffrey S. Evans & Associates

Bronze, Patina, Tapered & Reeded, 3-Part Base, Maitland-Smith, Late 1900s, 38 In., Pair....	531
Bronze, Pricket, Figural, Kneeling Young Man, Holding Torch, 1900s, 18 x 4 x 6 In.	58
Bronze, Veiled Prophet, Square Shape, Leaves, Stem, Engraved, c.1909, 6¾ In., Pair............	180
Chamber, Sheffield Plate, Starburst Hallmarks, Matthew Boulton, c.1810, 3 x 7 In., Pair	413
Chamber, Silver, Engraved, 2 Armorials, Bobeche, Emma Dear, Victorian, 1845, 5½ In. *illus*	281
Chamber, Silver, Stork Scene, Engraved, Handle, Footed, Repousse, Continental, 3 x ¾ In....	100
Copper, Renaissance Revival, Footed, France, Mid 1800s, 10 In.	65
Copper, Spiral Twist, Stepped Circular Foot, 24¼ In., Pair...	148
Cut Glass, Intaglio, Bronze Mount, Engraved, 11½ In., Pair...	219
Ebonized, Figural, Caryatid, Footed, Square Base, Continental, 1800s, 6½ In., Pair	100
Glass & Metal, Gilt Pricket, Molded, Bobeche & Fluted Column, Square Base, 21 In., Pair	295
Glass, Green, Cut To Clear, Bull's-Eye, Silver Plate Base & Top, 8¾ x 3¾ In., Pair.................	275
Glass, Holder, Signed, Tapio Wirkkala, Finland, 1954, 5¾ In., Pair .... *illus*	1188
Iron, Art Nouveau, Woman, Flower Shape Bobeche, Gilt, 12 In., Pair...................................	136
Iron, Hog Scraper, Domed Base, Shaped Hanger, Push-Up, c.1850, 6¼ In., Pair	6888
Iron, Scrolled Stem, Gert Rasmussen, 26¾ In., Pair	90
Jade, Nephrite, Silver Mount, Swag, Tassel Trim, Pedestal, 3 Dolphins, Button Feet, 7 x 3 In., Pair	2223
Majolica, Dolphin Stem, Shell, Seaweed, Footed, T.C. Brown Westhead Moore & Co., 10 In., Pair....	961
Patinated Metal, Figural Branch Shape, Aesthetic, Naturalistic, Leaf Base, 9¾ x 5 In., Pair	200
Patinated Metal, Fluted, Pricket Top, Marked, Obaso Bronze, Oscar Bach, c.1920, 15 In., Pair .*illus*	438
Pewter, Arts & Crafts, 4 Pillar Legs, Egg Shape Cups, Flat Rim, 3¾ In., Pair	270
Pewter, Reeded Stem, Tapered Domed Base, Britain, c.1850, 7¼ In., Pair	64
Pewter, Tall Sockets, Wide Drip Catcher, Stepped Base, Continental, 1700s, 11 In., Pair........	500
Porcelain, Elephants, White, Curled Trunk, Saddle Blankets, Blanc De Chine, 5 x 6 In., Pair	1476
Porcelain, Figural, Partially Nude Putti Standing, Holding Cornucopia, Royal Heidelberg, 9 In...	45
Porcelain, Painted, Gilt, Leaves, 4 Scroll Feet, Marked, Dresden, Germany, 12 In., Pair	2250
Pottery, Clear Orange Glaze, Curved Waist, Ben Owen Master, 13¼ In.	89
Sheffield Plate, Telescopic, Reeded Banding, Removable Bobeche, Early 1800s, 6¾ In., Pair.	305
Silver Plate, Grapes & Leaves, Footed, Fraget Warszawie, Poland, Late 1800s, 12 In., 3 Piece..	406
Silver, Acanthus Leaf, Flower Swag, Repousse, J.D. Schleissner & Sohne, 8 x 4 In., 4 Piece.....	585
Silver, Acanthus Leaves, Geometric, Elaborate Base, Shaft, Engraved, Russia, 13¾ In., Pair	750
Silver, Art Deco Style, Leather Case, Marked Goudji, Sterling Paris, 10½ In., Pair..................	8960
Silver, Brass, Scalloped Edge, Hexagonal Fluted Shaft, Bobeche, 1700s, 10 x 5 In., Pair........	293
Silver, Cactus, Fluted Rim, Round Base, Georg Jensen, 1945, 1¾ In.	875
Silver, Corinthian Columns, Removable Bobeches, Britton, Gould & Co., 1929, 12 In., Pair...	938
Silver, Diamond Shape, Bobeche, Engraved, A.C.E.-E.E.E., 1893-1918, 8 In............................	281
Silver, Flared Rim, Weighted, Scalloped Base, Wallace, 11½ In., Pair..................................	240
Silver, Flowers, Leaves, Engraved, Embossed, Monogram, Stieff, 9½ In., Pair.........................	1121
Silver, George II, Columnar, Fluted Stem, Engraved Crest, L.C, 1772, 12 In., 4 Piece..............	6875
Silver, Grape Pattern, Flared Rim, Domed Base, Footed, Hallmarked, Russia, c.1790, 14 In., Pair...	600
Silver, Hexagonal, Beaded Decor, Removable Bobeche, Footed, Gorham, 9½ In., Pair...........	354
Silver, Leaves, Scrolls, Shells, Nozzles, Embossed, Marked, Buccellati, Italy, 1900s, 11 In.	2520
Silver, Louis XV, 6 Flowers, Detachable Nozzle, Pierre-Nicolas Somme, 1762, 10 In., Pair *illus*	6048
Silver, Paneled Stems, Monogram, Mark, RTH, 10 In., Pair	150
Silver, Pantheon, Tapered, Pitch Loaded, Square Base, Monogram, LMK, c.1950, 11 In., Pair..	156
Silver, Repousse Castle Pattern, Marked, Loring Andrews, Early 1900s, 12 x 5¼ In., Pair *illus*	2944
Silver, Repousse, Flowers, Engraved, Embossed, Sheffield, TB & Co., c.1840, 9 In.	502
Silver, Repousse, Grapevine Design, Mauser, 1800s, 9⅜ In., Pair .... *illus*	160
Silver, Ribbed Stem, Swirl, Round Base, Weighted, 11¾ In., Pair	147
Silver, Rococo Style, Figural, Putto, Leafy Stem, Spreading Base, 1900s, 15¼ In., Pair........	594
Silver, Rococo Style, Stems, Flower Swirls, Nozzles, Domed Base, New York, 11 In., Pair	1599
Silver, Spiral Stem, Plastic, Marion Anderson Noyes, Towle Silversmiths, c.1950, 8¼ In., Pair *illus*	750
Silver, Typical Shape, Repousse, Spreading Feet, Poland, 1900s, 13½ In., Pair	688
Silver, Victorian, Figural, Rococo Base, Charles & George Fox, 1846, 7 In. .... *illus*	1250
Silver, Victorian, Knopped Stem, Ribbed, 10½ In., Pair...	225
Silver, Weighted Base, Marked, International, 12 In., 4 Piece	319
Steel, Vulcan, Blackened, Disc Foot, Albert Paley, 1994, 20¼ In., Pair...............................	3900
Tin, Hog Scraper, Wedding Band Shaft, Square Nut, Push-Up, Shaped Pusher Tab, 1800s, 10 In., Pair.	502
Wood, Carved, Wilhelm Schimmel Style, Central Ball, Tapered Sections, 1900s, 10 In., Pair.	95

Wood, Pricket, Carved, Turned & Block, Brass, Bobeche, Stepped Base, 25 In., Pair 83
Wrought Iron, Hand Forged, Rattail Twist Arm, Rush Reed, Spiral Foot, Early 1700s, 11 In. 288
Wrought Iron, Pierced Drip Plate, Tripod Feet, Impressed, Samuel Yellin, c.1910, 12 In. 4788

CANDLEWICK GLASS *items may be listed in the Imperial Glass and Pressed Glass categories.*

CANDY CONTAINER

Candy containers have been popular since the late Victorian era. Collectors have long favored the glass containers, but now all types, including tin and papier-mache, are collected. Probably the earliest glass container sold commercially was the Liberty Bell made in 1876 for sale at the Centennial Exposition. Thousands of designs were made until the cost became too high in the 1960s. By the late 1970s, reproductions were being made and sold without the candy. Containers listed here are glass unless otherwise described. A Belsnickle is a nineteenth-century figure of Father Christmas. Some candy containers may be listed in Toy or in other categories.

Airplane, Tin Wings, Fuselage, Propeller, Wheels, Lithograph, Liberty Motor, c.1920, 3 x 5 In. .... *illus* 1521
Basket, Bunnies, Chicks, Strap Handle, Hinged Lid, Multicolor, Tin Lithograph, 1952, 6 x 3 x 2 In. 49
Cat, Roly Poly, Blue & Yellow Suit, Red Trim, White Hat, Holds Mouse, Composition, 10¾ In... 500
Dog, Bulldog, Celluloid, Brown, Red Collar, c.1952, 3½ In......................... 145
Duck, Papier-Mache, Flocked Body, Glass Eyes, Germany, 7 x 7½ In......................... 95
Egg, Papier-Mache, Red Flowers, Germany, 1900s, 2 x 4 In. 70
George Washington, On White Horse, Blue Coat, Red Trim, Composition, Germany, 8½ In. *illus* 513
Girl, Long Robe, Hood, Muff, Bisque Face, Blue Glass Eyes, Victorian, 6½ In. 395
Greyhound Bus, Snap-On Closure, Stamped Tin Wheels, Victoria Glass Co., c.1930, 1 x 5 In. *illus* 263
Guitar, Cardboard, Silk Strap, Dresden, Germany c.1890, 3½ x 1 In.......................... 295
Halloween, Pumpkin Head, Glass, Metal Bail Handle, Screw Closure, c.1920, 4½ In. . *illus* 439
Halloween, Pumpkin Man, Cardboard, Pressed, Painted, 1930s, 7 In. .... *illus* 450
Iron Shape, Glass, Dem Artigen Kinde, Engraved, 2¾ In......................... 111
Jack-O'-Lantern, Alien, Spring Arms, 4 Spring Antennae, Mini Jack-O'-Lanterns, Composition, 5 In. 9600
Lantern, Bail Handle, Jeannette Glass, Paper Label, 3¾ In. 16
Penny Candy Jar, Glass, Tin Lid, c.1925, 8 x 5 In. 40
Pig, Pressed Paper, Painted, Glass Eyes, Plug In Belly, 3 x 5¼ x 2 In. .... *illus* 146
Pocket Watch, Stamped Tin Fob, Eagle, Leather Strap, Screw Closure, Embossed, c.1914, 2 In. 322
Polar Bear, On Snowball, White Fur, Glass Eyes, Open Mouth, Germany, 7 In....................... 366
Rabbit, Accordion, Glasses, Head & Ears On Springs, Papier-Mache, Composition, Germany, 15 In. 462
Rabbit, On Stump, Holding Bag, Composition, Blue, Green, Germany, 5½ In....................... 275
Rooster, Papier-Mache, Yellow, Green, Red, 4¾ In......................... 38
Santa Claus In Sleigh, Wood, 1950s, 5¾ In......................... 75
Santa Claus, Plastic, Red, White, c.1950, 4½ In......................... 28
Suitcase, Tin, Embossed, Faux Leather Straps & Handles, Green, 4 x 2 In......................... 48
Toadstool, Figural, Dwarf, Standing, Metal, Painted, 2½ In. .... *illus* 96
Turkey, Composition, Multicolor, Iridescent Highlights, Germany, 8 In. 185
Veggie Man, Bartender, Blue Apron, Pint, Turnip Head, Multicolor, Composition, Germany, 7 In. *illus* 5400
Watering Can, Tin Lithograph, Children Gardening, 3 x 2¾ In......................... 195

CANE

Canes and walking sticks were used by every well-dressed man in the nineteenth century, but by World War I the style had changed. Today canes are used by few but the infirm. Collectors prize old canes made with special features, like hidden swords, whiskey flasks, or risqué pictures seen through peepholes. Examples with solid gold heads or made from exotic materials are among the higher-priced canes. See also Scrimshaw.

Cabinet, Display, Oak, Leaded Glass Panel, 1900s, 39 x 31 x 16 In. .... *illus* 344
Carved Bone Grip, Bust Of Gentleman, Tapered Rosewood Shaft, c.1885, 36¼ In................ 122

Candy Container, Halloween, Pumpkin Head, Glass, Metal Bail Handle, Screw Closure, c.1920, 4½ In.
$439

Jeffrey S. Evans & Associates

Candy Container, Halloween, Pumpkin Man, Cardboard, Pressed, Painted, 1930s, 7 In.
$450

Bertoia Auctions

Candy Container, Pig, Pressed Paper, Painted, Glass Eyes, Plug In Belly, 3 x 5¼ x 2 In.
$146

Forsythes' Auctions

This is an edited listing of current prices. Visit **Kovels.com** to check thousands of prices from previous years and sign up for free information on trends, tips, reproductions, marks, and more.

Candy Container, Toadstool, Figural, Dwarf, Standing, Metal, Painted, 2 ½ In.
$96

Fox Auctions

Candy Container, Veggie Man, Bartender, Blue Apron, Pint, Turnip Head, Multicolor, Composition, Germany, 7 In.
$5,400

Bertoia Auctions

Cane, Cabinet, Display, Oak, Leaded Glass Panel, 1900s, 39 x 31 x 16 In.
$344

Cowan's Auctions

Cane, Novelty, Enamel, Manicure Scissors, Ivory Shaft, 5 Sections, Oak Case, c.1880, 40 In.
$1,968

Morphy Auctions

Cane, Novelty, Mother-Of-Pearl, Opera Glass In Shaft, Chestnut, Horn, c.1880, 36 In.
$984

Morphy Auctions

Cane, Novelty, Wineglass, Tipplers, Glass Tube, Maple Shaft, c.1920, 36 In.
$523

Morphy Auctions

Cane, Parasol Handle, Ivory, Snake Shape, Carved, Cylindrical Shaft, Hexagonal Collar, 1800s, 7 ½ In.
$1,063

Eldred's

Cane, Walking Stick, Carved Bone Top, Hidden Compass, Silver Guilloche Cover, Fleur-De-Lis, 36 In.
$1,404

Thomaston Place Auction Galleries

Cane, Walking Stick, Carved Horse Head Handle, Garnet Eyes, Wood Shaft, 36 In.
$225

Woody Auction

Doctor's, Surgical, 3 Tools, Snake Design Shaft, Engraved, Adams Germany, c.1880, 29 In. .	615
Mahogany, Tapered, Silver Knob, Inset 1904 Liberty Head Coin, Tiffany & Co., 36 In.	1353
Novelty, Brass, Music Stand, Hamilton Patented Jan'y 25 1898, 34 ½ In.	1152
Novelty, Enamel, Manicure Scissors, Ivory Shaft, 5 Sections, Oak Case, c.1880, 40 In. . *illus*	1968
Novelty, Horn, Blowdart, Wood Shaft, Hand Grained, c.1880, 37 In.	800
Novelty, Ivory, Carved, Mark Twain, 3 Cutlery Sets, Wood-Like Graining, c.1880, 36 In.	1152
Novelty, Ivory, Flick, Cruciform Blade, Full Bark Malacca Shaft, c.1860, 35 In.	1764
Novelty, Ivory, Lion, 12 Bottles Crane's Liniment Oil, Salesman's Sample, c.1890, 36 In........	738
Novelty, Mother-Of-Pearl, Opera Glass In Shaft, Chestnut, Horn, c.1880, 36 In. .... *illus*	984
Novelty, Periscope, Military, See Around Corners, Oak Shaft, Brass Ferrule, c.1917, 36 In......	1024
Novelty, Wineglass, Tipplers, Glass Tube, Maple Shaft, c.1920, 36 In. .... *illus*	523
Onyx, Handle Only, Blackamoor Head, Gold & Enamel Mount, Fredrik Kekly, c.1890, 3 In. ..	7560
Parasol Handle, Ivory, Snake Shape, Carved, Cylindrical Shaft, Hexagonal Collar, 1800s, 7½ In. *illus*	1063
Picker End, Bamboo, Maple, Brass, Fruit, Flower, Underwood, Haymarket, London, c.1875, 43 In.	190
Presentation, Gold Filled Repousse, Flower Handle, Engraved, Robt. Nesbitt, 1886, 33 ½ In...	120
Swagger Stick, Nude Woman Handle, Mahogany, Carved, 25 In.	270
Walking Stick, 18K Gold, Handle, Brass Ferrule, Inscribed Willie, Child's, 24 In..	615
Walking Stick, Ball Handle, Carved, Intertwined Snake, Painted, Early 1900s, 34 ½ In........	732
Walking Stick, Bamboo, Silver Cap, Signed, Geo Parker & Sons, London, 37 ½ In..............	259
Walking Stick, Bird Grip, Canvas Wrapped Shaft, Schtockschnitzler Simmons, 1885, 38 In.	1220
Walking Stick, Carved Bone Top, Hidden Compass, Silver Guilloche Cover, Fleur-De-Lis, 36 In *illus*	1404
Walking Stick, Carved Horse Head Handle, Garnet Eyes, Wood Shaft, 36 In. .... *illus*	225
Walking Stick, Carved Ram's Head, Brass Tipped, Composition, 36 In................................	83
Walking Stick, Duck & Eagle Head, Brass Handle, 1900s, 35 In., Pair	236
Walking Stick, Gold Filled Handle, Ebony, Scrolled Leaves, Engraved, JPY, 36 In................	472
Walking Stick, Gold, Silver, Bronze, Bird, Flower, Ebony Shaft, Japan, Late 1900s, 35 ½ In..	184
Walking Stick, Greyhound Carved Handle, Glass Eyes, Blond Wood, Early 1900s, 34¾ In....	101
Walking Stick, Horn Handle, Shepherd's Crook, Polished, 57 In. .... *illus*	238
Walking Stick, Hound's Head Grip, L-Shape Handle, Wood, Carved, c.1890, 33 In.	260
Walking Stick, Ink Calligraphy, Stylized Names, Figures, 1886, 34 ½ In.......................	793
Walking Stick, Inset Glass Marbles On Grip, Twisted Shaft, c.1900, 55 ½ In........................	113
Walking Stick, Ivory Handle, Carved, Ruffled & Spiral Cuffs, Wood Shaft, 1800s, 36 In........	406
Walking Stick, Silver Plate, Lion's Head Handle, Bamboo Shaft, Metal Tip End, 1910s, 35 In.	207
Walking Stick, Warriors, Wood, Carved, Japan, 36 In..	58
Walking Stick, Whalebone, Ball Handle, Incised Bands, Turned Stem, Abalone Dots, c.1850, 33 In.	3125
Walking Stick, Whalebone, Clenched Fist, Carved, Fingers, Shirt Cuff, Rope Band, 1800s, 34 ½ In.	1875
Walking Stick, Whalebone, Clenched Fist, Spiral Carving, Baleen Inlay, 1800s, 35 In..........	688
Walking Stick, Wood, Clenched Fist Handle, Hearts, Diamond, Black Branch Shaft, 1800s, 35 In..	750
Whalebone, Ball Shape Handle, Spiral Carved Shaft, 1800s, 34¾ In............................	688
Whalebone, Inlaid, Walnut & Ebony Handle, 1800s, 35 In.	281
Wood, Animal's Head Grip, Elongated Ear, Rustic Textured Shaft, c.1910, 35 In..............	790
Wood, Carved Animal's Head Grip, Elongated Ear, Rustic Shaft, c.1910, 35 In.	793
Wood, Carved Face, Nail Eyes, Snake, Civil War Soldier, 36¾ In.	406
Wood, Carved Fist Hand Grip, Tapered Shaft, c.1900, 32 ½ In....................................	153
Wood, Dog's Head, Carved, Nose, Eyes, Mouth, Painted, 1800s, 35¾ x 4 In	215
Wood, Knob End, Coiled Carved & Painted Rattlesnake, c.1900, 34 In.......................	504
Wood, Knob Grip, Spiraling Wraparound Snake, Painted, c.1910, 34 In.	183
Wood, L-Shape Handle, Carved Hound's Head Grip, c.1890, 32 ½ In...........................	259
Wood, Rosewood Shaft, Aluminum Handle, Engraved, Victorian, 33 In..........................	92
Wood, Silver, Urn Shape Handle, Gorham, Black Wood Shaft, 36 In	138
Wood, Snake, Carved, Ebonized Shaft, John Worsham Caswell Co., c.1880, 38 In..............	325
Wood, T-Shape Handle, Carved Bird Grip, c.1885, 37 ¼ In...	397
Wood, USS Lawrence, 8-Sided, Engraved, Commodore Perry's Flagship, 35¾ In.	3125

CANTON CHINA

Canton china is blue-and-white ware made near the city of Canton, in China, from about 1795 to the early 1900s. It is hand decorated with a landscape, pagoda, bridge, boats, trees, and a special border. There is never a person

Cane, Walking Stick, Horn Handle, Shepherd's Crook, Polished, 57 In.
$238

Pook & Pook

Canton, Platter, Octagonal, Landscape, 1850s, 14 ¼ x 17 ¼ In.
$215

Locati Auctions

Canton, Serving Dish, Scalloped Oval Rim, Shallow Bowl, 1800s, 3 x 11 ½ In.
$156

Charlton Hall Auctions

Canton, Tureen, Boar's Head, Handles, 1800s, 8 In.
$281

Eldred's

Capo-Di-Monte, Plaque, Wall, Classical Relief, Mythological Figures, Molded, Giltwood Frame, 18 x 22 In.
$277

Rich Penn Auctions

Captain Marvel, Comic Book, Captain Marvel Jr., No. 13, Fawcett, Nov. 1943, 12¾ x 8 In.
$450

Bruneau & Co. Auctioneers

---

on the bridge. The "rain and cloud" border was used. It is similar to Nanking ware, which is listed in this book in its own category.

Charger, House, Trees, 1800s, 14½ In.		200
Ginger Jar, Cream Shade, Carved, Wood Base, Mounted As Lamp, 1800s, 18 In.		325
Platter, Octagonal, Landscape, 1850s, 14¼ x 17¼ In.	*illus*	215
Platter, Octagonal, Village Landscape, 8 In., Pair		207
Serving Dish, Scalloped Oval Rim, Shallow Bowl, 1800s, 3 x 11½ In.	*illus*	156
Tureen, Boar's Head, Handles, 1800s, 8 In.	*illus*	281
Tureen, Dome Lid, Boar's Head Handles, 1800s, 9 x 12 In.		600
Vase, Landscape, Leaf Shape Lappets, 1800s, 13 x 8⅜ In.		1112

CAPO-DI-MONTE

Capo-di-Monte porcelain was first made in Naples, Italy, from 1743 to 1759. The factory was started by Charles VII, King of Naples, who lived in the Palace of Capodimonte. He became King Charles III of Spain in 1759 and the factory moved near Madrid, Spain. Charles' son, Ferdinand, reopened the factory in Italy in 1771 and it operated until 1821. The Ginori factory of Doccia, Italy, acquired the molds and began using the crown and *N* mark. In 1896 the Doccia factory combined with Societa Ceramica Richard of Milan. It eventually became the modern-day firm known as Richard Ginori, often referred to as Ginori or Capo-di-Monte. This company also used the crown and *N* mark. Richard Ginori was purchased by Gucci in 2013. The Capo-di-Monte mark is still being used. "Capodimonte-style" porcelain is being made today by several manufacturers in Italy, sometimes with a factory name or mark. The Capo-di-Monte mark and name are also used on cheaper porcelain made in the style of Capo-di-Monte.

Casket, Multicolor Raised Figures, Scrolled, Leafy, 7 x 10 x 14 In.		246
Centerpiece, Flowers, In Bowl, Handles, Painted, Footed, Marked, 1900s, 12 x 12 In.		23
Group, Provincial Woman, Sheep, Signed, D. Polo Uiato, Italy, 1950s, 38½ In.		207
Plaque, Adam & Eve, Gilt, Mounted, Inset Stones, Octagonal Frame, Late 1800s		313
Plaque, Octagonal, Embossed, Classical Figural Scene, N With Crown Mark, 19 In.		315
Plaque, Wall, Classical Relief, Mythological Figures, Molded, Giltwood Frame, 18 x 22 In. *illus*		277
Vase, Roses, Pastel, Leafy Designs, Marked, 1900s, 11¼ In.		29

CAPTAIN MARVEL

Captain Marvel was introduced in February 1940 in Whiz comic books. An orphan named Billy Batson met the wizard, Shazam, and whenever he said the magic word he was transformed into a superhero. A movie serial was released in 1940. The comic was discontinued in 1954. A second Captain Marvel appeared in 1966, a third in 1967. Only the original was transformed by shouting "Shazam."

Comic Book, Captain Marvel Jr., No. 13, Fawcett, Nov. 1943, 12¾ x 8 In.	*illus*	450
Comic Book, Shazam, No. 1, DC Comics, 1973	*illus*	88

CAPTAIN MIDNIGHT

Captain Midnight began as a network radio show in September 1940. The first comic book appeared in July 1941. Captain Midnight was really the aviator Captain Albright, who was to defeat the Nazis. A movie serial was made in 1942 and a comic strip was published for a short time. The comic book version of Captain Midnight ended his career in 1948. Radio premiums are the prized collector memorabilia today.

Badge, Secret Squadron, Photomatic, Ovaltine Premium, c.1942, 2 x 2 In.		175
Book, No. 48, Fawcett, February 1947		75

Patch, Secret Squadron Member, Embroidered, Red Letters, Plane, Blue Ground, Round, 1989, 3 In.   44
Pin, American Flag, Engraved Back, Loyalty Pledge Slip, Ovaltine Premium, 1941, 1⅜ In. ...   188

CARAMEL SLAG, see Imperial Glass category.

CARD

Cards listed here include advertising cards (often called trade cards), baseball cards, playing cards, and others. Color photographs were rare in the nineteenth century, so companies gave away colorful cards with pictures of children, flowers, products, or related scenes that promoted the company name. These were often collected and stored in albums. Baseball cards also date from the nineteenth century, when they were used by tobacco companies as giveaways. Gum cards were started in 1933, but it was not until after World War II that the bubble gum cards favored today were produced. Today over 1,000 cards are issued each year by the gum companies. Related items may be found in the Christmas, Halloween, Movie, Paper, and Postcard categories.

Advertising, Lance Parfum, Rodo, Color Lithograph, Alphonse Mucha, Frame, 1896, 9½ x 8 In..   1652
Advertising, Lion Coffee, Woman, Birds, Snow, Woolson Spice Co., Toledo, Oh., 1885-1900, 6¾ x 4 In.   19
Advertising, Sanella, Netball Game, Outdoors, Multicolor, Germany, 1930s   7
Advertising, Wheaties, Babe Ruth Photo, The Breakfast Of Champions, Orange Ground   75
Baseball, Babe Ruth, Sport Kings, No. 2, 1933 .... illus   2000
Baseball, Cleveland Indians, Team, No. 85, Dated, Topps, 1956   940
Baseball, Cy Young, Boston Am., American Caramel Co., 1909   3276
Baseball, Derek Jeter, No. 279, Foil, 1993 SP   188
Baseball, Hank Aaron, Topps, No. 20, 1957 .... illus   125
Baseball, Joe Tinker, Hands On Knees, Cubs Jersey, Piedmont, T206, c.1911   1260
Baseball, Triple Fold, Archer, Reulbach, Evers, Chicago Cubs, Hassan Cigarettes, 1912.........   96
Basketball, Topps Wax Pack, Unopened, 10 Cards, Sticker, Gum Stick, Blue Wrapper, 1973-74   646
Birthday, 2 Dutch Children, Blue, Gold Lettering, Marcus Greiner, Germany, 3 Piece   25
Football, Brett Favre, Atlanta Falcons, Quarterback, Rookie, Spanish, Mexico, No. 262, Pro Set, 1991 .   11
Greeting, Valentine, Pop-Up, Rose Garden, Windmill, Putti, 3 Layers, Multicolor, Early 1900s   14
Hockey, Topps, Box Of 36 Wax Packs, Unopened, 1976-77   1232
Playing, Salvador Dali Design, Light Blue Box, Paris, Draeger, Deck, c.1969 .... illus   344
Trading, Pokemon, Pocket Monsters, Basic Charizard, Holographic, Japanese Text, 1996   1080

CARDER, see Steuben category.

CARLSBAD

Carlsbad is a mark found on china made by several factories in Germany, Austria, and Bavaria. Many pieces were exported to the United States. Most of the pieces available today were made after 1891.

Dish, Conch Shell Shape, White, Gilt Trim, Red Crown Mark, Art Nouveau, 11½ x 6½ In.......   125
Plate, Green, Gilt Center Medallion, Raised Scene, Tree, Fairies, Marked, JKW Carlsbad, 12 In.   88

CARLTON WARE

Carlton ware was made at the Carlton Works of Stoke-on-Trent, England, beginning about 1890. The firm traded as Wiltshaw & Robinson until 1957. It was renamed Carlton Ware Ltd. in 1958. The company was bought and sold several times. Production stopped in 1992. Frank Salmon bought the trademark, molds, and pattern books in 1997. Production was outsourced to other potteries. Carlton Ware production ceased by 2016.

Compote, Foxglove, 2 Overlapping Yellow Leaves, Pink Flower, Footed, c.1940, 2½ x 6¼ x 4⅛ In..   35

Captain Marvel, Comic Book, Shazam, No. 1, DC Comics, 1973
$88

Potter & Potter Auctions

Card, Baseball, Babe Ruth, Sport Kings, No. 2, 1933
$2,000

Bruneau & Co. Auctioneers

Card, Baseball, Hank Aaron, Topps, No. 20, 1957
$125

Bruneau & Co. Auctioneers

Card, Playing, Salvador Dali Design, Light Blue Box, Paris, Draeger, Deck, c.1969
$344

Potter & Potter Auctions

Carlton Ware, Pitcher, Spangled Tree, Multicolor, Angled Handle, Footed, c.1936, 5 ¼ In.
$63

Lion and Unicorn

Carnival Glass, Apple Blossom Twigs, Bowl, Ruffled Edge, Amethyst, Dugan, 8 ¾ In.
$57

Strawser Auction Group

Carnival Glass Sets

Some carnival glass patterns were made in full sets that include bowls, plates, and accessories in numerous sizes. Other patterns were for novelties made in only one shape.

Figure, Butterfly Girl, Nude, Standing, Garden, Light Blue, Signed, England, 1900s, 9 ½ In.. 115
Figurine, Garden Fairy, Yellow & Black Wings, Butterfly, Artwave Collectables, 20th Century, 9 ½ In. 63 to 75
Pitcher, Spangled Tree, Multicolor, Angled Handle, Footed, c.1936, 5 ¼ In. .... *illus* 63
Sugar & Creamer, Teal, Pink Interior, Raised Scroll Leaf, Gilt Trim, Footed, Silver Plate Stand, 4 In. 37
Vase, Oval, Black Ground, Multicolor Enamel, Peacock Feathers, Flowers, Gilt Trim, Marked, 7 x 3 In.. 342

CARNIVAL GLASS

Carnival glass was an inexpensive, iridescent pressed glass made from about 1907 to about 1925. More than 1,000 different patterns are known. Carnival glass is currently being reproduced. Here are three marks used by companies that have made 20th-century carnival glass.

Cambridge Glass Co.
1901–1954, 1955–1958

Imperial
1910–1924

Northwood Glass Co.
1910–1918

Apple Blossom Twigs, Bowl, Ruffled Edge, Amethyst, Dugan, 8 ¾ In. .... *illus* 57
Blackberry, Bowl, Crimped & Ruffled Edge, Amethyst, Millersburg, 5 ½ In. 59
Butterfly & Fern, Pitcher, Water, Amethyst, Ruffled Edge, Handle, Fenton, 9 ¾ In. ...... *illus* 90
Butterfly & Fern, Pitcher, Water, Marigold, Clear Handle, Fenton, 9 ½ In. .... *illus* 60
Cherry, Chop Plate, White, Engraved, Ruffled Edge, Fenton, 10 ¾ In.......................... 431
Crackle, Candlestick, Hexagonal Base, Marigold, Unmarked, Jeannette, 7 x 4 In., Pair 6
Crackle, Candy Jar, Lid, Pedestal, Marigold, Unmarked, Jeannette, 7 ¾ x 3 ½ In. 13
Dandelion, Pitcher, Water, Tankard, Amethyst, Flowers, Handle, Northwood, 13 ½ In. *illus* 158
Fantail, Bowl, Butterfly & Berry Exterior, Blue, Footed, Fenton, 10 ¼ In. 100
Figurine, Alley Cat, Blue, Fenton, 11 In.. 172
Fluffy Peacock, Pitcher, Water, Ruffled Edge, Green Handle, Fenton, c.1910, 10 In. 200
Good Luck, Bowl, Blue, Piecrust Edge, Ribbed Exterior, Horseshoe, Northwood, 9 In. .. *illus* 125
Grape & Cable, Bowl, Fruit, Amethyst, 3 Curled Feet, Northwood, 5 ¼ x 10 ¾ In. 100
Grapevine, Pitcher & Bowl, Blue, Oval Bowl, Scalloped Rim, Footed Pitcher, 10 ¾ In. 60
Harvest, Bowl, Oval, 4-Footed, Turquoise, Indiana, 1970s, 4 ½ x 12 ½ x 8 ½ In. 62
Peacock & Urn, Bowl, Electric Purple, Fence, Ruffled Edge, Flowers, Leaves, Northwood, 8 ½ In. 283
Peacock & Urn, Bowl, Ice Cream, Ruffled Edge, White, 10 In. .... *illus* 100
Peacock At The Fountain, Punch Bowl, Purple Iridescent, Northwood, 10 x 11 ½ In. *illus* 250
Peacocks On Fence, Bowl, Green, Piecrust Edge, Ribbed Exterior, Northwood, 8 ¾ In. *illus* 150
Rose Show, Plate, Blue, Scalloped Rim, 9 ½ In.. 200
Stag & Holly, Bowl, Footed, Amethyst, Iridescent, Fenton, 8 In. 34
Wildflower, Bowl, Ruffled Edge, Marigold, Dugan, 1930s, 2 ¼ x 7 ½ In. 31
Wishbone, Epergne, Amethyst, Scalloped Rim, Footed, Basketweave, Lily Base, 9 x 8 In. *illus* 300
Zipper Loop, Lamp, Kerosene, Mottled, Powder Blue Base, White Chimney, 1876, 6 x 4 x 2 In. *illus* 211

CAROUSEL

Carousel or merry-go-round figures were first carved in the United States in 1867 by Gustav Dentzel. Collectors discovered the charm of the hand-carved figures in the 1970s, and they were soon classed as folk art. Most desirable are the figures other than horses, such as pigs, camels, lions, or dogs. A stander has all four feet on the carousel platform; a prancer has both front feet in the air and both back feet on the platform; a jumper has all four feet in the air and usually moves up and down. Both old and new animals are collected.

Centaur, Carved, Painted, Wood, Hinged Upper Body, Signed, Woody, Late 1900s, 51 x 64 In.. 443
Horse, Black, Paddle Seat, Glass Eyes, Silver Trimmings, Charles Looff, 63 x 60 x 10 In. 2457
Horse, Galloping, Carved, Painted, Inset Eyes, Multicolor, Mid 1900s, 55 x 50 In. .... *illus* 431
Horse, Jumper, Ball Top Brass Pole, Glass Eyes, Daniel Carl Muller, 1903, 42 x 44 x 10 In. *illus* 3510

Carnival Glass, Butterfly & Fern, Pitcher, Water, Amethyst, Ruffled Edge, Handle, Fenton, 9¾ In.
$90

Strawser Auction Group

Carnival Glass, Butterfly & Fern, Pitcher, Water, Marigold, Clear Handle, Fenton, 9½ In.
$60

Woody Auction

Carnival Glass, Dandelion, Pitcher, Water, Tankard, Amethyst, Flowers, Handle, Northwood, 13½ In.
$158

Strawser Auction Group

TIP

Do not display carnival glass made before 1910 in direct sunlight. The glass will turn purple or brown and the iridescent finish may fade.

Carnival Glass, Good Luck, Bowl, Blue, Piecrust Edge, Ribbed Exterior, Horseshoe, Northwood, 9 In.
$125

Woody Auction

Carnival Glass, Peacock & Urn, Bowl, Ice Cream, Ruffled Edge, White, 10 In.
$100

Woody Auction

Carnival Glass, Peacock At The Fountain, Punch Bowl, Purple Iridescent, Northwood, 10 x 11½ In.
$250

Woody Auction

Carnival Glass, Peacocks On Fence, Bowl, Green, Piecrust Edge, Ribbed Exterior, Northwood, 8¾ In.
$150

Woody Auction

Carnival Glass, Wishbone, Epergne, Amethyst, Scalloped Rim, Footed, Basketweave, Lily Base, 9 x 8 In.
$300

Woody Auction

Carnival Glass, Zipper Loop, Lamp, Kerosene, Mottled, Powder Blue Base, White Chimney, 1876, 6 x 4 x 2 In.
$211

Jeffrey S. Evans & Associates

Carousel, Horse, Galloping, Carved, Painted, Inset Eyes, Multicolor, Mid 1900s, 55 x 50 In.
$431

Rich Penn Auctions

Carousel Ladies

All horses on a carousel are mares.

Carousel, Horse, Jumper, Ball Top Brass Pole, Glass Eyes, Daniel Carl Muller, 1903, 42 x 44 x 10 In.
$3,510

Thomaston Place Auction Galleries

Carousel, Horse, Jumper, Fiberglass, Multicolor, Brass Pole, Wood Stand, 58 In.
$207

Richard D. Hatch & Associatesb

Horse, Jumper, Carved Mane, Jeweled, Custom Stand, Early 1900s, 66 x 70 In.		9375
Horse, Jumper, Carved, Painted, Saddle, Wooden Stand, c.1910, 49 In.		1464
Horse, Jumper, Fiberglass, Multicolor, Brass Pole, Wood Stand, 58 In.	*illus*	207
Horse, Jumper, Inside Row, Carved, Painted, Early 1900s, 48 In.		1708
Horse, Jumper, Multicolor, Mounted, Iron Base, C.W. Parker Company, c.1917, 64 x 64 x 11 In.		688
Horse, Jumper, Outer Row, Glass Eyes, Breast Collar, Betty, Parker, c.1920, 33 x 60 x 12 In.		3390
Lion, Standing, Saddle, Glass Eyes, Charles Looff, c.1900, 53 x 58 x 14 In.		11115

CARRIAGE

Carriage means several things, so this category lists baby carriages, buggies for adults, horse-drawn sleighs, and even strollers. Doll-sized carriages are listed in the Toy category.

Carriage, Baby, Folding Top, White, Red, Gilt, New Haven Folding Chair Co., 1800s, 45 x 50 x 23 In.		120
Sleigh, Painted, Push, Turned Handle, Wood, Child's, 32 x 18 In.	*illus*	567

CASH REGISTER

Cash registers were invented in 1883 because an eye on the cash was a necessity in stores of the nineteenth century, too. John and James Ritty invented a large model that resembled a clock and kept a record of the dollars and cents exchanged in the store. John Patterson improved the cash register with a paper roll to record the money. By the early 1900s, elaborate brass registers were made. More modern types were made after 1920. Cash registers made by National Cash Register Company are the most popular with collectors.

Brandt Automatic Cashier, Black Paint, Number Keys, Coin Dispenser, Marked, 14 x 11 In.		86
Brandt Automatic Cashier, Coin Vendor, Cast Aluminum, Embossed, Griffin, 11 x 16 In.		215
Hallwood, Naked Woman, Red Bronze, Sign, Eagle, Amount Purchased, 27 x 18 In.	*illus*	3690
Hallwood, Red Bronze, Pullout Drawer, Wood Base, 18 ½ x 10 ¼ x 17 In.		1080
National, Drawer, White Metal, Brass Box, Marble Counter, Wood Base, c.1915, 27 x 13 In.		413
National, Model 0, Candy Store, Nickel Plated, Amount Purchased, Rope Rail, 29 x 9 x 15 In.		5120
National, Model 5, Red Bronze, Fleur-De-Lis Pattern, Marble Plate, 21 x 16 In.	*illus*	1968
National, Model 6, Nickel Plated, Scrolls, Oak Base, Sign, Amount Purchased, 21 In.		5228
National, Model 15, Nickel Plated, Chicken Scratch Pattern, 22 x 19 In.	*illus*	1200
National, Model 79, Red Brass, Amount Purchased, Marquee, c.1907, 26 x 18 In.	*illus*	1107
National, Model 91, Red Bronze, Oak Base, Double Bank, Sign, 66 x 22 In.		4305
National, Model 92, Brass, Embossed Decor, Drawer, 15 x 22 In.		480
National, Model 135, Brass, Embossed, Leaves, 16 x 17 x 15 In.		215
National, Model 216, Oxidized Copper, Embossed, Fleur-De-Lis, Oak Stand, 44 x 13 In.	*illus*	1353
National, Model 332, Brass, Hinged Lift-Up Lid, 22 Push Down Keys, 1910s, 17 x 17 x 16 In.	*illus*	263
National, Model 347, Brass, Amount Purchased Sign, Marble Top, Oak Base, 22 x 19 x 16 In.		406
Union, Metal, Money Drawer, Oak Case, 16 x 18 In.		1320

CASTOR JAR

Castor jars for pickles are glass jars about six inches in height, held in special metal holders. They became a popular dinner table accessory about 1890. Each jar had a top that was usually silver or silver plate. The frame, also of a silver metal, had a handle that arched above the jar and a hook that held a pair of tongs. The glass jar was often painted. By 1900, the pickle castor was out of fashion. Many examples found today have reproduced glass jars in old holders. Additional pickle castors may be found in the various Glass categories.

Pickle, Cranberry Glass, Thumbprint, Enamel, Floral Stand, Forbes, Late 1800s, 9 ½ x 5 In.		98
Pickle, Cranberry, Enameled Flowers, Red Ground, Plated Frame, 12 ½ In.		113
Pickle, Rubina, Tree Bark Mold, Coralene Flowers, Silver Plate Lid, Bail, Victorian, 6 In.	*illus*	150

Carriage, Sleigh, Painted, Push, Turned Handle, Wood, Child's, 32 x 18 In.
$567

Fontaine's Auction Gallery

Cash Register, Hallwood, Naked Woman, Red Bronze, Sign, Eagle, Amount Purchased, 27 x 18 In.
$3,690

Morphy Auctions

Cash Register, National, Model 5, Red Bronze, Fleur-De-Lis Pattern, Marble Plate, 21 x 16 In.
$1,968

Morphy Auctions

Cash Register, National, Model 15, Nickel Plated, Chicken Scratch Pattern, 22 x 19 In.
$1,200

Morphy Auctions

Cash Register, National, Model 79, Red Brass, Amount Purchased, Marquee, c.1907, 26 x 18 In.
$1,107

Rich Penn Auctions

Cash Register, National, Model 216, Oxidized Copper, Embossed, Fleur-De-Lis, Oak Stand, 44 x 13 In.
$1,353

Rich Penn Auctions

Cash Register, National, Model 332, Brass, Hinged Lift-Up Lid, 22 Push Down Keys, 1910s, 17 x 17 x 16 In.
$263

Jeffrey S. Evans & Associates

Castor Jar, Pickle, Rubina, Tree Bark Mold, Coralene Flowers, Silver Plate Lid, Bail, Victorian, 6 In.
$150

Woody Auction

Castor Jar, Pickle, Thumbprint, Cranberry Glass, Rococo Webster Frame, Footed, Victorian, 10 ½ In.
$246

Rich Penn Auctions

89

Castor Set, 4 Bottles, Cut Glass, Shaded Cased Cranberry, Silver Plate Stand, T. Fattorini, Late 1800s, 9 In. $150

Jeffrey S. Evans & Associates

Celadon, Jar, Octagonal, Carved, Wood Stand, Joseon Dynasty, Korea, 3 ½ In. $767

Leland Little Auctions

Celadon, Lamp, 2-Light, Faux Handled Body, Flowers, Foo Dog Finial, Pierced Base, 1900s, 24 x 6 In. $156

Bruneau & Co. Auctioneers

Pickle, Thumbprint, Cranberry Glass, Rococo Webster Frame, Footed, Victorian, 10 ½ In. *illus* ... 246
Pickle, White, Gold, Polished Pontil Mark, Hobbs, Brockunier, c.1886, 5 ⅛ In. 129

CASTOR SET

Castor sets holding just salt and pepper castors were used in the seventeenth century. The sugar castor, mustard pot, spice dredger (shaker), bottles for vinegar and oil, and other spice holders became popular by the eighteenth century. These sets were usually made of sterling silver with glass bottles. The American Victorian castor set, the type most collected today, was made of silver plated Britannia metal. Colored glass bottles were introduced after the Civil War. The sets were out of fashion by World War I. Be careful when buying sets with colored bottles; many are reproductions. Other castor sets may be listed in various porcelain and glass categories in this book.

4 Bottles, Cut Glass, Greek Key Etching, Ball Feet, Silver Plate, S.J. Levi & Co., c.1915, 10 x 7 In.... 303
4 Bottles, Cut Glass, Shaded Cased Cranberry, Silver Plate Stand, T. Fattorini, Late 1800s, 9 In. ...*illus* 150
4 Bottles, Opalescent Glass, Cylindrical, Silver Plate Stand, Ring Handle, Ball Feet, c.1900, 8 In... 100
4 Bottles, Round Stand, Center Handle, Arched Top, Round Foot, Silver Plate, Victorian, 14 x 7 In. 48
5 Bottles, Cut Glass, Silver Stand, Horizontal Handle, 5-Footed, Hallmarks, Russia, 10 ½ In. . 953
5 Bottles, Etched Fern, Silver Plate Frame, Reticulated Top Handle, Footed, Victorian, 15 ¾ x 7 ½ In.. 30
5 Bottles, Etched, Silver Plate, Spins, Footed, Flowers, Leaves, Reed & Barton, 1800s, 16 x 6 In..... 139
5 Bottles, Thumbprint, Argus, Lead Glass, Britannia Stand, Bakewell, Pears & Co., Late 1800s, 9 In.... 82
7 Bottles, Cut Glass, Basket Shape Holder, Center Handle, Figural Stem, Gilt, 12 x 8 x 6 In. .. 64

CATALOGS *are listed in the Paper category.*

CAUGHLEY

Caughley porcelain was made in England from 1772 to 1814. Caughley porcelains are very similar in appearance to those made at the Worcester factory. See the Salopian category for related items.

Bowl, 3 Flowers, Butterfly On Reverse, Blue Transfer, c.1780, 2 ½ x 4 ⅞ In............................. 89
Plate, Kakiemon, Multicolor, Animal, Flowers, Basketweave Border, c.1790, 10 In. 256

CAULDON

Cauldon Limited worked in Staffordshire, Great Britain, and went through many name changes. John Ridgway made porcelain at Cauldon Place, Hanley, until 1855. The firm of John Ridgway, Bates and Co. of Cauldon Place worked from 1856 to 1859. It became Bates, Brown-Westhead, Moore and Co. from 1859 to 1862. Brown-Westhead, Moore and Co. worked from 1862 to 1904. About 1890, this firm started using the words *Cauldon* or *Cauldon Ware* as part of the mark. Cauldon Ltd. worked from 1905 to 1920, Cauldon Potteries from 1920 to 1962. Related items may be found in the Indian Tree category.

Plate, Ridgwood, Square, Black Transfer, Dog, Molded Rim, Marked, 20th Century, 8 ½ In., 12 Piece.. 378
Plate, The Water Jump, Hunter On Horseback, Dogs, Raised Scrolled Border, Marked, c.1950, 11 ¼ In.. 46
Platter, Greek Temple, Chariot Rider, Acanthus Leaf Border, Blue, White, Marked, 6 x 8 In.. 38

CELADON

Celadon is the name of a velvet-textured green-gray glaze used by Chinese, Japanese, Korean, and other factories. This section includes pieces covered with celadon glaze with or without added decoration.

Bowl, Blue Design, White Ground, Oriental, 13 ½ In. 107
Bowl, Curved Sides, Flared Rim, Tapered Foot, Blue Green Glaze, 6 In. 600

Bowl, Flowers, Trees, Leaves, Glaze, Enamel, Signed, Japan, 1900s, 3 In.	8
Bowl, Lotus, Glaze, Fluted, Footed, Sawankhalok, 3 ¼ In.	106
Brushpot, Cylindrical, Crackle Design, Glazed, Mark, Yongzheng, 6 x 4 ¾ In.	594
Censer, Tripod Shape, Glazed, Brown, Embossed, Footed, 2 ⅞ x 6 ¾ In.	250
Charger, Flowers & Leaves, Sloped Sides, Underfoot, Chinese, 1800s, 13 ⅜ In.	177
Dish, Scalloped Rim, Peony-Like Flower, 8 Characters, Footed, Chinese, 10 ½ In.	140
Figurine, Duck, Green, Hairline, Standing, Marked, Chinese, 9 In., Pair	83
Jar, Octagonal, Carved, Wood Stand, Joseon Dynasty, Korea, 3 ½ In. .... *illus*	767
Jardiniere, Peking Glass, Bonsai Tree, Multicolor, Flowers, Wood Planter, 19 x 27 In.	160
Lamp, 2-Light, Faux Handled Body, Flowers, Foo Dog Finial, Pierced Base, 1900s, 24 x 6 In. *illus*	156
Plate, Potted, Carved, Peony Design, Longquan, Chinese, 8 ½ In.	480
Pot, Hardstone Tree, White, Pink, Lavender, Flowers, Wood Stand, Chinese, Early 1900s, 16 In. *illus*	443
Vase, Blue, Figural, Flared Rim, Applied Handles, Wood Stand, 17 ¼ In. .... *illus*	177
Vase, Cong Shape, Rectangular, Sea Green, Glazed, Embossed, Footed, Chinese, 9 ½ In. *illus*	688
Vase, Incised Bamboo, Carved Stone Finial, Wood Base, Mounted As Lamp, 1910s, 32 x 13 x 7 In.	185
Vase, Moon Flask, Glazed, 2 Handles, Blue Archaic Mark, 1800s, 8 x 5 ¾ x 3 ¼ In.	875
Vase, Mounted As Lamp, Figural Scene, Fan Dance, Carved Wood Base, 29 ½ In.	150
Vase, Twisted Relief, Applied Gangly Dragon Encircling Neck, Mouth Agape, 1800s, 6 ⅞ In. *illus*	322

CELLULOID

Celluloid is a trademark for a plastic developed in 1868 by John W. Hyatt. Celluloid Manufacturing Company, the Celluloid Novelty Company, Celluloid Fancy Goods Company, and American Xylonite Company all used celluloid to make jewelry, games, sewing equipment, false teeth, and piano keys. The name *celluloid* was often used to identify any similar plastic. Celluloid toys are listed under Toy.

Button, Photo, Cowboy, Black, Flowers, Wooly Chaps, Easel Back, Early 1900s, 9 In. .... *illus*	118
Dresser Box, Lid, Pierced, Spartan Soldier & Dog, Red, Square, Hickock, Art Deco, 1 ¾ x 3 ¾ In.	30
Glove Stretcher, White, Silver Handles, Repousse Flowers, Vines, Scrolls, Art Nouveau, c.1905, 8 In.	69
Hair Receiver, Lid, Carved, Brown, Marbleized, 1900s, 1 ¾ x 4 ½ In.	27
Jewelry Box, Lid, Yellow, Rectangular, Gray Felt Interior, 3 Ring Slots, 1930s, 1 ½ x 3 ½ x 4 ½ In.	25
Jewelry Box, Ring, Lid, Cream, Silver Leaves, Apple Juice Base, Gray Interior, Dennison, 1 x 2 ¾ In.	45
Placecard Holder, Flower & Bud, Cream, Green Leaves, Yellow Base, Unmarked, 1 ⅛ x 1 ¾ In. ...	15
Trinket Box, Lid, Girl, Blue Flowers, Flower Side Borders, Metal Clasp, 1 ¼ x 3 x 4 ½ In.	35

CELS *are listed in this book in the Animation Art category.*

CERAMIC ART COMPANY

Ceramic Art Company of Trenton, New Jersey, was established in 1889 by Jonathan Coxon and Walter Scott and was an early producer of American belleek porcelain. It became Lenox, Inc. in 1906. Do not confuse this ware with the pottery made by the Ceramic Arts Studio of Madison, Wisconsin.

Bowl, Lily Pad, Pink & Yellow Interior, Gilt, 3-Footed, American Belleek, 3 ¾ x 7 In.	48
Pitcher, Cider, Chrysanthemum, Leaves, Beaded Handle, Marked, American Belleek, 6 x 8 In.	60
Pitcher, Cider, Pink Rose, Brown, Cream Ground, Applied Handle, American Belleek, 5 x 8 In. *illus*	90
Tea Set, Teapot, Sugar & Creamer, Shell Shape, Gilt Flowers, Handle, American Belleek, c 1900	216

CERAMIC ARTS STUDIO

Ceramic Arts Studio was founded about 1940 in Madison, Wisconsin, by Lawrence Rabbitt and Ruben Sand. Their most popular products were molded figurines. The pottery closed in 1955. Do not confuse these products with those of the Ceramic Art Co. of Trenton, New Jersey.

Figurine, Pete & Polly Parrot, Pink, Shelf Sitter, 8 In.	225
Figurine, Wall Hanging, Zor & Zorina, Dancers, Green Draping, c.1960, 9 x 5 In., Pair	37

CERAMIC ARTS STUDIO

Celadon, Pot, Hardstone Tree, White, Pink, Lavender, Flowers, Wood Stand, Chinese, Early 1900s, 16 In.
$443

Leland Little Auctions

Celadon, Vase, Blue, Figural, Flared Rim, Applied Handles, Wood Stand, 17 ¼ In.
$177

Austin Auction Gallery

Celadon, Vase, Cong Shape, Rectangular, Sea Green, Glazed, Embossed, Footed, Chinese, 9 ½ In.
$688

Susanin's Auctioneers & Appraisers

Celadon, Vase, Twisted Relief, Applied Gangly Dragon Encircling Neck, Mouth Agape, 1800s, 6 7/8 In.
$322

Jeffrey S. Evans & Associates

Celluloid, Button, Photo, Cowboy, Black, Flowers, Wooly Chaps, Easel Back, Early 1900s, 9 In.
$118

Austin Auction Gallery

Ceramic Art Co., Pitcher, Cider, Pink Rose, Brown, Cream Ground, Applied Handle, American Belleek, 5 x 8 In.
$90

Woody Auction

CHALKWARE

Chalkware is really plaster of Paris decorated with watercolors. One type was molded from Staffordshire and other porcelain models and painted and sold as inexpensive decorations in the nineteenth century. This type is collected today. Figures of plaster, made from about 1910 to 1940 for use as prizes at carnivals, are also known as chalkware. Kewpie dolls made of chalkware will be found in the Kewpie category.

Bust, Young Man, Plaster, Mounted, Yellow Pine Base, 1900s, 23 x 10 x 10 In.	154
Figurine, Cat, Biting Mouse, Red Ears, Oval Base, 1800s, 3 1/2 x 4 In.	4880
Figurine, Cat, Seated, Molded Body, Black, Yellow, Brown, 1800s, 13 1/2 In.	1800
Figurine, Deer, Reclining, Brown, Multicolor, Rectangular Base, 1850s, 11 1/2 x 4 x 9 In.	115
Figurine, Dog, Spaniel, Seated, White, Black Ears, Brown Collar, Mounted, 1800s, 12 In.	2440
Figurine, Frog, Seated, Gilt, Dotted, Platform Base, 1800s, 3 1/2 x 5 1/4 In.	671
Figurine, Poodle, Standing, Hollow Body, Platform Base, 1850s, 7 x 5 x 3 In. .... *illus*	105
Fruit Basket, Applied Paper Leaves, Multicolor, 1800s, 10 1/2 In.	519
Garniture, Fruit, Leaves, Green, Red, Yellow, Pedestal Base, 1800s, 13 1/2 In.	549
Garniture, Fruits, Lovebird Finial, White Basket, Painted, Plinth Base, 1850s, 11 In., Pair	1440
Sculpture, Hound, Seated, Painted, Rectangular Base, 1950s, 32 In. .... *illus*	148

CHARLIE CHAPLIN

Charlie Chaplin, the famous comedian, actor, and filmmaker, lived from 1889 to 1977. He made his first movie in 1913. He did the movie *The Tramp* in 1915. The character of the Tramp has remained famous, and in the 1980s appeared in a series of television commercials for computers. Dolls, candy containers, and all sorts of memorabilia with the image of Charlie's Tramp are collected. Pieces are being made even today.

Bottle, Figural, Hat Lid, Holds Walking Stick, Glass, 1940s, 11 5/8 x 4 3/8 In.	348
Poster, Movie, Great Dictator, Red Ground, Yellow Lettering, 1960 Re-Release, Italy, 37 3/4 x 26 3/4 In.	633
Toy, Walker, Windup, Metal Legs, Period Clothing, Key Wind, Painted, c.1920, 11 3/4 In. *illus*	140

CHARLIE McCARTHY

Charlie McCarthy was the ventriloquist's dummy used by Edgar Bergen from the 1930s. He was famous for his work in radio, movies, and television. The act was retired in the 1970s. Mortimer Snerd, another Bergen dummy, is also listed here.

Charm, Sitting, Mechanical, Head Pivots, Bale On Back, Sterling Silver, Marked, EB, 7/8 In.	42
Fur Clip, Bust, Mechanical, Mouth Moves, Brass, Goldtone, Pre-Production, Coro, 1930s, 1 1/4 x 3/4 In.	87
Game, Topper, 7 Wood Hats, Cards, Score Sheet, Instructions, Box, Whitman, 1938, 9 x 8 In.	44
LP, Lessons In Ventriloquism, Edgar Bergen, Charlie McCarthy, Mortimer Snerd	13
Photograph, With Edgar Bergen, Black & White, Philadelphia Record, 1938, 9 1/2 x 7 1/4 In.	20
Toy, Charlie Driving Car, Tin Lithograph, Black, White, Windup, Marx, 8 In.	225
Toy, Drummer Boy, Here Comes Charlie, Tin Litho, Windup, Marx, Box, 8 in. ....*illus*	458
Toy, Mortimer Snerd, Crazy Car, Tin Litho, Windup, Marx, Box, 1938, 7 x 7 In.	554
Toy, Mortimer Snerd, Hometown Band, Tin Lithograph, Windup, Marx, Box, 8 1/2 In.	458

CHELSEA

Chelsea porcelain was made in the Chelsea area of London from about 1745 to 1769. Some pieces made from 1770 to 1784 are called Chelsea Derby and may include the letter *D* for *Derby* in the mark. Ceramic designs were borrowed from the Meissen models of the day. Pieces were made of soft paste porcelain. The gold anchor was used as the mark, but it has been copied by many other factories. Recent copies of Chelsea have been made from the original molds. Do not confuse Chelsea porcelain with Chelsea Grape, a white pottery with luster grape decoration. Chelsea Keramic is listed in the Dedham category.

Plate, Exotic Bird, Painted, Gilt, Scalloped Rim, Gold Anchor, Marked, 1756, 9 In., 4 Piece ...*illus*	472

Chalkware, Figurine, Poodle. Standing, Hollow Body, Platform Base, 1850s, 7 x 5 x 3 In. $105

Jeffrey S. Evans & Associates

Chalkware, Sculpture, Hound, Seated, Painted, Rectangular Base, 1950s, 32 In. $148

Leland Little Auctions

TIP
"Never invest your money in anything that eats or needs repainting." Wise words from Billy Rose, a successful showman and art collector of the 1930–1940s.

Charlie Chaplin, Toy, Walker, Windup. Metal Legs, Period Clothing, Key Wind, Painted, c.1920, 11 ¾ In. $140

Jeffrey S. Evans & Associates

Charlie McCarthy, Toy, Drummer Boy, Here Comes Charlie, Tin Litho, Windup, Marx, Box, 8 In. $458

Pook & Pook

Chelsea, Plate, Exotic Bird. Painted, Gilt, Scalloped Rim, Gold Anchor, Marked, 1756, 9 In., 4 Piece $472

Leland Little Auctions

Chelsea, Tureen, Dome Lid, Undertray, Rococo Style, Birds & Leaves, Artichoke Finial, 10 ½ In. $207

Leland Little Auctions

TIP
Need a quick measurement at an antiques show? A penny is ¾ inch in diameter; a dollar bill is almost 6 inches long.

Chelsea, Tureen, Lid, Ladle, Swan Shape, Painted, Late 1900s, 19 x 23 In. $767

Leland Little Auctions

TIP
If you have glue from a label or piece of tape still stuck on your collectible, it may be possible to remove it by dabbing it with the sticky side of the same kind of label.

Chinese Export, Basin, Irish Armorial, Gilt Leaf, Shell & European Scrolling Border, c.1752, 14 In. $625

Charlton Hall Auctions

Chinese Export, Bowl, Vegetable, Lid, Fitzhugh, Blue, White, Fruit Shape Finial, Twisted Handles, 1830s, 12 In. $500

Eldred's

Chinese Export, Cider Jug, Blue & White, Squat Body, Dome Lid, Foo Dog Finial, 1800s, 6 In. $125

Eldred's

Chinese Export for Europe and America

The porcelains wanted in Europe and the United States were different from those made for Asians. Dishes with family coats of arms, figures in European clothes, American flags, ships, and biblical and mythological scenes were made for the European and American markets.

Plate, Painted, Flowers, Birds, Gilt Rim, White Porcelain, 9 ½ In., Pair		270
Tureen, Dome Lid, Undertray, Rococo Style, Birds & Leaves, Artichoke Finial, 10 ½ In. *illus*		207
Tureen, Lid, Ladle, Swan Shape, Painted, Late 1900s, 19 x 23 In. *illus*		767

CHELSEA GRAPE

Chelsea grape pattern was made before 1840. A small bunch of grapes in a raised design, colored with purple or blue luster, is on the border of the white plate. Most of the pieces are unmarked. The pattern is sometimes called Aynsley or Grandmother. Chelsea Sprig is similar but has a sprig of flowers instead of the bunch of grapes. Chelsea Thistle has a raised thistle pattern. Do not confuse these Chelsea patterns with Chelsea Keramic Art Works, which can be found in the Dedham category, or with Chelsea porcelain, the preceding category.

Bowl, Footed, Embossed, 6 x 3 In.	105
Plate, Paneled Edge, Blue Luster, 9 In.	26
Plate, Paneled Edge, Copper Luster, 8 In.	28
Sugar & Creamer, Blue Luster	30

CHELSEA SPRIG

Chelsea Sprig is similar to Chelsea Grape, a pattern made before 1840, but has a sprig of flowers instead of the bunch of grapes. Chelsea Thistle has a raised thistle pattern. Do not confuse these Chelsea patterns with Chelsea Keramic Art Works, which can be found in the Dedham category, or with Chelsea porcelain.

Plate, Paneled Edge, Copper Luster, c.1840, 9 In.	40

CHINESE EXPORT

Chinese export porcelain comprises the many kinds of porcelain made in China for export to America and Europe in the eighteenth, nineteenth, and twentieth centuries. Other pieces may be listed in this book under Canton, Celadon, Nanking, Rose Canton, Rose Mandarin, and Rose Medallion.

Basin, Irish Armorial, Gilt Leaf, Shell & European Scrolling Border, c.1752, 14 In. *illus*		625
Basket, Fruit, Blue, White, Fitzhugh, Underplate, c.1800, 4 x 10 ¼ In.		369
Basket, Fruit, Flowers, Branches, Birds, Lobed Openwork Rim, c.1750, 3 x 8 In.		1625
Bowl, Famille Rose, Flowers, Patina, Footed, Marked, 3 ¼ In., Pair		889
Bowl, Famille Rose, Flowers, People, Green Ground, Gilt Rim, 11 In.		73
Bowl, Famille Rose, Lotus, Flowers, Stems, Painted, Footed, 3 ½ x 5 ½ In.		861
Bowl, Footed, White Ground, Hand Painted Cow, Floral Interior, c.1800, 4 ½ x 10 ½ In.		1560
Bowl, Vegetable, Lid, Fitzhugh, Blue, White, Fruit Shape Finial, Twisted Handles, 1830s, 12 In. *illus*		500
Bowl, Vegetable, Lid, Gilt Highlight, Chestnut Shaped Knop, 1800s, 6 In., Pair		500
Cachepot, Famille Rose, Flowers, Scalloped Rim, Applied Handle, 1750s, 8 In., Pair		761
Candleholder, Famille Rose, Elephant, Standing, Multicolor, 7 ½ x 5 In., Pair		375
Cider Jug, Blue & White, Squat Body, Dome Lid, Foo Dog Finial, 1800s, 6 In. *illus*		125
Coffeepot, Tapered Shape, George Washington Portrait, Raised Flowers, Gilt, 10 ¼ In. *illus*		4063
Creamer, Armorial, Helmet Shape, Twig Handle, Gilt, Cobalt Blue Medallion, c.1850, 4 x 6 In.		19
Cup & Saucer, Tea, Famille Rose, Flower Feet, Painted, 2 x 2 ½ x 4 ¼ In.		1599
Cup, Engraved Flowers, Berries, Applied Handle, Reeded Rim, 1900s, 5 In.		1125
Dish, Famille Rose, Fish, Bulging Eyes, Flower Border, Red, Footed, 1800s, 2 x 6 x 6 In. *illus*		380
Dish, Famille Rose, Lotus Petal, Pink, Chrysanthemum Spray, 1700s, 10 In. *illus*		1968
Figurine, Foo Dog & Guardian, Plinths, 1900s, 8 ¼ In.		75
Fishbowl, Iron Red, Goldfish, Interlocking Waves, 6-Character Xianfeng Mark, 3 In.		344
Fishbowl, Woman, Dark Blue, Scrolled Leaves, Greek Key Border, 16 In. *illus*		325
Ginger Jar, Famille Rose, Bulbous Body, White Ground, 1700s, 11 x 9 In.		1440
Jar, Lid, Famille Rose, Figures, Peonies, Butterflies, 1800s, 24 ½ In., Pair		7560
Jar, Lid, Famille Rose, Multicolor Scene, Long Tailed Bird, Wood Stand, 1790s, 15 In., Pair		234
Jar, Lid, Landscape, Mountains, Pagoda, Painted, c.1700, 10 x 3 ¼ In., Pair		1046

Jardiniere, Figural, White Ground, Gilt, Wood Stand, Tripod Base, 31 In., Pair	3840
Pillow, Famille Rose, Painted, Women, Reticulated Side, 1900s, 5 x 6¾ In. *illus*	266
Plate, Armorial, Marriage Arms, Dozy & Blondeel Accolle, Flower Border, c.1785, 9 In., Pair	3375
Plate, Armorial, Painted Crest, Marquess Of Tweeddale, Gilded Rim, 1700, 7 In., Pair	1404
Plate, Famille Rose, Fish, Flowers, Butterfly, 1800s, 8½ In., Pair	4480
Plate, Hexagonal, Painted, Armorial, Diaper Border, Cartouches, c.1735, 9¾ In. *illus*	1386
Platter, Clobbered, White Ground, Blue Flowers, Leafy Rim, Late 1700s, 11⅝ In., Pair	1280
Platter, Oval, Fitzhugh, Flowers, Blue & White, 1830s, 14½ x 12½ In. *illus*	406
Platter, Round, Blue, White, Fitzhugh, Flowers, c.1800, 14½ x 11½ In.	338
Pot De Creme, Lid, Strawberry Finial, Armorial Cartouche, Red, Green, Gilt, 3½ In., 7 Piece	212
Punch Bowl, Famille Rose, Panels, Flowers, Carved Wood Stand, 12 x 5 x 8½ In.	250
Punch Bowl, Famille Rose, People, Flowers, Multicolor, 6⅛ In.	128
Serving Dish, Famille Rose, Figural Scenes, Central Bird, Flower Vignettes, 14½ In.	336
Tankard, Famille Verte, Barrel Shape, Silver Mount, Loop Handle, 6 In. *illus*	1890
Teapot, Lid, Famille Rose, Chrysanthemum, Lotus Flowers, Painted, 4¾ x 6 In.	861
Teapot, Lid, Famille Verte, Jug Shape, Spout, Landscape Scene, Figure, 12 x 10 In., Pair	671
Tray, Hot Water, Flowers, Handles, Blue & White, Fitzhugh, 1830s, 3 x 11 In.	469
Tureen, Lid, Boar's Head, Flower Sprays, Handle, c.1765, 9 x 12½ In. *illus*	800
Tureen, Lid, Tobacco Leaf Pattern, Patchwork, Flower Handles, Bud Finial, c.1775, 14 In.	6875
Tureen, Lid, Underplate, Famille Noire, Flowers, Berries, Gilt Handles, Finial, 1700s, 12 x 13 In.	558
Tureen, Soup, Lid, Blue & White, Fitzhugh, Strawberry Shape Finial, Twist Handles, 1830s, 9 In.	625
Urn, Lid, Flowers, Foo Dog, 2 Handles, Painted, 11 x 4½ In., Pair	1230
Vase, Blue & White, Rouleau Shape, 18½ x 7½ In., Pair *illus*	649
Vase, Famille Rose, Enamel, Flower, Gilt, Dragon, 1800s, 20½ In., Pair	2250
Vase, Famille Rose, Foo Dog Handles, Applied Dragons, Figural Scenes, Flower Border, 16 In. *illus*	567
Vase, Famille Rose, Lotus Mouth Bottle, Blue Jiaqing, Gilt, Millefleur, 9 x 4 In.	7995
Vase, Famille Rose, Multicolor Images, Orange Red Ground, Gilt Rim, 1730s, 21⅝ x 4 In. *illus*	1638
Vase, Famille Rose, Palace Scene, Carved Stand, 12 x 36½ x 15½ In.	531
Vase, Famille Verte, Rouleau, Landscape, Court Ladies, Mounted As Lamp, 18 In.	1342
Vase, Famille Verte, Trumpet, Sleeve Shape, Painted Deer, Figural Landscape, 16 In.	508
Vase, Lid, Famille Rose, Pheasant, Rocks, Peony, Butterfly, 1700s, 17 In., Pair	976
Vase, Monumental, Mother-Of-Pearl, Bird, Flowers, Stand, Painted, 1900s, 72 In.	430
Vase, Pear Shape, Flower Sprays, Exotic Birds, Palmette Design, Late 1800s, 8¼ In.	1722
Vase, Teal, Song Style, Dragon Handles, Mark, 11½ In.	188

CHINTZ

Chintz is the name of a group of china patterns featuring an overall design of flowers and leaves, similar to the design on chintz fabric. The design became popular with English makers about 1928. A few pieces are still being made. The best known are designs by Royal Winton, James Kent Ltd., Crown Ducal, and Shelley. Crown Ducal and Shelley are listed in their own sections.

Atlas China Co.
c.1934–1939

Old Foley/James Kent
c.1955

Royal Winton
c.1951+

Black Beauty, Cup & Saucer, Elijah Cotton Ltd.	75
Hazel, Plate, Luncheon, Scalloped Corners, Royal Winton, 10 In.	125
Heather, Stacking Teapot, Creamer, Sugar, Lid, Lord Nelson, 6 In.	345
June, Black, Cup & Saucer, Scalloped Edges, 22K Gold Trim, Rosina	22
Kew, Bowl, Footed, Scalloped Edge, Gold Trim, Royal Winton, 3 x 4 In.	24
Marina, Cake Plate, 2 Tab Handles, Scalloped Edge, Lord Nelson Ware, c.1938, 10 x 9 In.	45
Old Cottage, Relish, 4 Parts, Royal Winton, 11½ x 6¾ In.	28
Pansy, Sweetmeat, Rolled Sides, Gold Trim, Pierced Handles, 6 x 5 In.	42
Rosalynde, Teapot, Finial, James Kent, 9 x 6 x 6 In.	325

Chinese Export, Coffeepot, Tapered Shape, George Washington Portrait, Raised Flowers, Gilt, 10¼ In.
$4,063

Heritage Auctions

TIP
Don't put china with gold designs in the dishwasher. The gold will wash off.

Chinese Export, Dish, Famille Rose, Fish, Bulging Eyes, Flower Border, Red, Footed, 1800s, 2 x 6 x 6 In.
$380

Jeffrey S. Evans & Associates

Chinese Export, Dish, Famille Rose, Lotus Petal, Pink, Chrysanthemum Spray, 1700s, 10 In.
$1,968

Alderfer Auction Company

Chinese Export, Fishbowl, Woman, Dark Blue, Scrolled Leaves, Greek Key Border, 16 In.
$325

Austin Auction Gallery

Chinese Export, Pillow, Famille Rose, Painted, Women, Reticulated Side, 1900s, 5 x 6¾ In.
$266

Leland Little Auctions

Chinese Export, Plate, Hexagonal, Painted, Armorial, Diaper Border, Cartouches, c.1735, 9¾ In.
$1,386

Sotheby's

Chinese Export, Platter, Oval, Fitzhugh, Flowers, Blue & White, 1830s, 14½ x 12½ In.
$406

Eldred's

Chinese Export, Tankard, Famille Verte, Barrel Shape, Silver Mount, Loop Handle, 6 In.
$1,890

Sotheby's

Chinese Export, Tureen, Lid, Boar's Head, Flower Sprays, Handle, c.1765, 9 x 12½ In.
$800

Alderfer Auction Company

Chinese Export, Vase, Blue & White, Rouleau Shape, 18½ x 7½ In., Pair
$649

Bunch Auctions

Chinese Export, Vase, Famille Rose, Foo Dog Handles, Applied Dragons, Figural Scenes, Flower Border, 16 In.
$567

Fontaine's Auction Gallery

Chinese Export, Vase, Famille Rose, Multicolor Images, Orange Red Ground, Gilt Rim, 1730s, 21⅝ x 4 In.
$1,638

Jeffrey S. Evans & Associates

Summertime, Jelly Jar, Silver Plate Lid, 7 Spoons, 4-Sided, Royal Winton	65
Summertime, Salt & Pepper, 4-Sided, Royal Winton	85
Turquoise Blue Paisley, Cup & Saucer, Footed, D Shape Handle, Radfords	60

CHOCOLATE GLASS

Chocolate glass, sometimes mistakenly called caramel slag, was made by the Indiana Tumbler and Goblet Company of Greentown, Indiana, from 1900 to 1903. It was also made at other National Glass Company factories. Fenton Art Glass Co. made chocolate glass from about 1907 to 1915. More recent pieces have been made by Imperial and others.

Cactus, Compote, Streaks, Swirls, Scalloped Rim, Greentown, 8 In.	23
Cactus, Syrup, No. 375, Shaped Handle, Period Lid, Greentown, 1910s, 6 1/8 In.	105
Fighting Cocks, Dish, Lid, Beaded Rim, Basketweave Base, Greentown, c.1902, 3 x 4 x 5 In.	2691
Indoor Drinking Scene, Tankard, Pitcher, Applied Handle, Greentown, Early 1900s, 8 x 4 In.	190
Squirrel, Pitcher, Water, Scalloped Rim, Round Foot, Greentown, Early 1900s, 8 5/8 x 4 3/4 In. ..illus	293

CHRISTMAS

Christmas collectibles include not only Christmas trees and ornaments listed below, but also Santa Claus figures, special dishes, and even games and wrapping paper. A Belsnickle is a nineteenth-century figure of Father Christmas. A kugel is an early, heavy ornament made of thick blown glass, lined with zinc or lead, and often covered with colored wax. Christmas cards are listed in this section under Greeting Card. Christmas collectibles may also be listed in the Candy Container category. Christmas trees are listed in the section that follows.

Belsnickle, Dark Yellow Coat, Glitter, Red Chenille Face, Brush Tree, 9 1/2 In.	330
Candy Containers are listed in the Candy Container category.	
Creche, Nativity Scene, Arch, Birds, Flowers, Angel, Pottery, Ocumicho, Mid 1900s, 14 In. illus	443
Lamp, Figural, Santa Claus, Standing Snow Mound, Nutmeg Burner, c.1894, 9 1/2 x 3 3/8 In . illus	3042
Mug, Santa Claus Head, Sack Of Toys Handle, M. Abberley, Royal Doulton, 1983, 7 In.	60
Pin, Batterman's Santa's Headquarters, Celluloid, Santa Claus Picture, 1 3/8 In.	50
Santa Claus, Vinyl Face, Red Hat, White Beard, Jointed, Steiff, 1953, 12 In. illus	246
Tin, Biscuit, Chimney Shape, Santa Claus & Toy Sack, Lithograph, c.1925, 4 In.	536
Tin, Biscuit, Manger Shape, Nativity Scene, Lithograph, Germany, 10 x 12 In. illus	1130
Toy, Santa Claus, Walker, Wooden Rollers, Clockwork, Ives, 1800s, 10 x 5 x 4 In. illus	5700

CHRISTMAS TREES

Christmas trees made of feathers and Christmas tree decorations of all types are popular with collectors. The first decorated Christmas tree in America is claimed by many states, including Pennsylvania (1747), Massachusetts (1832), Illinois (1833), Ohio (1838), and Iowa (1845). The first glass ornaments were imported from Germany about 1860. Paper and tinsel ornaments were made in Dresden, Germany, from about 1880 to 1940. Manufacturers in the United States were making ornaments in the early 1870s. Electric lights were first used on a Christmas tree in 1882. Character light bulbs became popular in the 1920s, bubble lights in the 1940s, twinkle bulbs in the 1950s, plastic bulbs by 1955. In this book a Christmas light is a holder for a candle used on the tree. Other forms of lighting include light bulbs. Other Christmas collectibles are listed in the preceding section.

Aluminum, Silvered Finish, 91 Branches, Tripod Stand, Box, Evergleam, 1960s, 72 In.	240
Feather, 5 Tiers, Metal Candleholders, Turned Wood Base, Tabletop, 1900s, 29 1/2 In. .. illus	211
Feather, Green, Wood Base, 46 In.	600
Fence, Iron, Gate, Green Paint, Gold Accent, Mounted On Board, Early 1900s, 5 x 23 x 23 In. .	504
Kugel, Cluster Of Grapes, Beehive Cap, Green Glass, Germany, 5 In.	225

Chocolate Glass, Squirrel, Pitcher, Water, Scalloped Rim, Round Foot, Greentown, Early 1900s, 8 5/8 x 4 3/4 In. $293

Jeffrey S. Evans & Associates

Christmas, Creche, Nativity Scene, Arch, Birds, Flowers, Angel, Pottery, Ocumicho, Mid 1900s, 14 In. $443

Austin Auction Gallery

Christmas, Lamp, Figural, Santa Claus, Standing Snow Mound, Nutmeg Burner, c.1894, 9 1/2 x 3 3/8 In. $3,042

Jeffrey S. Evans & Associates

C

Christmas, Santa Claus, Vinyl Face, Red Hat, White Beard, Jointed, Steiff, 1953, 12 In. $246

Apple Tree Auction Center

Christmas, Tin, Biscuit, Manger Shape, Nativity Scene, Lithograph, Germany, 10 x 12 In. $1,130

Hartzell's Auction Gallery Inc.

Christmas, Toy, Santa Claus, Walker, Wooden Rollers, Clockwork, Ives, 1800s, 10 x 5 x 4 In. $5,700

Morphy Auctions

Christmas Tree, Feather, 5 Tiers, Metal Candleholders, Turned Wood Base, Tabletop, 1900s, 29 ½ In. $211

Jeffrey S. Evans & Associates

Chrome, Compote, Figural Stem, Nude Dancer, Bakelite Bowl, Handles, Art Deco, Early 1900s, 9 ½ In. $210

Blackwell Auctions

Chrome, Lamp, 3-Light, Koch & Lowy, Square Base, Marked, Otto Meinzer Iserlohn, c.1950, 62 In., Pair $366

Neal Auction Company

Chrome, Siphon, Soda, Brass, Enameled Aluminum, Plastic, Lawrence Ward, Sparklets Corp., 1936, 11 In. $1,250

Wright

Chrome, Teapot, Plated Brass, Glazed Ceramic, Bakelite, Ever-Hot, England, c.1940, 5 ¾ In. $438

Wright

Cigar Store Figure, Indian Chief, Cigars, Tobacco, Carved, Multicolor, Wood, Ralph Gallagher, 79 In. $1,353

Rich Penn Auctions

Ornament, Minnie Mouse, Santa Claus Outfit, Glass, Multicolor, Swarovski, 3 In.	288
Stand, Cast Iron, Leaves, Green, 3 Screws, Footed, 15 In.	100
Stand, Cast Iron, Oxidized Silver Finish, Embossed Swags, Tassels, 9 x 24 In.	45
Stand, Cast Iron, Wood Platform, Picket Fence, North Bros., Black & Gold Paint, 17 x 17 In.	163
Stand, Feather Tree, White Pine, Flowers, Green Ground, Cutout Base, c.1890, 8 x 18 x 8 In.	207

CHROME

Chrome items in the Art Deco style became popular in the 1930s. Collectors are most interested in high-style pieces made by the Connecticut firms of Chase Brass & Copper Co., Manning-Bowman & Co., and others.

Appetizer Tray, Brass Kromex Center, Midcentury Modern, 6 x 12 ½ In.	6
Cocktail Set, Gaiety, Shaker, Black Banding, 4 Cups, Tray, Marked, Chase, 11 ½ In.	125
Cocktail Set, Shaker, Rectangular Tray, 5 Goblets, Ruby Glass, Chrome Stem & Foot.	108
Cocktail Shaker, Black Top, Moor Face, 5 ½ In.	375
Coffee Set, Urn, Sugar, Creamer, Tray, Bakelite, Von Nessen, Chase, c.1940, 12 x 20 In.	1280
Compote, Figural Stem, Nude Dancer, Bakelite Bowl, Handles, Art Deco, Early 1900s, 9 ½ In. *illus*	210
Dresser Box, Black Lacquer Lid, Inset Stone, Suede Interior, Gene Jonson & Marcius, 6 x 11 x 9 ⅝ In.	189
Lamp, 3-Light, Koch & Lowy, Square Base, Marked, Otto Meinzer Iserlohn, c.1950, 62 In., Pair *illus*	366
Lamp, 3-Light, White, Plastic Globes, Circular Foot, Italy, c.1970, 99 In.	354
Lamp, Adjustable, Cantilevered Style, Lucite Base, Support Leg, Robert Sonneman, 1960, 16 In.	177
Lamp, Electric, Retro Cone Shape Top, White Satin Glass, 22 x 17 x 17 In., Pair	563
Lamp, Grasshopper, 2 Parts, Adjustable, Weighted Base, Alsy, 1970, 74 x 9 In.	354
Lamp, Melon Shape Base, Fiberglass Shade, France, c.1970, 49 In.	375
Lamp, Polished, Tall Plinth Shape, Vertical Split Side, Round, Black Base, 72 In., Pair	240
Lamp, Robert Sonneman Style, 5-Orb Socket, Columnar Stem, Faux Burl Base, c.1965, 30 In.	100
Pitcher, Red, Variegated Glaze, Exterior & Interior, 1940s, 6 In.	266
Sculpture, Abstract, Column, Ridges, Chrome Over Bronze, Signed, Edgar Tarfur, 12 ¾ x 4 x 3 ¾ In.	400
Siphon, Soda, Brass, Enameled Aluminum, Plastic, Lawrence Ward, Sparklets Corp., 1936, 11 In. *illus*	1250
Sugar & Creamer, Lid, Red Bakelite Handles, Art Deco, 6 In. & 4 In.	18
Teapot, Plated Brass, Glazed Ceramic, Bakelite, Ever-Hot, England, c.1940, 5 ¾ In. *illus*	438

CIGAR STORE FIGURE

Cigar store figures of carved wood or cast iron were used as advertisements in front of the Victorian cigar store. The carved figures are now collected as folk art. They range in size from counter type, about three feet, to over eight feet tall.

Indian Chief, Cigars, Tobacco, Carved, Multicolor, Wood, Ralph Gallagher, 79 In. *illus*	1353
Indian Maiden, Standing, Arm Up, Samuel Robb, c.1900, 58 In. *illus*	24400
Indian, Bust, Carved, Painted, Wood, Late 1800s, 23 ½ In.	4063
Man, Sitting, Cast Metal, Gilt Accent, Platform Base, 18 x 28 x 38 In.	1599

CINNABAR

Cinnabar is a vermilion or red lacquer. Pieces are made with tens to hundreds of thicknesses of the lacquer that is later carved. Most cinnabar was made in the Orient.

Box, Carved, Filigree, Village Scene, Structures, Trees & Figures, Chinese, 2 x 6 In.	189
Box, Carved, Flowers, Birds, Wood, Chinese, Early 1900s, 3 ½ x 5 ¼ In. *illus*	300
Box, Lid, Red, 2 Figures, Trees, Carved, Footed, Chinese, 3 x 5 In.	63
Vase, Carved, Red, Green Interior, Flowers, Leaves, Chinese, 4 ¼ In.	88

CIVIL WAR

Civil War mementos are important collectors' items. Most of the pieces are military items used from 1861 to 1865. Be sure to avoid any explosive munitions. Pictures are listed in this book in Photography.

Badge, 1st Corps, Silver, Circular, Elijah Devore, 13th Iowa Infantry, 1 In.	1063

Cigar Store Figure, Indian Maiden, Standing, Arm Up, Samuel Robb, c.1900, 58 In.
$24,400

Cowan's Auctions

Cinnabar, Box, Carved, Flowers, Birds, Wood, Chinese, Early 1900s, 3 ½ x 5 ¼ In.
$300

Garth's Auctioneers & Appraisers

Civil War, Broadside, Advertising, Two Musicians, Wagoner, Eagle Brigade, c.1861, 13 ½ x 20 ½ In.
$813

Cowan's Auctions

Civil War, Broadside, Recruitment, Regiment Of Riflemen, To Act As Sharp-Shooters, c.1861, 13 x 19 In.
$1,250

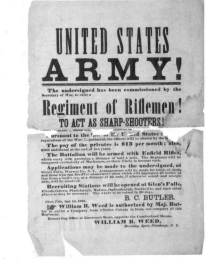

Cowan's Auctions

Civil War, Flask, Major General George H. Thomas, Silver Plate, Dixon & Son, c.1863, 10 In.
$2,750

Cowan's Auctions

Civil War, Pike, Hardwood Frame, Steel Mount, Retractable Blade, c.1860, 87 In.
$2,375

Eldred's

Civil War, Pipe, Carved, Laurel Root, Hand Shape, Holding Bowl, J.F. Randlett, 1862, 1¾ x 2½ x 1 In.
$1,375

Cowan's Auctions

Civil War, Print, Our Heroes And Our Flags, Memorial, 16 Confederate Generals, Lithograph, 1895, 22 x 17 In.
$293

Jeffrey S. Evans & Associates

Civil War, Relic, Wood Fragment, From USS Constellation, Tag, Piece Of Old Frigate, 6¾ In.
$113

Cowan's Auctions

Belt, Eagle, Wreath, Brass, Silver Overlay Buckle, Plate & Sword, 1830s, 2 7/16 x 3 In.	920
Box, Coffin Shape, Wood Hinge, Compass, Signed, Don F. Bingham, 1861, 1 3/4 x 5 In.	431
Broadside, Advertising, Two Musicians, Wagoner, Eagle Brigade, c.1861, 13 1/2 x 20 1/2 In. *illus*	813
Broadside, Recruitment, Regiment Of Riflemen, To Act As Sharp-Shooters, c.1861, 13 x 19 In. *illus*	1250
Broadside, Recruits Wanted, First Regiment, Grey Reserves, Frame, c.1861, 32 x 24 In.	1875
Canteen, Fabric Cover, Cloth Sling, Hadden, Porter & Booth, Phila., c.1850, 8 In.	256
Canteen, Wood, Drum Shape, Cork Stopper, Pewter Spout, 2 Iron Bands, Woven Sling, 7 1/2 x 2 In.	1875
Drum, Ash, Bentwood Hoops, Copper Tacks, North Carolina Seal, Leather Strap, 15 x 17 In..	7345
Flask, Major General George H. Thomas, Silver Plate, Dixon & Son, c.1863, 10 In. .... *illus*	2750
Pike, Hardwood Frame, Steel Mount, Retractable Blade, c.1860, 87 In. .... *illus*	2375
Pipe, Carved, Laurel Root, Hand Shape, Holding Bowl, J.F. Randlett, 1862, 1 3/4 x 2 1/2 x 1 In. *illus*	1375
Powder Tester, Flintlock, Walnut Grip, Carved Ramrod, Iron, 5 x 12 In...............	826
Print, Our Heroes And Our Flags, 16 Confederate Generals, Lithograph, 1895, 22 x 17 In. ..*illus*	293
Relic, Wood Fragment, From USS Constellation, Tag, Piece Of Old Frigate, 6 3/4 In. .... *illus*	113
Sword, Brass Handle, Gilt Twisted Wire, Stamped Ricasso, 1863, 39 In. .... *illus*	187
Sword, Cavalry, 3-Branch Brass Guard, Wire Wrapped Grip, Pommel Cap, Ames Mfg. Co., 1850, 35 In.	561
Sword, Cavalry, Engraved, Flowers, Flags, Eagle, Leather & Brass Scabbard, 38 In.................	443
Sword, Saber, Cavalry, Confederate, Memphis Novelty Works, Thomas Leech & Co., 1861, 35 In..	2816
Telegraph, Dial Format, Mahogany Case, Brass Dial, Charles T. Chester, 5 x 9 x 9 In., Pair ..	6435
Tumbler, Embossed, Union For Ever, Clasped Hands, Wreath, American Flag, 1880s, 3 x 2 3/4 In. ..*illus*	187
Watch, Presentation, Surgeon David B. Rice, 102nd Illinois Volunteers, LHM & Co., Pocket ..	2176

CKAW, *see Dedham category.*

CLARICE CLIFF

Clarice Cliff was a designer who worked in several English factories, including A.J. Wilkinson Ltd., Wilkinson's Royal Staffordshire Pottery, Newport Pottery, and Foley Pottery after the 1920s. She is best known for her brightly colored Art Deco designs, including the Bizarre line. She died in 1972. Pieces of some of her early work have been made again by Wedgwood.

Bizarre, Pitcher, Geometric, Multicolor, Green Outlines, Marked, Art Deco, 5 1/4 x 7 In. *illus*	572
Bizarre, Vase, Solid Handle, Orange, White Ground, Landscape, Square Foot, Box, 7 1/2 In....	520
Ophelia, Plate, Flowers, White Ground, Royal Staffordshire, c.1930, 8 In., 12 Piece...............	177
Pitcher, Light Blue, Applied Flower Handle, White, Footed, 9 In.	8
Toby Jug, Man, Seated, Drinking Beer, Red Coat, Yellow Trim, Black Handle, 9 In.	18
Vase, Circles, Squares, Yoyo, White Ground, Orange, Green, Blue, Yellow, Wedgwood, 1980s, 9 x 4 In.	86
Vase, Landscape, Multicolor, White Ground, Globular, Short Neck, Marked, 234 L/S, 4 3/4 x 6 In.	250

CLEWELL

Clewell was made in limited quantities by Charles Walter Clewell of Canton, Ohio, from 1902 to 1955. Pottery was covered with a thin coating of bronze, then treated to make the bronze turn different colors. Pieces covered with copper, brass, or silver were also made. Mr. Clewell's secret formula for blue patinated bronze was burned when he died in 1965.

Jardiniere, Bowl Shape, Copper Clad, Verdigris Patina, Signed, 3 x 7 In..................................	111
Vase, Art Pottery, Copper Overlay, Dark Green Ground, Curved Neck, 13 1/2 In. .... *illus*	791

CLIFTON POTTERY

Clifton Pottery was founded by William Long in Newark, New Jersey, in 1905. He worked there until 1909 making lines that included Crystal Patina and Clifton Indian Ware. Clifton Pottery made art pottery until 1911 and then concentrated on wall and floor tile. By 1914, the name had been changed to Clifton Porcelain and Tile Company. Another firm, Chesapeake Pottery, sold majolica marked *Clifton Ware.*

Vase, Blue Green, Marked, 1904, 3 1/4 In.	75
Vase, Crystal Patina, Yellow, Green Drip, Incised Mark, 1907, 11 1/2 In.	649

Civil War, Sword, Brass Handle, Gilt Twisted Wire, Stamped Ricasso, 1863, 39 In.
$187

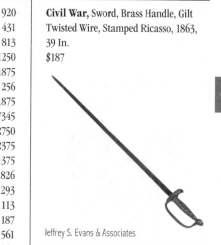

Jeffrey S. Evans & Associates

Civil War, Tumbler, Embossed, Union For Ever, Clasped Hands, Wreath, American Flag, 1880s, 3 x 2 3/4 In.
$187

Jeffrey S. Evans & Associates

Clarice Cliff, Bizarre, Pitcher, Geometric, Multicolor, Green Outlines, Marked, Art Deco, 5 1/4 x 7 In.
$572

DuMouchelles

Clewell, Vase, Art Pottery, Copper Overlay, Dark Green Ground, Curved Neck, 13 ½ In.
$791

Strawser Auction Group

Clock, Advertising, Budweiser, Round, Birds, Bat, Numbers, Multicolor Neon, 33 ¼ In.
$1,173

Selkirk Auctioneers & Appraisers

Clock, Banjo, Howard, E., Painted, Roman Numerals, No. 5, Boston, c.1860, 29 x 12 In.
$938

Eldred's

CLOCK

Clocks of all types have always been popular with collectors. The eighteenth-century tall case, or grandfather's, clock was designed to house a works with a long pendulum. The name on the clock is usually the maker but sometimes it is a merchant or other craftsman. In 1816, Eli Terry patented a new, smaller works for a clock, and the case became smaller. The clock could be kept on a shelf instead of on the floor. By 1840, coiled springs were used and even smaller clocks were made. Battery-powered electric clocks were first made in the late 1800s but the average household in the United States did not use a battery-operated clock until the 1930s. A garniture set can include a clock and other objects displayed on a mantel.

Advertising, 7Up Likes You, Metal, Glass Face, Logo, Bubbles, Pam Clock Co., Brooklyn, 15 In....	677
Advertising, Ask For Hood's Dairy Foods, Double Bubble, White Dial, Green Numerals, 15 ½ In.	748
Advertising, Bud Light, Round, White, Red, Blue, Numbers, Circular Red Neon, 1900s, 19 In.	110
Advertising, Budweiser, Round, Birds, Bat, Numbers, Multicolor Neon, 33 ¼ In. .... *illus*	1173
Advertising, Cadillac Authorized Service, Multicolor Dial, Blue Steel Case, 1980s, 20 x 6 In.	92
Advertising, Nestle's, Swiss Milk For All Time, Black & Red Text, Tin Front Case, c.1930, 19 In....	378
Advertising, Ringling Bros. Circus, Next Free Show, Paint On Board, Sun, Rainbow, 1960s, 24 In.	500
Advertising, Smoke Dog's Head Cigars, St. Bernard, Child Blowing Horn, Cast Iron, 11 x 12 ½ In..	1140
Advertising, Thirsty Just Whistle, Bubble Glass Cover, Aluminum Case, c.1950, 15 In.	554
Advertising, Wink, Grapefruit, Canada Dry, Square, Glass, Pam Clock Co., New York, 15 x 15 In.	276
Alarm, Travel, Brass, Square, White Dial, Swiss Quartz Movement, Tiffany & Co., 1970, 4 In. .	115
Alarm, Travel, LeCoultre, Goldtone Case, Black Enamel, Silvertone Dial, 2 x 1 ½ In.	207
Animated, Kit-Cat, Black, Earl Arnault, Allied Mfg. Co., Washington, c.1940s, 9 x 4 x 2 In....	325
Anniversary, Victorian Gazebo Shape, Enamel Dial, Finial, Germany, 14 ½ In........................	354
Ansonia, Kitchen, Walnut, Roman Numerals, Hinged Glass Door, Gilt, Late 1800s, 25 In.	177
Ansonia, Regulator, Crystal, Bronze, Scroll & Leaves Case, c.1905, 19 x 10 ½ x 9 In..............	1920
Ansonia, Regulator, Wall, Carved, Oak Case, Gilt, Pendulum, 39 x 15 In.	158
Ansonia, Shelf, Gold Accents, Pendant & Key, Cast Iron, Victorian, 10 In.	115
Ansonia, Silver Plated Metal, Paper Dial, Bisque Figure, c.1900s, 15 In..............................	510
Art Deco, Figural, Woman, Kneeling, Geometric Design, Onyx & Colored Marbles, c.1930, 10 In.	236
Banjo, Chelsea Ship's Bell, Brass, Eagle Finial, Painted Dial, Wood Case, c.1920	826
Banjo, Elnathan Taber, Federal, Mahogany, Roman Numeral Dial, White Face, Early 1800s, 32 In. ...	3172
Banjo, Gilt Finial, Painted Metal Dial, Hinged Glass Door, Early 1800s, 33 x 10 x 3 In...........	351
Banjo, Howard & Davis, Mahogany, Painted, Roman Numerals, No. 4, Marked, Boston, 1800s, 32 In.	4375
Banjo, Howard, E., Painted, Roman Numerals, No. 5, Boston, c.1860, 29 x 12 In. .... *illus*	938
Banjo, Mahogany, Mount Vernon, Finial, New Haven, Early 1900s, 18 x 5 In.	177
Banjo, Mahogany, Veneer, Pine, Squared Element, Wood, Pendulum, Early 1800s, 35 x 13 ½ In...	900
Banjo, Ornate, Giltwood, Eagle Case, Eglomise Acorn, Oak Leaves, Federal, 42 In.	615
Banjo, Waltham, Constitution & Guerriere, Eagle Finial, Weight Driven, 1910s, 39 x 11 x 5 In.	1152
Banjo, Waltham, Eagle Finial, Giltwood, Brass, Painted Glass, Signed, Early 1900s, 22 ½ In...	819
Blinking Eye, Topsy, Black Girl, Roman Numeral Dial, White Face, Round Base, 17 x 11 x 7 In.	1750
Bracket, Mahogany, Line Inlay, Brass Lion's Mask Handles, Painted Dial, Early 1800s, 15 In..	2074
Bracket, Robinson, F., Oak, Fusee, Roman Numerals, Pendulum, George II, London, 17 In. ..*illus*	1888
Bradley & Hubbard, Figural, Napoleonic Soldier, Blinking Eye, Holds Dial, Cast Iron, 17 In...	940
Bradley & Hubbard, Gambrinus, King Of Beers, Blinking Eye, Cast Iron, c.1859, 12 x 7 In..	5100
Bronze, Angel, Flying, Globe, Roman Numerals, Pendulum, Key, 20 ½ x 14 ½ x 6 ½ In........	3383
Caldwell, E.F., Desk, Ribbon Crest, Gilt Bronze, Porcelain, Marble Base, Early 1900s, 10 In. .	693
Calendar, National, 2 Metal Dials, Maple, Time & Strike Movement, Late 1800s, 27 x 15 In. .	148
Carriage, Benson, J.W., Brass Case, Swing Handle, White Face, London, Early 1900s, 7 In. . *illus*	512
Carriage, Brass, Beveled Glass, Porcelain Dial, 8-Day Time & Strike, 7 ½ In.	960
Carriage, Brass, Beveled Glass, Roman Numerals, Key, Miniature, 4 x 3 x 2 ½ In.	123
Carriage, Henley Anglaise, Brass, 8-Day, Roman Numerals, Glass Front, Key, 5 ¼ x 3 ¼ In...	148
Carriage, Sonnerie, Porcelain Dial, Beveled Glass Panels, Gilt, Brass, c.1880, 7 x 4 x 4 In. .*illus*	2691
Carriage, Wood, Beveled Glass, Numbers, Marked, France, 5 ½ In.	161
Carriage, Wuba, Roman Numerals, 2 Jewel, Engraved, Key, Holland, 10 x 6 In......................	92
Cartel, Louis XVI Style, Bronze, Enamel, Cornucopia Sides, Early 1900s, 26 x 14 x 6 In.	600

C

Clock, Bracket, Robinson, F., Oak, Fusee, Roman Numerals, Pendulum, George II, London, 17 In.
$1,888

Bunch Auctions

Clock, Carriage, Benson, J.W., Brass Case, Swing Handle, White Face, London, Early 1900s, 7 In.
$512

Cowan's Auctions

Clock, Carriage, Sonnerie, Porcelain Dial, Beveled Glass Panels, Gilt, Brass, c.1880, 7 x 4 x 4 In.
$2,691

Jeffrey S. Evans & Associates

Clock, Cartier, 18K Gold, Swiveling, Sword Shape, Alarm, Signed, c.1945
$5,625

Wright

Clock, Chelsea, Tambour, Bronze, Kennard & Co., Boston, c.1918, 12 x 23 ½ In.
$1,375

Eldred's

Clock, Colonial Mfg. Co., Empire, Mahogany, Fluted Columns, Roman Numerals, Michigan, 68 x 22 In.
$354

Austin Auction Gallery

Clock, Cuckoo, Black Forest, Landscape, Roman Numerals, Painted, Germany, c.1875, 14 x 9 ½ In.
$1,180

Austin Auction Gallery

Clock, Desk, 8-Day, Man & Woman, Seated, Roman Numerals, Gilt Metal, Footed, Swiss, 1900s, 4 In.
$288

Hindman

CLOCK

Clock, Desk, Owl, Spread Wings, Archangel Michael Standing, Ebony, Gray Onyx Case, 12 x 9 In.
$200

Woody Auction

Clock, Enamel, Key Wind, Marked, Argent 0935 Repose, Miniature, 4 x 4 In.
$923

Morphy Auctions

Clock, Forestville, Wall, Brass, Walnut, Leaf Shape Petals, Round, France, 23 x 23 In.
$148

Alderfer Auction Company

Clock, Gilbert, Regulator, Gilt Brass Case, Beveled Glass, Porcelain Dial, c.1900, 16 In.
$480

Cottone Auctions

Clock, Howard Miller, Digital, Floor, Red LED Lights, Wallace Interiors, Florida, 1970, 56 x 13 In.
$374

Blackwell Auctions

Clock, Howard Miller, Outdoor, Painted, Aluminum, Mounted, Stone Plinth Base, Late 1900s, 90 In.
$1,121

Leland Little Auctions

Clock, Howard Miller, Pretzel, No. 4774A, Maple, Enameled Steel, 1952, 17¼ In.
$938

Toomey & Co. Auctioneers

Clock, Howard, E. & Co., School, Oak, Enamel Face, Black, Roman Numerals, 31 x 15½ In.
$540

Michaan's Auctions

Clock, Ithaca, Mahogany, Hall, Time & Strike, Paper Dial, Painted, 87 In.
$106

Bunch Auctions

Cartier, 18K Gold, Swiveling, Sword Shape, Alarm, Signed, c.1945 .... *illus*	5625
Cartier, Desk, Green Nephrite Ground, Side Sleeves, Silver Mounts, c.1920, 3 x 4 x 1 In.	4095
Chelsea, Shelf, Beehive, String Inlaid, Dial Marked, Shreve & Co., 11 7/8 x 7 3/4 In......	236
Chelsea, Shelf, Gothic, Arched Door, Silvered Face, Marked, Smith, Patterson Co., 5 x 3 x 2 In....	688
Chelsea, Tambour, Bronze, Kennard & Co., Boston, c.1918, 12 x 23 1/2 In. .... *illus*	1375
Colonial Mfg. Co., Empire, Mahogany, Fluted Columns, Roman Numerals, Michigan, 68 x 22 In. *illus*	354
Cuckoo, Black Forest, Fusee, Grapevine, Tiered Fence, Carved Wood, 17 In.	1770
Cuckoo, Black Forest, Landscape, Roman Numerals, Painted, Germany, c.1875, 14 x 9 1/2 In. *illus*	1180
Dent, Swinging Fusee, Engraved, Brass & Silver, Corinthian Columns, Paw Feet, 1800s, 15 x 12 In.....	3068
Desk, 8-Day, Man & Woman, Seated, Roman Numerals, Gilt Metal, Footed, Swiss, 1900s, 4 In. *illus*	288
Desk, Mounted, Sterling Silver, Cut Glass Inkwell, Cross, 4 In.	288
Desk, Owl, Spread Wings, Archangel Michael Standing, Ebony, Gray Onyx Case, 12 x 9 In. *illus*	200
Electric, Mystery, Marc Newson, Disc, Carbon Fiber, Teflon, 2 Round White Markers, 32 In..	77500
Electric, Skyscraper, Manning-Bowman, Chrome, Orange Bakelite Panels, Art Deco, 17 x 8 In.	403
Elgin, Shelf, Brass, Glass, Roman Numerals, Square Stand, 10 x 7 In.	128
Enamel, Key Wind, Marked, Argent 0935 Repose, Miniature, 4 x 4 In. .... *illus*	923
Figural, Angel, Seated, Gilt, Bronze, Porcelain Dial, 8-Day Time & Strike, Footed, 16 x 25 In..	1320
Figural, Woman, Seated, Gilt, Bronze, Flower Vase Finial, 18 1/2 In......................	226
Forestville, Wall, Brass, Walnut, Leaf Shape Petals, Round, France, 23 x 23 In. .... *illus*	148
Gallery, Mahogany, White Face, Roman Numerals, Round Frame, Early 1900s, 30 1/2 In.	608
Gilbert, Regulator, Calendar, Oak, Carved, Painted, Black, Gold Tablet, 33 x 16 x 4 In.	238
Gilbert, Regulator, Gilt Brass Case, Beveled Glass, Porcelain Dial, c.1900, 16 In. .... *illus*	480
Gilbert, Wall, Porcelain, Pendulum, Key & Weights, Wood Case, c.1915, 49 In.	468
Godon, F.L., Shelf, White Marble, Woman, Cherub, Enamel, Numbers, Signed, France, 16 x 16 In..	1888
Gustav Becker, Free Swinger, Half & Hour Striking, Spiral Gong, c.1910, 37 x 15 5/8 In.	316
Gustav Becker, Wall, Freischwinger, Time & Strike Movement, Brass Pendulum, Late 1800s, 46 In...	150
Hanging, Shaker, Pine, Hanging, Roman Numerals, Battery Movement, c.1830, 45 In.....	688
Herman Miller, Table, Walnut Burl, Enameled Dial, Aluminum, Glass, Gilbert Rohde, 1934, 8 3/4 In..	3500
Herschede, Tall Case, 5 Tubes, 3-Weight, Mahogany Case, Silver Dial, 1900s, 78 x 21 In......	1260
Howard Miller, Asterisk, Enameled Steel, Aluminum, G. Nelson, 1953, 10 In.	500
Howard Miller, Ball, Wire Mesh, Birch Ball Numbers, G. Nelson, 12 In.	530
Howard Miller, Basket, Rattan, Birch, Steel, G. Nelson, c.1952, 12 In.	438
Howard Miller, Digital, Floor, Red LED Lights, Wallace Interiors, Florida, 1970, 56 x 13 In. . *illus*	374
Howard Miller, Outdoor, Painted, Aluminum, Mounted, Stone Plinth Base, Late 1900s, 90 In. ...*illus*	1121
Howard Miller, Pretzel, No. 4774A, Maple, Enameled Steel, 1952, 17 1/4 In. .... *illus*	938
Howard Miller, Steering Wheel, Brass, Steel, Aluminum, Vinyl, Enamel, 1949, 12 In.	875
Howard Miller, Sunflower, Laminated Walnut, Brass, G. Nelson, 29 In. Dia.	2125
Howard Miller, Tile, Glass, Walnut, G. Nelson, 1957, 13 1/2 In.	750
Howard Miller, Wall, Roman Numerals, Hexagonal Case, 1950s, 20 In...........................	86
Howard Miller, Wall, Sunflower, Ash, Brass, Aluminum, Signed, 1958, 29 x 2 In.	2125
Howard, E. & Co., School, Oak, Enamel Face, Black, Roman Numerals, 31 x 15 1/2 In. . *illus*	540
Ithaca, Calendar, Walnut, 2 Dials, Paneled Burl Front, Roman Numerals, 1865, 23 x 13 x 5 In..	546
Ithaca, Mahogany, Hall, Time & Strike, Paper Dial, Painted, 87 In. .... *illus*	106
Jaeger-LeCoultre, Atmos, 13 Jewel, Gilt Metal, Glass Case, Swiss, 9 x 8 x 6 In........................	826
Jaeger-LeCoultre, Atmos, Gold Plated Brass Case, c.1950, 8 3/4 In.	469
Jaeger-LeCoultre, Atmos, Torsion Pendulum, Bronze, Lapis Lazuli Dial, 1900s, 9 In. *illus*	1512
Jaeger-LeCoultre, Atmos, White Dial, Gilt Brass Case, Swiss, 1900s, 9 1/4 In.	375
Jaeger-LeCoultre, Desk, Blue, Lapis Lazuli Top & Bottom, 4 Fluted Corner Columns, 3 7/8 In.	2268
Jaeger-LeCoultre, Desk, Gilt Brass, Square Face, Swiss, c.1970, 9 x 8 x 6 In. .... *illus*	720
Jaeger-LeCoultre, Travel, Alarm, Recital, 8-Day, Beaded, Wood Frame, 3 1/2 In....................	165
Japy Freres, Regulator, Brass Movement, Porcelain Face, Tiffany & Co., c.1900, 11 x 6 x 5 In..	168
Japy Freres, Shelf, Champleve, Alabaster Case, Enamel, Pendulum, Late 1800s, 12 x 14 x 6 In. . *illus*	118
Japy Freres, Shelf, Gilt Bronze, Maiden & Child, White Dial, Roman Numerals, c.1860, 13 x 17 In.	469
Japy Freres, Shelf, Gilt, Fluted Columns, Plinth Base, Late 1800s, 15 3/4 x 18 1/2 In.	148
Junghans, Wall, Berliner Style, 8-Day Time & Strike, Victorian, c.1890 .... *illus*	425
Kieninger Kessels, Wall, Weight-Driven, Moon Phase, Silver Plate Dial, 36 x 12 x 8 In. ..*illus*	2925
Lantern, Brass, Dome Top, Fusee Movement, Signed, Ed Hemins Bisiter, 1800s, 17 x 8 1/2 In.	347
LeCoultre, Atmos, Gold, Numbers, Glass Case, 8 3/4 x 7 x 5 In.	375

Clock, Jaeger-LeCoultre, Atmos, Torsion Pendulum, Bronze, Lapis Lazuli Dial, 1900s, 9 In.
$1,512

Fontaine's Auction Gallery

TIP
Wind the clock fully each time you wind it.

Clock, Jaeger-LeCoultre, Desk, Gilt Brass, Square Face, Swiss, c.1970, 9 x 8 x 6 In.
$720

Michaan's Auctions

Clock, Japy Freres, Shelf, Champleve, Alabaster Case, Enamel, Pendulum, Late 1800s, 12 x 14 x 6 In.
$118

Leland Little Auctions

Clock, Junghans, Wall, Berliner Style, 8-Day Time & Strike, Victorian, c.1890 $425

Pook & Pook

Clock, Kieninger Kessels, Wall, Weight-Driven, Moon Phase, Silver Plate Dial, 36 x 12 x 8 In. $2,925

Thomaston Place Auction Galleries

Clock, Maitland-Smith, Figural, Bird, Brass, Clutching Quartz Timepiece, Enamel, Black Base, 6 x 7 In. $94

Bunch Auctions

Lighthouse, Industrial Animated, Brass, Silver Plate, Roman Numerals, France, 9¾ In.......	4720
Linden, Figural, Diana, Classical Dress, Holding Swinger Pendulum, 8-Day, Marked, Japan, 14 In.	127
Lovell Mfg. Co., Meridian, Rosewood, Brass, 8-Day Movement, Calendar Dial, Late 1800s, 24 In.	234
Mahogany, Chippendale, Brass Finial, Rosettes, Roman Numerals, Painted, 1900s, 59 x 11 In....	250
Maitland-Smith, Bronze, Monkey, Leaf Umbrella, Elephant, Rocky Plinth, 24 x 20 x 15 In..	431
Maitland-Smith, Figural, Bird, Brass, Clutching Quartz Timepiece, Enamel, Black Base, 6 x 7 In. *illus*	94
Marti, Samuel, Portico, Pink Marble, Enamel Face, Bronze Lion, 1900, 22 x 10 x 5 In. ....*illus*	840
Morbier, Pine, Flower, Roman Numerals, Bracket Feet, Painted, Marked, c.1850, 95½ x 19 In....	354
Morbier, Tall Case, Oak, Cornice Top, Roman Numerals, Bracket Feet, 1800s, 91 In.	531
Morbier, Wall, Brass, Flowers, Black Roman Numerals, Pendulum, 2-Weight, Late 1800s, 16 In.	325
Morrell, B., Mirror, Flowers, Gold, Roman Numerals, Signed, Boscawen, N.H., 1800s, 30 x 14 In..	4063
Mougin, Shelf, Gilt Brass, Enamel Face, Hinged Glass Door, Elaborate Case, c.1890, 22 In.	266
Mystery, Cartier, Glass Face, Gilt, Brass, Diamond Shape Hours, c.1945, 7¼ In.	4063
Mystery, Jefferson, Golden Hour, Gilt Metal & Glass, 1950, 9 x 7½ In. ....*illus*	89
New Haven, Mahogany, 30-Hour, Roman Numerals, Pendulum, Signo Vinces, 25¾ In.........	47
New Haven, Shelf, Mission, Los Santos, Oak Frame, Brass, Gong, c.1904, 13¾ x 12 x 5½ In. .	250
Novelty, Umbrella Shape, Dark Blue, Enamel, Silver Rim, Early 1900s, 3 x 3½ In. ..... *illus*	504
Peddler, Wag-On-Wall, Cast Iron, Spring Driven Movement, Marked, J.V.E., 15 x 5 x 8 In.	489
Portico, Rosewood & Marquetry, Bronze, Mounted, Leafy Bezel, Harp Pendulum, 20½ In. ..	384
Portico, Wood Case & Base, Enamel, Roman Numerals, Napoleon III, France, 1800s, 17 x 8 In. .*illus*	207
Recorder, International Time, Pendulum & Key, Oak Case, c.1920, 44 In.............................	199
Regulator, Crystal, Bronze Case, Gilt Hands, Porcelain Dial, Marble Base, Urn Finial, 17½ In..	630
Regulator, Satinwood, Mahogany, Gilt, Pendulum, Weight, White Dial, Wood Case, 1850s, 35 In.	896
Regulator, Vienna, 2 Porcelain Dials, Calendar, Urn Finial, Black, Jadeite, 40 In..................	472
Regulator, Wall, Wood, Roman Numerals, Beveled Glass, Door, Carved, 17 In.......................	74
Rosenbach, Wall, Brass, Time, Strike Movement, Gilt Case, Marked, Early 1900s, 17 In. *illus*	236
Sawin, J., Lyre, Mahogany, Carved Leaves, Roman Numerals, Signed, Boston, c.1815, 39 In. *illus*	4063
Schlabaugh & Sons, Shelf, Arts & Crafts, Oak, Motawi, Majolica Tile, Copper, 15½ In.	339
Sessions, Shelf, Brass Columnar, Architectural Wood Case, Late 1800s, 10 x 16 x 6 In...........	96
Sessions, Wall, Oak Case, Regulator, Pendulum & Key, Carved Border, c.1915, 38½ In.........	117
Seth Thomas, Gallery, Hebrew Writing, White Face, Mahogany Case, Early 1900s, 23 In. *illus*	375
Seth Thomas, Regulator, 8-Day Time & Strike Movement, Brass, Beveled Case, 11 x 4 In.	100
Seth Thomas, Regulator, Crystal, Beveled, Mythological Lion, Faux Mercury Pendulum, 16 In.	322
Seth Thomas, Regulator, Jeweler's, 8-Day, Enameled Face, Oak Case, 57 x 27 x 13 In.	775
Seth Thomas, Regulator, Long Drop, Octagonal, Wood, Brass, 31 In.................................	246
Seth Thomas, School, Wall, Oak Case, Octagonal Top, Hinged Door, c.1910, 31 In.................	234
Seth Thomas, Shelf, Black Paint, Numbers, Adamantine, 11 In.	49
Seth Thomas, Shelf, Cathedral, Inlaid Mahogany Case, Silvered Dial, Early 1900s, 15 x 7 x 10 In..	86
Seth Thomas, Shelf, Wood, Black, Faux Marble, 10¾ x 16 In..	71
Shelf, Brass Hardware, Enameled Dial, Resin & Wood Case, Late 1900s, 24 In., Pair	216
Shelf, Bronze Dore, Eros, Roman Numerals, Bun Feet, Signed, 1800s, 16 x 13 x 5 In............	1652
Shelf, Bronze Dore, Louis Philippe Style, Pierced Rococo Base, 1800s, 18 x 13 x 7 In.	500
Shelf, Bronze, Figural, Wine Barrel Shape, Metal Dial, Octagonal Base, 1800s, 13 x 12 In. ..*illus*	1408
Shelf, Bronze, Woman, Slate Architectural Case, Plinth Base, Winged Paw Feet, 18 x 16 In...	250
Shelf, Cavalier Topper, Gilt, Metal, Onyx, Cloche, France, 19¼ x 19 In.............................	531
Shelf, Chimento Rock, Glass, Globular Case, Gilt Metal Frame, Marble Base, 1950s, 9 x 13 In.	1500
Shelf, Cloisonne, Door, Enamel-On-Copper Portrait, Brass Frame, Late 1800s, 16 x 7 x 6 In. .*illus*	322
Shelf, Demeter, Gilt Metal, Figural, Roman Numerals, Pendulum, Stamped 188, 1800s, 17½ In. *illus*	585
Shelf, Figural, Frieze Symbols, Tall Plinth Base, Gilt, Bronze, 1800s, 16½ x 13¾ x 5 In........	1152
Shelf, Gilt, Metal Mounts, Roman Numerals, Pendulum, Key, Portico, France, 17 x 9 x 5 In..	313
Shelf, H&F, Urn Finial, Lion Handles, Roman Numeral Dial, Brass Works, 1880s, 15 x 9 x 7 In.	132
Shelf, Hercules, Ornate Bezel, Convex Dial, Roman Numerals, Early 1800s, 19 x 14 In.	2457
Shelf, Hunter's, Oak, Carved, Grouse, Chicks, Flowers, Leaves, Rocks, Black Forest, c.1878, 22 In. *illus*	1320
Shelf, Louis XIV, Urn Shape, Roman Numerals, Finial, Rectangular Base, Paw Feet, 22 x 19 In.	433
Shelf, Louis XVI Style, Gilt Bronze, Putto, Rooster On Top, Marble Base, 1800s, 12 x 11 In. ...	295
Shelf, Louis XVI, Ormolu, Marble, Gilt Bronze, Imbert L'Aine A Paris, Late 1700s, 25 In. *illus*	2832
Shelf, Marble Inset, Flowers, Brass Face Ring, Bailey, Banks & Biddle, Late 1800s, 12 x 12 In..	245
Shelf, Napoleon III, Gilt, Bronze, Allegorical Figure, Grain, Grapes, 1800s, 15½ In.	896

Clock, Marti, Samuel, Portico, Pink Marble, Enamel Face, Bronze Lion, 1900, 22 x 10 x 5 In.
$840

Garth's Auctioneers & Appraisers

Clock, Mystery, Jefferson, Golden Hour, Gilt Metal & Glass, 1950, 9 x 7 ½ In.
$89

Leland Little Auctions

Clock, Novelty, Umbrella Shape, Dark Blue, Enamel, Silver Rim, Early 1900s, 3 x 3 ½ In.
$504

Fontaine's Auction Gallery

Clock, Portico, Wood Case & Base, Enamel, Roman Numerals, Napoleon III, France, 1800s, 17 x 8 In.
$207

Austin Auction Gallery

Clock, Rosenbach, Wall, Brass, Time, Strike Movement, Gilt Case, Marked, Early 1900s, 17 In.
$236

Leland Little Auctions

Clock, Sawin, J., Lyre, Mahogany, Carved Leaves, Roman Numerals, Signed, Boston, c.1815, 39 In.
$4,063

Eldred's

Clock, Seth Thomas, Gallery, Hebrew Writing, White Face, Mahogany Case, Early 1900s, 23 In.
$375

Cowan's Auctions

Clock, Shelf, Bronze, Figural, Wine Barrel Shape, Metal Dial, Octagonal Base, 1800s, 13 x 12 In.
$1,408

Brunk Auctions

Clock, Shelf, Cloisonne, Door, Enamel-On-Copper Portrait, Brass Frame, Late 1800s, 16 x 7 x 6 In.
$322

Jeffrey S. Evans & Associates

Clock, Shelf, Demeter, Gilt Metal, Figural, Roman Numerals, Pendulum, Stamped 188, 1800s, 17 ½ In.
$585

Jeffrey S. Evans & Associates

Clock, Shelf, Hunter's, Oak, Carved, Grouse, Chicks, Flowers, Leaves, Rocks, Black Forest, c.1878, 22 In.
$1,320

Cottone Auctions

Clock, Shelf, Louis XVI, Ormolu, Marble, Gilt Bronze, Imbert L'Aine A Paris, Late 1700s, 25 In.
$2,832

Cottone Auctions

Clock, Shelf, Rococo Style, 2 Cherubs, Urn, Flower Garlands, Gilt Rocaille Case, 24 x 30 ¾ In.
$2,655

Austin Auction Gallery

Clock, Shelf, Roman Soldier, Seated, Eagle Top, Circular Case, Marble Base, 1800s, 13 x 20 x 7 In.
$207

Austin Auction Gallery

Clock, Shelf, Sevres Style, Gilt, Bronze, Porcelain Dial, 8-Day Time & Strike, Late 1800s, 15 In.
$369

Brunk Auctions

Clock, Skeleton, Brass, Open Moon Hands, Sub Second Dial, Roman Numerals, Ball Feet, 1800s, 15 In.
$756

Fontaine's Auction Gallery

Clock, Tall Case, Chippendale, Walnut, Poplar, Carved, 8-Day, c.1790, 93 x 10 In.
$3,690

Morphy Auctions

Shelf, Painted Dial, Roman Numerals, Marked, 1800s, 13½ x 7⅜ x 4¾ In. 512
Shelf, Pediment Top, Carved Detail, Roman Numeral Dial, Early 1900s, 17 x 13 x 9 In. 219
Shelf, Putti, Playing Violin, Patina, 8-Day Time & Strike, Marble Base, Signed, Rousseau, 21 In. 180
Shelf, Rococo Style, 2 Cherubs, Urn, Flower Garlands, Gilt Rocaille Case, 24 x 30¾ In. ..*illus* 2655
Shelf, Roman Soldier, Seated, Eagle Top, Circular Case, Marble Base, 1800s, 13 x 20 x 7 In. ..*illus* 207
Shelf, Rustic, Octagonal, Stepped Rectangular Base, Germany, 12 In. 158
Shelf, Secessionist, Mahogany, Inlaid Fruitwood, Copper Dial, 18 x 6 x 10 In. 1250
Shelf, Sevres Style, Gilt, Bronze, Porcelain Dial, 8-Day Time & Strike, Late 1800s, 15 In. *illus* 369
Shelf, Walnut, Mailbox Shape, Marked Letters, Brass Slot, Roman Numerals, 16 x 10 In. 281
Skeleton, Brass, Open Moon Hands, Sub Second Dial, Roman Numerals, Ball Feet, 1800s, 15 In. .*illus* 756
Solari & Co., Calendar, Solar, Plastic, Metals, Gino Valle, Italy, 12½ x 12½ In. 1063
Steeple, Mahogany, Landscape Scene, Roman Numerals, Door, Victorian, 19 In. 74
Stennes, Elmer, Mahogany, Painted, 8-Day Time & Strike, Spring Movement, 1900s, 29 x 16 In... 625
Tall Case, Chippendale, Walnut, Poplar, Carved, 8-Day, c.1790, 93 x 10 In. .... *illus* 3690
Tall Case, David Blasdel, Coffin Style, Pine, Roman Numerals, Signed, 1700s, 85½ x 17 In.. 4688
Tall Case, David Wood, Federal, Mahogany, Brass, 8-Day Weight, Bracket Feet, c.1795, 92 In.. 2600
Tall Case, Disc Polyphon, Music Box, Walnut, Brass Dial, 8-Day Time & Strike, 87 x 21 In.... 3240
Tall Case, Elgin, Mahogany, Roman Numerals, Pendulum, 1950s, 82 x 19 In. .... *illus* 205
Tall Case, Federal, Cherry, Fretwork Top, Roman Numerals, Brass Finials, c.1800, 84½ In.. 1680
Tall Case, Furtwangler, Brass Movement, Pendulum, c.1920, 78 x 20 x 11 In. 125
Tall Case, Halbert, Mahogany, 8-Day, Brass Finial, Scottish, Signed, Glasgow, 92 x 22 In 1845
Tall Case, Hazelnut, Pine Wood, Numbers, 2-Bell Chime, Sweden, c.1870, 79 x 18 In. 1188
Tall Case, Herschede Clock Co., Walnut Case, Numbers, Marked, 1900s, 87 x 24 In. 2276
Tall Case, Herschede, 3 Chimes, Tubular Bells, Christopher Columbus, c.1980, 87 In. 1408
Tall Case, Herschede, Mahogany, 9 Tubes, Shaped Crest, Finial, Pendulum, 1900s, 86 x 25 x 16 In ... 1920
Tall Case, Howard Miller, Westminster Chime, Sun & Moon Dial, 79 In. 118
Tall Case, Jacob Handel, Walnut, Poplar, Flat Top, Columns, Carlisle, Pa., c.1800, 96 x 28 In. .*illus* 6150
Tall Case, James Ivory, Oak Case, Swan's Neck Pediment, Carved Leaves, Late 1700s, 18 x 10 In. .. 266
Tall Case, John Cole, Roman Numerals, Flowers, Stepped Base, Bracket Feet, 1750s, 77 x 11 x 9 In. 750
Tall Case, John Williams, Georgian, Mahogany, Silver Dial, Moon Phase, England, 1800s, 96 In. *illus* 1020
Tall Case, Lemuel French, Mahogany, Bonnet, Ball & Steeple Finials, Bracket Feet, 1800s, 94 In. .. 5000
Tall Case, Mahogany, Brass, Moon Dial, Urn Finial, 1800s, 88 In. 207
Tall Case, Mahogany, Gilt, Roman Numerals, Tempus Fugit, Georgian, 1800s, 85 x 19 In.... 649
Tall Case, Mahogany, Gracie Fields, Broken Arch, Column Support, Bracket Feet, c.1840, 95 In. . *illus* 1625
Tall Case, Mahogany, Numbers, Carved, Marked, Tiffany & Co., 96½ x 24½ x 17 In. 1063
Tall Case, Mora, Removable Hood, Pine, Painted Flowers, Sweden, 1848, 77 x 22 x 8 In. 438
Tall Case, Morbier, Pine, Paint, Brass Dial, Bracket Feet, French Provincial, Late 1800s, 91 In. ... *illus* 1121
Tall Case, Oak, Black, Numbers, Brass, Pendulum, Arts & Crafts, c.1910, 78 x 20 In. .. *illus* 125
Tall Case, Riley Whiting, Arched Hood, Turned Finial, Wood Dial, Sponge Ground, c.1825, 90 In. 5625
Tall Case, Riley Whiting, Red Pine Case, Weight Driven, Arched Top, c.1810, 83 x 18 x 9 In... 644
Tall Case, Rudolf Korfhage, Mahogany, Chiming, Dome Top, Ball Base, 1904, 90 x 24 In. 590
Tall Case, Tiger Maple, Broken Arched Crest, Finial, Flowers, White Dial, c.1820, 96½ In..... 5368
Tall Case, Walnut, Brass, Numbers, Velvet, Enameled Aluminum, 71½ x 17 In. 1625
Tall Case, Walnut, Inlay, Rosettes, 3 Finials, 8-Day, Uniontown, Pa., c.1810, 100 x 18 In. *illus* 3383
Tall Case, Wetherell Of Cannock, Mahogany, Broken Arch, Moon Dial, William IV, c.1835, 100 In. *illus* 2375
Tall Case, White Face, Roman Numerals, Wood Case, Pendulum, 84½ In. 263
Tall Case, Winterhalder & Hofmeier, Bonnet, Pendulum, Germany, c.1950, 78¾ x 15 x 12 In. 330
Tall Case, Wm. Toleman, Mahogany Case, 8-Day, 1790, 96 x 20½ x 9½ In. 1750
Terry & Andrews, Steeple, Mahogany, 30-Hour, Roman Numerals, Pendulum, Key, 20 In. .. 71
Terry, Eli, Shelf, Pillar & Scroll, Mahogany Case, Wood Dial, c.1825, 30 x 17 x 4 In. .... *illus* 293
Tiffany & Co., Regulator, Crystal, Enameled Dial, Roman Numerals, Brass, Late 1800s, 10 In. 322

Tiffany clocks that are part of desk sets made by Louis Comfort Tiffany are listed in the Tiffany category. Clocks sold by the store Tiffany & Co. are listed here.

Toki, Stick, Wood, Brass, Drawer, Key, Japan, Early 1800s, 13 In. 1180
Walker, J., Dwarf, Cherry, Brass Finials, Roman Numerals, Early 1800s, 47¾ x 11¼ In. 5936
Wall, Act Of Parliament, Painted, Wood, Roman Numerals, Brass, Weights, Pendulum, 1800s, 58 x 27 1062
Wall, Quartz Movement, Verneuil Tole, Painted, Gilt, Leaf & Vine, Hanging Loop, 26 In. *illus* 106

Clock, Tall Case, Elgin, Mahogany, Roman Numerals, Pendulum, 1950s, 82 x 19 In.
$205

Hindman

Clock, Tall Case, Jacob Handel, Walnut, Poplar, Flat Top, Columns, Carlisle, Pa., c.1800, 96 x 28 In.
$6,150

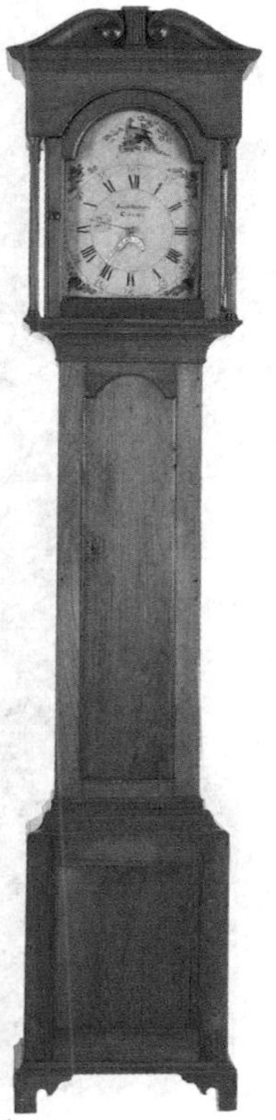

Morphy Auctions

Clock, Tall Case, John Williams, Georgian, Mahogany, Silver Dial, Moon Phase, England, 1800s, 96 In.
$1,020

Clock, Tall Case, Morbier, Pine, Paint, Brass Dial, Bracket Feet, French Provincial, Late 1800s, 91 In.
$1,121

Clock, Tall Case, Walnut, Inlay, Rosettes, 3 Finials, 8-Day, Uniontown, Pa., c.1810, 100 x 18 In.
$3,383

Selkirk Auctioneers & Appraisers

Austin Auction Gallery

Morphy Auctions

Clock, Tall Case, Mahogany, Gracie Fields, Broken Arch, Column Support, Bracket Feet, c.1840, 95 In.
$1,625

Clock, Tall Case, Oak, Black, Numbers, Brass, Pendulum, Arts & Crafts, c.1910, 78 x 20 In.
$125

Clock, Tall Case, Wetherell Of Cannock, Mahogany, Broken Arch, Moon Dial, William IV, c.1835, 100 In.
$2,375

Charlton Hall Auctions

Kamelot Auctions

Charlton Hall Auctions

Wall, Wood, Cuckoo Type, Roman Numerals, Enamel, Porcelain, Late 1800s, 11¾ In.	94
Waterbury, Wall, Oak Case, Regulator, Pendulum, 38¾ x 16½ x 4 In.	1408
Welch, Briggs Rotary, Glass Dome, Flying Ball Pendulum, Wood Base, Germany, c.1976, 7 In. *illus*	263

CLOISONNE

Cloisonne enamel was developed during the tenth century. A glass enamel was applied between small ribbons of metal on a metal base. Most cloisonne is Chinese or Japanese. Pieces marked *China* were made after 1900.

Bowl, 5-Claw Dragon, Black Ground, Gilt Rim & Base, Chinese, 1800s, 4 x 8¾ In.	177
Bowl, Brass Flared Rim, Multicolor Running Horse, Aqua Ground, Footed, 6 x 11½ In.	1170
Bowl, Lotus Leaf Shape Lid, Green, Metal Finial, Chinese, 1900s, 6½ x 17 In. *illus*	150
Box, Bronze Lid, Round, Intricate Flowers, Light Blue Ground, 3 x 5 In. *illus*	225
Box, Dome Lid, Green, Peonies, Butterflies, Chinese, 1950s, 6 In.	384
Box, Dome Lid, Knopped Finial, Enamel, Flowers, Butterflies, Green Ground, Chinese, 1950s, 6 In.	148
Box, Fitted Lid, Flowers, Butterflies, Multicolor, Blue Ground, Round, Chinese, 2⅝ In.	207
Box, Lid, Blue, Scrolled Leaves, Flower Medallion, Multicolor, Chinese, 6 In.	177
Box, Lid, Circular Celadon Jade Plaque, Carved Flowers, Early 1900s, 2 x 6 In.	4800
Box, Turtle Shape, Gilt, Copper, Carved Wood Base, Chinese, Early 1900s, 7 x 11 In. *illus*	125
Candlestand, Globular Lotus Mouth, Elaborate Stem, Splayed, Tripod Feet, Chinese, 21½ In., Pair	1098
Candlestick, Pricket, Light Blue Ground, Leaves, Urn, Wood Base, Chinese, 15½ In., Pair.	266
Censer, Bronze, Ding, Scrolling & Flower Designs, Signed, Chinese, 4½ In.	50
Charger, 2 Koi, Squid, Gold Rim, Black Paint, Japan, 12 In. *illus*	366
Charger, Bat & Flowers, Circular, Goldstone Panels, Japan, 1800s, 12 In.	416
Charger, Blue, Swimming, Fish, Bird & Flowers, Japan, 12 In. *illus*	177
Charger, Copper, Scalloped Edge, Central Chrysanthemum, Red Ground, 33½ In. *illus*	1287
Charger, Maroon Ground, Flowers, Birds Center, Rows Border, Scalloped Rim, 24 In. *illus*	693
Charger, Scalloped Rim, Brass, Phoenix, Butterflies, Dragon, Japan, 1800s, 14 In.	527
Cigarette Case, Flowers, Gilt Silver, Gustav Klingert, Moscow, 1890s, 3⅜ x 3 In.	1093
Figure, Woman, Carved Head, Hands, Feet, Teakwood Stand, 11½ x 15 In.	650
Figurine, Horse, Standing, Coat, Turquoise Blue Ground, Chinese, 18½ In., Pair	450
Ginger Jar, Green, Flowers, Bird, Dome Lid, Wood Stand, 7½ In., Pair	384
Jar, Double Dome Lid, Multicolor Butterflies, Gilt Foo Dog Finial, 1900s, 7¼ In.	118
Jardiniere, Flower Landscape, Cranes, Dog Ring Handles, Teak Stands, Chinese, 22 In., Pair	472
Jardiniere, Rectangular, Cut Corner, Flared Rim, Lotus Blossom, 1900s, 4 x 13 x 8 In. *illus*	497
Lamp, Oil, Converted Vase, Brass Burner, Japan, 1900s, 33 In.	256
Pitcher, Dragon, Fish Scale Style Handle, Bulbous, Flared Rim, Chinese, 11 In.	445
Pitcher, Multicolor Dragon, Swan Neck Handle, Bulbous Body, Chinese, 1800s, 10 In. *illus*	420
Planter, Hardstone Tree, Flowers, Turquoise, 13 In., Pair	330
Teapot, Lotus Flower Shape, Yellow, Frog Finial, Footed, Chinese, 1900s, 5 x 8 In. *illus*	649
Vase, 6-Sided, Foo Dog Design, Flared Circular Rim, Footed, Chinese, 20¼ In., Pair	960
Vase, Archaic Style, Landscape Scene, 3 Handles, Painted, Late 1800s, 18 In. *illus*	320
Vase, Art Nouveau Flowers, Gold Ground, Bronze, Jung, 1800s, 14 x 4 x 3 In., Pair	875
Vase, Bird, Leaves, Gilt Rim, Multicolor, Blue Interior, Chinese, 13½ In.	384
Vase, Blue, Scrolled Leaves, Geometric, Wood Stand, Chinese, 24 In.	590
Vase, Bronze Elliptical Rim, Turquoise Ground, Banded Conical Foot, Chinese, 1750s, 12 x 6 In. *illus*	600
Vase, Bulbous, Flowers, Blue, Black, Red, Gilt, Chinese, 10⅝ In.	115
Vase, Bulbous, Lilies, Yellow Ground, Painted, 7 x 3 In., Pair	148
Vase, Butterfly, Dark Green Ground, Gilt Rim & Base, Early 1900s, Japan, 5 In.	148
Vase, Cobalt Black, Rooster, Hen, Multicolor Flowers, Scalloped Band, c.1850, 14 x 5¾ In.	1112
Vase, Cylindrical, Bronze, Bamboo Motif Rim, Tortoise Feet, Japan, Late 1800s, 11 In., Pair.	1062
Vase, Gourd, Birds, Dragon, Blue, Painted, 18½ In.	308
Vase, Leaves, Multicolor, Turquoise Blue Ground, Brass, Chinese, 1800s, 9 In., Pair	325
Vase, Molded Rim, Multicolor, Carp Fish, Glazed, 7 In., Pair	537
Vase, Red, Silver, Fish Scale, Wirework Inlay, Wood Stand, Japan, Early 1900s, 6½ In., Pair.	150
Vase, Scrolling Leaves, Turquoise Blue Ground, Brass Mounts, Multicolor, 1800s, 9 In., Pair	531
Vase, Shouldered, Flared Rim, Samurai Warrior, Chrysanthemum, 1800s, 18 x 8 x 6 In. *illus*	1872
Vase, White Ground, Blue Leaves, Flowers, Molded Rim, Footed, Marked, Chinese, 10½ In., Pair	71
Vase, White, Songbird, Flowering Branches, Ruyi Band, Circular Foot, 1950s, 10¼ In., Pair.	413

Clock, Terry, Eli, Shelf, Pillar & Scroll, Mahogany Case, Wood Dial, c.1825, 30 x 17 x 4 In.
$293

Thomaston Place Auction Galleries

Clock, Wall, Quartz Movement, Verneuil Tole, Painted, Gilt, Leaf & Vine, Hanging Loop, 26 In.
$106

Bunch Auctions

Clock, Welch, Briggs Rotary, Glass Dome, Flying Ball Pendulum, Wood Base, Germany, c.1976, 7 In.
$263

Jeffrey S. Evans & Associates

CLOISONNE

Cloisonne, Bowl, Lotus Leaf Shape Lid, Green, Metal Finial, Chinese, 1900s, 6 ½ x 17 In.
$150

Eldred's

Cloisonne, Box, Bronze Lid, Round, Intricate Flowers, Light Blue Ground, 3 x 5 In.
$225

Ripley Auctions

Cloisonne, Box, Turtle Shape, Gilt, Copper, Carved Wood Base, Chinese, Early 1900s, 7 x 11 In.
$125

Bruneau & Co. Auctioneers

Cloisonne, Charger, 2 Koi, Squid, Gold Rim, Black Paint, Japan, 12 In.
$366

Nadeau's Auction Gallery

Cloisonne, Charger, Blue, Swimming, Fish, Bird & Flowers, Japan, 12 In.
$177

Bunch Auctions

Cloisonne, Charger, Copper, Scalloped Edge, Central Chrysanthemum, Red Ground, 33 ½ In.
$1,287

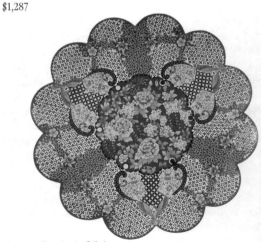

Thomaston Place Auction Galleries

Cloisonne, Charger, Maroon Ground, Flowers, Birds Center, Rows Border, Scalloped Rim, 24 In.
$693

Fontaine's Auction Gallery

Cloisonne, Jardiniere, Rectangular, Cut Corner, Flared Rim, Lotus Blossom, 1900s, 4 x 13 x 8 In.
$497

Thomaston Place Auction Galleries

Cloisonne, Pitcher, Multicolor Dragon, Swan Neck Handle, Bulbous Body, Chinese, 1800s, 10 In.
$420

Selkirk Auctioneers & Appraisers

Cloisonne, Teapot, Lotus Flower Shape, Yellow, Frog Finial, Footed, Chinese, 1900s, 5 x 8 In.
$649

Leland Little Auctions

Cloisonne, Vase, Archaic Style, Landscape Scene, 3 Handles, Painted, Late 1800s, 18 In.
$320

Hindman

Cloisonne, Vase, Bronze Elliptical Rim, Turquoise Ground, Banded Conical Foot, Chinese, 1750s, 12 x 6 In.
$600

Selkirk Auctioneers & Appraisers

Cloisonne, Vase, Shouldered, Flared Rim, Samurai Warrior, Chrysanthemum, 1800s, 18 x 8 x 6 In. $1,872

Thomaston Place Auction Galleries

Clothing, Belt, Officer's, Leather, Brass Buckle, Box, Marked, England, 3 x 2 In. Buckle $175

Cowan's Auctions

Clothing, Cap, Pillbox Style, Blue, GAR, Embroidered, Delegate, Augustus Thomas & Co., Phila., 1920, 7 In. $150

Cowan's Auctions

Zippers Tell

Vintage clothing clues: If an item has a metal zipper, it dates from before 1970. A side zipper on a dress was used in the 1940s or '50s. No zipper usually means before the 1940s.

CLOTHING

Clothing of all types is listed in this category. Dresses, hats, shoes, underwear, and more are found here. Other textiles are to be found in the Coverlet, Movie, Quilt, Textile, and World War I and II categories.

Christian Dior PARIS	NORMAN NORELL NEW YORK	Scaasi
Christian Dior 1947–present	Norman Norell 1958–1972	Arnold Scaasi 1956–2015

Belt, Officer's, Leather, Brass Buckle, Box, Marked, England, 3 x 2 In. Buckle.............. *illus*	175
Boots, Flight, Leather, Black, Dunlop, Fur Lined, Marked, 1936, 14 ½ In. High, Size 10	313
Boots, Officer's, Black, Leather, Sewn Soles, Marked, Size 9 ½	125
Boots, Victorian, Lace-Up, Black Leather, Lined, Pointed Toe, Block Heel, 10 x 9 In..............	110
Cap, Pillbox Style, Blue, GAR, Embroidered, Delegate, Augustus Thomas & Co., Phila., 1920, 7 In. *illus*	150
Cape, Gold, Silver, Embroidered, Flowers, Applique Style, 1800s, 57 x 65 In.	563
Cape, Mourning, Black Silk, Chantilly Floral Lace Overlay, c.1900, 15 ½ In.	245
Coat, Cowhide, Fringe At Arms, Silver Coin Buttons, Hand Sewn, 1950s, 47 In......................	207
Coat, Leather, Shearling, Oversized Shawl Collar, Waist Length, Men's, 1960s, Small	50
Coat, Silk, Embroidered, 2 Pockets, Center Split, Oscar De La Renta, Saks Fifth Ave., c.2000, Size 8	320
Coat, Winter, Fur, Purple, Leather, Callot Soeurs, 1927-28, 32 ½ In.	1280
Dress, Black Lace, Peach Silk, On Dressmaker's Form, Hallborghery, Victorian, 58 x 16 In. .. *illus*	246
Dress, Black, Drop Waist, Full Skirt, Rhinestone Beading, Diane Freis, 1980s, Size 8/10........	125
Dress, Evening, Black Velvet, Dramatic Sleeve, Bodice, Bias Cut Skirt, 1940s, Size 6/8...........	118
Dress, Strapless, Blue, Silk, Square Black Sequins, Angel Sanchez, 2014, 58 In. .... *illus*	192
Hat, Stetson, Brown, Feathered Band, Box, Size 7...	37
Jacket, Artillery, Blue, 12 Buttons, Cuffs, Mark, F.H. Shafer, 25 ½ In...........................	1536
Jacket, Green, Gold Tone, Pockets, Cuffed Sleeves, 1993, Size 36	416
Robe, Flowers, Butterflies, Symbols, Blue, Green, Embroidered, Chinese, 47 In.	344
Robe, Kimono, Blue, Guanyin, Dragons, Gold, Silk, Embroidery, Lishui Border, 42 In. . *illus*	1651
Scarf, Cuillers D'Afrique Pattern, Silk Twill, Caty Latham, Hermes, 35 x 35 In. .... *illus*	295
Scarf, Les Pivoines, Silk, Pale Pink Peonies, Celadon Basketweave Ground, Hermes, 35 x 35 In.	213
Scarf, Silk, Green, Tigre Royal, Sitting, Hermes, Frame, 35 x 35 In...............................	375
Scarf, Silk, Jacquard, White & Blue, Henry D'Origny, Hermes, 36 x 36 In.........................	756
Scarf, Silk, Mythiques Phoenix, Bird, Laurence Bourthoumieux, Hermes, 2016, 36 x 36 In. .	378
Scarf, Silk, Pink, Blue, Ecole Francaise D'Equitation, Hermes, Frame, 90 x 90 In.	250
Scarf, Silk, Print, Green, Picasso, Paris, 29 x 29 In. .... *illus*	173
Scarf, Silk, Royal Blue, White, Equestrian, Meadow Flowers, Hugo Grygkar, Hermes, 36 x 36 In.....	378
Scarf, Silk, Twill, Coupe De Gala, Black, Orange, Wlodek Kaminski, Hermes, 36 x 36 In.......	378
Scarf, Silk, Wildlife, Kermit Oliver, Hermes, Frame, 36 ¼ x 36 ¼ In................................	2242
Shako, Green, Leather Crown, Marked, Fa. A.A. Janssen & Co., Denmark, 10 x 7 x 5 ¾ In......	125
Shawl, Graffiti, Cashmere, Silk, Purple, Orange, Cyri Konga Phan, Hermes, Square, 2011, 55 In..	1134
Shawl, Wool, Paisley Pattern, Machine Woven, Scotland, c.1865, 67 x 65 In......................	310
Skirt, Pencil, Brown Leather, Ruffle, Lined, Self Belt, Yves Saint Laurent, 1980s, Size 10	735
Suit, Chanel, Wool Blend Tweed, Pink, Green, Lined Jacket, Wrap Skirt, 1970s, Size 6-8 *illus*	1250
Top Hat, Beaver, Leather Travel Case, Knox, Marked, HJS, Size 7 ½.....................................	266
Uniform, African Legion, Jacket, Black, 6 Buttons, 2 Pockets, Red & Black Border, Marcus Garvey *illus*	2875
Uniform, West Point Cadet, Jacket, Trousers, Gold Plated Buttons, c.1971, 20 x 23 In............	502

CLUTHRA

Cluthra glass is a two-layered glass with small bubbles and powdered glass trapped between the layers. The Steuben Glass Works of Corning, New York, first made it in 1920. Victor Durand of Kimball Glass Company in Vineland, New Jersey, made a similar glass from about 1925. Durand's pieces are listed in the Durand category. Related items are listed in the Steuben category.

Vase, Jade, Shouldered, Bulbous Body, Internal Bubbles, Steuben, c.1929, 8 ¼ In. .... *illus*	439
Vase, Smoky Green, 2 Applied Tab Handles, Signed, Charles Schneider, France, 7 ½ x 5 ½ In..	487

Clothing, Dress, Black Lace, Peach Silk, On Dressmaker's Form, Hallborghery, Victorian, 58 x 16 In.
$246

Clothing, Dress, Strapless, Blue, Silk, Square Black Sequins, Angel Sanchez, 2014, 58 In.
$192

Clothing, Robe, Kimono, Blue, Guanyin, Dragons, Gold, Silk, Embroidery, Lishui Border, 42 In.
$1,651

Clothing, Scarf, Cuillers D'Afrique Pattern, Silk Twill, Caty Latham, Hermes, 35 x 35 In.
$295

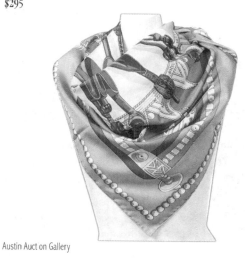

Clothing, Scarf, Silk, Print, Green, Picasso, Paris, 29 x 29 In.
$173

Clothing, Suit, Chanel, Wool Blend Tweed, Pink, Green, Lined Jacket, Wrap Skirt, 1970s, Size 6-8
$1,250

CLUTHRA

Clothing, Uniform, African Legion, Jacket, Black, 6 Buttons, 2 Pockets, Red & Black Border, Marcus Garvey
$2,875

Cowan's Auctions

Cluthra, Vase, Jade, Shouldered, Bulbous Body, Internal Bubbles, Steuben, c.1929, 8¼ In.
$439

Jeffrey S. Evans & Associates

Coalport, Cup & Saucer, Gold Ground & Interior, Blue Bird, Bamboo, Scalloped Rim
$150

Woody Auction

COALBROOKDALE

 Coalbrookdale was made by the Coalport porcelain factory of England during the Victorian period. Pieces are decorated with floral encrustations.

Basket, Potpourri, U-Shape Handle, Lid, Green, Multicolor Flowers, 6¼ In.	300
Candleholder, Flower Encrusted, Butterfly, Loop Handle, c.1930, 4½ x 3 In.	185
Vase, Flowers, Leaves, Cornucopia, Multicolor, c.1820, 5½ In.	245

COALPORT

Coalport ware was made by the Coalport Porcelain Works of England beginning about 1795. Early pieces were unmarked. About 1810–1825 the pieces were marked with the name *Coalport* in various forms. Later pieces also had the name *John Rose* in the mark. The crown mark was used with variations beginning in 1881. The date 1750 is printed in some marks, but it is not the date the factory started. Coalport was bought by Wedgwood in 1967. Coalport porcelain is no longer being produced. Some pieces are listed in this book under Indian Tree.

Coalport Porcelain Manufactory 1820	 Coalport Porcelain Manufactory c.1881	Coalport Porcelain Manufactory 1960

Bowl, Salad, Ming Rose, Gilt Rim, White Ground, Footed, 10¼ In.	47
Cup & Saucer, Gold Ground & Interior, Blue Bird, Bamboo, Scalloped Rim .... *illus*	150
Figurine, Flowers, Girl Holding Bouquet Of Roses, Jack Glynn, 1994, 9 x 7½ In.	115
Figurine, Man, Riding, Horse, Glaze, Painted, Wood Base, Timothy Potts, 12¾ In.	690
Vase, Lid, Flower Sprays, Gilt, Jewels, Blue Ground, c.1851-61, 14½ x 6 In., Pair	738

COBALT BLUE

Cobalt blue glass was made using oxide of cobalt. The characteristic bright dark blue identifies it for the collector. Most cobalt glass found today was made after the Civil War. There was renewed interest in the dark blue glass in the late 1930s and glass dinnerware was made.

Bowl, 12 Diamonds, Footed, Pittsburgh, Mid 1800s, 3 x 4¾ In. .... *illus*	375
Bowl, Swirling Flower, Geometric Designs, Undulated Rim, Shallow, 3½ x 10¼ In.	31
Salt, Gilt, Molded, Footed Base, Pittsburgh, Mid 1900s, 2½ In.	250
Urn, Gilt Bronze Mounts, Acanthus Leaves, Flower Sprays, Finials, 20 x 8½ In., Pair	1250
Vase, Rectangular, Neoclassical Style, Silver Plate Mount, 12 In., Pair .... *illus*	281

COCA-COLA

Coca-Cola was first served in 1886 in Atlanta, Georgia. It was advertised through signs, newspaper ads, coupons, bottles, trays, calendars, and even lamps and clocks. Collectors want anything with the word *Coca-Cola,* including a few rare products, like gum wrappers and cigar bands. The famous trademark was patented in 1893, the *Coke* mark in 1945. Many modern items and reproductions are being made.

Advertisement, Santa Claus, Photo Album, Red, 12 x 11 In.	31
Bookmark, Owl Holding Book, What Shall We Drink, Die Cut, Celluloid, c.1905, 3 In.	615
Bottle, Syrup, Silver Lid, Glass, Enameled, Drink Coca-Cola, Wreath, c.1910, 12½ In. . *illus*	554
Calendar, 1913, June Page, Garden Scene, Girl Drinking, Frame, 37 x 21¾ In.	7995
Clock Radio, Cooler Shape, Red Plastic, c.1950, 9½ x 12 In.	1169
Clock, Drink Coca-Cola, Rocking Bottle, Neon, Swihart, 1940s, 20 x 20 x 5½ In.	3690
Clock, Gilt Metal, Glass Face, Electric, Synchron, Price Brothers, 1960, 12 x 11 In.	431
Cooler, Drink Coca-Cola, Red Ground, 5 Cent, Spin Top, Vendo, 44 In. .... *illus*	819

Cobalt Blue, Bowl, 12 Diamonds, Footed, Pittsburgh, Mid 1800s, 3 x 4¾ In. $375

Cowan's Auctions

Cobalt Blue, Vase, Rectangular, Neoclassical Style, Silver Plate Mount, 12 In., Pair $281

Susanin's Auctioneers & Appraisers

Coca-Cola, Bottle, Syrup, Silver Lid, Glass, Enameled, Drink Coca-Cola, Wreath, c.1910, 12½ In. $554

Rich Penn Auctions

Coca-Cola, Cooler, Drink Coca-Cola, Red Ground, 5 Cent, Spin Top, Vendo, 44 In. $819

Fontaine's Auction Gallery

Coca-Cola, Cuff Links, Figural, Double Bottle, Sterling Silver, Traces Of Gold Plating, ¾ x ¼ In. $71

AntiqueAdvertising.com

Coca-Cola, Door Push, Thanks, Call Again For A Coca-Cola, Red, Yellow, Porcelain, Canada, 13½ In. $492

Rich Penn Auctions

Coca-Cola, Plate, Sandwich, Scalloped Edge, Sample, Wellsville China Co., c.1940, 7½ In. $492

Rich Penn Auctions

Coca-Cola, Sign, Drink Coca-Cola, Triangular, Wood, Metal Top Trim, Kay Displays, c.1930, 19 x 20 In. $1,230

Rich Penn Auctions

Coca-Cola, Sign, Policeman, Hand Up, Slow, School Zone, Die Cut Steel, Iron Base, 64 In., 2-Sided $3,383

Rich Penn Auctions

Coca-Cola, Sign, Take Home A Carton, Easy To Carry, Cardboard, Snyder & Black, Frame, 36 x 18⅝ In.
$1,408

Morphy Auctions

Coca-Cola, Tip Tray, 1910, Coca-Cola Girl, Drink Delicious Coca-Cola, 6 x 4⅜ In.
$400

Blackwell Auctions

Coca-Cola, Tray, 1928, Girl With Bobbed Hair, Lithograph, American Art Works, 13 x 10½ In.
$800

Rich Penn Auctions

Coffee Mill, Arcade, No. 2, Lid, Glass, Embossed, Wall Mount, Cast Iron, 19 In.
$277

Rich Penn Auctions

Old Stoves
Enameled gas stoves for the kitchen made in the 1920s and 1930s are selling quickly at flea markets. Be sure they have been inspected by an expert gas stove company before you use them. They can be used with a gas line or a butane gas tank.

Coffee Mill, Arcade, Telephone, Ornate Cast Scroll, Iron Cover, Oak Base, c.1893, 13 x 8 In.
$677

Rich Penn Auctions

Coffee Mill, Enterprise, No. 3, 2 Wheels, Cast Iron, Red, Decals, Grip Handle, Drawer, 14 In.
$600

Pook & Pook

Cuff Links, Figural, Double Bottle, Sterling Silver, Traces Of Gold Plating, ¾ x ¼ In. ... *illus*	71
Door Push, Thanks, Call Again For A Coca-Cola, Red, Yellow, Porcelain, Canada, 13 ½ In. . *illus*	492
Plate, 50th Anniversary, Gold Trim, Lenox, 1950s, 10 ½ In.	300
Plate, Sandwich, Scalloped Edge, Sample, Wellsville China Co., c.1940, 7 ½ In. . ... *illus*	492
Postcard, Motor Girl, Drink Bottled Coca-Cola, 1911, 5 ½ x 3 ½ In.	677
Rack, Please Place Empties Here, 3-Case, 1960s, 48 x 22 x 19 In.	120
Sign, Cap, Porcelain, Script Logo With Bottle, Red Ground, Mounting Holes, 36 In.	1476
Sign, Cap, Sign Of Good Taste, Red Ground, White, Yellow Lettering, 1948, 15 ¾ In.	431
Sign, Drink Coca-Cola, Triangular, Wood, Metal Top Trim, Kay Displays, c.1930, 19 x 20 In. *illus*	1230
Sign, Drink Coca-Cola, White Text, Red Ground, Aluminum Frame, 34 x 68 In.	226
Sign, Policeman, Hand Up, Slow, School Zone, Die Cut Steel, Iron Base, 64 In., 2-Sided *illus*	3383
Sign, Santa Claus, Cardboard, Die Cut, Lithograph, c.1950, 48 In.	13
Sign, Take Home A Carton, Easy To Carry, Cardboard, Snyder & Black, Frame, 36 x 18 ⅝ In. *illus*	1408
Thermometer, For Quality You Can Taste, Tin, Wood, North Hills Dairy, 1900s, 36 In.	448
Tip Tray, 1904, Exhibition Girl, Oval, 6 x 4 In.	498
Tip Tray, 1910, Coca-Cola Girl, Drink Delicious Coca-Cola, 6 x 4 ⅜ In. .... *illus*	400
Tip Tray, 1964, Girl With Flower, Le Da Mucho Mas, Mexico, 7 ¾ x 5 ½ In.	125
Toy, Truck, Delivery, Orange, Aluminum Cab, Smith Miller, 1900s, 8 x 13 ½ In.	1968
Toy, Truck, Delivery, Volkswagen, Tin Lithograph, Logo, Friction, Western Germany, 5 x 9 In.	600
Tray, 1913, Hamilton King Girl, Holding Glass, 13 ¼ x 10 ¾ In.	110
Tray, 1926, The Golfers, Red Border, 13 x 10 In.	175
Tray, 1928, Girl With Bobbed Hair, Lithograph, American Art Works, 13 x 10 ½ In. ...... *illus*	800
Tray, 1953, Menu Girl, Thirst Knows No Season, Have A Coke, 13 x 10 In.	60

COFFEE MILL

Coffee mills are also called coffee grinders, although there is a difference in the way each grinds the coffee. Large floor-standing or counter-model coffee mills were used in the nineteenth-century country store. Small home mills were first made about 1894. They lost favor by the 1930s. The renewed interest in fresh-ground coffee has produced many modern electric mills, hand mills, and grinders. Reproductions of the old styles are being made.

Arcade, No. 2, Lid, Glass, Embossed, Wall Mount, Cast Iron, 19 In. .... *illus*	277
Arcade, Telephone, Ornate Cast Scroll, Iron Cover, Oak Base, c.1893, 13 x 8 In. .... *illus*	677
Charles Parker Co., No. 1200, 2 Wheels, Cast Iron, Red, Blue, Late 1800s, 30 In.	550
Cherry, Pine, Cast Iron, Dovetailed Box, Drawer, A. Klein, York Cty., Pa., c.1820	1065
Elgin National, 2 Wheels, Eagle Finial, Hopper, Cast Iron, 67 x 28 x 22 In.	1845
Enterprise, 2 Wheels, Painted, Red, Drawer, Wood Handle, 12 In.	540
Enterprise, Black, Decals, Turned Grip Handle, Wood Base, Late 1800s, 13 x 6 x 10 In.	154
Enterprise, No. 2, 2 Wheels, Drawer, Wood Handle, Blue, Red, 10 ½ x 10 ¼ x 7 ½ In.	622
Enterprise, No. 3, 2 Wheels, Cast Iron, Red, Decals, Grip Handle, Drawer, 14 In. .... *illus*	600
Enterprise, No. 9, Cast Iron, 2 Wheels, Red, Drawer, Metal Stand, 60 x 24 x 22 In.	2750
Enterprise, No. 16, 2 Wheels, Eagle Finial, Swivel Lid, Cast Iron Base, Late 1800s, 65 x 30 In. *illus*	2808
Enterprise, No. 512, 2 Wheels, Cast Iron, Red, Tin Coffee Receptacle, 27 ½ x 17 x 17 In.	1250
Golden Rule, Cast Iron, Glass & Wood, Catch Cup, Citizens Wholesale Supply, 18 x 5 ½ In. ..	554
Golden Rule, Wall Mount, Cast Iron, Glass Bottle, Wood Back, c.1900, 18 In. .... *illus*	200
Grand Union, Cast Iron, Red Paint, Wood Base, Grand Union Tea Co., 1800s, 11 x 7 In. *illus*	677
Landers, Frary & Clark, Iron, Crank Handle, Red Paint, Wood Base, 12 ½ In.	219
Peugeot, Green, Painted, Iron & Wood, Lower Drawer, 1800s, 17 x 15 x 8 In. .... *illus*	236

COIN-OPERATED MACHINE

Coin-operated machines of all types are collected. The vending machine is an ancient invention dating back to 200 BC, when holy water was dispensed from a coin-operated vase. Smokers in seventeenth-century England could buy tobacco from a coin-operated box. It was not until after the Civil War that the technology made modern coin-operated games and vending machines plentiful. Slot machines, arcade games, and dispensers are all collected.

Arcade, Deluxe Super Slugger, Baseball, United Mfg. Co., c.1955, 81 x 77 x 26 In.	6765

Coffee Mill, Enterprise, No. 16, 2 Wheels, Eagle Finial, Swivel Lid, Cast Iron Base, Late 1800s, 65 x 30 In.
$2,808

Jeffrey S. Evans & Associates

Coffee Mill, Golden Rule, Wall Mount, Cast Iron, Glass Bottle, Wood Back, c.1900, 18 In.
$200

Pook & Pook

Coffee Mill, Grand Union, Cast Iron, Red Paint, Wood Base, Grand Union Tea Co., 1800s, 11 x 7 In.
$677

Rich Penn Auctions

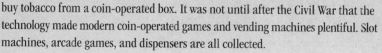

Coffee Mill, Peugeot, Green, Painted, Iron & Wood, Lower Drawer, 1800s, 17 x 15 x 8 In.
$236

Leland Little Auctions

Coin-Operated, Music Box, Symphonium, Disc, 12 Bells, Carved Mahogany Case, Late 1800s, 84 x 21 In.
$9,360

Jeffrey S. Evans & Associates

Coin-Operated, Shooting Game, Challenger, 1 Cent, Wood Base, A.B.T. Manufacturing Co., c.1930, 15 x 10 In.
$378

Fontaine's Auction Gallery

Automaton, 2 Birds In Cage, Wire, Giltwood, Ball Finial, Swing Handle, 25 x 12 x 12 In.	2337
Gambling, H.C. Evans Co., Dice, Aluminum Side, Glass Top, Green, Wood, Oval, 24 x 12 In.	1046
Gumball, Carousel, Red, Glass Bubble, Ebonized, Metal Stand, Leaf Inc., Illinois, 1985, 37 In.	39
Gumball, The Master, 1 Cent, Silver, Glass Panels, 1900s, 15¾ In.	594
Gumball, Victor, 1 Cent, Glass, Cast Iron, Mid 1900s, 17 x 6½ In.	76
Horse Race, Buckley Mfg. Co., Long Shot, Graphic Top Glass, Cabinet, 18¾ x 45 x 40 In.	2214
Joke Phone, Telephone Receiver, Wood Grain Box, 19 x 14 x 15 In.	490
Music Box, Symphonium, Disc, 12 Bells, Carved Mahogany Case, Late 1800s, 84 x 21 In. *illus*	9360
Pinball, Ball, Wood, Painted, Williams Dealers Choice, Illinois, 22 x 52 x 68½ In.	177
Pinball, Cowboy, Chicago Coin, 4 Players, Yellow, Hang Glider, 52 x 29 x 72 In.	246
Sculptoscope, Whiting's, American Novelty Co., Cincinnati, Oh, c.1900, 15 In.	660
Shooting Game, Challenger, 1 Cent, Wood Base, A.B.T. Manufacturing Co., c.1930, 15 x 10 In. *illus*	378
Skill, Target Practice, Wood, Brass, Key, 18 In.	330
Slot, Aristocrat, Espirit Super 22, Pull Crank, 25 Cent, 1950s, 31 x 16 In.	163
Slot, Art Deco, Copper Case, 3 Wheel Windows, Score Sheet, 1900s, 10½ x 11 x 10 In.	207
Slot, Brownie, Jackpot, Coin, Silver, Wood Case, 26 x 16 In.	1680
Slot, Caille Bros., 5 Cents, Gambling Wheel, Cast Iron Hardware, 1915, 21 x 17 x 64 In. *illus*	11070
Slot, Mills, Castle Front, 5 Cent, Blue Ground, Wood Base, c.1930, 26 x 16 In. *illus*	1169
Slot, Mills, Golden Nugget, Oak Mounts, Metal Label, 26 x 16 x 15½ In. *illus*	1020
Slot, Mills, Mobster, Figural, Holds Machine, 25 Cents, c.1950, 72 x 22 In.	2750
Slot, Watling, 5 Cents, Gooseneck Coin Slot, Keys, Painted, Wood Base, c.1930, 24 x 15 In. *illus*	938
Stamp, American Vending Machine Co., Beveled Mirror, Oak Case, c.1915, 22 x 9 x 18 In.	4305
Strength Tester, Pull The Tiger's Tail, Exhibit Supply Co., 1928, 58 x 29¾ x 18 In.	5440
Trade Stimulator, Cigarette, Zephyr, 1 Cent, 3-Reel, Paper Label, 1930s, 10½ x 9 x 8½ In.	348
Trade Stimulator, Fairest Wheel, Coin Drop, Wheel Spins For Payoff, Oak Case, 21 x 5 x 14 In. *illus*	602
Trade Stimulator, Groetchen, Mercury, Harley-Davidson Fantasy Theme, Black, Red, c.1940, 11 In.	338
Trade Stimulator, Horse Racing, Gee-Whiz, 6 Horses & Riders, Tin Lithograph, Wolverine, 29 In.	59
Trade Stimulator, Oshkosh Novelty Co., 1 Cent, Cigar, Cast Iron Stand, 1895, 71 x 14 x 14 In.	7200
Vending, Cigarette, Metal, Key, 61½ x 23 x 12½ In. *illus*	344
Vending, Matches, Advance Machine Co., 1 Cent, Cast Iron, Glass Globe, 17 x 9 In. *illus*	984
Vending, Nut, Silver King Hot Nut Dispenser, Painted, Chrome Plated, Glass Globe, 1950, 15 In.	295
Vending, Peanut, Advance Machine Co., Climax, Iron, Hourglass Globe, c.1915, 20 x 8 x 9 In. *illus*	1968
Vending, Peanut, North Western Corp., Glass, Metal, Morris, Illinois, 15½ In.	450
Vending, Perfume, Whiffs Of Fragrance, Cast Cupid, Flowers, Wood Base, 17 x 13¾ x 10 In.	9225
Vending, Stamp, American Postmaster, White & Blue, Iron Base, 43 In.	197

COMIC ART

Comic art, or cartoon art, includes original art for comic strips, magazine covers, book pages, and even printed strips. The first daily comic strip was printed in 1907. The paintings on celluloid used for movie cartoons are listed in this book under Animation Art.

Cartoon, Lucky Luke, Lithograph, In Color, Wood Frame, Morris, 1990, 15½ x 23½ In. *illus*	413
Drawing, Henry, Playing Guitar, Signed, John Lindy, 14 x 10¾ In.	6
Panel, Heroes Are Made, Ink, Paper, Pencil Marks, Frame, J.R. Williams, 1930, 19 x 19 In.	87
Panel, New Yorker, 2 Women On Street, Ink, Paper, Hank Ketcham, 11½ x 9 In.	144
Panel, New Yorker, Bar Scene, 2 Men, Ink, Paper, Virgil Franklin Partch, 9½ x 11½ In.	132
Strip, Beetle Bailey, Pen & Ink, Signed, Mort Walker, Frame, 10 x 14 In.	266
Strip, Winnie The Pooh, Ink On Illustration Board, Pub. Sept. 2, 1979, Frame, 24¼ x 30¼ In.	132

COMMEMORATIVE

Commemorative items have been made to honor members of royalty and those of great national fame. World's Fairs and important historical events are also remembered with commemorative pieces. Related collectibles are listed in the Coronation and World's Fair categories.

Beaker, Silver, Canted Sides, Applied Handle, Elizabeth Regina 1601, Birmingham, 1937, 5 In. *illus*	270
Knife, Bicentennial, 3 Blade, Stockman, Eagle, 1976, 4 In.	95

C

Coin-Operated, Slot, Caille Bros., 5 Cents, Gambling Wheel, Cast Iron Hardware, 1915, 21 x 17 x 64 In.
$11,070

Morphy Auctions

Coin-Operated, Slot, Mills, Castle Front, 5 Cent, Blue Ground, Wood Base, c.1930, 26 x 16 In.
$1,169

Rich Penn Auctions

Coin-Operated, Slot, Mills, Golden Nugget, Oak Mounts, Metal Label, 26 x 16 x 15 ½ In.
$1,020

Michaan's Auctions

Coin-Operated, Slot, Watling, 5 Cents, Gooseneck Coin Slot, Keys, Painted, Wood Base, c.1930, 24 x 15 In.
$938

Selkirk Auctioneers & Appraisers

Coin-Operated, Trade Stimulator, Fairest Wheel, Coin Drop, Wheel Spins For Payoff, Oak Case, 21 x 5 x 14 In.
$602

AntiqueAdvertising.com

Coin-Operated, Vending, Cigarette, Metal, Key, 61 ½ x 23 x 12 ½ In.
$344

Kamelot Auctions

Coin-Operated, Vending, Matches, Advance Machine Co., 1 Cent, Cast Iron, Glass Globe, 17 x 9 In.
$984

Rich Penn Auctions

Coin-Operated, Vending, Peanut, Advance Machine Co., Climax, Iron, Hourglass Globe, c.1915, 20 x 8 x 9 In.
$1,968

Morphy Auctions

Comic Art, Cartoon, Lucky Luke, Lithograph, In Color, Wood Frame, Morris, 1990, 15 ½ x 23 ½ In.
$413

Leland Little Auctions

Commemorative, Beaker, Silver, Canted Sides, Applied Handle, Elizabeth Regina 1601, Birmingham, 1937, 5 In.
$270

Garth's Auctioneers & Appraisers

Commemorative, Plate, University Of Texas, White Ground, Gold, Wedgwood, 1890, 10½ In., 2 Piece
$944

Austin Auction Gallery

Commemorative, Trinket Box, Lid, H.M. Queen Mary, Gilt, 1900s, 1½ In.
$29

Lion and Unicorn

Dishwasher Damage

Be careful about putting antique china or glass in the dishwasher. Glass will sometimes crack from the heat. Porcelains with gold overglaze decoration often lose the gold. Damaged or crazed glaze will sometimes pop off the plates in large pieces.

Medal, Thomas Jefferson, Portrait, History, Reeded Edge, Bronze		7
Plate, Prince Charles & Lady Diana, Marriage, Portraits, Bells, Canada, 1981, 9 In.		30
Plate, Prince William V & Princess Wilhelmina Of Prussia, Creamware, c.1790, 10 In.		625
Plate, University Of Texas, White Ground, Gold, Wedgwood, 1890, 10½ In., 2 Piece	*illus*	944
Serving Tray, Hawaiian Statehood, State, Map, Icons, Plastic, Open Handles, 17 x 11 In.		50
Trinket Box, Lid, H.M. Queen Mary, Gilt, 1900s, 1½ In.	*illus*	29
Tumbler, Chinese Theatre, Hollywood, California, 22K Gold, Glass, 1960s, 5½ In.		15

COMPACT

Compacts hold face powder. A woman did not powder her face in public until after World War I. By 1920, the beauty parlor, permanent waves, and cosmetics had become acceptable. A few companies sold cake face powder in a box with a mirror and a pad or puff. Soon the compact was designed by jewelers and made of gold, silver, and precious materials. Cosmetic companies began to sell powder in attractive compacts of less valuable metal or plastic. Collectors today search for Art Deco designs, famous brands, compacts from World's Fairs or political events, and unusual examples. Many were made with companion lipsticks and other fittings.

Boucheron, Gold Openwork Top, Birds, Flowers, Pearls, Silver Frame, Puff, 3 x 2¼ In.		677
Cartier, 18K Gold, Square, Basketweave, Mirror, Plastic Lining, 2⅞ In.		5330
Georg Jensen, Silver, Powder, Mirror, Round, Pineapple, Engraved, Embossed, Puff, 3 x 2 In.		142
Guilloche, Courting Scene, White Lobed Border, Mirror, Austria, Early 1900s, 2½ In.		100
Henriette, Silvertone Airplane, Rhinestones, Red, White & Blue, Brass Tone Ground, Puff, 3¼ In.		30
Marchak, 18K Gold, Textured, Woven, Diamond Push Button, Mirror, 3 x 2¼ In.		6875
Ripley & Gowen, Guilloche, Scene, Bridge, Swan, Silver Frame, Mirror, Lipstick Tube, c.1930, 2¼ In.		154
Silver, Enamel, Women Dancing Scene, Cupid, Heart Shape, 3 x 3¾ In.	*illus*	350
Silver, Engine Turned Lines, Gold Fan Clasp, 5 Ruby Cabochons, Diamonds, Inset Comb, 3 In.		1500
Silver, Flower Basket, Rectangular, Black Enamel Lid, Mirror, Chain, W & S Blackinton, 3 x 2 In.		160
Silver, Mirror, Rectangular, Flower, Engraved, Green Bag, Jack Lewis, 3 x 2½ In.		71
Vanity Case, 14K Gold, Engine Turned, Diamonds, Hinged, Chain, Art Deco, c.1930, 3⅝ In.	*illus*	3125

CONSOLIDATED LAMP AND GLASS COMPANY

Consolidated Lamp and Glass Company of Coraopolis, Pennsylvania, was founded in 1894. The company made lamps, tablewares, and art glass. Collectors are particularly interested in the wares made after 1925, including black satin glass, Cosmos (listed in its own category in this book), Martele (which resembled Lalique), Ruba Rombic (1928–1932 Art Deco line), and colored glasswares. Some Consolidated pieces are very similar to those made by the Phoenix Glass Company. The colors are sometimes different. Consolidated made Martele glass in blue, crystal, green, pink, white, or custard glass with added fired-on color or a satin finish. The company closed for the final time in 1967.

Bowl, Five Fruits, Yellow, Martele, Cone Shape, Footed, 2½ x 4½ In.		65
Dish, Ruba Rombic, 3 Sections, Handles, Jungle Green, Reuben Haley, 8 x 6¼ In.	*illus*	625
Lamp, Figural, Fruit Basket, Painted Glass, Mid 20th Century, 8 In.		313
Lamp, Kerosene, Quilt, Florette, Cased Pink Font, Clear Base, c.1894, 9⅜ In.		125
Lamp, Parlor, Glass Bonnet Shade, White Column, Raised Pink Flowers, Domed Base, 1800s, 26 In.		163
Night-Light, Figural, Brown Owl, Mounted, Black Glass Base, 8½ In.	*illus*	250
Sugar Shaker, Bulging Loops, Pigeon Blood, Metal Lid, c.1894, 5½ In.		162
Sugar Shaker, Guttate, Cased Cranberry Glass, Metal Lid, Late 19th Century, 5⅝ In.		88
Syrup, Guttate, Squat, Cased Pink Glass, Satin, Applied Handle, Metal Lid, c.1894, 4 In.		137
Vase, Nude Woman, Dancing, Green, Bulbous, Embossed, 12 In.		192
Vase, Pinecone, Black, Molded Rim, Footed, Bulbous Body, 1930s, 6⅞ In.		105

CONTEMPORARY GLASS, *see Glass-Contemporary.*

COOKBOOK

Cookbooks are collected for various reasons. Some are wanted for the recipes, some for investment, and some as examples of advertising. Cookbooks and recipe pamphlets are included in this category.

Anne Of Green Gables, Kate MacDonald, Softcover, McClelland-Bantam, 1988	22
Betty Crocker Picture Cookbook, Red & White, 1950, 449 Pages, 10 x 6 ½ x 1 In.	58
Betty Crocker, Dinner For Two, Spiral Bound, Red, Brown, White, 1974, 180 Pages	10
Cox's Gelatine, Softcover, Stapled Wraps, Art Deco, 1933, 30 Pages, 4 x 7 In.	16
Favorite Amish Family Recipes, White, Black, 1976, 254 Pages	15
From Julia Child's Kitchen, Hardcover, Dust Jacket, 1975, 687 Pages	30
New Good Housekeeping Cookbook, Hardcover, 1963, 895 Pages	24
Pillsbury's Bake-Off Cook Book, 1970, 111 Pages	10
Pillsbury's Best 10th Grand National Bake-Off, Softcover, 1958, 104 Pages	8
Texas Cookbook, Little, Brown & Co., Hardback, 1965, 489 Pages	45
Twelve Days Of Christmas, Softcover, Spiral Bound, Quail Ridge Press, 1978, 80 Pages	40
White House Chef Cookbook, Rene Verdon, Doubleday & Co., Signed, 1967	65

COOKIE JAR

Cookie jars with brightly painted designs or amusing figural shapes became popular in the mid-1930s. They became very popular again when Andy Warhol's collection was auctioned after his death in 1987. Prices have gone down since then and are very low. Many companies made them and collectors search for cookie jars either by design or by maker's name. Listed here are examples by the less common makers. Major factories are listed under their own names in other categories of the book, such as Abingdon, Brush, Hull, McCoy, Metlox, Red Wing, and Shawnee. See also the Disneyana category. These are marks of three cookie jar manufacturers.

Brush Pottery Co. 1925–1982	Fitz and Floyd Enterprises LLC 1960–1980	Twin Winton Ceramics 1946–1977

Baby Elephant, Closed Eyes, Trunk Up, Blue Bib, American Bisque, c. 1950, 12 In.	150
Barrel Shape, Santa Fe Pattern, Mikasa, 8 In.	28
Bunny, In Basket, White, Red Ears, Blue Bows, Pottery, 11 ½ In.	30
California Faience, Lid, Top & Side Handles, Brown, Blue Figure, Holding Dish, 1927, 6 x 8 In. *illus*	188
Car, Classic, White, Pink Trim, Open Top, Red Seats, Appleman, 1981, 15 ½ x 9 In.	375
Cookies, Stoneware, Brown, Marked, Monmouth, 8 x 8 In.	18
Dog On Drum, Brown, Yellow, Sierra Vista, 8 ½ In.	95
Goldilocks & Baby Bear, Regal China, 13 In.	110
Kitten On Beehive, Flowers, Butterflies, Pottery, USA, c.1950, 11 x 8 In.	110
Old Gray Woman, Green Scarf, Knob Handles, Ceramic, 6 ½ x 6 ¾ In.	46
Rabbit, Seated, Paw Up, Vines, Fitz & Floyd, c.1990, 11 x 7 In.	275
Sgraffito, Lid, Twisted Handles, Yellow, Flowers, Hearts, Leaves, Breninger Pottery, 1974, 10 In.	246
Skier, Hat & Scarf, Ceramic, Red, Blue, Green, 11 In.	22
Smiling Mammy, Brown & White, 10 In.	185
Sugar & Spice & Everything Nice, Basket Of Flowers, 1970s, 13 x 13 x 10 In.	35

COORS

Coors dinnerware was made by the Coors Porcelain Company of Golden, Colorado, a company founded with the help of the Coors Brewing Company. Its founder, John Herold, started the Herold China and Pottery Company in 1910 on the site of a glassworks owned

Compact, Silver, Enamel, Women Dancing Scene, Cupid, Heart Shape, 3 x 3 ¾ In.
$350

Pook & Pook

Compact, Vanity Case, 14K Gold, Engine Turned, Diamonds, Hinged, Chain, Art Deco, c.1930, 3 ⅝ In.
$3,125

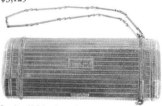

Charlton Hall Auctions

Consolidated, Dish, Ruba Rombic, 3 Sections, Handles, Jungle Green, Reuben Haley, 8 x 6 ¼ In.
$625

Toomey & Co. Auctioneers

Consolidated, Night-Light, Figural,
Brown Owl, Mounted, Black Glass Base,
8½ In.
$250

Woody Auction

Cookie Jar, California Faience, Lid, Top
& Side Handles, Brown, Blue Figure,
Holding Dish, 1927, 6 x 8 In.
$188

California Historical Design

Copeland, Bust, Princess Alexandra,
Thebes Jewel, Parian, Signed, England,
Late 1800s, 14¾ In.
$207

Lion and Unicorn

---

by Adolph Coors, the founder of the Coors brewery. The company began making art pottery using clay from nearby mines. Adolph Coors Company bought Herold China and Pottery Company in early 1915. Chemical porcelains were made beginning in 1915. The company name was changed to Coors Porcelain Company in 1920, when Herold left. Several lines of dinnerware were made in the 1920s and 1930s. Marks on dinnerware and cookware made by Coors include Rosebud, Glencoe Thermo-Porcelain, Colorado, and other names. Coors stopped making nonessential wares at the start of World War II. After the war, the pottery made ovenware, teapots, vases, and a general line of pottery, but no dinnerware—except for special orders. In 1986 Coors Porcelain became Coors Ceramics. In 2000, Coors Ceramics changed its name to CoorsTek. The company is still in business making industrial porcelain. For more prices, go to kovels.com.

Coors Porcelain Co.	Coors Porcelain Co.	Coors Porcelain Co.
1920s	1934–1942	1934–1942

Mortar & Pestle, White, Blue Mark, 1¾ x 2¾ In.	19
Vase, Green Matte Glaze, White Interior, 10-Sided, Scrolled Handles, Art Deco, Mark, 6 In. ...	12

COPELAND

Copeland pieces listed here are those that have a mark including the word *Copeland* used between 1847 and 1976. Marks include *Copeland Spode* and *Copeland & Garrett.* See also Copeland Spode, Royal Worcester, and Spode.

Bust, Ophelia, Porcelain Socle, Parian, 1800s, 11¼ In.	384
Bust, Princess Alexandra, Thebes Jewel, Parian, Signed, England, Late 1800s, 14¾ In. *illus*	207
Bust, Roman Statesman, Philosopher, Cicero, Parian, Signed, T.E. King, 1800s, 18 x 12 x 8 In.	1170
Figurine, Maidenhood, Standing, Circular Base, Parian, c.1865, 21¾ In.	344

 ## COPELAND SPODE

Copeland Spode appears on some pieces of nineteenth-century English porcelain. Josiah Spode established a pottery at Stoke-on-Trent, England, in 1770. In 1833, the firm was purchased by William Copeland and Thomas Garrett and the mark was changed. In 1847, Copeland became the sole owner and the mark changed again. W.T. Copeland & Sons continued until a 1976 merger when it became Royal Worcester Spode. The company was bought by the Portmeirion Group in 2009. Pieces are listed in this book under the name that appears in the mark. Copeland, Royal Worcester, and Spode have separate listings.

Plate, Service, Painted, Flower Cluster, Sky Blue, Gilt Rim Border, 10½ In., 9 Piece .... *illus*	384
Platter, Turkey, Field, Red & White Flower Border, Gadroon Edge, 23 x 18 In.	195
Service Set, Florence, White Ground, Light Blue & Gilt, Scalloped Edge, Lusterware, 1879, 88 Piece..	390

COPPER

Copper has been used to make utilitarian items, such as teakettles and cooking pans, since the days of the early American colonists. Copper became a popular metal with the Arts & Crafts makers of the early 1900s, and decorative pieces, like desk sets, were made. Copper pieces may also be found in Arts & Crafts, Bradley & Hubbard, Kitchen, Roycroft, and other categories.

POTTER
STUDIO

Chase Brass and Copper Co.,
Inc.
1930s

Craftsman Workshop
Mark of Gustav Stickley
c.1900–1915

Potter Studio
c.1900–1929

Bowl, Hammered, Rolled Rim, 2 Handles, 9 ½ In.	177
Bowl, Peacock Feather Motif, Hammered, Alvin J. Tuck Sr., 1910s, 2 ¾ x 9 ¾ In. .... *illus*	313
Bowl, Scalloped Edge, Hammered, Stamped, Hector Aguilar, Mexico, 1950s, 1 x 7 ½ In........	150
Box, Hinged Lid, Leather Insert, Monogram WTB, Kalo Shop, 2 ¹⁄₁₆ x 6 x 8 In..................	813
Bucket, Bail Handle, Molded Rim, Paul Beyer, 1800s, 10 x 11 In............	185
Cauldron, Continental, Handles, Tripod Legs, Oxidized, 26 ½ In., Pair......................	148
Cauldron, Hammered, Iron Handle & Stand, 18 ½ x 29 In....................................	384
Cauldron, Lid, Cylindrical, 2 Handles, 13 ¾ In...	177
Chamberstick, Hammered, Bobeche, Applied Handle, G. Stickley, 9 x 7 In. .... *illus*	594
Charger, Hammered, Flowers, Embossed, John Pearson, England, 30 In........	9375
Chocolate Pot, Hinged Dome Lid, Brass Finial, Turned Wood Side Handle, Late 1700s, 13 In.	443
Chocolate Pot, Lid, Dovetailed, Wood Handle, 1800s, 7 In. .... *illus*	325
Cistern, Water, Bucket Shape, Handle, 1900s, 18 In., Pair .... *illus*	256
Container, Lid, Modular Oval, Handles, 15 In..	43
Cuspidor, Hammered, Panels, Flared Rim, Weighted, Jos. Heinriches, Paris, N.Y., c.1910, 16 In.	225
Dispenser, Hot Water, Iron Stand, Brass Spigot, Bramhall, Deane & Co., Late 1800s, 25 x 13 In..	443
Dispenser, Toothpick, Log Cabin Shape, 4 ½ x 5 x 4 In....................................	98
Figure, Bonsai Tree, Bronze, Wood Base, Marked, Pang, Japan, c.1960, 12 x 18 In.......	128
Figure, Elephant, Standing, Upraised Trunk, Applied Tusks, Brown Glaze, c.1920, 9 In. *illus*	129
Finial, Architectural, Star Shape, Verdigris Surface, Custom Stand, Late 1800s, 9 ½ In.........	531
Footbath, Oval, 2 Brass Handles, Dovetailed, 1800s, 10 x 24 In. .... *illus*	413
Frame, Honeycomb Texture, Hammered, Old Mission Kopperkraft, 4 ½ x 9 In. .... *illus*	274
Ice Bucket, Aesthetic Movement, Brass Finial, Handles, Base, Glass Liner, Early 1900s, 12 In. ....*illus*	225
Jar, Bulbous Body, Round Rim, Hammered, Cast Bronze Handles, 16 x 11 In.	150
Jardiniere, Hammered, Scalloped Top Border, Dark Patina, G. Stickley, 8 x 11 ½ In.	2016
Jardiniere, Stand, Wrought Iron, Triangular Legs, 2 Handles, Arts & Crafts, 12 ½ x 11 ¾ In. .	3750
Kettle, Apple Butter, Crimped Seams, Iron Bail Handle, Rolled Rim, 1800s, 16 x 27 In.	363
Kettle, Apple Butter, Dovetailed, Swing Handle, Iron Tripod Frame, 1800s, 27 x 24 In............	369
Kettle, Apple Butter, Iron, Bail Handle, J.P. Schaum, Early 1800s, 18 In.	384
Kettle, Apple Butter, Iron, Handle, Stand, Stir Paddle, Mark, J.P. Schaum, c.1850, 30 In. *illus*	430
Kettle, Rolled Rim, Iron Swing Handle, Dovetailed, 16 ½ In.................................	57
Lamp Base, Hammered, Domed Base, Arts & Crafts, 18 In..................................	1140
Lavabo, Fountain, Repousse, Fleur-De-Lis, Oval Lid, Brass Spigot, Early 1900s, 24 x 13 In....	325
Lavabo, Wall Mounted, Brass Handles, Shaped Walnut Backboard, Late 1800s, 42 x 20 In. ..*illus*	649
Milk Can, Lid, Strap Style Finial, Swing Handle, 11 In...............................	98
Molds are listed in the Kitchen category.	
Planter, Brass Ring Handles, Repousse Foot, Early 1900s, 19 In.	649
Planter, Bulbous Body, 2 Side Swing Handles, Footed, Stamped, Stickley Brothers, 8 ¾ x 10 In..	1125
Planter, Iron Handles, Rounded Bottom, 11 ½ In..	236
Plaque, Cats, Orgonite, Resin, Quartz Crystal, Signed, E.M. Bo Long, 10 ½ x 7 ½ In. ...._	24
Plaque, Wall, Seed Pod, Hammered, Stamped Mark, G. Stickley, 20 In. .... *illus*	8125
Pot, Dovetailed, Wrought Iron Handles, V. Clad, 1800s, 9 ½ x 13 ½ In............................ ..	215
Pot, Removable Lid, Brass Ring Pull, Iron Bail Handle, c.1850, 10 In.	266
Sculpture, Metal, Free-Form, Black, Round Base, Curtis Jere, 23 ¼ x 13 ½ x 5 In.	183
Sculpture, Sounding, Beryllium, Brass, Rectangular Base, Val Bertoia, 41 x 8 x 10 In.	7423
Sculpture, Wall, Lobster, Brass, 8 Pointed Legs, 2 Claws, c.1940, 34 x 27 In. .... *illus*	1140
Serving Dish, Lid, Pig Shape, Wood, Plated, White Plastic Insert, 1900s, 12 x 26 In.	2124
Teakettle, Gooseneck, Finial, Swing Handle, Wm. A. Lewis & Co., 1800s, 12 In...................	549
Teakettle, Gooseneck, Loop Handle, Brass Finial, Kepner, Pittsburgh, c.1819, 12 In.	704
Teakettle, Gooseneck, Swing Handle, Finial, Stamped, W. MC., Pa., 1800s, 7 ½ In.	1342
Teakettle, Lid, Brass Handle & Finial, c.1810, 4 x 3 ¾ In...................................	40
Tray, Oval, Hammered Handles, G. Stickley, Impressed Mark, 1 ³⁄₁₆ x 11 x 23 In.	813

Copeland Spode, Plate Service, Painted, Flower Cluster, Sky Blue, Gilt Rim Border, 10 ½ In., 9 Piece
$384

Leland Little Auctions

Copper, Bowl, Peacock Feather Motif, Hammered, Alvin J. Tuck Sr., 1910s, 2 ¾ x 9 ¾ In.
$313

Toomey & Co. Auctioneers

TIP
Don't display copper on bare wooden shelves. The wood should be sealed with varnish to avoid allowing the acids in the wood and the acid vapors to attack the copper.

Copper, Chamberstick, Hammered, Bobeche, Applied Handle, G. Stickley, 9 x 7 In.
$594

Toomey & Co. Auctioneers

COPInER

Copper, Chocolate Pot, Lid, Dovetailed, Wood Handle, 1800s, 7 In.
$325

Pook & Pook

Copper, Cistern, Water, Bucket Shape, Handle, 1900s, 18 In., Pair
$256

Hindman

Copper, Footbath, Oval, 2 Brass Handles, Dovetailed, 1800s, 10 x 24 In.
$413

Leland Little Auctions

Copper, Frame, Honeycomb Texture, Hammered, Old Mission Kopperkraft, 4 1/2 x 9 In.
$274

Treadway

TIP
Decorators say you should think in threes. Accessories on a table look best when grouped in odd numbers.

Copper, Figure, Elephant, Standing, Upraised Trunk, Applied Tusks, Brown Glaze, c.1920, 9 In.
$129

Jeffrey S. Evans & Associates

Copper, Ice Bucket, Aesthetic Movement, Brass Finial, Handles, Base, Glass Liner, Early 1900s, 12 In.
$225

Pook & Pook

Copper, Kettle, Apple Butter, Iron, Handle, Stand, Stir Paddle, Mark, J.P. Schaum, c.1850, 30 In.
$430

Selkirk Auctioneers & Appraisers

Copper, Lavabo, Wall Mounted, Brass Handles, Shaped Walnut Backboard, Late 1800s, 42 x 20 In.
$649

Austin Auction Gallery

Tray, Oval, Hammered, 2 Handles, Embossed Flowers, Raised Border, 22 In. .... *illus*	158
Tray, Reticulated Edge, Chased, Bird, Flower Interior, 1950s, 38½ In.	325
Vase, Hammered, Aladdin Shape, Arts & Crafts, c.1900, 13¾ In.	427
Vase, Hammered, Braided Center, Embossed, 9½ x 10 In.	156
Vase, Santa Clara Del Cobre, Lower Tapered Panels, Signed, Abdon Punzo A., 6 In. .... *illus*	148
Wine Chiller, Brass Rim, Handles & Base, 4-Bottle, Art Deco Style, Global Views, 12 In.	201

COPPER LUSTER *items are listed in the Luster category.*

CORALENE

Coralene glass was made by firing many small colored beads on the outside of glassware. It was made in many patterns in the United States and Europe in the 1880s. Reproductions are made today. Coralene-decorated Japanese pottery is listed in the Japanese Coralene category.

Bowl, Sculpted Rim, Amber, Gilt, Iridescent, 2¾ x 6 In..	81
Vase, Blossom, Blue, Yellow, Brown Tones, Royal Kinjo, 1910, 8 x 4 In. .... *illus*	350
Vase, Poppy, Yellow & Blue Ground, Cobalt Blue Trim, Mark, Japan, 1909, 10 x 4 In. .... *illus*	700

CORDEY

Cordey China Company was founded by Boleslaw Cybis in 1942 in Trenton, New Jersey. The firm produced gift shop items. In 1969 it was acquired by the Lightron Corp. and operated as the Schiller Cordey Co., manufacturers of lamps. About 1950 Boleslaw Cybis began making Cybis porcelains, which are listed in the Cybis category in this book.

Bust, Woman, Blue Hat, Pink Roses, Curly Hair, White Dress, 9 In..	18
Bust, Woman, Hat, Pink Flowers, Large Blue Collar, 7 In.	29
Figurine, Woman, Hat, Pink Ruffles, Curled Wig, Pink & Blue Flowers, Lace, 8 In.	63
Shoe, White, Low Heel, Upturned Toe, Blue Lace Ring, Raised Scrolls, 2½ x 6 x 2 In.	12
Tray, Dresser, Shell Shape, Scrolled Handle, 2 Pink Flowers, Gilt Trim, 5 x 5 In.	30

CORKSCREW

Corkscrews have been needed since the first bottle was sealed with a cork, probably in the seventeenth century. Today collectors search for the early, unusual patented examples or the figural corkscrews of recent years.

Barrel Shape, Bone, Forged Metal Helix, Baluster Shape Shaft, 5½ x 3¼ In.	75
Boar's Tusk, Carved Bulldog's Head On End, Stone Eyes, Metal Collar, 3¾ x 4½ In.	400
Brush Handle, Thomason-Type, Brass Barrel, Seated Lion & Unicorn, England, 1800s, 7 In. *illus*	222
Ivory, Dog's Head On End, Carved, Glass Eye, Ink Highlights, Silver Cap, 7 In. .... *illus*	150
Key Shape, Brass, Carl Aubock, c.1950, 4¾ x 2¾ In..	625
Stag's Head, Bone, Carved, Closed Bell, 8 In.	234

CORONATION

Coronation souvenirs have been made since the 1800s. Pottery, glass, tin, silver, and paper objects with a picture of the monarchs and date have been sold at many coronations. The pieces that mention King Edward VIII, the king who was never crowned, are not rare; collectors should be sure to check values before buying. Related pieces are found in the Commemorative category.

Doll, Queen Elizabeth II, Ottenberg, Composition, Mohair Wig, Painted Face, 12 In., Box	136
Figurine, King George VI, Coronation Robes, Painted, No. 1493, Britains, 1937	250
Medal, King Chulalongkorn, Silver, Thailand, c.1873, 2½ In...	1464
Plate, Multicolor, Coat Of Arms, Gilt Lettering, King Edward VIII, 1937, Paragon, 10¾ In. .... *illus*	75
Saucer, Tsar Alexander III, Double Headed Eagle, Gilt Edge, Marked, Kuznetsov, Russia, 5 In.	225
Tyg, King George V & Queen Mary, Stoneware, Blue Rim, Handles, Royal Doulton, 1911, 6½ x 4½ In..	250

Copper, Plaque, Wall, Seed Pod, Hammered, Stamped Mark, G. Stickley, 20 In.
$8,125

Toomey & Co. Auctioneers

Copper, Sculpture, Wall, Lobster, Brass, 8 Pointed Legs, 2 Claws, c.1940, 34 x 27 In.
$1,140

Garth's Auctioneers & Appraisers

Copper, Tray, Oval, Hammered, 2 Handles, Embossed Flowers, Raised Border, 22 In.
$158

Fontaine's Auction Gallery

TIP
To hang copper molds in your kitchen, try this method: Mount a solid brass or wooden curtain rod across the top of the hanging area. Molds can then be hung by hooks and easily moved when new ones are added.

Copper, Vase, Santa Clara Del Cobre, Lower Tapered Panels, Signed, Abdon Punzo A., 6 In.
$148

C

Leland Little Auctions

Coverlet Markings

Woven coverlets often have a woven corner block with the name of the weaver or the name of the owner, the county or city, or the date. Sometimes weavers used logos or special designs—a sailboat, a flower, an eagle, or a star—or wove slogans, like "United We Stand, Divided We Fall," in the corner or border.

Coralene, Vase, Blossom, Blue, Yellow, Brown Tones, Royal Kinjo, 1910, 8 x 4 In.
$350

Woody Auction

COSMOS

Cosmos is a pressed milk glass pattern with colored flowers made from 1894 to 1915 by the Consolidated Lamp and Glass Company. Tablewares and lamps were made in this pattern. A few pieces were also made of clear glass with painted decorations. Other glass patterns are listed under Consolidated Lamp and also in various glass categories. In later years, Cosmos was also made by the Westmoreland Glass Company.

Bowl, Raised Flower Rim, Painted, Milk Glass, 8 In.	6
Creamer, Milk Glass, Painted Flowers, Pink Neck, 5 x 3 ¾ In.	9
Pitcher, Water, Milk Glass, Painted Flowers, Pink Neck, 8 ½ In.	79
Sugar, Open, Painted Flowers, Milk Glass, 4 x 3 ¼ In.	12
Water Set, Milk Glass, Painted Flowers, 9 ¼ In. Pitcher, 3 ¾ In. Tumbler	18

COVERLET

Coverlets were made of linen or wool during the nineteenth century. Most of the coverlets date from 1800 to the 1880s. There was a revival of hand weaving in the 1920s and new coverlets, especially geometric patterns, were made. The earliest coverlets were made on narrow looms, so two woven strips were joined together and a seam can be found. The weave structures of coverlets can include summer and winter, double weave, overshot, and others. Jacquard coverlets have elaborate pictorial patterns that are made on a special loom or with the use of a special attachment. Makers often wove a personal message in the corner. Quilts are listed in this book in their own category.

John Henry Meily (1817–1884)   Matthew Rattray (1796–1872)   Samuel Stinger (c.1801–1879)
1842–1850s   1822–1872   1838–1879

Double Weave, Indigo Blue, Ivory, Checkerboard, c.1820, 85 x 70 In.	125
Homespun, Blue, White, Eagles, Stars, Flowers, Signed, A. Hovey, 1832, 75 x 83 In.	259
Jacquard, Red & White, Starburst Medallion, Swags, S. Hausman, Trexlertown, 1848, 76 x 96 In. *illus*	118
Jacquard, Red Ground, White, Eagle, Union Shield, Patriotic, Ira Hadsell, 1872, 80 x 84 In.	281
Jacquard, Red, Black, Yellow, Flowers, Leaves, Signed, S. Hausman, Trexlertown, 1837, 100 x 74 In..	250
Jacquard, Red, Black, Yellow, White, Roses, Wool, Single Panel, Corner Block, H. Haeseler, 80 x 80 In.	168
Jacquard, Red, Navy Blue, White, Checkerboard Pattern, Flower Blossom, 1800s, 73 x 84 In. ....*illus*	113
Overshot, Blue On Blue, Geometric, Fringe, 73 x 90 In.	375
Overshot, Cobalt, Red, White, Blue, Stars Center, Tree Border, Fringe, 2 Panel, c.1825, 79 x 96 In.	273
Overshot, Dark Blue Wool, Cotton, Diamonds, Border On 3 Sides, 2 Panel, c.1880, 69 x 98 In.	47
Overshot, Red, White, Blue, Snowflakes, Pine Tree Border, Wool, Early 1800s, 71 x 80 In.	173
Summer & Winter, Blue, White, Flower Medallion, Vines, Flower Border, Wool, 2 Panel, 78 x 89 In..	384
Summer & Winter, Blue, White, Flowers, House Border, Ships In Corners, 2 Panel, 1838, 73 x 87 In.	492

COWAN POTTERY

Cowan Pottery made art pottery and wares for florists. Guy Cowan made pottery in Rocky River, Ohio, a suburb of Cleveland, from 1913 to 1931. A stylized mark with the word *Cowan* was used on most pieces. A commercial, mass-produced line was marked *Lakeware.* Collectors today search for the Art Deco pieces by Guy Cowan, Viktor Schreckengost, Waylande Gregory, Thelma Frazier Winter, and other artists.

Bowl, Jazz, Melon Green Glaze, Flared, Footed, c.1931, 8 ¼ x 13 ¼ In. ....*illus*	27500
Bowl, Oval, Blue, Side Handles, 10 Facets, Footed, 3 ½ x 11 ½ In.	18
Candlestick, Pink Luster, c.1920, 5 ⅜ x 4 ½ In., Pair	63

Coralene, Vase, Poppy, Yellow & Blue Ground, Cobalt Blue Trim, Mark, Japan, 1909, 10 x 4 In.
$700

Woody Auction

Corkscrew, Brush Handle, Thomason-Type, Brass Barrel, Seated Lion & Unicorn, England, 1800s, 7 In.
$222

Jeffrey S. Evans & Associates

Corkscrew, Ivory, Dog's Head On End, Carved, Glass Eye, Ink Highlights, Silver Cap, 7 In.
$150

White's Auctions

Coronation, Plate, Multicolor, Coat Of Arms, Gilt Lettering, King Edward VIII, 1937, Paragon, 10¾ In.
$75

Lion and Unicorn

Coverlet, Jacquard, Red & White, Starburst Medallion, Swags, S. Hausman, Trexlertown, 1848, 76 x 96 In.
$118

Leland Little Auctions

Coverlet, Jacquard, Red, Navy Blue, White, Checkerboard Pattern, Flower Blossom, 1800s, 73 x 84 In.
$113

Eldred's

Cowan, Bowl, Jazz, Melon Green Glaze, Flared, Footed, c.1931, 8 ¼ x 13 ¼ In. $27,500

Rago Arts and Auction Center

Crackle Glass, Vase, Pink, Flowers, Iridescent, Art Nouveau, c.1900, 11 In. $230

Blackwell Auctions

Crackle Glass, Vase, Pitcher, Vaseline, Flowers, Enamel, Bulbous, Applied Handle, 8 In. $125

Woody Auction

Charger, Green Glaze, Raised Scene, Woman, Dog, Dancing, Medallions On Rim, Holzinger, 15 In. .	384
Console, Oval, Pterodactyl Handles, Ivory, Apple Blossom Interior, Footed, 6 x 10 x 6 ¾ In....	202
Decanter, King & Queen, Red, Alice Through The Looking Glass, W. Gregory, c.1930, 11 In., Pair..	473
Figurine, Margarita, Clair De Lune Glaze, Waylande Gregory, 1929, 15 ½ x 11 In.................	3750
Plate, Sea, Blue, Underwater Scene, Fish Rim, Seaweed, Shells, Starfish, Thelma Frazier, 11 In.	360
Vase, Fish, Bubbles, Waves, Creamy Yellow, Green Ground, V. Schreckengost, c.1931, 6 x 5 In.....	4225
Vase, Lid, Dark Blue, Fish, Waves, Seaweed, Drypoint, Stand, V. Schreckengost, c.1931, 8 ¼ x 5 ¼ In.	3000
Vase, Oval, Light Green, Fish, Waves, Seaweed, Sgraffito, V. Schreckengost, c.1931, 6 ½ x 5 ¼ In..	4225
Vase, Squat, Light Brown, Blue Band, White Clouds, Brown Airplanes, Bogatay, 1930, 6 ½ x 9 In..	3500

CRACKER JACK

Cracker Jack, the molasses-flavored popcorn mixture, was first made in 1896 in Chicago, Illinois. A prize was added to each box in 1912. Collectors search for the old boxes, toys, and advertising materials. Many of the toys are unmarked. New toys are usually paper, older toys are tin, paper, or plastic.

Button, Pinback, Ki Cuyler, Chicago Cubs, Blue, White, 1930, 1 In.	125
Charm, Robber Guy, I'm No Santa Claus, Celluloid, 2-Sided, c. 1950, 1 In.	20
Container, Lid, Tin, 4 Scenes, Embossed Logo, 1990, 8 x 6 In.	15
Doll, Sailor Jack, Plastic, Bat, 16 In.	80
Mug & Bowl, Plastic, Logo, Red, White, Blue, c.1950...........................	14
Stock Certificate, Eagle Vignette, 1 Share, Canceled, Illinois, June 23, 1939..........	50
Trinket Box, Porcelain, Black, Blue, Brown, c.1970, 2 ½ x 1 ½ x 1 In.	30

CRACKLE GLASS

Crackle glass was originally made by the Venetians, but most of the wares found today were made since the 1800s. The glass was heated, cooled, and refired so that many small lines appeared inside the glass. Most was made from about 1930 to 1980, although some is made today. The glass is found in many colors, but collectors today pay the highest prices for amberina, cranberry, or ruby red. Cobalt blue is also popular. More crackle glass may be listed in those categories in this book.

Vase, Pink, Flowers, Iridescent, Art Nouveau, c.1900, 11 In.	*illus*	230
Vase, Pitcher, Vaseline, Flowers, Enamel, Bulbous, Applied Handle, 8 In.	*illus*	125

CRANBERRY GLASS

Cranberry glass is an almost transparent yellow-red glass. It resembles the color of cranberry juice. The glass has been made in Europe and America since the Civil War. It is still being made, and reproductions can fool the unwary. Related glass items may be listed in other categories, such as Rubina Verde.

Barber Bottle, Opalescent, Bitters, Seaweed, Square Shape, Polished Pontil Mark, c.1890, 8 x 2 In. *illus*		152
Barber Bottle, Opalescent, Bulbous, Tooled Mouth, Pouring Stopper, Stick Neck, 9 In..........		45
Decanter, Bottle Shape, Allover Gilt, Leaves, Stopper, 2 Handles, 1800s, 15 ¾ In....................		313
Dish, Sweetmeat, Lid, Etched To Clear Grape, Gilt, Faceted Finials, Square Feet, 9 In., Pair...		438
Jewelry Box, Hinged Lid, Enamel, Flowers, Gilt Trim, 2 ½ x 4 ¼ In.........................		90
Pitcher, Water, Elongated, Polished Pontil, Applied Clear Handle, 10 In. .... *illus*		90
Vase, Air Bubbles, Pin, Squat Base, Embossed, Victorian, 1800s, 31 ½ In.		156
Vase, Trumpet, Feather, Ruffled Rim, Gilt Figural Metal Base, Cherub Playing Mandolin, 14 In.		150
Wine, Stem, Cut To Clear, Triple Miter & Hob Button, Scalloped Foot, 4 ¾ In..........		650

CREAMWARE

Creamware, or queensware, was developed by Josiah Wedgwood about 1765. It is a cream-colored earthenware that has been copied by many factories. Similar wares may be listed under Pearlware and Wedgwood.

Basket, Reticulated, Molded Acorn, Oak Leaf Design, Scalloped Rim, Oval, 1700s, 11 x 9 In.	439

Bowl, Marble Field, Slip, Green Glazed Reeded Band, England, c.1780, 2½ x 5⅞ In.	531
Charger, Liverpool Birds, Transfer Print, Royal Shape Rim, Staffordshire, c.1780, 17 In. *illus*	644
Jug, Mother, 3 Children, Eye Of Providence, Verse, Transfer, c 1780, 8⅝ In.	410
Mug, Engine Turned, Bands, Brown Slip, Black Dot, Strap Handle, Early 1800s, 3½ In.	406
Pitcher, Dipped Fan Slip, White, Brown, Black Band Rim, Applied Strap Handle, 1800s, 6 In. .	2750
Pitcher, Poem, Maidenhead, Happy Is The Man, Scenes, Elephants, Castle, c.1780, 9½ In.....	176
Plate, Molded Relief, 2-Headed Eagle, Crossed Arrows, Flower Clusters, Marked, 1800s, 8¾ In.	369
Plate, Sailing Ship, American Flag, Transfer, Scalloped Rim, Flower Border, c.1780, 9 In., Pair .	878
Tankard, Farming Couple, Amorous, Barn, Workers, Transfer, Black, White Ground, c.1780, 6 In. *illus*	293
Urn, Lid, Painted, Red Band, Plinth Base, 1700s, 9¼ In., Pair..	195

CREIL

Creil, France, had a faience factory as early as 1794. The company merged with a factory in Montereau in 1819. It made stoneware, mocha ware, and soft paste porcelain. The name *Creil* appears as part of the mark on many pieces. The Creil factory closed in 1895.

Compote, Pearlware, Black Transfer, Interior Scene, Grapevine Border, Footed, 4 x 8½ In., Pair	875
Plate, Multicolor, Woman Dancing, Tambourine, Musician Seated On Floor, Wood Frame, 19 In. ..	2500
Plate, Yellow Ground, Brown Transfer, Woman & Boy In Boat, Flower Border, c.1830, 8⅜ In., Pair	84
Platter, Oval, Center Scene, Village Dance, Flower Border, Faience, Marked, 18¾ In.	150
Vase, Black Ground, Draped Figure, Grapes, Leaves, Gilt Trim, Turquoise Top & Base, 5½ x 3 In., Pair	63

CROWN DERBY, *see Royal Crown Derby category.*

CROWN DUCAL

Crown Ducal is the name used on some pieces of porcelain made by A.G. Richardson and Co., Ltd., of Tunstall and Cobridge, England. The name has been used since 1916. Crown Ducal is a well-known maker of chintz pattern dishes. The company was bought by Wedgwood in 1974.

Cup & Saucer, Espresso, Red & Orange Fruit, Green Leaves, White Ground, 2 x 3⅞ In.	13
Dinnerware Set, Bristol, Red Transfer, 49 Piece	60
Plate, Colonial Times, Blue Transfer, 10½ In., 12 Piece...	25
Platter, Turkey Dish, Black Transfer, Oval, Flowers Around Rim, 17 x 21 In...........................	197

CROWN MILANO

Crown Milano glass was made by the Mt. Washington Glass Works about 1890. It was a plain biscuit color with a satin finish decorated with flowers and often had large gold scrolls. Not all pieces are marked.

Biscuit Jar, Cream Tones, Enamel, Blossom & Leaf, Silver Plate Lid & Bail, Marked, 7 x 5 In..	350
Biscuit Jar, Flowers, Silver Plate Mouth & Lid, Opal, Tan Ground, 1880s, 6 In.	199
Biscuit Jar, Lid, Butterfly Finial, Gilt, Beaded Jewels, Marked, 6 In. .... *illus*	308
Biscuit Jar, Pastel Flower, Satin, Gold Finish, Metal Top, Swing Handles, 6 In.	92
Dish, Sweetmeat, Cream & Orange, Starfish, Silver Plate Bail, Turtle Finial, 4 x 6 In. .. *illus*	275
Dish, Sweetmeat, Zipper Mold, Blue & White, Wild Rose, Jewel, Silver Plate Bail & Lid, 4 x 5 In.	300
Lamp, Kerosene, Globular Peg, Flowers, Student Shade, Brass Collar, 1893, 17 x 5 In. .. *illus*	644
Vase, Central Reserve, Cherubs, Scrolling Frame, Opal, Tan, Gilt, 1880s, 8 In. .... *illus*	878
Vase, Melon Ribbed, Tulip, Cream & White Tones, Trifold Ears Rim 13 x 6¾ In.	200

CROWN TUSCAN *pattern is included in the Cambridge glass category.*

CRUET

Cruets of glass or porcelain were made to hold vinegar, oil, and other condiments. They were especially popular during Victorian times and have been made in a variety of styles since the eighteenth century. Additional cruets may be found in the Castor Set category and also in various glass categories.

Cranberry Glass, Barber Bottle, Opalescent, Bitters, Seaweed, Square Shape, Polished Pontil Mark, c.1890, 8 x 2 In.
$152

Jeffrey S. Evans & Associates

Cranberry Glass, Pitcher, Water, Elongated, Polished Pontil, Applied Clear Handle, 10 In.
$90

Woody Auction

Creamware, Charger, Liverpool Birds, Transfer Print, Royal Shape Rim, Staffordshire, c.1780, 17 In.
$644

Jeffrey S. Evans & Associates

Creamware, Tankard, Farming Couple, Amorous, Barn, Workers, Transfer, Black, White Ground, c.1780, 6 In. $293

Jeffrey S. Evans & Associates

Crown Milano, Biscuit Jar, Lid, Butterfly Finial, Gilt, Beaded Jewels, Marked, 6 In. $308

Rich Penn Auctions

Crown Milano, Dish, Sweetmeat, Cream & Orange, Starfish, Silver Plate Bail, Turtle Finial, 4 x 6 In. $275

Woody Auction

Cased Glass, Pink, Orange Applied Vine, Twist Handle, 3 Curved Feet, Murano, 9½ x 3½ In.	55
Cranberry Glass, Frosted Stopper, Icicle Overlay, 7-Footed Base, 9½ x 3¼ In.	48
Cut Glass, Faceted Stopper, Round, Fan & Starburst, 5½ In.	25
Glass, Green Cut To Clear, Thistle, Silver Stopper, Gorham, Applied Handle, c.1920, 7½ x 5 In.	889
Glass, Opaque, Green, Marbled Neck, Stopper, Applied Handle, Satin, New England Glass Co., 6 In.	556
Glass, Panel Optic, Teal To Cranberry, Enamel Flowers, Applied Handle, Stopper, Victorian, 7 In.	497

CT GERMANY

CT Germany was first part of a mark used by a company in Altwasser, Germany (now part of Walbrzych, Poland), in 1845. The initials stand for C. Tielsch, a partner in the firm. The Hutschenreuther firm took over the company in 1918 and continued to use the *CT* until 1952.

Creamer, Pink & Yellow Flowers, Gilt Trim, Altwasser, 5⅜ In.	7
Plate, Flowers, Scrolls, Embossed, Scalloped Edge, Marked, 9½ In.	21
Plate, Pink & Yellow Roses, Blue Ground, Openwork Rim, Gilt, 9 In.	35
Platter, Fish, Pink Rose Border, 21 x 9 In.	189
Shaving Mug, Occupational, Carriage Driver, H. Dutton, Gilt Trim, Lettering, 3½ In. *illus*	185
Syrup, Black-Eyed Susan, Brown To Yellow, 5 In.	165
Vase, Flared, White Ground, Flowers, Gilt Trim Around Foot, Silesia, c.1920, 4 In.	35

CUP PLATE

Cup plates are small glass or china plates that held the cup while a diner of the mid-nineteenth century drank coffee or tea from the saucer. The most famous cup plates were made of glass at the Boston and Sandwich factory located in Sandwich, Massachusetts. There have been many new glass cup plates made in recent years for sale to gift shops or collectors of limited editions. These are similar to the old plates but can be recognized as new.

Early American Pattern Glass, Scroll & Flute, Scalloped Rim, Teal Green, 3¾ In., Pair	87
Pressed Glass, Sulphide, Cameo, Man's Portrait, Facing Left, Scalloped Rim, France, 3¼ In.	431
Spatterware, Peafowl, Red, Green, Blue, Red Border, c.1840, 3¾ In., Pair	114

CURRIER & IVES

Currier & Ives made the famous American lithographs marked with their name from 1857 to 1907. The mark used on the print included the street address in New York City, and it is possible to date the year of the original issue from this information. Earlier prints were made by N. Currier and use that name from 1835 to 1847. Many reprints of the Currier or Currier & Ives prints have been made. Some collectors buy the insurance calendars that were based on the old prints. The words *large, small,* or *medium folio* refer to size. The original print sizes were very small (up to about 7 x 9 in.), small (8⅘ x 12⅘ in.), medium (9 x 14 in. to 14 x 20 in.), and large (larger than 14 x 20 in.). Other sizes are probably later copies. Copies of prints by Currier & Ives may be listed in Card, Advertising and in the Sheet Music category. Currier & Ives dinnerware patterns may be found in the Adams or Dinnerware categories.

Fashionable Turn-Outs In Central Park, Color, Worth, Frame, 1869, 20 x 29 In.	1536
General Tom Thumb, Barnum's Travelling Museum, Frame, 1849, 16¾ x 12½ In.	351
Queen Of The Turf, Maud S, Harold Dam Miss Russell, Frame, 1800s, 34 x 41 In.	625
Star Spangled Banner, Woman With Flag, Frame, c.1860, 14½ x 12½ In.	136

CUSTARD GLASS

Custard glass is a slightly yellow opaque glass. It was made in England in the 1880s and was first made in the United States in the 1890s. It has been reproduced. Additional pieces may be found in the Cambridge, Fenton, and Heisey categories. Custard glass is called *Ivorina Verde* by Heisey and other companies.

Apple Blossoms, Biscuit Jar, Lid, 8 In.	54
Argonaut, Spooner, Footed, c.1890, 4 In.	50
Cut Block, Toothpick Holder, Towner, North Dakota, 2 ½ In.	24
Lamp Shade, Light Green Rings, 3 Tiered Edges, Art Deco, 1920s, 11 x 9 In.	495

Maize is its own category in this book.

Martele, Planter, Nuthatch Birds, Phoenix, 1920s, 10 x 5 x 4 In.	145

CUT GLASS

Cut glass has been made since ancient times, but the large majority of the pieces now for sale date from the American Brilliant period of glass design, 1875 to 1915. These pieces have elaborate geometric designs with a deep miter cut. Modern cut glass with a similar appearance is being made in England, Ireland, Poland, the Czech Republic, and Slovakia. Chips and scratches are often difficult to notice but lower the value dramatically. A signature on the glass, usually on the smooth inside of a bowl, adds significantly to the value. Other cut glass pieces are listed under factory names, like Hawkes, Libbey, Pairpoint, Sinclaire, and Stevens & Williams.

Basket, Thistle, Monumental, Notched Handle, Lip, Pontil, c.1900, 21 In.	504
Bonbon, Lid, Kalana Lily, Acid Etched Pattern, Inverted Baluster Finial, c.1910, 7 x 5 In.	187
Bowl, Clear Blank, Wheel Pattern, Signed, Tuthill, 3 ¼ x 8 ¼ In.	125
Bowl, Diamond Pattern, Bronze Mounted Frame, Putti Handles, 1900s, 19 ½ In.	313
Bowl, Hobstars, Hand Cut, Scalloped Rim, 4 In.	46
Bowl, Neoclassical Style, Centerpiece, Molded, Cobalt Blue, Stepped Base, 10 x 9 ⅜ In., Pair	144
Bowl, Reticulated Floral Rim, Silver Mounted, Redlich, Early 1900s, 14 In.	750
Butter, Cover, Plate, Diamond, Ruffled Edge, Handle, 5 In.	115
Cake Stand, Sawtooth Rim, 2-Step Hexagonal Base, Opaque, White, 1860s, 7 x 11 In.	585
Celery Tray, Nailhead & Strawberry Diamond, Fan, Hobstar, Vesica, 11 x 5 ¾ In.	50
Celery Tray, Sultana, Clear, Dorflinger, 1880s, 4 ½ x 12 ½ In.	176
Centerpiece, Diamond, Sawtooth, 2 Handles, Mounted, Gilt Bronze, Claw Feet, 6 In.	630
Chamberstick, Air Trap Body, Flute Panels, Notched Edges, Hobstar Base, J. Hoare, 5 In.	750
Cheese Dish, Dome Lid, Oxford Pattern, Flared, Notched Rim, J. Hoare, 8 x 9 In.	230
Claret Jug, Flowers & Leaves, Mounted, Silver Plate Lid & Handle, 10 ¾ In., Pair ... illus	561
Claret Jug, Sunburst & Diamond, Silver, Spout, Handle, Lid, Berlin, J.H Werner, 10 ½ In.	130
Cologne Bottle, Columbia, Stopper, Embossed, Bergen, 7 x 5 In.	225
Cologne Bottle, Cut Overlay, Ruby, 3-Step Shoulder, Dorflinger, c.1850, 7 x 5 x 2 In. ... illus	439
Compote, 24-Point Rim, Concave Ribbed Stem, Stepped Domed Foot, 1860s, 7 ⅜ x 7 ¼ In. ...illus	439
Compote, Blue Cut To Clear, Brass, Reticulated Rim, Pedestal, Boy, Jug, Slate Base, Late 1900s, 24 In.	156
Compote, Buzz Saws & Hobstars, Bulbous Shape, Domed Base, 1950s, 18 ½ In.	215
Compote, Cased, Clear Stem & Foot, White, Folded Rim, Pittsburgh, 1830s, 8 ½ x 10 ½ In.	1320
Decanter Set, Oak, Tantalus, Silver Plate, England, 14 x 11 In.	150
Decanter, Barrel Shape, Diamond, Silver Plate, Faucet & Wagon, 10 ½ x 16 In.	693
Decanter, Electra, Stopper, 3-Ring Neck, Hobstar, File, Star, Fan, Straus, 12 In.	275
Decanter, Honeycomb, Stopper, 3-Ring Neck, Dorflinger, 12 x 5 In., Pair	875
Dish, Round, Royal Cutting, Star Cut Center, Dorflinger, 7 ⅜ In., Pair	31
Dish, Shell Shape, Enamel, Shepherds, Satyr, Clear Pedestal Base, Lobmeyr, 4 x 5 In. .. illus	850
Dish, Sweetmeat, Pear Shape, Tiered Prism Lid, Serrated Rim, Decagonal Base, 13 In., Pair	1046
Dispenser, Liquor, Lid, Labeled, Scotch & Bourbon, Brass Spouts, 1900s, 30 In., Pair	295
Egg, Faberge Style, Cut & Gilt Laurel, Bow Garlands, Pedestal Base, 1900s, 4 ¾ In.	384
Ewer, Cloisonne Stopper, Silver Mounted, Muted Pastel Palette, Early 1900s, 13 In.	3375
Goblet, Rock Crystal, Fruit Garland, Notched Stem, 7 In.	60
Humidor, Electra, Cut Base, Cherub, Monogram, Marked, Dominick & Haff, Straus, 6 x 6 In.	400
Humidor, Richelieu, Hobstar Cut Lid, Ray, J. Hoare, 8 x 5 In.	1610
Ice Tub, Hobstar, Prism, Strawberry Diamond & Fan, Pedestal, 2 Handles, 5 ¼ x 10 ¾ In.	275
Ice Tub, Underplate, Carolyn Pattern, Notched Edges, 6 ¼ x 10 In.	748
Jar, Hinged Lid, Cut Overlay, Cylindrical, Hob & Lace, Blue, Dorflinger, c.1900, 8 x 7 x 7 In. ...illus	176
Jar, Star Cut, Silver Lid, Frank M. Whiting, 7 In.	118
Jewelry Box, Strawberry Diamond, Hobstar Base, 3 x 5 In.	200

Crown Milano, Lamp, Kerosene, Globular Peg, Flowers, Student Shade, Brass Collar, 1893, 17 x 5 In.
$644

Jeffrey S. Evans & Associates

Crown Milano, Vase, Central Reserve, Cherubs, Scrolling Frame, Opal, Tan, Gilt, 1880s, 8 In.
$878

Jeffrey S. Evans & Associates

CT Germany, Shaving Mug, Occupational, Carriage Driver, H. Dutton, Gilt Trim, Lettering, 3 ½ In.
$185

Rich Penn Auctions

SELECTED CUT GLASS MARKS WITH DATES USED

J.D. Bergen & Co.
1885–1922
Meriden, Conn.

Tuthill Cut Glass Co.
1902–1923
Middletown, N.Y.

Pairpoint Corporation
1880–1938
New Bedford, Mass.

Libbey Glass Co.
1888–1925
Toledo, Ohio

C. Dorflinger & Sons
1852–1921
White Mills, Pa.

T.B. Clark and Co.
1884–1930
Honesdale, Pa.

Majestic Cut Glass Co.
1900–1916
Elmira, N.Y.

Wright Rich Cut Glass Co.
1904–1915
Anderson, Ind.

T.G. Hawkes & Co.
1880–1962
Corning, N.Y.

H.C. Fry Glass Co.
1901–1934
Rochester, Pa.

H.P. Sinclaire & Co.
1905–1929
Corning, N.Y.

House of Birks
c.1894–1907+
Montreal, Quebec, Canada

Laurel Cut Glass Co.
1903–1920
Jarmyn, Pa.

J. Hoare & Co.
1868–1921
Corning, N.Y.

L. Straus & Sons
c.1894–1917
New York, N.Y.

Jug, Whiskey, Crosscut Diamond, Strawberry Diamond, Fan, Stopper, Hobstar Base, 9 In.	350
Lamp, Cone Shape Shade, Baluster Stem, Hanging Prisms, Dome Base, 1900s, 33 x 11 In.	410
Lamp, Geometric, Fruit Pattern Panels, Domed Shade, Brass, 1900s, 18 ½ In.	207
Lamp, Gilt Bronze, Greek Key Border, Leaf Tiered Support, Square Base, 1800s, 17 In., Pair..	9225
Lamp, Luster Style, Prisms, Bronze, Glass Shade, Mirrored Base, Electric, 24 ½ In.	161
Lamp, Mushroom, Embossed, Prisms, Late 1800s, 25 In. .... *illus*	128
Nappy, Hobstar, Scalloped Edge, 2 Handles, 3 In.	316
Nappy, Trellis Pattern, Scalloped & Notched Edge, Egginton, c.1890, 6 In.	575
Perfume Holder, Diamond, Egg & Dart Banding, Bowl Center, Gilt Bronze, Claw Feet, 9 ¼ In.	284
Pitcher, Cider, Vertical Cut Ribs, Barrel Shape, Notched Handle, Ray Base, 7 In.	316
Pitcher, Expanding Star Pattern, Double Notched Handle, 8 ¼ In.	70
Pitcher, Marlboro, Clear, Bulbous, 20-Point Star, Dorflinger, c.1900, 8 ⅞ In. .... *illus*	322
Pitcher, Milk, Mirror Block, Oval, Pinched Neck, Mt. Washington, 8 In.	201
Pitcher, Water, Waffle & Snake, Frosted Blocks, Bakewell, c.1880, 10 ¼ x 4 ⅞ In. .. .. *illus*	1755
Plate, Diamond & Star, Ruby To Turquoise, 6 In., Pair	1024
Plate, Hobstar, Vesica, Cane, Strawberry Diamond, Notched Fan, 5 In.	25
Pokal, Goblet, Lid, Coat Of Arms, Crown, Flower Clusters, Cane Stem, 1800s, 15 ¾ In., Pair..	960
Powder Box, Hobstar & Fan, Signed, Egginton, 4 x 4 ¼ In.	125
Punch Bowl, Champion Pattern, Notched Rim, Skirted Base, J. Hoare, 12 x 12 In.	805
Punch Bowl, Hobstar, Alpenglow, Pedestal Base, T.B. Clark, 1908, 14 x 12 In.	281
Punch Bowl, Hobstars, Scalloped Edge, Embossed, Pedestal Base, 15 ½ In.	250
Punch Bowl, Marlboro, Hemispherical, Pointed Rim, Hobstar Peg, Dorflinger, c.1900, 7 x 14 In..	322
Punch Bowl, Stand, 6 Pentagonal Panels, Hobstars, Geometric Patterns, 11 x 10 In.	354
Punch Bowl, Sunburst, Diamond, Clear, Crystal Base, Continental, 1910s, 10 ¾ In. .... *illus*	204
Rose Bowl, Hobstar, Circular, Dorflinger, 5 ¾ x 7 In.	450
Rose Bowl, Persian Pattern, Round, Notched Rim, Ray Base, 2 x 3 In.	94
Sherbet, Kalana Lily, Peg Extension, Marked, R. Wallace & Sons, c.1910, 4 x 3 ⅝ In.	497
Tobacco Jar, Lift Lid, Grapes & Leaf, Tuthill, 5 ½ x 4 In.	225
Tumble-Up Set, Hindoo Pattern, Vertical Ribs, Tumbler Top, J. Hoare, 7 ½ In.	805
Urn, French Empire, Diamond, Gilt Bronze, Serpent Handle, Flame Finial, 1900s, 9 In., Pair .. *illus*	693
Urn, Sweetmeat, Tall Spire Shape Lid, Star Cut Foot, Anglo-Irish Style, 1900s, 14 In., Pair	472
Vase, Alternating Blocks, Hobstars, 1950s, 24 In. .... *illus*	369
Vase, Cobalt Blue To Clear, Sawtooth Rim, 11 ½ In. .... *illus*	106
Vase, Diamond & Star, Round Foot, 14 x 9 ¼ In.	448
Vase, Flashed Hobstar, Strawberry Diamond, Ray Cut Foot, Pedestal, 8 x 3 ½ In.	70
Vase, Kalana, Bud Shape, Panel Optic Interior, Zippered Rim, Dorflinger, c.1910, 16 x 5 In...	152
Vase, Mushroom, Seesaw Rim, Gourd, 1800s, 17 In.	384
Vase, Palladio, Diamond Band, Waisted Neck & Body, Rogaska, Etched Mark, 13 x 5 x 6 In...	236
Vase, Propeller Pattern, Oval, Horizontal Ribs, Notched Handles, Marshall Field, 10 In.	460
Vase, Star, Crosshatch & Zipper, Circular Foot, Late 1800s, 16 In.	492
Vase, Urn Shape, Pedestal, Hobstar, Vesica, Prism, Strawberry Diamond, Fan, 13 ¾ In.	450
Wine, Cranberry Cut To Clear, Miter Cutting, Hobnails, 5 In., Pair	1840
Wine, Grapes, Gold Border, Clear Stem, Circular Base, Dorflinger, 7 ½ In., Pair	73
Wine, Rhine, Clear Crystal, Enamel Peacock, Gold Highlights, 7 ¾ In.	275
Wine, Rock Crystal, Wheel Cut, Flowers, Air Trap, St. Louis, Early 1900s, 6 In., 11 Piece	649
Wine, Strawberry Diamond & Fan, Yellow Amber, Clear, Footed, Dorflinger, c.1896, 4 ½ In...	164

CYBIS

Cybis porcelain is a twentieth-century product. Boleslaw Cybis came to the United States from Poland in 1939. He started making porcelains in Long Island, New York, in 1940. He moved to Trenton, New Jersey, in 1942 as one of the founders of Cordey China Co. and started his own company, Cybis Porcelains, about 1950. Boleslaw died in 1957. It appears Cybis made porcelains until the 1990s and old ones are still selling. See also Cordey.

CYBIS

Bust, Madonna, With Bluebird, Wood Base, Marked, 1900s, 11 x 8 In.	230
Plaque, Holy Child Of Prague, Lusters & Gold, Signed, Frame, 23 x 19 In. .... *illus*	840

Cut Glass, Claret Jug, Flowers & Leaves, Mounted, Silver Plate Lid & Handle, 10 ¾ In., Pair
$561

Austin Auction Gallery

Cut Glass, Cologne Bottle, Cut Overlay, Ruby, 3-Step Shoulder, Dorflinger, c.1850, 7 x 5 x 2 In.
$439

Jeffrey S. Evans & Associates

Cut Glass, Compote, 24-Point Rim, Concave Ribbed Stem, Stepped Domed Foot, 1860s, 7 ⅜ x 7 ¼ In.
$439

Jeffrey S. Evans & Associates

Cut Glass, Dish, Shell Shape, Enamel, Shepherds, Satyr, Clear Pedestal Base, Lobmeyr, 4 x 5 In.
$850

Woody Auction

Cut Glass, Jar, Hinged Lid, Cut Overlay, Cylindrical, Hob & Lace, Blue, Dorflinger, c.1900, 8 x 7 x 7 In.
$176

Jeffrey S. Evans & Associates

Cut Glass, Lamp, Mushroom, Embossed, Prisms, Late 1800s, 25 In.
$128

Hindman

Cut Glass, Pitcher, Marlboro, Clear, Bulbous, 20-Point Star, Dorflinger, c.1900, 8 ⅞ In.
$322

Jeffrey S. Evans & Associates

Cut Glass, Pitcher, Water, Waffle & Snake, Frosted Blocks, Bakewell, c.1880, 10 ¼ x 4 ⅞ In.
$1,755

Jeffrey S. Evans & Associates

Cut Glass, Punch Bowl, Sunburst, Diamond, Clear, Crystal Base, Continental, 1910s, 10 ¾ In.
$204

Selkirk Auctioneers & Appraisers

Cut Glass, Urn, French Empire, Diamond, Gilt Bronze, Serpent Handle, Flame Finial, 1900s, 9 In., Pair
$693

Fontaine's Auction Gallery

Cut Glass, Vase, Alternating Blocks, Hobstars, 1950s, 24 In.
$369

Rich Penn Auctions

Cut Glass, Vase, Cobalt Blue To Clear, Sawtooth Rim, 11 ½ In.
$106

Bunch Auctions

CZECHOSLOVAKIA

Czechoslovakia is a popular term with collectors. The name, first used as a mark after the country was formed in 1918, appears on glass and porcelain and other decorative items. Although Czechoslovakia split into Slovakia and the Czech Republic on January 1, 1993, the name continues to be used in some trademarks.

CZECHOSLOVAKIA GLASS

Ashtray, Pegasus, Art Deco, Frosted, Curt Schlevogt, 1930, 3 x 4¾ In., Pair		177
Candlestick, Jade Green, Petal Socket, Dolphin Shape Stem, Stepped Base, c.1924, 10 In., Pair		875
Candlestick, Orange, Black Trim, Round Base, 3¾ x 4¼ In., Pair		60
Perfume Bottle, Amber Glass, 2 Nudes, Gilt Metal Fittings, Medallion Inset, 5 x 4 In. . *illus*		350
Plate, Red Border, White Ground, Flower Center, 8 Piece		58
Vase, Iridescent Green, Art Glass, Silver Overlay, Art Nouveau, c.1920, 8¼ In. *illus*		125

CZECHOSLOVAKIA POTTERY

Dish, Figural, Polar Bear, 7½ In.		113
Figurine, Bird Of Prey, Perched, On Stone, No. 8326, Amphora, 12½ In. *illus*		367
Figurine, Nude Woman, In Flower, White Glaze, 10 In.		107

DANIEL BOONE

Daniel Boone, a pre–Revolutionary War folk hero, was a surveyor, trapper, and frontiersman. A television series, which ran from 1964 to 1970, was based on his life and starred Fess Parker. All types of Daniel Boone memorabilia are collected.

Book, Pioneer Of Kentucky, Red Cover, Illustrated, John Abbot, Dodd, Mead & Co., c.1877		246
Coin, Commemorative, Half Dollar, Silver, Daniel Boone Bicentennial Pioneer Year, 1934		177
Lunch Box, Fess Parker, Metal, Signed By D. Hinton, King-Seeley, 1965 *illus*		75
Mold, Chocolate, Hinged, 5½ In., Pair		80
Print, Protects His Family, Color Lithograph, Black Border, Gold Text, H. Schile, 1874, 22 x 28 In.		625
Sculpture, Fur Hat, Rifle, Relief Carved, Pine, Unsigned, 20th Century, 34½ x 11¾ In.		59
Sculpture, Rifle, Dog, Bronze, Wood Base, James Earle Fraser, 1969, 11½ x 6 x 5¼ In.		250
Toy, Fort Boone Playset, Box, Blue & Orange Graphics, Fess Parker As Daniel Boone, 16 x 24 In.		132

D'ARGENTAL

D'Argental is a mark used in France by the Compagnie des Cristalleries de St. Louis. The firm made multilayered, acid-cut cameo glass in the late nineteenth and twentieth centuries. Cameo glass was made with the D'Argental mark from 1919 to 1925. D'Argental is the French name for the city of Munzthal, home of the glassworks. Later the company made enameled etched glass.

Vase, Brown, Raspberries, Leaves, Footed, Cameo, Signed, 6 x 3 In. *illus*		448
Vase, Yellow Ground, Orange Cameo, Carved Lily Pad & Blossom Overlay, Signed, 2½ x 4 In.		300

DAUM

Daum, a glassworks in Nancy, France, was started by Jean Daum in 1878. The company, now called *Cristalleries de Nancy,* is still working. The *Daum Nancy* mark has been used in many variations. The name of the city and the artist are usually both included. The term *martele* is used to describe applied decorations that are carved or etched in the cameo process.

Daum	Daum	Daum
1890	1960–1971	1960–1971

Bowl, Daffodil, Pate-De-Verre, Green & Yellow Glass, Air Trap, Signed, Late 1900s, 2 x 4 In.		266
Bowl, Mushrooms, Enamel, Notched Rim, Etched Base, 1¾ x 6 In.		2646

Cybis, Plaque, Holy Child Of Prague, Lusters & Gold, Signed, Frame, 23 x 19 In.
$840

Garth's Auctioneers & Appraisers

Czechoslovakia Glass, Perfume Bottle, Amber Glass, 2 Nudes, Gilt Metal Fittings, Medallion Inset, 5 x 4 In.
$350

Woody Auction

Czechoslovakia Glass, Vase, Iridescent Green, Art Glass, Silver Overlay, Art Nouveau, c.1920, 8¼ In.
$125

Bruneau & Co. Auctioneers

Czechoslovakia Pottery, Figurine, Bird Of Prey, Perched, On Stone, No. 8326, Amphora, 12 ½ In.
$367

Strawser Auction Group

Daniel Boone, Lunch Box, Fess Parker, Metal, Signed By D. Hinton, King-Seeley, 1965
$75

Pook & Pook

D'Argental, Vase, Brown, Raspberries, Leaves, Footed, Cameo, Signed, 6 x 3 In.
$448

Treadway

Bowl, Orange, Yellow, Signed, Pedestal Foot, Art Deco, 8 ½ x 11 x 11 In. .... *illus*	554
Bowl, Strawberries, Gilt Trim, Ruffled Rim, Footed, Cameo, 3 ½ x 8 ¹³⁄₁₆ In.	1625
Chandelier, Cameo Glass Shade, Leaves & Flowers, Gilt Bronze, Majorelle, 37 In.	5355
Cruet, Panel Optic, Thistle Engraved, Reeded Handle, Gilt, c.1915, 7 ½ x 6 In.	82
Ewer, Mythological Figure, Man, Handle, Pate-De-Verre, Red, Orange, Purple, Late 1900, 12 In.	920
Figurine, Car, Limousine, Clear Glass, Signed, c.1987, 4 ¾ x 17 x 5 ½ In. .... *illus*	896
Figurine, Dolphin, Molded Glass, Chrome Stand, Signed, 1950s, 17 In.	148
Figurine, Elephant, Red, Wood Base, Signed, Jean Francois Leroy, 13 ½ x 8 ¼ In.	2375
Figurine, Elephant, Trunk Up, Gray, Amber Pate-De-Verre, Petit Modele, 5 x 6 x 3 In. *illus*	288
Figurine, Legendre Nocturne, Plinth Base, 11 In.	236
Figurine, Prowling Tiger, Amber, Acid Cut Stripes, Pate-De-Verre, Late 1900s, 4 ½ In.	1180
Inkwell, Lid, Leaves, Applied Glass Insects, Acorns, Cube Shape, Metal Insert, 5 x 4 In. *illus*	2337
Lamp, Desk, Wishbone, Electrified, Art Nouveau, Signed, 15 x 7 x 5 In., Pair	2400
Lamp, Frosted, Etched Glass Shade, Reeded Stem, Edgar Brandt, c.1925, 11 x 5 In., Pair *illus*	4032
Paperweight, Conch Shell Shape, Art Glass, Signed, France, 2 ½ In.	71
Plate, Royal Blue, Gold Designs, Pate-De-Verre, Salvador Dali, c.1975, 10 ½ In.	150
Powder Box, Lid, Pink Top, White Bottom, 5 ½ In.	118
Rose Bowl, Mottled Green, Forest Scene, Folded-In Rim, Marked, Cross Of Lorraine, c.1920, 3 In.	1250
Vase, Bulbous, Orange, Yellow & Lavender Mottled Ground, Signed, Nancy, 4 ½ x 7 In. *illus*	175
Vase, Carved Leaves, Berries, Reddish-Brown, Mottled Pink, Bronze Coral Base, 1810s, 13 In.	336
Vase, Flowers, Carved, Multicolor Ground, Etched, Art Nouveau, Signed, 5 ½ In. ..... *illus*	1845
Vase, Flowers, Yellow, Brown, Mottled Ground, Cameo, Signed, 8 x 4 ³⁄₈ In.	813
Vase, Green, Blue Leaves, Pate-De-Verre, Lozenge Shape, Late 1900s, 6 ¾ In. ...... *illus*	266
Vase, Lake Scene, Trees, Shoreline, Footed, Signed, Cameo, 10 ¾ x 4 ½ In.	1544
Vase, Lierre, 2 Handles, Leaves, Etched, Cameo, Incised, Croix De Lorraine, c.1900, 7 In. *illus*	7560
Vase, Mottled Amber Ground, Brown, White, Enamel, Signed, Daum Nancy, Late 1800s, 2 In.	878
Vase, Poppy, Wheel Carved, White, Black, Cameo, Incised, Croix De Lorraine, c.1910, 12 In.	3528
Vase, Soliflor Roses, Tapered Rim, Clear, Pate-De-Verre Base, Signed, 9 x 4 In.	236
Vase, Spiral Body, Molded Rim, Bulbous, Croix De Lorraine, Early 1900s, 8 ½ x 11 ½ In.	305
Vase, Trumpet, Amber Glass, Square Base, Art Deco, 16 ½ x 12 x 12 In.	1536

DAVENPORT

Davenport pottery and porcelain were made at the Davenport factory in Longport, Staffordshire, England, from 1793 to 1887. Earthenwares, creamwares, porcelains, ironstone, and other ceramics were made. Most of the pieces are marked with a form of the word *Davenport*.

Cup & Saucer, Green Stripe, White Ground, Pink Flowers, Gilt, c.1880, 2 x 6 In.	75
Cup & Saucer, Imari Style, Flowers, Red & Cobalt Blue, White Ground, Gilt, 1870s, 2 x 5 In.	70
Platter, Blue & White, Country Scene, House, Trees, Animals, Flower Vine Border, 8-Sided, 19 x 14 In.	113
Platter, Castle & River Scene, Scrolled Flower Border, White Ground, Transferware, 19 x 16 In. *illus*	45
Platter, Flow Blue, Amoy, 8-Sided, 16 x 12 In.	138
Tureen, Lid, Underplate, Persian, Multicolor Flowers, Oval, Scrolled Handles, 1800s, 12 x 16 In.	188

DAVY CROCKETT

Davy Crockett, the American frontiersman, was born in 1786 and died in 1836. The historical character gained new fame in 1954 when the Walt Disney television show ran a series of episodes featuring Fess Parker as Davy Crockett. Coonskin caps and buckskins became popular and hundreds of different Davy Crockett items were made.

Bank, Bust, Copper Color, Name On Base, 5 In.	48
Book, Life Of David Crockett, Illustrations, A.L. Burt & Co., N.Y., 1903, 7 ½ x 5 In.	11
Comic Book, Davy Crocket Frontier Fighter, No. 1, 1955, 11 x 8 In.	6
Jacket, Tan, Vinyl, Green & Brown Graphic On Back, Fringe, Buckaroo, Child's, Size 12	18
Lamp, Ceramic Base, Tree Trunk, Crockett Hunting Bear, Multicolor Shade, 1950s ...... *illus*	138

DECORATED TUMBLERS *may be listed by maker or design or in Advertising, Coca-Cola, Pepsi-Cola, Sports, and other categories.*

Daum, Bowl, Orange, Yellow, Signed, Pedestal Foot, Art Deco, 8 ½ x 11 x 11 In.
$554

Morphy Auctions

Daum, Figurine, Car, Limousine, Clear Glass, Signed, c.1987, 4 ¾ x 17 x 5 ½ In.
$896

Morphy Auctions

Daum, Figurine, Elephant, Trunk Up, Gray, Amber Pate-De-Verre, Petit Modele, 5 x 6 x 3 In.
$288

Blackwell Auctions

Daum, Inkwell, Lid, Leaves, Applied Glass Insects, Acorns, Cube Shape, Metal Insert, 5 x 4 In.
$2,337

Morphy Auctions

Daum, Lamp, Frosted, Etched Glass Shade, Reeded Stem, Edgar Brandt, c.1925, 11 x 5 In., Pair
$4,032

Sotheby's

Daum, Vase, Bulbous, Orange, Yellow & Lavender Mottled Ground, Signed, Nancy, 4 ½ x 7 In.
$175

Woody Auction

> **TIP**
> *Think about the sig-*
> *nature on glass. Acid*
> *etched marks can be*
> *added. So can signa-*
> *tures. Be sure the mark*
> *seems appropriate.*

Daum, Vase, Flowers, Carved, Multicolor Ground, Etched, Art Nouveau, Signed, 5 ½ In.
$1,845

Morphy Auctions

Daum, Vase, Green, Blue Leaves, Pate-De-Verre, Lozenge Shape, Late 1900s, 6 ¾ In.
$266

Leland Little Auctions

Daum, Vase, Lierre, 2 Handles, Leaves, Etched, Cameo, Incised, Croix De Lorraine, c.1900, 7 In.
$7,560

Sotheby's

Davenport, Platter, Castle & River Scene, Scrolled Flower Border, White Ground, Transferware, 19 x 16 In. $45

Strawser Auction Group

Davy Crockett, Lamp, Ceramic Base, Tree Trunk, Crockett Hunting Bear, Multicolor Shade, 1950s $138

Keystone Auctions LLC

TIP

Don't put wood or paper or textiles near heating vents or fireplaces. Heat will harm them.

Decoy, Black Duck, Glass Eyes, Larry McLaughlin, Pa., c.1930, 6½ In. $250

Cowan's Auctions

DECOY

Decoys are carved or turned wooden copies of birds, fish, or animals. The decoy was placed in the water or propped on the shore to lure flying birds to the pond for hunters. Some decoys are handmade; some are commercial products. Today there is a group of artists making modern decoys for display, not for use in a pond. Many sell for high prices.

Black Duck, Cedar, Worn Paint, Gunning Wear, L. & S. Ward, Crisfield, Md., 1930, 18 In.	4059
Black Duck, Glass Eyes, Larry McLaughlin, Pa., c.1930, 6½ In. .... *illus*	250
Black Duck, Glass Eyes, Robert Turk, Levittown, Pa., c.1950, 7½ In.	281
Black Duck, Hollow Carved, Glass Eyes, Ron Marino, Milford, 1900s, 16½ In.	281
Black Duck, Hollow, Glass Eyes, Head Turned Left, Martin Collins, Mass., 1900s, 14 In. *illus*	500
Black Duck, Painted, Carved, Mounted, Driftwood Base, Signed, Stan Sparre, Mass., 4 In.	406
Black Duck, Steel Plate, Turned Head, Marked, Marcel Dufour, Canada, 7 In.	313
Blue Warbler, Glass Eyes, Mounted, Driftwood Base, Elmer Crowell, c.1948, 3½ In. ... *illus*	3500
Bluebill Drake, Football Shape, Carved, Painted, Metal Eyes, Paddle Tail, 1930, 13 In.	561
Bluebill Duck, Cast Iron, Sink Box, Painted, c.1900, 7 x 13 x 5½ In.	367
Bluebill Hen, Mallard, Carved, Painted, E.E. Avann, Canada, c.1905, 14 x 16½ In.	313
Blue-Winged Teal Drake, Painted, Glass Eyes, Signed, R.W. Means, 1932, 6½ In.	500
Bufflehead, Drake, Glass Eyes, Black & White, Signed, Ron Marino, 1800s, 11 In. ...... *illus*	125
Canada Goose, Carved Neck, Weighted Yellow Pine Keel, Plywood Bottom Board, 21 x 32 x 15 In.	226
Canada Goose, Carved, Bent Neck, Glass Eyes, Multicolor, Stamped V, 23 x 15 x 26 In.	150
Canada Goose, Carved, Painted, Glass Eyes, Signed, French Broad River Co., 1982, 27 In. *illus*	177
Canada Goose, Cast Iron, Black, Sink Box, 1989, 8½ x 24 x 8 In.	1921
Canada Goose, Flight Position, Glass Eyes, Carved, Painted, Gary Gibson, 24 x 29 In. . *illus*	313
Canada Goose, Hissing, Old Paint, Tack Eyes, M. Hancock, Chincoteague, Va., 1940s, 21 In.	602
Canada Goose, Painted, Black & White, Wire Frame, 9 x 23½ In.	236
Canada Goose, Swimming, Canvas Covered, Glass Eyes, Wood Base, Early 1900s, 35½ In...	1220
Canvasback Duck, Carved, Glass Eyes, Painted, Evans Decoy Company, c.1927-34, 7¼ x 14½ In.	206
Common Tern, Glass Eyes, Mounted, Shell Shape Base, James Lapham, 1909, 12 In.	625
Crow, Perching On Turned Wood Post Finial, Glass Eyes, Black, Carved, 17½ x 14¼ In.	374
Curlew, Carved, Painted, Square Base, Virginia, c.1890, 12 In.	313
Duck, Carved, Brown, Signed, Dan Cobb, 5¾ In. .... *illus*	313
Duck, Carved, Painted, Black, Brown, White, Branded, ELW, 14½ In.	100
Duck, Carved, Painted, Metal Tack Eyes, Leather Pull, 1930, 16 In.	826
Duck, Flying, Carved, Feather Details, Turned Pine Pedestal, Painted, 1900s, 20 x 24 In.	413
Duck, Glass Bead Eyes, Fine Feather Detail, Carved, Painted, 1900s, 16 In.	500
Duck, New Jersey, Preening, Tack Eyes, Painted, Black, c.1940, 14 In.	200
Eider Duck, Painted, Inset Eyes, Horseshoe, Shot Scars, c.1950, 13½ In.	100
Fish, Wood, Sheet Metal Fins, Painted Eyes, Black Speckles, 6½ In.	125
Goldeneye Duck, Carved Naive, Glass Eyes, Painted, Shot Scar, New England, 1910s, 10½ In.	108
Goose, Brown, Black, White, Signed, Raymond E. Hornick, 1984, 26 In.	71
Goose, Swimming Position, Black & White, Lake Champlain, Large .... *illus*	172
Heron, Carved, Painted, Inset Eyes, Mounted, Wood Base, Late 1900s, 31 In.	502
Mallard Drake, Alcide Carmadel Style, Carved, Bayou Gauche, 17 In.	352
Mallard Drake, Black & White, Yellow Beak, Glass Eyes, Ken Harris, Woodville, 1906, 15 In.	113
Mallard Drake, Wood, Tacked Eyes, Brown Beak, Green Head, Multicolor, 6¾ x 5 x 17½ In.	58
Mallard Duck, Crowell Style, Perched, Domed Base, Signed, Frank Adamo, Late 1900s, 4 In. *illus*	250
Mallard Hen, Brown, Black, Glass Eyes, Marked, A. Elmer Crowell, Mass., 1930s, 4¾ In. *illus*	1063
Mallard Hen, Carved, Glass Eyes, Painted, Marked, Ben Schmidt, 8 In.	250
Mallard Hen, Glass Eyes, Painted, Tube Dawson, 6½ x 15 In.	236
Merganser Duck, Painted, Brown, Black & White, Glass Eyes	55
Merganser Hen, Painted, Glass Eyes, Detroit, c.1900, 17 In.	5313
Pheasant, Carved, Painted, Mounted, Birch Base, Maine, 1900s, 7 In. .... *illus*	313
Pigeon, Cast Iron, Standing, Cube Shape, Plinth Base, 1800s, 7¼ x 10 In.	1582
Pintail Drake, Glass Eyes, Stand, Signed, Steve & Leon Ward, Maryland, 1948, 18 x 7 In.	1625
Quail, Flying Shape, Painted, Brown & Gray, James Lapham, 1909, 9½ In.	406
Quail, On Trunk, Carved & Painted, Metal Beak, Bob Booth, 25 In., 4 Piece	63
Rainbow Trout, Wood, Painted, Green, Pink, Teal, Tack Eyes, Miles Smith, c.1973, 9 x 32 In..	281

Decoy, Black Duck, Hollow, Glass Eyes, Head Turned Left, Martin Collins, Mass., 1900s, 14 In.
$500

Eldred's

Decoy, Blue Warbler, Glass Eyes, Mounted, Driftwood Base, Elmer Crowell, c.1948, 3 ½ In.
$3,500

Eldred's

Decoy, Bufflehead, Drake, Glass Eyes, Black & White, Signed, Ron Marino, 1800s, 11 In.
$125

Eldred's

Decoy, Canada Goose, Carved, Painted, Glass Eyes, Signed, French Broad River Co., 1982. 27 In.
$177

Leland Little Auctions

Decoy, Canada Goose, Flight Position, Glass Eyes, Carved. Painted, Gary Gibson, 24 x 29 In.
$313

Pook & Pook

Decoy, Duck, Carved, Brown, Signed, Dan Cobb, 5 ¾ In.
$313

Cowan's Auctions

Decoy, Goose, Swimming Position, Black & White, Lake Champlain, Large
$172

Apple Tree Auction Center

Decoy, Mallard Duck, Crowell Style, Perched, Domed Base, Signed, Frank Adamo, Late 1900s, 4 In.
$250

Eldred's

Decoy, Mallard Hen, Brown, Black, Glass Eyes, Marked, A. Elmer Crowell, Mass., 1930s, 4 ¾ In.
$1,063

Elcred's

Decoy, Pheasant, Carved, Painted, Mounted, Birch Base, Maine, 1900s, 7 In.
$313

Eldred's

Decoy, Shorebird, Glass Eyes, Long Legged, Wood, Carved, Stand, Signed, Mark McNairy, 16 In.
$1,098

Nadeau's Auction Gallery

Decoy, Turkey, Male, Glass Eyes, Mount, Wood Base, Signed, Bud Talpey, Massachusetts, 4½ In.
$406

Eldred's

Redhead Drake, Wood, 3 Holes, Painted, Russell Ayde, Wisconsin, 6¼ In., Pair	375
Ruddy Turnstone, Painted, Driftwood Base, A. Elmer Crowell, Massachusetts, 1930s, 3 In..	1250
Shorebird, Carved, Painted, Stump Base, Stamped, Sacket, 9 In.	50
Shorebird, Feather Details, Glass Eyes, Carved, Painted, Wooden Base, Signed, Perkins, 7¾ In.	75
Shorebird, Glass Eyes, Long Legged, Wood, Carved, Stand, Signed, Mark McNairy, 16 In. .... *illus*	1098
Shorebird, Sanderling, Carved, Painted, Metal Legs, Cherry Plinth, Ora A. Anderson, 1985, 7 x 7 In....	295
Sink Box, Sleeper Position, Cast Iron, 1800s, 11 In.	185
Swan, Sleeping, Laminated Construction, Black, Carved, 1900s, 17 In.	94
Tern, Black & White, Glass Eyes, Mounted, Square Base, 15 In.	75
Turkey, Male, Glass Eyes, Mount, Wood Base, Signed, Bud Talpey, Massachusetts, 4½ In. *illus*	406
Widgeon, St. Clair Flats, Carved, Painted, Inset Glass Eyes, L.A. McIves, 12½ In.	89
Wood Duck, Carved, Old Mottled Paint, Cleve Dabler, Barnegat Bay, N.J., c.1935, 17 In.	63

DEDHAM POTTERY

Dedham Pottery was started in 1895. Chelsea Keramic Art Works was established in 1872 in Chelsea, Massachusetts, by members of the Robertson family. The factory closed in 1889 and was reorganized as the Chelsea Pottery U.S. in 1891. The firm used the marks *CKAW* and *CPUS*. It became the Dedham Pottery of Dedham, Massachusetts, in 1896. The factory closed in 1943. It was famous for its crackleware dishes, which picture blue outlines of animals, flowers, and other natural motifs. Pottery by Chelsea Keramic Art Works and Dedham Pottery is listed here.

Elephant, Plate, Center Medallion, Elephants & Calf Rim, Blue Ink Stamp, 7½ In.	563
Grapevine, Bowl, Fruit, Blue, White Crackle Glaze, Blue Ink Stamp, c.1910, 4 x 9 In.	219
Grapevine, Plate, Blue & White, Blue Rabbit Mark, c.1910, 8¼ In. .... *illus*	125
Magnolia, Plate, Blue Ink Stamp, c.1910, 8¼ In.	94
Rabbit, Pitcher, White Crackle Glaze, C Handle, c.1900, 9 x 4½ x 6 In. .... *illus*	338
Snow Tree, Plate, Blue & White, Blue Rabbit Mark, c.1910, 8½ In. .... *illus*	219
Turtle, Cup & Saucer, Blue & White, Blue Mark, 2 x 6 In. .... *illus*	160
Vase, Blue Flowers, Leaves, White Crackle Glaze, H. Robertson, 1896-1908, 9 x 5¼ In.	12500
Vase, Copper Red, Green Glaze, Bulbous, Experimental, Hugh C. Robertson, c.1900, 8 In.	1500
Vase, Oxblood Paint, Green Glaze, Stoneware, Squat Base, H. Robinson, 1896-1908, 8½ In..	6875
Vase, Oxblood, Mottled Glaze, Drip, Experimental, H. Robertson, 1896-1908, 8 x 8 In.	4688

DEGUE

Degue is a signature acid etched on pieces of French glass made by the Cristalleries de Compiegne beginning about 1925. Cameo, mold blown, and smooth glass with contrasting colored rims are the types most often found. The factory closed in 1939.

Lamp, Glass, Yellow, Geometric, Puffy Flower Designs, Frosted, Signed, 4 x 13⅝ In. .... *illus*	230
Vase, Urn Shape, 5 Stylized Flowers, Red To Maroon, Mottled Pink Ground, c.1930, 17 x 7 In. .. *illus*	644

DELATTE

Delatte glass is a French cameo glass made by Andre Delatte. It was first made in Nancy, France, in 1921. Lighting fixtures and opaque glassware in imitation of Bohemian opaline were made.

Vase, Dark Purple Flowers, Orange Ground, Shouldered Flared Neck, Signed, 6 In.	192
Vase, Flared Rim, Mottled Blue, Trees, Signed, Footed, 6⅞ x 5 In.	313
Vase, Lavender Flowers, White Ground, Wide Foot, Pink Base, Signed, 5¾ In.	270
Vase, Squat, Brown Thistles & Leaves, Yellow Ground, Signed, 6 x 6 In.	576
Vase, Tall, Mottled Blue, Iron Mounted, Footed, Marked, c.1925, 4¼ In., Pair	3250
Vase, White Mottled Ground, Lavender Cameo, Carved Flower Overlay, 5¾ In.................*illus*	225

DELDARE, *see Buffalo Pottery Deldare.*

Dedham, Grapevine, Plate, Blue & White, Blue Rabbit Mark, c.1910, 8 1/4 In.
$125

California Historical Design

Dedham, Rabbit, Pitcher, White Crackle Glaze, C Handle, c.1900, 9 x 4 1/2 x 6 In.
$338

Locati Auctions

Dedham, Snow Tree, Plate, Blue & White, Blue Rabbit Mark, c.1910, 8 1/2 In.
$219

California Historical Design

Dedham, Turtle, Cup & Saucer, Blue & White, Blue Mark, 2 x 6 In.
$160

Nadeau's Auction Gallery

Degue, Lamp, Glass, Yellow, Geometric, Puffy Flower Designs, Frosted, Signed, 4 x 13 5/8 In.
$230

Blackwell Auctions

Degue, Vase, Urn Shape, 5 Stylized Flowers, Red To Maroon, Mottled Pink Ground, c.1930, 17 x 7 In.
$644

Jeffrey S. Evans & Associates

Delatte, Vase, White Mottled Ground, Lavender Cameo, Carved Flower Overlay, 5 3/4 In.
$225

Woody Auction

Delft, Charger, Blue & White, Flowers, Leafy Border, Scalloped Rim, Faience, Late 1700s, 14 In., Pair
$1,003

Austin Auction Gallery

Delft, Clock, Porcelain, Blue & White, Numbers, Enamel, Ansonia, 11 1/4 x 10 1/4 In.
$160

Hartzell's Auction Gallery Inc.

Delft, Cuspidor, Squat Shape, Scalloped Funnel, Flowers, Blue, White, 3 Loop Handles, 1700s, 3 x 5 In.
$1,107

Brunk Auctions

Delft, Plaque, Wall, Light Green & Blue Cage, Yellow Bird, White Ground, 1900s, 20 In.
$250

Pook & Pook

Delft, Plate, Royal Portrait, William III, Tulips, White Ground, c.1690, 8 5/8 In.
$2,928

Pook & Pook

Dental, Cabinet, Iron, Curved Glass Doors, Revolving Marble Top, France, 1930, 34 1/2 x 27 In.
$3,000

Kamelot Auctions

Dental, Cabinet, Mahogany, Rectangular Top, 22 Drawers, Knob Handle, 45 1/2 x 35 x 12 In.
$1,150

Stevens Auction Co.

DELFT

Delft is a special type of tin-glazed pottery. Early delft was made in Holland and England during the seventeenth century. It was usually decorated with blue on a white surface, but some was multicolor, decorated with green, yellow, and other colors. Most delftware pieces were dishes needed for everyday living. Figures were made from about 1750 to 1800 and are rare. Although the soft tin-glazed pottery was well-known, it was not named delft until after 1840, when it was named for the city in Holland where much of it was made. Porcelain became more popular because it was more durable, and Holland gradually stopped making the old delft. In 1876 De Porceleyne Fles factory in Delft introduced a porcelain ware that was decorated with blue and white scenes of Holland that reminded many of old delft. It became popular with the Dutch and tourists. By 1990 all of the blue and white porcelain with Dutch scenes was made in Asia, although it was marked *Delft*. Only one Dutch company remains that makes the traditional old-style delft with blue on white or with colored decorations. Most of the pieces sold today were made after 1891, and the name *Holland* usually appears with the Delft factory marks. The word *Delft* appears alone on some inexpensive twentieth- and twenty-first-century pottery from Asia and Germany that is also listed here.

Bowl, Flowers, Multicolor, White Ground, Initials, PK, 1700s, 5 1/2 x 9 3/4 In.	671
Charger, Blue & White, Flowers, Leafy Border, Scalloped Rim, Faience, Late 1700s, 14 In., Pair ....*illus*	1003
Charger, Man On Horseback, Tulip Border, Blue, Yellow, Green, Marked, Jacobus De Milde, 16 In..	720
Charger, White Ground, Blue, Flowers, Urn, Scalloped Rim, Early 1700s, 2 1/2 x 13 In., Pair..	660
Charger, William & Mary Portrait, Blue & White, Initials, KW KM, c.1690, 11 3/4 In.	2196
Clock, Porcelain, Blue & White, Numbers, Enamel, Ansonia, 11 1/4 x 10 1/4 In. ....*illus*	160
Cuspidor, Squat Shape, Scalloped Funnel, Flowers, Blue, White, 3 Loop Handles, 1700s, 3 x 5 In. *illus*	1107
Dish, Man, Bearded, Riding Horse, Blue, Green, Yellow, Ruffled Rim, c.1680, 2 3/4 x 13 In......	615
Plaque, Wall, Light Green & Blue Cage, Yellow Bird, White Ground, 1900s, 20 In. ....*illus*	250
Plate, Blue & White, Chinoiserie, Garden Landscape, Gilt Rim, Faience, 12 In., 5 Piece	2360
Plate, Royal Portrait, William III, Tulips, White Ground, c.1690, 8 5/8 In. ....*illus*	2928
Platter, Presentation, Blue & White, Flowers, Early 1900s, 11 1/4 In.	50
Porringer, Flowers, Blue & White, 2 Handles, 1700s, 2 3/4 x 8 1/2 In......................	397
Posset Pot, Lid, Blue & White, Flowers, Dashes, 2 Handles, Bristol, England, c.1720, 8 x 11 In.	3300
Tankard, Hinged Pewter Lid, Traveler, Landscape, Erfurt Type, 1750s, 8 In.	469
Tea Caddy, Pewter Screw Top, Blue Scrolled Flowers, 1700s, 7 x 3 x 3 In..................	140
Tile, Picture, Bull, Tree, Blue & White, Ebonized, Oak Frame, 1700s, 16 x 11 In., 6 Piece.......	2006
Urn, Dome Lid, Foo Dog Finial, Blue & White, Flowers, Earthenware, Late 1700s, 17 In.	561
Vase, Faience, Multicolor, Chinoiserie, Garden Ground, Late 1700s, 8 3/4 In.	472
Vase, Flowers, Octagonal Base, Painted, Signed JV, 1800s, 22 In., Pair.....................	813
Vase, Garniture, Blue, Windmill, Lion Finial, Marked, Joost Thooft & Labouchere, 11 In., Pair	81
Vase, Ribbed Body, Flared Rim, Windmill, Landscape, Blue & White, 1700s, 17 In.........	2125

DENTAL

Dental cabinets, chairs, equipment, and other related items are listed here. Other objects may be found in the Medical category.

Cabinet, Girator, Round, Green Body, Rotating Top, 4 Legs, Casters, Leon Martin, France, 35 x 27 In.	625
Cabinet, Iron, Curved Glass Doors, Revolving Marble Top, France, 1930, 34 1/2 x 27 In. *illus*	3000
Cabinet, Mahogany, Bird's-Eye Maple, 22 Drawers, Marble Top, Door, c.1910, 48 x 36 In.	500
Cabinet, Mahogany, Rectangular Top, 22 Drawers, Knob Handle, 45 1/2 x 35 x 12 In. ... *illus*	1150
Cabinet, Oak, Octagonal, 2 Layers, Revolving, 56 x 22 1/2 In.	4420
Furnace, Steeles, Electric, White, Columbus Dental Mfg. Co., 1920s, 12 x 6 1/2 x 9 In........	183
Teaching Model, Manikin, Metal, Stand, Square Base, Columbia Dentoform, New York, 1920s, 18 In.	704

DENVER

Denver is part of the mark on an American art pottery. William Long of Steubenville, Ohio, founded the Lonhuda Pottery Company in 1892. In 1900 he moved to Denver, Colorado, and organized the Denver China and

DENVER
C T &
P T Co

Denver, Pitcher, Lid, Pale Green Glaze, Mottled, Brown Ground, 5 3/4 x 4 1/2 In.
$210

Ruby Lane

Depression Glass, American Sweetheart, Bowl, Monax, 8 3/4 In.
$59

saffronsmile on eBay

Depression Glass, Mayfair Open Rose, Candy Dish, Lid, Pink, Footed, 9 In.
$30

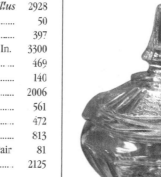

Homestead Auctions

This is an edited listing of current prices. Visit **Kovels.com** to check thousands of prices from previous years and sign up for free information on trends, tips, reproductions, marks, and more.

DENVER

Pottery Company. This pottery, which used the mark Denver, worked until 1905, when Long moved to New Jersey and founded the Clifton Pottery. Long also worked for Weller Pottery, Roseville Pottery, and American Encaustic Tiling Company. Do not confuse this pottery with the Denver White Pottery, which worked from 1894 to 1955 in Denver.

Pitcher, Lid, Pale Green Glaze, Mottled, Brown Ground, 4¾ x 4½ In. .... *illus* 210
Vase, Light Blue Matte, White Lace Band Around Shoulder, 5 x 4 In. 48

DEPRESSION GLASS

Depression glass is an inexpensive glass that was manufactured in large quantities during the 1920s and early 1930s. It was made in many colors and patterns by dozens of factories in the United States. Most patterns were also made in clear glass, which the factories called *crystal.* If no color is listed here, it is clear. The name *Depression glass* is a modern one and also refers to machine-made glass of the 1940s through 1970s. Sets missing a few pieces can be completed through the help of a matching service.

1700 Line, Sugar, Royal Ruby, Open, Anchor Hocking, c.1940, 2¾ x 3¼ In. 13
Adam, Grill Plate, Green, Divided, 3 Sections, Jeannette, 1930s, 9¼ In., 6 Piece 42
American Sweetheart, Bowl, Monax, 8¾ In. .... *illus* 59
American Sweetheart, Sherbet, Clear, Metal Holder, Cone Shape Foot, Macbeth-Evans, 3⅝ x 4 In. . 8
American Sweetheart, Soup, Cream, Monax, 2 Handles, Macbeth-Evans, 2 x 5 In. 46
Balda, Plate, Luncheon, Orchid, Central Glass Works, 1930s, 8½ In. 25
Balda, Sherbet, Tall, Pink, Clear Bowl, Twisted Stem, Central Glass Works, c.1940, 5½ In. ... 37
Balda, Tray, Serving, Amber, Etched, Round, Central Glass Works, 1930s, 14½ In. 34
Bamboo Optic, Cup, Pink, Liberty Works, 1920s, 2½ x 3¼ In., 4 Piece 33
Block Optic, Butter, Cover, Green, Anchor Hocking, c.1930, 4 x 7 x 4 In. 66
Bubble, Bowl, Jade-Ite, Anchor Hocking, 2 x 8½ In. 40
Bubble, Bowl, Vegetable, Milk White, Round, Anchor Hocking, 8 In. 12
Bubble, Saucer, Forest Green, 5¾ In. 6
Cameo, Pitcher, Hocking, 10 In. 68
Colonial, Tumbler, Clear, Footed, Anchor Hocking, 3 Oz., 3¼ In. 6
Cubist, Custard Cup, Clear, Deep, Jeannette, 2½ x 4½ In. 6
Delphite, Relish, Blue, 3 Sections, Flower Shape, Leaf Handle, Jeannette, 7 x 6 In. 15
Diana, Bowl, Console, Clear, Round, Scalloped Edge, Federal, 12¼ In. 12
Doric & Pansy, Cake Plate, Ultramarine, 2 Handles, Jeannette, 9 In. 9
Doric, Butter, Pink, Rectangular, Tab Handles, Jeannette, 9 x 3 In. 10
Doric, Pitcher, Pink, Footed, Jeannette, 48 Oz., 7 In. 700
Fire-King, Butter, Clear Cover, Jade-Ite Base, Rectangular, Tab Handles, Anchor Hocking, 6⅞ In. . 165
Fire-King, Mixing Bowl, 4 Colors, White Interior, Graduated, 9 To 6 In., Set of 4 100
Fire-King, Vase, Deco, Yellow, Fired-On Color, 5¼ x 3¼ In. 28
Floral, Bowl, Poinsettia, Green, Jeannette, 2¾ x 7½ In. 22
Fruits, Cup & Saucer, Green, Hazel-Atlas, 4 Piece 18
Iris, Champagne, Frosted, Jeannette, 4 In. 8
Jubilee, Cake Plate, Side Handles, Topaz, Lancaster Glass, 13 In. 20
Madrid, Saltshaker, Blue, Metal Lid, Footed, Federal, 3½ In. 100
Mayfair Open Rose, Candy Dish, Lid, Pink, Footed, 9 In. .... *illus* 30
Mayfair Open Rose, Celery Dish, Oval, Tab Handles, Pink, 11¼ x 5⅝ In. 5
Mayfair Open Rose, Sandwich Server, Center Handle, Blue, Hocking, 11⅞ In. 40
Miss America, Saltshaker, Green, Metal Lid, Footed, Anchor Hocking, 4⅛ In. 240
Moderntone Platonite, Berry Bowl, Red, Blue, Yellow, Green, Rimmed, Hazel-Atlas, 5 In., 4 Piece 20
Moderntone, Tumbler, Juice, Amethyst, Transparent, Hazel-Atlas, 3¾ In. 65
No. 615, Creamer, Square, Footed, Yellow, Indiana Glass, 4½ In. 7
Old Cafe, Olive Dish, Oblong, Scrolled Handles, Pink, 6 In. 7
Old Colony, Cookie Jar, Lid, Pink, Hocking, 1935-38, 7¼ x 6¼ In. 10
Patrick, Tumbler, Topaz, Footed, Lancaster, 8 Oz. 5⅞ x 2⅞ In. 80
Petalware, Plate, Luncheon, Monax, Pastel Bands, 8 In. 31
Princess, Cookie Jar, Lid, Green, 7½ x 6 In. .... *illus* 24

Depression Glass, Princess, Cookie Jar, Lid, Green, 7½ x 6 In.
$24

Homestead Auctions

Mayfair Open Rose
Mayfair Open Rose was made by Hocking Glass Company from 1931 to 1937. It was made primarily in light blue and pink, with a few green and yellow pieces. Crystal examples are rare. The cookie jar and the whiskey glass have been reproduced since 1982.

Depression Glass, Rosemary, Grill Plate, Amber, Federal Glass, 9½ In.
$20

Ruby Lane

Dick Tracy, Game, Stand-Up Target, Multicolor, Dart Gun, 2 Suction Cup Darts, Box, Marx, 1951, 10 In.
$177

Stony Ridge Auction

Ripple, Plate, Platonite, Pink Ruffled Rim, Hazel-Atlas, 1930s, 9 In.	31
Rose Cameo, Tumbler, Green, Cone Shape, Footed, Belmont Tumbler Co., 5⅛ In., 3 Piece	13
Rosemary, Grill Plate, Amber, Federal Glass, 9½ In. .... *illus*	20
Sandwich, Decanter, Amber, Stopper, Indiana Glass, 10½ In.	150
Sportsman Series, Ice Bucket, Sailboat, Cobalt Blue, White Enamel, Hazel-Atlas, 1930s, 4¼ x 4⅝ In.	45
Swirl, Refrigerator Dish, Lid, Ultramarine, Round, Jeannette, 70 Oz., 7½ In.	35
Thistle, Cup & Saucer, Pink, Macbeth-Evans, Set Of 4	6

DERBY, *see Royal Crown Derby category.*

DICK TRACY

Dick Tracy, the comic strip, started in 1931. Tracy was also the hero of movies from 1937 to 1947 and again in 1990, and starred in a radio series in the 1940s and a television series in the 1950s. Memorabilia from all these activities are collected.

Comic Art, Sketch, Pencil On Board, Signed, Chester Gould, Frame, 16 x 14 In.	407
Comic Art, Strip, 4 Panels, Ink On Paper, Chester Gould, Frame, 1955, 9 x 20½ In.	554
Comic Book, No. 27, Flattop Escapes Prison, Harvey Comics	44
Comic Book, No. 49, Chester Gould, Harvey Comics	313
Game, Stand-Up Target, Multicolor, Dart Gun, 2 Suction Cup Darts, Box, Marx, 1951, 10 In. *illus*	177
Poster, Movie, Vs. Crime Inc., Chapter 1, The Fatal Hour, Linen Back, 1 Sheet, 42 x 27 In.	150
Suspenders, Dick Tracy Junior, Braces For Smart Boys & Girls, On Card, Deluxe, 1950s	59
Toy, Car, Sparkling Riot Car, Blue, Yellow, Faces, Windows, Siren, Tin Litho, Friction, Marx, Box, 6 In.	175
Toy, Click Gun, Dick Tracy Jr., Black, Tin Lithograph, Box, Marx, 4 In.	75
Toy, Squad Car No. 1, Green, Characters In Windows, Tin Lithograph, Wood Wheels, 6¾ In.	138
Toy, Squad Car No. 1, Green, Yellow Lettering, Faces In Windows, Tin, Windup, Marx, 1949, 11 In.	156
Toy, Squad Car, Police, Blue, Tin, Friction, Marx, 6 In.	115
Wristwatch, AM Radio, Blue Band, Integrated Circuit, Earpiece, Creative Creations, Japan, Box, 1975.	88

DICKENS WARE *pieces are listed in the Royal Doulton and Weller categories.*

DINNERWARE

Dinnerware used in the United States from the 1930s through the 1950s is listed here. Most was made in potteries in southern Ohio, West Virginia, and California. A few patterns were made in Japan, England, and other countries. Dishes were sold in gift shops and department stores, or were given away as premiums. Many of these patterns are listed in this book in their own categories, such as Autumn Leaf, Azalea, Coors, Fiesta, Franciscan, Hall, Harker, Harlequin, Red Wing, Riviera, Russel Wright, Vernon Kilns, Watt, and Willow. For more prices, go to kovels.com. Sets missing a few pieces can be completed through the help of a matching service. Three examples of dated dinnerware marks are shown here.

W.S. George Pottery Co. Late 1930s–1940	Royal China Co. 1950s+	Salem China Co. 1940s–1960

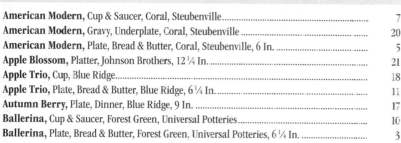

American Modern, Cup & Saucer, Coral, Steubenville	7
American Modern, Gravy, Underplate, Coral, Steubenville	20
American Modern, Plate, Bread & Butter, Coral, Steubenville, 6 In.	5
Apple Blossom, Platter, Johnson Brothers, 12¼ In.	21
Apple Trio, Cup, Blue Ridge	18
Apple Trio, Plate, Bread & Butter, Blue Ridge, 6¼ In.	11
Autumn Berry, Plate, Dinner, Blue Ridge, 9 In.	17
Ballerina, Cup & Saucer, Forest Green, Universal Potteries	10
Ballerina, Plate, Bread & Butter, Forest Green, Universal Potteries, 6¼ In.	3

D

Dinnerware, Barnyard King, Plate, Dinner, Turkey, Johnson Brothers, 10¾ In.
$41

Ruby Lane

Dionne Quintuplets, Doll, Madame Alexander, Composition, Sleep Eyes, Human Hair Wig, Name Pin, 12 In., 5 Piece
$420

Apple Tree Auction Center

Dirk Van Erp, Trivet, Round, Copper, Tile, Blue Ground, Flower Basket, California Faience, c.1920, 5¼ In.
$1,750

Rago Arts and Auction Center

Disneyana, Doll, Mickey Mouse, Felt Ears, Corduroy Pants, Velvet Tail, Novelty Co., c.1940, 21 In.

$117

Jeffrey S. Evans & Associates

White Gloves for Mickey

Mickey Mouse first appeared in 1928. He had black hands and no fingers. In about 1929, he was given white gloves because they were easier to draw and they stood out against his black body.

Disneyana, Figure, Minnie Mouse, Cloth, Original Hang Tag, Dean's Rag Book Co., 8 ¼ In.

$300

Pook & Pook

Bamboo, Plate, Bread & Butter, Harmony House, 6 ¼ In.		8
Barnyard King, Plate, Dinner, Turkey, Johnson Brothers, 10 ¾ In.	*illus*	41
Bellamy, Plate, Salad, Mikasa, 7 ½ In.		21
Blossom Time, Cup & Saucer, Royal Albert		32
Blossom Time, Plate, Dessert, Royal Albert, 7 In.		17
Blue Daisies, Bowl, Vegetable, Mikasa, 9 ¾ In.		25
Blue Daisies, Plate, Dinner, Mikasa, 10 ¾ In.		20
Blue Daisies, Plate, Salad, Mikasa, 8 In.		11
Blue Nordic, Plate, Dinner, Johnson Brothers, 9 ¾ In.		24
Bluebird, Platter, Oval, Salem, 13 ½ x 10 In.		19
Boutonniere, Cup & Saucer, Taylor, Smith & Taylor		5
Boutonniere, Plate, Bread & Butter, Taylor, Smith & Taylor, 6 ¾ In.		4
Boutonniere, Plate, Dinner, Taylor, Smith & Taylor, 10 ¼ In.		7
Carol's Roses, Platter, Round, Blue Ridge, 11 In.		65
Cherry, Plate, Dinner, Harmony House, 10 In.		15
Clarence, Bowl, Vegetable, Oval, Royal Albert, 10 In.		62
Continental, Bowl, Soup, Mikasa, 8 In.		12
Country Charm, Bowl, Cereal, Royal China, 6 ¾ In.		5
Country Charm, Plate, Dinner, Royal China, 10 In.		10
Country Charm, Saucer, Royal China		2
Country Sage, Bowl, Cereal, Homer Laughlin, 6 ¼ In.		5
Country Sage, Cup & Saucer, Homer Laughlin		6
Country Sage, Dish, Butter, Cover, Homer Laughlin		18
Country Strawberry, Plate, Dinner, Homer Laughlin, 10 In.		12
Dairy Maid, Bowl, Fruit, Crooksville, 5 ⅜ In.		11
Dairy Maid, Cup & Saucer, Crooksville		21
Dairy Maid, Plate, Bread & Butter, Crooksville, 6 In.		10
Dazzleplate, Bread & Butter, Blue Ridge, 6 In.		8
Desert Sand, Plate, Bread & Butter, Johnson Brothers, 6 ½ In.		5
Desert Sand, Plate, Dinner, Johnson Brothers, 10 ½ In.		13
Desert Sand, Saucer, Johnson Brothers		3
Dogwood, Cup & Saucer, Royal Albert		28
Dresden, Plate, Imperial Blue, 10 In.		5
Falling Leaves, Gravy Boat, Blue Ridge		35
Falling Leaves, Platter, Blue Ridge, 13 In.		25
Falling Leaves, Platter, Royal China, 13 In.		20
Family Affair, Bowl, Fruit, Steubenville, 5 In.		7
Family Affair, Plate, Bread & Butter, Steubenville, 6 ¼ In.		6
Flower Fest, Plate, Dinner, Mikasa, 10 ¾ In.		13
Fruit Fantasy, Saucer, Blue Ridge		4
Garland, Cup & Saucer, Impromptu Line, Iroquois China, Ben Seibel		8
Golden Apple, Plate, Dinner, Johnson Brothers, 10 In.		16
Golden Wheat, Bowl, Fruit, Homer Laughlin, 5 In.		4
Golden Wheat, Plate, Bread & Butter, Homer Laughlin, 6 In.		4
Golden Wheat, Plate, Salad, Homer Laughlin, 7 In.		5
Golden Willow, Cup & Saucer, Crooksville		9
Golden Willow, Plate, Bread & Butter, Crooksville		7
Granite, Bowl, Vegetable, Taylor, Smith & Taylor, 9 In.		10
Greendawn, Bowl, Vegetable, Johnson Brothers, 8 ¼ In.		21
Greendawn, Cup & Saucer, Johnson Brothers		8
Greendawn, Gravy Boat, Footed, Johnson Brothers		25
Greendawn, Plate, Bread & Butter, Johnson Brothers, 6 In.		6
Harvest Time, Creamer, Ben Seibel, Iroquois China, 6 In.		14
Harvest, Platter, Serving, Octagonal, Rounded Corners, Steubenville, 11 x 8 ¼ In.		10
Heritage Hall, Plate, Bread & Butter, Johnson Brothers, 6 ¾ In.		8
Heritage Hall, Plate, Dinner, Johnson Brothers, 9 ¾ In.		16
Indian Tree, Bowl, Cereal, Johnson Brothers, 6 In.		12
Indian Tree, Cup & Saucer, Johnson Brothers		10
Indian Tree, Platter, Johnson Brothers, 12 ¼ In.		24
Ivy Lea, Cup & Saucer, Royal Albert		25

Just Flowers, Cup & Saucer, Mikasa	15
Kate, Creamer, Blue Ridge	14
Kate, Cup & Saucer, Blue Ridge	21
Lavender Rose, Cup & Saucer, Royal Albert	30
Lavender Rose, Plate, Bread & Butter, Royal Albert, 6 3/8 In.	12
Lavender Rose, Sugar, Lid, Footed, Royal Albert	80
Lazy Daisy, Dish, Vegetable, Lid, Taylor, Smith & Taylor, 2 1/2 Qt.	45
Lazy Daisy, Plate, Dinner, Taylor, Smith & Taylor, 10 5/8 In.	12
Mainstreet, Plate, Dinner, Peach, Harmony House, 10 In.	12
Mexicana, Baking Dish, Homer Laughlin, 9 1/2 In.	42
Morning Light, Creamer, Pfaltzgraff, 4 1/2 In.	15
Mt. Vernon, Bowl, Vegetable, Lid, Harmony House	72
Mt. Vernon, Gravy Boat, Footed, Harmony House	25
Naturewood, Plate, Dinner, Pfaltzgraff, 9 3/4 In.	14
Old Country Roses, Mug, Flat Ribbed, Royal Albert, 3 3/4 In.	22
Oven Serve, Serving Bowl, Yellow, Green Flowers, Homer Laughlin, 8 x 5 1/2 In.	9
Petunias, Bowl, Soup, Mikasa, 8 1/2 In.	8
Poppy, Cup & Saucer, Harmony House	17
Quaker Apple, Bowl, Cereal, Blue Ridge, 6 In.	12
Quaker Apple, Plate, Bread & Butter, Blue Ridge, 6 In.	10
Rocky Plaid, Plate, Bread & Butter, Blue Ridge, 6 In.	6
Skytone, Cup & Saucer, Homer Laughlin	12
Sophisticate, Plate, Bread & Butter, Mikasa, 6 3/4 In.	6
Sophisticate, Plate, Salad, Mikasa, 7 1/2 In.	7
Sweet Pea, Bowl, Cereal, Blue Ridge, 7 In.	12
Sweet Pea, Plate, Dinner, Blue Ridge, 10 In.	22
Symphony, Plate, Dinner, Harmony House, 10 In.	12
The Old Mill, Charger, Johnson Brothers, 11 3/8 In.	24
Trend, Gravy, Underplate, Steubenville	15
Tulip Eggshell Nautilus, Bowl, Vegetable, Homer Laughlin, 8 In.	27
Tulip Eggshell Nautilus, Cup & Saucer, Homer Laughlin	11
Tulip Eggshell Nautilus, Plate, Bread & Butter, Homer Laughlin, 6 In.	5
Tulip Eggshell Nautilus, Plate, Dinner, Homer Laughlin, 9 7/8 In.	8
Tulip Eggshell Nautilus, Platter, Homer Laughlin, 13 In.	30
Village, Bowl, Vegetable, Oval, Tab Handles, Pfaltzgraff, 9 1/2 In.	15
Village, Butter, Cover, Pfaltzgraff	15
Village, Plate, Dinner, Pfaltzgraff, 10 3/8 In.	6
Village, Relish, 3 Sections, Pfaltzgraff, 12 In.	15
Village, Salt & Pepper, Pfaltzgraff	10
Wild Strawberry, Plate, Dinner, Blue Ridge, 10 1/4 In.	12
Woodfield, Console, Golden Fawn, Asymmetrical, Steubenville, 12 In.	40
Yellow Nocturne, Platter, Blue Ridge, 11 7/8 In.	25
Yorktowne, Bread Basket, Pfaltzgraff, 12 1/2 In.	12
Yorktowne, Butter, Cover, Pfaltzgraff	21
Yorktowne, Cup & Saucer, Pfaltzgraff	5
Yorktowne, Plate, Dinner, Pfaltzgraff, 10 1/4 In.	10

DIONNE QUINTUPLETS

Dionne quintuplets were born in Canada on May 28, 1934. The publicity about their birth and their special status as wards of the Canadian government made them famous throughout the world. Visitors could watch the girls play; reporters interviewed the girls and the staff. Thousands of special dolls and souvenirs were made picturing the quints at different ages. Emilie died in 1954, Marie in 1970, Yvonne in 2001. Annette and Cecile still live in Canada.

Doll Set, Composition, Molded & Painted Features, Bibs, c.1937, 8 In., 5 Piece	450
Doll, Madame Alexander, Composition, Sleep Eyes, Human Hair Wig, Name Pin, 12 In., 5 Piece ...*illus*	420
Toy, Furniture, Crib, Playpen, Scooter, Highchair, Play Chair, Wood, Painted, Fits 8-In. Dolls	196

Disneyana, Tape Measure, Minnie Mouse, Figural, Retracting Tape, England, 4 x 2 x 2 In.
$338

Morphy Auctions

Disneyana, Toy, Disneyland, Ferris Wheel, Windup, 6 Gondolas, Mickey, Donald, Chein, c.1950, 16 x 10 In.
$492

Rich Penn Auctions

Disneyana, Toy, Goofy, Cyclist, Tin Lithograph, Windup, Key Wind, Bell, Linemar, 7 x 5 In.
$984

Rich Penn Auctions

Disneyana, Toy, Mickey Mouse, Riding Horse, Jumps Up & Down, Windup, Japan, 4 x 6 x 3 In.
$1,140

Morphy Auctions

Disneyana, Wristwatch, Mickey Mouse, 1st Version, Ingersoll, Box, Century Of Progress, 1933
$11,422

Hake's Auctions

Doll, Bruno Schmidt, Bisque Head, Human Hair, Glass Eyes, Wood, Jointed, Peach Dress, 23 In.
$98

Apple Tree Auction Center

DIRK VAN ERP

Dirk Van Erp was born in 1860 and died in 1933. He opened his own studio in 1908 in Oakland, California. He moved his studio to San Francisco in 1909 and the studio remained under the direction of his son until 1977. Van Erp made hammered copper accessories, including vases, desk sets, bookends, candlesticks, jardinieres, and trays, but he is best known for his lamps. The hammered copper lamps often had shades with mica panels.

Bowl, Brass, Straight Sides, Rim, Hallmarks, 2 3/4 x 9 3/4 In.	352
Bowl, Copper, Hammered, Segmented Rim, Joined Brass Rings Foot, Early 1900s, 5 x 10 1/2 In.	375
Bowl, Fruit, Brass, Hammered, Open Box Mark, 11 In.	339
Cigarette Box, Hinged Lid, Rectangular, 3 Sections, Brass, Stamped, 11 In.	63
Fire Screen, Hammered Copper, 2 Airplanes, Flight Path, Center Propeller, 1939, 44 1/2 x 45 In.	9600
Tray, Silvered Metal, Rectangular, Scalloped Edge, 4 Ball Feet, Hand Wrought, 17 1/4 x 11 5/8 In.	420
Trivet, Round, Copper, Tile, Blue Ground, Flower Basket, California Faience, c.1920, 5 1/4 In. *illus*	1750

DISNEYANA

Disneyana is a collectors' term. Walt Disney and his company introduced many comic characters to the world. Mickey Mouse first appeared in the short film *Steamboat Willie* in 1928. Collectors search for examples of the work of the Disney Studios and the many commercial products modeled after his characters, including Mickey Mouse and Donald Duck, and well-known films, like *Beauty and the Beast, The Little Mermaid*, the *Toy Story* series, and *Frozen.*

Bank, Mickey & Minnie Mouse, Post Office, Tin, Happynak Series, 6 x 2 3/4 x 2 3/4 In.	270
Cane, Mickey Mouse Handle, Fun-E-Flex Body, Orange Shaft, Geo. Borgfeldt, c.1930, 34 In.	199
Cel, see Animation Art category.	
Doll, Mickey Mouse, Felt Ears, Corduroy Pants, Velvet Tail, Novelty Co., c.1940, 21 In. ... *illus*	117
Figure, Minnie Mouse, Cloth, Original Hang Tag, Dean's Rag Book Co., 8 1/4 In. *illus*	300
Game, Mickey Mouse Scatter Ball, Character Images, 2 Piece Box, 1930, 11 x 11 In.	155
Lantern, Tinker Bell, Hanging, Pixie In Peril, Peter Pan, 10 1/2 x 5 1/4 In.	58
Pin, Mickey Mouse, Walking, Trembler, Spring Mounted Hand Waves, Goldtone, Marked, 2 In.	40
Sculpture, Fantasia, Magical Fairy, Octagonal Shape, Artist's Proof, 4 x 5 1/2 In.	35
Shovel, Snow, Mickey & Pluto, Shoveling, Building Snowman, Decal, c.1950, 26 In.	144
Snow Globe, Tinker Bell, Peter Pan, Musical, Painted, Light-Up, 7 1/2 x 7 In.	35
Tape Measure, Minnie Mouse, Figural, Retracting Tape, England, 4 x 2 x 2 In. *illus*	338
Toy, Car, Dipsy, Mickey Mouse, Tin Lithograph, Windup, Marx, Box, 5 1/2 In.	336
Toy, Disneyland, Ferris Wheel, Windup, 6 Gondolas, Mickey, Donald, Chein, c.1950, 16 x 10 In. *illus*	492
Toy, Goofy, Cyclist, Tin Lithograph, Windup, Key Wind, Bell, Linemar, 7 x 5 In. *illus*	984
Toy, Mickey & Minnie Mouse, Handcar, Tin Lithograph, Windup, Lionel, Box, 8 In.	915
Toy, Mickey Mouse, Dipsy Car, Tin Lithograph, Windup, Marx, Box, 5 1/2 In.	336
Toy, Mickey Mouse, Nifty Jazz Drummer, Tin Litho, Spring Plunger, Germany, 1930s, 7 In.	840
Toy, Mickey Mouse, Race Car, Litho Frame, Yellow, Rubber Wheels, Lindstrom, 1936, 1 3/4 x 4 In.	264
Toy, Mickey Mouse, Riding Horse, Jumps Up & Down, Windup, Japan, 4 x 6 x 3 In. *illus*	1140
Toy, Pluto, Musical, Horn In Mouth, Bell & Cane, Tin Lithograph, Linemar, Japan, 6 x 3 In.	130
Toy, Pluto, Stretchy, Tin Lithograph, Mechanical, Linemar, Box, 7 x 4 In.	480
Treasure Box, Heart Shape, Tinker Bell, Gilt, Disney Showcase, Lenox, 6 3/4 In.	46
Wristwatch, Mickey Mouse, 1st Version, Ingersoll, Box, Century Of Progress, 1933 *illus*	11422

DOCTOR, *see Dental and Medical categories.*

DOLL

Doll entries are listed by marks printed or incised on the doll, if possible. If there are no marks, the doll is listed by the name of the subject or country or maker. Notice that Barbie is listed under Mattel. G.I. Joe figures are listed in the Toy section. Eskimo dolls are listed in the Eskimo section and Indian dolls are listed in the Indian section. Doll clothes and accessories are listed at the end of this section. The twentieth-century clothes listed here are in mint condition.

A.M., Floradora, Bisque Socket Head, Sleep Eyes, Jointed Composition, Lace Pinafore, 24 In.	111

Doll, Handwerck, 109, Bisque Socket Head, Blue Eyes, Brown Hair, Composition, c.1900, 30 In.
$164

Doll, Heubach, 310, Bisque, Glass Sleep Eyes, Mohair Wig, Jointed Kid Body, Early 1900s, 11 In.
$1,250

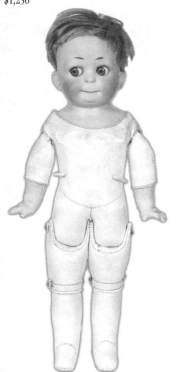

Doll, Jumeau, Bisque Socket Head, Blue Sleep Eyes, Blond Hair, Bebe, 1880s, 21 ¼ In.
$211

Doll, Kestner, Bisque Head, Mohair Wig, Glass Eyes, Burgundy Skirt, Jacket, Fur Hat, 22 In.
$369

Doll, Kestner, China Shoulder Head, Blue Eyes, Cloth Body, Leather Arms, 1850s, 30 In.
$556

Doll, Madame Alexander, Indian Boy, Brown Skin, Bent-Knee Body, Beaded Costume, 1961, 8 In.
$115

Doll, Madame Alexander, Margot, Ballerina, Plastic, Brunette Hair, Teal Tutu, Tag, 1953, 15 In.
$517

SELECTED DOLL MARKS WITH DATES USED

Effanbee Doll Co.
1922+
New York, N.Y.

Lenci
1922+
Turin, Italy

Hertwig & Co.
1864–c.1940
Katzhütte, Thuringia, Germany

K ☆ R
39

Kämmer & Rheinhardt
1886–1932
Waltershausen, Thüringia, Germany

J.D. Kestner Jr.
1805–1938
Waltershausen, Thuringia, Germany

IDEAL

Ideal Novelty & Toy Co.
1961
New York, N.Y.

L.A.& S.

Louis Amberg & Son
1909–1930
Cincinnati, Ohio; New York, N.Y.

BRU. J^{NE} R
11

Bru Jne. & Cie
c.1879–1899
Paris, France

Armand Marseille
c.1920
Köppelsdorf, Thüringia, Germany

DÉPOSE
TÊTE JUMEAU
ᴗ

Maison Jumeau
1886–1899
Paris, France

Bähr & Pröschild
1871–1930s
Ohrdruf, Thüringia, Germany

DÉPOSE
S.F.B.J.

S.F.B.J. (Société Française de Fabrication de
Bébés & Jouets)
1905–1950+
Paris and Montreuil-sous-Bois, France

ALBEGO
10
Made in Germany

Alt. Beck & Gottschalck
1930–1940
Nauendorf, Thuringia, Germany

Schoenau & Hoffmeister
1901–c.1953
Sonneberg, Thuringia, Germany

Gebruder Heubach
1840–1938
Lichte, Thuringia, Germany

A.M., Our Pet, Boy, Bisque Socket Head, Sleep Eyes, Mohair, Composition Body, Monkey, 11 In.	160

Alexander dolls are listed in this category under Madame Alexander.

Alt Beck & Gottschalck, Bisque Head, Human Hair, Glass Sleep Eyes, Jointed, Dress, 24 In.	135
American Miniature, Toni, Cheerleader, Vinyl Head, Auburn Hair, Plastic Body, Box, 10 In.	123

Armand Marseille dolls are listed in this category under A.M.

Automaton, Girl, Picnic Basket, Bisque, Music Box Inside, France, 16 In.	1792
Babyland Rag, Girl, Cloth, Face Printed On Silk, Painted Features, Stitch-Jointed, Dress, 14 In.	221

Barbie dolls are listed in this category under Mattel, Barbie.

Bergmann, Bisque Head, Open Mouth, Teeth, Pierced Ears, Jointed Composition, 29 In.	138
Bing, Cloth, Molded & Painted, Mohair Braids, Cloth Body, Green Dress, White Shoes, 10½ In.	49
Brooke Shields, World's Most Glamorous, Plastic, Posable, Outfits, LJN Toys, Box, 1982	50
Bruckner, Topsyturvy, Cloth, Black & White Mask Faces, Painted Features, Mohair, 13 In.	86
Bruno Schmidt, Bisque Head, Human Hair, Glass Eyes, Wood, Jointed, Peach Dress, 23 In *illus*	98
Chad Valley, Felt, Cloth, Painted, Side-Glancing Eyes, Red Curly Mohair Wig, Yellow Coat, 14 In.	185
China Head, Beaded Cloth Costume, Inscribed By Giver, England, 1845, 11 In.	2375
Cloth, Oil Painted Features, Stitch-Jointed Body, Navy & White Checked Dress, 14 In.	43
Cosmopolitan, Little Miss Ginger, Vinyl, Rooted Hair, Sleep Eyes, Hat, Shoes, Box, 8 In.	111
Door Of Hope, Asian Boy, Wood, Carved & Painted, Cloth Body, Original Costume, 9 In.	338
Door Of Hope, Asian Man, Wood, Human Hair Queue, Cloth Body, Original Costume, 11 In.	308
Door Of Hope, Asian Woman, Wood, Carved Chignon, Gold Clip, Original Costume, 11 In.	308
Effanbee, Honey, Plastic, Blond Hair, Bangs, Sleep Eyes, Party Dress, Shoes, Bows, 1951, 18 In.	374
Effanbee, Patsy Joan, Composition, Molded Hair, Painted Features, Check Skirt, Sweater, 16 In.	49
Effanbee, Patsy Lou, Composition, Green Sleep Eyes, Painted Red Hair, Dress, Bonnet, 1930s, 22 In.	192
Effanbee, Patsy, Composition, Blue Jumper, Cardboard Trunk, Outfits, 13 In.	111
Farnell, King George VI, Felt, Painted, Stuffed Cloth, Crown, Velvet & Faux Fur Cape, Tag, 15 In.	308
Fashion, Bisque Swivel Head, Brunette Mohair Curls, Jointed Wood, Wool Suit, Boots, 15 In.	3000
Fashion, Bisque, Shoulder Head, Blue Eyes, Blond Hair, France, 1850s, 13 In.	187
French, Bisque Head, Glass Eyes, Blond Mohair, Kid Body, Dress, Hat, Dog On Leash, 16 In.	1008

G.I. Joe figures are listed in the Toy category.

Gebruder Heubach dolls may also be listed in this category under Heubach.

German, Bisque Head, Blue Googly Eyes, Mohair Curls, Jointed Papier-Mache Toddler Body, 15 In.	2700
German, Bisque Head, Side-Glancing Googly Eyes, Composition Body, Clown Suit, 8 In.	338
German, Bisque Head, Sleep Eyes, Blond Hair, Open Mouth, Composition, Period Dress, 24 In.	150
German, Bisque, Blond Mohair Bob, Googly Eyes, Papier-Mache Body, Blue Dress, 12 In.	840
German, Bisque, Mohair Wig, Glass Eyes, Jointed, Folk Costume, 3½ In.	98
German, Lady & Gentleman, Bisque, Shoulder Head, Mohair Wig, Cloth Body, 7 In., Pair	360
German, Parian Shoulder Head, Painted Blond Braid, Blue Eyes, Cloth Body, Red Gown, 19 In.	360

Half-Dolls are listed in the Pincushion Doll category.

Handwerck, 109, Bisque Socket Head, Blue Eyes, Brown Hair, Composition, c.1900, 30 In. *illus*	164
Hasbro, Little Miss No Name, Round Eyes, Sad Mouth, Patched Burlap Dress, 1965, 15 In.	135
Heubach, 310, Bisque, Glass Sleep Eyes, Mohair Wig, Jointed Kid Body, Early 1900s, 11 In. *illus*	1250
Heubach, 7246, Bisque Head, Pouty Face, Brown Human Hair Bob, Composition & Wood, 19 In.	584
Heubach, Bisque Shoulder Head, Molded & Painted Face, Intaglio Eyes, Kid Body, Pink Dress, 13 In.	197
Huret, Fashion, China Head, Blue Eyes, Human Hair, Leather Over Wood Body, Silk Dress, 17 In.	6000
Ideal, Little Miss Revlon, Vinyl, Blond Updo, Evening Gown, Stockings, High Heels, c.1958, 10 In.	86
Ideal, Patti Playpal, Plastic, Straight Auburn Hair, Checked Dress, Pinafore, 1959, 35 In.	135
Ideal, Toni, Hard Plastic, Brown Nylon Curls, Blue Sleep Eyes, Red Corduroy Coatdress, 14 In.	43

Indian dolls are listed in the Indian category.

J.D.K., 257, Baby, Bisque Socket Head, Sleep Eyes, Mohair, Composition Body, Dress, 14½ In.	135

J.D.K. dolls are also listed in this category under Kestner.

Jane Zidjunas, Elise, Porcelain, Curly Hair, Lavender Costume, Purse, 22 In.	25
Jumeau, Bisque Head, Blue Eyes, Brown Curls, Jointed Papier-Mache, Organdy Dress, Bebe, 27 In.	6600
Jumeau, Bisque Socket Head, Blue Sleep Eyes, Blond Hair, Bebe, 1880s, 21¾ In. *illus*	211
Jumeau, Bisque Socket Head, Open Mouth, Blue Glass Eyes, Dark Brown Wig, 25½ In.	896
Jumeau, Girl With 2 Faces, Smiling, Screaming, Papier-Mache, Mohair, Wood, Says Mama, 18 In.	4920
K * R, Bisque Head, Glass Eyes, Jointed, Wood, Yellow Dress, 18 In.	196
Kathe Kruse, Boy & Girl, Hanne, Plastic, Painted, Human Hair, Cloth & Wire Body, Tags, 10 In., Pair	86
Kathe Kruse, Little German Child, Cloth Swivel Head, Painted, Mohair, Disc-Jointed, 14 In.	197
Kathe Redmond, British Nanny, Porcelain Head & Limbs, Mohair, Cloth, Dress, Hat, Bag, 13 In.	49

Doll, Madame Alexander, Polly Pigtails, Maggie Face, Red Braids, Pedal Pushers, Tam, 1952, 18 In.
$373

Theriault's

Doll, Madame Alexander, Wendy-Kins, Plastic, Brunette Hair, Bent-Knee Body, Jeans, 1956, 8 In.
$345

Theriault's

Doll, Mattel, Barbie, Color Magic, Scarlet Flame & Golden Blond Hair, Box, 1960s, 12 x 5 In.
$2,700

Morphy Auctions

Doll, Simon & Halbig, 949, Bisque Socket Head, Blue Eyes, Composition, Wood, Jointed, c.1888, 29 In. **$351**

Jeffrey S. Evans & Associates

Doll, Steiff, Policeman, Skating, Felt, Fat, Blue Uniform, Windup, 10¼ In. **$915**

Pook & Pook

Doll, Wood, Carved, Jointed, Blue Eyes, Closed Mouth, Brown & Cream Body, Black Head, 1800s, 15 In. **$105**

Jeffrey S. Evans & Associates

Kestner dolls are also in this category under J.D.K.

Kestner, Bisque Head, Mohair Wig, Glass Eyes, Burgundy Skirt, Jacket, Fur Hat, 22 In. *illus*	369
Kestner, China Shoulder Head, Blue Eyes, Cloth Body, Leather Arms, 1850s, 30 In. ..... *illus*	556

Kewpie dolls are listed in the Kewpie category.

Kley & Hahn, Walkure, Bisque Head, Open Mouth, Teeth, Jointed Composition Body, 30 In.	175
Lenci, 450, Girl, Felt, Pressed & Painted, Rooted Mohair Wig, Big Bow, Striped Dress, 13 In...	234
Lenci, Cupid, Felt, Painted Face, Knotted Hair, Costume With Hearts, Wings, Bow & Arrows, 8 In.	861
Lenci, Mozart, Felt, Pressed & Painted Features, Mohair Wig, Aqua Felt Coat, Tag, 14½ In. ..	861
Lewis Sorensen, Colonial Man, Wax, White Hair, Cloth Body, Period Clothes, 25½ In..........	55
Liberty Of London, King Henry VIII, Cloth, Full King Regalia, Cloth Label, 11½ In.	160
Luts, Ani, Girl Body, Big Green Glass Eyes, Black Hair, Ball-Jointed, Striped Leggings, Box, 17 In...	160
Madame Alexander, Cinderella, Plastic, Tosca Wig, Taffeta Gown, Crown, Rhinestones, 1955, 8 In.	920
Madame Alexander, Cissy, Blond Curls, Ice Blue Satin Gown, Rhinestones, Box, 1955, 20 In.	4830
Madame Alexander, Elaine, Plastic, Tosca Wig, Walking Body, Organdy Gown, Hat, 1954, 18 In.	1093
Madame Alexander, Indian Boy, Brown Skin, Bent-Knee Body, Beaded Costume, 1961, 8 In. *illus*	115
Madame Alexander, Lady, Rhinestone Beauty Mark, Plastic, Ash Blond, Satin Gown, 1951, 21 In.	5750
Madame Alexander, Lissy, Plastic, Blond Hair, Bangs, Yellow Dress, Pinafore, Shoes, 1956, 12 In.	431
Madame Alexander, Margaret, Ballerina, Coiled Braids, Tutu, Flowers, Tag, 1946, 14 In.....	600
Madame Alexander, Margaret, Bride, Plastic, Blond Mohair Curls, Tulle Gown, Veil, 1950, 21 In..	690
Madame Alexander, Margot, Ballerina, Plastic, Brunette Hair, Teal Tutu, Tag, 1953, 15 In. *illus*	517
Madame Alexander, Medici Bride, Auburn Curls, Lace, Pearls, Tulle Skirt, Cap, Veil, 1956, 20 In.	633
Madame Alexander, Polly Pigtails, Maggie Face, Red Braids, Pedal Pushers, Tam, 1952, 18 In. ..*illus*	373
Madame Alexander, Princess Margaret Rose, Plastic, Walking Body, Court Gown, 1953, 18 In.	1093
Madame Alexander, Sonja Henie, Skater, Madeline Head, Sleep Eyes, 1951, 18 In.................	70
Madame Alexander, Wendy, Garden Party, Titian Hair, Bent-Knee Body, Organdy Dress, 1956, 8 In.	345
Madame Alexander, Wendy-Kins, Plastic, Brunette Hair, Bent-Knee Body, Jeans, 1956, 8 In. *illus*	345
Maggie Iacono, Annie, Felt, Paint, Red Mohair Curls, Ball Joints, Dress, Embroidered Apron, 16 In...	431
Marx, Myra, Breakfast In Bed, Vinyl Head, Rooted Hair, Bed, Mattress, Bedding, 8½ In.......	209
Mary Hartline, Plastic, Red Dress, Holding Baton, White Boots, 16 In.....................................	62
Mattel, Barbie, Color Magic, Scarlet Flame & Golden Blond Hair, Box, 1960s, 12 x 5 In. *illus*	2700
Mattel, Francie, Plastic, Black Skin, Bathing Suit Outfit, No. 1100, 1967, 11¼ In.	475
Milliner's, Papier-Mache, Woman, Wearing Cap, Yellow Dress & Shawl, Late 1800s, 15 In.	780

Paper dolls are listed in their own category.

Pincushion dolls are listed in their own category.

Puppet, Folk Art, Wood, Carved, Painted, Tin Breastplate, Velvet Skirt, 1850s, 20 In.	351
Ravca, Old Peasant Man & Woman, Stockinet, Painted, Wooden Shoes, Walking Stick, 17 In., Pair	74
Schoenhut, Boy, Wood, Carved, Painted, Intaglio Eyes, Jointed, Suede Sherpa Costume, 14½ In.	438
Schoenhut, Child, Composition, Painted, Jointed, Blond Hair, Blush Cheek, White Dress, 17 In.	175
Schoenhut, Miss Dolly, Wood, Carved, Painted, Mohair Wig, Drop Waist Dress, 21½ In.........	308

Shirley Temple dolls are included in the Shirley Temple category.

Simon & Halbig, 949, Bisque Socket Head, Blue Eyes, Composition, Wood, Jointed, c.1888, 29 In. *illus*	351
Simon & Halbig, 1159, Bisque Socket Head, Brunette Mohair, Composition & Wood, Gown, 24 In.	677
Simon & Halbig, Bisque, Wood, Mohair Wig, Glass Eyes, Jointed, Print Cotton Dress, 24 In..	677
Steiff, Policeman, Skating, Felt, Fat, Blue Uniform, Windup, 10¼ In. .... *illus*	915
Steiner, Bisque Head, Blue Eyes, Brunette Mohair, Jointed Wood & Composition, Bebe, 25 In..	1088
Ventriloquist Dummy Head, Wood, Carved, Pegged, Stepped Base, Late 1800s, 7¼ In.	1140
Vogue, Ginny, Hard Plastic, Blond Mohair, Blue Eyes, 4 Costumes, Box, Tiny Miss, 1953, 7 In..	234
Vogue, Ginny, Miss 1910, Plastic, Mohair Wig, Brown Sleep Eyes, Dotted Swiss Dress, 1950, 8 In.	288
Vogue, Jan, Vinyl, Rooted Red Hair, Swivel Waist, Pink Dress, Tag, Box, c.1958, 10½ In.	49
Vogue, Marge, Ginny Series, Plastic, Auburn Wig, Dress, Faux Fur Coat, Tam, Muff, 1952, 8 In. ..	489
Wax, Over Composition, Shoulder Head, Flirty Side-Glancing Eyes, Blond Mohair, Dress, 16 In...	277
Wood, Carved, Jointed, Blue Eyes, Closed Mouth, Brown & Cream Body, Black Head, 1800s, 15 In. *illus*	105
WPA, Girl, Stockinet, Painted Features, Tab Jointed Limbs, Folk Dress, Milwaukee, 22 In.	172

DOLL CLOTHES

Cissy, Dress, Yellow Nylon, Flocked Bluebells, Lace, Straw Hat, Madame Alexander, Box, c.1956...	978
Dress, Full Skirt, Pink Stripes, Black Bodice, Black Trim, Flowers At Hem, Mary Hoyer, 1950s, 8½ In.	45
Gown, Red Taffeta, Cap Sleeves, Flared Skirt, Rhinestones, Madame Alexander, 1956............	863
Set, Boy's, Vest, Shorts, Hat, Scarf, White & Maroon, Fits 8-In. Doll.......................................	21

DONALD DUCK *items are included in the Disneyana category.*

DOORSTOPS

Doorstops have been made in all types of designs. The vast majority of the doorstops sold today are cast iron and were made from about 1890 to 1930. Most of them are shaped like people, animals, flowers, or ships. Reproductions and newly designed examples are sold in gift shops. These are three marks used by vintage doorstop makers.

Bradley & Hubbard
Manufacturing Co.
1854–1940

HUBLEY

Hubley Manufacturing Co.
1894–1965

WILTON PRODUCTS INC
WRIGHTSVILLE
PA.

Wilton Products, Inc.
c.1935–1989

Aunt Jemima, Standing, White Apron, Red Bandanna, Cast Iron, Littco, 7 ½ In.	1293
Boar, Standing, Cast Iron, Copper Finish, Ebersbach, 1900s, 4 In.	72
Buffalo Bill, Western, Flowers, Leaves, Oblong Base, Cast Iron, 12 ¼ x 10 ½ In.	154
Cat, Persian, Gray, Cast Iron, Hubley Foundry, Lancaster, Pa., c.1920, 9 ½ In.	236
Cat, Seated, Painted, Cast Iron, Black Ribbon, Early 1900s, 7 ½ In.	225
Cat, Seated, Scary Stare, Plinth, Bronze, 12 ½ In. *illus*	123
Charleston Dancers, Stylized Art Deco Man & Woman, Paint, Cast Iron, Hubley, 8 ¾ In.	310
Clown, 2-Sided, Molded Features, Rectangular Base, Cast Iron, Hubley, Early 1900s, 10 In.	500
Cow, Dairy, Black & White, Standing, Fence, Cast Iron, 8 ¼ In.	62
Cow, Standing, Painted, Black & White, Cast Iron, 10 ½ x 17 In.	43
Dapper Dan, Figural, Flat, Embossed, Wedge Style, Cast Iron, Judd Co., 8 ½ In. *illus*	540
Dog, Boston Terrier, Standing, Facing Right, Painted, Cast Iron, 10 ¼ x 9 ½ In.	109
Dog, Bull Terrier, Standing, Looking Up, Rubber Bumper, Cast Iron, c.1900, 9 ¾ In.	650
Dog, Bulldog, Standing, Facing Right, Cast Iron, Black & White Paint, 9 In.	46
Dog, French Bulldog, Black & White Paint, Cast Iron, 10 In.	62
Dog, French Bulldog, Glass, Jeweled Eyes, Dorflinger, 2 ½ x 2 ½ In.	150
Dog, Sealyham Terrier, Standing, Multicolor, Cast Iron, Hubley, c.1930, 9 x 13 In. *illus*	468
Dog, Spaniel, Seated, Column & Star On Base, Pottery, Rockingham Glaze, Ohio, 1800s, 12 In.	375
Dog, Terrier, Seated, Cast Iron, Hubley, 1920s, 7 x 6 x 2 In.	504
Drummer, Civil War, Confederate, Gray, White & Red Drum, Cast Iron, 8 In.	148
Duck, Painted, Cast Iron, 8 ½ In.	172
Dutch Boy, Bronze, Hands In Pockets, Standing, Cast Iron, 20 x 7 ½ In.	69
Flower, Purple Iris, Green Leaves, White Base, Cast Iron, Hubley, 10 ¾ In. *illus*	175
Fox, Sleeping, Painted, Black, Cast Iron, Late 1900s, 1 ½ x 7 In.	148
Frog, Green, Painted, Cast Iron, 6 In.	43
Frog, Seated, Cast Iron, c.1920, 5 In.	177
Frog, Standing, Holding White Tray, Painted, Cast Iron, 21 ½ In.	79
Fruit Basket, Handle, Variety Of Fruits, Painted, 12 In. *illus*	450
Gardener, Woman, Yellow Hat, White & Blue Clothes, Cast Iron, 12 ½ In.	90
Geese, Painted, Cast Iron, Fred Everett, Hubley, c.1930, 8 ¾ In.	204
Golfer, Standing, Multicolor, Green Base, Cast Iron, Hubley, Early 1900s, 10 ½ In.	313
Golfer, Swinging, Knickers & Jacket, Cap On Ground, Paint, Cast Iron, Hubley, c.1920, 10 In.	177
Goose, Head, Painted, Cast Iron, Marked, Clancey, Needham, 11 ¼ In.	86
Horse, Leaping, Man Riding, Folk Art, National Foundry, Early 1900s, 5 ½ In.	420
Horse, Standing, Black Paint, Cast Iron, Marked Hunter On Front, 1949, 10 ½ x 12 In.	236
Lion, Laurel Wreath, Tail Handle, Black, Cast Iron, 12 x 3 ¼ x 6 ½ In.	184
Little Red Riding Hood, Wolf, Nuydea, Embossed, Patented, 9 In. *illus*	420
Owl, Pedestal Base, Painted, Cast Iron, Signed, Bradley & Hubbard, Early 1900s, 15 ¾ In.	1250
Parrot, Multicolor, Painted, Perched, Green Base, Cast Iron, 14 In. *illus*	502
Parrot, Standing, Multicolor Paint, Square Base, Cast Iron, 6 ¾ In.	106
Penguin, Standing, Hollow Body, Black, White, Cast Iron, 10 x 5 In.	572
Rabbit, 2-Piece Construction, Full Figure, Seated, Painted, Cast Iron, 12 In.	468

Doorstop, Cat, Seated, Scary Stare, Plinth, Bronze, 12 ½ In.
$123

Hartzell's Auction Gallery Inc.

Doorstop, Dapper Dan, Figural, Flat, Embossed, Wedge Style, Cast Iron, Judd Co., 8 ½ In.
$540

Bertoia Auctions

Doorstop, Dog, Sealyham Terrier, Standing, Multicolor, Cast Iron, Hubley, c.1930, 9 x 13 In.
$468

Jeffrey S. Evans & Associates

DOORSTOP

Doorstop, Flower, Purple Iris, Green Leaves, White Base, Cast Iron, Hubley, 10¾ In.
$175

Pook & Pook

Doorstop, Fruit Basket, Handle, Variety Of Fruits, Painted, 12 In.
$450

Bertoia Auctions

Doorstop, Little Red Riding Hood, Wolf, Nuydea, Embossed, Patented, 9 In.
$420

Bertoia Auctions

Doorstop, Parrot, Multicolor, Painted, Perched, Green Base, Cast Iron, 14 In.
$502

Cottone Auctions

Doorstop, Sailor, Yellow, Dark Green, Black Base, Cast Iron, Littco, 11¼ In.
$1,050

Pook & Pook

Doulton, Bibelot, Match Stand, Lifebuoy, Man's Head, Saved, Stoneware, 1894, 3 x 4½ In.
$489

Lion and Unicorn

Doulton, Centerpiece, Aesthetic Movement, Sea Sprite, Shell, Glazed Vellum, Burslem, c.1895, 4 x 7 In.
$1,380

Lion and Unicorn

Doulton, Jardiniere, Children, Patent Silicon Chine Ware, Ada Dennis, 1885, 10 x 9 In.
$4,600

Lion and Unicorn

Doulton, Planter, Hexagonal, Stoneware, Birds, Flowers, Cobalt Blue, Brown, Signed, EW, 1900s, 8 x 7 In.
$92

Lion and Unicorn

Rabbit, Eating Cabbage, Wearing Sweater, Standing, Painted, Round Base, 1920, 8 In.	214
Rabbit, Sitting On Hind Legs, Brown, Leaves, Paint, Cast Iron, Bradley & Hubbard, 15 In.	1230
Rabbit, Wearing Hat, Green Domed Base, Cast Iron, Early 1900s, 10 In.	531
Sailor, Yellow, Dark Green, Black Base, Cast Iron, Littco, 11 1/4 In. *illus*	1050
Soldier, Standing, Painted, Red Shirt & Cap, Blue Pants, Cast Iron, c.1920, 11 3/4 In.	207
Toby, Standing, Tricorn Hat, Painted, Black & White, Cast Iron, Early 1900s, 15 In.	625
Turtle, Orange, Painted, Cast Iron, Marked, 7 1/2 In.	277
Turtle, Water, Spread Feet, Cast Iron, Wilton, 8 1/2 In.	188

DORCHESTER POTTERY

DORCHESTER
POTTERY WORKS
BOSTON, MASS.

Dorchester Pottery was founded by George Henderson in 1895 in Dorchester, Massachusetts. At first, the firm made utilitarian stoneware, but collectors are most interested in the line of decorated blue and white pottery that Dorchester made from 1940 until it went out of business in 1979. Even in the 1970s, automated machines were not used; pieces were hand-formed and hand-dipped, and handles were applied individually.

Bowl, Blueberries, White Ground, Blue Rim & Base, N. Ricci, C.A.H., 9 1/2 In.	32
Cup, Blueberry Spray, White, Blue Interior Signed, C.A.H., 1930s, 2 x 3 3/4 In.	32
Dish, Star Shape, 5 Points, Pine Needle Pattern, Blue, White Ground, 7 1/2 In.	21
Foot Warmer, Stoneware, Brown Glazed Top, c.1890, 11 1/2 In.	40
Mug, 8 Bells, Cobalt Blue Ship's Bell, Lettering, Stoneware, Signed, Knesseth Denison, 4 5/8 In., Pair	225
Mug, Pinecone, Cobalt Blue, Signed, C.A.H., 2 7/8 x 3 3/8 In.	25
Sugar & Creamer, Lids, Apple Branch, Blue, White, Striped Handles, N. Ricci, C.A.H., 4 1/2 In.	30
Sugar, Lid, Witch On Broomstick, Blue Trim, White Ground, 3 1/4 In.	45
Syrup, Lid, Spouting Whale, Seagulls On Reverse, Blue, Striped Handle, White Ground, C.A.H., 5 1/2 In.	40

DOULTON

Doulton was founded about 1858 in Lambeth, England. A second factory was opened in Burslem, England, by 1871. The name *Royal Doulton* appeared on the company's wares after 1902 and is listed in the Royal Doulton category in this book. Other Doulton ware is listed here. Doulton's Lambeth factory closed about 1956.

Doulton and Co.
1869–1877

Doulton and Co.
1880–1912, 1923

Doulton and Co.
1885–1902

Ashtray, Hummingbird, Cobalt Blue, Brown, Green, Stoneware, Lambeth, 1900s, 5 3/4 In.	230
Beaker, Sgraffito Design, Deer, Silver Mounted, Applied Jewels, Marked, 1800s, 5 1/4 In., Pair	431
Bibelot, Match Stand, Lifebuoy, Man's Head, Saved, Stoneware, 1894, 3 x 4 1/2 In. *illus*	489
Biscuit Jar, Lid, Barrel Shape, Rim, Handle, Stoneware, Lambeth, c.1881, 7 In.	259
Biscuit Jar, Silver Plate Lid, Barrel Shape, Sgraffito Deer, Handle, Marked, c.1878, 5 x 4 1/2 In.	374
Bottle, Old JRD Scotch Whisky, Stoneware, Brown, Cream, Lambeth, 1900s, 8 In.	35
Candlestick, Neoclassical, Stoneware, Cobalt Blue, Putti Holding Candleholder, Footed, 10 In.	1265
Centerpiece, Aesthetic Movement, Sea Sprite, Shell, Glazed Vellum, Burslem, c.1895, 4 x 7 In. *illus*	1380
Charger, Wall, Man, Blue, Flowers, Marked, Lambeth, 1900s, 15 1/2 In.	3795
Dispenser, Liquor, Toby, Stoneware, Seated, Barrel, Stand, Lambeth, c.1925, 10 1/2 x 5 1/4 In.	403
Jardiniere, Children, Patent Silicon Chine Ware, Ada Dennis, 1885, 10 x 9 In. *illus*	4600
Jardiniere, Pedestal, Raised Flowers, Leaves, Stoneware, Glazed, Lambeth, Late 1800s, 30 In.	1063
Jardiniere, Sailing Ships, Leaves, Backstamp, Lambeth, 1900s, 5 x 4 3/4 In.	184
Jug, Ball Shape, Flowers, White, Pink, Cream Tones, Gold Stencil, Burslem, 5 In.	60
Pitcher, Deer, Grazing, Applied Flowers, Brown, Stoneware, 1900s, 9 1/4 In.	316
Pitcher, Jug, Central Portrait Image, Burslem, Victorian, c.1890, 10 1/2 x 4 1/2 In.	1265

Doulton, Punch Bowl, Blue, White, Transfer, Flowers, Leaves, Lambethware, 9 x 17 3/4 In.
$100

Pook & Pook

Doulton, Teapot, Blue, Romeo & Juliet, Handle, Footed, Backstamp, Burslem, 1900s, 8 3/4 x 11 In.
$259

Lion and Unicorn

Doulton, Vase, Embossed Tapestry, Enamel, Slater's Patent, Gilt, c.1915, 11 3/4 In., Pair
$295

Leland Little Auctions

157

Doulton, Vase, Flowers, Leaves, Blue, Backstamp, Lambeth, c.1880, 11 ½ In., Pair
$633

Lion and Unicorn

Doulton, Vase, Luscian, Pegasus & Perseus Rescuing Andromeda, Burslem, c.1890, 16 x 7 In.
$6,325

Lion and Unicorn

Dresden, Cup & Saucer, Cream Ground, Gilt Rim & Handle, Medallion Portrait, Herzog Burgund
$400

Woody Auction

Pitcher, Lid, Pansies, Dragon Handle, Burslem, c.1880, 14 ¼ In.	488
Planter, Hexagonal, Stoneware, Birds, Flowers, Cobalt Blue, Brown, Signed, EW, 1900s, 8 x 7 In. *illus*	92
Plaque, Wall, Flowers & Insects, Green Grass, Backstamp, Lambeth, 1900s, 14 In.	316
Plate, Highland Cattle, Birds, Flowers, Scalloped Rim, Burslem, 11 In.	125
Punch Bowl, Blue, White, Transfer, Flowers, Leaves, Lambethware, 9 x 17 ¾ In. *illus*	100
Salt & Pepper, Stoneware, Silver Top, Flowers, Beaded, Blue, Emily Stormer, 1875, 4 ¼ In., Pair	103
Slop Jar, Flow Blue, Flowers, Filigree, Earthenware, Burslem, England, c.1890, 15 x 13 ½ In.	756
Tankard, Leather Ware, Blackjack Flagon, Dark Brown, Silver Rim, Marked, c.1890s, 6 In.	69
Tazza, Lake Como, Flowers, Scalloped Edge, Gilt, Painted, Signed, C. Hart, Late 1800s, 2 ¼ In.	127
Tea Caddy, Kingsware Dame, Elderly Woman Drinking Tea, Glaze, Backstamp, Late 1800s, 5 In.	58
Teapot, Blue, Romeo & Juliet, Handle, Footed, Backstamp, Burslem, 1900s, 8 ¾ x 11 In. *illus*	259
Teapot, Stoneware, Cobalt Blue, Tulips, Backstamp, Lambeth, 1900s, 6 ½ x 7 ½ In.	29
Tobacco Jar, Lid, Figural, Salt Glaze, Stoneware, Lambeth, 1894, 7 ½ x 4 ¾ In.	2300
Vase, Bulbous Oval, Blue, Women, Dog, Scalloped Rim, Backstamp, Burslem, 6 ¾ In.	150
Vase, Embossed Tapestry, Enamel, Slater's Patent, Gilt, c.1915, 11 ¾ In., Pair *illus*	295
Vase, Flowers, Leaves, Blue, Backstamp, Lambeth, c.1880, 11 ½ In., Pair *illus*	633
Vase, Luscian, Pegasus & Perseus Rescuing Andromeda, Burslem, c.1890, 16 x 7 In. *illus*	6325
Vase, Painted, Deer, Woods, Painted, Burslem, 1900s, 8 ¼ x 5 ¾ In.	431
Water Filter, Lid, Band Of Child Musicians, Stoneware, Brown, Blue, Cylindrical, 13 ½ In.	230

DRESDEN

Dresden and Meissen porcelain are often confused. Porcelains were made in the town of Meissen, Germany, beginning about 1706. The town of Dresden, Germany, has been home to many decorating studios since the early 1700s. Blanks were obtained from Meissen and other porcelain factories. Some say porcelain was also made in Dresden in the early years. Decorations on Dresden are often similar to Meissen, and marks were copied. Some of the earliest books on marks confused Dresden and Meissen, and that has remained a problem ever since. The Meissen "AR" mark and crossed swords mark are among the most forged marks on porcelain. Meissen pieces are listed in this book under Meissen. German porcelain marked "Dresden" is listed here. Irish Dresden and Dresden made in East Liverpool, Ohio, are not included in this section. These three marks say "Dresden" although none were used by a factory called Dresden.

Karl Richard Klemm
c.1891–1914

Ambrosius Lamm
c.1887+

Carl Thieme / Saxon Porcelain Manufactory
c.1903

Compote, Applied Flowers & Figures, Marked, c.1900, 17 ¾ In.	500
Creamer, Double Courting Scene, Gold Trim, Applied Handle, Marked, Miniature, 2 ¼ In.	175
Cup & Saucer, Cream Ground, Gilt Rim & Handle, Medallion Portrait, Herzog Burgund *illus*	400
Cup & Saucer, Woman, Gold, Blue Iridescent, Footed, Marked, 4 x 5 ⅞ In.	325
Etagere, 3 Glass Shelves, Floral Finials, 4 Columns, Early 1900s, 22 ¾ x 26 In.	354
Figurine, Andre Massena, First Duke Of Rivoli, Carl Thieme, 11 ½ In. *illus*	316
Figurine, Cat, Seated, Brown, White, 5 x 5 In.	94
Figurine, Monkey, Seated, Tree Trunk, White, Painted Vines, Flowers, Marked, 16 x 12 In.	1150
Figurine, Pug, Gilt Ball Shape Collar, Hand Painted, Carl Thieme, 8 ½ x 8 ½ In., Pair *illus*	936
Group, Horse Team & Carriage, Painted, Flowers & Gilt, Sandizell, Germany, 10 In. *illus*	1230
Group, Lace, Woman, Peacock, Gilt Metal Leaves, Faux Handles, Mounted As Lamp, 11 x 11 x 5 In.	325
Jar, Dome Lid, Men On Horseback Scene, Underglaze Blue Mark, Helena Wolfsohn, 15 In.	144
Plaque, Gentleman, Painted, Gilt Gesso Frame, Franz Till, 7 x 5 ¼ In.	94
Plate, Biblical Scene, Ruth, Pale Blue Border, Scroll, Butterfly, Marked, 9 ½ In.	500
Plate, Bird, Insect, Butterfly, Painted, Gilt Border, Rim, Richard Kleman, 8 ½ In., 11 Piece	510
Plate, Gilt, Scalloped Rim, Painted, Flowers, Marked, C. Tielsch & Co., 6 ½ In., 11 Piece	246

D

Dresden, Figurine, Andre Massena, First Duke Of Rivoli, Carl Thieme,
11 1/2 In.
$316

Blackwell Auctions

Dresden, Figurine, Pug, Gilt Ball Shape Collar, Hand Painted,
Carl Thieme, 8 1/2 x 8 1/2 In., Pair
$936

Thomaston Place Auction Galleries

Dresden, Group, Horse Team & Carriage, Painted, Flowers & Gilt,
Sandizell, Germany, 10 In.
$1,230

Rich Penn Auctions

Durand, Vase, Moorish Crackle, Gold Iridescent Ground, Blue, Opal,
Luster, 1924, 9 3/8 x 4 1/2 In.
$761

Jeffrey S. Evans & Associates

Durand, Vase, Tricorner, Dimpled Sides, Gold Iridescent, Pinkish King
Tut, Signed, 6 x 4 1/2 In.
$300

Woody Auction

Enamel, Box, Nude, Applied Chain, Round, Hammered Copper,
Boston, 1 x 3 1/4 In.
$1,719

Treadway

159

D

Enamel, Box, Peacock, Copper, Bezel Set, Boston School, 3 x 6¼ In. $2,125

Treadway

Enamel, Box, Peacock, Mahogany, 8-Sided, Frank Marshall, Mass., 2½ x 5½ In. $1,950

Treadway

TIP
Never put hot glass in cold water, or cold glass in hot water. The temperature change can crack the glass.

Enamel, Box, Ship, Sterling Silver, Marked, Mildred Watkins, Cleveland, 1 x 2 In. $2,000

Treadway

DUNCAN & MILLER

Duncan & Miller is a term used by collectors when referring to glass made by the George A. Duncan and Sons Company or the Duncan and Miller Glass Company. These companies worked from 1893 to 1955, when the use of the name *Duncan* was discontinued and the firm became part of the United States Glass Company. Early patterns may be listed under Pressed Glass.

Dish, Swan Shape, Citron, 11¼ x 8½ In.	45
Mint Tray, Sandwich Pattern, Ring Handle, Scroll Design, 6 In.	20
Vase, Ruby, Swirl Pattern, Rolled Rim, c. 1940, 5 x 3 In.	95

DURAND

Durand art glass was made from 1924 to 1931. The Vineland Flint Glass Works was established by Victor Durand and Victor Durand Jr. in 1897. In 1924 Martin Bach Jr. and other artisans from the Quezal glassworks joined them at the Vineland, New Jersey, plant to make Durand art glass. They called their gold iridescent glass Gold Luster.

Goblet, Opal Bowl, Applied Blue Coil, Ground Pontil Mark, 1924, 6⅞ In.	527
Lamp, 2-Light, Applied Threads, Gold Iridescent, Gilt Metal Base, Early 1900s, 14 x 7 In.	413
Lamp, Moorish Crackle, Oval Shade, Marble & Metal Base, Gold Iridescent, 1924, 67 x 8 In.	468
Plate, Cranberry Shading To Lavender, White Pulled Feather, 8 In.	80
Torchere, Trumpet Shape, Gold Iridescent, Green, Wrought Iron Base, 15½ In., Pair	819
Vase, Blue Hooked Feather, Opalescent Ground, Flared Rim, Gold Luster Stem & Foot, 7½ In.	1008
Vase, Gold Luster, Pontil, Signed, 7⅞ x 4¾ x 4¾ In.	288
Vase, King Tut Pattern, Cobalt Blue Iridescent, Pulled Vines, Trifold Rim, 5 x 7 In.	1875
Vase, Moorish Crackle, Gold Iridescent Ground, Blue, Opal, Luster, 1924, 9⅜ x 4½ In. *illus*	761
Vase, Pulled Feather, Trumpet Shape, Gold Iridescent, Flared Rim, Bulbous Base, 9½ In.	315
Vase, Threaded, Gold Iridescent, Oval Shouldered, Flared Rim, c.1903, 7 In.	192
Vase, Tricorner, Dimpled Sides, Gold Iridescent, Pinkish King Tut, Signed, 6 x 4½ In. *illus*	300

 ## DURANT KILNS

Durant Kilns was founded by Jean Durant Rice in 1910 in Bedford Village, New York. He hired Leon Volkmar to oversee production. The pottery made both tableware and artware. Rice died in 1919, leaving Leon Volkmar to run the business. After 1930 the name *Durant Kilns* was changed and only the *Volkmar* mark was used. See the Volkmar category.

Bowl, Fruit, Purple Glaze, Light Blue Interior, Lobed, Footed, Signed, Volkmar, 1920, 3¼ x 13½ In.	875
Bowl, Robin's Egg Blue Glaze, Flared, Brown Foot, Signed, Volkmar, c.1927, 4 x 4½ In.	208

ELVIS PRESLEY

Elvis Presley, the well-known singer, lived from 1935 to 1977. He became famous by 1956. Elvis appeared on television, starred in 27 movies, and performed in Las Vegas. Memorabilia from any of the Presley shows, his records, and even memorials made after his death are collected.

Badge, Prop, Chief Deputy, Shelby County, Tennessee, Star, Smith & Warren, 2½ In.	1560
Menu, Black & White Photo, Yellow Curtain, Las Vegas International Hotel, 1971, 12 x 9 In.	38
Photo Album, Souvenir, Color Photo On Cover, Blue Suit, Microphone, Signed, 11 x 8½ In.	900
Poster, Movie, Frankie & Johnny, United Artists, 1966, 3 Sheet, 81 x 41 In.	75
Print, Press Photograph, Black & White, With Guitar, Autographed, 11 x 8½ In.	402
Ticket, Concert, November 25, 1976, Pink, Black Lettering	55 to 168
Toy, Guitar, Plastic, Decals, Love Me Tender, Hound Dog, Emenee, Box, 13 x 33 In.	256

ENAMEL

Enamels listed here are made of glass particles and other materials heated and fused to metal. In the eighteenth and nineteenth centuries, workmen from Russia, France, England, and other countries made small boxes and table pieces of enamel on metal. One form of English enamel is called *Battersea* and is listed under that name. There was a revival of interest in artist-made enameling in the 1930s and a new style evolved. There is a recently renewed interest in the artistic enameled plaques, vases, ashtrays, and jewelry. Enamels made since the 1930s are usually on copper or steel, although silver was often used for jewelry. Graniteware, the factory-made household pieces made of tin or iron, is a separate category in this book. Enameled metal kitchen pieces may be included in the Kitchen category. Cloisonne is a special type of enamel using wire dividers and is listed in its own category. Descriptions of antique glass and ceramics often use the term *enamel* to describe paint, not the glass-based enamels listed here. Marks used by three important enamelists are shown here.

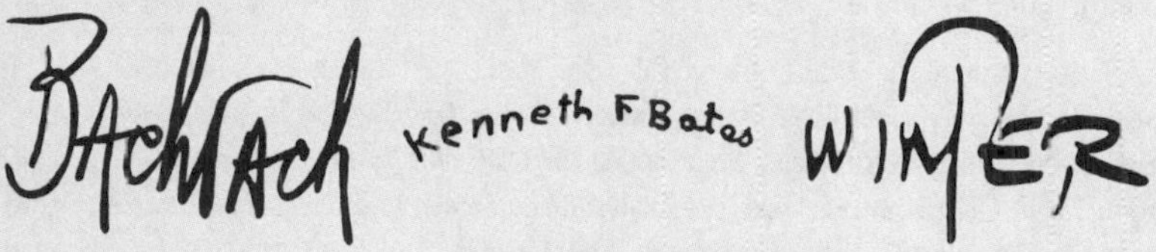

Lilyan Bachrach	Kenneth Bates	Edward Winter
1955–2015	1920s–1994	1932–1976

Bowl, Oval, Glass, Winter Scene, Gilt, Scalloped Rim, France, 2 ¾ x 8 In.	63
Box, Nude, Applied Chain, Round, Hammered Copper, Boston, 1 x 3 ¼ In. .... *illus*	1719
Box, Peacock On Square Plaque, Hammered Copper, Boston School, 2 x 6 ¾ In.	531
Box, Peacock, Copper, Bezel Set, Boston School, 3 x 6 ¼ In. .... *illus*	2125
Box, Peacock, Mahogany, 8-Sided, Frank Marshall, Mass., 2 ½ x 5 ½ In. .... *illus*	1950
Box, Peacock, Round, Lid, Copper, Patina, Frank J. Marshall, Mass., 2 x 4 ½ In.	3594
Box, Ship, Sterling Silver, Marked, Mildred Watkins, Cleveland, 1 x 2 In. .... *illus*	2000
Box, Stylized Flower, Copper, Hammered, Bezel Set, Boston School, 1 ¼ x 3 ¼ In.	500
Censer, Filigree Body, Dragon Shape Handles, Scrolled Feet, Chinese, 1900s, 7 x 3 x 7 In.	461
Dish, Copper, Multicolor, Signed, Saara Hopea, Finland, c.1975, 1 ¼ In.	375
Dish, Multicolor Flowers On Copper, Rust & Green Accents, Faure, 7 x 7 In.	861
Planter, Jade Tree, Figural, Enamel, Silver, Copper, Chinese, c.1900, 4 ½ x 5 ¼ x 4 In.	154
Plaque, Oval, Wall, Courting Couples, Gilt Bronze Frame, Painted, Signed, France, 11 x 8 In.	325
Plaque, Seated Man In Tavern, Gilt Bronze Frame, France, 1800s, 10 ¼ x 7 ½ In.	375
Plate, Copper, God Of Thunder, Cherub, Renaissance Style, Limoges, 9 ⅝ In.	349
Plate, Stylized Figures, Copper, Signed, Karl Drerup, c.1945, 7 ¼ In. .... *illus*	1125
Sconce, Peacock, Copper, Patina, Octagonal, Arts & Crafts, England, 13 ½ x 13 ½ In. .... *illus*	1563
Tray, Cherry Tree In Blossom, Rectangular, 4-Character Mark, Ando Studio, Japan, 7 x 9 In.	63
Vase, Bud, Leaves, Multicolor, Waisted Neck, Wood Base, Champleve, 10 In., Pair	266
Vase, Red Ground, Western Fashion, Gilt Mask Handles, Copper, Chinese, 1800s, 5 ½ In.	188

ERPHILA

Erphila is a mark found on Czechoslovakian and other pottery and porcelain made after 1920. This mark was used on items imported by Ebeling & Reuss, Philadelphia, a giftware firm that was founded in 1866 and out of business sometime after 2002. The mark is a combination of the letters *E* and *R* (Ebeling & Reuss) and the first letters of the city, Phila(delphia). Many whimsical figural pitchers and creamers, figurines, platters, and other giftwares carry this mark.

Corbel, Shell Shape, Scalloped, White, Germany, 5 ¾ In., Pair........................	75
Perfume Bottle, Stopper, 4-Sided, Flowers, Gilt Scrolls, Porcelain, Marked, Germany, c.1910, 4 ½ In.	25
Pitcher, Lid, Sussex Cheery Chintz, White Handle & Finial, Bavaria, 40 Oz., 7 ½ In.	280
Pitcher, Tavern Scene, 2 Cavaliers, Woman Serving, White Ground, Footed, Czechoslovakia, 3 Liter.	15

E

Enamel, Plate, Stylized Figures, Copper, Signed, Karl Drerup, c.1945, 7 ¼ In. $1,125

Wright

Enamel, Sconce, Peacock, Copper, Patina, Octagonal, Arts & Crafts, England, 13 ½ x 13 ½ In. $1,563

Treadway

Erphila, Reamer, Figural, Yellow Flower, Green Leaves, Loop Handle, Germany, 2 ½ x 8 In. $34

newenglandchris on eBay

ERPHILA

ES Germany, Vase, Bottle Shape, Maroon Iridescent, Portrait, Woman, Gilt, 2 Handles, Royal Saxe, 6 x 4 In. **$96**

Woody Auction

TIP

Keep packing materials in your car just in case you find an antiques store. Have a blanket, bungee cord, labels, tape, flashlight, and some boxes. Always carry parking meter change.

Eskimo, Amulet, Walrus Ivory, Toothy Grimace, Carved, 1910s, 6 In. **$406**

Eldred's

162

Plate, 2 Birds, Grape Leaves, Turquoise Ground, Majolica, Germany, 7¾ In.	8
Reamer, Figural, Yellow Flower, Green Leaves, Loop Handle, Germany, 2½ x 8 In. ...... *illus*	34
Sandwich Tray, Mayfair, Oval, Cheery Chintz Center, White Embossed Rim, Bavaria, 10½ x 7 In.	160
Teapot, Lid, Dorset Cheery Chintz, White Handle & Finial, Gilt Trim, 1 Cup, 2⅝ In.	180
Vase, Flared, Multicolor Flowers, Raised Bands, Gilt Trim, Marked, Germany, 6 x 6 In., Pair.	24
Vase, White Crackle Glaze, Turquoise Dripped Rim, Ribbed, Footed, Czechoslovakia, 8¼ In. .	40

ES GERMANY

ES Germany porcelain was made at the factory of Erdmann Schlegelmilch from 1861 to 1937 in Suhl, Germany. The porcelain, marked *ES Germany* or *ES Suhl*, was sold decorated or undecorated. Other pieces were made at a factory in Saxony, Prussia, and are marked *ES Prussia*. Reinhold Schlegelmilch also made porcelain. There is no connection between the two factories. Porcelain made by Reinhold Schlegelmilch is listed in this book under RS Germany, RS Poland, RS Prussia, RS Silesia, RS Suhl, and RS Tillowitz.

Bowl, Flowers Around Rim, White Ground, Gilt Trim, Marked, Prov. Saxe, 2¾ x 10 In.	18
Cake Plate, Woman's Portrait, Green Ground, Maroon Rim, Gilt, Open Handles, Royal Saxe, 10 In.	24
Chocolate Pot, Pink Flowers, Garland, White Ground, Gilt Trim, Lid, Open Finial, Royal Saxe, 8 In.	30
Plaque, Napoleon, Portrait, Scalloped Rim, Forest Green Border, 10 In.	169
Shaving Mug, Swallows, Violets, Blue Ground, c.1890, 3½ In.	85
Tray, Clover Shape, Yellow Flowers, Leaves, Gilt Rim & Handle, 8 x 7 In.	175
Vase, Bottle Shape, Maroon Iridescent, Portrait, Woman, Gilt, 2 Handles, Royal Saxe, 6 x 4 In. *illus*	96

ESKIMO

Eskimo artifacts of all types are collected. Carvings of whale or walrus teeth are listed under Scrimshaw. Baskets are in the Basket category. All other types of Eskimo art are listed here. In Canada and some other areas, the term *Inuit* is used instead of Eskimo. It is illegal to sell some whale parts that are used to made decorative items. The law has changed several times, so check the legality before you buy or sell.

Amulet, Walrus Ivory, Toothy Grimace, Carved, 1910s, 6 In. *illus*	406
Cribbage Board, Walrus Tusk, Carved & Engraved, Seal Shape Feet, 16½ In.	469
Figure, Animal Head, Walrus Tusk, Carved, Early 1900s, 4 In. *illus*	313
Figure, Polar Bear, Inuit, Carved, Black Accent, Walrus Tusk, Black Wood Stand, 3 x 2 x 1 In.	148
Moccasins, Beaded, Upper Part Lined With Fur, 1930s, 9 In., Pair *illus*	106
Sculpture, Inuit, Holding Bowl, Dark Green Ground, Soapstone, Marked, 11¼ x 8 x 7 In.	288
Snowshoes, Bear Paw, Natural Bent Wood, Animal Hide Weaving, c.1925, 36 x 18 In., Pair .	250

ФАБЕРЖЕ FABERGE
КФ

Faberge was a firm of jewelers and goldsmiths founded in St. Petersburg, Russia, in 1842, by Gustav Faberge. Peter Carl Faberge, his son, was jeweler to the Russian Imperial Court from about 1870 to 1917. The rare Imperial Easter eggs, jewelry, and decorative items are very expensive today. The name *Faberge* is also used for art made of precious metals and jewels by Peter Carl Faberge's grandson. Theo Faberge launched a collection of artistic things made of expensive materials in 1985. He made jeweled eggs in several sizes. The collection is sold in several museums.

Candy Dish, Round, Basket Shape, Articulated Handle, Footed, Silver, Hallmarks, c.1894, 2 x 4 In.	861
Chess Set, Imperial Jeweled, Marble Board, Rosewood, Stone Pieces, Igor Faberge, 15½ In.	5200
Figurine, Mouse, Silver, Ruby Eyes, Head Raised, Signed, Hallmarked, c.1900, 2 In.	2560
Letter Opener, Red Guilloche Handle, Nephrite Jade Blade, Finial, Wood Case, 12 x 2 x 1 In. .	1287
Wine Cooler, Bronze, Mounted, Face Handle, Gilt Rim, Etched, Tatiana, 8¾ In. *illus*	1000

E

FAIENCE

Faience refers to tin-glazed earthenware, especially the wares made in France, Germany, and Scandinavia. It is also correct to say that faience is the same as majolica or Delft, although usually the term refers only to the tin-glazed pottery of the three regions mentioned.

Bust, Apollo, Flower Crown, Gold Hair, Blue Draped Garment, Socle Base, 1800s, 23 In. *illus*		472
Cachepot, Chinoiserie, Lion Mask Handles, Red Band, France, 7¾ In. .... *illus*		502
Ewer, Narrow Spout, Top & Side Handles, Painted, Flowers, Birds, Signed, M. Clerc, 16 In. *illus*		236
Flowerpot, Yellow Ground, Half Round, Sceaux, France, 4 x 8⅛ In., Pair		238
Inkstand, Cherub Decor, Gilt, Cream Ground, Paw Foot, 10¾ In.		83
Lavabo, Blue & White, Tin Glaze, Carved, Wood Bracket, Continental, Late 1800s, 37 x 18 In.		313
Tile, Coat Of Arms, Squeezebag Outline, Glazed, Square, 6 x 6 In.		121

FAIRING

Fairings are small souvenir boxes and figurines that were sold at country fairs during the nineteenth century. Most were made in Germany. Reproductions of fairings are being made, especially of the famous *Twelve Months after Marriage* series.

Dresser Box, Lid, Girl, Doves, Seated On Vanity, Painted, Porcelain, Victorian, 4 x 1¾ x 4 In.	32
Figure, Girl, Hood, Green Cloak, Muff, Red Skirt, Staffordshire, 6 In.	50
Group, 3 Pug Dogs, Chair, The Orphans, 4 x 3½ x 1¾ In. .... *illus*	148
Match Striker, Cat, On Hind Legs, Pink Dress, Holds Kitten, Basket On Back, Germany, 6 In.	69
Match Striker, Man, Gray Suit, Hat, Black Coat, Bags, I Am Starting For A Long Journey, 5¾ In.	32
Match Striker, Ready To Start, Girl, Pink Coat, Open Satchel, Conta Boehme, 6 x 3⅜ In. ... *illus*	100
Trinket Box, Child, Lying In Bed, Red Pillow, Striped Cat, Gilt Trim, Conta Boehme, 4¾ x 3 x 2 In.	48
Trinket Box, Figural, Boy, Sitting In Rowboat, Holds Oar, Molded Waves On Base, 2½ x 3 In.	50
Trinket Box, Lid, Girl, Kittens, Hand Painted, Porcelain, Conta Boehme, Late 1800s, 3½ x 3¾ x 2 In.	44
Trinket Box, Lid, Half Doll, Woman, Blond, Flower, Ruffled Pink Dress, Holds Book, Germany, 2 In.	65
Trinket Box, Open Loop On Lid, Figures, Goose Biting Girl, Conta Boehme, Late 1800s, 5 x 3 x 2 In.	60

FAIRYLAND LUSTER *pieces are included in the Wedgwood category.*

FAMILLE ROSE, *see Chinese Export category.*

FAN

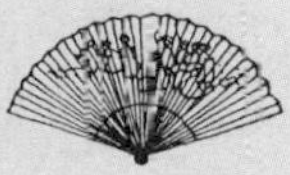

Fans have been used for cooling since the days of the ancients. By the eighteenth century, the fan was an accessory for the lady of fashion and very elaborate and expensive fans were made. Sticks were made of ivory or wood, set with jewels or carved. The fans were made of painted silk or paper. Inexpensive paper fans printed with advertising were giveaways in the late nineteenth and early twentieth centuries. Electric fans were introduced in 1882. There are collectors of electric fans who like to buy damaged ones to repair.

Carved, Sandalwood, Silk, Folding, Painted, Chinese, Early 1900s, 20 In. .... *illus*	283
Electric, 4 Blades, Aluminum, Wire Cage, Oscillating, 3-Speed, 12 In. Blades, Table	72
Electric, 4 Blades, Wire Cage, Cast Iron Base, Blue Paint, No. 5219, Dominion, Art Deco, 12 In. Blades	34
Electric, 4 Blades, Wire Cage, Red Logo In Center, Blue Base, Zero, Midcentury, Table, 16 x 12 In.	325
Electric, Air Flight, Hassock, Bakelite, W.W. Welch Co., c.1950, 14 x 15 In. .... *illus*	563
Electric, Ceiling, The Islander, Metal, Hanging Light, Italian Style, 44 In.	35
Electric, Handy-Fannett, Battery, Juice Mixer Attachment, Nihonkako Corp., Japan, Box, 7 x 3 In.	24
Electric, Safe Flex, 4 Blades, Rubber, Brown, Painted Stand, No. 146N, Samson, 10 In. Blades	63
Electric, Whiz, 4 Brass Blades, Cage, Metal Stand, Felt Base, No. D74869, General Electric, 12½ In.	166
Electric, Zephair, 4 Blades, Aluminum, Wire Cage, Hunter, 16 In. Blades, Table	72
Lacquer, Figures In Rooms, Folding, Painted, Box, Chinese, Late 1800s, 18¼ In. .... *illus*	832

FAST FOOD COLLECTIBLES *may be included in several categories, such as Advertising, Coca-Cola, Toy, etc.*

Eskimo, Figure, Animal Head, Walrus Tusk, Carved, Early 1900s, 4 In. $313

Eldred's

Eskimo, Moccasins, Beaded, Upper Part Lined With Fur, 1930s, 9 In., Pair $106

Austin Auction Gallery

Faberge, Wine Cooler, Bronze, Mounted, Face Handle, Gilt Rim, Etched, Tatiana, 8¾ In. $1,000

Hindman

TIP
Ask a new bride if she would like an antique, then pick one that goes with modern like brass or glass candlesticks or a set of silver salad serving pieces, a large spoon and fork.

Faience, Bust, Apollo, Flower Crown, Gold Hair, Blue Draped Garment, Socle Base, 1800s, 28 In.
$472

Austin Auction Gallery

Faience, Cachepot, Chinoiserie, Lion Mask Handles, Red Band, France, 7¾ In.
$502

Leland Little Auctions

Faience, Ewer, Narrow Spout, Top & Side Handles, Painted, Flowers, Birds, Signed, M. Clerc, 16 In.
$236

Austin Auction Gallery

Fairing, Group, 3 Pug Dogs, Chair, The Orphans, 4 x 3½ x 1¾ In.
$148

Ruby Lane

Fairing, Match Striker, Ready To Start, Girl, Pink Coat, Open Satchel, Conta Boehme, 6 x 3⅜ In.
$100

Ruby Lane

Fan, Carved, Sandalwood, Silk, Folding, Painted, Chinese, Early 1900s, 20 In.
$288

Hindman

Fan, Electric, Air Flight, Hassock, Bakelite, W.W. Welch Co., c.1950, 14 x 15 In.
$563

Wright

Fan, Lacquer, Figures In Rooms, Folding, Painted, Box, Chinese, Late 1800s, 18¼ In.
$832

Hindman

Fenton, Cranberry Opalescent, Lampshade, Umbrella Shape, For Hanging Lamp, 13½ In.
$690

Blackwell Auctions

FEDERZEICHNUNG, *see Loetz category.*

FENTON

Fenton Art Glass Company was founded in 1905 in Martins Ferry, Ohio, by Frank L. Fenton and his brother, John W. Fenton. They painted decorations on glass blanks made by other manufacturers. In 1907 they opened a factory in Williamstown, West Virginia, and began making glass. The company stopped making art glass in 2011 and assets were sold. A new division of the company makes handcrafted glass beads and other jewelry. Copies are being made from leased original Fenton molds by an unrelated company, Fenton's Collectibles. The copies are marked with the Fenton mark and Fenton's Collectibles mark. Fenton is noted for early carnival glass produced between 1907 and 1920. Some of these pieces are listed in the Carnival Glass category. Many other types of glass were also made. Spanish Lace in this section refers to the pattern made by Fenton.

Fenton Art Glass Co. 1970–1975	Fenton Art Glass Co. 1980s

Fenton Art Glass Co. 1983+

Black Rose Crest, Vase, Hand, White Opalescent, Pink Double Ruffled, 11 In.	34
Blue Opalescent, Pitcher, Ruffled Rim, Bulbous, Applied Handle, c.1910, 9 ¼ In.	80
Burmese, Vase, Painted, Shells, Seahorse, Cream Ground, Pink Spout, 8 In.	148
Cranberry Opalescent, Lampshade, Umbrella Shape, For Hanging Lamp, 13 ½ In. ... *illus*	690
Custard, Basket, Scalloped Rim, Hanging Heart Design, U-Shape Handle, Footed, 10 In.	197
Daisy & Fern, Lamp, Brass, White Opalescent, Footed, 18 In.	74
Dusty Rose, Epergne, Iridescent, Ruffled Rim, Disc Foot, 7 In.	102
Favrene, Vase, Blue Iridescent, Rose Bowl Shape, Draped Flowers, 1980s, 5 ⅜ In.	82
Figurine, Alley Cat, Yellow Custard, Iridescent, Seated, Smiling, 11 In.	170
Hanging Hearts, Vase, Sweet Pea, Applied Amethyst Rim, Teal, Iridescent, c.1926, 4 x 6 In. *illus*	761
Mosaic, Vase, Urn Shape, Flared Rim, Orange, Red & Amber Spots, 1925, 11 In. *illus*	2016
Poppy, Lamp, Gone With The Wind Style, Brass Plated Fittings, Pink, 1980s, 24 In. *illus*	432
Rose, Lamp, Kerosene, Banquet, Burmese Shade, Brass Plated Base, 1980s, 38 In.	396
Silver Crest, Epergne, 3 Vases, Bowl, 11 In.	62
Vase, Jack-In-The-Pulpit, Hand Painted Flower, Green Leaves, Clear Opaque, 11 In.	57

FIESTA

Fiesta, the colorful dinnerware, was introduced in 1936 by the Homer Laughlin China Co., redesigned in 1969, and withdrawn in 1973. It was reissued again in 1986 in different colors and is still being made. New colors, including some that are similar to old colors, have been introduced. One new color is introduced in March every year. The simple design was characterized by a band of concentric circles beginning at the rim. Cups had full-circle handles until 1969, when partial-circle handles were made. Harlequin and Riviera were related wares. For more prices, go to kovels.com.

Fiesta 1936–1970	Fiesta Kitchen Kraft 1939–c.1943	Fiesta Casual 1962–c.1968

Beige, Pitcher, Disc, Concentric Rings, Only Known Example, 1948, 6 In. ... *illus* 10350

Fenton, Hanging Hearts, Vase, Sweet Pea, Applied Amethyst Rim, Teal, Iridescent, c.1926, 4 x 6 In. $761

Jeffrey S. Evans & Associates

Fenton, Mosaic, Vase, Urn Shape, Flared Rim, Orange, Red & Amber Spots, 1925, 11 In. $2,016

Fontaine's Auction Gallery

Fenton, Poppy, Lamp, Gone With The Wind Style, Brass Plated Fittings, Pink, 1980s, 24 In. $432

Garth's Auctioneers & Appraisers

FIESTA

Fiesta, Beige, Pitcher, Disc, Concentric Rings, Only Known Example, 1948, 6 In.
$10,350

Fiesta, Cobalt Blue, Compote, Sweets, Circular Base
$136

Fiesta, Cobalt Blue, Relish, Red Center, Green, Yellow, Ivory, Turquoise Inserts
$254

Fiesta, Dark Green, Casserole, Lid, Curved Tab Handles, 9¾ x 8 x 5¾ In.
$173

Fiesta, Medium Green, Bowl, Salad, Individual
$62

Fiesta, Red, Candleholder, Bulb Shape, Plinth Base, Pair
$68

Fiesta, Red, Candleholder, Tripod, Art Deco, 1935-1942, 4½ x 4½ x 3½ In., Pair
$230

Fiesta, Tidbit, 3 Tiers, Red, Yellow & Green Plates, Center Looped Handle
$98

Fiesta, Turquoise, Soup, Onion, Lid, Curved Tab Handles, 1938, 6 x 4½ In.
$3,450

Brown, Coffeepot, Amberstone, Dome Lid, Spout & Handle	62
Celadon Green, Pitcher, Juice, Disc, Wide Spout.....................................	136
Chartreuse, Casserole, Lid, Triangular Finial, Foot	113
Cinnabar, Butter, Cover, Rectangular, Urn Shape Finial, Underplate.............	96
Cobalt Blue, Compote, Sweets, Circular Base.............................*illus*	136
Cobalt Blue, Relish, Red Center, Green, Yellow, Ivory, Turquoise Inserts .... *illus*	254
Cobalt Blue, Syrup, Lid With Pour Sliding Spout & Handle, 1938-40, 5 ¾ In.	173
Cobalt Blue, Tidbit, 3 Tiers, Red, Green	57
Dark Green, Casserole, Lid, Curved Tab Handles, 9 ¾ x 8 x 5 ¾ In. .... *illus*	173
Dark Green, Eggcup, Domed Base...	96
Dark Green, Jug, Water, Glaze, Wide Spout, Handle	90
Gray, Pitcher, Water, Disc, Handle, Wide Spout...................................	68
Green, Tumbler, Water, Medium	1582
Ivory, Candleholder, Tripod, Pair..	226
Ivory, Compote, Sweets, Marked, HLC...	136
Ivory, Mug, Ovaltine, Handle, Green Band Rim	113
Juniper, Tray, Round, 12 ½ In.	85
Mauve Blue, Teapot, Lid, Triangular Finial & Handle, Molded Rim	40
Medium Green, Bowl, Salad, Individual .... *illus*	62
Medium Green, Soup, Cream, 2 Molded Handles, Underfoot	735
Periwinkle, Sugar & Creamer, Underplate, Concentric Rings, Post 1986, Tray 10 In.	39
Red, Candleholder, Bulb Shape, Plinth Base, Pair .... *illus*	68
Red, Candleholder, Tripod, Art Deco, 1935-42, 4 ½ x 4 ½ x 3 ½ In., Pair .... *illus*	230
Red, Cup & Saucer, After Dinner	62
Red, Syrup, Lid, Pointed Spout	181
Rose, Bowl, Fruit, 4 ¾ In., 10 Piece	62
Rose, Jug, Pointed Spout, Handle, 2 Pt...	90
Sapphire Blue, Pitcher, Water, Disc, 60th Anniversary, Wide Spout, Handle	62
Spruce Green, Letter Opener, Elephant, 6 ¾ In.	7910
Tidbit, 3 Tiers, Red, Yellow & Green Plates, Center Looped Handle .... *illus*	98
Turquoise, Candleholder, Bulb, Square Base, Pair.................................	45
Turquoise, Soup, Onion, Lid, Curved Tab Handles, 1938, 6 x 4 ½ In. .... *illus*	3450
Yellow, Bowl, Fruit, 11 ¾ In.	73
Yellow, Chop Plate, Gold Cherry, Scenic, 15 In...................................	40

FINCH, *see Kay Finch category.*

FINDLAY ONYX AND FLORADINE

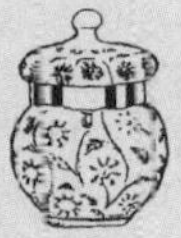

Findlay onyx and Floradine are two similar types of glass made by Dalzell, Gilmore and Leighton Co. of Findlay, Ohio, about 1889. Onyx is a patented yellowish white opaque glass with raised silver daisy decorations. A few rare pieces were made of rose, amber, orange, or purple glass. Floradine is made of cranberry-colored glass with an opalescent white raised floral pattern and a satin finish. The same molds were used for both types of glass.

Bowl, Floradine, Ruby, Lid, Frosted, Clear Finial, Satin Finish, c.1889, 5 ¾ In.	1989
Creamer, Floradine, Ruby, White Flower, Factory Polished Rim, Frosted, Clear Handle, c.1889, 4 ⅝ In.	702
Spooner, Floradine, Ruby, Factory Polished Rim, White Flower, Satin Finish, c.1889, 4 ⅜ In. ..	351
Mustard, Period Lid, Ivory, Platinum Flowers, c.1889, 3 ⅝ In.	263
Pitcher, Ivory Opalescent Handle, Raised Silver Flowers, c.1889, 7 ⅞ In..........	679
Tumbler, Carafe Fitted, Baluster Shape, Ivory, Flowers, c.1889, 8 ⅜ x 3 ⅝ In. .... *illus*	1170

FIREFIGHTING

Firefighting equipment of all types is collected, from fire marks to uniforms to toy fire trucks. It is said that every little boy wanted to be a fireman or a train engineer 75 years ago and the collectors today reflect this interest.

Bucket, Brass, Banded Wood, Removable Brass Liner, Handle, 13 x 13 ½ In. .... *illus*	555

Findlay Onyx, Tumbler, Carafe Fitted, Baluster Shape, Ivory, Flowers, c.1889, 8 ⅜ x 3 ⅝ In.
$1,170

Jeffrey S. Evans & Associates

F

Firefighting, Bucket, Brass, Banded Wood, Removable Brass Liner, Handle, 13 x 13 ½ In.
$555

Alderfer Auction Company

Firefighting, Extinguishing Kit, 6 Extinguishers, Iron Hinged Box, Red, Shur-Stop, 10 x 12 x 7 In.
$156

Kamelot Auctions

Firefighting, Fire Mark, Insurance, Protector, Fireman, Holding Hose, Stamped, Painted, Copper, c.1825, 9 In. $468

Firefighting, Grenade, Hayward's Hand, Pat Aug. 8 1871, Lime Green, Diamond Panels, Contents, 6¼ In. $450

Fireplace, Andirons, Brass, Faceted Diamond Top, Chippendale, 1700s, 5 In. $5,612

TIP

Don't overclean hardware, andirons, or other old brass objects. Clean off the worst, but don't try to make them look brand new.

Bucket, Hand Stitched, Leather Bail Handle, 11½ x 7½ In.	94
Bucket, Leather, British Coat Of Arms, Lion & Unicorn, Swing Handle, 1800s, 13 In.	443
Bucket, Leather, Copper, Metal Rim, 2 Ring Handles, 12¼ In.	115
Bucket, Leather, Green Ground, Black Lettering, L. Batchelder, Applied Strap Handle, 20 In.	813
Bucket, Leather, Red Ground, Painted, Ringed Bail Handle, Mid 1800s, 15¼ In.	527
Extinguishing Kit, 6 Extinguishers, Iron Hinged Box, Red, Shur-Stop, 10 x 12 x 7 In. *illus*	156
Fire Mark, Fireman's Alliance Plaque, Cast Iron, c.1850, 11½ x 7¼ In.	175
Fire Mark, Insurance, Protector, Fireman, Holding Hose, Stamped, Painted, Copper, c.1825, 9 In. *illus*	468
Fire Mark, Lumberman's Insurance Company, Log Shape Frame, Cast Iron, c.1890, 11 x 11 In.	125
Grenade, Hayward's Hand, Pat Aug. 8 1871, Lime Green, Diamond Panels, Contents, 6¼ In. *illus*	450
Helmet, Chapman Steamer, White Leather, John Olson Co., N.Y., c.1860, 9 x 14 In.	1625
Helmet, Overlay Shield, La Plata Volunteer Fire Dept., Red, Cairns & Brothers, 1910s, 6 In.	176
Sign, Harmony Voluntary Fire Dept, Honor Roll, Painted, 1900s, 43¾ x 13 In.	1063
Siren, Iron Frame, Nickel Plated, Crank, Sterling Fire Alarm Co., c.1920, 13 x 8 In.	554

FIREPLACE

Fireplaces were used to cook food and to heat the American home in past centuries. Many types of tools and equipment were used. A pair of andirons held the logs in place, firebacks reflected the heat into the room, and tongs were used to move either fuel or food. Many types of spits and roasting jacks were made and may be listed in the Kitchen category.

Andirons, Brass, Cannonball Finial, Ring Turned Supports, Spur Knee, Early 1900s, 26 In.	502
Andirons, Brass, Chippendale, Paneled Lemon Top, Spur Knee, Pad Feet, 1700s, 21 x 12 In..	443
Andirons, Brass, Classical Style, Lidded Urn Shape, 4 Turned Feet, Early 1900s, 16 x 11 In.	384
Andirons, Brass, Faceted Diamond Top, Chippendale, 1700s, 5 In. *illus*	5612
Andirons, Brass, Federal, Lemon Top, Ball Feet, Stepped Bar, Early 1800s, 22 x 12 x 19 In.	861
Andirons, Brass, Heraldic Style, Central Knight Helmet, Crested Shield, 1800s, 27¾ In.	281
Andirons, Brass, Iron Ring Stem, Spurred Cabriole Legs, Ball Feet, Early 1800s, 20 In.	344
Andirons, Brass, Iron, Steeple Top, Spurred Cabriole Legs, Early 1800s, 25 x 12 x 20 In.	281
Andirons, Brass, Neoclassical Style, Lion Mask, Ring Handle, Serpent Feet, c.1900s, 25 In. *illus*	207
Andirons, Brass, Silver Plate, Pierced, Filigree, Late 1800s, 24½ x 10 In. *illus*	126
Andirons, Brass, Spread Legs, Ball Feet, Federal, 19 x 11 In.	219
Andirons, Cast Bronze, Figural, Lion, Grotesque Mask, Log Rest, 34 x 21 x 22 In.	410
Andirons, Cast Iron, Brownie Sitting On Wall, Copper Patina, Dated, 1969, 18 x 19 In. *illus*	762
Andirons, Cast Iron, Duck Decoy Shape, Black, 1900s, 11 x 14½ x 22 In.	213
Andirons, Cast Iron, George Washington, Left Hand At Back, 15 x 7 x 17 In.	200
Andirons, Cast Iron, George Washington, Painted, Black, Marked, Mid 1900s, 20 x 9 In.	295
Andirons, Cast Iron, Goose Head, Curved Feet, 1800s, 17½ In. *illus*	443
Andirons, Cast Iron, Hand Forged, Brass Rosette Tops, 29 In.	86
Andirons, Cast Iron, Horse Head Finial, Horseshoe Legs, American, Early 1900s, 12 x 19 In.	168
Andirons, Cast Iron, Horse Head, Ring Bale, Hoof Base, Early 1900s, 17 x 5 In. *illus*	313
Andirons, Cast Iron, Leaf Shape, Hinged, Arts & Crafts Style, 19 In.	63
Andirons, Cast Iron, Man, Full Body, 16½ x 10 In. *illus*	374
Andirons, Cast Iron, Mask, Bootjack Legs, Gothic Revival, 22½ x 10 In.	207
Andirons, Copper, Iron, Cattail, Stamped Mark, Martin Rose, 26 x 30 x 11 In.	297
Andirons, Gilt Bronze, Gothic Revival, Trefoil Finial, Octagonal Column, Arched Leg, 33 In. .	567
Andirons, Nickel Plated, Urn Shape, Engraved, Paw Feet, 1900s, 21 In. *illus*	281
Andirons, Silvered Bronze, Figural, Cobra, Stamped E Brandt, c.1925, 12 x 14 In. *illus*	6400
Andirons, Wrought Iron, Brass Loop, Melchiorre Bega, c.1942, 13½ In.	5000
Andirons, Wrought Iron, Cross Stick Golf Clubs, Hearts, c.1915, 24 In.	1560
Andirons, Wrought Iron, Faceted Tapered Columns, Fire Dogs, Ball Ends, 1880s, 11 x 12 x 9 In.	46
Andirons, Wrought Iron, Knob Tops, 3 Spit Hooks, Arched Feet, 1700s, 22 x 25 In.	375
Bellows, Mechanical, Hand Crank, Brass, Ornate Base, 22 In. *illus*	160
Bellows, Turtleback, Red Flowers, Brass Nozzle, Tacks, 1810s, 7 x 18 In.	138
Bellows, Wood, Leather, Handles, Numerical Stamp, Blacksmith, France, 1800s, 7 x 12 In. ..	384
Brass, Folding Screen, Tools, Hearth Stand, 1900s, 32 In.	125
Chenets, Andirons, Brass, Pan Shape, 2 Putti, Holding Horn, 11 x 13 In.	125
Chenets, Andirons, Bronze, Louis XV Style, Scrolled Leaves, France, 1800s, 17 x 13 In. *illus*	266

Fireplace, Andirons, Brass, Neoclassical Style, Lion Mask, Ring Handle, Serpent Feet, c.1900s, 25 In.
$207

Leland Little Auctions

Fireplace, Andirons, Brass, Silver Plate, Pierced, Filigree, Late 1800s, 24 ½ x 10 In.
$126

Fontaine's Auction Gallery

Fireplace, Andirons, Cast Iron, Brownie Sitting On Wall, Copper Patina, Dated, 1969, 18 x 19 In.
$762

Rafael Osona Nantucket Auctions

Fireplace, Andirons, Cast Iron, Goose Head, Curved Feet, 1800s, 17 ½ In.
$443

Copake Auction

Fireplace, Andirons, Cast Iron, Horse Head, Ring Bale, Hoof Base, Early 1900s, 17 x 5 In.
$313

Bruneau & Co. Auctioneers

F

Fireplace, Andirons, Cast Iron, Man, Full Body, 16 ½ x 10 In.
$374

Stevens Auction Co.

Fireplace, Andirons, Nickel Plated, Urn Shape, Engraved, Paw Feet, 1900s, 21 In.
$281

Eldred's

Fireplace, Andirons, Silvered Bronze, Figural, Cobra, Stamped E Brandt, c.1925, 12 x 14 In.
$6,400

Morphy Auctions

Fireplace, Bellows, Mechanical, Hand Crank, Brass, Ornate Base, 22 In.
$160

Hartzell's Auction Gallery Inc.

Fireplace, Chenets, Andirons, Bronze, Louis XV Style, Scrolled Leaves, France, 1800s, 17 x 13 In.
$266

Austin Auction Gallery

Fireplace, Chenets, Andirons, Louis XVI Style, Gilt Bronze, Urn & Pinecone Finials, Late 1800s, 18 In.
$192

Brunk Auctions

Fireplace, Coal Bin, Pine, Metal, Mounted, 12 x 12 In.
$128

Roland Auctioneers & Valuers

Fireplace, Coal Scuttle, Ebonized Metal, Brass Handle & Hinges, Footed, Late 1800s, 16 x 10 x 16 In.
$50

Pook & Pook

Fireplace, Coal Scuttle, Lid, Copper, Iron, 2 Handles, Footed, W.A.S. Benson, England, 27 x 16 In.
$569

Treadway

Fireplace, Fender, Brass, Curved, Paw Foot, 10 In.
$594

Charlton Hall Auctions

Fireplace, Fender, Club, Brass, Leather Seats, Button Tufted, Brown, 1910s, 22 x 70 In.
$1,416

Austin Auction Gallery

Fireplace, Fender, Iron, Wirework, Curved, Black, Turned Brass Feet, Late 1800s, 11 x 29 In.
$118

Leland Little Auctions

Fireplace, Fireback, Iron, Scrollwork, Fleur-De-Lis, 2 Beasts, France, 1700s, 18 ½ x 18 In.
$354

Austin Auction Gallery

Chenets, Andirons, Bronze, Neoclassical Style, Pierced, Leaves, Urn & Griffin, 1800s, 12 In..	443
Chenets, Andirons, Bronze, Seated Putti Blowing Horn, Leafy, Brass Tools, 1800s, 11 In......	375
Chenets, Andirons, Cast Iron, Female Sphinx, Central Cartouche Base, Patina, 1800s, 21 ½ In..	236
Chenets, Andirons, Figural, Louis XV Style, Gilt, Bronze, Chinoiserie, Early 1900s, 12 In.	375
Chenets, Andirons, Louis XVI Style, Gilt Bronze, Urn & Pinecone Finials, Late 1800s, 18 In. ..illus	192
Coal Bin, Pine, Metal, Mounted, 12 x 12 In. .... illus	128
Coal Bucket, Stickley Brothers, Stave, Fluted Rim, Brass, Copper, 13⅜ x 15¼ In.	1500
Coal Grate, Arched Cast Iron Fireback, Brass Knob Finials, Fender, 1800s, 27 x 23 x 13 In. ..	431
Coal Scuttle, Brass, Rococo Style, Leafy, Scrolled Feet, Removable Scoop, 1800s, 19 ½ In.....	344
Coal Scuttle, Copper, Brass, Bail Top Handle, Domed Foot, 1800s, 13 In......................	148
Coal Scuttle, Copper, Handle, Stamped, 15 In..	58
Coal Scuttle, Dome Lid, Black, Crackled, Gold Bands, Tapered Rectangle, Ball Feet, 17 x 18 In.	46
Coal Scuttle, Ebonized Metal, Brass Handle & Hinges, Footed, Late 1800s, 16 x 10 x 16 In. ..illus	50
Coal Scuttle, Hinged Slant Top, Ring Handles, Cabriole Legs, Copper, 1900s, 16 x 16 x 11 In..	59
Coal Scuttle, Lid, Copper, Iron, 2 Handles, Footed, W.A.S. Benson, England, 27 x 16 In. illus	569
Coal Scuttle, Quartersawn Oak, Brass Trim, Flame Shape Knob, Paw Feet, 1800s, 19 x 19 x 24 In.	245
Coal Scuttle, Walnut, Hinged Lid, Gilt Handle & Knob, Victorian, 14 In......................	58
Fender, 2 Cherubs, Seated, Brass, Patina, 13 ½ In.	352
Fender, Brass Rail, Finials, Scroll, Wire, Federal, 1810s, 13 ½ x 33 x 13 In.	230
Fender, Brass, Curved, Paw Foot, 10 In. .... illus	594
Fender, Brass, Figural, Fleur-De-Lis, Lion's Head, Continental, 1800s, 25 ¾ In.	176
Fender, Brass, Georgian, Serpentine, Pierced Flowers, 1800s, 6 x 48 ½ In.	175
Fender, Brass, Louis XV Style, Flower Basket Finial, Paw Feet, Late 1800s, 19 x 43 x 12 In.	259
Fender, Brass, Pierced, Convex Applied Buttons, Paw Feet, Georgian Style, 14 x 20 x 45 In. ...	24
Fender, Brass, Pierced, Openwork, Leaves, Ball Feet, 8¾ x 38½ x 12 In.	163
Fender, Bronze, Brass, Frieze Panels, Harvest & Geometric, 1800s, 9 x 61 x 15 In.	671
Fender, Club, Brass, Leather Seats, Button Tufted, Brown, 1910s, 22 x 70 In. .... illus	1416
Fender, Iron, Serpentine Fence, Brass Acorn Finials, Hairy Paw Feet, 1800s, 16 x 49 In.	345
Fender, Iron, Wirework, 2 Brass Ball Finial, Shaped Feet, Early 1800s, 14 ½ In.	300
Fender, Iron, Wirework, Curved, Black, Turned Brass Feet, Late 1800s, 11 x 29 In. ...... illus	118
Fire Rail, Brass, Wire, Turned Post, Openwork, 14 x 50 x 10 ½ In.	183
Fireback, Cast Iron, 2 Soldiers, Carrying Grapes, Engraved, Embossed, England, 34 x 24 In. .	127
Fireback, Cast Iron, Classical Figure, Holding Scales, Sword, Arched Top, 1800s, 32 x 26 In.	293
Fireback, Cast Iron, Raised Text, Virginia Metalcrafters, 1737, 24 x 20 ½ In.	185
Fireback, Iron, Scrollwork, Fleur-De-Lis, 2 Beasts, France, 1700s, 18 ½ x 18 In. .... illus	354
Firkin, Vertical Slats, Blue Paint, Flattened Handle, So. Hingham, Mass. On Lid, 1800s, 6 In..	3172
Hearth Crane, Wrought Iron, Tapered Legs, Top Bar, Upright Tabs, 1800s, 30¾ x 15¾ In...	439
Kettle Tilter, Scroll Handle, 2 Kettle Hooks, Wrought Iron, 1800s, 19 In............	140
Mantel is listed in the Architectural category.	
Panel, Cast Iron, Shield, Lion Rampant, Sunburst, 5 Fleur-De-Lis, Faux Stud Border, 1700s, 35 In.	649
Pot Hanger, Metal, 10 Hooks, Painted, Grapevines & Leaves, 1900s, 22 ½ x 44 x 21 In. illus	236
Pot, Boiling, Copper, Hammered, Steel Handle, 12 In.	92
Pot, Brass, Molded Rim, Swing Handle, 16 ½ In................................	35
Screens are also listed in the Architectural and Furniture categories.	
Screen, 3-Panel, Folding, Clear, Blue & Green, Leaded Glass, Iron Frame...............	338
Screen, 5-Panel, Brass & Mesh, Handles, 38 x 65 In.	138
Screen, Brass, Flower Garland, Trifold, Handle, Footed, France, 30 x 48 In.	288
Screen, Bronze Dore, Lovebirds, Ram's Head, Louis XVI Style, France, 31¾ x 42½ In.........	502
Screen, Bronze, Louis XV Style, Scrolling Leafy Frame, Mesh, Late 1800s, 29 In. .... illus	413
Screen, Candle, 12 Holders, Peacocks, Elephants, Figures, Iron, 25 x 19 In., Pair	767
Screen, Cast Iron, 3-Panel, Folding, Engraved, 22 ½ In.	104
Screen, Cast Iron, Monumental, Oak Leaf, Acorn Panel, Flower Finial, 57 ½ x 88 x 10 In.	400
Screen, Empire, Mahogany, Needlepoint, Flowers, Carved Crest, Tripod Feet, 46 x 24 In. illus	201
Screen, Gilt Brass, Belgian Tapestry, Scenic, Stick & Ball, Victorian, 39 x 30 In. .... illus	492
Screen, Iron, Wirework, Scroll, England, Early 1800s, 31 x 39 x 15 In.	406
Screen, Louis XV Style, Giltwood, Silk Tapestry Inset, Frame, 1800s, 46⅝ x 31 In................	544
Screen, Louis XVI, Hardwood, Carved, Flower Crest, Needlepoint, Late 1700s, 45 x 17 In. illus	330
Screen, Mahogany, Carved, Bowknot Crest, Leafy Finial, Fabric Panels, 41 x 21 x 15 In........	250
Screen, Pole, Mahogany, Needlepoint Panel, Spiral Finial, Tripod Base, Paw Feet, 57 In. illus	160
Screen, Pole, Mahogany, Needlework, Brown Ground, Rope Twist, Cabriole Legs, c.1900s, 58 In. .	132

Fireplace, Pot Hanger, Metal, 10 Hooks, Painted, Grapevines & Leaves, 1900s, 22 ½ x 44 x 21 In.
$236

Austin Auction Gallery

Top Ten Categories
Hundreds of thousands of users visit our website Kovels.com each month. The ten categories that are the most popular among our visitors are:
1. Pottery & Porcelain
2. Glass & Bottles
3. Antique & Modern Furniture
4. Toys & Dolls
5. Silver & Other Metals
6. Design
7. Advertising & Packaging
8. Lamps & Lighting
9. Prints
10. Photographs & Paper Ephemera

Fireplace, Screen, Bronze, Louis XV Style, Scrolling Leafy Frame, Mesh, Late 1800s, 29 In.
$413

Austin Auction Gallery

FIREPLACE

Fireplace, Screen, Empire, Mahogany, Needlepoint, Flowers, Carved Crest, Tripod Feet, 46 x 24 In.
$201

Stevens Auction Co.

Fireplace, Screen, Gilt Brass, Belgian Tapestry, Scenic, Stick & Ball, Victorian, 39 x 30 In.
$492

Rich Penn Auctions

Fireplace, Screen, Louis XVI, Hardwood, Carved, Flower Crest, Needlepoint, Late 1700s, 45 x 17 In.
$330

Garth's Auctioneers & Appraisers

Fireplace, Screen, Pole, Mahogany, Needlepoint Panel, Spiral Finial, Tripod Base, Paw Feet, 57 In.
$160

Neal Auction Company

Fireplace, Screen, Walnut, Carved Flowers, Leaf, Shakespearean Scene, Late 1800s, 49¾ x 26½ x 16 In.
$1,063

Cowan's Auctions

Fishing, Creel, Rattan, Willow, Leather Bound, Metal Snap Closure, 13 x 8 In.
$35

Copake Auction

F

Screen, Pole, Mahogany, Oval Silk Panel, Leaf Pedestal, Federal Style, Late 1800s, 64 In.	92
Screen, Pole, Queen Anne, Mahogany, Needlework, Spiral Turned Knop, Cabriole Legs, 1700s, 57 In.	225
Screen, Tin, Painted, Red Flowers, Green Pot, 31 x 30 In.	207
Screen, Walnut, Carved Flowers, Leaf, Shakespearean Scene, Late 1800s, 49¾ x 26½ x 16 In. *illus*	1063
Screen, Walnut, Figural Tapestry, Young Girl, Carved, Tripod Legs, 55 In.	504
Stand, Cresset, Melting Pot, Bail Handle, Wrought Iron, 3 Tapered Legs, 1800s, 5⅝ In.	164
Tongs, Ember, Wrought Iron, 4 Scissors Hinges, Spiral Twisted Clamps, 1800s, 16⅓ In.	3000
Tongs, Ember, Wrought Iron, Spring Tension, Penny Pincers, Pipe Stamp, Screen, 1700s, 19½ In.	750
Trammel, Wrought Iron, Sawtooth, Heart At Top, 1800s, 42 In.....................................	375

FISCHER, *see Herend category.*

FISHING

Fishing reels of brass or nickel were made in the United States by 1810. Bamboo fly rods were sold by 1860, often marked with the maker's name. Lures made of metal, or metal and wood, were made in the nineteenth century. Plastic lures were made by the 1930s. All fishing material is collected today and even equipment of the past 30 years is of interest if in good condition with original box.

Creel, Rattan, Willow, Leather Bound, Metal Snap Closure, 13 x 8 In. .... *illus*	35
Creel, Wicker, Leather Lid Ties & Strap, 14 x 7 x 8 In.	195
Line Winder, Brass, Wood, c.1925, 16 x 3½ In.	75
Lure, Carved, Hand Painted, Blue, Signed, Danny Chebra, 7 In....................................	20
Reel, Abu-Matic 155, 1960s...	172
Reel, Daiwa Mini Cast, 1 Spin, Seiko Co., Japan..	39
Reel, English Nottingham Starback, Wood, Brass Frame, c.1890, 5 In.	295
Reel, Kosmic, Casting, Model 935, Square Pillar, Nickel Silver Foot, 1⅜-In. Spool..........	500
Reel, Pfluger Akron, 1893...	22
Tackle Box, Fly Fishing, Metal, 15 Numbered Compartments, Hardy Bros Alnwick................	645
Tackle Box, Marbleized Plastic, Green, USA, 15 x 6 x 4 In..	35

FLAGS *are included in the Textile category.*

FLASH GORDON

Flash Gordon appeared in the Sunday comics in 1934. The daily strip started in 1940. The hero was also in comic books from 1930 to 1970, in books from 1936, in movies from 1938, on the radio in the 1930s and 1940s, and on television from 1953 to 1954. All sorts of memorabilia are collected, but the ray guns and rocket ships are the most popular.

Pistol, Signal, Green & Red, Tin Lithograph, Marx, Box, 7 In. .... *illus*	3172
Print, Flash Gordon & Woman In Space Suits, Rocket, King Features, Mat, 1951, 14 x 9 In. ..	191
Rocket Fighter, Flash Gordon In Cockpit, Tin Lithograph, Windup, King Features, 5 x 12 In....	385
Toy, Click Pistol, Radio Repeater, Tin Lithograph, Marx, Box, 9¾ In..............................	580
Toy, Rocket Fighter Ship 5, Tin Litho, Red, Yellow, Die Cast, Windup, c.1950, 4½ x 12 In. *illus*	516
Wallet, Red, ID Card, Badge, Flash Gordon Space Club, Original Package, 1979, 9 x 6 In.........	12

FLORENCE CERAMICS

Florence Ceramics were made in Pasadena, California, from the 1940s to 1977. Florence Ward created many colorful figurines, boxes, candleholders, and other items for the gift shop trade. Each piece was marked with an ink stamp that included the name *Florence Ceramics Co.* The company was sold in 1964 and although the name remained the same, the products were very different. Mugs, cups, and trays were made.

Figurine, Adeline, Woman, Green Dress, Pink Scarf, Blond Hair, Gilt Trim, Marked, 8½ In.	38

Flash Gordon, Pistol, Signal, Green & Red, Tin Lithograph, Marx, Box, 7 In. $3,172

Pook & Pook

Flash Gordon, Toy, Rocket Fighter Ship 5, Tin Litho, Red, Yellow, Die Cast, Windup, c.1950, 4½ x 12 In. $516

Garth's Auctioneers & Appraisers

Florence Ceramics, Figurine, Woman, Glamorous, White Dress, Gilt, Applied Pompons, Marked, 8¾ In. $100

Lion and Unicorn

F

Flow Blue, Teapot, Lid, Gooseneck Spout, Shaped Handle, Scalloped Base, Grindley, 7 ½ In.
$158

Strawser Auction Group

Folk Art

Some think that folk art, like antiques, must be old, but the work now refers to amateur art, both antique and vintage. Tramp art can be seen as one of the original "turning trash into treasure" movements.

Folk Art, Alligator, Painted, Multicolor, Long Jaws, Nail Teeth, Disc Eyes, Metal Scales, Claws, 16 In.
$266

Leland Little Auctions

Folk Art, Cage, Squirrel, Tin, Wood, Church Shape, Hinged Door, Painted, c.1880, 27 ¼ x 9 In.
$234

Jeffrey S. Evans & Associates

TIP
A brisk rubbing with olive oil will remove most alcohol stains from wood.

Figurine, Woman, Glamorous, White Dress, Gilt, Applied Pompons, Marked, 8 ¾ In. ... *illus* — 100
Plaque, Cameo, Woman, Blond Hair, Brown Hat, White Ground, Brown Trim, Oval, 7 In.... — 22

FLOW BLUE

Flow blue ceramics were made in England and other countries about 1830 to 1900. The dishes were printed with designs using a cobalt blue coloring. The color flowed from the design to the white body so that the finished piece has a smeared blue design. The dishes were usually made of ironstone china. More Flow Blue may be found under the name of the manufacturer. These three marks are used on flow blue dishes.

W.H. Grindley & Co. (Ltd.) c.1880–1891	Johnson Brothers c.1913+	Wood & Son(s) (Ltd.) 1891–1907

Pitcher, United States Capitol Building, Flowers, Applied Handle, 5 ¼ In. .... — 350
Plate, Florence, Turkey, Flowers, White Ground, Bishop & Stonier, 10 ¼ In. .... — 70
Plate, Turkey Center, White Ground, Cauldin, 9 ¾ In., 9 Piece .... — 424
Platter, Temple, Octagonal, White Ground, Podmore & Walker, 18 x 14 In. .... — 85
Platter, Whampoa, River Scene, Floral Border, England, Octagonal, 1800s, 15 In. .... — 313
Teapot, Lid, Gooseneck Spout, Shaped Handle, Scalloped Base, Grindley, 7 ½ In. .... *illus* — 158
Tureen, Bleeding Heart, White Ground, Shaped Base, 8 In.................................... — 73
Tureen, Lid, Egerton, Scalloped Rim, Gold Trim, Footed, 5 ½ x 11 ½ In.......................... — 40

FLYING PHOENIX, *see Phoenix Bird category.*

FOLK ART

Folk art is also listed in many categories of this book under the actual name of the object. See categories such as Box, Cigar Store Figure, Paper, Weather Vane, Wooden, etc.

Alligator, Painted, Multicolor, Long Jaws, Nail Teeth, Disc Eyes, Metal Scales, Claws, 16 In. *illus* — 266
Bird, Carved, Painted, Mounted, Square Wood Base, 1900s, 5 ¼ In.................................. — 263
Bird, Egret, Carved, Painted, Wood, Glass Eyes, Green Plinth, Late 1900s, 56 x 30 In. .... — 561
Bird, Standing Over Nest, Piece Of Gnarled Root, 20 x 16 In. .... — 266
Birdhouse, Cast Iron, Windows, Finial, Red Paint, 3 Pegs On Bottom, c.1910, 9 x 12 x 18 In. — 780
Birdhouse, Wood, Carved, Old Red Paint, Asymmetric Asphalt Shingle Roof, Dormer, Window.. — 30
Butler, Card Holder, Black, Holding Oval Tray, Carved, Wood, Early 1900s, 17 ½ In. .... — 780
Caddy, Spool, Hanging, Pocket, Cutout Crest, Baby Face, Painted, Early 1900s, 15 x 8 In. ...... — 420
Cage, Squirrel, Tin, Wood, Church Shape, Hinged Door, Painted, c.1880, 27 ¼ x 9 In. .. *illus* — 234
Cat, Seated, Limestone, Carved, Blocky Base, William Edmondson, 18 x 7 x 4 ½ In............... — 2486
Cat, Standing, Carved, Black & White Striped, Open Mouth, 19 x 24 ½ In. .... — 236
Chain, Whimsy, Pine, Carved, Figure, Man, Standing, Early 1900s, 47 In. .... *illus* — 288
Chair, Sam The Dot Man McMillan, Painted, Multicolor, Dots, Birds, Animals, 29 x 15 In. *illus* — 354
Chest, Red, Lid Mount, Beveled Top, 1800s, 6 ¾ x 7 ½ x 6 In.......................... — 254
Church, Log, Wood, Painted, 20 In.. — 86
Cowboy, Rodeo, African American, Carved Face & Limbs, Leather, Willie M. Pickett, 19 In.... — 502
Crane In Flight, Spread Wings, Driftwood, Signed, N.E. Dan West, 2011, 64 x 68 In............. — 117
Diorama, Revolutionary War, Battle Of Saratoga, Hand Painted, c.1930, 12 x 14 In. .... *illus* — 222
Eagle, Spread Wings, Carved, Oval Wood Base, 1910s, 10 In....................... — 117
Figurehead, Ship's, Demeter, Goddess Of Harvest, Grains, Wood, Carved, c.1880, 25 ½ x 16 In. *illus* — 8125
Fish, Carved, Tin Fin, Distressed Tan Paint, Silhouettes, Wood Base, 1950, 29 x 41 x 7 In. ..... — 168
Frame, Carved Hardwood, Flowers, Scroll Relief, Black Woman, c.1910, 14 x 10 In. .... — 259
Frame, Patriotic, Red, White, Blue, Stars, Crest, Painted, Chicken Top, Early 1900s, 23 x 16 In. — 600
Lady Liberty, Standing, Blond Hair, Patriotic Dress, Carved, 1900s, 19 In....................... — 270

F

Folk Art, Chain, Whimsy, Pine, Carved, Figure, Man, Standing, Early 1900s, 47 In.
$288

Pook & Pook

Folk Art, Chair, Sam The Dot Man McMillan, Painted, Multicolor, Dots, Birds, Animals, 29 x 15 In.
$354

Leland Little Auctions

Folk Art, Diorama, Revolutionary War, Battle Of Saratoga, Hand Painted, c.1930, 12 x 14 In.
$222

Jeffrey S. Evans & Associates

Folk Art, Figurehead, Ship's, Demeter, Goddess Of Harvest, Grains, Wood, Carved, c.1880, 25 ½ x 16 In.
$8,125

Eldred's

Folk Art, Ram, Standing, Black & White Glaze, Molded Resin, J. Hartfield, 1987, 24 x 40 In.
$123

Brunk Auctions

Folk Art, Retablo, St. James Matamoros, Moor Slayer, Horseback, Raised Sword, Tin, 1800s, 10 In.
$1,298

Austin Auction Gallery

Folk Art, Rug, Hooked, Stylized Horse, Elongated Design, On Stretcher, Velcro, c.1920, 20 x 38 In.
$469

New Haven Auctions

Folk Art, Shield, American Flag, 13 Stars, Scroll Cut, Wood Panel, Vertical Stripes, c.1876, 30 x 20 In.
$6,215

Soulis Auctions

Folk Art, Toy, Dancing Man, Jointed, Repurposed Tin Clock Dials, Wire, Wood Handle, 14 In.
$163

New Haven Auctions

Folk Art, Toy, Steam Engine, Black, Red Brown Trim & Wheels, Tin & Wood, 26 ½ In.
$62

Apple Tree Auction Center

Folk Art, Whirligig, Figural, Man, Bucksaw, Cutting Wood, Cut Out & Painted, 1910s, 16 ¾ In.
$164

Jeffrey S. Evans & Associates

Folk Art, Whirligig, Soldier In Uniform, Carved, Wood, Signed, J.C. Ursch, 1986, 35 In.
$420

Garth's Auctioneers & Appraisers

Mermaid, Playing Stringed Instrument, Pottery, Painted, Josefina Aguilar, 20¾ x 23 In.	236
Mirror, Hand, Make-Do, Wood, Chip Carved, Teardrop Glass, Pa., 1800s, 11 x 6 In.	438
Musician, Black Man, Playing Banjo, Iron, Bradley & Hubbard, c.1880, 10½ x 4¾ x 16 In.	677
Owl, Perched, Carved, Burl, 11½ In.	35
Owl, Spook, Wood, Carved, Metal, Hanger, Wire, Painted, Early 1900s, 18½ x 6½ In.	4294
Penguin, Carved, Wood, White, Black, Square Base, 33 x 16 In.	635
Plaque, Blind Bartimaeus, Carved, Wood, Relief Figures, Elijah Pierce, 1892, 16 x 14 In.	4200
Plaque, Patriotic, Eagle, Multicolor, Gilt, E Pluribus Unum Banner, 1950s, 7 x 45 In.	805
Portrait, L. Philipp, King Louis Philippe, Uniform, Wood Frame, c.1815, 12 x 9½ In.	164
Ram, Standing, Black & White Glaze, Molded Resin, J. Hartfield, 1987, 24 x 40 In. *illus*	123
Retablo, Christ, Pierced Hand, Chromolithograph, Crucifix Finial, Early 1900s, 30 x 6 x 16 In.	288
Retablo, Madonna & Child, Oil On Tin, Wreath Of Roses, 1800s, 13 x 9 In.	531
Retablo, St. James Matamoros, Moor Slayer, Horseback, Raised Sword, Tin, 1800s, 10 In. *illus*	1298
Rooster, Standing, Carved, Wood, Painted, Yellow, Green, Gesso Ground, c.1950, 23½ x 16 In.	180
Rug, Hooked, Stylized Horse, Elongated Design, On Stretcher, Velcro, c.1920, 20 x 38 In. *illus*	469
Sheep, Carved, Applied Wool, Wood Ears, Snout, Feet, Early 1900s, 30 x 17 x 35 In.	6875
Shield, American Flag, 13 Stars, Scroll Cut, Wood Panel, Vertical Stripes, c.1876, 30 x 20 In. *illus*	6215
Table, Sam The Dot Man McMillan, Painted, Multicolor, Lyre Supports, 19 x 25 In.	472
Toy, Dancing Man, Jointed, Repurposed Tin Clock Dials, Wire, Wood Handle, 14 In. *illus*	163
Toy, Steam Engine, Black, Red Brown Trim & Wheels, Tin & Wood, 26½ In. *illus*	62
Wall Pocket, Pine, Reeded Mirror Frame, Leafy Corner, Walter Ullery, 1966, 20 x 18 In.	36
Weather Vane, Patriotic, Carved, Painted, Eagle, Shield & Anchor, Wood Base, 1900s, 24 In.	936
Whimsy, Juggler, Standing, Barber Pole, Stars On Base Corner, Carved, Painted, 1900s, 41 In.	761
Whirligig, 2 Men & Mule, Painted, Wood, Custom Stand, 33½ In.	106
Whirligig, Adam, Bearded Man, Holding Leaf Paddle, Wood Stand, Frank Finney, Late 1900s, 16 In.	1188
Whirligig, Bathing Beauty, Pine, Paddle Arms, Carved, Painted, 1900s, 16½ In.	263
Whirligig, Figural, Man, Bucksaw, Cutting Wood, Cut Out & Painted, 1910s, 16¾ In. *illus*	164
Whirligig, Man On Bike, Wood, Carved, Painted Tin Bike, Stand, c.1910, 13 x 20 In.	500
Whirligig, Man, Painted, Wood, Brushed Steel Stand, Square Base, Mid 1900s, 75 x 33 x 12 In.	295
Whirligig, Owl, Carved, Copper Paddles, Speckled Surface, Painted, Late 1800s, 9½ In.	2928
Whirligig, Pine, Carved, Black Man, White Shirt, Paddle Hands, Mounted, 28½ In.	188
Whirligig, Sea Captain, Wearing Hat, Painted, Black Shoes, 45½ In.	438
Whirligig, Soldier In Uniform, Carved, Wood, Signed, J.C. Ursch, 1986, 35 In. *illus*	420
Whirligig, Windmill, Wood, 4 Blades, Painted Blue, Yellow & Burgundy, c.1915, 14 x 19 In.	85
Whirligig, Windmill, Wood, Painted, Blue Base, Brown Roof, Early 1900s, 14 x 19 In. *illus*	125
Woman, Skeleton, Standing, Calaca, Square Base, La Candelaria, Juan Torres, 31 x 8 In.	826

FOOT WARMER

Foot warmers solved the problem of cold feet in past generations. Some warmers held charcoal, others held hot water. Pottery, tin, and soapstone were the favored materials to conduct the heat. The warmer was kept under the feet, then the legs and feet were tucked into a blanket, providing welcome warmth in a cold carriage or church.

Wood Case, Dovetailed, Pierced Top & Sides, Base Molding, Wire Bail Handle, 6 x 8 In.	163
Wood, Molded, Overhanging Top, Carved, Pierced, Iron Swing Handle, 1776, 6 x 9 x 7 In. *illus*	1170

FOOTBALL *collectibles may be found in the Card and the Sports categories.*

FOSTORIA

Fostoria glass was made in Fostoria, Ohio, from 1887 to 1891. The factory was moved to Moundsville, West Virginia, and most of the glass seen in shops today is a twentieth-century product. The company was sold to Lancaster Colony Corporation in 1983 and closed in 1986. Additional Fostoria items may be listed in the Milk Glass category. Original Fostoria Coin pattern was made in amber, blue, crystal, green, olive green, and red. Reproduction colors include crystal, dark green, pale blue, and red. All coins on original Fostoria are frosted or gold decorated. The

Folk Art, Whirligig, Windmill, Wood, Painted, Blue Base, Brown Roof, Early 1900s, 14 x 19 In.
$125

Pook & Pook

F

Foot Warmer, Wood, Molded, Overhanging Top, Carved, Pierced, Iron Swing Handle, 1776, 6 x 9 x 7 In.
$1,170

Thomaston Place Auction Galleries

Fostoria, American, Strawholder, Dome Lid, Ball Finial, 12½ In.
$431

Rich Penn Auctions

Fostoria, Colony, Candlestick, Twist Stem, Clear Bobeches, Sapphire Blue, c.1920, 14 In., Pair
$225

Woody Auction

Franciscan, Apple, Pitcher, Water, Ice Lip, 8¾ In.
$18

Woody Auction

Franciscan, Coronado, Vase, Rose Bowl, Turquoise, 2¾ x 6½ In.
$28

mehann-59 on eBay

TIP

Black lights can detect repairs to antiques that are invisible to the eye, but be sure you use a longwave black light. A shortwave black light could injure your eyes or skin.

---

coins on new Lancaster Colony pieces are not frosted. Some of these unfrosted coins are being frosted—with either acid or sandblasting—after they are purchased.

American, Strawholder, Dome Lid, Ball Finial, 12½ In. .... *illus*	431
American, Vase, Ruffled Rim, Round Base, 10 x 8 In.	40
Colony, Candlestick, Twist Stem, Clear Bobeches, Sapphire Blue, c.1920, 14 In., Pair ... *illus*	225
Jamestown, Pitcher, Brown, Mid 20th Century, 40 Fluid Oz., 7 x 8¾ In.	68
Myriad, Set, Vase, 2 Double Candlesticks, 1941, 7 In. Vase, 2½-In. Candlesticks.............	54
Victoria, Celery Vase, Clear, Frosted, Metal Stands, Marked, 8¾ In., Pair............................	156

FOVAL, *see Fry category.*

FRAMES *are included in the Furniture category under Frame.*

FRANCISCAN

Franciscan is a trademark that appears on pottery. Gladding, McBean and Company started in 1875. The company grew and acquired other potteries. It made sewer pipes, floor tiles, dinnerware, and art pottery with a variety of trademarks. It began using the trade name *Franciscan* in 1934. In 1936, dinnerware and art pottery were sold under the name *Franciscan Ware.* The company made china and cream-colored, decorated earthenware. Desert Rose, Apple, El Patio, and Coronado were best sellers. The company became Interpace Corporation and in 1979 was purchased by Josiah Wedgwood & Sons. The plant closed in 1984, but production of a few patterns shifted to China and Thailand. For more prices, go to kovels.com.

GMB	FRANCISCAN WARE	Franciscan EARTHENWARE
Gladding, McBean & Co. 1934–1963	Gladding, McBean & Co. c.1940	International Pipe and Ceramics 1963+

Apple, Butter, Cover, Apple Finial, c.1950, 7 x 3¾ In.	50
Apple, Pitcher, Water, Ice Lip, 8¾ In. .... *illus*	18
Apple, Relish, 10 x 4 x 1 In...	35
Coronado, Vase, Rose Bowl, Turquoise, 2¾ x 6½ In. .... *illus*	28
Desert Rose, Platter, 14 x 10 In...	39
Ivy, Platter, 13 x 10 In..	30
Oasis, Plate, Salad, Crescent Shape, 1950s, 9½ x 4½ In.............................	125
Silver Pine, Sugar, Lid, Handles, 2⅜ x 5⅛ In..	49
Starburst, Bowl, Vegetable, Oval, 8 In..	64
Starburst, Pepper Mill, Metal Top, 7 In.	415
Strawberry Fair, Sugar & Creamer, c.1980..	40

FRANCISWARE

Francisware is the name of a glassware made by Hobbs, Brockunier and Company of Wheeling, West Virginia, in the late 1800s. It is a clear or frosted hobnail or swirl pattern glass with an amber-stained rim. Some pieces were made by a pressed glass method, others were mold blown.

Bowl, Oval, Hobnail, Silver Plate Stand, Top Handle, Scroll Feet, Rockford, c.1886, 10 In. *illus*	88
Bowl, Square, Hobnail, Satin Frost, 1880s, 3 x 7 In..................................	64
Dish, Clover Shape, 12½ In..	26
Sugar, Lid, Amber Finial, Hobnail, Frosted, 5½ x 5 In...............................	455
Water Set, Pitcher, 5 Tumblers, Spot-Optic, Frosted Base, 1890s, 8½ In. Pitcher..................	212

FRANKART

Frankart Inc., New York, New York, mass-produced nude "dancing lady" lamps, ashtrays, and other decorative Art Deco items in the 1920s and 1930s. They were made of white lead composition and spray painted. *Frankart Inc.* and the patent number and year were stamped on the base.

Ashtray, Hunter, Stylized Figure, Hat, Snowshoes, Holds Long Rifle, Green, 7 1/4 x 9 1/2 In.	123
Ashtray, Metal, Nude Woman, Kneeling, Pillow, Missing Bowl, Green, 5 3/4 x 4 In. .... *illus*	259
Ashtray, Nude, Seated On Pedestal, Square, Fluted, Green, 9 x 4 3/4 x 7 1/4 In.	892
Bookends, Sailor Boy, Sitting Dog, L Shape Mount, Marked, 7 x 3 1/2 x 5 1/2 In.	50
Bookends, Woman's Head, Flower Headband, Stepped Base, 6 1/2 x 5 x 3 3/4 In.	115
Lamp, 2 Nude Women, Amber, Skyscraper Glass Shade, Art Deco, Marked, 20 1/2 In. .... *illus*	633
Lamp, Electric, Airplane, DC-9, Blue Glass Shade, Chrome Base, 7 3/4 x 13 1/2 x 11 3/4 In.	896
Lamp, Figural, 2 Nude Women, Legs Up, Crackle Glass Shade, Signed, 1928, 19 x 8 x 5 In.	863
Sculpture, Cowboy, Astride Horse, Hollow, Cast Spelter, Embossed, 1928, 7 1/2 x 5 1/3 In.	92
Smoking Stand, Nude Woman, Holding Ashtray, Steel Globe, 24 In.	431

FRANKOMA POTTERY

Frankoma Pottery was originally known as The Frank Potteries when John F. Frank opened shop in 1933. The name "Frankoma," a combination of his last name and the last three letters of Oklahoma, was used beginning in 1934. The factory moved to Sapulpa, Oklahoma, in 1938. Early wares were made from a light cream-colored clay from Ada, Oklahoma, but in 1956 the company switched to a red clay from Sapulpa. The firm made dinnerware, utilitarian and decorative kitchenwares, figurines, flowerpots, and limited edition and commemorative pieces. John Frank died in 1973 and his daughter, Joniece, inherited the business. Frankoma went bankrupt in 1990. The pottery operated under various owners for a few years and was bought by Joe Ragosta in 2008. It closed in 2010. The buildings, assets, name, and molds were sold at an auction in 2011.

Bean Pot, Lid, Plainsman, Peach Mountain, Closed Side Handles, 5 x 8 In.	32
Bean Pot, Lid, Woodland Moss, Leaf Shape Finial, 2 Side Handles, 8 In.	12
Casserole, Lid, Plainsman, Cinnamon, Round, Tab Handles, 4 1/2 In.	16
Casserole, Lid, Westwind, Flame, Round, 2 Qt., 10 In.	70
Ewer, Mottled Pale Green, 8 In.	24
Pitcher, Lazybones, Prairie Green, Sapulpa Clay, No. 4D, 2 Qt., 6 5/8 x 9 In.	55
Soup, Coupe, Plainsman, Woodland Moss, 6 1/8 In.	14
Tumbler, Wagon Wheel, Prairie Green, 10 Oz., 4 5/8 In.	20
Tureen, Soup, Lid, Plainsman, Desert Gold, 3 Qt., 6 x 11 x 9 In.	75
Vase, Spiral, Prairie Green, 11 1/2 x 6 In.	39
Vase, V5, Red Orange, Loop Base, Black Foot, Signed, Grace Lee Frank, 13 x 3 In.	48

FRATERNAL

Fraternal objects that are related to the many different fraternal organizations in the United States are listed in this category. The Elks, Masons, Odd Fellows, and others are included. Also included are service organizations, like the American Legion, Kiwanis, and Lions Club. Furniture is listed in the Furniture category. Shaving mugs decorated with fraternal crests are included in the Shaving Mug category.

Knights Templar, Sword, Straight Blade, Bone Grip, Brass Cross, 1850s, 29 1/2 In. .... *illus*	413
Masonic, Chair, Oak, Upholstered, Alligatored Varnish, Arms, Late 1800s, 69 x 40 x 34 In.	120
Odd Fellows, Apron, Cotton, All-Seeing Eye, Classical Figures, Ribbon, 1800s, 17 x 16 In.	60
Odd Fellows, Drawing, Birds, Watercolor, Crayon, Graphite, Frame, Signed, A. Thoman, 20 x 26 In.	960
Odd Fellows, Lectern, Painted, Pine, Beveled Edge, Motto, Gilt, c.1900, 41 x 30 x 17 In.	123
Odd Fellows, Lodge Staff, Wood, Painted, Red, c.1900, 34 1/2 In.	60
Odd Fellows, Pedestal, Plinth, Pine, Painted, Molded Edge Panels, Lavender, 30 x 24 In.	1200

F

Francisware, Bowl, Oval, Hobnail, Silver Plate Stand, Top Handle, Scroll Feet, Rockford, c.1886, 10 In.
$88

Jeffrey S. Evans & Associates

Frankart, Ashtray, Metal, Nude Woman, Kneeling, Pillow, Missing Bowl, Green, 5 3/4 x 4 In.
$259

Blackwell Auctions

Frankart, Lamp, 2 Nude Women, Amber, Skyscraper Glass Shade, Art Deco, Marked, 20 1/2 In.
$633

Blackwell Auctions

Fraternal, Knights Templar, Sword, Straight Blade, Bone Grip, Brass Cross, 1850s, 29 ½ In.
$413

Leland Little Auctions

Fry, Finger Bowl, Underplate, Cut Glass, Hobstar, Arch, Crosscut Diamond, Engraved Flower, 3 x 6 In.
$540

Woody Auction

TIP

A small chip in a glass goblet or vase can be ground off by a glass-repair expert, but there is little that can be done for cracks.

Fry Foval, Iced Tea, Delft Festooning, Applied Handle, Footed, c.1922, 5 ⅛ In.
$263

Jeffrey S. Evans & Associates

FRY GLASS

Fry glass was made by the H.C. Fry Glass Company of Rochester, Pennsylvania. The company, founded in 1901, first made cut glass and other types of glasswares. In 1922 it patented a heat-resistant glass called Pearl Ovenglass. For two years, 1926–1927, the company made Fry Foval, an opal ware decorated with colored trim. Reproductions of this glass have been made. Depression glass patterns made by Fry may be listed in the Depression Glass category. Some pieces of cut glass may also be included in the Cut Glass category.

FRY

Bowl, Bubbles, Green Threaded Rim, Ruffled, 14 In.	94
Bowl, Cut Glass, Pinwheel, Crosscut Diamond, Strawberry Diamond & Fan, Sawtooth Rim, 4 x 9 In.	96
Celery Dish, Hobstar, Crosshatch, Sawtooth Rim, 10 ½ x 4 ¼ In.	13
Cocktail, Flared, Etched Flowers & Vines, Stem, Round Foot, 1920s, 8 Oz., 4 ½ In.	26
Finger Bowl, Underplate, Cut Glass, Hobstar, Arch, Crosscut Diamond, Engraved Flower, 3 x 6 In. *illus*	540
Pitcher, Lid, 5 Goblets, Black Handle, Finial, Foot, Cut Fan, 10 ⅝ In.	75
Punch Bowl, Removable Stand, Cut Glass, Keystone, 11 ½ x 12 In.	330
Sherbet, Etched, Grape Leaves, Footed, 3 ¼ x 3 ½ In., 6 Piece	30
Soup, Cream, Handles, Footed, Amethyst, 2 ⅛ x 5 ⅛ In.	18

FRY FOVAL

Candlestick, Delft Threading, Wafer, Polished Pontil Mark, c.1922, 12 In., Pair	527
Iced Tea, Delft Festooning, Applied Handle, Footed, c.1922, 5 ⅛ In. *illus*	263
Vase, Jack-In-The-Pulpit, Delft Blue Rim, Polished Pontil Mark, c.1922, 10 In.	380

FULPER

Fulper Pottery Company was incorporated in 1899 in Flemington, New Jersey. It made art pottery from 1909 to 1929. The firm had been making bottles, jugs, and housewares since 1805. Vasekraft is a line of art pottery with glazes similar to Chinese art pottery that was introduced in 1909. Doll heads were made about 1928. The firm became Stangl Pottery in 1929. Stangl Pottery is listed in its own category in this book.

Centerpiece, Scalloped Rim, Underfoot, 3 x 15 In.	270
Fishbowl, Brown Flambe, Flemington Green Matte, Vasekraft Paper Label, 1909, 2 x 11 In.	1875
Lamp, 2-Light, Domed Shade, Caramel, Leaded Glass, Bulbous Bottom, Vasekraft, 17 In.	11340
Vase, Bullet, Black Mirror Glaze, Silver Crystals, Marked, 10 In.	726
Vase, Cucumber, Crystalline, Glaze, Oval, Incised Racetrack Mark, 17 x 7 In. *illus*	2625
Vase, Drip Glaze, Pale Blue, Bulbous, Rolled Rim, 5 Loop Handles, Early 1900s, 10 ½ In.	438
Vase, Multicolor, Short Neck, Molded Rim, 2 Handles, Pinched Base, 18 ½ In.	450
Vase, Yellow Flambe, Ring Handle, Glaze, 12 ½ x 8 In.	1000

FURNITURE

Furniture of all types is listed in this category. Examples dating from the seventeenth century to 2010 are included. Prices for furniture vary in different parts of the country. Oak furniture is most expensive in the West; large pieces over eight feet high are sold for the most money in the South, where high ceilings are found in the old homes. Modern is popular in New York, California, and Chicago. Condition is very important when determining prices. These are NOT average prices but rather reports of unique sales. If the description includes the word *style,* the piece resembles the old furniture style but was made at a later time. It is not a period piece. Small chests that sat on a table or dresser are also included here. Garden furniture is listed in the Garden Furnishings category. Related items may be found in the Architectural, Brass, and Store categories.

Armchairs are listed under Chair in this category.

Armoire, Colonial Style, Hardwood, 2 Paneled Fold Back Doors, Shelf Interior, 74 x 43 In. ..	1098
Armoire, French Provincial, Walnut, Carved, Doors, Bracket Feet, 1700s, 112 x 79 In. . . illus	5605
Armoire, Louis XV, Carved, Mirrored Door, Cabriole Legs, Continental, 1800s, 105 x 60 In..	840
Armoire, Louis XV, Provincial Style, Walnut, 2 Doors, Carved Crest, 1880s, 93 x 51 In...........	1920
Armoire, Louis XV, Walnut, Arched, 2 Doors, Shaped Panels, France, c.1825, 80 x 70 In........	375
Armoire, Mahogany, 2 Paneled Doors, Shelves, Drawers, Louisiana, c.1850, 96 In.	1750
Bar Cart, 3 Tiers, Teak, Black Laminate Shelf, Caster Feet, c.1960, 27 x 18 In.......................	500
Bar Cart, Edward Wormley, Drop Leaf, Bleach Mahogany, Applied Caster, 1960s, 33 x 49 In. ..illus	531
Bar Cart, Wicker, Iron Frame, 2 Circular Tiers, 16 Rings, Wheels, Mid 1900s	148
Bar, Marcel Guillemard, Amboyna, Art Deco Design, Drawers, Doors, c.1930, 40 x 69 In. illus	900
Barstool, Leather, Patchwork Seat, Whiskey Barrel Back, Schubert, c.1979, 44 x 21 In.. Pair	469
Bed Canopy, Crown, French Style, Gilt, Sheer Curtain, Late 1900s, 9 x 24 x 14 In...................	472
Bed Steps, Chippendale Style, Mahogany, Hinged Top, Suter's, c.1980, 17 x 18 In. .... illus	472
Bed, Brass, Ball Finials, Iron Rails, Caster Feet, Half Size, 60 x 79 In...........................	144
Bed, Burl Walnut Veneer, Attached Nightstands, Steel Hardware, Italy, c.1950, 48 x 105 x 88 In.	840
Bed, Cherry, Curly Maple, Gooseneck Head &Foot, Cannonball Finial, c.1850, 50 x 54 x 72 In.	120
Bed, Colonial Style, Mahogany, Ball Finials, Headboard, Turned Feet, Suter's, c.1950, Twin..	1062
Bed, Custom, Steel, Aluminum, Gisue Hariri & Mojgan Hariri, c.1985, 98 x 108 In. ...... illus	5625
Bed, Directoire Style, Female, Headboard, Footboard, Turned Legs, France, 1800s, 72 x 47 In.	354
Bed, Ebonized Bentwood Headboard, Red Leather Rails, Normand Couture, Late 1900s, Queen .	443
Bed, Four-Poster, Chippendale Style, Mahogany, Acanthus, Lion's Head Leg, c.1885, 86 x 68 x 81 In.	567
Bed, Four-Poster, Federal Style, Urn Finials, Shaped Headboard, c.1880, 80 x 56 x 80 In.	177
Bed, Four-Poster, Mahogany, Carved, Cluster Columns, Scroll Crest, Post Base, 1810s, 112 x 78 In. illus	3328
Bed, Four-Poster, Sheraton Style, Canopy, Reeded, Leafy, Finials, Queen, 72 x 66 In.	1872
Bed, Four-Poster, Sheraton, Mahogany, Birch, Reeded Foot, New Hampshire, 1800s, 58 x 62 In. . illus	3500
Bed, Half-Tester, Walnut, Rosewood, Headboard, Removable Crest, Poster, c.1890, 108 x 66 In. illus	1920
Bed, Iron, Center Cartouche, Scrolled, Leafy Frame, 1900s, 97 x 98½ In. .... illus	443
Bed, Louis XVI Style, Wreath Crown, Carved, Gilt, Fluted Legs, Painted, France, 63 x 77 In....	590
Bed, Mahogany, Carved, France, 1930, Twin, 45 x 43½ x 81 In......................................	1750
Bed, Panel, Louis Philippe, Carved, Head & Footboard, Bun & Bracket Feet, 1800s, 73 x 81 In.	472
Bed, Rococo Revival, Footboard, Headboard, Walnut, Carved, Leaves, Rocaille, c.1880, 71 In..	1534
Bed, Shaker, Poplar, Chestnut, Shaped Headboard, Turned Legs, 1850s, 30 x 29 x 70 In. illus	497
Bed, Walnut, Carved, Crown Headboard, Urn Finials, Queen Size, 1800s, 87 x 60 In.	768
Bench, B&B Italia, Wood, Metal, Incurvate Plank Top, Parsons Base, 15 x 35 x 16 In.	671
Bench, Bucket, Pine, 1800s, 36 x 49¾ In..	500
Bench, Bucket, Shallow Top Shelf, Shaped Sides, Gray, Blue, Early 1800s, 36 x 31 x 10 In......	1625
Bench, Butterfly, Pedro Friedeberg, Wood, Carved, Painted, Human Form Feet, 18 x 39 In. illus	6875
Bench, Carved, Embossed, Silver Gilt, Scrolls, Swags, Faux Snake Upholstery, 33 x 86 x 28 In.	420
Bench, Carved, Gilt, Shell & Leaves Decor, Green Seat, Stretcher Base, Mid 1900s, 22 x 19 In. ....illus	708
Bench, Cast Aluminum, Oak Slats, Paint, Cedar Point Amusement Park, Ohio, 1900s, 30 x 48 In.	595
Bench, Church, Rustic, Pine, Scalloped Rail, Plank Seat, Trestle Base, 1800s, 33 x 90 x 18 In.	531
Bench, Finn Juhl, Rosewood, Enamel Steel, Brass, Bovirke, Denmark, 1959, 16 x 17 In.	5938
Bench, G. Nelson, Slats, Black, Herman Miller, 14 In. .... illus	531
Bench, H. Bertoia, Teak Slats, Black Iron Leg, Knoll, c.1960, 15 x 18 x 66 In...........................	1375
Bench, Mixed Wood, Spindle Back, Rectangular Crest, Turned Post, 1830s, 32 x 13 x 46 In..	403
Bench, Pine, Latticework Back, Plank Seat, Turned Tapered Legs, Continental, 35 x 72 In. illus	671
Bench, Pine, Mortised Legs, Cutout Feet, Blue, 1800s, 19 x 83¼ x 11½ In........................	549
Bench, Pine, Scalloped Apron, Mortised Legs, Black, 1800s, 21 x 84 In.	2440
Bench, Rocker, Mammy's, Tablet Crest Rail, 11 Spindles, Shaped Plank Seat, c.1850, 31 x 45 In..	761
Bench, Rosewood, Plank Seat, Reticulated Skirt, Brackets, Stanchions, Chinese, 18 x 72 x 11 In. .	2574
Bench, Rustic, Wood, Old Paint, New Mexico, 17 x 72 x 18½ In. .... illus	600
Bench, Vanity, Iron, Gilt, Faux Leopard Skin, Scimitar Supports, Verona, c.1920, 18 x 21 In.	472
Bench, Vanity, Leather, Black & White, Vinyl Cushion, Contemporary, 24 x 22 In.	59
Bench, Wagon Seat, Iron Construction, Wood, 24 x 51 x 15½ In.	277
Bench, Window, Cornucopia Arms, Mahogany, Gadroon Seat, Paw Feet, c.1880, 27 x 47 In. . illus	512
Bench, Window, Inlay, Flowers, Scrolled Legs, Spherule Feet, Continental, 1800s, 25 x 47 In.	3250
Bench, Window, Mahogany, Upholstered, Curved Back, Barrel Ends, 29 x 45 In.................	230
Bench, Windsor, Bamboo Turned Back, Maple Crest, Splayed Legs, 36 x 72 x 20 In.	688
Bookcase, 2 Parts, Walnut, Glass Door, Drawers, Bracket Feet, Continental, Late 1700s, 74 In.	1125
Bookcase, 5 Shelves, Black Steel Frame, Trestle Base, Pad Feet, Italy, c.1960s, 74 x 30 In.	236

Fulper, Vase, Cucumber, Crystalline, Glaze, Oval, Incised Racetrack Mark, 17 x 7 In.
$2,625

Tocmey & Co. Auctioneers

Furniture, Armoire, French Provincial, Walnut, Carved, Doors, Bracket Feet, 1700s, 112 x 79 In.
$5,605

Austin Auction Gallery

This is an edited listing of current prices. Visit **Kovels.com** to check thousands of prices from previous years and sign up for free information on trends, tips, reproductions, marks, and more.

181

FURNITURE

Furniture, Bar Cart, Edward Wormley, Drop Leaf, Bleach Mahogany, Applied Caster, 1960s, 33 x 49 In.
$531

Toomey & Co. Auctioneers

TIP
Don't move a bed all by yourself unless the bed is on wheels. You may cause stress on one of the bed's joints and break it. Of course, you could also stress your own joints.

Furniture, Bar, Marcel Guillemard, Amboyna, Art Deco Design, Drawers, Doors, c.1930, 40 x 69 In.
$900

Michaan's Auctions

Furniture, Bed Steps, Chippendale Style, Mahogany, Hinged Top, Suter's, c.1980, 17 x 18 In.
$472

Leland Little Auctions

Furniture, Bed, Custom, Steel, Aluminum, Gisue Hariri & Mojgan Hariri, c.1985, 98 x 108 In.
$5,625

Wright

Furniture, Bed, Four-Poster, Mahogany, Carved, Cluster Columns, Scroll Crest, Post Base, 1810s, 112 x 78 In.
$3,328

Neal Auction Company

Furniture, Bed, Four-Poster, Sheraton, Mahogany, Birch, Reeded Foot, New Hampshire, 1800s, 58 x 62 In.
$3,500

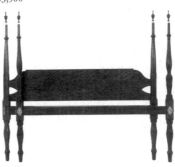

Eldred's

Furniture, Bed, Half-Tester, Walnut, Rosewood, Headboard, Removable Crest, Poster, c.1890, 108 x 66 In.
$1,920

Garth's Auctioneers & Appraisers

Furniture, Bed, Iron, Center Cartouche, Scrolled, Leafy Frame, 1900s, 97 x 98 ½ In.
$443

Austin Auction Gallery

Furniture, Bed, Shaker, Poplar, Chestnut, Shaped Headboard, Turned Legs, 1850s, 30 x 29 x 70 In.
$497

Jeffrey S. Evans & Associates

Bookcase, Arts & Crafts, Oak, Overhanging Top, Backsplash, 2 Doors, Limbert, 57 x 48 In...	1230
Bookcase, Barrister, 4 Stack, Oak, Lead Glass, Globe Wernicke Co., 58 In. .... *illus*	1280
Bookcase, Barrister, Mahogany, Bracket Base, 4 Parts, Macey, 56 x 35 x 12 In...........	246
Bookcase, Barrister, Oak, 6 Stack, Flip-Up Glass, Globe-Wernicke, c.1910, 92 x 34 In._____	900
Bookcase, Biedermeier, Ebonized Details, 2-Tone, 1800s, 71 x 48 x 22 In...............	1000
Bookcase, Breakfront, Molded Cornice, 3 Doors, Cabinet, Turned Feet, Early 1900s, 91 x 65 In..	590
Bookcase, Cabinet, 3 Shelves & Drawers, Tapered Legs, Bornholm Nobler, c.1960, 71 x 39 In..	1000
Bookcase, Cherry, Faux Bamboo, 5 Shelves, Ethan Allen, Late 1900s, 81 x 35 In., Pair *illus*	767
Bookcase, G. Stickley, Oak, 2 Doors, Glass, Panel, Iron Pulls, 56 x 12 x 62 In .... *illus*	7500
Bookcase, G. Stickley, Oak, Glass, Copper Pulls, Hinged Door, Shelves, 56 x 13 x 35 In..........	3250
Bookcase, George III Style, Mahogany, Breakfront, Broken Arch Crest, 1800s, 10 x 83 x 22 In. ...	2900
Bookcase, Georgian Style, Mahogany, 3 Doors, 5 Drawers, Maitland-Smith, c.1980, 91 x 43 In. ...*illus*	885
Bookcase, Gilt Metal, 6 Wood Shelves, Contemporary, 1900s, 93 x 39 In.	480
Bookcase, Grand Rapids, Quartersawn Oak, 3 Doors, Adjustable Shelves, Early 1900s, 42 x 62 In..	3250
Bookcase, Macey, Mahogany, 4 Stack, Sectional, Early 1900s, 62 x 17 In............................	1071
Bookcase, Mahogany, 4 Doors, Adjustable Shelves, 87 x 84 In....................................	2500
Bookcase, Mahogany, Doors, Shelves, Plinth Base, Late 1900s, 53 ½ x 60 In...................	1180
Bookcase, Mahogany, Gallery Top, Leaded Stained Glass Door, c.1890, 65 In................	995
Bookcase, Mahogany, Glass Front, 2 Drawers, Carved Column, 1800s, 60 x 54 In. .... *illus*	1053
Bookcase, Mahogany, Routed Edge Top, 2 Shelves, Slat Ends, Casters, 1910s, 36 x 23 x 23 In..	210
Bookcase, Oak, Molded Cornice, Cabinet Doors, Plinth Base, Bun Feet, Brenton, 74 x 87 In.	708
Bookcase, Renaissance Revival, Carved, Shelves, Footed, Early 1900s, 70 x 38 In.................	767
Bookcase, Renaissance Revival, Walnut, Arched, Tombstone Glass Doors, c.1870, 110 x 56 In. ...	3198
Bookcase, Revolving, 2 Tiers, Oak, Collapsible Bookstand, Brass Casters, 36 x 21 In. ... *illus*	500
Bookcase, Revolving, Brass Gallery, Side Slats, Casters, c.1900, 35 x 20 In. .... *illus*	330
Bookcase, Revolving, Edwardian, Rosewood, 2 Shelves, Caster Feet, Late 1800s, 34 x 19 In..	561
Bookcase, Revolving, Fruitwood, 2 Shelves, Caster Feet, Late 1900s, 31 x 18 In.............	472
Bookcase, Revolving, Georgian Style, Burl Veneer Top, 4 Shelves, Bracket Feet, 1900s, 24 In...	180
Bookcase, Shaker, Butternut, Divider, 3 Shelves, Painted, c.1840, 36 x 27 In. .... *illus*	615
Bookcase, Starbay, 2 Parts, 3 Adjustable Shelves, Brass Flush-Mount Pulls, 80 x 39 x 16 In..	1404
Bookcase, Teak, 3 Open Shelves, 3 Drawers, Tapered Legs, Denmark, c.1950, 62 x 30 x 17 In..	384
Bookcase, Tim Mackaness, Tree Frog, Black Walnut, Koa, c.1975, 87 x 49 In. .... *illus*	6250
Bookcase, William & Mary Style, Mirror Doors, Ball Feet, 1800s, 89 x 40 In. .... *illus*	6765
Bookrack, Black Forest, Swiss Carved, Walnut, Cockerel, Folding Panels, c.1900, 8 x 26 In...	98
Bookstand, Dictionary, Adjustable, Wood, Cast Iron Base, Arched Legs, Harvard, 45 In. *illus*	266
Bookstand, Gilt, Adjustable Reading Shelf, Enamel, Ball & Claw Feet, Belle Epoque, 5 x12 In	590
Bookstand, Oak, Folding, Carved, Scrolled Leaves, Monogram, Holland, 1700s, 22 In....... .	1500
Buffet, French Provincial, Deux Corps, Cherry, Carved, Panel Doors, 1800s, 98 x 64 In.	2944
Buffet, Louis XV Style, Oak, Pink, Gray, Marble Top, Drawers, 1800s, 38 x 70 In...................	756
Buffet, Mahogany, Demilune Shape, Brass Serpentine Shelf, Tapered Legs, Late 1900s, 43 x 48 In.	354
Bureau, Chippendale, Mahogany, 2 Sets Of 4 Drawers, Back Door, c.1750, 29 x 31 In.......	5315
Bureau, Louis XVI Style, Cylinder, Cherubs, Ormolu, Medallion, Brass, 43 x 46 x 24 In........	5250
Bureau, Mahogany, Serpentine Front, 5 Drawers, Brass Bail Handles, 1800s, 37 x 42 In.	625
Bureau, Neoclassical, Sponge Painted, Step Back Top, 5 Drawers, c.1830, 10 x 9 In.............	313
Bureau, Sheraton, Tiger Maple, Turret Corner Top, Drawers, Ball Feet, c.1815, 41 In........	1625
Bureau, Slant Front, 6 Drawers, Oak, Arched Openings, c.1914, 12 x 13 In.	384
Bureau, Slant Front, Chippendale Style, 5 Drawers, Late 1800s, 19 x 17 ½ x 10 In. ...... *illus*	352
Bureau, Walnut, Serpentine, 3 Drawers, Inlay, 1800s, 16 x 18 In........	502
Cabinet, 2 Doors, Oak, Glass Shelves, Mirrored Back, Light-Up Interior, 78 x 44 In.............	123
Cabinet, 2 Tiers, Octagonal, Pine Drawers, Revolving, Rectangular Base, 66 x 30 x 30 In.. *illus*	3390
Cabinet, 6 Drawers, Rosewood, Oak, Brass, Mogens Lysell, Denmark, c.1955, 32 x 30 In. *illus*	3000
Cabinet, American Aesthetic, Walnut, Ebonized, Carved, Parcel Gilt, Bun Feet, c.1890, 60 In. *illus*	8320
Cabinet, Art Deco Style, Walnut, Flowers, Shelves, Cabriole Legs, c.1910, 62 x 37 In..............	156
Cabinet, Bar, Teak, 4 Doors, Slide-Out Top, Laminate, Denmark, c.1960, 32 x 43 In. ... *illus*	500
Cabinet, Boule, Inlay, Ebonized, Walnut, Brass, Marble Top, c.1865, 44 x 41 In. .... *illus*	2460
Cabinet, Chinoiserie, 2 Doors Over Drawers, Carved, Berkey & Gay, 1930s, 70 x 43 In............	240
Cabinet, Console, Wood, Vine Design, Marble Top, Shelves, c.1890, 43 x 18 In., Pair..............	1000
Cabinet, Corner, Hanging, Chinoiserie, Convex Shape, Doors, c.1910, 42 x 17 In. .... *illus*	502
Cabinet, Corner, Teak, 2 Doors, Shelves, 3 Drawers, Inset Footboard, 1900s, 69 x 39 In........	936
Cabinet, Demilune Console, Mirror, Marble Top, Blue, Painted, Reeded Legs, c.1930, 92 x 31 In...	384

Furniture, Bench, Butterfly, Pedro Friedeberg, Wood, Carved, Painted, Human Form Feet, 18 x 39 In.
$6,875

New Orleans Auction Galleries

Furniture, Bench, Carved, Gilt, Shell & Leaves Decor, Green Seat, Stretcher Base, Mid 1900s, 22 x 19 In.
$708

Leland Little Auctions

F

Furniture, Bench, G. Nelson, Slats, Black, Herman Miller, 14 In.
$531

Eldred's

> **TIP**
> *Different types of fur-niture polish give dif-ferent finishes. Liquid, oil polish, and paste wax leave a high luster. Cream polish and spray wax leave a medium luster.*

Furniture, Bench, Pine, Latticework Back, Plank Seat, Turned Tapered Legs, Continental, 35 x 72 In.
$671

Neal Auction Company

FURNITURE

Furniture, Bench, Rustic, Wood, Old Paint, New Mexico, 17 x 72 x 18 ½ In. $600

Santa Fe Art Auction

TIP

Lick a clean cotton swab and use it to remove dirt from small carvings on furniture. Saliva has enzymes that help dissolve the dirt.

Furniture, Bench, Window, Cornucopia Arms, Mahogany, Gadroon Seat, Paw Feet, c.1880, 27 x 47 In. $512

Brunk Auctions

Furniture, Bookcase, Barrister, 4 Stack, Oak, Lead Glass, Globe Wernicke Co., 58 In. $1,280

Roland Auctioneers & Valuers

Cabinet, Display Case, 2 Doors, Brass Hinges, Ebonized, Chinoiserie, 64 x 33 In.	512
Cabinet, Display, Cherry, 2 Doors, Mirror Back, Fretwork Crest, 85 x 45 x 15 In.	135
Cabinet, Display, Italian Style, Walnut, Gilt, 2 Glass Shelves, Velvet Base, 56 In.	165
Cabinet, Display, Jacobean Style, Mahogany, Walnut Veneer, Drawers, 77 x 64 In.	625
Cabinet, Display, Louis XV Style, Mahogany, Plexiglas Panels, Spain, Late 1900s, 59 x 26 In. *illus*	432
Cabinet, Display, Walnut, Burl Veneer, Pane Doors, Flush Base, 91 x 47 In.	1770
Cabinet, Federal, Cherry, 4 Drawers, 2 Doors, French Feet, c.1790, 76 x 40 In.	732
Cabinet, Filing, Cherry, Leather Top, 4 Drawers, Metal Pulls, Bracket Feet, 30 x 36 In.	118
Cabinet, Filing, Oak, 10 Drawers, Porcelain Pulls, 1900s, 34 x 46 x 35 In. *illus*	649
Cabinet, Filing, Stacking, 3 Sections, Mahogany, Square Feet, Weiss, 59 In.	367
Cabinet, Gio Ponti, Poplar, Beech, Steel, Geometric, Label, Italy, 29 x 88 In. *illus*	55000
Cabinet, Hanging, Wood Peg, Door, Shelves, Knob Handle, Painted, 1800s, 42 x 10 x 30 In.	961
Cabinet, Henredon, Campaign Style, Walnut, 2 Doors, c.1970, 28 x 32 In., 4 Piece	1416
Cabinet, Jewelry, Beveled Glass, Ormolu Frame, Velvet Lined, France, 9 x 5 In. *illus*	144
Cabinet, Lacquer, Multicolor, Painted, 2 Hinged Doors, Chinese, 1900s, 60 x 36 In. *illus*	384
Cabinet, Mahogany, Carved, 2 Drawers, 2 Doors, Early 1800s, 93 x 52 In.	688
Cabinet, Memphis Style, Pine, Door, Painted Geometric Shapes, 4 Legs, David Marsh, 34 In.	225
Cabinet, New Hope School, Mixed Wood, Tambour Doors, 1970s, 23 x 26 x 40 In.	1040
Cabinet, Oak, 2 Drawers, 2 Doors, 1800s, 37 x 50 ½ In.	531
Cabinet, Oak, Tambour Door, Brass Pulls, 8 Interior Shelves, c.1910, 59 x 16 In.	363
Cabinet, Pedestal, Mahogany, Marble Top, Door, Flush Base, 1800s, 31 x 14 In.	266
Cabinet, Peter Hunt, 4 Seasons, 2 Paneled Doors, Anno 50, Ovince, 1950s, 72 x 41 In. *illus*	2091
Cabinet, Pine, Red Brown, 9 Drawers, Grained Burl Panels, 1850s, 38 x 22 In.	450
Cabinet, Pine, Tabletop, 12 Cubbyholes, Molded Cornice, Green, 1800s, 14 x 26 In.	1098
Cabinet, Quartersawn Oak, Lion's Head, 4 Shelves, Glass, Carved, Chinese, 76 x 56 In. *illus*	516
Cabinet, R. Whitley, Revolving Bar, Walnut, Maple, Carved, Doors, 1960, 35 x 29 In. *illus*	4225
Cabinet, Record, Cylinder, Oak, Drawers, Brass, 1899, 36 x 20 x 17 In. *illus*	431
Cabinet, Renaissance Revival, Bedside, Walnut, Pompeo Toniutti, Bologna, c.1880, 31 x 20 In. *illus*	354
Cabinet, Renaissance Revival, Walnut, Carved, Luigi Frullini, 1800s, 70 x 92 In. *illus*	30000
Cabinet, Sewing, Shaker, Pine, Maple & Cherry, Drawers, Hinged Door, c.1850, 28 x 33 In.	750
Cabinet, Spice, Mahogany, Oak, Dovetailed, White Pine, 6 Drawers, Scalloped Skirt, c.1950, 19 In.	148
Cabinet, Spice, Pine, 8 Drawers, Porcelain Knobs, Cutout Bracket Base, 15 x 10 x 14 In.	150
Cabinet, Storage, White Walnut, 2 Doors, Carved, 78 x 40 In.	130
Cabinet, Swingline, Lacquer, Masonite, Walnut, Henry P. Glass, 1952, 33 In.	9375
Cabinet, Tabernacle, Carved, Painted, Wood, Gilt, Tombstone Door, c.1910, 20 x 18 In. *illus*	295
Cabinet, Tole, Grain Painted, Bouquets, Marble Top, Scroll Feet, 1850s, 32 x 16 In. *illus*	240
Cabinet, Wall, Paolo Buffa, Drop Front, Walnut, Silvered Glass, Brass, Italy, 1940s, 54 x 50 In.	1375
Cabinet, Walnut, 2 Drawers, Door, Continental, 1800s, 33 ½ x 22 In.	128
Cabinet, Walnut, Chrome Plated Steel, Metal Legs, Herman Miller, c.1955, 80 x 31 In.	2860
Cabinet, Walnut, Urn Design Panel, Tapered Legs, Continental, c.1890, 36 x 24 In.	469
Cabinet, Wood, Blue Paint, Drawer Over Door, Towel Bar, Mirror, New Mexico, 28 x 19 In. *illus*	552
Candlestand, 2 Candleholders, Oak, Adjustable, Threaded Post, Tripod, 1800s, 15 In.	936
Candlestand, Black Paint, Flowers, Gilt, Scrolled Feet, 1800s, 25 x 16 In.	413
Candlestand, Chippendale, Mahogany, Columnar Pedestal, Cabriole Legs, c.1790, 27 x 17 In.	1200
Candlestand, George III, Tilt Top, Mahogany, Carved, Ball & Claw Feet, 1700s, 27 ½ In.	1375
Candlestand, Queen Anne, Tiger Maple, Square Top, Turned Pedestal, Pad Feet, c.1790, 25 In.	163
Candlestand, Tilt Top, Mahogany, Flower, Bird, Pedestal, Slipper Feet, c.1890, 27 In. *illus*	225
Candlestand, Tilt Top, Mahogany, Rectangular, Canted Corners, 22 x 16 x 28 In.	43
Candlestand, Tilt Top, Walnut, Cabriole Legs, Snake Feet, New England, 1750s, 25 ½ In.	875
Canterbury, Burl Walnut Veneer, Mahogany, Lion's Head Pulls, Caster Feet, 20 x 22 In.	313
Canterbury, Mahogany, Baluster Turnings, Raised Pierced Handle, 1810s, 20 x 18 In. *illus*	222
Canterbury, Regency Style, Mahogany, Turned Post, Brass Pull, c.1890, 18 x 20 x 14 In.	281
Canterbury, Regency, Burl, Mahogany, Openwork, Removable Posts, Caster Feet, 15 x 22 In. *illus*	1968
Canterbury, Victorian, Walnut, Jigsaw Cutout Ends, Turned Handle, 1880s, 28 x 18 x 11 In.	158
Canterbury, Walnut, Carved, Leaf Design, Turned Legs, Brass Casters, 21 x 20 In. *illus*	469
Cart, G. Nelson, Steel Frame, Grasscloth Top, Herman Miller, 1950s, 24 x 17 In. *illus*	438
Cart, Regency, Mahogany, Gallery Top, Frieze Drawer, Shelves, Casters, c.1890, 41 x 44 In.	1830
Cart, Serving, Edwardian, Mahogany, Drop Leaf, 3 Drawers, Casters, c.1910, 26 x 26 In. *illus*	236
Case, Shaker, 23 Drawers, Red, Painted, Knob Pulls, Dovetailed, Mid 1800s, 29 x 31 In.	4375
Cellarette, Mahogany, Dovetailed Box, Hinged Lid, Cock-Beaded, Early 1900s, 39 x 19 In. *illus*	1416

Furniture, Bookcase, Cherry, Faux Bamboo, 5 Shelves, Ethan Allen, Late 1900s, 81 x 35 In., Pair
$767

Leland Little Auctions

Furniture, Bookcase, Georgian Style, Mahogany, 3 Doors, 5 Drawers, Maitland-Smith, c.1980, 91 x 43 In.
$885

Leland Little Auctions

Furniture, Bookcase, Mahogany, Glass Front, 2 Drawers, Carved Column, 1800s, 60 x 54 In.
$1,053

Thomaston Place Auction Galleries

Furniture, Bookcase, Revolving, 2 Tiers, Oak, Collapsible Bookstand, Brass Casters, 36 x 21 In.
$500

Eldred's

Furniture, Bookcase, Revolving, Brass Gallery, Side Slats, Casters, c.1900, 35 x 20 In.
$330

Garth's Auctioneers & Appraisers

Furniture, Bookcase, Shaker, Butternut, Divider, 3 Shelves, Painted, c.1840, 36 x 27 In.
$615

Morphy Auctions

Furniture, Bookcase, Tim Mackaness, Tree Frog, Black Walnut, Koa, c.1975, 87 x 49 In.
$6,250

Wright

Furniture, Bookcase, William & Mary Style, Mirror Doors, Ball Feet, 1800s, 89 x 40 In.
$6,765

Brunk Auctions

Furniture, Bookstand, Dictionary, Adjustable, Wood, Cast Iron Base, Arched Legs, Harvard, 45 In.
$266

Bunch Auctions

FURNITURE

Furniture, Bureau, Slant Front, Chippendale Style, 5 Drawers, Late 1800s, 19 x 17 ½ x 10 In.
$352

Hindman

Furniture, Cabinet, 2 Tiers, Octagonal, Pine Drawers, Revolving, Rectangular Base, 66 x 30 x 30 In.
$3,390

Soulis Auctions

Furniture, Cabinet, 6 Drawers, Rosewood, Oak, Brass, Mogens Lysell, Denmark, c.1955, 32 x 30 In.
$3,000

Wright

Furniture, Cabinet, American Aesthetic, Walnut, Ebonized, Carved, Parcel Gilt, Bun Feet, c.1890, 60 In.
$8,320

Neal Auction Company

Furniture, Cabinet, Bar, Teak, 4 Doors, Slide-Out Top, Laminate, Denmark, c.1960, 32 x 43 In.
$500

Kamelot Auctions

Furniture, Cabinet, Boule, Inlay, Ebonized, Walnut, Brass, Marble Top, c.1865, 44 x 41 In.
$2,460

Morphy Auctions

Furniture, Cabinet, Corner, Hanging, Chinoiserie, Convex Shape, Doors, c.1910, 42 x 17 In.
$502

Leland Little Auctions

Furniture, Cabinet, Display, Louis XV Style, Mahogany, Plexiglas Panels, Spain, Late 1900s, 59 x 26 In.
$432

Garth's Auctioneers & Appraisers

Furniture, Cabinet, Filing, Oak, 10 Drawers, Porcelain Pulls, 1900s, 34 x 46 x 35 In.
$649

Austin Auction Gallery

Furniture, Cabinet, Gio Ponti, Poplar, Beech, Steel, Geometric, Label, Italy, 29 x 88 In.
$55,000

Palm Beach Modern Auctions

Furniture, Cabinet, Jewelry, Beveled Glass, Ormolu Frame, Velvet Lined, France, 9 x 5 In.
$144

Blackwell Auctions

Furniture, Cabinet, Lacquer, Multicolor, Painted, 2 Hinged Doors, Chinese, 1900s, 60 x 36 In.
$384

Leland Little Auctions

Furniture, Cabinet, Peter Hunt, 4 Seasons, 2 Paneled Doors, Anno 50, Ovince, 1950s, 72 x 41 In.
$2,091

Brunk Auctions

Furniture, Cabinet, Quartersawn Oak, Lion's Head, 4 Shelves, Glass, Carved, Chinese, 76 x 56 In.
$516

Stevens Auction Co.

Furniture, Cabinet, R. Whitley, Revolving Bar, Walnut, Maple, Carved, Doors, 1960, 35 x 29 In.
$4,225

Freeman's

Furniture, Cabinet, Record, Cylinder, Oak, Drawers, Brass, 1899, 36 x 20 x 17 In.
$431

Hartzell's Auction Gallery Inc.

Furniture, Cabinet, Renaissance Revival, Bedside, Walnut, Pompeo Toniutti, Bologna, c.1880, 31 x 20 In.
$354

Austin Auction Gallery

Furniture, Cabinet, Renaissance Revival, Walnut, Carved, Luigi Frullini, 1800s, 70 x 92 In.
$30,000

Cottone Auctions

Furniture, Cabinet, Tabernacle, Carved, Painted, Wood, Gilt, Tombstone Door, c.1910, 20 x 18 In.

$295

Leland Little Auctions

Furniture, Cabinet, Tole, Grain Painted, Bouquets, Marble Top, Scroll Feet, 1850s, 32 x 16 In.

$240

Garth's Auctioneers & Appraisers

Furniture, Cabinet, Wood, Blue Paint, Drawer Over Door, Towel Bar, Mirror, New Mexico, 28 x 19 In.

$552

Santa Fe Art Auction

Cellarette, Regency, Carved Mahogany, Hinged Lid, Medallion, Early 1800s, 29 x 28 x 22 In.	2750
Cellarette, Regency, Mahogany, Carved, Brass Ring Handles, c.1820, 22 x 28 In. .... *illus*	854
Chair Set, Chippendale, Owl Splats, Trapezoid Slip Seats, Mass., c.1890, 37 In., 4	1065
Chair Set, Folding, Bamboo, Rattan, Slat Back & Seat, Stretcher, 1900s, 34 In., 8	767
Chair Set, G. Stickley, Side, Oak, Leather Seat, Rear Stretchers, c.1905, 36 In., 4	975
Chair Set, Niels Koefoeds, Teak, Upholstered Seat, Straight Legs, c.1960, 35 In., 4	1652
Chair Set, Rush Seats, Turned Legs, Stretcher Base, L. Hitchcock, c.1950, 34 In., 4	767
Chair, Adam Style, Slip Seat, Turned Legs, Arms, Angelica Kaufman, 32½ In., Pair	1216
Chair, Banister Back, Pierced Crest, Heart, Crown, Turned Stretchers, 1745, 47 x 17 In.........	4688
Chair, Barcelona, Brown Leather, Stainless Steel Frame, Knoll, 29 x 29 x 31 In., Pair	4688
Chair, Baseball Glove, Leather, Steel, Casters, De Pas Lomazzi & D'Urbino Joe, 39 x 73 In. .....*illus*	2360
Chair, Bergere, Carved, Crest & Stiles, Upholstered, Closed Arms, 1800s, 45 In., Pair.............	400
Chair, Bergere, Louis XV Style, Fruitwood, Upholstered, Closed Arms, c.1980, 34 In., Pair *illus*	2006
Chair, Bergere, Louis XV Style, Wing, Walnut, Cabriole Legs, Closed Arms, 43 x 28 In. .. *illus*	352
Chair, Bergere, Louis XVI Style, Carved, Upholstered, Closed Arms, c.1910, 33 In., Pair	708
Chair, Billiards Room, Adjustable, Metal & Wood, 40 In. .... *illus*	240
Chair, Black Forest, Walnut, Carved, Upholstered Panel, Open Arms, 1800s, 37 In., Pair *illus*	3500
Chair, Celestial, Lacquer, Painted, Gilt, Pedro Friedeberg, 15 x 22 x 7 In. ...... *illus*	6175
Chair, Chippendale, Lolling, Mahogany, Open Arms, Upholstered, Mass., c.1790, 45 In.........	530
Chair, Chippendale, Mahogany, Carved, Pierced Splat, Ball & Claw Feet, c.1765, 38 In., Pair.	1220
Chair, Chippendale, Ribbonback, Mahogany, Serpentine Seat, Molded Legs, c.1780, 37 In.	4305
Chair, Corner, Georgian, Mahogany, X-Stretcher, Carved Back, Late 1700s, 33 In.	225
Chair, Desk, Ettore Sottsass, Plastic, Upholstered, Steel, Casters, Italy, c.1968, 32 x 20 In. *illus*	1000
Chair, Eames Style, Wood, Swivel, Side, Caster Feet, 35 x 18 In...	128
Chair, Eames, Aniline Dyed Ash, Plywood, Rubber, Herman Miller, c.1950, 27 In., Pair *illus*	1625
Chair, Edwardian, Inlaid, Mahogany, Plush Upholstery, Paw Feet, c.1900, 35 In.	767
Chair, Edwardian, Satinwood, Downswept Arms, Padded Seat, Saber Legs, c.1900, 35 In. *illus*	938
Chair, Federal, Walnut, Upholstered, Pierced Splats, 1750s, 39 In., Pair	4375
Chair, Frank Lloyd Wright, Walnut, Black, Leather, Avery Coonley Playhouse, 34 In. ..... *illus*	10000
Chair, Gazelle, Bronze, Cane, Restrained Arms, Shaped Seat & Rail, Dan Johnson, 31 In. *illus*	2500
Chair, Gehry, Laminated Cardboard, Masonite, Easy Edges, Wiggle, c.1970, 38 In.	1500
Chair, George III, Carved, Mahogany, Library, Square Legs, Stretcher, Arms, Late 1700s, 39 In. .*illus*	1250
Chair, George III, Mahogany, Blue, Upholstered, Arms, c.1810, 33 In...........................	64
Chair, Ghost, Polycarbonate, Circle Back, Philippe Starck, 1900s, 37 In...............................	207
Chair, Gio Ponti, Walnut, Upholstered, Label, Italy, 40 x 26 x 28 In., Pair .... *illus*	10000
Chair, Gothic Revival Style, Oak, Carved Panels, Lift Seat, Arms, 1900s, 75 x 30 In.	3250
Chair, Gothic Revival, Needlepoint, Upholstered, Caster Feet, Victorian, 30 In., Child's..........	201
Chair, Hardwood, Carved, Phoenix, Dragons, Flowers, Arms, Chinese, 1950s, 34 In. .... *illus*	590
Chair, Hardwood, Reticulated Back, Paneled Plank Seat, Chinese, 1800s, 36 x 24 In., Pair ...	510
Chair, High Back, Walnut, Cane, Crown Crest Rail, Putti, Carved Armrest, 46 x 23 x 24 In....	813
Chair, Hill House, Black Lacquer, Wood, Upholstered, Mackintosh, Late 1900s, 55 In., Pair .*illus*	960
Chair, Horseshoe Shape, Carved, Square Legs, Stretcher Base, Chinese, c.1910, 37 In. .. *illus*	148
Chair, Jonathan Whitney, Spindle Back, Shaped Crest, Bamboo Turned Legs, 1828, 35 In., Pair.	438
Chair, Ladder Back, Splats, Ribbon Arms, Turned Supports, Signed T.L., 45 In.	244
Chair, Leather, Buttoned Cushion Back, Swiveling, Chromed Steel Base, c.1950, 40 In. *illus*	207
Chair, Lolling, Federal, Mahogany, Upholstered, Block Legs, c.1800, 45 In. .... *illus*	1250
Chair, Louis XVI Style, Gilt, Cane Seat, Damask Upholstery, Arms, c.1890, 38 In., Pair . *illus*	2124
Chair, Louis XVI, Fruitwood, Carved, Needlework, Arms, 47 In. .... *illus*	250
Chair, Lounge, Finn Juhl, Upholstered, Green, Yellow, Teak, Brass, Denmark, 1953, 29 In.....	7500
Chair, Lounge, Frank Gehry, Rocking, Walnut, Easy Edges, Inc., 1972, 25 In. .... *illus*	4688
Chair, Lounge, H. Probber, High Back, Walnut, Plinth, c.1970, 37½ x 34 In...........................	200
Chair, Lounge, Hans Wagner, Oak, Flat Armrest, Tapered Legs, Cord Seat, 28 In. .... *illus*	3510
Chair, Lounge, Leather, Cantilever, Chrome, Tufted Upholstery, 31 In., Pair .... *illus*	384
Chair, Lounge, Maple Frame, Button Back, Tweed Upholstery, Milo Baughman, 29 x 30 In. ..*illus*	461
Chair, Lounge, Richard Schultz, White & Brown, Knoll, 1900s, 36 x 25½ x 76 In., Pair........	1300
Chair, Lounge, Upholstered, Ball Feet, Damask, Ethan Allen, 36 In...................................	266
Chair, Mahogany, Cane Seat, Carved, Gilt, Regency, Side, 33 In., Pair	125
Chair, Mahogany, Carved, Shield Back, Tapered Legs, Spade Feet, Federal, N.Y., 38 In............	554
Chair, Mahogany, Egyptian, Gesso, Woven Seat, Paw Feet, Baker Furniture, c.1950, 33 In. *illus*	875
Chair, Mahogany, Hepplewhite, Shield Back, Carved Splat, Side, Late 1700s, 19 In., Pair	156

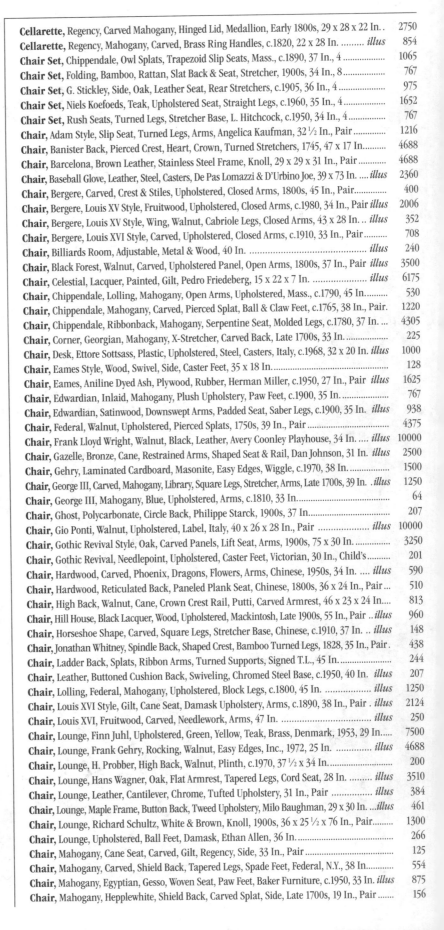

F

Furniture, Candlestand, Tilt Top, Mahogany, Flower, Bird, Pedestal, Slipper Feet, c.1890, 27 In.
$225

Eldred's

Furniture, Canterbury, Mahogany, Baluster Turnings, Raised Pierced Handle, 1810s, 20 x 18 In.
$222

Jeffrey S. Evans & Associates

Furniture, Canterbury, Regency, Burl, Mahogany, Openwork, Removable Posts, Caster Feet, 15 x 22 In.
$1,968

Rich Penn Auctions

Furniture, Canterbury, Walnut, Carved, Leaf Design, Turned Legs, Brass Casters, 21 x 20 In.
$469

Eldred's

Furniture, Cart, G. Nelson, Steel Frame, Grasscloth Top, Herman Miller, 1950s, 24 x 17 In.
$438

Eldred's

Furniture, Cart, Serving, Edwardian, Mahogany, Drop Leaf, 3 Drawers, Casters, c.1910, 26 x 26 In.
$236

Leland Little Auctions

Furniture, Cellarette, Mahogany, Dovetailed Box, Hinged Lid, Cock-Beaded, Early 1900s, 39 x 19 In.
$1,416

Leland Little Auctions

Furniture, Cellarette, Regency, Mahogany, Carved, Brass Ring Handles, c.1820, 22 x 28 In.
$854

Neal Auction Company

Furniture, Chair, Baseball Glove, Leather, Steel, Casters, De Pas Lomazzi & D'Urbino Joe, 39 x 73 In.
$2,360

Austin Auction Gallery

FURNITURE

Furniture, Chair, Bergere, Louis XV Style, Fruitwood, Upholstered, Closed Arms, c.1980, 34 In., Pair
$2,006

Leland Little Auctions

Furniture, Chair, Bergere, Louis XV Style, Wing, Walnut, Cabriole Legs, Closed Arms, 43 x 28 In.
$352

Crescent City Auction Gallery

Furniture, Chair, Billiards Room, Adjustable, Metal & Wood, 40 In.
$240

Cottone Auctions

Furniture, Chair, Black Forest, Walnut, Carved, Upholstered Panel, Open Arms, 1800s, 37 In., Pair
$3,500

New Orleans Auction Galleries

Furniture, Chair, Celestial, Lacquer, Painted, Gilt, Pedro Friedeberg, 15 x 22 x 7 In.
$6,175

Freeman's

Furniture, Chair, Desk, Ettore Sottsass, Plastic, Upholstered, Steel, Casters, Italy, c.1968, 32 x 20 In.
$1,000

Toomey & Co. Auctioneers

Furniture, Chair, Eames, Aniline Dyed Ash, Plywood, Rubber, Herman Miller, c.1950, 27 In., Pair
$1,625

Wright

Furniture, Chair, Edwardian, Satinwood, Downswept Arms, Padded Seat, Saber Legs, c.1900, 35 In.
$938

New Orleans Auction Galleries

Furniture, Chair, Frank Lloyd Wright, Walnut, Black, Leather, Avery Coonley Playhouse, 34 In.
$10,000

Wright

F

Furniture, Chair, Gazelle, Bronze, Cane, Restrained Arms, Shaped Seat & Rail, Dan Johnson, 31 In.
$2,500

Neal Auction Company

Furniture, Chair, George III, Carved, Mahogany, Library, Square Legs, Stretcher, Arms, Late 1700s, 39 In.
$1,250

Charlton Hall Auctions

Furniture, Chair, Gio Ponti, Walnut, Upholstered, Label, Italy, 40 x 26 x 28 In., Pair
$10,000

Palm Beach Modern Auctions

Furniture, Chair, Hardwood, Carved, Phoenix, Dragons, Flowers, Arms, Chinese, 1950s, 34 In.
$590

Leland Little Auctions

Furniture, Chair, Hill House, Black Lacquer, Wood, Upholstered, Mackintosh, Late 1900s, 55 In., Pair
$960

Brunk Auctions

Furniture, Chair, Horseshoe Shape, Carved, Square Legs, Stretcher Base, Chinese, c.1910, 37 In.
$148

Leland Little Auctions

Furniture, Chair, Leather, Buttoned Cushion Back, Swiveling, Chromed Steel Base, c.1950, 40 In.
$207

Austin Auction Gallery

Furniture, Chair, Lolling, Federal, Mahogany, Upholstered, Block Legs, c.1800, 45 In.
$1,250

Eldred's

Furniture, Chair, Louis XVI Style, Gilt, Cane Seat, Damask Upholstery, Arms, c.1890, 38 In., Pair
$2,124

Austin Auction Gallery

F

FURNITURE

Furniture, Chair, Louis XVI, Fruitwood, Carved, Needlework, Arms, 47 In.
$250

Charlton Hall Auctions

Furniture, Chair, Lounge, Frank Gehry, Rocking, Walnut, Easy Edges, Inc., 1972, 25 In.
$4,688

Wright

Furniture, Chair, Lounge, Hans Wagner, Oak, Flat Armrest, Tapered Legs, Cord Seat, 28 In.
$3,510

Thomaston Place Auction Galleries

Furniture, Chair, Lounge, Leather, Cantilever, Chrome, Tufted Upholstery, 31 In., Pair
$384

Neal Auction Company

Furniture, Chair, Lounge, Maple Frame, Button Back, Tweed Upholstery, Milo Baughman, 29 x 30 In.
$461

Alderfer Auction Company

Furniture, Chair, Mahogany, Egyptian, Gesso, Woven Seat, Paw Feet, Baker Furniture, c.1950, 33 In.
$875

Eldred's

Furniture, Chair, Mahogany, Shell Design, Saber Legs, Maitland-Smith, Late 1900s, 32 In.
$207

Austin Auction Gallery

Furniture, Chair, Marc Newson, Molded Polypropylene, Marked, W & LT Shop, 32 In., Pair
$2,375

Wright

Furniture, Chair, Queen Anne Style, Mahogany, Wing, Upholstered, Kittinger, Mid 1900s, 46 ½ In.
$250

Eldred's

Furniture, Chair, Reading, Leather Upholstery, Queen Anne Legs, Caster Feet, 1800s, 35 x 31 In.
$2,928

Neal Auction Company

2021 Furniture Changes
New furniture in 2021 is often made in sections that can be moved to fit in different size places. Most chairs and sofas have thick padded seats and backs. Fabrics are muted earth tones or bright colored prints.

Furniture, Chair, Sheraton, Wing, Burgundy, Upholstered, Shield Crest, New Hampshire, c.1820, 41 In.
$4,688

Eldred's

Furniture, Chair, Sling, Olive Green, Chrome, Plated Metal Tubing, Germany, 1900s, 31 In.
$188

Bruneau & Co. Auctioneers

Furniture, Chair, Tim Mackaness, Stylized Chicken, Black Walnut, Koa, c.1975, 40 In.
$6,250

Wright

Furniture, Chair, Upholstered, Needlepoint, Carved, Victorian, 29 x 16 In., Child's
$144

Stevens Auction Co.

Furniture, Chair, W. McArthur, Leather Upholstery, Aluminum, Arms, c.1930, 34 In.
$2,772

Sotheby's

Furniture, Chair, W. Platner, Nickel Plated Steel, Upholstered Seat, Arms, Knoll, 29 In.
$1,708

Neal Auction Company

Furniture, Chair, Wendell Castle, Oak, Leather, Inscription, In God We Trust, 1964, 46 x 42 In.
$140,000

Furniture, Chair, Wharton Esherick, Hessian Hills, Red Oak, Leather, 1931, 26 x 16 In., Child's
$36,000

Furniture, Chair, William & Mary, Leaf Carved, Scroll Crest, Upholstered Seat, c.1715, 47 In.
$9,840

Brunk Auctions

Furniture, Chair, Windsor, Bow Back, 7 Spindles, Bamboo Turnings, Pine Seat, Arms, c.1790, 36 In.
$1,356

Soulis Auctions

Chair, Mahogany, Leather Upholstery, Scroll Arms, Ball & Claw Feet, 35 In.	570
Chair, Mahogany, Shell Design, Saber Legs, Maitland-Smith, Late 1900s, 32 In. .... *illus*	207
Chair, Maple, Pine, Comb Back, Serpentine Crest, Saddle Seat, Turned Legs, c.1790, 42 In. ..	1500
Chair, Maple, Rush Seats, Circular Legs, Arms, CM-Haarby, 28 x 23 ½ In., Pair	148
Chair, Marc Newson, Felt, White Leather, Aluminum, Organic Shape, 1989, 32 x 26 In.	8125
Chair, Marc Newson, Molded Polypropylene, Marked, W & LT Shop, 32 In., Pair .... *illus*	2375
Chair, Milo Baughman, Barrel Shape, Walnut Base, Thayer Coggin, 1900s, 28 In.	875
Chair, Mischievous, Jacaranda, Brown Leather, Sergio Rodrigues, Brazil, 1963, 29 x 36 In. ...	5000
Chair, Morris, L. & J.G. Stickley, Oak, Paddle Arms Leather Seat, 39 In.	2000
Chair, Neoclassical Style, Upholstered, Brass Casters, Carved Swan Arms, 41 In., Pair	1353
Chair, Neoclassical, Fruitwood, Carved Swan Arms, Silk Brocade, 1800s, 31 In., Pair	885
Chair, Oak, Embossed Leather Back, Casters, Arms, England 1800s, 39 In.	406
Chair, Ottoman, Papa, Stylized Wing, Wood, Upholstered, Hans Wegner, c.1952	7500
Chair, Ox, Ottoman, Wegner, Tan Leather, Chrome, Elongated Headrest, c.1990, 35 x 39 In.	6875
Chair, Paolo Buffa, Leather Upholstery, Zebra Design, Tapered Legs, c.1960, 33 In., Pair	2000
Chair, Plywood, Rubber, Molded Birch, Herman Miller, 1945, 27 x 22 In., Pair	1625
Chair, Prayer, Napoleon III, Flowers, Upholstered, Turned Legs, 1800s, 34 In.	295
Chair, Provincial Style, Shield Shape, Wicker Back, Padded, Cabriole Legs, Arms, 1960s, 38 In.	16
Chair, Queen Anne Style, Mahogany, Wing, Upholstered, Kittinger, Mid 1900s, 46 ½ In. *illus*	250
Chair, Ralph Lauren, Leather, Brown, Winged & Tufted Back, Bun Feet, Arms, 36 In., Pair ..	3835
Chair, Reading, Leather Upholstery, Queen Anne Legs, Caster Feet, 1800s, 35 x 31 In. .. *illus*	2928
Chair, Recliner, Black Leather, Whiskey Barrel Back, Carved Legs, Schubert, 38 In.	125
Chair, Renaissance Revival, Positive & Negative, Bone Inlay, Arrow Feet, c.1850, 49 In., Pair	944
Chair, Renaissance Revival, Walnut, Carved, Upholstered, Hunzinger, c.1880, 38 In.	293
Chair, Risom, Maple, High Flattened Armrests, Striped Wool Upholstery, Knoll, 30 x 24 In.	184
Chair, Rootwood & Hardwood, Plank Seat, Arms, 1900s, 23 In., Child's	295
Chair, Russian Style, Scroll Shape, Saber Legs, Gilt, Arms, 40 x 24 In., Pair	813
Chair, Scandinavian, Curved, Upholstered, Splayed Teak Legs, N. Ditzel, 1953, 27 In.	3000
Chair, Sgabello, Carved, Shell Masque, Caryatids, Octagonal Seat, Italy, 42 In., Pair	295
Chair, Shaker, 3 Arched Slats, Caned Seat, Tilter, Melinda Hubbard, c.1820, 41 In.	813
Chair, Shaker, Cane Seat, Tilters, Acorn Finials, c.1840, 40 ½ In.	1375
Chair, Shaker, Ladder Back, Maple, Wool Tape Seat, Turned Finials, 1850s, 51 In.	1872
Chair, Sheraton, Carved, Mahogany, Cane Back, Satinwood Inset, Striped Silk, 33 In.	1476
Chair, Sheraton, Wing, Burgundy, Upholstered, Shield Crest, New Hampshire, c.1820, 41 In. ..*illus*	4688
Chair, Sling, Olive Green, Chrome, Plated Metal Tubing, Germany, 1900s, 31 In. .... *illus*	188
Chair, Slipper, E. Wormley, Mahogany, Lacquer, Tufted Upholstery, Dunbar, c.1965, 32 In., Pair	1250
Chair, Spindle Back, Orange Striped Upholstery, Slip Seat, Arms, c.1940, 29 x 22 In.	2655
Chair, Swing, Red Leather Upholstery, Swivel Base, Denis Santachiara, Italy, 35 In.	295
Chair, Tim Mackaness, Stylized Chicken, Black Walnut, Koa, c.1975, 40 In. .... *illus*	6250
Chair, Upholstered, Needlepoint, Carved, Victorian, 29 x 16 In., Child's .... *illus*	144
Chair, Victorian, Spindle Back, Splayed Legs, Late 1800s, 52 In., Pair	984
Chair, W. McArthur, Leather Upholstery, Aluminum, Arms, c.1930, 34 In. .... *illus*	2772
Chair, W. Platner, Nickel Plated Steel, Upholstered Seat, Arms, Knoll, 29 In. .... *illus*	1708
Chair, Walnut, Carved, Red, Upholstered, Turned, Block Stretcher Base, 1600s, 49 In.	207
Chair, Walnut, Openwork Urns & Leaves, Upholstered Seat, Bun Feet, D. Marot Style, 52 In., Pair.	1188
Chair, Wegner, Shell, Model CH07, Painted & Laminated Wood, Leather, 2004, 29 x 36 In.	1063
Chair, Wegner, Wishbone, Model CH24, Oak, Paper Cord, Turned Legs, c.1950, 29 In., Pair...	1040
Chair, Wendell Castle, Oak, Leather, Inscription, In God We Trust, 1964, 46 x 42 In. ....*illus*	140000
Chair, Wharton Esherick, Hessian Hills, Red Oak, Leather, 1931, 26 x 16 In., Child's .... *illus*	36000
Chair, William & Mary, Leaf Carved, Scroll Crest, Upholstered Seat, c.1715, 47 In. .... *illus*	9840
Chair, William & Mary, Yoke Back, Splayed Scroll Arms, Stretchers, Rush Seat, 43 In.	1112
Chair, Windsor, Bow Back, 7 Spindles, Bamboo Turnings, Pine Seat, Arms, c.1790, 36 In. *illus*	1356
Chair, Windsor, Brace Back, Turnings, Carved Seat, Arms, Nantucket, c.1790, 44 In.	7500
Chair, Windsor, Braced Fan Back, Knuckle Handholds, Turned Legs, Nantucket, c.1790, 44 In.	7500
Chair, Windsor, Comb Back, Tiger Maple, Writing Arm, Knuckles, D.R. Dimes, 47 In. .. *illus*	1755
Chair, Windsor, Fan Back, 7 Swollen Spindles, Shaped Arms, Mass., c.1790, 39 In.	5940
Chair, Windsor, Sack Back, Spindles, Shaped Seat, Turned Legs, Arms, 1700s, 39 In.	250
Chair, Windsor, Saddle Back, Scroll Ears, Scroll Arms, Turned Legs, 1900s, 47 In. .... *illus*	460
Chair, Windsor, Spindle Back, Mixed Wood, Scroll Arms, David T. Smith, 39 In. .... *illus*	259
Chair, Windsor, Upholstered Seat, H-Stretcher, Duckbill, c.1790, 35 ½ In.	600

F

Chair, Wing, Louis XV Style, Cowhide, Leather, Arms, Our House Designs, Late 1900s, 49 In. ... 1298
Chair, Wing, Queen Anne, Leather Cushion Seat, Cabriole Legs, Pad Feet, Arms, 42 x 26 In. . 472
Chair, Wood, Carved, Splat, Upholstered, Block Feet, Arms, Early 1900s, 38 x 26 In............. 649
Chair, Wormley, Gray Blue, Leather, Upholstered, Dunbar, Arms, 30 x 24 In., Pair 437
Chair, Rocker, is listed under Rocker in this category.
Chaise Longue, Eames, Leather Cushion, Aluminum Frame, c.1960, 27 x 76 In. 3540
Chaise Longue, Louis XVI Style, Oak, Caned Seat & Back, Carved Crown Design, 38 x 62 In. . 216
Chaise Longue, Louis XVI Style, Velvet Upholstery, Gilt Frame, 6 Legs, Late 1800s, 36 x 59 In. 1003
Chaise Longue, Maarten Van Severen, LCP, Molded, Clear Plastic, 25 In. 502
Chest, 17 Drawers, Stepped, Burl Roof, Architectural, Plinth Base, Luca Scacchetti, 59 In. 8260
Chest, 2 Drawers, Pintel Hinged Top, Ball Feet, Early 1700s, 41 x 38 In. 3500
Chest, 3 Drawers, Walnut, Parquetry, Continental, Late 1700s, 47 x 23 In. 620
Chest, 4 Drawers, Molded Base, Ogee Bracket Feet, Brass Handle, Late 1700s, 37 x 45 In. 1375
Chest, Althorp Regency Style, Mahogany, 4 Drawers, Theodore Alexander, 1990s, 36 x 38 In. 1180
Chest, Bachelor's, 4 Drawers, Bracket Feet, Henkel Harris, 1900s, 34 x 34 In. 469
Chest, Black Lacquer, Flowers, Gilt & Copper, Footed Stand, Chinese Export, 1800s, 13 In. 512
Chest, Black Lacquer, Jade & Mother-Of-Pearl, Glass Top, Brass, Bracket Feet, Japan, 24 x 22 In. . 73
Chest, Blanket, 4-Panel Front, Bootjack Cutout Ends, Pyro Flowers, Late 1800s, 5 x 4 x 11 In. . 184
Chest, Blanket, Fitted Interior, Dovetailed, French Feet, 27 x 41 In. 221
Chest, Blanket, Pine, Hinged Lid, Painted, Black Sponge, Bootjack Feet, c.1810, 23 x 37 In..... 500
Chest, Blanket, Pine, Hinged Lid, Red Ground, Stenciled, Leaping Stag, 1800s, 10 x 18 In...... 2196
Chest, Blanket, Pine, Poplar, Open Interior, Till, Red Paint, Pa., c.1910, 18 x 25 In. 550
Chest, Blanket, Pine, Slide Lid, Footed, Rectangular, Blue, 1800s, 30 x 49 In. 671
Chest, Blanket, Pine, Stenciled, Silver Sailboat On Lid, Ball Feet, 1800s, 5 ½ x 10 In............. 900
Chest, Blanket, Queen Anne, Lift Top, Molded Edge, Drawers, Wood Pulls, 42 x 38 In. 2223
Chest, Blanket, Tiger Maple & Pine, Fishtail Hinges, Turned Feet, Early 1800s, 24 x 41 In. ... 502
Chest, Blanket, Walnut, 6-Board Case, Iron Strap Handle, Late 1700s, 24 x 48 x 21 In. 240
Chest, Blanket, William & Mary, Pine, Drawer, Compartment, c.1715, 29 x 33 In. 4063
Chest, Blanket, Wood, Painted, Hunt Scenes, Crests, French Motto, Strap Hinges, 18 x 34 In. . 1000
Chest, Bombe, Louis XV, Mahogany, Drawers, Cast Pulls, Late 1700s, 32 x 47 In. .... *illus* 1320
Chest, Bombe, Yellow, Flowers, Drawers, Adolfo Genoveses, c.1950, 30 x 31 x 17 In. ...... *illus* 375
Chest, Burl, Oak, Inlay, Marble Top, 6 Drawers, Brass, c.1900, 60 x 36 In. .... *illus* 1003
Chest, Butler, Georgian Style, Walnut, 7 Drawers, 59 x 28 x 17 In. 375
Chest, Campaign, Anglo-Colonial, Bowfront, Brass Mounts, 4 Drawers, 1800s, 38 x 49 In. 1216
Chest, Campaign, Camphorwood, 2 Parts, 8 Drawers, Brass Pull, Footed, c.1810, 43 x 46 In. . 1989
Chest, Campaign, Mahogany, Drawers, Brass Mounts, 1800s, 48 x 42 In........................... 2304
Chest, Campaign, Rosewood, Drawers, Brass String Inlay, Block Feet, 35 x 33 In. 2360
Chest, Cherry, 6 Drawers, Twisted Column, Turned Legs, 53 x 47 In................................. 403
Chest, Cherry, 9 Drawers, Hepplewhite Style Foot, Baker Furniture, 70 x 19 x 34 In............... 172
Chest, Cherry, Pine, 4 Drawers, Turned Pulls, Reeded Corner Posts, 1800s, 42 x 40 x 21 In... 295
Chest, Chippendale Style, Carved, Mahogany, Cabriole Legs, Claw Feet, c.1890, 84 x 24 In. ... 369
Chest, Chippendale Style, Mahogany, Hinged Lid, Fretwork, Casters, 1800s, 38 x 52 In. *illus* 354
Chest, Classical Revival, Mahogany, Horizontal Bank, Drawers, Scrolled Pilasters, 46 x 44 In... 384
Chest, Copeland, Cherry, 10 Drawers, Chrome Pulls, Bracket Base, 42 x 57 In. 1404
Chest, Dome Lid, Pine, Hinged, Red, Scandinavia, 1800s, 16 x 28 In................................. 125
Chest, Dower, Molded Hinged Top, Turned Feet, Mustard Yellow Paint, c.1825, 27 x 49 x 22 In. ... 688
Chest, Dresser, Ebony Papier-Mache, Inlaid Abalone, Velvet Lined Interior, Gilt, 10 x 16 In. .. 275
Chest, Dressing, Chippendale Style, Carved, Mahogany, 4 Drawers, 32 x 42 x 22 In. 63
Chest, Dressing, Queen Anne, Cherry, Fan Carved, Cabriole Legs, 1700s, 32 x 33 x 21 In........ 1125
Chest, Dutch Style, Oak, Burl Veneer, Ormolu Pulls, Front Paw Feet, 1950s, 39 x 29 In.......... 510
Chest, Ebonized Wood, Inlaid Bone Stars, Heavy Carving, Drawer Over 2 Doors, 40 x 43 In. . 1875
Chest, Empire, Curly Maple, Cherry, 4 Drawers, Peaked Crest, Scroll Feet, Mid 1800s, 15 x 9 In... 720
Chest, Federal, Birch, Tiger Maple, 6 Drawers, Brass Pulls, Turned Legs, Ball Feet, c.1820, 46 In. 497
Chest, Federal, Bowfront, Flame Mahogany, 4 Inlaid Drawers, New England, c.1800, 37 x 36 In. . 6100
Chest, Federal, Cherry, Fan & String Inlay, 2 Short & 3 Long Drawers, c.1790, 44 x 40 In. 1952
Chest, French Provincial Style, Walnut, Drawers, Polo, Ralph Lauren, c.1985, 35 x 55 In. 885
Chest, Fruitwood, String Inlaid Drawers, Turned Legs, 1800s, 35 x 51 x 21 In..................... 1188
Chest, G. Nakashima, Cherry, Walnut, 8 Drawers, New Hope, 1961, 46 x 16 In. .... *illus* 10400
Chest, G. Nelson, White Top, Drawers, Herman Miller, 1950s, 29 In., Pair........................ 1500
Chest, Hat Box, Mahogany, Mirror, 5 Drawers, Brass Pulls, Paw Feet, 68 x 21 In.................... 201

Furniture, Chair, Windsor, Comb Back, Tiger Maple, Writing Arm, Knuckles, D.R. Dimes, 47 In.
$1,755

Thomaston Place Auction Galleries

Furniture, Chair, Windsor, Saddle Back, Scroll Ears, Scroll Arms, Turned Legs, 1900s, 47 In.
$460

Forsythes' Auctions

Furniture, Chair, Windsor, Spindle Back, Mixed Wood, Scroll Arms, David T. Smith, 39 In.
$259

Forsythes' Auctions

F

Furniture, Chest, Bombe, Louis XV, Mahogany, Drawers, Cast Pulls, Late 1700s, 32 x 47 In.
$1,320

Garth's Auctioneers & Appraisers

Furniture, Chest, Bombe, Yellow, Flowers, Drawers, Adolfo Genoveses, c.1950, 30 x 31 x 17 In.
$375

Bruneau & Co. Auctioneers

Furniture, Chest, Burl, Oak, Inlay, Marble Top, 6 Drawers, Brass, c.1900, 60 x 36 In.
$1,003

Leland Little Auctions

Furniture, Chest, Chippendale Style, Mahogany, Hinged Lid, Fretwork, Casters, 1800s, 38 x 52 In.
$354

Leland Little Auctions

Furniture, Chest, G. Nakashima, Cherry, Walnut, 8 Drawers, New Hope, 1961, 46 x 16 In.
$10,400

Freeman's

Furniture, Chest, Henkel Harris, Cherry, Hinged Lid, Ebony Trim, Late 1900s, 40 x 21 In.
$1,180

Leland Little Auctions

Furniture, Chest, Spice, Cherry, 24 Drawers, Molded Cornice, Shoe Foot, Countertop, 35 x 23 x 8 In.
$410

Thomaston Place Auction Galleries

F

Furniture, Chest, Walnut, 5 Drawers, Brass Pulls & Escutcheons, 1700s, 31 x 33 x 18 In.
$938

Eldred's

Furniture, Chest-On-Chest, George III, Walnut, 6 Drawers, Brass Pulls, c.1800, 70 x 40 In.
$2,500

Charlton Hall Auctions

Furniture, Chest-On-Frame, Doors, Drawer, Chinoiserie, Lacquer, Tapered Legs, Late 1900s, 46 In.
$708

Austin Auction Gallery

Furniture, Chiffonier, Regency, Rosewood, Panel Doors, Brass, Bun Feet, c.1815, 35 x 53 In.
$4,000

Charlton Hall Auctions

Furniture, Coat Rack, Oak, Stick & Ball, Brass Fittings, Hooks, Mirror, 1890s, 33 x 25 In.
$537

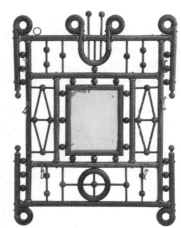

Soulis Auctions

> **TIP**
> Use silicone, not soap, on the bottom of drawers that stick.

Furniture, Commode, Bombe, Louis XV Style, Inlay, Marble Top, 2 Drawers, Brass, c.1910, 34 x 40 In.
$649

Austin Auction Gallery

Furniture, Commode, Georgian, Satinwood, Inlay, Mahogany, D Shape, Crossbanded, c.1780, 35 x 48 In.
$2,500

Charlton Hall Auctions

F

Furniture, Commode, Louis XV Style, Oval, Brass Gallery, Drawers, Saber Legs, 1900s, 28 In., Pair
$320

Brunk Auctions

Furniture, Commode, Louis XVI Style, Mahogany, Marble Top, 3 Drawers, Brass, 32 x 32 x 16 In.
$1,000

Kamelot Auctions

Furniture, Cradle, Hooded, Pine, Red & Black Paint, New England, 1810s, 28 x 24 In.
$250

Eldred's

Furniture, Credenza, Travertine, Brass, Herringbone Design, Hinged Doors, Ello, 1970, 30 x 63 In.
$649

Leland Little Auctions

TIP
Refinished Mission furniture is worth 10 to 25 percent less than furniture with the original finish.

Furniture, Cupboard, Bonnetiere, Burl, Inlay, Canted Cornice, Drawer, Scrolled Toes, 93 x 47 In.
$1,250

Neal Auction Company

Chest, Henkel Harris, Cherry, Hinged Lid, Ebony Trim, Late 1900s, 40 x 21 In. .... *illus*	1180
Chest, Jewelry, Calamander, Drop Down Door, Drawers, Mirrored Pulls, 1800s, 10 x 13 x 10 In...	277
Chest, Mahogany, 4 Drawers, Barber Pole Inlay, Ogee Bracket Feet, Late 1700s, 31 x 38 In. ...	2768
Chest, Mahogany, 5 Drawers, Bracket Feet, 38 ½ x 38 x 21 In.	438
Chest, Mahogany, Marble Top, 6 Drawers, Columns, Bronze Mount, 1800s, 56 x 39 x 18 In...	625
Chest, Mahogany, Overhanging Top, 3 Drawers, Turned Pulls, Cove Molded Base, 10 x 6 x 10 In.	374
Chest, Marriage, Walnut, Carved, Medallion, Molded Edge, Paw Feet, 1700s, 24 x 60 x 24 In.	585
Chest, Mother-Of-Pearl Inlay, Brass, Deer & Crane Landscape, Korea, 22 x 31 In....................	2040
Chest, Oak, 8 Drawers, Ring Turned Edge, Geometric Panel, Bun Front Feet, 38 x 37 x 23 In..	3125
Chest, Poplar, Painted, Yellow, Flowers, Pinwheels, Jacob Wherley, Ohio, c.1850, 24 x 40 In. .	9760
Chest, Renaissance Revival, Carved Mask Handle, 7 Drawers, 1850s, 59 x 25 x 20 In.............	813
Chest, Rosewood, Brass Bound, Cartouche, Inlay, Bracket Feet, Late 1800s, 11 ½ x 23 In.	472
Chest, Sheraton, Cherry, Drawers, Brass Handles, 46 ½ x 43 In.	560
Chest, Sheraton, Cherry, Poplar, 6 Drawers, Beaded Edges, Turned Legs, 1830s, 52 x 41 x 20 In....	936
Chest, Spice, Cherry, 24 Drawers, Molded Cornice, Shoe Foot, Countertop, 35 x 23 x 8 In. *illus*	410
Chest, Storage, Dome Top, Lid, Red Stain, Iron Handles, 1800s, 14 x 25 x 13 In.	622
Chest, Storage, Renaissance Revival, Hinged Top, Carved Edges, Early 1900s, 22 x 51 x 17 In...	885
Chest, Sugar, Walnut, Hinged Lid, Drawers, Carved, Key, South Carolina, c.1815, 34 In.	600
Chest, Tansu, Metal Hardware, 7 Drawers, Applied Handles, Japan, 1963, 17 x 24 x 13 In.	187
Chest, Walnut, 4 Drawers, Brass Pulls, Vine & Urn, Turned Feet, Shinnston, c.1815, 40 In.....	2000
Chest, Walnut, 5 Drawers, Brass Pulls & Escutcheons, 1700s, 31 x 33 x 18 In. .... *illus*	938
Chest, Walnut, Bonnet Door, Drawers, Lion's Head, Carved, Paw Foot, c.1880, 67 x 36 In.......	1416
Chest, William & Mary Style, Oak, 4 Drawers, Brass Pulls, Bun Feet, 1900s, 36 x 39 In.	1063
Chest, William & Mary, Hinged Lid, Brass Pulls, Turned Feet, Painted, 34 x 37 In..................	1169
Chest, Wood, Dovetailed Construction, 2 Lift Lids, 1800s, 19 x 61 In...................................	197
Chest-On-Chest, George III, Walnut, 6 Drawers, Brass Pulls, c.1800, 70 x 40 In. .... *illus*	2500
Chest-On-Frame, Doors, Drawer, Chinoiserie, Lacquer, Tapered Legs, Late 1900s, 46 In. *illus*	708
Chiffonier, Regency, Rosewood, Panel Doors, Brass, Bun Feet, c.1815, 35 x 53 In. .... *illus*	4000
Chifforobe, Mahogany, Cedar Compartment, 5 Drawers, Brass Pulls, Splayed Feet, 58 x 36 In.	144
Coat Rack, Machine Age, Chrome Plated Steel, Enamel, 6 Hooks, 74 x 16 In..........................	313
Coat Rack, Oak, Stick & Ball, Brass Fittings, Hooks, Mirror, 1890s, 33 x 25 In. .... *illus*	537
Commode, Bodart, 4 Drawers, Glossy Black, Gold, Cabriole Legs, 1900s, 32 x 42 x 19 In.	390
Commode, Bombe, Burl, Banded Top, 3 Drawers, Bracket Feet, c.1910, 32 x 40 x 22 In.	1062
Commode, Bombe, Louis XV Style, Inlay, Marble Top, 2 Drawers, Brass, c.1910, 34 x 40 In. *illus*	649
Commode, Bombe, Louis XV Style, Inlay, Marble Top, Cabriole Legs, 1900s, 35 x 46 In..........	472
Commode, Burl, Curved, Bombesque Cabinet, 2 Doors & Drawers, Late 1800s, 28 x 29 In. ...	720
Commode, Charles X, Mahogany, Marble Top, Ogee Drawer, Block Feet, 1800s, 39 x 51 x 24 In.	1062
Commode, Empire Style, Mahogany, Burl Veneer, Marble Top, Mirror, c.1985, 41 x 54 In.	1875
Commode, Georgian, Satinwood, Inlay, Mahogany, D Shape, Crossbanded, c.1780, 35 x 48 In. *illus*	2500
Commode, Lift Top, Painted Design, Shaped Base, Ralph Eugene Cahoon Jr., 29 In..............	3125
Commode, Louis XV Style, Heart Shape Lid, Inlay, Early 1900s, 29 x 16 x 14 In.	615
Commode, Louis XV Style, Marble Top, 2 Drawers, 1800s, 29 x 24 In.	416
Commode, Louis XV Style, Marble Top, Flower, 2 Drawers, Bracket Feet, c.1890, 31 x 38 In...	531
Commode, Louis XV Style, Oval, Brass Gallery, Drawers, Saber Legs, 1900s, 28 In., Pair *illus*	320
Commode, Louis XV, Kingwood, Tulipwood, Bronze Mounted, Marble Top, 33 x 51 x 26 In....	4410
Commode, Louis XVI Style, Mahogany, Marble Top, 3 Drawers, Brass, 32 x 32 x 16 In. .. *illus*	1000
Commode, Mahogany, Marble Top, Lion Pulls, Claw Feet, Continental, 1800s, 34 ½ x 45 In.	938
Commode, Marble Top, Multicolor, 3 Drawers, Fluted Corners, 1900s, 34 x 46 In..................	2655
Commode, Neoclassical Style, Mahogany, Brass Pulls, Bracket Feet, 1900s, 34 x 46 In.	650
Commode, Pine, Green Paint, Fruit & Swags, Bracket Feet, Late 1800s, 27 x 30 In.	875
Cradle, Hooded, Pine, Red & Black Paint, New England, 1810s, 28 x 24 In. .... *illus*	250
Cradle, Rocking, Pine, Iron, Dovetailed, 24 x 38 In.	83
Cradle, Wicker, Canoe Shape, Turned Feet, 36 ½ x 20 x 36 In.	126
Cradle, Wood, Old Blue Paint, Arched Headboard, Cutout Hearts, Pa., c.1840, 38 x 17 In.......	83
Credenza, Empire Style, Mahogany, Marble Top, Pullout Drawers, Early 1900s, 36 x 72 x 18 In..	1000
Credenza, Haller, Steel, Charcoal Enamel, 3 Tiers, Labeled, USM, Swiss, 30 x 60 x 15 In.	1298
Credenza, Travertine, Brass, Herringbone Design, Hinged Doors, Ello, 1970, 30 x 63 In. *illus*	649
Credenza, Victorian, Walnut, Pullout Desk Drawer, 2 Doors, Side Shelves, 37 x 65 x 20 In.	345
Credenza, Walnut, Drawers, Rectangular Top, Alma Castilian, Mid 1900s, 29 x 78 x 21 In. ..	1125

Cupboard, 2 Sections, Open Shelves, Glass Doors, 3 Drawers, Metal Pulls, c.1850, 80 x 60 In..	480
Cupboard, Bonnetiere, Burl, Inlay, Canted Cornice, Drawer, Scrolled Toes, 93 x 47 In. *illus*	1250
Cupboard, Cherry, Arched Glazed Doors, Keystone Crest, Bracket Feet, 1900s, 85 x 42 In.	354
Cupboard, Chimney, Pine, Plank Top, 2 Doors, Brass Button Knobs, c.1890, 85 x 26 In.	8190
Cupboard, Corner, 2 Sections, Cherry, Glass Doors, Shelves, Drawers, Doors, c.1820, 60 In. .*illus*	2337
Cupboard, Corner, 2 Sections, Pine, 12-Pane Arched Doors, Bracket Feet, 91 x 56 In............	384
Cupboard, Corner, Chippendale, Pine, Stain, Glazed & Paneled Doors, Pa., c.1780, 103 x 72 In.	768
Cupboard, Corner, Hanging, Chippendale Style, Cherry, Brass H-Hinges, 37 x 35 x 19 In.	448
Cupboard, Corner, Hanging, Mahogany, Heart Cutouts, 3 Shelves, c.1890, 37 x 16 In. .. *illus*	1464
Cupboard, Corner, Walnut, Pine, 2 Paneled Doors, Inlay, Shelves, c.1790, 84 x 55 In. .. *illus*	4920
Cupboard, Gothic Revival, Carved, Drawers, Bracket Feet, Early 1900s, 94 x 79 x 22 In.........	2360
Cupboard, Hanging, 2 Doors, Dovetailed Construction, 17 x 12 In.	123
Cupboard, Hanging, Beaded Edge, Open Top, Paneled Door, Vermont, 1830s, 87 x 38 x 20 In.	2160
Cupboard, Hanging, Chippendale Style, Tiger Maple, Wall Bracket, 39 In.	704
Cupboard, Hanging, Paneled Door, Wrought Iron Hook, c.1850, 46 x 40 x 10 In.	390
Cupboard, Hanging, Pine, Poplar, 3 Shelves, 4 Drawers, 1800s, 29 x 23 In. .... *illus*	100
Cupboard, Hanging, Shaker, Pine, 2 Doors, Knob Pulls, Interior Shelves, c.1830, 49 x 24 In.	1625
Cupboard, Jelly, Hepplewhite, Drawer, 2 Doors, Chamfered Panels, c.1810, 43 x 43 In. *illus*	613
Cupboard, Linen, 4 Drawers, Panel Doors, Shelved Interior, Squat Bun Feet, 1900s, 79 x 56 In. .	480
Cupboard, Oak, Carved, Gadrooned Frieze Drawer, 2 Doors, Fans, Putti, Bun Feet, 50 x 59 In.	2250
Cupboard, Pine, Ocher Grain Painted, 2 Hinged Doors, Rectangular Top, 1800, 63 x 46 In..	4636
Cupboard, Shaker, 2 Paneled Doors, 5 Molded Drawers, Yellow, 1840, 78 x 35 x 20 In.	9375
Cupboard, Shaker, Pine, Doors, Molding, Shelves, c.1830, 49 x 24 x 8 In.	1300
Cupboard, Spice, Step Back, 3 Drawers, Shelves, c.1900, 21 x 7 x 17 In.	374
Cupboard, Step Back, Butternut, Grain Painted Trim, 2 Sections, Doors, Drawers, Pa., 84 In.	445
Cupboard, Step Back, Pine, Painted, 2 Shelves, 2 Doors, 1800s, 79 x 38 ½ x 16 In. ...... *illus*	469
Cupboard, Step Back, Walnut, Poplar, 4 Shelves, 2 Plank Doors, Shoe Feet, c.1850, 83 x 44 x 14 In..	600
Cupboard, Trastero, Wood, Green Paint, New Mexico, 56 x 33 ½ In. .... *illus*	2880
Daybed, B. Mathsson, Brown, Laminated, Plywood, Sweden, 1957, 16 x 30 In.........................	5625
Daybed, Federal, Walnut, Serpentine Crest, Spindles, Finial, 1810s, 29 x 76 x 31 In...............	1664
Daybed, G. Nelson, Leather Upholstery, Birch, Herman Miller, 1950s, 24 In.	1063
Daybed, Lucca, Burr Maple, Parcel Gilt, Paw Feet, Rectangular Base, c.1820, 59 x 116 x 68 In.	8820
Daybed, Walnut, Black, Stainless Steel, Chromed Steel, Herman Miller, c.1950, 27 In. . *illus*	2500
Desk Caddy, Compartments, Drawers, Brass Pulls, Bracket Feet, Johnathan Charles, 10 x 16 In...	192
Desk, Arts & Crafts, Oak, 5 Drawers, Early 1900s, 30 x 66 In.	664
Desk, Bamboo, 3 Drawers, Leather Lined, Continental, c.1900, 54 ½ x 32 In.	938
Desk, Bombe Boudoir, Slant Front, Inlay, Brass Pulls, Saber Legs, 1900s, 34 x 19 In. .... *illus*	708
Desk, Bonheur Du Jour, Louis XVI Style, Mahogany, Marble Top, Fluted Legs, c.1890, 46 x 31 In.	1003
Desk, Campaign Style, 9 Drawers, Gold Metal Mounts, 30 x 54 In.	354
Desk, Campaign Style, Drop Front, Lower Door, Shelves, Drawers, Custom, 50 x 24 In.	142
Desk, Chair, Convertible, Mahogany, Carved, Flip Top, Leather, c.1854, 30 x 32 In. .... *illus*	1586
Desk, Chippendale Style, Mahogany, 3 Drawers, Brass Pulls, Council, Chinese, 30 x 55 In. ...	325
Desk, Chippendale, Slant Front, Cherry, Pine, Drawers, Brass Pulls, c.1770, 44 In.	1200
Desk, Chippendale, Walnut, Slant Front, Drawers, Brass Bracket Feet, Pa., c.1770, 31 x 41 In. .	413
Desk, Frankl, Kidney Shape, Oak, Lacquer, Johnson Furniture Co., c.1950, 28 x 48 x 24 In. ..	4788
Desk, G. Stickley, Drop Front, 4 Drawers, Copper Pulls, 45 x 15 x 37 In. .... *illus*	2625
Desk, G. Stickley, Drop Front, c.1900, 52 x 26 In. .... *illus*	3900
Desk, G. Stickley, Drop Front, Oak, 3 Drawers, 2 Doors, Marked Red Decal, 48 x 14 x 32 In. ..	5000
Desk, Gio Ponti, Walnut, Metal, Label, Giordano Chiesa, Italy, 36 x 48 In. .... *illus*	5938
Desk, Glass Top, Open Shelves, Adjustable, 2 Drawers, Steel Frame, c.1960, 86 x 46 In.	590
Desk, Governor Winthrop Style, Comparted Top, Maple, 71 x 34 x 15 In.............................	148
Desk, Hepplewhite, Slant Front, Drawers, Brass Eagle Pulls, 1800s, 40 x 42 In. .... *illus*	438
Desk, Jacobean, 2 Parts, Drawers, Doors, Carved, Brass Handles, Ball Feet, 64 x 40 In..........	531
Desk, Karl Springer, Segmented, Goatskin Leather Covered, Dated 1982, 29 x 28 x 64 In......	2125
Desk, Kneehole, Walnut, Black Laminate Top, Brass Handles, 29 x 46 In.	94
Desk, Louis XV Style, Bronze Dore, Mounted, Inlay, Bombe, 39 x 36 In. .... *illus*	360
Desk, Louis XV Style, Drop Front, Mahogany, Marble Top, c.1910, 35 x 45 In.	1003
Desk, Louis XV Style, Flowers, 4 Drawers, Carved, Late 1800s, 37 x 36 In. .... *illus*	512
Desk, McCobb, Birch, 5 Drawers, Kneehole, Planner Group, c.1960, 29 x 53 In. .... *illus*	438
Desk, Oak, Lacquered Wood, Metal Tag, Key, Giuseppe Pagano, Italy, 1940s, 31 x 59 In.	2750

F

Furniture, Cupboard, Corner,
2 Sections, Cherry, Glass Doors, Shelves,
Drawers, Doors, c.1820, 60 In.
$2,337

Morphy Auctions

Furniture, Cupboard, Corner, Hanging,
Mahogany, Heart Cutouts, 3 Shelves,
c.1890, 37 x 16 In.
$1,464

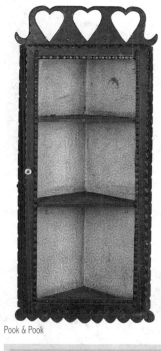

Pook & Pook

FURNITURE

Furniture, Cupboard, Corner, Walnut, Pine, 2 Paneled Doors, Inlay, Shelves, c.1790, 84 x 55 In.
$4,920

Morphy Auctions

Furniture, Cupboard, Hanging, Pine, Poplar, 3 Shelves, 4 Drawers, 1800s, 29 x 23 In.
$100

Pook & Pook

Furniture, Cupboard, Jelly, Hepplewhite, Drawer, 2 Doors, Chamfered Panels, c.1810, 43 x 43 In.
$613

Soulis Auctions

Furniture, Cupboard, Step Back, Pine, Painted, 2 Shelves, 2 Doors, 1800s, 79 x 38 ½ x 16 In.
$469

Eldred's

Furniture, Cupboard, Trastero, Wood, Green Paint, New Mexico, 56 x 33 ½ In.
$2,880

Santa Fe Art Auction

Furniture, Daybed, Walnut, Black, Stainless Steel, Chromed Steel, Herman Miller, c.1950, 27 In.
$2,500

Wright

Furniture, Desk, Bombe Boudoir, Slant Front, Inlay, Brass Pulls, Saber Legs, 1900s, 34 x 19 In.
$708

Cottone Auctions

Furniture, Desk, Chair, Convertible, Mahogany, Carved, Flip Top, Leather, c.1854, 30 x 32 In.
$1,586

Neal Auction Company

Desk, Pietra Dura Top, Birds, Squares, Rosewood, Movable Shelf, Bronze Feet, 31 x 33 In.	3375
Desk, Queen Anne Style, Drop Front, Walnut, Writing, c.1890, 39 x 27 In. .... *illus*	562
Desk, Queen Anne, Lady's, Burr Walnut, Slant Front, Simulated Books, 1800s, 46 x 27 In *illus*	192
Desk, Roll Top, C Roll, Oak, Mirror, Brass Pulls, 3 Drawers, 37 x 22 ½ x 58 In.	224
Desk, Roll Top, Inlay, Angels, Turned Legs, c.1910, 9 ½ x 8 In. .... *illus*	513
Desk, Roll Top, Louis XVI Style, 6 Small Drawers, c.1900, 43 x 30 x 20 In.	313
Desk, Rosewood, Drawers, Marked, Denmark, 1950-60, 28 x 69 In.	4425
Desk, Schoolmaster's, Pine, Slant Front, Red, Black, New England, 1800s, 37 x 22 In. . *illus*	238
Desk, Sewing, Shaker, 9 Drawers, Knob Pulls, Concave Side, Bracket Base, c.1840, 36 x 23 In.	8750
Desk, Shaker, Cherry, Cabinet Top, 6 Drawers, Prospect Door, 1830s, 38 x 24 x 24 In. .. *illus*	390
Desk, Sheraton Style, Mahogany, Leather Top, Drawers, Spade Feet, 1900s, 31 x 54 In. .—....	500
Desk, Slant Front, Cherry, Bird's-Eye Maple, Fitted Interior, Turned Feet, 1829, 48 x 41 In.....	9150
Desk, Slant Front, Rosewood, 2 Parts, Brass, 6 Drawers, Late 1900s, 43 x 37 x 15 In.	313
Desk, Slant Front, Walnut, Pine, Fitted Interior, Bracket Feet, c.1790, 44 x 42 In. .... *illus*	3383
Desk, Stand, Gothic Style, Walnut, Hinged Lid, Trestle, Belgium, c.1950, 50 x 44 In..........	590
Desk, Stickley, Arts & Crafts, Slant Front, Quartersawn Oak, Square Legs, c.1890, 42 In.	375
Desk, Teak, Floated Top, 6 Drawers, Kneehole, Tampered Legs, c.1960, 29 x 57 In.	594
Desk, Vargueno, Stand, Baroque Style, Carved, Brass, Bun Feet, 1800s, 68 x 43 In.	5310
Desk, Walnut, Kneehole, Cylinder, 2 Banks, 5 Drawers, c.1875, 57 x 54 x 31 In..................	504
Desk, Wooton, Walnut, Renaissance Revival, Carved, 72 x 44 x 31 In. .... *illus*	5228
Dresser, Bachelor's, Mahogany, Column Support, Mirror, Hidden Drawer, c.1850, 80 x 36 In. *illus*	1725
Dresser, Burl Walnut, 4 Drawers, Marble Top, France, c.1870, 38 x 52 In..........................	1750
Dresser, Cherry, Walnut, Mirror Back, 2 Doors, Drawer, Heart, Pinwheel, Late 1800s, 75 x 41 In..	7320
Dresser, Chestnut, 4 Drawers, Carved Pulls, Bracket Feet, Victorian, 39 x 17 x 36 In.	472
Dresser, Federal, Cherry, Mahogany, Bowfront, 2-Door Upper Case, Drawers, c.1800, 59 In..	2500
Dresser, Kitchen, Reclaimed Pine, Carved & Pierced Frieze, Molded Shoe Base, 1900s, 85 x 64 In.	1298
Dresser, Mahogany, Mirror, Serpentine Front, 3 Drawers, Splayed Legs, Caster Feet, 68 x 44 In..	288
Dresser, Mahogany, Revolving Mirror, 3 Drawers, Ivory Finial, Ball Feet, c.1800, 20 x 23 In.	225
Dresser, Mirror, 7 Burl Drawers, Angled Legs, Metal Capped Feet, c.1950, 69 x 61 In.	649
Dresser, Mixed Wood, Drawers, Beveled Edge Mirror, Carved Crest, Late 1800s, 24 x 15 x 7 In.	480
Dresser, P. Evans, Patchwork, Olive Burl, 8 Drawers, 33 x 73 In.................................	3125
Dresser, Rococo Revival, Rosewood, Arched Mirror, Marble Top, 3 Drawers, c.1875, 87 x 48 In.	1500
Dresser, Rosewood, 6 Drawers, Tapered Legs, Chrome Pulls, c.1960, 27 x 67 In.	3000
Dresser, Walnut, 6 Drawers, Tapered Legs, Calvin Furniture Co., 30 x 72 In..........................	1015
Dry Sink, Pine, 2 Hinged Doors, Rectangular, Bracket Feet, 1800s, 28 x 47 In. .... *illus*	425
Dry Sink, Rounded Backsplash, 2 Doors, 3 Drawers, Gray Blue, c.1900, 32 x 66 In................	1300
Dumbwaiter, Chippendale, Mahogany, 3 Tiers, Carved, Tripod Base, Ireland, c.1900, 41 In.	2805
Dumbwaiter, Federal Style, Drop Leaf, 2 Tiers, Mahogany, Scimitar Legs, 1910s, 37 x 25 In	168
Dumbwaiter, Regency, 3 Turned Columns, Dish Top, Scrolled Legs, Casters, c.1820, 43 x 23 In..	207
Easel, Artist's, Adjustable, Oak, France, c.1910, 69 ¾ x 20 ¾ x 17 In.	688
Easel, Artist's, Walnut, Adjustable, Rope Pulley, Crank Handle, Casters, Early 1900s, 87 In. ..	1003
Easel, Eastlake, Adjustable Shelf, Scrolled Legs, 75 In...	236
Easel, Eastlake, Walnut, Carved Scrolls, Ball Feet, Victorian, 73 In. .... *illus*	431
Easel, Lyre Shape, Wood, Adjustable, Splayed Legs, 58 In.	189
Easel, Renaissance Revival Style, Cherry, Tripod, Carved, Shelf, Adjustable, c.1890, 7 In.	375
Etagere, 3 Glass Shelves, Brass Supports, Italy, c.1970, 42 x 34 ½ x 14 In.	295
Etagere, Art Deco Style, Mahogany, Shield Shape, Open Shelves, 1900s, 34 x 38 In. ...... *illus*	502
Etagere, Hardwood, Open Shelves, Drawer, Carved Crest, Chinese, 81 x 39 x 14 In.	4063
Etagere, Metal, 4 Glass Shelves, Painted, 81 x 36 In.	95
Etagere, Walnut, Bronze, Mounted, Mirror, Cabriole Legs, 66 x 38 In.	1890
Footstool, Abercrombie & Fitch, Lion, Leather, Dmitri Omersa, c.1970, 19 x 31 In. .... *illus*	3159
Footstool, Abercrombie, Leather, Horse, Display, 34 In..	492
Footstool, Empire Style, Upholstered, Diamond Pattern, Caster Feet, 17 x 26 In.	201
Footstool, George II, Walnut, Upholstered Seat, Cabriole Legs, c.1750, 18 In., Pair	3250
Footstool, Neoclassical, Upholstered Seat, Carved, Hoof Feet, Italy, c.1900, 19 x 25 In. . *illus*	270
Footstool, Oval, Needlepoint Top, Splayed Legs, 12 ½ In. .... *illus*	55
Footstool, Poplar, Flowers, Brown Ground, Turned Splayed Legs, c.1850, 8 x 12 ½ In.	397
Footstool, Upholstered, Curved Birch Legs, Circular Base, Heywood-Wakefield Co., 18 x 18 In...*illus*	62
Frame, Pine, Painted, Green, Black, Red Corner Blocks, Stenciled Designs, 1800s, 17 ½ x 16 In..	2196
Frame, Plasterwork, Carved, Leaves, Gold Ground, 1800s, 22 ½ x 18 ½ In.............................	413

F

Furniture, Desk, G. Stickley, Drop Front, 4 Drawers, Copper Pulls, 45 x 15 x 37 In.
$2,625

Toomey & Co. Auctioneers

Furniture, Desk, G. Stickley, Drop Front, c.1900, 52 x 26 In.
$3,900

Cottone Auctions

Furniture, Desk, Gio Ponti, Walnut, Metal, Label, Giordano Chiesa, Italy, 36 x 48 In.
$5,938

Palm Beach Modern Auctions

This is an edited listing of current prices. Visit **Kovels.com** to check thousands of prices from previous years and sign up for free information on trends, tips, reproductions, marks, and more.

Furniture, Desk, Hepplewhite, Slant Front, Drawers, Brass Eagle Pulls, 1800s, 40 x 42 In.
$438

Eldred's

Furniture, Desk, Louis XV Style, Bronze Dore, Mounted, Inlay, Bombe, 39 x 36 In.
$360

Michaan's Auctions

Furniture, Desk, Louis XV Style, Flowers, 4 Drawers, Carved, Late 1800s, 37 x 36 In.
$512

Hindman

Furniture, Desk, McCobb, Birch, 5 Drawers, Kneehole, Planner Group, c.1960, 29 x 53 In.
$438

Kamelot Auctions

Furniture, Desk, Queen Anne Style, Drop Front, Walnut, Writing, c.1890, 39 x 27 In.
$562

Charlton Hall Auctions

Is It a Marriage?

If you have a two-part piece of furniture like a highboy or secretary-desk, the two parts should match in every way: wood grain, dovetailing, and other construction details. If they do not, it is possible that the piece is a "marriage." The parts originally came from two different pieces later joined together by a dealer. Recently we saw a "divorce"—a Victorian dresser split into a mirror and two small chests of drawers.

Furniture, Desk, Queen Anne, Lady's, Burr Walnut, Slant Front, Simulated Books, 1800s, 46 x 27 In.
$192

Morphy Auctions

Furniture, Desk, Roll Top, Inlay, Angels, Turned Legs, c.1910, 9 ½ x 8 In.
$513

Pook & Pook

Furniture, Desk, Schoolmaster's, Pine, Slant Front, Red, Black, New England, 1800s, 37 x 22 In.
$238

Pook & Pook

Furniture, Desk, Shaker, Cherry, Cabinet Top, 6 Drawers, Prospect Door, 1830s, 38 x 24 x 24 In.
$390

Garth's Auctioneers & Appraisers

Furniture, Desk, Slant Front, Walnut, Pine, Fitted Interior, Bracket Feet, c.1790, 44 x 42 In.
$3,383

Morphy Auctions

Furniture, Desk, Wooton, Walnut, Renaissance Revival, Carved, 72 x 44 x 31 In.
$5,228

Morphy Auctions

Furniture, Dresser, Bachelor's, Mahogany, Column Support, Mirror, Hidden Drawer, c.1850, 80 x 36 In.
$1,725

Stevens Auction Co.

Furniture, Dry Sink, Pine, 2 Hinged Doors, Rectangular, Bracket Feet, 1800s, 28 x 47 In.
$425

Pook & Pook

TIP
Spool-turned furniture or "Jenny Lind" pieces with sharp corners are older than those with rounded corners.

Furniture, Easel, Eastlake, Walnut, Carved Scrolls, Ball Feet, Victorian, 73 In.
$431

Rich Penn Auctions

F

Furniture, Etagere, Art Deco Style, Mahogany, Shield Shape, Open Shelves, 1900s, 34 x 38 In.
$502

Austin Auction Gallery

Furniture, Footstool, Abercrombie & Fitch, Lion, Leather, Dmitri Omersa, c.1970, 19 x 31 In.
$3,159

Jeffrey S. Evans & Associates

Furniture, Footstool, Neoclassical, Upholstered Seat, Carved, Hoof Feet, Italy, c.1900, 19 x 25 In.
$270

Michaan's Auctions

Furniture, Footstool, Oval, Needlepoint Top, Splayed Legs, 12 ½ In.
$55

Hartzell's Auction Gallery Inc.

Frame, Wood, Dutch Style, Black Paint, Ebonized, Continental, c.1940, 23 ⅕ x 19 ½ In. *illus*	938
Frame, Wood, Flower, Leaves & Scroll Design, Gilt, Gesso, 1800s, 32 ½ x 28 ¾ In.	320
Frame, Wood, Hudson River School, Gesso, Gold Paint, Gilt, 1800s, 16 x 22 In.	406
Hall Seat, Carved, Spindle Back, Hinged Seat, Bun Feet, Brittany, Late 1800s, 60 x 46 In. *..illus*	1652
Hall Seat, Provincial, Walnut, X-Shape Back Slats, Hinged Seat, Early 1900s, 33 x 62 x 15 In.	767
Hall Seat, Shaped Crest Rail, Spindle Back, Curved Arms, 1800s, 37 x 77 x 21 In.	439
Hall Stand, Marble Top, Mirror, 6 Hooks, Ball Feet, Victorian, 81 x 35 In.	148
Hall Stand, Mission Style, Oak, Mirror, Lift Seat, 8 Hooks, Splayed Legs, 79 x 33 In.	288
Hall Tree, 4 Parts, Bentwood, White, Painted, Peg Hooks, Round Stone Base, c.1960, 69 In..	207
Hall Tree, Black Forest, Bears, Branch Umbrella Stand, Late 1800s, 82 x 29 x 24 In. ... *illus*	7995
Hall Tree, Black Forest, Carved, Bear & 2 Cubs, Glass Eyes, c.1877, 84 In.	5400
Hall Tree, Lion Heads, Umbrella Rail, Gilt, Italian Renaissance Revival, 1800s, 77 x 41 In. *..illus*	413
Hall Tree, Longhorn Steer Rack, Shaped Finial, Curved Feet, 1900s, 60 x 24 x 20 In.	148
Hall Tree, Maple, 6 Hanging Sticks, Circular Domed Base, Nana Ditzel, 66 x 24 In.	413
Hall Tree, Spanish Renaissance Revival, Oak, Carved, Hooks, Hinged Seat, 1800s, 72 x 52 In. *illus*	944
Hat Rack, Mahogany, Reeded Stem, Flame Finial, Claw Feet, 70 In.	316
Hat Rack, Mahogany, Wolf Head, Open Mouth, Holding Round Bar, c.1870, 5 x 15 In., Pair *illus*	1020
Hat Rack, Wood, 12 Pegs, Porcelain Knobs, Adjustable, 28 x 30 In.	62
Hat Tree, Street Signs, Hano Rd., San Felipe Ave., Turned Wood Base, Hooks, 1930s, 90 In.	380
Headboard, Italianate, 2-Board, Carved, Painted, White Ground, 60 x 78 In.	590
Headboard, Teak, Grass Panels, 2 Drawers & Table Ends, Denmark, c.1960, 50 x 104 In.	438
Highboy, Mahogany, 2 Parts, 10 Drawers, Brass Pulls, Buds Finial, 1900s, 83 ½ x 22 In.	118
Highboy, Queen Anne Style, Painted, Brass Pulls, Splayed Legs, Dixie, 1950s, 62 ½ In. *illus*	176
Highboy, Queen Anne, 10 Drawers, Grain Painted, Brass Pulls, Cabriole Legs, 36 x 20 x 59 In.	177
Highboy, William & Mary, Mahogany, Brass Knobs, Maitland-Smith, 58 x 17 In. .... *illus*	690
Highchair, 2-Slat Back, Woven, Oak, Splint Seat, Turned Legs, Arms, c.1870, 36 In. .... *illus*	82
Huntboard, Federal, Cherry, Pine, Geometric Carved, Drawers, 1800s, 42 x 47 In. ...... *illus*	5535
Kneeler, Prie-Dieu, Cutout Feet, Square Head Nails, 1800s, 7 x 57 ½ In.	175
Kneeler, Prie-Dieu, Fruitwood, Openwork Back Splat, Padded Top Rail, Seat, 1800s, 36 x 18 In.	384
Lap Desk, Campaign, Wood Veneers, Brass Inlays, Hinged Lid, 1800s, 8 x 18 x 11 In.	384
Lap Desk, George III, Mahogany, Brass Medallion & Band, Stand, Late 1700s, 21 x 21 x 11 In.	1235
Lap Desk, Hinged Writing Surface, Roll Top, Tambour Lid, c.1810, 7 x 12 x 10 In.	313
Lap Desk, Roll Top, Camphorwood, Campaign Style, Drawer, Brass, Chinese, 1800s, 9 x 18 In.	531
Lap Desk, Rosewood, Carved, Gilt, Compartment, Campaign Style, Late 1800s, 6 x 18 In.	188
Lap Desk, Traveling, Mahogany, Brass Inlay, Hinged Lid, E. Turner, 1800s, 5 x 13 In.	384
Lap Desk, Victorian, Sloped Writing Surface, 2 Compartments, 1800s, 8 x 20 x 12 In.	374
Lectern, Eagle, Spread Wings, Brass, Pedestal Stand, 3 Applied Feet, 1800s, 58 In. ...... *illus*	1053
Lectern, Slant Front, Scrollwork Page Rests, 2-Sided, Wrought Iron, 1800s, 66 In. .... *illus*	384
Library Ladder, William IV, Mahogany, Leather Treads, Pole, c.1830, 32 x 18 x 24 In. *illus*	4388
Library Steps, Arts & Crafts, Oak, Leather, England, c.1900, 35 x 17 In.	630
Library Steps, Brass Mounted, Mahogany, Leather Clad Feet, England, 1800s, 80 x 11 In. ...	4920
Library Steps, Regency, Mahogany, Folding, Leather Treads, Turned, England, 1800s, 55 In.	2090
Linen Press, Georgian, Mahogany, 3 Drawers, Brass Pulls, Bracket Feet, 1800s, 84 x 52 x 22 In.	263
Linen Press, Hepplewhite, Mahogany, Molded Cornice, 2 Doors, 1700s, 76 x 43 x 20 In. *illus*	2457
Linen Press, Mahogany, Drawers, Doors, Bracket Feet, Georgian, c.1810, 80 x 54 In.	885
Linen Press, Molded Cornice, 2 Doors, Shelves, Drop Front Panel, 92 x 45 x 18 In.	1003
Love Seat, Asymmetrical, Cherry Wood, Silver Frosted, Red, Ceccotti, Italy, 17 x 23 In.	2375
Love Seat, Colonial Scene Painted Back, Yellow Upholstery, Wood Tones, 1900s, 44 In. *illus*	123
Love Seat, Curved Back, Acorn & Leaf Upholstery, Tufted, Skirted Base, 30 x 69 x 35 In.	527
Love Seat, Wing, Southwest Style, Leather, Cowhide Yoke, Late 1900s, 73 x 68 In.	1888
Lowboy, Chippendale Style, Mahogany, Molded Top, Marlboro Legs, c.1960, 28 x 18 x 30 In..	127
Lowboy, Edwardian, Walnut, Banded, 5 Drawers, Claw Feet, c.1900, 28 x 32 In. .... *illus*	561
Lowboy, Queen Anne, Mahogany, 3 Dovetailed Drawers, Pad Feet, 1700s, 28 x 17 x 30 In.	338
Lowboy, William & Mary, Pine, Molded Edge, 2 Drawers, Turned Legs, 1700s, 29 x 33 x 21 In.	936
Mirror, 6 Split Tusks, Turned Button Lap Joints, Beveled Glass, 1800s, 34 x 25 In.	1872
Mirror, Aesthetic Revival, Anglo-Japonesque, Brass, Fan Shape, Carved, c.1890, 14 x 21 In. *..illus*	96
Mirror, Arts & Crafts, Square, Copper Clad, Engraved, Embossed, c.1900, 18 x 18 In.	141
Mirror, Bamboo, Wrapped Corners, 43 x 33 In.	106
Mirror, Black Forest, Carved, Crescent Shape, 2 Bears, Glass Eyes, c.1925, 29 In. .... *illus*	3720
Mirror, Black Iron, Stick Figures, Animals, Rectangular, Frederick Weinberg, 1950, 31 x 24 In.	708

Furniture, Footstool, Upholstered, Curved Birch Legs, Circular Base, Heywood-Wakefield Co., 18 x 18 In.
$62

Alderfer Auction Company

Furniture, Frame, Wood, Dutch Style, Black Paint, Ebonized, Continental, c.1940, 23 ⅓ x 19 ½ In.
$938

Kamelot Auctions

Furniture, Hall Seat, Carved, Spindle Back, Hinged Seat, Bun Feet, Brittany, Late 1800s, 60 x 46 In.
$1,652

Austin Auction Gallery

Furniture, Hall Tree, Black Forest, Bears, Branch Umbrella Stand, Late 1800s.
82 x 29 x 24 In.
$7,995

Brunk Auctions

Furniture, Hall Tree, Lion Heads, Umbrella Rail, Gilt, Italian Renaissance Revival, 1800s, 77 x 41 In.
$413

Austin Auction Gallery

Furniture, Hall Tree, Spanish Renaissance Revival, Oak, Carved, Hooks, Hinged Seat, 1800s, 72 x 52 In.
$944

Austin Auction Gallery

Furniture, Hat Rack, Mahogany, Wolf Head, Open Mouth, Holding Round Bar, c.1870, 5 x 15 In., Pair
$1,020

Cottone Auctions

Furniture, Highboy, Queen Anne Style, Painted, Brass Pulls, Splayed Legs, Dixie, 1950s, 62 ½ In.
$176

Jeffrey S. Evans & Associates

FURNITURE

Furniture, Highboy, William & Mary, Mahogany, Brass Knobs, Maitland-Smith, 58 x 17 In.
$690

Forsythes' Auctions

Furniture, Highchair, 2-Slat Back, Woven, Oak, Splint Seat, Turned Legs, Arms, c.1870, 36 In.
$82

Jeffrey S. Evans & Associates

Furniture, Huntboard, Federal, Cherry, Pine, Geometric Carved, Drawers, 1800s, 42 x 47 In.
$5,535

Brunk Auctions

Furniture, Lectern, Eagle, Spread Wings, Brass, Pedestal Stand, 3 Applied Feet, 1800s, 58 In.
$1,053

Jeffrey S. Evans & Associates

Furniture, Lectern, Slant Front, Scrollwork Page Rests, 2-Sided, Wrought Iron, 1800s, 66 In.
$384

Austin Auction Gallery

Furniture, Library Ladder, William IV, Mahogany, Leather Treads, Pole, c.1830, 32 x 18 x 24 In.
$4,388

Thomaston Place Auction Galleries

Furniture, Linen Press, Hepplewhite, Mahogany, Molded Cornice, 2 Doors, 1700s, 76 x 43 x 20 In.
$2,457

Thomaston Place Auction Galleries

Furniture, Love Seat, Colonial Scene Painted Back, Yellow Upholstery, Wood Tones, 1900s, 44 In.
$123

Apple Tree Auction Center

Furniture, Lowboy, Edwardian, Walnut, Banded, 5 Drawers, Claw Feet, c.1900, 28 x 32 In.
$561

Leland Little Auctions

Mirror, Blue, Yellow Green, Fish Design, Tiles Frame, 31 x 30 In.............................	83
Mirror, Buddha, Seated, Circular, Bronze, Wood Stand, 4 ¼ In.	138
Mirror, Cast Iron, Giltwood, Painted, Eagle & Shield, Admiral Dewey, 19 ½ In.	185
Mirror, Chippendale Style, Mahogany, Carved, Parcel Gilt, Phoenix Crest, 1900s, 52 In *illus*	960
Mirror, Chippendale Style, Mahogany, Rectangular, 42 x 21 In...........................	31
Mirror, Chippendale, Giltwood, Oval Shape, Draped Flower Vine, 47 x 27 In...............	633
Mirror, Chippendale, Mahogany Frame, Phoenix, Giltwood Crest, c.1790, 40 x 21 In........	1375
Mirror, Circular, Chimera Shape Stand, Lying Down, Horned Qilin, Bronze, 1800s, 16 In. ...	4800
Mirror, Circular, Tin, Lizard Surrounding Frame, Mexico, 32 x 32 In. .... *illus*	472
Mirror, Classical Style, Bull's-Eye, Giltwood, Eagle, Oakleaf Finial, c.1950, 34 x 24 In.	708
Mirror, Classical, Carved, Giltwood, Rectangular, 2-Part Mirror Plate, 58 x 31 In..............	2706
Mirror, Dresser, Arts & Crafts Style, Revolving, 3 Drawers, Early 1900s, 36 In..................	69
Mirror, Dresser, Mahogany, Shield Shape, Drawers, Key, Late 1700s, 18 x 8 x 24 In.	207
Mirror, Edgar Brandt, Wrought Iron, Patina, Impressed, c.1925, 50 x 24 In.	6930
Mirror, Empire Style, Wall, Beveled Glass, John Richard, France, 50 x 31 ½ In.	236
Mirror, Empire, Flame Mahogany, Figured Trim, American, 1800s, 26 ½ x 17 ½ In.	25
Mirror, Federal Style, Giltwood, Bull's-Eye, Eagle Finial, Late 1800s, 35 x 21 In.	313
Mirror, Federal, Carved Eagle, Giltwood, Reeded, Ebonized, Leaf Shape Pendant, 41 x 24 In..	1708
Mirror, Federal, Giltwood, Reverse Painted, Cornice Spherules, 1810s, 36 In................	100
Mirror, Federal, Mahogany, Giltwood, Arch Pediment, Urn Crest, Leaf Swags, c.1790, 54 In.	3125
Mirror, Federal, Mahogany, River Scene, Applied Molding, Early 1800s, 33 x 16 ½ In..........	113
Mirror, Federal, Reverse Painted, Courting Scene, Blue Flower, c.1800, 12 x 7 In.	750
Mirror, Federal, Shaving, Shield Shape, Drawers, Bracket Feet, New Hampshire, c.1800, 23 In.	1375
Mirror, Gilt Gesso Carved, Peacock, Foster Brothers Badge, 1880s-90s, 55 x 34 In. ...... *illus*	1150
Mirror, Giltwood, 8-Sided, Eglomise, Jansen, 1950, 32 ¾ x 25 ½ In.	1375
Mirror, Giltwood, Carved Crest, Flowers, Birds, Swags, 1800s, 60 x 26 In....................	2250
Mirror, Giltwood, Carved, Oval Frame, Tabletop, Marble Base, Mid 1800s, 22 x 18 In.	375
Mirror, Giltwood, Crest, Carved, Flowers, Basket, Italy, 1900s, 50 x 26 In. .... *illus*	1180
Mirror, Giltwood, Scrolling Leafy Design, Carved, Spain, Early 1900s, 61 ½ x 41 In. .... *illus*	325
Mirror, Girandole, Convex, Giltwood, Eagle Crest, 2 Candle Sockets, c.1900, 38 x 21 In. *illus*	420
Mirror, Girandole, Giltwood Frame, Beveled, 55 x 26 In.	336
Mirror, Hanging, Lacquer, Parcel Gilt Frame, Late 1900s, 40 x 29 In......................	384
Mirror, Jester, Holding Face, Oak & Pine, Late 1800s, 19 x 10 In...........................	472
Mirror, Louis XV Style, Giltwood, Flowers, Basket, Garlands, Late 1900s, 63 x 31 In.	540
Mirror, Louis XVI, Giltwood, Oval, Engraved, Late 1700s, 51 x 33 In. .... *illus*	2176
Mirror, Mahogany, Horse, Chariot, Leaves, Carved, Giltwood, Lion's Paw Feet, 1800s, 76 x 30 In..	563
Mirror, Mira Nakashima, Walnut, Glass, 1993, 27 x 47 x 3 ⅝ In.	1560
Mirror, Neoclassical Style, Giltwood, Gold, Leaves, Gesso, 54 ½ x 32 ½ In.	344
Mirror, Neoclassical, Convex, Giltwood, Eagle, Swags, 2-Light Sconce, 47 x 31 In.........	2375
Mirror, Oak, Carved Leafy Crest, Scrolled Openwork Frame, Early 1900s, 47 x 32 In.......	384
Mirror, Oscar Bach, Patinated, Enameled Tin, Glass, Scrolls, c.1925, 37 x 22 In. .... *illus*	313
Mirror, Oval, Giltwood, Carved, Italy, c.1940, 49 x 32 ¾ In., Pair	2000
Mirror, Pencil Reeds, Leaves Shape, Gabriella Crespi, c.1970s, 46 x 33 In.	502
Mirror, Pier, Giltwood, Flowers, Painted, Art Deco, 48 x 26 ¼ In..........................	288
Mirror, Pier, Louis XVI Style, Painted, Musical Instruments, 1800s, 73 x 50 In................	2006
Mirror, Pier, Louis XVI Style, Painting, Woman, Cherub, Parcel Giltwood, 60 x 34 In. . *illus*	390
Mirror, Pier, Neoclassical Style, Man, Woman, Children, Giltwood, 1800s, 81 x 7 In...........	256
Mirror, Queen Anne, Scroll Cutout Crest, Molded Sides, David T. Smith, 15 x 8 In.........	58
Mirror, Queen Anne, Walnut, Scrolled Crest, Shaped Pendant Bottom, 1700s, 37 x 18 In.......	345
Mirror, Regency Style, Convex, Giltwood, Dragon Shape, 43 x 23 In.	2125
Mirror, Regency, Convex, Bull's-Eye, Spread Wing Eagle, Giltwood, c.1825, 50 x 27 In.	3218
Mirror, Reliquary, Carved, Giltwood, Scrolling Leaves Frame, Circular Base, c.1900, 19 In..	236
Mirror, Rococo Revival, Giltwood, Flower & Shell Crest, Pierced, Italy, 1800s, 33 x 26 In., Pair	1952
Mirror, Round, Mussel Seashell, Painted, Gold, Metal Frame, Label, Thomas Boog, 43 In.	1250
Mirror, Rustic, Wood, Split Logs, Salmon Paint, c.1950, 34 x 34 In.........................	154
Mirror, Shaving, Beveled, Adjustable, Iron, 7 In.. ..	31
Mirror, Shaving, Mahogany, Arched, Rope Twist, Serpentine Marble Base, Victorian, 31 x 28 In. ..	125
Mirror, Shaving, Renaissance Revival Style, Iron, Oval, Griffins, Frame, 1800s, 19 x 13 In...	246
Mirror, Sheraton, Reverse Painted, Adam & Eve, Stars, Anchors, Carved Bird, 1800s, 18 x 12 In.	580
Mirror, Split Baluster, Cavalry Trooper, Rosette Block Corner, Giltwood, 1850s, 22 x 12 In...	225

F

FURNITURE

Furniture, Mirror, Circular, Tin, Lizard Surrounding Frame, Mexico, 32 x 32 In.
$472

Austin Auction Gallery

Furniture, Mirror, Gilt Gesso Carved, Peacock, Foster Brothers Badge, 1880s-90s, 55 x 34 In.
$1,150

Blackwell Auctions

Furniture, Mirror, Giltwood, Crest, Carved, Flowers, Basket, Italy, 1900s, 50 x 26 In.
$1,180

Austin Auction Gallery

Furniture, Mirror, Giltwood, Scrolling Leafy Design, Carved, Spain, Early 1900s, 61½ x 41 In.
$325

Austin Auction Gallery

Furniture, Mirror, Girandole, Convex, Giltwood, Eagle Crest, 2 Candle Sockets, c.1900, 38 x 21 In.
$420

Garth's Auctioneers & Appraisers

Furniture, Mirror, Louis XVI, Giltwood, Oval, Engraved, Late 1700s, 51 x 33 In.
$2,176

Hindman

Furniture, Mirror, Oscar Bach, Patinated, Enameled Tin, Glass, Scrolls, c.1925, 37 x 22 In.
$313

Rago Arts and Auction Center

Furniture, Mirror, Pier, Louis XVI Style, Painting, Woman, Cherub, Parcel Giltwood, 60 x 34 In.
$390

Michaan's Auctions

Furniture, Ottoman, Tufted Leather, Mahogany Legs, Brass Casters, Late 1900s, 15 x 40 In.
$649

Leland Little Auctions

F

Mirror, Teak, Hexagonal, Leather Hanging Strap, Italy, 22 x 22 ¼ x 2 In.	767
Mirror, Victorian, Bronze, Applied Trim, Ornate, 36 x 23 In.	374
Mirror, Wood, Organic Shape, Dragons, Brown Paint, Carved, Nepal, 17 ¼ x 28 ½ x 3 In.	94
Ottoman, Bombay, Carved Apron, Serpentine, Cabriole Legs, Hoof Feet, Upholstered, 1800s, 18 In.	180
Ottoman, Button Tufted Cushion, Tapered Square Legs, Caps & Casters Feet, 14 In.	366
Ottoman, Mahogany, Silk Upholstery, Scroll & Leaf Carved Support, c.1825, 15 x 21 x 15 In.	2100
Ottoman, Pierre Paulin, Upholstered, Artifort, 1960, 14 x 20 In.	585
Ottoman, Tufted Leather, Mahogany Legs, Brass Casters, Late 1900s, 15 x 40 In. .... illus	649
Overmantel Mirror, see Architectural category.	
Parlor Set, Secessionist, Settee, 2 Chairs, 2 Armchairs, Shaped Back, Slats, c.1910, 5 Piece ..	1250
Pedestal, Aesthetic Revival, Mahogany, Round, Incised Rosettes, Victorian, 37 In. .... illus	277
Pedestal, Baroque Style, Walnut, Trailing Flowers, Early 1900s, 38 x 19 x 9 In.	649
Pedestal, Birch, Mahogany, Stick & Ball Top, Spiral Post, Brass, 1800s, 32 x 11 In.	693
Pedestal, Black Marble, Blue & White, Flowers, Octagonal, Pietra Dura, 36 In., Pair	3150
Pedestal, Carved, Gilt, Gesso, Swivel Square Top, Fluted Column, 1900s, 39 In. .... illus	413
Pedestal, Columnar, Ebonized, Reeded, Italy, 1800s, 48 x 14 x 14 In.	544
Pedestal, Deco Style, Wood, Marble Base, Chrome Feet, Painted, 35 ½ x 14 In., Pair.	165
Pedestal, Green Marble, Neoclassical Style, Bronze Ormolu Mounts, Flowers, 46 x 13 x 13 In.	497
Pedestal, Louis XV Style, Wood, Gilt Metal, Vernis Martin, c.1915, 52 x 14 In., Pair .... illus	704
Pedestal, Mahogany, 4 Columns, Mounted, Brass, Baker Furniture, 40 ½ In.	266
Pedestal, Mahogany, Column Shape, White Marble Top, Door, 28 ½ x 15 In.	315
Pedestal, Mahogany, Flower Tendrils, Circular Top, Acanthus Leaves, Hairy Paw Feet, c.1880 illus	375
Pedestal, Mahogany, Spiral Turned Column, Round Top & Base, 3 Raised Feet, 37 In.	189
Pedestal, Marble Veneered, Gilt Corinthian Capital, Stepped Base, 51 x 14 x 14 In.	750
Pedestal, Marble, Carved, Black, Gold, Gilt Caps, Base Rings, 37 x 10 In., Pair	546
Pedestal, Marble, Circular Molding, Plain Shaft, Square Base, Early 1900s, 47 x 8 x 8 In.	154
Pedestal, Marble, Columnar, Circular Top, Fluted Shaft, Stepped Octagonal Base, 42 x 11 In.	688
Pedestal, Oak, Molded Circular Top, Turned Shaft, Polka Dots, Late 1800s, 36 x 14 ½ In.	129
Pedestal, Oak, Round Top, Footed, Empire, 30 ½ x 14 In., Pair.	633
Pedestal, Pine, White Marble Top, Column, Carved, Late 1800s, 32 x 12 In.	266
Pedestal, Rectangular Top, Mounted, Onyx & Brass, Footed, 37 ½ In.	780
Pedestal, White Marble, 6 Sections, Turned, Carved Leaves, 1910s, 42 In.	216
Pedestal, Wood, Ebonized, Marble Top, Downswept Legs, Platform Base, 34 x 16 In.	219
Pew, Oak, Acanthus Leaf, Carved, Painted, Scrolled Armrest, 34 x 45 In.	354
Pie Safe, 2 Doors, Punched Tin Panels, Gray Overpaint, c.1850, 49 x 42 x 17 In. .... illus	510
Pie Safe, Pine, Oyster White Painted, Screened Hinged Door, Late 1800s, 13 x 19 In. ... illus	1755
Pie Safe, Poplar, Punched Tin Panels, Iron Tacks, Shenandoah Valley, 49 x 16 x 39 In.	7910
Pie Safe, Walnut, Pine, Punched Tin Panels, Drawers, 1800s, 50 x 50 In. .... illus	2952
Pie Safe, Walnut, Punched Tin Panels, Drawers, Turned Legs, 1800s, 52 x 38 x 17 In. . illus	2074
Pie Safe, Wood, Brown Stain, 12 Punched Tin Panels, Cornice, 2 Doors, Drawer, 60 x 41 In.	540
Plateau, Mirror, Bronze, Glass, Jay Strongwater, France, 1 x 14 In.	416
Press, Jackson, Pine, Red Washed, Glass Doors, Drawers, Doors, c.1810, 84 x 42 In. ..... illus	1220
Rack, Baking, Brass, 5 Shelves, Glass Insert, Oak Wood Support, Late 1900s, 79 x 53 In. illus	472
Rack, Baking, Openwork, Scroll, 3 Shelves, Iron, Brass Corner, 83 x 25 In., Pair .... illus	266
Rack, Magazine, Bullet, Enamel, Steel, James Waring Carpenter, c.1935, 13 x 21 In.	2006
Rack, Mahogany, Brass Hooks, 4 Queen Anne Legs, 75 x 18 In.	201
Rack, Plate, Hardwood, Spurred Cornice, 4 Galleried Shelves, Continental, 45 x 48 In.	214
Recamier, Mahogany, Scrolled Backrest, Reeded Arms, Rosette Terminals, 33 x 80 In., Pair	7380
Recamier, Rococo Revival, Rosewood, Upholstered, Carved Crest, 43 x 71 x 22 In. ...... illus	5750
Recamier, Walnut, Upholstered, Cushion, Scroll Feet, France, Late 1800s, 33 x 56 x 25 In. .. illus	1652
Rocker, A. Pearsall, Walnut, Triangular Sides Continue To Rocker, Tufted Upholstery, 31 In. .	805
Rocker, Eames, Fiberglass, Metal Base, Wood Rocker Rails, 1957, 28 x 25 In.	531
Rocker, Hunzinger, Oak, Twist Carved Supports, Upholstered, Spring Base, Victorian, 42 In. illus	369
Rocker, L. & J.G. Stickley, Oak, Leather Seat, Flat Armrest, Marked, 37 x 31 x 28 In.	750
Rocker, Lounge, G. Nakashima, Figured Black Walnut, Hickory, 9 Spindles, 1989, 35 In.	8125
Rocker, No. 7, Applied, Mushroom Grips, Acorn Finials, 41 x 21 In. ....illus	882
Rocker, Shaker, Maple, Ladder Back, Acorn Finial, Turned Legs, New Lebanon, N.Y., c.1850, 46 In.	281
Rocker, V. Kagan, Faux Leather, Wood, Rounded Form, Stuffed, Curved Arms, 25 x 27 In. .. .	173
Screens are also listed in the Architectural and Fireplace categories.	
Screen, 2-Panel, Art Nouveau Style, Pond Lily, Leaded Glass, Wood, 64 x 34 In.	3625

Furniture, Pedestal, Aesthetic Revival, Mahogany, Round, Incised Rosettes, Victorian, 37 In.
$277

Rich Penn Auctions

Furniture, Pedestal, Carved, Gilt, Gesso, Swivel Square Top, Fluted Column, 1900s, 39 In.
$413

Leland Little Auctions

Furniture, Pedestal, Louis XV Style, Wood, Gilt Metal, Vernis Martin, c.1915, 52 x 14 In., Pair
$704

Hindman

F

FURNITURE

Furniture, Pedestal, Mahogany, Flower Tendrils, Circular Top, Acanthus Leaves, Hairy Paw Feet, c.1880
$375

Bruneau & Co. Auctioneers

Furniture, Pie Safe, 2 Doors, Punched Tin Panels, Gray Overpaint, c.1850, 49 x 42 x 17 In.
$510

Garth's Auctioneers & Appraisers

Furniture, Pie Safe, Pine, Oyster White Painted, Screened Hinged Door, Late 1800s, 13 x 19 In.
$1,755

Jeffrey S. Evans & Associates

Furniture, Pie Safe, Walnut, Pine, Punched Tin Panels, Drawers, 1800s, 50 x 50 In.
$2,952

Brunk Auctions

Furniture, Pie Safe, Walnut, Punched Tin Panels, Drawers, Turned Legs, 1800s, 52 x 38 x 17 In.
$2,074

Pook & Pook

Furniture, Press, Jackson, Pine, Red Washed, Glass Doors, Drawers, Doors, c.1810, 84 x 42 In.
$1,220

Neal Auction Company

Furniture, Rack, Baking, Brass, 5 Shelves, Glass Insert, Oak Wood Support, Late 1900s, 79 x 53 In.
$472

Leland Little Auctions

Furniture, Rack, Baking, Openwork, Scroll, 3 Shelves, Iron, Brass Corner, 83 x 25 In., Pair
$266

Bunch Auctions

Screen, 2-Panel, Carved, Brown, Gilt, Wall Bracket, 68 x 46 In.	118
Screen, 3-Panel, Dressing, Oak Frame, Stick & Ball Borders, Crest, 66 x 58 In.	252
Screen, 3-Panel, Folding, Teak, Linen, Rubber, Steel, Pierre Jeanneret, c.1957, 67 In. *illus*	7500
Screen, 3-Panel, Mahogany, Women, Man, Painted, France, c.1890, 37 x 30 In. *illus*	480
Screen, 3-Panel, Oak, Carved Leaves, Ribbon Crest, Glass, Continental, c.1910, 64 x 60 In.	281
Screen, 3-Panel, Provincial Style, Carved, Painted, Pink Moire Silk, 1910s, 73 x 66 In.	295
Screen, 4-Panel, Birds, Trees, Painted, Coromandel, Chinese, 36 x 42 ½ In.	219
Screen, 4-Panel, Brass Hinges, Inlaid Oval Starbay Bone Plaque, 75 x 79 In.	761
Screen, 4-Panel, Carved, Ebonized, Red Silk, Gilt, Embroidery, Chinese Export, 1800s, 73 x 20 In.	5760
Screen, 4-Panel, Coromandel, Stylized Bamboo, Embroidered Silk, Chinese, 1950s, 65 x 94 In. *illus*	234
Screen, 4-Panel, Hardwood, Cloud Carvings, Birds, Flowers, Chinese, 1900s, 53 x 72 In.	246
Screen, 4-Panel, Louis XV, Arched, Multicolor, Sanguine Pastoral Reserves, 1700s, 82 In.	960
Screen, 4-Panel, Painted, Plum Blossom Tree, Cream Ground, 1900s, 36 x 72 In.	266
Screen, 4-Panel, Palm Shape, Rattan, Whitewashed, Plastic Tie Hinges, 1980, 72 x 88 In. *illus*	826
Screen, 4-Panel, Rosewood, Teak, Landscape, Carved, 74 x 70 In. *illus*	266
Screen, 4-Panel, Silk, Flowers, Leaves, Birds, Painted, 60 x 74 In.	469
Screen, 4-Panel, Temples & Pavilions Landscape, Gold Ground Japan, 1900s, 36 x 72 In.	113
Screen, 6 Panel, Ochre Lacquer, Chinoiserie, Botanical, Phoenix, 4 Fans, 78 x 126 In.	4000
Screen, 6-Panel, Dressing, Oak, Gothic, Spanish Style, c.1940, 61 x 59 ½ In.	531
Screen, 6-Panel, Painted, Battle Scene, Body Of Water, Japan, 68 x 137 In.	756
Screen, 6-Panel, Silk Kesi, Male Figures, Carved Dragon, Chinese, 1800s, 66 x 36 In.	207
Screen, 8-Panel, Blue & White, Porcelain, Landscapes, Table, Chinese, 1800s, 32 x 56 In.	2600
Screen, 8-Panel, Lacquer, Carved, Painted, Women, Garden, Reverse, Birds, Chinese, 96 x 145 In.	650
Screen, Aalto, Model 100, Pine, Flexible Slats, Finmar, Finland, 1938, 59 x 78 In.	4375
Screen, Pole, Papier-Mache, Landscape, Lacquer, Border, Painted, Bun Feet, c.1890, 56 x 16 In.	443
Secretary, 3 Drawers, Painted, Harbor Scenes, Bracket Feet, Early 1900s, 92 x 46 In.	7965
Secretary, Chinoiserie, Slant Front, Bracket Feet, Mid 1900s, 79 x 23 In.	885
Secretary, Chippendale Style, Slant Front Lid, Bracket Feet, 2 Parts, 1900s, 77 x 18 x 28 In.	215
Secretary, Chippendale, Walnut, Urn Finial, Glazed Doors, Ogee Bracket Feet, 93 x 39 In.	5228
Secretary, Drop Front, Burl, Veneered, Gray Marble Top, Early 1900s, 58 x 39 x 16 In.	625
Secretary, Drop Front, Teak, Open Shelves, 3 Drawers, c.1960, 80 x 65 In.	649
Secretary, Federal, Mahogany, 2 Sections, Flip Top, 4 Drawers, c.1800, 87 x 40 In.	732
Secretary, French Style, Fitted Interior, 2 Parts, 88 x 42 In.	325
Secretary, Georgian, Drawers, Doors, Bracket Feet, Edwards & Roberts, 1800s, 91 x 42 In.	480
Secretary, Hepplewhite, Mahogany, 3 Drawers, Arch Glass Door, Brass Pulls, 1800s, 75 ½ In.	325
Secretary, Louis XV Style, Drop Front, Marble Top, Bombe Case, Early 1900s, 54 x 28 In.	826
Secretary, Louis XVI Style, Slant Front, Carved, Drawers, Cylindrical Legs, 40 x 41 In.	594
Secretary, Louis XVI Style, Tambour Door, 3 Drawers, Pulls, France, c.1940, 44 x 12 In. *illus*	1625
Secretary, Queen Anne, Walnut, Double Dome, Slant Front, Drawers, 1700s, 77 x 39 In. *illus*	11700
Secretary, Renaissance Revival, Drop Front, Walnut, Carved, Retail Label, c.1880, 70 x 36 In.	250
Secretary, Venetian Paint, Drawers, Door, Bracket Feet, 1800s, 88 x 42 In. *illus*	1770
Secretary, Venetian, Slant Front, 3 Drawers, Bracket Feet, 1900s, 39 x 47 x 18 In.	649
Semainier, Louis XVI Style, Mahogany, Marble Top, 7 Drawers, 1900s, 47 x 26 In. *illus*	590
Server, Empire Style, Flame Mahogany, Canted Drawer, Bronze Mount, c.1880, 39 x 57 In.	1000
Server, Hepplewhite, Mahogany, Dovetailed Drawers, Brass Knob, Tapered Legs, 39 x 30 In.	207
Server, Jacobean Style, Oak, Carved, Mask Pull, Side Stretchers, c.1900, 38 x 41 In.	384
Server, Marble Top, Concave, 3 Drawers, 4 Doors, Filigree Borders, 6 Legs, 37 x 52 x 20 In.	630
Server, Sheraton, Mahogany, Shaped Front, 2 Drawers, Reeded Legs, c.1820, 31 x 19 x 37 In.	349
Server, Step Back, Pine, Brass Wire, 3 Shelves, 2 Drawers, Stretcher, c.1985, 64 x 75 In. *illus*	826
Serving Cart, 2 Tiers, Painted, Reeded Legs, Casters, 31 x 22 In., Pair	3000
Serving Cart, Edwardian, Mahogany, Circular Tray, Brass Gallery, 3 Wheels, c.1885, 32 x 20 In.	563
Serving Cart, Poul Hundevad, Rosewood, Removable Shelf, c.1960, 23 x 29 In.	200
Settee, Adam Style, Cane Back, Painted, Arms, Upholstered Seat, 1900s, 35 x 41 In. *illus*	128
Settee, Adam Style, Slip Seat, Turned Legs, Arms, Angelica Kaufman, 33 x 43 In.	3520
Settee, Double Back, Upholstered, Italy, Early 1900s, 38 ½ In. *illus*	192
Settee, Edwardian, Mahogany, Inlay, Padded Seat, Open Arms, 35 x 45 x 26 In.	75
Settee, Federal, Mahogany, Carved, Scroll Arms, 1800s, 32 x 54 In.	708
Settee, G. Nakashima, Black Walnut, Conoid Cushion, Velvet Upholstery, 1971, 30 x 48 In.	6300
Settee, G. Stickley Style, Oak, Black Leather, Early 1900s, 41 x 48 In.	488
Settee, George III, Hepplewhite, Parcel Gilt, Caned Seat, Multicolor, c.1800, 45 x 72 In.	8190

Furniture, Recamier, Rococo Revival, Rosewood, Upholstered, Carved Crest, 43 x 71 x 22 In.
$5,750

Stevens Auction Co.

Furniture, Recamier, Walnut, Upholstered, Cushion, Scroll Feet, France, Late 1800s, 33 x 56 x 25 In.
$1,652

Leland Little Auctions

Furniture, Rocker, Eames, Fiberglass, Metal Base, Wood Rocker Rails, 1957, 28 x 25 In.
$531

Austin Auction Gallery

Furniture, Rocker, Hunzinger, Oak, Twist Carved Supports, Upholstered, Spring Base, Victorian, 42 In.
$369

Rich Penn Auctions

Furniture, Rocker, No. 7, Applied, Mushroom Grips, Acorn Finials, 41 x 21 In. $882

Fontaine's Auction Gallery

Furniture, Screen, 3-Panel, Folding, Teak, Linen, Rubber, Steel, Pierre Jeanneret, c.1957, 67 In. $7,500

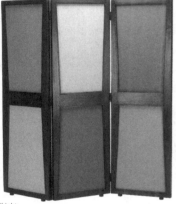

Wright

Furniture, Screen, 3-Panel, Mahogany, Women, Man, Painted, France, c.1890, 37 x 30 In. $480

Hindman

Furniture, Screen, 4-Panel, Coromandel, Stylized Bamboo, Embroidered Silk, Chinese, 1950s, 65 x 94 In. $234

Jeffrey S. Evans & Associates

> **TIP**
> Never use spray polish on antique furniture. It will leave a gray haze and attracts dirt.

Furniture, Screen, 4-Panel, Palm Shape, Rattan, Whitewashed, Plastic Tie Hinges, 1980, 72 x 88 In. $826

Leland Little Auctions

Furniture, Screen, 4-Panel, Rosewood, Teak, Landscape, Carved, 74 x 70 In. $266

Bunch Auctions

Furniture, Secretary, Louis XVI Style, Tambour Door, 3 Drawers, Pulls, France, c.1940, 44 x 12 In. $1,625

Kamelot Auctions

Furniture, Secretary, Queen Anne, Walnut, Double Dome, Slant Front, Drawers, 1700s, 77 x 39 In. $11,700

Cottone Auctions

Settee, Georgian Style, C-Scrolls, Acanthus, Claw Feet, London, c.1890, 40 x 51 In.	768
Settee, Georgian, Mahogany, Double Carved Back, Cabriole Legs, Pad Feet, 37 x 33 In.	702
Settee, Georgian, Queen Anne Style, Mahogany, Cabriole Legs, 1750s, 51 x 51 In. .... *illus*	3803
Settee, Louis XV Style, Fruitwood, Upholstered, Cabriole Legs, 1900s, 34 x 47 In.	413
Settee, Louis XVI, Painted, Brown Leather Upholstery, 1900, 34 x 47 x 26 In.	2375
Settee, Mahogany, Cushion Seat, Curved Arms, Paw Feet, Casters, 1800s, 49 x 24 In. ... *illus*	177
Settee, Meridienne, Rococo Revival, Carved, Rosewood, Scrolled Feet, c.1850, 36 In. ... *illus*	1280
Settee, Oak, Woven, Edward Durell Stone, Fulbright, 1945, 31 x 34 In.	7500
Settee, Rococo Revival, Mahogany, Carved, Upholstered, Cabriole Legs, 1800s, 45 x 82 In.....	2000
Settee, Sheraton Style, 3-Shield Back, Painted, Upholstered Seat, Arms, c.1915, 56 In.	960
Settee, Sheraton, Black Paint, Flowers, Cane Seat, Turned Legs, Partial Back, 27 x 76 In.	1500
Settee, W. Platner, Bronze, Patina Steel, Cream Upholstery, Knoll, c.1970, 31 x 70 In. .... *illus*	7800
Settee, Wicker, Painted, Splayed Feet, 25 ½ x 32 In., Child's .... *illus*	98
Settee, Windsor, Maple, Crest, Upswept Arms, Slab Seat, Tapered Legs, 1800s, 32 x 17 x 83 In.	904
Settle, Jacobean, Hinged Lid, Carved, 59 x 64 In.	1792
Shelf, 5 Tiers, Painted, Yellow, Blue, Turned Supports & Legs, Late 1800s, 60 ½ In....	600
Shelf, Curio, Metal, Black, Faux Rattan Wrap, Glass Shelves, 75 x 43 In. .... *illus*	47
Shelf, Hanging, Pine, 3 Shelves, Brown Finish, Scalloped Sides, 32 ½ In. .... *illus*	224
Shelf, Hanging, Pine, 3 Shelves, Sectioned, Scalloped Cornice, 23 x 34 x 6 ½ In.	88
Shelf, Hanging, Pine, Walnut, Scroll Cut Sides, Red Washed, Late 1800s, 32 x 15 In.	489
Shelf, Hanging, Vertical, Blue & Red Paint, 4 Boards, 2 Shelves, 1800s, 44 x 8 x 25 In.........	678
Shelf, Hanging, Wood, Carved, Rope & Tassels, Leaves, Gilt, 7 ½ x 5 In., Pair......................	81
Shelf, Mahogany, Flowers, Tile Panel, Bracket, Continental, Late 1800s, 12 x 85 ½ In	125
Shelf, Mahogany, Whale Side, 3 Shelves, 2 Drawers, Wood Pulls, 1800s, 34 x 25 In............	375
Shelf, Marc Newson, Voronoi, Gray Marble, Openwork Base, 29 ⅝ x 111 In........................	106250
Shelf, Stepped Shape, Chrome Plated Frame, Mirror Back, Glass Shelves, 75 x 42 In.	512
Shelf, Wall, Walnut, Cherub's Head, Wings, Acanthus & Scrolling Design, 18 ¾ In.	693
Shelf, Wood, Carved, Mythical Animals, 51 x 29 x 11 ½ In. .... *illus*	123
Sideboard, 2 Tiers, Oak, Marble Top, Drawers, Cabinet, Brass, Footed, Early 1900s, 85 x 63 In..	472
Sideboard, 6 Drawers, Open Shelf, Metal Legs, Gianfranco Frattini, c.1960, 31 x 74 In	1180
Sideboard, Art Nouveau, Walnut, Carved, Leaded Glass Doors, c.1900, 93 x 62 ½ In............	625
Sideboard, Burl, Ebonized Trim, Backsplash, Turned Feet, Saint Hubert, 1800s, 80 x 57 In.	531
Sideboard, Cherry, 2 Drawers, 4 Paneled Doors, Thomas Moser, 1993, 37 x 60 In.	2394
Sideboard, Duncan Phyfe, Mahogany, 6 Drawers, 2 Cabinets, Brass Pulls, Bracket Feet, 35 x 62 In.	201
Sideboard, Empire Style, Mahogany, Marble Top, Drawers, Cup Feet, Early 1900s, 40 x 78 In.	1838
Sideboard, Federal Style, Mahogany, Serpentine Shape, Drawers, Doors, 1900s, 39 x 72 In. *illus*	615
Sideboard, French Style, Chinoiserie, Demilune, Marble Top, 1900s, 35 x 59 In. .... *illus*	1000
Sideboard, Gothic Revival, Bull's-Eye Glass Doors, Painted, c.1910, 95 x 87 In.	4130
Sideboard, Hepplewhite Style, Mahogany, Cabinet Doors, Tapered Legs, 1933, 40 x 70 In. *illus*	800
Sideboard, Hepplewhite Style, Mahogany, Serpentine Front, Inlaid Legs, 37 x 68 In.............	497
Sideboard, Hepplewhite Style, Serpentine, Quarter Fan, String Inlay, Late 1800s, 42 x 69 In..	813
Sideboard, Hepplewhite Style, Tiger Maple, Tapered Legs, Eldred Wheeler, 39 x 63 In.	3744
Sideboard, Hepplewhite, Mahogany Veneer, Tapered Legs, Late 1700s, 32 x 44 In.	780
Sideboard, Louis XV Style, Marble Top, Walnut, Drawers, Cabriole Legs, 1900s, 42 x 97 In. .. *illus*	1062
Sideboard, Louis XVI, Satinwood, Marble Top, Reticulated Gallery, 36 x 85 In.	1664
Sideboard, Oak, Claw Feet, Curved Glass End Cabinet, 1900s, 52 x 48 In.	677
Sideboard, Pencil Reeds, Rectangular, Drawers, Gabriella Crespi, Late 1990s, 30 x 60 In.	649
Sideboard, Regency, Mahogany, Inlaid, Pedestal Ends, Bowfront, 4 Drawers, c.1820, 35 x 95 In...	750
Sideboard, Renaissance Revival, Oak, Carved, Backsplash, Bun Feet, c.1910, 66 x 72 In. *illus*	1062
Sideboard, Renaissance Revival, Oak, Carved, Mask & Griffins, Paw Feet, 1910s, 51 x 100 In.	2242
Sideboard, Renaissance Revival, Walnut, Black Marble, Drawers, Doors, c.1910, 40 x 84 In.	826
Sideboard, Renaissance Revival, Walnut, Carved, Female, Lion Heads, 1800s, 84 x 90 In.....	5900
Sideboard, Sheraton Style, Mahogany, Concave, Tapered Legs, Turned Feet, 1800s, 46 x 70 In...	708
Sideboard, Sheraton Style, Mahogany, Inlay, Satinwood, Drawer, c.1910, 31 x 72 In. ... *illus*	531
Sideboard, Sheraton, Mahogany, Drawers, String Inlay, c.1890, 43 In.	230
Sideboard, Teak, Sliding Doors, Compartments, Drawers, Denmark, c.1960, 31 x 82 In. *illus*	2375
Sideboard, Venetian Paint, Marble Top, Doors, Bracket Feet, Early 1900s, 32 ½ x 51 In. *illus*	2124
Sideboard, Walnut, Drawers, Doors, Bracket Feet, Italy, Late 1900s, 39 x 93 In..................	767
Silver Chest, Henkel Harris, Hepplewhite Style, Walnut, Hinged Lid, 1900s, 40 x 21 In. *illus*	1475
Silver Chest, Hinged Lid, Quartersawn Oak, Lined, Brass Plaque, Presentation, 6 x 14 x 9 In. *illus*	175

Furniture, Secretary, Venetian Paint, Drawers, Door, Bracket Feet, 1800s, 88 x 42 In.
$1,770

Austin Auction Gallery

Furniture, Semainier, Louis XVI Style, Mahogany, Marble Top, 7 Drawers, 1900s, 47 x 26 In.
$590

Austin Auction Gallery

Furniture, Server, Step Back, Pine, Brass Wire, 3 Shelves, 2 Drawers, Stretcher, c.1985, 64 x 75 In.
$826

Leland Little Auctions

F

Furniture, Settee, Adam Style, Cane Back, Painted, Arms, Upholstered Seat, 1900s, 35 x 41 In.
$128

Morphy Auctions

Furniture, Settee, Double Back, Upholstered, Italy, Early 1900s, 38 ½ In.
$192

Hindman

Furniture, Settee, Georgian, Queen Anne Style, Mahogany, Cabriole Legs, 1750s, 51 x 51 In.
$3,803

Jeffrey S. Evans & Associates

214

Furniture, Settee, Mahogany, Cushion Seat, Curved Arms, Paw Feet, Casters, 1800s, 49 x 24 In.
$177

Copake Auction

Furniture Made Here
The center of furniture manufacturing in the United States in the late nineteenth century was Grand Rapids, Michigan.

Furniture, Settee, Meridienne, Rococo Revival, Carved, Rosewood, Scrolled Feet, c.1850, 36 In.
$1,280

Neal Auction Company

Furniture, Settee, Wicker, Painted, Splayed Feet, 25 ½ x 32 In., Child's
$98

Hartzell's Auction Gallery Inc.

Furniture, Shelf, Curio, Metal, Black, Faux Rattan Wrap, Glass Shelves, 75 x 43 In.
$47

Bunch Auctions

Furniture, Shelf, Hanging, Pine, 3 Shelves, Brown Finish, Scalloped Sides, 32 ½ In.
$224

Bunch Auctions

Furniture, Shelf, Wood, Carved, Mythical Animals, 51 x 29 x 11 ½ In.
$123

Hartzell's Auction Gallery Inc.

Furniture, Sideboard, Federal Style, Mahogany, Serpentine Shape, Drawers, Doors, 1900s, 39 x 72 In.
$615

Brunk Auctions

Furniture, Sideboard, French Style, Chinoiserie, Demilune, Marble Top, 1900s, 35 x 59 In.
$1,000

Bruneau & Co. Auctioneers

TIP
Large mirrors should not be taken down to be cleaned. Get an assistant to hold the mirror steady while it is being wiped.

Furniture, Sideboard, Hepplewhite Style, Mahogany, Cabinet Doors, Tapered Legs, 1933, 40 x 70 In.
$800

Locati Auctions

Furniture, Sideboard, Louis XV Style, Marble Top, Walnut, Drawers, Cabriole Legs, 1900s, 42 x 97 In.
$1,062

Austin Auction Gallery

TIP
When moving a large chest, always remove the top drawers first. If you pull out the bottom drawers and then move the chest, it is likely to tip over.

Furniture, Sideboard, Renaissance Revival, Oak, Carved, Backsplash, Bun Feet, c.1910, 66 x 72 In.
$1,062

Austin Auction Gallery

Furniture, Sideboard, Sheraton Style, Mahogany, Inlay, Satinwood, Drawer, c.1910, 31 x 72 In.
$531

Kamelot Auctions

Furniture, Sideboard, Teak, Sliding Doors, Compartments, Drawers, Denmark, c.1960, 31 x 82 In.
$2,375

Kamelot Auctions

Furniture, Sideboard, Venetian Paint, Marble Top, Doors, Bracket Feet, Early 1900s, 32 ½ x 51 In.
$2,124

Austin Auction Gallery

FURNITURE

Furniture, Silver Chest, Henkel Harris, Hepplewhite Style, Walnut, Hinged Lid, 1900s, 40 x 21 In.
$1,475

Handles
Many Victorian chests had mushroom-turned wooden knobs. But by the later part of the Victorian era, the leaf-carved handle or the molded, mass-produced leaf handle was used.

Furniture, Silver Chest, Hinged Lid, Quartersawn Oak, Lined, Brass Plaque, Presentation, 6 x 14 x 9 In.
$175

Furniture, Sofa, 4 Seats, Leather, Patchwork, Whiskey Barrel, Schubert, c.1979, 32 x 97 x 32 In.
$1,000

Furniture, Sofa, Baroque Style, Carved, Parcel Gilt, Upholstered, Cabriole Legs, 1900s, 49 x 70 In.
$767

Furniture, Sofa, Chippendale, Camelback, Red Velvet Upholstery, 35 x 84 In.
$118

Furniture, Sofa, Teak, Upholstered, Chrome Legs, Jydsk Mobelvaerk, Denmark, c.1970, 28 x 88 x 30 In.
$1,375

Sofa, 3 Seats, Teak, Wool, Tove & Edvard Kindt-Larsen, c.1960, 33 x 81 x 31 In. 520
Sofa, 4 Seats, Leather, Patchwork, Whiskey Barrel, Schubert, c.1979, 32 x 97 x 32 In. . . *illus* 1000
Sofa, Baroque Style, Carved, Parcel Gilt, Upholstered, Cabriole Legs, 1900s, 49 x 70 In. *illus* 767
Sofa, Camelback, Brown Leather, Block Legs, Old Hickory Tannery, Late 1900s, 38 x 97 In. .. 4130
Sofa, Chesterfield, Oxblood, Leather Upholstery, Button Tufted, c.1985, 28 x 72 In. 1770
Sofa, Chesterfield, Tufted Burgundy Leather, Roll Arms, G. Smith, England, 35 x 80 In......... 5760
Sofa, Chippendale, Camelback, Red Velvet Upholstery, 35 x 84 In. .... *illus* 118
Sofa, Compact, White, Upholstered, Enamel, Chrome Plated Steel, 34 x 72 In.......... 1950
Sofa, Leather, Brown, Sheepskin, Walnut, Steel, Denmark, c.1945, 64 In. 4063
Sofa, Louis XVI Style, Painted, Upholstered, Concave Frame, France, 36 x 73 In. 2000
Sofa, Mahogany, Carved, Swan Back, Upholstered, Turned Feet, 70 x 27 In.......... 531
Sofa, Neoclassical, Mahogany, Leather, Flared Arms, Paw Feet, W. Camp, Md., c.1820, 35 x 94 In.. 2250
Sofa, Sectional, Home Theater, Brown Leather, Cupholders, 3 Sections, Palliser, 90 In......... 325
Sofa, Stickley, Mission, Oak, William Morris Style, Upholsteed, Late 1900s, 29 x 84 In. 3540
Sofa, Teak, Upholstered, Chrome Legs, Jydsk Mobelvaerk, Denmark, c.1970, 28 x 88 x 30 In. *illus* 1375
Stand, 2 Doors, Painted, Porcelain Plaques, Bronze Mounts, Early 1900s, 28 x 19 In. 480
Stand, Baroque Style, Burl, Plaque, 3 Drawers, Bracket Feet, Late 1900s, 28 x 29 In., Pair..... 384
Stand, Basin, Oscar Bach, Patinated Metal, Copper Basin, c.1925, 43 x 18 In. .... *illus* 1125
Stand, Birch, Drawer, Door, Stainless Steel, Herman Miller, c.1954, 24 x 18 In., Pair.......... 1690
Stand, Brass, Rue Marble Top, Cherubs, Cabriole Legs, France, 1800s, 31 x 19 In. .... *illus* 3240
Stand, Cherry, Poplar, Drawer, Painted, Soap Hollow, Initialed, P.L., 1872, 30 x 22 ½ In. 7930
Stand, Cherry, Walnut, Drawer, Turned Legs, Rectangular Top, c.1830, 29 x 21 In. 1952
Stand, Crock, Pine, 3 Tiers, Rotating Shelves, Green, 36 x 30 In.. 438
Stand, Empire, 3 Drawers, Cylinder Stem, Glass Pulls, Caster Feet, 28 ½ x 18 In. 173
Stand, Federal Style, Cherry, Beaded Edge Drawers, Eldred Wheeler, 27 x 18 x 17 In., Pair 1170
Stand, Federal, Tiger Maple, Square Top, Icicle Inlaid, Tapered Legs, c.1800, 25 x 21 x 21 In. *illus* 344
Stand, Fern, American Aesthetic, Parcel Ebonized, Gilt, Onyx Top, Splayed Legs, 1800s, 38 In. *illus* 793
Stand, Fern, Mahogany, Carved, Woman's Bust, Knopped Stem, Round Base, 34 x 13 In. 125
Stand, Fern, Victorian, Brass, Twisted Column, Cast Legs, Paw Feet, 1880s, 32 x 17 ½ In. 156
Stand, G. Nelson, Walnut, Cubic Tower Shape, 3 Shelves, c.1950, 40 x 17 In., Pair .... *illus* 1037
Stand, George III, Mahogany, Carved, Tripod, Ribbed, Splayed Legs, c.1785, 25 x 10 In......... 4000
Stand, Louis Philippe, Walnut, Marble Top, Drawer, Door, c.1850, 30 x 16 In. .... *illus* 383
Stand, Louis XV Style, Mahogany, Marble, Flowers, Drawers, Cabriole Legs, 1900s, 28 x 20 x 13 In. 224
Stand, Magazine, Eastlake, Walnut, Gilt, 2 Fold-Out Doors, Victorian, 36 In. .... *illus* 861
Stand, Mahogany, 3 Layers, Doors, Round Foot, 16 ½ x 11 ½ x 43 In. 83
Stand, Mahogany, Bowfront Case, 3 Drawers, Saber Legs, 1900s, 25 ½ x 19 In., Pair.......... 2655
Stand, Mahogany, Marble Top, Column, Hexagonal Base, France, 1800s.......... 531
Stand, Music, Art Nouveau Style, Wood, Leaves, Carved, 1900s, 53 In.......... 448
Stand, Music, Mahogany, Adjustable, Brass Mounts, 2-Sided, Late 1900s, 47 In.......... 266
Stand, Music, Victorian Style, Mahogany, Carved, Openwork Crest, Adjustable, 62 In.......... 215
Stand, Neoclassical, Glass Top, Open Bronze Base, X-Form, Continental, 1900s, 56 In., Pair. 1000
Stand, Painted, Classical Landscape, Hinged Door, Stepped Plinth, c.1950, 32 x 16 In.......... 413
Stand, Plant, 3 Tiers, Pine, Painted, c.1900, 37 ½ x 60 In. 338
Stand, Plant, Caribbean Style, Rattan, 4 Coiled Wicker Baskets, Tripod Base, 1900s, 45 In.... 118
Stand, Plant, Hardwood, Carved, Black, Ebonized, Chinese, c.1950, 29 ¼ In. 79
Stand, Plant, Mahogany, String Inlay, 2 Tiers, Round Shelves, Elongated Legs, 16 x 12 In..... 71
Stand, Plant, Metal, Wirework Gallery, Stretchers, Casters, 1880s, 33 x 17 In. 380
Stand, Plant, Oak, Turned Column, Vertical Ribs, Footed, 1800s, 21 x 12 ½ In.......... 76
Stand, Plant, Square Top, Stick & Ball Design, Early 1900s, 31 x 15 In.......... 55
Stand, Plant, Walnut, Checkerboard Top, Victorian, 29 ½ In.......... 46
Stand, Red Brown, Painted, Glass Pull, Turned Legs, Ball Feet, 1800s, 28 ½ In. .... *illus* 313
Stand, Rosewood, High Foot, Lacquer, Niels Clausen, Denmark, c.1960, 21 x 16 In., Pair....... 10000
Stand, Rouge Marble Top, Gilt, Oak, Stepped Square Base, Pedestal, Late 1800s, 38 ½ In... .. 472
Stand, Shaker, Cherry, Drawer & Shelf, Union Village, Ohio, c.1830, 28 ¾ x 21 ½ In. 813
Stand, Shaving, Mahogany, Mirror, Drawer, Inlay, 16 In.......... 31
Stand, Shaving, Oval Mirror, Walnut, Carved, Adjustable, Tripod Base, Victorian, 70 x 16 In. .....*illus* 369
Stand, Sheraton, Bird's-Eye Maple, Drawer, Painted, New Hampshire, 1850s, 28 x 17 In........ 1625
Stand, Sheraton, Mahogany, Drawers, Glass Pulls, Turned Legs, Ball Feet, Early 1800s, 29 x 23 In..... 148
Stand, Smoking, Ashtray, Steel, Domed Foot, Smokador Manufacturing Co., c.1930s-40s, 25 In. . *illus* 236
Stand, Smoking, Maid Butler, Ashtray, Painted, Wood, Early 1900s, 33 ½ In. .... *illus* 138

Furniture, Stand, Basin, Oscar Bach, Patinated Metal, Copper Basin, c.1925, 43 x 18 In.
$1,125

Raço Arts and Auction Center

Furniture, Stand, Brass, Rue Marble Top, Cherubs, Cabriole Legs, France, 1800s, 31 x 19 In.
$3,240

Cottone Auctions

Furniture, Stand, Federal, Tiger Maple, Square Top, Icicle Inlaid, Tapered Legs, c.1800, 25 x 21 x 21 In.
$344

Nadeau's Auction Gallery

F

Furniture, Stand, Fern, American Aesthetic, Parcel Ebonized, Gilt, Onyx Top, Splayed Legs, 1800s, 38 In.
$793

Neal Auction Company

Furniture, Stand, G. Nelson, Walnut, Cubic Tower Shape, 3 Shelves, c.1950, 40 x 17 In., Pair
$1,037

Neal Auction Company

Furniture, Stand, Louis Philippe, Walnut, Marble Top, Drawer, Door, c.1850, 30 x 16 In.
$383

Austin Auction Gallery

Stand, Writing, Sheraton, Mahogany, Porringer Top, Drawers, Spool Turned Feet, c.1815, 29 In.	594
Stool, 2 Tiers, Blue Paint, Canted, 1800s, 20 x 6¾ x 15¾ In.	311
Stool, Ashanti, Carved, Wood, Rectangular Base, Ghana, 1900s, 14½ x 21½ x 11½ In. *illus*	266
Stool, Carved, Lotus Seed Pod, Painted, Pink Sides, Footed, Chinese, 1900s, 12 x 18 In.	177
Stool, Chinese Style, Drum Shape, Patina, Lacquered Brass, Mastercraft, c.1980, 18 x 18 In.	845
Stool, Chippendale, Mahogany, Flower Cover, Ball & Claw Feet, c.1790, 18 x 22 x 19 In.	4680
Stool, Coronation, Blue Velvet, Removable Cover, Square Legs, 1937, 18½ x 18 In.	600
Stool, Cricket, Limbert, Oak, Shelf, Through Tenon, Leather Seat, Tacks, 18 x 16 x 21 In.	1000
Stool, Esherick Style, Walnut, Kidney Shape Seat, 3 Splayed Legs, 20 In.	549
Stool, Maple, Spray Of Grapes, Leaves, Turned Splayed Legs, 1800s, 7 x 12 x 8 In.	531
Stool, Mira Nakashima, Black Walnut, Tri-Footed Splayed Legs, Signed, 1991, 12 x 18 x 15 In.	3024
Stool, Piano, Italian Grotto Style, Walnut, Carved, Shell Shape Seat, c.1890, 25 In.	2500
Stool, Sori Yanagi Style, Walnut, Butterfly Shape, Bentwood, 15 x 17 In., Pair	625
Stool, Sori Yanagi, Butterfly Shape, Rosewood, Plywood, Brass, Tendo Mokko, c.1954, 15 In., Pair	5000
Stool, Thebes, Oak, Slatted Seat, Spindle Supports, Turned Legs, c.1890, 15 x 16 In.	384
Stool, Thebes, Walnut, Cherry, Lacquered, Liberty & Co., c.1910, 14 x 16 In. *illus*	1500
Stool, Walnut, Curved, Upholstered, Pedestal Base, Turned Feet, Baker Furniture, c.1970, 17 x 24 In.	649
Stool, Windsor, Circular Top, Turned Legs, Bulbous Stretchers, Black, c.1801, 13 x 14 x 16 In.	2486
Stool, Windsor, Round Seat, Splayed Legs, Wood, 1800s, 17 x 16 In.	732
Stool, Wood, Mushroom Shape, Carved, Bulbous Sturdy Base, c.1960, 20 x 15 x 17 In. *illus*	250
Table, 2 Tiers, Renaissance Revival, Grotesque Masks, Winged Griffins, Late 1800s, 26 In.	2655
Table, A. Mangiarotti, Marble, Round, Tapered Base, Tisettanta, Italy, 30 x 51 In. *illus*	14080
Table, Acrylic, Robert Loughlin, Blue Ground, Turned Legs, 22½ x 29 In.	2750
Table, Altar, Hardwood, 6 Drawers, Carved Skirts, Chinese, Early 1900s, 32 x 62 In. *illus*	708
Table, Altar, Hardwood, Fretwork Apron, Splayed Legs, Chinese, 36 x 99 x 11½ In.	250
Table, Altar, Rectangular Shape, Compartment, Sliding Doors, Chinese, 1800s, 32 x 66 In.	875
Table, Ash Plywood, Zinc Plated Steel, Lacquered Masonite, Herman Miller, 1950, 20 x 24 In.	1625
Table, Baroque Style, Walnut, 3 Drawers, Spiral Legs, H-Stretcher, 1800s, 31 x 90 In. *illus*	2124
Table, Bedside, Glass Top, Gilt Pull, Curved Tripod Base, Italy, c.1690, 25 x 22 In., Pair	443
Table, Biedermeier, Birch, Ebonized, Oval, Flared Legs, Gilt Painted, 1800s, 31 x 40 In.	1125
Table, Biedermeier, Tilt Top, Walnut, Inlaid Medallion, Pedestal, Vienna, c.1810, 30 x 43 In.	3245
Table, Bistro, Marble Top, Cast Iron Trestle Base, France, 1900s, 27 x 39 x 23 In. *illus*	443
Table, Black Forest, Bear, Standing, Glass Eyes, Hand Carved, Painted, 37 x 15 x 17 In. *illus*	1404
Table, Card, Empire, Mahogany, Carved Pedestal Base, Claw Feet, 28 x 18 x 36 In. *illus*	153
Table, Card, Federal, Cherry, Pine, Shaped Top & Apron, Reeded Legs, 1810s, 29 x 36 x 17 In. *illus*	450
Table, Card, Rococo, Mahogany, Oak, Drawer, C-Scrolls, Claw Feet, c.1770, 28 x 31 x 32 In.	5760
Table, Center, Arts & Crafts Style, Oak, Pedestal Shape, Early 1900s, 30 x 16 In.	110
Table, Center, Octagonal, Faux Bamboo, Caster Feet, France, c.1870, 28 x 31 In.	1560
Table, Center, Renaissance Revival, Oak, Carved, Griffin, Caster Feet, Late 1900s, 29 x 32 In.	502
Table, Center, Walnut, Marble Top, Victorian, 29 x 38 In. *illus*	316
Table, Chippendale Style, Drop Leaf, Walnut, Ball & Paw Feet, 31 x 23 x 48 In.	188
Table, Coffee, Adrian Pearsall, Glass Top, Walnut, Crisscross Base, 16 x 59 In.	923
Table, Coffee, Blond Wood, Rectangular, Glass Top, 18 x 54 x 38 In.	94
Table, Coffee, Burl, Hinged Leaves, Plinth Base, c.1950, 20 x 28 x 55 In.	472
Table, Coffee, Gilt Iron, Wood, Asian Design, c.1910, 18 x 65 x 32 In.	5000
Table, Coffee, Gio Ponti, Etched Glass, Walnut, Brass, Singer & Sons, Italy, 13 x 41 In. *illus*	12800
Table, Coffee, Gio Ponti, Parchment, Wood, Steel, Label, Italy, 15 x 43 In. *illus*	16250
Table, Coffee, Glass Top, Gilt Iron, Flower Center, Silas Seandel, 14 x 41 In.	625
Table, Coffee, Ib Kofod-Larsen, Rosewood, Teak, Turned Legs, Denmark, c.1960, 19 x 63 x 22 In.	845
Table, Coffee, Karl Springer, Embossed Leather, Signed, Germany, 1989, 18 x 32 In. *illus*	2500
Table, Coffee, Philip & Kelvin LaVerne, Chin Ying, Enameled, Pewter, c.1970s, 17 x 70 x 30 In.	4875
Table, Coffee, Rectangular, Slatted Top, Turned Support, Ball Feet, 18 x 30 In.	71
Table, Coffee, Regency Style, Brass, Mottled Mirror Top, France, c.1950, 17 x 40 x 18 In.	688
Table, Coffee, Ribbon, Bent Rattan, Waterfall Design, Round Edges, Betty Cobonpue, c.1980s.	590
Table, Coffee, Triangular, Rosewood, Circular Glass Top, c.1950, 16 In.	188
Table, Coffee, Wagon Wheel, Glass Top, Twisted Wrought Iron Legs, Horseshoe Feet, 22 In. *illus*	590
Table, Coffee, Wormley, Walnut, Recessed Base, Shelf Tier, Dunbar, 1950s, 22 x 48 x 28 In.	563
Table, Console, Balcony Surround, Scrollwork, Glass Top, Wrought Iron, 1900s, 28 x 43 In., Pair	1180
Table, Console, Directoire Style, Gilt, Carved, White Marble Top, 37 x 19 x 16 In., Pair	2520
Table, Console, Federal Style, Mahogany, Inlaid, Brass Pulls, Hekman, 30 x 52 In.	325

F

Furniture, Stand, Magazine, Eastlake, Walnut, Gilt, 2 Fold-Out Doors, Victorian, 36 In.
$861

Rich Penn Auctions

Furniture, Stand, Red Brown, Painted, Glass Pull, Turned Legs, Ball Feet, 1800s, 28 ½ In.
$313

Eldred's

Furniture, Stand, Shaving, Oval Mirror, Walnut, Carved, Adjustable, Tripod Base, Victorian, 70 x 16 In.
$369

Rich Penn Auctions

Furniture, Stand, Smoking, Ashtray, Steel, Domed Foot, Smokador Manufacturing Co., c.1930s-40s, 25 In.
$236

Austin Auction Gallery

Furniture, Stand, Smoking, Maid Butler, Ashtray, Painted, Wood, Early 1900s, 33 ½ In.
$138

Pook & Pook

Furniture, Stool, Ashanti, Carved, Wood, Rectangular Base, Ghana, 1900s, 14 ½ x 21 ½ x 11 ½ In.
$266

Austin Auction Gallery

Furniture, Stool, Thebes, Oak, Slatted Seat, Spindle Supports, Turned Legs, c.1890, 15 x 16 In.
$384

Neal Auction Company

F

FURNITURE

Furniture, Stool, Thebes, Walnut, Cherry, Lacquered, Liberty & Co., c.1910, 14 x 16 In. $1,500

Wright

Furniture, Stool, Wood, Mushroom Shape, Carved, Bulbous Sturdy Base, c.1960, 20 x 15 x 17 In. $250

Bruneau & Co. Auctioneers

Furniture, Table, A. Mangiarotti, Marble, Round, Tapered Base, Tisettanta, Italy, 30 x 51 In. $14,080

Hindman

Furniture, Table, Altar, Hardwood, 6 Drawers, Carved Skirts, Chinese, Early 1900s, 32 x 62 In. $708

Leland Little Auctions

Furniture, Table, Baroque Style, Walnut, 3 Drawers, Spiral Legs, H-Stretcher, 1800s, 31 x 90 In. $2,124

Austin Auction Gallery

Furniture, Table, Bistro, Marble Top, Cast Iron Trestle Base, France, 1900s, 27 x 39 x 23 In. $443

Austin Auction Gallery

Furniture, Table, Black Forest, Bear, Standing, Glass Eyes, Hand Carved, Painted, 37 x 15 x 17 In. $1,404

Thomaston Place Auction Galleries

Furniture, Table, Card, Empire, Mahogany, Carved Pedestal Base, Claw Feet, 28 x 18 x 36 In. $153

Nadeau's Auction Gallery

Furniture, Table, Card, Federal, Cherry, Pine, Shaped Top & Apron, Reeded Legs, 1810s, 29 x 36 x 17 In. $450

Garth's Auctioneers & Appraisers

Furniture, Table, Center, Walnut, Marble Top, Victorian, 29 x 38 In.
$316

Stevens Auction Co.

Furniture, Table, Coffee, Gio Ponti, Etched Glass, Walnut, Brass, Singer & Sons, Italy, 13 x 41 In.
$12,800

Hindman

Furniture, Table, Coffee, Gio Ponti, Parchment, Wood, Steel, Label, Italy, 15 x 43 In.
$16,250

Palm Beach Modern Auctions

Furniture, Table, Coffee, Karl Springer, Embossed Leather, Signed, Germany, 1989, 18 x 32 In.
$2,500

Abington Auction Gallery

Furniture, Table, Coffee, Wagon Wheel, Glass Top, Twisted Wrought Iron Legs, Horseshoe Feet, 22 In.
$590

Austin Auction Gallery

Furniture, Table, Console, Louis XVI Style, Gilt, Marble Top, Demilune, c.1910, 36 x 47 x 19 In.
$531

Kamelot Auctions

Furniture, Table, Console, Louis XVI, Gilt, Demilune Top, Tapered Legs, Early 1900s, 60 x 23 x 33 In., Pair
$1,000

Bruneau & Co. Auctioneers

Furniture, Table, Console, Oscar Bach, Demilune, Bronze, Marble, Iron, Enamel, c.1925, 34 x 29 In.
$625

Rago Arts and Auction Center

Furniture, Table, Demilune, Grain Painted, Stretcher, 1860s, 30 x 50 x 25 In., Pair
$1,200

Garth's Auctioneers & Appraisers

FURNITURE

Furniture, Table, Dining, L. & J. G. Stickley, No. 720, Oak, 4 Leaves, c.1915, 96 In.
$2,210

Freeman's

Furniture, Table, Dining, Peter McCarthy, Oak, Pierced Legs, American Studio, 30 x 74 In.
$475

Neal Auction Company

Furniture, Table, Dining, Regency Style, E.J. Victor, Mahogany, Pedestal, Casters, Late 1900s, 29 x 60 In.
$7,375

Leland Little Auctions

Furniture, Table, Dressing, Louis XV Style, Marquetry, 3 Drawers, Late 1800s, 31 x 32 In.
$288

Hindman

Furniture, Table, Dressing, Queen Anne, Mahogany, Brass, Drawers, Cabriole Legs, 1800s, 27 x 29 In.
$306

Brunk Auctions

Table, Console, Gilt, Marble Top, Eagle, Georgian, William Kent, 1800s, 32 x 39½ In., Pair..	8850
Table, Console, Glass Top, 2 Swans, Steel Base, Silver Gilt, 1900s, 30 x 53 x 18 In.	295
Table, Console, Italian Style, Iron, Marble Top, Grape & Vine Design, 33 x 74 In.	177
Table, Console, Louis XV Style, Mirror, Gilt, Marble Top, Whorl Feet, 1900s, 95 x 48 In.	885
Table, Console, Louis XVI Style, Gilt, Marble Top, Demilune, c.1910, 36 x 47 x 19 In. .... *illus*	531
Table, Console, Louis XVI Style, Marble Top, Carved, Flower Panel, Fluted Legs, 1800s, 32 x 40 In.	1298
Table, Console, Louis XVI, Gilt, Demilune Top, Tapered Legs, Early 1900s, 60 x 23 x 33 In., Pair *illus*	1000
Table, Console, Lower Shelf, Olive Paint, Drawer, 37 x 12 x 31 In.	62
Table, Console, Mahogany, Marble, Serpentine Top, X-Stretcher Base, Late 1900s, 31 x 41 In. .	561
Table, Console, Oscar Bach, Demilune, Bronze, Marble, Iron, Enamel, c.1925, 34 x 29 In. *illus*	625
Table, Console, Oscar Bach, Marble Top, Bronze, Iron, Painted Steel, c.1924, 35 x 48 In.	2596
Table, Console, Oscar Bach, Marble Top, Cabriole Legs, Cast Iron, c.1927, 32 x 47 x 14 In.	8750
Table, Console, Rococo Style, Carved, Painted, Marble Top, Mid 1900s, 28 x 32 In.	1534
Table, Console, Tiger Oak, Beveled, Pier Mirror, Shelf, c.1900, 84 x 55 x 10 In.	266
Table, Console, Wood, Carved, Marble Top, Wall Mount Top, Italy, c.1940, 41 x 42 x 19 In	281
Table, Console, Wood, Leather, Plated, Glass, Tecno, Osvaldo Borsani, Italy, c.1970, 33 x 95 In.	1250
Table, Demilune, Grain Painted, Stretcher, 1860s, 30 x 50 x 25 In., Pair .... *illus*	1200
Table, Dining, L. & J. G. Stickley, No. 720, Oak, 4 Leaves, c.1915, 96 In. .... *illus*	2210
Table, Dining, Lazy Susan, Heart Pine Boards, Circular Top, Turned Legs, 30 x 48 In	944
Table, Dining, Mahogany, 3 Pedestal Tripod Bases, Casters, England, 1800s, 29 x 97 In.......	800
Table, Dining, Mahogany, 3 Pedestals, Reeded Legs, Early 1900s, 29 x 108 x 49 In.	2375
Table, Dining, Mahogany, Oblong, Fluted Legs, Bun Feet, Ralph Lauren, 30 x 86 In.	1050
Table, Dining, Neoclassical, Mahogany, Leaves, Extendable, Continental, 1800s, 29 In.........	3780
Table, Dining, Oak, Draw Leaf, Geometric Inlay, Carved, Shoe Base, 1900s, 30 x 86 In	1298
Table, Dining, Parzinger, Walnut, Ebonized, Brass, 2 Leaves, 1950s, 29 x 108 x 42 In.	3380
Table, Dining, Peter McCarthy, Oak, Pierced Legs, American Studio, 30 x 74 In. .... *illus*	475
Table, Dining, Regency Style, E.J. Victor, Mahogany, Pedestal, Casters, Late 1900s, 29 x 60 In. *illus*	7375
Table, Dining, Regency Style, Round, Rosewood, Brass, Dolphin Supports, 1950s, 28 In........	3780
Table, Dining, Teak, Drop Leaf, 3-Panel Top, Late 1900s, 30 x 36 x 18 In.......................... .	556
Table, Dining, Walnut, 3 Drop Leaves, Turned Legs, Caster Feet, 1850s, 29 x 42 In.	293
Table, Draw Leaf, Oak, Carved Trestle Base, 1900s, 38½ x 108 x 33 In.	615
Table, Dressing, Chippendale Style, Mahogany, Cabriole Legs, Ball & Claw Feet, 31 x 36 In. ..	1830
Table, Dressing, Chippendale, Walnut, 4 Drawers, Claw Feet, Pa., c.1780, 30 x 35 In........	1890
Table, Dressing, Louis XV Style, Marquetry, 3 Drawers, Late 1800s, 31 x 32 In. .... *illus*	288
Table, Dressing, Queen Anne, Mahogany, Brass, Drawers, Cabriole Legs, 1800s, 27 x 29 In. *illus*	306
Table, Dressing, Queen Anne, Mahogany, Fan Carved, 4 Drawers, Mass., 1700s, 33 x 29 In....	1415
Table, Dressing, William & Mary Style, Cross Stretcher, Drexel, Late 1900s, 31 x 63 In. *illus*	270
Table, Drop Leaf, Carved, Curved Legs, Ball & Pad Feet, 25 In.	73
Table, Drop Leaf, Filigree, Musical Design, Fluted Legs, Bronze, Mounted, Stretcher, 29 x 32 x 23½ In.	1638
Table, Drop Leaf, Flame Mahogany, Turned Legs, Teardrop Feet, Early 1800s, 27 x 12 x 33 In.	995
Table, Drop Leaf, G. Nakashima, Black Walnut, Trestle, 1957, 30 x 60 x 49 In.	8820
Table, Drop Leaf, George III, Walnut, Turned Legs, Pad Foot, 28½ x 49 x 18½ In.	688
Table, Drop Leaf, Georgian Style, Mahogany, Cabriole Legs, Hoof Feet, 1900s, 30 x 16 In.. *illus*	1188
Table, Drop Leaf, Henkel Harris, Side, Banded Mahogany, Brown, Drawer, 28 x 23 x 24 In.	148
Table, Drop Leaf, Louis Philippe, Rosewood, Inlay, Drawers, A. Giroux, c.1850, 26 x 28 In.....	730
Table, Drop Leaf, Maple, Butterfly, Splayed Legs, Box Stretcher, New England, 1700s, 26 In....	1000
Table, Drop Leaf, Maple, Oval Top, Ring Turned Legs, Stretchers, c.1750, 28 x 49 x 39 In.......	938
Table, Drop Leaf, Queen Anne Style, Mahogany, Turned Legs, Brass Pulls, c.1970, 30 x 36 In..	184
Table, Drop Leaf, Queen Anne, Mahogany, Pad Feet, Handkerchief, 1700s, 27 x 36 x 19 In. . *illus*	148
Table, Drop Leaf, Queen Anne, Mahogany, Scalloped Skirts, Cabriole Legs, 28 x 19 x 54 In. ....*illus*	1230
Table, Drop Leaf, Queen Anne, Maple, Cabriole Legs, Pad Feet, c.1740, 28 x 36 x 34 In.	1375
Table, Drop Leaf, Regency Style, Mahogany, Triple Pedestal, Early 1800s, 29 x 57 In.............	2242
Table, Drop Leaf, Sheraton, Cherry, Spiral Turned Legs, 29½ x 15 In.	59
Table, Drop Leaf, Sheraton, Dining, Cherry, Casters, 28½ x 25 x 47 In.	175
Table, Drop Leaf, Sunderland, Burl Walnut, Caster Feet, 1800s, 29 x 40½ x 36½ In...............	531
Table, Drop Leaf, Wake, Oak, Ring Turned, Inset Gate Legs, 1900s, 33½ x 20 x 60 In............	1170
Table, Drum, David Wider, Ebony, Pearwood, Veneer Top, Tapered Legs, c.1965, 24 x 24 In... *illus*	1220
Table, Drum, Mahogany, Drawers, Pine, Leather Top, Casters, New York, c.1810, 30 In. *illus*	590
Table, D-Shape, Mahogany, Drop Leaf, Continental, Late 1800s, 29¼ x 25 In.	219

Furniture, Table, Dressing, William & Mary Style, Cross Stretcher, Drexel, Late 1900s, 31 x 63 In.
$270

Garth's Auctioneers & Appraisers

F

Cocktail or Coffee?
The coffee table was named and designed about 1933, when Prohibition ended. The low table was first called a cocktail table, but "coffee" seemed less sinful.

Furniture, Table, Drop Leaf, Georgian Style, Mahogany, Cabriole Legs, Hoof Feet, 1900s, 30 x 16 In.
$1,188

Eldred's

Furniture, Table, Drop Leaf, Queen Anne, Mahogany, Pad Feet, Handkerchief, 1700s, 27 x 36 x 19 In.
$148

Leland Little Auctions

This is an edited listing of current prices. Visit Kovels.com to check thousands of prices from previous years and sign up for free information on trends, tips, reproductions, marks, and more.

Furniture, Table, Drop Leaf, Queen Anne, Mahogany, Scalloped Skirts, Cabriole Legs, 28 x 19 x 54 In.
$1,230

Brunk Auctions

Furniture, Table, Drum, David Wider, Ebony, Pearwood, Veneer Top, Tapered Legs, c.1965, 24 x 24 In.
$1,220

Neal Auction Company

Marquetry

Furniture with marquetry designs is always expensive. Best are pieces made of walnut, then mahogany, then oak. Flower marquetry designs are more common than bird or insect designs.

Furniture, Table, Drum, Mahogany, Drawers, Pine, Leather Top, Casters, New York, c.1810, 30 In.
$590

Copake Auction

Table, Empire Style, Round Marble Top, Tripod Base, Portrait Plaques, 1900s, 25 In.	219
Table, Enamel Steel, Round Top, Laminate, Knoll International, 1953, 20 In.	1125
Table, French Neoclassical, Black Marble Top, Gilt, Bronze, Round, Paw Feet, 29 x 27 In., Pair	2684
Table, Fruitwood, Marble, Bronze Mount, 2 Drawers, France, c.1910, 28 x 11 x 14 In., Pair	281
Table, Gae Aulenti, Jumbo, Marble, Square, Label, Knoll USA, 14 x 44 In. *illus*	7500
Table, Game, Checkers, Tray Top, Turned Shaft, Cabriole Legs, 1800s, 21 x 19 x 26 In. *illus*	156
Table, Game, Gio Ponti, Mahogany, Teak, Flip Top, Felt, Drink Rests, Italy, 29 x 35 In. . *illus*	2500
Table, Game, Louis XV Style, Boule, Ormolu, Mounted, Saber Legs, 1800s, 29 x 36 x 18 ½ In. .	1003
Table, Game, Marquetry, Bronze, Mounted, Saber Legs, France, 1900s, 31 x 32 x 23 In. *illus*	472
Table, Game, Regency, Mahogany, Baize Top, Inlaid Bands, Swivels & Folds, 29 x 34 In.	1408
Table, Game, Renaissance Revival, Mahogany, Flip Top, Carved, 4-Pedestal Base, Casters, 29 x 35 In.	240
Table, Game, Theodore Alexander, Castle Bromwich, Walnut, 2 Drawers, Stretcher, 1900s, 31 x 42 In.	594
Table, George I, Gateleg, Oak, 2 Drop Sides, Turned & Painted Legs, 28 x 12 x 32 In.	3416
Table, George II, Mahogany, Tilt Top, Carved, Tripod Base, Scroll Feet, c.1755, 30 In. ... *illus*	375
Table, Giacometti Style, Patina, Bronze, Rectangular, Male & Female Figures, 27 In., Pair	1652
Table, Glass Top, Painted, Black Canines, Bronze Base, Maitland-Smith, 16 x 30 In. .... *illus*	338
Table, Good Boy, Stylized Dog, Mixed Wood, Tommy Simpson, 2011, 25 x 33 In. .... *illus*	1750
Table, I. Noguchi, Laminated Plywood, Steel, Label, Knoll Assoc., 20 x 24 In. .... *illus*	1500
Table, I. Noguchi, Rudder, Birch, Steel, Asymmetric, Herman Miller, 1949, 26 x 50 In. . *illus*	69000
Table, Ice Cream, Cast Iron, 4 Attached Seats, Display Case Top, c.1900, 33 x 44 In. ..... *illus*	1476
Table, J. Wade Beam, Zephyr, Marble, Chrome, Glass, Brueton, 23 x 51 In. .... *illus*	704
Table, Jules Leleu, Rosewood, Oblong, 5-Pedestal Base, Ball Feet, c.1940, 22 x 47 x 31 In. *illus*	708
Table, Le Corbusier, Rectangular Forged Glass Top, Aluminum Base, c.1980, 30 x 33 x 80 In. .	600
Table, Library, Chippendale Style, Mahogany, Drawers, Cabriole Legs, Early 1900s, 31 ½ In.	885
Table, Library, Hunzinger, Mahogany, Drawers, Twisted Legs, 30 x 46 x 30 In. .... *illus*	748
Table, Library, Limbert, Oak, Lower Shelf, Copper Pull, 20 x 30 x 42 In. .... *illus*	938
Table, Library, Mahogany, Carved, Twisted Legs, Ball & Claw Feet, Victorian, 31 x 42 x 28 In. *illus*	234
Table, Library, Rectangular, Carved, Trestle Shape Base, Scrolled Feet, c.1920, 32 x 70 x 33 In.	1534
Table, Lift Top, Easel Back, Carved, Pirate's Head, Hands & Feet, c.1910, 16 x 6 In. .... *illus*	688
Table, Louis XV Style, Oak, Drawer, Cabriole Legs, Early 1990s, 29 x 59 In.	944
Table, Louis XV Style, Porcelain, Mahogany, Carved, Ormolu, Cabriole Legs, 1900s, 22 In.	406
Table, Louis XV, Provincial, Fruitwood, 3 Drawers, Brass Fittings, 1750s, 24 x 16 x 11 In.	252
Table, Louis XVI Style, Mahogany, Ormolu Mount, Brass, Paw Feet, Round, 31 x 27 x 23 In. .	938
Table, Mahogany, 2 Drawers, Saber Legs, Bamboo Turned Stretchers, 30 x 22 x 64 In.	369
Table, Mahogany, 2 Pedestals, Tripod Legs, Ball & Claw Feet, England, c.1815, 30 x 60 x 48 In.	563
Table, Mahogany, Flower Design, Circular Top, Drawers, Maitland-Smith, Late 1900s, 31 ½ In.	413
Table, Maple, Oval Top, Drawer, Brass Accents, Baker Furniture, c.1950, 25 x 28 In. ..... *illus*	200
Table, Neoclassical Style, Mahogany Veneer, Pedestal, Dolphin, Late 1900s, 30 x 100 x 64 In. .	640
Table, Nesting, Edwardian, Mahogany, Inlaid Burl, Oval, Trestle, c.1910, 27 x 19 In., 4 Piece	425
Table, Nesting, Regency, Rosewood, Rectangular, Turned Legs, c.1810, 29 In., 4 Piece	1125
Table, Oak, Tuckaway, Octagonal, 3-Board Top, Stretcher, Turned Legs, 27 x 27 ½ x 21 In.	1000
Table, P. Evans, Dining, Smoked Glass, Chromed Metal, Wood Base, c.1980, 29 x 72 x 42 In..	50
Table, Painted, Blue, Green, Brown, Red, Base, Ball Feet, Martin's Mill, Early 1900s, 29 x 40 x 40 In.	3125
Table, Pembroke, Federal, Mahogany, Tapered Legs, 1790, 28 ½ x 20 x 33 In.	1024
Table, Pembroke, Georgian, Inlaid Mahogany, Drawer, 1800s, 27 x 39 x 33 In.	832
Table, Pembroke, Mahogany, Drawer, Cross Stretcher, Hearts, Late 1700s, 27 x 21 In. *illus*	7500
Table, Philip & Kelvin LaVerne, Etched, Patinated Bronze, Signed, Label, 16 x 48 In. ... *illus*	3250
Table, Pine, Removable Top, Shelf, Turned Legs, Cutout Bootjack Ends, 29 x 70 x 29 In.	633
Table, Pub, Iron, Green Marble Top, Tripod Base, Caskell & Chambers, Victorian, 31 x 30 In. .*illus*	720
Table, Queen Anne, Tiger Maple, Scalloped Apron, Tapered Legs, 1700s, 26 x 31 x 25 In.	2500
Table, R. Wyland, Round, Glass Top, Brass Dolphin & Coral Reef Base, c.1985, 33 x 43 In.	4212
Table, Regency, Hardwood, Shaped Top, Drawer, Trestle, Casters, 1800s, 29 x 36 In.	575
Table, Rococo Revival, Walnut, Carved, Marble, Drawer, Meeks, c.1875, 22 x 59 In. ...... *illus*	2375
Table, Rosewood, Tooled Leather Top, Gilt, Bronze, Mounted, 31 x 42 ½ In.	420
Table, Sewing, Bamboo, Flowers, Square Top, Splayed Legs, Late 1800s, 29 ½ x 18 In.	88
Table, Sewing, Brass, Hinged Lid, Silk Lined Interior, Lion Mask Handles, Flowers, c.1885, 31 ½ In..	2223
Table, Sewing, Drop Leaf, Mahogany, Carved, 2 Drawers, Applied Caster, 29 x 19 x 19 ½ In..	188
Table, Sewing, Eastlake, Walnut, Hinged Lid, Yarn Holder, Caster Feet, Victorian, 33 In. *illus*	431
Table, Sewing, Empire, Chestnut, 2 Drawers, Knob Handles, Scroll Feet, 29 x 22 x 16 In.	345

F

Furniture, Table, Gae Aulenti, Jumbo, Marble, Square, Label, Knoll USA, 14 x 44 In.
$7,500

Hindman

Furniture, Table, Game, Checkers, Tray Top, Turned Shaft, Cabriole Legs, 1800s, 21 x 19 x 26 In.
$156

Bruneau & Co. Auctioneers

Furniture, Table, Game, Gio Ponti, Mahogany, Teak, Flip Top, Felt, Drink Rests, Italy, 29 x 35 In.
$2,500

Palm Beach Modern Auctions

Furniture, Table, Game, Marquetry, Bronze, Mounted, Saber Legs, France, 1900s, 31 x 32 x 23 In.
$472

Cottone Auctions

Furniture, Table, George II, Mahogany, Tilt Top, Carved, Tripod Base, Scroll Feet, c.1755, 30 In.
$375

Charlton Hall Auctions

Furniture, Table, Glass Top, Painted, Black Canines, Bronze Base, Maitland-Smith, 16 x 30 In.
$338

Alderfer Auction Company

Furniture, Table, Good Boy, Stylized Dog, Mixed Wood, Tommy Simpson, 2011, 25 x 33 In.
$1,750

Rago Arts and Auction Center

Furniture, Table, I. Noguchi, Laminated Plywood, Steel, Label, Knoll Assoc., 20 x 24 In.
$1,500

Hindman

F

FURNITURE

Furniture, Table, I. Noguchi, Rudder, Birch, Steel, Asymmetric, Herman Miller, 1949, 26 x 50 In.
$69,000

Furniture, Table, Ice Cream, Cast Iron, 4 Attached Seats, Display Case Top, c.1900, 33 x 44 In.
$1,476

Rich Penn Auctions

Furniture, Table, J. Wade Beam, Zephyr, Marble, Chrome, Glass, Brueton, 23 x 51 In.
$704

Hindman

Furniture, Table, Jules Leleu, Rosewood, Oblong, 5-Pedestal Base, Ball Feet, c.1940, 22 x 47 x 31 In.
$708

Cottone Auctions

Furniture, Table, Library, Hunzinger, Mahogany, Drawers, Twisted Legs, 30 x 46 x 30 In.
$748

Stevens Auction Co.

Furniture, Table, Library, Limbert, Oak, Lower Shelf, Copper Pull, 20 x 30 x 42 In.
$938

Toomey & Co. Auctioneers

Furniture, Table, Library, Mahogany, Carved, Twisted Legs, Ball & Claw Feet, Victorian, 31 x 42 x 28 In.
$234

Hartzell's Auction Gallery Inc.

Furniture, Table, Lift Top, Easel Back, Carved, Pirate's Head, Hands & Feet. c.1910, 16 x 6 In.
$688

Eldred's

Furniture, Table, Maple, Oval Top, Drawer, Brass Accents, Baker Furniture, c.1950, 25 x 28 In.
$200

Eldred's

Furniture, Table, Nesting, Regency, Rosewood, Rectangular, Turned Legs, c.1810, 29 In., 4 Piece
$1,125

New Orleans Auction Galleries

Hang-Ups
Plain wooden dressing-table mirrors with handles have a new use. Decorators are hanging groups of the mirrors in powder rooms, partly as decoration and partly to be used as mirrors. Dealers at shows find the mirrors are selling again.

Furniture, Table, Pembroke, Mahogany, Drawer, Cross Stretcher, Hearts, Late 1700s, 27 x 21 In.
$7,500

Eldred's

Furniture, Table, Philip & Kelvin LaVerne, Etched, Patinated Bronze, Signed, Label, 16 x 48 In.
$3,250

Hindman

Furniture, Table, Pub, Iron, Green Marble Top, Tripod Base, Caskell & Chambers, Victorian, 31 x 30 In.
$720

Michaan's Auctions

Furniture, Table, Rococo Revival, Walnut, Carved, Marble, Drawer, Meeks, c.1875, 22 x 59 In.
$2,375

New Orleans Auction Galleries

Furniture, Table, Sewing, Eastlake, Walnut, Hinged Lid, Yarn Holder, Caster Feet, Victorian, 33 In.
$431

Rich Penn Auctions

Furniture, Table, Side, 3 Tiers, Wood, Black, Bombay Co., 27 x 21 ½ In.
$35

Bunch Auctions

FURNITURE

Furniture, Table, Tavern, Maple, Oval, Cabriole Legs, Pad Feet, New Hampshire, 1710s, 26 ½ In.
$6,875

Eldred's

Furniture, Table, Telephone, Karl Springer, Snakeskin, Casters, 1987, 20 x 15 In., Pair
$1,020

Michaan's Auctions

Furniture, Table, Tilt Top, Lacquer, Man, Woman, Circular Base, Scrolled Feet, 1800s, 27 ¼ In.
$443

Austin Auction Gallery

Furniture, Table, Tilt Top, Papier-Mache, Mother-Of-Pearl, Tripod Base, Late 1800s, 27 x 21 In.
$502

Austin Auction Gallery

Furniture, Table, Turtleback, Walnut, Marble Top, Carved, Scroll & Finial Base, c.1880, 28 x 34 In.
$738

Rich Penn Auctions

Furniture, Table, Wagon Seat, Converted, Oak, Iron Hardware, Tapered Legs, 26 x 52 x 3 In.
$192

Michaan's Auctions

Furniture, Table, Wood, Old Blue Paint, New Mexico, 20th Century, 20 x 24 x 22 In.
$132

Santa Fe Art Auction

Furniture, Table, Work, Neoclassical, Mahogany, Inlay, Drawer, Writing Surface, Pedestal, 1800s, 31 In.
$1,342

Neal Auction Company

Furniture, Tabouret, Louis XV Style, Metallic Thread Embroidery, Upholstered, 1900s, 19 x 22 x 19 In.
$896

Hindman

Table, Sewing, Federal, Mahogany, String Inlay, Turned, Reeded Legs, c.1810, 29 x 18 In......	2925
Table, Sewing, Mahogany, Martha Washington Style, 3 Drawers, Reeded Legs, 29 x 28 In.	71
Table, Sewing, Sheraton, Mahogany Drawers, Rope Turned Legs, Swelled Feet, 1700s, 28½ In...	406
Table, Sewing, Walnut, Caster, Burl Trim, Victorian Style, 31½ In.	316
Table, Side, 3 Tiers, Wood, Black, Bombay Co., 27 x 21½ In. .... *illus*	35
Table, Side, Blue Lacquer, Brass Hardware, 2 Drawers, 27 x 16 x 22 In., Pair..............	625
Table, Side, Gilt Metal, Cartouche Shape, Marble Top, Pierced Apron, Curved Legs, c.1950, 29 In.	472
Table, Side, Ib Kofod-Larsen, Rosewood, Rectangular, Flower, Brass Feet, c.1970s, 20 x 30 In..	384
Table, Side, Karl Springer, 6-Sided, Leather, Embossed, Marked, Germany, 18 x 18 In.	813
Table, Side, Mahogany, Dolphin Mounts, Ball & Claw Feet, c.1900, 28 x 36 x 21 In.	472
Table, Side, Old Hickory, Round Top, Green Paint, Tripod Feet, 30 x 24 In.	369
Table, Side, Rootwood, Round Top, Cloisonne Plate, Birds, Flowers, Stand, c.1890, 23 x 14 In.	590
Table, Side, Rosewood, Bookmatch Veneer, Round, Stepped Base, c.1930, 23½ x 23 In....	800
Table, Side, Round Glass Top, Mirror, Green Stripes, Flared Supports, c.1960, 19 x 26 In.	236
Table, Side, Theodore Alexander, Louis XV Style, Mahogany, Kidney Shape, Drawer, 29 x 26 x 16 In. ..	767
Table, Side, Walnut, Slatted X-Base, Savonarola, Italy, Early 1900s, 28 x 29 In......................	207
Table, Tavern, Maple, Oval, Cabriole Legs, Pad Feet, New Hampshire, 1710s, 26½ In. .. *illus*	6875
Table, Tavern, Queen Anne, Pine, Maple, Porringer Top, Tapered Legs, 1700s, 28 x 27 In......	405
Table, Tavern, Round, Straight Skirt, Turned Leg & Stretchers, 1900s, 26 x 29 In................	595
Table, Tavern, William & Mary, Cherry, Ash, Oak, Inlaid Compass Star, N.Y., 20 x 38 In.	960
Table, Tea, Mahogany, Tilt Top, Piecrust, Claw Feet, 30 In.	230
Table, Telephone, Karl Springer, Snakeskin, Casters, 1800s, 20 x 15 In., Pair .... *illus*	1020
Table, Theodore Muller, Marble Top, Black Geometric Base, Kittinger, 1950s, 14 x 42 In........	316
Table, Tilt Top, Lacquer, Man, Woman, Circular Base, Scrolled Feet, 1800s, 27¼ In. ... *illus*	443
Table, Tilt Top, Papier-Mache, Mother-Of-Pearl, Tripod Base, Late 1800s, 27 x 21 In. ... *illus*	502
Table, Tole, Wrought Iron, Painted, Classical, Greek Key Frieze, Swan Mounts, 18 x 37 In.	2125
Table, Tray, Majorelle, Wood, Handles, Inlay, Metal Base, Shelf, c.1900, 31 x 38 In.	5935
Table, Tray, Rectangular, Lacquered, X-Stretcher, Chinoiserie, 35 x 22 x 20 In.	600
Table, Tray, Teak Plywood, Chrome-Plated Steel, Enamel, 17 x 18 In.	650
Table, Tulip, White, 6 Fiberglass Swivel Chairs, Aluminum Base, Burke, 29 x 60 x 45 In	984
Table, Turtleback, Walnut, Marble Top, Carved, Scroll & Finial Base, c.1880, 28 x 34 In. *illus*	738
Table, Victorian, Walnut, White, Marble Turtle Top, Dog On Base, Scrolled Legs, 27 x 32 In..	489
Table, Wagon Seat, Converted, Oak, Iron Hardware, Tapered Legs, 26 x 52 x 3 In. .... *illus*	192
Table, William & Mary, Yellow Pine, White Cedar, Baluster Turned Base, Early 1700s, 28 x 39 In.	1968
Table, Wood, Old Blue Paint, New Mexico, 20th Century, 20 x 24 x 22 In. .... *illus*	132
Table, Wood, Rectangular Top, Rustic, 22 x 13 x 14 In.	25
Table, Work, Federal, Maple, Carved, Drawers, Spiral Legs, c.1820, 29 In.	625
Table, Work, Mahogany, 2 Drawers, Turret, Reeded Legs, 28 x 19½ In..............................	369
Table, Work, Neoclassical, Mahogany, Inlay, Drawer, Writing Surface, Pedestal, 1800s, 31 In. *illus*	1342
Table, Writing, Art Deco, Rectangular Top, Painted, Ebonized, 1910s, 29¾ x 55 In.	250
Table, Writing, Drawer, Mahogany, Inlay, Continental, 1800s, 30½ x 34 In.	544
Tabouret, Empire, White, X-Frame, Flowers, 1800s, 21 x 27 x 20 In., Pair..............................	7560
Tabouret, Louis XV Style, Metallic Thread Embroidery, Upholstered, 1900s, 19 x 22 x 19 In. *illus*	896
Tabouret, Louis XVI Style, Cream Cushion, Painted, Parcel Gilt, 1800s, 19½ x 21 In.	1105
Tea Cart, 2 Drawers, Drop Sides, Carved Apron, 38 x 19 x 30 In.	74
Tea Cart, 2 Tiers, Oak, Metamorphic, Carved, Trestle Base, Bun Feet, 1800s, 39 x 48 In........	896
Tea Cart, Aalto, Birch, Lacquer, Wood, O.Y. Huonekalu, Finland, 1936, 21 x 35 In. .... *illus*	8750
Tea Cart, Louis XV Style, Removable Tray Top, Cabriole Legs, Casters, 1950s, 29 x 31 In. ...	266
Tea Cart, Mahogany, Plywood, 3 Tiers, Chrome, Silver Plated Fittings, Casters, 1900s, 55 x 24 In.	2625
Teapoy, Mahogany, Hinged Top, Leather Lined, Scrolled Legs, Casters, 1800s, 31 x 19 In.......	531
Umbrella Stand, Aldo Tura, Parchment, Brass, Stained Maple, Italy, c.1950, 23 x 12½ In...	875
Umbrella Stand, Bronze, Bamboo Bundle Shape, Verdigris, 1920s, 24¾ In., Pair................	938
Umbrella Stand, Cylindrical, Geometric, Multicolor, Italy, c.1960s, 19½ In.................... .	384
Umbrella Stand, Spindles, Turned Ball Ornaments, Light Green, Gray, Late 1800s, 25 In. ...	125
Umbrella Stand, Terra-Cotta, Cast Dragon Design, Gold, Painted, Chinese, 24 In. ..... *illus*	165
Umbrella Stand, Victorian, Cast Iron, Figural, Fisherman, Molded Seashells, 26 x 14 In. *illus*	468
Valet, Gentleman's, Hanger, Pants Rail, Casters, Fratelli Reguitti, 1960s, 42 x 17 In. .... *illus*	207
Valet, Paul Dupre Lafon, Oak, Brass, Leather, Hermes, France, c.1935, 54 In.........................	6875
Vanity, Glass Top, 5 Drawers, Flowers, Tapered Legs, 46 x 17 x 30½ In.	98
Vanity, Heart Shape Beveled Mirror, Silver Mounted, William Comyn & Sons, 1884, 12 In. ...	200

Furniture, Tea Cart, Aalto, Birch, Lacquer, Wood, O.Y. Huonekalu, Finland, 1936, 21 x 35 In.
$8,750

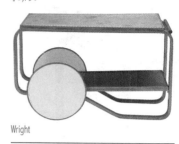

Wright

Furniture, Umbrella Stand, Terra-Cotta, Cast Dragon Design, Gold, Painted, Chinese, 24 In.
$165

Garth's Auctioneers & Appraisers

Furniture, Umbrella Stand, Victorian, Cast Iron, Figural, Fisherman, Molded Seashells, 26 x 14 In.
$468

Thomaston Place Auction Galleries

Furniture, Valet, Gentleman's, Hanger, Pants Rail, Casters, Fratelli Reguitti, 1960s, 42 x 17 In.
$207

Austin Auction Gallery

Furniture, Vitrine, Chippendale Style, Mahogany, Step Back, Glass Lift Top, 70 x 26 x 19 In.
$995

Thomaston Place Auction Galleries

Vanity, Louis XV Style, Burl, Elm, Ormolu, Drawers, Cabriole Legs, 1900s, 34 x 37 In.	469
Vitrine, Art Glass, Beveled Glass, Gilt, Mounted, 2 Cranberry Glass Vases, 14 x 15 x 7 In.	369
Vitrine, Bernhard Rohne, Metal, Glass, Acid Etched, Abstract Geometrics, 87 x 16 x 38 In.	625
Vitrine, Chippendale Style, Mahogany, Step Back, Glass Lift Top, 70 x 26 x 19 In. .... *illus*	995
Vitrine, George III Style, Wood, Gilt, 4 Drawers, Cabinet On Stand, 85 x 38 In.	7560
Vitrine, Josef Frank, Mahogany, Glass Sides, Doors, Svenskt Tenn, Late 1900s, 67 x 36 x 13 In.	5500
Vitrine, Louis XVI Style, Mahogany, Marble Top, Glass Shelves, c.1910, 57 x 25 x 14 In.	266
Vitrine, Vernis Martin, Louis XV Style, Bombe, Kingwood, Tulipwood, c.1890, 70 x 30 In. *illus*	3600
Vitrine, Wood, Gilt, Flowers, Door, Curved Glass, France, c.1900, 53 x 25 x 15 In.	531
Wall Unit, McCobb, 6 Parts, Walnut, Aluminum Legs, 10 Doors, 7 Drawers, 1960, 84 x 111 In.	590
Wardrobe, Cherry, Poplar, 2 Doors, Knob Pulls, Molded Cornice, 1800s, 72 x 44 In ..... *illus*	380
Wardrobe, Victorian, Oak, Ornate, Beveled Mirror Doors, Knockdown, 1880s, 82 x 58 x 21 In.	540
Washstand, Backsplash, Drawer, Metal Pull, Turned Legs & Stretcher, 34 In.	107
Washstand, Burnt Bamboo, Marble Top, Green Tiles, Hinged Door, c.1890, 44 x 35 In. *illus*	708
Washstand, Corner, Federal, Mahogany, Inlay, Maple Banded, Shelf, Boston, c.1800, 41 In. .	1125
Washstand, Corner, Federal, Mahogany, Tiger Maple, 3 Tiers, Inlaid, J. & T. Seymour, 41 In. .	1125
Washstand, Painted, Flowers, Brass Pulls, Caster Feet, Victorian, 30 x 15 ½ In. .... *illus*	59
Washstand, Shaped Marble Top, Carved, Hart, Malone & Co., Late 1800s, 31 x 38 x 18 In.....	266
Washstand, Sheraton, Pine, Faux Marble, 2 Shelves, Turned Legs, 1800s, 41 x 45 ½ In. *illus*	375
Washstand, Sheraton, Pine, Grain Painted, Red Wash, Rosettes, Drawer, c.1835, 37 x 18 In.	160
Washstand, Walnut, Marble, Drawer, Towel Rails, Top Shape Feet, France, 1800s, 31 x 31 In.	310

G. ARGY-ROUSSEAU

G. Argy-Rousseau is the impressed mark used on a variety of glass objects in the Art Deco style. Gabriel Argy-Rousseau, born in 1885, was a French glass artist. In 1921, he formed a partnership that made pate-de-verre and other glass. The partnership ended in 1931 and he opened his own studio. He worked until 1952 and died in 1953.

Coupe, Scene De Chasse, Molded, Eagle, Purple, Red, Pate-De-Verre, Signed, c.1925, 4 ⅜ In.	5040
Night-Light, Angular Leaves, Cone Shape, Purple, Pink, Red, Pate-De-Verre, Signed, 8 x 5 In. ... *illus*	6930
Night-Light, Bouquet Of Flowers, Maroon, Purple, Spiral, Metal Base, 1-Light, 5 ½ In. *illus*	5440
Vase, Molded Flowers, Leaves, Frosted, Pate-De-Verre, Signed, c.1910, 4 In.	925
Vase, White, Purple Flowers, Green Leaves, Pate-De-Verre, c.1900, 4 x 2 ½ In.	2000

GALLE

Galle was a designer who made glass, pottery, furniture, and other Art Nouveau items. Emile Galle founded his factory in France in 1874. After Galle's death in 1904, the firm continued to make glass and furniture until 1931. The *Galle* signature was used as a mark, but it was often hidden in the design of the object. Galle cameo and other types of glass are listed here. Pottery is in the next section. His furniture is listed in the Furniture category.

Berry Bowl, Leaves, Vines, Yellow Ground, Cameo, Pedestal Base, Signed, Galle Tip, 10 In. ..	252
Box, Lid, Pyramid Shape, Green Trees, Blue Mountains, Signed, 5 ¾ x 7 ½ In.	1152
Vase, 3 Colors, Mountain & Tree Scene, Cameo, Signed, 4 ½ x 3 ½ In. .... *illus*	400
Vase, Apple Blossom, Cream, Yellow Ground, Bulbous, Etched, Cameo, Signed, c.1900, 14 In...	5670
Vase, Bud, Pink, Banjo Shape, Hydrangea, White, Violet, Green Leaves, Signed, c.1900, 7 In.	750
Vase, Carved Overlay, Trees & Lake, White, Pink, Green Cameo, Signed, 12 ½ x 3 ¾ In. *illus*	600
Vase, Carved Tree, Lake Scene, White & Yellow Ground, Cameo, Signed, 11 In.	500
Vase, Clusters Of Blueberries, Leaves & Vines, Circular Base, Cameo, 21 ½ In.	5670
Vase, Cream, Blue, Green, Etched, Mountains, River, Bulbous, Footed, Cameo, 9 x 7 ½ In.....	976
Vase, Falling Japanese Maple Leaves, Rain, Red, Violet, Etched, Signed, c.1890, 7 In.	2125
Vase, Ferns, Bronze Green, Pale Green Ground, Narrow Elongated Neck, Signed, c.1900, 19 ¾ In..	675
Vase, Fish & Leaves, Frosted Glass, Blue Cameo, Marked, 1900s, 9 x 9 ½ In.	677
Vase, Flowers, Peach To Pink Over Clear, Pavot Case, Etched, Early 1900s, 8 ½ In. .... *illus*	230

Furniture, Vitrine, Vernis Martin, Louis XV Style, Bombe, Kingwood, Tulipwood, c.1890, 70 x 30 In.
$3,600

Cottone Auctions

TIP
Mother-of-pearl for inlays can be bought at a guitar factory. You may have to sand the back to make the inlay thinner.

Furniture, Wardrobe, Cherry, Poplar, 2 Doors, Knob Pulls, Molded Cornice, 1800s, 72 x 44 In

Jeffrey S. Evans & Associates

Furniture, Washstand, Burnt Bamboo, Marble Top, Green Tiles, Hinged Door, c.1890, 44 x 35 In.
$708

Leland Little Auctions

Furniture, Washstand, Painted, Flowers, Brass Pulls, Caster Feet, Victorian, 30 x 15 ½ In.
$59

Copake Auction

Furniture, Washstand, Sheraton, Pine, Faux Marble, 2 Shelves, Turned Legs, 1800s, 41 x 45 ½ In.
$375

Eldred's

G. Argy-Rousseau, Night-Light, Angular Leaves, Cone Shape, Purple, Pink, Red, Pate-De-Verre, Signed, 8 x 5 In.
$6,930

Morphy Auctions

G. Argy-Rousseau, Night-Light, Bouquet Of Flowers, Maroon, Purple, Spiral, Metal Base, 1-Light, 5 ½ In.
$5,440

Morphy Auctions

TIP
Never wash lacquered wood. Just wipe it clean with a damp cloth. Water could seep into the base wood and cause damage.

G

Galle, Vase, 3 Colors, Mountain & Tree
Scene, Cameo, Signed, 4 1/2 x 3 1/2 In.
$400

G

Woody Auction

Galle, Vase, Carved Overlay, Trees &
Lake, White, Pink, Green Cameo, Signed,
12 1/2 x 3 3/4 In.
$600

Woody Auction

Galle, Vase, Flowers, Peach To Pink Over
Clear, Pavot Case, Etched, Early 1900s,
8 1/2 In.
$230

Blackwell Auctions

Vase, Long Neck, White Ground, Purple Leaves, Fire Polished, Cameo, 20 In.	1200
Vase, Orchid, Gold & Cordovan, c.1905, 6 In.	472
Vase, Square, Blue Cameo, White Opaque Ground, Bulbous Base, 28 In. ..... *illus*	1197
Vase, White, Lavender, Carved Overlay, Flowers, Cameo, Signed, 3 1/2 x 3 In.	175

GALLE POTTERY

Galle pottery was made by Emile Galle, the famous French designer, after
1874. The pieces were marked with the initials *E. G.* impressed, *Em. Galle
Faiencerie de Nancy,* or a version of his signature. Galle is best known for his glass,
listed above.

Sauceboat, Rooster Shape, White Ground, Red, Black, Signed, Late 1800s, 3 3/4 x 7 1/2 In.	246
Vase, Raised Bees, Yellow Honeycomb Ground, Incised Signature, 8 x 10 1/2 In.	3198
Vase, Seascape, Harbor, Flowering Vine, Diagonal Spiral, Signed, c.1890, 6 1/2 In.	1063
Wall Pocket, Dragonfly Shape, Folded Wings, Multicolor, Red Mark, c.1880, 10 3/4 x 5 3/4 In.	1920

GAME

Game collectors like all types of games. Of special interest are any board
games or card games. Transogram and other company names are
included in the description when known. Other games may be found listed under
Card, Toy, or the name of the character or celebrity featured in the game. Gameboards
without the game pieces are listed in the Gameboard category.

Backgammon Pieces, Bakelite, Marbled, Red, Butterscotch, Catalin, Crisoid, Box, 1/2 x 2 In., 30 Piece	400
Backgammon Set, Leather, Bakelite, Velvet, Asprey & Co., UK, c.1965, 27 x 18 In.	3500
Bagatelle, Red Ryder Corral, Multicolor Board, Pieces, Red & Blue Box, Gotham, 1950, 16 1/2 x 9 In.	188
Bambino Baseball, Target Hole Bases, Outfield, Tin, Mansfield Products, Box, 1946, 12 x 20 In.	154
Bowling, 8 Penguin Shape Pins, 2 Striped Balls, Black & White, H.F. Kohaut, N.J., 1935, 12 In.	3250
Carnival, Throwing Skill, Painted, Wood, 6 Pickets, c.1940, 18 x 36 In. ..... *illus*	148
Chess, Backgammon, Lacquered Wood Box, 2-Sided, Jade Pieces, Chinese Export, 15 In.	3520
Chess, Revolutionary War Figures, Checkerboard, Drawer, Mahogany, Box, 17 x 23 x 16 In.	644
Chuck-A-Luck, Hourglass Shape, Metal Wire, 3 Bakelite Dice, c.1950, 17 3/4 In. ..... *illus*	63
Croquet, Boxwood Table Croquet, Box, Hinged Lid, Label, Late 1900s, 3 x 17 x 7 In. .... *illus*	129
Dice, Rotating Bowl, Bone Etched, Mahogany Finish, 9 1/2 x 18 1/2 x 18 1/2 In. ..... *illus*	960
Game Of Merry Christmas, Santa Claus Holding Toys, Parker Bros., Board, 1898, 17 x 24 x 2 In.	5228
Game Of The Wild West, 2 Spinners, 9 Cowboys & Indians, R. Bliss, Board, Box, 1889, 19 In.	2250
Game Of Yellowstone, Scenic, Buffalo, Yellow Flowers On Reverse, H.E. Klamer, Card, Box, 3 x 2 In.	123
Kentucky Derby, Dice, Horses, Wood Frame, 2 1/2 x 12 1/2 In.	780
Mahjong, Bone Inlay, 5 Drawers, 148 Tiles, Wood Case, Chinese, 6 1/2 x 9 1/2 In. ..... *illus*	826
Mahjong, Bone, Wood Case, Painted, Art Deco, Chinese, 1910s, 6 x 9 1/2 In.	204
Pinball, Tabletop, Hit The Deck, Card Theme, Oak Cabinet, 9 x 16 1/2 x 26 In.	832
Puzzle, Dissected Map Of The United States, Milton Bradley, c.1900 ..... *illus*	145
Puzzle, Planetary, Plastic, Movable Pieces, Metal Case, Vasarely, 20 x 20 In., 390 Pieces	738
Roulette Wheel, Maple & Mahogany, Vinyl Stand, Marked, Mason & Co., 35 In. ..... *illus*	793
Roulette Wheel, Traveling, Number Slots, Crate, Mahogany, George Mason, 34 x 35 x 10 In.	2091
Roulette Wheel, Wood, Merle & Heaney Mfg. Co., c.1900, 31 1/2 In.	1800
Soccer, 2 Boys Playing, Fenced Field, Flag, Tin Litho, Clockwork, Germany, 7 1/2 x 14 In.	1476
Target, Baseball Toss, Revolving Target, Player's Face, Canvas Covered, Easel Shape Stand, 48 x 36 In.	56
Target, Bull's-Eye, Bird, Embossed Letters, Square Base, Iron, Signed, Wurfflein, 12 x 10 In.	2486
Video, Super Mario Bros., Original Box, 1985	114000
Wheel, Gambling, Black Numbers, White Ground, Red, White, Blue, Stand, Late 1800s, 25 In.	425
Wheel, Gambling, Dice, Metal Spokes, Finial, Wood Stand, H.C. Evans, c.1920, 90 x 64 x 21 In. *illus*	2304
Wheel, Gambling, Numbered Slots, Multicolor, Wood, 2-Sided, Stand, Early 1900s, 27 x 20 In.	184
Wheel, Gambling, Red, White, Blue, Numbers, 8 Horses, Nickel Plated Mount, Early 1900s, 35 In.	2712
Wheel, Gambling, Stencil Numbers, Turned, Yellow, Blue Pole, Early 1900s, 74 In.	438
Wheel, Gambling, Wood, Carved, Painted, 3 Bands Of Dice Border, Tripod Base, c.1900, 31 In.	1830

Galle, Vase, Square, Blue Cameo, White Opaque Ground, Bulbous Base, 28 In.
$1,197

Fontaine's Auction Gallery

Game, Carnival, Throwing Skill, Painted, Wood, 6 Pickets, c.1940, 18 x 36 In.
$148

Leland Little Auctions

Game, Chuck-A-Luck, Hourglass Shape, Metal Wire, 3 Bakelite Dice, c.1950, 17¾ In.
$63

Bruneau & Co. Auctioneers

Game, Croquet, Boxwood Table Croquet, Box, Hinged Lid, Label, Late 1900s, 3 x 17 x 7 In.
$129

Jeffrey S. Evans & Associates

Game, Dice, Rotating Bowl, Bone Etched, Mahogany Finish, 9½ x 18½ x 18½ In.
$960

Morphy Auctions

> **TIP**
> It is not just ivory mahjong tiles that are wanted; collectors also like Bakelite tiles. Newer, plastic tiles are not selling well.

Game, Mahjong, Bone Inlay, 5 Drawers, 148 Tiles, Wood Case, Chinese, 6½ x 9½ In.
$826

Leland Little Auctions

Game, Puzzle, Dissected Map Of The United States, Milton Bradley, c.1900
$145

Ruby Lane

Game, Roulette Wheel, Maple & Mahogany, Vinyl Stand, Marked, Mason & Co., 35 In.
$793

Neal Auction Company

Millions of "Yahtzee"
Edwin Lowe, the man who first marketed Bingo, was asked to promote a new game called Yacht Game in 1956. Lowe renamed it Yahtzee. He filed for a trademark in April 1957 and eventually sold more than 40 million Yahtzee games.

G

Game, Wheel, Gambling, Dice, Metal Spokes, Finial, Wood Stand, H.C. Evans, c.1920, 90 x 64 x 21 In.
$2,304

Morphy Auctions

Game Plate, Platter, Pheasant, Grass, Flowers, Gilt, Scalloped Rim, Germany, c.1870, 12 x 17 In.
$32

Wiederseim Associates

Gameboard, Checkers, Parcheesi, Leaves, Painted, Wood, 2-Sided, Late 1800s, 16 1/8 x 16 1/4 In.
$1,220

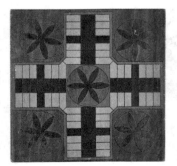

Pook & Pook

TIP
Bright sunlight may fade colors of gameboard boxes.

GAME PLATE

Game plates are plates of any make decorated with pictures of birds, animals, or fish. The game plates usually came in sets consisting of 12 dishes and a serving platter. These sets were most popular during the 1880s.

Birds, Outdoor Scene, Majolica, France, 9 In., 3 Piece	213
Charger, 3 Deer, Outdoor Scene, Blue Border, Gilt Trim, Beehive Mark, Bavaria	52
Platter, Pheasant, Grass, Flowers, Gilt, Scalloped Rim, Germany, c.1870, 12 x 17 In. .... *illus*	32
Wild Game, Birds, Hand Painted, Artist Signed, Royal Worcester, 1953, 10 1/2 In., 12 Piece	558

GAMEBOARD

Gameboard collectors look for just the board without the game pieces. The boards are collected as folk art or decorations. Gameboards that are part of a complete game are listed in the Game category.

Checkers, Backgammon, Hinged, Dovetail Case, Compass Star, Footed, Anno 1817, 5 x 8 x 2 In...	527
Checkers, Backgammon, Red Scroll, Green, Edge Molding, Late 1800s, 20 3/4 x 16 5/8 In.........	750
Checkers, Cribbage Counters, Card Suit Corners, Laminated, Painted, 1910s, 23 x 23 In.......	270
Checkers, Cribbage, Parquetry, Diamond Inlays, Late 1800s, 19 1/4 x 19 In.	275
Checkers, Decoupage Slate, Hound, Wildflower, Black, Red, c.1900, 20 x 20 In....................	580
Checkers, Green Square, Red Stars, Wood, Painted, 24 x 17 In.	48
Checkers, Home, Square Slate, Painted, Marbleized, Metal Frame, 1800s, 20 In., 2-Sided.....	1121
Checkers, Painted, Raised, Mustard Squares, 1800s, 52 1/2 x 17 1/8 In., 2-Sided...................	180
Checkers, Parcheesi, Leaves, Painted, Wood, 2-Sided, Late 1800s, 16 1/8 x 16 1/4 In. .... *illus*	1220
Checkers, Parcheesi, Painted, Wood, 2-Sided, Early 1900s, 22 In..................................	125
Checkers, Pine, Breadboard Ends, White Pinstripes, Red, Black, Late 1800s, 18 x 16 In.	1500
Checkers, Pine, Painted, Yellow, Black Squares, Varnished Ground, Late 1800s, 27 x 19 In...	222
Checkers, Pine, Red & Black Squares, Game Piece Trays, Late 1800s, 18 1/4 x 30 1/4 In...........	313
Checkers, Wood, Drawn Geometrics, White & Green, Carved, FLP, Late 1800s, 14 x 11 In......	281
Chess, Inlaid, Marble, Octagonal, Flowers, Leaves, White Ground, 1900s, 15 1/2 In. .... *illus*	123
Parcheesi, Black & Yellow Playing Grid, Salmon Ground, Late 1800s, 26 x 26 1/4 In.	439
Parcheesi, Red, Black, Green & Yellow Squares, Folk Art, c.1900, 18 x 21 In.	704
Parcheesi, Rosette Corners, Yellow, Applied Edge Molding, Late 1800s, 25 x 25 In................	875
Parcheesi, Walnut, Painted, Green & Gold, Brown Ground, 1800s, 20 x 25 In.	250
Parcheesi, Yellow Ground, Green, Red, White, Mahogany Panel, Late 1800s, 14 x 13 3/4 In....	750

GARDEN

Garden furnishings have been popular for centuries. The stone or metal statues, urns and fountains, sundials, small figurines, and wire, iron, or rustic furniture are included in this category. Many of the metal pieces have been made continuously for years.

Armillary, Sphere, Stand, Painted, Aluminum, Copper, Marked, Arts Mundi, Late 1900s, 46 In.	708
Bench, Aesthetic Style, Leaves, Branch, Cabriole Legs, Pad Feet, Cast Iron, 1900s, 41 x 72 In.	1088
Bench, Bird Design, White Paint, Engraved, Cast Iron, 43 x 72 1/2 In.	1495
Bench, Bird Head Armrests, Leafy Design, Pierced, Cabriole Legs, Cast Iron, c.1880, 32 x 37 In...	960
Bench, Black, Gothic Design, Rosette Seat, Cabriole Legs, Cast Iron, 1800s, 32 x 44 In. *illus*	1003
Bench, Curved Seat, Gadroon Border, 2 Pedestals Base, Stone, c.1950, 18 x 55 In.	708
Bench, Grapevine & Scrollwork, White, Painted, Iron, Tree Surround, 6-Footed, 1950s, 28 x 46 In....	236
Bench, Green, Cast Metal, 29 3/4 x 45 x 19 1/2 In.	250
Bench, Painted, Slatted, S-Curve Back & Seat, Wood, Iron Supports, Early 1900s, 31 x 78 In. .	708
Bench, Painted, Wood Plank Back & Seat, Scrolled Supports, Cast Iron, Early 1900s, 31 x 70 In.	472
Bench, Park, Cape Cod Design, Red, White, Blue, Wrought Iron, Polyurethane, 1900s, 32 In. .	500
Bench, Park, Green, Painted, Slat Back, Scrolled Feet, Iron, Late 1800s, 33 x 60 x 27 In........	561
Bench, Peacock, Pierced Back, Shells, Leaves, Slat Seat, Arms, Cast Iron, 37 x 47 In., Pair	2562
Bench, Pierced, Flowers & Urn, Painted, White, Cast Iron, Victorian, 27 x 15 In.....................	165
Bench, Reticulated, Center Fan Back, Serpentine Arms, Saber Legs, Iron, 30 x 46 x 23 In.	2340
Bench, Riveted Fasteners, Green Paint, Wrought Iron, Salesman's Sample, c.1900, 8 x 9 x 5 In. ..*illus*	86
Bench, Salterini Style, Openwork, Arms, Scroll, Flowers, White, 36 1/2 x 17 In.	71
Bench, Shell, Leaves, Slatted Seat, Outswept Legs, Iron, Coalbrookdale, 1800s, 37 x 47 In., Pair ..*illus*	2562

Bench, Swan, Cast Iron, 6 Wood Slats, Victorian, 33 x 63 x 21 In.	6780
Bench, Tete-A-Tete, Pierced Back, Metal, 29 x 42 x 16 In.	219
Bench, Victorian Style, Painted, Plaque, Slat Seat, Hoof Feet, Iron, Late 1900s, 40 x 64 In.	1888
Bench, Victorian, Openwork, Ornate Legs, Flower Skirt, Wrought Iron, c.1880, 33 x 44 x 15 In.	1035
Birdbath, Black, Painted, Aluminum & Iron, Virginia Metalcrafters, 1950s, 24 In. *illus*	413
Birdbath, Circular, Shallow Dish, Column, 3 Cherubs, Riding Dolphin, Stone, c.1950, 40 In.	354
Bucket, Strainer, Spout, Swing Handle, Tin, 12 In.	43
Chair, Arch Rail, Wood Slat Seat, Scroll Arms, Iron Frame, Early 1900s, 34 x 23 In., Pair *illus*	944
Chair, Black, Cabriole Legs, Paw Feet, Wrought Iron, Victorian, 30 x 13 x 14 In. *illus*	144
Chair, Fern, White, Painted, Aluminum, Coalbrookdale, 32 x 23 In., Pair	540
Chair, Gothic Revival, White, Painted, Arms, Iron, 36¾ In., Pair	320
Chair, Painted, Black, Fabric Lined, Seat Board, Wrought Iron, Late 1900s, 34 x 29 In., Pair	767
Chair, Salterini Style, Painted, Cream Ground, Green Leaves, Splayed Legs, Iron, 35 In., Pair *illus*	354
Cistern, Baroque, Embossed, Owner's Initials & Date, Lead, Continental, 1714, 29 x 60 x 20 In.	7560
Figure, Black Man, Standing, Red Hat, Shirt, White Pants, Cast Iron, 47½ x 16½ x 15 In	854
Figure, Cat, Seated, Plinth Base, Stone, 1900s, 18½ In. *illus*	1000
Figure, Cherub, Standing, Holding Branch, Bronze, Patina, 17¼ x 16 x 16 In.	813
Figure, Crane, Standing, Painted, Black, Cast Iron, Late 1900s, 30 In., Pair	708
Figure, Crane, Standing, Painted, Patina, Metal, Late 1900s, 49 In., Pair	443
Figure, Deer, Full Body, Painted, Cast Iron, Rectangular Base, Cove's End, 1800s, 48 x 16 In. *illus*	4680
Figure, Eagle, Spread Wings, Open Talons, Cast Iron, 62½ x 55 x 33 In.	938
Figure, Elf, Seated, Pointed Hat, Buttoned Shirt, Stone, 14½ x 15 In., Pair *illus*	236
Figure, Flamingo, Head Down Eating, Other Is Preening, Painted, Cast Iron, 23 In., Pair	1100
Figure, Geisha, Standing, Holding Fan, Plinth Base, Cement, 39 In.	106
Figure, Giraffe, Standing, Bronze, Patina, 1900s, 78 x 92 In., Pair	10000
Figure, Griffin, Seated, Open Wings, Scrolled Tail, Cast Iron, Late 1800s, 22 In., Pair *illus*	938
Figure, Lion, Gray, Walking, Paw On Ball, Rectangular Base, Cement, 23 x 28 In. *illus*	150
Figure, Man, Beard, Robe & Turban, Carved, Leaves, Terra-Cotta, Continental, 60½ In.	400
Figure, Reclining Mermaid, Painted, Green, Cast Iron, 17 In. *illus*	488
Figure, Roman Soldier, Standing, Pedestal Base, Stone, c.1950, 46½ In.	325
Figure, Rooster, Standing, Painted, Red, Cast Iron, 22 In. *illus*	244
Figure, Woman, Grecian Style, Pedestal, Fiberglass & Composition, Painted, 93 In. *illus*	472
Figure, Woman, Holding Planter, Faux Flowers, Pedestal Base, Late 1900s, 67 In., Pair *illus*	767
Fountain, 3 Putti, Playing Trumpet, Urn Center, Tripod Base, Bronze, 1900s, 40 x 48 In.	2000
Fountain, Crocodile, Raised Head & Tail, Open Mouth, Cast Metal, 1900s, 19⅝ x 48 In.	438
Fountain, Heron, Cattails, Verdigris Finish, Circular Base, Bronze, 42¼ In.	1062
Fountain, Lion, Open Mouth, Cartouche Shield, Cast Bronze, 1900s, 19 x 8 x 12 In. *illus*	738
Fountain, Wall, Carved Arched Top, Rosette, Shell Shape Base, Marble, 1800s, 26 x 15 x 4 In.	468
Gate, Flowers, Scroll, Handle, Metal, Painted, 77 x 49 In.	976
Gate, Scroll, Vine, Acanthus Leaf Sprays, Flowers, Butt Hinges, Forged Iron, 77 x 66 In., Pair	4095
Gate, Tole Style, Swans, Flower Lattice, Green Paint, Tin, 1900s, 53 x 14 In. *illus*	625
Hitching Post Finial, Horse Head, Iron, G. Menzel & Co., 16 In.	300
Hitching Post, Columnar Pedestal, Dark Green, Cast Iron, 42 In., Pair	238
Hitching Post, Horse Head, Black, 2 Movable Rings, Wood Base, Cast Iron, 1880s, 28 x 10 In. *illus*	105
Hitching Post, Horse Head, Ring In Mouth, Molded, Flowers & Scrolls, Black Paint, c.1875, 17 In.	750
Hitching Post, Horse Head, Rings, Iron Stand, Stepped Round Base, 1800s, 55 x 9 In., Pair	2040
Hitching Post, Jockey, Standing, Painted, Cast Iron, c.1950, 46 In.	360
Hitching Post, Lawn Jockey, Standing, Holding Metal Ring, Square Base, Early 1900s, 47 x 16 In. *illus*	1534
Hitching Post, Pine, Carved, 2 Parts, Iron Ring, Barnwood Base, Early 1900s, 43½ In.	354
Lamppost, Cherub, Holding Glass Globe, Square Plinth, Molded, Stone, Late 1900s, 65 In., Pair	944
Lawn Sprinkler, Turtle, Upturned Head, Cast Iron, Rotating, c.1915, 6 x 10 x 7 In. *illus*	2034
Lounge Chair, Radar, Cast Iron Mesh, Rounded, Leg Rest, 6 Legs, Tempestini, Salterini, 28 x 30 In.	374
Love Seat, Victorian, White, Scrolled Armrest, Painted, Spiraled Metal, Late 1800s, 48 x 56 In.	128
Ornament, Mushroom, Multicolor, Painted, Cast Cement, c.1950, 11 In. *illus*	188
Ornament, Pig, Standing, Painted, Stone, c.1920, 12 x 16 In.	236
Patio Set, Topiary, Orange Aluminum, Openwork, Rolled Arms, Bench, Knoll, 54 In., 3 Piece	1840
Plant Stand, see also Furniture, Stand, Plant.	
Plant Stand, 3 Platforms, Diamond Shape, Medallion, Nude, Iron, Art Deco, 1930s, 37 x 21 In.	313
Plant Stand, Corner, 3 Tiers, Painted, White & Green, Metal, 34 x 23½ In.	354
Plant Stand, Elephant, Happiness Symbol, Rectangular Base, Plaster, Chinese, 16½ x 15 x 9 In., Pair	413
Plant Stand, Green, Gold, Cable & Leaves, White Flowers, 3-Footed, Porcelain, 31½ In.	173

Gameboard, Chess, Inlaid, Marble, Octagonal, Flowers, Leaves, White Ground, 1900s, 15½ In.
$123

Locati Auctions

G

Garden, Bench, Black, Gothic Design, Rosette Seat, Cabriole Legs, Cast Iron, 1800s, 32 x 44 In.
$1,003

Leland Little Auctions

> **TIP**
> Lead garden sculptures should not be cleaned. The dirt and discoloration add to the beauty of the piece. Lead is so soft that most types of cleaning will harm the finish.

Garden, Bench, Riveted Fasteners, Green Paint, Wrought Iron, Salesman's Sample, c.1900, 8 x 9 x 5 In.
$86

Rich Penn Auctions

GARDEN

Garden, Bench, Shell, Leaves, Slatted Seat, Outswept Legs, Iron, Coalbrookdale, 1800s, 37 x 47 In., Pair
$2,562

Neal Auction Company

Garden, Birdbath, Black, Painted, Aluminum & Iron, Virginia Metalcrafters, 1950s, 24 In.
$413

Leland Little Auctions

Garden, Chair, Arch Rail, Wood Slat Seat, Scroll Arms, Iron Frame, Early 1900s, 34 x 23 In., Pair
$944

Austin Auction Gallery

Garden, Chair, Black, Cabriole Legs, Paw Feet, Wrought Iron, Victorian, 30 x 13 x 14 In.
$144

Stevens Auction Co.

Garden, Chair, Salterini Style, Painted, Cream Ground, Green Leaves, Splayed Legs, Iron, 35 In., Pair
$354

Bunch Auctions

Garden, Figure, Cat, Seated, Plinth Base, Stone, 1900s, 18 ½ In.
$1,000

Cowan's Auctions

Garden, Figure, Deer, Full Body, Painted, Cast Iron, Rectangular Base, Cove's End, 1800s, 48 x 16 In.
$4,680

Thomaston Place Auction Galleries

Garden, Figure, Elf, Seated, Pointed Hat, Buttoned Shirt, Stone, 14 ½ x 15 In., Pair
$236

Austin Auction Gallery

Garden, Figure, Griffin, Seated, Open Wings, Scrolled Tail, Cast Iron, Late 1800s, 22 In., Pair
$938

Charlton Hall Auctions

G

Garden, Figure, Lion, Gray, Walking, Paw On Ball, Rectangular Base, Cement, 23 x 28 In.
$150

Eldred's

Garden, Figure, Reclining Mermaid, Painted, Green, Cast Iron, 17 In.
$488

Neal Auction Company

TIP
A garden sculpture should be mounted at least 18 inches above the ground. It should be cleaned to keep off moss and algae.

Garden, Figure, Rooster, Standing, Painted, Red, Cast Iron, 22 In.
$244

Neal Auction Company

Garden, Figure, Woman, Grecian Style, Pedestal, Fiberglass & Composition, Painted, 93 In.
$472

Leland Little Auctions

Garden, Figure, Woman, Holding Planter, Faux Flowers, Pedestal Base, Late 1900s, 67 In., Pair
$767

Austin Auction Gallery

Garden, Fountain, Lion, Open Mouth, Cartouche Shield, Cast Bronze, 1900s, 19 x 8 x 12 In.
$738

Brunk Auctions

Garden, Gate, Tole Style, Swans, Flower Lattice, Green Paint, Tin, 1900s, 53 x 14 In.
$625

Bruneau & Co. Auctioneers

Garden, Hitching Post, Horse Head, Black, 2 Movable Rings, Wood Base, Cast Iron, 1880s, 28 x 10 In.
$105

Jeffrey S. Evans & Associates

GARDEN

Garden, Hitching Post, Lawn Jockey, Standing, Holding Metal Ring, Square Base, Early 1900s, 47 x 16 In.
$1,534

Bunch Auctions

Garden, Lawn Sprinkler, Turtle, Upturned Head, Cast Iron, Rotating, c.1915, 6 x 10 x 7 In.
$2,034

Soulis Auctions

Garden, Ornament, Mushroom, Multicolor, Painted, Cast Cement, c.1950, 11 In.
$188

Bruneau & Co. Auctioneers

Garden, Plant Stand, Wirework, 4 Tiers, Painted, White, Scrolled Feet, Late 1800s, 38 x 50 In.
$1,652

Leland Little Auctions

Garden, Planter, 2 Rabbits, White & Green, Center Basket, Cast Iron, 11 In.
$1,000

Pook & Pook

Garden, Planter, Circular Side Drops, Ball Feet, Square, Metal, 1800s, 19¾ x 19½ In., Pair
$594

Eldred's

Garden, Planter, Green Glaze, Flowers & Figures, Chinese, 24½ In.
$413

Austin Auction Gallery

Garden, Planter, Wall, Hanging, Wrought Iron, 38 x 21 In., Pair
$219

Kamelot Auctions

Garden, Sculpture, Powder Coated, Steel & Bronze, Post Modernist, c.1980s, 40 x 23 x 21 In.
$380

Thomaston Place Auction Galleries

Garden, Seat, Blue & White, Flower Vine, Phoenix Bird, Porcelain, Chinese, 1900s, 17 In.
$125

Bruneau & Co. Auctioneers

Garden, Seat, Peaches & Peacocks, Famille Rose, Yellow Ground, Porcelain, Chinese, 19 x 14 In., Pair
$5,100

Cottone Auctions

Garden, Stool, Circular, Porcelain Top, Wood Reticulated Base, Carved, Chinese, 1900s, 18 In.
$177

Leland Little Auctions

Garden, Stool, Green, Blue, Glazed, Pierced Panels, Hexagonal, Terra-Cotta, Chinese, Late 1900s, 16 In.
$295

Leland Little Auctions

Garden, Sundial, Horizontal, Octagonal, Scroll Gnomon, Compass Rose, Bronze, Georgian, 6 x 13 In.
$976

Neal Auction Company

Garden, Table, Circular Top, Patina, Iron Frame, Tree Shape Support, 3 Branches, Concrete, 30 x 29 In.
$1,534

Austin Auction Gallery

TIP
Don't store old paint rags. They may ignite spontaneously.

Garden, Table, Victorian, Pierced Round Top, Wrought Iron, Signed, Atlanta Stove Works, 26 x 40 In.
$345

Stevens Auction Co.

Garden, Urn, Classical Style, Flared
Rim, Black, Hexagonal Base, Cast Iron,
Late 1900s, 44 In., Pair
$1,408

Brunk Auctions

Garden, Urn, Figural Handles, Stepped
Pedestal Stand, Cast Iron, 27 In., Pair
$1,093

Stevens Auction Co.

Garden, Urn, Grotto, Seashells, Pyrite,
Rutilated Quartz, Rock Crystal,
Julia-Carr Bayler, 21 In.
$384

Leland Little Auctions

Plant Stand, Ornate, Cast Iron, Verdigris Patina, Griffin Tripod Base, 1880s, 30 In.	300
Plant Stand, Wirework, 4 Tiers, Painted, White, Scrolled Feet, Late 1800s, 38 x 50 In. . *illus*	1652
Planter, 2 Rabbits, White & Green, Center Basket, Cast Iron, 11 In. *illus*	1000
Planter, Campagna Shape, Melon Rib Body, Molded Edge, Square Pedestal Foot, Iron, 30 x 23 In.	413
Planter, Circular Side Drops, Ball Feet, Square, Metal, 1800s, 19¾ x 19½ In., Pair ..... *illus*	594
Planter, Copper, Bowl Top, Hammered, Iron Frame, 2 Curving Arms, 2 Handles, 58 In., Pair.	6300
Planter, Egyptian Pharaoh, Bowl On Top, Bronze, Marble Base, 39½ In.	1495
Planter, Elephant, Standing, Trunk Raised, Whimsical, Hammered Copper, 1900s, 13 x 6 In.	100
Planter, Face Shape, Stone, Signed, Nina Studios, Late 1900s, 19 x 22 In.	531
Planter, Fancy Rim, Swan Handles, Footed, Tole, 5½ x 10 x 7 In., Pair	460
Planter, Flame, Glazed Terra-Cotta, Painted, 15 x 27 In.	5938
Planter, Floor, Verde, Faux Loop Handles, Earthenware, 1900s, 24½ In., Pair	561
Planter, Frog Shape, Sitting, Rectangular Base, Cement, Early 1900s, 13 x 15 In.	1063
Planter, Green Glaze, Flowers & Figures, Chinese, 24½ In. *illus*	413
Planter, H-Stretcher, Porcelain Shards, Pine, Folk Art, c.1920, 26 x 30¾ x 9 In.	293
Planter, Leafy Scroll Corners, Multicolor, Claw Feet, Earthenware, Abigails, 1900s, 8 x 19 In. .	148
Planter, Oblong, Pierced Lattice Panels, Pad Feet, Metal Liners, Cast Iron, 12½ In., Pair	244
Planter, Oval, Acanthus Border, Black, Painted, Cabriole Legs, Cast Iron, 1800s, 23 x 14 In., Pair.	861
Planter, Reticulated Panels, Flowers, Footed, Black, Cast Iron, 12½ x 12½ In., Pair	156
Planter, Satinwood, Marquetry, Inlay, Adams Style, 39 In.	59
Planter, Turquoise, Flowers, Birds, Underplate, Red Chop Mark, Porcelain, Chinese, 15 x 16 In..	500
Planter, Urn Shape, Neoclassical Style, Octagonal Base, Marble, 19 x 15 In., Pair	4388
Planter, Urn Shape, Ribbed, 2 Handles, Square Base, Stone, 19 In., Pair	472
Planter, Urns, Fluted, Square Pedestal, Stone, Late 1900s, 42½ x 16 In., Pair	531
Planter, Wall, Hanging, Wrought Iron, 38 x 21 In., Pair *illus*	219
Sculpture, Cat Shape, Seated, Block Base, Cement, 1910s, 18 x 10 In., Pair	500
Sculpture, Children, Goat & Fawn, Patina, Bronze, Steven Bennett, Late 1900s, 56 In., Pair	7670
Sculpture, Elephant, Standing, 2 Tusks, Open Mouth, Bronze, 1900s, 52 x 42 In.	1500
Sculpture, Powder Coated, Steel & Bronze, Post Modernist, c.1980s, 40 x 23 x 21 In. ... *illus*	380
Seat, Barrel Shape, Pierced, Yellow, Pottery, Chinese, 17½ In.	448
Seat, Blue & White, Flower Vine, Phoenix Bird, Porcelain, Chinese, 1900s, 17 In. *illus*	125
Seat, Famille Rose, Painted Scene, Flowers, Butterflies, Porcelain, Chinese, 19 In.	2400
Seat, Hexagonal, Blue Transfer, Sobraon, Flowers, Porcelain, Staffordshire, 1850s, 19 x 10 In.	293
Seat, Peaches & Peacocks, Famille Rose, Yellow Ground, Porcelain, Chinese, 19 x 14 In., Pair ..*illus*	5100
Settee, Georgian Style, Distressed Wood, Circle & Slat Back, Slat Seat, Rockwood, 38 x 55 In. .	1046
Stand, Circular Top, Metal Skirt, Twisted Stem, Tripod Feet, Wrought Iron, 1900s, 40 In., Pair...	192
Stand, Wirework, Painted, Green, 3 Tiers, Pedestal Base, Iron, Late 1800s, 54 In.	295
Stool, Circular Top, Patina, Bronze, Gert Rasmussen, 17½ In.	170
Stool, Circular, Bamboo, Birds, Flower, Imari Palette, Porcelain, Japan, 20¼ In.	266
Stool, Circular, Porcelain Top, Wood Reticulated Base, Carved, Chinese, 1900s, 18 In. . *illus*	177
Stool, Green, Blue, Glazed, Pierced Panels, Hexagonal, Terra-Cotta, Chinese, Late 1900s, 16 In. .*illus*	295
Sundial, Figural, Folding Gnomon, Man On Horseback, Zodiac Signs, 1800s, 8½ In.	263
Sundial, Horizontal, Octagonal, Scroll Gnomon, Compass Rose, Bronze, Georgian, 6 x 13 In. ..*illus*	976
Sundial, Iron, Lancaster County, Pennsylvania, Dated 1840, 5½ x 10 In.	225
Sundial, Stand, Stoneware & Bronze, F. Barker & Sons., Late 1800s, 45 In.	1024
Sundial, Stone, Zinc Dial, Time Passes, Memories Remain, Roman Numerals, Pedestal, 36 In...	649
Table, Bamboo, Glass Top, Iron Frame, Planter Center, Tripod Feet, 22 x 20 In.	71
Table, Circular Top, Patina, Iron Frame, Tree Shape Support, 3 Branches, Concrete, 30 x 29 In. *illus*	1534
Table, Faux Bois, Circular Top, Tree Trunk Pedestal, Cast Concrete, c.1950, 32 x 38 In.	1003
Table, Marble Top, Wrought Iron Base, Secessionist, Vienna, c.1920, 30 x 25¾ In.	1750
Table, Victorian, Pierced Round Top, Wrought Iron, Signed, Atlanta Stove Works, 26 x 40 In. .*illus*	345
Topiary Frame, Inverted Cone Shape, Cross Shape Top, Iron, 52 In.	197
Topiary, Grotto, Shells, Carved, Mounted, Composition Base, Late 1900s, 30 In.	266
Urn, 2 Parts, Rolled Rim, Tapered Body, Fluted Plinth, Stepped Base, Cast Iron, 1800s, 28 In., Pair	885
Urn, Black Paint, Pedestal Base, Cast Iron, 29 In., Pair	460
Urn, Campagna Shape, Square Plinth Base, Cast Iron, 16¾ In., Pair	375
Urn, Classical Style, Egg & Dart Rim, Fluted, Stepped Plinth, Cast Iron, 1900s, 26 x 21 In., Pair..	1888
Urn, Classical Style, Flared Rim, Black, Hexagonal Base, Cast Iron, Late 1900s, 44 In., Pair ...*illus*	1408
Urn, Classical Style, Painted, Green, Egg & Dart Rim, Footed, Iron, Late 1900s, 25 In., Pair..	531
Urn, Figural Handles, Stepped Pedestal Stand, Cast Iron, 27 In., Pair *illus*	1093
Urn, Grotto, Seashells, Pyrite, Rutilated Quartz, Rock Crystal, Julia-Carr Bayler, 21 In. *illus*	384

G

Urn, Lava Stone, Tessellated Faux Agate, Short Neck, Bulbous Body, 1900s, 36 In., Pair *illus*	177
Urn, Lid, Finial, Louis XV Style, Putti Handles, Flowers, Cast Iron, 29 ½ x 20 In., Pair	1664
Urn, Pedestal, Cast Stone, Riprod Vietata, 37 ½ In., 4 Piece	2125
Urn, Roundel, Rose Swag, Terra-Cotta, Continental, 33 ¼ In.	850

GAUDY DUTCH

Gaudy Dutch pottery was made in England for the American market from about 1810 to 1820. It is a white earthenware with Imari-style decorations of red, blue, green, yellow, and black. Only sixteen patterns of Gaudy Dutch were made: Butterfly, Carnation, Dahlia, Double Rose, Dove, Grape, Leaf, Oyster, Primrose, Single Rose, Strawflower, Sunflower, Urn, War Bonnet, Zinnia, and No Name. Other similar wares are called Gaudy Ironstone and Gaudy Welsh.

Grape pattern 1810–1820   Single Rose pattern 1810–1820   War Bonnet pattern 1810–1820

Creamer, Butterfly, Wide Spout, White Ground, Handle, 4 ¾ In. *illus*	1708
Cup Plate, War Bonnet, Flowers, Yellow, Blue, Orange Border, 3 ½ In. *illus*	458

GAUDY IRONSTONE

Gaudy ironstone is the collector's name for the ironstone wares with the bright patterns similar to Gaudy Dutch. It was made in England for the American market after 1850. There may be other examples found in the listing for Ironstone or under the name of the ceramic factory.

Plate, Cut Sponge Lip, Blue Flowers, Stylized Interior, Multicolor, 12 ½ In.	35
Platter, Flowers & Bamboo, Blue Transfer, Tree & Well, Gilt, 1850s, 21 x 17 In.	59
Tureen, Lid, Oval, Flowers, Branch Shape Handle, Fruit Basket Finial, Gilt, c.1850, 11 In.	140

GAUDY WELSH

Gaudy Welsh is an Imari-decorated earthenware with red, blue, green, and gold decorations. Most Gaudy Welsh was made in England for the American market. It was made from 1820 to about 1860.

Bowl, Grapevine, Blue, Russet, Green, Copper Luster Sprays, Pedestal Base, c.1840, 8 In.	195
Tureen, Lid, White Ground, Leaves, Flowers, Gilt, Ram's Head Handle, Footed, 13 In. *illus*	106
Tureen, Soup, White, Blue, Undertray & Ladle, Imperial Stone, 1800s, 12 ¼ x 13 In.	63

GEISHA GIRL

Geisha girl porcelain was made for export in the late nineteenth century in Japan. It was an inexpensive porcelain often sold in dime stores or used as free premiums. Pieces are sometimes marked with the name of a store. Japanese ladies in kimonos are pictured on the dishes. There are over 125 recorded patterns. Borders of red, blue, green, gold, brown, or several of these colors were used. Modern reproductions are being made.

Cup & Saucer, 2 Women In Garden, Blue Border, Tashiro Shoten Ltd., 1930s, 2 x 5 ¼ In.	45
Cup & Saucer, Woman Sitting On Bench, Fan, Flared Rim Cup, Red Border, Gilt Trim, 1 x 4 ½ In.	18
Lamp, Oil, Porcelain Base, Handles, Woman With Umbrella, 3-Footed, Red, Gilt Trim, 5 ¾ x 3 ¾ In.	34

Garden, Urn, Lava Stone, Tessellated Faux Agate, Short Neck, Bulbous Body, 1900s, 36 In., Pair
$177

Austin Auction Gallery

Gaudy Dutch, Creamer, Butterfly, Wide Spout, White Ground, Handle, 4 ¾ In.
$1,708

Pook & Pook

Gaudy Dutch, Cup Plate, War Bonnet, Flowers, Yellow, Blue, Orange Border, 3 ½ In.
$458

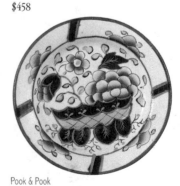

Pook & Pook

This is an edited listing of current prices. Visit Kovels.com to check thousands of prices from previous years and sign up for free information on trends, tips, reproductions, marks, and more.

Gaudy Welsh, Tureen, Lid, White Ground, Leaves, Flowers, Gilt, Ram's Head Handle, Footed, 13 In. $106

Apple Tree Auction Center

Girl Scout, Pin, Round, Blue Enamel Frame, 3 White Arms, Center Trefoil, Goldtone, Pendant Loop, 1 In. $30

Cordier Auctions

> **TIP**
> *Do not wipe gold or platinum decorated glasses while they are hot from the dishwasher. The metallic color will rub off.*

Glass, Bowl, Peking, Lid, Chinese Accents, Brown Vines, Yellow Base, Chinese, 3½ x 3½ In. $469

Abington Auction Gallery

242

GIBSON GIRL

Gibson Girl black-and-blue decorated plates were made in the early 1900s. Twenty-four different 10½-inch plates were made by the Royal Doulton pottery at Lambeth, England. These pictured scenes from the book *A Widow and Her Friends* by Charles Dana Gibson. Another set of twelve 9-inch plates featuring pictures of the heads of Gibson Girls had all-blue decoration. Many other items also pictured the famous Gibson Girl.

Cup & Saucer, Pedestal Cup, Portrait Inside, Cobalt Blue Border, Gilt Stencil, Germany	18
Illustration, Ink On Paper, Girl, Older Couple & 2 Men, Signed, Frame, c.1900, 19 x 28 In.	220
Plate, Black Transfer Portrait, Head Raised, Leaning, 1901, 9 In.	117
Plate, Sepia Transfer Scene, Day After Arriving At Her Journey's End, 1901, 10 In.	13

GIRL SCOUT

Girl Scout collectors search for anything pertaining to the Girl Scouts, including uniforms, publications, and old cookie boxes. The Girl Scout movement started in 1912, two years after the Boy Scouts. It began under Juliette Gordon Low of Savannah, Georgia. The first Girl Scout cookies were sold in 1928.

Bank, Brownie Gold, Elf Head, Logo On Hat, Porcelain, 6½ x 5 x 4 In.	25
Cutlery Set, Metal Knife, Fork & Spoon, Plastic Case, Emblem, 1950-60s, 7 In.	18
Pin, Figural, Bust, Brownie, Blond Hair, Brown Uniform, Red Bow & Tie, Plastic, 1⅞ x 1⅛ In.	24
Pin, Round, Blue Enamel Frame, 3 White Arms, Center Trefoil, Goldtone, Pendant Loop, 1 In. *illus*	30

GLASS

Glass factories that are well known are listed in this book under the factory name. This category lists pieces made by less well-known factories. Additional pieces of glass are listed in this book under the type of glass, in the categories Glass-Art, Glass-Blown, Glass-Bohemian, Glass-Contemporary, Glass-Midcentury, Glass-Venetian, and under the factory name.

Bowl, Brass, Birds & Flowers, Beveled Mirror, Ruffled Border, Stand, Victorian, 12½ In.	316
Bowl, Flower Shape, Turquoise, Opaque, Lobed Sides, Wood Stand, Chinese, c.1910, 4 x 10 In.	549
Bowl, Peking, Lid, Chinese Accents, Brown Vines, Yellow Base, Chinese, 3½ x 3½ In. *illus*	469
Celery Vase, Cranberry, Opalescent, Swirl Ribbed, Bulbous Base, Wilcox, Victorian, 9 In. *illus*	185
Compote, White Ground, Gilded Cobalt Blue Rim, Coiled Snake, Italy, 1900s, 10⅛ In.	313
Epergne, 5-Lily, Cranberry Opalescent, Vaseline, Ruffled Rim, Victorian, 21½ In.	805
Epergne, 6-Flute, Cranberry, Centerpiece, Ruffled Flute & Bowl, Late 1800s, 22½ In.	767
Epergne, Cranberry, Opalescent, Trumpet Vase, Quadruple Plated Stand, Victorian, 26 In. *illus*	123
Figurine, Bird, Frosted, Carved, Round Base, Warren Kessler, 4¼ x 7 x 3 In.	31
Goblet, Stipple, Bacchanalian Putto, White Twist Stem, Domed Foot, Dutch, 1700s, 7 In.	3250
Pitcher, Cobalt Blue, Pillar Mold, Rolled Neck Ring, 8 Pulled Prunt Feet, Pittsburgh, 8 In.	610
Vase, Birds, Flowers, Gilt Metal, Enamel, Painted, Late 1800s, 16½ In.	544
Vase, Bulbous Body, Square Rim, Acid Etched, Flowers, Erneste Baptiste, Leveille, 1880s, 8 In.	293
Vase, Clear, Ruffled Lip, Ribbed Body, Polished Pontil, Flared Flat Foot, 1800s, 16 In., Pair	156
Vase, Green, Iridescent, Indistinct Mark, Early 1900s, 4⅜ In.	192
Vase, Silver Overlay, Emerald Green, 2 Applied Handles, Trumpet Rim, Marked Sterling, 11¾ In.	756

GLASS-ART

Art glass means any of the many forms of glassware made during the late nineteenth or early twentieth century. These wares were expensive when they were first made and production was limited. Art glass is not the typical commercial glass that was made in large quantities, and most of the art glass was produced by hand methods. Later twentieth-century glass is listed under Glass-Contemporary, Glass-Midcentury, or Glass-Venetian. Even more art glass may be found in categories such as Burmese, Cameo Glass, Tiffany, and other factory names.

Bowl, Art Nouveau Style Frame, Fittings, Iridescent Green, Amethyst, Palme Koenig, 5 x 11 In.	400
Charger, Decoupage, Faberge Style Egg, Susan Ward, 13 ⅛ In., 8 Piece	148
Epergne, 1-Lily Basket, Clear Twist Arms, Cranberry, Opalescent, 21 ½ In.	2185
Figurine, Rooster, Blown & Applied, Multicolor Body, Gold Tail & Base, 9 In., Pair	31
Lamp, Amber, Cylindrical Body, White Shade, 16 In., Pair	83
Lamp, Gold, Pulled Feather Design, Gilt, Metal Base, 16 In. .... *illus*	1560
Lamp Base, Metal, Blue, Iridescent, Durand Style, Elgin, 25 In. .... *illus*	201
Lampshade, Gold, Pink, Bulbous, Iridescent, 5 x 5 In.	172
Lampshade, Mushroom Dome, Green Iridescent, Multicolor, Mottled, Fitter Ring, 5 ½ x 12 In.	175
Pitcher, Florentine Cameo, Cranberry Ground, White Enamel Bird, Flowers, 8 ¼ In	50
Salt Dip, Pink & Gold Opalescent, Crimpled Rim, Monot & Stumpf, c.1900, 1 ½ In.	150
Sculpture, Red, Yellow, Turquoise, Millefiori Shape, White Swirl Cased, Robert Willson, 22 In.	1792
Tumbler, Orange, Amethyst Carved Back Overlay, Mountain, Trees Scene, Signed, Lamiral, 4 In.	40
Vase, 4 Dimpled Sides, Leaf, Gold Stencil, Signed Honesdale, Dorflinger, 6 ½ x 4 In. ... *illus*	350
Vase, Blue, Pulled Feather, Jack-In-The-Pulpit, Signed, Correia, 10 ¼ In.	144
Vase, Blue, Silver Overlay, La Pierre, Marked, Early 1900s, 11 ¾ In.	896
Vase, Clad Frosted, Bronze, Gilt, Pedestal, 2 Handles, 6 In.	96
Vase, Clear, Sinuous Lines, Large, Molded, Alvar Aalto, Finland, 1936, 11 ¾ x 12 In.	5625
Vase, Deep Red With Clear Stem, Pedestal Vase, Bubble Stem, 11 ¾ x 7 In.	90
Vase, Geometric, Metallic Flecks, Blue Sommerso Interior, Cut To Clear Sides, 7 ¾ In.	144
Vase, Green & Orange, Mottled, Striped, Bulbous Body, Monart, c.1930, 9 ¾ x 8 In.	275
Vase, Green Design, Bronze Stick Shape Handles, Leaf Collar, Early 1900s, 16 In.	360
Vase, Molded, Leaf, Blue & Red, Metal Base, Louis Majorelle, c.1920, 11 ½ x 6 ¼ In.	546
Vase, Pale Opaque Green, Waisted Neck, Gray Mottled Band, Gilt Outline, Late 1800s, 6 ½ In.	615
Vase, Pulled Feather, Green, White, Iridescent, Correia, Signed, 10 In.	144
Vase, Red Orange Ground, Short Neck, Underfoot, Marked, Lorraine, Early 1900s, 8 In. *illus*	183
Vase, Ruffled Rim, Crackle, Brown Interior, Olive Green, 14 In.	34
Vase, Steuben Style, Trumpet Shape, Gold Iridescent, Scalloped Rim, Early 1900s, 7 ¾ In.	56
Vase, Trevaise, Opalescent, Green, Pulled Feather, Gold Iridescent Interior, Round Foot, 4 ¾ In. *illus*	1386
Vase, Yellow, Mounted, Wrought Iron Base, Footed, Early 1900s, 4 ¾ x 5 ½ In.	113
Wine, Green, Gold Ground, Enamel, Violet, Cut Hollow Stem, Moser Style, 7 In. .... *illus*	150

GLASS-BLOWN

Blown glass was formed by forcing air through a rod into molten glass. Early glass and some forms of art glass were hand blown. Other types of glass were molded or pressed.

Bottle, Bar, Cobalt Blue Stripes, Gray, Applied Neck Rings, Mid 1800s, 10 ¾ In., Pair	330
Bowl, Yellow Amber, Olive Tone, Flared, Outward Folded Rim, c.1825, 2 ½ x 7 ¼ In.	480
Box, Cobalt Blue Ground, Gold, Platinum Leaf, 4-Sided, Kyohei Fujita, 6 x 4 ½ x 4 ¾ In. *illus*	7320
Cake Cover, Clear, Pressed Star Shape, Knob Handle, Applied Bottom Lip, 12 x 14 ½ In.	518
Canister, Lid, Clear, 3 Applied Blue Rings, Shaped Finial, c.1860, 15 ½ In., Pair	344
Cannister, Clear, 2 Applied Cobalt Blue Rings, Pressed Glass Lid, Pittsburgh, c.1850, 11 In.	198
Carboy, Green, Bulbous Shape, Narrow Neck, France, 20 In. .... *illus*	236
Celery Vase, Pillar, Cobalt Stripes, Scalloped Rim, Baluster Stem, Mid 1800s, 9 ½ In.	4200
Compote, Green Wide Dish Top, Colorless Baluster Stem, Flared Base, 1850s, 7 x 8 ½ In.	406
Dish, Light Green, Swirl, Folded Rim, Early 1800s, 10 ¾ In.	469
Epergne, 3 Trumpets, Clear, Flared Rim, Ruffled Bowl, 19 ½ x 9 In.	144
Epergne, Clear, Etched Greek Key, 8-Point Stars, Shallow Dish, Corning, N.Y., 1800s, 14 In.	250
Ewer, Polished Pontil, Bulbous Stopper, Air Pocket, Early 1900s, 12 ⅜ In., 6 Piece	295
Fishbowl, Folded Edge Rim, Etched Interior, Footed, Flint Glass, Bakewell, Mid 1800s, 13 In.	420
Fishbowl, Molded Rim, Domed Base, Footed, 1800s, 16 ½ In.	1088
Marmalade, Light Amber, Cylindrical, Flared Mouth, Early 1800s, 4 ¼ x 3 In.	225
Pitcher, Shaded Light Green, Blue Gray Bands, Bulbous, 10 ⅝ In.	417
Pitcher, Water, 4 Molded Rings, Bulbous Body, Applied Strap Handle, 1840, 9 x 4 x 4 In. *illus*	234
Salt, Cobalt Blue, Ray & Diamond Panels, Wide Rim, Footed, 19th Century, 2 ½ x 2 ¾ In.	406
Sculpture, Fitted Shape, 3-Piece Mold, Light Brown, Olive, Green, Gray, Pablo Soto, 16 In.	369
Sculpture, Stork Like Bird, Rectangular Base, William Morris, Signed, 14 ½ In.	6000
Smoke Bell, Cobalt Blue, Hall Light, Metal Band, Hanging Fixture, 1840s, 10 x 8 In. ... *illus*	660

Glass, Celery Vase, Cranberry, Opalescent, Swirl Ribbed, Bulbous Base, Wilcox, Victorian, 9 In.
$185

G

Glass, Epergne, Cranberry, Opalescent, Trumpet Vase, Quadruple Plated Stand, Victorian, 26 In.
$123

Glass-Art, Lamp, Gold, Pulled Feather Design, Gilt, Metal Base, 16 In.
$1,560

Glass-Art, Lamp Base, Metal, Blue, Iridescent, Durand Style, Elgin, 25 In. $201

Blackwell Auctions

Glass-Art, Vase, 4 Dimpled Sides, Leaf, Gold Stencil, Signed Honesdale, Dorflinger, 6 ½ x 4 In. $350

Woody Auction

Glass-Art, Vase, Red Orange Ground, Short Neck, Underfoot, Marked, Lorraine, Early 1900s, 8 In. $183

Neal Auction Company

Smoother, Green Aqua, Long Neck, Circular Shape, 4 In.	123
Stringholder, Clear, Applied Piping, Openings, Cobalt Blue, Flint Glass, 1800s, 4 ¼ x 4 ¼ In.	123
Tazza, Paneled Column, Brass Top & Foot Rim, Clambroth, 1850s, 7 ½ x 7 In., Pair	330
Vase, Birth Of Venus, Classical Scene, Cylindrical, Engraved, 1900s, 16 x 3 ½ x 3 ⅜ In.	468
Vase, Etched, Pale Green, Air Bubbles, Pictorial Scene, Ships, 2 Loop Handles, 10 In., Pair	236
Vase, Multicolored Canes, Inverted Top, Gary Beecham & Mary Lynn White, 1987, 6 x 6 ¾ In.	427

GLASS-BOHEMIAN

Bohemian glass is an ornate overlay or flashed glass made during the Victorian era. It has been reproduced in Bohemia, which is now a part of the Czech Republic. Glass made from 1875 to 1900 is preferred by collectors.

Adolf Beckert
c.1914–1920s

Gräflich Schaffgotsch'sche
Josephinenhütte
c.1890

J. & L. Lobmeyr
1860+

Beaker, Medallion Portrait, Mozart, Clear, Diamond Band, 7 ¼ In.	300
Biscuit Jar, Blue Iridescent, Silver Lid, Rindskopf, 6 ¾ In. .... *illus*	111
Bowl, Underside Cut, Amber, Black, Gold, Enamel, 4-Horse Carriage, c.1915, 2 x 12 In.	222
Candlestick, Ruby, Cutback Girandoles, Hanging Prisms, Enamel Design, Circular Base, 9 In. .. *illus*	118
Candy Dish, Lid, Green Cut To Clear, Painted Flowers, Gilt, Knob Finial, 5 x 3 In.	60
Champagne, Tapered Bowl, Ornate, Scalloped Foot, Intaglio Cut, Green, 1910s, 5 x 4 In.	187
Cigar Holder, Cobalt Blue, Cut Glass, Trumpet Shape, 3 In. .... *illus*	69
Compote, Hemispherical Bowl, Stained, Fuchsia Petal, Green Leaves, Late 1800s, 7 x 5 In.	117
Cruet, Globular, Flowers, Period Stopper, Cranberry, Multicolor, Enamel, Late 1800s, 6 In.	234
Decanter, Parcel Gilt, Spire Shape Stopper, Multicolor, Flowers, Cabochons, Late 1800s, 19 In.	266
Dresser Box, Ruby Agate, Cylindrical, Lithyalin, Riedrich Ergermann, 3 x 3 In.	527
Epergne, Blue Cased, Ruffled Edges, White, Gilt Flowers, Funnel Shape, Footed, 15 In.	68
Goblet, Clear To Amber, Tapered Bowl, Flowers, Cut Stem, Hexagonal Foot, 1800s, 6 ¾ In. *illus*	236
Ice Bucket, Ruby Red, Hunt Scene, Gilt, Enamel, Side Handles, 1930s, 9 ¼ x 7 ½ In.	86
Pitcher, Blue & Clear, Colorful Blossoms, Blue Applied Handle, Drip Rim, Harrach, 6 ½ In.	150
Pitcher, Cranberry, Flowers, Scroll, Gold Highlights, Meyer's Neffe, 4 In.	100
Pitcher, Man Playing Violin, Enamel, Gold Stencil, Theodore Rossler, c.1920, 7 ½ In.	50
Pitcher, Shaded Green, Tankard, Scalloped Rim, Engraved, Flowers, Gilt, 1880s, 12 ½ In.	176
Tumbler, Blue Ground, Scroll Decorated, Flower, Meyer's Neffe, 3 ¾ In. .... *illus*	50
Tumbler, Cranberry, Hourglass Shape, Gilt & Enamel Design, 1800s, 4 ¾ In., 18 Piece	266
Vase, Bird, Flowers, Blue Satin, Ruffle Top, Footed, Ormolu Base, Signed, Harrach, 12 ¾ In. . *illus*	633
Vase, Blue Iridescent, Ruffled Rim, Pulled Design, Cobalt Blue & White Teardrops, 1950s, 9 In.	325
Vase, Blue Iridescent, Silver Art Nouveau Overlay, Early 1900s, 4 In.	207
Vase, Enamel, Shaded Green, Rose Bowl Shape, Flowers, Gilt Band, Footed, Late 1800s, 8 In.	263
Vase, Green Iridescent, Oil Spot, Tooled Rim, c.1890, 11 ½ In.	177
Vase, Light Amber, Satin, White, Enamel, 1800s, 12 In., Pair	89
Vase, Lithyalin, Marble, 14 Cut Panels, Green, Blue, 7 ¼ x 4 ¼ In. .... *illus*	950
Vase, Luster, Cut To Clear, Dangling Spear Prisms, Foil Label, 12 In., Pair	259
Vase, Oil Spot, Pink & White Pulled Loop, Kralik, 6 ½ x 3 In. .... *illus*	125
Vase, Ruby, Crystal, Cut To Clear, Hobstar, Flared Rim, Square Foot, 12 In. .... *illus*	325
Vase, Ruby, Cut To Clear, Rock Crystal Style, 1900s, 12 In., Pair .... *illus*	177
Wine, Cranberry Cup, Hobstar, Crystal Stem & Base, 1900s, 7 ½ x 3 In., 10 Piece	207

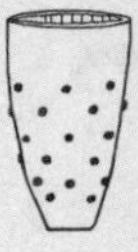

GLASS-CONTEMPORARY

Glass-Contemporary includes pieces by glass artists working after 1970. Many of these pieces are free-form, one-of-a-kind sculptures. Paperweights by contemporary artists are listed in the Paperweight category. Earlier studio glass may be found listed under Glass-Midcentury or Glass-Venetian.

Glass-Art, Vase, Trevaise, Opalescent, Green, Pulled Feather, Gold Iridescent Interior, Round Foot, 4¾ In.
$1,386

Fontaine's Auction Gallery

Glass-Art, Wine, Green, Gold Ground, Enamel, Violet, Cut Hollow Stem, Moser Style, 7 In.
$150

Woody Auction

Glass-Blown, Box, Cobalt Blue Ground, Gold, Platinum Leaf, 4-Sided, Kyohei Fujita, 6 x 4½ x 4¾ In.
$7,320

Neal Auction Company

Glass-Blown, Carboy, Green, Bulbous Shape, Narrow Neck, France, 20 In
$236

Austin Auction Gallery

Glass-Blown, Pitcher, Water, 4 Molded Rings, Bulbous Body, Applied Strap Handle, 1840, 9 x 4 x 4 In.
$234

Jeffrey S. Evans & Associates

Glass-Blown, Smoke Bell, Cobalt Blue, Hall Light, Metal Band, Hanging Fixture, 1840s, 10 x 8 In.
$660

Garth's Auctioneers & Appraisers

GLASS-CONTEMPORARY

Glass-Bohemian, Biscuit Jar, Blue Iridescent, Silver Lid, Rindskopf, 6¾ In.
$111

Rich Penn Auctions

> **TIP**
> Be sure to take any labels off your glass and save them. The acid in the labels will permanently etch the glass.

Glass-Bohemian, Candlestick, Ruby, Cutback Girandoles, Hanging Prisms, Enamel Design, Circular Base, 9 In.
$118

Apple Tree Auction Center

Glass-Bohemian, Cigar Holder, Cobalt Blue, Cut Glass, Trumpet Shape, 3 In.
$69

Blackwell Auctions

245

Glass-Bohemian, Goblet, Clear To Amber, Tapered Bowl, Flowers, Cut Stem, Hexagonal Foot, 1800s, 6¾ In.
$236

Austin Auction Gallery

Glass-Bohemian, Tumbler, Blue Ground, Scroll Decorated, Flower, Meyer's Neffe, 3¾ In.
$50

Woody Auction

Glass-Bohemian, Vase, Bird, Flowers, Blue Satin, Ruffle Top, Footed, Ormolu Base, Signed, Harrach, 12¾ In.
$633

Richard D. Hatch & Associates

Glass-Bohemian, Vase, Lithyalin, Marble, 14 Cut Panels, Green, Blue, 7¼ x 4¼ In.
$950

Woody Auction

Glass-Bohemian, Vase, Oil Spot, Pink & White Pulled Loop, Kralik, 6½ x 3 In.
$125

Woody Auction

Glass-Bohemian, Vase, Ruby, Crystal, Cut To Clear, Hobstar, Flared Rim, Square Foot, 12 In.
$325

Austin Auction Gallery

Glass-Bohemian, Vase, Ruby, Cut To Clear, Rock Crystal Style, 1900s, 12 In., Pair
$177

Leland Little Auctions

Glass-Contemporary, Bowl, Blue Wavy Rim, Mottled Green, Clear, Cut Pontil, Studio Art, 1997, 6½ In.
$266

Leland Little Auctions

Glass-Contemporary, Bowl, Blue, Brown, Orange, Signed, Labino, 1969, 2 x 6¾ In.
$550

Woody Auction

Glass-Contemporary, Sculpture, Abstract, Twisted Free Shape, Signed, John Lotton, 1986, 10½ x 11½ In.
$222

Jeffrey S. Evans & Associates

Basket, Seafoam Green, Red Lip Wrap, Dale Chihuly, Etched, 1981, 8 x 10 ¼ x 7 ¾ In.	2900
Bowl, Blue & Pink, Iridescent, Daniel Lotton, 1991, 12 In.	384
Bowl, Blue Wavy Rim, Mottled Green, Clear, Cut Pontil, Studio Art, 1997, 6 ½ In. *illus*	266
Bowl, Blue, Brown, Orange, Signed, Labino, 1969, 2 x 6 ¾ In. *illus*	550
Bowl, Marble, Feather Pattern, Blue & Red, Michael David & Kit Karbler, 1988, 9 ¼ In.	83
Bowl, Ruby, Platinum Threading, Free-Form, Abstract, Polished Base, c.2000, 6 x 11 ¼ In.	322
Bowl, Seaform, Clear, Pink & White Waves, Black Lip, Chihuly, 1981, 10 x 10 In.	3250
Candy Jar, White & Red Stripe, Cane Handle, Signed, 1975, 10 x 5 ¾ In.	70
Decanter, Multi Flora, White Flowers, Leaves, Stopper, Signed, Charles Lotton, 1983, 9 x 7 In.	439
Lamp, Iridescent, Pulled Feather, Green, Gold, Electric, Steven Correia, 1984, 18 ½ In.	345
Sculpture, Abstract, Twisted Free Shape, Signed, John Lotton, 1986, 10 ½ x 11 ½ In. *illus*	222
Sculpture, Cranberry & Amber, Twisted Exterior, Knotted Rope, 8 x 8 In. *illus*	275
Sculpture, Disc, Swirling Abstract, Green, Orange, Blue, Signed, Rollin Karg, 9 ½ x 3 In.	144
Sculpture, Large Loop, Swirled, Pink & Blues, Blown Cased, David Goldhagen, 1994, 15 In.	354
Sculpture, Orchid, Purple, Glass Base, Box, Signed, Liuli Gongfang, 2 ½ x 6 ½ x 4 ½ In.	94
Sculpture, Sunset Macchia, Black Base, Paperwork, Signed, Dale Chihuly, Box, 7 x 8 In.	2750
Tray, Quilt, 9 Interior Squares, Red, Yellow, Blue, Amethyst Bar, 1980s, 14 x 18 ¼ In.	23
Urn, Neoclassical Style, Pineapple Finial, Handles, Marble Base, Late 1900s, 58 x 22 In., Pair	2655
Vase, Bag, Blue Iridescent, Orient & Flume, Signed, Smallhouse, 8 x 6 ¾ In. *illus*	250
Vase, Blown, Pink Iridescent, Pulled Feather Design, Signed, Bertil Vallien Minos, 9 ¾ In.	106
Vase, Dark Amethyst, Iridescent Green, Gold, Eickholt, 1990, 6 ¾ In.	100
Vase, Flower Form, Blue Iridescent, Domed Base, Signed, Lundberg, 1900s, 13 ½ In. *illus*	284
Vase, Gold Heart, Vine, Pink Iridescent, Charles Lotton, 1987, 6 ¼ x 4 ¾ In.	400
Vase, Gold Iridescent, Acid Cut Back, Swirl Design, 1998, 7 ¾ In.	89
Vase, Green & Blue Iridescent, Bulbous, Elongated Neck, Orient & Flume, 9 In.	62
Vase, Horse Design, Blue, Dominick Labino, 5 ½ In. *illus*	325
Vase, Iridescent Green, Gold Opaque, Bulbous, Signed, Dominick Labino, 1971, 3 ¾ x 4 ½ In. *illus*	300
Vase, Jack-In-The-Pulpit, Iridescent, Brown, Blue Swirls, C. Lotton, 1981, 15 In.	2000
Vase, Macchia, Plexiglas Case, Dale Chihuly, 11 ¾ In. *illus*	3660
Vase, Noble Effort, Tapered Shape, Opaque Blue Ground, 2 Handles, Richard Marquis, 1985, 4 In.	439
Vase, Prunus Branch, Mottled, Metallic Ground, Round Rim & Base, John Nygren, c.1981, 9 ¼ In.	175
Vase, Pulled Feather, Green & Blue Iridescence, Orient & Flume, Signed, 1978, 7 ⅞ x 4 In.	173
Vase, Silver & Brown, Pulled Feather, Iridescent Caramel, Signed, Lundberg Studios, 1976, 5 In. *illus*	125
Vase, Swirling White Canes, Green, Richard Royal & Kathy Elliot, 1996, 12 ½ In. *illus*	793
Vase, Teal Hawthorne, Tooled, Millefiori Design, Orient & Flume, 1982, 8 In.	413
Vase, Trumpet, Blue, Iridescent, Bronze Base, Lundberg Studios, 19 x 5 In. *illus*	461

GLASS-CUT, *see Cut Glass category.*

GLASS-DEPRESSION, *see Depression Glass category.*

GLASS-MIDCENTURY

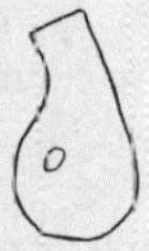

Glass-Midcentury refers to art glass made from the 1940s to the early 1970s. Some glass factories, such as Baccarat or Orrefors, are listed under their own categories. Earlier glass may be listed in the Glass-Art and Glass-Contemporary categories. Italian glass may be found in Glass-Venetian.

Bowl, Blue, Underfoot, Scandinavia, c.1955, 5 x 8 ½ In.	256
Bowl, Cone Shape, Alexandrite, Ruby, Blue, Signed, Dominick Labino, 1968, 2 ⅜ x 5 ½ In. *illus*	187
Bowl, Sapphire Blue, Etched, Per Lutken, Holmegaard, c.1950, 10 ¾ In.	71
Decanter, Etched, Leaves, Flowers & Bird, Silver Stopper & Collar, 10 In.	177
Gulvase, Cylindrical, Yellow, Flat Rim, Bottle Neck, Kastrup Holmegaard, c.1950, 15 In., Pair	384
Sculpture, Elfo III, Face, Yellow, Green, Signed, Max Ernst, Fucina Degli Angeli, 1966, 6 In. *illus*	2040
Vase, Green, Blue, Marbleized, Signed, Labino, 1966, 10 ½ x 3 ½ In. *illus*	650

GLASS-PRESSED, *see Pressed Glass category.*

Glass-Contemporary, Sculpture, Cranberry & Amber, Twisted Exterior, Knotted Rope, 8 x 8 In.
$275

Woody Auction

G

Glass-Contemporary, Vase, Bag, Blue Iridescent, Orient & Flume, Signed, Smallhouse, 8 x 6 ¾ In.
$250

Woody Auction

Glass-Contemporary, Vase, Flower Form, Blue Iridescent, Domed Base, Signed, Lundberg, 1900s, 13 ½ In.
$284

Fontaine's Auction Gallery

Glass-Contemporary, Vase, Horse Design, Blue, Dominick Labino, 5½ In. $325

Cottone Auctions

Glass-Contemporary, Vase, Iridescent Green, Gold Opaque, Bulbous, Signed, Dominick Labino, 1971, 3¾ x 4½ In. $300

Woody Auction

Glass-Contemporary, Vase, Macchia, Plexiglas Case, Dale Chihuly, 11¾ In. $3,660

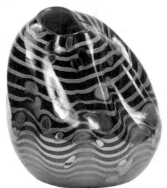

Neal Auction Company

GLASS-VENETIAN

Venetian glass has been made near Venice, Italy, since the thirteenth century. Thin, colored glass with applied decoration is favored, although many other types have been made. Collectors have recently become interested in the Art Deco, 1950s, and contemporary designs. Glass was made on the Venetian island of Murano from 1291. The output dwindled in the late seventeenth century but began to flourish again in the 1850s. Some of the old techniques of glassmaking were revived, and firms today make traditional designs and original modern glass. Since 1981, the name *Murano* may be used only on glass made on Murano Island. Other pieces of Italian glass may be found in the Glass-Contemporary and Glass-Midcentury categories of this book.

Bowl, Green, Blue, Marked, Fulvio Bianconi, Italy, 1950s, 2¼ In.	250
Bowl, Lid, Multicolor Flower Cluster, Ribbed, Metallic Pink, Italy, 1800s, 8 In.	2380
Bowl, Sommerso, Gold, Frosted Exterior, Polished Panel Side, 4 In.	35
Bowl, Underplate, Pink & White Caning, Gold Flecks, Latticinio, Murano, Mid 1900s, 3½ In., Pair	118
Bowl, White Ground, Gold Speckles, Bullicante Design, Alfredo Barbini, Murano, 10¼ In.	47
Bowl, Yellow Opaque, Scalloped Rim, Ribbed, Marked, Yalos Casa Murano, 5 x 10 In.	80
Candleholder, Amber, Clear Glass, Ercole Barovier, Italy, 3¼ In., Pair	531
Candleholder, Blackamoor, Colonial Garb, Waist Coat, Step Cupped Base, Murano, 9½ In.	242
Centerpiece, Bowl, Dolphin, Fish Handles, Gold Speckle, Swirling Quilted, Salviati, 3⅞ In.	201
Chandelier, 5-Light, Pink, Clear, Tooled & Blown Glass, Metal, Murano, Late 1900s, 24 x 16 In.	885
Figurine, Bird, Blown Cased, White & Gold Fleck, Murano, Mid 1900s, 18½ In., Pair .....*illus*	413
Figurine, Duck, Black & Silver, Glass Eyes, Murano, Italy, c.1950-60, 6½ x 12 x 5 In.	554
Figurine, Horse Head, Blue, Yellow, Red, Wood Base, Signed, Oggetti Murano, 13 x 16 In.	438
Figurine, Swordfish, Seesaw Fin, Crystal Base, Murano, 18 In.	57
Figurine, Tropical Bird On Perch, Cranberry Case, Gold Mica, Murano, 11½ In.	125
Jar, Lid, Lampworked Stopper, Aventurine, Swan Handles, Dabber, Murano, 1900s, 19 In., Pair *illus*	761
Lamp, Electric, Pyramid, Pink & White, Lino Tagliapietra, Murano, c.1980s, 27 x 10 In.	1770
Mirror, Wall, Round, Brass, Silvered Glass, Italy, 29¾ x 3½ In.	1500
Paperweight, Multicolor Filigree, Opaque Twist, Aventurine Bands, Murano, 1850s, 2¾ In.	293
Pitcher, Canne, Multicolor, Signed, Venini, Murano Italia, Gio Ponti, c.1958, 9¼ In. ... *illus*	1300
Sculpture, 2 Polar Bears, Ice Floe Base, Signed, Angelo Seguso, Murano, 9½ x 7½ In. *illus*	403
Sculpture, Abstract, Man & Woman Embracing, Signed, Roberto Moretti, Italy, 1968, 12½ In.	105
Sculpture, Abstract, Swirl Shape, Murano, 9½ In., Pair	156
Sculpture, Cockatoo, On Branch, Licio Zanetti, Murano, 29 In.	277
Sculpture, Double Fish, Curled Iron Base, Signed, Latticinio, Murano, 1990s, 24 x 8 x 25 In. *illus*	1125
Sculpture, Female Figure, Clear, Circular Glass Base, Murano, 30 x 5 x 4 In.	375
Sculpture, Horse Head, Pino Signoretto, Murano, Late 1900s, 19 x 14 x 5¼ In.	800
Sculpture, Modernist, Pale Blue, Studio Art, Livio Seguso, Murano, 1950s, 12½ x 13 In.	644
Sculpture, Pelican, Teal, Beak Up, Clear Gullet, Fish, Murano, c.1975, 22 In.	454
Sculpture, Purple, Knot Shape, Clear Glass Base, Livio Seguso, Murano, 11 x 12 x 4 In.	427
Sculpture, Spiral, Clear, Seguso Vetri D'Arte, Murano, 1970s, 16½ x 4 x 11 In.	313
Sculpture, The Kiss, 2 Figures, Reds & Blues, Etched, Dino Rosin, c.2000, 25 In. ...... *illus*	2645
Tray, Dresser, Gilt Handles, Etched Mirrored Center, Courting Scene, Fountain, Leaves, 23 In.	47
Vase, Amber, Tan Stripes, Squat, Flared Rim, L. Tagliapietra, Murano, 1982, 10 In.	1375
Vase, Art, Paper Label, Blue, Bulbous, Wavy Top, Artie, Murano, 14½ In.	28
Vase, Blown, Black Ground, Multicolor, Elongated Caning, Murrine, Murano, Late 1900s, 11 In. *illus*	148
Vase, Blown, Pink, Blue, Archimede Seguso, Italy, 9⅞ x 4⅞ In.	1125
Vase, Blue, Stylized Face, Etched Underfoot, Murano, Late 1900s, 12 In. ..... *illus*	384
Vase, Bottle Shape, Mottled Brown, Gino Cenedese, Scavo, Murano, 14 x 3¼ In.	259
Vase, Canne, Multicolor, Gio Ponti, Venini, Italy, c.1955, 11¼ In. .... *illus*	3250
Vase, Clear, Light Green & Violet, Murano, 7 In.	960
Vase, Handkerchief, Lavender, Green Lattice Striped, Murano, 4½ x 6½ In.	70
Vase, Inciso, Blue, Long Neck, Free-Blown, Paolo Venini, Murano, c.1960, 14 x 4¼ x 2½ In.	1755
Vase, Red, Gold Glitter, Side Handle, Signed, Pino Signoretto, Murano, 14 x 13 x 7 In., Pair ..	1063
Vase, Swan, White Ground, Orange Eyes, Green Domed Base, Murano, 11½ x 10 In. ... *illus*	1416
Vase, Tortoiseshell, Flared Rim, Murano, Italy, 12¼ In.	288

G

Glass-Contemporary, Vase, Silver & Brown, Pulled Feather, Iridescent Caramel, Signed, Lundberg Studios, 1976, 5 In.
$125

Woody Auction

Glass-Contemporary, Vase, Swirling White Canes, Green, Richard Royal & Kathy Elliot, 1996, 12 1/2 In.
$793

Neal Auction Company

Glass-Contemporary, Vase, Trumpet, Blue, Iridescent, Bronze Base, Lundberg Studios, 19 x 5 In.
$461

Alderfer Auction Company

Glass-Midcentury, Bowl, Cone Shape, Alexandrite, Ruby, Blue, Signed, Dominick Labino, 1968, 2 3/8 x 5 1/2 In.
$187

Jeffrey S. Evans & Associates

Glass-Midcentury, Sculpture, Elfo III, Face, Yellow, Green, Signed, Max Ernst, Fucina Degli Angeli, 1966, 6 In.
$2,040

Michaan's Auctions

Glass-Midcentury, Vase, Green, Blue, Marbleized, Signed, Labino, 1966, 10 1/2 x 3 1/2 In.
$650

Glass-Venetian, Figurine, Bird, Blown Cased, White & Gold Fleck, Murano, Mid 1900s, 18 1/2 In., Pair
$413

Leland Little Auctions

Glass-Venetian, Jar, Lid, Lampworked Stopper, Aventurine, Swan Handles, Dabber, Murano, 1900s, 19 In., Pair
$761

Woody Auction

Jeffrey S. Evans & Associates

G

Glass-Venetian, Pitcher, Canne, Multicolor, Signed, Venini, Murano Italia, Gio Ponti, c.1958, 9¼ In.
$1,300

Freeman's

Glass-Venetian, Sculpture, 2 Polar Bears, Ice Floe Base, Signed, Angelo Seguso, Murano, 9½ x 7½ In.
$403

Blackwell Auctions

Glass-Venetian, Sculpture, Double Fish, Curled Iron Base, Signed, Latticinio, Murano, 1990s, 24 x 8 x 25 In.
$1,125

Abington Auction Gallery

Glass-Venetian, Sculpture, The Kiss, 2 Figures, Reds & Blues, Etched, Dino Rosin, c.2000, 25 In.
$2,645

Blackwell Auctions

Glass-Venetian, Vase, Blown, Black Ground, Multicolor, Elongated Caning, Murrine, Murano, Late 1900s, 11 In.
$148

Leland Little Auctions

Glass-Venetian, Vase, Blue, Stylized Face, Etched Underfoot, Murano, Late 1900s, 12 In.
$384

Austin Auction Gallery

Glass-Venetian, Vase, Canne, Multicolor, Gio Ponti, Venini, Italy, c.1955, 11¼ In.
$3,250

Wright

Glass-Venetian, Vase, Swan, White Ground, Orange Eyes, Green Domed Base, Murano, 11½ x 10 In.
$1,416

Cottone Auctions

Glidden, Vase, Ball Shape, Pierced Top, Blue Green Glaze, Multicolor Stripes, c.1965, 10 x 11 In.
$688

New Haven Auctions

G

250

Vase, Wide Rim, Red Ground, Scavo, Signed, Cenedese, Murano, 5 ½ x 3 ⅛ In.	81
Vase, Yellow Vertical Canes, Scalloped Rim, Lino Tagliapietra, Murano, 10 ½ x 13 ¾ In.	€000
Wine, Blown, Ruby Red Glass, Gold Fleck Swan Stems, Rough Pontil, 1950s, 8 In., 8 Piece	413

GLASSES

Glasses for the eyes, or spectacles, were mentioned in a manuscript in 1289 and have been used ever since. The first eyeglasses with rigid side pieces were made in London in 1727. Bifocals were invented by Benjamin Franklin in 1785. Lorgnettes were popular in late Victorian times. Opera Glasses are listed in their own category.

Bifocals, Gold Plated, Glass Lenses, c.1930	20
Lorgnette, Gold Wash, Silver, Repousse, Flowers, Thumb Latch, Art Nouveau, c.1910, 4 ⅞ In.	475
Lorgnette, Octagonal Lenses, Silver Handle	120
Pinch Clip-On, Light Cream, Gold Plated, 1920s, 4 x 1 ½ In.	60
Saddle Bridge, Bow Side Arms, Flexible Side Loops, Gold Filled Frame, Late 1800s	85
Sun, Cat's-Eye, Red Plastic, Rhinestone Studded, France	45

GLIDDEN

Glidden Pottery worked in Alfred, New York, from 1940 to 1957. The pottery made stoneware, dinnerware, and art objects.

Box, Lid, Painted Fish, Rectangular, Black, Artist Signed, 2 x 8 ¾ x 3 ¾ In.	87
Candelabrum, 3-Light, Pierced, Gulf Stream Glaze, Cylindrical Stand, Fong Chow, 9 x 8 x 3 In.	450
Vase, Ball Shape, Pierced Top, Blue Green Glaze, Multicolor Stripes, c.1965, 10 x 11 In. *illus*	688
Vase, Cylindrical, Green & Blue Stripes, Stoneware, Fong Chow, 17 x 3 In.	413

GOEBEL

Goebel is the mark used by W. Goebel Porzellanfabrik of Oeslau, Germany, now Rodental, Germany. The company was founded by Franz Detleff Goebel and his son, William Goebel, in 1871. It was known as F&W Goebel. Slates, slate pencils, and marbles were made. Soon the company began making porcelain tableware and figurines. Hummel figurines were first made by Goebel in 1935. Since 2009 they have been made by another company. Goebel is still in business. Old pieces marked Goebel Hummel are listed under Hummel in this book.

Cordial, Friar Tuck, 4 Cups, Red, Brown, Blue, Green, White Oval Tray, Marked, Original Packaging	110
Doll, Cardinal Tuck, Red Robe, Karen Kennedy, Certificate, Stand, Box, 10 ½ In.	25
Figurine, Dove, White, Puffed Chest, Lowered Tail, Marked, Dated, 1978, 7 ½ In.	36
Figurine, Mallard Duck, Standing, Multicolor, Glazed, CV117, 11 In. *illus*	45
Figurine, Parakeet, On Leafy Branch, Head Turned, Missing Bee Mark, Dated, 1972, 7 ½ x 5 In.	88
Figurine, Rabbit, Bowling, Blue Skirt, Yellow Apron, Missing Bee Mark, 4 ¾ In.	13
Group, Canary Feeding Young, Marked, Dated, 1967, 6 x 5 ½ In.	63
Lamp, Perfume, Figural, Dog, Front Paws Raised, White, Stylized Bee Mark, 7 In.	48
Powder Dish, Half Doll, Powder Puff, Red & Black Dress, Red Chair, Art Deco, 1920s, 5 ½ In. *illus*	4688

GOLDSCHEIDER

Goldscheider was founded by Friedrich Goldscheider in Vienna in 1885. The family left Vienna in 1938 and the factory was taken over by the Germans. Goldscheider started factories in England and in Trenton, New Jersey. It made figurines and other ceramics. The New Jersey factory started in 1940 as Goldscheider-U.S.A. In 1941 it became Goldscheider-Everlast Corporation. From 1947 to 1953 it was Goldcrest Ceramics Corporation. In 1950 the Vienna plant was returned to Mr. Goldscheider, but it closed in 1953. The Trenton, New Jersey, business, called Goldscheider of Vienna, is a wholesale importer.

Bust, Woman, Flapper Style Hat, Terra-Cotta, Multicolor, Early 1900s, 26 In.	281

GOLDSCHEIDER

Goebel, Figurine, Mallard Duck, Standing, Multicolor, Glazed, CV117, 11 In.
$45

Strawser Auction Group

Goebel, Powder Dish, Half Doll, Powder Puff, Red & Black Dress, Red Chair, Art Deco, 1920s, 5 ½ In.
$4,688

Perfume Bottles Auction

Goldscheider, Figurine, Woman, Basket, Flowers, Pink, Yellow, Green, Backstamp, Austria, 1900s, 12 In.
$104

Lion and Unicorn

G

GOLDSCHEIDER

Goss, Cauldron, Shakespeare Verse, Bath Crest, Angled Handles, 3-Footed, 2¼ x 2 In.
$6

bakertowncollectables on eBay

Gouda, Tray, Trudy, Teal Ground, Stylized Leaves & Flowers, Orange, Blue, Shaped Rim, 13 x 10 In.
$120

Auctions at Showplace, NYC

Gouda, Vase, Bagdad, Pinched Neck, Orange Band, Eduard Antheunis, 12 In.
$95

Fontaine's Auction Gallery

TIP
To remove sediment in the bottom of a vase or pitcher, put salt and crushed ice into the vase and stir. The friction will remove the stain.

Clock, Man, Woman, Holding Hands, Temporis Menso Pulsus Cordis, Terra-Cotta, c.1901, 21 x 18 In.	708
Figurine, Duke Of Marlborough, Green Jacket, Blond Hair, Holds Sword, Stepped Base, 10⅜ In.	288
Figurine, Jester, Yellow & Blue Suit, Playing Flute, On Pillar, Green Draping, Oval Base, 12 In.	4125
Figurine, Woman & Sealyham Dog, Blue, Cream, Caramel, Glazed Luster, c.1936, 6¾ x 15 In.	2875
Figurine, Woman, Basket, Flowers, Pink, Yellow, Green, Backstamp, Austria, 1900s, 12 In. ...*illus*	104
Figurine, Woman, Sitting, Ruffled Dress, Purple, Flowers, Holds Mask, 6 x 5 In.	125
Lamp, Electric, 3-Light, Draped Woman, Arms Raised, Holds Vase Of Flowers, Signed, c.1900, 42 In.	5440
Wall Mask, Woman, Curly Blond Hair, White Face, Purple Collar, 12¼ x 7¾ In.	75

GOLF, *see Sports category.*

GONDER

Gonder Ceramic Arts, Inc., was opened by Lawton Gonder in 1941 in Zanesville, Ohio. Gonder made high-grade pottery decorated with flambe, drip, gold crackle, and Chinese crackle glazes. The factory closed in 1957. From 1946 to 1954, Gonder also operated the Elgee Pottery, which made ceramic lamp bases.

Lamp Base, Electric, Trojan Horse, Green Glaze, 12½ x 6½ In.	12
Vase, Bottle Shape, Yellow Glaze, 16¾ In., Pair	30
Vase, Cornucopia, Turquoise Glaze, Rectangular Base, 9 In., Pair	18

GOSS

Goss china has been made since 1858. English potter William Henry Goss first made it at the Falcon Pottery in Stoke-on-Trent. The factory name was changed to Goss China Company in 1934 when it was taken over by Cauldon Potteries. Production ceased in 1940. Goss China resembles Irish Belleek in both body and glaze. The company also made popular souvenir china, usually marked with local crests and names.

Cauldron, Shakespeare Verse, Bath Crest, Angled Handles, 3-Footed, 2¼ x 2 In. ...... *illus*	6
Cauldron, Welsh Crochon Shape, Aberystwyth Crests, Angled Handles, 3-Footed, 3 x 3½ In. .	28
Cup & Saucer, Port Erin Crest, Scalloped Rim, 1½ x 4¾ In.	28
Figurine, Pinecone, Bournemouth Crest, Impressed Mark, c.1910, 3½ In.	18
Hatpin Holder, Round, Squat, Beaumaris, Anglesea, Wales, Cinquefoil On Top, 3½ x 5 In..	52
Jar, Southwold, Bottle Shape, Round Base, East Anglia Crest, c.1910, 3½ In.	15
Vase, Exeter, Handles, Buxton Crest, Gilt Rim, c.1910, 2½ In.	15
Vase, Jar Shape, Llandudno Crest, 1920s, 3⅜ x 2⅜ In.	16

GOUDA

Gouda, Holland, has been a pottery center since the seventeenth century. Two firms, the Zenith pottery, established in 1749, and the Zuid-Hollandsche pottery, made the colorful art pottery marked *Gouda* from 1898 to about 1964. Other factories that made "Gouda" style pottery include Regina (1898–1979), Schoonhoven (1920– present), Ivora (1630–1965), Goedewaagen (1610–1779), Dirk Goedewaagen (1779–1982), and Royal Goedewaagen (1983–present). Many pieces featured Art Nouveau or Art Deco designs. Pattern names in Dutch are often included in the mark.

Gouda / Plateelbakkerij Zenith 1915

Gouda / Kon. Hollandsche Pijpen–en Aardewekfabriek Goedewaagen 1923–1928

Gouda / Zuid–Holland Plateelbakkerij 1926+

Bowl, Damascus III, Yellow Band, Blue Poppies, Green Ground, Footed, 1920-40, 9 x 6 In...	150

Charger, Avisa, Peacock, Red & Yellow Flowers, White Ground, Black Rim, Regina, 12¾ In.	124
Compote, Stylized Leaves & Flowers, Stepped Cone Shape, White, Green, Teal, Orange, Blue, 6 In..	54
Compote, Verona, Yellow Ground, Green & Blue Leaves, Black Exterior, Footed, Regina, 4¾ x 9 In.	62
Lantern, Hanging, Glazed, Ring Handle, Painted, 9½ In.	94
Tray, Trudy, Teal Ground, Stylized Leaves & Flowers, Orange, Blue, Shaped Rim, 13 x 10 In. *illus*	120
Vase, Bagdad, Pinched Neck, Orange Band, Eduard Antheunis, 12 In. *illus*	95
Vase, Flowers, Bulbous, Painted, Signed, Zuid Holland, 14 x 5¾ In. *illus*	144
Vase, Kawi, Geometric Bands, Multicolor, Black Ground, Shoulders, Footed, c.1923, 23¾ In.	188
Vase, Narrow, Waisted, Red & Purple Flowers, Stems, Leaves, Zuid Holland, Art Nouveau, 17 In., Pair.	436
Vase, Phylis, Multicolor Geometric, Orange, Yellow Stylized Flowers, Light & Dark Brown, Footed, 9 In.	63
Vase, Tulip, Geometric Bands, Green, Orange, Blue, Red, White, Footed, Double Triangle Mark, 9 In..	50

GRANITEWARE

Graniteware is enameled tin or iron used to make kitchenware since the 1870s. Earlier graniteware was green or turquoise blue, with white spatters. The later ware was gray with white spatters. Reproductions are being made in all colors.

Geuder, Paeschke & Frey Co. 1905–c.1972	Iron Clad Manufacturing Co. 1888–1913	Lalance & Grosjean Manufacturing Co. 1877–1955

Bathtub, Blue, 2 Side Handles, White Interior, Child's, 10½ x 24½ In.	266
Churn, Chrysolite, Dark Green, Wood Lid, Dasher, 2 Handles, 18 x 9 In.	590
Coffeepot, Hinged Lid, Gooseneck, Gray Speckled, 10¾ In.	30
Coffeepot, Lid, Blue & White Swirl, Bail Handle, Grip, 13 In.	31
Coffeepot, White Body, Multicolor Leaves & Acorns, Lid, Gooseneck Spout, Pewter, 11½ In.	50
Funnel, Rounded, Light Blue & White, Solid White Interior, c.1900, 9 x 8⅞ In.	148
Pail, Blue & White Swirl, White Interior, Bail Handle, 8¾ x 11½ In.	119
Pail, Lid, Raspberry Swirl, Bail Handle, Wood Grip, 1940s, 13 x 12 In. *illus*	236
Teapot, Lid, Brown & White, Relish Pattern, Round, Pewter Trim, 8½ In.	38

GREENTOWN

Greentown glass was made by the Indiana Tumbler and Goblet Company of Greentown, Indiana, from 1894 to 1903. In 1899, the factory became part of National Glass Company. A variety of pressed glass was made. Additional pieces may be found in other categories, such as Chocolate Glass, Holly Amber, Milk Glass, and Pressed Glass.

Racing Deer & Doe, Pitcher, Plain Rim, Pedestal, Early 1900s, 9 In.	222
Teardrop & Tassel, Pitcher Cobalt Blue, Round Foot, 8¾ In.	150
Teardrop & Tassel, Salt Shaker, Nile Green, Metal Lid, Footed, 3¼ In. *illus*	1245

GRUEBY

Grueby Faience Company of Boston, Massachusetts, was founded in 1894 by William H. Grueby. Grueby Pottery Company was incorporated in 1907. In 1909, Grueby Faience went bankrupt. Then William Grueby founded the Grueby Faience and Tile Company. Grueby Pottery closed about 1911. The tile company worked until 1920. Garden statuary, art pottery, and architectural tiles were made until 1920. The company developed a green matte glaze that was so popular it was copied by many other factories making a less expensive type of pottery. This eventually led to the financial problems of the pottery. Cuerda seca (dry cord) decoration uses a greasy pigment to separate different glaze colors during firing. Cuenca (raised

Gouda, Vase, Flowers, Bulbous, Painted, Signed, Zuid Holland, 14 x 5¾ In.
$144

Blackwell Auctions

Graniteware, Pail, Lid, Raspberry Swirl, Bail Handle, Wood Grip, 1940s, 13 x 12 In.
$236

Leland Little Auctions

Greentown, Teardrop & Tassel, Salt Shaker, Nile Green, Metal Lid, Footed, 3¼ In.
$1,245

Jeffrey S. Evans & Associates

Grueby, Tile, Yellow Tulip, Green
Leaves, Glaze, Wood Frame, Square,
7 In.
$1,719

Treadway

G

Grueby, Vase, Carved, Leaves, Flared
Rim, Green Matte Glaze, 12 In.
$2,880

Cottone Auctions

Grueby, Vase, Squat, Lobed, Blue Matte
Glaze, Incised Signature, LEH, Boston,
1800s, 4 In.
$594

Eldred's

line) decorations are impressed, leaving ridges that separate the glaze colors. The company
name was often used as the mark, and slight changes in the form help date a piece.

Bowl, Carved Leaf, Green Matte Glaze, Ruffled Rim, Low, Impressed, 2 x 6 In.		1250
Tile, Cherub, Cornucopia, Fruit, Raised, Painted, Initials E.M., Square, 6 In.		330
Tile, Yellow Tulip, Green Leaves, Glaze, Wood Frame, Square, 7 In.	*illus*	1719
Vase, 6 Broad Leaves, Flower Band, Green, Squat, Ruth Erickson, c.1905, 4 ¼ x 5 ½ In.		4063
Vase, Alternating Leaves, Green Matte Glaze, Lillian Newman, Faience Mark, 5 x 7 In.		3125
Vase, Carved, Leaves, Flared Rim, Green Matte Glaze, 12 In.	*illus*	2880
Vase, Jack-In-The-Pulpit, Green, Cylindrical, Flared Bottom & Rim, W. Post, c.1909, 12 In.		18750
Vase, Molded Flowers, Overlapping Leaves, Bronze Green Matte Glaze, c.1900, 13 ½ In.		4063
Vase, Squat, Lobed, Blue Matte Glaze, Incised Signature, LEH, Boston, 1800s, 4 In.	*illus*	594

GUN. *Only toy guns are listed in this book. See Toy category.*

GUNDERSEN *glass is listed in Pairpoint.*

GUSTAVSBERG

Gustavsberg ceramics factory was founded in 1827 near Stockholm, Sweden. It is best
known to collectors for its twentieth-century artwares, especially Argenta, a green
stoneware with metallic silver inlay. The company broke up and was sold in the 1990s
but the name is still being used.

GUSTAFSBERG	GUSTAVSBERG	GUSTAVSBERG
Gustavsberg	Gustavsberg	Gustavsberg
1839–1860	1940–1970	1970–1990s

Plaque, Face, Studiohand, Glazed, Stig Lindberg, 13 x 15 In.		840
Vase, Green, Bird, Glaze, Stoneware, Footed, Argenta, Wilhelm Kage, c.1930, 11 ½ In.	*illus*	1000
Vase, Sgrafitto, Powder Blue Glazed Base, Josef Ekberg, Sweden, 1918, 10 ¾ x 5 ¾ In.		293

HAEGER

Haeger Potteries, Inc., Dundee, Illinois, started making commercial
artwares in 1914. Early pieces were marked with the name *Haeger* written
over an *H*. About 1938, the mark *Royal Haeger* was used in honor of Royal Hickman,
a designer at the factory. The firm closed in 2016. See also the Royal Hickman category.

Ashtray, Horseshoe Shape, Horse Heads, Footed, Green, White, 8 In.	45
Figurine, Dog, German Shepherd, Laying, Black, Brown, Tan, 1940s, 11 ½ In.	108
Figurine, Matador, Red, c.1945, 11 x 9 x 5 In.	225
Vase, Feather, Red, 10 In.	75
Vase, Fish In Waves, Aqua, c.1947, 6 x 7 In.	40
Vase, Triple Cornucopia, Green Matte, Leaf Base, 9 x 13 In.	89

HALF-DOLL, *see Pincushion Doll category.*

HALL CHINA

HALL'S SUPERIOR QUALITY KITCHENWARE

Hall China Company started in East Liverpool, Ohio, in 1903. The firm
made many types of wares. Collectors search for the Hall teapots made
from the 1920s to the 1950s. The dinnerware of the same period, especially
Autumn Leaf pattern, is popular. The Hall China Company merged with Homer Laughlin
China Company in 2010. Autumn Leaf pattern dishes are listed in their own category
in this book.

Blue Garden, Casserole, Lid, 8 In.	48
Hercules, Pitcher, Glazed, Earthenware, J. Palin Thorley, 1940, 9 ¼ In., Pair	688

Poppy, Sugar & Creamer, c.1940...	90
Royal Rose, Salt & Pepper, Handles..	41
Silhouette, Mug...	21
Teapot, Individual, Army Green, Restaurant Ware, 3 ¼ x 6 In.	10
Teapot, Ronald Reagan, Big Nose, White Ground, 10 In. .... *illus*	71
Tomorrow's Classic, Bowl, Cereal, 6 In.	12

HALLOWEEN

Halloween is an ancient holiday that has changed in the last 200 years. The jack-o'-lantern, witches on broomsticks, and orange decorations seem to be twentieth-century creations. Collectors started to become serious about collecting Halloween-related items in the late 1970s. Old costumes and papier-mache decorations, now replaced by plastic, are in demand.

Figure, Black Cat, Paper Pulp, Painted, 8 In. .... *illus*	120
Figure, Veggie, Carrot Lady, Cloth, Gingham Dress, Flowers, Homemade, c.1945, 7 In. . . *illus*	108
Jack-O'-Lantern, 2 Faces, Paper Insert On One Side, 9 In. .... *illus*	270
Jack-O'-Lantern, Papier-Mache, Orange, Scary Face, Paper Insert Eyes & Teeth, Wire Handle, 9 In. .	192
Jack-O'-Lantern, Papier-Mache, Paper Insert, Wire Handle, 6 In.	94
Lantern, Owl, Black Cat Details, Papier-Mache, Wire Handle, 5 In.	300
Lantern, Parade, Jack-O'-Lantern, Tin, Painted, Ohio Art Co., Early 1900s, 17 x 6 In.	5700
Lantern, Parade, Orange, Pumpkin, Tin, Wood Handle, 27 In.	885
Lantern, Tree, Frowning, Composition, Wire & Wood Lift-Out Candleholder, Germany, 3 ½ In. *illus*	18000
Light Bulb, Jack-O'-Lantern Cover, 7 In. .... *illus*	36
Postcard, Girl, Covering Eyes, Witches, Embossed, Stecher..............................	59

HAMPSHIRE

Hampshire pottery was made in Keene, New Hampshire, between 1871 and 1923. Hampshire developed a line of colored-glaze wares as early as 1883, including a Royal Worcester–type pink, olive green, blue, and mahogany. Pieces are marked with the printed mark or the impressed name *Hampshire Pottery* or *J.S.T. & Co., Keene, N.H.* (James Scollay Taft). Many pieces were marked with city names and sold as souvenirs.

Bowl, Green Matte Glaze, Applied Leaves, Signed, 2 ½ x 10 In.	773
Bowl, Green Matte Glaze, Lily Pads, Buds, No. 57, 3 ¼ x 10 In.....................	500
Vase, Dripped Blue, White Glaze, Dark Blue Ground, Monogram, Cadmon Robertson, 8 x 10 In.	1750
Vase, Green Glaze, Yellow, Stylized Leaves, 7 ½ x 4 ¼ In. .... *illus*	1950

HANDBAG, *see Purse category.*

HANDEL

Handel glass was made by Philip Handel working in Meriden, Connecticut, from 1885 and in New York City from 1893 to 1933. The firm made art glass and other types of lamps. Handel shades were made not only of leaded glass in a style reminiscent of Tiffany but also of reverse painted glass. Handel also made vases and other glass objects.

Humidor, Apollo Silver Plate Lid, Green Ground, Pipe, Match, Pipe Finial, 6 In......................	125
Humidor, Lid, Knob Finial, 2 Owls, On Branch, Multicolor, 7 In..	1080
Lamp Base, 3-Light, Woman, Kneeling, Brown Patina, 24 In. .... *illus*	944
Lamp Base, Bronze, Japanese Baluster Vase, Molded, Birds, Blossom, Reticulated Base, 23 In. ..	225
Lamp, 2-Light, Domed Shade, Reverse Painted, Brown Patina Base, Marked, 23 In.............	3245
Lamp, 3-Light, Cattail, Slag Glass Shade, Brown, Green, Tree Trunk Base, 24 In. .... *illus*	9450
Lamp, Blossom, Bud, Vine, Leaded Glass, Bronze Tree Trunk Base, Early 1900s, 34 x 21 In...	6875
Lamp, Brown Chipped Ice Glass Shade, Round Base, Cloth Label, 57 x 9 x 14 In..................	1125

Gustavsberg, Vase, Green, Bird, Glaze, Stoneware, Footed, Argenta, Wilhelm Kage, c.1930, 11 ½ In.
$1,000

Wright

H

Hall, Teapot, Ronald Reagan, Big Nose, White Ground, 10 In.
$71

Bunch Auctions

Halloween, Figure, Black Cat, Paper Pulp, Painted, 8 In.
$120

Bertoia Auctions

Halloween, Figure, Veggie, Carrot Lady, Cloth, Gingham Dress, Flowers, Homemade, c.1945, 7 In.
$108

Halloween, Jack-O'-Lantern, 2 Faces, Paper Insert On One Side, 9 In.
$270

Halloween, Lantern, Tree, Frowning, Composition, Wire & Wood Lift-Out Candleholder, Germany, 3 ½ In.
$18,000

Halloween, Light Bulb, Jack-O'-Lantern Cover, 7 In.
$36

Hampshire, Vase, Green Glaze, Yellow, Stylized Leaves, 7 ½ x 4 ¼ In.
$1,950

Handel, Lamp Base, 3-Light, Woman, Kneeling, Brown Patina, 24 In.
$944

Handel, Lamp, 3-Light, Cattail, Slag Glass Shade, Brown, Green, Tree Trunk Base, 24 In.
$9,450

Handel, Lamp, Chipped Ice Domed Shade, Landscape Scene, Bronze Metal Base, 22 x 18 In.
$3,750

Handel, Lamp, Domed Shade, Chipped Ice Exterior, Apple Blossom, Butterfly, Signed, 18 In.
$4,025

Lamp, Brown Chipped Ice Shade, Harp, Bronze Base, Signed, 57 x 9¾ In.	1000
Lamp, Ceiling, 3-Light, Bronze, Painted Glass Domed Shades, Chains, Marked, 14 x 18 In.	2500
Lamp, Chipped Ice Domed Shade, Landscape Scene, Bronze Metal Base, 22 x 18 In. ... *illus*	3750
Lamp, Domed Shade, Chipped Ice Exterior, Apple Blossom, Butterfly, Signed, 18 In. ... *illus*	4025
Lamp, Domed Shade, Reverse Painted, Reticulated Base, Signed, 1900s, 22½ x 17¾ In.	2944
Lamp, Fall Landscape, Full Harvest Moon, Bronze Base, Flower Buds, Acorn Pulls, 23½ In.	3388
Lamp, Forest Landscape, Lotus Socket, Bronze Base, Signed, Henry Bedigie, Early 1900s, 24 In. *illus*	4480
Lamp, Landscape, Trees On Water, 3-Light, Electric, Painted, Signed, 25 In.	5843
Lamp, Painted Shade, Parrots, Domed Base, 13 In.	2280
Lamp, Reverse Painted, Aquarium, Trapezoid Shade, Textured, Mermaid Base, 23 In. . *illus*	11685
Lamp, Reverse Painted, Daffodil, Chipped Ice, Bronze Base, Handel Cloth Tag, 25 x 18 In. ...*illus*	5843
Lamp, Scenic Shade, Field, Cherry Blossom, Gilt Metal Base, Signed, 13½ x 7 In.	800
Lamp, Scenic Shade, Ribbed Body, Reticulated Bronze Base, Signed, Early 1900s, 24 x 18 In.	4200
Lamp, Student, Chipped Ice Shade, Brown Patina, Metal Base, 25 In.	960
Lamp, Teroca, Caramel Panel Shade, Green Leaf Overlay, Square Bronze Base, c.1920, 30 x 25 In.	2520
Lamp, Yellow, Brown, Green, Leaves, Nouveau Style, Electric, Signed, c.1920, 24½ In.	7500
Vase, Flowers, Acid Etched Tulips, Fluted Rim, Albert Parlow, c.1905, 10½ In.	375
Vase, Teroma, Etched & Painted, Trees, White Ground, Marked, 11 In.	1080
Vase, Teroma, Frosted Ice Chip, Tree, Lake Scene, 9¾ x 7½ In. *illus*	350

HARDWARE, *see Architectural category.*

HARKER

Harker Pottery Company was incorporated in 1890 in East Liverpool, Ohio. The Harker family had been making pottery in the area since 1840. The company made many types of pottery but by the Civil War was making quantities of yellowware from native clays. It also made Rockingham-type brown-glazed pottery and whiteware. The plant was moved to Chester, West Virginia, in 1931. Dinnerware was made and sold nationally. In 1971 the company was sold to Jeannette Glass Company, and all operations ceased in 1972. For more prices, go to kovels.com.

Amy, Bean Pot	10
Blue Mist, Plate, Bread & Butter, 5 In.	5
Cock O'Morn, Soup, Dish, 7¾ In.	9
Coronet, Cup & Saucer	5
Everglades, Plate, Dinner, 10¼ In.	15
Golden Dawn, Bowl, Vegetable, 8½ In.	12
Pink Cocoa, Gravy Boat, Underplate	15
Shell Pink, Plate, Bread & Butter, 5 In.	4
White Cap, Bowl, Vegetable, 6 In.	18
White Daisy, Plate, Dinner, 10 In.	24

HARLEQUIN

Harlequin dinnerware was produced by the Homer Laughlin Company from 1938 to 1964, and sold without trademark by the F. W. Woolworth Co. It has a concentric ring design like Fiesta, but the rings are separated from the rim by a plain margin. Cup handles are triangular in shape. Seven different novelty animal figurines were introduced in 1939. For more prices, go to kovels.com.

Gray, Bowl, Salad, 1950s, 7⅜ In.	40
Gray, Pitcher, 22 Oz., 5 In.	65
Mauve Blue, Eggcup, Double, 3¾ In.	29
Medium Green, Cup	15
Red, Pitcher, Water, Ball Shape	90
Rose, Bowl, Salad, 1940s, 7⅜ In.	36
Spruce Green, Platter, Oval, 11 x 9 In.	50
Spruce Green, Tumbler, 4⅜ In.	55
Turquoise, Platter, Oval, 11 In.	28

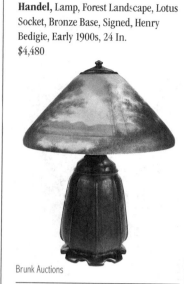

Handel, Lamp, Forest Landscape, Lotus Socket, Bronze Base, Signed, Henry Bedigie, Early 1900s, 24 In.
$4,480

Brunk Auctions

H

Handel, Lamp, Reverse Painted, Aquarium, Trapezoid Shade, Textured, Mermaid Base, 23 In.
$11,685

Morphy Auctions

Handel, Lamp, Reverse Painted, Daffodil, Chipped Ice, Bronze Base, Handel Cloth Tag, 25 x 18 In.
$5,843

Morphy Auctions

Handel, Vase, Teroma, Frosted Ice Chip, Tree, Lake Scene, 9 ¾ x 7 ½ In. $350

Woody Auction

Harlequin, Turquoise, Relish, 4 Red & Yellow Inserts, 1938-40 $489

Strawser Auction Group

Hatpin, Brass, Compact, Hinged Lid, Mirror, Lamb's Wool Puff, Art Nouveau, c.1900, 13 x 1 ⅝ In. $775

teacherwebb on eBay

Turquoise, Relish, 4 Red & Yellow Inserts, 1938-40 .... *illus* 489
Yellow, Cup & Saucer... 10

HATPIN

Hatpin collectors search for pins popular from 1860 to 1920. The long pin, often over four inches, was used to hold the hat in place on the hair. The tops of the pins were made of all materials, from solid gold and real gemstones to ceramics and glass. Be careful to buy original hatpins and not recent pieces made by altering old buttons.

14K Gold, Citrine Cabochon, Bulb Shape Bezel, Etruscan Style, Top Screws To Pin, 9 ⅞ In. ..	395
18K Gold, Sword Shape, Red & White Enamel, Diamond & Pearl Accents, Victorian, 6 ½ In.	462
Aluminum, Horizontal Head, Steel Pin, c.1900, 4 In.	8
Amethyst, Stylized Flower Setting, 14K Gold, 4 Small Pearls, Art Nouveau, 4 ½ x ⅝ In.	492
Bakelite, Dark Amber, Screw Shape, Brass Pin, c.1915, 8 ½ x 3 In.	46
Brass, Compact, Hinged Lid, Mirror, Lamb's Wool Puff, Art Nouveau, c.1900, 13 x 1 ⅝ In. .. *illus*	775
Brass, Round Head, 3 Rhinestone Rows, Blue & Clear, Glass Cabochon, Opalescent, 9 In. .. *illus*	45
Enamel Inlay, Cobalt Blue & Turquoise, 3 Lobes, Silver Setting, Steel Pin, c.1910, 8 ⁵⁄₁₆ x 1 In.	135
Peking Glass Cabochon, Turquoise, Silver Setting, 5 ½ In.	44
Rhinestones, Circular, Brass Setting, Victorian, 11 x 1 ½ In..	24

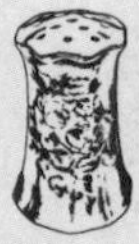

HATPIN HOLDER

Hatpin holders were needed when hatpins were fashionable from 1860 to 1920. The large, heavy hat required special long-shanked pins to hold it in place. The hatpin holder resembles a large saltshaker, but it often has no opening at the bottom as a shaker does. Hatpin holders were made of all types of ceramics and metal. Look for other pieces under the names of specific manufacturers.

Carnival Glass, Grape & Cable, Black Amethyst Base, Northwood, 6 ¾ In. .... *illus*	125
Porcelain, White, Pink Roses, Gold Trim, Attached Pin Box, RS Prussia, 4 ¾ In. .... *illus*	120
Porcelain, Petite Roses, Pink, White & Cream Ground, Gilt Trim, 3 Handles, RS Prussia, c.1900, 4 In.	159
Porcelain, Pink Flower Spray, Hexagonal Base, Goldtone Hatpins, Limoges, c.1910, 7 In.......	381
Porcelain, Romeo, Series Ware, Backstamp, Royal Doulton, 1900s, 5 ½ In...........................	46

HAVILAND

Haviland china has been made in Limoges, France, since 1842. David Haviland had a shop in New York City and opened a porcelain company in Limoges, France. Haviland was the first company to both manufacture and decorate porcelain. Pieces are marked *H & Co., Haviland & Co.,* or *Theodore Haviland.* It is possible to match existing sets of dishes through dealers who specialize in Haviland china. Other factories worked in the town of Limoges making a similar chinaware. Those porcelains are listed in this book under Limoges.

HAVILAND & Co.
Limoges
Haviland and Co.
1876–1878; 1889–1931

Théo Haviland
Limoges
FRANCE
Theodore Haviland
1893–early 1900s

Haviland
France
Haviland and Co.
c.1894–1931

Box, Lid, Figural, Fox, Lying Down, Head Raised, Brown Trim, E.M. Sandoz, Limoges, c.1921, 4 x 7 In.	100
Chocolate Pot, Lid, Melon Shape, Purple Flowers, Gilt Trim, Hand Painted, Limoges, 10 In.	71
Cup & Saucer, Pink Rose Garlands, Gilt Trim, Marked, Theodore Haviland, Limoges, 2 ¾ x 4 ¾ In. ..	24
Dinnerware Set, Claude Monet Giverny Pattern, Yellow Border, Blue Rim, 70 Piece ... *illus*	4480
Pitcher, Bulbous, Shaded Brown & Green, Leafy Branches, Fruits, Scrolled Handle, 8 x 9 ½ In.	23
Pitcher, Lid, Figural, Penguin, Green & White, Pink Beak, Feet, Edouard Marcel Sandoz, 5 ½ In. *illus*	188
Plate, Burgundy Rose Vine Rim, Signed, F.A. Bischoff, Early 20th Century, 9 ½ In.	407

H

Plate, Sea Life, Multicolor Enamel, Scalloped Rim, Gilt Trim, Marked, Haviland & Co., 8 In., 4 Piece 192
Tea Set, Teapot, Sugar, Creamer, Poppies, Green Ground, Gold Band, Handle, Finial, E. Merry... 180

HAVILAND POTTERY

Haviland Pottery began in 1872, when Charles Haviland decided to make art pottery. He worked with the famous artists of the day and made pottery with slip glazed decorations. Production stopped in 1885. Haviland Pottery is marked with the letters *H & Co.* The Haviland name is better known today for its porcelain.

HAVILAND & Cº
Limoges
Haviland and Co.
1875–1882

H & Cº
L
Haviland and Co.
1875–1882

C F H
G D M
FRANCE
Charles Field Haviland
1891+

Vase, Bottle Shape, Flat, Dog In Grass, White & Brown, Tree On Reverse, Faience, 9 x 6 ½ x 3 In... 495
Vase, Shaded, Flowers, 4-Footed, Terra-Cotta, Jules Habert-Dys, c.1880, 11 x 8 In., Pair *illus* 4278

HAWKES

Hawkes cut glass was made by T. G. Hawkes & Company of Corning, New York, founded in 1880. The firm cut glass blanks made at other glassworks until 1962. Many pieces are marked with the trademark, a trefoil ring enclosing a fleur-de-lis and two hawks. Cut glass by other manufacturers is listed under either the factory name or in the general Cut Glass category.

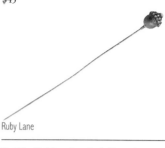

Bowl, Low, Maltese Cross, 1 ¾ x 9 ¾ x 8 ¾ In. 300
Carafe, Water, Venetian, Ray Cut, 1890, 7 ½ x 5 In. 100
Celery Tray, Folded, Venetian, 1890, 2 ¾ x 10 ¾ x 5 In........ 70
Cocktail Shaker, Cut Glass, Silver Cap, c.1955, 11 ½ In. .... *illus* 938
Cologne Bottle, Venetian, Stopper, Signed, 1890, 6 ½ x 3 ¾ In. 200
Compote, Hobstar, Strawberry Diamond & Fan, Ray Cut, Signed, 7 ¼ x 7 In. 25
Cruet, Venetian, Triple Notched Handle, Ray Base, 1890, 6 In. 125
Goblet, 8 Buckles, Diamond-Point Cut, Monogram D, Clear, c.1875, 6 ⅛ x 3 ¾ In., Pair *illus* 1112
Vase, Pairpoint Blank, Air Trap Orbs, Wheel Cut, Flowering Vines, Early 1900s, 12 ½ In........ 649

HEAD VASE

Head vases, generally showing a woman from the shoulders up, were used by florists primarily in the 1950s and 1960s. Made in a variety of sizes and often decorated with imitation jewelry and other lifelike accessories, the vases were manufactured in Japan and the U.S.A. Less elaborate examples were made as early as the 1930s. Religious themes, babies, and animals are also common subjects. Other head vases are listed under manufacturers' names and can be located through the index in the back of this book. Collecting head vases was a fad in the 1960s–1970s and prices rose. There is less interest now and only a few are high priced.

Mae West, Hand Raised, Eyes Closed, Yellow Hat, Pearls, Gilt Trim, Japan, 6 x 4 ½ In. . . *illus* 42
Woman, Blond Hair, Pearl Earrings, Light Blue Hat, High Collar, Marked, Napco, 1959, 5 ½ In..... 20
Woman, Bouffant Hair, Pearls, Green Dress, Knot At Shoulder, Napco, 7 ½ In. .... *illus* 98
Woman, Curly Blond Hair, Raised Hand, White Hat, Pearl Earrings & Necklace, Japan, 7 ½ In.. 690
Woman, Elegant, Short Blond Hair, Closed Eyes, Pearl Necklace, White Collar, Inarco, 1963, 7 In.. 48

HEINTZ

Heintz Art Metal Shop used the letters *HAMS* in a diamond as a mark. In 1902, Otto Heintz designed and manufactured copper items with colored enamel decorations under the name Art Crafts Shop. He took over the Arts & Crafts Company in Buffalo, New York, in 1903. By 1906 it had become the Heintz Art

Hatpin, Brass, Round Head, 3 Rhinestone Rows, Blue & Clear, Glass Cabochon, Opalescent, 9 In.
$45

Ruby Lane

Hatpin Holder, Carnival Glass, Grape & Cable, Black Amethyst Base, Northwood, 6 ¾ In.
$125

Woody Auction

Hatpin Holder, Porcelain, White, Pink Roses, Gold Trim, Attached Pin Box, RS Prussia, 4 ¾ In.
$120

Woody Auction

Haviland, Dinnerware Set, Claude Monet Giverny Pattern, Yellow Border, Blue Rim, 70 Piece
$4,480

Stair Galleries

Haviland, Pitcher, Lid, Figural, Penguin, Green & White, Pink Beak, Feet, Edouard Marcel Sandoz, 5 ½ In.
$188

Selkirk Auctioneers & Appraisers

Haviland Pottery, Vase, Shaded, Flowers, 4-Footed, Terra-Cotta, Jules Habert-Dys, c.1880, 11 x 8 In., Pair
$4,278

Ruby Lane

Metal Shop. It remained in business until 1930. The company made ashtrays, bookends, boxes, bowls, desk sets, vases, trophies, and smoking sets. The best-known pieces are made of copper, brass, and bronze with silver overlay. Similar pieces were made by Smith Metal Arts and were marked *Silver Crest*. Some pieces by both companies are unmarked.

Humidor, Hinged Lid, Patchwork, Silver Plated Bronze, Shagreen, Cedar, c.1925, 3 x 10 In...	1875
Lamp, Desk, Pierced, Flowers, Leaves, Green Ground, Silver On Copper, 10 In. .... *illus*	510
Lamp, Desk, Poppy Boudoir Shade, Bulbous, Metal On Bronze, Electric, 9 ½ x 8 ½ In.	489
Trophy Cup, Silver Deco Design, Rifleman, Badge, 2 Handles, Inlay, 10 ¼ In. .... *illus*	142

HEISEY

Heisey glass was made from 1896 to 1957 in Newark, Ohio, by A. H. Heisey and Co., Inc. The Imperial Glass Company of Bellaire, Ohio, bought some of the molds and the rights to the trademark. Some Heisey patterns have been made by Imperial since 1960. After 1968, they stopped using the *H* trademark. Heisey used romantic names for colors, such as Sahara. Do not confuse color and pattern names. The Custard Glass and Ruby Glass categories may also include some Heisey pieces.

Heisey
1900–1957

Heisey
Paper label

Heisey
Paper label

Animal, Pheasant, 6 In., Pair..	81
Aristocrat, Candlestick, Blue & Gold, 9 ¼ In., Pair..........................	98
Aristocrat, Candlestick, Square Base, 12 In.	31
Cabochon, Pitcher, Pt.	20
Cobel, Cocktail Shaker, Moon Glow Cutting, Clear, Stopper, Qt.........	95
Colonial, Basket, Round, U-Shape Handle, Scalloped Rim, Flower & Fern, Octagonal Base, 7 In..	49
Duquesne, Goblet, No. 868, Minuet Cutting, 10 Oz.	62
Empress, Plate, Square, 8 In.	5
Flat Panel, Jar, Crushed Fruit, Greek Key Lid, Clear, Qt..................	71
Locket On Chain, Butter, Cover, Ball Handle, Clear Glass, 1896, 5 ¼ In. .... *illus*	152
Locket On Chain, Goblet, No. 160, Green, Round Foot, 1896-1904, 5 ⅝ x 3 ⅛ x 3 In.............	468
Octagon, Ice Bucket, No. 500, Nimrod Carving, Handle .... *illus*	135
Orchid Etch, Cocktail Shaker, Stopper, Silver Base, 13 x 4 ¼ In...............................	115
Orchid Etch, Vase, No. 4198, 8 ½ In..	172
Paneled Cane, Tumbler	32
Peerless, Orchid, Vase, 5 In..	45
Trident, Candlestick, 2-Light, Sahara, Pair	50
Waverly, Jar, Cigarette Holder, Lid, Seahorse Handle	25
Whaley, Beer Mug, Equestrian Etch, 16 Oz.	160
Winged Scroll, Nappy, Custard, 7 ½ In..	32

HEREND

Herend is a mark used on porcelain made in Herend, Hungary. A pottery was established there in 1826. The pottery was bought by Moritz Fischer in 1839. Fischer made replacement pieces for German and Far Eastern dinnerware and later began making his own dinnerware patterns. Figurines were made beginning in the 1870s. The company became Herend Porcelain Works Co. in 1884. It was nationalized in 1948. Herend became an independent company in 1981. In 1993 it became Herend Porcelain Manufactory. It is the world's largest porcelain manufacturer.

Biscuit Barrel, Dome Lid, Rose Finial, Rothschild Bird, 7 x 6 In............................	649
Candy Box, Reticulated Body, Strawberry Finial, Painted, Flower Sprays, 6 ¾ x 7 In.............	325

H

Hawkes, Cocktail Shaker, Cut Glass, Silver Cap, c.1955, 11 ½ In.
$938

Wright

Hawkes, Goblet, 8 Buckles, Diamond-Point Cut, Monogram D, Clear, c.1875, 6 ⅛ x 3 ¾ In., Pair
$1,112

Jeffrey S. Evans & Associates

Head Vase, Mae West, Hand Raised, Eyes Closed, Yellow Hat, Pearls, Gilt Trim, Japan, 6 x 4 ½ In.
$42

Ruby Lane

Head Vase, Woman, Bouffant Hair, Pearls, Green Dress, Knot At Shoulder, Napco, 7 ½ In.
$98

Ruby Lane

Heintz Art, Lamp, Desk, Pierced, Flowers, Leaves, Green Ground, Silver On Copper, 10 In.
$510

Cottone Auctions

Heintz Art, Trophy Cup, Silver Deco Design, Rifleman, Badge, 2 Handles, Inlay, 10 ¼ In.
$142

Bunch Auctions

Heisey, Locket On Chain, Butter, Cover, Ball Handle, Clear Glass, 1896, 5 ¼ In.
$152

Jeffrey S. Evans & Associates

> **TIP**
> *Products that are used to remove lime buildup in showers will also work on glass vases.*

Heisey, Octagon, Ice Bucket, No. 500, Nimrod Carving, Handle
$135

Apple Tree Auction Center

Herend, Cup & Saucer, White Ground, Green, Flowers, Leaves, Scalloped Rim, Gold Highlights
$150

Woody Auction

Herend, Dish, Dragon Shape, Gold Fishnet, 24K Gold Embellishment, Black Dynasty, 3 ½ x 11 In.
$1,180

Leland Little Auctions

Herend, Figurine, Cat, Resting, Blue Fishnet, 24K Gold Accents, 4 x 8 ½ In.
$413

Leland Little Auctions

Herend, Figurine, Elephant, Standing, Black & Silver Fishnet, Multicolor, Lotus, 7 ¾ x 10 In.
$5,074

Leland Little Auctions

Herend, Figurine, Pelican, Blue Fishnet, 24K Gold Beak, 8 ½ x 6 x 3 ½ In.
$288

Blackwell Auctions

Herend, Plate, Dinner, Gilt Rim, White Ground, Chinese Bouquet Green, 10 In., 12 Piece
$1,416

Leland Little Auctions

Cup & Saucer, White Ground, Green, Flowers, Leaves, Scalloped Rim, Gold Highlights *illus*	150
Dish, Dragon Shape, Gold Fishnet, 24K Gold Embellishment, Black Dynasty, 3½ x 11 In. *illus*	1180
Dish, Shell Shape, Bronze Rim, White, Birds, Butterflies, 9 In.	94
Figurine, Boy, Holding Manger, Standing, Domed Base, 8½ In.	177
Figurine, Cat, Resting, Blue Fishnet, 24K Gold Accents, 4 x 8½ In. *illus*	413
Figurine, Cobra, Head Up, Blue Fishnet, 4½ In.	354
Figurine, Dragon Koi Fish, Porcelain, Hand Painted, Fischer, 1900s, 3¼ In.	127
Figurine, Duck, Fishnet, Blue, Gilt Beak, Vieux, 2¾ x 4 x 3¼ In., Pair	201
Figurine, Elephant, Standing, Black & Silver Fishnet, Multicolor, Lotus, 7¾ x 10 In. ... *illus*	5074
Figurine, Foo Dog, Siang Noir, Liberal Gold Highlights, 10 In.	413
Figurine, Lion & Lioness, Sitting, Green Fishnet, 6½ x 8½ In.	615
Figurine, Mouse, Fishnet, 24K Gold Trim, Pink Raspberry, Hand Painted, Signed, 2¼ In.	144
Figurine, Parrot, Green, Perched, Berries & Nuts, Rockery Base, 1900s, 9¾ In.	344
Figurine, Pelican, Beak Up, Gilt Catch At Feet, Black Fishnet, Striped Wings, Marked, 8 In.	307
Figurine, Pelican, Blue Fishnet, 24K Gold Beak, 8½ x 6 x 3½ In. *illus*	288
Figurine, Rabbit, Green Fishnet, Gold Feet & Nose, 5¼ In.	59
Figurine, Rabbit, Seated, Green Fishnet Ground, Gold Highlights, Marked, 12 In.	450
Figurine, Rooster, Sitting, Rust Fishnet, Gold Accents, 6 In.	71
Figurine, Scottie McDuff, Black Ground, Blue Fishnet, 2⅝ In.	295
Ice Bucket, Rothschild Bird, Insect, Blue Herend Hungary Shield, Gilt, 1900s, 6 x 10 In.	861
Plate, Dinner, Gilt Rim, White Ground, Chinese Bouquet Green, 10 In., 12 Piece *illus*	1416
Plate, Dinner, Morning Glory, Shaped Gilt Rim, 10¼ In., 6 Piece	561
Platter, Gilt, Scalloped Rim, Butterflies, Rothschild Bird, 15 In.	384
Soup, Dish, White Field, Basket Weave Pattern, 2 Gold Bands, 9⅝ In., 6 Piece	384
Tea Set, Christmas Holly & Berry, Plaid Ribbon, Gold Trim, c.1980, 10 Piece	313
Teapot, Dome Lid, Bird Finial, Gilt Spout, Child's, 6 In.	85
Tray, Hunter Trophies, Shaped Rectangle, Branch Shape Handles, Painted, 18½ In.	443
Tray, Rothschild Bird, Butterflies, Scalloped, Branch Handles, 11 In. *illus*	472
Tray, Rothschild Bird, Oval, Ribbon Wrapped Sheath, Wheat Handles, 1900s, 3 x 25 x 19 In.	800
Tray, Serving, Chinese Bouquet Green, Rectangular, Gilt Rim, Branch Handles, 16 In.	708
Tureen, Dome Lid, Dolphin Finial & Handles, Gilt Lappets, Underplate, 12 In. *illus*	1062
Urn, 2 Parts, Flowers, Blue Border, Square Plinths, Gilt, 1950s, 10¾ In., Pair	2250
Urn, Dome Lid, Rothschild Bird, Painted, Flowers, 14 In., Pair	2596
Vase, Rothschild Bird, Urn Shape, Gilt, White Ground, Paw Feet, 5 In.	118

HEUBACH

Heubach is the collector's name for Gebruder Heubach, a firm working in Lichten, Germany, from 1840 to 1925. It is best known for bisque dolls and doll heads, the principal products. The company also manufactured bisque figurines, including piano babies, beginning in the 1880s, and glazed figurines in the 1900s. Piano Babies are listed in their own category. Dolls are included in the Doll category under Gebruder Heubach and Heubach. Another factory, Ernst Heubach, working in Koppelsdorf, Germany, also made porcelain and dolls. These will also be found in the Doll category under Heubach Koppelsdorf.

Candy Container, Snowball, Holly, Berries, Applied Leaves, Cloth Over Wire, Christmas, 3 In.	63
Figurine, Dancing Girl, Green Pleated Dress, Pink Detail, Lace Collar, Intaglio Eyes, Bisque, 16 In.	156

HISTORIC BLUE, *see factory names, such as Adams, Ridgway, and Staffordshire.*

HOBNAIL

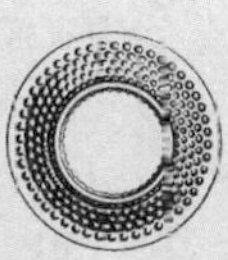

Hobnail glass is a style of glass with bumps all over. Dozens of hobnail patterns and variants have been made. Clear, colored, and opalescent hobnail have been made and are being reproduced. Other pieces of hobnail may also be listed in the Duncan & Miller and Fenton categories.

Bowl, Ruby, Opal Rim, Plate Stand, Dew Drop, Hobbs, Brockunier, c.1886, 3 x 7 x 11 In.	164
Cruet, Vaseline Handle, Facet Cut Stopper, Dew Drop, Hobbs, Brockunier, c.1886, 7½ x 6 In.	289

Herend, Tray, Rothschild Bird, Butterflies, Scalloped, Branch Handles, 11 In.
$472

Leland Little Auctions

Herend, Tureen, Dome Lid, Dolphin Finial & Handles, Gilt Lappets, Underplate, 12 In.
$1,062

Leland Little Auctions

Hobnail, Pitcher, Jug, Frosted Amberina, Dew Drop, Amber Handle, Hobbs, Brockunier, c.1886, 7 In.
$211

Jeffrey S. Evans & Associates

Holt-Howard, Desk Set, Professor Perch, Fish Shape, Pencil Sharpener & Holder, c.1958, 2½ In.
$97

Ruby Lane

Hopalong Cassidy, Sign, Hey Look Gang, Hoppy's Favorite Milk, Lehigh Valley Milk, Cardboard, 14 x 28 In.
$113

Pook & Pook

Horn, Chair, 8 Curved Steer Horns, Brown Suede Upholstery, Beaded Trim, Arms, 38 x 30 In.
$1,197

Fontaine's Auction Gallery

264

Lamp, Student, Pink, Shade, Opalescent, Electrified, 21 In.		81
Pitcher, Jug, Frosted Amberina, Dew Drop, Amber Handle, Hobbs, Brockunier, c.1886, 7 In. *illus*		211

HOLT-HOWARD

Holt-Howard was an importer that started working in New York City in 1949 and moved to Stamford, Connecticut, in 1955. The company sold many types of table accessories, such as condiment jars, decanters, spoon holders, and saltshakers. Its figural pieces have a cartoon-like quality. The company was bought out by General Housewares Corporation in 1968. Holt-Howard pieces are often marked with the name and the year or *HH* and the year stamped in black. The *HH* mark was used until 1974. The company also used a black and silver paper label. Holt-Howard production ceased in 1990 and the remainder of the company was sold to Kay Dee Designs. In 2002, Grant Holt and John Howard started Grant-Howard Associates and made retro pixie cookie jars marked *GHA* that sold from a mail-order catalog. Other GHA retro pixie pieces were made until 2006.

Bowl, Cantaloupe, Green Exterior, Yellow Interior, 6 In., 8 Piece		107
Candleholder, Coq Rouge, Rooster, Red, Yellow, 4¼ In.		34
Desk Set, Professor Perch, Fish Shape, Pencil Sharpener & Holder, c.1958, 2½ In. ...... *illus*		97
Mustard Jar, Pixie Ware, Yellow Stripes, c.1958, 2¾ x 4 In.		32
Salt & Pepper, Figural, Pear, Yellow, Foil Label, 3½ In.		19
Salt & Pepper, Four Seasons, 4-Sided, Blue, Brown, Cream, c.1964		27
Shaker, Siamese Cat, c.1961, 5 In.		20

HOPALONG CASSIDY

Hopalong Cassidy was a character in a series of 28 books written by Clarence E. Mulford, first published in 1907. Movies and television shows were made based on the character. The best-known actor playing Hopalong Cassidy was William Lawrence Boyd. His first movie appearance was in 1919, but the first Hopalong Cassidy film was not made until 1934. Sixty-six films were made. In 1948, William Boyd purchased the television rights to the movies, then later made 52 new programs. In the 1950s, Hopalong Cassidy and his horse, named Topper, were seen in comics, records, toys, and other products. Boyd died in 1972.

Sign, Hey Look Gang, Hoppy's Favorite Milk, Lehigh Valley Milk, Cardboard, 14 x 28 In. .*illus*		113
Toy, Box Only, Acme Cowboy Boots, Hoppy On Topper, Yellow, 11 x 9½ In.		50
Toy, Television, Brown & White Swirl, Plastic, Windup, Automatic Toy Co., Box, 5 x 5 x 5¾ In.		354
Tumbler, Milk Glass, Red & Black Graphic, Breakfast, Lunch, Dinner, Snacks, Box, 4¾ In., 4 Piece		100

HORN

Horn was used to make many types of boxes, furniture inlays, jewelry, and whimsies. The Endangered Species Act makes it illegal to sell many of these pieces. See also Powder Horn.

Chair, 8 Curved Steer Horns, Brown Suede Upholstery, Beaded Trim, Arms, 38 x 30 In. *illus*		1197
Vase, Drinking, Brown & Black, Silver Plate, Mounted, Russia, 1900s, 15 x 2¾ In.		101

HOWDY DOODY

Howdy Doody and Buffalo Bob were the main characters in a children's series televised from 1947 to 1960. Howdy was a redheaded puppet. The series became popular with college students in the late 1970s when Buffalo Bob began to lecture on campuses.

Book, Howdy Doody's Lucky Trip, Little Golden Book, 1953		22
Doll, HD 12, Moving Mouth, Pull String, Box, E.G. Dolls, Goldberger, 12 In.		44

Doll, Red, Blue, Yellow, Orange, Box, 12 In............	230
Earmuffs, Mouton Lamb Fur, Plastic, 1950s............	39
Pen, Figural, Jointed, Vinyl, Red, Blue, 6 In............	19
Toy, Delivery Wagon, Tricycle, Clarabell, Celluloid, Tin, Friction, Linemar, Box, 6 In............	780

HULL

Hull pottery was made in Crooksville, Ohio, from 1905. Addis E. Hull bought the Acme Pottery Company and started making ceramic wares. In 1917, A. E. Hull Pottery began making art pottery as well as the commercial wares. For a short time, 1921 to 1929, the firm also sold pottery imported from Europe. The dinnerware of the 1940s (including the Little Red Riding Hood line), the matte wares of the 1940s, and the high gloss artwares of the 1950s are all popular with collectors. The firm officially closed in March 1986.

Hull Pottery
c.1915

Hull Pottery
1930s

Hull Pottery
c.1950

Bow Knot, Vase, Flowers, Turquoise, Pink, Oval, 6 ½ In...........	39
Brown Drip, Pitcher, Ice Guard, 8 ½ In...........	18
Parchment & Pine, Vase, Black, Green, Turquoise, Yellow, c.1950, 7 x 4 In...........	45
Piggy Bank, Sitting, Brown, 6 x 5 ½ In...........	95
Sunglow, Planter, Embossed Daisies & Leaves, Green, Pink, Yellow, 4 ½ x 5 In...........	22
Tokay, Bowl, Console, Candleholder Handles, Grapevines, Footed, 16 x 4 x 5 In...........	40
Wild Flower, Vase, Side Handles, Pink Top, Blue Foot, White & Yellow Flowers, 9 ¾ In...........	19
Wild Flower, Vase, Urn Shape, 2 Handles, Petal Flared Top, Blue, Pink, Yellow, 5 ¾ In...........	79

HUMMEL

Hummel figurines, based on the drawings of the nun M.I. Hummel (Berta Hummel), were made by the W. Goebel Porzellanfabrik of Oeslau, Germany, now Rodental, Germany. They were first made in 1935. The *Crown* mark was used from 1935 to 1949. The company added the *bee* marks in 1950. The *full bee* with variations, was used from 1950 to 1959; *stylized bee,* 1957 to 1972; *three line mark,* 1964 to 1972; *last bee,* sometimes called *vee over gee,* 1972 to 1979. In 1979 the V bee symbol was removed from the mark. *U.S. Zone* was part of the mark from 1946 to 1948; *W. Germany* was part of the mark from 1960 to 1990. The Goebel *W. Germany* mark, called the *missing bee* mark, was used from 1979 to 1990; *Goebel, Germany,* with the crown and *WG,* originally called the *new mark,* was used from 1991 through part of 1999. A new version of the bee mark with the word *Goebel* was used from 1999 to 2008. A special *Year 2000* backstamp was also introduced. Porcelain figures inspired by Berta Hummel's drawings were introduced in 1997. These are marked *BH* followed by a number. They were made in the Far East, not Germany. Goebel discontinued making Hummel figurines in 2008 and Manufaktur Rodental took over the factory in Germany and began making new Hummel figurines. Hummel figurines made by Rodental are marked with a yellow and black bee on the edge of an oval line surrounding the words *Original M.I. Hummel Germany.* The words *Manufaktur Rodental* are printed beneath the oval. Manufaktur Rodental was sold in 2013 and new owners, Hummel Manufaktur GmbH, took over. It was sold again in 2017, but figurines continue to be made in the factory in Rodental. Other decorative items and plates that feature Hummel drawings were made by Schmid Brothers, Inc. beginning in 1971. Schmid Brothers closed in 1995.

Hummel, Figurine, No. 200/0, Little Goat Herder, Boy, 2 Goats, Full Bee, Germany, 1948, 5 In.
$115

Lion and Unicorn

Hummel, Figurine, No. 809, Bulgarian Girl Feeding Chickens, Blond Hair, Full Crown, 5 ⅛ In.
$2,185

Blackwell Auctions

Hutschenreuther, Figurine, Bremen Town Musicians, Brothers Grimm Folktale, 1900s, 7 ¾ In.
$230

Lion and Unicorn

Hutschenreuther, Plate, Gold Encrusted, Raised Scroll, Green Band, Royal Bavarian, 1900s, 10¾ In., 12 Piece
$2,006

Leland Little Auctions

Icon, Ascension Of Christ, Silver Oklad, Repousse, Andrey Antonovich Kovalsky, 1848, 12 x 10 In.
$1,112

Thomaston Place Auction Galleries

Icon, Mary & Baby Jesus, Renaissance Revival, Porcelain, Enamel, Frame, Late 1800s, 10 x 7 In.
$1,188

Charlton Hall Auctions

Hummel 1935–1949	Hummel 1950–1959	Hummel 2009–present

Ashtray, No. 675, Let's Sing, Seated Boy, Playing Accordion, Bird, 3 x 6 In. 37
Bell, No. 707, Girl Singing, Holding Music, Missing Bee, 1985, 5½ In. 89
Clock, No. 441, Tower, Children, Roman Numerals, Painted, Marked, 1988, 13¼ x 6 In. 92
Figurine, Adventure Bound, 7 Swabians, Children, Holding Spear, Last Bee, 7 In. 275
Figurine, No. 2, Little Fiddler, Boy With Brown Hat, Faience, Crown Mark, 1989, 10¾ In. 2280
Figurine, No. 7/1, Merry Wanderer, Faience Finish, Crown Mark, 7½ In. 2645
Figurine, No. 13, Meditation, Attached Flowerpot, Crown Mark, 5½ In. 2300
Figurine, No. 12/1, Chimney Sweep, Full Bee, 1940s, 5¾ In. 100
Figurine, No. 31, Silent Night, Baby, Angel, Black Child, A. Moeller, 1935, Crown Mark, 1935, 3½ In... 1840
Figurine, No. 123, Max & Moritz, Last Bee, c.1970, 5 In. 199
Figurine, No. 170/III, School Boys, Last Bee 158
Figurine, No. 172, Festival Harmony, Angel With Mandolin, R. Unger, 1947, 10¾ In. 805
Figurine, No. 189, Old Woman Knitting, Sample, Arthur Moeller, 1948, 7 In. 4888
Figurine, No. 200/0, Little Goat Herder, Boy, 2 Goats, Full Bee, Germany, 1948, 5 In. ... *illus* 115
Figurine, No. 231, Boy & Girl, Praying To Blessed Mary, Square Base, Full Bee, 7 In. 69
Figurine, No. 309, With Loving Greetings, Child & Inkwell, 2 Pens, Full Bee, 3½ In. 1180
Figurine, No. 329, Off To School, Boy & Girl With Schoolbags, A. Moeller, Stylized Bee, 1955, 5 In. 920
Figurine, No. 348, Ring Around The Rosy, Stylized Bee 424
Figurine, No. 363, Goose Girl, Modern Hummel Goebel Mark, 12½ In. 863
Figurine, No. 369, Follow The Leader, 3 Children, Dog, Last Bee, 1970s, 7 In. 318
Figurine, No. 370, Companions, 2 Boys, G. Skrobek, F. Kirchner, Stylized Bee, 1964, 5 In...... 1035
Figurine, No. 375, Morning Stroll, Girl, Baby Carriage, Dog, Three Line Mark, 1964, 4½ In. ... 1150
Figurine, No. 396, Ride Into Christmas, Boy On Sled, Tree, Last Bee, 1971, 6 x 5 x 3 In. 134
Figurine, No. 809, Bulgarian Girl Feeding Chickens, Blond Hair, Full Crown, 5⅛ In. .. *illus* 2185
Figurine, No. 825, Swedish Girl With Letter, International, Crown Mark, 5 In. 4025
Figurine, No. 832, Girl With Letter, Basket Over Arm, International, Crown Mark, 5½ In. 3450
Figurine, No. 854, Hungarian Girl, Holding Flowers, International, Crown Mark, 5 In. 1840
Figurine, Signs Of Spring, Girl, 4 Fence Posts, Full Bee Mark, 5½ In. 6490
Holy Water Font, No. 77, Raised Cross, Doves & Branches, Arched, R. Unger, Crown Mark, 1937, 6½ In... 805
Music Box, Umbrella Girl On Lid, Wood, Plays Raindrops Keep Falling, Anri, 1990, 6 x 4½ In. ... 173
Plaque, No. 134, Quartet, Missing Bee, 6½ x 6¼ In. 70
Plate, No. 267, Goose Girl, Last Bee, 1974, 7½ In. 37
Plate, No. 685, Umbrella Boy, Missing Bee, 1981, 7 In. 28

HUTSCHENREUTHER

Hutschenreuther Porcelain Factory was founded by Carolus Magnus in Hohenburg, Bavaria, in 1814. A second factory was established in Selb, Germany, in 1857. The company made fine quality porcelain dinnerware and figurines. The mark changed through the years, but the name and the lion insignia appear in most versions. Hutschenreuther became part of the Rosenthal division of the Waterford Wedgwood Group in 2000. Rosenthal became part of the Arcturus Group in 2009.

Figurine, Bremen Town Musicians, Brothers Grimm Folktale, 1900s, 7¾ In. .... *illus* 230
Figurine, Nude Woman, On Golden Ball, 2 Hands Raised, Germany, 13 In. 136
Figurine, Putti & Ram, Fighting, White, Marked, 10½ x 11 x 7 In. 313
Plate, Dinner, Flower Center, Gilt Rim, Maroon Border, Ovington's, 10¾ In., 12 Piece.......... 315
Plate, Gold Encrusted, Raised Scroll, Green Band, Royal Bavarian, 1900s, 10¾ In., 12 Piece .*illus* 2006

H

COLLECTING TRENDS:
TWENTIETH-CENTURY AMERICAN STUDIO JEWELRY

By Al Eiber

Museum shows were the first to highlight the important and innovative designs created by artists, jewelers, and sculptors in the late 1940s and 1950s. In 1946, the Museum of Modern Art (MOMA) in New York City opened an exhibition called Modern Handmade Jewelry, which presented modern jewelry as wearable art. The exhibit emphasized innovation over technical perfection, displaying creative designs that incorporated unusual materials, not the traditional precious stones and precious metals. The works revealed a strong reaction against the conventional design of commercial, costume, and traditional jewelry. The artists included sculptors, such as Alexander Calder and Harry Bertoia, and jewelers, such as Art Smith, Sam Kramer, Margaret De Patta, and Paul Lobel. They created bold new pieces where the materials were not as important as the forms and their value was aesthetic, not monetary. They used silver, brass, copper, wood, non-precious stones, and anything that would embellish their concept. Many had little or no formal training as jewelers, but their originality and inventive designs left a mark on personal ornamentation.

Two years later, in 1948, the Walker Art Center in Minneapolis showed a ground-breaking exhibit titled Modern Jewelry under Fifty Dollars. This was followed by other jewelry exhibits at the Walker in 1955 and 1959.

In 1956, the Museum of Contemporary Crafts opened in New York City. In 1979, the name was changed to the American Craft Museum and in 2002, it became the Museum of Arts and Design (MAD). MAD has held numerous jewelry exhibits since its founding, and it has a permanent encyclopedic collection where visitors can open drawers to see items in the collection that are not currently on display.

The Cleveland Museum of Art held an Annual Exposition of Cleveland Artists & Craftsmen starting in 1919. The show, which became known as the May Show, was open to any artist or craftsperson born or residing in the greater Cleveland area and later expanded to include the Western Reserve. This juried show was an important venue that showcased the work of many important modernist artists including jewelers and enamelists. In 1990, more than 1,000 artists applied and only 170 were juried in.

Alexander Calder and Harry Bertoia each created sculpture and jewelry that influenced an entire generation of jewelers, such as Ed Wiener, Margaret De Patta, and Merry Renk, that followed. Others, especially Sam Kramer and Art Smith, were influenced by surrealist painters such as Joan Miró, Man Ray, Marcel Duchamp, Yves Tanguy, and Hans Arp. Many of these surrealist painters also designed jewelry during their lifetimes.

Harry Bertoia (1915–1978) was a sculptor, designer, and jeweler. He learned metalworking at Cranbrook Academy in Detroit and later became head of the department. During World War II, when metal was scarce, Bertoia would find metal scraps to make jewelry and maquettes of his sculpture. His jewelry production during his lifetime was very small, estimated at only a few hundred pieces.

Left: Harry Bertoia pin, sterling silver, 3¼ in. by 1½ in.

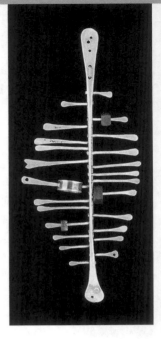

Left: Harry Bertoia necklace,
14-karat gold, 9 in., pendants
each 1¾ in. by 1⅛ in.

Right: Harry Bertoia Abacus pin,
sterling silver, ebony,
4¼ in. by 1⅞ in.

Alexander Calder (1898–1976) was one of the most influential sculptors/jewelers of this period. Although trained as a mechanical engineer, he took evening art classes at the Art Students League of New York to learn to draw. Wire, which was an important element in his sculptures, was also his preferred material for jewelry. He worked mostly in silver or brass, twisting or hammering the metal to achieve strong forms without using solder. Calder produced about 1,800 pieces of jewelry over his lifetime that were frequently given as gifts to his family and friends.

Above: Alexander Calder belt buckle, brass, 6 in.
by 2⅝ in.

Right: Alexander Calder cuff bracelet, sterling
silver, 2½ in. by 2⅛ in.

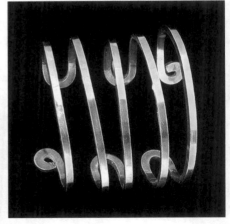

Left: Alexander Calder pendant, sterling
silver, 2½ in. diam.

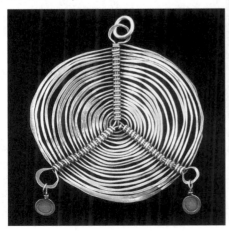

Betty Cooke (1924–) has been called an "icon within the tradition of modernist jewelry." Her work has been shown nationally and internationally and is included in many important museum collections, including the Museum of Modern Art in New York.

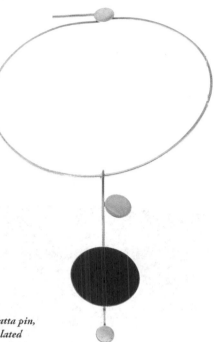

Right: Betty Cooke pendant necklace, c.1990, sterling silver, onyx disc drop, signed, pendant 5½ in., collar 6½ in.

Left: Margaret De Patta pin, sterling silver, articulated quartz, ebony, 2¼ in. by 2 in.

Margaret De Patta (1903–1964) is probably the most important maker to work in the modernist tradition of jewelry design. She studied under László Moholy-Nagy, a Bauhaus painter and sculptor who influenced her work throughout her career. De Patta's jewelry received more awards during her lifetime than probably any other American studio jeweler.

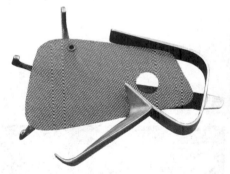

Above: Margaret De Patta pin, sterling silver, stainless steel mesh screen, 4⅝ in. by 1⅞ in.

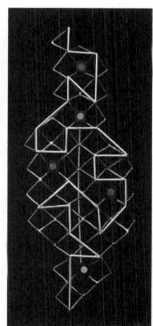

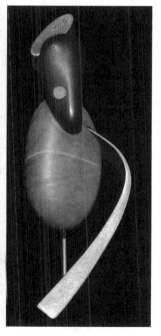

Left: Margaret De Patta pin, gold, onyx, jade, coral, 1¾ in. by 4⅝ in.

Right: Margaret De Patta pin, sterling silver, stone, ebony, turquoise

Claire Falkenstein (1908–1997) was an internationally recognized sculptor and jeweler. She made a large amount of jewelry while living in Paris in the early 1950s. Edgar Kaufmann Jr., then chairman of the Museum of Modern Art, saw Falkenstein's jewelry in Paris and purchased two pieces for MOMA. In 1960, Peggy Guggenheim commissioned Falkenstein to make front entrance gates at her villa, now the Guggenheim Venice. They were made of welded iron rods that formed a metal "web" embedded with chunks of glass.

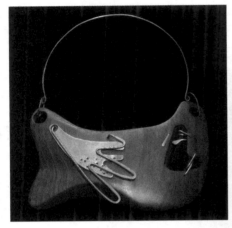

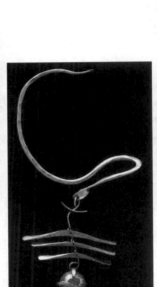

Left: Claire Falkenstein necklace, wood, brass, ebony

Right: Claire Falkenstein necklace, gold-plated brass, glass, 8½ in. by 5¼ in.

Above: Claire Falkenstein pendant necklace, brass and fused glass, 3½ in. by 4 in.

Elsa Freund (1912–2001) started working on jewelry in the 1940s. She experimented with firing clay with glass shards to make glazed ceramic beads of all sizes, which she called

"Elsaramics." By the 1950s, Freund became a significant figure in the studio jewelry movement, and her jewelry is in the permanent collection of many major museums.

Below: Peter Macchiarini pin, sterling silver, copper, brass, carnelian, 4 in. by 3⅜ in.

Left: Elsa Freund pendant necklace, sterling silver, glass, ceramic, pendant 3¾ in. by 3½ in., overall 21 in.

Sam Kramer (1913–1964) was the most avant-garde, individualist jeweler of the group. Heavily influenced by the surrealistic art movement, his jewelry was, at the same time, bizarre and beautiful.

Left: Two Sam Kramer pins, each sterling silver and glass, left: 2⅜ in. by ⅞ in., right: 2⅛ in. by 1½ in.

Below: Sam Kramer earrings, sterling silver, glass, taxidermy eyes, 2½ in. by 1¼ in.

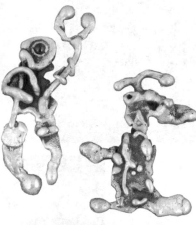

Above: Sam Kramer pin, sterling silver, taxidermy eye, 7 in. by 1½ in.

Below: Sam Kramer ring, stylized face, sterling silver, ruby eye, 1 in. by 1¼ in.

Right: Sam Kramer necklace, sterling silver, bone, coral, collar 11¼ in. diam., pendant 6¼ in. by 4⅜ in.

Peter Macchiarini (1909–2001) lived and worked in San Francisco and is considered one of the icons of the modernist jewelry movement. Macchiarini incorporated cubism, primitivism, and surrealism in his work. He worked with various non-precious metals, including silver, nickel, copper, brass, and iron. His sculpture and jewelry are represented in the collections of many museums, including the Oakland Museum, Montreal Museum, and Museum of Art and Design in NYC.

Right: Peter Macchiarini pin, sterling silver, Inconel, brass, copper, ivory, ebony, 4½ in. by 1⅝ in.

Earl Pardon (1926–1991) trained as a painter, and his work includes painting, drawing, and sculpture. He also made incredible jewelry throughout his career. He was a well-known teacher of enameling and jewelry at Skidmore College from 1951 to 1989.

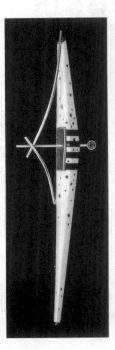

Right: Earl Pardon pin, sterling silver, brass, ivory, garnet, 5½ in. by 1½ in.

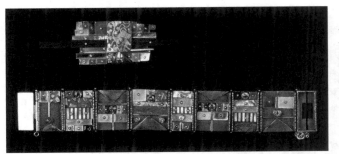

Above: Earl Pardon pin and bracelet, sterling silver, 14-karat gold, enamel, semiprecious stones, pin 3½ in. by 1 in., bracelet 6½ in. by 1 in.

Right: Earl Pardon pin, sterling silver, coral, 3⅝ in. by 1¾ in.

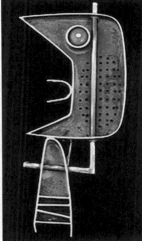

Above: Svetozar Radakovich pendant necklace, 14-karat gold, pendant 2¾ in. by 2⅞ in.

Right: Ruth Radakovich pendant necklace, sterling silver, moonstone, pendant 3 in. by 2⅞ in.

Ruth (1920–1975) **and Svetozar** (1918–1998) **Radakovich** were respected jewelers, sculptors, and teachers who spent most of their careers in Encinitas, California. They met in Belgrade, Yugoslavia, in 1946 when they were both working with the United Nations Relief and Rehabilitation Administration. They are included in almost every major publication on the history of modern metalworking.

Merry Renk (1921–2012) designed jewelry whose overriding concept was structure; it was frequently composed of several metal parts that moved or interlocked. She studied at the Institute of Design in Chicago and later moved to San Francisco, where she dedicated her career to jewelry.

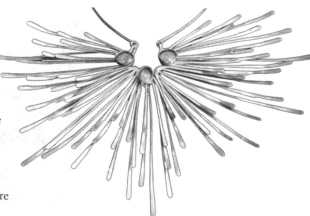

Above: Merry Renk In the Sky necklace, sterling silver, iridescent stones, 12 in. by 11¾ in.

Below: Ruth Roach Pod necklace, sterling silver, 3½ in. by 1¼ in.

Above: Ruth Roach Clarinet Key bracelet, sterling silver, ebony, 3 in. by 1¼ in.

Below: Ruth Roach Double Cuff bracelet, sterling silver, moss agate, 2½ in. by 1¼ in.

Ruth Roach (1913–1979) was a multitalented artist/craftsperson who made a significant impact on the art world during her relatively short career. In the late 1950s, Roach won many prizes for her jewelry and appeared in many important museum exhibitions.

Left: Art Smith Diminishing Spirals necklace, brass, 41 in. by 3 in.

Right: Art Smith Patina necklace, sterling silver, 11 in. by 6 in.

Below: Art Smith Lava Cuff bracelet, brass, copper, 6 in. by 2⅝ in.

Art Smith (1917–1982) designed the most desired jewelry of this period. He worked in silver, brass, and copper, frequently using three-dimensional biomorphic shapes that looked like miniature mobiles in his necklaces and earrings.

Ed Wiener (1918–1991) worked in New York after World War II and was well respected by his peers. He took a general crafts class at Columbia University in 1945 but was, otherwise, self-taught. Wiener typically worked in silver until about 1966, when he started using gold more frequently.

Above: Ed Wiener Abacus pin, silver, baroque beads, 2⅜ in. by 2 in.

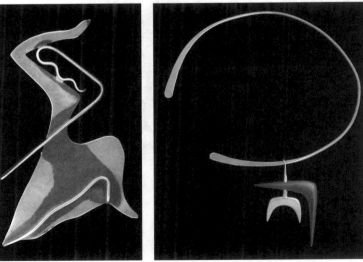

Left: Ed Wiener Dancer pin, sterling silver 3½ in. high

Right: Ed Wiener necklace, sterling silver, ebony, 7 in. by 4½ in.

ICON

Icons, special, revered pictures of Jesus, Mary, or a saint, are usually Russian or Byzantine. The small icons collected today are made of wood and tin or precious metals. Many modern copies have been made in the old style and are being sold to tourists in Russia and Europe and at shops in the United States. Rare, old icons have sold for over $50,000. The riza (oklad) is the metal cover protecting the icon. It is often made of silver or gold.

3 Saints, Engraved Silver Oklad, Traveler's Pendant, Hanging Loop, 1800s, 2 3/4 x 2 3/8 In. 322
4 Saints, Standing, Multicolor, Wood Panel, Gilt Ground, Molded Frame, Russia, 21 x 17 3/4 In. . 413
12 Saints, Gilt & Tempera, On Panel, Partial Sketch On Reverse, Greece, 16 7/8 In. 549
Ascension Of Christ, Silver Oklad, Repousse, Andrey Antonovich Kovalsky, 1848, 12 x 10 In. *illus* 1112
Christ Pantocrator, Oil On Walnut, Gilt Silver Oklad, Carved Edge, Frame, 1800s, 12 x 11 In. ... 585
Christ Pantocrator, Ornate Riza, Cloisonne, Enamel, Gilt Silver, Fedor Ivanov, 1880, 12 x 10 In. 8625
Christ Pantocrator, Painted, Carved, Gilt, Arch Shape, Russia, 1800s, 25 x 18 In. 720
Madonna & Child, Silver Oklad, Painted, Carved Wood Frame, Greece, 18 1/2 x 14 1/2 In. 938
Madonna & Child, Silver Plate, Gold Gilt Frame, Shadowbox Case, Russia, c.1900, 10 1/2 x 9 In. 750
Madonna & Child, Silver, Oil Painting, Engraved, Russian Orthodox, Embossed, 13 1/2 x 11 In. ... 938
Madonna & Child, Wood Panel, Chased Tin Riza, Enamel, Copper, Velvet, 1900s, 10 x 8 In. 132
Mary & Baby Jesus, Renaissance Revival, Porcelain, Enamel, Frame, Late 1800s, 10 x 7 In. *illus* 1188
Orthodox, 7 Saints, Painted, On Panel, Carved, Gilt, Show Box, Frame, Russia, 1800s, 20 x 18 In. . 540
Saint, Picture, Multicolor, Giltwood Panel, Russia, 1950s, 21 1/2 x 17 1/4 In. 89
St. Dionysios, Orthodox, Greek Island Of Zakynthos, Frame, 13 1/4 x 9 1/2 In. 761
St. George, Plaque, Bronze, Horseback, Slaying Dragon, Cast Iron Frame, Mid 1900s, 19 In. 219
St. John Chrysostom, Archbishop Of Constantinople, Gilt & Tempera, On Panel, 23 5/8 In. .. 671
Supplicant, Mother, Child, Cloisonne, Silver, Mark, A.C., Russia, c.1900, 12 1/2 x 10 1/2 In. 1180
Virgin Mary, Child, Silver, Repousse, Oklad, Byzantine, Frame, 1900s, 8 1/4 x 6 1/2 In. 177

IMARI

Imari porcelain was made in Japan and China beginning in the seventeenth century. In the eighteenth century and later, it was copied by porcelain factories in Germany, France, England, and the United States. It was especially popular in the nineteenth century and is still being made. Imari is characteristically decorated with stylized bamboo, floral, and geometric designs in orange, red, green, and blue. The name comes from the Japanese port of Imari, which exported the ware made nearby in a factory at Arita. Imari is now a general term for any pattern of this type.

Basin, Flowers, Chrysanthemums, 4 Shaped Panels, Kenjo, Apocryphal Mark, 1700, 11 In. ... 2394
Bowl, Panels, Alternating Figures & Gardens, Metal Hanger, c.1885, 15 1/2 In. 250
Charger, Armorial, Central Crest, Pomegranates, Blossoms, Flower Band, 1800s, 4 x 21 In. . 369
Charger, Center Medallion, Flowers, Scalloped Rim, Early 1900s, 13 1/4 In. ..... *illus* 108
Charger, Central Roundel, 3 Friends Of Winter, Cartouche, Flowers, Phoenix Birds, 16 1/4 In. 122
Charger, Cobalt Blue Ground, Scroll Shape Medallions, Japan, 1800s, 17 In. ..... *illus* 89
Charger, Cobalt Blue, Iron Red, Green, Gilt, Phoenix, Flowers, Shaped Medallion, 1800s, 14 In. ... 118
Charger, Iron Red, Leaves, Flowers, Cobalt Blue, 12 1/2 In. 30
Charger, Painted, Scroll & Fan, Figures, Cobalt Blue Ground, Late 1900s, 18 In. 148
Charger, Palette Colors, Ruffled Rim, Flowers, 1800s, 17 1/2 In. 594
Charger, Red Seal, Flowers, Ruffled Edge, Painted, 1800s, 17 In. 131
Dish, Shell Shape, Gilt, Scalloped Edge, Japan, 3 x 9 1/2 In., Pair 177
Punch Bowl, Flowers, Yellow, Orange, Blue, White, Bronze Ormolu Base, 9 7/8 x 14 1/2 In. 344
Urn, Converted To Lamp, Bronze Mounts, Flowers, Japan, c.1900, 25 In., Pair ..... *illus* 531
Vase, Bottle Shape, Flowers, Painted, Carved, Wood Stand, 8 1/2 In. 94
Vase, Japanese Style, Rectangular, Flared Rim, Tapered Neck, Figural, Flowers, 13 In., Pair. 118
Vase, Orange, Blue Blossom, Octagonal Frame, Flared Rim, 49 3/4 x 18 In. 761
Vase, Ribbed, Ruffled Edge, Painted, Late 1800s, 10 1/2 In., Pair ..... *illus* 192

Imari, Charger, Center Medallion, Flowers, Scalloped Rim, Early 1900s, 13 1/4 In.
$108

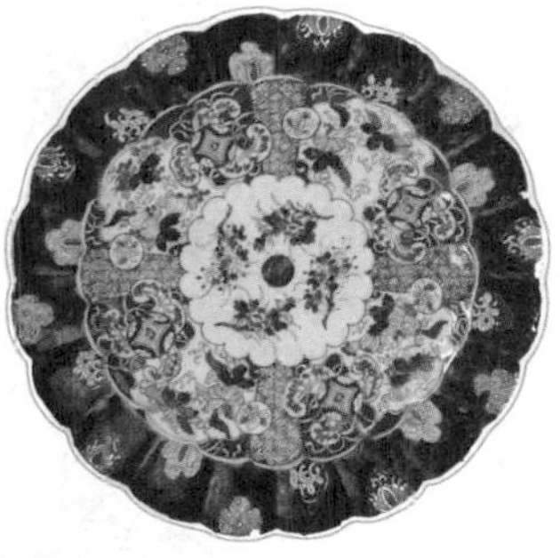

Garth's Auctioneers & Appraisers

Imari, Charger, Cobalt Blue Ground, Scroll Shape Medallions, Japan, 1800s, 17 In.
$89

Leland Little Auctions

Imari, Urn, Converted To Lamp, Bronze Mounts, Flowers, Japan, c.1900, 25 In., Pair
$531

Charlton Hall Auctions

I

Imari, Vase, Ribbed, Ruffled Edge, Painted, Late 1800s, 10 ½ In., Pair $192

Hindman

Imperial, Free Hand, Vase, Hearts & Vines, Transparent, Green Ground, Red, Cobalt Blue Rim, 6 ⅞ In. $945

Fontaine's Auction Gallery

Imperial, Free Hand, Vase, Urn Shape, Hearts & Vines, Deep Orange Iridescent Interior, c.1925, 5 ¾ In. $468

Jeffrey S. Evans & Associates

IMPERIAL

Imperial Glass Corporation was founded in Bellaire, Ohio, in 1901. It became a subsidiary of Lenox, Inc., in 1973 and was sold to Arthur R. Lorch in 1981. It was sold again in 1982, and went bankrupt in 1984. In 1985, the molds and some assets were sold. The Imperial glass preferred by the collector is freehand art glass, carnival glass, slag glass, stretch glass, and other top-quality tablewares. Tablewares and animals are listed here. The others may be found in the appropriate sections.

| Imperial Glass 1911–1932 | Imperial Glass 1913–1920s | Imperial Glass 1973–1981 |

Candlewick, Cake Plate, Footed, 11 In.	31
Free Hand, Vase, Jack-In-The-Pulpit, Drag Loop, Embossed Paper Label, Early 1900s, 10 ½ In...	1625
Free Hand, Vase, Hearts & Vines, Transparent, Green Ground, Red, Cobalt Blue Rim, 6 ⅞ In. ...*illus*	945
Free Hand, Vase, Urn Shape, Hearts & Vines, Deep Orange Iridescent Interior, c.1925, 5 ¾ In. *illus*	468
Lead Luster, Vase, Blue On White, Orange Rim, Polished Pontil, Early 1900s, 5 ¾ In.	313

 ## INDIAN

Indian art from North and South America has attracted the collector for many years. Each tribe has its own distinctive designs and techniques. Baskets, jewelry, pottery, and leatherwork are of greatest collector interest. Eskimo art is listed under Eskimo in this book.

Arrowheads, 80 Pieces, Radiating Pattern, Glass Frame, Wood Border, 31 ½ x 25 ¼ In. *illus*	561
Bag, Plains Style, Beaded Hide, Animal At Front, Metal Cones, 1950s, 8 ¼ x 3 ½ In.	177
Basket, Apache, Geometric, Stepped Diagonal Lines, Multicolor, Late 1800s, 7 ¾ x 14 In. *illus*	702
Basket, Apache, Woven, Cone Shape, Late 1800s, 16 In.	281
Basket, Cherokee, Carol Welch, North Carolina, 8 In.	59
Basket, Choctaw, Mississippi Bamboo, River Cane, Natural Dye, Diamonds, Squared, 18 x 19 In.	281
Basket, Hava Supai, Circular, Dish Shape, Devil's Claw, Leaves, 1920, 10 In.	148
Basket, Papago, Bold Geometric, Black, Red, c.1910, 4 ½ x 10 In.	104
Basket, Pima, Woven, Late 1800s, 5 In.	625
Basket, Storage, Attributed To Washo, Triangular Mountains, Lake Tahoe, Early 1900s, 2 ¾ x 6 ½ In.	625
Basket, Woodlands, Blue & Salmon Bands, Applied Handle, Late 1800s, 4 x 9 In. *illus*	1342
Belt, Crow, Leather, Beaded, c.1880-1900, 36 ½ x 2 ¾ In.	551
Blanket, Navajo, Germantown, Eye Dazzler, Red Ground, Wood Frame, Early 1900s, 51 x 29 In.	688
Blanket, Navajo, Red Eye Dazzler, Central Dragonfly, Pendleton Woolen Mills, 64 x 80 In.	413
Boots, Athabascan, Hide, Flower Beading, Medium High, c.1960-80, 10 In.	83
Bowl, Apache, Coiled, Woven Basketry, Geometric, Late 1800s, 4 x 14 ⅝ In.	293
Bowl, Apache, Woven, Red Yucca Root, Whirling Logs, Seedpod Husk, c.1900, 22 ½ In.	5504
Bowl, Hopi, Bird, Pottery, Painted, Distressed Finish, c.1970, 11 In.	708
Bowl, Hopi, Ear Of Corn Interior, Geometric Band, Signed, Fannie Nampeyo, 1900s, 2 x 6 In. *illus*	352
Bowl, San Ildefonso, Blackware, Signed, Maria Poveka, 3 ¾ x 6 ¾ In.	575
Bowl, San Ildefonso, Blue Corn, Black, Squat, 2 ¾ x 6 In.	908
Bowl, San Ildefonso, Matte Feather-Like Band, Maria Poveka Martinez, c.1923, 4 x 4 In. *illus*	995
Bowl, Santa Clara Pueblo, Blackware, Geometric Bands, Harrison Begay Jr., c.2002, 5 In. *illus*	497
Bowl, Santa Clara Pueblo, Step Design, Blackware, Ursulita Naranjo, c.1960, 3 In.	266
Canteen, Acoma, Birds, 2 Loop Handles, Cream Ground, Multicolor, c.1930, 7 x 5 In.	150
Canteen, Cochiti, Pottery, Whimsical, 2 Heads, Signed J. Ortiz, Late 1900s, 6 ¾ x 9 In. *illus*	352
Canteen, Zuni, Red & Brown, Zoomorphic Design, Leather Cord, c.1880, 11 ¼ In. *illus*	3200
Case, Plateau, Cylindrical, Geometric Design, Multicolor, c.1890-1910, 21 ½ In.	767
Club, Sioux, Floppy Head, Oval Stone Held By Deer Hide, Beaded Handle, 1880s, 39 In.	177
Cradle, Sioux, Hood, Quillwork, Willow Wood Frame, Moth Holes, 1890-1910, 9 ½ x 10 In.	1298
Doll, Navajo, Green Velour Dress, Beaded Earrings, Braids, Signed, Mary S. Chicharello, 9 In.	83
Dress, Plateau, Beaded, Fringed Hide, Long Sleeve, Cream Ground, c.1900, 54 x 60 In. *illus*	5000

I

Drum, Hand, Tesuque Pueblo, Painted, Dancers, Deerskin, Bentwood Frame, Late 1800s, 9 x 11 In..	354
Headstall, Blackfoot, Stitched, Navy, Yellow & Red Beads, White Ground, c.1920, 18 In.........	438
Jar, Acoma, Pottery, Geometric, White Ground, Lucy M. Lewis, Late 1900s, 3 ⅜ In...	2950
Jar, Hopi, Painted, Vignettes Of Birds, Dragonfly, Signed, Dee Stella, 1900s, 7 ¾ x 13 In.	960
Jar, Hopi, Seed, Oval, Geometric Images, Lizard, Turtles, Multicolor, Sylvia Naha, 1880s, 4 ⅝ In.	439
Jar, Mata Ortiz, Red, Black, Geometric, White Ground, Angel Amaya, Mexico, 3 ¾ x 7 ½ In. ..*illus*	148
Jar, Pueblo, Red Ground, Melon Shape, Alton Komolestewa, 6 In.	791
Jar, San Ildefonso, Black On Black, Feather, Coil Built, Maria Martinez, 1968, 8 x 9 ¾ In.	3750
Jar, Santo Domingo Pueblo, Bulbous, Geometric, Signed, Videl Aguilar SDP, 17 x 12 In.	460
Jar, Zia, Birds & Geometric Designs, Bulbous, Redware, Multicolor, Olla, c.1930s-40s, 7 ½ In..	531
Katsina, Hopi, Deer Hotevilla, Hand Carved, Multicolor, 1973, 6 x 5 x 6 In. .... *illus*	219
Katsina, Southwest, Carved, Painted, Wood, Leather, Fabric, Wilfred Tewawina, 19 In.........	89
Knife Sheath, Plains Style, Beaded Hide, Jingle Cones, 1950s, 15 ½ In.	266
Knife Sheath, Plains, Beaded, Blue, White, Geometrics, c.1900, 3 ¼ x 10 In.	138
Legging Strip, Northern Plains, Men's, Beaded, Multicolor, Geometrics, Yellow, 3 x 20 In.....	344
Mask, Iroquois, Wood, Carved, Reddish Brown, Black Stripes, c.1940-60, 12 ½ x 6 ½ In. *illus*	502
Moccasins, Northern Cree, Beaded, Flowers, Rabbit Fur, c.1940, 8 ½ In.	106
Moccasins, Plains, Sinew Sewn, Beadwork, Turquoise Ground, Child's, 1880, 7 In. ..... *illus*	322
Moccasins, Plains, Thread & Sinew Sewn, White, Navy, Sky Blue & Yellow Beads, 10 In. *illus*	594
Moccasins, Sioux, Thread Sewn, Beaded, Blue Tint, Turquoise, Purple, Leather, c.1890, 10 In...	690
Model, Canoe, Ojibwe Style, Birch Bark, Sewn, Stick Supports, Folk Art, 1930s, 17 ½ In........	39
Model, Canoe, Pacific Northwest, Carved, Painted, Wood, 1900s, 11 x 57 In. .... *illus*	1200
Olla, Acoma Pueblo, Geometrics, Orange & Black, Pottery, New Mexico, 9 In.	443
Olla, Acoma, Stylized Flowers, Geometrics, Multicolor, c.1900, 8 x 8 ¾ In.	690
Olla, Acoma, Tapered Neck & Shoulder, Geometric Design, c.1920, 9 ⅛ In. .... *illus*	1830
Olla, Cochiti Pueblo, Multicolor Bear, Deer, Geometric, Early 1900s, 16 ½ x 15 In.	7995
Olla, Hopi, Polished, Blackware, Alton Komalestewa, Late 1900s, 11 In. .... *illus*	510
Olla, Zia, Redware, Painted, Bird & 4 Color Design, Helen Gachupin, c.1980, 8 ¼ In.	413
Olla, Zuni, Frogs, Animals, Multicolor, 10 x 10 In.	2214
Pipe Bag, Sioux, Beaded, Hide, Red, White, Yellow, c.1950-80, 17 In............................. ...	148
Pipe Bag, Sioux, Multicolor, Metallic Beadwork, Slats, Fringe, 1880s, 35 ½ x 6 ½ In. ... *illus*	995
Pipe, Sioux, Red Catlinite, Lead Inlaid Arrow, Circle On Bowl & Shank, 4 x 7 ½ In..............	207
Pot, Acoma, Geometric Design, Cream Ground, 5 ½ x 7 ½ In. .... *illus*	144
Pot, Hopi, Brown Ground, Ted Howato, 8 In..	254
Pot, Mata Ortiz, Knife Blade, Black On Black, Signed, Jesus Tina, 6 ½ x 9 In..............	90
Pouch, Sioux, Beaded, Hide, Fringe, Red, Blue, Yellow, c.1890-1910, 5 x 7 In.	266
Pouch, Southern Plains, Beaded, Hide, Fringe, Drawstrings, Early 1900s, 9 In................... ..	308
Roach, Plains, Deer Hair, Porcupine Quills, Yarn, 1910-25, 17 In. .... *illus*	354
Rug, Navajo, Central Diamond, Gray Ground, Brown & Red Border, Early 1900s, 49 x 84 In.	375
Rug, Navajo, Ganado Storm Design, c.1925-40, 66 x 37 In. .... *illus*	531
Rug, Navajo, Geometric Stepped Mesa, Black Ground, c.1930, 66 x 51 In.........................	863
Rug, Navajo, Gray Field, 2 Cruciform Medallions, Black Border, 48 x 85 In....................	1003
Rug, Navajo, Gray Field, Gold Geometric Design, Marie Kee, 67 x 94 In.	1298
Rug, Navajo, Hand Woven, Red, Black, Gray, Wool, 60 x 41 ½ In. .... *illus*	266
Rug, Navajo, Ocher, White, Brown & Red Geometric Patterns, Black Border, c.1955, 60 x 34 In...	144
Rug, Navajo, Pictorial Weaving, Woven, Woman, Laverne Begay, 1900s, 40 x 27 In. ...... *illus*	576
Rug, Navajo, Red, Gray, White, Black, Woven, Square, 41 In.	590
Rug, Navajo, Storm Pattern, Black, Gray Ground, Brown & White Accents, 51 x 38 In.	425
Rug, Navajo, Teec Nos Pos, Woven, Geometric, Zigzag, Distinct Border, Helen Lee, 32 x 48 In..	374
Rug, Navajo, Yei, Wool, 4 Dancers, Colorful Costumes, c.1950, 30 x 40 In......................	570
Saddlebag, Sioux, Beads, Hide, Marked, U.S. Indian Dept, c.1900-20, 11 In	2242
Sampler, Navajo, Germantown, Eye Dazzler, Red, Green, c.1900, 29 x 36 In. .... *illus*	1320
Scoop, Iroquois, Pine, Carved Slot, Long Handle, Custom Stand, 1700s, 22 In.......................	188
Sculpture, Jemez, Maiden Holding Jar, Signed On Hem Of Skirt, Kathleen Wall, 1900s, 17 In. *illus*	960
Sculpture, Zuni, Pueblo Man, Traditional Headband, Stone, Carved, Freddie Leekya, 3 ¼ In.	81
Shirt, Ojibwa, Velvet, Black, Beaded, Flowers, Collar & Cuffs, Sleeves, c.1895-1915, 26 In. *illus*	708
Skirt, Apache, Beaded, Dyed, Yellow, Brown, Fringe, c.1925-45, 31 In.	531
Streamer, Comanche, Battle Honor, Red, 2 Black Silk Stripes, Nez Perce War, Frame, 2 ¾ x 48 In..	640
Tobacco Bag, Sioux, Beaded, Hide, Quilled, c.1895-1915, 6 x 23 In............................	944
Tomahawk Pipe, Plains Style, Iron, Spontoon Head, Brass Heart, Inlay, Wood Shaft, 1900s, 24 In.	406

Indian, Arrowheads, 80 Pieces, Radiating Pattern, Glass Frame, Wood Border, 31 ½ x 25 ¼ In.
$561

Austin Auction Gallery

Indian, Basket, Apache, Geometric, Stepped Diagonal Lines, Multicolor, Late 1800s, 7 ¾ x 14 In.
$702

Jeffrey S. Evans & Associates

Indian, Basket, Cherokee, Carol Welch, North Carolina, 8 In.
$59

Bunch Auctions

Indian, Basket, Woodlands, Blue & Salmon Bands, Applied Handle, Late 1800s, 4 x 9 In.
$1,342

Pook & Pook

Indian, Bowl, Hopi, Ear Of Corn Interior, Geometric Band, Signed, Fannie Nampeyo, 1900s, 2 x 6 In.
$352

Cowan's Auctions

Indian, Bowl, San Ildefonso, Matte Feather-Like Band, Maria Poveka Martinez, c.1923, 4 x 4 In.
$995

Jeffrey S. Evans & Associates

Indian, Bowl, Santa Clara Pueblo, Blackware, Geometric Bands, Harrison Begay Jr., c.2002, 5 In.
$497

Jeffrey S. Evans & Associates

Indian, Canteen, Cochiti, Pottery, Whimsical, 2 Heads, Signed J. Ortiz, Late 1900s, 6¾ x 9 In.
$352

Cowan's Auctions

Indian, Canteen, Zuni, Red & Brown, Zoomorphic Design, Leather Cord, c.1880, 11¼ In.
$3,200

Neal Auction Company

Indian, Jar, Mata Ortiz, Red, Black, Geometric, White Ground, Angel Amaya, Mexico, 3¾ x 7½ In.
$148

Austin Auction Gallery

Indian, Katsina, Hopi, Deer Hotevilla, Hand Carved, Multicolor, 1973, 6 x 5 x 6 In.
$219

Lion and Unicorn

Indian, Dress, Plateau, Beaded, Fringed Hide, Long Sleeve, Cream Ground, c.1900, 54 x 60 In.
$5,000

Charlton Hall Auctions

Indian, Mask, Iroquois, Wood, Carved, Reddish Brown, Black Stripes, c.1940-60, 12½ x 6½ In.
$502

Austin Auction Gallery

Indian, Moccasins, Plains, Sinew Sewn, Beadwork, Turquoise Ground, Child's, 1880, 7 In.
$322

Jeffrey S. Evans & Associates

Indian, Moccasins, Plains, Thread & Sinew Sewn, White, Navy, Sky Blue & Yellow Beads, 10 In.
$594

Charlton Hall Auctions

Indian, Model, Canoe, Pacific Northwest, Carved, Painted, Wood, 1900s, 11 x 57 In.
$1,200

Michaan's Auctions

Indian, Olla, Acoma, Tapered Neck & Shoulder, Geometric Design, c.1920, 9⅛ In.
$1,830

Neal Auction Company

Indian, Olla, Hopi, Polished, Blackware, Alton Komalestewa, Late 1900s, 11 In.
$510

Michaan's Auctions

Indian, Pipe Bag, Sioux, Multicolor, Metallic Beadwork, Slats, Fringe, 1880s, 35½ x 6½ In.
$995

Jeffrey S. Evans & Associates

Indian, Pot, Acoma, Geometric Design, Cream Ground, 5½ x 7½ In.
$144

Michaan's Auctions

What is Quillwork?

A box with a decoration made from rolled pieces of paper was sold recently as a "piece of quillwork." Quillwork has two meanings. Quillwork was used by American Indians to decorate moccasins, pincushions, and even small books and baskets made of thin wood or birch bark. Porcupine quills were stitched on in appropriate designs. The other quillwork is made of rolled paper. It was used to decorate boxes, tea caddies, mirrors and other pieces in the early 1800s in Europe. The roll of paper was inserted so the small end could be seen. These ends were often gilded and looked like gold "paper filigree."

Indian, Roach, Plains, Deer Hair, Porcupine Quills, Yarn, 1910-25, 17 In.
$354

Austin Auction Gallery

Indian, Rug, Navajo, Ganado Storm Design, c.1925-40, 66 x 37 In.
$531

Austin Auction Gallery

Indian, Rug, Navajo, Pictorial Weaving, Woven, Woman, Laverne Begay, 1900s, 40 x 27 In.
$576

Cowan's Auctions

Indian, Sampler, Navajo, Germantown, Eye Dazzler, Red, Green, c.1900, 29 x 36 In.
$1,320

Cottone Auctions

Indian, Rug, Navajo, Hand Woven, Red, Black, Gray, Wool, 60 x 41 ½ In.
$266

Austin Auction Gallery

Indian, Sculpture, Jemez, Maiden Holding Jar, Signed On Hem Of Skirt, Kathleen Wall, 1900s, 17 In.
$960

Cowan's Auctions

Indian, Shirt, Ojibwe, Velvet, Black, Beaded, Flowers, Collar & Cuffs, Sleeves, c.1895-1915, 26 In.
$708

Austin Auction Gallery

Totem Pole, Northwest Coast, Walrus Ivory, Multicolor, Carved, Wood Base, 9 ½ In. .... *illus*	313
Tray, Pima, Basketry, Akimel O'Odham, Rolling Log, Woven, c.1910, 5 x 15 In.	207
Vase, Hopi, Migration Pattern, Eagle Tail, Multicolor, Leah Garcia Nampeyo, 1920s, 11 x 8 In.	448
Vase, Laguna Pueblo, Ceremonial Dancer, Multicolor, Carved, Jr.-N-Diane, 1996, 21 In.	63
Vase, Pueblo, Blackware, Black Matte Glaze, Glossy Symbols, Squat, M. Martinez, 6 x 7 In.	708
Vase, Pueblo, Pottery, Shawna Garcia Rustin, 5 In.	311
Vase, Shipibo, Red Ground, Flared Rim, Geometric, South America, 14 In. .... *illus*	63
Vase, Shipibo Conibo, Effigy, Mask, Geometric Design, Peru, 18 In.	472
Vase, Wedding, Santa Clara Pueblo, Black, Double Spouted, Signed, 8 x 6 ½ x 6 In.	281
Vase, Wedding, Santa Clara Pueblo, Geometric, Signed, Glenda Naranjo, 7 ½ x 6 ¾ In. *illus*	202
Vest, Plateau, Beaded, Hide, Blue, Leafy Design, c.1880-1900, 17 x 23 ½ In. .... *illus*	944
Weaving, Navajo, Wide Ruins Runner, Woven, Green, Pink, Teal, Marie Begay, 1950s, 76 x 31 In. *illus*	320

INDIAN TREE

Indian Tree is a china pattern that was popular during the last half of the nineteenth century. It was copied from earlier Indian textile patterns that were very similar. The pattern includes the crooked branch of a tree and a partial landscape with exotic flowers and leaves. Green, blue, pink, and orange were the favored colors used in the design. Coalport, Spode, Johnson Brothers, and other firms made this pottery. Don't be confused by a pattern called India Tree made by Copeland.

Cup & Saucer, Pink Ground, Gold Enamel, Griffin, Marked, Aynsley	70
Platter, Oval, White Ground, Black Rim, Minton, 20 ½ In. .... *illus*	107

INKSTAND

Inkstands were made to be placed on a desk. They held some type of container for ink, and possibly a sander, a pen tray, a pen, a holder for pounce, and even a candle to melt the sealing wax. Inkstands date to the eighteenth century and have been made of silver, copper, ceramics, and glass. Additional inkstands may be found in these and other related categories.

Bronze & Marble, Napoleon III Style, Eagle, Hinged Lid, Fluted Feet, 1900s, 11 x 15 x 8 In. ...*illus*	266
Bronze, Jade, Dragon Buckle, Removable, Rectangular, Hinged Lid, Chinese, 3 ½ x 5 x 2 In.	3835
Bronze, Pen Nib Box, 2 Glass Inkwells, Mounted, Wood Case, Footed, 7 x 18 ½ In. .... *illus*	284
Glass, Chandelier Shape, Lid, Emry Davis, O'Hara Glass Co., c.1888, 4 ¼ In.	117
Porcelain, Gilt Bronze Mounted, Shell Shaped Tray, 3 Wells, Paris, 1800s, 12 x 7 In.	313
Porcelain, Limoges, Flowers, Victorian Dip Pen, Painted, Signed, 1906, 6 ½ x 10 In.	52
Rosewood, French Empire Style, Dolphin, Shell, Candleholders, Drawers, Footed, 5 ½ x 11 In.	127
Stoneware, Brushed Cobalt Blue, Ink Fountain, Beaded, Salt Glaze, Round, 1830s, 2 ¾ In.	497

INKWELL

Inkwells, of course, held ink. Ready-made ink was first made about 1836 and was sold in bottles. The desk inkwell had a narrow hole so the pen would not slip inside. Inkwells were made of many materials, such as pottery, glass, pewter, and silver.

Brass, Arts & Crafts, Hammered, c.1900, 3 x 8 ½ In.	240
Brass, Shell Shape, Lid, Glass Insert, 2 Penholders, Stone Stepped Base, Late 1800s, 4 x 5 In.	177
Bronze, Bust, Pen Wipe Lid, Bacchanalian, Claw Feet, F. Barbedienne, 11 ¾ x 19 In.	1890
Bronze, Dog, Seated, Holding Bag, 4 Puppies Inside, Black & Brown, Painted, 4 ½ In.	567
Bronze, Old Man, Animal Head, The Vanishing Race, Footed, Signed, Charles Plein, 7 x 8 In.	813
Bronze, Urn, Lid, Embossed Fruit, Lion's Head Handles, Pedestal Base, 4 ¼ x 4 In.	175
Cameo Glass, Gorham Silver Mounted Lid, White Flowers, Gold Ground, c.1887, 5 ¾ In.	1250
Cast Iron, Lid, Owl, Glass Eyes & Bottle, Victorian, 6 ½ In.	209
Champleve, Enamel Encrier, Tray, Handles, Pen Rest, Late 1800s, 4 x 11 x 7 In.	295
Copper, Hammered, Double, Riveted Trim & Hinges, Glass Inserts, Arts & Crafts, 3 x 11 In. *illus*	504
Copper, Hammered, Lid, Glass, Stamped Mark, G. Stickley, 2 ⅜ x 5 ⅝ In.	438
Cut Glass, Cane Pattern Base, Silver Flip Lid, Monogram & Crown, 4 ½ x 4 In.	80

Indian, Totem Pole, Northwest Coast, Walrus Ivory, Multicolor, Carved, Wood Base, 9 ½ In.
$313

Eldred's

Indian, Vase, Shipibo, Red Ground, Flared Rim, Geometric, South America, 14 In.
$63

Pook & Pook

Indian, Vase, Wedding, Santa Clara Pueblo, Geometric, Signed, Glenda Naranjo, 7 ½ x 6 ¾ In.
$202

Blackwell Auctions

Indian, Vest, Plateau, Beaded, Hide, Blue, Leafy Design, c.1880-1900, 17 x 23 ½ In.

$944

Austin Auction Gallery

TIP

Store vintage textiles flat or roll them. Don't fold. It makes creases.

Indian, Weaving, Navajo, Wide Ruins Runner, Woven, Green, Pink, Teal, Marie Begay, 1950s, 76 x 31 In.

$320

Cowan's Auctions

Gilt Bronze, Boulle, French Empire, Glass, Classical Figures, 6 x 4 ½ x 4 In.	406
Gilt Metal, Encrier, Hinged Lid, 2 Porcelain Parakeets, Desk Stand, Late 1800s, 11 ½ x 14 In.	649
Glass, Daisy & Button High Backed Chair, Amber, Canton Glass Co., Late 1800s, 3 ½ In.	117
Glass, Olive Green, 3-Piece Mold, New Hampshire, Early 1800s, 1 ¾ In.	281
Glass, Silver Lid, Panels, Etched Flowers, Love Dreams Pattern, Unger Bros., 1900s, 5 In.	185
Glass, Umbrella, 12-Sided, Aquamarine, Folded Mouth, Pontil, J.S. Dunham, c.1850, 2 In.	410
Metal, Race Car, 2 Drivers, Silvered, Signed, Wilhelm Zwick, Germany, 1900s, 6 x 15 In. *illus*	1512
Metalwork, Lily Pad Style, Painted, Germany, Art Nouveau, 6 x 4 ½ In.	58
Porcelain, Enamel, Molded, Shells, Cushion Shape Base, c.1820, 5 x 5 In.	293
Porcelain, Hinged Lid, Cherubs Scene, Gold & Blue Filigree, Gilt Bronze, Footed, 4 ¾ In.	315
Pressed Glass, Lid, Early Thumbprint, Hinged Brass Mount, Rays On Base, 1860s, 3 x 3 In. *illus*	117
Silver Mounted, Hinged Lid, Mahogany Base, Ball Feet, John Grinsell & Sons, 1910, 7 In.	200
Silver Plate, Figural, Woman, Art Nouveau, Shaped Dish, Relief Lily Tendril, WMF, c.1906 *..illus*	288
Silver, Cobalt Blue Insert, Clock, White Face, Roman Numeral Dial, Round, 3 ½ x 6 In.	214
Stoneware, White Slip, Cobalt Blue Design, 4-Footed, Earthenware, Billy Ray Hussey, 5 ⅛ In.	354
Wood, Dog, Black Forest, Seated, Carved, Hinged Head, 6 ¾ x 10 In.	531

INSULATOR

Insulators of glass or pottery have been made for use on telegraph or telephone poles since 1844. Billions of insulators in hundreds of styles have been made. Most common glass insulators are clear or aqua; the most common porcelain ones are chocolate brown. The most desirable are the threadless types made from 1850 to 1870. Collectors identify insulators by their shape. Glass insulators are identified by their CD (Consolidated Design) numbers and porcelain insulators by their U (Unipart) numbers. Information about these numbering systems can be found online.

CD 22, Battery Rest, Cobalt Blue, 1 ¼ x 2 ¼ In.	176
CD 155, Telecom, Double Petticoat, Straw, Colombia, 3 ⅞ x 3 ⅝ In.	16
CD 162, Hemingray, 19, Signal, Deep Groove, Double Petticoat, True Yellow, 3 ⅞ x 3 ¼ In. *illus*	7150
CD 254, Hemingray, No. 3 Cable, Bright Aqua, 5 ¾ x 4 ¼ In.	77
Thomas, Porcelain, Dry Process, Brown, Speckled, 3 ⅜ x 3 ¼ In.	12
U-320, Ohio Brass, Porcelain, Embossed O & B, Cobalt Blue, 3 ½ x 3 ¼ In.	12
U-1690, Porcelain, Brick Red, Poland, 3 ⅞ x 2 ¾ In. *illus*	105
Willington Glass Works, Inverted Cone Shape, 8-Sided, Threaded Shaft, Deep Olive, c.1870, 5 ¾ In.	805

IRISH BELLEEK, *see Belleek category.*

IRON

Iron is a metal that has been used by man since prehistoric times. It is a popular metal for tools and decorative items like doorstops that need as much weight as possible. Items are listed here or under other appropriate headings, such as Bookends, Doorstop, Kitchen, Match Holder, or Tool. The tool that is used for ironing clothes, an iron, is listed in the Kitchen category under Iron and Sadiron.

Bill Clip, Lady Liberty Head, Painted, 3 ½ In.	400
Birdhouse, Windows, Finial, Red Paint, 3 Pegs On Bottom, Early 1900s, 9 x 12 x 18 In. *illus*	780
Boot Scraper, Dachshund, Painted, Black, Mid 1900s, 8 x 22 In. *illus*	236
Boot Scraper, Dachshund, Standing, Painted, Black, Mid 1900s, 7 ½ x 20 In.	118
Boot Scraper, Duck Shape, Painted, Mounted, Cast Iron, Wood Base, 10 ¾ In.	37
Boot Scraper, Duck, Painted, Inset Eyes, Applied Brush, c.1950, 6 x 16 x 8 In.	266
Boot Scraper, Figural, Duck, Molded Body, Feather Detail, Scraping Blade, 17 ½ In.	345
Boot Scraper, Griffin Terminals, Fluted Pan, 4-Footed, Black, 7 x 9 ½ x 11 ½ In.	127
Boot Scraper, H-Shape, Curl Post Finial, Wrought, Limestone Block, 1800s, 5 In. *illus*	1169
Boot Scraper, Rooster, Standing, Square Base, Cast Iron, 12 x 10 In.	106
Boot Scraper, Scroll Forged Supports, Wrought, 1800s, 9 ½ x 12 ½ In.	250
Boot Scraper, Scroll, Black, Iron, Square Marble Base, 13 x 13 In.	463
Boot Scraper, Semicircular, Scrolled Ends, Inclined Granite Base, c.1820, 9 ¾ x 8 x 9 In.	438
Bootjack, Heart Cutout, Cast, Embossed, 1800, 13 In.	150
Bootjack, Naughty Nellie, Woman Lying Down, Legs Spread, 11 In. *illus*	55

I

Indian Tree, Platter, Oval, White Ground, Black Rim, Minton, 20½ In.
$107

Strawser Auction Group

Inkstand, Bronze & Marble, Napoleon III Style, Eagle, Hinged Lid, Fluted Feet, 1900s, 11 x 15 x 8 In.
$266

Leland Little Auctions

Inkstand, Bronze, Pen Nib Box, 2 Glass Inkwells, Mounted, Wood Case, Footed, 7 x 18½ In.
$284

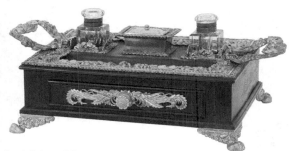

Fontaine's Auction Gallery

Inkwell, Copper, Hammered, Double, Riveted Trim & Hinges, Glass Inserts, Arts & Crafts, 3 x 11 In.
$504

Fontaine's Auction Gallery

Inkwell, Metal, Race Car, 2 Drivers, Silvered, Signed, Wilhelm Zwick, Germany, 1900s, 6 x 15 In.
$1,512

Fontaine's Auction Gallery

Inkwell, Pressed Glass, Lid, Early Thumbprint, Hinged Brass Mount, Rays On Base, 1860s, 3 x 3 In.
$117

Jeffrey S. Evans & Associates

Inkwell, Silver Plate, Figural, Woman, Art Nouveau, Shaped Dish, Relief Lily Tendril, WMF, c.1906
$288

Morphy Auctions

I

275

IRON

Insulator, CD 162, Hemingray, 19, Signal, Deep Groove, Double Petticoat, True Yellow, 3 ⅞ x 3 ¼ In.
$7,150

Bill and Jill Insulators

Insulator, U-1690, Porcelain, Brick Red, Poland, 3 ⅞ x 2 ¾ In.
$105

Bill and Jill Insulators

Iron, Birdhouse, Windows, Finial, Red Paint, 3 Pegs On Bottom, Early 1900s, 9 x 12 x 18 In.
$780

Morphy Auctions

Iron, Boot Scraper, Dachshund, Painted, Black, Mid 1900s, 8 x 22 In.
$236

Leland Little Auctions

New or Old Iron

New cast-iron copies of old doorstops, toys, and other collectibles are not as well-made as originals. The parts of the old ones fit together with no empty space between joints. Old cast-iron pieces are held together with flat-head screws, not Phillips-head screws. Rust on old pieces is dark brown. Rust on new pieces is reddish brown. Old cast iron has a smooth surface; newer pieces are rough and slightly bumpy.

Iron, Boot Scraper, H-Shape, Curl Post Finial, Wrought, Limestone Block, 1800s, 5 In.
$1,169

Brunk Auctions

Iron, Bootjack, Naughty Nellie, Woman Lying Down, Legs Spread, 11 In.
$55

Hartzell's Auction Gallery Inc.

Iron, Censer, Archaic Style, Zoomorphic Handles, Taotie Mask Decor, Chinese, 1900s, 8 x 10 In.
$207

Leland Little Auctions

Iron, Cuspidor, Top Hat Shape, Porcelain Liner, Standard Mfg., Pittsburgh, Pa., Late 1800s, 7 In.
$438

Eldred's

Bust, Man, African American, Wearing Shirt, Collar, Cylindrical Base, 1800s, 8 ½ x 3 ½ In..	1356
Cannon, Signal, Wood Wheels, Kilgore Manufacturing Co., c.1900, 8 x 18 In.	540
Censer, Archaic Style, Zoomorphic Handles, Taotie Mask Decor, Chinese, 1900s, 8 x 10 In. ..*illus*	207
Coffin, Child's, Sarcophagus Form, Molded Decoration, Glass Window At Head, Victorian, 9 x 55 In....	11250
Cross, Black, Mary, Vineyard, Monogram, France, 1800s, 63 In.	240
Cross, Crucifix, Virgin Mary & Saint John, Patina, Pierced, Leaves Design, Late 1800s, 78 In..	1652
Cross, Virgin Mary, Saint John, Mourning, Patina, Pierced, Leaves, Late 1800s, 80 ½ In.	1121
Crucifix, Wrought, Mounted, Church Steeple, Turned Wood Stand, 1900s, 27 x 11 ½ In	230
Cuspidor, Hat Shape, Zanesville Wine Co., 1800s, 6 ½ x 10 ½ In.	360
Cuspidor, Top Hat Shape, Porcelain Liner, Standard Mfg., Pittsburgh, Pa., Late 1800s, 7 In. *illus*	438
Cuspidor, Turtle, Mechanical Shell, Marked, Golden Novelty Co., Late 1800s, 4 x 13 ½ In.....	113
Dispenser, Cigarette, Elephant, Turned Trunk, Painted, Red .... *illus*	113
Door Mat, Folk Art, Heart Shape, Late 1800s, 24 x 15 In., Pair	439
Figure, Wall, Fox Head, Painted, Hanging Hook, 4 ½ In.	74
Gate, Hammered, Arched, Leaf Top, Stylized Flower Openwork, 70 x 58 In.	630
Heater, Water, Pierced, Patina, Tapered Legs, Lawson, Early 1900s, 13 ½ In.	106
Hopper, Rainwater, Gothic Revival, Parcel Gilt, Painted, Cross & Trefoil, Late 1800s, 21 In	236
Horse Bit, Scrolled Accents, Black, Metal Stand, Spanish Colonial, 1800s, 11 ¼ x 5 In	118
Lamp, Art Nouveau Style, Acanthus Leaves, Stained Glass, Circular Base, 1900s, 50 x 20 In..	590
Lamp, Coffee Mill Base, Brass, 2-Light, Enterprise Mfg. Co., Late 1800s, 29 ½ In., Pair	472
Mask, Neoclassical Style, Woman's Face, Engraved, Stand, 28 In.	375
Pitcher, Pump Shape, Green Paint, Marked, Hancock Gross, Philadelphia, 16 In.	98
Plaque, Bulldog, White, Red, Black Rim, Round, Holes For Hanging, 9 ½ In.	92
Plaque, Dog, Black, Rescue Cup, Chain, Wood, Hanging, 25 In.	35
Pot, Flared Rim, Domed Bottom, Louisiana, 1800s, 21 x 43 ½ In. .... *illus*	1586
Safe, Floor, Black Paint, Hinged Door, Bail Handles, Wheel Feet, Late 1800s, 29 x 22 x 20 In. *illus*	708
Safe, Marvin, Victorian, Boudoir, 3 Shelves, 2 Drawers, Stand, c.1870, 49 ¾ x 14 x 14 In......	9225
Sculpture, 3 Horses & Man, Sitting, Driver, Evgeny Ivanovich Naps, Russia, 10 ½ x 11 ½ In...*illus*	219
Sculpture, Abstract, Welded, Walnut Slab Base, Painted, 38 x 10 ½ x 8 In.	354
Sculpture, Dog, Dalmatian, Standing, Brown, White, 30 In.	6000
Sculpture, Dog, Whippet, Reclining, Black, Seated, 17 ½ In., Pair	2476
Sculpture, Mother Horse, Foal, Standing, Natural Ground Base, 12 x 15 In.	504
Sculpture, Peacock, Painted, Curved Tail, 1960, 15 In.	443
Stand, Flag, Oval Base, American Eagle & Stars, Threaded Bolt, 1900s, 15 In.	188
Taper Jack, Heart Shape Holder, Tripod Legs, Wrought, Late 1700s, 9 ½ In.	450
Target, Shooting Gallery, 12 Lollipops, Yellow Paint, Rotates, W. Mangels, 31 In. ....*illus*	6215
Target, Shooting Gallery, Clown Face, Old Paint, Lightbulbs In Eyes, W. Mangels, 26 In. *illus*	36160
Target, Shooting Gallery, Crocodile's Head, Paint, Bull's-Eye Gong, W. Mangels, 33 In. *illus*	22600
Target, Shooting Gallery, Indian Princess, War Bonnet, Signed, C.W. Parker, 1910, 13 x 4 In....	4068
Target, Shooting Gallery, Man In The Moon, Old White Paint, H.C. Evans, c.1920, 15 In. *illus*	16950
Target, Shooting Gallery, Owl, Old Paint, Bull's-Eye Center, Wings Flap, C.W. Parker, 1911, 16 In. *illus*	16950
Target, Shooting Gallery, Pierrot Clown, Silhouette, Red Paint, Germany, c.1930, 12 x 6 In.	961
Target, Shooting Gallery, Rooster, Painted, Bull's Eye, Spring Loaded Star, 13 In. ....*illus*	11300
Target, Shooting Gallery, Shorty, Cowboy, Old Paint, W. Mangels, c.1900, 53 x 28 In. ...*illus*	33900
Target, Shooting Gallery, Turkey, Bull's-Eye, Signed, Wurfflein Philad, c.1900, 11 x 22 ½ In. .*illus*	1582
Tractor Seat, Ornate, Black Paint, Metal, Champion, 18 x 14 In. ....*illus*	74
Windmill Weight, Bull, Boss, Red Lettering, Black, Dempster, Wood Base, 12 ¼ In.	1098
Windmill Weight, Chicken, Elgin, Mounted, Wood Base, 23 In.	519
Windmill Weight, Crescent Moon, Eclipse, Rusted Surface, 10 ½ In.	270
Windmill Weight, Eclipse, Crescent Moon, Wood Stand, 14 In.	671
Windmill Weight, Rooster, Elgin Nichols Mill, c.1890, 19 ½ x 18 x 7 ¾ In.	2260
Windmill Weight, Rooster, Hummer, Wood Base, Elgin Wind Power & Pump Co., c.1900, 13 In. *illus*	600
Windmill Weight, Spear, Round Base, Challenge Co., Batavia, 32 In.	305

IRONSTONE

Ironstone china was first made in 1813. It gained its greatest popularity during the mid-nineteenth century. The heavy, durable, off-white pottery was made in white or was decorated with any of hundreds of patterns. Much flow blue pottery was made of ironstone. Some of the decorations were raised. Many pieces of ironstone are unmarked, but some English and American factories included the word *Ironstone* in their marks.

Iron, Dispenser, Cigarette, Elephant, Turned Trunk, Painted, Red
$113

Bruneau & Co. Auctioneers

Iron, Pot, Flared Rim, Domed Bottom, Louisiana, 1800s, 21 x 43 ½ In.
$1,586

Neal Auction Company

Iron, Safe, Floor, Black Paint, Hinged Door, Bail Handles, Wheel Feet, Late 1800s, 29 x 22 x 20 In.
$708

Leland Little Auctions

Iron, Sculpture, 3 Horses & Man, Sitting, Driver, Evgeny Ivanovich Naps, Russia, 10 ½ x 11 ½ In.
$219

Abington Auction Gallery

Iron, Target, Shooting Gallery, 12 Lollipops, Yellow Paint, Rotates, W. Mangels, 31 In.
$6,215

Soulis Auctions

Iron, Target, Shooting Gallery, Clown Face, Old Paint, Lightbulbs In Eyes, W. Mangels, 26 In.
$36,160

Soulis Auctions

Iron, Target, Shooting Gallery, Crocodile's Head, Paint, Bull's-Eye Gong, W. Mangels, 33 In.
$22,600

Soulis Auctions

TIP

Ivory should never be washed. Collectors like the off-white color that comes with age.

Additional pieces may be listed in other categories, such as Chelsea Grape, Chelsea Sprig, Flow Blue, Gaudy Ironstone, Mason's Ironstone, Moss Rose, Staffordshire, and Tea Leaf Ironstone. These three marks were used by companies that made ironstone.

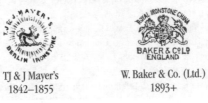

| TJ & J Mayer's | W. Baker & Co. (Ltd.) | Wood & Son(s) (Ltd.) |
| 1842–1855 | 1893+ | 1910+ |

Flask, Circular, Strap Loops, Spout With Cork, GAR Medal, Embossed, Painted, Cavalry, 7¾ In.	938
Footbath, Banded Design, Crackle White Ground, 2 Handles, Late 1800s, 7¾ x 18 In.	1003
Platter, Elongated Octagonal Shape, Stick Spatter, Sprig, England, 1860s, 11½ x 15 In. *illus*	230

 ISPANKY

Ispanky figurines were designed by Laszlo Ispanky, who began his American career as a designer for Cybis Porcelains. He was born in Hungary and came to the United States in 1956. In 1966 he went into business with George Utley in Trenton, New Jersey. Ispanky made limited edition figurines marked with his name and *Utley Porcelain Ltd.* The company became Ispanky Porcelains Ltd. in 1968 and moved to Pennington, New Jersey. Ispanky worked for Goebel of North America beginning in 1976. He worked in stone, wood, or metal, as well as porcelain. He died in 2010.

Bust, Young Woman, Gray Veil, Pink Flowers At Neckline, 12 In.	50
Figurine, Excalibur, Young Man, Medieval Dress, Book On Stand, Green Draping, 1970s, 12 In.	213
Figurine, King Arthur & Guinevere, Round Base, Goebel, 11 In., Pair	120
Figurine, Spirit Of The Sea, Kneeling Woman, Green Drape, Blond, Shell Shape Base, 13 In.	40
Group, Mallard Drake & Hen, Wood Base, American Wildlife Creation, 1980s, 9 x 13½ In. *illus*	113
Group, Seminude Man & Woman, Round Base, Heart Border, 12½ In.	120

 IVORY

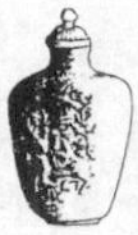

Ivory from the tusk of an elephant is thought by many to be the only true ivory. To most collectors, the term *ivory* also includes such natural materials as walrus, hippopotamus, or whale teeth or tusks, and some of the vegetable materials that are of similar texture and density. Other ivory items may be found in the Scrimshaw and Netsuke categories. Collectors should be aware of the recent laws limiting the buying and selling of elephant ivory and scrimshaw.

Censer, Lid, Deer, Tree, Chinese, Late 1800s, 5 In.	150
Cigar Cutter, Walrus Tusk Handle, Silver Mounted, Spring Shank, Marked, Pfeirling, 8 x 2 x 1 In.	819
Dipper, Coconut Shell, Bowl Mount, Wood Handle, Engraved, H.I.V., 1878, 14½ In. *illus*	531
Figurine, Carpenter, Holding Drawer Frame, Inscribe, Ich Saubres Bild, 1800s, 12 x 4 In.	1112
Figurine, Man, Seated, Wood, Whale Ivory Head & Hands, Hands Crossed, 1800s, 8¼ In.	1125
Figurine, Snake Shape, Inset Eyes, Baleen, Metal Stand, c.1850, 4½ In.	1250
Figurine, Village Scene, Trees, Temples, Glass Case, c.1950, 11½ x 18 x 4½ In. *illus*	5228
Figurine, Woman, Holding A Flower, Hand Mirror, Standing, Wood Stand, Chinese, 1800s, 12 In.	375
Group, Buddha, Laughing, Standing, 6 Children, Carved, 1644-1911, Chinese, 7½ In. *illus*	540
Group, Young Children, Riding Wave, Fish, Chinese, Early 1900s, 5¼ In.	540
Page Turner, Baleen, Handle, Carved, Lady's Leg & Boot, Engraved, T, 1800s, 10½ In.	531
Pendant, Dragon & Phoenix, Entangled, Carved, Mounted, Silver, Chinese, Late 1800s, 3 In.	63
Pie Crimper, Ring In Hand, Carved, Elliptical Shaft, Scrolled Yoke, Fluted Wheel, c.1850	3750
Pie Crimper, Walrus Tusk, 3-Tined Fork, Curved Handle, Maine, 9½ In.	351
Triptych, Egg Shape, Carved, Life Of Christ, Brass Hinges, Top Loop, 1600s, 2⅛ In.	819
Tusk, Carved, Painted, Figural Scene, Signed, Late 1900s, Pair	1134
Urn, Lid, Carved, Dragons, Foo Dog, Ring Handles, Signed, c.1950, 12 x 12½ x 4 In. *illus*	1890
Wax Seal, Terminal, Carved, Clenched Left Fist, Turned Stem, 1800s, 3 In. *illus*	250

Iron, Target, Shooting Gallery, Man In The Moon, Old White Paint, H.C. Evans, c.1920, 15 In.
$16,950

Soulis Auctions

Iron, Target, Shooting Gallery, Owl, Old Paint, Bull's-Eye Center, Wings Flap, C.W. Parker, 1911, 16 In.
$16,950

Soulis Auctions

Iron, Target, Shooting Gallery, Rooster, Painted, Bull's Eye, Spring Loaded Star, 13 In.
$11,300

Soulis Auctions

Iron, Target, Shooting Gallery, Shorty, Cowboy, Old Paint, W. Mangels, c.1900, 53 x 28 In.
$33,900

Soulis Auctions

Iron, Target, Shooting Gallery, Turkey, Bull's-Eye, Signed, Wurfflein Philad, c.1900, 11 x 22½ In.
$1,582

Soulis Auctions

Iron, Tractor Seat, Ornate, Black Paint, Metal, Champion, 18 x 14 In.
$74

Hartzell's Auction Gallery Inc.

Iron, Windmill Weight, Rooster, Hummer, Wood Base, Elgin Wind Power & Pump Co., c.1900, 13 In.
$600

Garth's Auctioneers & Appraisers

Ironstone, Platter, Elongated Octagonal Shape, Stick Spatter, Sprig, England, 1860s, 11½ x 15 In.
$230

Garth's Auctioneers & Appraisers

Ispanky, Group, Mallard Drake & Hen, Wood Base, American Wildlife Creation, 1980s, 9 x 13½ In.
$113

Lion and Unicorn

Ivory, Dipper, Coconut Shell, Bowl Mount, Wood Handle, Engraved, H.I.V., 1878, 14 ½ In.
$531

Eldred's

Ivory, Figurine, Village Scene, Trees, Temples, Glass Case, c.1950, 11 ½ x 18 x 4 ½ In.
$5,228

Morphy Auctions

TIP
Ivory expands and contracts in heat and cold, so it can crack or craze if the temperature and humidity do not remain moderate.

Ivory, Group, Buddha, Laughing, Standing, 6 Children, Carved, 1644-1911, Chinese, 7 ½ In.
$540

Selkirk Auctioneers & Appraisers

J.P. JACOB PETIT

Jacob Petit (1796–1868) was a porcelain painter who worked for the Sevres factory in France. He opened his own shop near Paris sometime after 1830 and took over a nearby factory in about 1834. The factory made ornamental vases, statues, clocks, inkwells, and perfume bottles. A specialty were figural veilleuses shaped like sultans or fortune tellers. These were meant for use in the bedroom. He used the cobalt blue initials *J.P.* as his mark, but many of his pieces were not marked. His customers wanted "antique" style china, so he made copies of Sevres vases, Meissen figurines, many patterns of English dinnerware, Chinese export porcelain, and more. Petit sold his factory to one of his employees in 1862, but he continued to work in Paris until 1866.

Ewer, Snowball Body, Encrusted Flowers, Gilt Framed Jewels, J.P., c.1850, 16 In., Pair .. *illus*	2000
Figurine, Leopard, Lying Down, Spotted Tawny Coat, Green Grass Base, Marked, 2 ¾ In.......	153
Perfume Bottle, Crown Shape, Encrusted Flowers, Gilt, Cross Shape Stopper, c.1850, 9 x 7 In. *illus*	2500
Vase, Spill, Robinson Crusoe & Friday, Standing, Signed J.P., c.1835, 11 In., Pair.....................	8745

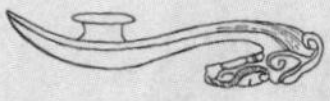

JADE

Jade is the name for two different minerals, nephrite and jadeite. Nephrite is the mineral used for most early Oriental carvings. Jade is a very tough stone that is found in many colors from dark green to pale lavender. Jade carvings are still being made in the old styles, so collectors must be careful not to be fooled by recent pieces. Jade jewelry is found in this book under Jewelry.

Box, Spinach Jade, Dragon Lid, Lobed, Mythical Beast Handles, 4 Short Legs, 1900s, 6 x 6 x 3 In.	448
Brush Washer, White, Carved, Wood Stand, 1 x 6 ¼ x 3 ½ In.	219
Figure, Horse, Nephrite, Marbled Tan, Brown, Black Streaks, Chinese, 6 ¾ x 8 In...................	207
Figurine, 2 Dogs, Lying Down, Mottled Celadon Stone, Carved Wood Stand, 11 x 3 x 2 In......	585
Figurine, Buddha, Seated, Carved, Celadon, Hardwood Stand, Chinese, 3 x 5 x 3 In..............	154
Figurine, Frog, Carved, Specimen, Signed, Georg O. Wild, Germany, 1894, 1 In. .... *illus*	375
Figurine, Hippopotamus, Specimen, Ruby Eyes, Georg O. Wild, 1894, 1 ¾ x 5 ½ In. .... *illus*	1250
Figurine, Mystical Phoenix, Celadon, Russet Tones, Flowering Sprig, Chinese, 2 x 2 ½ In.....	10000
Figurine, Mythological Bird, Variegated, Green, Red Wood Base, Carved, 5 x 6 x 3 In.	201
Figurine, Polar Bear, Walking, Carved, 4 ½ In...	240
Figurine, Woman, Holding Lotus Pod, Standing, Chinese, c.1950, 5 ½ In...............................	75
Group, Carved, Figural, Folktale Characters, Child Climbing Water Buffalo, 5 x 6 In.............	2125
Incense Burner, Pierced Lid, Nephrite, Carved, Stylized Dragon Handles, Late 1900s, 14 x 12 In.	43
Mirror, Dragon, Belt Hook Handle, Silver Mounted, Chinese, Late 1800s, 9 In. .... *illus*	270
Pendant, Ornament, Carved, 2 Dragons, Scrolled Designs, Chinese, 2 ⅝ In..........................	1003
Pendant, White, Round, Carved, Chilong & Lingzhi, 1800s, 2 ¼ In.	2730
Plaque, White, Birds, Baskets, Fruits, Carved, 12 x 12 In..	242
Table Screen, Hardwood, Carved, Plaque, Boat, Fretwork Designs, Chinese, 10 x 8 ⅜ In. *illus*	2006
Tea Bowl, Translucent Hardstone, Celadon Green, Underfoot, 1900s, 4 In.............................	266

JAPANESE WOODBLOCK PRINTS *are listed in this book in the Print category under Japanese.*

JASPERWARE

Jasperware can be made in different ways. Some pieces are made from a solid-colored clay with applied raised designs of a contrasting colored clay. Other pieces are made entirely of one color clay with raised decorations that are glazed with a contrasting color. Additional pieces of jasperware may also be listed in the Wedgwood category or under various art potteries.

Cake Plate, Dome Lid, Knot Shape Finial, Light Brown, Leaves, Marked, GP, England, 12 In. .	180
Cheese Dish, Lid, Blue, White, Acorn Finial, England, Dudson Brothers, 1800s, 10 ½ In. *illus*	469
Pitcher, Football Scene, Red Brown Ground, Grassy Borders, Copeland Spode, 6 x 4 In........	90

JASPERWARE

Ivory, Urn, Lid, Carved, Dragons, Foo Dog, Ring Handles, Signed, c.1950, 12 x 12 ½ x 4 In.
$1,890

Morphy Auctions

Ivory, Wax Seal, Terminal, Carved, Clenched Left Fist, Turned Stem, 1800s, 3 In.
$250

Eldred's

TIP
You can tell a piece of jade by the feel. It will be cold, even in warm weather.

Jacob Petit, Ewer, Snowball Body, Encrusted Flowers, Gilt Framed Jewels, J.P., c.1850, 16 In., Pair
$2,000

New Orleans Auction Galleries

Jacob Petit, Perfume Bottle, Crown Shape, Encrusted Flowers, Gilt, Cross Shape Stopper, c.1850, 9 x 7 In.
$2,500

New Orleans Auction Galleries

Jade, Figurine, Frog, Carved, Specimen, Signed, Georg O. Wild, Germany, 1894, 1 In.
$375

Charlton Hall Auctions

Jade, Figurine, Hippopotamus, Specimen, Ruby Eyes, Georg O. Wild, 1894, 1 ¾ x 5 ½ In.
$1,250

Charlton Hall Auctions

Jade, Mirror, Dragon, Belt Hook Handle, Silver Mounted, Chinese, Late 1800s, 9 In.
$270

Selkirk Auctioneers & Appraisers

281

Jade, Table Screen, Hardwood, Carved, Plaque, Boat, Fretwork Designs, Chinese, 10 x 8⅜ In.
$2,006

Austin Auction Gallery

Jasperware, Cheese Dish, Lid, Blue, White, Acorn Finial, England, Dudson Brothers, 1800s, 10½ In.
$469

Eldred's

Jewelry, Bracelet, Bakelite, Bangle, Yellow, Citrine Studs, 18K Gold Mounts, Mark Davis, 2½ In.
$1,375

Rago Arts and Auction Center

> **TIP**
> *Wear your old jewelry, especially the pieces that look old. You will be surprised how many will ask about it.*

JEWELRY

Jewelry, whether made from gold and precious gems or plastic and colored glass, is popular with collectors. Values are determined by the intrinsic value of the stones and metal and by the skill and fame of the craftsmen and designers. Although costume jewelry has been made since the 17th century, it became fashionable in the 1920s. Victorian and older jewelry has been collected since the 1950s. Edwardian and Art Deco jewelry were copied in the first half of the 1900s, then Modernist jewelry designs appeared. Bakelite jewelry was a fad from the 1930s to the 1990s. Copies of almost all styles are being made. American Indian jewelry is listed in the Indian category in this book. Tiffany jewelry is listed here.

Bracelet, 12 Rectangular Panels, Reticulated, Red Enamel, David Andersen, 7 In.	85
Bracelet, Bakelite, Bangle, Orange Juice, Clear Orange, Domed, Art Deco, c.1930, 2½ x ⅞ In.	250
Bracelet, Bakelite, Bangle, Yellow, Citrine Studs, 18K Gold Mounts, Mark Davis, 2½ In. *illus*	1375
Bracelet, Bangle, 6 Dangling Openwork Ball Charms, Nina Ricci, 7 In.	88
Bracelet, Bangle, Clic Clac, Hinged, H-Clasp, Steel, Enamel Band, Marked, Hermes K, 7 In.	366
Bracelet, Bangle, Hinged, 18K Gold, Spaced Diamonds & Emeralds, Cartier, 6 In.	2750
Bracelet, Bangle, Hinged, Modernist, Textured 14K Gold, 5 Sapphires, Ed Weiner, 6 In. Wide	2318
Bracelet, Bangle, Petate, Silver, 3 Hinged Textured Ovals, Shaped Ends, Spratling, 7 In.	1386
Bracelet, Bangle, Thin Mirror, Curled Band, Hammered 18K Gold, U. & M. Kaufmann, 8 In.	3750
Bracelet, Cuff, Goldtone, Inset Multicolor Gripoix Stones, Chanel, 2¼ In. Wide *illus*	1440
Bracelet, Cuff, Hinged, Mammoth Tusk, 5 Inset Citrines, 18K Gold, Seaman Schepps, 6½ In. *illus*	4688
Bracelet, Cuff, Poured Glass Stones, Green, Red, Blue, Amber, Gold Metal, Chanel, 6 x 2 In.	2125
Bracelet, Cuff, River Of Life, Silver, Flowing Form, W. Spratling, c.1940, 6 x 1½ In.	500
Bracelet, Cuff, Wire, Diamante, Rhinestones, Faceted Crystals, Fred Block, 2½ In. Wide *illus*	175
Bracelet, Happy Diamond, 18K Yellow Gold, Attached Heart, Chopard, 7 x 17 In.	2375
Bracelet, Link, Alternating Textured & Polished Rectangles, 18K Gold, Uno A Erre, 7 In.	3024
Bracelet, Modernist, 5 Goldtone Panels, Applied Balls, Sidney Carron, 7 In.	113
Bracelet, Modernist, Bangle, Silver, Textured Square, Tiger-Eye Cabochon, 2¼ In. Wide	100
Bracelet, Modernist, Cuff, Oxidized Silver, Opal & Yellow Metal Discs, Thor Selzer, 6¼ In. *illus*	500
Bracelet, Modernist, Silver, Openwork, Tiger-Eye Cabochon Ends, D. S. Denmark, 2 In. Wide.	100
Bracelet, Pearls Alternating With 14K Textured Gold Tubes, Lucien Piccard, 7½ In. *illus*	1000
Bracelet, Red Vase Design, Enamel, Marked, Hermes, Austria, 2½ In.	4578
Chatelaine, Victorian Style, Pinchbeck, Brass, Embossed, 5 Drops, 10 In. *illus*	338
Clip, Dress, Bakelite, Green, Translucent, Door Knocker Shape, Round, 2 x 1¾ In.	15
Clip, Dress, Diamonds, Openwork Mount, 14K White Gold, Scalloped Ends, Edwardian, 3 In., Pair	6875
Clip, Dress, Multicolored Rhinestones, Beads, Eisenberg Originals, 1930s, 3 In. *illus*	625
Cuff Links, Gemstones, Clear, Red & Orange, Pillow Shape, 18K Gold, Links, Trianon, ½ In. *illus*	610
Cuff Links, Lapis Tablet, 8-Sided, 18K Gold & Onyx Border, Tiffany & Co., ¾ x ¾ In.	1200
Cuff Links, Round Plaque, 2 Raised Lion's Heads Roaring, 14K Gold, Art Nouveau, ⅝ In.	366
Earrings, Checkerboard, Lapis, 18K Gold, Pillow Form, Angela Cummings, Tiffany, ¾ In.	3438
Earrings, Citrine, Rectangular, Faceted, Prong Set, 18K Gold Wire Mount & Posts, Retro, ½ In.	480
Earrings, Fly Shape, Banded Agate, Goldtone Antenna & Legs, Victorian, c.1880, 1 In.	938
Earrings, Gray Pearl, Surrounded By 7 Citrines & Diamonds, Seaman Schepps, 1 In.	4063
Earrings, Koi, Sea Shimmer, Goldtone, Blue Rhinestone Eyes, Eliz. Taylor, Avon, 1994, 1 In.	156
Earrings, Lily Pad, Gilt Aluminum, Clip-On, JAR, Leather Pouch, 1¼ In.	5938
Earrings, Quartz Drop, Oval, Silver Stem & Stud, Georg Jensen, 2⅜ In. *illus*	300
Earrings, Seashell, Textured Goldtone, 3 Blue Stones, Clip-On, K. Matsumoto, Trifari, 1 In.	73
Earrings, Shell, White Iridescent, Rubies, Emeralds, 14K Gold Ropetwist, Clip-On, MAZ, 1 In.	1107
Earrings, Square, Onyx, 8 Inset Diamonds, Coral Center, 14K Gold, Clip-On, Trianon, 1 In.	2500
Hair Comb, Horn Prongs, Bezel Set Diamonds, Pierced Mount, Edwardian, 4¾ In.	3750
Hairpin, Bakelite, Tortoiseshell, Rhinestone Head, 1970s, 6 In.	48
Hairpin, Flower & Wheat Sprays, Gold, Topaz, Garnets, Enamel, Steel Pin, c.1820, 7 In.	8125
Hatpins are listed in this book in the Hatpin category.	
Locket, Mourning, Flower Basket, Blue Enamel, 3 Diamond Circles, Hair, Victorian, 1¼ In.	1586
Necklace & Earrings, Bead, Blue Iridescent Glass, 3 Strands, Clip-On Earrings, Laguna, 18 In.	42
Necklace & Earrings, Fruit Salad Beads, Plastic, Marked, Austria, c.1955, 17 In.	79
Necklace & Earrings, Knotted Strands, 14K Gold, Bailey, Banks & Biddle, 17 & 1½ In.	2750
Necklace & Earrings, Link, Balls, Textured Clay, Oxidized Silver, F. Forlano, 22 & 1 In.	1875

J

Necklace, 41 Silver Balls, Graduated Sizes, Sterling Silver, Taxco, Mexico, 20 In. .... *illus*	154
Necklace, Beads, 3 Strands, Green, 6 Gilt Roses, Glass Clusters, Miriam Haskell, 16¾ In. ..*illus*	1130
Necklace, Beads, Amber, Faceted, Various Shapes & Shading, 1920s, 56 In.	272
Necklace, Beads, Tanzanite, Graduated, 5 Strands, Silver Clasp, Tiffany & Co., 17 In.............	1715
Necklace, Collar, 3 Rounded Bands, Sterling Silver, Los Ballesteros, 17 In.................	393
Necklace, Collar, 11 Starfish, Graduated, Goldtone, Blue Stones, K. Matsumoto, Trifari, 17 In. ...	230
Necklace, Fleurettes, Small Etched Glass Flowers, Elongated Barrels, Silk Cord, Lalique, 20 In.....	850
Necklace, Flower Disc, 2 Textured Discs, 3 Coil Collars, 18K Gold, Niessing, 18 In.	3000
Necklace, Kragen, Gold Band, Tapered, Curled, 18K Textured Gold, U. & M. Kaufmann, 15 In....	6250
Necklace, Lariat, Opaque White Rhinestones, 7 Strands, Long Fringe, Trigere, 48 In. .. *illus*	88
Necklace, Link, Stylized Buds, Sterling Silver, Marked, Taxco, 16¼ In.	156
Necklace, Link, Teardrops, Sideways, Silver, Vermeil Rope Accents, Taxco, Mexico, 17¼ In..	150
Necklace, Magnifying Glass, Diamond Frame, Platinum Chain, Black, Starr & Frost, 1920s, 16 In.	2813
Necklace, Modernist, Oval Tiger Eye, Silver Bar Fringe, Kaunis Koru, Finland, 1972, 31 In.	225
Necklace, Pearls, 6 Mother-Of-Pearl Plaques, Gemstones, Silver Chain, Toggle, Konstantino, 35 In....	305
Necklace, Pearls, Graduated, Single Strand, 3 Entwined CC Logos, Chanel, 42 In.	397
Necklace, Pendant, Fan Shape, Enamel & Gold Inlaid Scrolls, Twist Collar, M. Frey, 17 In....	1125
Necklace, Pendant, Fish, Green Agate, 14K Gold, Diamond Eye, Chain, Marked, KUL, 21 In..	300
Necklace, Pendant, Moonstone, Silver Mount & Chain, Quatrefoil Spacers, Konstantino, 36 In..	519
Necklace, Pendant, Opal, Pear Shape, Diamonds, Gold Mount & Chain, Burle Marx, 1⅔ In..	1260
Necklace, Pendant, Peace Sign, Sterling Silver, Chain, Marked, Tiffany & Co., Box, 17 In.	230
Necklace, Pendant, Rhinestones, Blues, Oval Center, Link Chain, Schreiner, c.1960, 2 In...	281
Necklace, Pendant, Shoe, Platform Base, 18K Gold, Gemstone Stripes, Ferragamo, 1938, 31 In..	2806
Necklace, Pendant, Stylized Dragon, Silver, Abalone Inlay, Modernist, M.G. Martinez, 22 In...	118
Necklace, Talosel & Red Mirror Fringe, White Metal Wire, Line Vautrin, 15 In. .... *illus*	1250
Necklace, Techno-Pollen, Perforated Geometric Shapes, Polymer, Gold Leaf, K. Dustin, 23 In.	813
Pendant, Beating Hearts, 5 Open, Graduated Sizes, Gold Over Brass, Yaacov Agam, 3 In......	504
Pendant, Eye Of Time, Watch In Eyeball, Diamond Teardrop, S. Dali, Joies, 2003, Box, 2 In. *illus*	938
Pendant, Glass, Intaglio, Goddess At Altar, 18K Gold Frame, 12 Moonstones, E. Locke, 2 In..	2000
Pendant, Glass, Intaglio, Woman Standing, Gold, Moonstones, Rectangular, E. Locke, 1⅝ In..	1875
Pendant, Japanese Woman, Painted Glass, Faux Bamboo Rod Frame, Tiffany, c.1880, 2 In.	18750
Pendant, King Tut's Head, 18K Gold, Sapphire Cabochon, Hieroglyph, Egyptian Revival, 2 In.	594
Pendant, Profile, Woman, Blue A-Jour Panels, Vine Frame, Diamond, Art Nouveau, 2 In...........	420
Pendant, Robot, 18K Gold, Round Head, Red Stone Eyes, Marked, Brev, Mid 1900s, 1¾ In... *illus*	330
Pin & Earrings, Pairs Of Dolphins, Sterling Silver, Marked, Georg Jensen, Pin 1½ In...	270
Pin & Earrings, Spiral Design, 18K Gold & Silver, Reiko Ishiyama, Pin 3¼ In.	1000
Pin & Earrings, Triangle, Silver, Yellow Enamel, Brushed Zigzags, A. Michelsen, Pin 2¾ In..	75
Pin, 3 Wise Monkeys, Curly Tails, Branch, 18K Gold, Gems, Van Cleef & Arpels, 1950s, 2 In..	13750
Pin, 4 Ribbed Leaves, 18K Gold, White Gold Stem, 3 Pearls, Buccellati, Italy, 2 x 1¼ In.	1140
Pin, American Flag, Platinum, Sapphire Canton, Diamond & Ruby Stripes, c.1910, 1 In.......	5313
Pin, Ballerina, Gold Over Silver, Rhinestones, Enamel, Eisenberg, c.1945, 3 In. .... *illus*	1000
Pin, Bird On Branch, Cloisonne, Guilloche, Blue, Green, 18K Gold, Marked, Starling, 2 In. ...	800
Pin, Bow, 5-Pearl Cluster, Sterling Silver, Beaded Ribbon Edge, Mikimoto, 2 In. .... *illus*	182
Pin, Bow, 15 Loops, Textured 18K Gold, Beaded Edges, 5 Diamond Accents, Retro, 1940s, 2 In.	875
Pin, Butterfly, Gold Over Silver, Topaz, Lacy Wings, Eisenberg, 1940s, 2¾ In. .... *illus*	438
Pin, Cameo, Shell, Woman's Bust, 1920s Hat, Applied Diamond Necklace, Earring, 1920s, 2 In.	938
Pin, Car, Jaguar XK120, Onyx, Diamond Hood, Ruby Wheels, Hinged Door, 1950s, 4 In.	5313
Pin, Child Holding Dog, 14K Gold, Sapphire Eyes, Pearl Base, William Ruser, 2½ In.	1200
Pin, Circle, 9 Amethysts, Oval, Faceted, 9 Diamonds, 9 Leaves, 14K Gold, Tiffany & Co., 1 In.	819
Pin, Circle, Overlapping Leaves, Openwork, 18K Gold, Mabe Pearl, Buccellati, 1½ In. Diam.	1800
Pin, Cornucopia, Diamonds, Tutti-Frutti Gems, Platinum, Art Deco, 2 In.	3750
Pin, Dog, Terrier, Doghouse With Clock, Link Chain, 14K Gold, Ruby Eyes, Retro, 1¼ In.	1250
Pin, Dragonfly, A-Jour Enamel Wings, Ruby, Diamonds, Gold, Art Nouveau, 3 In...................	7500
Pin, Enamel, Geometric Panels, Silver, Gold, Ebony, Gemstones, c.1985, Earl Pardon, 2 In. *illus*	1375
Pin, Fish, 18K Gold, Hammered, Disc Scales, Ruby Cabochon Eyes, David Webb, 2 In............	3000
Pin, Flowerpot, Silver, Garnet Cabochon Blossoms, Georg Jensen, 1940s, 2 x 1¾ In.	688
Pin, Fox, Celluloid, Black & Brown, Rhinestone Eye & Bushy Tail, 1940s, 1¾ In................... .	48
Pin, Holiday Tree, Green & Citrine Crystals, Rhinestones, Eisenberg Ice, 3½ In. .... *illus*	100
Pin, Hoop, 4 Twisted Circles, Textured Feathery Leaves, 6 Diamonds, Grosse, Germany, 2 In..	693
Pin, Horse, Prancing, Flowing Mane, Sterling Silver, Marked, Mexico Silver, c.1955, 2 In.	61
Pin, Horse, Running, Diamonds, Ruby Eye, Platinum, Edwardian, Marked, Tiffany & Co., 1 In.	3250

Jewelry, Bracelet, Cuff, Goldtone, Inset Multicolor Gripoix Stones, Chanel, 2¼ In. Wide
$1,440

Auctions at Showplace, NYC

Jewelry, Bracelet, Cuff, Hinged, Mammoth Tusk, 5 Inset Citrines, 18K Gold, Seaman Schepps, 6½ In.
$4,688

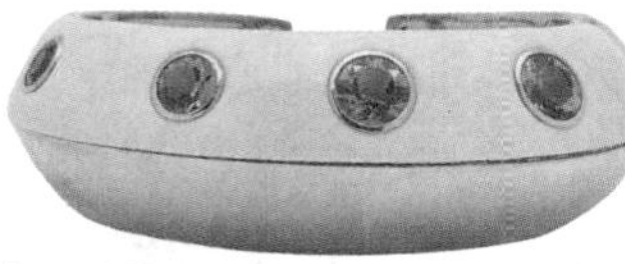

Grogan & Company

Jewelry, Bracelet, Cuff, Wire, Diamante, Rhinestones, Faceted Crystals, Fred Block, 2½ In. Wide
$175

Ripley Auctions

Jewelry, Bracelet, Modernist, Cuff, Oxidized Silver, Opal & Yellow Metal Discs, Thor Selzer, 6¼ In.
$500

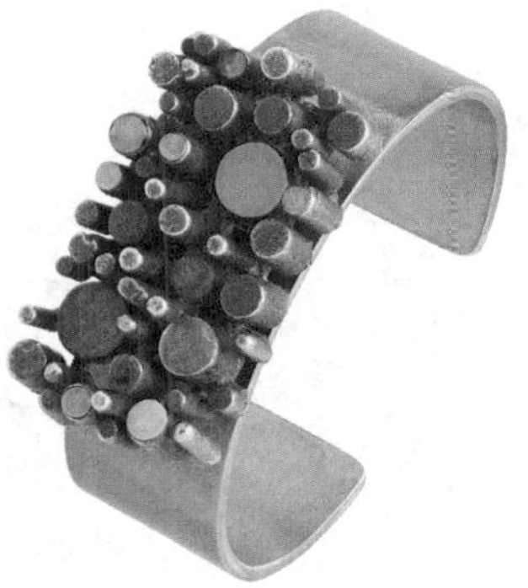

Rago Arts and Auction Center

JEWELRY

Jewelry, Bracelet, Pearls Alternating With 14K Textured Gold Tubes, Lucien Piccard, 7 ½ In.
$1,000

Ripley Auctions

Jewelry, Chatelaine, Victorian Style, Pinchbeck, Brass, Embossed, 5 Drops, 10 In.
$338

Rich Penn Auctions

Jewelry, Clip, Dress, Multicolored Rhinestones, Beads, Eisenberg Originals, 1930s, 3 In.
$625

Ripley Auctions

Jewelry, Cuff Links, Gemstones, Clear, Red & Orange, Pillow Shape, 18K Gold, Links, Trianon, ½ In.
$610

Hampton Estate Auction

Jewelry, Earrings, Quartz Drop, Oval, Silver Stem & Stud, Georg Jensen, 2 ⅜ In.
$300

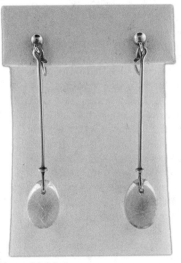

Hampton Estate Auction

Jewelry, Necklace, 41 Silver Balls, Graduated Sizes, Sterling Silver, Taxco, Mexico, 20 In.
$154

North American Auction Co.

Jewelry, Necklace, Beads, 3 Strands, Green, 6 Gilt Roses, Glass Clusters, Miriam Haskell, 16 ¾ In.
$1,130

Greenwich Auction

Jewelry, Necklace, Lariat, Opaque White Rhinestones, 7 Strands, Long Fringe, Trigere, 48 In.
$88

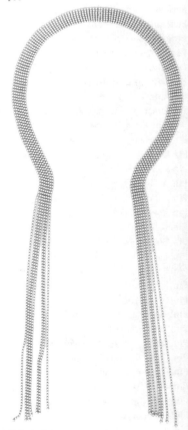

Ripley Auctions

J

Jewelry, Necklace, Talosel & Red Mirror Fringe, White Metal Wire, Line Vautrin, 15 In. $1,250

Rago Arts and Auction Center

Jewelry, Pendant, Eye Of Time, Watch In Eyeball, Diamond Teardrop, S. Dali, Joies, 2003, Box, 2 In. $938

Ripley Auctions

Jewelry, Pendant, Robot, 18K Gold, Round Head, Red Stone Eyes, Marked, Brev, Mid 1900s, 1¾ In. $330

Auctions at Showplace, NYC

Jewelry, Pin, Ballerina, Gold Over Silver, Rhinestones, Enamel, Eisenberg, c.1945, 3 In. $1,000

Ripley Auctions

Jewelry, Pin, Bow, 5-Pearl Cluster, Sterling Silver, Beaded Ribbon Edge, Mikimoto, 2 In. $182

Keystone Auctions LLC

Jewelry, Pin, Butterfly, Gold Over Silver, Topaz, Lacy Wings, Eisenberg, 1940s, 2¾ In. $438

Ripley Auctions

Jewelry, Pin, Enamel, Geometric Panels, Silver, Gold, Ebony, Gemstones, c.1985, Earl Pardon, 2 In. $1,375

Rago Arts and Auction Center

Jewelry, Pin, Holiday Tree, Green & Citrine Crystals, Rhinestones, Eisenberg Ice, 3½ In. $100

Ripley Auctions

Jewelry, Pin, Mermaid, Gold Over Silver, Aquamarine Crystals, Eisenberg, c.1945, 3 In. $4,500

Ripley Auctions

J

Jewelry, Pin, Modernist, 18K Gold, Bark Texture, Opal, Diamonds, Marked, Ed Wiener, 2⅝ In.
$5,938

Rago Arts and Auction Center

Jewelry, Pin, Modernist, Textured 18K Bicolor Gold, Green Tourmalines, Diamonds, La Triomphe, 2 In.
$1,375

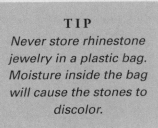

Rago Arts and Auction Center

Jewelry, Pin, Vase Of Flowers, Amethyst Crystals, Rhinestones, Eisenberg, 1940s, 4 In.
$1,125

Ripley Auctions

Jewelry, Ring, Band, 3 Tapering Braids, 18K Tricolor Gold, Buccellati, Size 5½
$688

Rago Arts and Auction Center

Jewelry, Ring, Modernist, Spinner, Kinetic Sphere, Ridged Gold, Diamond, N. Teufel, c.1972, Size 6½
$4,063

Rago Arts and Auction Center

Judaica, Kiddush Cup, Hexagonal, 6-Sided, Gold Wash, Hebrew Inscription, Engraved, 6½ In.
$2,750

Susanin's Auctioneers & Appraisers

John Rogers, Group, Uncle Ned's School, Painted, Plaster, Circular Base, Signed, 1866, 20 x 14 In.
$381

Fontaine's Auction Gallery

Pin, Jadeite Disc, 18K Gold Frame, 2 Dragons, Emerald Eyes, Chinese Character Mark, 1 In.	3438
Pin, Jadeite Plaque, Oval, Openwork Flowers, Birds, 14K Gold, Seed Pearls, Enamel, Cartier, 1 In.	1353
Pin, Leaf, Openwork, Polished 14K Gold, Cartier, 2½ In.	1750
Pin, Lizard, Silver Over 14K Gold, Rubies, Diamonds, Garnet Eyes, c.1890, 1¼ In.	625
Pin, Mermaid, Gold Over Silver, Aquamarine Crystals, Eisenberg, c.1945, 3 In. .... *illus*	4500
Pin, Micro Mosaic, Cross, Flower Tips, Blues, Round, Archaeological Revival, Castellani, 1 In.	6250
Pin, Micro Mosaic, Woman Standing By Fountain, Malachite Plaque, Gold Frame, Italy, 2 In.	688
Pin, Modernist, 18K Gold, Bark Texture, Opal, Diamonds, Marked, Ed Wiener, 2⅝ In. . *illus*	5938
Pin, Modernist, Boomerang Form, Silver, Black Enamel, Marked, Poul Warmind, Denmark, 1½ In..	85
Pin, Modernist, Oval Jet Plaque, Protruding Diamonds & Gold Beads, R. Greene, 2½ In.	1375
Pin, Modernist, Sticks, 14K Tricolor Gold, Tourmaline & Onyx Tips, 3½ In.	1408
Pin, Modernist, Textured 18K Bicolor Gold, Green Tourmalines, Diamonds, La Triomphe, 2 In. ... *illus*	1375
Pin, Mouton, Metal, Black & White Enamel, Francois-Xavier Lalanne, c.1990, 1 x 1¼ In.	2500
Pin, Oval, Beads, Gripoix Glass, Blue & Green, Pearls, Rhinestones, Chanel, 2¾ In.	1140
Pin, Pythagoras, Square, Concave Center, 18K Gold, Marked, Niessing, 2 In.	1375
Pin, Rooster, Ruby Comb, Diamonds, Emeralds, 18K Gold, France, Belle Epoque, c.1900, 1¼ In.	4063
Pin, Seahorse, Carved Resin, Goldtone Seaweed, Multicolor Stones, C. Lacroix, 3 In.	300
Pin, Starburst, Twisted 18K Gold, Opals, Rubies, LeCoultre, 1½ In.	625
Pin, Stylized Lizard, Embossed Words All Over, Gilt Bronze, Line Vautrin, 1945, 2½ In.	875
Pin, Toucan, Enamel, Yellow, Black & Red, Colorless Crystals, Marked, Swarovski, 2½ In.....	73
Pin, Turtle, 18K Gold, Diamonds On Shell, Ruby Eyes, Cartier, Paris, 1⅛ In.	7560
Pin, Vase Of Flowers, Amethyst Crystals, Rhinestones, Eisenberg, 1940s, 4 In. .... *illus*	1125
Ring, Amethyst, Rectangle Cut, White Gold Filigree Mount, Enamel, Art Deco, 1920s, Size 4¼....	688
Ring, Band, 3 Tapering Braids, 18K Tricolor Gold, Buccellati, Size 5½ .... *illus*	688
Ring, Band, Hand Holding 4 Diamonds, 18K Gold, CC For Carrera Y Carrera, Size 6¼..........	875
Ring, Flower Starburst, Layered Petals, Diamonds, Openwork, 18K Rose Gold, Leon, Size 7...	688
Ring, Modernist, Spinner, Kinetic Sphere, Ridged Gold, Diamond, N. Teufel, c.1972, Size 6½ . *illus*	4063
Ring, Tiger Eye Cabochon, 6 Pearls, Shaped Rose Gold Frame, Enamel, Victorian, Size 5¾ ..	175

Watches are listed in their own category.

Wristwatches are listed in their own category.

JOHN ROGERS

John Rogers statues were made from 1859 to 1892. The originals were bronze, but the thousands of copies made by the Rogers factory were of painted plaster. Eighty different figures were created. Similar painted plaster figures were produced by some other factories. Rights to the figures were sold in 1893, and the figures were manufactured until about 1895 by the Rogers Statuette Co. Never repaint a Rogers figure because this lowers the value to collectors.

Figure, Man With Gun, Fighting Bob, Plaster, Painted, 34 In.	407
Group, Traveling Magician, Painted, Plaster, Signed, 23 In.	1890
Group, Uncle Ned's School, Painted, Plaster, Circular Base, Signed, 1866, 20 x 14 In. .. *illus*	381

JUDAICA

Judaica is any memorabilia that refers to the Jews or the Jewish religion. Interests range from newspaper clippings that mention eighteenth- and nineteenth-century Jewish Americans to religious objects, such as menorahs or spice boxes. Age, condition, and the intrinsic value of the material, as well as the historic and artistic importance, determine the value.

Kiddush Cup, Double Walled, Triangular Base, Michael Jerry, c.1995, 8 In.	1690
Kiddush Cup, Hexagonal, 6-Sided, Gold Wash, Hebrew Inscription, Engraved, 6½ In. *illus*	2750
Kiddush Cup, Silver, Filigree, 4 Oval Cabochon Stones, Israel, 5¾ In.	224
Mezuzah, Figural, 2 Musicians, Patina, Bronze Case, Signed, Urinsin, 6¼ In. .... *illus*	256
Plate, Engraved Rim, Verses, Tablet Of The Covenant, Crown Of Torah, Flowers, Pewter, 1800s, 9 In.	384
Spice Box, Besamim, Silver, Tower Shape, Filigree, 1826, 10 x 2¾ x 2¾ In.	400
Spice Box, Hinged Lid, Figural, Ostrich, Stone Set Eyes, Marked SA, Dutch, c.1897, 4⅝ In. ...	938
Spice Tower, Silver, Flags, Engraved Star, Footed, 1800s, 8½ x 2¼ In.	120

Judaica, Mezuzah, Figural, 2 Musicians, Patina, Bronze Case, Signed, Urinsin, 6¼ In.
$256

Brunk Auctions

J

Jugtown, Platter, Round, Orange, Bear Profile In Tent, Yellow Slip, Stamped, 16 In.
$2,583

Leland Little Auctions

Jukebox, Selector, Buckley, Steel, Glass Front, Wall Mount, Red Labels, Dial Selector, 11½ In.
$282

Potter & Potter Auctions

Kay Finch, Pig, Winking, Green Ears, Yellow Hair, Strawberries On Back, 4 x 4½ In.
$24

Ruby Lane

Kay Finch, Plate, Blue Daisy, Square, White Ground, Rounded Corners, 7¾ In.
$15

nescia51 on eBay

Kelva, Humidor, Cigar, Pink Poppy, Mottled Green Ground, 6 x 4 In.
$350

Woody Auction

Kelva, Jewelry Box, Hinged Lid, Mottled Green Ground, Pink Flowers, Beaded, 3 x 4 In.
$125

Woody Auction

JUGTOWN POTTERY

Jugtown Pottery refers to many pottery pieces made in North Carolina as far back as the 1750s. In 1915, Juliana and Jacques Busbee set up a training and sales organization for what they named Jugtown Pottery. In 1921, they built a shop at Jugtown, North Carolina, and in 1923 hired Ben Owen as a potter. The Busbees moved the village store where the pottery was sold to New York City. Juliana Busbee sold the New York store in 1926 and moved into a log cabin near the Jugtown Pottery. The pottery closed in 1959. It reopened in 1960 and is still working near Seagrove, North Carolina.

Candlestick, Speckled Glaze, Brown, Flared Base, Round Cup, Signed, Vernon Owens, 12 x 5 In., Pair	160
Jar, Lid, Bulbous, Handles, Flared Top, Gray, Blue Flowers, Marked, Vernon Owen, 1986, 10½ x 10 In. .	32
Jug, Salt Glaze, Stylized Blue Flying Birds, White Ground, Incised Bands, Circular Mark, 10 In.	73
Platter, Round, Orange, Bear Profile In Tent, Yellow Slip, Stamped, 16 In. .... *illus*	2583
Vase, Blue Glaze, Earthenware, Red, Incised Bands, Shoulders, Flared Neck, c.1935, 11 x 7 In..	938
Vase, Oval, White Glaze, Brown Base, Stamped, Early 1900s, 7 In.	74

JUKEBOX

Jukeboxes play records. The first coin-operated phonograph was demonstrated in 1889. In 1906 the Automatic Entertainer appeared, the first coin-operated phonograph to offer several different selections of music. The first electrically powered jukebox was introduced in 1927. Collectors search for jukeboxes of all ages, especially those with flashing lights and unusual design and graphics.

Capehart, Model 100, Pierced Scrolled Front, Yellow Panels, Red Trim, Visible Mechanism	510
Mills, Model 880, Dance Master, Wood Cabinet, 12 Records, 78 RPM, 1935, 49 x 35 x 21 In....	1560
Rock-Ola Rocket, Clear Top, Visible Mechanism, Multicolor Lights, 60 x 30 In......................	295
Seeburg, Stereo, Rectangular, Top Hood, Blue & Pink Stripes On Front, 1970s, 49 x 40 x 28 In..	111
Selector, Buckley, Steel, Glass Front, Wall Mount, Red Labels, Dial Selector, 11½ In. .. *illus*	282
Selector, Seeburg Wall-O-Matic, Tabletop, 12½ x 5½ In.	189
Speaker Light, Rock-Ola, Tone-O-Lier, Spinning Color Wheel, Mirrors, Plastic, Chain, 14 x 22 In.	1560
Wurlitzer, Multi Selector, 5-10-25 Cents, 24 Records, 78 RPM, Art Deco, 1940s, 57 x 32 x 27 In..	4800
Wurlitzer, Super Star, Model 3600, Rectangular, Mottled Red Front Panels, 51 x 40 x 20 In.	480

Kay Finch KAY FINCH CERAMICS
CALIFORNIA

Kay Finch Ceramics were made in Corona del Mar, California, from 1935 to 1963. The hand-decorated pieces often depicted whimsical animals and people. Pastel colors were used.

Figurine, Dog, Whippet, Sitting, Flying Ears, Chain Collar, Cream, F. McFarlin, 12 In.	795
Pig, Winking, Green Ears, Yellow Hair, Strawberries On Back, 4 x 4½ In. .... *illus*	24
Planter, Baby Lamb, Book, Our Baby, Blue, White, Embossed Mark, 6¾ x 5 In......................	32
Plate, Blue Daisy, Square, White Ground, Rounded Corners, 7¾ In. .... *illus*	15

KAYSERZINN, *see Pewter category.*

KELVA KELVA

Kelva glassware was made by the C. F. Monroe Company of Meriden, Connecticut, about 1904. It is a pale, pastel-painted glass decorated with flowers, designs, or scenes. Kelva resembles Nakara and Wave Crest, two other glasswares made by the same company.

Dresser Box, Flower, Indigo Blue, Mottled Design, Art Glass, C.F. Monroe Co., 3½ In.	81
Humidor, Cigar, Pink Poppy, Mottled Green Ground, 6 x 4 In. .... *illus*	350
Jewelry Box, Hinged Lid, Mottled Green Ground, Pink Flowers, Beaded, 3 x 4 In. .... *illus*	125

KEW BLAS

Kew Blas is a name used by the Union Glass Company of Somerville, Massachusetts. The name refers to an iridescent golden glass made from the 1890s to 1924. The iridescent glass was reminiscent of the Tiffany glass of the period.

Vase, Hooked Feather, Gold Borders, Green Interior Scalloped Rim, Footed, 12 ¾ In. .....*illus*   1,512

KEWPIES

Kewpies, designed by Rose O'Neill (1874–1944), were first pictured in the *Ladies' Home Journal*. The figures, which are similar to pixies, were a success, and Kewpie dolls and figurines started appearing in 1911. Kewpie pictures and other items soon followed. Collectors search for all items that picture the little winged people. They are still popular with collectors.

Bank, Composition, Sitting, Wears Glasses, Coin Slot Front, A.N. Brooks, Chicago, 11 x 5 In.	100
Bisque, Head Tilted, Side-Glancing Eyes, Jointed Arms, Germany, 11 In. .....*illus*	861
Bisque, Lying Down, Head Up, Doodle Dog On Back, Side-Glancing Eyes, Marked, c.1915, 3 In.	1140
Bisque, Side-Glancing Eyes, Strung Arms, Paper Label On Chest & Back, Incised Name On Feet, 9 In.	450
Postcard, New Year, 3 Kewpies, Bell Tower, Birds, Ring In A Happy New Year, c.1926	6
Tray, Advertising, Arctic Ice Cream, Blue Ground, Ice Cream Block, Kewpie Golfer, Tin, 13 In. *illus*	87
Vase, Bud, Blue To Ivory, Kewpie Playing Guitar, Rectangular Base, Incised Goebel, Full Crown, 5 In.	197

KING'S ROSE, *see Soft Paste category.*

KITCHEN

Kitchen utensils of all types, from eggbeaters to bowls, are collected today. Handmade wooden and metal items, like ladles and apple peelers, were made in the early nineteenth century. Mass-produced pieces, like iron apple peelers and graniteware, were made in the nineteenth century. Also included in this category are utensils used for other household chores, such as laundry and cleaning. Other kitchen wares are listed under manufacturers' names or under Advertising, Iron, Tool, or Wooden.

Barrel, Wood, 4 Iron Bands, Hole, Oval Shape, 17 x 10 In. .....*illus*	49
Bin, Dough, Plank Top, Block Legs, France, 1800s, 29 x 70 In. .....*illus*	649
Biscuit Jar, Lid, Blue, Flower, Silver Plate Rim, 9 ½ In.	173
Board, Cutting, Circular, Carved, Eagle Top, Rectangular Base, Wood, 20 In. .....*illus*	431
Board, Cutting, Pine, Flowers, Tulips, Scandinavia, Anna Hegehlz, 1887, 25 ¾ x 20 ½ In.	234
Board, Dough, Poplar, Heart Cutout Handle, 1950, 24 x 17 ½ In.	88
Board, Dough, Walnut, Heart Cutouts, 1800s, 17 ¾ x 37 ¾ In.	3416
Bowl, Butter, Wood, 25 In.	226
Bowl, Krenit, Green Interior, Black Exterior, Enamel, Steel, Herbert Krenchel, 1953, 5 ½ In. ...*illus*	195
Box, Sugar, Hinged Lid, Pine, Iron Cutter, Painted, Dovetailed, c.1863, 8 ¼ x 14 ½ In. .. *illus*	380
Broiler, Hearth, Wrought Iron, 5 Bars, Curled Hook, Footed, 1800s, 10 x 18 ½ In. ..... *illus*	468
Broiler, Scotch, Hearth, Wrought Iron, Arched, 15 Ram's Horn Hooks, 1800s, 13 In.	263
Broiler, Wrought Iron, Round, Rotating Top, Stylized Fleur-De-Lis, Long Handle, 1880s, 22 In.	350
Butcher Block, 3 Splayed Legs, Round, Painted, 1800s, 25 ½ x 31 ½ In.	671
Butcher Block, Mixed Wood, Stainless Steel Brackets, Square Legs, 33 x 47 x 23 In.	384
Butcher Block, Oak, Parquetry, Metal Brackets, Carved Apron, Reeded Legs, 1800s, 34 x 47 In. .. *illus*	2360
Butcher Block, Wood, Triangular Side Handles, Turned Legs, Square Feet, 34 x 24 In.	173
Butter Stamp, Carved, Flowers, Rope Border, 1800s, 4 ¾ In.	469
Butter Stamp, Flying Fish, Carved, Turned, Wood, 1800s, 4 ⅝ In.	2074
Butter Stamp, Treen, 2-Sided, Carved, Bird Among Flowers, Geometric, 1850s, 4 ⅝ In. ..... *illus*	380
Butter Stamp, Turned Maple, Cow, Standing, Flowers, Patina, 6 x 4 ¼ In.	219
Cabinet, Spice, Wall, Hanging, 8 Drawers, Knob Pulls, Wood, 11 ¾ In.	62
Cake Plate, Dome Lid, Courtly Check, Wood Finial, Metal, Mackenzie-Childs, 15 ⅞ In.	177
Cauldron, Copper & Iron, Hand Forged Bail Handles, 1800s, 12 x 18 In. .....*illus*	295

Kew Blas, Vase, Hooked Feather, Gold Borders, Green Interior, Scalloped Rim, Footed, 12 ¾ In.
$1,512

Fontaine's Auction Gallery

Kewpie, Bisque, Head Tilted, Side-Glancing Eyes, Jointed Arms, Germany, 11 In.
$861

Apple Tree Auction Center

Kewpie, Tray, Advertising, Arctic Ice Cream, Blue Ground, Ice Cream Block, Kewpie Golfer, Tin, 13 In.
$87

Ron Rhoads Auctioneers

Kitchen, Barrel, Wood, 4 Iron Bands, Hole, Oval Shape, 17 x 10 In. $49

Hartzell's Auction Gallery Inc.

Kitchen, Bin, Dough, Plank Top, Block Legs, France, 1800s, 29 x 70 In. $649

Austin Auction Gallery

Kitchen, Board, Cutting, Circular, Carved, Eagle Top, Rectangular Base, Wood, 20 In. $431

Apple Tree Auction Center

Cauldron, Oval, Painted, Black, Bail Handle, Iron, Clark & Co., 1800s, 7 Gal., 22 In.	118
Chestnut Roaster, Wrought Iron, Sheet Metal, Handle, Stamped, Salem, 1800s, 40 In.	531
Churn, Barrel Shape, Iron Band, Lid & Plunger, Mid 1800s, 22 In.	148
Churn, Barrel Shape, Oak, Pressed Steel Legs, c.1900, 41 In. *illus*	123
Churn, Floor, Crank, Square, Tole Container, Dazey, Early 1900s, 25 In.	31
Churn, Glass, Wood Paddles, Cast Iron Crank, 14 In. *illus*	62
Churn, Jar, Cast Iron Crank, Wood Paddles, Early 1900s, 6 Qt., 15 x 6¾ In.	118
Churn, Lid, Milk Paint, Plunger, 1800s, 26 In. *illus*	688
Churn, Painted, Blue, Barrel Shape, Metal Band, 1800s, 29 In. *illus*	313
Churn, Stave, Tapered Shape, Sheet Metal Bands, Dasher, Blue, 1800s, 21 x 12 In.	537
Churn, Tabletop Style, Crank & Lid, Wood, 15 x 13 x 9½ In. *illus*	86
Churn, Tin, Metal Container, Hand Crank, Marked, Dazey, 25 In.	58
Churn, White Cedar, Cylinder, Crank, 15 In.	74
Coffee Grinders are listed in the Coffee Mill category.	
Coffee Maker, La Pavoni Europiccola, Metal Body, Plastic Fittings, 12 x 8 x 11 In. *illus*	325
Coffee Mills are listed in their own category.	
Coffeepot, Gooseneck Spout, Tin, Wriggle Work, Spread Wing Eagle, Flowers, Early 1800s, 11 In.	1625
Coffeepot, Hinged Lid, Brass Finial, Tin, Wriggle Ware, Pennsylvania, Early 1700s, 11⅛ In.	750
Coffeepot, Tin, Wriggle Work, Flowers, Eagle, Angled Spout, C-Shape Handle, Pa., c.1815, 11 In.	1625
Cookie Mold, Elephant, Tin, Rectangular, Late 1800s, 7⅝ x 10⅝ In.	531
Cranberry Scoop, Wood, Cherry, 18 Fingers, 6½ x 15 In.	35
Dough Box, Lid, 4 Handles, Primitive, Wood, 10 x 41 x 15 In. *illus*	197
Dough Box, Pine, Mustard Paint, Sloped Sides, Brace Handles, 1800s, 10 x 36 x 18 In. *illus*	123
Dough Box, Sheraton, Pine, Maple, Dovetailed Case, Splayed Turned Legs, c.1835, 29 x 18 x 44 In.	633
Dough Box, Slide Lid, Pine, Splayed Turned Legs, Red Stain, 1800s, 28 x 36 x 17 In. *illus*	904
Dough Box, Tabletop, Pine, Lift Lid, Signed, Esther Thompkins, 1850s, 11 x 15½ x 30 In.	234
Dough Scraper, Iron Blade, Ring Turned Brass Handle, Stamped, Peter Derr, 1842, 4 In.	732
Dough Scraper, Wrought Iron, Curved Blade, Turned Walnut Handle, 1800s, 5¾ x 3⅛ In.	813
Dutch Oven, Lid, Swing Handle, Erie, No. 6, Tite-Top, Trivet, 11 In.	288
Eggbeater, Wood Handle, Glass Base, Silver, No. 3 *illus*	136
Fish Roaster, Wrought Iron, 6 Curved Tines, Chamfered Cross Bar, Handle, c.1820, 20 x 15 In.	500
Flour Sifter, Plastic, Red & White, Ivy Design, Squeeze Handle, 5-Cup, c.1945, 5 x 4 In.	15
Grill, Side Burner, Black, Timer, 2 Doors, Caster, Weber Genesis, 49 x 56 In.	71
Grinder, Metal, Crank, Mount, Wood Block, 15 In.	86
Ice Cream Cone Holder, Pierced, 12 Holes, Turned Handle, Late 1800s, 17 x 10 x 8 In.	425
Icebox, Oak, Belding's National, Beveled Mirror, Henry N. Clark Co., 54 x 25 In. *illus*	3150
Icebox, Oak, Refrigerator, 3-Latch Door, Access Panel, Cavalier, 37 x 28 x 15 In. *illus*	113
Iron Heater, Stove Top, 2 Sadirons, Engraved, Handle, 6 In.	277
Iron, Charcoal, Brass, Head Latch, Trivet, Wood Handle, Footed, 7 In. *illus*	338
Iron, Charcoal, Bronze, Sole, Wood Handle, Asian, 5½ In.	37
Iron, Charcoal, Dragon Handle, Carved, Sole, Indonesia, 8¼ In. *illus*	400
Iron, Charcoal, Stainless, Griffin Latch, Engraved, 7½ In.	43
Iron, Electric, Enamel, White Handle, Trivet, Quality Appliance Co., 7 In.	62
Iron, Fluter, Slug, Brass Roller, Base, Elgin, 5 In. *illus*	135
Iron, Fluter, Slug, Revolving Combination, Wood Handle, 5 In.	209
Iron, Fuel, Tank, Wood Handle, Engraved, Embossed, Jubilee, 1904, 6¼ In. *illus*	135
Iron, Gas, Black Handle, Brass Tank, Albert Lea Minn, American Gas Machine Co., 1912, 6½ In. *illus*	43
Iron, Hat, Removable Brim Edge, Wood Handle, 3½ In.	55
Iron, Swan Shape, Cast Iron, Handle, Engraved, 3½ In.	308
Juicer, Silver Plate, Handle, Victorian, 8 In.	148
Kettle, Brass, Bell Shape, Wrought Iron, Swing Handle, Late 1800s, 9½ x 12 In. *illus*	26
Kettle, Copper, Gooseneck Spout, Swing Handle, Stamped, J. Upperman, Lancaster, 1800s, 3 In.	458
Kettle, Copper, Lid, Hammered, Gooseneck Spout, Swing Handle, Dayton, Stutsman, 1800s, 11 In.	375
Knife Sharpener, Rotary, Cast Iron, Wood, Cartouche, Brass Mount, Kent's, 1800s, 18 x 19 In. *illus*	492
Knife, Whalebone, Wood Handle, Engraved, 1800s, 11¼ In.	625
Ladle, Straining, Wrought Iron, Copper, Punched Pinwheel Design, 1800s, 25 In. *illus*	125
Mangle Board, Wood, Horse Head, Tulips, Geometric Design, Engraved, Painted, 1800s, 24 In. *illus*	197
Match Holders can be found in their own category.	
Match Safes can be found in their own category.	
Measure, Nested, Bent Hickory, Varnished, Marked, E.B. Frye & Son, Wilton N.H., 8 x 14 In. *illus*	374

K

Mixing Bowl, Wood, Oval, Cream & Green Paint, Patina, 2½ x 7¾ In.	181
Mixing Bowl, Wood, Shallow, On Stand, Spoon, Fork, 34 In.	35
Mold, Candy, Chocolate, Black, Bear Shape, Standing, Tin, 11 In.	400
Mold, Chocolate, Rabbit, Basket Backpack, Standing, Marked, 14¾ In., Pair .... *illus*	98
Mold, Ice Cream, see Pewter category.	
Molds may also be found in the Pewter and Tinware categories.	
Mortar & Pestle, Bronze, Relief Design, Masks, Floral Swags, Continental, 5 x 6 In. ... *illus*	30
Mortar & Pestle, Turned Wood, Cylindrical, Thick Walls, Lignum Vitae, 1700s, 7 x 8 In.	576
Mortar & Pestle, Wood, Turned Urn Shape, Red Ground, 1800s, 7½ In. .... *illus*	213
Pan, Bronze, Iron, Oriental Design, Engraved, 2¼ In.	55
Pantry Box, Bentwood, Iron Staple Bands, Finger Lap Seams, Red Stain, 1800s, 3 x 5 In. *illus*	226
Pantry Box, Lid, Bent Hickory, Wire Bail Handle, Stamped, N. & J. Howe & Co., 12 In........	316
Pantry Box, Red, Yellow, Black Ground, Straight Seam, Iron Tacks, 1800s, 3¾ x 6 In.	138
Pantry Box, Round, Bentwood, Laced Seam Base, Finger Seam Lid, Dark Brown, 1850s, 3 x 11 In.	192
Peeler, Apple, Yellow Pine, Poplar, Metal Blade, Mortise & Tenon Frame, 1800s, 12 x 24 In. ..*illus*	82
Pepper Grinder, Barrel Shape, Sterling, Peugeot Freres, France, Mid 1900s, 3¾ In. ... *illus*	108
Pie Lifter, Thick Wire Extension, Turned Handle, Brass Collar, Shaker, c.1820, 14½ In.... ...	75
Pot, Cooking, Brass, Squat, 3-Legged Shape, Iron Swing Handle, 1800s, 12¼ In. .... *illus*	177
Pot, Double Boiler, Lid, White Enamel, Cobalt Blue Handles, 1930-40s, 8¾ x 6 In.	15
Press, Cider, Maple, Cast Iron Fittings, Stave Bucket, 1910s, 36 x 17½ x 17½ In............	216
Rack, Baking, Metal, Black, 3 Tiers, 75 x 35 x 18 In.	75
Reamers are listed in their own category.	
Refrigerator, Electrolux, Red & Black, Wine, Door, Window, 33 x 23½ In. .... *illus*	130
Roaster, Hearth, Wrought Iron, Brass, 4 Meat Hooks, Tripod Base, 1800s, 11 In................	556
Roasting Oven, Hearth, Sheet Iron, Open Handles, Hinged Door, 4 Legs, 1800s, 7½ In........	497
Rolled Oats Press, Iron, Wood Crank Handle & Base, Drawer .... *illus*	51
Rolling Pin, Glass, Red, White Stripes, 17 In. .... *illus*	59
Salt & Pepper Shakers are listed in their own category.	
Salt Grinder, Twergi, Lacquered, Red, Black, Brown, Wood, Alessi, Ettore Sottsass, 4 In. *illus*	688
Scoop, Ice Cream, Cone Clipper, Spring Loaded, Metal, Geer Mfg. Co., Pat. 1906, 9 x 3 In. *illus*	83
Scoop, Ice Cream, Gilchrist, No. 30, Nickel & Brass, 11 In.	49
Scoop, Ice Cream, Silver & Brass, Wood Handle, Cylindrical Bowl, Fisher Motor Co., c.1920, 9 In.	246
Scoop, Maple, Turned, Bent Handle, 1800s, 11¾ In.	375
Skillet, Bronze, Round, Tripod Legs, Handle, Molded, John Fathers, c.1700, 6½ x 19½ In....	1875
Skillet, Griswold, No. 12, Cast Iron, Heat Ring, Block Logo .... *illus*	277
Spatula, Wrought Iron, Pierced 3 Hearts, Flattened Handle, Early 1800s, 13½ In................	305
Spice Box, Hanging, 4 Drawer, Wooden, Marked, Tidewater Crafts Of Virginia, 16 x 8 In.	74
Spice Box, Pine, 4 Drawers, Knob Pulls, Black, Painted, 1860s, 8¾ In. .... *illus*	187
Spice Box, Wood, 2 Tombstone Shape Back Panels, Lift Lid, 2 Drawers, 1800s, 13 x 16 x 7 In..	380
Spice Chest, 12 Drawers, Gray, Red Label, Brass Knob Handle, 1850s, 18 x 14½ x 6 In.	688
Spice Chest, Countertop, Tin, Painted, Gilt, Removable Lid, Early 1800s, 15⅝ x 24¼ In.	2944
Spice Chest, Maple, 8 Drawers, Turned Pulls, Shaped Backsplash, Late 1800s, 17 x 10 x 5 In. ..*illus*	125
Spice Chest, Pine, Painted, 4 Drawers, Shaped Backsplash, 8¼ x 7¾ In. .... *illus*	122
Spit Jack, Brass, Clockwork, Embossed Label, John Linwood Warranted, 1800s, 14 In. *illus*	84
Spoon Rack, Hanging, Oak, 1800s, 26½ x 21½ In.	113
Spoon Rack, Wall, Backboard, 2 Pierced Rails, Slant Top Box, Brass Hinges, Early 1900s, 29 In..	94
Strainer, Heart Shape, Canted & Rolled Sides, Punchwork, Patina, 14½ x 13½ In. ... *illus*	625
Strawholder, Amber Glass, Thumbprint, Quadruple Plated Lid, 12 In. .... *illus*	338
Toaster, Wrought Iron, Rotating Holder, Ram's Horn End, 1880s, 14 In................	140
Trammel, Wrought Iron, Sawtooth, Candleholder, Hook Hanger, 1800s, 28 In.	425
Tray, Cutlery, Poplar, Vinegar Painted, Cutout Handle, 1800s, 7 x 12 x 9¼ In................	125
Tray, Cutlery, Wood, Pierced Handle, Deep Canted, Nail Construction, Red, Early 1800s, 10 x 12 In.	344
Trencher, Burl, Oblong, Incised Rim, Footed, 1800s, 4½ x 20¼ In.	1320
Trencher, Oval, Maple, Brown Ground, Patina, 1800s, 3½ x 13¼ x 24½ In.	196
Trencher, Wood, Oval, 2 Handles, 1900s, 6 x 26¼ x 15¾ In.	500
Trivet, see Trivet category.	
Wafer Iron, Round Plates, Incised Eagles, Handle, Cast Iron, No. 2, c.1810, 27 In................	565
Wafer Iron, Wrought Iron, Spread Wing Eagle, Shield, Closing Loop, Molded, Early 1800s, 29 In.	600
Waffle Iron, Griswold, No. 18, Heart & Star, Cast Iron, Stamped, Pa., 17 In. .... *illus*	184
Water Dispenser, Crystal Spring Water, Glass, Iron, Ceramic, 55 x 15½ x 20 In.	500

Kitchen, Bowl, Krenit, Green Interior, Black Exterior, Enamel, Steel, Herbert Krenchel, 1953, 5½ In.
$195

Wright

Kitchen, Box, Sugar, Hinged Lid, Pine, Iron Cutter, Painted, Dovetailed, c.1863, 8¼ x 14½ In.
$380

Jeffrey S. Evans & Associates

K

Kitchen, Broiler, Hearth, Wrought Iron, 5 Bars, Curled Hook, Footed, 1800s, 10 x 18½ In.
$468

Jeffrey S. Evans & Associates

Kitchen, Butcher Block, Oak, Parquetry, Metal Brackets, Carved Apron, Reeded Legs, 1800s, 34 x 47 In.
$2,360

Austin Auction Gallery

Kitchen, Butter Stamp, Treen, 2-Sided, Carved, Bird Among Flowers, Geometric, 1850s, $4\frac{5}{8}$ In.
$380

Jeffrey S. Evans & Associates

Kitchen, Cauldron, Copper & Iron, Hand Forged Bail Handles, 1800s, 12 x 18 In.
$295

Leland Little Auctions

Kitchen, Churn, Barrel Shape, Oak, Pressed Steel Legs, c.1900, 41 In.
$123

Rich Penn Auctions

Kitchen, Churn, Glass, Wood Paddles, Cast Iron Crank, 14 In.
$62

Apple Tree Auction Center

Kitchen, Churn, Lid, Milk Paint, Plunger, 1800s, 26 In.
$688

Eldred's

Kitchen, Churn, Painted, Blue, Barrel Shape, Metal Band, 1800s, 29 In.
$313

Cowan's Auctions

Kitchen, Churn, Tabletop Style, Crank & Lid, Wood, 15 x 13 x $9\frac{1}{2}$ In.
$86

Hartzell's Auction Gallery Inc.

Kitchen, Coffee Maker, La Pavoni Europiccola, Metal Body, Plastic Fittings, 12 x 8 x 11 In.
$325

Austin Auction Gallery

K

Kitchen, Dough Box, Lid, 4 Handles, Primitive, Wood, 10 x 41 x 15 In.
$197

Apple Tree Auction Center

Kitchen, Dough Box, Pine, Mustard Paint, Sloped Sides, Brace Handles, 1800s, 10 x 36 x 18 In.
$123

Rich Penn Auctions

Kitchen, Dough Box, Slide Lid, Pine, Splayed Turned Legs, Red Stain, 1800s, 28 x 36 x 17 In.
$904

Soulis Auctions

Kitchen, Eggbeater, Wood Handle, Glass Base, Silver, No. 3
$136

Strawser Auction Group

Kitchen, Icebox, Oak, Belding's National, Beveled Mirror, Henry N. Clark Co., 54 x 25 In.
$3,150

Fontaine's Auction Gallery

K

KITCHEN

Kitchen, Icebox, Oak, Refrigerator, 3-Latch Door, Access Panel, Cavalier, 37 x 28 x 15 In.
$113

Kitchen, Iron, Charcoal, Brass, Head Latch, Trivet, Wood Handle, Footed, 7 In.
$338

Kitchen, Iron, Charcoal, Dragon Handle, Carved, Sole, Indonesia, 8¼ In.
$400

Kitchen, Iron, Fluter, Slug, Brass Roller, Base, Elgin, 5 In.
$135

Kitchen, Iron, Fuel, Tank, Wood Handle, Engraved, Embossed, Jubilee, 1904, 6¼ In.
$135

Kitchen, Iron, Gas, Black Handle, Brass Tank, Albert Lea Minn, American Gas Machine Co., 1912, 6½ In.
$43

Kitchen, Kettle, Brass, Bell Shape, Wrought Iron, Swing Handle, Late 1800s, 9½ x 12 In.
$26

Kitchen, Knife Sharpener, Rotary, Cast Iron, Wood, Cartouche, Brass Mount, Kent's, 1800s, 18 x 19 In.
$492

Kitchen, Ladle, Straining, Wrought Iron, Copper, Punched Pinwheel Design, 1800s, 25 In.
$125

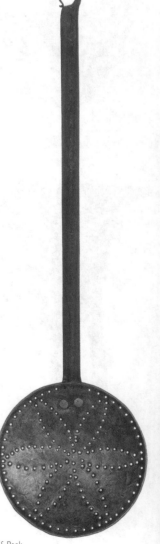

Kitchen, Mangle Board, Wood, Horse Head, Tulips, Geometric Design, Engraved, Painted, 1800s, 24 In.
$197

Hartzell's Auction Gallery Inc.

> **TIP**
> *Restoring and reusing old things is the purest form of recycling.*

Kitchen, Measure, Nested, Bent Hickory, Varnished, Marked, E.B. Frye & Son, Wilton N.H., 8 x 14 In.
$374

Forsythes' Auctions

Kitchen, Mold, Chocolate, Rabbit, Basket Backpack, Standing, Marked, 14¾ In., Pair
$98

Hartzell's Auction Gallery Inc.

Kitchen, Mortar & Pestle, Bronze, Relief Design, Masks, Floral Swags, Continental, 5 x 6 In.
$30

Leland Little Auctions

Kitchen, Mortar & Pestle, Wood, Turned Urn Shape, Red Ground, 1800s, 7½ In.
$213

Pook & Pook

Kitchen, Pantry Box, Bentwood, Iron Staple Bands, Finger Lap Seams, Red Stain, 1800s, 3 x 5 In.
$226

Soulis Auctions

Kitchen, Peeler, Apple, Yellow Pine, Poplar, Metal Blade, Mortise & Tenon Frame, 1800s, 12 x 24 In.
$82

Jeffrey S. Evans & Associates

Kitchen, Pepper Grinder, Barrel Shape, Sterling, Peugeot Freres, France, Mid 1900s, 3¾ In.
$108

Selkirk Auctioneers & Appraisers

> **TIP**
> *Don't put a hot iron pan in cold water; the pan could warp or even crack.*

K

Kitchen, Pot, Cooking, Brass, Squat, 3-Legged Shape, Iron Swing Handle, 1800s, 12¼ In.
$177

Leland Little Auctions

Kitchen, Refrigerator, Electrolux, Red & Black, Wine, Door, Window, 33 x 23½ In.
$130

Bunch Auctions

Kitchen, Rolled Oats Press, Iron, Wood Crank Handle & Base, Drawer
$51

Strawser Auction Group

Kitchen, Rolling Pin, Glass, Red, White Stripes, 17 In.
$59

Apple Tree Auction Center

Kitchen, Salt Grinder, Twergi, Lacquered, Red, Black, Brown, Wood, Alessi, Ettore Sottsass, 4 In.
$688

Wright

Kitchen, Scoop, Ice Cream, Cone Clipper, Spring Loaded, Metal, Geer Mfg. Co., Pat. 1906, 9 x 3 In.
$83

AntiqueAdvertising.com

Cast-Iron Kitchen Utensils

Cast-iron kitchen utensils are used for three reasons: to put heat in (skillets), to take heat out (molds), and to apply pressure (for example, to crush nuts or candy).

Kitchen, Skillet, Griswold, No. 12, Cast Iron, Heat Ring, Block Logo
$277

Hartzell's Auction Gallery Inc.

Kitchen, Spice Box, Pine, 4 Drawers, Knob Pulls, Black, Painted, 1860s, 8¾ In.
$187

Jeffrey S. Evans & Associates

Kitchen, Spice Chest, Maple, 8 Drawers, Turned Pulls, Shaped Backsplash, Late 1800s, 17 x 10 x 5 In.
$125

Eldred's

Kitchen, Spice Chest, Pine, Painted, 4 Drawers, Shaped Backsplash, 8¼ x 7¾ In.
$122

Neal Auction Company

K

KNIFE

Knife collectors usually specialize in a single type. In the 1960s, the United States government passed a law that required knife manufacturers to mark their knives with the country of origin. This seemed to encourage the collectors, and knife collecting became an interest of a large group of people. All types of knives are collected, from top quality twentieth-century examples to old bone- or pearl-handled knives in excellent condition.

Antler Handle, Steel Blade, Brass, Stag, Turquoise, Pommel With Mask, Late 1900s, 9 In. *illus*	118
Bowie, Crown Stag Handle, Brown, Leather Sheath, Marked, Patton, 9¼ In. .... *illus*	369
Bowie, Forged Blade, Damascus Fittings, Walnut Handle, Burt Foster, Marked, 10 In.......	819
Bowie, German Silver, Stag Handles, Engraved, 8 In.	125
Bowie, Sheffield, Tooled Leather Case, R.H. Alexander, 9¾ In..	708
Dagger, Confederate Style, Civil War, Wood Handle, 17 x 3½ In.	1250
Dagger, Koummya, Curved Blade, Wood Grip, Brass, Morocco, 1900s, 16¾ In. .... *illus*	148
Dagger, Scabbard, Koftgari Design, Wood Handle, Covered, Indian, Early 1800s, 6½ x 12 In.	200
Dagger, Stag Handle, Brass Quillion Guard, Leather, Brown Sheath, Randall, c.1960, 11⅝ In.	281
Dagger, Tribal, Cassowary Bird Bone, Shell, Feathers, Papua New Guinea, 1910s, 12 In........	118
Dagger, Tribal, Tuareg, Silver, Leather, Brass Sheath, Pommel, North Africa, 1800s, 9¼ In.	235
Dagger, Wood Grip, Engraved, Animals, Kozuka, Japan, 7⅜ In.	173
Dirk, Naval, Double Edge Blade, Gilt, Eagle Head Pommel, Early 1800s, 14½ In.	800
Dirk, Silver Ferrule, Eagle Pommel, Spiral Handle, Leather Sheath, Marked, Germany, 7 In.	250
Fighting, Rabbit Ear Design, Brass, Double Edge, Revolutionary War Era, 12¾ In. ...... *illus*	554
Hatchet, Case XX, Faux Horn Handle, Ruler Case, 8½ In.	325
Hunting, Clip Point Blade, Stag Handle, Leather Sheath, Frank Centofante, 9⅜ In. ....-..	431
Hunting, Fixed Blade, Double Edge, Trailing Point Blade, Nylon Sheath, Walter Brend, 8⅝ In...	2185
Hunting, Fixed Blade, Skinner, Stag Grip, Padded Zipper Case, Marked Randall, Orlando, 6 In.	1152
Pocket, Buffalo Horn, 8 Blades, Steel, Signed, Hermes, c.1950, 5½ In.	1875
Scabbard, Silver, Flowers, Carved, Marked, Dufour, 9½ In.	813

KNOWLES, TAYLOR & KNOWLES *items may be found in the KTK and Lotus Ware categories.*

KOSTA

Kosta, the oldest Swedish glass factory, was founded in 1742. During the 1920s through the 1950s, many pieces of original design were made at the factory. Kosta and Boda merged with Afors in 1964 and created the Afors Group in 1971. In 1976, the name Kosta Boda was adopted. The company merged with Orrefors in 1990 and is still working.

Bowl, Pedestal, Carved Interior Overlay, Green Cameo, Signed, Ajors B. Vallien, 7 x 6 In. *illus*	80
Paperweight, Circling Sharks, Internal Controlled Bubble, Vicke Lindstrand, 4¼ In.............	225
Vase, Indian Head Shape, Orange, Green, Yellow, Zigzag, Marked, Boda, 15 x 4½ In. .... *illus*	225
Vase, Open Minds, Ear Handle, Wood Plinth, Ulrica Hydman-Vallien, Late 1900s, 10 x 5½ In.	190

KPM

K.P.M

KPM refers to Berlin porcelain, but the same initials were used alone and in combination with other symbols by several German porcelain makers. They include the Konigliche Porzellan Manufaktur of Berlin, initials used in mark, 1823–1847; Meissen, 1723–1724 only; Krister Porzellan Manufaktur in Waldenburg, after 1831; Kranichfelder Porzellan Manufaktur in Kranichfeld, after 1903; and the Krister Porzellan Manufaktur in Scheibe, after 1838.

Cachepot, White, Bow Shape Handles, 4¼ x 6¼ In., Pair	125
Compote, Gilt, Center Medallion, 3 Egyptian Winged Griffins Base, 5½ In. .... *illus*	504
Lithophane, see also Lithophane category.	
Plaque, Oval, Flower Girl, Signed, Wagner, Berlin, Late 1800s, 13⅜ x 11⅛ In.	1638
Plaque, Royal Family Member, Oval Portrait, Wagner, Shadowbox Frame, 12⅜ x 11⅜ In....	575
Plaque, Royal Family Member, Portrait, Signed, Wagner, Giltwood Frame, 5 x 3½ In...........	460

Kitchen, Spit Jack, Brass, Clockwork, Embossed Label, John Linwood Warranted, 1800s, 14 In.
$84

Garth's Auctioneers & Appraisers

Kitchen, Strainer, Heart Shape, Canted & Rolled Sides, Punchwork, Patina, 14½ x 13½ In.
$625

Eldred's

Kitchen, Strawholder, Amber Glass, Thumbprint, Quadruple Plated Lid, 12 In.
$338

Rich Penn Auctions

K

KPM

Kitchen, Waffle Iron, Griswold, No. 18, Heart & Star, Cast Iron, Stamped, Pa., 17 In.
$184

Richard D. Hatch & Associates

Pointed Knives
An early knife with a pointed end was used to get food to your mouth. Forks were invented in the 18th century and after that table knife ends were rounded.

Knife, Antler Handle, Steel Blade, Brass, Stag, Turquoise, Pommel With Mask, Late 1900s, 9 In.
$118

Austin Auction Gallery

Knife, Bowie, Crown Stag Handle, Brown, Leather Sheath, Marked, Patton, 9¼ In.
$369

Brunk Auctions

Knife, Dagger, Koummya, Curved Blade, Wood Grip, Brass, Morocco, 1900s, 16¾ In.
$148

Leland Little Auctions

Knife, Fighting, Rabbit Ear Design, Brass, Double Edge, Revolutionary War Era, 12¾ In.
$554

Brunk Auctions

Kosta, Bowl, Pedestal, Carved Interior Overlay, Green Cameo, Signed, Ajors B. Vallien, 7 x 6 In.
$80

Woody Auction

Kosta, Vase, Indian Head Shape, Orange, Green, Yellow, Zigzag, Marked, Boda, 15 x 4½ In.
$225

Woody Auction

KPM, Compote, Gilt, Center Medallion, 3 Egyptian Winged Griffins Base, 5½ In.
$504

Fontaine's Auction Gallery

298

Plaque, Ruth Wearing Flowing Robe, Holding Wheat, Charles Landelle, Frame, 1850s, 11 x 8 In.	644
Plaque, Woman, Long Brown Hair, Oval, Gilt Frame, 17 x 14¾ In. .... illus	2142
Plaque, Young Woman, On Bed, Cherub, Curtain, Gilt Frame, Emil Ens, c.1860, 18 x 15 In...	2875
Platter, Fish, Oval, Gilt Border, White Ground, Signed, M. Radloff, 1800s, 25½ In..	205
Tray, Quatrefoil Shape, Nude Figures, Fruit Garland, Pierced Rim, Parcel Gilt, 1800s, 8½ In. *illus*	313

KTK

KTK are the initials of the Knowles, Taylor & Knowles Company of East Liverpool, Ohio, founded by Isaac W. Knowles in 1853. The company made many types of utilitarian wares, hotel china, and dinnerware. It made belleek and the fine bone china known as Lotus Ware from 1891 to 1896. The company merged with American Ceramic Corporation in 1928. It closed in 1934. Lotus Ware is listed in its own category in this book.

Creamer, Blue Bird, 6 Oz., 2 In.	38
Jar, Lid, Moss Rose, Open Finials, Side Handles, Footed, Square Shape, c.1879, 7 In.	76
Plate, Luncheon, Flower Swags Around Rim, Multicolor Paneled Edge, Red Trim, 8¾ In......	8
Relish, Duchess, Orange & Blue Poppies, Gilt Trim, Side Handles, 7¾ In.	16
Syrup, Hinged Lid, Angled Handle, White, Ironstone, c.1880, 6 x 4 In.	148

KUTANI

Kutani porcelain was made in Japan after the mid-seventeenth century. Most of the pieces found today are nineteenth century. Collectors often use the term *Kutani* to refer to just the later, colorful pieces decorated with red, gold, and black pictures of warriors, animals, and birds.

Biscuit Jar, Lid, Red Finial, 2 Panels, Children Playing, Side Handles, Late 19th Century, 7 x 5 In..	416
Bowl, Footed, Red Ground, Cartouche Scenes Around Exterior, Koi Fish Interior, 4½ x 6 In.	38
Figurine, Jurojin Scholar, Standing, Holding Staff, White & Blue Robes, 18¾ In.	295
Figurine, Shishi Lion, Aubergine Purple Glaze, Yellow Ball, Japan, 1800s, 6½ In. .... *illus*	118
Okimono, Cat, Lying Down, Sleeping, Gold Luster Spots, Orange & Blue Bow, c.1900, 10 In..	127
Tea Caddy, Lid, Red, White Cartouches, Flowers, Birds, Gilt, Marked, c.1880, 4¾ x 3¾ In....	54
Vase, Green Foo Dog Handles, Peacock, Landscape, Flowers, Birds, Blue, White, Box, 1900s, 21 In.	2188
Vase, Green Iridescent, Silver Overlay Flower, Crisscross, 8 x 4½ In.	938
Vase, Gold Iridescent, Art Nouveau Style, Silver Overlay, Flowers, Leaves, Vines, 5 In.	252
Vase, Maeander, Light Yellow Iridescent, Tooled, Figure Rim, Tapered Body, c.1900, 10 In.....	295
Vase, Metallin, Green, Silver Overlay, Flowers, 4 In.	125
Vase, Mottled Gold Iridescent, Silberiris, Ruffled Rim, Twisted Body, Square Base, 11 In......	125
Vase, Multicolor Iridescent, Bronze Deco Holder, 13 x 8 In..................................	3383
Vase, Outdoor Scene, Traveling Group, Trees, Orange & Gilt Borders, 20th Century, 18 In., Pair..	205
Vase, Purple Iridescent Shaded To Red, Oil Spot, Pinched, Spiral Ribs, Folded Rim, 1902, 8 In.	201
Vase, Red Ground, Parcel Gilt, Birds, Flowers, Women, Bird On Reverse, Metal Base, 1900s, 16 x 7 In..	99
Vase, Yellow Iridescent, Amber, Bronze Mount Handle, Footed, Signed, 7¾ In.	690

L.G. WRIGHT

L.G. Wright Glass Company of New Martinsville, West Virginia, started selling glassware in 1937. Founder "Si" Wright contracted with Ohio and West Virginia glass factories to reproduce popular pressed glass patterns like Rose & Snow, Baltimore Pear, and Three Face, and opalescent patterns like Daisy & Fern and Swirl. Collectors can tell the difference between the original glasswares and L.G. Wright reproductions because of colors and differences in production techniques. Some L.G. Wright items are marked with an underlined *W* in a circle. Items that were made from old Northwood molds have an altered Northwood mark—an angled line was added to the *N* to make it look like a *W*. Collectors refer to this mark as "the wobbly W." The L.G. Wright factory was closed and the existing molds sold in 1999. Some of the molds are still being used.

KPM, Plaque, Woman, Long Brown Hair, Oval, Gilt Frame, 17 x 14¾ In.
$2,142

Fontaine's Auction Gallery

KPM, Tray, Quatrefoil Shape, Nude Figures, Fruit Garland, Pierced Rim, Parcel Gilt, 1800s, 8½ In.
$313

Hindman

L

Kutani, Figurine, Shishi Lion, Aubergine Purple Glaze, Yellow Ball, Japan, 1800s, 6½ In.
$118

Leland Little Auctions

TIP
A mixture of flour and olive oil can sometimes remove a dull film from a lacquered piece. Rub on the paste, then wipe and polish with a soft cloth.

L.G. Wright, Stars & Bars, Barber
Bottle, Cranberry Opalescent,
Reproduction, 20th Century, 7 In.
$105

Jeffrey S. Evans & Associates

Lacquer, Egg, Rorik Of Dorestad, Rurik
Dynasty, Kingdom Of Ruthenia, Russia,
9 In.
$47

Bunch Auctions

Lacquer, Tray, Serving, Birds, Flower
Branches, Fan Design, Japan, 28 x 22 In.
$118

Austin Auction Gallery

Coin Dot, Lamp, Oil, Cranberry Opalescent, Ball Shade, Elongated Font, Chimney, 1950s, 8 x 2 In..	312
Cranberry Opalescent, Tumbler, Windows, 20th Century, 3¾ In., 5 Piece	150
Spot Optic, Lamp, Cranberry, Umbrella Shape Shade, Nutmeg Burner, 7¼ In.	75
Stars & Bars, Barber Bottle, Cranberry Opalescent, Reproduction, 20th Century, 7 In. *illus*	105

LACQUER

Lacquer is a type of varnish. Collectors are most interested in the Chinese and Japanese lacquer wares made from the Japanese varnish tree. Lacquer wares are made from wood with many coats of lacquer. Sometimes the piece is carved or decorated with ivory or metal inlay.

Bowl, Landscape, Center Character, Multicolor, Hand Painted, Chinese, 1800s, 4 x 10 In.	293
Box, Golden Cockerel, Round, Red Interior, Lift-Up Lid, Signed, Palekh, 1978, 4 In.	288
Box, Lid, Gold Color, Bird & Flower, Marked, Sato Seijo, Japan, 1900s, 1 x 3 x 2 In.	63
Box, Ruslan & Ludmilla, Rectangular, Hinged Lid, Palekh, 1975, 1¾ x 5 x 7 In.	489
Egg, Rorik Of Dorestad, Rurik Dynasty, Kingdom Of Ruthenia, Russia, 9 In. *illus*	47
Model, Airplane, Wood, Black & White, Metal Stand, Louis Vuitton, c.1985, 4 x 21 In.	5625
Screen, 3-Panel, Red, Folding, Bamboo, Birds, Landscape Scene, Painted, Late 1900s, 78 x 48 In.	207
Table, Center, Round, Black, Gilt, Modern Design, 28 x 30 In.	47
Tray, Serving, Birds, Flower Branches, Fan Design, Japan, 28 x 22 In. *illus*	118

LADY HEAD VASE, *see Head Vase.*

LALIQUE

Lalique glass and jewelry were made by Rene Lalique (1860–1945) in Paris, France, between the 1890s and his death in 1945. Beginning in 1921 he had a manufacturing plant in Alsace. The glass was molded, pressed, and engraved in Art Nouveau and Art Deco styles. Most pieces were marked with the signature *R. Lalique.* Lalique glass is still being made. Most pieces made after 1945 bear the mark *Lalique.* After 1978 the registry mark was added and the mark became *Lalique ® France.* In the prices listed here, this is indicated by Lalique (R) France. Some pieces that are advertised as ring dishes or pin dishes were listed as ashtrays in the Lalique factory catalog and are listed as ashtrays here. Names of pieces are given here in French and in English. The Lalique brand was bought by Art & Fragrance, a Swiss company, in 2008. Lalique and Art & Fragrance both became part of the Lalique Group in 2016. Lalique is still being made. Jewelry made by Rene Lalique is listed in the Jewelry category.

R. LALIQUE.FRANCE	LALIQUE FRANCE	*Lalique ® France*
Lalique c.1925–1930s	Lalique 1945–1960	Lalique 1978+

Ashtray, Quail, Frosted, Feather Details, Clear Bowl, Oval, 2¼ x 4 In.	40
Ashtray, Woman's Head, Frosted Glass, Chrome Tray, 1928, 4 x 9 x 7¾ In.	461
Bookends, Sobek, Crocodile, Frosted & Clear Glass, 8 x 3 In.	813
Bowl, Actina, Shallow, Marked R. Lalique, c.1930s, 10¼ In.	500
Bowl, Cendrier, Sculptural Design, Frosted & Clear Glass, Signed, 2½ x 8½ In. *illus*	325
Bowl, Champs Elysees, Engraved, Frosted & Clear Glass, Leaves, 1951, 10 x 7¼ In.	688
Bowl, Champs Elysees, Frosted & Clear Glass, Oak Leaves, Signed, 7½ x 18 In.	920
Bowl, Champs Elysees, Frosted & Clear, Circular Foot, Marc Lalique, 7½ In. *illus*	767
Bowl, Cote-D'Or, Female Nudes, Grapevines, Engraved, Signed, France, 15¾ In.	492
Bowl, Entwined Serpents, Applied, Amber Glass, Clear, Marie-Claude Lalique, 3 x 9 In.	649
Bowl, Lierre, Ivy, Green, Frosted & Clear, France, Late 1900s, 3½ x 8½ In. *illus*	708
Bowl, Nemours, Flower Heads, Black Enameled Center Dots, 4 x 10 In.	275
Bowl, Nemours, Flower Heads, Frosted Glass, Signed, 4 x 10 In.	281
Bowl, Pinsons, Finches & Vines, Frosted & Clear Glass, Signed, 1950s, 3½ x 9¼ In.	274
Bowl, Roscoff, Fish, Bubbles, Clear, Engraved, 13¾ x 2¾ In.	460
Candlestick, Mesanges, Band Of Birds, Flowers, Frosted & Clear, Signed, 1950s, 6 In., Pair...	590

L

Lalique, Bowl, Cendrier, Sculptural Design, Frosted & Clear Glass, Signed, 2 1/2 x 8 1/2 In.
$325

Austin Auction Gallery

Lalique, Bowl, Champs Elysees, Frosted & Clear, Circular Foot, Marc Lalique, 7 1/2 In.
$767

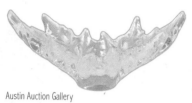

Austin Auction Gallery

Lalique, Bowl, Lierre, Ivy, Green, Frosted & Clear, France, Late 1900s, 3 1/2 x 8 1/2 In.
$708

Leland Little Auctions

Lalique, Figurine, Deux Danseuses, 2 Dancers, Frosted & Clear, Signed, Late 1900s, 10 In.
$767

Leland Little Auctions

Lalique, Figurine, Naiade, Water Nymph, Nude, Frosted, Signed, 3 3/4 x 2 3/16 In.
$92

Blackwell Auctions

Lalique, Hood Ornament, Chrysis, Nude Woman, Kneeling, Frosted, 1925, 5 1/4 x 6 1/2 In.
$375

Neal Auction Company

Lalique, Hood Ornament, Tete D'Aigle, Eagle Head, Frosted, 1950s, 4 3/8 In.
$380

Jeffrey S. Evans & Associates

Lalique, Hood Ornament, Tete De Belier, Ram's Head, Frosted & Clear, Signed R. Lalique, 4 In.
$904

Strawser Auction Group

Lalique, Hood Ornament, Victoire, Androgynous Figure, Frosted, c.1928, 6 1/2 In.
$2,142

Fontaine's Auction Gallery

L

LALIQUE

Lalique, Paperweight, Bird, Head Up, Frosted, Label On Base, Signed, 3 1/4 x 4 1/2 In.
$200

Lalique, Perfume Bottle, Ambre D'Orsay, Tapered, Rectangular, Opaque Black, Signed, c.1912, 5 1/4 In.
$936

Lalique, Vase, Bacchantes, Nudes, Cone Shape, Frosted, Engraved, 1900s, 9 x 7 In.
$1,638

Lalique, Vase, Epis, Leaves & Flared Ribs, Frosted, Etched, c.1946, 6 1/2 x 6 3/8 In.
$316

> **TIP**
> If garage windows are painted, burglars won't be able to tell if cars are home or not. Use translucent paint to get light in the closed garage.

Lamp, 2-Light, Moe Bridges, Reverse Painted Shade, River Landscape, Metal Base, 1920s, 20 3/4 In.
$750

L

Compote, Coupe Nogent, 4 Satin Birds, Circular Foot, Marc Lalique, 3 ¼ In.	354
Compote, Elizabeth, Frosted, Leaves, Square Base, Signed, 5 ¼ x 4 ¾ In.	118
Cooler, Champagne, Ganymede, Entwined Nudes, Grapevines, Embossed, Late 1900s, 9 In.	563
Cruet, Bourgueil, Triangular Design, Frosted, Geometric, Fitted Stand, Late 1900s, 6 In., Pair	649
Decanter, Bulbous Body, Doughnut Shape Stopper, Flat Edge, 1950s, 10 ½ In.	202
Decanter, Femmes, Women, Swirl Stopper, Frosted Images, 9 ½ x 5 ½ In.	200
Decanter, Phalsbourg, Vine & Fruit Stopper, Signed, France, 1900s, 10 In.	708
Decanter, Scarab, Frosted & Clear Panels, Flared Rim, Stopper, Lalique France, 9 x 5 In.	406
Figurine, Ariane, 2 Doves, Frosted Glass, Circular Base, 8 ½ x 6 ¾ In.	529
Figurine, Chat Assis, Cat, Sitting, Frosted Glass, Signed, 8 ¼ In.	375
Figurine, Daphnis, Bird, Frosted Glass Foot Rim, Marie-Claude Lalique, Late 1900s, 9 In., Fair	148
Figurine, Deux Danseuses, 2 Dancers, Frosted & Clear, Signed, Late 1900s, 10 In. *illus*	767
Figurine, Elephant, Frosted, Trunk Up, Clear Glass Base, 6 ½ In.	147
Figurine, Fish, Frosted, Clear Glass, Signed, 4 x 6 ¼ x 2 ⅝ In., Pair	125
Figurine, Gedeon Canard, Duck, Clear, Frosted, Mounted, Round Base, Signed, 5 x 5 ¼ In.	173
Figurine, Leopard, Black, Crawling, Signed, 4 x 14 ½ In.	949
Figurine, Madonna & Child, Molded, Frosted Glass, Black Plinth Base, Signed, 14 ½ In.	158
Figurine, Naiade, Water Nymph, Nude, Frosted, Signed, 3 ¾ x 2 ³⁄₁₆ In. *illus*	92
Figurine, Pisces, 2 Fish, Frosted Accents, Signed, France, Late 1900s, 11 ¼ In.	1298
Figurine, Quail, Frosted Glass, Paper Label, Signed, France, 5 ¼ In., 2 Piece	192
Goblet, 6 Figurines Exterior, Tan, Stained, Signed, R. Lalique, 1900s, 4 In.	293
Hood Ornament, Chrysis, Nude Woman, Kneeling, Frosted, 1925, 5 ¼ x 6 ½ In. *illus*	375
Hood Ornament, Tete D'Aigle, Eagle Head, Frosted, 1950s, 4 ⅜ In. *illus*	380
Hood Ornament, Tete De Belier, Ram's Head, Frosted & Clear, Signed R. Lalique, 4 In. *illus*	904
Hood Ornament, Victoire, Androgynous Figure, Frosted, c.1928, 6 ½ In. *illus*	2142
Paperweight, Bird, Head Up, Frosted, Label On Base, Signed, 3 ¼ x 4 ½ In. *illus*	200
Paperweight, Coq Nain, Rooster, Round Base, Engraved, 8 x 5 ½ x 2 ¾ In.	207
Perfume Bottle, Ambre D'Orsay, Tapered, Rectangular, Opaque Black, Signed, c.1912, 5 ¼ In. *illus*	936
Perfume Bottle, Deux Fleurs, 2 Flowers, Frosted, Petals Shape, 4 x 3 ½ In.	123
Perfume Bottle, Nina Ricci, Grande Pomme, Apple Shape, Frosted, Leaves Stopper, 5 ½ In	130
Plate, Annual, Etched, 1966, 8 ½ In., 11 Piece	201
Plate, Ondines, Nude Sea Nymph, Opalescent, Wheel Engraved, 1921, 10 ¾ In.	700
Platter, Chene, Oak Leaves, Frosted, Oval, Signed, 24 ¼ x 13 ¾ In.	949
Platter, Piriac, Medial Band Of Fish & Waves, Frosted, Oval, Scalloped Edge, 10 ¾ In.	384
Urn, Dampierre, Protruding Sparrows, Clear, Frosted, Signed, France, 4 ¾ In., Pair	266
Vase, Andromeda, Fish Scales, Embossed, Clear & Frosted, Signed, 5 ¾ x 5 ¾ In.	375
Vase, Bacchantes, Nudes, Cone Shape, Frosted, Engraved, 1900s, 9 x 7 In. *illus*	1638
Vase, Bagatelle, Fledglings, Frosted, Olive Branches, Embossed, Signed, 6 ¾ In.	100 to 345
Vase, Bali, Frosted Glass, Molded, Acid Etched, Lalique France, 7 ¼ In.	320
Vase, Bud, Etched Grass Leaf, Cream Ground, Marked, c.1910, 6 ¾ In.	1000
Vase, Chevreuse Style, Tapered Shape, 5 Encircling Rings, Frosted, 1900s, 6 ¼ In.	284
Vase, Dampierre, Protruding Sparrows, Vines, Frosted, Signed, 5 x 4 ½ In.	83
Vase, Elisabeth, Protruding Birds, Leaves, Frosted, Engraved, Box, 5 ¼ In.	313
Vase, Epis, Leaves & Flared Ribs, Frosted, Etched, c.1946, 6 ½ x 6 ⅜ In. *illus*	316
Vase, Ornis, Bird Handles, Frosted, Circular Base, c.1915, 7 ¾ In.	1046
Vase, Spiraling Leaves, Frosted Glass, Embossed, 1900s, 7 ½ In.	266
Vase, Vibration, Globe Shape, Raised Wave, Frosted & Clear, Engraved, 11 x 11 In.	502

LAMP

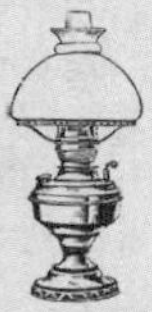

Lamps of every type, from the early oil-burning Betty and Phoebe lamps to the recent electric lamps with glass or beaded shades, interest collectors. Fuels used in lamps changed through the years; whale oil (1800–1840), camphene (1828), Argand (1830), lard (1833–1863), solar (1843–1860s), turpentine and alcohol (1840s), gas (1850–1879), kerosene (1860), and electricity (1879) are the most common. Early solar or astral lamps burned fat. Modern solar lamps are powered by the sun. Other lamps are listed by manufacturer or type of material.

2-Light, Electric, Arts & Crafts, 4-Sided Caramel Slag Glass Shades, Metal Base, 19 x 20 In.	700
2-Light, Gilt Metal, Faux Candle Cover, 3 Curved Legs, France, 71 In.	94

Lamp, Aladdin, Burmese, Brass Collar, Model 23 Burner, Flowers, Fenton, Kerosene Stand, 1997, 22 In.
$527

Jeffrey S. Evans & Associates

Lamp, Argand, 2-Light, Brass, 2 Perched Birds, Cut Glass Prisms & Shades, 24 In.
$1,260

Fontaine's Auction Gallery

Lamp, Argand, 2-Light, Classical, Gilt, Bronze, Leaves & Scrolls, c.1830, 21 In.
$1,152

Neal Auction Company

Lamp, Argand, Bronze, Gilt & Patina, Prisms, Paw Feet, J & I Cox, Electrified, c.1834, 19 In., Pair
$768

Neal Auction Company

L

Lamp, Argand, Cut Glass, Faceted, Spear Prisms, Bronze, Marble Base, Mid 1800s, 23 In., Pair
$350

Neal Auction Company

2-Light, Moe Bridges, Reverse Painted Shade, River Landscape, Metal Base, 1920s, 20¾ In. *illus*	750
2-Light, Neoclassical Style, Gilt Bronze, France, Early 1900s, 61 In.	768
3-Light, Glass, Copper, Flower, Green Shade, Trumpet Shape Base, Marked, 23 x 18 In.	1500
Advertising, Shaeffer Pens, Gilt Metal, Toggle Switch, c.1950, 14 x 18 x 6 In.	177
Aladdin, Bronze, Oil, Aurene Glass Shade, Trifoot Base, Marked, 54 x 19 x 12 In.	1250
Aladdin, Burmese, Brass Collar, Model 23 Burner, Flowers, Fenton, Kerosene Stand, 1997, 22 In. *illus*	527
Argand, 2-Light, Brass, 2 Perched Birds, Cut Glass Prisms & Shades, 24 In. *illus*	1260
Argand, 2-Light, Classical, Gilt, Bronze, Leaves & Scrolls, c.1830, 21 In. *illus*	1152
Argand, 2-Light, Frosted Glass Globe, Bronze, American Empire, Baldwin Gardiner, 1840, 19 In.	1062
Argand, Bronze, Beaded Pendant, Cut, Frosted Glass Shade, c.1840, 12½ x 13 x 8½ In.	550
Argand, Bronze, Gilt & Patina, Prisms, Paw Feet, J & I Cox, Electrified, c.1834, 19 In., Pair *illus*	768
Argand, Cut Glass, Faceted, Spear Prisms, Bronze, Marble Base, Mid 1800s, 23 In., Pair *illus*	350
Argand, Gilt Bronze, Lobed Bell Shape, Glass Base, Mounted, Lewis Vernon & Co., 25 x 21 In.	3444
Argand, Gilt, Bronze, Fluted Urn Shape, Cylindrical Base, Frosted Shade, 1800s, 17 In., Pair	2337
Art Deco, Silvered Bronze, Figural, Dancer, Holding Glass Globe, Late 1900s, 22 In.	472
Art Glass, Dinanderie, Globe Shape, Painted, Celluloid Shade, c.1930, 13 In.	320
Banquet, Brass, Cupped Shades, White, Leafy Base, Stiffel, c.1950, 29 In., Pair	300
Banquet, Brass, Onyx, Doric Column, Stepped Base, Etched Ball Shade, Fleur-De-Lis, 1880s, 37 In.	240
Banquet, Clear Swirled Glass, Globe Shape, Frosted Shades, 17¾ In., Pair	142
Banquet, Glass Globe, Gilt Bronze, Filigree, Cartouche Shields, Victorian, 35 x 12 In.	5040
Banquet, Oil, Ceramic, Stylized Flowers, Leaves, Textured Ground, 1900s, 21 x 10 x 10 In.	94
Banquet, Oil, Onyx Shaft, Globular Shade, Reticulated Base, Victorian, Electrified, 34 In.*illus*	230
Banquet, Oil, Thermidor Lampe Belge, Silver Brass, Cranberry Hobnail, c.1890, 29 x 8 In.	281
Banquet, Victorian, Brass Base, Frosted Shade, Black Trim, 32 In.	259
Betty, Copper, Hinged Lid, Peened Knop, Shaped Hanging Arm, Peter Derr, c.1836, 5½ In.	2000
Betty, Wrought Iron, Swivel Lid, Key Shape Finial, Serrated Hanger, 1910s, 7 In. *illus*	132
Bouillotte, 2-Light, Brass, 2 Horn Candelabra, Tole Shade, Ring Finial, Wildwood Base, 1900s, 26 In.	354
Bouillotte, 3-Light, Adjustable Shade, Swan Shape Candle Arms, Urn Shaft, 31 In.	305
Bouillotte, 3-Light, Tole Peinte Shade, Dish Base, France, 1900s, 27 x 13½ In.	488
Bouillotte, French Tole Peinte, Brass, Black Adjustable Shade, 1900s, 25 In. *illus*	732
Bradley & Hubbard lamps are included in the Bradley & Hubbard category.	
Brass, 3-Light, Empire Style, Corinthian Column, Claw Feet, Early 1900s, 66 In.	410
Brass, Moorish Revival, Pierced, Cone Shape Shade, Domed Circular Foot, Early 1900s, 73 In.	649
Bronze, Art Nouveau Style, Woman, Nude, Black Marble Base, 21 x 7 In.	188
Bronze, Electric, Cast Figurine, Whistler Boy, Slag Glass, c.1940, 25¾ In. *illus*	230
Bronze, Mermaid, Trumpet, Glass Shade, Signed, A. Boucher, 54¾ In. *illus*	406
Bronze, Woman, Dress, Arms Outstretched, Gilt, Octagonal Base, Marked, AG Paris, 24¾ x 11 In.	406
Candlestick Base, Yellow Resin, Table, Dorothy Thorpe, 29 x 8 x 4 In., Pair	406
Ceiling, Brass, Frosted Glass, Paavo Tynell, Finland, c.1945, 11½ x 10½ In.	1000
Chandelier, 2 Tiers Of Candle Sockets, Leaves, Scrolled, Sheet Metal, Late 1900s, 56 x 61 In.	300
Chandelier, 3-Light, Boudoir, Lead Cut Crystal Prisms, Ceiling Cap, Late 1900s, 10 In.	413
Chandelier, 3-Light, Bronze, Blue Glass, Gilt, Neoclassical, 1800s, 43 In.	882
Chandelier, 3-Light, Bronze, Glass, Basket Shape, Ribbon Decor, c.1910, 28 x 20½ x 20½ In.	4750
Chandelier, 3-Light, Twig & Leaf, Wrought Iron, Rustic	246
Chandelier, 4-Light, Brass, Multicolor Metal, Perforated Shades, Italy, 23 In. *illus*	1000
Chandelier, 4-Light, Colonial Style, Wire Arms, Wood, 22½ In.	148
Chandelier, 4-Light, Empire Style, Gilt Canopies, Crystal Swags, Early 1900s, 29 x 20 x 15 In. *...illus*	443
Chandelier, 4-Light, French Empire Style, Candle Sockets, Metal Drop Link Chain, 1900s, 42 x 27 In.	761
Chandelier, 4-Light, Iron, Curved Glass, 40 x 20 In.	366
Chandelier, 4-Light, Pewter, Scroll Arms, Mid Drip Pan, Candleholder, 1700s, 17 x 14 In.	3904
Chandelier, 5-Light, Black Forest Style, Oak, Carved, Early 1900s, 32 In.	1680
Chandelier, 5-Light, Brass, Scrolled Leafy Arms, Orb, Ring, Dutch, 1700s, 15 In.	1375
Chandelier, 5-Light, Brass, Tapered Linen Shades, Paavo Tynell, Taito Oy, No. 9030, 33 In.	1300
Chandelier, 5-Light, Chrome, Eyeball, Hanging, c.1950-60, 30 In.	125
Chandelier, 5-Light, Cut Glass Prisms, 41 x 27 In.	250
Chandelier, 6-Light, Brass, Curved Arms, Reeded Stem, Leafy, Finial, 1880s, 34 x 20 In.	202
Chandelier, 6-Light, Brass, Glass, Candleholder, Louis XV Style, 1900s, 33 In. *illus*	448
Chandelier, 6-Light, Candle, Cast Brass Pin, Hanging Ring, Dutch, 1700s, 22 x 28 In.	2457
Chandelier, 6-Light, Candle, Iron, Scrollwork Frame, Electrified, 1800s, 34 x 36 x 18 In.	761
Chandelier, 6-Light, Cone Shape, Iron, Profuse Punch Design, Candlecups, 1800s, 18 In.	625

Lamp, Banquet, Oil, Onyx Shaft, Globular Shade, Reticulated Base, Victorian, Electrified, 34 In.
$230

Stevens Auction Co.

Lamp, Betty, Wrought Iron, Swivel Lid, Key Shape Finial, Serrated Hanger, 1910s, 7 In.
$132

Garth's Auctioneers & Appraisers

Lamp, Bouillotte, French Tole Peinte, Brass, Black Adjustable Shade, 1900s, 25 In.
$732

Neal Auction Company

Lamp, Bronze, Electric, Cast Figurine, Whistler Boy, Slag Glass, c.1940, 25 ¾ In.
$230

Blackwell Auctions

Lamp, Bronze, Mermaid, Trumpet, Glass Shade, Signed, A. Boucher, 54 ¾ In.
$406

Charlton Hall Auctions

Lamp, Chandelier, 4-Light, Brass, Multicolor Metal, Perforated Shades, Italy, 23 In.
$1,000

Kamelot Auctions

Lamp, Chandelier, 4-Light, Empire Style, Gilt Canopies, Crystal Swags, Early 1900s, 29 x 20 x 15 In.
$443

Austin Auction Gallery

Lamp, Chandelier, 6-Light, Brass, Glass, Candleholder, Louis XV Style, 1900s, 33 In.
$448

Hindman

305

Lamp, Chandelier, 6-Light, Iron, Horse, Deer, Scrollwork, Naos Forge, 31 x 43 In.
$1,298

Austin Auction Gallery

Lamp, Chandelier, 8-Light, Art Deco, White, Alabaster Stone Panes, Iron, Leaves, Scroll, 24 x 35 In.
$885

Austin Auction Gallery

Lamp, Chandelier, 10-Light, Cut Glass, George III Style, 49 x 34 In.
$3,780

Sotheby's

Chandelier, 6-Light, French Style, Gilt Metal, Crystal Beads, 15 x 21 In.	83
Chandelier, 6-Light, Gilt, Glass, Scroll Arms, Embellished, Beads, 32 In.	768
Chandelier, 6-Light, Hanging, Scroll Arms, 25 In.	236
Chandelier, 6-Light, Iron, Horse, Deer, Scrollwork, Naos Forge, 31 x 43 In. .... *illus*	1298
Chandelier, 6-Light, Iron, Tole, Green Ground, Gilt, Hanging Prisms, Early 1900s, 32 x 30 In.	1536
Chandelier, 6-Light, Steel Frame, 3 Blue Glass Shades, Italy, c.1970, 11 x 10 ¼ In.	325
Chandelier, 6-Light, Venetian, Carved, Giltwood, Hanging Crystal, 30 x 29 In.	288
Chandelier, 6-Light, White, Painted Metal, Faux Coral Branches, 75 In.	375
Chandelier, 6-Light, Wrought Iron, Art Deco, Frosted Glass Shade, Flowers, 24 x 20 x 34 In.	3125
Chandelier, 6-Light, Wrought Iron, Scrolled Frame, Bobeche, Sun Pendant, Late 1900s, 54 In.	354
Chandelier, 7-Light, Circular Shade, Fabric Lining, Tassels, Pierced, Faux Candles, 1900s, 53 In.	561
Chandelier, 8-Light, 2 Tiers, Wire Frame Canopy, Gilt Metal, Teardrop Prism, 1900s, 27 x 24 In.	443
Chandelier, 8-Light, Art Deco, White, Alabaster Stone Panes, Iron, Leaves, Scroll, 24 x 35 In. *illus*	885
Chandelier, 8-Light, Gilt Bronze, Baccarat Crystal Beads, Swags & Prisms, c.1910, 41 In.	13125
Chandelier, 8-Light, Glass, Bronze, Ormolu Sculptural, Signed, Baccarat, 38 x 30 In.	2875
Chandelier, 8-Light, Metal, Parchment Shades, Eric Schmitt, Germany, c.1992, 46 x 30 In.	2000
Chandelier, 8-Light, Neoclassical Style, Clear & Amethyst Glass, Gilt Metal, 40 x 28 In.	300
Chandelier, 8-Light, Neoclassical Style, Leafy, Pinecone Pendant, Early 1900s, 25 x 24 In.	1875
Chandelier, 8-Light, White Porcelain Roses, Gilt Leaves, Ceiling Cap, Mid 1900s, 28 x 26 In.	1003
Chandelier, 9-Light, Scroll Arms, Cut Glass Beads, Metal, Patina, 1900s, 35 x 38 In.	4270
Chandelier, 10-Light, Brass, 2 Dragons, 48 x 35 x 16 In.	344
Chandelier, 10-Light, Cut Glass, George III Style, 49 x 34 In. .... *illus*	3780
Chandelier, 10-Light, Empire Gilt, Bronze, Crown Hung, Basket Base, Central Ball, 48 x 33 In.	9840
Chandelier, 12-Light, Neoclassical, Gilt Bronze, Teardrop Finial, c.1825, 26 x 24 In.	2772
Chandelier, 12-Light, Rope Twist Arms, Cranberry Glass Shades, Monumental, 64 x 40 In.	3163
Chandelier, 15-Light, Regency, Bronze, 5 Arms, Swags, Flowers, Leaves, c.1845, 33 x 39 In. *illus*	12188
Chandelier, Alabaster, Dish Shape, Bronze, Ram's Head, 3 Ropes, France, c.1940, 26 x 14 x 15 In.	1188
Chandelier, Art Deco, Molded, Frosted Glass Shade, Fruit & Geometrics, c.1930, 13 ¾ In.	358
Chandelier, Bronze, Swirling Filigree, Acanthus, Etched Glass Shade, 25 x 28 In. ...... *illus*	5355
Chandelier, Gilt Metal, Glass, Basket Shape, Hall Fixture, 26 In. .... *illus*	469
Chandelier, Hall, Glass, Wrought Iron, Carved, Art Deco, Signed, Daum Nancy, 36 x 17 x 17 In.	5120
Chandelier, Iron, Lemons, Candleholders, Tole, Painted, Italy, c.1940, 22 x 21 In.	313
Chandelier, Leaded Shade, Caramel Slag Glass, Pierced Metal Trim, Hanging, 1950s, 12 x 20 In.	293
Chandelier, Poul Henningsen, Pendant, Copper, Enamel, Aluminum, Denmark, 1927, 12 In., Pair	5313
Desk, Brass, Red, Enameled Steel, Marked, Roberto Giulio Rida, Italy, 2000s, 22 x 7 In., Pair.	1500
Desk, Duffner & Kimberly, Flower Blossom, Leaves, Bronze Base, Early 1900s, 25 ½ x 20 In.	8750
Electric, 2-Light, Arts & Crafts, Oak, Caramel & Green Slag Glass Shade, 23 x 20 In.	938
Electric, 2-Light, Brass, Wrought Iron, Tripod Base, Floor, 57 x 17 In.	75
Electric, 2-Light, Central Font, 2 Tin Shades, 22 x 14 In.	75
Electric, 2-Light, Desk, Louis XVI Style, Gilt Bronze, Pleated Silk Shade, 1800s, 20 In.	756
Electric, 2-Light, Mica Shades, Wood Base, Signed, William Morris Studio, 19 In. ...... *illus*	237
Electric, 2-Light, Murano Glass, Yellow, Copper Ring Base, Marbro, 39 x 7 In., Pair	344
Electric, 2-Light, Neoclassical Urn, Robin's-Egg Blue Enamel, Gilt Brass, Acorn Finial, 24 In.	71
Electric, 2-Light, Paris, Pink, Handle, Circular Base, 29 In., Pair	316
Electric, 2-Light, Parrot, Perch, Fabric Shade, Stepped Base, Frederick Cooper, Late 1900s, 31 In. *illus*	325
Electric, 2-Light, Reverse Painted Shade, Fields & Trees, Signed, Jefferson, 20 x 14 In. *illus*	500
Electric, 2-Weight, Matching Finial, Flowers, St. Clair, 29 ½ In.	147
Electric, 4-Light, Duffner & Kimberly, Peacock, Bronze Base, c.1906, 27 In. ....*illus*	27060
Electric, 4-Light, Tiffany Style, Twisted Vine Base, 25 In.	4200
Electric, 5-Light, Bronze, Renaissance Revival, Satin Glass, Flame Shape Shade, Early 1900s, 66 In.	1298
Electric, 5-Light, Flower Shape, Art Glass Shade, Wrought Metal, Patina, Early 1900s, 69 In.	2750
Electric, 6 Panels, Dome Top, Brass, Flowers, Bronze Base, Victorian, 22 x 18 In.	840
Electric, 6-Light, Bronze, Circular Shade, Pierced, Pedestal Base, Early 1900s, 70 In.	885
Electric, 6-Light, Wheel Feet, Martine Bedin, Memphis Milano, 1981, 13 ½ x 23 x 6 ½ In. *illus*	1180
Electric, 12-Light, Hanging, Fixture, Moravian Star, Ball Shape Finial, 1900s, 16 ½ In.	497
Electric, 15-Light, Mottled, Lily Art Glass Shades, Metal Base, Late 1900s, 21 In. .... *illus*	431
Electric, Adjustable, Enameled & Nickel Plated Brass, Frosted Glass, Angelo Lelii, c.1954, 10 In.	6875
Electric, Adjustable, Swivel, Steel Base, Rectangular, Signed, Cedric Hartman, 41 x 11 In.	5000
Electric, Akari, Isamu Noguchi, Cotton, Bamboo, Enamel Steel, Ozeki & Co. Ltd., c.1970, 76 In.	5938
Electric, Anodized Aluminum & Steel, Glass, Kem Weber, Miller Co., c.1935, 15 In. ...... *illus*	2500

Electric, Architectural, Wood, Green, Gold, Painted, Mounted, Ball Feet, 1800s, 38 In., Pair *illus* ... 708
Electric, Arredoluce, Triennale, Aluminum, Chrome Plated, Brass, Angelo Lelii, 1947, 65 In. *illus* ... 5000
Electric, Art Deco Style, Nude Woman Figure, Stepped Cone Shade, Oval Base, 13 ½ In. 230
Electric, Art Deco Style, Skyscraper, Opaque, White Glass Shade, Black, Wood Base, 17 ¾ In. .. 270
Electric, Art Deco, Figural, Woman, Silvered, Pulled Feather Shade, Art Glass, 16 In. 254
Electric, Art Glass, Millefiori, Painted, Signed, Cenedese, 18 In. 265
Electric, Art Nouveau, Brass Shade, Multicolor Jewels, Flower Swag, Round Base, 22 In 1121
Electric, Art Nouveau, Caramel & Red Slag Glass, Flowers, 16 Panels, Bronze Base, c.1920, 24 In. ... 188
Electric, Arts & Crafts Style, Gilt Metal, Slag Glass Shade, Landscape, c.1950, 23 In. 219
Electric, Arts & Crafts Style, Leaded Glass Shade, Tree Trunk Metal Base, 22 x 12 In. 100
Electric, Banker's, Star Emblem, Art Deco, Brass, Marble Base, Michel Decoux, c.1920, 29 In. 1298
Electric, Bergman Style, Cossack, Horse, Tree, Figural, Glass Cutouts, Spelter, 26 In. 531
Electric, Bernini Style, Carved Wood, Plaster Faux Stone Base, 52 x 10 In., Pair 458
Electric, Blanc De Chine, Reticulated, Bamboo, Cherry Blossom, Wood Base, Mid 1900s, 27 In., Pair 354
Electric, Boudoir, Domed Shade, Faceted Glass Flowers, Gilt Metal, Early 1900s, 14 x 9 In., Pair. 443
Electric, Brass, Faux Bamboo, Brass Circular Base, Italy, 33 x 8 x 8 In., Pair 406
Electric, Brass, Lily Flower, Art Glass Shade, Art Nouveau, 49 x 10 In. .... *illus* 531
Electric, Brass, Paper, Plastic, Kaare Klint, Denmark, 1945, 17 In., Pair 1750
Electric, Brass, White, Sphere Shape Shade, 3 Legs, Circular Base, Nessen, 25 In. 500
Electric, Bronze, Black Marble, Gilt, France, 1800s, 17 ¼ x 6 ½ In., Pair 563
Electric, Bronze, Figural, Female, Nude, Holding Flower Aloft, Circular Stand, Paw Feet, 21 In... 244
Electric, Bronze, Figural, Woman, Seated, Crops, Neoclassical, France, 26 In. 58
Electric, Bronze, Urn Shape, 3 Minogame Turtles, Key Motif Rim, Japan, Early 1900s, 25 In. . 207
Electric, Bronze, Woman, Nude, Seated, Denmark, 1900s, 9 ¼ In. 128
Electric, Brushed Metal, Square Shade, Contemporary, 35 x 10 In. 125
Electric, Burlwood, Bronze, Acorn Final, Cream Shade, Theodore Alexander, 1800s, 28 In., Pair 649
Electric, Candlestick Shape, 8-Panel Shade, Slag Glass, Gilt, Metalwork, c.1920, 24 In. 390
Electric, Candlestick Shape, Silver Sticks, Cabochon, Silk Shades, Sweden, 1860, 9 ½ In., Pair... 142
Electric, Caramel Slag Glass Shade, Brass Frame, Flowers, Square Base, 16 In. .... *illus* 135
Electric, Caramel Slag Glass Shade, Flowers, Spelter Base, Early 1900s, 24 x 16 In................ 154
Electric, Cast Iron, Brass Base, Marble Ornament, 57 ½ In. 31
Electric, Ceiling, 6-Light, Palm Leaf, Brass, Cut Glass, Late 1800s, 23 ½ x 19 In.................... 1664
Electric, Ceiling, Hanging, Daum Cameo Glass Shade, Berries, Chipped Ice, 8 x 6 In. .. *illus* 1088
Electric, Chapman, Tobacco Leaf, Painted, Chinese Export Style, Wood Plinths, 1970, 29 In., Pair ... 649
Electric, Chrome, Molded Shade, Metal Diffuser, Vertical Rods, Circular Base, c.1970, 65 In. *illus* 266
Electric, Chrome, Mushroom Shade, Glass Rods, Round Stepped Base, 16 x 14 In., Pair *illus* 345
Electric, Chrome, Stacked & Formed Sheet Metal, Round Base, C. Jere, 39 In. 142
Electric, Contemporary, Asian Style, Ceramic, Fruit & Butterfly Motif, 21 ½ In...................... 49
Electric, Copper, Brown Finish, Adjustable Lights, Weighted Cone Shape Base, 71 In., Pair .. 738
Electric, Cork, Wood, String Shades, Mid Century, 28 ½ In., Pair 148
Electric, Cut Glass, Bedroom, Clear, Trumpet Base, Mushroom Shape Shade, c.1915, 16 ½ In. 129
Electric, Cut Glass, Disc Shape Shade, Leaves & Star, Mounted, Gilt Base, c.1940, 8 In., Pair. 148
Electric, Cut Glass, Hobstar & Diamond, Domed Shade, Metal Rim, Crystal Prisms, 26 In. *illus* 266
Electric, Doe & Deer, Black, Lacquer Base, Cream Shade, 28 In................................ 212
Electric, Domed Glass Shade, Summer Landscape, River, Trees, Houses, Painted, Early 1900s, 25 In... 219
Electric, Dragon, Carved, Black, Lantern Shade, 69 ½ In. 295
Electric, Driftwood, c.1970, 26 In., Pair.. 406
Electric, Duffner & Kimberly, Thistle, Leaded Glass Shade, Early 1900s, 22 x 20 In. 9900
Electric, Edgar Brandt, Iron, Grapevine, Alabaster Shade, Early 1900s, 68 x 15 In. 1024
Electric, Emeralite, Cast Spelter Base, Adjustable Arm, Bellova Glass Shade, c.1916, 13 In. *illus* 704
Electric, Enameled Steel, Aluminum, Bakelite, Middletown Mfg. Co., 48 x 12 In. 200
Electric, Exterior Light, Lacquered Wood, Frosted Glass, Frank Lloyd Wright, 1912, 37 In. 9375
Electric, Figural, Horse Head, White Glaze, Lucite Base, 25 x 8 ½ x 20 In., Pair.................... 369
Electric, Figural, Man, Seated, Playing Flute, Dog, Bronze, Gilt, Continental, 19 In. 94
Electric, Figural, Young Roma Woman, Bronze Domed Shades, Hanging Beads, 19 x 9 x 12 In. . 518
Electric, Flame Finial, Octagonal Base, Visual Comfort & Co., 16 ½ In., Pair..................... 443
Electric, Funeral Parlor, Brass, Spiral Standard, Green Glass, 1900s, 67 ½ In...................... 200
Electric, G. Magnusson, Grasshopper, Enameled Steel, Aluminum, Sweden, c.1947, 50 In. . *illus* 4063
Electric, Giltwood, Carved, Baluster Shape, Domed Foot, Continental, Early 1900s, 74 In. 413
Electric, Glass Fruit Basket, Beaded, Czechoslovakia, 11 x 11 In. .... *illus* 225

Lamp, Chandelier, 15-Light, Regency, Bronze, 5 Arms, Swags, Flowers, Leaves, c.1845, 33 x 39 In.
$12,188

New Orleans Auction Galleries

Lamp, Chandelier, Bronze, Swirling Filigree, Acanthus, Etched Glass Shade, 25 x 28 In.
$5,355

Fontaine's Auction Gallery

Lamp, Chandelier, Gilt Metal, Glass, Basket Shape, Hall Fixture, 26 In.
$469

Charlton Hall Auctions

L

Lamp, Electric, 2-Light, Mica Shades, Wood Base, Signed, William Morris Studio, 19 In.
$237

Eldred's

Lamp, Electric, 2-Light, Parrot, Perch, Fabric Shade, Stepped Base, Frederick Cooper, Late 1900s, 31 In.
$325

Austin Auction Gallery

Lamp, Electric, 2-Light, Reverse Painted Shade, Fields & Trees, Signed, Jefferson, 20 x 14 In.
$500

Woody Auction

Lamp, Electric, 4-Light, Duffner & Kimberly, Peacock, Bronze Base, c.1906, 27 In.
$27,060

Morphy Auctions

Lamp, Electric, 6-Light, Wheel Feet, Martine Bedin, Memphis Milano, 1981, 13 ½ x 23 x 6 ½ In.
$1,180

Austin Auction Gallery

Lamp, Electric, 15-Light, Mottled, Lily Art Glass Shades, Metal Base, Late 1900s, 21 In.
$431

Rich Penn Auctions

Lamp, Electric, Anodized Aluminum & Steel, Glass, Kem Weber, Miller Co., c.1935, 15 In.
$2,500

Wright

Lamp, Electric, Architectural, Wood, Green, Gold, Painted, Mounted, Ball Feet, 1800s, 38 In., Pair
$708

Leland Little Auctions

Lamp, Electric, Arredoluce, Triennale, Aluminum, Chrome Plated, Brass, Angelo Lelii, 1947, 65 In.
$5,000

Wright

Lamp, Electric, Brass, Lily Flower, Art Glass Shade, Art Nouveau, 49 x 10 In.
$531

Bruneau & Co. Auctioneers

Lamp, Electric, Caramel Slag Glass Shade, Brass Frame, Flowers, Square Base 16 In.
$135

Apple Tree Auction Center

Lamp, Electric, Ceiling, Hanging, Daum Cameo Glass Shade, Berries, Chipped Ice, 8 x 6 In.
$1,088

Morphy Auctions

Lamp, Electric, Chrome, Molded Shade, Metal Diffuser, Vertical Rods, Circular Base, c.1970, 65 In.
$266

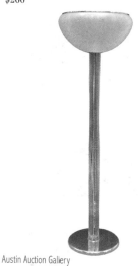

Austin Auction Gallery

Lamp, Electric, Chrome, Mushroom Shade, Glass Rods, Round Stepped Base, 16 x 14 In., Pair
$345

Blackwell Auctions

Lamp, Electric, Cut Glass, Hobstar & Diamond, Domed Shade, Metal Rim, Crystal Prisms, 26 In.
$266

Austin Auction Gallery

L

LAMP

Lamp, Electric, Emeralite, Cast Spelter Base, Adjustable Arm, Bellova Glass Shade, c.1916, 13 In.
$704

Brunk Auctions

Lamp, Electric, G. Magnusson, Grasshopper, Enameled Steel, Aluminum, Sweden, c.1947, 50 In.
$4,063

Wright

Lamp, Electric, Glass Fruit Basket, Beaded, Czechoslovakia, 11 x 11 In.
$225

Woody Auction

Lamp, Electric, Hanging, Apothecary Show Globe, Stained & Leaded Glass, Teardrop Shape, 17 x 11 In.
$1,107

Rich Penn Auctions

Lamp, Electric, Laurel Lamp Co., Mushroom Frosted Shade, Anodized Aluminum Base, 1950s, 14¾ In.
$263

Jeffrey S. Evans & Associates

Lamp, Electric, Monkey, Holding Book, Maitland Smith, Late 1900s, 23 x 14 In.
$944

Austin Auction Gallery

Lamp, Electric, Oak, Hammered Metal, Signed, G. Stickley, Early 1900s, 56 In.
$4,200

Cottone Auctions

Lamp, Electric, Pendant, P. Henningsen, PH 4/3, Copper, Denmark, c.1980, 12 x 18 In., Pair
$5,313

Wright

L

Electric, Glass, Blue, Stone, Signed, Keith Haring & Toshiyuki Kita, 1988, 21 x 12 In.	1375
Electric, Glass, Metal, Flowers, Frosted, Triangular Shade, Scalloped Edge, Art Deco, 25 In., Pair.	242
Electric, Glass, Millefiori, Mushroom Shape Shade, Baluster Base, 1900s, 14 ½ In.	512
Electric, Hanging, Apothecary Show Globe, Stained & Leaded Glass, Teardrop Shape, 17 x 11 In. .illus	1107
Electric, Hanging, Leaded Glass, Leaves & Grapes, Cream Ground, Brass Chain, 20 In.	75
Electric, Hanging, Painted, Porcelain, Flowers, Brass, Crystal Prisms, Victorian, 38 In.	189
Electric, Harlequin, Painted, Bronze, Mounted, Marble Arch & Plinth Base, 24 x 16 In.	420
Electric, Isamu Noguchi, Bamboo Shaft, Brass Fittings, Japan, c.1950, 55 x 5 ½ In.	1100
Electric, Italian Style, Brass, Reeded Column, Trapezoidal Black Shade, 65 In.	384
Electric, Laurel Lamp Co., Mushroom Frosted Shade, Anodized Aluminum Base, 1950s, 14 ¾ In. illus	263
Electric, Leaded Glass Shade, Fruit & Flowers, Wood Stem, Circular Base, 1920s, 69 x 20 In.	83
Electric, Mahogany, Barley Twist, Central Dish Tray, Later Shade, 1900s, 59 In.	767
Electric, Mahogany, Punched Brass, Column Stem, Square Base, 39 x 6 ½ In.	31
Electric, Marble & Alabaster, Tripod, Lion Heads & Paw Feet, Early 1900s, 16 x 8 In.	599
Electric, Marble, Carved, Corinthian Capitals, Fluted Columns, c.1930, 23 In., Pair	1000
Electric, Metal, Candlestick Cup, Man, Nude, Engraved, Slag Glass Shade, 18 In.	690
Electric, Metal, Censer Shape, Black, White Shade, Carved, Japan, 22 In., Pair	188
Electric, Metal, Shell, Fleur-De-Lis, Square Base, Theodore Alexander, 28 In., Pair	165
Electric, Midcentury Modern, Brass, Floor, Cantilevered Base, 65 x 33 In.	406
Electric, Monkey, Holding Book, Maitland Smith, Late 1900s, 23 x 14 In. illus	944
Electric, Murano Glass, Ribbed, Tapered Lucite, Stepped Base, 22 In., Pair	250
Electric, Oak, Hammered Metal, Signed, G. Stickley, Early 1900s, 56 In. illus	4200
Electric, Pear Wood, Bronze, Italy, 34 In.	635
Electric, Pendant, P. Henningsen, PH 4/3, Copper, Denmark, c.1980, 12 x 18 In., Pair . illus	5313
Electric, Piano, Brass, Gilt, Filigree Decor, Spiral Center Post, Tripod Base, Victorian, 51 In.	630
Electric, Pittsburgh, Reverse & Obverse Painted, Woodland Scene At Night, Matching Base, 25 In. illus	1792
Electric, Porcelain, Urn Shape, Sevres Style, Pink Ground, Gilt, Philippe Mourey, 17 ½ In. illus	177
Electric, Pressed Shade, Onyx Glass, Scroll Arm, Brass Supports, 1930s, 59 In.	219
Electric, Red Alligator Leather, Fiberglass Shade, Cone Shape Base, c.1950s, 16 In., Pair.	325
Electric, Red, Eyeball Shade, Adjustable, 2 Chrome Rods, Circular Base, c.1960, 23 In. illus	282
Electric, Rosewood Trays, White Shade, Brass, Adjustable, Retractable, 49 x 12 In., Pair	938
Electric, Sculptural, Lucite Shapes, 6 Piece, Chrome Rod, Finial, c.1970, 32 In.	94
Electric, Sfumato Glass, 7 Stacking Parts, Brass Base, Mazzega, Carlo Nason, c.1969, 52 In. illus	4800
Electric, Silver, Stacked Geometric Slices, Oval Resin Shade, Late 1900s, 39 In., Pair ... illus	531
Electric, Slag Glass Shade, Bronze, 22 ¼ In.	416
Electric, Slag Glass Shade, Brown, Brass Mount, 23 ½ x 19 In.	406
Electric, Slag Glass, Octagonal, Spelter, Circular Base, Salem Brothers, New York, 22 In.	608
Electric, Soholm Stentoj, Stoneware, Glazed, Brass, Linen Shade, Denmark, 65 x 16 In. illus	1875
Electric, Stig Lindberg, Earthenware, Glazed, Sweden, c.1960, 23 ¼ x 3 ½ In., Pair ..... illus	3000
Electric, Tahiti, Enamel, Steel, Laminate Base, Ettore Sottsass, 1981, 24 ¾ x 15 x 4 In. illus	1652
Electric, Teak, Steel, Brass, Plastic, Svend Aage Holm Sorensen, Denmark, c.1955, 60 x 36 In. ...	5850
Electric, Telescoping, Metal Pole, Black Enamel, Plastic Diffuser Shade, Lightolier, 51 In. ...	161
Electric, Tiffany Style, Bronze Base, Dome Shape Leaded Shade, Late 1800s, 19 x 12 In.	1989
Electric, Tiffany Style, Leaded Glass Shade, Turtle Medallion, Bronze Base, Late 1900s, 46 In. ...	1200
Electric, Tiffany Style, Scarab Shape Glass Shade, Iridescent, Bronze Metal Base, 9 ½ In.	469
Electric, Tiger's-Eye Panels, Black Metal Base, 40 In., Pair	94
Electric, Tole, Canister Shape, Tea, Gold & Black Decor, White Shade, Early 1900s, 25 In., Pair ..illus	1003
Electric, Torchiere, Faux Bamboo Pole, Spread Base, Flared Brass Shade, Russel Wright, 65 In..	150
Electric, Tripod, T. Robsjohn Gibbings, Chrome, 3 Supports, Widdicomb, c.1950, 47 In., Pair .	1875
Electric, Urn Shape, Metal, Marble Base, Gilt Feet, 1960s, 5 ¼ x 5 ¼ In.	31
Electric, Walnut, Brass, Linen, Phillip Lloyd Powell, 1960s, 33 In., Pair	2250
Electric, White, Painted, Removable Top, Flowers, Ormolu Leaves, Porcelain, 1930s, 18 In., Pair	192
Electric, Wicker, Brown, Bent Tripod Iron Legs, c.1970, 13 x 7 In., Pair	281
Electric, Wood, Dove, Orange, Square Base, Clark Voorhees, 1950, 25 ½ In.	502
Electric, Wood, Palm Tree, Monkey, Rattan Shade, Painted, 27 In. illus	142
Electric, Yellow, Scavo Glass, Copper, Vetri Soffiati Muranese Venini & Co., Italy, 1990s, 13 In.	531
Fairy, Hanging, Satin Glass, Apricot, Rolled Rim Base, Gilt Metal Frame, 13 x 7 In. ..... illus	400
Fat, Peter Derr, Copper, Iron, Turned Wood Stand, Stamped, P.D., 1834, 13 In. illus	4148
Figural, 2-Light, Classical, Ruffled Rim, Glass Shade, Gilt, 30 In., Pair	144
Figural, Nude Woman, Seashell Shade, Metal, Reservoir Base, McClelland Barclay, 18 In.	313

Lamp, Electric, Pittsburgh, Reverse & Obverse Painted, Woodland Scene At Night, Matching Base, 25 In.
$1,792

Morphy Auctions

Lamp, Electric, Porcelain, Urn Shape, Sevres Style, Pink Ground, Gilt, Philippe Mourey, 17 ½ In.
$177

Austin Auction Gallery

Lamp, Electric, Red, Eyeball Shade, Adjustable, 2 Chrome Rods, Circular Base, c.1960, 23 In.
$282

Bruneau & Co. Auctioneers

LAMP

Lamp, Electric, Sfumato Glass, 7 Stacking Parts, Brass Base, Mazzega, Carlo Nason, c.1969, 52 In.
$4,800

Neal Auction Company

Lamp, Electric, Silver, Stacked Geometric Slices, Oval Resin Shade, Late 1900s, 39 In., Pair
$531

Leland Little Auctions

Lamp, Electric, Soholm Stentoj, Stoneware, Glazed, Brass, Linen Shade, Denmark, 65 x 16 In.
$1,875

Wright

Lamp, Electric, Stig Lindberg, Earthenware, Glazed, Sweden, c.1960, 23¼ x 3½ In., Pair
$3,000

Wright

Lamp, Electric, Tahiti, Enamel, Steel, Laminate Base, Ettore Sottsass, 1981, 24¾ x 15 x 4 In.
$1,652

Austin Auction Gallery

Lamp, Electric, Tole, Canister Shape, Tea, Gold & Black Decor, White Shade, Early 1900s, 25 In., Pair
$1,003

Leland Little Auctions

Lamp, Electric, Wood, Palm Tree, Monkey, Rattan Shade, Painted, 27 In.
$142

Figural, Rose Quartz, Guanyin, Phoenix Birds, Carved, Metal Base, Chinese, 28 x 22 In., Pair....	671
Figural, Sailor, Holding Pipe, Vines, Spelter, Electric, Signed, France, Early 1900s, 23 In	330
Fluid, Molded, Milk Glass, Golden Footed, Electric, 25 In.	38
Gas, Brass, Glass, Bulbous Shape, Marked, Hudson, 13 In., Pair...........................	59
Gasolier, 2-Light, Rococo, Bronze, Portrait Bust, Scroll Arms, 1800s, 58 x 34 x 8 In.	610
Gasolier, 6-Light, Brass, Curved Arms, Reticulated, Leafy, Electric, 1880s, 50 x 20 In...........	324
Gasolier, 6-Light, Rococo Revival, Gilt, Patina, Bronze, France, Mid 1800s, 52 x 42 In. *illus*	3712
Gilt Bronze, Candlestick, Empire, Leaf Border, Flowers, 1800s, 22 x 16 In., Pair........	2268
Gone With The Wind, Kerosene, Globe, Floral, Green, Pink Tones, 11 x 11 x 4 In..............	275
Gone With The Wind, Kerosene, Red Satin, Glass Chimney, Brass, 24 In. .... *illus*	158
Gone With The Wind, Painted, Porcelain, Pink Roses, Brass, Electric, 29 x 12 In.	115
Gone With The Wind, Umbrella Shape Shade, Brass, Stencil, Late 1800s, 19 In.	105
Grease, Sheet Iron, Tin, Fat, Ringed, Cylindrical, Crimped Saucer Base, c.1850, 7½ In........	199
Handel lamps are included in the Handel category.	
Hanging, 2-Light, Stained, Tiffany Style, Flowers, Domed Shade, Cabochons, Late 1900s, 11 x 18 In.	207
Hanging, 6-Light, Half Frosted Shade, Brass, 16 x 22 In.	83
Hanging, 16-Light, Fixture, Saporiti Style, 8 Chrome Shades, Italy, 1950s, 30 x 24 In. ...._	200
Hanging, Beehive Shape, Enamel Steel, Acrylic, Nessen Studio, Inc., 1960, 14 In. .... *illus*	8125
Hanging, Blown Glass Shade, Iron Wire Frame, France, Early 1900s, 17 x 11¼ In.	325
Hanging, Brass, Multicolor, Glass Beads Strung, 1950, 10 x 6½ In.	295
Hanging, Bronze Dore, Amber, Clear & Blue Stained Glass Panels, Late 1800s, 31 x 11½ In.	826
Hanging, Bronze, Beveled Glass Inserts, Art Deco, France, c.1930, 108 x 25 x 19½ In.	1625
Hanging, Bronze, Pierced, Filigree, Multicolor, Jewels, Early 1900s, 15 x 9 In., Pair........ ...	536
Hanging, Embossed Shell, Umbrella Shade, Brass Frame, Pink Ground, Gilt, c.1900, 10 In....	322
Hanging, Grape Shape, Green, Blown Glass, Late 1800s, 12 In. .... *illus*	154
Hanging, Hall, Covered Urn Shape, Frosted Opaque Glass, Floral Leaf, Brass Fittings, 15 In..	275
Hanging, Hook Top, Heart Shape Stem, Wrought Iron, 1800s, 27 In. .... *illus*	175
Hanging, Leaded & Stained Glass, Teardrop Shape, Red Tulips, Brass, 10 x 33 In., 3 Piece..	1512
Hanging, Leaded Glass, Multicolor, Flower Border, Electric, 14 In...........................	35
Hanging, Swag, Blue Spaghetti Style, Plastic, Brass Chain, Round, 13 In. .... *illus*	86
Hanging, Tiffany Style, Stained, Leaded Glass, Dragonfly, Beaded Trim, Chain, 11 In.	1121
Hanging, Tiffany Style, Wire Twist, Art Glass Shade, c.1900, 16 In................................	1200
Hanging, Tin Shade, Glass Chimney, Loop Handle, 1800s, 29 In.	83
Hurricane, Matched, Chimney, Sheffield, Paul Revere Silver Co., 18¾ x 5 In., Pair...........	150
Kerosene, Banquet, Brass, Glass Shade, Porcelain Base, Victorian, Electrified, 31 In.	504
Kerosene, Banquet, Ornate, Winged Griffin, Cherub, Globe Shade, Brass, Onyx, 40 In.	800
Kerosene, Flowers, Rose Ground, Gilt Metal, Painted, Rococo Style, Electrified, 1800s, 26 In..	125
Kerosene, Globe Shape, Hanging, Glass, Brass, Embossed, Perkins, c.1920, 15 In., Pair *illus*	1625
Kerosene, Kitchen, Opaque White Shade, Iron Frame, Chains, Hanging, 14 In.................... ..	60
Kerosene, Vase Style, Swirl Body, Lion's Head Handle, 4 Paw Feet, Blue, 1880s, 7 x 4 In. *illus*	556
Kerosene, Wall, Quilted, Pink Glass Shade & Chimney, Ruffled Rim, Victorian, 16 In. *illus*	504
Leaded Glass, Green, Tulip, Schlitz Furnaces & Studios, Milwaukee, Late 1900s, 17 In. *illus*	5888
Leaded Glass, Stained, Green, Red, Engraved, Round Base, 23 In.	104
Newel Post, Figural, 5-Light, Leafy Scroll Arms, Brown & Green Patina, Cast Metal, 42 In. ..*illus*	984
Oil, Beaded Panel, Chimney Shade No. 1, Plume & Atwood Hornet Burner, Green, 1880s, 9 x 2 In. *illus*	263
Oil, Brass Twist Shade, Rose Painted, Putti Stand, Tri-Point Base, Plume & Atwood Burner, 42 In..	236
Oil, Brevete, Gilt, Bronze, Mounted, Moderator, Cylindrical, Stamped, Late 1800s, 21 In........	1169
Oil, Cast Iron, Floor, Twisted, Black Paint, 25 In.	62
Oil, Cranberry Glass, Brass, Corinthian Column, Ring Handles, Stepped Base, 1800s, 32 In..	118
Oil, Gilt Bronze, Square Base, Frosted Glass Shade, Etched Flowers, 1800s, 21 x 14 In.	1169
Oil, Glass, Diamond Design, Spiraling, Metal Collar, Early 1800s, 21 In.	88
Oil, Neoclassical Style, Urn Shape, Black, Late 1800s, 19 In., Pair.............................	448
Oil, Pressed Rib, Mother-Of-Pearl, Air Trap, Crimped Rim, Kosmos Burner, 1880s, 9 x 4 In. *illus*	263
Oil, Sanctuary, Baluster Shape, 3 Chains, Domed Canopy, Silver, Joseph Jackson, 1782, 36 In.	5040
Oil, Toleware, Grapevine Designs, Glass Shades, Frosted, France, 24½ In., Pair	469
Oil, White, Hobnail Glass Shade, Globe, Burner, Round Base, 26 In.	135
Pairpoint lamps are in the Pairpoint category.	
Perfume, Blue, Shaded Night-Light, Hammered, Wrought Iron Base, Robj Paris, 1926, 4½ In..	575
Piano, 3-Light, Brass, Onyx Top, Spiral Columns, Paw Feet, 65 In.......................	173
Piano, Brass, Globe Shade, Filigree, Spiral Post, Acanthus Legs, Paw Feet, Late 1800s, 66 In. ..*illus*	410

Lamp, Fairy, Hanging, Satin Glass, Apricot, Rolled Rim Base, Gilt Metal Frame, 13 x 7 In.
$400

Woody Auction

Lamp, Fat, Peter Derr, Copper, Iron, Turned Wood Stand, Stamped, P.D., 1834, 13 In.
$4,148

Pook & Pook

Lamp, Gasolier, 6-Light, Rococo Revival, Gilt, Patina, Bronze, France, Mid 1800s, 52 x 42 In.
$3,712

Neal Auction Company

L

Lamp, Gone With The Wind, Kerosene, Red Satin, Glass Chimney, Brass, 24 In. $158

Strawser Auction Group

Lamp, Hanging, Beehive Shape, Enamel Steel, Acrylic, Nessen Studio, Inc., 1960, 14 In. $8,125

Wright

The Drilled Hole

In the 1930s, lamps were often assembled using antique porcelain or glass pieces. Some lamps were mounted on a stand with a rod at the back that went up to hold the bulb and the shade. Others were drilled. A hole lowers the value of the antique part of a lamp. Many of these lamps have been dismantled, and the separated vases and figurines have hit the auction market with holes that lower their value.

Piano, Kerosene, Opaque Blue, Ball Shade, Brass, 3 Looping Legs, Claw Feet, Late 1800s, 56½ In.	322
Piano, Telescopic, Gilt Metal, Onyx, Adjustable, Leaves, Victorian, Electric, 63½ In.	177
Pittsburgh, Domed Shade, Oak Leaves, Owl Shape Base, Gold Finish, 22 x 20 In. .... *illus*	2337
Sconce, 2-Light, Adam Style, Carved, Giltwood, Rope Twist, Tassel Design, 32 In., Pair	875
Sconce, 2-Light, Bagues Style, Mirrored, Giltwood Frame, Italy, 23½ x 9½ x 5¾ In., Pair	840
Sconce, 2-Light, Bird, Rock Crystal, Gilt Iron Frame, Molded Glass Vase, 19 x 12 x 4 In., Pair *illus*	2000
Sconce, 2-Light, Brass, Hurricane Glass Shades, 14¼ In.	113
Sconce, 2-Light, Candlecups, Louis XVI Style, Giltwood, Carved, Stamped, Italy, 41 x 16 In.	1260
Sconce, 2-Light, Ceramic, Signed, Bjorn Wiinblad, c.1956, 18½ In.	207
Sconce, 2-Light, Drapery Drop, Quiver, Arrow, Scrolled Leafy Arms, Electric, 1900s, 22 In.	200
Sconce, 2-Light, Iron, Dragon Heads, In The Manner Of Samuel Yellin, 1920, 15 x 12 x 8 In.	531
Sconce, 2-Light, Leaves, Wrought Iron, 19 x 9 In., Pair	450
Sconce, 2-Light, Louis XV Style, Brass, Nickel Plated, Urn Finial, 1900s, 14 x 10 x 4 In., Pair	207
Sconce, 2-Light, Neoclassical Style, White Paint, Metal, Mirror, Late 1900s, 24 x 11 In.	50
Sconce, 2-Light, Shaped Mirror, Gilt Frame, Octagonal, Cut Glass Bobeche, 1800s, 15 In., Pair	502
Sconce, 2-Light, Torch Shape, Frosted Shell Globe, Brass Bracket, Early 1900s, 17 In., Pair	561
Sconce, 3-Light, Bronze & Glass, Feather Shape Shade, c.1940, 16 In.	406
Sconce, 3-Light, Bronze, Louis XVI Style, Ribbon Shape, Fluted Arms, 1900s, 33 x 16 In., Pair	708
Sconce, 3-Light, Gilt, Bronze, Wax Candle Covers, Fabric Shade, France, 1800s, 25½ In.	1416
Sconce, 4-Light, Rococo Style, Bronze, Oval, Moonlit Landscape, Scrolls, 16 In., Pair .. *illus*	315
Sconce, 5-Light, Louis XVI Style, Bronze, Teardrop Finials, c.1920, 16 x 14 x 8 In., Pair	188
Sconce, 5-Light, Wrought Iron, Leaves, 24 x 27 In., Pair	177
Sconce, 7-Light, Hanging Crystal, Brass, Gilt, Flower Shape Bobeches, 22 In., Pair	192
Sconce, 7-Light, Rococo, Bronze, Lion's Head, Acanthus Leaves, France, 1800s, 10 x 18 In., Pair	313
Sconce, Brass, Candleholder, Dorlyn Silversmiths, Tommi Parzinger, 1950s, 23 x 21 In., Pair.	563
Sconce, Brass, Wall, Arts & Crafts Style, Scroll Arms, c.1950, 17 x 4¼ In., Pair	71
Sconce, Bronze, Old Man, Candleholders, 29 x 11 In.	156
Sconce, Brutalist Style, Rock Crystal Quartz Diffuser, Bronze, 1900s, 14¾ x 5½ In., Pair .... *illus*	2242
Sconce, Candle, Silver, Bronze Figural, Velvet Mounts, 8½ In., Pair	644
Sconce, Classical Style, Carved, Giltwood, Scroll Arms, Mid 1900s, 38 x 11 In., Pair	531
Sconce, Eagle, Carved, Wood, 2 Candleholders, Gesso, 1800s, 13½ x 19 In., Pair	1586
Sconce, Empire Style, Cornucopia Shape Candlestick, Ribbon & Torch, Brass, 1900s, 13 In., Pair	113
Sconce, Enamel, Aluminum, Brass, Gino Sarfatti, Arteluce, Italy, 1951, 7 In., Pair	2500
Sconce, Gilt, Bronze, Acanthus Decor, Green Striated Marble, 1900s, 21 In., Pair	284
Sconce, Green Glass, Multicolor, Leaf Shape, Metal Decor, 9 x 9½ In., 4 Piece	224
Sconce, Hammered Copper, Glass Shade, Michael Adams, Aurora Studios, 14 x 10 x 5 In., Pair .	3625
Sconce, Hand Shape, Torchiere, Twist Pricket, Wood, Carved, Continental, 1910s, 21 In., Pair	180
Sconce, Metal, Cherubs, Scroll Arms, Louis XIV Style, France, 1800s, 16 x 8 In., Pair	295
Sconce, Metal, Gilt, Scroll & Leaves, Ring Held By Hand, 1900s, 25 In., 4 Piece .... *illus*	704
Sconce, Mirror Back, Tin, Early 1800s, 9 In., Pair	813
Sconce, Neoclassical, Face, Flowers, Engraved, Gilt Bronze, Early 1900s, 20 In., Pair ... *illus*	320
Sconce, Oval, Sheet Iron, Drip Pans, Piecrust Edge, Embossed Design, 1800s, 12 In., Pair .. *illus*	750
Sconce, Punched Tin, Detachable Candleholder, Crimped Bobeche, 1900s, 17 x 10 x 4 In., Pair..	1112
Sconce, Tin, Candle Socket, Arched Top, Tall Back, Punched Heart, Geometric, 1800s, 13½ In..	150
Sconce, Tin, Mirrored Center, Fluted Surround, Drip Pan, 14¼ x 10½ In., Pair	575
Sconce, Tin, Spread Wing Eagle, Arrows, Triangular Base, Early 1900s, 12⅜ In., Pair	594
Sconce, Torch Shape, Frosted, Cone Shape Shades, Tapered Metal Base, 1900s, 24 In., Pair..	177
Sconce, Wall, Carved, Giltwood, Scrolling Leaves, Late 1900s, 16 In., Pair	177
Sconce, White Sphere, Adjustable, Curved, Blue Base, c.1960, 5 x 8½ x 2½ In., Pair	148
Sinumbra, Reeded Column, Marble Base, Frosted Cut Glass Shade, Prisms, 1800s, 29 In. *illus*	1071
Sinumbra, Tole, Classical, Brass Caduceus, Crossed Torches, Octagonal Base, 1830s, 22 x 10 In.	1560
Solar, Gilt Bronze, Brass, Cut Prisms, Marble Base, Starr, Fellows & Co., c.1850, 20½ In.	610
Student, 2-Light, Brass, Adjustable, Tole Shade, Frederick Cooper, 24 In.	472
Student, 2-Light, Burmese Glass Shades, Cast Brass Weighted Base, Late 1800s, 19 x 4 In.	164
Student, 2-Light, Electric, Manhattan Brass Co., Cone Shape Milk Glass Shade, 1879, 26 In.	216
Student, Bisque Porcelain Lithophane Shade, Landscape Scene, Brass Base, 19 x 12 x 5 In. .	384
Student, Electric, Brass, Green Shades, Twist Arms, Stepped Base, 30 x 29 x 10 In.	316
Student, Emeralite, Electric, Green Glass Shade, Iron Base, Early 1900s, 14 x 8 x 7 In. *illus*	207
Student, Fuel Feed Tank, Gilt, Smoke Shade, Circular Base, Electrified, Late 1800s, 28 In.	188
Student, Milk Glass Shade, Chrome Plated Brass, Victorian, Electric, 20¾ x 8 In.	115
Student, Opal Shade, Chimney, Brass, Adjustable Shaft, Weighted Base, Late 1800s, 21¾ In..	82

Lamp, Hanging, Grape Shape, Green, Blown Glass, Late 1800s, 12 In.
$154

Locati Auctions

Lamp, Hanging, Hook Top, Heart Shape Stem, Wrought Iron, 1800s, 27 In.
$175

Pook & Pook

Lamp, Hanging, Swag, Blue Spaghetti Style, Plastic, Brass Chain, Round, 13 In.
$86

Alderfer Auction Company

Lamp, Kerosene, Globe Shape, Hanging, Glass, Brass, Embossed, Perkins, c.1920, 15 In., Pair
$1,625

Eldred's

Lamp, Kerosene, Vase Style, Swirl Body, Lion's Head Handle, 4 Paw Feet, Blue, 1880s, 7 x 4 In.
$556

Jeffrey S. Evans & Associates

Lamp, Kerosene, Wall, Quilted, Pink Glass Shade & Chimney, Ruffled Rim, Victorian, 16 In.
$504

Fontaine's Auction Gallery

Lamp, Leaded Glass, Green, Tulip, Schlitz Furnaces & Studios, Milwaukee, Late 1900s, 17 In.
$5,888

Hindman

Lamp, Newel Post, Figural, 5-Light, Leafy Scroll Arms, Brown & Green Patina, Cast Metal, 42 In.
$984

Fich Penn Auctions

Lamp, Oil, Beaded Panel, Chimney Shade No. 1, Plume & Atwood Hornet Burner, Green, 1880s, 9 x 2 In.
$263

Jeffrey S. Evans & Associates

LAMP

Lamp, Oil, Pressed Rib, Mother-Of-Pearl, Air Trap, Crimped Rim, Kosmos Burner, 1880s, 9 x 4 In.
$263

Jeffrey S. Evans & Associates

Lamp, Piano, Brass, Globe Shade, Filigree, Spiral Post, Acanthus Legs, Paw Feet, Late 1800s, 66 In.
$410

Fontaine's Auction Gallery

Lamp, Pittsburgh, Domed Shade, Oak Leaves, Owl Shape Base, Gold Finish, 22 x 20 In.
$2,337

Morphy Auctions

> **TIP**
> *Reverse-painted lampshades should never be washed. Just dust them.*

Lamp, Sconce, 2-Light, Bird, Rock Crystal, Gilt Iron Frame, Molded Glass Vase, 19 x 12 x 4 In., Pair
$2,000

Abington Auction Gallery

Lamp, Sconce, 4-Light, Rococo Style, Bronze, Oval, Moonlit Landscape, Scrolls, 16 In., Pair
$315

Fontaine's Auction Gallery

Lamp, Sconce, Brutalist Style, Rock Crystal Quartz Diffuser, Bronze, 1900s, 14¾ x 5½ In., Pair
$2,242

Austin Auction Gallery

Lamp, Sconce, Metal, Gilt, Scroll & Leaves, Ring Held By Hand, 1900s, 25 In., 4 Piece
$704

Neal Auction Company

Lamp, Sconce, Neoclassical, Face, Flowers, Engraved, Gilt Bronze, Early 1900s, 20 In., Pair
$320

Hindman

Lamp, Sconce, Oval, Sheet Iron, Drip Pans, Piecrust Edge, Embossed Design, 1800s, 12 In., Pair
$750

Eldred's

Lamp, Sinumbra, Reeded Column, Marble Base, Frosted Cut Glass Shade, Prism, 1800s, 29 In.
$1,071

Fontaine's Auction Gallery

Lamp, Student, Emeralite, Electric, Green Glass Shade, Iron Base, Early 1900s, 14 x 8 x 7 In.
$207

Austin Auction Gallery

Lamp, Torchere, Scrolled Lantern Style, Tinted Glass, Dragon's Head, Tripod Base, 1900s, 72 In., Pair
$677

Locati Auctions

Lamp, Whale Oil, Turned Column, Acorn Shape Font, Brass Double Spout, Sellew & Co., 9 1/2 x 4 3/4 In.
$431

Forsythes' Auctions

Lamp Base, 2-Light, Brass, Blue & White, People, Rectangular, Chinese Export, 37 In., Pair
$9,600

Roland Auctioneers & Valuers

Lamp Base, Electric, Blue & White, Landscape, Wood Base, Chinese 29 3/4 In.
$207

Austin Auction Gallery

L

Lampshade, Hanging, Daffodil, Leaded Glass, Blue Ground, Somers, 11 ½ x 20 In.
$3,276

Fontaine's Auction Gallery

Lampshade, Leaded Glass, 10 Panels, Caramel Slag, 1910s, 23 ½ In.
$64

Hindman

Lantern, Bronze, Figural, Removable Lid, Stylized Bamboo Handle, Fern, 1800s, 26 ½ In.
$263

Jeffrey S. Evans & Associates

Lantern, Dietz, Red Globe, Painted, Swing Handle, Monarch, 13 ½ In.
$62

Hartzell's Auction Gallery Inc.

Lantern, Hanging, Bell Jar, Ruby Glass, Crystals, Brass Chain, 24 x 14 ½ In.
$1,152

Roland Auctioneers & Valuers

Lantern, Hanging, Dietz, Little Wizard, Blue, Red, Globe Shape, Oil, 12 In.
$31

Hartzell's Auction Gallery Inc.

Lantern, Hanging, Iron, Glass Hexagonal Shade, Spiral, Scrollwork Elements, Spain, 28 In.
$148

Austin Auction Gallery

Lantern, Onion Shape, Whale Oil, Blown Glass Shade, Hanging Loop, 18 x 10 In.
$325

Cottone Auctions

Lantern, Reverse Painted, Wood, Glass Panels, Painted Figures, Carved, Chinese, c.1925, 28 In.
$2,125

New Orleans Auction Galleries

Tiffany lamps and Tiffany style lamps are listed in the Tiffany category.

Tole, Equestrian Style, Horse, Cast Metal, Metal Shade, Electric, 24 x 13 In.	531
Torchere, 19-Light, Gilt, Bronze, Flower Form, Cluster Column, 1800s, 55 ½ In., Pair...........	1664
Torchere, Art Deco, Silvered Metal, Glass Shade, Vellum, c.1930, 71 ⅝ x 22 ½ In., Pair	4410
Torchere, Bronze, Nude Maidens, Dancing, Glass Shade, 71 x 16 ½ In., Pair	1500
Torchere, Brutalist, Aluminum & Metal, Hammered Open Top, Tripod Base, 52 In., Pair.....	281
Torchere, Scrolled Lantern Style, Tinted Glass, Dragon's Head, Tripod Base, 1900s, 72 In., Pair ...*illus*	677
Whale Oil, 2 Burners, Flint Glass, Lyre, Tin, Sheet Iron Base, 1800s, 11 In............................	425
Whale Oil, Glass, Cylindrical Fonts, Metal Burners, Brass, Candlesticks, c.1850, 14 ¾ In., Pair....	531
Whale Oil, Turned Column, Acorn Shape Font, Brass Double Spout, Sellew & Co., 9 ½ x 4 ¾ In. *illus*	431
Vase, Rouleau, Blue, White, Columnar Neck, Narrative Scene, 1800s, 17 In.	1260

LAMP BASE

2-Light, Brass, Blue & White, People, Rectangular, Chinese Export, 37 In., Pair .... *illus*	9600
Electric, Blue & White, Landscape, Wood Base, Chinese, 29 ¾ In. .... *illus*	207

LAMPSHADE

Art Glass, Iridescent Calcite, Gold Interior, 7 In...	62
Globe, Deep Red Glass, Ball Shape, Gilt Dragon & Bats, Victorian, 11 ¾ In.	1080
Gold Iridescent Glass, Pearlescent Whites, Ribbed Aurene, Quezal Style, 5 In., Pair...........	144
Hanging, Daffodil, Leaded Glass, Blue Ground, Somers, 11 ½ x 20 In. .... *illus*	3276
Hanging, Yellow, Leaded Glass, Metal Border, Brown Fringe, 7 In.	180
Hurricane, Glass, Cobalt Blue, Folded Top Rim, Engraved, Flowers, 23 x 9 In......................	2074
Leaded Glass, 10 Panels, Caramel Slag, 1910s, 23 ½ In. .... *illus*	64
Leaded Glass, Green, Orange, White & Red, Scalloped Finial, Iron Frame, 19 ½ In.	49

LANTERN

Lanterns are a special type of lighting device. They have a light source, usually a candle, totally hidden inside the walls of the lantern. Light is seen through holes or glass sections.

Arts & Crafts, Pink Flowers, 4 Leaded & Slag Glass Panels, Bronze Chain, 34 In.	693
Bronze, Figural, Removable Lid, Stylized Bamboo Handle, Fern, 1800s, 26 ½ In. .... *illus*	263
Candle Lamp, Emerald Green Glass Globe, Metal Fittings, Ring Top, 1800s, 13 ½ In...........	960
Candle, 6-Sided, Wood Frame, Glass Panels, Wire Bail Handle, Early 1800s, 11 x 10 x 10 In.	1074
Candle, Pierced & Punched, Iron, Cylindrical, Strap Handle, Hinged Door, 1800s, 19 ½ In...	211
Candle, Punched Tin, Cylindrical, Cone Shape Cap, Hanging Ring, c.1850, 18 In.	2457
Candle, Tin, Glass, 4 Windows, Cone, Band Top, Triangular Feet, 1850s, 11 In..................	200
Carriage, Beveled Glass, Cobalt Blue, Cut To Clear, Ruby, Brass, 7 ¼ In., Pair.......................	316
Dietz, Gas, Street Lamp, Glass Globe, Black, Metal Frame, 22 In.	209
Dietz, Red Globe, Painted, Swing Handle, Monarch, 13 ½ In. .... *illus*	62
Glass, White, Gilt Bronze, Carved, Neoclassical, Late 1800s, 39 ½ In.	128
Hanging, 3-Light, Gilt Bronze, Chains, Ram's Head, Teardrop Finial, Early 1900s, 36 x 12 In.....	2520
Hanging, Bell Jar, Ruby Glass, Crystals, Brass Chain, 24 x 14 ½ In. .... *illus*	1152
Hanging, Dietz, Little Wizard, Blue, Red, Globe Shape, Oil, 12 In. .... *illus*	31
Hanging, Iron, Glass Hexagonal Shade, Spiral, Scrollwork Elements, Spain, 28 In. ..... *illus*	148
Hanging, Iron, Leaded Glass Panels, Gothic Style, Hexagonal, Late 1800s, 17 x 12 x 12 In.	1287
Hanging, Terra-Cotta, Cord, Malcolm Leland, c.1961, 27 In.	4375
Hanging, Tole, Blue, Chinoiserie, Bell Tassels, 31 x 15 ¾ x 14 In.	3250
Kerosene, Princess Charlotte, 4 Glass Windows, Vertical Bars, Handle, c.1890, 15 In.	150
Metal, Hanging, Black, Hexagonal, Chinese, 13 ¼ x 9 ¼ In..	156
Onion Shape, Whale Oil, Blown Glass Shade, Hanging Loop, 18 x 10 In. .... *illus*	325
Pendant, Aluminum, Hanging, Black Enamel, 12 Fins, Machine Age Style, 24 ½ x 20 In., Pair ..	791
Reverse Painted, Wood, Glass Panels, Painted Figures, Carved, Chinese, c.1925, 28 In. *illus*	2125
Skater's, Kerosene, Clear Glass, Bulbous, Brass Handle, 7 In. .... *illus*	43
Tin, Arched Back, Glass Window Front, Cylindrical Chimney Vent, Handle, 1800s, 15 x 7 In..	275
Tin, Peaked Top, Smoke Vents, Ring Handle, Flared Foot, Brass Burner, c.1860, 16 x 5 ½ In..	173
Tin, Pyramidal Top, Shaped Loop Hanger, Punched, c.1925, 14 ¼ In.	250
Toleware, Arched Case, Chimney Style Top, Gilt, Glass Inserts, Sarreid Ltd., 1900s, 22 x 8 In.....	325
Wall, Brass, Glass, Pane Shape Fronts, Pair, 17 x 5 ½ In..	125

Lantern, Skater's, Kerosene, Clear Glass, Bulbous, Brass Handle, 7 In.
$43

Apple Tree Auction Center

Le Verre Francais, Bowl, Orange & White, Cameo, Circular Foot, Art Deco, Signed, Early 1900s, 4 ½ In.
$567

Fontaine's Auction Gallery

Le Verre Francais, Vase, Footed, Amber Ground, Amethyst, Carved, Cameo, Art Deco, Signed, 5 ½ x 3 In.
$225

Woody Auction

L

Leather, Bag, Satchel, Brown, Adjustable, Pocket, Buckle, 10 x 12 In. $148

Austin Auction Gallery

TIP
Scratches on leather may be partially hidden by polishing the leather with saddle soap.

Leather, Belt, Hermes, Black, Goldtone, H Buckle, Hook Closure, 41 ½ In. $832

Crescent City Auction Gallery

Leather, Saddle, Western, Blossoming Roses, Scrolled Leaves, Custom Stand, 19 ½ x 15 x 11 In. $431

Rich Penn Auctions

LE VERRE FRANCAIS

Le Verre Francais is one of the many types of cameo glass made by the Schneider Glassworks in France. The glass was made by the C. Schneider factory in Epinay-sur-Seine from 1918 to 1933. It is a mottled glass, usually decorated with floral designs, and bears the incised signature *Le Verre Francais*.

Bowl, Orange & White, Cameo, Circular Foot, Art Deco, Signed, Early 1900s, 4 ½ In. ... *illus*	567
Vase, Footed, Amber Ground, Amethyst, Carved, Cameo, Art Deco, Signed, 5 ½ x 3 In. . *illus*	225
Vase, Marrons, Mottled Yellow, Orange Ground, Bulbous, Domed Foot, Signed, 12 ¼ In........	1071

LEATHER

Leather is tanned animal hide and has been used to make decorative and useful objects for centuries. Leather objects must be carefully preserved with proper humidity and oiling or the leather will deteriorate and crack. This damage cannot be repaired.

Bag, Fiber Shot, Intricate Heart & Dot, Woven Cloth Shoulder Strap, Geometric, 1900s, 9 x 7 In..	94
Bag, Golf, Travel, Red, Gerald Ford, RAM, 50 ¾ x 24 ¼ In.	358
Bag, Satchel, Brown, Adjustable, Pocket, Buckle, 10 x 12 In. .... *illus*	148
Bag, U.S. Mail, Canvas, Leather Straps, Patrick's & Co., Wells Fargo & Co., 20 x 24 In............	708
Belt, Hermes, Black, Goldtone, H Buckle, Hook Closure, 41 ½ In. .... *illus*	832
Book Cover, Green Ground, 22K Gold Tooled, Morocco, Mid 1900s, 14 x 10 In.	180
Camera Bag, Red, Goldtone, Rockstud Cross, Valentino, 2017, 5 ½ In.........................	500
Case, Brown, Rectangular, Handles, Ball Feet, George Rex, 7 x 28 x 10 In..............................	125
Figure, Camel, Brown, Resting, Down On Its Knees, 8 ½ In..................................	48
Saddle, Western, Basket Weave, Concha Accents, Stirrup Tapaderos, Light Brown, 15 ¾ In....	561
Saddle, Western, Blossoming Roses, Scrolled Leaves, Custom Stand, 19 ½ x 15 x 11 In. *illus*	431
Side Saddle, Tooled, Cinch Straps, Engraved, Marked, E. Heinrich, Texas, Late 1800s..........	354
Wallet, Blue, 10 Card Holders, 4 Bill Compartments, Zipper, Logo, Chanel, 4 x 6 In...............	576

LEEDS
LEEDS POTTERY

Leeds pottery was made at Leeds, Yorkshire, England, from 1774 to 1878. Most Leeds ware was not marked. Early Leeds pieces had distinctive twisted handles with a greenish glaze on part of the creamy ware. Later ware often had blue borders on the creamy pottery. A Chicago company named Leeds made many Disney-inspired figurines. They are listed in the Disneyana category.

Candlestick, Classical Figure, Draped, Carrying Lamb, Square Base, Creamware, c.1770, 11 In., Pair	928
Plate, Pansy, Blue & Yellow Flowers, Green & Brown Leaves, Green Leaf & Scale Border, 8 ¾ In. .	413
Plate, Umbrella Flower, Multicolor, Green Leaf & Scale Border, Soft Paste, 8 ¾ In.	384
Tureen, Lid, Finial, Twisted Handles, Footed, Creamware, Marked, 1770s, 8 x 13 ½ x 9 In....	384
Waste Bowl, Stylized Leaves, Brown & Orange, Flowering Vine Inner Border, Soft Paste, 3 x 7 In.	224

LEFTON

Lefton is a mark found on pottery, porcelain, glass, and other wares imported by the Geo. Zoltan Lefton Company. The company started in 1941. George Lefton died in 1996 and members of the family continued to run the company. Lefton was sold to OMT Enterprises of Gardena, California, in 2005 and is now a division of that company. The name "Lefton" is still used. The company mark has changed through the years and a mark is usually used for a long period of time.

Lefton China
1948–1953

Lefton China
1950–1955

Lefton China
1949–2001

Birthday Angel, January, Paper Label, 4 ½ In.	12

L

Lefton, Group, Bull, 3 Putti, Grapevine, Oval Base, Meissen Style, 20th Century, 8½ x 12 x 5½ In.
$320

Crescent City Auction Gallery

Legras, Carafe, 3 Colors, Branch, Leaf & Berry, Cameo, 9 x 5½ In.
$300

Woody Auction

Legras, Vase, Art Deco, Flowers, Enamel, Cameo, Signed, Early 1900s, 12½ In.
$189

ontaine's Auction Gallery

Lenox, Figurine, Nefertiti, Hand Painted, Applied Gold, Glazed, 8½ x 3½ x 3 In.
$138

Lion and Unicorn

Lenox, Plate, Rose Banded Border, Gilt Rim, Monogram, Early 1900s, 9 In., 12 Piece
$708

Leland Little Auctions

Lenox, Stein, Golfer, Blue & White, Silver Lid, Painted Under Glaze, ½ Liter
$510

Fox Auctions

Letter Opener, Rabbit Head Top, Cast Brass, c.1915, 11¾ In.
$590

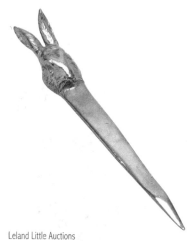

Leland Little Auctions

Lighter, Cigar, Figural, Dandy, Multicolor, Metal, Brass Fittings, Amber Shade, Victorian, 19½ In.
$338

Rich Penn Auctions

L

321

Lighter, Cigar, The Wireless, No. 12, Oak Case, Portraits, John Carr, Dante, 15 x 7 x 9 In.
$500

Woody Auction

Lighter, Dunhill, Tinder Pistol, Wood Handle, c.1930, 4 x 6 ¼ In.
$207

Leland Little Auctions

Lighter, Nude, Art Deco, Goldtone Metal, Electric, c.1935, 6 ½ In.
$111

Rich Penn Auctions

Cup & Saucer, Pink, Yellow, Red Roses, Reticulated Handle, Footed	47
Dog, Collie & Pup, Sable & Rust, c.1950, 5 In.	55
Figurine, Southern Belle, Maroon Dress, Flowers, Rhinestones, c.1956, 5 ½ In.............	42
Group, Bull, 3 Putti, Grapevine, Oval Base, Meissen Style, 20th Century, 8 ½ x 12 x 5 ½ In. .. *illus*	320
Head Vase, Carmen Miranda, White Turban, Fruit, Gold Hoop Earrings, Flower Necklace, 4 In..	96
Head Vase, Woman, Brown Hair, Raised Hand, Wide Brim Hat, Collar, White, Purple Flowers, 6 In.	81
Planter, Rabbit, Albino, Pink Ears, Nose & Eyes, Foil Label, 7 x 5 In...............................	36
Ring Holder, Bouquets, Multicolor, Gilt Trim, 2 ¾ x 3 In...	20

LEGRAS

Legras was founded in 1864 by Auguste Legras at St. Denis, France. It is best known for cameo glass and enamel-decorated glass with Art Nouveau designs. Legras merged with Pantin in 1920 and became the Verreries et Cristalleries de St. Denis et de Pantin Reunies.

Bowl, Amber, Acid Cut, Art Deco Fan, Signed, 3 ½ x 9 ¾ In.	90
Bowl, Berries & Leaves, Yellow Stained Ground, Multicolor, Enamel, 1910s, Signed, 2 x 4 In.	117
Bowl, Rectangular, Inverted Corners, Waterscape, Marked, 3 ½ x 8 ½ In................................	185
Bowl, Tricornered, Tortoiseshell Glass, Enamel, Flower, Signed, 3 x 4 ½ In.	225
Carafe, 3 Colors, Branch, Leaf & Berry, Cameo, 9 x 5 ½ In. .... *illus*	300
Vase, Art Deco, Flowers, Enamel, Cameo, Signed, Early 1900s, 12 ½ In. .... *illus*	189
Vase, Mottled, Yellow & Orange, Enamel, Flowers, Shaped Neck, Bulbous Base, Signed, 7 ¾ In....	221
Vase, Tapered Sides, Landscape, Square Foot, Cameo, Signed, c.1920, 14 x 2 ¾ In.................	369
Vase, White Opal Overlay, Cameo Carved Trees, Lake Scene, Signed, 6 x 3 In.	225

LENOX

Lenox porcelain is well-known in the United States. Walter Scott Lenox and Jonathan Coxon founded the Ceramic Art Company in Trenton, New Jersey, in 1889. In 1896 Lenox bought out Coxon's interest, and in 1906 the company was renamed Lenox, Inc. The company makes porcelain that is similar to Irish Belleek. In 2009, after a series of mergers, Lenox became part of Clarion Capital Partners. The marks used by the firm have changed through the years, so collectors can date the ceramics. Related pieces may also be listed in the Ceramic Art Co. category.

Figurine, Nefertiti, Hand Painted, Applied Gold, Glazed, 8 ½ x 3 ½ x 3 In. .... *illus*	138
Figurine, Tinker Bell, Fiery Fairy, Standing, Arms Crossed, Leafy Base, 1900s, 6 ½ In...........	35
Plate, Rose Banded Border, Gilt Rim, Monogram, Early 1900s, 9 In., 12 Piece .... *illus*	708
Stein, Golfer, Blue & White, Silver Lid, Painted Under Glaze, ½ Liter .... *illus*	510

LETTER OPENER

Letter openers have been used since the eighteenth century. Ivory and silver were favored by the well-to-do. In the late nineteenth century, the letter opener was popular as an advertising giveaway and many were made of metal or celluloid. Brass openers with figural handles were also popular.

Anchor With Rope, Brass, Patina, 8 ½ In...	14
Baccarat, Barracuda Shape, Brass, Fruitwood Base, Francois Xavier Lalanne, 1 ½ x 10 In...	1875
Dachshund, Standing, Pointed Tail, Silver, Signed, Hermes, c.1955, 1 x 9 In.	4063
Penguin, Pelican, Bronze, 2-Sided, Marked, E.T. Hurley, 8 ⅜ In.	847
Rabbit Head Top, Cast Brass, c.1915, 11 ¾ In. .... *illus*	590
Silver, Pointed Tip, Knot Handle, Van Cleef & Arpels, France, c.1955, 7 ½ In...........................	1250
Silver, Tapered, Teardrop End, Incised Bands, Sheffield Steel Blade, c.1950, 9 In.	42

LIBBEY

Libbey Glass Company has made many types of glass since 1888, including the cut glass and tablewares that are collected today. The stemwares of the 1930s and

1940s are once again in style. The Toledo, Ohio, firm was purchased by Owens-Illinois in 1935 and is still working under the name Libbey Inc. Maize is listed in its own category.

Bowl, Star & Feather, Signed, Cut Glass, 4 x 8 In.	225
Bowl, Tricornered, Diamonds, Modified Pinwheels, Notched Rim, Marked, 3 x 8½ In.	36
Bowl, Wedgemere, Notched Rim, American Brilliant, 4 x 8 In.	1495
Jar, This Little Pig Went To Market, Coin, Brown, 1900s, 5 Gal., 19½ x 10 x 9 In.	31
Plate, Wedgemere, Cut Glass, Clear, 7 In.	400
Platter, Kingston, Rounded Square, 4 Points, Sawtooth Edge, 1900s, 12 In.	275
Vase, Ellsmere, Flower Center, Signed, Facet Cut, Ring Neck, 6 x 8 In.	550
Vase, Flute & Star Block, Pedestal Base, Ray Cut Foot, Marked, 10 In.	150
Vase, Nash Spot-Optic, Pink Threading, Footed, Polished Pontil, 1930s, 8½ x 5¾ In.	176

LIGHTER

Lighters for cigarettes and cigars are collectible. Cigarettes became popular in the late nineteenth century, and with the cigarette came matches and cigarette lighters. All types of lighters are collected, from solid gold to the first disposable lighters. Most examples found were made after 1940.

Cigar, Ball In Hand, Porcelain Burner, Blue Globe, Wood Base, 14 x 8 x 12 In.	1107
Cigar, Figural, Dandy, Multicolor, Metal, Brass Fittings, Amber Shade, Victorian, 19½ In. *illus*	338
Cigar, Midland, Wood Case, Nickel Plated Brass Mounts, Countertop, 1920, 15 x 7¼ In.	219
Cigar, National Manufacturing Co., 2 Front Panels, Pull Down Spark, 13 x 7 x 11 In.	960
Cigar, The Wireless, No. 12, Oak Case, Portraits, John Carr, Dante, 15 x 7 x 9 In. *illus*	500
Dunhill, Jumbo, Alligator, Shagreen Panel, Silver Plate, Marked, c.1940, 4 x 3 In.	1750
Dunhill, Swing Arm, Silver, Blue Enamel Columns, Clock Face, Mother-Of-Pearl, 2 In.	1875
Dunhill, Tinder Pistol, Wood Handle, c.1930, 4 x 6¼ In. *illus*	207
Nude, Art Deco, Goldtone Metal, Electric, c.1935, 6½ In. *illus*	111
S.T. Dupont, Silver Plate, Vertical Ridges, Brass Top & Base, Jeroboam, France, c.1975, 4 x 3 In.	2000
Silver, 18K Gold Incan Inspired Design, Llama, Peru, 2¼ x 1½ In. *illus*	177
Striker, Painted, 2 Dogs, Silver, Guilloche Enamel, P.G.R., Early 1900s *illus*	366
Van Cleef & Arpels, 18K Gold, Ribbed Body, Hinged Lid, Marked SAM, c.1950, 2 In.	2625
Zippo, 14K Gold, Monogram, 20th Century, 2¼ x 1½ In.	1476

LIGHTNING ROD AND LIGHTNING ROD BALL

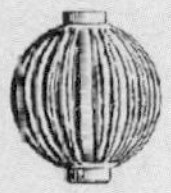

Lightning rods and lightning rod balls are collected. The glass balls were at the center of the rod that was attached to the roof of a house or barn to avoid lightning damage. The balls were made in many colors and many patterns. Collectors prefer examples made before 1940.

LIGHTNING ROD

Copper Rod, Twisted, Patina, Milk Glass Ball, 44 In.	30
Copper, Milk Glass Ball, 8-Sided, Tripod Legs, Mounted On Board, 26½ In.	132
Copper, Patina, Brass Ball, 2-Footed, Hawkeye, 30 In. *illus*	148
Copper, Twisted, Forked Barbed Finial, Tripod Base, 1890s	175

LIGHTNING ROD BALL

Diddie Blitzen, 8-Sided, Blue Milk Glass, Embossed Letters, 4 x 3⅝ In.	78
Electra, Faceted, Embossed, Purple, Sun Colored Glass, 5¼ In.	80
Fenton For Harger, Purple Glass, Embossed H In Trapezoid, 5 x 4½ In.	99
Geo. E. Thompson, Ribbed, Ruby Glass, Amberina Ridge, Metal End Caps, 1910-30, 4½ In. *illus*	110
Mercury Glass, Silver, Brass Caps, 4½ In.	29
Milk Glass, Blue, Globular, 5 In. Diam., Pair	132
Milk Glass, D & S, Cylindrical, 10-Sided	40
Milk Glass, Globular, 5 In., Pair	75
Vaseline Glass, Ear Of Corn Shape, Metal End Caps, 3¾ x 2⅞ In. *illus*	153

Lighter, Silver, 18K Gold Incan Inspired Design, Llama, Peru, 2¼ x 1½ In.
$177

Lighter, Striker, Painted, 2 Dogs, Silver, Guilloche Enamel, P.G.R., Early 1900s
$366

Lightning Rod, Copper, Patina, Brass Ball, 2-Footed, Hawkeye, 30 In.
$148

This is an edited listing of current prices. Visit Kovels.com to check thousands of prices from previous years and sign up for free information on trends, tips, reproductions, marks, and more.

L

Lightning Rod Ball, Geo. E. Thompson, Ribbed, Ruby Glass, Amberina Ridge, Metal End Caps, 1910-30, 4 ½ In.
$110

turnlove on eBay

Lightning Rod Ball, Vaseline Glass, Ear Of Corn Shape, Metal End Caps, 3 ¾ x 2 ⅞ In.
$153

marros-67 on eBay

Limoges, Charger, Hand Painted, Basket, Poppies, Gold Trim, Coronet, Signed, Duval, 15 ½ In.
$400

Woody Auction

Limoges, Humidor, Stag Scene, Pinecone, Branch Highlights, Brown, Blue Tones, Marked, 7 In.
$150

Woody Auction

Limoges, Plaque, Landscape, Windmill, Fisherman, Multicolor, Giltwood Frame, 1910s, 20 x 15 In.
$410

Jeffrey S. Evans & Associates

Limoges, Tray, Kingfisher, Shell, Signed, Edouard Marcel Sandoz, 6 x 9 In.
$272

Humler & Nolan

LIMOGES

Limoges porcelain has been made in Limoges, France, since the mid-nineteenth century. Fine porcelains were made by many factories, including Haviland, Ahrenfelct, Guerin, Pouyat, Elite, and others. Modern porcelains are being made at Limoges. The word *Limoges* as part of the mark is not an indication of age. Porcelain called "Limoges" was also made by Sebring China in Sebring, Ohio, in the early 1900s. The company changed its name to American Limoges China Company after the Limoges Company in France threatened to sue. American Limoges China Company went out of business in 1955. Haviland, one of the Limoges factories, is listed as a separate category in this book. These three marks are for factories in Limoges, France.

A. Klingenberg	D & Co.	M. Redon
c.1880s–1890s	c.1881–1893	c.1882–1896

Apothecary Jar, Lid, Pink & Gold Paint, Bee, Eagle, Marked, A. Tallec, 1900s, 9 ½ In.	163
Bowl, 2 Handles, Gilt Grapevine, Green Matte Ground, Base Stamp, 1900s, 10 ½ In.	308
Charger, Hand Painted, Basket, Poppies, Gold Trim, Coronet, Signed, Duval, 15 ½ In. . *illus*	400
Charger, Hand Painted, Fruit, Gold Trim, Signed, Luc, 10 ¼ In.	190
Charger, Painted, Orchids, White Ground, Gilt Rim, Signed, S.D. Hall, 12 ¼ In.	423
Charger, Young Fisherman, Boy, Cane Pole, Basket, Gold Trim, Signed, Baumy, 12 ½ In.	81
Chocolate Pot, Lid, White Ground, Scattered Pink Roses, Gold Rim & Handle, 3 In.	50
Cup & Saucer, Pink Ground, Gold Flowers, Lattice, G.D. & Co.	200
Dresser Box, Hinged Lid, Circular, Allegorical Scenes, Gilt, Mounted, 1900s, 7 ½ In.	72
Dresser Box, Painted, Asian Motif, Gilt, White Ground, Tiffany & Co., 1969, 2 x 5 ½ In.	180
Humidor, Stag Scene, Pinecone, Branch Highlights, Brown, Blue Tones, Marked, 7 In. *illus*	150
Plaque, 2 Greeks, European Women, Hand Painted, Oval Frame, 19 ¼ x 15 ¼ In.	144
Plaque, Landscape, Windmill, Fisherman, Multicolor, Giltwood Frame, 1910s, 20 x 15 In. *illus*	410
Plate, White Center, Cobalt Blue Band, Gilt Rim, 10 ⅜ In., 12 Piece	443
Plate, White Ground, Gold, Encrusted Border, Swags & Urns, Pouyat, 10 ⅞ In., 6 Piece	130
Punch Bowl, Grapes, Gilt Rim, Green Interior, Marked, Jean Pouyat, Late 1800s, 6 x 13 In.	118
Tray, Kingfisher, Shell, Signed, Edouard Marcel Sandoz, 6 x 9 In. *illus*	272
Vase, Art Nouveau, Gourd, Cinched Neck, Pale Flowers, Mauve Glaze, 3 Handles, Late 1800s, 8 In.	325
Vase, Gilt Rim & Handle, Leaves, Dark Blue Ground, J.P., 22 ½ In., Pair *illus*	420
Vase, Multicolor Flowers, Leaves, Ivory Ground, Elephant Handles, 1800s, 12 ¾ In., Pair	238
Vase, Pate-Sur-Pate, White Slip, Pale Blue Ground, Maiden, Auguste Riffaterre, c.1895, 12 In.	5040
Vase, Pillow, Brown, Swallows, Berries, Faience, Signed, France, c.1880, 16 ½ x 11 x 4 ½ In. *illus*	594
Vase, Woman, Gilt, Leafy Handles, Painted, White & Green Ground, Footed, 12 In.	51

LINDBERGH

Lindbergh was a national hero. In 1927, Charles Lindbergh, the aviator, became the first man to make a nonstop solo flight across the Atlantic Ocean. In 1932, his son was kidnapped and murdered, and Lindbergh was again the center of public interest. He died in 1974. All types of Lindbergh memorabilia are collected.

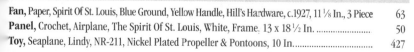

Fan, Paper, Spirit Of St. Louis, Blue Ground, Yellow Handle, Hill's Hardware, c.1927, 11 ⅛ In., 3 Piece	63
Panel, Crochet, Airplane, The Spirit Of St. Louis, White, Frame, 13 x 18 ½ In.	50
Toy, Seaplane, Lindy, NR-211, Nickel Plated Propeller & Pontoons, 10 In.	427

LITHOPHANE

Lithophanes are porcelain pictures made by casting clay in layers of various thicknesses. When a piece is held to the light, a picture of light and shadow is seen through it. Most lithophanes date from the 1825–1875 period. A few are

Limoges, Vase, Gilt Rim & Handle, Leaves, Dark Blue Ground, J.P., 22 ½ In., Pair
$420

Cottone Auctions

L

TIP
Don't scrub gilding and gold edges on porcelains.

Limoges, Vase, Pillow, Brown, Swallows, Berries, Faience, Signed, France, c.1880, 16 ½ x 11 x 4 ½ In.
$594

Bruneau & Co. Auctioneers

Lithophane, Candle Shield, Tile, Madonna & Child, Cast Iron Tripod Base, 1800s, 22 x 10 x 5 In. $148

Austin Auction Gallery

Lithophane, Lampshade, 5 Panels, Multicolor Scenes, Gold Stamped Metal Frame, PPM, 6 5/8 x 6 In. $64

Nye & Company

Lithophane, Stein, Porcelain, Pewter Top, Missile, Nude On Base, F. Jones, Germany, 8 1/2 In. $69

Richard D. Hatch & Associates

still being made. Many lithophanes sold today were originally panels for lampshades.

Candle Shield, Girl With Pup, Tripod Base, 4 1/2 In.	875
Candle Shield, Street Scene, Church In Center, Metal Frame, Gothic Style, Scrolls, Adjustable, 17 In.	750
Candle Shield, Tile, Madonna & Child, Cast Iron Tripod Base, 1800s, 22 x 10 x 5 In. .. *illus*	148
Lampshade, 5 Panels, Multicolor Scenes, Gold Stamped Metal Frame, PPM, 6 5/8 x 6 In. *illus*	64
Panel, 2 Children, Dog, At Base Of Tree, Cast Metal Stand, PPM, Victorian, 18 x 6 In.	123
Sleeping Boy, Chickens, c.1887, 4 x 5 In.	175
Stein, Porcelain, Pewter Top, Missile, Nude On Base, F. Jones, Germany, 8 1/2 In. *illus*	69
Tea Warmer, 4 Paneled Scenes, Brass, Footed, Bail Handle, 1890s, 5 In. Diam.	110

LIVERPOOL

Liverpool, England, has been the site of many pottery and porcelain factories since the eighteenth century. Color-decorated porcelains, transfer-printed earthenware, stoneware, basalt, figurines, and other wares were made. Sadler and Green made print-decorated wares starting in 1756. Many of the pieces were made for the American market and feature patriotic emblems, such as eagles and flags. Liverpool pitchers are called Liverpool jugs by collectors.

Bowl, George Washington, 2 Angels, Verse, Herculaneum, Gray Transfer, c.1795, 3 x 7 In.	2684
Bowl, The World In Planisphere, 3 Outdoor Scenes On Exterior, Black Transfer, c.1780, 5 x 13 1/2 In. ..	2250
Jug, George Washington, Crowned Laurel, Eagle, Union Shield, Transfer, F. Morris, 8 In.	2109
Jug, Hunting Scene, Hound Dog Handle, Rockingham Glaze, Harker Taylor, 10 In.	375
Jug, Masonic Design, 2-Masted Ship, Pointed Spout, Black Transfers, 1800s, 7 3/4 In.	344
Jug, Success To America, John Adams, Transfer, Creamware, Late 1700s, 9 x 8 In. .... *illus*	2706
Punch Bowl, George Washington, Horseback, 3-Masted Ship Inside, American Flag, 15 Stars, 11 In.	2500
Tankard, George Washington On Horseback, Directing Troops, Transfer, 1780s, 5 In. . *illus*	4063

LLADRO

LLADRÓ® Lladro is a Spanish porcelain. Brothers Juan, Jose, and Vicente Lladro opened a ceramics workshop in Almacera in 1951. They soon began making figurines in a distinctive, elongated style. In 1958 the factory moved to Tabernes Blanques, Spain. The company makes stoneware and porcelain figurines and vases in limited and unlimited editions. Dates given are first and last years of production. Marks since 1977 have the added word *Daisa,* the acronym for the company that holds the intellectual property rights to Lladro figurines.

Bowl, Centerpiece, Mermaid, Antonio Ballester, 1971, 16 1/4 In.	325
Bust, Clown, Painted, No. 5612, Jose Puche, 1988-94, Box, 9 1/2 In.	173
Figurine, Artist's Model, Nude, Reading Book, Seated, White Matte, No. 5417, 1987-90, 11 7/8 In. . *illus*	384
Figurine, Circus Serenade, Harlequin, Playing Violin, No. 5694, Jose Puche, 1990-94, Box, 7 In.	196
Figurine, Far Away Thoughts, Woman On Balcony, No. 1798, Joan Coderch, 1995-97, Box, 14 1/2 In.	4025
Figurine, Intermezzo Chaise Lounge, Woman, Sitting, No. 5424, 1987-89, 8 1/2 x 11 In. *illus*	207
Figurine, Little Bo Peep, Sitting Girl, Bottle Feeding Lamb, No. 1312, 1974-85, 6 3/4 x 7 In. *illus*	90
Figurine, Tea Time, Woman, Holding Cup Of Tea, No. 5470, Juan Huerta, 1988-97, Box, 14 1/4 In..	115
Figurine, Tree Topper, Angel, Flowing Dress, Cape, No. 5875, Francisco Catala, 1992, 7 In.	46
Group, Debutantes, 2 Young Women, No. 5486, Jose Puche, 1988-97, Box, 8 1/2 In.	431
Group, Elephants, Mother & Calf, Trunks Up, Gloss Finish, No. 1151, 1971-99, 11 x 10 In. *illus*	288
Group, Jester's Serenade, Jester & Ballerina, Wood Base, No. 5932, 1993-94, 16 x 15 1/4 In.	920
Group, Old Man, Cane, Boy, Lute, Walking, Painted, Round Base, No. 4652, 1969-78, 14 In. *illus*	224
Group, Once Upon A Time, Mother, Boy, Reading, No. 5721, 1990-97, Box, 10 1/4 In.	345
Tray, Lily Pad & Frog, Bisque Glaze, Shaped Lozenge, 15 1/8 In.	207

LOETZ

Loetz Austria Loetz glass was made in many varieties. Johann Loetz bought a glassworks in Klostermuhle, Bohemia (now Klastersky Mlyn, Czech Republic), in 1840. He died in 1848 and his widow ran the company; then in 1879, his grandson

Liverpool, Jug, Success To America, John Adams, Transfer, Creamware, Late 1700s, 9 x 8 In.
$2,706

Brunk Auctions

Liverpool, Tankard, George Washington On Horseback, Directing Troops, Transfer, 1780s, 5 In.
$4,063

Heritage Auctions

Lladro, Figurine, Artist's Model, Nude, Reading Book, Seated, White Matte, No. 5417, 1987-90, 11 7/8 In.
$384

eland Little Auctions

Lladro, Figurine, Intermezzo Chaise Lounge, Woman, Sitting, No. 5424, 1987-89, 8 1/2 x 11 In.
$207

Leland Little Auctions

Lladro, Figurine, Little Bo Peep, Sitting Girl, Bottle Feeding Lamb, No. 1312, 1974-85, 6 3/4 x 7 In.
$90

Woody Auction

Lladro, Group, Elephants, Mother & Calf, Trunks Up, Gloss Finish, No. 1151, 1971-99, 11 x 10 In.
$288

Lion and Unicorn

Lladro, Group, Old Man, Cane, Boy, Lute, Walking, Painted, Round Base, No. 4652, 1969-78, 14 In.
$224

Bunch Auctions

Loetz, Lamp, Greenish Brown Patina, Bronze Base, Gustav Gurschner, Early 1900s, 13 In.
$1,560

Cottone Auctions

Loetz, Vase, Cobalt Blue Iridescent, Wavy Bands, Spot Design, Neurot Ground, 9¾ In.
$1,890

Fontaine's Auction Gallery

took over. Most collectors recognize the iridescent gold glass similar to Tiffany, but many other types were made. The firm closed during World War II.

Bowl, Esmerelda Pattern, Bright Yellow Iridescent, Curled Rim, c.1904, 3¾ In.	148
Inkwell, Gold Iridescent, Bronze Mounted, Round Top, Square Base, 3¾ x 4 x 4 In.	230
Lamp, Domed Shade, Jeweled, Bronze Women's Heads Base, Electric, Gustav Gurschner, 21 In.	1130
Lamp, Green Iridescent, Glass Body, Bronze Mount, Flame Finial, Early 1900s, 27 x 5 In.	527
Lamp, Greenish Brown Patina, Bronze Base, Gustav Gurschner, Early 1900s, 13 In. .... *illus*	1560
Lamp, Hanging, Bronze Rope Style, Green, Yellow Iridescent, 21 x 12 x 12 In.	4920
Vase, Argonaut, Shell Shape, Amber, Gold Iridescent, 5¾ x 7½ In.	350
Vase, Candia Phaenomen, Silver Pulled Threads, Iridescent, Blue Prunts, c.1901, 9½ In.	970
Vase, Carneol, Gold Enamel Highlights, Bulbous, c.1888, 6¼ x 5¼ In., Pair	275
Vase, Cobalt Blue Iridescent, Wavy Bands, Spot Design, Neurot Ground, 9¾ In. .... *illus*	1890
Vase, Enamel, Green, Flower Design, Iridescent, Gilt, Loetz Style, France, 4½ In. .... *illus*	58
Vase, Gold Aurene Iridescent, Stick, Bulbous Body, Pink Ground, Signed, 10 In.	115
Vase, Gold Iridescent, Art Nouveau Style, Silver Overlay, Flowers, Leaves, Vines, 5 In.	252
Vase, Green Iridescent, Silver Overlay Flower, Crisscross, 8 x 4½ In. .... *illus*	938
Vase, Maeander, Light Yellow Iridescent, Tooled, Figure Rim, Tapered Body, c.1900, 10 In.	295
Vase, Metallin, Green, Silver Overlay, Flowers, 4 In. .... *illus*	125
Vase, Mottled Gold Iridescent, Silberiris, Ruffled Rim, Twisted Body, Square Base, 11 In.	125
Vase, Multicolor Iridescent, Bronze Holder, 13 x 8 In. .... *illus*	3383
Vase, Purple Iridescent Shaded To Red, Oil Spot, Pinched, Spiral Ribs, Folded Rim, 1902, 8 In. ..	201
Vase, Yellow Iridescent, Amber, Bronze Mount Handle, Footed, Signed, 7¾ In. .... *illus*	690

LONE RANGER

Lone Ranger, a fictional character, was introduced on the radio in 1932. Over three thousand shows were produced before the series ended in 1954. In 1938, the first Lone Ranger movie was made. The latest movie was made in 2013. Television shows were started in 1949 and are still seen on some stations. The Lone Ranger appears on many products and was even the name of a restaurant chain from 1971 to 1973 that gave out silver bullets and other souvenirs.

Game, Board, Playing Pieces, Spinners, Box, Parker Brothers, 1938 .... *illus*	38
Guitar, Supertone, 6-String, Black, White, Red, Cowboy, 35½ In.	88
Radio, Bakelite, Brown, Celluloid Window, Pilot, Handle, 9 x 15 In.	150
Saddle, Leather, Fender, Black, Stirrups, Initial LR, Silver, Beaded, Child's, 19 In.	388
Toy, Pistol, Black, Decal On Side, Marx, Box	88

LONGWY WORKSHOP

Longwy Workshop of Longwy, France, first made ceramic wares in 1798. The workshop is still in business. Most of the ceramic pieces found today are glazed with many colors to resemble cloisonne or other enameled metal. Many pieces were made with stylized figures and Art Deco designs. The factory used a variety of marks.

Longwy Faience Co.
1880–1939

Longwy Faience Co.
1890–1948

Longwy Faience Co.
1951–1962

Charger, 3 Cranes, Flowers, Stems, Leaves, Multicolor, Marked, Rehausse, 14 In.	128
Charger, Red Nose Knight, Bottle, Wine Cup, Coat Of Arms, Multicolor, 1703, 14½ In. *illus*	424
Moon Flask, Chinoiserie Cloisonne Design, Faience, Mark, c.1880, 9⅝ In., Pair .... *illus*	813
Vase, Art Deco, Aux Baigneuses, To The Bathers, Atelier Primavera, Faience, c.1935, 13 In. ...	1220
Vase, Cylindrical, Flowers, Painted, Cobalt Blue, Elephant's Head Handles, 13½ In.	400
Vase, Pinched Neck, Crackle, White Ground, Full Moon, 11½ In.	192

Loetz, Vase, Enamel, Green, Flower Design, Iridescent, Gilt, Loetz Style, France, 4 ½ In.
$58

Blackwell Auctions

Loetz, Vase, Green Iridescent, Silver Overlay Flower, Crisscross, 8 x 4 ½ In.
$938

Treadway

Loetz, Vase, Metallin, Green, Silver Overlay, Flowers, 4 In.
$125

Woody Auction

Loetz, Vase, Multicolor Iridescent, Bronze Holder, 13 x 8 In.
$3,383

Morphy Auctions

Loetz, Vase, Yellow Iridescent, Amber, Bronze Mount Handle, Footed, Signed, 7 ¾ In.
$690

Blackwell Auctions

Lone Ranger, Game, Board, Playing Pieces, Spinners, Box, Parker Brothers, 1938
$38

Pook & Pook

329

Longwy, Charger, Red Nose Knight, Bottle, Wine Cup, Coat Of Arms, Multicolor, 1703, 14 ½ In.
$424

Humler & Nolan

Longwy, Moon Flask, Chinoiserie Cloisonne Design, Faience, Mark, c.1880, 9 ⅝ In., Pair
$813

Charlton Hall Auctions

Lonhuda, Vase, Wild Grapes, Standard Glaze, Short Neck, Monogram, Charles J. Dibowski, 10 ½ In.
$333

Humler & Nolan

LONHUDA

LONHUDA

Lonhuda Pottery Company of Steubenville, Ohio, was organized in 1892 by William Long, W. H. Hunter, and Alfred Day. Brown underglaze slip-decorated pottery was made. The firm closed in 1896. The company used many marks; the earliest included the letters *LPCO*.

Jug, 2 Handles, Roses, Mottled Light Green Ground, Faience, Albert Haubrich, 4 x 6 ½ x 5 In.... 227
Vase, Wild Grapes, Standard Glaze, Short Neck, Monogram, Charles J. Dibowski, 10 ½ In. *.illus* 333

LOSANTI

Losanti was made by Mary Louise McLaughlin in Cincinnati, Ohio, about 1899. It was a hard-paste decorative porcelain. She stopped making it in 1906.

Vase, Blue Flowers & Scrolling Stems, White Ground, Oval, M.L. McLaughlin, c.1900, 5 x 3 In..... 4063
Vase, Peacock Feathers, Green, Blue Eye, Cylindrical, M.L. McLaughlin, c.1900, 6 x 2 ½ In. .. 10000

LOTUS WARE

Lotus Ware was made by the Knowles, Taylor & Knowles Company of East Liverpool, Ohio, from 1890 to 1900. Lotus Ware, a thin porcelain that resembles Belleek, was sometimes decorated outside the factory. Other types of ceramics that were made by the Knowles, Taylor & Knowles Company are listed under KTK.

Bowl, Shell Shape, Portrait, Woman, Profile, Handle, Scalloped Rim, Gilt Trim, 5 In. .. *illus* 99
Cup, Twisted, Green, Peach Highlights, Vines, Flowers, Butterfly, 3 ¾ In. 165
Teapot, Globe Shape, Lid, Finial, Bamboo Handle, Ribbed Spout, White, 4 x 7 x 3 In. 198
Teapot, Raised Flowers, White, Gold Bands, Marked, 4 x 3 In... 279
Vase, 2 Handles, Footed, Moriage, Transfer, Portrait, Woman, Cupid & Psyche, 17 x 9 In. 711

J. & J. G. LOW   ## LOW

Low art tiles were made by the J. and J. G. Low Art Tile Works of Chelsea, Massachusetts, from 1877 to 1902. A variety of art and other tiles were made. Some of the tiles were made by a process called "natural," some were hand-modeled, and some were made mechanically.

Fireplace, Yellow Tiles, Raised Figures, Scrolls On Sides, Copper, Iron, c.1900, 46 x 34 x 26 In. *illus* 688
Tile, Fireplace, Sunflower Top Panel, Cobalt Blue Glaze, 6 x 5 ¼ In... 5
Tile, Square, Portrait, Woman, Profile, Earring, Lace Collar, Leafy Ground, Blue, 4 In., Pair 120
Tile, Teal, Raised Bust, Allegorical Figure, Summer, Autumn, Winter, Spring, 1885, 6 x 4 In., 4 Piece 585

LOY-NEL-ART, *see McCoy category.*

LUNCH BOX

Lunch boxes and lunch pails have been used to carry lunches to school or work since the nineteenth century. Today, most collectors want either early tin tobacco advertising boxes or children's lunch boxes made since the 1930s. These boxes are made of metal or plastic. Vinyl lunch boxes were made from 1959 to 1982. Injection molded plastic lunch boxes were made beginning in 1972. Legend says metal lunch boxes were banned in Florida in 1972 after a group of mothers claimed children were hitting each other with them and getting injured. This is not true. Metal lunch boxes stopped being made in the 1980s because they were more expensive to make than plastic lunch boxes. Boxes listed here include the original Thermos bottle inside the box unless otherwise indicated. Movie, television, and cartoon characters may be found in their own categories. Tobacco tin pails and lunch boxes are listed in the Advertising category.

Annie Oakley & Tagg, Bucking Horse, White Rim, Blue Handle, Metal, Aladdin	100
Fireball X15, Rocket Launch, Man, Woman, Metal, Yellow Rim, No Thermos, King-Seeley..	38
Gunsmoke, Matt Dillon U.S. Marshall, Double L, Metal, Aladdin, 1959 .... *illus*	150
Rough Rider, Motorcyclist, Multicolor, Red Lettering, Green Border, Metal, Aladdin	32
Sesame Street, Bert & Ernie, Other Characters, Metal, Thermos, 1983, 8 x 7 In.	25
ABC Wild World Of Sports, Metal, Yellow, Orange Cup, Top Handle, King-Seeley, 1976, 13 In.	36
Flintstones, Metal, Yellow Ground, Red Cup, Closed Handle, Aladdin, 1960s	52
Hot Wheels, Yellow Ground, Green Car, Redline Era, No. 2804, 1968-77	46
Orbit, Blue Ground, Rocket, Space Capsules, Parachutes, Red Cup, 1963, 8 In.	42
Tom Corbett Space Cadet, Metal, Red Cup, 6 ¼ x 3 ¼ In.	23
Warner Bros. Looney Tunes, Characters, Metal, Light Green, Red Cup, Holtemp, 1959, 8 In. ...	48
Wild Bill Hickock & Jingles, Multicolor, Red Cup, Aladdin, 1955	35

LUNEVILLE

Luneville, a French faience factory, was established about 1730 by Jacques Chambrette. It is best known for its fine bisque figures and groups and for large faience dogs and lions. The early pieces were unmarked. The firm was acquired by Keller and Guerin and is still working.

Bowl, Purple & White, Mottled Ground, Signed, Muller Freres, 2 ½ x 9 ¼ In.	125
Vase, Cherry, Flowers, Red & White, Green Ground, Underfoot, 12 In. .... *illus*	98

LUSTER

Luster glaze was meant to resemble copper, silver, or gold. The term *luster* includes any piece with some luster trim. It has been used since the sixteenth century. Some of the luster found today was made during the nineteenth century. The metallic glazes are applied on pottery. The finished color depends on the combination of the clay color and the glaze. Blue, orange, gold, and pearlized luster decorations were used by Japanese and German firms in the early 1900s. Fairyland Luster was made by Wedgwood in the 1900s. Copies made by modern methods started appearing in 1990. Tea Leaf pieces have their own category.

Copper, Charger, Reflejo, Hispano-Moresque Revival, Early 1900s, 17 ¼ In.	354
Copper, Pitcher, Andrew Jackson, Transfer Portrait, Blue Ground, Wide Spout, 1824, 5 ¼ In.	977
Copper, Pitcher, Lafayette, Surrender Of Cornwallis, Bulbous, Yellow Ground, Transfer, 5 In. *illus*	286
Fairyland Luster is included in the Wedgwood category.	
Pink, Pitcher, Black Ship Design, Naval Battles, Green, Handle, Staffordshire, c.1820, 4 In. ..	1778
Pink, Pitcher, Hand Colored, Transfers, c.1815, 8 ½ In.	300
Sunderland Luster pieces are in the Sunderland category.	
Teapot, Lamp Shape, Spout, Handle, Painted, Mount On Wood, England, 9 ¾ In.	64
Vase, Blue, Parcel Gilt, Flared Neck, Blue, Gold, 1900s, 9 ½ In.	25

LUSTRES

Lustres are mantel decorations or pedestal vases with many hanging glass prisms. The name really refers to the prisms, and it is proper to refer to a single glass prism as a lustre. Either spelling, luster or lustre, is correct.

Blue Opaque, Art Glass, 5 Hanging Prisms, Scalloped Rim, 5 ¼ In., Pair .... *illus*	90
Cranberry, Flowers, Hanging Pendants, Bohemian, 13 In., Pair .... *illus*	123
Emerald Green, Flowers, Cut Glass Drop Prisms, Bohemia, 14 ½ In., Pair .... *illus*	118
Pink, Candlestick, Hanging Prisms, Gilt, Stepped, Circular Base, 11 In., Pair	173
Ruby Glass, Cut To Clear, Glass Drop Prisms, Bohemia, 1900s, 13 ¼ In., Pair	472
Ruby Glass, Flower, Hatchwork Panels, Scalloped Rims, Circular Base, 12 ¾ In., Pair	256
White, Cut Prisms, Ruffled Edge, Marble Base, 10 ½ In., Pair	173

MACINTYRE, *see Moorcroft category.*

Lotus Ware, Bowl, Shell Shape, Portrait, Woman, Profile, Handle, Scalloped Rim, Gilt Trim, 5 In.
$99

Ruby Lane

Low, Fireplace, Yellow Tiles, Raised Figures, Scrolls On Sides, Copper, Iron, c.1900, 46 x 34 x 26 In.
$688

Rago Arts and Auction Center

Lunch Box, Gunsmoke, Matt Dillon U.S. Marshall, Double L, Metal, Aladdin, 1959
$150

Pook & Pook

Luneville, Vase, Cherry, Flowers, Red & White, Green Ground, Underfoot, 12 In.
$98

Hartzell's Auction Gallery Inc.

Luster, Copper, Pitcher, Lafayette, Surrender Of Cornwallis, Bulbous, Yellow Ground, Transfer, 5 In.
$286

Heritage Auctions

Lustres, Blue Opaque, Art Glass, 5 Hanging Prisms, Scalloped Rim, 5 ¼ In., Pair
$90

Woody Auction

Lustres, Cranberry, Flowers, Hanging Pendants, Bohemian, 13 In., Pair
$123

Rich Penn Auctions

Lustres, Emerald Green, Flowers, Cut Glass Drop Prisms, Bohemia, 14 ½ In., Pair
$118

Leland Little Auctions

Maize, Pitcher, Water, Oval, Opaque White, Green Leaves, Applied Handle, 8 ¾ In.
$75

Jaremos

Maize, Toothpick Holder, Custard, Blue, Gilt, Polished Rim, c.1889, 2 ¼ In.
$556

Jeffrey S. Evans & Associates

Majolica, Carafe, Water, Bulbous Shape, Elongated Neck, Molded Pineapple, Impressed O, 1880s, 8 In.
$105

Jeffrey S. Evans & Associates

Majolica, Dish, Sardine, Lid, Gilt Rim, Cobalt Blue, Flowers, Underplate, George Jones, 1800s, 6 x 8 In.
$300

Cottone Auctions

M

MAIZE

Maize glass was made by W.L. Libbey & Son Company of Toledo, Ohio, after 1889. The glass resembled an ear of corn. The leaves were usually green, but some pieces were made with blue or red leaves. The kernels of corn were light yellow, white, or light green.

Bowl, Amber, Clear Husks, 9 In.	38
Pickle Castor, White, Green, Brown Leaves, Silver Plate, Pierced, Spoon, Gorham, 12 In.	157
Pitcher, Water, Oval, Opaque White, Green Leaves, Applied Handle, 8¾ In. *illus*	75
Sugar Shaker, Custard, Yellow Stained Husks, Gilt Trim, Metal Lid, Late 1800s, 5½ In.	100
Toothpick Holder, Custard, Blue, Gilt, Polished Rim, c.1889, 2¼ In. *illus*	556

MAJOLICA

Majolica is a general term for any pottery glazed with an opaque tin enamel that conceals the color of the clay body. It has been made since the fourteenth century. Today's collector is most likely to find Victorian majolica. The heavy, colorful ware is rarely marked. Some famous makers include George Jones & Sons, Ltd.; Griffen, Smith and Hill; Joseph Holdcroft; and Minton. Majolica made by Wedgwood is listed in the Wedgwood category. These three marks can be found on majolica items.

George Jones, George Jones & Sons, Ltd. 1861–1873	Griffen, Smith and Hill c.1879–1889	Joseph Holdcroft, Sutherland Pottery 1865–1906

Basket, Lid, Fish, 2 Molded Handles, Green Ground, Continental, 5 In.	311
Bowl, Reticulated, White Elephant, Yellow Base, Eichwald, 8 In.	136
Butter, Cover, Cow Finial, Pineapple Shape, Underplate	283
Cachepot, Cobalt Blue, Nesting Birds, Bamboo Rim & Bands, Domed Base, Forester, 7½ In.	226
Carafe, Water, Bulbous Shape, Elongated Neck, Molded Pineapple, Impressed O, 1880s, 8 In. *illus*	105
Charger, Lobster, Shell Border, Sand Ground, Palissy, 12½ In.	124
Clock, Shelf, 8-Day Time & Strike, Porcelain Dial, Short Splayed Feet, c.1900, 11 In.	120
Dish, Game, Lid, Painted, Duck, Rabbits, Brown Ground, Late 1900s, 7 x 13 x 8 In.	207
Dish, Rectangular, Basket & Leaves Design, Sunflower, Handle, Painted, 1800s, 8 x 10 In.	219
Dish, Sardine, Lid, Gilt Rim, Cobalt Blue, Flowers, Underplate, George Jones, 1800s, 6 x 8 In. *illus*	300
Ewer, Figural, Dolphin Shape, Handle, Round Base, Glaze, Marked, Japan, 12¼ In.	40
Figurine, Cockatiel, Green, On Tree Shape Base, Marked Paul Manson, 1800s, 17 In., Pair	1046
Figurine, Dog, Front Feet Crossed, Brown Glazed, St. Clement, 11 In.	79
Figurine, Monkey, Dark Brown Glaze, Seated, Holding Banana, 1900s, 16½ In.	148
Garden Seat, Cylindrical, Turquoise, Birds, Water Lilies, George Jones, c.1875, 18 x 12 In. *illus*	3164
Humidor, Figural, Dog, Seated, Ribbon, Pink Glazed Interior, Late 1800s, 8 In.	236
Jardiniere, Barbotine, Flowers, Fruits, Turquoise Interior, Paw Feet, France, 9½ x 18½ In. *illus*	472
Jardiniere, Pan Head, Berries, Oak Leaves, Animal Handles, Hugo Lonitz, 1800s, 13 x 15 In., Pair	590
Jardiniere, Passion Flower, Lion's Head Handles, Turquoise Glaze, Minton, 13 x 17 x 13 In.	2925
Jardiniere, Pedestal, Hearts, Scrolls, Multicolor, Austria, c.1900, 43 x 15 In.	1188
Jardiniere, Scalloped Leafy Rim, Pink, Fish Scales Pattern, Underfoot, Wardle, 11 In.	215
Jardiniere, Stand, Blue & Brown Glaze, Grapevine Motif, Early 1900s, 28 In.	177
Jardiniere, Winged Putto, Holding Vase On Head, Blue, White, Wall Mounted, Cantagalli, 1800s, 18 In.	443
Jug, Palissy, Green Ground, Lizard Handle, Turtle, Frog, Salamanders, Stand, 10 In.	424
Jug, Tower, Lid, Jester Finial, Pewter Mount, Branch Handle, Minton, Late 1800s, 13 x 7 x 5 In.	351
Oyster Plate, 6 Wells, Light Blue Shell, Bowl Center, Minton, 9 In.	735
Oyster Server, 4 Tiers, Revolving, 3 Fish Shape Finial, Impressed, Minton, c.1870, 10 x 12 In.	9945
Oyster Server, Revolving, 5 Tiers, Sardines, Snake Shape Top Handle, Minton, 1800s, 12 x 12 In.	4095
Pedestal, Classical, Adams Style, Olive Green Glaze, Embossed, England, 1880s, 43 In.	780

Majolica, Garden Seat, Cylindrical, Turquoise, Birds, Water Lilies, George Jones, c.1875, 18 x 12 In. $3,164

Soulis Auctions

Majolica, Jardiniere, Barbotine, Flowers, Fruits, Turquoise Interior, Paw Feet, France, 9½ x 18½ In. $472

Austin Auction Gallery

M

Majolica, Pitcher, Calla Lilies, Rope Twist Frame, Handle & Foot Ring, George Jones, 6½ In. $708

Strawser Auction Group

TIP
Most old majolica pieces have a colored bottom. The newer pieces have white bottoms.

Majolica, Pitcher, Frog, Green Glaze, Lily Pad Foot, 6 ¾ In.
$118

Strawser Auction Group

Majolica, Teapot, Figural, Isle Of Man, Seated, Brown Hat & Base, Glazed, 10 In.
$396

Strawser Auction Group

Majolica, Umbrella Stand, Minton Style, Bird, Heron, Painted, Modeled, 7 ½ In.
$165

Bunch Auctions

Majolica, Urn, Dragon Handles, Cartouches, Romantic Scene, Landscape, Angelo Minghetti, 27 In., Pair
$2,500

Charlton Hall Auctions

Majolica, Wall Plaque, Istoriato, Satyr Pursuing Nymph, Cherubs, Leaves, Round, 1700s, 16 In.
$293

Thomaston Place Auction Galleries

Malachite, Figurine, Guanyin, Robed Woman, Wood Stand, Inlaid Silver Wire, Chinese, 4 ½ x 5 In.
$173

Blackwell Auctions

Map, Amsterdam, Americae Pars Meridionalis, Hendrick Hondius II, Matted, Frame, 1638, 18 x 21 In.
$512

Neal Auction Company

Map, Cape Cod, Blue, White, F.J. Miller, Massachusetts, Frame, c.1940, 24 x 35 In.
$438

Eldred's

Map, Globe, Terrestrial, Ebonized, Walnut Stand, Rand McNally, c.1925, 39 x 24 In.
$2,040

Michaan's Auctions

M

Pitcher, Calla Lilies, Rope Twist Frame, Handle & Foot Ring, George Jones, 6 1/2 In.	*illus*	703
Pitcher, Frog, Green Glaze, Lily Pad Foot, 6 3/4 In.	*illus*	118
Pitcher, Lilies, Overlapping Leaves, Footed, Curved Tendril Handle, Minton, 8 In.		2596
Pitcher, Sunflower, Blue Textured Ground, Branch Handle, Etruscan, 4 1/2 In.		384
Planter, Frolicking Figures, Branch Handles, Glazed, Roped Rim, 9 x 16 1/2 x 10 1/4 In.		125
Planter, Window Box, Rectangular, Embossed, Bird & Branch, Red Interior, 6 x 10 x 5 In.		400
Shaker, Owl Shape, Standing, Yellow Eyes, Domed Base, 4 In.		113
Teapot, Figural, Isle Of Man, Seated, Brown Hat & Base, Glazed, 10 In.	*illus*	396
Teapot, Monkey On Coconut, Curved Tail Handle, Branch Spout, Minton, 8 1/2 In.		413
Tureen, Lid, Blue Glaze, Winged Putti, Landscape, Albisola, Italy, 1900s, 9 x 17 x 11 In.		207
Tureen, Lid, Coconut Shape, Parakeets, Orange Ground, Flowers, Green Base, Minton, 1868, 7 In.		5368
Tureen, Lid, Fish, Painted, Bordallo Pinheiro, Portugal, Early 1900s, 17 1/2 In.		1008
Umbrella Stand, Art Nouveau, Herons, Cattails, Flowers, Green & Pink Ground, Early 1900s, 21 In.		384
Umbrella Stand, Green & Brown Ground, Embossed, 19 In.		58
Umbrella Stand, Minton Style, Bird, Heron, Painted, Modeled, 7 1/2 In.	*illus*	165
Urn, Art Nouveau, Stand, Green & Brown Glaze, Acanthus Leaf & Scroll, Late 1800s, 31 In.		148
Urn, Dragon Handles, Cartouches, Romantic Scene, Landscape, Angelo Minghetti, 27 In., Pair	*illus*	2500
Urn, Ormolu, Mounted, Putto, Pedestal, Shields & Wreaths, Continental, 1800s, 28 In., Pair		443
Vase, Cobalt Blue Glaze, Flowers, 2 Elephant Mask Handles, Late 1800s, 30 In.		118
Vase, Gilt Rim, Mocha Ground, White Flowers, Signed, c.1900, 38 1/2 In.		960
Vase, Glazed, Flowers, Yellow Ground, 2 Handles, Underfoot, 18 1/2 In.		51
Vase, Glazed, Ribbed, Frogs & Grape Clusters, 4 Rope Handles, 11 In.		106
Vase, Owl Shape, Brown Eyes, Light Green Top, Dark Green Base, Bretby, 11 In., Pair		79
Vase, Red & Blue, Cherubs, Dragonflies, Flowers, Square Base, Marked, H.V., 1900s, 18 1/2 In.		920
Wall Plaque, Istoriato, Satyr Pursuing Nymph, Cherubs, Leaves, Round, 1700s, 16 In.	*illus*	293

MALACHITE

Malachite is a green stone with unusual layers or rings of darker green shades. It is often polished and used for decorative objects. Most malachite comes from Siberia or Australia. Copies are made of molded glass.

Figurine, Guanyin, Robed Woman, Wood Stand, Inlaid Silver Wire, Chinese, 4 1/2 x 5 In.	*illus*	173

MAP

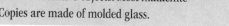

Maps of all types have been collected for centuries. The earliest known printed maps were made in 1478. The first printed street map showed London in 1559. The first road maps for use by drivers of automobiles were made in 1901. Collectors buy maps that were pages of old books, as well as the multifolded road maps popular in the twentieth century. Terrestrial globes are spherical maps of the earth. Celestial globes show the position of the stars and the constellations in the sky.

Amsterdam, Americae Pars Meridionalis, Hendrick Hondius II, Matted, Frame, 1638, 18 x 21 In.	*illus*	512
Amsterdam, Nova Persia, Armenia, Arabia, Engraved, Frederick De Wit, Frame, c.1710, 32 x 29 In.		316
Cape Cod, Blue, White, F.J. Miller, Massachusetts, Frame, c.1940, 24 x 35 In.	*illus*	438
Carolina, Colored, Engraving, On Thick Laid Paper, Pierre Mortier, Frame, 1696, 31 x 27 In.		1968
Carolina, Hand Colored, Engraving, Laid Paper, John Speed, Wood Frame, 1676, 17 x 23 In.		984
Cheshire, Atlas, Outline Color, C.F. Cruchley, Wood Frame, Gilt Liner, c.1890, 15 x 17 In.		177
Florence, Hand Colored, Italian, German, Matthaus Seuter, Augsburg, Frame, c.1800, 24 x 27 In.		450
Georgia, Wove Paper, Engraved, Hand Colored, Anthony Finley, Frame, 1831, 12 1/4 x 9 3/4 In.		554
Globe, Terrestrial, Blue, Black, Stand, Round Base, Denoyer Geppert, Mid 1900s, 56 In.		896
Globe, Terrestrial, Brass Stand, Replogle World Classic, 35 In.		83
Globe, Terrestrial, Brass, Cast Iron, Replogle Comprehensive, Tripod Iron Base, 1900s, 51 In.		256
Globe, Terrestrial, Cram's Ideal, Wood Stand, 18 1/2 In.		135
Globe, Terrestrial, Ebonized, Walnut Stand, Rand McNally, c.1925, 39 x 24 In.	*illus*	2040
Globe, Terrestrial, Edwardian Style, Georama, Mahogany Stand, Fluted Legs, c.1985, 48 x 26 In.		1287
Globe, Terrestrial, Glass, 2 Figures On Wood Base, George F. Cram Co., c.1940, 15 x 15 In.		882
Globe, Terrestrial, Iron, Scrollwork Stand, Rand McNally, Mid 1900s, 35 In.	*illus*	295
Globe, Terrestrial, Library, Metal Meridian, Quadruped Wood Stand, Replogle, c.1930, 36 In.		325

Map, Globe, Terrestrial, Iron, Scrollwork Stand, Rand McNally, Mid 1900s, 35 In. $295

Leland Little Auctions

Map, Ohio, Indiana, Sectional, Hand Colored, Engraved, H.S. Tanner, 1848, 22 x 27 1/2 In. $300

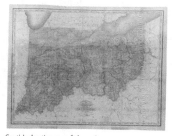

Garth's Auctioneers & Appraisers

Map, World, Explorers' Routes, Hand Colored, Hendrik De Leth, France, Frame, c.1750, 20 x 28 In. $1,250

Early American History Auctions

M

Marble, Swirl, Divided Core, Red, Yellow, Orange, Black, White, 2 ½ In. $400

Morphy Auctions

Marble Carving, Bust, Child, Classical Style, Curly Hair, Circular Base, 1910s, 17 In. $826

Leland Little Auctions

Marble Carving, Bust, Man, Classical Attire, Continental School, 1850s, 21 In. $2,106

Jeffrey S. Evans & Associates

Globe, Terrestrial, Lithograph, Mounted, Ring Turned Legs, Wilson's, 1836, 18 x 16 In.	800
Globe, Terrestrial, Revolving, Graduated Stand, Replogle, c.1950, 33 In.	31
Globe, Terrestrial, Silver, Gilt Continents, Dolphin Stand, c.1950, 10 ½ x 7 x 6 In.	4875
Globe, Terrestrial, Stand, Paw Feet, Kittinger Company, New York, 1893, 37 In.	236
Globe, Terrestrial, Table, Circular Plinth Base, Silver, Tiffany & Co., c.1975, 8 ½ In.	6875
Globe, Terrestrial, Wood Base, Replogle World Classic, 12 In.	49
Globe, Terrestrial, Wood Stand, 3 Paw Feet, Rand McNally, c.1940, 25 x 16 In.	236
Globe, Terrestrial, Wrought Iron Stand, Germany, 1900s, 38 ¾ In.	1003
Great Britain, Needlepoint, Frame, 27 ¼ x 22 ¼ In.	94
Kentucky & Tennessee, State House, Nashville, Johnson's, Mat, Frame, 1865, 25 x 30 In.	82
Mexico, Diego Province, Antonio Ysarti, 12 x 14 ¼ In.	75
Middle East, Hand Colored, Engraved, Nicolaes Visscher, Dutch, c.1650, 16 x 20 In.	443
North & South America, Copper Engraved, Atlas Page, M. L'Abbe Expilly, France, 1765, 8 ¼ x 5 In.	532
North America, Color, Engraving, On Laid Paper, Robert Sayer & John Bennett, Frame, 48 x 55 In.	2091
Ohio, Engraved, On Paper, Canals, William Woodruff, Frame, 1837, 21 ¾ x 17 ¾ In.	600
Ohio, Indiana, Sectional, Hand Colored, Engraved, H.S. Tanner, 1848, 22 x 27 ½ In. ... *illus*	300
Rome, Black & White, Beaded, Wood Frame, 1748, 26 ¾ x 36 In.	688
Rugen Island, Coat Of Arms, Willen Blaeu, Theatrum Orbis Terrarum, 1600s, Frame, 24 x 28 In.	95
Vermont, Engraved, Colored, D.F. Stozmann, Frame, 1797, 33 x 23 ¾ In.	2032
Virginiae Partis Australis, Et Floridae, Willem Janszoon Blaeu, Frame, 1640, 24 x 28 In.	1968
World, Explorers' Routes, Hand Colored, Hendrik De Leth, France, Frame, c.1750, 20 x 28 In. ... *illus*	1250

MARBLE

Marble collectors pay highest prices for glass and sulphide marbles. The game of marbles has been popular since the days of the ancient Romans. American children were able to buy marbles by the mid-eighteenth century. Dutch glazed clay marbles were least expensive. Glazed pottery marbles, attributed to the Bennington potteries in Vermont, were of a better quality. Marbles made of pink marble were also available by the 1830s. Glass marbles seem to have been made later. By 1880, Samuel C. Dyke of South Akron, Ohio, was making clay marbles and The National Onyx Marble Company was making marbles of onyx. The Navarre Glass Marble Company of Navarre, Ohio, and M. B. Mishler of Ravenna, Ohio, made the glass marbles. Ohio remained the center of the marble industry, and the Akron-made Akro Agate brand became nationally known. Other pieces made by Akro Agate are listed in this book in the Akro Agate category. Sulphides are glass marbles with frosted white figures in the center.

Comic Strip Characters, Multicolor, Bennett, Box, 12 Piece	125
Slag, Swirled, Black, Brown, White, Machine Made, Early 20th Century, 60 Piece	25
Sulphide, Horse, Running, 1 ½ In.	50
Sulphide, Ram, 1 9/16 In.	48
Swirl, Divided Core, Red, Yellow, Orange, Black, White, 2 ½ In. ... *illus*	400

MARBLE CARVING

Marble carvings, such as large or small figurines, groups of people or animals, and architectural decorations, have been a special art form since the time of the ancient Greeks. Reproductions, especially of large Victorian groups, are being made of a mixture using marble dust. These are very difficult to detect and collectors should be careful. Other carvings are listed under Alabaster.

Bowl, Black & White, Molded Rim, Shaped Handle, 23 ¼ In.	236
Bust, Augustus Caesar, Wearing Cloak, 1900s, 20 In.	594
Bust, Child, Classical Style, Curly Hair, Circular Base, 1910s, 17 In. ... *illus*	826
Bust, Female Figure, Hair Pulled Up, Bun, White, Continental, Late 1800s, 20 In.	720

M

Bust, Havelock, Mounted On Waisted Circular Socle, E.W. Wyon, c.1860, 15 In.		250
Bust, Henry Wadsworth Longfellow, Pedestal Base, American School, 1800s, 16 In.		935
Bust, Man, Classical Attire, Continental School, 1850s, 21 In. .... *illus*		2106
Bust, Portrait Of Dante's Beatrice, Integral Base, 17½ x 14 x 7 In.		1287
Bust, Sarah Amelia Day Lodert, White Carrera Marble, c.1850, 22 x 15 x 8 In.		4920
Bust, Woman, Flowers In Hair, Art Nouveau, Continental, 1890s, 11 x 10¼ In.		300
Bust, Woman, Sitting, Pedestal, Wavy Hair, Italy, 24 In.		2125
Bust, Woman, Wearing Fancy Hat, White Ground, 16 In.		113
Bust, Woman, White, Round, Beveled, Signed, George Simonds, Italy, Frame, 23½ In.		2125
Bust, Woman, White, Veil Across, Starburst, Signed, Emilio P. Fiaschi, 15½ In.		469
Bust, Young Boy, Eyes Closed, Smiling, Socle, 1800s, 16½ In.		649
Bust, Young Woman, Bronze, Rouge Marble Base, Emile Boudon, 1930, 6¾ x 22½ In.		1000
Bust, Young Woman, Wearing Necklace, Olive Branch, Dark Stone Base, 14 x 15 In. .... *illus*		175
Feet, Wearing Sandals, Roman Style, 8 x 15½ x 5½ In., Pair .... *illus*		625
Jardiniere, Ironstone, Pedestal, Flowering Vine, Blue, Gold Trim, 38 In.		138
Lamp, Red Shades, Acanthus Leaf Urn, Stepped Base, 1910s, 28 In., Pair		384
Obelisk, Bronze Mounted, Tortoise Support, Continental, c.1900, 17¼ x 3¾ In., Pair		384
Obelisk, Louis XVI, Portico Clock Shape, Gilt Bronze Mounted, c.1785, 24 x 8 x 7 In., Pair		5040
Obelisk, Multicolor, Geometric, White Ground, Stepped Base, 24 In., Pair		540
Obelisk, White Ground, Gray Veining, Round Olive Accents, Metal Finial, 19 In., Pair		708
Pedestal, 3-Part Pillar, Roman Style Column, White, Gray Veined, Italy, 38 x 8¾ In..		189
Pedestal, Black, Octagonal Base, Continental, Late 1800s, 41½ In. .... *illus*		179
Pedestal, Black, Round Top, Octagonal Base, 32½ x 15 In.		250
Pedestal, Brown, Variegated, Rounded Corners, Square Top & Base, Continental, 32 In., Pair		2250
Pedestal, Columnar, Black Amazonian, White & Brown, Square Base, 36¾ x 14 In., Pair .. *illus*		960
Pedestal, Green, Classical, Spiral Twist, Incised, Octagonal Base, c.1920, 41 x 10 In...........		649
Pedestal, Mother-Of-Pearl, Circular Top, Gilt, Paw Feet, Empire Style, 1900s, 42½ In., Pair		1298
Pedestal, Onyx, White, Ormolu Mount, 1930s, 42 x 12½ x 10½ In..........................		219
Pedestal, Rouge, Gilt, Bronze, Mounted, Reverse Tapered, Brown Ground, Plinth Base, 43¼ In		576
Pedestal, Turned Support, Octagonal Top & Base, Continental, Early 1900s, 41 x 11 In.		188
Pedestal, Verde, Circular, Octagonal Base, Continental, Late 1800s, 45 In........................		210
Pedestal, White, Flowers, 2 Sections, Stepped Base, Round Top, 10¾ In.		286
Pedestal, White, Octagonal Base, Reeded Column, Leafy, Italy, Early 1900s, 31 In.		375
Plaque, Angel, Cherub Holding Torch, Flowers, Round, 2 x 20 In.		625
Plaque, Feathered Serpent, Slate, Jose Magana, 9¾ In.		92
Statue, Abstract Shape, Wood Plinth Base, 20 x 6½ In.		177
Statue, Abstract, Circular Plinth Base, 51 In.		625
Statue, Allegory Of Love, 2 Putti Embracing, Gilt Bronze Base, 1800s, 20 x 18 x 11 In. .. *illus*		4800
Statue, Bather, Nude Woman, Braided Hair, Draped Cloth, Etienne-Maurice Falconet, 1900s, 32 In...		1063
Statue, Caryatid, Classical Style, Nude Women, Flowers, Acanthus Scroll, 1900s, 44 In., Pair		561
Statue, Christ, Praying, Square Base, Marked, Signed, Koren, 1900s, 36 x 9 x 6 In................		188
Statue, Cupid, Curly Hair, Standing, Arrow Back, Circular Base, 27 In...........................		1890
Statue, Dog, Male, Seated, Rectangular Plinth Base, Continental, 13½ In. .... *illus*		1464
Statue, Female Torso, Bathing Suit, White, Wood Base, 1950s, 24 In.		316
Statue, Female Torso, Plinth Base, Signed, James MacGill, 24 In.............................. ..		375
Statue, Foo Dog, Seated, White, Square Base, Chinese, 19 In., Pair.............................		600
Statue, Grand Tour Lion, Lying Down, Egyptian Marble Base, 1800s, 5 x 8 In., Pair ..... *illus*		1952
Statue, Horse Head, Gray Veined, Cropped Mane, Art Deco, 1930, 10¼ In........................		266
Statue, Nude Roman Male, Carved, Torso, Travertine Base, 50 x 19 x 10 In.		5000
Statue, Roman Boy, Sitting, Pulling Thorn, Italy, Early 1900s, 19 In.		508
Statue, Torso, Roman Soldier, Mount, Travertine Base, 48 x 21 In...............................		2500
Statue, Woman, Life-Size Figure, Standing, Round Base, Carrara, 67 x 22 In. .... *illus*		2125
Statue, Woman, Seminude, Side Glancing, Drape, Round Base, 31 In.		850
Statue, Woman's Face, Square Base, Signed, J. Goldsack, 1900s.................................		281
Statue, Young Boy, Holding Bird, Apple, Sitting, Octagonal Base, Continental, 23¾ x 16 In..		769
Statue, Young Woman, Carrier Belleuse, Socle Base, Albert Ernest, 24 In.		3480
Statue, Young Woman, Flowing Dress, Round Base, Signed, A. Batacchi, Italy, 1800s, 32 x 10 In.		2875
Urn, Lid, Leafy Handles, Brown, Brass Mounted, Continental, 12 In.		94
Urn, Neoclassical Style, Painted, Gilt Bronze Rim & Stand, Paw Feet, Italy, 20 x 6 In., Pair ...		840

Marble Carving, Bust, Young Woman, Wearing Necklace, Olive Branch, Dark Stone Base, 14 x 15 In.
$175

Woody Auction

Marble Carving, Feet, Wearing Sandals, Roman Style, 8 x 15½ x 5½ In., Pair
$625

Kamelot Auctions

Marble Carving, Pedestal, Black, Octagonal Base, Continental, Late 1800s, 41½ In.
$179

M

Hindman

Marble Carving, Pedestal, Columnar, Black Amazonian, White & Brown, Square Base, 36¾ x 14 In., Pair
$960

Michaan's Auctions

Marble Carving, Statue, Allegory Of Love, 2 Putti Embracing, Gilt Bronze Base, 1800s, 20 x 18 x 11 In.
$4,800

Brunk Auctions

Marble Carving, Statue, Dog, Male, Seated, Rectangular Plinth Base, Continental, 13½ In.

Neal Auction Company

> **TIP**
> When buying antiques, beware of stickers, Magic Marker numbers, or other dealer-added labels that may damage the antique. Any type of sticky tape or label will leave marks on paper or paint finishes. Metal with an oxidized finish is damaged when ink marks are removed. Pencil or pen notations often leave indentations. All of these "scars" lower the value.

Marble Carving, Statue, Woman, Life-Size Figure, Standing, Round Base, Carrara, 67 x 22 In.
$2,125

Abington Auction Gallery

Marble Carving, Statue, Grand Tour Lion, Lying Down, Egyptian Marble Base, 1800s, 5 x 8 In., Pair
$1,952

Neal Auction Company

MARBLEHEAD POTTERY

Marblehead Pottery was founded in 1904 by Dr. J. Hall as a rehabilitative program for the patients of a Marblehead, Massachusetts, sanitarium. Two years later it was separated from the sanitarium and it continued operations until 1936. Many of the pieces were decorated with marine motifs.

Vase, Art Pottery, Light Blue Ground, Peaked Rim, 10 In.	540
Vase, Carved Flowers, Matte Green Glaze, Paneled, Marked, HT, MP & Ship, 6 In. .... *illus*	150000
Vase, Grapevine Band, Tan Speckled Glaze, Oval, Marked M & Ship, c.1915, 5 x 4 In.	1040
Vase, Squat, Blue Matte Glaze, Marked, Early 1900s, 4¾ x 5½ In. .... *illus*	111
Vase, Squat, Bulbous Body, Matte Curdled, Glazed, Seagull Mark, 4⅝ x 2¹¹/₁₆ In.	2250
Vase, Stylized Peacock Feathers, Matte Glaze, Bulbous, Tapered, A. Baggs, 1908, 11 x 10 In.	9375
Vase, Stylized Plants, Carved, Brown Glaze, A. Hennesey, S. Tutt, Initials, 3½ x 4¾ In. *illus*	3906

MARDI GRAS

Mardi Gras, French for "Fat Tuesday," was first celebrated in seventeenth-century Europe. The first celebration in America was held in Mobile, Alabama, in 1703. The first krewe, a parading or social club, was founded in 1856. Dozens have been formed since. The Mardi Gras Act, which made Fat Tuesday a legal holiday, was passed in Louisiana in 1875. Mardi Gras balls, carnivals, parties, and parades are held from January 6 until the Tuesday before the beginning of Lent. The most famous carnival and parades take place in New Orleans. Parades feature floats, elaborate costumes, masks, and "throws" of strings of beads, cups, doubloons, or small toys. Purple, green, and gold are traditional Mardi Gras colors. Mardi Gras memorabilia ranges from cheap plastic beads to expensive souvenirs from early celebrations.

Mask, White, Gilt Flowers, Jester's Hat, Bells, Blue & Gold Ribbons, Scepter, Ermes Ferrari, Venice	48
Pin, Twelfth Night Revelers, Figure, Arms Raised, Enamel Scrolls, Red, Yellow, Orange, 1923	366
Poster, May You Find Peace, Putto, White Drape, D'Ann Potts, Ed Rahaim, Frame, 1982, 25 x 19 In.	625

MARTIN BROTHERS

Martin Brothers of Middlesex, England, made Martinware, a salt-glazed stoneware, between 1873 and 1915. Many figural jugs and vases were made by the four brothers. Of special interest are the fanciful birds, usually made with removable heads. Most pieces have the incised name of the artists plus other information on the bottom.

Jar, Bird, Lid, Glazed, Stoneware, Wood Base, Incised, 1899, 14 In. .... *illus*	8190
Jug, Cobalt Blue, Man's Face, 2-Sided, Gray, Stoneware, 1900, 6¼ x 6 In.	7763
Pitcher, Flowers, Brown Dip Glaze Rim, Semigloss, Incised Martin London, c.1876, 10 In.	484

MARY GREGORY

Mary Gregory is the name used for a type of glass that is easily identified. White figures were painted on clear or colored glass as the decoration. The figures chosen were usually children at play. The first glass known as Mary Gregory was made in about 1870. Similar glass is made even today. The traditional story has been that the glass was made at the Boston & Sandwich Glass Company in Sandwich, Massachusetts, by a woman named Mary Gregory. Recent research has shown that none was made at Sandwich. In fact, all early Mary Gregory glass was made in Bohemia. Beginning in 1957, the Westmoreland Glass Co. made the first Mary Gregory–type decorations on American glassware. These pieces had simpler designs, less enamel paint, and more modern shapes. France, Italy, Germany, Switzerland, and England, as well as Bohemia, made this glassware. Children standing, not playing, were not pictured until after the 1950s.

Marblehead, Vase, Carved Flowers, Matte Green Glaze, Paneled, Marked, HT, MP & Ship, 6 In.
$150,000

Rago Arts and Auction Center

Marblehead, Vase, Squat, Blue Matte Glaze, Marked, Early 1900s, 4¾ x 5½ In.
$111

Locati Auctions

Marblehead, Vase, Stylized Plants, Carved, Brown Glaze, A. Hennesey, S. Tutt, Initials, 3½ x 4¾ In.
$3,906

Treadway

This is an edited listing of current prices. Visit **Kovels.com** to check thousands of prices from previous years and sign up for free information on trends, tips, reproductions, marks, and more.

Martin Brothers, Jar, Bird, Lid, Glazed, Stoneware, Wood Base, Incised, 1899, 14 In.
$8,190

Sotheby's

Mary Gregory, Dresser Box, Hinged Lid, Girl, Grasshopper, Amethyst, Meriden Silver Plate Fittings, 5 x 10 In.
$840

Woody Auction

Mason's, Cider Jug, Chinese Export Style, River Scene, Pagodas, Blue, White Handle, c.1790, 10 In.
$320

Alex Cooper Auctioneers

Bottle, Girl, Holding Twig, Boy, Hand Outstretched, Square, Faceted Stopper, 8 x 2 ¼ In., Pair	62
Comb Glass, Barber's, Boy & Girl, Playing Badminton, Cobalt Blue, c.1890, 7 ⅛ x 5 ⅛ In.	200
Dresser Box, Hinged Lid, Girl, Grasshopper, Amethyst, Meriden Silver Plate Fittings, 5 x 10 In. *illus*	840
Powder Jar, Hinged Lid, Round, Woman, Playing Harp, Gilt Flowers, Green, Moser, 3 ½ x 6 In..	63
Tankard, Girl, Jumping Rope, Amber, Applied Blue Handle, Round Foot, c.1900, 13 ¼ In......	30
Tumble-Up, Girl, Painting, Cranberry Glass, 7 In., 2 Piece..	54
Vase, Cherubs, Gilt Scrolls, Blown Glass, Green, Fan Shape, Ruffled Rim, Footed, c.1970, 12 In., Pair	155
Vase, Cranberry, White Enamel, Forest, Gold Trim, 12 In., Pair...	138
Vase, Girl, Boy, Under Branch, Green, Clear Rigaree On Sides, 10 x 4 ¾ In., Pair.....................	270
Vase, Mantel, Boy, Sitting, Reading, Blue, Gilt Trim, Footed, Silver Plate Frame, Tufts, 9 In..	107

MASONIC, *see Fraternal category.*

MASON'S IRONSTONE

Mason's Ironstone was made by the English pottery of Charles J. Mason after 1813. Mason, of Lane Delph, was given a patent for this improved earthenware. He usually called it *Mason's Patent Ironstone China.* It resisted chipping and breaking, so it became popular for dinnerware and other table service dishes. Vases and other decorative pieces were also made. The ironstone was decorated with orange, blue, gold, and other colors, often in Japanese-inspired designs. The firm had financial difficulties but the molds and the name *Mason* were used by many owners through the years, including Francis Morley, Taylor Ashworth, George L. Ashworth, and John Shaw. Mason's joined the Wedgwood group in 1973 and the name was used for a few years and then dropped.

Bowl, Imari, Flowering Branch, Bird, Perched, Multicolor, Blue Trim, 10 ½ In., Pair............	84
Cider Jug, Chinese Export Style, River Scene, Pagodas, Blue, White Handle, c.1790, 10 In. *illus*	320
Ewer, Putti, Scrolls, Acanthus Leaves, Satyr Masks, Flowers, Gilt, On Base, 1820s, 24 In. *illus*	630
Plate, Flower Sprays, Navy Border, Gilt Leafy Vine, Tiffany & Co., 10 In., 5 Piece....................	125
Platter, Imari Style, Flowers, White Ground, Late 1800s, 20 In. .... *illus*	443
Platter, Imari, Center Scene, Flowering Branch, Buildings, Scalloped Edge, Late 1800s, 20 In. ...	443
Platter, Meat, Oval, Flowers, Birds, Geometric Border, Mahogany Stand, 20 x 22 In. .... *illus*	254
Platter, Prince Of Wales, Crown, Flower Basket Border, Transfer, Blue Mark, 1813-26, 17 x 14 In.	175
Tureen, Flow Blue Lid, Chinoiserie, Flower Finial, Gilt, Hexagonal, 1830, 8 In., Pair..............	254

MASSIER

Massier, a French art pottery, was made by brothers Jerome, Delphin, and Clement Massier in Vallauris and Golfe-Juan, France, in the late nineteenth and early twentieth centuries. It has an iridescent metallic luster glaze that resembles the Weller Sicardo pottery glaze. Most pieces are marked *J. Massier.* Massier may also be listed in the Majolica category.

Charger, Landscape, Golfe-Juan On The Cote D'Azur, Metallic, Signed, 9 ¾ In.	1475
Jardiniere, Pedestal, Butterflies, Flowers, Cream Ground, Marble Foot, Delphin, 48 In. ..*illus*	4410

MATCH HOLDER

Match holders were made to hold the large wooden matches that were used in the nineteenth and twentieth centuries for a variety of purposes. The kitchen stove and the fireplace or furnace had to be lit regularly. One type of match holder was made to hang on the wall, another was designed to be kept on a tabletop. Of special interest to collectors today are match holders that have advertisements as part of the design.

Basket, Hinged Lids, Cast Iron, Brass Handle, Painted, Scalloped Base, 5 ½ In.......................	135
Bear, Seated, Holding Stump, Wearing Harness, Inset Eyes, Bronze, Russia, Late 1800s, 2 ¾ In. *illus*	210
Brass, Ornate Shape, Man & Woman Faces, 11 In...	277

Mason's, Ewer, Putti, Scrolls, Acanthus
Leaves, Satyr Masks, Flowers, Gilt,
On Base, 1820s, 24 In.
$630

Brunk Auctions

Mason's, Platter, Imari Style, Flowers, White
Ground, Late 1800s, 20 In.
$443

Leland Little Auctions

Mason's, Platter, Meat, Oval, Flowers, Birds,
Geometric Border, Mahogany Stand,
20 x 22 In.
$254

Rafael Osona Nantucket Auctions

Massier, Jardiniere, Pedestal, Butterflies,
Flowers, Cream Ground, Marble Foot,
Delphin, 48 In.
$4,410

Fontaine's Auction Gallery

> **TIP**
> *The less you handle an
> antique or collectible
> the better. Always pick it
> up with two hands.*

Match Holder, Bear, Seated, Holding Stump,
Wearing Harness, Inset Eyes, Bronze, Russia,
Late 1800s, 2¾ In.
$210

Match Holder, Fly, Figural, Cast Iron,
Richard H. Adams & Co., Importers Of
Tailors Trimmings, 2 x 4 x 3 In.
$307

AntiqueAdvertising.com

Match Holder, Hand, Holding Goblet,
Cast Iron, Drink C. Feigenspans Lager,
Countertop, 5 In.
$246

M

Hartzell's Auction Gallery Inc.

Match Safe, Cat, Seated, Figural, Painted,
Gold, Striker Base, 3¼ In.
$221

Hartzell's Auction Gallery Inc.

Selkirk Auctioneers & Appraisers

Medical, Box, Cocaine, Hinged Lid, 2 Handles, Gilt Lettering, Maritime, 1911, 14 x 22 ½ In.
$1,008

Fontaine's Auction Gallery

Medical, Cabinet, Apothecary, 20 Drawers, Poplar, Pine, Porcelain Knobs, Late 1800s, 21 x 35 x 14 In.
$761

Jeffrey S. Evans & Associates

Medical, Cabinet, Specimen, 7 Drawers, 2 Doors, White Pulls, Square Feet, 27 ½ x 18 In.
$400

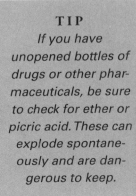

Pook & Pook

TIP
If you have unopened bottles of drugs or other pharmaceuticals, be sure to check for ether or picric acid. These can explode spontaneously and are dangerous to keep.

Fly, Figural, Cast Iron, Richard H. Adams & Co., Importers Of Tailors Trimmings, 2 x 4 x 3 In. ..*illus* 307
Hand, Holding Goblet, Cast Iron, Drink C. Feigenspans Lager, Countertop, 5 In. .... *illus* 246
Knight, Head, Armor, Mounted, Egyptian Design Backing, Hanging, 9 ¾ In. 209
Nakara, Blue Flowers, Pink Shaded Ground, 8-Sided Base, Gilt Rim, 2 x 2 ¼ In. 72

MATCH SAFE

Match safes were designed to be carried in the pocket or set on a table. Early matches were made with phosphorus and could ignite unexpectedly. The matches were safely stored in the tightly closed container. Match safes were made in sterling silver, plated silver, or other metals. The English call these "vesta boxes."

Cat, Seated, Figural, Painted, Gold, Striker Base, 3 ¼ In. .... *illus* 221
Factory, Flat Roof, 2 Smokestacks, Applied Letters Ohio, Late 1800s, 5 ½ x 7 x 7 In.............. 188
House Shape, Cast Iron, Painted, Black, Square Base, Marked, 1883, 4 ¼ x 4 ½ x 5 In. 74
Indian, Chief, Silver, Engraved, Embossed, 6 In.. 708
J.H. Lesher & Co., Tailors, Chicago, Turtle Shape, Iron, Shell Lid, 5 In. 207
Nude Female, Silver, Repousse, High Relief, Floral, Marked, Gorham, 2 x 1 x ¼ In. 201

McCOY

McCoy

McCoy pottery was made in Roseville, Ohio. Nelson McCoy and J.W. McCoy established the Nelson McCoy Sanitary and Stoneware Company in Roseville, Ohio, in 1910. The firm made art pottery after 1926. In 1933 it became the Nelson McCoy Pottery Company. Pieces marked *McCoy* were made by the Nelson McCoy Pottery Company. Cookie jars were made from about 1940 until December 1990, when the McCoy factory closed. Since 1991 pottery with the McCoy mark has been made by firms unrelated to the original company. Because there was a company named Brush-McCoy, there is great confusion between Brush and Nelson McCoy pieces. See Brush category for more information.

Bowl, Brown Drip, c.1970, 10 ½ x 3 In... 31
Cookie Jar, Cinderella's Pumpkin Coach, Mice Finial, Gray, Green, Orange, 9 ½ x 8 x 8 In... 88
Mixing Bowl, Green, Window Pane, Marked, No. 9, 9 x 6 In.................................... 75
Pitcher, Angel Fish, Blue, c.1930, 6 In... 140
Pitcher, Ribbed Base, Green, 1940s, 5 ½ x 6 ½ In.. 125
Planter, Figural, Cowboy Boots, Brown & Tan, c.1955, 6 ¾ In.................................. 55
Planter, Humpty Dumpty, Pink Glaze, 4 ½ x 4 ½ x 2 ½ In...................................... 40
Planter, Saucer, Handle, Holly, Berries, Fluted, Ribbed, 5 In. 20
Planter, Spinning Wheel, Dog, Cat, Brown, Green, 1950s, 7 x 4 ½ In.......................... 160
Vase, Magnolia Blossom Shape, Asymmetrical, Leaves, Stems, Pink, 8 ¼ x 7 In. 250

McKEE

McKee is a name associated with various glass enterprises in the United States since 1836, including J. & F. McKee (1850), Bryce, McKee & Co. (1850 to 1854), McKee and Brothers (1865), and National Glass Co. (1899). In 1903, the McKee Glass Company was formed in Jeannette, Pennsylvania. It became McKee Division of the Thatcher Glass Co. in 1951 and was bought out by the Jeannette Corporation in 1961. Pressed glass, kitchenwares, and tablewares were produced. Jeannette Corporation closed in the early 1980s. Additional pieces may be included in the Custard Glass and Depression Glass categories.

McKee
McKee Glass Co.
c.1870

PRESCUT
McKee Glass Co.
c.1904–1935

McKee Glass Co.
1935–1940

Cake Plate, Pedestal, Scalloped Edge, Rum Ring, c.1894, 10 x 8 ½ In.......................... 110

M

Compote, Lid, Fan Shaped Shells, Diamond Design, c.1880, 11 In.	95
Reamer, Sunkist, Jade, c.1930, 8 x 5 In.	50
Relish, Deer & Pine, c.1890, 5 x 8 In.	35
Sugar Shaker, Jade, Square, 2½ In.	68

MECHANICAL BANKS *are listed in the Bank category.*

MEDICAL

Medical office furniture, operating tools, microscopes, thermometers, and other paraphernalia used by doctors are included in this category. Veterinary collectibles are also included here. Medicine bottles are listed in the Bottle category. There are related collectibles listed under Dental.

Box, Cocaine, Hinged Lid, 2 Handles, Gilt Lettering, Maritime, 1911, 14 x 22½ In. .... *illus*	1008
Cabinet, Apothecary, 9 Drawers, Pine & Poplar, Bracket Feet, Late 1900s, 25 x 29 In.	390
Cabinet, Apothecary, 9 Drawers, Porcelain Pulls, Bracket Feet, c.1900, 35¾ x 37 x 11¾ In.	234
Cabinet, Apothecary, 12 Drawers, Poplar, Knob Handle, Pa., 1800s, 30 x 18¾ In.	488
Cabinet, Apothecary, 20 Drawers, Poplar, Pine, Porcelain Knobs, Late 1800s, 21 x 35 x 14 In. *illus*	761
Cabinet, Apothecary, 24 Drawers, Wood Knob, Mustard Paint, 1800s, 57 x 46 In.	2712
Cabinet, Apothecary, 27 Drawers, Pine & Poplar, Painted, Black, 1800s, 46 x 60 In.	688
Cabinet, Apothecary, 42 Drawers, Elmwood, Carved, Chinese Letters, 46 x 33 In.	413
Cabinet, Apothecary, Spanish Style, Pine, Flat Top, Molded Front Shoe Feet, 74 x 47 x 14 In.	1404
Cabinet, Filing, Laboratory, Oak, 16 Drawers, Paneled Sides, Back, Brass Tag & Pulls, 52 x 2 In.	615
Cabinet, Oak, 2 Parts, 4 Drawers, Hinged Doors, Casters, W.D. Allison Co., c.1890, 68 x 32 In.	1121
Cabinet, Oak, Metal Handle, Carved, Flowers, Drawer, Late 1800s, 29 x 15 In.	221
Cabinet, Specimen, 7 Drawers, 2 Doors, White Pulls, Square Feet, 27½ x 18 In. .... *illus*	400
Case, Apothecary, Mahogany, Traveling, Brass Handle, Bottles, 1800s, 10½ x 8½ In.	500
Case, Pharmacy, Steel, Glass, Adjustable Shelves, Belgium, 38 In. .... *illus*	768
Chair, Invalid's, Rolling, Oak, Caned Seat, Writing Surface, Reclines, 1800s, 50 x 29 In.	99
Chart, Mechanical Stimulation, Nerves, Vibrator Instrument Co., Frame, 1902, 27 x 33 In.	94
Crutches, Wood, Carved, Cutout Hearts At Top & Base, c.1860, 51⅝ In.	200
Cupboard, Apothecary, 9 Drawers, Knob Pulls, Painted, Signed, R Zucati, 1998, 38 x 73½ In. ...*illus*	322
Figurine, Doctor, Young Woman, Sitting, Blood Pressure, Painted, Signed, Moretto, 9 x 8 In. ....*illus*	81
Lancet, Spring, Brass Case, Marked, Wiegand & Snowden, Philadelphia, Fitted Box, 2 In., Pair	173
Leg Splint, Molded, Mahogany, Plywood, Charles & Ray Eames, 1943, 42 In.	845
Massager, Roller, Vita Master VMRL-1, Seafoam Green, Multiple Speeds, 24 In.	59
Medicine Cabinet, Tansu Style, 16 Small Drawers, Metal Fittings, 1900s, 26 x 21 x 10 In.	118
Model, Human Male, Acupuncture Body, Rubberized, Plastic, Standing, Wood Base, 20 In. *illus*	288
Pill Roller, 2 Piece, Walnut, Grooved Brass Plates, 19th Century, 2½ x 13¾ x 12 In.	152
Saddlebag, Leather, Brown, Tin Lined, 30 Bottles, Elliot's Patent, A.A. Mellier, 16 x 6¾ x 6 In.	484
Scale, Height & Weight, Light Green, Howe Scale Company, Rutland, Ver., Late 1800s, 53 In.	50
Show Globe, Apothecary, Glass, Cast Filigree, Iron Eagle Flange Bracket, 24 x 6 x 17 In. *illus*	246
Wall Bracket, Show Globe, Apothecary, Gothic Dragon, Recast Metal, 10 x 15 x 1 In., Pair	861
Wall Bracket, Show Globe, Apothecary, Victorian Style, Bronze, Winged Griffin, 15 In., Pair	1353

MEISSEN

Meissen is a town in Germany where porcelain has been made since 1710. Any china made in the town can be called Meissen, although the famous Meissen factory made the finest porcelains of the area. The crossed swords mark of the great Meissen factory has been copied by many other firms in Germany and other parts of the world. Pieces of Meissen dinnerware in the Onion pattern are listed in their own category in this book.

Basket, Oval, Basketwork, 2 Handles, 2 Cockerels, c.1735, 7⅛ In., Pair	3024
Basket, Rococo Style, Flowers, Reticulated Sides, Splayed Twig Legs, c.1900, 5 x 14 x 9 In.	330
Bell, Table, Flowers, Parcel Gilt, Painted, Blue Crossed Swords Mark, Late 1800s, 4¼ In.	141
Box, Oval, Bronze Mounted, Landscape Scenes, Painted, 1700s, 1¼ x 2 In.	1125

Medical, Case, Pharmacy, Steel, Glass, Adjustable Shelves, Belgium, 38 In.
$768

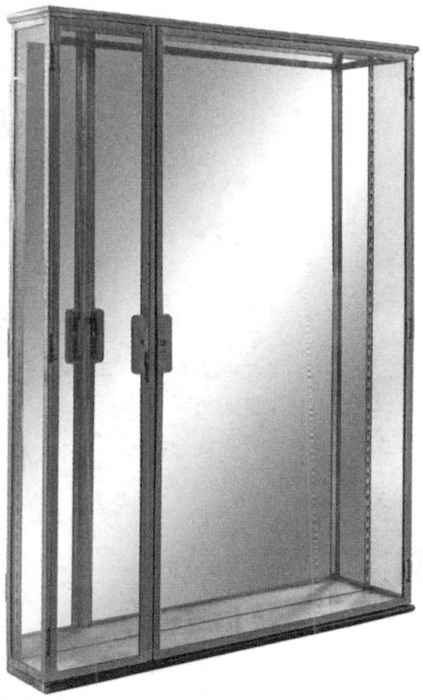

Hindman

Medical, Cupboard, Apothecary, 9 Drawers, Knob Pulls, Painted, Signed, R Zucati, 1998, 38 x 73½ In.
$322

Jeffrey S. Evans & Associates

M

Medical, Figurine, Doctor, Young Woman, Sitting, Blood Pressure, Painted, Signed, Moretto, 9 x 8 In.
$81

Blackwell Auctions

Medical, Model, Human Male, Acupuncture Body, Rubberized, Plastic, Standing, Wood Base, 20 In.
$288

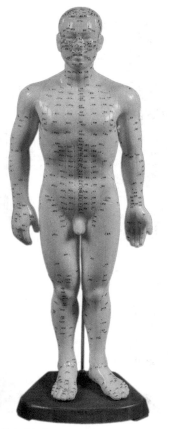

Blackwell Auctions

Medical, Show Globe, Apothecary, Glass, Cast Filigree, Iron Eagle Flange Bracket, 24 x 6 x 17 In.
$246

Morphy Auctions

Cake Plate, Gilt, Leaves, Scalloped Rim, Flower Center, Crossed Swords Mark, 13 In.	177
Cake Stand, Porcelain, Pink, Flowers, Gilt, Scalloped Rim, 4 ½ In.	46
Candelabrum, 5-Light, Sitting, Putti, Flower Heads, Scroll Feet, 1800s, 26 ¾ x 27 ⅛ In., Pair	3024
Centerpiece, Putti, Fish, Eel, Seaweed, Shell, Fishing Net, Marble Base, 1800s, 12 ¾ In. *illus*	7560
Chamber Pot, Gilt Bronze Mount, 5 Chinoiserie Figures, 2 Winged Insects, c.1735, 5 In.	3276
Charger, Round, Man, Woman, Trees, Sitting, Ruffled Rim, Marked, 1900s, 11 ¾ In., Pair	256
Cup & Saucer, White Ground, Multicolor, Flowers, Gold Highlights, Footed *illus*	175
Cup, High Relief Bust & Trim, Ornate, Gilded, Patriotic Eagle, Footed, 1830s, 5 ¼ In.	1094
Figurine, Cherub, Hand Painted, Arrows, Ribbon, Te Prends Mon Essor, Marked, 1850s, 5 ¼ In.	439
Figurine, Cherub, Standing, Un Me Suffit, Flower, Hexagonal Base, 5 ½ x 2 ½ In.	277
Figurine, Creeping Fox, Stalking Pose, Schleichender Fuchs, Marked, 2 ¾ x 9 ¾ In.	236
Figurine, Fisherman, Holding Net, Brown Hat, Standing, Wavy Base, Painted, 6 ¼ x 3 x 5 In.	215
Figurine, Malabar Musician, Crossed Swords, Blue Underglaze, Late 1700s, 7 ⅜ In.	1375
Figurine, Nodding Head, Asian Man, Open Mouth, Tongue & Hands Move, Wood Base, 11 In.	3250
Figurine, Nodding Pagoda, Articulated Tongue, Hands, Crossed Swords Mark, Late 1800s, 7 In.	6300
Figurine, Woman, Yellow Dress, Flowers, Gold Gilt, Round Base, Germany, 1860-1924, 7 ¾ In.	525
Group, 3 Putti, Holding Flute, Lyre, Trumpet, Music Stand, Rocky Plinth Base, c.1900, 8 In. *illus*	1320
Group, Capture Tritons, Seminude Woman, 2 Babies, Blue Crossed Swords, 1800s, 13 x 11 x 7 In.	1140
Plate, Flowers, Ruffled Rim, Blue Crossed Swords Underglaze, Parcel Gilt, 1900s, 10 ⅝ In.	288
Plate, Flowers, Trailing Vine, Shaped Gilt Rim, Crossed Swords Mark, c.1770, 9 In., Pair	207
Plate, Flowers, White Ground, Cobalt Blue Border, Gold Trim, Blue Crossed Swords Mark, 11 In.	225
Plate, Painted, European Hunting Scenes, Insects, Flowers, Gilt, c.1725, 8 ⅝ In. *illus*	6300
Potpourri, Pierced Lid, Applied Putti, Courting Scene, 1850s, 12 x 8 x 4 In., Pair	1521
Saucepan, Blue, White, Lambrequin, Diaper Borders, Handle, Henry H. Arnhold, c.1730, 8 In.	3024
Scent Bottle, Applied Leaves & Flowers, White Ground, Footed, 8 ¼ In. *illus*	366
Stein, Crown Orb, Crossed Swords, Underglaze Blue Cell Border, Silver Mount, c.1900, 5 In.	688
Tea Canister, Lid, Hexagonal, Strapwork Panels, Gilt Ribs, Acanthus Leaves, c.1720, 3 In.	4043
Teapot, Chained Lid, Gilt Metal Mount, Pastoral Scene, Crossed Swords Mark, c.1720, 5 In.	3024
Tray, Flowers, Shell Corners, Cobalt Blue Rim, Gilt, Hand Painted, Rococo, Late 1800s, 15 ¾ In.	330
Tray, Oval, Lovers In Garden, Fish Scale Border, Gilt Handle, C. Teichert, c.1880, 11 x 15 In. *illus*	215
Urn, Figural Handles & Finial, Multicolor, Flowers, 26 In., Pair	688
Urn, Tapering Shape, Cobalt Blue, Scrolled Handles, Gilt, Leaves, 1800s, 25 ¼ x 12 ½ In.	1024
Vase, Augustus Rex Style, Bottle Shape, Romantic Vignette, Flowers, Early 1900s, 12 In., Pair.	188

MERCURY GLASS

Mercury glass, or silvered glass, was first made in the 1850s. It lost favor for a while but became popular again about 1910. It looks like a piece of silver but it is a hollow glass piece with mercury coloring inside. It was copied in the 1990s.

Gazing Ball, Butler's, Attached Pedestal, Round Foot, 9 ½ In.	68
Gazing Ball, Stem, Metal Stand, 3 Satyr Shape Feet, Patina, 15 ½ x 9 In.	118
Scent Bottle, Double Overlay, Emerald To Clear To Silver, Hinged Lid, Late 1800s, 3 ⅞ In.	100
Vase, Bottle Shape, Gadrooned, Applied Clear Handles, 17 x 11 ¾ In.	369
Vase, Cup Shape, Short Stem, Round Foot, 15 ¾ x 11 In.	123

METLOX POTTERIES

Metlox Potteries was founded in 1927 in Manhattan Beach, California. Dinnerware was made beginning in 1931. Evan K. Shaw purchased the company in 1946 and expanded the number of patterns. Poppytrail (1946–1989) and Vernonware (1958–1980) were divisions of Metlox under Shaw's direction. The factory closed in 1989.

Antique Grape, Sugar & Creamer	32
Autumn Berry, Cup & Saucer	8
California Apple, Plate, Salad, 9 In.	20
California Rose, Plate, Dinner, 10 ⅜ In.	14
Pepper Tree, Platter, 15 In.	21

Meissen, Centerpiece, Putti, Fish, Eel, Seaweed, Shell, Fishing Net, Marble Base, 1800s, 12 ¾ In.
$7,560

Sotheby's

Meissen, Cup & Saucer, White Ground, Multicolor, Flowers, Gold Highlights, Footed
$175

Woody Auction

Meissen, Group, 3 Putti, Holding Flute, Lyre, Trumpet, Music Stand, Rocky Plinth Base, c.1900, 8 In.
$1,320

Michaan's Auctions

Meissen, Plate, Painted, European Hunting Scenes, Insects, Flowers, Gilt, c.1725, 8 ⅝ In.
$6,300

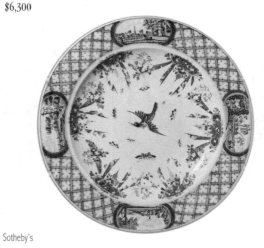

Sotheby's

Meissen, Scent Bottle, Applied Leaves & Flowers, White Ground, Footed, 8 ¼ In.
$366

Neal Auction Company

Meissen, Tray, Oval, Lovers In Garden, Fish Scale Border, Gilt Handle, C. Teichert, c.1880, 11 x 15 In.
$215

Locati Auctions

M

345

METTLACH

Mettlach, Coaster, No. 1032, Dwarf, Plays Bagpipes To Radish, Print Under Glaze, 5 In.
$72

Fox Auctions

Mettlach, Compote, No. 2895, Flowers, Art Nouveau, Etched
$720

Fox Auctions

TIP

Milk glass can now be repaired by black light–proof methods. Be very careful when buying antiques.

Mettlach, Plaque, No. 1044/411, Bavarian Girl, Beer Stein, Print Under Glaze, 17½ In.
$144

Fox Auctions

Mettlach, Plate, No. 2148, Snow White, Dwarfs, Etched, 16 In.
$192

Fox Auctions

Mettlach, Stein, No. 2958, Boy Bowling, Multicolor, Metal Lid, Bowling Pin Style Thumb Rest, c.1910, 15 In.
$263

Jeffrey S. Evans & Associates

Milk Glass, Candle Lamp, Figural, Bee Skep, Basket Weave, Brass Vent Cap, Hanger, 8½ x 3½ In.
$230

Forsythes' Auctions

Milk Glass, Dish, Lid, Figural, Fainting Couch, Green Quilted Top, Red Base, 1800s, 2 x 5 In.
$187

Jeffrey S. Evans & Associates

Milk Glass, Photograph, Opalotype, Glass Pane, Young Woman, Hand Colored, Frame, 3½ x 2¾ In.
$42

Charleston Estate Auctions

Milk Glass, Vase, Portrait, Young Girl, Green, Frosted, Gilt, Geometric Designs, Britain, 1900s, 17 In.
$288

Lion and Unicorn

M

346

METTLACH

Mettlach, Germany, is a city where the Villeroy and Boch factories worked. Steins from the firm are marked with the word *Mettlach* or the castle mark. They date from about 1842. *PUG* means painted under glaze. The steins can be dated from the marks on the bottom, which include a date-number code that can be found online. Other pieces may be listed in the Villeroy & Boch category.

Coaster, No. 1032, Dwarf, Plays Bagpipes To Radish, Print Under Glaze, 5 In. .... *illus*	72
Compote, No. 2895, Flowers, Art Nouveau, Etched ....*illus*	720
Jar, Lid, Blue & White, Flowers, Lion's Head, 7 x 7 In..	31
Plaque, No 1044/411, Bavarian Girl, Beer Stein, Print Under Glaze, 17 ½ In. .... *illus*	144
Plate, No. 2148, Snow White, Dwarfs, Etched, 16 In. .... *illus*	192
Stein, No. 1758, Gray Ground, Policeman Portrait, Black Lid, 9 In....................................	107
Stein, No. 2075, Telegrapher, Eagle, Steam Locomotive, Inlay, Engraved, 7 ¾ In.	575
Stein, No. 2401, Operatic Tannhauser, Venusberg Scene, Etched, Thumblift Lid, 10 ¼ In.	363
Stein, No. 2581, Women, Singing, Playing Harp, Lid, ½ Liter, 8 In.	138
Stein, No. 2958, Boy Bowling, Multicolor, Metal Lid, Bowling Pin Style Thumb Rest, c.1910, 15 In. *illus*	263
Stein, Pewter Steeple Lid, Dragon Handle, Etched, St. Florian, Verse To One Side, 1899, 8 In.	213

MILK GLASS

Milk glass was named for its milky white color. It was first made in England during the 1700s. The height of its popularity in the United States was from 1870 to 1880. It is now correct to refer to some colored glass as blue milk glass, black milk glass, etc. Reproductions of milk glass are being made and sold in many stores. Related pieces may be listed in the Cosmos, Vallerysthal, and Westmoreland categories.

Bell, Ruffled Rim, Raised Scrolls, 6 ½ In.	23
Candle Lamp, Figural, Bee Skep, Basket Weave, Brass Vent Cap, Hanger, 8 ½ x 3 ½ In. *illus*	230
Cruet, Hobnail, Stopper, Pontil..	16
Dish, Lid, Figural, Fainting Couch, Green Quilted Top, Red Base, 1800s, 2 x 5 In. .... *illus*	187
Dish, Lid, Figural, Rooster, Blue, White Head, Comb, Ribbed Base, 20th Century, 5 x 6 In.	25
Egg, Blown, Hand Painted, Pink Flowers, Green Leaves, Easter, Victorian, 7 x 4 In.	65
Jar, Metal Lid, Red, Spiced Fish, Green Body, Wire Handle, 6 ½ In..	160
Photograph, Opalotype, Glass Pane, Young Woman, Hand Colored, Frame, 3 ½ x 2 ¾ In. *illus*	42
Rolling Pin, Wood Handles, 19 ¼ x 2 ½ In.	42
Salt Dip, Chickens, Opalescent Edge, c.1915...	42
Vase, Bottle Shape, Opaline Foot, Marked, Sevres, France, 9 ½ x 3 ¼ In.	63
Vase, Ivy, Flared, Footed, Kemple, 1950s, 9 ½ In..	20
Vase, Portrait, Young Girl, Green, Frosted, Gilt, Geometric Designs, Britain, 1900s, 17 In. *illus*	288

MILLEFIORI

Millefiori means, literally, a thousand flowers. Many small pieces of glass resembling flowers are grouped together to form a design. It is a type of glasswork popular in paperweights and some are listed in that category.

Decanter, Ball Shape Stopper, Flared Base, Multicolor, 10 In.	210
Lamp, Electric, Multicolor, Egg Shape Shade, Heat Hole, Pedestal Base, 16 x 6 ½ In. .... *illus*	480
Lamp, Multicolor, Mushroom Shape Shade, Baluster Shape Base, 10 ½ x 6 In.	600
Salt, Open, Flared Rim, Red & Blue Canes, 2 ¼ In., Pair	219
Wine, Multicolor Cane Bowl, Figural Stem, Dolphins, Signed, Dan Schreiber, 1994, 10 ½ In.	80

MINTON

Minton china was made in the Staffordshire region of England beginning in 1796. The firm became part of the Royal Doulton Tableware Group in 1968, but the wares continued to be marked *Minton*. In 2009 the brand was bought by KPS Capital Partners of New York and became part of WWRD Holdings. The company no longer makes

Millefiori, Lamp, Electric, Multicolor, Egg Shape Shade, Heat Hole, Pedestal Base, 16 x 6 ½ In.
$480

Woody Auction

Minton, Figurine, Arthur, Once & The Future King, Multicolor, Gilt, John Ablitt, 1993, 15 x 8 In.
$1,610

Lion and Unicorn

Minton, Plate, Dessert, Fruit, Raised Border, Gold Trim, Marked, 9 ¼ In., 15 Piece
$2,944

Stair Galleries

Minton, Vase, Pate-Sur-Pate, Peacock, Blue Ground, White Slip, Cupid, Signed, L. Solon, c.1895, 8 In. $4,410

Sotheby's

Mocha, Bowl, Earthworm Design, Blue, White, Turned Band, Pearlware, England, 3 x 5½ In. $270

Nadeau's Auction Gallery

Mocha, Bowl, Marbleized, Green Incised Bands, Footed, Cream Color, Early 1800s, 2½ x 4¾ In. $431

Locati Auctions

Minton china. Many marks have been used. The word *England* was added in 1891. Minton majolica is listed in this book in the Majolica category.

Minton
c.1822–1836

Minton
c.1863–1872

Minton
1951–c.2009

Bowl, Hadden Hall, Pastel, Flowers, Lattice Pattern Exterior, Gilt Rim, 3 x 9¾ In.	89
Figurine, Arthur, Once & The Future King, Multicolor, Gilt, John Ablitt, 1993, 15 x 8 In. *illus*	1610
Figurine, Colin Minton Campbell, Standing, Majolica Stand, Parian, 1886, 19 In.	148
Figurine, Miranda, Seated, Rocky Base, Inscribed, John Bell, Parian, 1850s, 5 In.	225
Figurine, Woman, Carrying Grapes, Child, Parian, Circular Base, England, 1800s, 23¼ In.	575
Plate, Aesthetic, Blue, Reticulated Border, Bird & Fan Center, 9 In.	396
Plate, Dessert, Fruit, Raised Border, Gold Trim, Marked, 9¼ In., 15 Piece .... *illus*	2944
Plate, Dinner, Landscapes, Yellow Flower Border, Gold Trim, 9 In., 6 Piece	448
Plate, Ornate, Gilt, Flower Vine Pattern, Puce Printed, White Ground, 10 In., 12 Piece	375
Vase, Moon Flask, White Decor, Gilt Handles & Highlight, 11 In.	153
Vase, Pate-Sur-Pate, Peacock, Blue Ground, White Slip, Cupid, Signed, L. Solon, c.1895, 8 In. *illus*	4410

MIRRORS *are listed in the Furniture category under Mirror.*

MOCHA

Mocha pottery is an English-made product that was sold in America during the early 1800s. It is a heavy pottery with pale coffee-and-cream coloring. Designs of blue, brown, green, orange, black, or white were added to the pottery and given fanciful names, such as Tree, Snail Trail, or Moss. Mocha designs are sometimes found on pearlware. A few pieces of mocha ware were made in France, the United States, and other countries.

Bowl, Earthworm Design, Blue, White, Turned Band, Pearlware, England, 3 x 5½ In. *illus*	270
Bowl, Earthworm, Blue, Black Bands, Brown Ground, 3⅛ x 6¼ In.	1159
Bowl, Lid, Underplate, Marbleized Brown, Tan & Blue, 2 Fan Handles, Acorn Finial, 1800s, 7 In.	9150
Bowl, Marbleized, Green Incised Bands, Footed, Cream Color, Early 1800s, 2½ x 4¾ In. *illus*	431
Coffeepot, Dome Lid, Blue Speckled Ground, Dipped Fan Design, Don Carpentier, c.1996, 11 In. *illus*	702
Coffeepot, Dome Lid, Bulbous, Tree, Applied Strap Handle, Flared Base, Early 1800s, 11 In.	281
Jug, Pearlware, Dentil Design, Bulbous, Navy Edge, Lines, Handle, 5¾ In.	1220
Loving Cup, Marbleized, 3 Green Roulette Bands, 2 Handles, 4¾ In.	427
Mug, Bands On Looped Cable, Tricolor Cable, Orange, Footed, 6 In.	635
Mug, Seaweed, Squat, Green Band, Applied Handle, 2¾ In.	580
Pepper Pot, Dome Lid, Geometric Bands, Bulbous, Footed, 3½ In. .... *illus*	854
Pitcher, Earthworm, Double Bands, Curved Handle, Wide Spout, 1800s, 6½ In. .... *illus*	976
Pitcher, Trees, Machine Turned Band, Central Gray Slip, Creamware, Early 1800s, 6¾ In. ..	600
Pitcher, Water, Cat's-Eye, 4 Wavy Lines, Pearlware, 8½ In.	420
Salt, Earthworm, Ocher, Brown Bands, Cream Interior, Footed, Early 1800s, 2⅛ x 3 In.	316
Salt, Earthworm, Orange Bands, Footed, Pearlware, 1910s, 2 In.	556
Sugar, Lid, Seaweed, Ball Finial, Brown, Tan Ground, Footed, 5¼ In. .... *illus*	519

MONMOUTH

Monmouth Pottery Company started working in Monmouth, Illinois, in 1892. The pottery made a variety of utilitarian wares. It became part of Western Stoneware Company in 1906. The maple leaf mark was used until about 1930.

Birdbath, Brown, Green, Relief Leaves, Flowers On Rim, Western Stoneware Co., 25 x 17 In. ..*illus*	173
Vase, Blue, Yellow Leaves Around Shoulder, Arts & Crafts, 14 In.	95

MONT JOYE, *see Mt. Joye category.*

Mocha, Coffeepot, Dome Lid, Blue Speckled Ground, Dipped Fan Design, Don Carpentier, c.1996, 11 In.
$702

Jeffrey S. Evans & Associates

Mocha, Pepper Pot, Dome Lid, Geometric Bands, Bulbous, Footed, 3 ½ In.
$854

Pook & Pook

Mocha, Pitcher, Earthworm, Double Bands, Curved Handle, Wide Spout, 1800s, 6 ½ In.
$976

Pook & Pook

Mocha, Sugar, Lid, Seaweed, Ball Finial, Brown, Tan Ground, Footed, 5 ¼ In.
$519

Pook & Pook

Monmouth, Birdbath, Brown, Green, Relief Leaves, Flowers On Rim, Western Stoneware Co., 25 x 17 In.
$173

Richard Opfer Auctioneering, Inc.

Moorcroft, Ewer, Giraffes, Cream Ground, Handle, Multicolor, 12 In.
$502

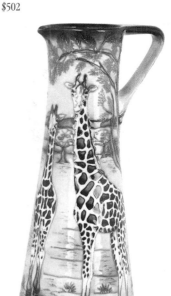

Cottone Auctions

Moorcroft, Lamp Base, Electric, Flower, Glaze, Painted, Early 1900s, 26 In., Pair
$403

Blackwell Auctions

M

349

Moorcroft, Vase, Melon, Green Glaze, Mushrooms, Art Nouveau, c.1910, 7 x 6¾ In. $3,450

Lion and Unicorn

Moorcroft, Vase, Tubeline Trees, Blue Ground, Moonlit Blue, Pewter Base, Tudric, c.1925, 9 In. $2,875

Lion and Unicorn

Moriage, Pitcher, Cylindrical, Flowers, Nippon, 11¾ In. $88

Eldred's

MOORCROFT

Moorcroft pottery was first made in Burslem, England, in 1913. William Moorcroft had managed the art pottery department for James Macintyre & Company of England from 1898 to 1913. The Moorcroft pottery continues today, although William Moorcroft died in 1945. The earlier wares are similar to the modern ones, but color and marking will help indicate the age.

W. Moorcroft Ltd. 1898–c.1905	W. Moorcroft Ltd. 1898–1913	W. Moorcroft Ltd. 1928–1978

Ewer, Giraffes, Cream Ground, Handle, Multicolor, 12 In. .... *illus*	502
Lamp, Electric, Baluster Shape, Raised, Painted, Fruit, 1900s, 22 In.	207
Lamp, Electric, Poppies, Flambe Glaze, 34 x 7½ In.	345
Lamp Base, Electric, Flower, Glaze, Painted, Early 1900s, 26 In., Pair .... *illus*	403
Urn, Lid, Pomegranate, Dark Blue Ground, Oval, 10½ In.	702
Vase, Anemone, Cobalt Blue, Red Flowers, Shouldered, Flared Rim, Marked, 1950s, 6 x 5¾ In....	318
Vase, Flowers, Leaves, Painted, Multicolor, Bulbous, Flared Rim, Footed, 15 In.	531
Vase, Leaves & Berries, Shaded Yellow, Red, Orange, Burgundy, Tapered Neck, 10 In..............	1001
Vase, Melon, Green Glaze, Mushrooms, Art Nouveau, c.1910, 7 x 6¾ In. .... *illus*	3450
Vase, Toadstools, Green Blue Ground, Multicolor, Mounted As Lamp, 1910s, 23¼ In.	3276
Vase, Tubeline Trees, Blue Ground, Moonlit Blue, Pewter Base, Tudric, c.1925, 9 In. .... *illus*	2875

MORIAGE

Moriage is a special type of raised decoration used on some Japanese pottery. Sometimes pieces of clay were shaped by hand and applied to the item; sometimes the clay was squeezed from a tube the way we apply cake frosting. One type of moriage is called Dragonware by collectors.

Bowl, Crescent Shape, Flower Design, 4-Footed Base, Nippon, 5 In..	25
Bowl, Trees, Flowers, Sea, Ship, Footed, Embossed, Painted, Nippon, 7 x 4½ In.	86
Candlestick, Flower Cartouche, Beaded Ground, Embossed, Painted, Nippon, 9 In..............	50
Jar, Lid, Melon Shape, Flowers, Cherry Blossom, Mark, Nippon, 5 In...............................	25
Jug, Claret, Wheat Design, Stopper, Handle, Painted, Nippon, Mark, 9 In.	313
Lamp, Oil, Flowers, Green Ground, Silver Overlay, Nippon, 11 In..	96
Pitcher, Cylindrical, Flowers, Nippon, 11¾ In. .... *illus*	88
Tray, Dresser, Rectangular, Flower Cartouche, Painted, Nippon, Mark, 9¾ In.	50
Vase, Flowers, Ring Handles, Painted, Nippon, 6¼ x 7½ In.	561

MOSAIC TILE COMPANY

Mosaic Tile Company of Zanesville, Ohio, was started by Karl Langerbeck and Herman Mueller in 1894. Many types of plain and ornamental tiles were made until 1959. The company closed in 1967. The company also made some ashtrays, bookends, and related giftwares. Most pieces are marked with the entwined MTC monogram.

Box, Lid, Figural, Turtle, Green, Brown Trim, 4 In..	72
Cat, Fishbowl, Wood Frame, 10 x 10 In.	250
Figurine, Dog, German Shepherd, Drip Glaze, Logo On Collar, 9 x 8 x 4 In., Pair.................	250
Figurine, Dog, Lying Down, Head Raised, White, 6 x 3 x 10¼ In. .... *illus*	132
Figurine, Grizzly Bear, Standing, Mouth Open, Black Glaze, Signed, c.1920, 6 x 9½ x 5 In...	407
Tile, Art Deco, Swirls, Dots, Lavender, Mint, 1920s, 5 x 5 In..	145
Tile, Elephant, Standing On Ball, Red Logo, Yellow Ground, Green Border, Impressed, 6 In. *illus*	2646
Tile, Leaping Deer, Cupids Arrow, 6 x 6 In.	75

M

Mosaic Tile Co., Figurine, Dog, Lying Down, Head Raised, White, 6 x 3 x 10 ¼ In.
$132

Martin Auction Co.

Mosaic Tile Co., Tile, Elephant, Standing On Ball, Red Logo, Yellow Ground, Green Border, Impressed, 6 In.
$2,646

Humler & Nolan

Moser, Dresser Box, Hinged Lid, Cranberry, Enamel Design, Ormolu, Footed Base, 6 ½ In.
$492

Rich Penn Auctions

Moser, Pitcher, Blue Panels, Cabochon, Ray Cut Base, Notched Handle, Gold Stencil, Early 1900s, 12 In.
$275

Woody Auction

Moser, Vase, Amberina, Enamel Leaf, Applied Acorn, Footed, 5 ½ x 3 In.
$550

Woody Auction

Moser, Vase, Blue, Blown Glass, Seashore & Castle, 3-Footed, 6 ¼ In.
$192

Fox Auctions

M

351

Mother-Of-Pearl, Pitcher, Butterscotch, White Satin, Ruffled Rim, Ribbed Handle, 8 ½ In.
$150

Woody Auction

Mother-Of-Pearl, Pitcher, Cranberry, Quilted, Satin, Handle, 8 ½ In.
$69

Richard D. Hatch & Associates

Mother-Of-Pearl, Vase, Raindrop, Honeycomb, 4 Dimpled Edges, Pastel Pink, Blue, 12 ¾ In.
$125

Woody Auction

MOSER

Moser glass is made by a Bohemian glasshouse founded by Ludwig Moser in 1857. Art Nouveau–type glassware and iridescent glassware were made. The most famous Moser glass is decorated with heavy enameling in gold and bright colors. The firm, Moser Glassworks, is still working in Karlovy Vary, Czech Republic. Few pieces of Moser glass are marked.

Cologne Bottle, Green Shading To Clear, Engraved, Flowers, Stopper, 5 ½ x 4 ¾ In.	150
Dresser Box, Hinged Lid, Cranberry, Enamel Design, Ormolu, Footed Base, 6 ½ In. .... *illus*	492
Ewer, Silver Plate Lid, Glass Base, Art Nouveau, Flowers, Cabochons, Early 1900s, 11 In.	177
Goblet, Pale Blue, Stylized Butterfly, Bee, Flowers, Multicolor, c.1885, 5 ¾ In.	164
Perfume Bottle, Cobalt Blue, Atomizer, Gold Gilt, Circular Base, 9 ½ In.	85
Pitcher, Blue Panels, Cabochon, Ray Cut Base, Notched Handle, Gold Stencil, Early 1900s, 12 In. *illus*	275
Pitcher, Cranberry, Enamel Flowers, Straight, Gold Rim & Handle, 6 ¾ In.	181
Vase, Amberina, Enamel Leaf, Applied Acorn, Footed, 5 ½ x 3 In. *illus*	550
Vase, Black, Flowers, Ruffled Rim, Amethyst Base, 15 ¾ x 5 ¾ x 5 ¾ In.	461
Vase, Blue, Blown Glass, Seashore & Castle, 3-Footed, 6 ¼ In. *illus*	192
Vase, Clear, Flowers, Acid Etched, Gilt, Cylindrical, Polished Pontil Mark, Late 1800s, 15 ¾ In.	105
Vase, Green, Glass, Young Maiden, Gilt, Round Base, Painted, 14 ¾ In.	148
Wine, Cranberry, Faceted Stem, Red, Gold Enameled, Clear Base, L.C. Tiffany, 8 ¼ In.	40

MOTHER-OF-PEARL GLASS

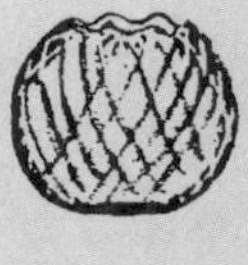

Mother-of-pearl glass, or pearl satin glass, was first made in the 1850s in England and in Massachusetts. It was a special type of mold-blown satin glass with air bubbles in the glass, giving it a pearlized color. It has been reproduced. Mother-of-pearl shell objects are listed under Pearl.

Cup, Tea, Diamond Quilted, Red To Pink Satin, Applied Frosted Handle, Victorian, 2 ½ In.	23
Ginger Jar, Herringbone, Cranberry Satin, Lid, Opalescent Insert, Late 19th Century, 5 ⅛ In.	177
Pitcher, Butterscotch, White Satin, Ruffled Rim, Ribbed Handle, 8 ½ In. *illus*	150
Pitcher, Cranberry, Quilted, Satin, Handle, 8 ½ In. *illus*	69
Pitcher, Water, Coin Spot, Butterscotch To White, Ruffled Rim, Applied Frosted Handle, 8 ½ In.	180
Vase, Diamond Quilted, Lavender Satin, Flared Ruffled Rim, Long Neck, c.1960, 13 In.	36
Vase, Dimpled Gourd Shape, Seaweed, Air Trap, Citron Green, Late 1800s, 8 In.	234
Vase, Herringbone, Rainbow Satin, Pastel Colors, Bottle Shape, 8 ¼ In.	108
Vase, Quilted, Blue Satin, Gooseneck Shape, Mike & Mary Ann Callahan, 9 In.	40
Vase, Raindrop, Blue Satin, Bulbous, Pulled Lip, 7 ¾ x 6 ¾ In.	84
Vase, Raindrop, Honeycomb, 4 Dimpled Edges, Pastel Pink, Blue, 12 ¾ In. *illus*	125

MOTORCYCLE

Motorcycles and motorcycle accessories of all types are being collected today. Examples can be found that date back to the early twentieth century. Toy motorcycles are listed in the Toy category.

Harley-Davidson, Dealer Photo, Store Front View, Hartford, Frame, c.1920, 7 x 15 ½ In. *illus*	351
Helmet, Yoder Pacer 79x, Orange Metallic, Rubber Lip, Black Padding, 1966, 9 x 10 x 8 In. ..	74
Jacket, Excelled, Leather, Black, Zippered Pockets & Sleeves, Size 40	57

MOUNT WASHINGTON, *see Mt. Washington category.*

MOVIE

Movie memorabilia of all types are collected. Animation Art, Games, Sheet Music, Toys, and some celebrity items are listed in their own section. A lobby card is usually 11 by 14 inches, but other sizes were also made. A set of lobby cards includes seven scene cards and one title card. An American one sheet, the standard movie poster, is 27 by 41 inches. A three sheet is 40 by 81 inches. A half sheet is 22 by 28 inches. A window card, made of cardboard, is 14 by 22 inches.

Motorcycle, Harley-Davidson, Dealer Photo, Store Front View, Hartford, Frame, c.1920, 7 x 15 ½ In.
$351

Jeffrey S. Evans & Associates

Movie, Lobby Card, Pawnee, George Montgomery, Photographic, Artwork, 1957, 22 x 28 In.
$201

Stevens Auction Co.

Movie, Poster, Cleopatra, Elizabeth Taylor, Richard Burton, Paper Lithograph, c.1950, 40 x 81 In.
$204

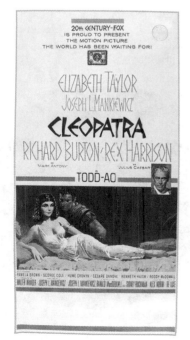

Selkirk Auctioneers & Appraisers

Movie, Poster, Le Mans, Steve McQueen, Glossy, Fotobusta, Rotograph Roma, Frame, 1971, 36 x 48 In.
$192

Brunk Auctions

Movie, Poster, The Revolt Of Mamie Stover, Jane Russell, Richard Egan, Printed, 1956, 27 x 41 In.
$92

Stevens Auction Co.

Movie, Poster, Woman Of The River, Sophia Loren, Man, Kissing, 1957, 22 x 28 In.
$69

Stevens Auction Co.

Mt. Joye, Vase, Amethyst, Acid Cameo Cut, Flowers, Pinched Spiral Shape, Gold Highlights, 8 x 5 In.
$250

Woody Auction

Mt. Washington, Biscuit Jar, Cream Exterior, Multicolor Gold Bamboo, Silver Plate Lid, Bail, 7 x 5 In.
$350

Woody Auction

Mt. Washington, Biscuit Jar, Lid, Hand Painted, Flying Duck, Metal Collar, Swing Handle, 1800s, 6½ In.
$1,664

Brunk Auctions

Mt. Washington, Bride's Bowl, Cameo, Square, Ruffled Rim, Griffins, Flowers, Opaque Pink, c.1885, 4 x 8 In.
$761

Jeffrey S. Evans & Associates

Mt. Washington, Pickle Castor, Ribbed Body, Brown Texture Column, Flowers, 6½ x 4¼ In.
$100

Woody Auction

Mt. Washington, Vase, Lava, Squat, Waisted Neck, Applied Reeded Scroll Handles, 1878, 3 x 2 In.
$1,755

Jeffrey S. Evans & Associates

M

An insert is 14 by 36 inches. A herald is a promotional item handed out to patrons. Press books, sent to exhibitors to promote a movie, contain ads and lists of what is available for advertising, i.e., posters, lobby cards. Press kits, sent to the media, contain photos and details about the movie, i.e., stars' biographies and interviews.

Insert, Here Come The Co-Eds, Bud Abbott, Lou Costello, Artwork Style, 1945, 14 x 36 In.	58
Lobby Card, Hercules, Woman, Steve Reeves, Card Stock Paper, Photographs, 1959, 22 x 28 In.	115
Lobby Card, Joe Palooka In Winner Take All, Joe Kirkwood Jr., Elyse Knox, 1948, 22 x 28 In.	46
Lobby Card, Pawnee, George Montgomery, Photographic, Artwork, 1957, 22 x 28 In. .. *illus*	201
Lobby Card, Princess Of The Nile, Debra Paget, Jeffery Hunter, Michael Rennie, 1954, 22 x 28 In.	35
Lobby Card, Ride Beyond Vengeance, Chuck Connors, Michael Rennie, Horse, 1965, 22 x 28 In.	58
Poster, Caddyshack, Chevy Chase, Rodney Dangerfield & Others, Autographs, 1980, 16 x 11 In.	70
Poster, Cleopatra, Elizabeth Taylor, Richard Burton, Paper Lithograph, c.1950, 40 x 81 In. .. *illus*	204
Poster, Goldfinger, James Bond, Kissing Shirley Eaton, Frame, 38 ½ x 24 ½ In.	118
Poster, Goliath & The Sins Of Babylon, Mark Forest, Printed, Thin Paper, 1963, 27 x 41 In.	46
Poster, Good Times, Sonny & Cher, George Sanders, Norman Alden, Paper Stock, 1974, 27 x 41 In.	56
Poster, Harte Manner Aus Wildwest, James Ellison, Russell Hayden, c.1958, 33 x 23 ½ In.	94
Poster, Hey There It's Yogi Bear, Dancing, Helicopter, Silk Screen, 1964, 60 x 40 In.	288
Poster, Le Mans, Steve McQueen, Glossy, Fotobusta, Rotograph Roma, Frame, 1971, 36 x 48 In. .. *illus*	192
Poster, LG Trapped In Tangiers, Edmund Purdom, Genevieve Page, Gino Cervi, 1960, 66 x 51 In.	125
Poster, Little Wise Quacker, Dogs, Pony, Printed, Thin Paper Stock, 1952, 27 x 41 In.	81
Poster, Love & Bullets, Charles Bronson, Jill Ireland, Rod Steiger, 1979, 41 x 27 In.	25
Poster, Papillon, S. McQueen, D. Hoffman, Greatest Adventure Of Escape, 1976, 41 x 27 In.	83
Poster, The Charge Of The Light Brigade, Wood Frame, 22 x 28 In.	118
Poster, The Revolt Of Mamie Stover, Jane Russell, Richard Egan, Printed, 1956, 27 x 41 In. *illus*	92
Poster, The Three Stooges In Orbit, Carol Christiansen, Edson Stroll, 1962, 60 x 40 In.	173
Poster, Trader Horn, Ethelreda Lewis, W.S. Van Dyk, Man, Kissing, Elephants, 1931, 27 x 41 In.	58
Poster, Wizard Of Oz, Judy Garland, Ira Roberts Publication, MGM, 1939, c.1950, 24 x 18 In.	88
Poster, Woman Of The River, Sophia Loren, Man, Kissing, 1957, 22 x 28 In. .... *illus*	69
Window Card, The Silencers, Dean Martin, Stella Stevens, Daliah Lavi, Signed, 1966, 14 x 22 In.	104

MT. JOYE

Mt. Joye is an enameled cameo glass made in the late nineteenth and twentieth centuries by Saint-Hilaire Touvier de Varraux and Co. of Pantin, France. This same company made De Vez glass. Pieces were usually decorated with enameling. Most pieces are not marked.

Bowl, Amber, Acid Cut Ground, Branch, Leaf & Blossom, Rectangular, Signed, 3 x 11 x 7 In.	175
Vase, Amethyst, Acid Cameo Cut, Flowers, Pinched Spiral Shape, Gold Highlights, 8 x 5 In. *illus*	250
Vase, Art Nouveau Style, Enamel, Flowers, Gold Design, Purple & Clear Ground, 20 In.	158
Vase, Cylindrical, Clear Crystal, Flowers, 10 ¼ x 4 ½ In.	100

MT. WASHINGTON

Mt. Washington Glass Works started in 1837 in South Boston, Massachusetts. In 1870 the company moved to New Bedford, Massachusetts. Many types of art glass were made there until 1894, when the company merged with Pairpoint Manufacturing Co. Amberina, Burmese, Crown Milano, Cut Glass, Peachblow, and Royal Flemish are each listed in their own category.

Biscuit Jar, Cream Exterior, Multicolor Gold Bamboo, Silver Plate Lid, Bail, 7 x 5 In. .. *illus*	350
Biscuit Jar, Dimpled Sides, Silver Plate Mount & Lid, Gilt, Signed, Napoli, 1894, 5 ¾ In.	140
Biscuit Jar, Lid, Hand Painted, Flying Duck, Metal Collar, Swing Handle, 1800s, 6 ½ In. *illus*	1664
Biscuit Jar, Pansies, White, Silver Plate Top, Swing Handle, 6 ½ In.	92
Bride's Bowl, Cameo, Square, Ruffled Rim, Griffins, Flowers, Opaque Pink, c.1885, 4 x 8 In. *illus*	761
Pickle Castor, Ribbed Body, Brown Texture Column, Flowers, 6 ½ x 4 ¼ In. .... *illus*	100
Salt & Pepper, Fig Shape, Brown & White Ground, Yellow & Pink Flowers, 2 ½ In.	84
Salt & Pepper, Flowers, Yellow Ground, Squat Fig Shape, 2 ¾ In.	96
Sugar Shaker, Cut Glass, Strawberry Diamond, Star, Fan, Silver Cap, Egg Shape, 4 In.	780

Muller Freres, Lamp, Frosted, Orange & Green Glass Shade, Art Nouveau, Wrought Iron, Early 1900s, 2 In.
$512

Brunk Auctions

M

Muller Freres, Vase, Roses, Ruby Thorny Vines, Scattered Leaves, Blue Cameo, Signed, 1910s, 9 x 8 In.
$1,638

Jeffrey S. Evans & Associates

Music, Banjo, 5-String, Slim Maple Finish Neck, Aria, Hardshell Case, Marked, Japan, 14 x 11 In.
$173

Blackwell Auctions

Music, Banjo, Grover Patent Presto, Ebonized, Stenciled Design, Case, 34 In. $504

Fontaine's Auction Gallery

Music, Box, Cylinder, 8 Tunes, Inlaid Lid, Grain Painted, 4 Bells, 1850s, 11½ x 22 x 13 In. $480

M

Garth's Auctioneers & Appraisers

Music, Box, Cylinder, George Baker & Co., 8 Tunes, Steel Comb, Mahogany Case, 1880s, 37 x 43 x 21 In. $4,388

Jeffrey S. Evans & Associates

Vase, Lava Glass, Black Ground, Pink, Blue, Green, Handles, Flared Neck, 1800s, 6 x 4¾ In., Pair	960
Vase, Lava, Squat, Waisted Neck, Applied Reeded Scroll Handles, 1878, 3 x 2 In. .... *illus*	1755

MULBERRY

Mulberry ware was made in the Staffordshire district of England from about 1850 to 1860. The dishes were decorated with a reddish brown transfer design, now called mulberry. Many of the patterns are similar to those used for flow blue and other Staffordshire transfer wares.

Pitcher & Bowl, Flowers, Transferware, 13 x 13½ In.	65
Pitcher & Bowl, Octagonal, Wide Spout, Shaped Handle, Flowers, Transferware, 13 In........	62
Plate, Flowers, White Ground, Shaped Rim, Transferware, 9¾ In., 6 Piece	51

MULLER FRERES

Muller Freres, French for Muller Brothers, made cameo and other glass from about 1895 to 1933. Their factory was first located in Luneville, then in nearby Croismare, France. Pieces were usually marked with the company name.

Lamp, Frosted, Orange & Green Glass Shade, Art Nouveau, Wrought Iron, Early 1900s, 2 In. *illus*	512
Potpourri Jar, Lid, Decorative Brass, Cameo, Embossed, Bulbous, Luneville, 6¼ In.	90
Vase, Roses, Ruby Thorny Vines, Scattered Leaves, Blue Cameo, Signed, 1910s, 9 x 8 In. *illus*	1638
Vase, Satin, Mottled Hues, Amethyst Purple, Pink & Green, Art Glass, Luneville, 9 In.	148

MUNCIE

Muncie Clay Products Company was established by Charles Benham in Muncie, Indiana, in 1918. The company made pottery for the florist and gift-shop trade. Art pottery was made beginning in 1922. Rombic is pottery made by this company and Ruba Rombic is glass made by the Consolidated Glass Company. Both were designed by Reuben Haley. The company closed by 1939. Pieces are marked with the name *Muncie* or just with a system of numbers and letters, like *1A*.

Lamp Base, Art Deco, 5 Panels, High Relief, Veiled Nude Dancers, Pink, Green, Incised, 10 In....	135

MURANO, *see Glass-Venetian category.*

MUSIC

Music boxes and musical instruments are listed here. Phonograph records, jukeboxes, phonographs, and sheet music are listed in other categories in this book.

Accordion, Black Ground, Gilt, Special Excelsior Model, New York, 18½ In.	148
Amplifier, AC15, Celestion, G12 Blue Speakers, Vox, c.1964	3250
Amplifier, Bassman, Black Face, Model AB165, 50 Watts, Fender, 1967, 8½ x 22 x 10 In.	1053
Banjo, 5-String, Hardshell Case, Ibanez Artist, c.1976	1375
Banjo, 5-String, Slim Maple Finish Neck, Aria, Hardshell Case, Marked, Japan, 14 x 11 In. . *illus*	173
Banjo, Granada, Mastertone, Resonator, Flame Maple Body, Gibson, Hardcase, 1994, 26 In.	4095
Banjo, Grover Patent Presto, Ebonized, Stenciled Design, Case, 34 In. .... *illus*	504
Banjo, Maple, Gambling Theme, Billet Aluminum, Signed, Tony Tanzi, c.1950, 39½ In........	688
Banjo, Tenor, Fretboard, Celluloid Covered Headstock, Resonator, Case, c.1950, 33½ In.	188
Box, Aeola, Symphonian Style, 84 Teeth, Walnut Case, Lithograph, 22½ x 13½ x 29¼ In....	2280
Box, Calliope, Spindle, Crank, Chromolithoprint, Disc, Wood, Germany, 16 x 15 In...............	775
Box, Cigarette Dispenser, Cherubs, Porcelain, Gilt Metal, Swiss Movement, Italy, c.1950, 13 In.	204
Box, Clock In Top, Drum Shape, Swiss Movement, Brass, c.1900, 4 x 3 In................................	240
Box, Cylinder, 12 Tunes, Rosewood, Damper, Swiss, c.1890, 6¾ x 26 In..................................	469
Box, Cylinder, 73 Disc, Mahogany Case, Crank, Stella, No. 64, Storage Cabinet, c.1898, 30 x 31 x 24 In.	4388
Box, Cylinder, 8 Tunes, 3 Bells, Tune Cord, String Inlay, Ebonized Trim, Swiss, 9 x 17¾ In. .	354
Box, Cylinder, 8 Tunes, 3 Bells, Wood Case, Swiss, Late 1800s, 16¾ In..................................	625

Music, Box, Singing Bird, 2 Birds, Brass Cage, Embossed Base, Early 1900s, 20 x 11 In.
$1,353

Rich Penn Auctions

Music, Box, Singing Bird, Cage, Flowers, Standing, Hanging, Marked, Reuge, Swiss, 10 ½ In.
$338

Hartzell's Auction Gallery Inc.

Music, Box, Singing Bird, Green, Red & Black Plumage, Hinged Lid, Karl Griesbaum, 1 x 4 x 2 In.
$767

Leland Little Auctions

Music, Guitar, Acoustic & Electric, Yamaha, FGX700SC Cutaway, Bound Spruce Top, Mahogany
$266

Leland Little Auctions

Music, Guitar, Gibson, Lap Slide, Black Lacquer, Golden Hue, Lucite Knobs, Case, c.1950, 32 ½ In.
$813

Bruneau & Co. Auctioneers

Music, Guitar, Martin, 12-String, Spruce Top, Acoustic, Mahogany, 1965
$1,888

Leland Little Auctions

Music, Harmonica, Wood & Aluminum, Sextet, M. Hohner, Box
$172

Apple Tree Auction Center

Music, Horn, Copper, Silver Plate, Antoine Courtois, France, 1900s, 23 In.
$219

Bruneau & Co. Auctioneers

MUSIC

Music, Loudspeaker, B & W, Mounted, Model DM1400, Labeled, 31 x 10 x 11¾ In., Pair
$200

Selkirk Auctioneers & Appraisers

Music, Mandolin, Mahogany, Fretboard, 8-String, Case, Signed, C.F. Martin, Early 1900s, 23¾ In.
$750

Bruneau & Co. Auctioneers

Music, Organ, Pump, Empire, Rosewood, Carved Knees, Cabriole Legs, Xavier Spang, 32 x 54 x 24 In.
$288

Stevens Auction Co.

Box, Cylinder, 8 Tunes, Inlaid Lid, Grain Painted, 4 Bells, 1850s, 11½ x 22 x 13 In. ...... *illus*	480
Box, Cylinder, George Baker & Co., 8 Tunes, Steel Comb, Mahogany Case, 1880s, 37 x 43 x 21 In. *illus*	4388
Box, Cylinder, Inlaid Rosewood, Single Comb, Hinged Lid, Brass, 1800s, 6 x 21 x 8½ In........	563
Box, Cylinder, Marquetry Flower, Wood Case, Etouffoirs En Acier Aoit A Spiraux, 5 x 19 In. ...	492
Box, Cylinder, Mermod Freres, Rosewood, Gilt, Metal Border, Swiss, Late 1800s, 4½ x 14 In.	441
Box, Cylinder, Organcleide, Hinged Lid, Inlaid Case, 7 x 21½ x 9 In...........................	400
Box, Cylinder, Reuge, Hungarian Rhapsody, Flower Inlay, Saint Croixe, Swiss, 9 x 5 x 3 In.....	403
Box, Cylinder, Tabletop, Carved Mahogany, Hinged Lid, Trestle Base, Late 1800s, 9 x 24 x 16 In. .	2952
Box, Cylinder, Trophy Inlaid Case, Wood, Late 1800s, 5½ x 16½ In..........................	125
Box, Mahogany, Carved, Soprano, Cylinder, Tabletop, Switzerland, 1880, 40 x 16 x 13 In.	5750
Box, Miniature Organ, Mirror, Wood, Marked, Winder, 5½ x 4¼ In.	62
Box, Regina, Double Comb, Crank, 10 Disc, Wood Case, 15½ In.	1150
Box, Singing Bird, 2 Birds, Brass Cage, Embossed Base, Early 1900s, 20 x 11 In. .... *illus*	1353
Box, Singing Bird, Cage, Flower Trim, Winding Key, Circular Base, Karl Griesbaum, 11 x 6 In.....	708
Box, Singing Bird, Cage, Flowers, Standing, Hanging, Marked, Reuge, Swiss, 10½ In. ....*illus*	338
Box, Singing Bird, Cage, Swing Handle, Germany, 11 In.................................	175
Box, Singing Bird, Cardinal On Stand, Brass Wire, Ken-D, Germany, 1910s, 11 In.	144
Box, Singing Bird, Feathers, Perch, Gilt Brass Cage, c.1920, 11¾ x 6½ In.	443
Box, Singing Bird, Flower Garland, Cage, Platform Base, Embossed, France, 1800s, 11 In.	189
Box, Singing Bird, Gilt Bronze, Scrollwork, Hinged Lid, Germany, c.1925, 2 x 4 In.	2125
Box, Singing Bird, Green, Red & Black Plumage, Hinged Lid, Karl Griesbaum, 1 x 4 x 2 In. ..*illus*	767
Box, Singing Bird, Hinged Lid, Silver, Repousse, Bun Feet, Germany, 4¼ x 3 In.....................	649
Box, Singing Bird, Shell & Gold, Black Case, 1800s, 1½ x 3¾ In.	3300
Box, Stella, Double Comb, Mahogany Case, Carved, 13 x 28 In.............................	2040
Chair, Oak, Filigree, Carved, Crest & Back, Saddle Seat, Cabriole Legs, 1800s, 44 x 17 In.......	189
Clarinet, Blue, Ergonomic Finger Rest, 24K Gold Plate, Stainless Steel Spring, Venus, 22 In.	88
Drum, Barrel Shape, Red Painted Body, Metal, Ring Handles, 18½ x 17 In......................	183
Drum, Marching, String, Wood, Abner Stevens, Pittsfield, Massachusetts, 1800s, 16 In.........	438
Drum, Wood, Carved, Painted Base, Africa, 28½ In.	177
Flute, Silver, Case, Wm. S. Haynes Co., Boston, c.1954, 26⅝ In............................	1375
Flute, Sonare SF-7000, B Foot, Gizmo Key, 5 Open Hole, Verne Q. Powell, Case, 13 x 3 x 2 In.	1053
Guitar, Acoustic & Electric, Yamaha, FGX700SC Cutaway, Bound Spruce Top, Mahogany *illus*	266
Guitar, Acoustic, Gibson, 6-String, Epiphone V, Spruce Top, Rosewood Fretboard, 41½ In....	585
Guitar, Acoustic, Goya, Mahogany, Thumb Spots, 13 Strings & Music Book, Japan, 1900s	188
Guitar, Acoustic, Taylor, 6-String, Big Baby, Case, Mexico, 5½ x 42 x 16 In.	384
Guitar, Amplifier, Epiphone, Studio Acoustic, Chorus 15C, 2 Channel, Bass, 12 x 13½ x 8½ In..	31
Guitar, Electric, Epiphone, Riviera, Turquoise, Hardshell Case, 1966	590
Guitar, Electric, Fender, Mustang, Blue, Hardshell Case, c.1970......................	1625
Guitar, Electric, Fender, Stratocaster, Squier, 6-String, Red, White, Hard Case, 38 x 12 In.....	100
Guitar, Gibson, Lap Slide, Black Lacquer, Golden Hue, Lucite Knobs, Case, c.1950, 32½ In. ..*illus*	813
Guitar, Martin, 12-String, Spruce Top, Acoustic, Mahogany, 1965 .... *illus*	1888
Guitar, Wood, 6-String, Western, Cowboy, Signed Goodluck Buck Jones, Silver, 37 In............	138
Harmonica, Wood & Aluminum, Sextet, M. Hohner, Box .... *illus*	172
Horn, Copper, Silver Plate, Antoine Courtois, France, 1900s, 23 In. .... *illus*	219
Loudspeaker, B & W, Mounted, Model DM1400, Labeled, 31 x 10 x 11¾ In., Pair .... *illus*	200
Mandolin, 3-String, Triangular Base, Wood, 27 In..	74
Mandolin, HM390 F-5 Style, Serial No. 10-79, Pickguard, Hang Tag, Hohner, Case, 1979	2000
Mandolin, Mahogany, Fretboard, 8-String, Case, Signed, C.F. Martin, Early 1900s, 23¾ In. *illus*	750
Organ, Pump, Empire, Rosewood, Carved Knees, Cabriole Legs, Xavier Spang, 32 x 54 x 24 In.*illus*	288
Organ, Roller, Chautauqua, Fruitwood, Tabletop, Stencil, Crank, Late 1800s, 12½ x 18 In.......	313
Piano, Baby Grand, Kawai, Model KG-1, 3-Pedal, Black Lacquered, Bench, 60 In.	512
Piano, Baby Grand, W.M. Kimball, Black, Bench, 36½ x 55½ x 53½ In.........................	625
Piano, Baby Grand, Wurlitzer, Ebony, Bench, 53 In.	472
Piano, Grand, Collard & Collard, Rosewood, 1800s, 69 In. .... *illus*	352
Piano, Spinet, Wurlitzer, Oak, Carved Floral, Turned Spindles, Bench, 1980s, 42 x 58 x 25 In.	158
Piano, Upright, Young Chang, Console, Polished, Ebony Wood Case & Bench, 43 x 56 In.......	576
Saxonette, Clariphon, Silver, Buescher, Elkhart, c.1920...................................	688
Saxophone, Alto, Brass, Neck Stamped, Selmer Mark VI, 1958................................	7500
Speaker, Filigree, Walnut Case, Turned, Pedestal Base, Tripod Feet, Early 1900s, 36 x 18 In.	347
Trumpet, Super Deluxe, Brass, Mother-Of-Pearl Buttons, Case, Getzen, Wisc., c.1950, 5½ x 20 In.	207

M

Ukulele, 4-String, Wood Case, Marked, Cuffs Martin & Co., 1833, 21 x 6 ½ In.	882
Violin Case, Brown, Blue Velvet Interior, W.E. Hill & Sons, c.1980	688
Violin Case, Yellow Flowers, Brown Ground, Gentleman Riding Chicken, Cummins, 1800s, 32 In.	1037
Violin, 3-String, Heinrich E. Heberlein Jr., Germany, 24 In.	819
Violin, Cherry, Red Varnish, Bow, Case, Labeled J.T.L., 1970, 23 In.	797
Violin, Lion's Head, Peghead, Painted, Red Tongue, Aubert, Mirecourt Bridge, Case, 23 In. *illus*	384
Violin, Mittenwald, Nickel Mounted Bow, 2-Piece Back, Red Brown, 1823, 3 x 10 x 31 In.	554
Zither, American Alpine, Case, Franz Schwarzer, c.1920	813

MUSTACHE CUP

Mustache cups were popular from 1850 to 1900 when the large, flowing mustache was in style. A ledge of china or silver held the hair out of the liquid in the cup. This kept the mustache tidy and also kept the mustache wax from melting. Old left-handed mustache cups are rare and have been reproduced since the 1960s.

Advertising, J&P Coats, Black Lettering, Colonial Soldiers, White Ground, 3 ⅞ x 3 ⅜ In.	42
Art Nouveau Lines, Flower Petals, Pastels, c.1900, 3 ½ In.	54
Castle Scenes, 6-Sided, Gold Handle, Royal Bayreuth, 1890s, 3 In.	95
Christmas Holly & Berry, Saucer, Germany	100
Flowers, Cream, Green Ground, Pink Border, Gilt Stencil, Ruffled Rim, Saucer, 3 x 6 In.	84
Pink Rose, Yellow Shaded Ground, Red Border, Gilt, Saucer, R.S. Prussia, 2 ¾ x 6 ½ In. *illus*	120
White Flower, Green To White Ground, Gilt, Swirl Mold, Marked, R.S, Prussia, 3 In.	48

MZ AUSTRIA

MZ Austria

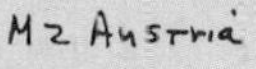

MZ Austria is the wording on a mark used by Moritz Zdekauer on porcelains made at his works in Altrolau, Austria, from 1884 to 1909. The mark was changed to *MZ Altrolau* in 1909, when the firm was purchased by C.M. Hutschenreuther. The firm operated under the name Altrolau Porcelain Factories from 1909 to 1945. It was nationalized after World War II. The pieces were decorated with lavish floral patterns and overglaze gold decoration. Full sets of dishes were made as well as vases, toilet sets, and other wares.

Butter, Cover, Domed, Round, White, Gold Trim, 7 x 4 In.	40
Humidor, Lid, Brown Ground, Pinecones, Gilt Stencil, Monogram, 6 ½ In. *illus*	48
Humidor, Lid, Yellow Roses, White Ground, Pink, Green, Marked, 6 ¾ In.	36
Plate, Blue Jay, Branch, Open Handles, c.1916, 6 In.	145
Plate, Flower Border, Central Bouquet, Multicolor, c. 1920, 8 ½ In.	185
Ramekin, Underplate, Pink Flower Garland, Gilt Trim, Scalloped Rim, 2 x 5 In., 12 Piece.	113
Tray, Flowers, Purple, Leaves, 2 Gold Handles, c.1910, 19 x 6 In.	295

NAILSEA

Nailsea glass was made in the Bristol district in England from 1788 to 1873. The name also applies to glass made by many different factories, not just the Nailsea Glass House. Many pieces were made with loopings of either white or colored glass as decoration.

Fairy Lamp, 4 Arms, Blue, Opal Loops, Pedestal Stand & Lamp Cups, Late 1800s, 16 x 12 In.	527
Fairy Lamp, Venetian Thread, Yellow, 3 Tiers, Shallow Bowl, Crimped Rim, 1880s, 11 x 9 In. *illus*	1989
Flask, White Loops, Applied Rigaree, Oval, Double, 9 x 4 In.	30
Mug, Aqua Blue & White, Ribbed Optic, 5 ½ In.	80
Pipe, Whimsy, Pulled Blue & White, 19 In.	650
Pitcher, Tankard, Blue, Opalescent Loops, Cylindrical, Applied Blue Handle, 11 ¾ In. *illus*	875
Rolling Pin, Cobalt Blue, Flowers, Knopped Ends, c.1860, 13 ¾ In.	132
Scent Bottle, Brass Hinged Lid, Blue & White Loops, Late 1800s, 3 ½ In.	62

NAKARA

Nakara is a trade name for a white glassware made about 1900 by the

Music, Piano, Grand, Collard & Collard, Rosewood, 1800s, 69 In.
$352

Hindman

Music, Violin, Lion's Head, Peghead, Painted, Red Tongue, Aubert, Mirecourt Bridge, Case, 23 In.
$384

Austin Auction Gallery

N

Mustache Cup, Pink Rose, Yellow Shaded Ground, Red Border, Gilt, Saucer, R.S. Prussia, 2 ¾ x 6 ½ In.
$120

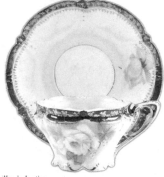
Woody Auction

MZ Austria, Humidor, Lid, Brown Ground, Pinecones, Gilt Stencil, Monogram, 6 ½ In.
$48

Woody Auction

Nailsea, Fairy Lamp, Venetian Thread, Yellow, 3 Tiers, Shallow Bowl, Crimped Rim, 1880s, 11 x 9 In.
$1,989

Jeffrey S. Evans & Associates

N

> **TIP**
> *Do not light a closed cabinet filled with glass with light bulbs over 25 watts. Strong bulbs generate too much heat. Some new types of bulbs are brighter and give off less heat.*

C. F. Monroe Company of Meriden, Connecticut. It was decorated in pastel colors. The glass was very similar to another glass, called Wave Crest, made by the company. The company closed in 1916. Boxes for use on a dressing table are the most commonly found Nakara pieces. The mark is not found on every piece.

Biscuit Jar, Blue, Cream, Plume Type Mold, Pink Flowers, Gilt Metal Bail & Rim, 7 x 6 In. *illus*	450
Dish, Open, Blue Tones, Pink Flowers, Gilt Metal Rim, 2 ¼ x 6 In.	80
Dresser Box, Girls, Garden, Satin, Peach Field, Art Glass, Marked, 6 In.	230
Humidor, Hunting Dog, Outdoor Scene, Green To Cream, Hinged Lid, Metal Collar, Marked, 6 x 4 In.	1020
Jewelry Box, Hinged Lid, Apricot, Yellow Ground, Lavender Iris, 3 ½ x 6 In.	400

NANKING

Nanking is a type of blue-and-white porcelain made in China from the late 1700s to the early 1900s. It was shipped from the port of Nanking. It is similar to Canton wares (listed here in the Canton category). The blue design was almost the same, a landscape, building, trees, and a bridge. But a person was sometimes on the bridge on a Nanking piece. The "spear and post" border was used, sometimes with gold added.

Bowl, Blue & White, Cut Corner, 19th Century, 10 x 10 x 4 In.	265
Cider Jug, Lid, Foo Dog Knop, Geometric Border, Double Strap Handle, 1760s, 9 In. .... *illus*	960
Plate, Boatman Pattern, 6 Flowers Around Rim, Nanking Cargo, 18th Century, 9 ⅛ In. *illus*	625
Serving Dish, Blue & White, Detailed Edge, Oval, c.1860, 7 ½ x 6 ¼ In.	125
Tankard, Strap Handle, Spear & Post Border, 7 ½ In.	180
Teapot, Lid, Round, Gold Trim, c.1760, 5 ½ x 9 In.	640

NAPKIN RINGS

Napkin rings were in fashion from 1869 to about 1900. They were made of silver, porcelain, wood, and other materials. They are still being made today. Collectors pay the highest prices for the silver plated figural examples. Small, realistic figures were made to hold the ring. Good and poor reproductions of the more expensive rings have been made since the 1950s and collectors must be very careful.

Figural, Silver Plate, Boy Pulling Cart, Wheels Turn, 2 ⅝ x 4 In. *illus*	185
Figural, Silver Plate, Cat, Red Glass Eyes, Meriden Britannia Co., Late 1800s, 3 In. *illus*	644
Figural, Silver Plate, Girl Pulling Cart, Wheels Turn, 2 ¾ x 3 ¾ In.	369
Figural, Silver Plate, Girl With Muff, Marked, Meriden B Co., 2 ¾ x 4 In. *illus*	270
Figural, Silver Plate, Goat, Pulling Cart, Meriden Britannia Co., Late 1800s, 4 x 3 In. .. *illus*	263
Figural, Silver Plate, Whistler, Boy, Hands In Pockets, Marked, Barbour Silver Co., 4 x 2 ¾ In.	150
Lacquer, Forest Scene, People, Horses, Marked, Vishnyakov, Russia, 1800s, 2 ¼ In.	90
Pewter, Applied Owl Figure To Side, Marked, 2 In., Pair	63
Silver Plate, Sailor, Anchor, Bud Vase On Ring, Rectangular Base, Leaf Feet, 5 x 4 In.	315

NATZLER

Natzler pottery was made by Gertrud Amon and Otto Natzler. They were born in Vienna, met in 1933, and established a studio in 1935. Gertrud threw thin-walled, simple, classical shapes on the wheel, while Otto developed glazes. A few months after Hitler's regime occupied Austria in 1938, they married and fled to the United States. The Natzlers set up a workshop in Los Angeles. After Gertrud's death in 1971, Otto continued creating pieces decorated with his distinctive glazes. Otto died in 2007.

Bowl, Blue Glaze, Straight-Sided, Brown Rim, Signed, c.1960, 3 ⅝ x 5 In.	617
Bowl, Brown Glaze, Shallow, Signed, Gertrud & Otto Natzler, 1950s, 2 ½ In.	1375
Bowl, Shallow, Red Glaze, Black Shading At Rim, Ink Mark, 1950s, 2 x 10 ¾ In.	950
Bowl, Short Cylindrical Foot, Sang Black Nocturne Glaze, 1961, 3 x 7 In.	1875
Vase, Crater Glaze, White, Brown, Blue Rim, Cylindrical, Signed, c.1960, 5 ½ x 7 ¼ In.	3000

Nailsea, Pitcher, Tankard, Blue, Opalescent Loops, Cylindrical, Applied Blue Handle, 11¾ In.
$875

Nanking, Cider Jug, Lid, Foo Dog Knop, Geometric Border, Double Strap Handle, 1760s, 9 In.
$960

Napkin Ring, Figural, Silver Plate, Cat, Red Glass Eyes, Meriden Britannia Co., Late 1800s, 3 In.
$644

Jeffrey S. Evans & Associates

Napkin Ring, Figural, Silver Plate, Girl With Muff, Marked, Meriden B Co., 2¾ x 4 In.
$270

Alex Cooper Auctioneers

Nanking, Plate, Boatman Pattern, 6 Flowers Around Rim, Nanking Cargo, 18th Century, 9⅛ In.
$625

Jaremos

Nakara, Biscuit Jar, Blue, Cream, Plume Type Mold, Pink Flowers, Gilt Metal Bail & Rim, 7 x 6 In.
$450

Mid-Hudson Auction Galleries

Napkin Ring, Figural, Silver Plate, Boy Pulling Cart, Wheels Turn, 2⅝ x 4 In.
$185

Morphy Auctions

Napkin Ring, Figural, Silver Plate, Goat, Pulling Cart, Meriden Britannia Co., Late 1800s, 4 x 3 In.
$263

Woody Auction

Morphy Auctions

Jeffrey S. Evans & Associates

N

NAUTICAL

Nautical, Bell, Yacht, Brass, Mahogany Stand, Late 1800s, 19 x 9 In.
$469

Eldred's

Nautical, Billethead, White Pine, Carved, Flower, Bellflower, Acanthus Leaves, Gilt, 1800s, 12 x 6¾ In.
$5,000

Eldred's

Nautical, Buoy, Metal, Ocean, Red & Black Paint, No. 2, 79 x 32 In.
$500

Susanin's Auctioneers & Appraisers

Nautical, Cannon, Yacht, Mahogany, Brass, Carriage, Marked, 1800s, 10 x 10½ In.
$4,375

Eldred's

> **TIP**
>
> *Look through the wrong end of a telescope you plan to buy. If it can be focused, all of the parts are there.*

Nautical, Chronometer, Brass, Silver Clock Dial, Mahogany Case, John Bliss & Co., 1800s, 7 x 7 x 7 In.
$1,375

Selkirk Auctioneers & Appraisers

Nautical, Clock, Chelsea, Ship's, Roman Numerals, Nickel Plated, Round, J.E. Caldwell, 15 In.
$266

Bunch Auctions

Nautical, Clock, Silver, Square, Wood Case, 120th Anniversary, Hamilton, 4¾ x 5¼ In.
$313

Pook & Pook

Nautical, Diorama, Sailing Ship, Town, Lighthouse, Canvas, Gesso, Painted, Frame, 1900s, 26 x 36½ In.
$5,100

Garth's Auctioneers & Appraisers

Nautical, Harpoon, Twisted Wedge Shape, Barbs, Marked, C.F. Brown, Warren, R.I., 1850, 33 In.
$1,875

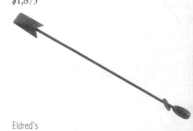

Eldred's

> **TIP**
>
> *Don't store your college graduation diploma in a cedar chest. The aromatic oils will soften ink and cause serious damage.*

N

NAUTICAL

Nautical antiques are listed in this category. Any of the many objects that were made or used by the seafaring trade, including ship parts, models, and tools, are included. Other pieces may be found listed under Scrimshaw.

Beckets, Braided Rope, Red, White, Blue Green, Turk's Head Knots, 1800s, 9 x 5 In., Pair.....	644
Bell, Navy, Brass, Rope, Engraved, U.S.N., 1900s, 11 ½ In........	544
Bell, Yacht, Brass, Mahogany Stand, Late 1800s, 19 x 9 In. .... *illus*	469
Billethead, White Pine, Carved, Flower, Bellflower, Acanthus Leaves, Gilt, 1800s, 12 x 6 ¾ In. . *illus*	5000
Binnacle, Ship's, Gimballed Dry Mount Compass, Brass Column, c.1900, 48 x 24 x 19 In......	117
Binnacle, Submarine, Brass Plaque, Royal Navy, England, c.1950, 19 In	625
Boat Motor, Johnson Seahorse, 1 ½ Horsepower, Waukegan, Ill., 1937, 35 In.........	500
Bollard, Brass, Cylindrical, Round Cap, 4 Bolt Holes, c.1930, 17 ½ x 30 ½ In., Pair...........	4375
Box, Ship's Desk, Scene On Lid, Sperm Oil, Tools, Native American Indian, 7 ½ x 15 In.	450
Buoy, Metal, Ocean, Red & Black Paint, No. 2, 79 x 32 In. .... *illus*	500
Cannon, Signal, Black, Painted, Cast Iron, Wood Carriage, 25 In.	896
Cannon, Yacht, Mahogany, Brass, Carriage, Marked, 1800s, 10 x 10 ½ In. .... *illus*	4375
Canoe, Old Town, Canvas, Painted, Green, Wood Frame, Salesman's Sample, c.1915, 48 In.....	11250
Chest, Sea, Captain's, Pine, Painted, Red, Brass Hinges, Knobs, Bail Handles, 1800s, 11 x 17 In..	225
Chronometer, Brass, Silver Clock Dial, Mahogany Case, John Bliss & Co., 1800s, 7 x 7 x 7 In.. *illus*	1375
Clock, Chelsea, Ship's Bell, Bronze Finished Case, Silvered Dial, 17 x 14 x 5 In......................	1404
Clock, Chelsea, Ship's, Brass Case, Steel, L.A. Karcher & Co., Boston, c.1907, 14 In.	7500
Clock, Chelsea, Ship's, Roman Numerals, Nickel Plated, Round, J.E. Caldwell, 15 In. . . *illus*	266
Clock, Chelsea, Ship's, U.S. Government, Black, Numbers, Box, 6 In..........................	299
Clock, Gilt, Silver, Industrial, Bronze Rope, Anchors, Porcelain Dial, France, 17 x 10 In.	7245
Clock, Seth Thomas, U.S. Navy Course, Cast Iron, Bakelite Lid, Pine Box, 1940s, 8 x 11 In. ...	590
Clock, Ship's Bell, Roman Numerals, Ball Feet, Spaulding & Co., Early 1900s, 6 x 6 In...........	438
Clock, Silver, Square, Wood Case, 120th Anniversary, Hamilton, 4 ¾ x 5 ¼ In. .... *illus*	313
Compass, Brass, Dry Card, Ebonized, Box, Lid, Dovetailed, Robert Merrill, 1900s, 6 x 11 In..	125
Desk, Captain's, Sheraton, Mahogany, Slant, 5 Drawers, Tapered Reeded Legs, 1823, 36 In...	1250
Diorama, 2 Clipper Ships, Rigged, 4-Masted, Cotton, Wool, Wood Case, 1800s, 20 x 30 x 11 In. ..	1170
Diorama, Sailing Ship, Town, Lighthouse, Canvas, Gesso, Painted, Frame, 1900s, 26 x 36 ½ In. *illus*	5100
Diorama, Ship, American Flag, Rope Bordered Frame, Signed, P.E. Heggeland, 1800s, 17 x 24 In..	488
Diorama, Shipbuilder's Shop, Wood Frame, Signed Patrick Richard, 2007, 12 x 30 x 4 In.....	2106
Engine, Ship's, Repeater, Wheelhouse, Clan Mackenzie, c.1954, 46 x 16 ¼ x 10 ½ In.............	615
Figurehead, Man, Bust Portrait, Green Frock Coat, Carved, Early 1700s, 38 x 16 x 18 In.......	1872
Flag, Yacht, American, 14 Stars, Anchor, Hand Sewn, Blue, c.1915, 30 ½ x 48 In.	250
Half-Model, Cabin Cruiser, Carved, Painted, Green & Cream, Mounted, Wood, c.1940, 11 x 36 In .	540
Harpoon, Twisted Wedge Shape, Barbs, Marked, C.F. Brown, Warren, R.I., 1850, 33 In. *illus*	1875
Harpoon, Whaling, Iron, Wood Shaft, Rope Loop, 1800s, 89 In.	488
Helmet, Diving, Copper & Brass, Black Formica Stand, Stepped Brass Base, 50 In. .... *illus*	854
Hull, Painted, Cabins, Hatches, Capstans, Canton Packet Cohota, William Webb, c.1843, 9 x 29 ½ In..	5625
Lamp, Clock & Barometer, 8-Day, 2-Light, Brass, Circular Base, Salem & Co., 21 ½ In............	177
Lamp, Ship's, Globe Shape, Red, Glass, Nickel Frame, Hanging, Perko, 22 ¾ In......................	625
Lantern, Electric, Hanging, Beveled Glass, Brass, Bail Top Handle, 1800s, 16 ¾ In., Pair........	590
Lantern, Marine, Ruby Globe, Bail Handle, Brass, Perko, 1910s, 15 In., Pair	293
Lantern, Ship's, Cabin, Brass, Bail Handle, Bullpit & Sons Ltd., Birmingham, 1941, 16 ½ In.	250
Lantern, Ship's, Gimbal, Oval, Wall Mount, Scroll Arms, Brass, 1800s, 13 x 4 x 12 In., Pair ...	702
Light, Anchor, Copper & Brass, Clear Glass, Bail Handle, Kerosene, Early 1900s, 18 ½ In.......	561
Masthead, Risque, Breasted Beauty, Hands Behind Head, Leafy Mount, Alfco, Ca., 1970, 35 In...	664
Model, Bluenose II, Schooner, 2-Masted, Sidney Culverwell Oland, Case, 1980s, 27 x 35 x 12 In.	351
Model, Builder's, Coastal Freight Schooner, Full Hull, Raised Poop, Planked, 1800s, 64 x 14 x 9 In.	878
Model, Clipper Ship, Wood, Painted, Oak & Glass Case, 1800s, 27 x 39 In.	378
Model, Fishing Boat, White, Green, Red, c.1950, 26 x 11 ¾ In. .... *illus*	563
Model, Frigate, Glass Cloche, Wood, Composition Ground, Early 1900s, 16 x 14 In.............	236
Model, Gaff Cutter, Cotton Sails, White Painted Gunwale, Matched Stand, 48 x 47 In.	201
Model, Garvey Sloop, Canvas Sails, Mounted, Wood Base, Lucite Case, c.1990, 25 x 28 In.	128
Model, HMS Victory 1805, Wood, Sheathed Copper Hull, Stephens & Kenau, 1900s, 29 x 41 In. *illus*	6400
Model, Riva Aquarama, Blue & White Upholstery, Wood Hull, Black Lacquered Stand, 9 x 35 x 10 In.	2124
Model, Sailboat, Glass Hull, Lucite, 18 In.	43
Model, Sailboat, Gloriana II, Swan 82, Sparksman & Stephens, Case, 1979, 43 x 37 x 10 In...	3510
Model, Sailboat, Wood, Lead Weighted Keel, Painted, 34 In.	94

Nautical, Helmet, Diving, Copper & Brass, Black Formica Stand, Stepped Brass Base, 50 In.
$854

Neal Auction Company

Nautical, Model, Fishing Boat, White, Green, Red, c.1950, 26 x 11 ¾ In
$563

N

Eldred's

Nautical, Model, HMS Victory 1805, Wood, Sheathed Copper Hull, Stephens & Kenau, 1900s, 29 x 41 In.
$6,400

Brunk Auctions

Nautical, Model, Spanish Galleon, 2 Eagle Heads, Glass Paneled Case, Wood Base, 34 x 43 In.
$384

Austin Auction Gallery

Nautical, Model, Whaleship, Mahogany Base, Glass Cover Not Shown, Charles Morgan, c.1950, 31 x 14 In.
$8,125

Eldred's

Nautical, Pennant, Cotton, Adelaide II, White Font, Blue Ground, c.1929, 47 In.
$406

Eldred's

> **TIP**
> *It is safe to wash shells, but use distilled or salt-free water.*

Nautical, Pond Boat, Yacht, On Stand, Painted, New England, c.1920, 51¾ x 42 In.
$219

Charlton Hall Auctions

Nautical, Porthole, Mounted, Brass, Glass Center, X-Shape Base, 1900s, 23½ x 23½ In.
$688

Eldred's

Nautical, Sailor's Valentine, Shells, White, Purple, Octagonal Frame, Debra Callaway, 2005, 10 x 2 In.
$531

Bruneau & Co. Auctioneers

Nautical, Ship's Wheel, Wood, 10 Spokes, Turned, Brass Hub, Inlay, 1800s, 65 In.
$1,000

Eldred's

Nautical, Sternboard, Zanzibar, Carved, Elephant Heads, Blue Ground, Gilt, 10 In.
$344

Eldred's

Nautical, Telegraph, Ship's Engine Order, Brass Case, Marked, J.W. Ray & Co. Ltd., 41 x 15 x 11 In.
$1,112

Thomaston Place Auction Galleries

Model, Sailboat, Wood, Rectangular Base, Contemporary, 42 x 39 x 11 In.		63
Model, Scale, Mahogany, Painted, Glazed Cased, L.D. Taylor, Great Britain, 1900s, 32 x 15½ In.		3125
Model, Scandinavian Drakkar, Silver, Wood Base, Marked, Mexico, 6½ x 5½ In.		230
Model, Schooner, Benjamin W. Latham, Hull, Painted, Black & Red, 1900s, 28 x 32 In.		250
Model, Ship, Fabric Sails, Tricolor Flag, Mounted Cannons, Oak Case, 1900s, 33 x 36 In.		590
Model, Spanish Galleon, 2 Eagle Heads, Glass Paneled Case, Wood Base, 34 x 43 In.	*illus*	384
Model, U.S. Navy, Battleship, Marine Warship, Painted, 11½ In.		94
Model, Yacht, Tank, Wood, Interior Hollowed, Lou Banks Jr., New Jersey, c.1961, 10¾ In.		3250
Model, Whaleship, Mahogany Base, Glass Cover Not Shown, Charles Morgan, c.1950, 31 x 14 In.	*illus*	8125
Octant, Browning, Brass, Ebony, 3 Swing Filters, Boston, c.1820, 11½ In.		1708
Paddle, Canoe, Wood, Tintype Image, Center Block Building In Ottawa, 21½ In., 3 Piece		213
Paddle, Painted, Lake Scene, Figure, Rowboats & Steamboat, Shadowbox Frame, 1909, 3 x 23 In.		438
Pelorus, Bendix Aviation Corp., Brass Disc, Sights & Levels, Wood Case, c.1950, 8 x 17 In.		413
Pennant, Cotton, Adelaide II, White Font, Blue Ground, c.1929, 47 In.	*illus*	406
Pond Boat, Sailboat, Green, Cream, Wood Cockpit, Cabin, Stand, Neptune Phila, Early 1900s, 48 In.		94
Pond Boat, Wood Hull, Cotton Sails, Weighted Racing Keel, Display Stand, c.1900, 87 x 80 In.		1404
Pond Boat, Yacht, On Stand, Painted, New England, c.1920, 51¾ x 42 In.	*illus*	219
Porthole, Mounted, Brass, Glass Center, X-Shape Base, 1900s, 23½ x 23½ In.	*illus*	688
Sailor's Valentine, Shells, White, Purple, Octagonal Frame, Debra Callaway, 2005, 10 x 2 In.	*illus*	531
Sailor's Valentine, Think Of Me, Shells, Octagonal, 2-Sided, Hinged, Wood Case, 1800s, 9 x 9 In.		2750
Sea Chest, Pine, Dovetail, Sailor & Lady, Star, Rope Handles, Black, 1900s, 16 x 31½ In.		1375
Sextant, Roth Brothers Chronometer Co, No. 553, Mahogany Case, Lid.		413
Sextant, Stanley, Brass, Nickel, Magnifier, Leather Case, Embossed, 1900s, 3 x 5 x 4¾ In.		144
Ship Model , see Nautical, Model.		
Ship's Wheel, 8 Spokes, Wood, Brass Hub & Inlay, 1800s, 30 In.		225
Ship's Wheel, Wood, 10 Spokes, Turned, Brass Hub, Inlay, 1800s, 65 In.	*illus*	1000
Sign, Directional, To Life Boats, Arrow Base, Brass, 2½ x 19 In.		443
Sign, Walnut, Wood, Carved, Welcome Aboard, Flower, Eagle, Spread Wings, Late 1900s, 17 In.		2750
Sternboard, Wood, Carved, Benjamin S. Wright, Blue, Black Ground, Gilt, Contemporary, 10 In.		375
Sternboard, Zanzibar, Carved, Elephant Heads, Blue Ground, Gilt, 10 In.	*illus*	344
Stove, Yacht, Little Cod, Molded, Charles Fawcett Manufacturing Co., Early 1900s, 11 x 17 In.		688
Telegraph, Ship's Engine Order, Brass Case, Marked, J.W. Ray & Co. Ltd., 41 x 15 x 11 In.	*illus*	1112
Telegraph, Ship's Engine, Room, Brass, Round Base, 51½ In.		500
Tiller Yoke, Brass, Rectangular Slot, Openwork Arms, c.1880, 16½ In.		531
Trophy, Dome Lid, Yachting, George II Style, Handles, Tiered Foot, Engraved, 1902, 11½ In.		2500
Trunk, Sea Captain's, Camphorwood, Leather Covered, Bail Handle, Early 1800s, 13 x 29 x 15 In.		1521
Trunk, Sea Captain's, Rope Side Handles, Painted, Morning Star, 1800s, 36 x 16½ In.	*illus*	266

NETSUKE

Netsukes are small ivory, wood, metal, or porcelain pieces used as toggles on the end of the cord that held a Japanese money pouch or inro. The earliest date from the sixteenth century. Many are miniature carved works of art. This category also includes the ojime, the slide or string fastener that was used on the inro cord. There are legal restrictions on the sale of ivory. Check the laws in your state.

Bone, Man Riding Fish, 2 In.		135
Boxwood, Nut Shape, 2 Figures, 1⅝ In.		398
Inro, Hardwood, Dragon, Oval Medallion, Carved, 1800s, 3¼ x 2¾ In.		106
Ivory, Seated Man & Woman, Erotic, Inked Engraving, Signed, 1900s, 2¼ In.	*illus*	144
Jade, Man, Carved, Gray Green, 1¾ In.		295
Wood, Boy With Fan, Japan, 2½ In.		54
Wood, Rat Perched On Bale Of Hay, Carved, Japan, 1900s, 1⅝ In.		59
Wood, Shishi Lion, Open Mouth, Sharp Teeth, Bulging Eyes, 1900s, 2 In., Pair	*illus*	59

NEW HALL

New Hall Porcelain Works was in business in Shelton, Hanley, Staffordshire, England, from 1781 to 1835. Simple decorated wares were made. Between 1810 and 1825, the factory made a glassy bone porcelain sometimes

New Hall

Nautical, Trunk, Sea Captain's, Rope Side Handles, Painted, Morning Star, 1800s, 36 x 16½ In.
$266

Copake Auction

Netsuke, Ivory, Seated Man & Woman, Erotic, Inked Engraving, Signed, 1900s, 2¼ In.
$144

Garth's Auctioneers & Appraisers

N

Netsuke, Wood, Shishi Lion, Open Mouth, Sharp Teeth, Bulging Eyes, 1900s, 2 In., Pair
$59

Leland Little Auctions

New Hall, Pitcher & Bowl, Blue Bird, Flowering Branch, Clouds, Scrolled Handle, White Interior, 16 In.
$99

Hartzell's Auction Gallery Inc.

New Hall, Tea Set, Chinoiserie, Garden Scene, Teapot, Cup & Saucer, Red Mark, c.1805
$351

Jeffrey S. Evans & Associates

Newcomb, Bowl, Japanese Quince Design, Matte Glaze, Blue, Green, Pink Underglaze, 1923, 3 x 9 In.
$1,792

Neal Auction Company

marked with the factory name. Do not confuse New Hall porcelain with the pieces made by the New Hall Pottery Company, Ltd., a twentieth-century firm working from 1899 to 1956 at the New Hall Works.

Cream Jug, Ewer Shape, Garden, 2 Figures, Windmill, Multicolor Leaves At Base, c.1785, 3 x 5 In. .	1003
Cup, Coffee, Blue Transfer, 2 Doves, Tree, Flowering Branch, Gilt Rim, 2½ In.	142
Pitcher & Bowl, Blue Bird, Flowering Branch, Clouds, Scrolled Handle, White Interior, 16 In. *illus*	99
Plate, Dessert, Fruit Basket, Blue Rim, White Molded Roses, c.1820, 8 In.	84
Tea Set, Chinoiserie, Garden Scene, Teapot, Cup & Saucer, Red Mark, c.1805 .... *illus*	351

NEWCOMB POTTERY

Newcomb Pottery was founded at Sophie Newcomb College, New Orleans, Louisiana, in 1895. The work continued through the 1940s. Pieces of this art pottery are marked with the printed letters *NC* and often have the incised initials of the artist and potter as well. A date letter code was printed on pieces made from 1901 to 1941. Most pieces have a matte glaze and incised decoration. From 1942 to 1952 the Newcomb mark was revived and put on pieces of pottery from the college. New names were used.

Bowl, Japanese Quince Design, Matte Glaze, Blue, Green, Pink Underglaze, 1923, 3 x 9 In. *illus*	1792
Charger, 3 Crayfish, Water Ripples, Painted, Marie Levering Benson, 1907, 7½ In.	2180
Jar, Lid, Landscape, Live Oak Trees, Acorns, Bulbous, Blue & Green, A. Simpson, 1915, 6 In...	3250
Pitcher, Art Pottery, White Flowers, Pointed Spout, 5¾ In.	904
Plaque, Chapel, Matte Glaze, Blue, Green, Pink Underglaze, Frame, Sadie Irvine, 1915, 6 x 10 In...	16470
Plate, Yellow, Green, Flowers, Circular, Signed, Amelie Roman, 10¾ In...................................	3750
Tyg, Stylized Wisteria, Green Underglaze, 2 Handles, Harriet Joor, 1903, 8 In. .... *illus*	19520
Vase, Blue Matte Glaze, Pink Dogwood Shoulder, Sadie Irvine, 1931, 5 x 6 In.	819
Vase, Cherokee Roses, Blue, Green, Margaret Sterling Lea, 1907, 7½ In....................	6100
Vase, Cherokee Roses, Blue, Green, Yellow Underglaze, 1907, 6 In.	6100
Vase, Expansive Scene, Live Oak, Spanish Moss, Marked, 5½ In. .... *illus*	1063
Vase, Full Moon Scene, S. Irvine, 7 In..	3108
Vase, Landscape, Pine Trees, Crescent Moon, Blue & Green Matte, Oval, A. Simpson, 7 In.	5313
Vase, Spanish Moss & Moon, Blue Matte Glaze, Sadie Irvine, 1927, 6¾ x 4½ In.	4063

NILOAK POTTERY

Niloak Pottery (*Kaolin* spelled backward) was made at the Hyten Brothers Pottery in Benton, Arkansas, between 1910 and 1947. Although the factory did make cast and molded wares, collectors are most interested in the marbleized art pottery line made of colored swirls of clay. It was called Mission Ware. By 1931 the company made castware, and many of these pieces were marked with the name *Hywood*.

NILOAK	NILOAK	NILOAK
Niloak 1910	Niloak c.1910–1920s	Niloak 1930s–1947

Ewer, Flying Eagle, Stars, Blue Over Rose, Marked, c.1940, 10 In...	58
Strawberry Planter, Green Teal Glaze, Leaves, Raised Mark, 1930s, 7 x 4 In.........................	38
Vase, Globular, Marbleized, Brown, Blue, Cream, 4 In.	145
Vase, Marbleized, Earth Tones, Marked, 6 In.	95
Vase, Marbleized, Jar Shape, Red, White, Blue, Signed, 4 x 3¼ In. .... *illus*	375
Vase, Marbleized, Oval, Wide Flared Rim, Tan, Blue, Brown, Cream, 6½ In...........................	84

NIPPON

Nippon porcelain was made in Japan from 1891 to 1921. *Nippon* is the Japanese word for "Japan." The McKinley Tariff Act of 1891 mandated that goods imported to the United States had to be marked with the country of origin. A few firms continued to use the word *Nippon* on ceramics after 1921 as a part of the company name and not to identify things as made in Japan. More pieces marked *Nippon* will be found in the Dragonware, Moriage, and Noritake categories.

Nitto
1890–1921

Nippon
1894–1920

Morimura/Noritake
c.1911–1921

Ashtray, 3 Embossed Dogs, Blown-Out Mold, Brown Tones, 2 1/4 x 6 1/2 In.	100
Ashtray, Circular, Egyptian Design, 3 Handles, Mark, 5 In.	50
Ashtray, Indian, Beaded Green, Browns, Yellow, Painted, Blue M Wreath, 5 1/4 In.	184
Ashtray, Raccoon, Tree Trunk, Carved, Painted, 4 1/2 In., Pair	173
Biscuit Jar, Lid, Middle East Scene, Camels, Mountain, 2 Handles, Marked, 5 1/4 x 9 In.	25
Box, Enameled Lid, Rectangular, Lion Crest, Painted, Marked, 4 1/2 In.	75
Candlestick, Art Deco Style, Square Base, Painted, Marked, 7 1/2 In.	38
Chocolate Pot, Art Deco Style, Flowers, Gold Trim, Signed, 9 1/2 In.	46
Humidor, Diamond Shape, Playing Cards, Pipe, Cigarette, Poker Chips, Marked, 4 1/2 x 4 1/2 In. *illus*	125
Humidor, Native American, Horseback, Brown, Carved, 6 1/2 In.	368
Humidor, Rectangular, Egyptian Design, Flowers, Painted, 4 3/4 In.	50
Pitcher, River Scene, Handle, Ruffled Bottom, Painted, 7 1/2 In.	1115
Plaque, Round, Horse, Molded, Painted, Marked, 10 1/2 In.	238
Plate, Round, Coastal Scene, Cottage, Sailboat, Marked, 10 In.	25
Plate, Round, Lion & Lioness, Tree, Sitting, Painted, 10 1/2 In.	230
Vase, Blown-Out Decor, Man & Dogs, Gilt, Cream Ground, Scrolled Handle, 9 In.	367
Vase, Cylindrical, Sparrow & Pine Tree Design, Painted, 9 3/4 In.	281
Vase, Flowers, House, Trees, Handles, Gilt, Painted, 15 1/2 In.	29
Vase, Hand Painted, Gilt, Flowers, Handles, 9 x 8 In. *illus*	94
Vase, Lobed, Hand Painted, Gold Trim, High Square Handles, 10 x 6 In.	173
Vase, Pheasant Scene, Red Border, Gold Trim, 2 Handles, Marked, 12 3/4 x 7 1/2 In.	90

NODDER

Nodders, also called nodding figures or pagods, are figures with heads and hands that are attached to wires. Any slight movement causes the parts to move up and down. They were made in many countries during the eighteenth, nineteenth, and twentieth centuries. A few Art Deco designs are also known. Copies have been made. A more recent type of nodder is made of papier-mache or plastic. These often represent sports figures or comic characters. Sports nodders are listed in the Sports category.

Chinese Woman, Seated, Inset Clock In Belly, Porcelain, Meissen Style, 9 1/2 x 8 x 8 In.	2125
Chinese Woman, Tongue & Hands Move, Blue Crossed Swords, Meissen, 1800s, 7 x 7 In. *illus*	3000
Lion, Chalk, Standing, Flocked Body, Fur Mane, Glass Eyes, c.1915, 8 In.	120
Salt & Pepper Shakers are listed in the Salt & Pepper category.	

NORITAKE

Noritake porcelain was made in Japan after 1904 by Nippon Toki Kaisha. A maple leaf mark was used from 1891 to 1911. The best-known Noritake pieces are marked with the *M* in a wreath for the Morimura Brothers, a New York City distributing company. This mark was used primarily from 1911 to 1921 but was last used in the early 1950s. The *N* mark was used from 1940 to the 1960s, and *N Japan* from 1953 to 1964. Noritake made dinner sets with pattern names. Noritake Azalea is listed in the Azalea category in this book.

Basket, Flared, Chinoiserie, Green Rim, Gilt Top Handle, Red M In Wreath, 4 1/2 In.	57
Bowl, Cereal, Angela, 6 In.	21
Bowl, Cereal, Bright Side, 5 1/2 In.	8

Newcomb, Tyg, Stylized Wisteria, Green Underglaze, 2 Handles, Harriet Joor, 1903, 8 In.
$19,520

Neal Auction Company

Newcomb, Vase, Expansive Scene, Live Oak, Spanish Moss, Marked, 5 1/2 In.
$1,063

Charlton Hall Auctions

Niloak, Vase, Marbleized, Jar Shape, Red, White, Blue, Signed, 4 x 3 1/4 In.
$375

California Historical Design

Nippon, Humidor, Diamond Shape, Playing Cards, Pipe, Cigarette, Poker Chips, Marked, 4 ½ x 4 ½ In.
$125

Woody Auction

Nippon, Vase, Hand Painted, Gilt, Flowers, Handles, 9 x 8 In.
$94

Bunch Auctions

Nodder, Chinese Woman, Tongue & Hands Move, Blue Crossed Swords, Meissen, 1800s, 7 x 7 In.
$3,000

Cottone Auctions

Noritake, Celery Dish, Shell Shape, Celery & Radish Interior, Gilt, Red M In Wreath, 13 ¼ In.
$63

Eldred's

Noritake, Plate, Dinner, Imperial Hotel, Frank Lloyd Wright, Red N In Wreath, c.1950, 10 ½ In.
$500

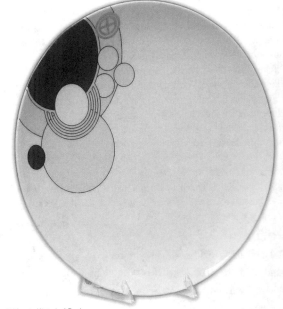

California Historical Design

Norse, Vase, No. 24, Fern, 4 Handles, Bulbous Body, Black Ground, 8 ¾ In.
$787

Humler & Nolan

Bowl, Fruit, Adagio Fruit, 5 ½ In.	20
Bowl, Fruit, Blue Moon, 5 In.	18
Bowl, Fruit, Isabella, 5 ½ In.	6
Bowl, Vegetable, Oval, Shelby, 10 ⅝ In.	35
Celery Dish, Shell Shape, Celery & Radish Interior, Gilt, Red M In Wreath, 13 ¼ In. .... *illus*	63
Creamer, Colburn, 2 ⅝ In.	15
Creamer, Milburn	8
Cup & Saucer, Angela	10
Cup & Saucer, Blue Moon	7
Cup & Saucer, Colburn	12
Cup & Saucer, Sunny Side	7
Gravy Boat, Dutch Treat	28
Gravy Boat, Pacific	21
Gravy Boat, Underplate, Goldston	25
Plate, Bread & Butter, Blue Haven, 6 In.	4
Plate, Bread & Butter, Bright Side, 6 ¼ In.	8
Plate, Bread & Butter, Goldston, 6 ¼ In.	5
Plate, Christmas Ball, Gold Enamel Around Rim, 10 In., 17 Piece	113
Plate, Dinner, Blue Haven, 10 In.	20
Plate, Dinner, Century, 10 ⅜ In.	16
Plate, Dinner, Imperial Hotel, Frank Lloyd Wright, Red N In Wreath, c.1950, 10 ½ In. .. *illus*	500
Plate, Dinner, Isabella, 10 ½ In.	13
Plate, Salad, Century, 8 ¼ In.	9
Platter, Goldston, 12 In.	20
Platter, Isabella, 12 In.	15
Salt & Pepper, Blue Moon	28
Saucer, Century	3
Sugar & Creamer, Cartouche, Lake, Tree, Flowers, Cobalt Blue, Gilt, Green M In Wreath, 5 ¾ In.	24
Sugar, Angela, Footed	9
Vase, Hand Painted, Galleon Ship, Gilt Trim, Signed, 8 ¼ x 3 ¾ In.	90

NORSE POTTERY

Norse Pottery Company started in Edgerton, Wisconsin, in 1903. In 1904 the company moved to Rockford, Illinois. The company made a black pottery, which resembled early bronze relics of the Scandinavian countries. The firm went out of business in 1913.

Mug, Cylindrical, Black Brown Glaze, Circle Design Base, 5 In.	225
Pitcher, Geometric Designs, Black Brown Glaze, Green Accents, 9 ¼ In.	795
Vase, No. 24, Fern, 4 Handles, Bulbous Body, Black Ground, 8 ¾ In. .... *illus*	787

NORTH DAKOTA SCHOOL OF MINES

North Dakota School of Mines was established in 1898 at the University of North Dakota. A ceramics course was established in 1910. Students made pieces from the clays found in the region. Although very early pieces were marked *U.N.D.*, most pieces were stamped with the full name of the university. After 1963 pieces were only marked with students' names.

U. N. D.

North Dakota School of Mines
1910–1963

North Dakota School of Mines
c.1913–1963

Bowl, Red, Tan Trim, Geometrics Interior, Wave Exterior, Flared Rim, 1936, 4 x 9 In.	1125
Decanter, Melon Shape Lid, Gourd, Long Neck, Light Blue Ground, 9 In.	396
Vase, Cowboys, Brown Glaze, Carved Relief Band, Lasso, Horse, Mattson, 7 x 4 ½ In.	1950
Vase, Cream Glaze, Shoulders, Incised Bands Around Neck, Stamped, 6 ⅝ In.	88

North Dakota, Vase, Openwork Flower Panels, Signed, Jarvis, 10 ⅝ x 5 ⅝ In. $875

John Moran Auctioneers

North Dakota, Vase, Oval, Blue Ground, Underglaze Cats & Grapevines, Marked, Lila M. Ague, 7 ⅛ In. $441

Homestead Auctions

North Dakota, Vase, Tan To Green, Incised Geometric Bands, Earthenware, Margaret Cable, 8 x 5 In. $1,080

Cottone Auctions

Northwood, Leaf Umbrella, Creamer, Sapphire, Blue, Clear Handle, Polished Rim, c.1889, 4 In.
$293

Jeffrey S. Evans & Associates

Northwood, Swirl, Pitcher, Water, White Opalescent, Square Ruffled Top, Clear Handle, 8 ½ In.
$70

Woody Auction

TIP
Always buy the best you can afford. It will keep its value better than less expensive items.

Nutcracker, Dog, Cast Iron, Nickel Plated, Small Squirrel Base, 12 ½ In.
$123

Hartzell's Auction Gallery Inc.

Vase, Cylindrical, Pink & Blue Flowers, Blue Ring Collar, Signed, Viola Thomas, 1935, 7 ½ In.	385
Vase, Green To Brown, Matte Glaze, Marked, Freida Hammers, 6 ½ In.	252
Vase, Green, Stylized Flowers, 3 High Glaze Colors, Julia Mattson, 3 ⅜ x 6 In.	2898
Vase, Openwork Flower Panels, Signed, Jarvis, 10 ⅝ x 5 ⅝ In. .... *illus*	875
Vase, Orange Glaze, Cylindrical, Signed, 4 ½ x 2 ¾ In.	282
Vase, Oval, Blue Ground, Underglaze Cats & Grapevines, Marked, Lila M. Ague, 7 ⅛ In. *illus*	441
Vase, Stick, Footed, Brown, Light To Dark, Cable, c. 1939, 10 In.	225
Vase, Tan To Green, Incised Geometric Bands, Earthenware, Margaret Cable, 8 x 5 In. *illus*	1080
Vase, Turquoise To Purple, Red Base, Marked, JM, c.1932, 3 ½ x 3 In.	300
Vase, Winter Berries, Green To Brown Ground, Earthenware, Marked, Eggers, 6 ¾ x 4 ¾ In. .	4063

NORTHWOOD

Northwood glass was made by one of the glassmaking companies operated by Harry C. Northwood. His first company, Northwood Glass Co., was founded in Martins Ferry, Ohio, in 1887 and moved to Ellwood City, Pennsylvania, in 1892. The company closed in 1896. Later that same year, Harry Northwood opened the Northwood Co. in Indiana, Pennsylvania. Some pieces made at the Northwood Co. are marked "Northwood" in script. The Northwood Co. became part of a consortium called the National Glass Co. in 1899. Harry left National in 1901 to found the H. Northwood Co. in Wheeling, West Virginia. At the Wheeling factory, Harry Northwood and his brother Carl manufactured pressed and blown tableware and novelties in many colors that are collected today as custard, opalescent, goofus, carnival, and stretch glass. Pieces made between 1905 and about 1915 may have an underlined *N* trademark. Harry Northwood died in 1919, and the plant closed in 1925.

Northwood Glass Co. 1905–c.1915	Northwood Glass Co. 1905–c.1915	Northwood Glass Co. 1905–c.1915

Acorn Burrs, Punch Set, Pedestal Base, Green Iridescent, 6 Cups, 11 x 11 ½ In.	425
Coin Spot, Pitcher, Water, Blue Opalescent, Star Crimped Top, Shaped Handle, 8 ¾ In.	51
Leaf Umbrella, Creamer, Sapphire, Blue, Clear Handle, Polished Rim, c.1889, 4 In. .... *illus*	293
Maple Leaf, Toothpick Holder, Custard, Green Stain, Gilt, c.1900, 2 ⅜ In.	164
Reverse Swirl, Pitcher, Water, Graniteware, Blue, Opal Frit, Handle, 1880s, 9 In.	94
Swirl, Pitcher, Water, White Opalescent, Square Ruffled Top, Clear Handle, 8 ½ In. ..... *illus*	70

NU-ART *see Imperial category.*

 ## NUTCRACKER

Nutcrackers of many types have been used through the centuries. At first the nutcracker was probably strong teeth or a hammer. But by the nineteenth century, many elaborate and ingenious types were made. Levers, screws, and hammer adaptations were the most popular. Because nutcrackers are still useful, they are still being made, some in the old styles.

Alligator, Cast Iron, Lift Tail, Black, Painted, 12 In.	308
Dog, Bronze, Brown, Standing, Black Base, 10 In.	47
Dog, Cast Iron, Nickel Plated, Small Squirrel Base, 12 ½ In. .... *illus*	123
Dragon, Cast Iron, Spiny Back, 14 In.	277
Elephant, Cast Iron, Painted, Red Ground, Trunk Handle, 1800s, 9 ½ x 5 In.	106
Elephant, Cast Iron, Whimsical, Orange, Painted, Trunk Handle, 5 x 10 In.	62
Elephant, Hinged Trunk, Stylized, Red & Black Paint, Iron, Vindex, 5 x 9 ¾ In.	92
Gnome, Wood, On Tree Stump, Carved, Late 1800s, 11 In.	86
Hippo, Cast Iron, 8 In. .... *illus*	1200
Squirrel, Cast Iron, Figural Handle, Bell Shape Stand, Wood Base, Late 1800s, 7 In. ... *illus*	263

N

NYMPHENBURG, *see Royal Nymphenburg.*

OCCUPIED JAPAN

Occupied Japan was printed on pottery, porcelain, toys, and other goods made during the American occupation of Japan after World War II, from 1947 to 1952. Collectors now search for these pieces. The items were made for export. Ceramic items are listed here. Toys are listed in the Toy category in this book.

Casserole, Lid, Flowers, Leaves, Multicolor, Footed, Scroll Handles, 11 x 9 In.	28
Creamer, Cow, Brown, Tan, 4 ¼ x 3 In.	53
Figurine, Bird, Crane, Picking Feather, Black, Cream, Red, 5 x 3 ¼ In.	74
Figurine, Girl, Selling Apples, Bonnet, Green, Red, White, 3 ¾ In.	18
Wall Pocket, Cherubs, Wings, Porcelain, 5 ½ x 5 ¼, Pair	120

OFFICE TECHNOLOGY

Office technology includes office equipment and related products, such as adding machines, calculators, and check-writing machines. Typewriters are in their own category in this book.

Envelope Sealer, Cast Iron, Chain Drive, Mechanical, Reynold's, Chicago, c.1910, 8 x 19 In.	154
Ticker Tape Machine, Wall Street Journal, Octagonal Base, Dow Jones & Co., 1950, 49 In. *illus*	189

OHR

Ohr pottery was made in Biloxi, Mississippi, from 1883 to 1906 by George E. Ohr, a true eccentric. The pottery was made of very thin clay that was twisted, folded, and dented into odd, graceful shapes. Some pieces were lifelike models of hats, animal heads, or even a potato. Others were decorated with folded clay "snakes." Reproductions and reworked pieces are appearing on the market. These have been reglazed, or snakes and other embellishments have been added.

Card Holder, Seashell Shape, Glazed, Impressed, G.E. Ohr, Biloxi, 2 x 3 x 4 In.	625
Mug, Bronze Metallic Glaze, Black Spatters, Loop Handle, Signed, G.E. Ohr, 4 x 2 ¾ In.	1159
Teapot, Inverted Lid, Green Glaze, Speckles, Mustard Interior, 4 ¼ In. *illus*	9500
Vase, Coupe, Mottled Brown To Tan To Green, Folded Rim, 2 Asymmetric Handles, c.1900, 7 x 7 In.	27500
Vase, Green Speckled Glaze, Incised Bands, 2 Shaped Asymmetric Handles, Signed, c.1898, 4 x 5 In.	18750
Vase, Green, Gunmetal, Yellow & Raspberry Glazes, Pinched & Folded, Signed, 6 x 6 In.	62500
Vase, Lid, Scalloped Rim, Umber Glaze, Black Spattering, 4 ¼ In.	1100
Vase, Pinched Rim, Green, Orange, Speckle Glaze, Base Impressed, 4 x 5 x 3 ¾ In. *illus*	3660
Vase, Pinched Waist, Green, Red Speckled Glaze, Umber Interior, 7 ¾ In. *illus*	8750
Vase, Speckled & Sponged On Green & Brown Glaze, Crumpled, Signed, 1897-1900, 3 x 4 ½ In.	8750

OLD PARIS, *see Paris category.*

OLD SLEEPY EYE, *see Sleepy Eye category.*

OLYMPICS

Olympics memorabilia include commemorative pins, posters, programs, patches, mascots, and other items from the Olympics, even the torch carried before the games. The Olympics are thought to have started as a religious festival held in Olympia, Greece, in 776 BC. It included a foot race in the stadium. After that games were held every four years until 393 AD and more athletic events were added. The games were revived in 1896 when the first modern Olympics were held in Athens, Greece, with fourteen countries participating. The Olympics were held only in the summer until 1924 when the first Winter Olympics were held in Chamonix, France. The current schedule of an Olympics every two years, alternating between Summer

Nutcracker, Hippo, Cast Iron, 8 In. $1,200

Bertoia Auctions

Nutcracker, Squirrel, Cast Iron, Figural Handle, Bell Shape Stand, Wood Base, Late 1800s, 7 In. $263

Jeffrey S. Evans & Associates

Office, Ticker Tape Machine, Wall Street Journal, Octagonal Base, Dow Jones & Co., 1950, 49 In. $189

Fontaine's Auction Gallery

O

Ohr, Teapot, Inverted Lid, Green Glaze, Speckles, Mustard Interior, 4 ¼ In.
$9,500

Neal Auction Company

Ohr, Vase, Pinched Rim, Green, Orange, Speckle Glaze, Base Impressed, 4 x 5 x 3 ¾ In.
$3,660

Neal Auction Company

Ohr, Vase, Pinched Waist, Green, Red Speckled Glaze, Umber Interior, 7 ¾ In.
$8,750

Neal Auction Company

and Winter Olympics, began in 1994. The Olympic flag was introduced in 1908; official Olympics posters were first commissioned in 1912; the Olympic torch first appeared in 1928; and the first relay to light the torch was held in 1936 at the Olympics in Berlin.

Jacket, Coach's, Winter Olympics, Sarajevo, 1984, Hockey, Team USA, Blue Nylon, Size L . *illus*	303
Medal, Paris, 1900, Gold Plated Silver, 2 ½ In.	192
Medal, Silver, Summer Olympics, Los Angeles, 1984, Seated Victory, Ribbon, Case .... *illus*	6400
Medal, Silver, Summer Olympics, Seoul, 1988, Seated Victory Dove, Ribbon, Case, 2 ½ In.	6250
Torch, Summer Olympics, Mexico City, 1968, Type 1, Mexico 68 On Rim, White Metal, 18 In.	2309
Torch, Winter Olympics, Lake Placid, 1980, Metal, Silver Ring, Cleanweld, 1980, 28 ½ In. *illus*	43750

ONION PATTERN

Onion pattern, originally named bulb pattern, is a white ware decorated with cobalt blue or pink designs of a vine with buds that look like onions. Although it is commonly associated with Meissen, other companies made the pattern in the late nineteenth and the twentieth centuries. A rare type is called *red bud* because there are added red accents on the blue-and-white dishes.

Coffee Mill, Eagle Mark, J.S., 10 x 5 ¼ In. .... *illus*	62
Cup & Saucer, Blue & White, Hutschenreuther	20
Double Salt, Boy, Hat, Holding Baskets, 5 ½ x 5 In.	225
Gravy Boat, 2 Spouts, Lid, Handles, Finial, Meissen, 6 ¾ x 5 In.	184
Oyster Plate, 5 Wells, Wave Design, Scalloped Edge, Stamped, T Germany, c.1900, 8 In.	235
Plate, Blue & White, Scalloped Edge, Gilt, Meissen, 7 ¾ In.	150
Teapot, Lid, Handle & Spout, Blue, White Ground, Bud Finial, Meissen, 1900s, 5 ¼ In. *illus*	305
Trivet, Blue & White, Porcelain, Wood, 8 ½ In. Diam.	13

OPALESCENT GLASS

Opalescent glass is translucent glass that has the tones of the opal gemstone. It originated in England in the 1870s and is often found in pressed glassware made in Victorian times. Opalescent glass was first made in America in 1897 at the Northwood glassworks in Indiana, Pennsylvania. Some dealers use the terms *opaline* and *opalescent* for any of these translucent wares. More opalescent pieces may be listed in Hobnail, Pressed Glass, and other glass categories.

Buttons & Braids, Pitcher, Green, Applied Handle, Jefferson Glass Co., 10 In.	100
Crisscross, Toothpick Holder, Cranberry, c.1894, 2 ⅜ In.	152
Crisscross, Tumbler, Cranberry, Satin Finish, Factory Polished Rim, c.1888, 3 ¾ In. .. *illus*	176
Double Greek Key, Pitcher, Ruffled Rim, Nickel Plate Glass Co., 8 ¼ In. .... *illus*	275
Swirl, Pitcher, Water, Cranberry, Ruffled Star Crimped Top, 8 ½ In.	150
Swirl, Toothpick Holder, Oval, Blue, Late 1800s, 2 ¼ In.	47
Windows Swirl, Cruet, Cranberry, Clear Handle, Hobbs, Brockunier & Co., c.1888, 6 In.	164

OPALINE

Opaline, or opal glass, was made in white, green, and other colors. The glass had a matte surface and a lack of transparency. It was often gilded or painted. It was a popular mid-nineteenth-century European glassware.

Compote, Neoclassical Style, Green Glass, Ormolu, Fruit Finial, Claw Feet, Late 1800s, 9 In. ..*illus*	502
Cruet, Brocade, Spanish Lace, Pressed Facet Stopper, Vaseline, Northwood, c.1899, 7 x 5 In.	176
Vase, Sky Blue Ground, Painted, Flowers, Polished Pontil, Late 1800s, 14 In.	177

OPERA GLASSES

Opera glasses are needed because the stage is a long way from some of the seats at a play or an opera. Mother-of-pearl was a popular decoration on many French glasses.

O

Olympics, Jacket, Coach's, Winter Olympics, Sarajevo, 1984, Hockey, Team USA, Blue Nylon, Size L
$303

RR Auction

Olympics, Medal, Silver, Summer Olympics, Los Angeles, 1984, Seated Victory, Ribbon, Case
$6,400

Julien's Auctions

Olympics, Torch, Winter Olympics, Lake Placid, 1980, Metal, Silver Ring, Cleanweld, 1980, 28 ½ In.
$43,750

RR Auction

Onion, Coffee Mill, Eagle Mark, J.S., 10 x 5 ¼ In.
$62

Ron Rhoads Auctioneers

Onion, Teapot, Lid, Handle & Spout, Blue, White Ground, Bud Finial, Meissen, 1900s, 5 ¼ In.
$305

Neal Auction Company

Opalescent, Crisscross, Tumbler, Cranberry, Satin Finish, Factory Polished Rim, c.1888, 3 ¾ In.
$176

Jeffrey S. Evans & Associates

Opalescent, Double Greek Key, Pitcher, Ruffled Rim, Nickel Plate Glass Co., 8 ¼ In.
$275

Woody Auction

Opaline, Compote, Neoclassical Style, Green Glass, Ormolu, Fruit Finial, Claw Feet, Late 1800s, 9 In.
$502

Leland Little Auctions

Opera Glasses, Porcelain, Flowers, Cobalt Blue, Opaline, Gilt, Mother-Of-Pearl Eye Rings, Late 1800s, 2 In.
$168

Garth's Auctioneers & Appraisers

O

Orrefors, Bowl, Clear, Brown Ribbon, Footed, Signed, Edvin Ohrstrom, 1985, 3 x 6 In.
$100

Woody Auction

Overbeck, Figurine, Southern Belle, Blue Dress, Bouquet, Hat, Signed, 1944, 4 x 2 x 3 In.
$531

Ripley Auctions

Overbeck, Vase, 3 Stylized Praying Mantis, Green Matte Glaze, Blue Gray Highlights, 4¾ In.
$6,050

Humler & Nolan

Enamel, Green & White, Flowers, Gilt, Chavance & Co., Dustis Bros., Velvet Bag, 2 x 4 In.	256
Gilt Bronze, Mother-Of-Pearl, Telescoping, Handle, Graviere, Fabt., Paris, c.1875	250
Mother-Of-Pearl, Paneled, Optiker Ruhke, Germany, 1920s	280
Porcelain, Flowers, Cobalt Blue, Opaline, Gilt, Mother-Of-Pearl Eye Rings, Late 1800s, 2 In. ..*illus*	168
Tortoiseshell, Telescoping Handle, c.1860, 3½ x 1½ In.	195

ORPHAN ANNIE

Orphan Annie first appeared in the comics in 1924. The last strip ran in newspapers on June 13, 2010. The redheaded girl, her dog Sandy, and her friends were on the radio from 1930 to 1942. The first movie based on the strip was produced in 1932. A second movie was produced in 1938. A Broadway musical that opened in 1977, a movie based on the musical and produced in 1982, and a made-for-television movie based on the musical produced in 1999 made Annie popular again, and many toys, dishes, and other memorabilia have been made. An adaptation of the movie based on the musical opened in 2014.

Big Book, The Story Of Little Orphan Annie, Harold Gray, First Edition, Whitman, 9½ x 7½ In.	48
Big Little Book, Little Orphan Annie In The Movies, No. 1416, Harold Gray, Whitman, 1937	12
Comic Strip, 3 Panels, Signed, Harold Gray, Frame, 1960, 7⅜ x 20⅞ In.	462
Cup, Plastic, Annie, Sandy, Shaking Cup Of Ovaltine, 1940s, 3¾ In.	28
Doll, Red Dress, Effanbee, Box, 10¾ In.	12
Mug, Annie, Raising Cup, Porcelain, Wander Co., 3 In.	56
Mug, Ovaltine, Annie & Sandy, Jumpin' Grasshoppers!, Beetleware, The Wander Co., 1930s, 3 In.	45
Mug, Shake-Up, Ovaltine, Red Cap, Multicolor Annie & Sandy Graphics, Beetleware, 5 Piece	57
Toothbrush Holder, Annie & Sandy, Seated, Blue Chair, Bisque, Japan, 1930s, 3 x 3 In.	53
Toothbrush Holder, Bisque, Annie, Sandy On Hind Legs, Marked, Japan, 1930s, 3⅞ In.	20
Toy, Sandy, Carrying Bag, Tin Lithograph, Black, Yellow, Windup, 1930s, 4 x 1½ x 5 In.	114

ORREFORS

Orrefors

Orrefors Glassworks, located in the Swedish province of Smaaland, was established in 1898. The company is still making glass for use on the table or as decorations. There is renewed interest in the glass made in the modern styles of the 1940s and 1950s and after. In 1990, the company merged with Kosta Boda and is still working as Orrefors. Most vases and decorative pieces are signed with the etched name *Orrefors*.

Bowl, 8 Ribbed Petals, Center Green Splash, Signed, 5 x 6¾ In.	50
Bowl, Clear, Brown Ribbon, Footed, Signed, Edvin Ohrstrom, 1985, 3 x 6 In. ....*illus*	100
Bowl, Green, Ariel, Signed, Edvin Ohrstrom, Sweden, 1950, 3¼ x 6¾ In.	813
Bowl, Irregular Panel Cutting, Crystal, Anne Nilsson, 1980s, 6½ x 10½ In.	101
Vase, Nude Maiden, Octagonal, Simon Gate, c.1930, 9 x 5½ In.	488
Vase, Nude Man, Playing A Harp, Signed, Vicke Lindstrand, 8⅝ x 5½ x 5½ In.	156

OTT & BREWER

Ott & Brewer Company operated the Etruria Pottery at Trenton, New Jersey, from 1871 to 1892. It started making belleek in 1882. The firm used a variety of marks that incorporated the initials *O & B*.

Biscuit Jar, Dandelions, Orange, Pinched Sides, Handles, Lid, c.1876, 7 x 6 In.	256
Coffeepot, Blue, White, Oak Leaves, Acorns Gold Sponge Decoration, c.1880, 9 In.	165

OVERBECK POTTERY

Overbeck Pottery was made by four sisters named Overbeck at a pottery in Cambridge City, Indiana. They started in 1911. They made all types of vases, each one of a kind. Small, hand-modeled figurines are the most popular pieces with today's collectors. The factory continued until 1955, when the last of the four sisters died.

Figurine, Southern Belle, Blue Dress, Bouquet, Hat, Signed, 1944, 4 x 2 x 3 In. ....*illus*	531

Vase, 3 Stylized Praying Mantis, Green Matte Glaze, Blue Gray Highlights, 4¾ In. .... *illus* 6050

OWENS POTTERY

Owens Pottery was made in Zanesville, Ohio, from 1891 to 1928. The first art pottery was made after 1896. Utopian Ware, Cyrano, Navarre, Feroza, and Henri Deux were made. Pieces were usually marked with a form of the name *Owens*. The company continued to make tiles but production of art pottery was discontinued about 1907 and the company was sold. The new owners went bankrupt in 1909. J.B. Owens started the J.B. Owens Floor & Wall Tile Company in 1909. It closed in 1928.

Owens Pottery
1896–1907

Owens Pottery
1896–1907

Owens Pottery
1905+

Vase, Apple Blossom, Silver Overlay, Incised 894, Cypher, 5¾ In. .... *illus* 303
Vase, Dark Green Ground, Art Pottery, Geometric Design, 9 In. 367
Vase, Keg Shape, Multicolor Glass Panel, Ruth Wolf Smith, 1972, 13 x 9 In. 100

OYSTER PLATE

Oyster plates were popular from 1840 to 1900. Each course at dinner was served in a special dish. The oyster plate had indentations shaped like oysters. Usually six oysters were held on a plate. There is no greater value to a plate with more oysters, although that myth continues to haunt antiques dealers. There are other plates for shellfish, including cockle plates and whelk plates. The appropriately shaped indentations are part of the design of these dishes.

5 Wells, Rutherford B. Hayes, White House China, 8½ In. .... *illus* 4063
5 Wells, Turkey Style, Sea Life, White Ground, Gilt Rim, Haviland, 8½ In. 147
5 Wells, White, Gilt Trim, Leafy Border, Haviland, J.E. Caldwell & Co., Early 1900s, 7¾ In., 12 Piece.. 270
6 Wells, Porcelain, Shell Shape, Gilt, White Ground, Early 1900s, 9½ In., 6 Piece .... *illus* 384

PAIRPOINT

Pairpoint Manufacturing Company was founded by Thomas J. Pairpoint in 1880 in New Bedford, Massachusetts. It soon joined with the glassworks nearby and made glass, silver-plated pieces, and lamps. Reverse-painted glass shades and molded shades known as "puffies" were part of the production until the 1930s. The company reorganized and changed its name several times. It became the Pairpoint Glass Company in 1957. The company moved to Sagamore, Massachusetts, in 1970 and now makes luxury glass items. Items listed here are glass or glass and metal. Silver-plated pieces are listed under Silver Plate. Three marks are shown here.

Pairpoint Corp.
1894–1939

Gunderson–Pairpoint Glass
Works
1952–1957

Pairpoint Manufacturing Co.
1972–present

Biscuit Jar, Cherry Blossoms, Yellow Ground, Metal Lid, 7½ In. .... *illus* 123
Biscuit Jar, Ornate Scrolls, Flowers, Molded Bottom Edge, Gilt, Signed, Late 1800s, 8 x 7 In. 263
Biscuit Jar, Square, Pink, White Tones, Gold Enamel Flowers, Silver Plate Lid & Bail, 8 x 5 In. ..*illus* 200

Owens, Vase, Apple Blossom, Silver Overlay, Incised 894, Cypher, 5¾ In. $303

Humler & Nolan

Oyster Plate, 5 Wells, Rutherford B. Hayes, White House China, 8½ In. $4,063

Heritage Auctions

Oyster Plate, 6 Wells, Porcelain, Shell Shape, Gilt, White Ground, Early 1900s, 9½ In., 6 Piece $384

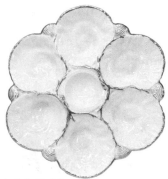

Austin Auction Gallery

P

Pairpoint, Biscuit Jar, Cherry Blossoms, Yellow Ground, Metal Lid, 7 ½ In.
$123

Rich Penn Auctions

Pairpoint, Biscuit Jar, Square, Pink, White Tones, Gold Enamel Flowers, Silver Plate Lid & Bail, 8 x 5 In.
$200

Woody Auction

Pairpoint, Box, Hinged Lid, Heart Shape, Cream Tones, Pink & Yellow Flowers, 3 x 6 In.
$100

Woody Auction

Bowl, Oval, Clear Blank, Cut Glass, Silver Leaf, 3 ½ x 10 ¾ x 7 ½ In.		200
Box, Hinged Lid, Heart Shape, Cream Tones, Pink & Yellow Flowers, 3 x 6 In.	*illus*	100
Candlestick, Cobalt Blue, Hollow Stem, Engraved, Polished Pontil Mark, c.1925, 16 In., Pair		468
Compote, Tazza, Green, Wide Bowl, Colias, Spherical Air Trap Connector, c.1925, 6 x 6 In., Pair		263
Compote, Vaseline Glass, Engraved, 4 ¼ x 8 ¼ In.		100
Dish, Apple Green Vaseline, Wafer Ray Cut, Miter Border, 1 ¾ x 5 ¼ In.		90
Fairy Lamp, Puffy, Grapes & Butterfly Shade, Turned Mahogany Pedestal Base, c.1920, 7 x 3 In.		351
Lamp, Bullet Shape Shade, Sycamore Branch, Marked, 14 ¼ x 5 In.		500
Lamp, Desk, Harbor Scene, Domed Shade, Reverse Painted, Turned Wood Base, c.1910, 20 In.		1750
Lamp, Exeter Shade, Reverse Painted, Autumnal Trees, Ball Chain Pulls, 21 x 17 ¼ In.		605
Lamp, Flowers, Reverse Painted Shade, Brass Stem & Base, Marked, 24 In.	*illus*	531
Lamp, Puffy, 4-Light, Rose Bonnet, Red, Pink, Green Leaves, Butterflies, 21 In.	*illus*	34440
Lamp, Puffy, Apple Tree, Apples, Leaves, Branches, Tree Trunk Base, 21 In.	*illus*	12300
Lamp, Puffy, Multicolor, Brass Finial, Domed Base, Signed, 14 In.		720
Lamp, Puffy, Oxford Shade, Medallions, Green Striated Ground, Art Nouveau Style Base, 22 In.		3780
Lamp, Puffy, Reverse Painted, Pedestal Base, Shade Signed, 1900s, 19 x 14 In.		2944
Lamp, Puffy, Rose & Butterfly, Square Shade, Metal Tree Trunk Base, Signed, 24 x 17 In.		3840
Lamp, Puffy, Stratford Shade, Cranberry Ground, Silvered Base, 15 In.	*illus*	567
Lamp, Radio, Reverse Painted Glass Panel, Sailing Ship, Stormy Sunset, Gilt Base, 10 ½ In.	*illus*	2142
Lamp, Reverse Painted Shade, Row Of Trees, Loving Cup Base, Silver Trim, W. Macy, 27 In.		832
Lamp, Seagull, Copley Style Shade, Turned Mahogany, Signed, F. Rae, Early 1900s, 25 x 20 In.		1755
Lamp, Swedish Oil, Candle Shape Swirled Shade, String Burner, Pink Ground, 1897, 8 x 4 In.	*illus*	439
Paperweight, Air Trap, Clear, Blue Swirl, Circular Foot, 3 Floral Reserves, c.1920, 3 x 2 In.		322
Urn, Lid, Sweetmeat, Napoleon III Style, Satin Glass, Gilt Brass Base, 1900s, 8 ½ In.	*illus*	118
Vase, Clear Controlled, Bubble Stem, Apple Green Vaseline, Colias, 11 ¾ x 6 ¼ In.		225
Vase, Cream Tones, Guba Duck Scene, 2 Handles, Limoges, 15 x 6 ½ In.	*illus*	175

PALMER COX, *Brownies, see Brownies category.*

PAPER

Paper collectibles, including almanacs, catalogs, children's books, some greeting cards, stock certificates, and other paper ephemera, are listed here. Paper calendars are listed separately in the Calendar category. Paper items may be found in many other sections, such as Christmas and Movie.

Bond, State Of South Carolina, Reconstruction, 1000 Dollar, Wood Frame, 1874, 18 x 14 In.		295
Book, Glinda Of Oz, L. Frank Baum, J.R. Neill, First Edition, Partial Dust Jacket, 1920	*illus*	923
Book, Life & Adventures Of Santa Claus, L. Frank Baum, Signed By M. Hague, First Edition, 2003	*illus*	150
Book, Scarecrow Of Oz, L. Frank Baum, J.R. Neill, First Edition, First State, 1915	*illus*	210
Book, Wizard Of Oz, L. Frank Baum, Movie Edition, First Printing, 1939	*illus*	2460
Book, Wonderful Wizard Of Oz, L. Frank Baum, W.W. Denslow, First Edition, 1899	*illus*	3383
Fraktur, Birth & Baptism, John Wiestling, Watercolor & Ink, 1816, 18 x 15 In.		82
Fraktur, Birth & Baptism, Watercolor, Flowers, Sarah Opellinger, Frame, c.1802, 12 x 15 In.		4063
Fraktur, Birth, Ink & Watercolor, Johan Frederick Schumacher, Frame, 8 ¼ x 13 In.		1342
Fraktur, Birth, Jacob Schapbell, Ink, Watercolor, Martin Brechal, 12 x 15 In.		388
Fraktur, Birth, Johann Heinrich Gerbrich, Ink & Watercolor, 12 x 15 ¾ In.		7930
Fraktur, Drawing, Lovebirds & Tulips, Wood Frame, Late 1800s, 10 x 14 ¼ In.		263
Fraktur, Scherenschnitte, Cutwork, Watercolor, Pa., 1910s, Frame, 10 x 8 In.		6710
Fraktur, Valentine, Cutwork, Birds, Tulips, Stars, Painted, Frame, c.1820, 18 ¾ x 19 In.		2500
Fraktur, Watercolor, Black Frame, Montgomery Country, Pennsylvania, 1700s, 13 x 16 In.		832
Fraktur, Wedding, Watercolor, Wood Frame, Westmoreland County, Pennsylvania, c.1824	*illus*	4480

PAPER DOLL

Paper dolls were probably inspired by the pantins, or jumping jacks, made in eighteenth-century Europe. By the 1880s, sheets of printed paper dolls and clothes were being made. The first paper doll books were made in the 1920s. Collectors prefer uncut sheets or books or boxed sets of paper dolls. Prices are about half as much if the pages have been cut.

P

Pairpoint, Lamp, Flowers, Reverse Painted Shade, Brass Stem & Base, Marked, 24 In. $531

Cottone Auctions

Pairpoint, Lamp, Puffy, 4-Light, Rose Bonnet, Red, Pink, Green Leaves, Butterflies, 21 In. $34,440

Morphy Auctions

Pairpoint, Lamp, Puffy, Apple Tree, Apples, Leaves, Branches, Tree Trunk Base, 21 In. $12,300

Morphy Auctions

Pairpoint, Lamp, Puffy, Stratford Shade, Cranberry Ground, Silvered Base, 15 In. $567

Fontaine's Auction Gallery

Pairpoint, Lamp, Radio, Reverse Painted Glass Panel, Sailing Ship, Stormy Sunset, Gilt Base, 10 ½ In. $2,142

Fontaine's Auction Gallery

Pairpoint, Lamp, Swedish Oil, Candle Shape Swirled Shade, String Burner, Pink Ground, 1897, 8 x 4 In. $439

Jeffrey S. Evans & Associates

Pairpoint, Urn, Lid, Sweetmeat, Napoleon III Style, Satin Glass, Gilt Brass Base, 1900s, 8 ½ In. $118

Leland Little Auctions

Pairpoint, Vase, Cream Tones, Guba Duck Scene, 2 Handles, Limoges, 15 x 6 ½ In. $175

Woody Auction

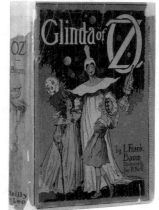

Paper, Book, Glinda Of Oz, L. Frank Baum, J.R. Neill, First Edition, Partial Dust Jacket, 1920 $923

Turner Auctions + Appraisals

P

Paper, Book, Life & Adventures Of Santa Claus, L. Frank Baum, Signed By M. Hague, First Edition, 2003
$150

Turner Auctions + Appraisals

Paper, Book, Scarecrow Of Oz, L. Frank Baum, J.R. Neill, First Edition, First State, 1915
$210

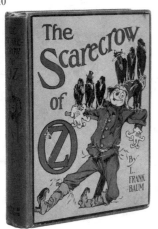

Turner Auctions + Appraisals

Paper, Book, Wizard Of Oz, L. Frank Baum, Movie Edition, First Printing, 1939
$2,460

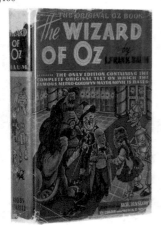

Turner Auctions + Appraisals

Paper, Book, Wonderful Wizard Of Oz, L. Frank Baum, W.W. Denslow, First Edition, 1899
$3,383

Turner Auctions + Appraisals

Paper, Fraktur, Wedding, Watercolor, Wood Frame, Westmoreland County, Pennsylvania, c.1824
$4,480

Cowan's Auctions

Paperweight, Buzzini, Chris, Angelfish, Flowers, Underwater Scene, Signed, 2 ½ In.
$69

Blackwell Auctions

Paperweight, Clichy, Zachary Taylor, Military Bust, Cobalt Blue Ground, Domed, c.1848, 2 ½ In.
$781

Heritage Auctions

Paperweight, Eckstrand, Aquatic, Skeletal Fish, Seaweeds, Multicolor, 1991, 4 ¾ In.
$650

Woody Auction

Paperweight, Kaziun, Jr., Charles, Miniature, Clear, White, Cranberry Blossom, Lampwork, 1950s, 2 x 1 x 1 In.
$234

Jeffrey S. Evans & Associates

PAPERWEIGHT

Paperweights must have first appeared along with paper in ancient Egypt. Today's collectors search for every type, from the very expensive French weights of the nineteenth century to the modern artist weights or advertising pieces. The glass tops of the paperweights sometimes have been nicked or scratched, and this type of damage can be removed by polishing. Some serious collectors think this type of repair is an alteration and will not buy a repolished weight; others think it is an acceptable technique of restoration that does not change the value. Printie is the flat or concave surface formed when a paperweight is shaped on a grinding wheel. Baccarat paperweights are listed separately under Baccarat.

Abelman, Orange Blossom, Mirror Finish Ground, 1980, 3 In........................	150
Advertising, Buffalo, Figural, Cast Iron, Buffalo Tank Corp., BT Brand On Side, 2 ½ In..... ...	42
Advertising, R.T. Crane Brass & Bell Foundry, Building Shape, 1855, 2 ½ x 4 x 3 In.............	98
Bronze, Bulldog, Standing, Leashed, Marble & Rectangular Base, 5 ½ x 3 x 3 ½ In.	71
Buzzini, Chris, Angelfish, Flowers, Underwater Scene, Signed, 2 ½ In. .... *illus*	69
Cartier, Panthere, Silver Panther On Blue Ball, Marked, Spain, 2 In.	400
Cast Iron, Frog, Seated, Painted, Early 1900s, 35 ¼ x 6 ¼ In..............................	177
Clichy, Zachary Taylor, Military Bust, Cobalt Blue Ground, Domed, c.1848, 2 ½ In. ..... *illus*	781
Deacons, John, Flower Bouquet, Clear, Pink, Green Stem, Yellow Spiral, Lampwork, c.1981, 2 In.	234
Eckstrand, Aquatic, Skeletal Fish, Seaweeds, Multicolor, 1991, 4 ¾ In. .... *illus*	650
Kaziun, Jr., Charles, Miniature, Clear, White, Cranberry Blossom, Lampwork, 1950s, 2 x 1 x 1 In. *illus*	234
Lewis, John, Moon Vase, Mountain Lake, Blue Swirls, Signed, 1976, 4 ½ In.	173
Lundberg, Steven, Yellow Trumpet Flower, Clear, Cobalt Blue Ground, Lampwork, c.1990, 3 In. .	761
Millefiori, Concentric, Central Tube Cane, Cogs, Floral, White & Teal, 1800s, 2 ⅝ In. .. *illus*	527
Millefiori, Glass, Round, Multicolor, Flowers, 3 ¾ In.....................................	55
New England Glass Co., 3-Millefiori Floral Cane, Nosegay, 4 Leaves, Clear, Lampwork, 1800s, 1 In.	222
New England Glass Co., Fruit Bouquet, 5 Apples, Lampwork, Latticinio, Concave, 1870s, 2 ½ In. *illus*	234
New England Glass Co., Pear Shape, Blown Glass, Clear Cookie Base, 2 x 3 In. .... *illus*	720
Orient & Flume, Bird, Perched, Pulled Feather, Iridescent, Multicolor, 1978, 3 In.	81
Perthshire, White Latticinio Ground, Scattered Millefiori, Animal Silhouette, 1972, 2 ½ In.	125
Pressed Glass, Early Thumbprint, Cut Facet Finial, Rayed Base, Bakewell, Pears & Co., 3 In..	105
Ritter, Richard, Glass, Multicolor Glaze, Signed, 3 ¼ x 2 ¼ In................................	31
Sandwich Glass, Poinsettia, Lutz Rose Cane Center, Bubbles, Clear Ground, 2 ⅝ In. ... *illus*	390
St. Louis, 13 Filigree Twist, Green, Ruby, Opaque, Blue Central Cane, 1800s, 2 ⅝ In. ... *illus*	1053
St. Louis, Blue Clematis, White Latticinio Cushion, 2 ¾ In. .... *illus*	1800
St. Louis, Millefiori Center, Green, Opal Jasper Ground, Factory Polished Base, 1800s, 2 In..	702
St. Louis, Nympheas De Monet, Lotus, Lily Pads, Faceted, Date Cane, 1884, 3 ¼ In. ..... *illus*	480
Trabucco, Victor, Clear, Flower Bouquet, Faceted, 6 Leaves, Opaque White Base, c.1979, 2 In...	439
Ysart, Paul, Clematis, Lampwork, Blue, White Petals, Central Cane, Box, 1950s, 2 ¾ In........	380

PAPIER-MACHE

Papier-mache is made from paper mixed with glue, chalk, and other ingredients, then molded and baked. It becomes very hard and can be painted. Boxes, trays, and furniture were made of papier-mache. Some of the nineteenth-century pieces were decorated with mother-of-pearl. Papier-mache is still being used to make small toys, figures, candy containers, boxes, and other giftwares. Furniture made of papier-mache is listed in the Furniture category.

Dish, Swing Handle, Scalloped Rim, Black & Gilt Lacquer, Maritime Scene, 10 ⅜ In............	148
Figure, Skeleton, Cowboy, Accordion, Battery Operated, Eyes & Base Light, Mexico, 18 ½ In	148
Hat Stand, Figural, Woman's Head, Painted, 1800s, 16 In. .... *illus*	1586
Mask, Goliath, Horsehair Detail, Multicolor Finish, Early 1900s, 17 x 12 In	115

Paperweight, Millefiori, Concentric, Central Tube Cane, Cogs, Floral, White & Teal, 1800s, 2 ⅝ In.
$527

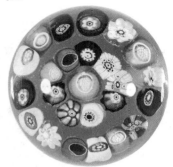

Jeffrey S. Evans & Associates

TIP
You cannot fix a cracked snowdome paperweight.

Paperweight, New England Glass Co., Fruit Bouquet, 5 Apples, Lampwork, Latticinio, Concave, 1870s, 2 ½ In.
$234

Jeffrey S. Evans & Associates

Paperweight, New England Glass Co., Pear Shape, Blown Glass, Clear Cookie Base, 2 x 3 In.
$720

Santa Fe Art Auction

P

PAPIER-MACHE

Paperweight, Sandwich Glass, Poinsettia, Lutz Rose Cane Center, Bubbles, Clear Ground, 2 ⅝ In.
$390

Santa Fe Art Auction

Paperweight, St. Louis, 13 Filigree Twist, Green, Ruby, Opaque, Blue Central Cane, 1800s, 2 ⅝ In.
$1,053

Jeffrey S. Evans & Associates

Paperweight, St. Louis, Blue Clematis, White Latticinio Cushion, 2 ¾ In.
$1,800

Santa Fe Art Auction

Paperweight, St. Louis, Nympheas De Monet, Lotus, Lily Pads, Faceted, Date Cane, 1884, 3 ¼ In.
$480

Santa Fe Art Auction

Papier-Mache, Hat Stand, Figural, Woman's Head, Painted, 1800s, 16 In.
$1,586

Pook & Pook

Papier-Mache, Tray, Chippendale Shape, Gilt Faux Bamboo Stand, C.R. Fenton & Co., 1800s, 20 x 22 x 17 In.
$322

Thomaston Place Auction Galleries

Paris, Basket, Navette Shape, Oval Reticulated, Gilt & Bleu De Roi, 1800s, 10 In.
$549

Neal Auction Company

Paris, Cachepot, Trumpet Shape, Rose, Central Gilt Panel, Inscribed, Early 1800s, 5 In.
$738

Brunk Auctions

Paris, Vase, Magenta Ground, Painted, Empire Design, Plinth Base, Darte Freres, c.1818, 18 In.
$640

Neal Auction Company

P

Sculpture, Standing, 2 Men, Mixed Media & Plexiglas, Willie Birch, 1992, 25 ⅝ In........	1024
Tray, Chippendale Shape, Gilt Faux Bamboo Stand, C.R. Fenton & Co., 1800s, 20 x 22 x 17 In. ..*illus*	322

PARASOL, *see Umbrella category.*

PARIAN

Parian is a fine-grained, hard-paste porcelain named for the marble it resembles. It was first made in England in 1846 and gained favor in the United States about 1860. Figures, tea sets, vases, and other items were made of Parian at many English and American factories.

Bust, Young Woman, Eyelashes, Bonnet, Flower Buds, 9 x 7 In...	255
Figurine, Chastity, Woman, Wearing Robe, Standing, Circular Base, 1900s, 24 ½ In.	58
Figurine, Washington, Standing, Wrapped In His Cloak, Holding Scroll, 13 ½ In.................	2188
Sculpture, Little Bo Peep, Lamb, c.1880, 27 In..	115

PARIS

Paris, Vieux Paris, or Old Paris, is porcelain ware that is known to have been made in Paris in the eighteenth or early nineteenth century. These porcelains often have no identifying mark but can be recognized by the whiteness of the porcelain and the lines and decorations. Gold decoration is often used.

Basket, Navette Shape, Oval Reticulated, Gilt & Bleu De Roi, 1800s, 10 In. .... *illus*	549
Cachepot, Trumpet Shape, Rose, Central Gilt Panel, Inscribed, Early 1800s, 5 In. .... *illus*	738
Candlestick, Castle Tower Shape, Gilt, Multicolor, Footed, 14 In...	158
Compote, 3 Tiers, Gilt, Decorated Scalloped Rim, Trifid Base, 17 x 10 In.	800
Lamp, Enamel, White Shade, Boy, Playing, Electrified, 32 In...	172
Plate, Shells, Insects Amongst Ferns, Gilt Leafy Border, Darte, c.1820, 9 In...........................	1260
Vase, Downward Flange Rim, Bird, Gilt, Tapered Base, 1800s, 15 ½ In...........................	384
Vase, Fruit & Flowers In Cartouche, Green Ground, Ormolu Mounts, J. Petit, 23 In., Pair......	6000
Vase, Magenta Ground, Painted, Empire Design, Plinth Base, Darte Freres, c.1818, 18 In. *illus*	640
Vase, Mantel, Scenic, Blue Ground, Black Rim Border, Round Base, 13 In., Pair .... *illus*	316
Vase, Putto, Cupid, Psyche, Blue Base, Cartouche, Scroll Feet, Gilt, 1850s, 13 x 7 In..............	256

PATENT MODEL

Patent models were required as part of a patent application for a United States patent until 1880. In 1926 the stored patent models were sold by the U.S. Patent Office. Some were given to the Smithsonian, some were returned to inventors' descendants, and the rest were sold as a group. As groups changed hands in later years in unsuccessful attempts to start a museum, individual models started appearing in the marketplace. A model usually has an official tag.

Brick Kiln, Mixed Wood, Tag, Label, John Eisele, Ann Arbor, Michigan, c.1870, 8 x 6 In.......	65
Press, Cider & Wine, Wood, Rectangular, 4-Footed, R.J. Leaks, 7 x 6 x 5 In.............................	240
Refrigerator, Hinged Lid, Side Door, Wood, Metal Interior, Spout, Tag, J.K. Ludlow, 1879 *illus*	1000
Sawmill, Mechanized, Metal Saw & Gears, Wood Base & Supports, c.1850, 17 x 10 x 5 In.	625

PATE-DE-VERRE

Pate-de-verre is an ancient technique in which glass is made by blending and refining powdered glass of different colors into molds. The process was revived by French glassmakers, especially Galle, around the end of the nineteenth century.

Bowl, Blue, Ribbed, Flared Rim, Pedestal Foot, Decorchemont, c.1925, 5 ⅞ x 6 In.	1625
Bowl, Cone Shape, Folded Side, Light Blue, Purple, Tessa Clegg, 1987, 5 ½ x 11 In. .... *illus*	625
Bowl, Round Top Opening, Swirls, Copper Trim, Keith Clayton, 6 x 17 In. .... *illus*	2560
Panel, Light Blue, Cats, Raised Borders, Liz Marx Studios, Late 1900s, 6 ½ x 4 ½ In.	59
Paperweight, Yellow Ground, Applied Flower, Leaves, Decorchemont, c.1890, 1 ¾ x 3 ¾ In. ...	715

Paris, Vase, Mantel, Scenic, Blue Ground, Black Rim Border, Round Base, 13 In., Pair $316

Stevens Auction Co.

TIP
Clean chrome with white vinegar or tea.

Patent Model, Refrigerator, Hinged Lid, Side Door, Wood, Metal Interior, Spout, Tag, J.K. Ludlow, 1879 $1,000

Fairfield Auction

P

Pate-De-Verre, Bowl, Cone Shape, Folded Side, Light Blue, Purple, Tessa Clegg, 1987, 5 ½ x 11 In. $625

Heritage Auctions

Pate-De-Verre, Bowl, Round Top Opening, Swirls, Copper Trim, Keith Clayton, 6 x 17 In. $2,560

Alex Cooper Auctioneers

Pate-Sur-Pate, Plaque, Art Nouveau Style, Semi-Clad Nude, White, Blue Ground, Translucent, Frame, 17 x 21 In. $460

Blackwell Auctions

P

Plaque, Square, Blue Pedestal, Fruit, In Yellow Circle, Ribbed Orange Ground, Frame, 26 x 26 In..	594
Plaque, White Flowering Plants, Dark Brown Ground, Curved Top, France, c.1890, 5 x 4 In..	163
Urn, Mottled Brown, Snake Handles, Flared Rim, Copper Electroplated Base, Seth Randal, 12 In.	1375
Vase, Squat, Flared, Leafy Tendrils, Gree n, Pedestal Foot, Signed, Charlie Miner, 5 x 8 In. ...	1003

PATE-SUR-PATE

Pate-sur-pate means paste on paste. The design was made by painting layers of slip on the ceramic piece until a relief decoration was formed. The method was developed at the Sevres factory in France about 1850. It became even more famous at the English Minton factory about 1870. It has since been used by many potters to make both pottery and porcelain wares.

Jardiniere, Figural, Frog Shape, White, Textured Skin, Bulging Eyes, Chinese, c.1790, 7 x 11 x 8 In...	780
Plaque, Art Nouveau Style, Semi-Clad Nude, White, Blue Ground, Translucent, Frame, 17 x 21 In. *illus*	460
Plaque, Terpsichore, Blue, White Figures, Frame, Mabel G. Lewis, University City, 1913, 6 ½ x 4 In..	2250
Vase, Brown, Cartouche, Young Woman, Putto, Fishing, Gilt Trim, Ring Handles, 6 x 5 x 3 In., Pair	1200

PAUL REVERE POTTERY

Paul Revere Pottery was made at several locations in and around Boston, Massachusetts, between 1906 and 1942. The pottery was operated as a settlement house program for teenage girls. Many pieces were signed *S.E.G.* for Saturday Evening Girls. The artists concentrated on children's dishes and tiles. Decorations were outlined in black and filled with color.

Bowl, Landscape, Dark Blue Ground, Saturday Evening Girls, Albina Mangini, 1910s, 2 x 8 In....	2125
Bowl, Lotus Band, F. Levine, A. Mangini, S.E.G., 1911, 2 x 4 ½ In. .... *illus*	563
Bowl, Rabbits, Lettuce Patch, Graphite & Dappled Outline, Gray Glaze, 2 ¼ x 5 ½ In.	206
Plate, Bunnies On Border, Marked, S.E.G., 1916, 6 ¼ In. .... *illus*	813
Plate, Cabbage Border, Fannie Levine, S.E.G., 1914, 7 ¾ In. .... *illus*	344
Plate, Landscape Border, Eva Geneco, S.E.G., 1917, 6 ⅜ In. .... *illus*	531
Plate, Rabbits, Eating Cabbage, Yellow Matte Glaze, Rose Bacchini, 1911, 7 ⅝ In. .... *illus*	1500
Trivet, Landscape, Mustard Matte Glaze, Multicolor, Saturday Evening Girls, 5 ¾ In.	625
Vase, Tulip Band, Green, Dark Blue Ground, Glazed, Signed, JMD, 1926, 4 ⅜ x 3 ⅝ In. *illus*	688
Vase, Turquoise Glaze, Signed, Saturday Evening Girls, c.1925, 6 ¾ In.	59

PEACHBLOW

Peachblow glass was made by several factories beginning in the 1880s. New England Peachblow is a one-layer glass shading from red to white. Mt. Washington Peachblow shades from pink to bluish-white. Hobbs, Brockunier and Company of Wheeling, West Virginia, made Coral glass that it marketed as Peachblow. It shades from yellow to peach and is lined with white glass. Reproductions of all types of peachblow have been made. Related pieces may be listed under Webb Peachblow.

Biscuit Jar, Pink, Flowers, Silver Plate Top, Swing Handle, Satin, Enamel, Victorian, 7 ½ In..	127
Bride's Bowl, Compressed Shape, Ruffled Rim, Flowers, Glossy, Gilt, 1800s, 4 x 10 In.	211
Cruet, Coral, Glossy, Tricorner Mouth, Amber Handle, Hobbs, Brockunier, c.1886, 6 x 5 In. *illus*	234
Decanter, Red, Glossy, Twisted Reed Style Handle, Stopper, Art Glass, c.1890, 9 ½ In............	127
Lamp, Embossed Rib & Scroll, Flared Scalloped Rim, Slip Burner, Gloss, 1880s, 10 x 3 In. . *illus*	351
Vase, Bird, Branch & Blossom, Bulbous, 9 ¼ x 6 In. .... *illus*	125
Vase, Lily, 3-Petal Rim, Plush, Footed, Polished Pontil Mark, New England, 1800s, 14 x 5 In.	410
Vase, Narrow Spout, Dark Red, Orange, Cream Ground, Imperial, 10 ½ In............................	62
Vase, New England, Cased, 5-Griffin Stand, Satin Finish, 10 In. .... *illus*	649
Vase, Pink, Bird, Flowers, Satin, 7 ½ In.	219
Vase, Ribbed, Flared Top, Ruffled Rim, Bulbous, Mt. Washington, 5 In.	452
Vase, Stick, Wheeling, Bulbous Body, Long Necked, Gloss Glaze, 8 ½ In.	275

Paul Revere, Bowl, Lotus Band, F. Levine, A. Mangini, S.E.G., 1911, 2 x 4½ In.
$563

Paul Revere, Plate, Landscape Border, Eva Geneco, S.E.G., 1917, 6⅜ In.
$531

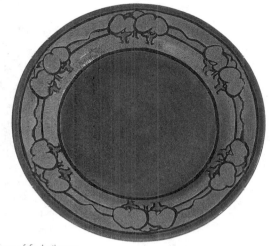

Toomey & Co. Auctioneers

Paul Revere, Plate, Bunnies On Border, Marked, S.E.G., 1916, 6¼ In.
$813

Toomey & Co. Auctioneers

Paul Revere, Plate, Rabbits, Eating Cabbage, Yellow Matte Glaze, Rose Bacchini, 1911, 7⅝ In.
$1,500

Toomey & Co. Auctioneers

Paul Revere, Plate, Cabbage Border, Fannie Levine, S.E.G., 1914, 7¾ In.
$344

Toomey & Co. Auctioneers

Paul Revere, Vase, Tulip Band, Green, Dark Blue Ground, Glazed, Signed, JMD, 1926, 4⅜ x 3⅝ In.
$688

oomey & Co. Auctioneers

Toomey & Co. Auctioneers

Peachblow, Cruet, Coral, Glossy, Tricorner Mouth, Amber Handle, Hobbs, Brockunier, c.1886, 6 x 5 In.
$234

Jeffrey S. Evans & Associates

Peachblow, Lamp, Embossed Rib & Scroll, Flared Scalloped Rim, Slip Burner, Gloss, 1880s, 10 x 3 In.
$351

Jeffrey S. Evans & Associates

Peachblow, Vase, Bird, Branch & Blossom, Bulbous, 9 ¼ x 6 In.
$125

Woody Auction

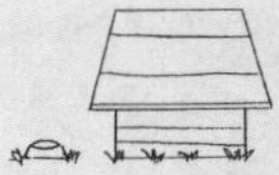

PEANUTS

Peanuts is the title of a comic strip created by cartoonist Charles M. Schulz (1922–2000). The strip, drawn by Schulz from 1950 to 2000, features a group of children, including Charlie Brown and his sister Sally, Lucy Van Pelt and her brother Linus, Peppermint Patty, and Pig Pen, and an imaginative and independent beagle named Snoopy. The Peanuts gang has also been featured in books, television shows, and a Broadway musical. The comic strip is being rerun in some newspapers.

Bank, Snoopy, Sailboat, Porcelain, Red, Yellow, Green, United Syndicate, 4½ In.	44
Book, He's Your Dog Charlie Brown, Hardcover, World Publishing, 1968	52
Cookie Cutter, Linus, Green, Plastic, Hallmark, 4¾ In.	12
Lunch Box, Dome Top, Have Lunch With Snoopy, American Thermos, 1968	75
Mobile, Wood, Musical, Charlie, Lucy, Snoopy, Linus, Sally, Nursey Originals, 1965, 16 x 14 In.	48
Pendant, Snoopy, Standing, 18K Gold, Top Loop, Signed, Cartier, Box, 1 x ¾ In. ...... *illus*	10625
Poster, Movie, Bon Voyage Charlie Brown, Paramount, 1980, 41½ x 27 In.	38
Toy, Sally, Blond, Pink Dress, Vinyl, Squeak, 1984, 6 In.	20
Toy, Snoopy Astronaut, Clear Bubble Helmet, Box, United Feature Syndicate, 9 In. ...... *illus*	216

PEARL

Pearl items listed here are made of the natural mother-of-pearl from shells. Such natural pearl has been used to decorate furniture and small utilitarian objects for centuries. The glassware known as mother-of-pearl is listed by that name. Opera glasses made with natural pearl shell are listed under Opera Glasses.

Box, Table, Arabesque, Bone, Mother-Of-Pearl, Star, Red Lined Interior, 3 x 8½ In., Pair	325
Magnifying Glass, Handle, Gilt, Marked, Donegan Optical, 17¼ In. ...... *illus*	305
Tie Clip, Mother-Of-Pearl, Surfboard Shape, 2¼ In.	16
Trinket Box, Mother-Of-Pearl, Brass, Round, 1950s, 2 In.	45

Pearl PEARLWARE

Pearlware is an earthenware made by Josiah Wedgwood in 1779. It was copied by other potters in England. Pearlware is only slightly different in color from creamware and for many years collectors have confused the terms. Wedgwood pieces are listed in the Wedgwood category in this book. Most pearlware with mocha designs is listed under Mocha.

Bowl, Brown & White Splotches, Orange Ground, Green Rim, Late 1700s, 2⅜ x 4½ In.	380
Bowl, Chinoiserie, Footed, Blue Style Pagoda Exterior, Floral Interior, c.1780, 4⅝ In.	187
Bowl, Flowering Vine, Multicolor, Purple Luster Trim, England, Early 1800s, 5 x 9⅞ In.	50
Creamer, Cow, Milkers, Spatterware, Painted, 5½ In., Pair	762
Figurine, Deer, Lying Down, Bocage Back, Molded Green Base, Staffordshire, c.1815, 4⅜ In. *illus*	468
Figurine, St. Mark, Holding Book, Blue Flowers, Green Base, Staffordshire, 7½ In.	113
Jug, Farmer, Hand Painted, Agricultural Tools, Applied Handle, Early 1800s, 6½ In.	469
Mug, Brown & Salmon Bands, Wavy Lines, Slip, Molded Handle, Early 1800s, 5 x 5 In.	344
Mug, Trailed Slip, Branches, Brown, Black, White, Olive Field, Strap Handle, Early 1800s, 3 In.	688
Plate, Eagle, Union Shield, Arrows, Yellow Border, Octagonal, 1800s, 6 In.	5856
Salt, White, Brown, Black Cable, Blue Slip Ground, Flared Foot, Early 1800s, 2⅛ In.	813
Tankard, Wavy Blue Lines, Flower Border, White, 1776, 4 In.	1270
Vase, Spill, 3 Sheep, Tree Trunk, Flowers, Greenery, England, Early 1800s, 7 x 7¾ x 4 In.	293

PEKING GLASS

Peking glass is a Chinese cameo glass first made popular in the eighteenth century. The Chinese have continued to make this layered glass in the old manner, and many new pieces are now available that could confuse the average buyer.

Bowl, Green Water Lilies, White Ground, Ruffled Rim, Footed, 1950s, 3 x 7 In.	9

Bowl, Green, White, Carved, Lotus Petal, Wood Stand, 3 ¼ In., Pair .... *illus* 671
Snuff Bottle, Silver Mounted Cabochon, Apple Green Ground, Early 1900s, 2 ²³⁄₆₄ In. 150
Snuff Bottle, White, Yellow, Gray, Relief Crickets, Oval, Beaded Metal Lid, c.1880, 3 In. 148
Vase, Baluster, Marbleized, Swirling Red, Molded Rim, 1800s, 10 ¼ In., Pair....................... 266
Vase, Baluster, Opaque White, Red Overlay, Flowers, Rocks, 1900s, 11 x 4 In. 125
Vase, White Ground, Sapphire Blue Design, Mythical Animals, Chinese, 1900s, 14 In., Pair *illus* 177

PEN

Pens replaced hand-cut quills as writing instruments in 1780, when the
first steel pen point was made in England. But it was 100 years before the commercial
pen was a common item. The fountain pen was invented in the 1830s but was not made
in quantity until the 1880s. All types of old pens are collected, everything from quill
pens to fountain pens. Float pens feature small objects floating in a liquid as part of
the handle. Advertising pens are listed in the Advertising section of this book.

Cartier, Ballpoint, Les Must De Cartier, Gold Plate, Flat, Vertical Ridges, Box...................... 350
Chesterfield, Fountain, 2 Tone, 18K M Nib, Inkwell, Tiger's Eye Style Case, Krone, 4 ¾ In..... 89
Dupont, Fountain, Montaparnasse Chairman, Amber Lacquer, 18K Gold Nib, 1989, 5 ½ In. *illus* 561
Eversharp, Fountain, Wahl Oxford, Marbleized Ruby, Celluloid Barrel, 14K Nib, 5 In........... 59
Montblanc, Ballpoint, Orange & Black Resin, Ernest Hemmingway, 5 ¼ In........................... 561
Montblanc, Fountain, Louis XIV, 18K Nib Size F, Vermeil Silver Case, 5 ½ In. .... *illus* 2360
Montblanc, Fountain, Meisterstuck, Black, Nib Stamped, 4810, Case, c.1980, 5 In. 380
Parker, Fountain, Art Deco Style, Vermeil Silver Cap, Jewel Ends, 5 ¼ In........................... 443
Parker, Fountain, Duofold Spider Web, 18K Gold Nib, Wood Case, 5 ¼ In............................. 708
Pelikan, Fountain, Vermeil Silver, Oxidized Relief Decor, 18K Gold Nib, 5 ½ In. 1180
Waterman, Fountain, Edson, Gold Plated, 18K Gold Nib, Hard Case, 6 In. .... *illus* 590

PEN & PENCIL
Montblanc, Mechanical Pencil, Fountain Pen, Meisterstuck, 14K Gold, Germany, c.1950, 5 In. .. 1440

PENCIL

Pencils were invented, so it is said, in 1565. The eraser was not added
to the pencil until 1858. The automatic pencil was invented in 1863. Collectors today
want advertising pencils or automatic pencils of unusual design. Boxes and sharpeners
for pencils are also collected. Advertising pencils are listed in the Advertising category.
Pencil boxes are listed in the Box category.

Cartier, Retractable, Bamboo, 18K Gold, Marked, Box, France, c.1940, 4 ½ In. 438
Mechanical, 14k Gold, Bail At Top, Extendible, c.1900, 3 ¼ In. 395

PENNSBURY POTTERY

Pennsbury Pottery worked in Morrisville, Pennsylvania, from 1950 to
1971. Full sets of dinnerware as well as many decorative items were made. Pieces are
marked with the name of the factory.

Pennsbury Pottery

Figurine, Wood Duck, Head Raised, Leafy Base, 10 In. 180
Pie Plate, Sgraffito, 2 Birds, Flowers, Text Around Rim, Shoo Fly Pie, 9 ½ In. .... *illus* 44

PEPSI-COLA

Pepsi-Cola, the drink and the name, was invented in 1898 but was
not trademarked until 1903. The logo was changed from an elaborate
script to the modern block letters in 1963. Several different logos have been used. Until
1951, the words *Pepsi* and *Cola* were separated by two dashes. These bottles are called
"double dash." In 1951 the modern logo with a single hyphen was introduced. All types
of advertising memorabilia are collected, and reproductions are being made.

Clock, The Light Refreshment, Plastic, Light-Up, Dualite Displays Inc., c.1960, 16 ½ In. *illus* 1169

Peachblow, Vase, New England, Cased,
5-Griffin Stand, Satin Finish, 10 In.
$649

Peanuts, Pendant, Snoopy, Standing,
18K Gold, Top Loop, Signed, Cartier, Box,
1 x ¾ In.
$10,625

Peanuts, Toy, Snoopy Astronaut, Clear
Bubble Helmet, Box, United Feature
Syndicate, 9 In.
$216

P

PEPSI-COLA

Pearl, Magnifying Glass, Handle, Gilt, Marked, Donegan Optical, 17¼ In.
$305

Neal Auction Company

Pearlware, Figurine, Deer, Lying Down, Bocage Back, Molded Green Base, Staffordshire, c.1815, 4⅜ In.
$468

Jeffrey S. Evans & Associates

Peking Glass, Bowl, Green, White, Carved, Lotus Petal, Wood Stand, 3¼ In., Pair
$671

Nadeau's Auction Gallery

TIP
Keep your collection of glassware away from the speakers of your sound system. Heavy bass and high-pitched sounds can crack the glass.

Peking Glass, Vase, White Ground, Sapphire Blue Design, Mythical Animals, Chinese, 1900s, 14 In., Pair
$177

Leland Little Auctions

Pen, Dupont, Fountain, Montaparnasse Chairman, Amber Lacquer, 18K Gold Nib, 1989, 5½ In.
$561

Leland Little Auctions

Pen, Montblanc, Fountain, Louis XIV, 18K Nib Size F, Vermeil Silver Case, 5½ In.
$2,360

Leland Little Auctions

Pen, Waterman, Fountain, Edson, Gold Plated, 18K Gold Nib, Hard Case, 6 In.
$590

Leland Little Auctions

Pennsbury, Pie Plate, Sgraffito, 2 Birds, Flowers, Text Around Rim, Shoo Fly Pie, 9½ In.
$44

Conestoga Auction Company

Fast-Food Glasses
If you collect the decorated glasses from fast-food restaurants, never wash them in the dishwasher. The heat and detergent will change the coloring and lower the value.

Pepsi-Cola, Clock, The Light Refreshment, Plastic, Light-Up, Dualite Displays Inc., c.1960, 16½ In.
$1,169

Rich Penn Auctions

Cooler, Aluminum, Square Shape, Handle, Engraved, Marked, 16 x 17 x 9 In. .... *illus*	184
Cooler, Can. Thermo-Keep, Cylindrical, Vinyl, Insulated, Nappy......................................	17
Dispenser, Chromed Metal, Celluloid, Press Pump Plays Jingle, 1920s, 20 In.......................	230
Sign, A Nickel Drink Worth A Dime, 5 Cents, Double Dash, 1930s, 12 ⅜ x 5 ⅜ In....................	1107
Sign, Bottle Cap, Drink Pepsi-Cola, 3-D, Stout Sign Co., St. Louis, Missouri, 30 In. .... 120 to 170	
Sign, Bottle Cap, Stout Sign Co., 20 In...	615
Thermometer, Embossed, Bottle Cap Logo, Yellow Ground, 1955, 27 In. .... *illus*	554
Thermometer, Weather Cold Or Weather Hot, Double Dash, Embossed. Rounded Rim, 27 x 7¼ In..	3075
Tip Tray, 1909 Calendar Girl, Tin Lithograph, Soda Fountain Scene, 6 x 4 In.	1935
Vending Machine, Drink Pepsi-Cola, Hits The Spot, Vendo 81, Script Logo, 59 x 27 In.........	6875

PERFUME BOTTLE

Perfume bottles are made of cut glass, pressed glass, art glass, silver, metal, jade, enamel, and even plastic or porcelain. Although the small bottle to hold perfume was first made before the time of ancient Egypt, it is the nineteenth- and twentieth-century examples that interest today's collector. DeVilbiss Company has made atomizers of all types since 1888 but no longer makes the perfume bottle tops so popular with collectors. These were made from 1920 to 1968. The glass bottle may be by any of many manufacturers even if the atomizer is marked *DeVilbiss*. The word *factice,* which often appears in ads, refers to large store display bottles. Glass or porcelain examples may be found under the appropriate name such as Lalique, Czechoslovakia, Glass-Bohemian, etc.

Cut Glass, Cranberry To Clear, Arched Step, Bull's-Eye Highlights, Stopper. 10¾ In. ... *illus*	400
Cut Glass, Double Miter & Hobnail, Hinged Cap, Gilt, Silver, Monogram, London, Late 1800s, 11 In..	63
Daniel Lotton, Ruffled Collar, Turquoise Blue Flower, Opal Teardrop Stopper, 9 ⅝ x 5 ¾ In...	847
Double Miters, Hobnail, Hinged Gilt Silver Cap, Lay Flat, Late 1870s, 11 In.	63
Francis Whittemore, Paperweight, Millville Rose Style, Yellow Rose, Stopper, 1950s, 4 In..	199
Glass, Gilt Stopper, Round Gilt Brass Holder, Crest, Eagle, Leaves, 1890s, 5 x 4 In...........	313
Glass, Purple & Green, Faceted, Clear Stopper, Signed, 1989, 5 ½ In. .... *illus*	75
Glass, White Iridescent, Round, Applied Green Threading, Green Stopper, Dabber, 3 ½ x 3 In.	180
Hattie Carnegie, Bust, Woman, Goldtone, Short Curly Hair, Art Deco, France, 4 ½ In. *illus*	37
Josh Simpson, Ball Shape Stopper, Signed, 1986, 4 ½ In..	35
Porcelain, Aqua, Dotted Circles, Stopper, Chain, Ormolu Mounts, Continental, 7 ¾ In. *illus*	310
Satin Glass, Round, Shaded Blue, Loops, Chased Silver Cap, England, 2 ½ In........................	124

PETERS & REED

Peters & Reed Pottery Company of Zanesville, Ohio, was founded by John D. Peters and Adam Reed in 1897. Chromal, Landsun, Montene, Pereco, and Persian are some of the art lines that were made. The company, which became Zane Pottery in 1920 and Gonder Pottery in 1941, closed in 1957. Peters & Reed pottery was unmarked.

Bowl, Moss Aztec, Dragonfly, 5 ¾ In..	125
Tankard, Grape & Leaf Sprig, Amber, Green, Dark Blue, 5 ½ In.	79
Vase, Chromal, Scenic, 2 People Walking, Red Headed Woman In Blue Dress, 5 ¾ In. .. *illus*	605
Vase, Shouldered, Drip, Tan & Green, 8 ¾ In.	176

PEWABIC POTTERY

PEWABIC

Pewabic Pottery was founded by Mary Chase Perry Stratton in 1903 in Detroit, Michigan. The company made many types of art pottery, including pieces with matte green glaze and an iridescent crystalline glaze. The company continued working until the death of Mary Stratton in 1961. It was reactivated by Michigan State University in 1968.

Tile, Turquoise, 2 Birds, Branch, Gold Luster Backdrop, Carved, Wood Frame, 10 ½ In. *illus*	182

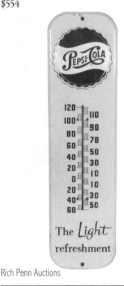

Pepsi-Cola, Cooler, Aluminum, Square Shape, Handle, Engraved, Marked, 16 x 17 x 9 In.
$184

Richard D. Hatch & Associates

Pepsi-Cola, Thermometer, Embossed, Bottle Cap Logo, Yellow Ground, 1955, 27 In.
$554

Rich Penn Auctions

Perfume Bottle, Cut Glass, Cranberry To Clear, Arched Step, Bull's-Eye Highlights, Stopper, 10¾ In.
$400

Woody Auction

Perfume Bottle, Glass, Purple & Green, Faceted, Clear Stopper, Signed, 1989, 5 ½ In.
$75

Julien's Auctions

Perfume Bottle, Hattie Carnegie, Bust, Woman, Goldtone, Short Curly Hair, Art Deco, France, 4 ½ In.
$37

Ron Rhoads Auctioneers

Perfume Bottle, Porcelain, Aqua, Dotted Circles, Stopper, Chain, Ormolu Mounts, Continental, 7 ¾ In.
$310

John McInnis Auctioneers

Peters & Reed, Vase, Chromal, Scenic, 2 People Walking, Red Headed Woman In Blue Dress, 5 ¾ In.
$605

Humler & Nolan

Pewabic, Tile, Turquoise, 2 Birds, Branch, Gold Luster Backdrop, Carved, Wood Frame, 10 ½ In.
$182

Humler & Nolan

Pewabic, Vase, Metallic Glaze, Bulbous, Round Rim, Obscured Mark, 5 ½ x 4 In.
$1,563

Treadway

Vase, Metallic Glaze, Bulbous, Round Rim, Obscured Mark, 5 ½ x 4 In. .... *illus* 1563

PEWTER

Pewter is a metal alloy of tin and lead. Some of the pewter made after 1840 has a slightly different composition and is called Britannia metal. This later type of pewter was worked by machine; the earlier pieces were made by hand. In the 1920s pewter came back into fashion and pieces were often marked *Genuine Pewter*. Eighteenth-, nineteenth-, and twentieth-century examples are listed here. Marks used by three pewter workshops are pictured.

Thomas Danforth
1727–1733

Timothy Boardman
1822–1825

William Will
1764–1798

Basin, Stephen Barnes, Molded Rim, Middletown, c.1800, 2¾ x 10¼ In.	976
Bowl, Sugar & Creamer, Napier Co., Nickel Plated, Brass, c.1935, 3 In. .... *illus*	750
Box, Hinged Lid, Sugar Bowl, Fluid Shape, Germany, Early 1900s, 3 x 4½ In.	48
Candlestick, Homan, Fluted Rim, Shape Column, Round Base, 1840s, 7 In., Pair	288
Chalice, H. Yale & Co., Domed, Stepped Base, Wallingford, c.1824, 7½ In.	192
Chocolate Pot, Lid, Acorn Finial, Wood Handle, August & Marie, 1868, 9 In.	177
Compote, Archibald Knox, Liberty & Co., Arts & Crafts, 3 Legs, Pierced, Glass Liner, 5 In.	1400
Dipper, Coconut, Shell Bowl, Concentric Swag Design, Wood Handle, Inlay, c.1850, 14½ In.	406
Figure, Soldiers, Standing, Engraved, Round Base, Continental, 18 In., Pair	256
Flagon, Boardman & Co., C-Scroll Handle, Thumblift, 8¼ x 5 In.	288
Flagon, Hinged Lid, Thumb Rest, Scroll Handle, Monogram, 1700s, 12½ In.	236
Flagon, Thomas D. & Sherman Boardman, Swelled Ribbed Finial, Scrolling Handle, c.1810, 11 In. ...	594
Flagon, Wine, Ludwig Roder, Spout, Lid, Engraved Vmbwertsg Ana Graf I, c.1798, 13 In........	125
Lamp, Oil, Disc Shape, 2 Magnifying Lenses, Eagle Touchmark, American, 1910s, 10¾ In., Pair	840
Mold, Candle, 24 Tubes, Bench Style, Red, Painted, Hardwood Frame, Late 1700s, 18 x 20½ In. *illus*	527
Mold, Ice Cream, Black Boy Choking Turkey, Early 1800s, 4 x 4 In.	123
Plate, Beaded Rim, Blakeslee Barns, 1812, 8 In., 4 Piece	380
Porringer, William Billings, Reticulated Handle, Rhode Island, c.1800, 5½ In....................	976
Tea Set, Gene Theobald, Wilcox Silver Plate Co., Black Handle, Bakelite, c.1928, 4 In............	2750
Teapot, Hexagonal, Gooseneck Spout, Foo Dog Finial, Cartouche, Chinese Export, 1900s, 7½ In.	59
Tray, Jade & Carnelian Stones, Birds, Flowers, Handles, Painted, 2 x 8 In.	406
Tray, Lily Pad Shape, 3 Frog Feet, Marked, 4½ In...	25
Trophy, Yacht Racing, Vase Shape, Leaves & Flowers, Mahogany Base, 1902, 15 In..........	213
Vase, Woman In Relief, Tree, Flowers, Flared, Handles, Art Nouveau, Germany, c.1905, 14 x 8 In.	840

PHOENIX GLASS

Phoenix Glass Company was founded in 1880 in Pennsylvania. The firm made commercial products, such as lampshades, bottles, and glassware. Collectors today are interested in the "Sculptured Artware" made by the company from the 1930s until the mid-1950s. Some pieces of Phoenix glass are very similar to those made by the Consolidated Lamp and Glass Company. Phoenix made Reuben Blue, lavender, and yellow pieces. These colors were not used by Consolidated. In 1970 Phoenix became a division of Anchor Hocking, which was sold to the Newell Group in 1987. The factory is still working.

Cruet, Clear Handle, Frosted, Applied Thread, Polished Pontil, 1880s, 6 In............................	140
Lamp, Bell Shape Shade, Skirted Ringed Base, Opalescent Stripe, Acorn Burner, 1880s, 7 x 3 In. *illus*	410
Lamp, Peacock, Blue Iridescent, Flared Glass Shade, Chain Pull, Carl Radke, 1979, 21 x 14 In. *illus*	527
Pitcher, Water, Pink Blossom, Branch, Blue, Yellow, White, Mottled Ground, 10 In..............	175
Tumbler, Honeycomb, Optic, Ruby Cased, Opal Glass, Factory Polished Rim, Red, c.1883, 3⅞ In. *illus*	293

Pewter, Bowl, Sugar & Creamer, Napier Co., Nickel Plated, Brass, c.1935, 3 In. $750

Wright

Pewter, Mold, Candle, 24 Tubes, Bench Style, Red, Painted, Hardwood Frame, Late 1700s, 18 x 20½ In. $527

Jeffrey S. Evans & Associates

Phoenix Glass, Lamp, Bell Shape Shade, Skirted Ringed Base, Opalescent Stripe, Acorn Burner, 1880s, 7 x 3 In. $410

Jeffrey S. Evans & Associates

P

Phoenix Glass, Lamp, Peacock, Blue Iridescent, Flared Glass Shade, Chain Pull, Carl Radke, 1979, 21 x 14 In. $527

Thomaston Place Auction Galleries

Phoenix Glass, Tumbler, Honeycomb, Optic, Ruby Cased, Opal Glass, Factory Polished Rim, Red, c.1883, 3 7/8 In. $293

Jeffrey S. Evans & Associates

Phonograph, Columbia, Graphophone, Oak, Horn, Disc, St. Louis, 1904, 12 3/4 x 12 3/4 In. $554

Hartzell's Auction Gallery Inc.

PHONOGRAPH

Phonographs, invented by Thomas Edison in 1877, have been made by many firms. This category also includes other items associated with the phonograph. Jukeboxes and Records are listed in their own categories.

Columbia, Graphophone, Oak, Horn, Disc, St. Louis, 1904, 12 3/4 x 12 3/4 In. .... *illus*	554
Continental, Suitcase Model, Faux Snakeskin, Portable, Windup, Side Crank, 7 x 13 3/4 x 10 1/2 In.	123
Edison, Amberola, Model 50, Cylinder, Hand Crank, Hinged Lid, Oak Case, c.1920, 16 1/2 In..	351
Edison, Amberola, Model BVIII, Cylinder, Tabletop, Crank, Marked, 15 1/2 x 13 1/4 x 16 In. *illus*	277
Edison, Standard, Cylinder, Oak Cabinet, Metal Horn, 1905, 11 1/2 x 13 In. .... *illus*	649
Edison, Standard, Cylinder, Oak Cabinet, Tall Crane, Painted, Morning Glory Horn, 1903, 37 In..	413
Edison, Standard, Oak, Japanned Plate, Nickel Trim, Black Paneled Horn, c.1920, 28 x 13 In.	438
Horn, Morning Glory, Red Interior, Early 1900s, 30 x 22 In.	300
Regina, Hexaphone, Model 101, 5 Cent, 6 Discs, Key, Coin-Operated, 1909, 26 x 49 x 18 In. ..	6765
Regina, Hexaphone, Model 104, 6 Cylinder, Oak Cabinet, Coin-Operated, 1915, 65 x 26 x 19 In..	8610
Silvertone, Mahogany Case, Tabletop, Disc, Early 1900s, 15 x 18 In. .... *illus*	50
Victor III, Oak Case, Molded Columns, Spear Tip Horn, Felt Turntable, c.1920, 32 x 16 In.....	2000
Victor III, Oak Case, Spear Tip Horn, Exhibition Reproducer, Felt Table, 1915, 32 In............	1600
Victor, Monarch, Gramophone, HMV Manor, Morning Glory Horn, Oak Cabinet, c.1910, 29 In.	502
Victrola, Model VV89, Oak, Cabinet, Extra Records, 1920s, 46 x 25 x 19 In.	400

PHONOGRAPH NEEDLE CASE

Phonograph needle cases of tin are collected today by music and phonograph enthusiasts and advertising addicts. The tins are very small, about 2 inches across, and often have attractive graphic designs lithographed on the top and sides.

Edison Bell, Sympathetic Chromic, Semi Permanent Needles, Brown, Blue, 1 1/2 In.	20
Embassy, Radiogram, Long Playing, Orange Lid, Sealed, England, 1950s, 1 1/2 In.	35
Happy, Mickey Mouse, Betty Boop, Felix The Cat, Green, Japan, 1930s, 2 1/4 x 1 3/5 In.............	100
Helvetia, Swiss Needles, B.1, Mountain Illustration, Red Border, 200 Needles, 1950, 1 3/8 x 2 In.	51
Songster, Soft Tone, Blue, Gold Sun, Bird On Branch, Paper Insert, J. Stead & Co., 1 3/8 x 2 In.	20

PHOTOGRAPHY

Photography items are listed here. The first photograph was a view from a window in France taken in 1826. The commercially successful photograph started with the daguerreotype introduced in 1839. Today all sorts of photographs and photographic equipment are collected. Albums were popular in Victorian times. Cartes de visite, popular after 1854, were mounted on 2 1/2-by-4-inch cardboard. Cabinet cards were introduced in 1866. These were mounted on 4 1/4-by-6 1/2-inch cards. Stereo views are listed under Stereo Card. Stereoscopes are listed in their own section.

Albumen, Abraham Lincoln, Portrait, Oval, Mat, Henry D. Warren, Frame, 1865, 8 x 6 1/2 In. ..	5938
Albumen, Infantryman, Harden West, Holding Rifle, Co. H., E. Jacobs, c.1862, 7 1/4 x 5 1/4 In.	938
Ambrotype, Confederate Lieutenant, Sidney A. Hinton, North Carolina, 1861, 1/6 Plate.........	1121
Ambrotype, Confederate Soldier, Thermoplastic Union Case, Octagonal, Early 1860s, 1/6 Plate *illus*	2500
Ambrotype, Occupational, Ironsmith, Posed, Holding, Hammer, Gilt Frame, c.1860, 3 3/4 x 3 1/4 In.	177
Cabinet Card, Strong Man, Lifting 4 Men On Barrel, Sword Bros., York, Pa., c.1890, 6 x 4 In..	385
Camera, Folmer & Schwing, R.B. Tele Graflex, Box Shape, 2 Photo Plates, 8 x 6 1/2 x 8 In......	75
Camera, Leica, 35 mm, Serial No. S7625, Black, Silver Hardware	861
Camera, Movie, Paillard Bolex, Leather Case, Switzerland, 1940, 13 x 10 In.	875
Carte De Visite, Carpetbagger, Holding Pouch & Umbrella, Twining & Twifords, c.1866	500
Carte De Visite, George Armstrong Custer, Brigadier General, Brady, c.1864 .... *illus*	938
Carte De Visite, Group Of Officers, Maine, Oval, Wood Frame, 12 1/4 x 14 1/2 In.	406
Carte De Visite, Kit Carson, Mountain Man, Black Of Boston, c.1868 ....*illus*	2500
Carte De Visite, Private Everard I. Drisko, Bugler, Standing, California Battalion, c.1863	127
Carte De Visite, Robert E. Lee, Autographed, C.E. Jones & Vannerson .... *illus*	4375
Carte De Visite, Stone Church, Centreville, Albumen, Barnard & Gibson, 12 x 14 In.	438
Carte De Visite, Union Civil War Soldier, Seated, Holding Violin, 10 x 14 In..........................	406

Phonograph, Edison, Amberola, Model
BVIII, Cylinder, Tabletop, Crank, Marked, 15
½ x 13 ¼ x 16 In.
$277

Hartzell's Auction Gallery Inc.

Phonograph, Edison, Standard, Cylinder,
Oak Cabinet, Metal Horn, 1905, 11 ½ x 13 In.
$649

Leland Little Auctions

Phonograph, Silvertone, Mahogany Case,
Tabletop, Disc, Early 1900s, 15 x 18 In.
$50

elkirk Auctioneers & Appraisers

Photography, Ambrotype, Confederate
Soldier, Thermoplastic Union Case,
Octagonal, Early 1860s, ⅙ Plate
$2,500

Cowan's Auctions

Photography, Carte De Visite, George
Armstrong Custer, Brigadier General, Brady,
c.1864
$938

Cowan's Auctions

Photography, Carte De Visite, Kit Carson,
Mountain Man, Black Of Boston, c.1868
$2,500

Cowan's Auctions

Photography, Carte De Visite, Robert E. Lee,
Autographed, C.E. Jones & Vannerson
$4,375

Cowan's Auctions

Photography, Photograph, Gerald R. Ford,
Betty Ford, Signed, Frame, 10 x 8 In.
$195

Freeman's

Photography, Tintype, Abraham Lincoln,
Cheeks & Lips Tinted, Beardstown Portrait,
c.1860, ⅙ Plate
$18,750

Cowan's Auctions

P

Piano Baby, Baby, Sitting, Toe To Mouth, Knees Bent, Blond, Nude, Bisque, Heubach, 8 x 10 x 7 In.
$400

Richard Opfer Auctioneering, Inc.

TIP

Rearrange your furniture so valuable silver or paintings can't be seen from the street.

Piano Baby, Girl, Sitting, Hand Raised, Yellow Dress, Gold Dots, Blue Trim, Bisque, 9 ½ x 11 In.
$62

Kodner Galleries, Inc.

Pickard, Mug, Ginko, Cream Ground, Gold Trim, Signed, Max Rost Leroy, c.1903, 4 ¾ In.
$225

Woody Auction

Carte De Visite, W.T. Sherman & His Generals, Mathew Brady, 1865, 19 x 24 In.	1500
Carte De Visite, William Watts Davis, Brigadier General, Albumen, 4 x 6 In.	250
Daguerreotype, U.S. Marines Officer, Mexican War, Hair Reliquary, Oval, c.1846, 2 ½ x 2 In.	761
Photograph, Bement Barber Shop, 2 Chairs, Mug Racks, Frame, c.1895, 12 x 15 In.	98
Photograph, Certificate, Colorado Senators, Signed, Dwight D. Eisenhower, 1950s, 8 x 10 In.	325
Photograph, Gerald R. Ford, Betty Ford, Signed, Frame, 10 x 8 In. .... *illus*	195
Photograph, Lincoln, Bust, Oval, George B. Ayers, Wood Frame, 12 x 14 In.	1750
Photograph, Lou Henry Hoover, Inscription, Signed, Harris & Ewing, Washington, D.C., 11 x 8 In.	260
Tintype, Abraham Lincoln, Cheeks & Lips Tinted, Beardstown Portrait, c.1860, ⅙ Plate *illus*	18750
Tintype, Elliot Rice, Union Officer, Horse, Open Tent, Leather Case, ¼ Plate	3375
Tintype, Oliver & Rufus Caldwell, Brothers, Confederate, Tennessee, Frame, 4 ¼ In.	413
Tintype, Sergeant Jacob Darst, Color Bearer, 80th Ohio Volunteers	813

PIANO BABY

Piano baby is a collector's term. About 1880, the well-decorated home had a shawl on the piano. Bisque figures of babies were designed to help hold the shawl in place. They usually range in size from 6 to 18 inches. Most of the figures were made in Germany. Reproductions are being made. Other piano babies may be listed under manufacturers' names.

Baby, Lying, On Back, Touching Toes, White Gown, Blue Trim, Bisque, Heubach, 5 ¼ x 8 ½ In.	150
Baby, On Stomach, Rosy Cheeks, Brown Molded Hair, Puppy, Bisque, Germany, 9 x 4 In.	71
Baby, Sitting, Legs Crossed, Curly Blond Hair, Yellow Dress, Porcelain, 12 In.	148
Baby, Sitting, Reaching For Toe, Blond Hair, White Smock, Sunburst Mark, Heubach, 10 In.	96
Baby, Sitting, Toe To Mouth, Knees Bent, Blond, Nude, Bisque, Heubach, 8 x 10 x 7 In. *illus*	400
Girl, Sitting, Hand Raised, Yellow Dress, Gold Dots, Blue Trim, Bisque, 9 ½ x 11 In. ..... *illus*	62

PICKARD

Pickard China Company was started in 1893 by Wilder Pickard. Hand-painted designs were used on china purchased from other sources. In the 1930s, the company began to make its own china wares in Chicago, Illinois. The company made a line of limited edition plates and bowls in the 1970s and 1980s. It now makes many types of porcelains.

Pickard/Edgerton Art Studio 1893–1894   Pickard/Pickard Studios, Inc. 1925–1930   Pickard, Inc. 1938–present

Bowl, Stylized Tulips, Luster, White Center, Gold Border, Signed, Fish, c.1905, 9 In.	90
Cake Plate, Twin Tulip, Cream Ground, Leaf, Gold Trim, Signed, Skoner, c.1905, 11 ¾ In.	150
Dish, Italian Garden, Roses, Lake, Gold Trim, Pierced Bird Handles, Signed, Gasper, 8 In.	125
Gravy Boat, Attached Underplate, Orange Poppies, Gold Trim, Scalloped Rim, 3 ¾ x 6 ¾ In.	108
Mug, Ginko, Cream Ground, Gold Trim, Signed, Max Rost Leroy, c.1903, 4 ¾ In. .... *illus*	225
Pitcher, Cherries On Branch, Rococo Handle, Gilt, Hand Painted, Early 1900s, 7 ½ In.	219
Pitcher, Cider, Strawberries, Leaves, Blossom, Gold Trim, Signed, J. Beitler, 8 In.	450
Planter, Aura Argenta Linear, Cream, Gold Panels, Silver Trim, Marked, 5 ½ x 5 ½ In. *illus*	250
Vase, Cornflower, Leaves, Gold Ground, Cobalt Blue, 2 Handles, Frank Yeschek, c.1905, 8 x 5 In..	700
Vase, Gold Painted, Landscape On Shoulder, Scattered Pink Roses, Artist Signed, 7 x 3 ¾ In.	360
Vase, Vellum, Walled Garden, Signed, Curtis Marker, Early 1900s, 9 In. .... *illus*	89

PICTURE

Pictures, silhouettes, and other small decorative objects framed to hang on the wall are listed here. Some other types of pictures are listed in the Print and Painting categories.

Calligraphy, Leaping Stag, Pen & Ink, 1800s, 16 x 20 ¼ In. .... *illus*	26
Collage, 3-D, Mixed Media, Plastic, Glass, Wire Screening, Ceramic, Jo Warner, 1966, 4 x 5 In.	2
Collage, Horse Blinders East, Silkscreen, James Rosenquist, Dated, 1972, 37 x 69 In.	175

Diorama, 2-Masted Sloop, White Sails, Orange & White Hull, Painted, Early 1900s, 20 x 16 In...	200
Drawing, Architectural, Pen & Ink, Arched Doorway, Signed, William B. Halliday, 1920, 17 x 10¼ In..	94
Drawing, Friendship, Heart & Poem, Frame, Thomas Jefferson & Rebecca Ritchards, 1862, 10 x 8 In..	105
Drawing, Gothic Revival House, Bucolic, Watercolor, Giltwood Frame, 1800s, 11 x 14 In.	1638
Drawing, Locomotive, Lackawanna & Western Railroad, John W. Elder, Wood Frame, 25 x 56 In.	1512
Drawing, Sanctuary Lamp, Colored Pencil, St. Francis Xavier Church, Alfonso Iannelli, 19 In. ..	938
Drawing, Texas Shield, Charcoal, On Paper, Jesus Bautista Moroles, Frame, 41 x 29 In.........	531
Drawing, The Boxer & The Fight, Ink & Watercolor, Signed, John Groth, 27¼ x 40½ In.	325
Drawing, Woman & Child, Raphael Soyer, Wood Frame, 13 x 8½ In.	118
Drawing, Woman & Horse, Colored Pencil, Signed, Carlo Canevari, Frame, 18 x 15 In..........	1500
Etching, Vedute Di Roma, Mat, Frame, Giovanni Battista Piranesi, 1800s, 18 x 28 In.	502
Featherwork, Eagle, Spread Wings, Union Shield, Patriotic, Wood Frame, 15½ x 19 In........	163
Needlework, Girl Holding Cat, Dog To Right, Landscape, Silk, Wool, c.1810, Frame, 9 x 5½ In.	213
Needlework, God Bless America, Eagle, Flag, Morris Edelman, Frame, 1900s, 18 x 18 In. *illus*	313
Needlework, Hunter, 2 Dogs, Silk Tent Stitch, Wool, Queen Anne, Frame, Early 1700s, 13 x 11 In. *illus*	6150
Needlework, Man Riding Large Dog, 2 Cats, Wool, Gilt Molded Frame, 1880s, 18½ x 19¾ In.	439
Needlework, Memorial, Silk & Chenille, George Washington, Frame, Early 1800s, 11 x 12 In.	2440
Needlework, Memorial, Silk, Woman, Painted Face, House, 2 Trees, Frame, Early 1800s, 15 x 17 In.	625
Needlework, Memorial, Young Woman Mourns At Monument, Giltwood Frame, Early 1800s, 12 In.	2700
Needlework, Orpheus Playing Lyre, Animals, Frame, 1700s, 7¾ x 10¾ In.	4392
Needlework, Paradise, Adam & Eve, Embroidery, Wool, Silk, Mary Tombafon, c.1811, 20 x 15¾ In.	861
Needlework, Pastoral, Oval, Oak, Arts & Crafts, Carved, Frame, 1894, 11 x 9 In....................	177
Needlework, Pastoral, Sheep, Sitting, Tree, Silk, Painted, Frame, 1800s, 11½ x 10 In..........	325
Needlework, Patriotic, Eagle, Spread Wings, Flag, Silk, Wood Frame, 1910s, 15¼ x 14½ In. ..*illus*	176
Needlework, Religious, Moses, Presenting 10 Commandments, Wood Frame, 32 x 30 In.	378
Needlework, Ship, Flowering Vine, Sailor & Wife, Swagged Curtain, Woolwork, Frame, 1800s, 17 In.	750
Needlework, Stumpwork, Silk, Woman, Lambs, England, Frame, 1800s, 20 x 17 In.	344
Needlework, Tree, Castle, Embroidery, Silk, Metallic Thread, Frame, 1600s, 11½ x 17 In.	1830
Needlework, Young Woman, Playing Piano, Sheep, Barn, Embroidery, Silk, Gilt Frame, 13 x 10 In.	246
Pastel, On Paper, Portrait, Redheaded Boy, Holding Book, Black Frame, 1800s, 14 x 12 In....	266
Pen & Ink, On Paper, Squirrel, On Branch, Spencerian, E.L. Burnett, Frame, 8¾ x 9 In. ... *illus*	570
Pencil, On Paper, Gouache, 2 Women, Signed, Alphonse Maria Mucha, Czechia, Frame, 25 x 19 In.	6563
Scherenschnitte, Scalloped, Medallion, Turquoise Blue Ground, Frame, 9 x 13 In. .... *illus*	177
Scroll, Hanging, Ink & Color, Landscape, Hermit Scholars, Shen Xiang Xie, 1941, 51 x 13 In..	1500
Silhouette, Mr. & Mrs. Samuel Dyer, Standing, Face To Face, August Edouart, 12¼ x 10 In...	277
Silhouette, Woman, Hollow Cut, Wood Frame, 1800s, 15½ x 11¼ In. .... *illus*	63
Theorem, Oil, On Velvet, Basket Of Fruit, Painted Pine Frame, 1800s, 15 x 17 In............	229
Wall Sculpture, Pompon Design, Metal, Gold, Curtis Jere, 60 x 20 In..............................	219
Watercolor & Gouache, On Paper, Portrait, Folk Art, Josiah Lyttleton, Frame, 5½ x 4¾ In. .	188
Watercolor, Jazz Band, 4 Men, Playing Instruments, Leo Meiersdorff, Frame, 1966, 19 x 25 In..	438
Watercolor, Lord & Lady John Sackville, Duke Of Dorset, S. Cooper, Frame, 1700s, 6 x 9 In. ..*illus*	1250
Watercolor, Madonna, Red Dress, Blue Mantle, Landscape, Brass Frame, 1800s, 3⅝ x 3 In.	89
Watercolor, Portrait, Man, Monogram, WWW, Oval Locket Frame, c.1830, 3⅜ x 2⅞ In. ..*illus*	1534
Watercolor, Sailing Rig With Lifeboat, Ernest C. Towler, Wood Frame, 18 x 21 In.	266
Watercolor, Wedding Memorial, Landscape, Pennsylvania, Carved Frame, 19¼ x 23¾ In...	1125
Wax, Lovers Scene, Seated, Beneath Tree, Germany, Gilt Frame, Early 1900s, 6¼ In.............	24

PICTURE FRAMES *are listed in this book in the Furniture category under Frame.*

PILLIN

W + P

Pillin

Pillin pottery was made by Polia (1909–1992) and William (1910–1985) Pillin, who set up a pottery in Los Angeles in 1948. William shaped, glazed, and fired the clay, and Polia painted the pieces, often with elongated figures of women, children, flowers, birds, fish, and other animals. The company closed in 2014. Pieces are marked with a stylized Pillin signature.

Vase, 3 Women, Birds, Glazed, Signed, 1960s, 5¼ x 6⅝ In. .... *illus*	500
Vase, Bottle Shape, Blue Ground, Woman's Portrait On Front & Back, Signed, 7½ In.	308
Vase, Horse, Brown Glaze, Earthenware, Footed, Signed, c.1960, 5¾ x 4½ In. .... *illus*	563

Pickard, Planter, Aura Argenta Linear, Cream, Gold Panels, Silver Trim, Marked, 5½ x 5½ In.
$250

Woody Auction

Pickard, Vase, Vellum, Walled Garden, Signed, Curtis Marker, Early 1900s, 9 In.
$89

Leland Little Auctions

Picture, Calligraphy, Leaping Stag, Pen & Ink, 1800s, 16 x 20¼ In.
$263

Pook & Pook

P

Picture, Needlework, God Bless America, Eagle, Flag, Morris Edelman, Frame, 1900s, 18 x 18 In.
$313

Eldred's

Picture, Needlework, Hunter, 2 Dogs, Silk Tent Stitch, Wool, Queen Anne, Frame, Early 1700s, 13 x 11 In.
$6,150

Brunk Auctions

Picture, Needlework, Patriotic, Eagle, Spread Wings, Flag, Silk, Wood Frame, 1910s, 15 ¼ x 14 ½ In.
$176

Jeffrey S. Evans & Associates

Picture, Pen & Ink, On Paper, Squirrel, On Branch, Spencerian, E.L. Burnett, Frame, 8 ¾ x 9 In.
$570

Garth's Auctioneers & Appraisers

Picture, Scherenschnitte, Scalloped, Medallion, Turquoise Blue Ground, Frame, 9 x 13 In.
$177

Leland Little Auctions

Shadow Portraits
Silhouettes were called "shadow portraits," "black profiles," "shadowgraphs," or "skiagrams."

Picture, Silhouette, Woman, Hollow Cut, Wood Frame, 1800s, 15 ½ x 11 ¼ In.
$63

Pook & Pook

Picture, Watercolor, Lord & Lady John Sackville, Duke Of Dorset, S. Cooper, Frame, 1700s, 6 x 9 In.
$1,250

Charlton Hall Auctions

Picture, Watercolor, Portrait, Man, Monogram, WWW, Oval Locket Frame, c.1830, 3 ⅜ x 2 ⅞ In.
$1,534

Leland Little Auctions

Pillin, Vase, 3 Women, Birds, Glazed, Signed, 1960s, 5 ¼ x 6 ⅝ In.
$500

Toomey & Co. Auctioneers

PINCUSHION DOLL

Pincushion dolls are not really dolls and often were not even pincushions. Some collectors use the term "half-doll." The top half of each doll was made of porcelain. The edge of the half-doll was made with several small holes for thread, and the doll was stitched to a fabric body with a voluminous skirt. The finished figure was used to cover a hot pot of tea, powder box, pincushion, whiskbroom, or lamp. They were made in sizes from less than an inch to over 9 inches high. Most date from the early 1900s to the 1950s. Collectors often find just the porcelain doll without the fabric skirt.

Woman, Blond Mohair Wig, Nude Torso, Reading Letter, Lace Skirt, Karl Schneider, Germany, 4½ In.	108
Woman, Bonnet, Feathers, Gold Silk Pincushion, Gilt Shoes, Schneider, Germany, c.1915, 11 In.	180
Woman, Molded Blond Hair, Feather Headdress, Pink Dress, Hands Raised, Germany, 6½ In. *illus*	156
Woman, Nude, Arms Extended, Rose, Bisque, Germany, Dressel & Kister, c.1910, 5½ In.	270
Woman, Nude, Head Raised, Hands Together, Art Deco, Germany, Dressel & Kister, c.1900, 5 In. *illus*	122
Woman, Purple Lined Bonnet, Folded Hands, White Ruffled Skirt, Purple Bow, 6 x 6 In. *illus*	36

PIPE

Pipes have been popular since tobacco was introduced to Europe. Carved wood, porcelain, ivory, and glass pipes and accessories may be listed here.

Box, Curly Maple, Scrolled Edges & Crest, Dovetailed, Eldred Wheeler, Late 1900s, 16 x 4 In.	216
Box, Mahogany, Drawer, Grooved Border, Signed, Simeon Folger, Nantucket, 1700s, 16 x 6 In. *illus*	4688
Box, Pine, Cutout Heart Design, New England, 1800s, 22¼ In.	625
Box, Tiger Maple, Shaped Back, Sides & Front Panel, Drawer, Metal Pull, 1900s, 21 In. *illus*	225
Briar, Cylindrical Bowl, Rough Cut, Vulcanite Stem, Marked, Willmer, England, 6 In.	36
Briar, Shell Finish, Black Stain, Sandblasted, Marked, 59 F/T, Dunhill, 5½ In.	138
Folk Art, Figural, Man's Head, Wearing Cap, Carved, Brass Lined Rim, 1800s, 5 In.	125
Meerschaum, Carved Well-Dressed Woman, Carrying Basket, 5¾ In. *illus*	518
Meerschaum, Figural, Bull's Head, Amber Stem, Case, 6¾ x 3¼ In.	500
Porcelain, George Washington Portrait, Metal Cap, Splitter, Fritzche, Germany, c.1880, 4¾ In.	407
Rack, Wood, Shield Shape, Hanging Plaque, Drawer, Shelf, Turtle, Fish, Folk Art, c.1950, 22 In.	180
Wood, Football Shape Bowl, Carved, Marked, Jonson, 4½ x 3 In.	23

PIRKENHAMMER

Pirkenhammer is a porcelain manufactory started in 1803 by Friedrich Holke and J. G. List. It was located in Bohemia, now Brezova, Czech Republic. The company made tablewares usually decorated with views and flowers. Lithophanes were also made. It became Manufaktura Pirkenhammer I.S. Original Porcelan Fabrik Brezova s.r.o. in 2002. The mark of the crossed hammers is easy to remember as the Pirkenhammer symbol.

Bowl, Basket Weave, Multicolor Flowers, Open Handles, Marked, 10 x 8 In.	35
Cachepot, Footed, Figures, Greek Key Band, Fischer & Mieg, Late 1800s, 8½ In., Pair	375
Dresser Box, Dome Lid, Courting Couple, Gilt Band, Magenta Border, 5 x 4 In.	125
Egg Server, Hen Shape Lid, 12 Cups, Side Handles, Blue, Gilt Trim, Footed, 12 x 15 In.	236
Figurine, Dog, Borzoi, Lying Down, 12 x 5 In.	600
Figurine, Dog, Brittany Springer, Pointing, Brown & White, 8 In.	199
Plate, Flowers, Birds, Insects, Reticulated Rim, Gilt Trim, 9 In., 12 Piece	1000
Plate, Woman's Portrait, Red Flower In Hair, Green Rim, Gilt Leaves, Fischer & Mieg, 9 In.	63
Platter, Oval, Gilt Fish, Shaded Blue Ground, Leafy Trim, Scalloped Border, Footed, 26 In.	1140
Tea Set, Teapot, Lid, Cup, Sugar & Creamer, Red Stripes, Flowering Vine, 1918-38, 9½ In. *illus*	312

PISGAH FOREST

Pisgah Forest Pottery was made in North Carolina beginning in 1926. The pottery was started by Walter B. Stephen, who had been making pottery in that location since 1914. The pottery continued in operation after his death in 1961. It closed in 2014. The most

Pillin, Vase, Horse, Brown Glaze, Earthenware, Footed, Signed, c.1960, 5¾ x 4½ In.
$563

Toomey & Co. Auctioneers

Pincushion Doll, Woman, Molded Blond Hair, Feather Headdress, Pink Dress, Hands Raised, Germany, 6½ In.
$156

Apple Tree Auction Center

Pincushion Doll, Woman, Nude, Head Raised, Hands Together, Art Deco, Germany, Dressel & Kister, c.1900, 5 In.
$122

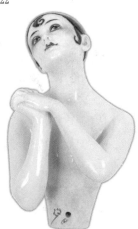

Selkirk Auctioneers & Appraisers

Pincushion Doll, Woman, Purple
Lined Bonnet, Folded Hands, White
Ruffled Skirt, Purple Bow, 6 x 6 In.
$36

Martin Auction Co.

Pipe, Box, Mahogany, Drawer, Grooved
Border, Signed, Simeon Folger,
Nantucket, 1700s, 16 x 6 In.
$4,688

Eldred's

Pipe, Box, Tiger Maple, Shaped Back,
Sides & Front Panel, Drawer, Metal Pull,
1900s, 21 In.
$225

Eldred's

famous Pisgah Forest ware are the turquoise crackle glaze wares and the cameo type with designs made of raised glaze.

Pisgah Forest Pottery
1926+

Pisgah Forest Pottery
Late 1940s

Pisgah Forest Pottery
1961+

Bowl, Green & Blue, Cameo, Covered Wagon, Teepee, Pink Interior, 1942, 3 x 11 In. .... *illus*	246
Pitcher, Turquoise, Pink Interior Glaze, Impressed Mark, c.1942, 8 ½ In.	146
Vase, Blue, Dark Purple, Loop Handle, 5 In..	75
Vase, Urn Shape, Crackled Turquoise, 1930s, 4 ½ In.	85

PLANTERS PEANUTS

Planters peanuts memorabilia are collected. Planters Nut and Chocolate Company was started in Wilkes-Barre, Pennsylvania, in 1906. The Mr. Peanut figure was adopted as a trademark in 1916. National advertising for Planters Peanuts started in 1918. The company was acquired by Standard Brands, Inc., in 1961. Standard Brands merged with Nabisco in 1981. Nabisco was bought by Kraft Foods in 2000. Kraft merged with H.J. Heinz Company in 2015. Planters brand is now owned by Kraft Heinz. Some of the Mr. Peanut jars and other memorabilia have been reproduced and, of course, new items are being made.

Bag, Burlap, Mr. Peanut, Planters Salted In Shell Roasted Peanuts, 5 Lb................................	23
Bank, Mr. Peanut, Cast Iron, Painted, Round Base, Coin Slot In Back, 11 ½ In.	62
Cards, Playing, Linen Finish, Original Box, Full Deck, c.1932, 4 x 2 ¼ In................................	390
Cookie Jar, Lid, Peanut Finial, Figural, Mr. Peanut, Glass, Green, Pink, 13 x 5 x 7 In., Pair..	95
Jar, Glass, Clear, Round, Flat Panels, Mr. Peanut, 5 Cent Salted Peanut, Red Pennant Bags, 10 In.	25
Jar, Lid, Peanut Finial, Cobalt Blue, 4 Raised Peanuts, 14 ½ In.	56
Jar, Lid, Red Finial, Painted, Blue Lettering, Red Ground, Mr. Peanut, Toms, 10 x 7 In.	144
Sign, Planters, The Name For Quality!, Mr. Peanut, Planters Nut Dept., 2-Sided, 12 x 24 In. ....*illus*	1088

PLASTIC

Plastic objects of all types are being collected. Some pieces are listed in other categories; gutta-percha cases are listed in the Photography category. Celluloid is in its own category. Some bakelite may also be found in the Jewelry category.

Cocktail Shaker, Bakelite, Master Incolor, Black, Silver, Recipes, England, 1930s, 11 In. ... *illus*	23750
Figure, Civil War Soldier, Hand Painted, Blue, 20 In..	25

PLATED AMBERINA

Plated amberina was patented June 15, 1886, by Joseph Locke and made by the New England Glass Company. It is similar in color to amberina, but is characterized by a cream colored or chartreuse lining (never white) and small ridges or ribs on the outside.

Cruet, Globular, 12 Vertical Ribs, Pale Amber, New England Glass Co., c.1886, 6 x 5 In..........	1170
Punch Cup, Opal Case, Maroon Fuchsia, Applied Handle, New England Glass Co., c.1886, 2 In. . *illus*	995

PLIQUE-A-JOUR

Plique-a-jour is an enameling process. The enamel is laid between thin raised metal lines and heated. The finished piece has transparent enamel

Pipe, Meerschaum, Carved Well-Dressed Woman, Carrying Basket, 5¾ In.
$518

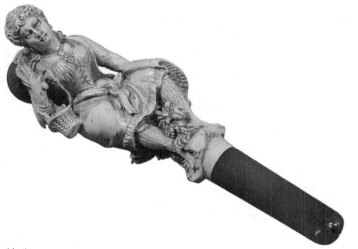

Blackwell Auctions

Pirkenhammer, Tea Set, Teapot, Lid, Cup, Sugar & Creamer, Red Stripes, Flowering Vine, 1918-38, 9½ In.
$312

Freeman's

Pisgah Forest, Bowl, Green & Blue, Cameo, Covered Wagon, Teepee, Pink Interior, 1942, 3 x 11 In.
$246

Brunk Auctions

Planters Peanuts, Sign, Planters, The Name For Quality!, Mr. Peanut, Planters Nut Dept., 2-Sided, 12 x 24 In.
$1,088

Morphy Auctions

Plastic, Cocktail Shaker, Bakelite, Master Incolor, Black, Silver, Recipes, England, 1930s, 11 In.
$23,750

Sotheby's

Plated Amberina, Punch Cup, Opal Case, Maroon Fuchsia, Applied Handle, New England Glass Co., c.1886, 2 In.
$995

Jeffrey S. Evans & Associates

Plique-A-Jour, Bowl, Blue Fish Scale Ground, Flowering Branches, Brass Feet, Chinese, 3 x 5½ In.
$95

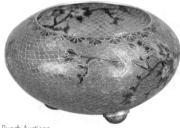

Bunch Auctions

Plique-A-Jour, Caddy Spoon, Geometric, Silver Wires, Pierced Scrolled Handle, Marked, Norway, 4½ In.
$384

Treasureseeker Auctions

TIP
Keep your keys on a pull-apart chain so the house keys and car keys can be separated when you leave the car in a parking lot.

Plique-A-Jour, Goblet, Stylized Flowers, Red, Blue, White, Ruby Panel Rim, Vermeil, Silver, 4 x 3½ In.
$532

P

Kaminski Auctions

PLIQUE-A-JOUR

Political, Bandanna, Alton B. Parker, Henry G. Davis, Busts, Draped Flag, Glass Frame, 1904, 28 x 27 In.
$351

Jeffrey S. Evans & Associates

Political Ribbons
Mass-produced printed ribbons for political campaigns were first manufactured in the United States in 1813.

Political, Bandanna, Cleveland & Thurman, For President, Red Cotton, Jugate, 1888, 26 x 28 In.
$1,131

Cowan's Auctions

Political, Bandanna, Harrison & Morton Campaign, Our Choice, Stars, Cotton, Jugate, 1888, 26 x 28 In.
$175

Cowan's Auctions

---

held between the thin metal wires. It is different from cloisonne because it is translucent.

Bowl, Blue Fish Scale Ground, Flowering Branches, Brass Feet, Chinese, 3 x 5 ½ In. .... *illus*	95
Bowl, Flared Rim, Fish Scale Ground, Multicolor Flowers, Ring Foot, 2 ¾ x 5 ½ In.	51
Bowl, White Fish Scale Ground, Pink, Orange Flowering Branch, Red & Blue Rim, Chinese, 2 x 5 In.	186
Box, Hinged Lid, Egg Shape, Blue Ground, Multicolor Scrolls, Flowers, Crosses, 2 ¾ x 2 In. ...	1020
Caddy Spoon, Geometric, Silver Wires, Pierced Scrolled Handle, Marked, Norway, 4 ½ In. .*illus*	384
Goblet, Stylized Flowers, Red, Blue, White, Ruby Panel Rim, Vermeil, Silver, 4 x 3 ½ In. .*illus*	532
Lamp, Desk, Electric, Gooseneck, Blue Fish Scale Shade, Grapevines, Cloisonne Base, Chinese, 16 In.	128
Snuffbox, Hinged Lid, Diamond Shape Medallion, Flowers, Pierced Silver, Russia, 1800s, 3 x 2 In.	984
Tea Strainer, Silver, Pierced Scrolled Frame, Multicolor, 5 x 3 In.	520
Vanity Box, Hinged Lid, Landscape, Figures, Pewter, Gilt Interior, France, Early 1900s, 2 x 6 x 3 ½ In..	2813
Vase, Blue & White Peonies, Pink Fish Scale Ground, Round, Flared Neck, Chinese, 4 In.	111

POLITICAL

Political memorabilia of all types, from buttons to banners, are collected. Items related to presidential candidates are the most popular, but collectors also search for material related to state and local offices. Memorabilia related to social causes, minor political parties, and protest movements are also included here. Many reproductions have been made. A jugate is a button with photographs of both the presidential and vice presidential candidates. In this list a button is round, usually with a straight pin or metal tab to secure it to a shirt. A pin is brass, often figural, sometimes attached to a ribbon.

Bandanna, Alton B. Parker, Henry G. Davis, Busts, Draped Flag, Glass Frame, 1904, 28 x 27 In. *illus*	351
Bandanna, Cleveland & Thurman, For President, Red Cotton, Jugate, 1888, 26 x 28 In. *illus*	1131
Bandanna, Harrison & Morton Campaign, Our Choice, Stars, Cotton, Jugate, 1888, 26 x 28 In. *illus*	175
Banner, James A. Garfield, Portrait, Stars & Stripes, Blue, Red Border, Cotton, 18 x 24 In.	4063
Banner, Our President Dwight D. Eisenhower, Bunting, Grommets, 1964, 36 x 108 In.	288
Bookends, Teddy Roosevelt, Gilt, Bronze, 6 ¼ In. .... *illus*	94
Bust, George Washington, Toga Like Drape, Plaster, Jean-Antoine Houdon, 1785, 26 In.	1563
Button, Cox & Roosevelt, 1920 Campaign, Celluloid, Jugate, ⅞ In. .... *illus*	35695
Button, Harry S. Truman, President, Portrait, Celluloid, 1949, 1 ¾ In. .... *illus*	156
Button, T. Roosevelt, Portrait, Rebus, Rose & Velt, Celluloid, 1 ¼ In. .... *illus*	130
Button, Taft & Sherman, Pin, W.F. Miller Back Paper, Jugate, 1908, 1 ¾ In. .... *illus*	11719
Button, Theodore Roosevelt, American Flag, Presidential Campaign, Painted, 1904, 1 x 2 In.	845
Button, Washington, Presidential Inauguration, GW, Long Live The President, Brass, 1 ¼ In. ..	2340
Button, William Howard Taft, Theodore Roosevelt, U-N-I-TED, You & I Ted, 1908, 1 In.	455
Cane, Jimmy Carter, For President, 2 Stars, Metal Handle, 1976, 35 ½ In. .... *illus*	81
Cane, Presentation, Hon. Grover Cleveland, Gold Knob, Wood Shaft, Engraved, 1884, 35 In..	1328
Cane, Walking Stick, Carved, President Woodrow Wilson Holding Pencil, Eagle, 1917, 34 In. *illus*	527
Ferrotype, Campaign, Tassel, Circular Frame, Ulysses S. Grant, 1868, 1 In.	520
Handkerchief, Printed Cotton, 39 Stars, National Banner Co., Frame, c.1890, 30 x 28 ½ In.	293
Lantern, McKinley & Roosevelt, Full Dinner Pail, Tin, Punched-Out Stars, 1900, 9 x 6 In. ...*illus*	2969
License Plate, No. 1, Dist. Of Columbia, 1957 Presidential Inaugural, Metal, 6 x 12 In.	7995
License Plate Topper, Alf Landon, 1936 Presidential Campaign, Republican, Tin Litho, 6 x 3 In. *illus*	531
Lithophane, Zachary Taylor, Spyglass, Gothic, Openwork Frame, Brass & Marble Stand, 6 x 8 In.	2891
Medal, Chang Kai Shek, Chinese Script, Engraved, Painted, 3 ½ x 1 ¾ In.	188
Mug, James Monroe, Portrait, Misspelled Munroe, Patriotic Eagle, Transfer, 1825, 2 x 2 In. ..*illus*	7813
Photograph, Seymour & Blair, Presidential, Albumen, Jugate, Brass Frame, 1868, 1 x ¾ In.	128
Plate, Service, Benjamin Harrison, Eagle, Corn & Goldenrod, White House China, 8 ½ In. ..*illus*	875
Plate, Soup, Rutherford B. Hayes, Frog, Lily Pad, White House China, 9 In.	1719
Poster, I Am A Black Woman, Angela Davis, Printed, Richard McCrary, 1971, 23 x 29 In. *illus*	531
Poster, John F. Kennedy, Kennedy For President, Leadership For The 60's, 1960, 42 ½ x 30 In. *illus*	423
Poster, Kennedy, Pictures Robert Kennedy, Black & White, 24 ½ x 38 In., 12 Copies	443
Scale, Benjamin Harrison & Grover Cleveland, Bisque, Wood, Metal, 1888, 5 ½ In. .... *illus*	4316
Stickpin, Lincoln & Hamlin, Ferrotype, Jugate, Gilt Brass Frame, ⅞ In.	31250
Tapestry, In Memoriam U.S. Grant, Casket, Flag, Angels, Silk, Needlework, c.1885 .... *illus*	1625
Token, Lincoln, Campaign, Brass, Ferrotype, Marked, Hannibal Hamlin, 1860, 1 In.	1280

Political, Bookends, Teddy Roosevelt, Gilt, Bronze, 6 ¼ In.
$94

Copake Auction

Political, Button, Cox & Roosevelt, 1920 Campaign, Celluloid, Jugate, ⅞ In.
$35,695

Hake's Auctions

Political, Button, Harry S. Truman, President, Portrait, Celluloid, 1949, 1 ¾ In.
$156

Hake's Auctions

"On the Curl"

For a political collector, "on the curl" has a special meaning. It indicates that the name of the maker is printed on the curled edge of a celluloid or tin campaign button.

Political, Button, T. Roosevelt, Portrait, Rebus, Rose & Velt, Celluloid, 1 ¼ In.
$130

Hake's Auctions

Political, Button, Taft & Sherman, Pin, W.F. Miller Back Paper, Jugate, 1908, 1 ¾ In.
$11,719

Heritage Auctions

Political, Cane, Jimmy Carter, For President, 2 Stars, Metal Handle, 1976, 35 ½ In.
$81

Blackwell Auctions

Political, Cane, Walking Stick, Carved, President Woodrow Wilson Holding Pencil, Eagle, 1917, 34 In.
$527

Jeffrey S. Evans & Associates

Political, Lantern, McKinley & Roosevelt, Full Dinner Pail, Tin, Punched-Out Stars, 1900, 9 x 6 In.
$2,969

Heritage Auctions

P

Political, License Plate Topper, Alf Landon, 1936 Presidential Campaign, Republican, Tin Litho, 6 x 3 In.
$531

AntiqueAdvertising.com

Political, Mug, James Monroe, Portrait, Misspelled Munroe, Patriotic Eagle, Transfer, 1825, 2 x 2 In.
$7,813

Heritage Auctions

Political, Plate, Service, Benjamin Harrison, Eagle, Corn & Goldenrod, White House China, 8 1/2 In.
$875

Cowan's Auctions

Political, Poster, I Am A Black Woman, Angela Davis, Printed, Richard McCrary, 1971, 23 x 29 In.
$531

Cowan's Auctions

Political, Poster, John F. Kennedy, Kennedy For President, Leadership For The 60s, 1960, 42 1/2 x 30 In.
$423

Freeman's

Political, Scale, Benjamin Harrison & Grover Cleveland, Bisque, Wood, Metal, 1888, 5 1/2 In.
$43,161

Heritage Auctions

Political, Tapestry, In Memoriam U.S. Grant, Casket, Flag, Angels, Silk, Needlework, c.1885
$1,625

Cowan's Auctions

POMONA

Pomona glass is a clear glass with a soft amber border decorated with pale blue or rose-colored flowers and leaves. The colors are very, very pale. The background of the glass is covered with a network of fine lines. It was made from 1885 to 1888 by the New England Glass Company. First grind was made from April 1885 to June 1886. It was made by cutting a wax surface on the glass, then dipping it in acid. Second grind was a less expensive method of acid etching that was developed later.

Cruet, Cornflower, Scalloped Base, Faceted Stopper, New England Glass Works, 1880s, 7 x 5 In. . *illus*	117
Pickle Castor, Cornflower, Silver Plate Caddy, Meriden, 12 In.	282

POOLE POTTERY

Poole Pottery was founded by Jesse Carter in 1873 in Poole, England, and has operated under various names since then. The pottery operated as Carter & Co. for several years and established Carter, Stabler & Adams as a subsidiary in 1921. The company specialized in tiles, architectural ceramics, and garden ornaments. Tableware, bookends, candelabra, figures, vases, and other items have also been made. *Poole Pottery Ltd.* became the name in 1963. The company went bankrupt in 2003 but continued under new owners. Poole Pottery became part of Burgess & Leigh Ltd. in 2012. It is still in business, now making pottery in Middleport, Stoke-on-Trent.

Poole Pottery
1921–1924

Poole Pottery
1924–1950

Poole Pottery Ltd.
1990–1991

Bowl, Yellow Border, Orange Stylized Flowers, 10 In.	80
Charger, Yachts, Red Sunset Sky, c.1972, 13¾ In.	131
Cup, Delphis, Orange, Red, c.1960, 3¾ x 2¾ In.	32
Figurine, Penguin, Black, White, Yellow, c.1980, 8½ In.	103
Plate, Delphis, Bow Design, Blue, Red, 1960s, 8 In.	95
Vase, Bottle Shape, PRB Pattern, Brown, White Bands, Alfred Burgess Read, c.1950, 15 x 6 In.	75
Vase, Delphis, Squat, Tapered Top, Hand Painted, Outlined Shapes, Red, Yellow, 4 x 7 In.	42
Vase, Delphis, Squat, Tapered Top, Red, Orange Circles, Green Triangles, Marked, MA, 4 x 6¼ In.	42
Vase, Oval, Flower Spray Panels, Yellow Bird, Multicolor, 1930s, 15 In.	171

POPEYE

Popeye was introduced to the Thimble Theatre comic strip in 1929. The character became a favorite of readers. In 1932, an animated cartoon featuring Popeye was made by Paramount Studios. The cartoon series continued and became even more popular when it was shown on television starting in the 1950s. The full-length movie with Robin Williams as Popeye was made in 1980. KFS stands for King Features Syndicate, the distributor of the comic strip.

Face Mask, Molded, Rubber, Mesh Eyes, Stand, 17 In. *illus*	431
Pail, Popeye & Kids At Beach, Smiling Sun, Shovel, Tin Lithograph, J. Chein, 1932, 6 x 6 In..	1680
Poster, Popeye Film Festival, Paramount, J. Lichitert & Phils., Brussels, 18 x 13½ In.	100
Toy, Airplane, Popeye The Pilot, Tin Lithograph, Windup, Marx, 1940, 6 x 7 In.	575
Toy, Eccentric Airplane, Tin Lithograph, Windup, Marx, Box, 7 In.	580
Toy, Handcar, Popeye & Olive Oyl, Tin Lithograph, Springs, Cord, Linemar, Japan, 7 In. *illus*	748
Toy, Pistol, Popeye Pirate, Tin Lithograph, Marx, Box, 9¾ In.	580
Toy, Popeye Express, Blow Me Down Airport, Tin Lithograph, Marx, Box, 9 In.	1159

Pomona, Cruet, Cornflower, Scalloped Base, Faceted Stopper, New England Glass Works, 1880s, 7 x 5 In.
$117

Jeffrey S. Evans & Associates

Popeye, Face Mask, Molded, Rubber, Mesh Eyes, Stand, 17 In.
$431

Rich Penn Auctions

Popeye, Toy, Handcar, Popeye & Olive Oyl, Tin Lithograph, Springs, Cord, Linemar, Japan, 7 In.
$748

Rich Penn Auctions

This is an edited listing of current prices. Visit Kovels.com to check thousands of prices from previous years and sign up for free information on trends, tips, reproductions, marks, and more.

Popeye, Toy, Popeye, Basketball Player, Tin Lithograph, Windup, Linemar, Japan, 1950s, 9 In.
$3,738

Rich Penn Auctions

Popeye, Toy, Popeye, Carrying Parrot Cages, Tin Lithograph, Windup, Marx, Box, 8 In.
$510

Bertoia Auctions

> **TIP**
> *Don't repaint old metal toys. It lowers the value*

Toy, Popeye Express, Tin Lithograph, Marx, Box, 8¼ In.	610
Toy, Popeye Overhead Bag Puncher, Tin Lithograph, Windup, J. Chein, Box, 1932, 10 In.	1840
Toy, Popeye, Aeroplane, Pilot, Smoking Pipe, Lithograph, Windup, Marx, c.1936, 7¾ x 6 x 6¼ In.	1792
Toy, Popeye, Basketball Player, Tin Lithograph, Windup, Linemar, Japan, 1950s, 9 In. .. *illus*	3738
Toy, Popeye, Carrying Parrot Cages, Tin Lithograph, Windup, Marx, Box, 8 In. .... *illus*	510
Toy, Popeye, Heavy Hitter, Rings Bell, Tin Lithograph, Windup, Box, J. Chein, c.1932, 12 In. *illus*	3450
Toy, Popeye, Mechanical Roller Skater, Tin Lithograph, Windup, Linemar, Box, 6 In. ... *illus*	920
Toy, Popeye, Olive Oyl, Jiggers Dancing, On Rooftop, Tin Lithograph, Windup, Marx, 1930, 9½ x 6 In.	677
Toy, Popeye, Rowboat, Remote Control, Tin Litho, Moving Oars, Linemar, 10 In.	2337
Toy, Popeye, Unicyclist, Tin Lithograph, Linemar, Box, Color Graphics, 6 x 3 In.	1152
Toy, Truck, Hauler & Trailer, Popeye Transit Co., Moving, Tin Lithograph, Box, 1958, 6 x 9 In.	1476

🫖 PORCELAIN

Porcelain factories that are well known are listed in this book under the factory name. This category lists pieces made by the less well-known factories. Additional pieces of porcelain are listed in this book in the categories Porcelain-Asian, Porcelain-Chinese, Porcelain-Contemporary, Porcelain-Midcentury, and under the factory name.

Basket, Lovers, Flowers, Gilt, Bronze Mounted, Sevres Style, Signed, Aurele, 1800s, 10 x 9 In. .	500
Bust, French Maiden, Blue & White, Glazed, Signed, G. Levy, France, 17¼ x 8½ In.	431
Centerpiece, 2 Winged Cupids, Holding Bowl, Claw Feet, 12 x 12 In.	144
Centerpiece, Louis XV Style, Reticulated Basket, 4 Putti, Gilt Borders, Tiche, 1900s, 27¼ In.	512
Centerpiece, Transfer, Renaissance Scene, Gilt, Bronze Handle, Flowers, c.1900, 15¾ x 23 In. *illus*	431
Charger, Central Cartouche, Lovers, Cupid Border, Multicolor, Continental, 1800s, 15 In.	188
Dish, Sevres Style, Holder, Scrolled, Handles, Signed, L. Pastin, c.1900, 8 x 15 In. ...... *illus*	236
Ewer, Cobalt Blue Ground, Bulbous Body, Leafy Mounts, France, 1850s, 19 x 37 In., Pair	1320
Figurine, Cockatoo, Standing, Painted, Germany, 12 In.	69
Figurine, Gardener, Delft Style, Blue & White, Holding Basket, Stepped Base, 18 In.	59
Figurine, Horse & Rider, Hofborg Wien Courbette, Augarten, Austria, 1900s, 11¾ In.	708
Figurine, Horse, Chinese, Aqua Blue Crackle Glaze, Rectangular Stand, 1900s, 15 In. . *illus*	413
Figurine, Monkey, Seated, Brown, White & Black, Crossed Lines Mark, 8 In. .... *illus*	305
Figurine, Putti, Holding Fish, Blanc De Chine, Continental, 9 In.	35
Figurine, Rider On Stallion, Wood, Plinth Base, Augarten, Austria, 1900s, 11⅜ In. ..... *illus*	295
Figurine, Spanish Woman, No. 1124, Dahl Jensen, Copenhagen, Denmark, 9½ In.	295
Footbath, Flowers, Canted Corners, Painted, Gilt Rim & Base, Early 1900s, 5 x 16 In.	118
Group, Equestrian, White Horse, Galloping, Luigi Fabris, 1800s, 20 x 18 In.	431
Group, Hunt Scene, Man, Dogs, Von Schierholz, Germany, 14 In.	106
Jar, Apothecary, Grecian Fight Scene, Greek Key Borders, Finial, France, 1900s, 12 In., Pair..	168
Lamp, Chinoiserie, Birds, Flowers, Fruit Trees, Wood Base, Continental, Early 1900s, 15 In., Pair	531
Lavabo, Flowers, Cistern, Lid, Metal Spigot, Blue Anchor Mark, Walnut Board, 1800s, 34 x 18¾ In.	62
Pitcher, Gilt, Flowers, Leaf Molded Spout, Tucker Porcelain Factory, U.S.A., c.1830, 9 x 5 x 7 In. . *illus*	615
Pitcher, White Ground, Gilt, Painted, Flowers, Mercer County, 1800s, 9¼ In., Pair	160
Planter, Multicolor, Cat Family, Mother, Baby Kitten, Playing Drum & Seated, 6¾ In.	35
Plaque, At Shrine Of Venus, Carved, Wood Frame, Signed, H. Goruar, Vienna, 20 x 21 In.	850
Plaque, Finding Of Moses, Bulrushes, River, Basket, Brass Frame, 9 x 7 In.	756
Plaque, Mignon, Portrait, Woman, Holding Mandolin, Germany, 1900s, 6 x 4¼ In.	118
Plaque, Painted, Man & Woman, Seated, Fountain, Tree Ground, Gilt Frame, 23 x 21 In.	315
Plaque, Painted, Woman, Reticulated Border, Signed, Gilt Frame, Vienna, 23 In. .... *illus*	126
Plaque, Polish Countess, Sophie Potocka, Blue Dress, Giltwood Frame, Late 1800s, 13 x 11 In.	380
Plaque, Portrait, Savonarola, Oil, Oval, Hardwood Frame, c.1900s, 5¾ In.	118
Plaque, Woman, Holding Baby, Carved, Plaster Pane, Gilt, Painted, Wood Frame, 21 x 9 In..	1599
Plaque, Woman, Standing, Tambourine, Signed, E. Fengar, Continental, Frame, 1911, 17 In. *illus*	281
Plate, Dinner, Robin's-Egg Blue, Gilt Band, Monogram, Boyer, Mid 1800s, 9 In., 10 Piece	976
Plate, Gentleman In Wig, Ruffled Edge, Painted, Signed, F. Amblet, 9¾ In.	83
Plate, Portrait, Woman, White Ground, Flowers, Leaves, Gold Border, Franz Dorfl, 10 In., Pair	945
Plate, Tropical Bird, Green, White, Chelsea, 1800s, 9¾ In., Pair	200
Sculpture, Venus, Nude, Bathing, Standing, Classical, Octagonal Base, Italy, 49¼ In.	413
Tray, Gilt Metal Mounted, Central Garden Scene, Leafy Handles, Early 1900s, 3 x 20 x 10 In.	177
Tray, Multicolor, Flowers, Handles, Wood Frame, Brass Feet, Germany, c.1900s, 3 x 23 x 13 In.	177

P

Popeye, Toy, Popeye, Heavy Hitter, Rings Bell, Tin Lithograph, Windup, Box, J. Chein, c.1932, 12 In.
$3,450

Popeye, Toy, Popeye, Mechanical Roller Skater, Tin Lithograph, Windup, Linemar, Box, 6 In.
$920

TIP
To avoid break-ins, be sure the hinges for your exterior doors are on the interior side of the door.

Porcelain, Centerpiece, Transfer, Renaissance Scene, Gilt, Bronze Handle, Flowers, c.1900, 15¾ x 23 In.
$431

Porcelain, Dish, Sevres Style, Holder, Scrolled, Handles, Signed L. Pastin, c.1900, 8 x 15 In.
$236

Porcelain, Figurine, Horse, Chinese, Aqua Blue Crackle Glaze, Rectangular Stand, 1900s, 15 In.
$413

Porcelain, Figurine, Monkey, Seated, Brown, White & Black, Crossed Lines Mark, 8 In.
$305

Porcelain, Figurine, Rider On Stallion, Wood, Plinth Base, Augarten, Austria, 1900s, 11⅜ In.
$295

TIP
You can use an empty vase as a bookend if you weight it. Put a resealable plastic bag in the vase. Fill the bag with sand, then seal it. The vase should be about half full. This is also a good way to keep a vase with an irregular base from tipping.

Porcelain, Pitcher, Gilt, Flowers, Leaf Molded Spout, Tucker Porcelain Factory, U.S.A., c.1830, 9 x 5 x 7 In.
$615

Brunk Auctions

Porcelain, Plaque, Painted, Woman, Reticulated Border, Signed, Gilt Frame, Vienna, 23 In.
$126

Fontaine's Auction Gallery

Porcelain, Plaque, Woman, Standing, Tambourine, Signed, E. Fengar, Continental, Frame, 1911, 17 In.
$281

Charlton Hall Auctions

Tureen, Lemon Shape, Leaves, Yellow, Green, Italy, 1900s, 10 In.	31
Tureen, Soup, Lid, Gnome, Impressed 758, Germany, 12½ In.	71
Urn, Asian Hunters, Gilt, Handle, Paris, 1800s, 10½ In., Pair	420
Urn, Campagna Shape, Flared Rim, Building & Landscape Scene, 1850s, 10 In., Pair	384
Urn, Faux Shagreen, Gilt, Dolphin Shape Handles, Pedestal Foot, Late 1900s, 16 In., Pair	2655
Urn, Gilt, Mounted, Bronze Base, Swag Handles, Bud Finial, Giulia Mangani, 29 In., Pair	1792
Urn, Inset Lid, Pierced Fleur-De-Lis Finial, Lion Mask Handle, Flowers, Gilt Bands, 1800s, 14 In.	1968
Urn, Lid, Mounted, Brass, Acorn Finial, Putti Portrait, 1800s, 18 In., Pair	540
Urn, Lid, Sevres Style, Cobalt Blue Ground, Gilt, Leaves & Classical Figures, 1800s, 18 In.	360
Urn, Napoleon, Czar Alexander, Parcel Gilt, Swan Shape Handles, Signed Boz, 18 In., Pair ... *illus*	767
Urn, Tree, Turkey, Chicken Scenes, Bird, Scroll, Flower, Gilt, Painted, 10¾ In.	71
Urn, Triangular Lid, Blue Transfer, Pineapple, Mottahedeh, U.S.A., 1900s, 10½ In., Pair	111
Urn, Woman, Cupid, Sevres, Ormolu Mounted, Champleve Lid, Signed, Roche, 12 In., Pair	575
Urn, Woman, Yellow Dress, Brass Handles, Floral Champleve Base, France, Late 1800s, 12 In.	240
Vase, Bottle Shape, Flower Sprays, Painted, 14 x 5 In., Pair	246
Vase, Butterfly, Bird, Fruit & Flowers, White Ground, Continental, 13 In.	59
Vase, Lid, Hexagonal Body, Gold Insects, Cobalt Blue, Finial, c.1875, 15 In., Pair	1625
Vase, Lobe Shape, Gilt Metal, Leaves, Light Blue, Castilian, Late 1900s, 24¼ x 11½ In.	266
Vase, Mantel, Gilt, Gray Ground, Cartouches, Flower Cluster, 1850s, 13½ In., Pair ... *illus*	325
Vase, Mauve Ground, Flowers, Oval, Square Base, Early 1800s, 10 In.	1107
Vase, Neoclassical Style, Black Ground, Campana Shape, Le Tallec, Late 1900s, 9 In.	1020
Vase, Painted, Vienna Style, Woman, Dark Green Ground, Gilt Rim & Base, c.1900, 8½ In.	1105
Vase, Portland, Blue Ground, Applied White Classical Figures, Handles, c.1880, 10½ In.	105
Vase, Portrait, Little Girl, Pink Dress, Green & White Ground, 2 Handles, Footed, 12 In.	83
Vase, Reticulated Rim, Floral Diamonds Border, Mark, Von Schierholz, Germany, c.1900, 5¾ In.	177
Wall Pocket, Child, Seated, Holding Books, Flowers, Painted, Continental, 1800s, 8½ x 8 In.	94

Porcelain-Asian includes pieces made in Japan, Korea, and other Asian countries. Asian porcelain is also listed in Canton, Chinese Export, Imari, Japanese Coralene, Moriage, Nanking, Occupied Japan, Porcelain-Chinese, Satsuma, Sumida, and other categories.

Bowl, Scalloped Rim, Alternating Panels, Painted, Sea Creature, Vietnam, 1800s, 7 In.	313
Fishbowl, Flowers, Fish Design Interior, Painted, Mark, 13¾ In.	59
Garden Seat, Blue & White, Flowers, Wood Pedestal, 11 x 18 In.	59
Ginger Jar, Removable Lid, Figures, Tree, Flowers, Leaves, White Ground, 13 In., Pair . *illus*	630
Incense Burner, Rectangular, Reticulated, Yellow Ground, Bronze Lid & Base, 18½ In.	2520
Jar, Melon, Lid, Iman Design, Kabuki Samurai Warrior, Flowers, Gilt Finial, 14 In., Pair	71
Planter, White Ground, Trees, Flowers, Berries, Teakwood Stand, 27½ In., Pair .... *illus*	1512
Vase, Cream Crackle, Gilt Black Dragon, Embossed, 24 In.	59
Vase, Curved Neck, Red Ground, Carved, Landscape, Flowers, 19 In.	177
Vase, Cylindrical, Raised Bird, Bamboo, Flowers, Makuzo Kozan, Japan, 1800s, 17 x 5 In. *illus*	995
Vase, Flowers, Leaves, Birds, Gilt Rim, Scrolled Feet, Japan, c.1900, 11 In., Pair	1075
Vase, Green, Glazed, Rolled Rim, Black Design, Embossed, 11 In.	24

Porcelain-Chinese is listed here. See also Canton, Chinese Export, Imari, Moriage, Nanking, and other categories.

Bowl, Blue & White, Bell Shape, Flowers, Vine Design, 8 In.	159
Bowl, Bulb, Teal, Lotus Scalloped Rim, Cherry Blossoms, Bats, Early 1900s, 3¼ In.	150
Bowl, Butterflies, Flowers, Fruit, Painted, Marked, 7½ In.	162
Bowl, Famille Rose, Flowers, Leaves, Footed, Marked, 1800s, 2¼ x 4¾ In.	188
Bowl, Kangxi Style, Upturned Bell Shape, Gilt Landscape, Powder Blue, 3¾ x 7⅝ In.	3000
Bowl, Lid, Ecuelle, 2 Handles, Red, Chrysanthemum Blooms, 6 In., Pair	3528
Bowl, Octagonal, Teal Glaze, Wave Pattern, Flowers, Famille Rose, Footed, Late 1800s, 8 In.	250
Bowl, Russet Splashed, Lustrous Black Glaze, Indented Rim, Splayed Foot, 8¼ In.	600
Bowl, White Ground, Blue Dragon, Rounded Side, Flared Rim, Painted, 10 In. .... *illus*	2160
Box, Lid, Blue & White, Geometric Pattern, Landscape Scene, 2½ x 7 In., 3 Piece	384
Box, Lid, Butterflies, Round, Painted, 1800s, 7 x 10½ In.	125
Box, Lid, Famille Rose, Peach, Flowers, Lotus Flower On Base, Mark, Yongzheng, 4 x 7½ In.	1500

Porcelain, Urn, Napoleon, Czar Alexander, Parcel Gilt, Swan Shape Handles, Signed Boz, 18 In., Pair
$767

Austin Auction Gallery

Porcelain, Vase, Mantel, Gilt, Gray Ground, Cartouches, Flower Cluster, 1850s, 13 ½ In., Pair
$325

Leland Little Auctions

Porcelain-Asian, Ginger Jar, Removable Lid, Figures, Tree, Flowers, Leaves, White Ground, 13 In., Pair
$630

Fontaine's Auction Gallery

> **TIP**
> Quick cure for a leaking flower vase: Coat the outside and inside with clear silicone household glue. Coat again if it still leaks.

Porcelain-Asian, Planter, White Ground, Trees, Flowers, Berries, Teakwood Stand, 27 ½ In., Pair
$1,512

Fontaine's Auction Gallery

Porcelain-Asian, Vase, Cylindrical, Raised Bird, Bamboo, Flowers, Makuzo Kozan, Japan, 1800s, 17 x 5 In.
$995

Thomaston Place Auction Galleries

Porcelain-Chinese, Bowl, White Ground, Blue Dragon, Rounded Side, Flared Rim, Painted, 10 In.
$2,160

Michaan's Auctions

Porcelain-Chinese, Brushpot, Green Ground, Leaves, Flowers, Painted, 5 ½ In.
$480

P

Cottone Auctions

405

Porcelain-Chinese, Charger, 4 Women, Playing Go, Black Geometric Pattern Rim, 1900s, 12⅞ In.
$443

Leland Little Auctions

> **TIP**
> *Keep basement windows locked at all times.*

Porcelain-Chinese, Charger, Famille Rose, Round, Painted, 1900s, 23½ In., Pair
$448

Hindman

Porcelain-Chinese, Creamer, Helmet Shape, Gilt Handle, 2 Figures, Flowers, Domed Foot Base, 4 x 5 x 2 In.
$322

Thomaston Place Auction Galleries

Porcelain-Chinese, Dish, Square, Blue & White, Central Scroll, Taotie Masks, c.1700, 7⅝ In.
$590

Leland Little Auctions

Porcelain-Chinese, Ewer, Lid, Copper, Red Leafy Design, 6 Characters, Ming Style, Mark, 15 In.
$625

Susanin's Auctioneers & Appraisers

Porcelain-Chinese, Figurine, Dragon Boat, Carrying 3-Story Pagoda, 12 x 11 In.
$201

Blackwell Auctions

Porcelain-Chinese, Figurine, Foo Dog, Blanc De Chine, Seated, Plinth Base, 1900s, 14 x 6 x 4 In., Pair
$325

Austin Auction Gallery

Porcelain-Chinese, Figurine, Foo Dog, Mottled, Multicolor, Bulging Eyes, Reticulated Ball, 1900s, 16 In., Pair
$590

Leland Little Auctions

Porcelain-Chinese, Figurine, Woman, Lying On Bed, Blue Robe, Brown Flower Pants, 1900s, 17 In.
$156

Bruneau & Co. Auctioneers

Porcelain-Chinese, Ginger Jar, Lid, Famille Rose Palette, Scholar Motif, Gilt Finial, 1800s, 14 In.
$472

Porcelain-Chinese, Jar, Dome Lid, Famille Rose, Temple, Flowers, Peacock, Vase Design, Gilt Base, 16 In., Pair
$325

Porcelain-Chinese, Lamp, Guanyin, Flower Bundle, Oval Linen Shade, Blue Leaves, Wood Base, 30 In., Pair
$295

Leland Little Auctions

Austin Auction Gallery

Porcelain-Chinese, Group, 2 Figures, Seated On Rock, Multicolor Enamel, c.1925, 10 In.
$325

Porcelain-Chinese, Jar, Lid, Wucai, Transitional Style, Qilin, Chimera, Foo Dog, Wood Stand, 18 In.
$750

Leland Little Auctions

Austin Auction Gallery

> **TIP**
> Almost all the
> eighteenth-century
> porcelain figures had
> brown eyes.

Porcelain-Chinese, Jar, Chrysanthemum, Lotus Flower Panel, Blue, White, Cracked Ice Ground, c.1700, 7 In.
$671

Porcelain-Chinese, Tureen, Famille Rose, Hen, Multicolor, Painted, Early 1900s, 9 ½ x 13 ½ x 8 In.
$125

Neal Auction Company

Neal Auction Company

Porcelain-Chinese, Jardiniere, Frog, Green, White, Glazed, Bulging Eyes, Wood Base, 8 In.
$960

Bruneau & Co. Auctioneers

Nadeau's Auction Gallery

Porcelain-Chinese, Umbrella Stand, Seurat Park Scene, Transfer, Marked, Late 1900s, 18½ In.
$118

Leland Little Auctions

Porcelain-Chinese, Vase, Blue & White, Red, Late 1800s, 9½ In.
$1,416

Bunch Auctions

Brush Box, Rectangular, White & Blue, Temple Landscape, 3 x 7 x 4 In., 3 Piece	413
Brushpot, Blue & White, 2 Dragons, Light Celadon Glaze Interior, 6 In.	177
Brushpot, Green Ground, Leaves, Flowers, Painted, 5½ In. .... *illus*	480
Cachepot, Famille Verte, Hexagonal Shape, Figures, Painted, 7½ x 8½ x 9½ In.	63
Charger, 4 Women, Playing Go, Black Geometric Pattern Rim, 1900s, 12⅞ In. .... *illus*	443
Charger, Blue & White, Lotus Blossom, Fish, Sunburst Border, 18¼ In., Pair	236
Charger, Famille Rose, Enamel, 2 Women, Child, Garden Setting, Fruit, Flowers, 1700s, 12 In. *illus*	800
Charger, Famille Rose, Round, Painted, 1900s, 23½ In., Pair .... *illus*	448
Charger, Red Dragon, Flowers, Copper, Leafy Shape Rim, 2¾ x 16¼ In.	813
Creamer, Helmet Shape, Gilt Handle, 2 Figures, Flowers, Domed Foot Base, 4 x 5 x 2 In. *illus*	322
Cup, Blue & White, Stem, Dragon, 6 Characters, Late 1800s, 4¾ x 7¼ In.	1375
Dish, Central Dragon Roundel, Blue, White, Bisque Base, Ming Style, 1¾ x 8¼ In.	336
Dish, Octagonal, Rose Foot, Gilt Trim, Orange Peel Glaze, Red Seal Mark, 1860s, 1 x 4 x 4 In.	210
Dish, Square, Blue & White, Central Scroll, Taotie Masks, c.1700, 7⅝ In. .... *illus*	590
Ewer, Lid, Copper, Red Leafy Design, 6 Characters, Ming Style, Mark, 15 In. .... *illus*	625
Figurine, Dragon Boat, Carrying 3-Story Pagoda, 12 x 11 In. .... *illus*	201
Figurine, Foo Dog, Blanc De Chine, Seated, Plinth Base, 1900s, 14 x 6 x 4 In., Pair ..... *illus*	325
Figurine, Foo Dog, Mottled, Multicolor, Bulging Eyes, Reticulated Ball, 1900s, 16 In., Pair . *illus*	590
Figurine, Foo Dog, Yellow Ground, Paw On Ball & Cub, Openwork Base, 11¾ In., Pair	472
Figurine, Phoenix Bird, Blue, Yellow, Glaze, 1900s, 18½ x 6 In., Pair	207
Figurine, Tailor, Riding, Goat, Iron On Horn, Painted, Marked, 6¾ In.	246
Figurine, Woman, Lying On Bed, Blue Robe, Brown Flower Pants, 1900s, 17 In. .... *illus*	156
Food Warmer, Dome Lid, 4 Tiers, Blue, Cranes, Bats, White Ground, Wire Handle, 7 x 7 In..	585
Ginger Jar, Lid, Famille Rose Palette, Scholar Motif, Gilt Finial, 1800s, 14 In. .... *illus*	472
Ginger Jar, Lid, Scrolling Flowers, Text Blocks, Blue Underglaze, 9 x 8 In.	92
Group, 2 Figures, Seated On Rock, Multicolor Enamel, c.1925, 10 In. .... *illus*	325
Jar, 4 Panels, Red Multicolor, Painted, Birds, Flowers, Animal Head Handles, 15½ In., Pair..	366
Jar, Chrysanthemum, Lotus Flower Panel, Blue, White, Cracked Ice Ground, c.1700, 7 In. .. *illus*	671
Jar, Dome Lid, Bulbous Body, Exotic Birds, Flowers, Blue & White, 1800s, 10 x 8 In.	190
Jar, Dome Lid, Famille Rose, Temple, Flowers, Peacock, Vase Design, Gilt Base, 16 In., Pair *illus*	325
Jar, Lid, Blue & White, Birds, Flowers, 14½ x 9 In.	188
Jar, Lid, Multicolor, Peacocks, Lotus, Leaves, White Ground, 10 In., Pair	236
Jar, Lid, Wucai, Transitional Style, Qilin, Chimera, Foo Dog, Wood Stand, 18 In. .... *illus*	750
Jar, Melon, Red, Sang De Boeuf, Glaze, Knopped Finial, 12¾ x 8¼ In.	561
Jar, Scene, Noble Figures, Horseback, Wucai, Blossoming Tree, 10¾ In.	1652
Jar, Temple, Dome Lid, Knopped Finial, Deer, Crane, Peonies, Pine Branches, 16 In., Pair.....	325
Jardiniere, Blue & White, 2 Men, Seated, Talking, Greek Key, 7¼ x 9 In.	500
Jardiniere, Frog, Green, White, Glazed, Bulging Eyes, Wood Base, 8 In. .... *illus*	960
Jardiniere, Octagonal, Birds, Flowers, Square Rim, Late 1800s, 3¼ x 8¾ In.	132
Lamp, Bisque, Woman, Long Dress, Robe, Multicolor, Electrified, 27½ In.	390
Lamp, Guanyin, Flower Bundle, Oval Linen Shade, Blue Leaves, Wood Base, 30 In., Pair *illus*	295
Pillow, Neck, Blue & White, Flowers, Multicolor, 5 x 9¾ In., Pair	94
Plaque, Old Man, Seated, Painted, 21 x 12½ In.	63
Plaque, Painted, Longevity Figure, Landscape, White Ground, Wood Frame, 32 x 59 In........	148
Platter, Blue & White, Reticulated, Pierced Rim, Pagoda Scene, Late 1900s, 18 x 15½ In.	531
Punch Bowl, Cobalt Blue, Central Medallion, Scrolling Vine, Wood Stand, 1900s, 8 x 18 In..	384
Teapot, Lid, Blue, White, Rotund Shape, Red Clay Mark, 8¼ x 8¼ In.	156
Tureen, Famille Rose, Hen, Multicolor, Painted, Early 1900s, 9½ x 13½ x 8 In. .... *illus*	125
Umbrella Stand, Flowers, Bird, Hand Painted, 19 In.	94
Umbrella Stand, Seurat Park Scene, Transfer, Marked, Late 1900s, 18½ In. .... *illus*	118
Urn, Lid, Painted 3-Claw Dragon, Phoenix Bird, Bulbous, 25 In.	366
Vase, Birds & Flowers, White Ground, Hand Painted, Footed, 1900s, 14¼ x 7 In.	173
Vase, Blue & White, Red, Late 1800s, 9½ In. .... *illus*	1416
Vase, Blue Ground, Dragons, Yellow, White Interior, Bulbous, 17½ In., Pair	305
Vase, Blue Tiger, White Ground, Long Neck, Underfoot, Late 1700s, 8¼ In.	1080
Vase, Bottle, Cobalt Blue, Glaze, Elongated Neck, Bulbous Body, 1900s, 14 x 7½ In., Pair......	1638
Vase, Cobalt Blue Ground, White, Flowers & Leaves, 12½ In., Pair	1134
Vase, Cylindrical, Landscape, Molded Rim, Famille Rose, 9¼ In.	531

Porcelain-Chinese, Vase, Famille Noire, Enamel, Leaves, Bird, Gilt, Deer Head Handles, 12 x 9 ½ In., Pair
$207

Austin Auction Gallery

Porcelain-Chinese, Vase, Gilt Rim, Blue & White, 2 Handles, Mottahedeh, Reproduction, 7 In.
$128

Roland Auctioneers & Valuers

Porcelain-Chinese, Vase, Iron Red, Birds, Phoenix, Flower Garden, Plum Blossoms, Ruyi Rim Border, 1800s, 17 In.
$354

eland Little Auctions

Porcelain-Chinese, Vase, Peacock's Eye, Lavender, Blue, Oxblood Flambe Spots, Brown Ground, 1700s, 15 ¾ In.
$1,220

Neal Auction Company

Porcelain-Chinese, Washbasin, Blue & White, Islamic, Rounded Sides, Flared Rim, Flat Base, 10 In.
$7,200

Michaan's Auctions

Porcelain-Contemporary, Vase, Euphrates, Glazed, Ettore Sottsass, Memphis, Italy, 1983, 15 ½ In.
$1,250

Wright

Postcard, Photograph, Woody
Hedspath, L'Albatros, American Bicyclist,
Black & White, France
$125

Cowan's Auctions

Postcard, Valentine, Baby Suffragette,
Love Me Love My Vote, Ellen H.
Clapsaddle
$105

Matthew Bullock Auctioneers

Poster, Circus, Buffalo Bill's Wild West,
Lithograph, Chaix, Paris, Frame, 1890s,
31 x 42 ¼ In.
$625

Cowan's Auctions

Vase, Famille Noire, Enamel, Leaves, Bird, Gilt, Deer Head Handles, 12 x 9 ½ In., Pair . *illus*	207
Vase, Famille Noire, Yen Yen, Black Ground, Royal Hunting Party Scene, 1900s, 25 In., Pair.	610
Vase, Famille Rose, Enamel, Multicolor, Festival Scene, Flared Rim, 14 ¼ In., Pair	384
Vase, Famille Rose, Man, Holding Cane, Multicolor, Marked, 9 In., Pair	813
Vase, Famille Verte, Figural Design, Wood Base, Paper Shade, Lamp Mounted, 33 In.	531
Vase, Flared Rim, Gilt, Pierced Handles, Mountain Landscape, Horseback, Wood Base, 24 In.	384
Vase, Flared Rim, Scrolled, Leaves, Geometric Designs, Blue Ground, 13 In., Pair	944
Vase, Flowers, Swan, Horse, Blue Rim, Painted, 11 ½ In.	94
Vase, Gilt Rim, Blue & White, 2 Handles, Mottahedeh, Reproduction, 7 In. *illus*	128
Vase, Gu Shape, Blue & White, Flowers, 9 x 4 ⅜ In.	313
Vase, Iron Red, Birds, Phoenix, Flower Garden, Plum Blossoms, Ruyi Rim Border, 1800s, 17 In. *illus*	354
Vase, Mountain, Horseback, Attendants, Gilt, Handles, Wood Stand, 24 ½ In.	354
Vase, Ornate, Blue & White, Flowers, 10 In., Pair	81
Vase, Peacock's Eye, Lavender, Blue, Oxblood Flambe Spots, Brown Ground, 1700s, 15 ¾ In. *illus*	1220
Vase, Pear Shape, Waisted Neck, Flared Rim, Black Glaze, 12 ¼ In.	1440
Vase, Sang De Boeuf, Red, Garlic Mouth, Blue Archaic, Mark, 1800s, 8 ¾ In.	625
Washbasin, Blue & White, Islamic, Rounded Sides, Flared Rim, Flat Base, 10 In. *illus*	7200

Porcelain-Contemporary lists pieces made by artists working after 1975.

Charger, Flower, Blue, Brown, Marked, Birger Kaipiainen, Finland, c.1985, 14 x 1 ¾ In.	1250
Eggcup, Hen, Spread Wings, Claude Lalanne, c.1990, 3 In., Pair	3750
Figurine, Boxer, Standing, Glazed, Signed, Lars Calmar, Denmark, 2008, 23 ⅛ x 8 ½ In.	2000
Plate, Flowers, Round, Brown, Glaze, Fiori, Birger Kaipiainen, Finland, 1983	2250
Plate, Gilt Rim, Multicolor, White Ground, Mottahedeh, U.S.A., 10 In., 8 Piece	325
Tray, Change, Burgundy, White, Wrought Iron, Velvet Goatskin Base, H Deco Series, Hermes, 8 x 7 In..	630
Vase, Euphrates, Glazed, Ettore Sottsass, Memphis, Italy, 1983, 15 ½ In. *illus*	1250

Porcelain-Midcentury includes pieces made from the 1940s to about 1975.

Figurine, Mother, Child, Flowers, Gold Detailing, Luigi Fabris, Italy, 1940s, 8 ½ x 9 In.	633
Plate, Round, Flowers, Ceramic Decal, Seeing Is Believing, Howard Kottler, c.1972, 10 ¼ In..	250
Vase, Lid, Incised Design, Multicolor, Gilt, La Maitrise De Nimy, c.1940, 19 ¼ In.	427

POSTCARD

Postcards were first legally permitted in Austria on October 1, 1869. The United States passed postal regulations allowing the card in 1872. Most of the picture postcards collected today date after 1910. The amount of postage can help to date a card. The rates are: 1872 (1 cent), 1917 (2 cents), 1919 (1 cent), 1925 (2 cents), 1928 (1 cent), 1952 (2 cents), 1958 (3 cents), 1963 (4 cents), 1968 (5 cents), 1971 (6 cents), 1973 (8 cents), 1975 (7 cents), 1976 (9 cents), 1978 (10 cents), March 1981 (12 cents), November 1981 (13 cents), 1985 (14 cents), 1988 (15 cents), 1991 (19 cents), 1995 (20 cents), 2001 (21 cents), 2002 (23 cents), 2006 (24 cents), 2007 (26 cents), 2008 (27 cents), 2009 (28 cents), 2011 (29 cents), 2012 (32 cents), 2013 (33 cents), 2014 (34 cents), 2016 (35 cents beginning January 17 and back to 34 cents beginning April 10, 2016), 2018 (35 cents beginning January 21, 2018). Collectors search for early or unusual postmarks, picture postcards, or important handwritten messages (that includes celebrity autographs). While most postcards sell for low prices, a small number bring high prices. Some of these are listed here.

Bons Baisers, Photo, Baby In Airplane, French Flag Tail, Multicolor Flowers, France, c.1900 .	16
Musee Du Louvre, Old Master Paintings, Black & White Prints, Box, Early 1900s, 48 Piece .	37
New Year, 1909, Happy New Year, 2 Children In Snow, Hold-To-Light, Multicolor	50
Photograph, Maiden, 2 Horses, 1914	17
Photograph, Small Girl, Standing, Large Dog, Sitting, Black & White, 5 ½ x 3 ½ In.	15
Photograph, Woody Hedspath, L'Albatros, American Bicyclist, Black & White, France . *illus*	125
Rock Island Plow Co. Exhibit, 1907	7
St. Patrick's Day, Family, Driving In Car, Nothing Slow For The Like Of Us, Embossed, 1910	30
Thanksgiving, Boy Riding Turkey, Blue Outfit, White Hat, 1917	15

Poster, Concert, Doors & Yardbirds, July 1967, Lithograph, B. MacLean, 22 x 14 In.
$8,125

Stephenson's Auctioneers & Appraisers

Poster, Concert, Grateful Dead, Aoxomoxoa, Jan. 1969, Lithograph, R. Griffin, 26 x 22 In.
$16,250

Stephenson's Auctioneers & Appraisers

Poster, Show, Hoyt's, Trip To Chinatown, Musical Comedy, Lithograph, Frame, 1891, 44½ x 34¾ In.
$125

Susanin's Auctioneers & Appraisers

Poster, Travel, Pistany Spa, Czechoslovakia, Village Background, Hempel, 42 x 26½ In.
$523

Alderfer Auction Company

411

Potlid, Cherry Tooth Paste, Patronized By The Queen, Multicolor, John Cosnell, London, 3 In.
$24

Strawser Auction Group

Potlid, Taylor's Saponaceous Compound, Man In Mirror, Purple Transfer, Base, 3⅝ x 1⅞ In.
$300

Blackwell Auctions

Pottery, Centerpiece, Fish, Swimming, Ruffled Rim, Green Ground, Foley Intarsio, 6 x 16 In.
$513

Pook & Pook

Pottery, Dish, Blue & White, Earthenware, Leafy Border, Underfoot, Persia, 9 In.
$207

Austin Auction Gallery

Pottery, Dish, Game, Hatching Chicks, Lid, Underplate, Caneware, William Schiller & Sons, c.1880, 6 In.
$354

Leland Little Auctions

Pottery, Humidor, Golfers, Swing Handle, Brass Base, W. Wood & Co., 1895, 6¾ x 6½ In.
$502

Leland Little Auctions

Pottery, Roof Tile, Figural, Warrior, Tiger, Glaze, Wood Stand, Marked, 14¼ x 14½ In.
$944

Austin Auction Gallery

Pottery, Vase, Earthenware, Silver Collar, Painted, Blue Flowers, Talavera, Mexico, 8 In.
$236

Austin Auction Gallery

Valentine, Baby Suffragette, Love Me Love My Vote, Ellen H. Clapsaddle .... *illus* 105
YMCA Building, Omaha, Nebraska, Linen, 1944 5

POSTER

Posters have informed the public about news and entertainment events since ancient times. Nineteenth-century advertising and theatrical posters and twentieth-century movie and war posters are of special interest today. The price is determined by the artist, the condition, and the rarity. Posters may also be listed in Movie, Political, World War I and II, and other categories in this book.

American Red Cross, Roll Call, Mother, Carrying Child, Roringer, 1918, 42 x 28 In. 110
Bieres De La Meuse, Print, On Paper, Wood Frame, Portal Publications, Late 1900s, 42 x 30 In.. 118
Broadside, Grand Admiral Barber & His Bubbles, Oil On Canvas, Waldo Pierce, 36 x 26 In... 1404
Broadside, New Zealand Centennial Games, Paper Lithograph, Black Box Frame, 1940, 40 x 30 In... 468
Carnival, The Big Show Entrance, Hanging, Hand Painted, 30 ½ x 13 x 14 In. 2768
Circus, Buffalo Bill's Wild West, Lithograph, Chaix, Paris, Frame, 1890s, 31 x 42 ¼ In. *illus* 625
Circus, Harry Qubey's Dog, Riverside Printing Co., Milwaukee, Early 1900s, 27 ¾ x 41 ¾ In. 266
Circus, Ringling Bros. & Barnum & Bailey, Polar Bear, Red Ground, 1921, 22 x 32 In. 750
Circus, Ringling Bros. Barnum & Bailey, Combined Clown, Linen, Erie Litho, 1930s, 29 x 41 In. 295
Circus, Ringling Bros., World's Biggest Menagerie, Strobridge, Frame, 1916, 23 x 32 In. 863
Concert, Doors & Yardbirds, July 1967, Lithograph, B. MacLean, 22 x 14 In. .... *illus* 8125
Concert, Eric Burdon & The Animals, Oct. 1967, Lithograph, B. MacLean, 21 x 14 In........... 125
Concert, Grateful Dead, Aoxomoxoa, Jan. 1969, Lithograph, R. Griffin, 26 x 22 In. ...... *illus* 16250
Concert, Grateful Dead, Fillmore West, Feb. 1970, Lithograph, D. Singer, 22 x 14 In. 2745
Concert, Moody Blues, November 1968, Lithograph, A. Kelly, R. Griffin, 22 x 14 In.............. 375
Concert, Simon & Garfunkel, Jan. 22, 1967, Lincoln Center, Black Stylized Letters, 40 x 26 In.... 207
New Orleans Jazz Fest, Al Hirt, Blue Dog, Signed, George Rodrigue, Frame, 2000, 40 x 26 In. 920
Show, Hoyt's, Trip To Chinatown, Musical Comedy, Lithograph, Frame, 1891, 44 ½ x 34 ¾ In. *illus* 125
Stock Car Races, Pine Bowl Speedway, Troy, N.Y., White Ground, 27 ½ x 13 ½ In................. 177
Theater, New York State Theater, Lincoln Center, 23 Apr 64, Litho, Robert Indiana, 1964, 45 x 30 In. 156
Travel, Berk Place, 3 Women, Holding Globe, Boats, Frame, L. Peutier, Early 1900s, 63 x 47 In. .. 173
Travel, Pistany Spa, Czechoslovakia, Village Background, Hempel, 42 x 26 ½ In. .... *illus* 523
Travel, Vacation, Plymouth, Rowe's Wharf, Paper Lithograph, Frame, 900s, 25 x 18 In........ 200

POTLID

Potlids are just that, lids for pots. Transfer-printed potlids had their heyday from the 1840s to the early 1900s. The English Staffordshire potteries made ceramic containers with decorative lids for bear's grease, shrimp or meat paste, cold cream, and toothpaste. Printed advertising and pictures of historical events, portraits of famous people, or scenic views were designed in black and white or color. Reproductions have been made.

Beef Marrow, Eugene Roussel Pomatum, Cow, Transfer, c.1850, 3 In. 69
Cherry Tooth Paste, Patronized By The Queen, Multicolor, John Cosnell, London, 3 In. *illus* 24
Taylor's Saponaceous Compound, Man In Mirror, Purple Transfer, Base, 3 ⅝ x 1 ⅞ In.. *illus* 300
The Village Wedding, Tenier's Pink, Group Dancing, Multicolor, Base, Pratt, 1857, 4 ¼ In.. 24

POTTERY

Pottery and porcelain are different. Pottery is opaque; you can't see through it. Porcelain is translucent. If you hold a porcelain dish in front of a strong light, you will see the light through the dish. Porcelain is colder to the touch. Pottery is softer and easier to break and will stain more easily because it is porous. Porcelain is thinner, lighter, and more durable. Majolica, faience, and stoneware are all pottery. Additional pieces of pottery are listed in this book in the categories Pottery-Art, Pottery-Chinese, Pottery-Contemporary, Pottery-Midcentury,

Pottery, Vase, Green Matte Glaze, Lobed Petals, Arts & Crafts, Jemerick Pottery, 1900s, 7 ½ In.
$384

Austin Auction Gallery

Pottery-Art, Bowl, Reticulated Lid, Spout Shape Handles, Pierced Base, Vally Wieselthier, 7 ½ In.
$1,098

Neal Auction Company

TIP

Repairs on standing figures or pitchers should be made from the bottom up.

Pottery-Art, Bust, Omar Khayyam, Mahogany Glaze, Oscar Bachelder, 1913, 17 In.
$4,613

P

Brunk Auctions

Pottery-Art, Figurine, Mother & Child, Slip Cast, Glazed, Karoly Fulop, 21 ½ x 8 x 5 In.
$1,250

Toomey & Co. Auctioneers

Pottery-Art, Vase, Flowers, Multicolor, Glazed, Spiral Handles, Vally Wieselthier, c.1925, 8 In.
$1,037

Neal Auction Company

and under the factory name. For information about pottery makers and marks, see *Kovels' Dictionary of Marks—Pottery & Porcelain: 1650–1850* and *Kovels' New Dictionary of Marks—Pottery & Porcelain: 1850 to the Present.*

Bowl, Jun Ware, Lotus, Scalloped Rim, Lobed Exterior Wall, Pale Blue Glaze, 4¾ x 9 In.	150
Bowl, Shaving, Multicolor, Deep Well, Bird, Shell Pattern Rim, Earthenware, Late 1700s, 11 In.	354
Bowl, Stacking, Torso, Stoke-On-Trent, 12 x 18 In.	384
Bust, Indian, Headdress, Marbleized, Square Base, 1910s, 19 In.	266
Centerpiece, Fish, Swimming, Ruffled Rim, Green Ground, Foley Intarsio, 6 x 16 In. ... *illus*	513
Charger, Earthenware, Gadrooned Center, Molded Border, Tin Glazed, Continental, 1600s, 15 In.	923
Dish, Blue & White, Earthenware, Leafy Border, Underfoot, Persia, 9 In. ...... *illus*	207
Dish, Game, Hatching Chicks, Lid, Underplate, Caneware, William Schiller & Sons, c.1880, 6 In. *illus*	354
Figurine, Foo Dog, Seated, Jade Green, Glaze, Square Platform, 21 x 14½ x 23 In.	677
Figurine, Leopard, Seated, Black Spot, Gold Ground, Glazed, 10½ In.	207
Flowerpot, Shallow, Painted, Multicolor, Arts & Crafts, 7 In.	62
Ginger Jar, Dome Lid, Tin Glazed, Signed, Uriarte, Talavera Mexico, Late 1900s, 17 In.	354
Group, 4 Doves, On Branches, Tree Stumps, Circular Plinth, 10 In.	236
Humidor, Golfers, Swing Handle, Brass Base, W. Wood & Co., 1895, 6¾ x 6½ In. ...... *illus*	502
Jar, Cream Ground, Painted, Green Band, Multicolor, Leaves, Flared Rim, 23 In.	31
Jar, Storage, Martavan, Glazed, 1800s, 37 In.	832
Lamp, Blue Transfer, Asian Design, Gilt Metal, Mounted, White Shade, Castilian, 36 In.	130
Plate, Daffodil, Bee, White Ground, George Jones, Marked, H.O.J., c.1890, 9 In.	40
Roof Tile, Figural, Warrior, Tiger, Glaze, Wood Stand, Marked, 14¼ x 14½ In. ..... *illus*	944
Tray, Cream Center, Stylized Orange, Tulip, Gold Trim, Scalloped Rim, 7 x 6½ In.	25
Vase, 2 Handles, Rounded Lip, Speckled Blue Green Glaze, N.C., 14½ In.	325
Vase, Earthenware, Silver Collar, Painted, Blue Flowers, Talavera, Mexico, 8 In. ...... *illus*	236
Vase, Frog Shape, Open Mouth, Green Glaze, Brown Base, 6½ In., Pair	488
Vase, Green Matte Glaze, Lobed Petals, Arts & Crafts, Jemerick Pottery, 1900s, 7½ In. . *illus*	384
Vase, Green, Glaze, Scheurich, Germany, 18 In.	25
Vase, Marble Glaze, 2 Handles, Hiroshi Nakayama & Judy Glasser, 12¼ In.	177
Vase, Tree, Castle, Birds Flying, Multicolor, Foley Intarsio, 8¾ In.	288

 Pottery-Art. Art pottery was first made in America in Cincinnati, Ohio, during the 1870s. The pieces were hand thrown and hand decorated. The art pottery tradition continued until studio potters began making different artistic wares about 1930. American, English, and Continental art pottery by less well-known makers is listed here. Most makers listed in *Kovels' American Art Pottery,* such as Arequipa, Ohr, Rookwood, Roseville, and Weller, are listed in their own categories in this book. More recent pottery is listed under the name of the maker or in Pottery-Contemporary or Pottery-Midcentury.

Bowl, Reticulated Lid, Spout Shape Handles, Pierced Base, Vally Wieselthier, 7½ In. ... *illus*	1098
Bust, Omar Khayyam, Mahogany Glaze, Oscar Bachelder, 1913, 17 In. ...... *illus*	4613
Charger, Rustic Trellis, Orange, Yellow, Blue, Green, Charlotte Rhead, 12½ In.	103
Figurine, Mother & Child, Slip Cast, Glazed, Karoly Fulop, 21½ x 8 x 5 In. ...... *illus*	1250
Jar, Dream, Lid, Amethyst & Agate Slice Finials, Iridescent Glaze, Raku Fired, 12 In.	177
Vase, 2 Koi Fish, Red Flambe, Brown, Fluted, Signed, Bernard Moore, England, Early 1900s, 10 In.	1380
Vase, Black Gunmetal Glaze, Red, Yellow, Green Overrun, Oscar Bachelder, Monogram, Lobe, 4½ In.	2214
Vase, Brown, Black, Signed, Charles Catteau, France, 6½ In.	192
Vase, Earthenware, Mottled Marbleized Glaze, Stick Neck, Bretby, England, 12 In.	59
Vase, Floor, 2 Handles, Molded Rim, Burley Winter, 19½ In.	147
Vase, Flowers, Beige, Bisque, Painted, H.A. Graack & Son Pottery, Florida, 6¾ In.	92
Vase, Flowers, Multicolor, Glazed, Spiral Handles, Vally Wieselthier, c.1925, 8 In. ...... *illus*	1037
Vase, Green Matte, Floral, Molded Rim, 9½ In. ...... *illus*	540
Vase, Hadcote, Floral, Long Neck, Frederick Hurten Rhead, Wardle & Co., 12¼ x 5½ In.	1000
Vase, Lacquered Geometric Design, Dark Tortoise Blue Ground, Japan, c.1900, 31 x 11 In.	1638
Vase, Leathery Green, Fluted Rim, Footed, Marked, Strobl, 1907, 4¼ In.	1210
Vase, Leaves, Footed, Gourd Shape, Multicolor, Bretby, England, 1900s, 9 In.	50
Vase, Majolica Style, Blue Glaze, Oriental Motif, Theodore Deck, 10 In. ...... *illus*	509

P

Pottery-Art, Vase, Green Matte, Floral, Molded Rim, 9 ½ In.
$540

Cottone Auctions

Pottery-Art, Vase, Majolica Style, Blue Glaze, Oriental Motif, Theodore Deck, 10 In.
$509

Strawser Auction Group

Pottery-Art, Vase, Metallic Glaze, Reclining Nude, Jean Barol, c.1930, 7 ⅞ In.
$610

Leal Auction Company

Pottery-Contemporary, Candlestick, Praying Angel Shape, Glazed, Gilt, Mary Lou Higgins, 1996, 5 ¼ In.
$266

Leland Little Auctions

Pottery-Contemporary, Charger, 6 Parachuting Stick Figures, Hand Thrown, Beatrice Wood, 14 ⅝ In.
$968

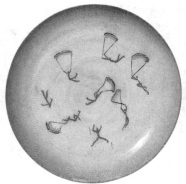

Humler & Nolan

Pottery-Contemporary, Dish, Rectangular, Dimpled Pattern, Black & Celadon Glaze, Peter Lane, 3 ½ In.
$354

Leland Little Auctions

Pottery-Contemporary, Pitcher, Garlic Bulb Shape, Yellow, Green, White, Makoto Yabe, Late 1900s, 4 ½ x 6 In.
$313

Eldred's

Pottery-Contemporary, Platter, Fish, Redware, Checkerboard, Flower, Oval, Mackenzie Childs, 19 x 10 In.
$130

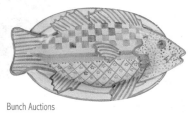

Bunch Auctions

P

Pottery-Contemporary, Dish, Casserole, 3-D Print, Micaceous Clay, R. Rael, V. San Fratello, 2020
$2,500

Pottery-Contemporary, Teapot, Lid, Finial, Black & Yellow Glaze, Wood Handle, Finial, Signed, Frith, 6 x 7 In.
$131

Susanin's Auctioneers & Appraisers

Pottery-Contemporary, Vase, Esperance, Resin Sheet, Colored & Folded, Gaetano Pesce, 2020, 65 x 42 In.
$120,000

Pottery-Contemporary, Vase, Raku Fired, Stephen Merritt, 1900s, 20 In.
$330

Cottone Auctions

Pottery-Midcentury, Bowl, Glazed, Footed, Incised, CB, Clyde Burt, Melrose, Ohio, 1960s, 2½ In.
$750

Toomey & Co. Auctioneers

Pottery-Midcentury, Charger, Green Rim, Sunflowers, Glazed, Yellow Ground, Mid 1900s, 20¾ In.
$236

Leland Little Auctions

TIP
Don't hide all your valuables in one place. Burglars may miss some hiding places.

Pottery-Midcentury, Figurine, Bird, Incised Design, Brass Legs, Square Base, Aldo Londi, Bitossi, 11 In.
$554

Locati Auctions

Vase, Metallic Glaze, Reclining Nude, Jean Barol, c.1930, 7 7/8 In. .... *illus*	610
Vase, Orange & Green Matte Glaze, Raised Vines, Markham Pottery, Ann Arbor, Mich., 7 In.	1700
Vase, Squat, Bulbous Body, Green Matte Glaze, 2 Handles, Merrimac, c.1905, 4 1/2 x 6 3/4 In. ..	527

Pottery-Contemporary lists pieces made by artists working about 1975 and later.

Bowl, Triangle Design, Jeff Oestreich, 12 1/2 In.	79
Candlestick, Praying Angel Shape, Glazed, Gilt, Mary Lou Higgins, 1996, 5 1/4 In. .... *illus*	266
Charger, 6 Parachuting Stick Figures, Hand Thrown, Beatrice Wood, 14 5/8 In. .... *illus*	968
Charger, Crete, Dancing Stick Figures, Blue Shaded To Mauve, Beatrice Wood, 14 5/8 In........	970
Charger, Golden Brown Ground, Lines Decoration, Warren Mackenzie, 17 1/2 In.....................	1074
Charger, Oval, Multicolor Design, Jun Kaneko, Japan, 1990, 28 x 22 In................	3673
Dish, Casserole, 3-D Print, Micaceous Clay, R. Rael, V. San Fratello, 2020 .... *illus*	2500
Dish, Rectangular, Dimpled Pattern, Black & Celadon Glaze, Peter Lane, 3 1/2 In. .... *illus*	354
Jardiniere, Eagle Reserves, Tan Border, Stand, Signed, Rick Wiscarver, 1989, 16 In.	346
Jug, Face, Light Bodied Clay, Cream Ground, Applied Eyes, Footed, Late 1900s, 5 In.	500
Jug, Face, Swirl, Brown, Cream, Broken Teeth, Applied Handle, Charles Lisk, 16 In.	281
Moon Pot, Rattle, Glazed Stoneware, Toshiko Takaezu, 5 In......................................	3380
Oil Jar, Lid, Flared Mouth, Inner Rim, White Slip, Brown Glaze, Archie Teague, 11 1/2 In.	118
Pitcher, Garlic Bulb Shape, Yellow, Green, White, Makoto Yabe, Late 1900s, 4 1/2 x 6 In. *illus*	313
Plate, Blue, Wavy Glaze, Makoto Yabe, Late 1900s, 11 In.	438
Plate, Male Nude II, Dark Brown Ground, Red Lines, R.C. Gorman, c.1980, 8 3/4 In.................	311
Platter, Fish, Redware, Checkerboard, Flower, Oval, Mackenzie Childs, 19 x 10 In. ...... *illus*	130
Pot, Fantasy, Pre-Columbian Style, Red Clay, Squat Ribbed Body, Wood Stand, 10 x 15 In.	148
Pot, Monumental, Raku Fired, Earthenware, Rick Dillingham, Signed, 1985, 15 x 16 In.	6300
Teapot, Lid, Finial, Black & Yellow Glaze, Wood Handle, Finial, Signed, Frith, 6 x 7 In. *illus*	131
Tumbler, Ethereal Beauty, Floats, Multicolor, Geometrics, Jane Peiser, 7 In.	502
Vase, Barro Negro, Bulbous, Flowers, Carved, Ruffled Rim, Signed, Reyna Simon Lopez, c.1900, 8 In...	71
Vase, Brown & White, Circles, Rob Pulleyn, Impressed Wired, Signed, 20 In.....................	678
Vase, Bubble Design, Hand Painted, Metallic Glazes, Carolyn Carroll, Late 1900s, 12 In.	89
Vase, Bud Shape, Earthenware, Terra Sigillata, Glass Base, Alice Ballard, c.1983, 27 In.	1003
Vase, Bud, Mottled Luster Glaze, Flared Rim, Marked, Beatrice Wood, 9 x 3 3/4 In.	2375
Vase, Esperance, Resin Sheet, Colored & Folded, Gaetano Pesce, 2020, 65 x 42 In. .... *illus*	120000
Vase, Lid, Monumental, Glazed, Val Cushing, Signed, 23 x 8 1/2 In................	1188
Vase, Metal Mounted, Ornate Gilded Spelter Handle, Glazed, Marked, Ecni, 24 x 10 x 6 In.....	351
Vase, Painted, Abstract Figures, Jonathan Nash Glynn, 1993, 10 1/2 In.	325
Vase, Raku Fired, Stephen Merritt, 1900s, 20 In. .... *illus*	330
Vase, Stoneware, Flared Rim, Green Abstract, Tan Glaze, Oval, Paul Chaleff, 15 1/2 x 16 In. ...	527
Watering Can, Elongated Spout, Shaped Handle, Marked SW, 17 In.	62

Pottery-Midcentury includes pieces made from the 1940s to about 1975.

Bowl, Glazed, Footed, Incised, CB, Clyde Burt, Melrose, Ohio, 1960s, 2 1/2 In. .... *illus*	750
Chalice, Mottled Luster Glaze, Flared, Dots, Buttressed Handles, B. Wood, 11 In.............	2750
Charger, Green Rim, Sunflowers, Glazed, Yellow Ground, Mid 1900s, 20 3/4 In. .... *illus*	236
Figurine, Bird, Incised Design, Brass Legs, Square Base, Aldo Londi, Bitossi, 11 In. ..... *illus*	554
Pitcher, Earthenware, Black Slip, White Ground, Pablo Picasso, 5 x 6 x 5 1/2 In. .... *illus*	3690
Pitcher, Hibou, Owl Shape, Cobalt Blue, White Earthenware, Pablo Picasso, 9 1/2 In. .... *illus*	6875
Plate, Bull Under Tree, Black, White, Dots, Picasso, Madoura, 1952, 8 In......................... ...	2124
Plate, Earthenware Glaze, White Ground, Black Slip, Pablo Picasso, 8 3/4 In. .... *illus*	3998
Plate, Stoneware, Engobe Wash, Pass-Through, P. Voulkos, 1974, 5 x 20 In.	4800
Plate, Visage Noir, Stylized Face, Black Ground, Picasso, 1948, 9 In......	4688
Plate, White Earthenware Clay, Engobes, Red, Green, Black Ground, Picasso, 1948, 9 1/2 In...	5625
Tray, Reticulated, Mottled Grayish Blue Glaze, Stoneware, Peter Lane, 3 x 15 x 15 In.	512
Urn, Stylized Horse, Orange Ground, White Glaze, Footed, Italy, 11 x 7 1/2 x 8 In.	74
Vase, 4-Sided, Blue, Bright Green, Volcanic Glaze, Rose Cabat, 3 1/4 In. .... *illus*	1210
Vase, Blackware, Bulbous, Flower, Leafy, Carved, Reed Stand, Signed, Dona Rosa, 16 3/4 In. ..	649
Vase, Coupe, Mottled Luster Glaze, Splayed Foot, Beatrice Wood, 6 x 6 In.	2750
Vase, Feelie, Vellum Glaze, Brown, Signed, Rose Cabat, 4 3/4 x 3 1/2 In. .... *illus*	704
Vase, Feelie, Yellow, Glaze, Stoneware, Signed, Rose Cabat, Arizona, 1980s, 3 3/8 In...............	688
Vase, Glaze Stoneware, Bulbous, Claude Conover, 1960s, 20 x 16 In. .... *illus*	3250

Pottery-Midcentury, Pitcher, Earthenware, Black Slip, White Ground, Pablo Picasso, 5 x 6 x 5 1/2 In. $3,690

Brunk Auctions

Pottery-Midcentury, Pitcher, Hibou, Owl Shape, Cobalt Blue, White Earthenware, Pablo Picasso, 9 1/2 In. $6,875

Charlton Hall Auctions

P

Pottery-Midcentury, Plate, Earthenware Glaze, White Ground, Black Slip, Pablo Picasso, 8 3/4 In. $3,998

Brunk Auctions

Pottery-Midcentury, Vase, 4-Sided, Blue, Bright Green, Volcanic Glaze, Rose Cabat, 3 ¼ In.
$1,210

Humler & Nolan

Pottery-Midcentury, Vase, Feelie, Vellum Glaze, Brown, Signed, Rose Cabat, 4 ¾ x 3 ½ In.
$704

Treadway

Pottery-Midcentury, Vase, Glaze Stoneware, Bulbous, Claude Conover, 1960s, 20 x 16 In.
$3,250

Toomey & Co. Auctioneers

Pottery-Midcentury, Vase, Il Sesante, Glazed, Earthenware, Ettore Sottsass, c.1966, 14 ⅜ In.
$1,260

Sotheby's

Pottery-Midcentury, Vase, Pink & Black Enamel, Tapered, Handle, Fausto Melotti, c.1950, 26 In.
$63,308

Sotheby's

Pottery-Midcentury, Vase, Stylized Sun Face, Enamel, Marked, Fausto Melotti, c.1955, 13 In.
$24,117

Sotheby's

Pottery-Midcentury, Vase, Vaso Luna, Stoneware, Iridescent Glaze, Fausto Melotti, 1950, 27 In.
$72,352

Sotheby's

Vase, Il Sesante, Glazed, Earthenware, Ettore Sottsass, c.1966, 14 3/8 In. .... *illus* 1260
Vase, Pink & Black Enamel, Tapered, Handle, Fausto Melotti, c.1950, 26 In. .... *illus* 63308
Vase, Pink & Blue Drip, Matte Glaze, Mounted, Lucite Plinth, c.1970, 27 In............................ 89
Vase, Purple Volcanic Luster Glaze, Tapered, Beatrice Wood, 5 x 4 In. 2750
Vase, Stylized Sun Face, Enamel, Marked, Fausto Melotti, c.1955, 13 In. .... *illus* 24117
Vase, Vaso Luna, Stoneware, Iridescent Glaze, Fausto Melotti, 1950, 27 In. .... *illus* 72352
Wall Plaque, Face, Round, Matte Glaze, Painted, CB, Clyde Burt, Melrose, Ohio, 1960s, 12 x 1/2 In. 2000

POWDER FLASK AND POWDER HORN

Powder flasks and powder horns were made to hold the gunpowder used in antique firearms. The early examples were made of horn or wood; later ones were of copper or brass.

POWDER FLASK

Copper, Soldered Construction, Stamped, Acanthus Decor, Brass Spout, 1850s, 8 1/4 In. 118
Velvet, Gilt Bronze Mounts, Triangular, Vase Shape Nozzle, Italy, 1800s, 8 1/2 x 7 1/2 In. 1063

POWDER HORN

Brown, Threaded & Faceted Spout, Accession Number, Marked, 13 In. .... *illus* 50
Engraved, Bone Cap, Carved, Leafy Design, Sailing Vessels, Fishermen, Wm. McKeath, 1837 594
Engraved, Ship, Anchor, Cannon, 2 Stars, Signed, IBR, 1812, 15 In.. 448
Hunter, Animals, Flower, House, Carved Spout, Brass Hanging Loop, John Wiltson, 1748, 13 In.. 3375
Incised, Sea Serpent, US Shield, Compass Rose, Capt. John Tobin His Horn, Civil War, 10 x 2 1/2 In 563
Sailing Ships, Birds, Flat Pine Base, Carved Spout, Inscribed, Peter Farnum, 1799, 13 In.... 1000
Scrimshaw, 2 Hippocamps, Eagle, Flags, Salmon Cove Conception Bay, Wood End Cap, 1869, 14 In. 400
Scrimshaw, Landscape, Castle, British Flag, Ship, Deer Hunt, Dog, House, David, 1700s, 12 In.... 6710
Silver Mount, Figural Base, Raised Stem, Weighted Foot, Sweden, 1850s, 16 1/2 In. 1000

PRATT

PRATT
FENTON

Pratt ware means two different things. It was an early Staffordshire pottery, cream colored with colored decorations, made by Felix Pratt during the late eighteenth century. There was also Pratt ware made with transfer designs during the mid-nineteenth century in Fenton, England. Reproductions of the transfer-printed Pratt are being made.

Box, Lid, Children Of Flora, White Ground, Round, 5 3/4 In....................... 34
Garniture Set, Neoclassical Style, Vase, 2 Candlesticks, Classical Figures, c.1890, 9 In. 705
Watch Hutch, Figural, Tall Case Clock Shape, Apollo, Ceres, Early 1800s, 9 1/4 x 6 x 2 In....... 322

PRESSED GLASS

Pressed glass, or pattern glass, was first made in the United States in the 1820s after the invention of glass pressing machines. Hundreds of patterns of pressed glass were made in complete table settings. Although the Boston and Sandwich Works was the most famous of the pressed glass factories, there were about sixteen other factories making pressed glass from 1830 to 1850, and still more from 1850 to 1900, when pressed glass reached its greatest popularity. It is now being widely reproduced. The pattern names used in this listing are based on the information in the book *Pressed Glass in America* by John and Elizabeth Welker. There may be pieces of pressed glass listed in this book in other categories, such as Lamp, Ruby Glass, Sandwich Glass, and Souvenir.

Amazon, Vase, Double Bud, Clear, Sawtooth Edge, Footed, Bryce Bros., c.1890, 9 x 7 1/2 x 4 In. 30
Ashburton, Goblet, 8-Sided Stem, Barrel, Vaseline, Canary Yellow, 6 3/8 x 3 1/2 x 3 3/8 In. 129
Barrel Excelsior, Goblet, Flint, Hexagonal Stem, Round Foot, c.1866, 5 5/8 x 2 5/8 x 3 In. 199
Beaver Band, Goblet, Block Lettering, St. Jean Baptiste, c.1880, 5 5/8 x 2 7/8 x 2 3/4 In. 644
Bellflower, Celery Vase, 2 Vine, 4 Cluster, Hexagonal Stem, 1860s, 8 1/2 In. .... *illus* 468

Powder Horn, Brown, Threaded & Faceted Spout, Accession Number, Marked, 13 In.
$50

Cowan's Auctions

Pressed Glass, Bellflower, Celery Vase, 2 Vine, 4 Cluster, Hexagonal Stem, 1860s, 8 1/2 In.
$468

Jeffrey S. Evans & Associates

Glass Patterns

The early 1840s were the time of pressed glass table settings. Early patterns were simple, with heavy loops or ribbed effects. The 1870s brought more elaborate naturalistic patterns. Clear and frosted patterns with figures were in style during the 1870s. Overall patterns that were slightly geometric in feeling were in style by 1880, and patterns such as Daisy and Button and Hobnail came into vogue. Colored pressed glass patterns became popular after the Civil War.

P

PRESSED GLASS

Pressed Glass, Bull's-Eye & Fleur-De-Lis, Decanter, 6 Panels, Flared Rim, Stopper, 1860s, 14 x 3¾ In.
$351

Pressed Glass, Esther, Pitcher, Water, Applied Handle, Amber Stained, Riverside, c.1896, 10 In.
$82

Pressed Glass, Shell & Tassel, Bride's Basket, Blue, Silver Plate Stand, Duncan & Sons., c.1881, 11 x 5 x 9 In.
$164

Jeffrey S. Evans & Associates

Pressed Glass, Waffle & Thumbprint, Spoon Holder, Palace, Sage Green, Circular Foot, 1850, 5 x 3 x 2⅞ In.
$2,223

Jeffrey S. Evans & Associates

Pressed Glass, Colonial, Sugar, Lid, 9-Sided Bowl, Rim Scallops, Robertson & Co., 1850, 9 x 5 x 3 In.
$1,404

Jeffrey S. Evans & Associates

Pressed Glass, Giant Prisms With Thumbprint Band, Compote, Scalloped Rim, Stem, 1860s, 8 x 9 x 5 In.
$211

Jeffrey S. Evans & Associates

Jeffrey S. Evans & Associates

Jeffrey S. Evans & Associates

Pressed Glass, King's Crown, Banana Stand, Excelsior, Ruby Stained, Adams & Co., c.1891, 8 x 7 x 10 In.
$878

Jeffrey S. Evans & Associates

Bull's-Eye & Fleur-De-Lis, Decanter, 6 Panels, Flared Rim, Stopper, 1860s, 14 x 3¾ In. *illus* ... 351
Bull's-Eye With Diamond Point, Tumbler, Whiskey, 1860s, 3⅜ x 3 In. 94
Colonial, Goblet, Hexagonal Bowl, Knopped Stem, Stepped Circular Foot, 1850s, 6 x 3 x 3 In. .. 410
Colonial, Sugar, Lid, 9-Sided Bowl, Rim Scallops, Robertson & Co., 1850, 9 x 5 x 3 In. *illus* 1404
Daisy & Button, Cheese Dish, Lid, Underplate, Amberina, Polka Dot, Hobbs, c.1884, 5 x 7 In. 117
Dakota, Pitcher, Water, Elk, Large Antlers, Applied Handle, 1885, 11¾ In. 152
Diamond, Compote, Blue, Scallop & Point Rim, McKee Bros., c.1880, 10 In. 83
Dragon, Goblet, Clear, Round Foot, McKee & Brothers, 1880s, 5⅝ x 3 x 3⅛ In. 497
Draped Window, Goblet, Knopped Stem, Round Foot, 1880s, 5¾ x 3 x 2⅞ In. 585
Esther, Pitcher, Water, Applied Handle, Amber Stained, Riverside, c.1896, 10 In. .... *illus* 82
Fine Rib, Goblet, Bellflower Border, Twist Stem Variation, 1870s, 5¾ x 3⅜ x 3¼ In. 497
Giant Prisms With Thumbprint Band, Compote, Scalloped Rim, Stem, 1860s, 8 x 9 x 5 In. *illus* 211
Heart With Thumbprint, Goblet, Ruby Stain, Knop Stem, Footed, Hartford, c.1898, 5 x 3 x 3 In. 936
Honeycomb, Tumbler, Ruby, Clear, Factory Polished Rim, Flint, Durand, c.1924, 5 In. 47
Horse, Cat & Rabbit, Goblet, Knopped Stem, Round Foot, 1880s, 6⅜ x 3¼ x 3 In. 263
King's Crown, Banana Stand, Excelsior, Ruby Stain, Adams & Co., c.1891, 8 x 7 x 10 In. *illus* 878
Klondike, Goblet, No. 175, Round Foot, Dalzell, 6¼ In. 117
Liberty Bell, Mug, Opaque White, Molded Rim, Applied Handle, Child's, Late 1800s, 2 In. 70
Magnet & Grape, Dispenser, Frosted Leaf, Brass Spigot, Tulip Shape Stopper, 1855, 20 x 5 In. 1755
Shell & Tassel, Bride's Basket, Blue, Silver Plate Stand, Duncan & Sons, c.1881, 11 x 5 x 9 In. *illus* 164
Stars & Bars, Bowl, Fruit, Railroad Car Shape, Bellaire Goblet Co., c.1896, 6 x 5 x 12 In. 1521
Waffle & Thumbprint, Spoon Holder, Palace, Sage Green, Circular Foot, 1850, 5 x 3 x 2⅞ In. *illus* 2223

PRINT

Print, in this listing, means any of many printed images produced on paper by one of the more common methods, such as lithography. The prints listed here are of interest primarily to the antiques collector, not the fine arts collector. Many of these prints were originally part of books. Other prints will be found in the Advertising, Currier & Ives, Movie, and Poster categories.

Audubon bird prints were originally issued as part of books printed from 1826 to 1854. They were issued in two sheet sizes, 26½ inches by 39½ inches and 11 inches by 7 inches. The height of a picture is listed before the width. The quadrupeds were issued in 28-by-22-inch prints. Later editions of the Audubon books were done in many sizes, and reprints of the books in the original sizes were also made. The words *After John James Audubon* appear on all of the prints, including the originals, because the pictures were made as copies of Audubon's original oil paintings. The bird pictures have been so popular they have been copied in myriad sizes using both old and new printing methods. This list includes originals and later copies because Audubon prints of all ages are sold in antiques shops.

J.W.Audubon

Audubon, Antelope Americana, Lithograph, Hand Colored, T. Bowen, 21 x 27 In............... ... 492
Audubon, Baltimore Orioles, Frame, 25 x 21 In. 100
Audubon, Douglass Squirrel, Hand Colored, 27 x 21 In. .... *illus* 448
Audubon, Florida Jays, Frame, 25 x 21 In.. 750
Audubon, Jager, Hand Colored, R. Havell, 1835, 16 x 21½ In. 861
Audubon, Long-Billed Curlew, Aquatint, R. Havell, Frame, 1834, 21 x 32 In. 840
Audubon, Passenger Pigeon, R. Havell, Birds Of America, 25 x 20 In. 128
Audubon, Red Backed Sandpiper, Lithograph, Hand Colored, Frame, 15 x 17 In. 492
Audubon, Tropic Bird, Etching, Aquatint, R. Havell, 1835, 21 x 31¾ In. 1800
Audubon, White-Crowned Pigeon, Hand Colored, R. Havell, Frame, 1834, 37¾ x 24¾ In..... 2813
Audubon, Wild Turkey, Plate 1, Gilt Frame, 32⅜ x 22 In... 313
Bad Dog, Color Screen Print, William Wegman, Signed, Dated, Stamp, Frame, 39 x 32 In. 938
Currier & Ives prints are listed in the Currier & Ives category.
Gould & Richter, Bird, On Branch, Loxia Curvirostra, Lithograph, Gilt Frame, 19¾ x 13¼ In. . *illus* 13
Hassall, John, 4 Golfing Scenes, Chromolithograph, Frame, c.1904, 25 x 13 In., Set Of 4 . *illus* 1560

Print, Audubon, Douglass Squirrel, Hand Colored, 27 x 21 In.
$448

Neal Auction Company

Print, Gould & Richter, Bird, On Branch, Loxia Curvirostra, Lithograph, Gilt Frame, 19¾ x 13¼ In.
$13

Pook & Fook

P

Print, Hassall, John, 4 Golfing Scenes, Chromolithograph, Frame, c.1904, 25 x 13 In., Set Of 4
$1,560

Morphy Auctions

Print, Marilyn Monroe, Serigraph, Red, Signed, Bert Stern, Wood Frame, 39 ½ x 39 x ½ In.
$469

Eldred's

Purse, Basket, Nantucket, Lid, Ebony Plaque, Carved Whale, Signed, Donna Cifranic, 1993, 9 In.
$1,500

Eldred's

TIP
Cracked plastic purses cannot be repaired.

Purse, Bucket, Duffle Sac, Green Leather, Brass Hardware, Coach, 15 x 12 x 9 In.
$197

Neue Auctions

Icart prints were made by Louis Icart, who worked in Paris from 1907 as an employee of a postcard company. He then started printing magazines and fashion brochures. About 1910 he created a series of etchings of fashionably dressed women, and he continued to make similar etchings until he died in 1950. He is well known as a printmaker, painter, and illustrator. Original etchings are much more expensive than the later photographic copies.

Icart, Autumn Grapes, Woman Picking, Etching, Hand Colored, Frame, 29 ¼ x 22 ½ In.	375
Icart, Charm Of Montmartre, Etching, Aquatint, Hand Colored, Signed, Frame, 1932, 31 x 24 In.	492
Icart, Cigarette Memories, Etching, Aquatint, Hand Colored, Frame, 1931, 25 x 28 In.	1169
Icart, Dancer, Seminude, Lithograph, Pastel, Hand Colored, Signed, Frame, 1928, 24 x 19 ¾ In.	350
Icart, Forbidden Fruit, Etching, Signed, Seal, c.1929, 17 ½ x 13 ½ In.	625
Icart, Joy Of Living, Woman & 2 Dogs, Etching, Aquatint, Signed, 23 ½ x 15 ¼ In.	531
Icart, Mealtime, Woman Feeding Puppies, Etching, Aquatint, 1927, 18 x 13 In.	677
Icart, Meditation, Reclining Nude Blonde Woman, 1930s, 14 ¾ x 18 ¾ In.	308
Icart, Springtime Promenade, 2 Women In Carriage, Aquatint, 1948, 13 x 16 In.	584
Icart, Thais, Woman & Leopards, Etching, Aquatint, Frame, 1927, 25 x 29 In.	984
Icart, Thoroughbreds, Woman On Horse, Etching, Drypoint, Aquatint, 1938, 17 ¾ x 34 In.	5535
Icart, Tosca, Etching, Aquatint, Signed, Windmill Stamp, Arched Gilt Frame, 1928, 29 x 21 In.	923
Icart, Woman In Dress Admiring Birdcage, Etching, Hand Tinted, 1927, 43 x 31 In.	317

Jacoulet prints were designed by Paul Jacoulet (1902–1960), a Frenchman who spent most of his life in Japan. He was a master of Japanese woodblock print technique. Subjects included life in Japan, the South Seas, Korea, and China. His prints were sold by subscription and issued in series. Each series had a distinctive seal, such as a sparrow or butterfly. Most Jacoulet prints are approximately 15 x 10 inches.

Jacoulet, 3 Koreans, Seoul, Color, Signed In Pencil, c.1935, 14 x 18 ¾ In.	313
Jacoulet, Butterflies, Tropics, Color, Signed, 15 ½ x 11 ¾ In.	531
Jacoulet, Flower Vendor, Seoul, Watercolor, Signed, Dated 1936, 9 ⅜ x 9 ¾ In.	5313
Jacoulet, Flowers Of Distant Islands, South Seas, Color, Signed, 14 ¼ x 18 ¼ In.	1188
Jacoulet, Flowers Of Winter, Oshima, Japan, Color, PJ Seal Edition, 1955, 15 ⅜ x 11 ¾ In.	1188
Jacoulet, Salt Merchant, Korea, Color, Signed, Good Luck Hammer Seal, 1936, 15 x 12 In.	375
Jacoulet, Sorrows Of Love, Kusale, East Caroline Islands, Color, Signed, 1940, 16 x 13 In.	375
Jacoulet, The Dead Parakeet, Celebes, Color, 1948, 15 ¼ x 11 ¾ In.	531
Jacoulet, The Nest, Korea, Color, Signed, PJ Seal, 1941, 15 ½ x 11 ¾ In.	750
Jacoulet, The Son's Letter, Seoul, Korea, Color, Embossed Garment, 1938, 15 x 11 ⅝ In.	500
Jacoulet, The Substitute, Mongolia, Woman & Rabbit, Color, Signed, 16 ⅜ x 3 In.	688

Japanese woodblock prints are listed as follows: Print, Japanese, name of artist, title or description, type, and size. Dealers use the following terms: *Tate-e* is a vertical composition. *Yoko-e* is a horizontal composition. The words *Aiban* (13 by 9 inches), *Chuban* (10 by 7 ½ inches), *Hosoban* (13 by 6 inches), *Koban* (7 by 4 inches), *Nagaban* (20 by 9 inches), *Oban* (15 by 10 inches), *Shikishiban* (8 by 9 inches), and *Tanzaku* (15 by 5 inches) denote approximate size. Modern versions of some of these prints have been made. Other woodblock prints that are not Japanese are listed under Print, Woodblock.

Japanese, Hasui, Kawase, Golden Pavilion In Snow, c.1930, 6 x 4 In.	19
Japanese, Hasui, Kawase, Harbor At Night, 1933, Shoichiro Watanabe, 15 ½ x 10 ½ In.	89
Japanese, Hasui, Kawase, Kasuga Shrine, Nara, Watanabe Seal, 1933, 15 ½ x 10 ½ In.	123
Japanese, Hasui, Kawase, Kenchoji Temple Gate, Watanabe Seal, 1933, 15 ¼ x 10 ¼ In.	112
Japanese, Hasui, Kawase, Rain At Shinagawa, Watanabe D-Seal, 1931, 15 x 10 ¼.	78
Japanese, Hiroshige, Fireworks At Ryogoku Bridge, Baba Nobuhiko, 1930s, 7 ½ x 5 In.	19
Japanese, Hiroshige, Little Owl In Moonlight, Later Edition, 4 ½ x 6 In.	44
Japanese, Ito, Sozan, Java Sparrow On Maple, Watanabe, 1925, 15 x 6 ½ In.	44
Japanese, Jinbo, Tomoyo, Rain, Beauty & Hydrangea, 1938, 15 x 10 In.	67

P

Japanese, Kasamatsu, Shiro, Snow At Matsushima, Unsodo, 1954, 15 1/4 x 10 3/4 In. 252
Japanese, Kasamatsu, Shiro, Spring Snow, Sparrows, Self-Published, 1955, 15 1/2 x 11 In. 392
Japanese, Kawase, Sunset At Ichinokura, Trees At Sunset, Seal, 1928, 10 3/8 x 15 In. 2214
Japanese, Koho, Shoda, Bridge In Rain, Nishinomiya, 1930s, 15 x 10 In. 504
Japanese, Koho, Shoda, Shrine Gate At Miyajima, Night Series, Hasegawa, 9 x 6 1/2 In. 392
Japanese, Koho, Shoda, Woman On Beach, Moonlight, Dark Version, Hasegawa, c.1910, 15 x 10 In. 336
Japanese, Koitsu, Tsuchiya, Asakusa Temple, Doi, 1933, 15 3/4 x 10 1/2 In. 1120
Japanese, Komura, Settai, Women, On Veranda, Ink, Settai Seal, Frame, 10 x 14 In. 188
Japanese, Koson, Ohara, Carp & White Lotus, Watanabe, 1933, 11 x 9 3/4 In. 560
Japanese, Koson, Ohara, Courtesan In Silhouette, Kokkeido, c.1910, 14 1/2 x 5 In. 504
Japanese, Koson, Ohara, Wading Egret In Reeds, Kawaguchi, c.1930, 9 3/4 x 9 1/4 In. 392
Japanese, Shodo, Kawarazaki, White Roses, Ink & Colors On Paper, Silk Mat, 1954, 20 x 15 In. 59
Japanese, Shotei, Takahashi, Fireworks At Ryogoku, Tokyo, Watanabe, 1927, 15 x 7 In. 1568
Japanese, Shotei, Takahashi, Five Story Pagoda, Watanabe, 1925-36, 15 x 6 1/2 In. 504
Japanese, Shotei, Takahashi, Inari Shrine At Oji, Watanabe, Before 1936, 15 x 6 1/2 In. 560
Japanese, Shotei, Takahashi, Inhume Pass, Watanabe, 1925-36, 15 x 6 1/2 In. 672
Japanese, Shotei, Takahashi, Sunset Glow At Tone River, Watanabe, c.1930, 10 x 7 In. 448
Japanese, Soseki, Komori, Birds On Persimmon, Kawaguchi & Sakai, c.1929, 15 x 8 3/4 In..... 672
Japanese, Utamaro, Beauty With A Teacup, Bokashi Shading, c.1965, 15 1/2 x 10 1/2 In.......... 67
Japanese, Yoshimoto, Gesso, Sailing Boats, Red Sunset, Hasegawa, 1930s, 5 1/2 x 13 In......... 280
Lithograph, Boston's Masonic Temple, J.H. Bufford, Gilt Frame, 1865, 26 x 31 In........... 594
Lithograph, Townsend's Oyster Catcher, Hand Colored, Mat, Frame, 1800s, 14 x 11 In........ 207
Lithograph, Triple Self-Portrait, Pencil Signed, Norman Rockwell, Frame, 42 x 35 In........... 940
Marilyn Monroe, Serigraph, Red, Signed, Bert Stern, Wood Frame, 39 1/2 x 39 x 1/2 In. *illus* 469

Nutting prints are popular with collectors. Wallace Nutting is known for his pictures, furniture, and books. Collectors call his pictures Nutting prints although they are actually hand-colored photographs issued from 1900 to 1941. There are over 10,000 different titles. Wallace Nutting furniture is listed in the Furniture category.

Nutting, A Garden Of Larkspur, Cottage, Garden, Frame, 22 1/2 x 19 3/4 In.................... 160
Nutting, Ash Row, Dirt Road, Trees, Wooden Fence, Hand Colored, Frame, 17 x 19 1/2 In. 128
Nutting, Autumn In America, Dirt Road, Blossoming Trees, Hand Tinted, Frame, 7 x 9 In..... 59
Nutting, Flowering Time, Hand Colored, 16 1/2 x 22 1/2 In................................. 115
Nutting, Going Forth Of Betty, Woman Leaving House, Hand Tinted, Frame, c.1915 73
Nutting, Grace, Hand Colored, 1920, 13 x 10 In.. 60
Nutting, Hollyhock Cottage, Thatch Roof, Hand Colored, 14 x 17 In. 38
Nutting, Honeymoon Drive, Hand Colored, 16 x 20 In. 54
Nutting, Honeymoon Stroll, Hand Colored, 7 1/2 x 9 1/2 In. 56
Nutting, Honeymoon Windings, Dirt Road, Rock Wall, Hand Tinted, Frame, 13 3/4 x 19 In..... 64
Nutting, Larkspur, Hand Colored, Frame, 17 x 14 In..................................... 50
Nutting, Recreation Of Our Foremothers, Frame, 1913, 20 1/2 x 24 1/2 In................. 30
Nutting, Reeling The Yarn, Woman Knitting In Parlor, Hand Colored, 1916, 15 x 18 In...... .. 56
Nutting, Road To Yesterday, Hand Colored, Frame, 25 x 44 In............................. 219
Nutting, Spring In The Dell, Hand Colored, Frame, 11 x 13 In............................ 30
Nutting, Sylvan Dell, Creek & Trees, Hand Colored, Frame, 20 3/4 x 17 3/4 In. 42
Nutting, Under Elm Arches, Hand Colored, Frame, 1910 59

Parrish prints are wanted by collectors. Maxfield Frederick Parrish was an illustrator who lived from 1870 to 1966. He is best known as a designer of magazine covers, posters, calendars, and advertisements. His prints have been copied in recent years. Some Maxfield Parrish items may be listed in Advertising.

Parrish, Cleopatra, Original Frame With Clipped & Shaped Corners, 24 x 28 In.................... 546
Parrish, Daybreak, Signed, Frame, 1922, 21 x 33 In.................................... 360
Parrish, Evening, Lithograph, Reinthal & Newman, Period Frame, 1922, 16 x 13 In. 188
Parrish, Garden Of Allah, Women Lounging In Garden, Trees, Large Urns, 18 x 33 In. 144
Parrish, Hilltop, 2 Women Reclining Under Tree, 11 x 7 1/4 In........................... 272
Parrish, Jack & The Beanstalk, Square, 10 3/4 In....................................... 175

Purse, Canvas, Tote, Rolled Shoulder Straps, Damier Ebene, Louis Vuitton, 10 x 20 x 5 3/4 In.
$590

Austin Auction Gallery

Purse, Leather, Beige Squares, Front Flap, CC Turn Lock, Goldtone Hardware, Chanel, 5 x 10 In.
$885

Austin Auction Gallery

Purse, Leather, Bleu Agate, 2 Zipper Pulls, Twist Lock, Handles, Strap, Hermes, 8 x 11 In.
$7,560

Sotheby's

Purse, Leather, Brown, Quilted, Double Flap, Mademoiselle Chain Strap, Chanel, c.1984, 7 In.
$3,500

Hindman

Purse, Leather, Tote, 2 Handles, Brown, Red Interior, Pocket, Zipper, Louis Vuitton, 14 In.
$748

Blackwell Auctions

Purse, Mesh, Flat, 2 Camels, Riders, Marked, Whiting & Davis, Egyptian Revival, c.1930, 7 x 4 In.
$384

Austin Auction Gallery

Parrish, Rubaiyat, C.A. Crane, Cleveland, Copyright 1917, Frame, 12 ½ x 34 ½ In.	590
Parrish, Stars, c.1920, 11 x 7 In.	311
Parrish, Triptych, Daybreak, Wild Geese, Canyon, Lithograph, c.1920, 21 x 55 In.	4250
Parrish, Under Summer Skies, 12 x 9 In.	325
Parrish, Wild Geese, Frame, c.1933, 16 x 13 In.	311
Woman, December 1922 Calendar, Newspaper Background, Frame, 1900s, 31 x 26 In.	31

 Woodblock prints that are not in the Japanese tradition are listed here. Most were made in England and the United States during the Arts and Crafts period. Japanese woodblock prints are listed under Print, Japanese.

Woodblock, Baskin, Leonard, Football, Football Player, Rice Paper, c.1960, 17 x 13 In.	120
Woodblock, Buthaud, Rene, 2 Friends With Dog, Art Deco Style, c.1980s, 23 ½ x 19 ½ In.	344
Woodblock, Dali, Salvador, Greatest Beauty Of Beatrice, Color, Frame, 1900s, 20 x 17 In.	375
Woodblock, Geritz, Franz, Mt. San Gorgonio, Trees Against Mountains, 1937, 13 x 10 In.	660
Woodblock, Horton, Ann V., Magnolia On Branch, Blossoms, Frame, 1930s, 9 ½ x 12 In.	693
Woodblock, Inagaki, Tomoo, Two Cats, Stylized, Color, Heavy Outlining, c.1970, 25 x 18 In.	1188
Woodblock, Inuit, Figure In Bear Fur Eating Salmon, Canada, 1965, 16 x 9 ½ In.	210
Woodblock, Lap, Engelbert, Ski Tracks On Snow, Mountain, Color, 1920s, 7 ½ x 10 In.	720
Woodblock, Lum, Bertha, Homeward, Birds Over Bridge, Minneapolis Handicraft Guild, 10 x 4 In.	750
Woodblock, Patterson, Margret, Guinea Boat, Color, Signed, Mid-1900s, 7 ½ x 10 In.	2280
Woodblock, Red Star, Kevin, Crow Family Portrait, Deep Color, Signed, 1980, 10 x 8 In.	861
Woodblock, Schmidt-Rottluff, Karl, Harbor On The Elbe, Stylized Harbor, 1950, 11 x 14 In.	4920
Woodblock, Shields, Alan, Martian Worm Village, Meandering Path, Black, Turquoise, 24 x 24 In.	354

Purinton Pottery PURINTON

Purinton Pottery Company was incorporated in Wellsville, Ohio, in 1936. The company moved to Shippenville, Pennsylvania, in 1941 and made a variety of hand-painted ceramic wares. By the 1950s Purinton was making dinnerware, souvenirs, cookie jars, and florist wares. The pottery closed in 1959.

Apple & Pear, Pitcher, 5 ½ In.	40
Apple, Cruets, Oil & Vinegar, Corks, 9 ¼ In.	24
Apple, Salt & Pepper, Loop Handle, 2 ½ In.	22

PURSE

Purses have been recognizable since the eighteenth century, when leather and needlework purses were preferred. Beaded purses became popular in the nineteenth century, went out of style, but are again in use. Mesh purses date from the 1880s and are still being made. How to carry a handkerchief, lipstick, and cell phone is a problem today for every woman, including the Queen of England.

Basket, Nantucket, Applied Carved Whale, Signed, Farnum, 1978, 7 In.	200
Basket, Nantucket, Lid, Ebony Plaque, Carved Whale, Signed, Donna Cifranic, 1993, 9 In. . *illus*	1500
Bucket, Duffle Sac, Green Leather, Brass Hardware, Coach, 15 x 12 x 9 In. *illus*	197
Canvas, Leather Band, Steel Lock Bars, Marked, Wells Fargo & Co., 30 x 18 In.	177
Canvas, Pockets, Handles, Zippers, Monogram, Trouville, Louis Vuitton, 12 In.	394
Canvas, Tote, Monogram, Leather, Brass, Zip Pocket, Neverfull, Louis Vuitton, 9 x 15 In.	1107
Canvas, Tote, Rolled Shoulder Straps, Damier Ebene, Louis Vuitton, 10 x 20 x 5 ¾ In. . *illus*	590
Canvas, Visetos, 2 Rolled Top Handles, Caramel & Black Monogram, MCM, 8 x 10 x 6 In.	32
Coated Canvas, Alma, Monograms, Tan Leather Handles, Goldtone Hardware, Louis Vuitton, 14 In.	67
Crocodile, Metallic Gray, Knotted Handle, Hobo, Nancy Gonzalez, 10 x 19 x 4 In.	94
Fabric, Black, Silk Lining, Coral Closure, Art Deco, Cartier, c.1910, 7 In.	200
Leather, Beige Squares, Front Flap, CC Turn Lock, Goldtone Hardware, Chanel, 5 x 10 In. *illus*	88
Leather, Bleu Agate, 2 Zipper Pulls, Twist Lock, Handles, Strap, Hermes, 8 x 11 In. *illus*	756
Leather, Brown, Gold Plated Brass Hardware, Hermes, 1979, 23 x 23 In.	625
Leather, Brown, Quilted, Double Flap, Mademoiselle Chain Strap, Chanel, c.1984, 7 In. *illus*	350

P

Purse, Mesh, White, Black, Silver Plate Clasp, Portrait, Charlie Chaplin, Whiting & Davis, 20 In.
$315

Purse, Tote, Business Carryall, Brown Leather, Palladium Hardware, Tag, Coach, 11 x 19 In.
$98

Purse, Wallet, Ostrich Leather, Red, Goldtone Hardware, Snap Closure, Gucci, 3 ½ x 7 x ¾ In.
$354

Austin Auction Gallery

Neue Auctions

Purse, Tote, Canvas, Fuchsia & Orange, Illustration Of Bonnie Cashin, Coach, 1962, 12 In.
$36

TIP

If you have an old evening bag with a fabulous frame and clasp and the bag is worn, keep the frame and have a new fabric bag made.

Purse, Wristlet, Campbell's Tomato Soup Can, Leather, Palladium Hardware, Zipper, Coach, 6 In.
$99

Fontaine's Auction Gallery

Neue Auctions

Neue Auctions

Purse, Silk, Embroidery, Phoenix, Butterfly, Flowers, Filigree Closure, Chain Handle, c.1900, 6 x 8 In.
$295

Purse, Wallet, Brick Stitch, Row Of Scales, Raspberry Glaze Wool Lining, William Long, 1785, 5 x 8 In.
$2,460

Purse, Wristlet, Flower Patch, Canvas, Coated & Printed, Palladium Hardware, 4 x 6 In.
$25

eland Little Auctions

Brunk Auctions

Neue Auctions

P

PURSE

Quezal, Lampshade, Dome Shape, Green, Pulled Feathers, Gold Iridescent Interior, Signed, 5 x 11 In.
$677

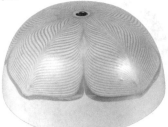

Rich Penn Auctions

Quezal, Vase, Blue Iridescent, Pulled Swirls, Signed, 11 x 6 In.
$900

Cottone Auctions

Quezal, Vase, Bulbous Body, Fluted Rim, Green Pulled Feather, Signed, 5 x 3 ½ In.
$1,020

Cottone Auctions

426

Leather, Clutch, Glycine, Rectangle, Front H, Pullover Tab, Jige Elan, Hermes, 6 x 11 ½ In. ..	2772
Leather, Handbag, Alligator, Brown, Head, Braided Straps, 1950, 7 ½ x 11 In.	70
Leather, Handbag, Black, Fur Lining, 2 Handles, Compartment, Pocket, Paolo Masi, Italy, 11 x 18 In.	325
Leather, Handbag, Brown, Geometrics, Satin Interior, Pocket, Leather Handle, Logo, Prada, 7 x 7 In.	750
Leather, Handbag, Brown, Padlock, Handles, Baradini, 12 x 15 x 8 In.	313
Leather, Pocket, Zipper, Strap, Petite Boite Chapeau Souple, Louis Vuitton, 8 In.	2268
Leather, Shoulder Bag, Argyle, Chaine D'Ancre, Strap, Palladium Hardware, Hermes, 2 x 7 x 5 In.	4400
Leather, Shoulder Bag, Black, Compartment, Strap, Salvatore Ferragamo, Late 1900s, 10 x 12 In..	313
Leather, Speedy 30, Damier Azur, Coated, Canvas, Brass Hardware, Louis Vuitton, 8 x 11 In.	590
Leather, Tote, 2 Handles, Brown, Red Interior, Pocket, Zipper, Louis Vuitton, 14 In. ..... *illus*	748
Leather, Tote, Bucket Bag, Black, YSL Charm, Saint Laurent, 12 In....................................	875
Leather, Yellow, Chevron Caviar, Goldtone, Le Boy CC, Chain, Pocket, Chanel, 6 x 10 In........	4410
Leatherette, Shoulder Bag, Tan, Cloth Bag, Gucci, Italy, 1900s, 8 x 7 x 3 In.........................	219
Mesh, Flat, 2 Camels, Riders, Marked, Whiting & Davis, Egyptian Revival, c.1930, 7 x 4 In. ..*illus*	384
Mesh, Silver, Flowers, Chain, 6 ½ In..	83
Mesh, Sterling Silver, Openwork Frame, Finger Ring, Chain, 6 In....................................	104
Mesh, White, Black, Silver Plate Clasp, Portrait, Charlie Chaplin, Whiting & Davis, 20 In. *illus*	315
Metal Frame, Loops, Silver, Crystal, Bugle Beads, Faux Pearls, Richere, 1960s, 7 In.............	65
Microbeaded, Violets, Silver Chain, Glass Drawstring, Late 1800s, 6 In............................	84
Needlepoint, Petit Point, Embroidery Genre Scene, Floral Frame, Gold Chain, c.1950, 9 In. .	36
Silk, Embroidery, Phoenix, Butterfly, Flowers, Filigree Closure, Chain Handle, c.1900, 6 x 8 In. ..*illus*	295
Silk, Gray, Embroidered Flowers, Silver & Blue Sequins, Beads, Metal Clasp, Lined, 9 x 7 In..	235
Snakeskin, Crossbody, Fuchsia, Quilted, Flap, CC Logo, Chain & Leather Strap, Chanel, 6 x 7 In.	2318
Tote Bag, Canvas, Woven Interior, Pocket, Leather Handles, Marked, Gucci, Italy, 12 x 13 In. .	625
Tote, Business Carryall, Brown Leather, Palladium Hardware, Tag, Coach, 11 x 19 In. . *illus*	98
Tote, Canvas, Fuchsia & Orange, Illustration Of Bonnie Cashin, Coach, 1962, 12 In. .... *illus*	36
Wallet, Brick Stitch, Row Of Scales, Raspberry Glaze Wool Lining, William Long, 1785, 5 x 8 In. *illus*	2460
Wallet, Flame Stitch, Twill Edging, New England, Late 1700s, 3 ¾ x 7 ½ In............................	1188
Wallet, Ostrich Leather, Red, Goldtone Hardware, Snap Closure, Gucci, 3 ½ x 7 x ¾ In. *illus*	354
Wool, Needlework, Flame Stitch, Pocketbook, Adam Churnlide, c.1792, 5 ½ x 8 ½ In.............	1800
Wristlet, Campbell's Tomato Soup Can, Leather, Palladium Hardware, Zipper, Coach, 6 In. .*illus*	99
Wristlet, Flower Patch, Canvas, Coated & Printed, Palladium Hardware, 4 x 6 In. .... *illus*	25

PYREX

pyrex

Pyrex glass baking dishes were first made in 1915 by the Corning Glass Works. Pyrex dishes are made of a heat-resistant glass that can go from refrigerator or freezer to oven or microwave and are nice enough to put on the table. Clear glass dishes were made first. Pyrex Flameware, for use on a stovetop burner, was made from 1936 to 1979. A set of four mixing bowls, each in a dfferent color (blue, red, green, and yellow), was made beginning in 1947. The first pieces with decorative patterns were made in 1956. After Corning sold its Pyrex brand to World Kitchen LLC in 1998, changes were made to the formula for the glass.

Baking Pan, Lime Green, 1 ½ Qt., 11 ½ x 6 ½ In..	34
Bowl, Vegetable, Milk Glass, Delphite Blue, Divided, 13 x 8 In...............................	20
Mixing Bowl, Harvest Wheat, Nesting, Tab Handles, 3 Piece..............................	48
Mixing Bowl, Yellow, 2 ½ Qt.	6

QUEZAL

Quezal

Quezal glass was made from 1901 to 1924 at the Queens, New York, company started by Martin Bach. Other glassware by other firms, such as Loetz, Steuben, and Tiffany, resembles this gold-colored iridescent glass. Martin Bach died in 1921. His son-in-law, Conrad Vahlsing Jr., went to work at the Lustre Art Company about 1920. Bach's son, Martin Bach Jr., worked at the Durand Art Glass division of the Vineland Flint Glass Works after 1924.

Lamp, Hanging, 8-Light, Bronze, Moorish, Pulled Feather Shades, c.1900, 30 x 16 In.	864

Lampshade, Bell Shape, Green Pulled Feather, Gold Aurene, Signed, 5 x 4 ¼ In.	144
Lampshade, Blown Golden Glass, Ribbed Design, Signed, Early 1900s, 5 ¼ In., 6 Piece	443
Lampshade, Dome Shape, Green, Pulled Feathers, Gold Iridescent Interior, Signed, 5 x 11 In. *illus*	677
Lampshade, Green, Gold Pulled Feathers, Latticework, Ruffled Rim, c.1915, 7 ¼ In., Pair	3720
Lampshade, Pearl Iridescent, Dome Shape, Pulled Feather, Green, Gold, Early 1900s, 4⅝ In., Pair	369
Salt Dip, Ribbed Body, Gold Iridescent, Molded Rim, 1 x 3 In.	90
Vase, Blue Iridescent, Pulled Swirls, Signed, 11 x 6 In. *illus*	900
Vase, Bulbous Body, Fluted Rim, Green Pulled Feather, Signed, 5 x 3 ½ In. *illus*	1020
Vase, Cordial Stem, Gold Iridescent, Round Base, Signed, 4 ¼ In.	70
Vase, Flower Shape, Gold Iridescent, Green Pulled Feather, Latticework, Cream Ground, 8 ½ In.	1386
Vase, Flower Shape, Green, Gold Iridescent, Feather, 9 ½ x 7 x 7 In. *illus*	1020
Vase, Jack-In-The-Pulpit, Blue Iridescent, White & Gold, Ruffled, Pulled Feathers, 15 x 7 In.	5860
Vase, King Tut, 4 Lobes, Flared Rim, Blue Iridescent, Paper Label, Early 1900s, 12 In.	512

QUILT

Quilts have been made since the seventeenth century. Early textiles were very precious and every scrap was saved to be reused. A quilt is a combination of fabrics joined to a filler and a backing by small stitched designs known as quilting. An appliqued quilt has pieces stitched to the top of a large piece of backing fabric. A patchwork, or pieced, quilt is made of many small pieces stitched together. Embroidery can be added to either type.

Album, Patchwork, Embroidered, Squares, Shamrocks, Geometric Border, Wool, c.1890, 70 x 72 In	780
Amish, 9-Patch Chain, Pieced, Embroidered, Diagonal Line, Flowers, Cotton, Rayon, 1938, 71 x 78 In.	423
Amish, Bars, Black & Maroon Stripes, 1950s, 84 x 84 In. *illus*	375
Amish, Log Cabin, Solid Blue, Purple, Shell, Late 1800s, 56 x 64 In.	780
Amish, Patchwork, Abstract Logs, Window Pane, Cotton, Chevrons, Ohio, c.1925, 75 x 68 In. *illus*	531
Amish, Patchwork, Diamond Sawtooth In Square, Cotton, Pa., 1910, 84 x 83 In. *illus*	563
Amish, Patchwork, Double Wedding Ring, Chinese Coins, Cotton, Pa., c.1945, 93 x 81 In. *illus*	1375
Amish, Patchwork, Floating Bars, Wool, Cotton, Lancaster Co., Pa., 79 x 68 In. *illus*	2813
Amish, Patchwork, Lady Of The Lake, Multicolor Blocks, Cables, Tulips, Ohio, 82 x 68 In.	594
Amish, Pieced, Sunshine & Shadow, Multicolor, Purple Border, Blue Back, c.1925, 76 x 78 In.	813
Amish, Tulip, Yellow Ground, Red, Pieced Cotton, Early 1900s, 71 x 88 In.	216
Appliqued, 16 Squares, Flower Basket, Wide Teal Border, Pa., c.1920, 88 x 88 In.	793
Appliqued, Album, Flower Blossom Pattern, Red, Green & Bright Yellow, 1900s, 68 x 86 In.	293
Appliqued, Birds, Trees, Grapevine Border, Signed, Beulah Shirts, 1925, 76 x 76 In. *illus*	1375
Appliqued, Blue & White, Flowers, Scalloped Edges, White Background, 88 x 84 In.	94
Appliqued, Embroidered, Animals, Birds, Figures, Hearts, Red Border, 1800s, 88 x 86 In.	358
Appliqued, Flower Basket, Green Shade, Label, H. Clark, Late 1800s, 86 x 86 In.	228
Appliqued, Princess Feather, Blue & White, Printed, Late 1800s, 98 x 100 In.	715
Appliqued, Princess Feather, Red, White, Cotton, c.1900, Crib, 44 x 46 In.	1464
Appliqued, Tree Of Life Center, Blue, Red Bird, Pinwheel Diamond, Tulips, 82 x 81 In.	489
Appliqued, Tulip Design, Pink, Green, White, 86 x 104 In.	81
Appliqued, White Ground, Salmon, Ruffled Border, c.1900, 72 x 84 In. *illus*	213
Crazy, Embroidered, Stitch Designs, Multicolor, Cotton & Wool, 1900s, 71 In.	177
Mennonite, Appliqued, Tobacco Leaf, Red, Yellow, Green, Pink, Cotton, Late 1800s, 91 x 86 In. *illus*	585
Mennonite, Patchwork, Multiple Pattern, Princess Feather, Burgundy, Green, 1910s, 86 x 86 In.	570
Mennonite, Windmill Variation, Black & Yellow, Wool, Backed, Red Flannel, 1900s, 58 x 74 In.	423
Patchwork & Appliqued, Cabin, Sunshine, Shadow Log, Diagonal Border, Late 1800s, 82 x 79 In.	1098
Patchwork & Appliqued, Red & White Stripes, Zigzag Pattern, Cotton, Pa., c.1915, 86 x 80 In.	815
Patchwork & Appliqued, Sunburst, Red, White, Polka Dot, Scalloped Border, c.1900, 80 x 76 In.	1105
Patchwork & Appliqued, Tulips, White Ground, Ann Sharper, Evershire, Cotton, 1850, 92 x 100 In	281
Patchwork & Appliqued, Whig Rose, Red, Green, Yellow, Feathered Wreath, c.1890, 79 x 66 In. *illus*	520
Patchwork, Friendship, Flying Crow, 42 Squares, Wide Green Border, James Maek, 1854, 97 x 87 In.	2684
Patchwork, Indian Wedding Ring, Green, White, Early 1900s, 80 x 64 In.	339
Patchwork, Irish Chain, Cream Ground, Geometric Border, Stitched, 1800s, 83 x 76 In.	62
Patchwork, Steeple Chase, Blue, White Prints, White Back, Cotton, c.1900, 56 x 82 In.	110
Stripes, Stars, Crescents, Lincoln Hidden Message, Cotton, Frame, 1863, 30 x 36 In. *illus*	5000
Trapunto, Floral Vine, Whitework, Initialed, E.A., 1819, 89 x 86 In.	1952

Quezal, Vase, Flower Shape, Green, Gold Iridescent, Feather, 9 ½ x 7 x 7 In. $1,020

Morphy Auctions

Quilt, Amish, Bars, Black & Maroon Stripes, 1950s, 84 x 84 In. $375

Pook & Pook

Quilt, Amish, Patchwork, Abstract Logs, Window Pane, Cotton, Chevrons, Ohio, c.1925, 75 x 68 In. $531

Q

John Moran Auctioneers

Quilt, Amish, Patchwork, Diamond Sawtooth In Square, Cotton, Pa., 1910, 84 x 83 In.
$563

John Moran Auctioneers

Quilt, Amish, Patchwork, Double Wedding Ring, Chinese Coins, Cotton, Pa., c.1945, 93 x 81 In.
$1,375

John Moran Auctioneers

Quilt, Amish, Patchwork, Floating Bars, Wool, Cotton, Lancaster Co., Pa., 79 x 68 In.
$2,813

John Moran Auctioneers

Quilt, Appliqued, Birds, Trees, Grapevine Border, Signed, Beulah Shirts, 1925, 76 x 76 In.
$1,375

New Haven Auctions

Quilt, Appliqued, White Ground, Salmon, Ruffled Border, c.1900, 72 x 84 In.
$213

Pook & Pook

Quilt, Patchwork & Appliqued, Whig Rose, Red, Green, Yellow, Feathered Wreath, c.1890, 79 x 66 In.
$520

Freeman's

Quilt, Stripes, Stars, Crescents, Lincoln Hidden Message, Cotton, Frame, 1863, 30 x 36 In.
$5,000

Cowan's Auctions

Quilt, Mennonite, Appliqued, Tobacco Leaf, Red, Yellow, Green, Pink, Cotton, Late 1800s, 91 x 86 In.
$585

Freeman's

Q

QUIMPER

Quimper pottery has a long history. Tin-glazed, hand-painted pottery has been made in Quimper, France, since the late seventeenth century. The earliest firm was founded in 1708 by Pierre Bousquet. In 1782, Antoine de la Hubaudiere became the manager of the factory and the factory became known as the HB Factory (for Hubaudiere-Bousquet), de la Hubaudiere, or Grande Maison. Another firm, founded in 1772 by Francois Eloury, was known as Porquier. The third firm, founded by Guillaume Dumaine in 1778, was known as HR or Henriot Quimper. All three firms made similar pottery decorated with designs of Breton peasants and sea and flower motifs. The Eloury (Porquier) and Dumaine (Henriot) firms merged in 1913. Bousquet (HB) merged with the others in 1968. The group was sold to an American holding company in 1984. More changes followed, and in 2011 Jean-Pierre Le Goff became the owner and the name was changed to Henriot-Quimper.

Cup & Saucer, Leaves, Blue Handle, Cream Ground, 9 Piece	254
Server, Lid, Yellow Glaze, Hat Shape Finial, 2 Handles, Footed, 1900s, 6 x 11 In. .... *illus*	74
Tray, Seafood Design, Scalloped Rim, Brown & Cream Ground, Footed, 19 x 15 In.	73
Vase, Farmer & Musician, Flared Rim, Curved Neck, Footed, 15 In., Pair	452
Vinaigrette, Portraits, Breton & Bretonne, Man, Woman, 2 Cylinders, Odetta, 5¾ In. . . *illus*	94

RADIO

Radio broadcast receiving sets were first sold in New York City in 1910. They were used to pick up the experimental broadcasts of the day. The first commercial radios were made by Westinghouse Company for listeners of the experimental shows on KDKA Pittsburgh in 1920. Collectors today are interested in all early radios, especially those made of Bakelite plastic or decorated with blue mirrors. Figural advertising radios and transistor radios are also collected.

Arborphone, Model 27, External Speaker, 5 Valves, 3 Dials, 1920s	185
Catalin Sentinel, Model 284, Marbleized, Butterscotch, Red Trim, c.1945, 11 x 7 x 7½ In. ..	704
Fada, Model 115, Catalin, Bullet, Streamliner, Yellow, Red Knobs, Handle, 6 x 10 x 5 In.	677
Fada, Model 1000, Catalin, Bullet, Butterscotch, Red, Handle, 6 x 10½ In. .... *illus*	738
General Electric, Black, Green, Handle, Knobs, Continental, Table Model, 6 x 8¾ x 5½ In. *illus*	461
Sign, Motorola, White Neon Script, America's Finest Radio On Base, 12 x 23 In.	1188

RAILROAD

Railroad enthusiasts collect any train memorabilia. Everything is wanted, from oilcans to whole train cars. The Chessie system has a store that sells many reproductions of its old dinnerware and uniforms.

Bell, Locomotive, PM RR, Pere Marquette, Brass, Air Operated, 12 In. .... *illus*	360
Bread Tray, Santa Fe, Silver Plate, Handles, Engraved, Harrison Bros. & Howson, 13 x 8 In. ... *illus*	170
Cabinet, Ticket, Oak, Tapering Roll Front, 2 Drawers, c.1880, 59 x 19 x 28 In.	480
Chime, Dining Car, 4 Tones, Music Booklet, Signed, J.C. Deagan Dinner, 12 x 8½ In.	192
Clock, Regulator, New Haven Railroad, Oak, Leaves, Roman Numerals, 1800s, 67 x 34 In. *illus*	3125
Coffeepot, Lid, Santa Fe, Silver Plate, Gadroon Design, Harrison Bros. & Howson, 7 x 8 In. .. *illus*	113
Hammer, Tie Marking, C & A RR, Chicago & Alton	48
Lamp, Adlake, Wood, Pedestal Base	142
Lamp, Bell Shape Shade, 2 Flower Medallions, Circular Base, Pullman Co., c.1920, 21 In.	688
Lantern, Amber Globe, Marked, Adams & Westlake Co., 9 In.	74
Lantern, Boston, Revere Beach & Lynn RR, Metal Cage, Glass Globe, 1875-1937 .... *illus*	120
Lantern, Brass, Blown Pyriform Fixed Globe, Bail Handle, Burner, Kelly Lamp Co., c.1865, 12 In.	878
Lantern, Brass, Clear Globe, Loop Handle, Dome Base, Kelly Lamp Co., 18 In. .... *illus*	502
Lantern, Oil Font, Tin Reflector, Glass Globe, Electric, Marked, Dietz Fitall, 1850s, 16 x 15 In.	187
Lantern, Red & Blue Lights, Non-Sweating Adlake Lamp, Chicago, 19 In.	420
Lantern, Steel, Barrel Shape, Candle Lit, Fluted Top Vent, Swing Handle, 15 x 8 x 5 In.	104
Lock, C ST L & P RR, Chicago, St. Louis & Pittsburgh, Brass, Chain, No Key .... *illus*	1920
Mail Pouch, Canvas, Leather, Railway Express Agency, Lock, Key, Stencil, Am. Ry. Ex. Co., 17 x 24 In.	205

Quimper, Server, Lid, Yellow Glaze, Hat Shape Finial, 2 Handles, Footed, 1900s, 6 x 11 In.
$74

Locati Auctions

Quimper, Vinaigrette, Portraits, Breton & Bretonne, Man, Woman, 2 Cylinders, Odetta, 5¾ In.
$94

Bunch Auctions

Radio, Fada, Model 1000, Catalin, Bullet, Butterscotch, Red, Handle, 6 x 10½ In.
$738

Hartzell's Auction Gallery Inc.

Radio, General Electric, Black, Green, Handle, Knobs, Continental, Table Model, 6 x 8¾ x 5½ In.
$461

Hartzell's Auction Gallery Inc.

R

Railroad, Bell, Locomotive, PM RR, Pere Marquette, Brass, Air Operated, 12 In.
$360

Chupp Auctions & Real Estate, LLC

Railroad, Bread Tray, Santa Fe, Silver Plate, Handles, Engraved, Harrison Bros. & Howson, 13 x 8 In.
$170

Soulis Auctions

Railroad, Clock, Regulator, New Haven Railroad, Oak, Leaves, Roman Numerals, 1800s, 67 x 34 In.
$3,125

Eldred's

Railroad, Coffeepot, Lid, Santa Fe, Silver Plate, Gadroon Design, Harrison Bros. & Howson, 7 x 8 In.
$113

Soulis Auctions

Railroad, Hammer, Tie Marking, C & A RR, Chicago & Alton
$48

Chupp Auctions & Real Estate, LLC

Railroad, Lantern, Boston, Revere Beach & Lynn RR, Metal Cage, Glass Globe, 1875-1937
$120

Chupp Auctions & Real Estate, LLC

> **TIP**
> Fakers sometimes "marry" a clock works and a clock case. Examine a clock carefully to be sure the parts are all original.

Railroad, Lantern, Brass, Clear Globe, Loop Handle, Dome Base, Kelly Lamp Co., 18 In.
$502

Cottone Auctions

Railroad, Lock, C ST L & P RR, Chicago, St. Louis & Pittsburgh, Brass, Chain, No Key
$1,920

Chupp Auctions & Real Estate, LLC

Railroad, Match Holder, Ashtray Base, Rock Island, Eiffel & Husted Chicago, Early 1800s, 3 x 5 In.
$308

Rich Penn Auctions

Match Holder, Ashtray Base, Rock Island, Eiffel & Husted Chicago, Early 1800s, 3 x 5 In. *illus*		308
Paperweight, Pennsylvania RR, Nickeled Brass, Keystone, 3 1/4 x 3 1/2 In.		86
Plate, B & O, Harper's Ferry, Blue & White, Buffalo China, 9 1/2 In.		29
Platter, B & O, Indian Creek, Scammells Lamberton, Blue & White, Oval, 16 In.		196
Server, Butter, Santa Fe, Silver Plate, Ice Insert, Footed, Harrison Bros. & Howson, 2 x 6 In.		254
Sign, Cast Bronze, North Side Station, Pittsburgh, Pennsylvania, 1900s, 53 1/2 x 14 In.		480
Sign, Crossing, Black Text & Border, White Ground, Metal, 1900s, 48 x 48 In.		128
Sign, Crossing, Embossed Lettering, Cast Iron, c.1920, 48 x 48 In.		250
Sign, Railroad Crossing, Crossbuck, Cat's-Eye Reflectors, 48 In. *illus*		180
Sign, Railroad Crossing, Painted, Embossed, Plastic Reflector Buttons, c.1960, 40 In. *illus*		277
Signal, Red, Yellow, Green Ground, 42 In.		240
Step, Coach, Cast Iron & Wood, Luther, Early 1900s, 14 x 26 In. *illus*		154
Syrup, Santa Fe, Silver Plate, Lines, Leaves, Attached Underplate, International Silver Co., 5 x 4 In.		113
Tray, Santa Fe, Silver Plate, Round, Lines, Leaves, International Silver Co., 12 In.		113
Tureen, Lid, Santa Fe, Handles, Silver Plate, Engraved, GM Company, 6 x 8 1/2 In.		283
Whistle, Steam, Brass, 12 x 2 1/2 In. *illus*		330

RAZOR

Razors were used in ancient Egypt and subsequently wherever shaving was in fashion. The metal razor used in America was made in Sheffield, England, until about 1870. After 1870, machine-made hollow-ground razors were made in Germany or America. Plastic or bone handles were popular. The razor was often sold in a set of seven, one for each day of the week. The set was often kept by the barber who shaved the well-to-do man each day in the shop.

Gillette, Double Edge, Red Tip Safety Razor, Twist Open, 1956	47
Schick Injector, Marbleized Plastic Handle, Brass Head, Case, c.1931	83
Straight, Faux Bamboo Handle, 6 In.	35

REAMERS

Reamers, or juice squeezers, have been known since 1767, although most of those collected today date from the twentieth century. Figural reamers are among the most prized.

Aluminum, Handle, Foley Food Mill, 1950s, 8 1/2 In.	13
Clear, Crisscross, Swirled Rib Cone, Raised Ring Foot, 1930s, 6 In.	48
Clown, Blue, Orange, Yellow, Handle, Japan, 4 1/2 x 4 1/2 In.	35
Depression Glass, Green, Ribbed, 8 3/4 In.	25
Milk Glass, c.1960, 8 1/4 x 3 1/2 x 5 In.	32
Silver Plate, Shell Shape Handle, Spout, 2 Piece, 3 x 4 1/2 In.	768
Silver, Gold Wash, Curled Handle, Rope Like Edge, Fuchs, c.1891, 4 3/4 x 4 In.	550
Stoneware, Blue & Brown Border, Blue Flowers, Handle, Spout, 2 Piece, Yamato, Norden, 7 In.	2

RECORD

Records have changed size and shape through the years. The cylinder-shaped phonograph record for use with the early Edison models was made about 1889. Disc records were first made by 1894, the double-sided disc by 1904. High-fidelity records were first issued in 1944, the first vinyl disc in 1946, the first stereo record in 1958. The 78 RPM became the standard in 1926 but was discontinued in 1957. In 1932, the first 33 1/3 RPM was made but was not sold commercially until 1948. In 1949, the 45 RPM was introduced. Compact discs became available in the United States in 1982 and many companies began phasing out the production of phonograph records. Vinyl records are popular again. People claim the sound is better on a vinyl recording, and new recordings are being made. Some collectors want vinyl picture records. Vintage albums are collected for their cover art as well as for the fame of the artist and the music.

Barbie Birthday Album, Barbie, Ken, Friends, Cake, Gifts, Mattel, 33 1/3 RPM, 1981	12

Railroad, Sign, Railroad Crossing, Crossbuck, Cat's-Eye Reflectors, 48 In. $180

Chupp Auctions & Real Estate, LLC

Railroad, Step, Coach, Cast Iron & Wood, Luther, Early 1900s, 14 x 26 In. $154

Rich Penn Auctions

R

Railroad, Whistle, Steam, Brass,
12 x 2½ In.
$330

Chupp Auctions & Real Estate, LLC

Red Wing, Bowl, Stoneware, Brown &
Tan Salt Glaze, North Star, 11 In.
$225

Seeck Auctions

Redware, Birdhouse, Cone Shape Top,
Piecrust Rim, Pronounced Finial, 1910s,
6³⁄₈ In.
$497

Jeffrey S. Evans & Associates

Bob Segar & Silver Bullet Band, Stranger In Town, 33⅓ RPM, Capitol Records, 1978		15
Don Ellis & The Survival, Star Wars Main Title Theme, 45 RPM, Atlantic Records..............		9
Johnny Cash, At Folsom Prison, Columbia Records, 1968		40
Santa Claus Is Coming To Town, 45 RPM, Peter Pan Records..		20
Supremes A' Go-Go, 33⅓ RPM, Columbia, 1966		60

RED WING

Red Wing Pottery of Red Wing, Minnesota, was a firm started in 1877. The company first made utilitarian pottery, including stoneware jugs and canning jars. In 1906, three companies combined to make the Red Wing Union Stoneware Company and began producing flowerpots, vases, and dinnerware. Art pottery was introduced in 1926. The name of the company was changed to Red Wing Potteries in 1936. Many dinner sets and vases were made before the company closed in 1967. R. Gillmer bought the company in 1967 and operated it as a retail business. The name was changed again, to Red Wing Pottery. The retail business closed in 2015. Red Wing Stoneware Company was founded in 1987. It was sold to new owners in 2013. They bought Red Wing Pottery and combined the two companies to become Red Wing Stoneware & Pottery. The company makes stoneware crocks, jugs, mugs, bowls, and other items with cobalt blue designs. Rumrill pottery made by the Red Wing Pottery for George Rumrill is listed in its own category. For more prices, go to kovels.com.

Bowl, Stoneware, Brown & Tan Salt Glaze, North Star, 11 In. .... *illus*		225
Crock, Lid, Molded Handles, Cobalt Blue, Stoneware, Leaf Mark, 5 Gal., 17 In........................		124
Jar, Pantry, Cobalt Blue Bands, Wing, Stoneware, 3 Gal.		4750
Pig, Standing, Black, Gold Highlights, Albany Slip, Stoneware...		575

REDWARE

Redware is a hard, red stoneware that has been made for centuries and continues to be made. The term is also used to describe any common clay pottery that is reddish in color. American redware was first made about 1625.

Basket, Presentation, Urn Shape, Twisted Handle, Slip, Saucer, Ruth Scarbrouth, 1824, 8 In..		117
Birdhouse, Cone Shape Top, Piecrust Rim, Pronounced Finial, 1910s, 6³⁄₈ In. .... *illus*		497
Bowl, Fluted Rim, Brown & Yellow Slip, Inscribed, BK, 1800s, 3½ x 12½ In...........................		519
Bowl, Shallow, Yellow Slip Design, Pennsylvania, 1800s, 7¾ In., Pair .... *illus*		288
Canteen, Applied Grapevines & Leaves, Yellow, Green Slip Accent, 1850s, 6 In........................		420
Charger, Coggled Rim, Trailing Decoration, Copper Slip, 1880s, 13¼ In. .... *illus*		1440
Charger, Running Stag, Cream Glaze, Brown, Green Slip Decoration, 1828, 21½ In. .. *illus*		450
Charger, Yellow Slip, Bird, Coggled Rim, Montgomery County, 1800s, 12⅛ In.		7320
Charger, Yellow Slip, Coggled Rim, Trailed Loop Designs, Lead Glaze Interior, 13¼ In.		187
Dish, Bread Loaf, Yellow Slip Waves & Stems, Oval, Pennsylvania, 1800s, 10 x 13 In.		2196
Dish, Loaf, Yellow Slip, Coggled Rim, Breininger, 11½ x 17½ In..		138
Dish, Round, Piecrust Rim, Orange, Yellow Horse, Signed, Ned Foltz Reinholds, Pa., 10 In....		17
Dish, Scalloped Rim, Mottled Manganese & Lead Glaze, c.1860, 4⅞ In....................................		439
Figurine, Cat, Seated, Lead Glaze, Curled Tail, Oval Base, Bell Family, 1845, 4¼ In. ... *illus*		1872
Figurine, Dog, Spaniel, Sitting On Rug, Manganese & Yellow Splashes, 19th Century, 5 In. ..		5856
Flask, 4 Applied Horizontal Loops, Oval Foot, Manganese Glaze, 1800s, 6⅝ x 6⅞ In............		94
Flowerpot, Molded Rim, Integral Water Base, Glaze, Marked, John Bell, c.1860, 5 x 5¼ In...		375
Flowerpot, Undertray, Molded Rim, Pennsylvania, 1800s, 6¾ In. .... *illus*		263
Jar, Double Rim, 2 Shaped Handles, Waisted Base, 1800s, 8 In.		75
Jar, Flared Rim, Turtlecreek, Crackle Cream Ground, Black Band, Leaves, Bird, 9¾ In.........		88
Jar, Storage, 3-Line Slip Trailed White Bands, 4 Semi-Lunate Handles, Late 1800s, 15 x 13 In.		46
Jar, Storage, Cylindrical, Green Paint, Concave Neck, Sloped Shoulder, 1800s, 7 x 5½ In......		36?
Jar, Storage, Lid, Moss Green, Rust Red Glaze, 1810s, 5¾ In. .... *illus*		68?
Jug, Bulbous, Rolled Rim, Applied Strap Handle, Black Glaze, Early 1800s, 6 In......................		13?
Jug, Cream, Lead Glaze, Strap Handle, Molded Rim & Base, J. Buck, Woodstock, c.1840, 4 In. .		497?
Jug, Handle, Mottled Rust, Moss Green Glaze, Signed, 1810s, 8¾ In. .... *illus*		40?

Redware, Bowl, Shallow, Yellow Slip Design, Pennsylvania, 1800s, 7¾ In., Pair
$288

Pook & Pook

Redware, Charger, Coggled Rim, Trailing Decoration, Copper Slip, 1880s, 13¼ In.
$1,440

Crocker Farm, Inc.

Redware, Charger, Running Stag, Cream Glaze, Brown, Green Slip Decoration, 1828, 21½ In.
$450

Garth's Auctioneers & Appraisers

Redware, Figurine, Cat, Seated, Lead Glaze, Curled Tail, Oval Base, Bell Family, 1845, 4¼ In.
$1,872

Jeffrey S. Evans & Associates

Redware, Flowerpot, Undertray, Molded Rim, Pennsylvania, 1800s, 6¾ In.
$263

Pook & Pook

Redware, Jar, Storage, Lid, Moss Green, Rust Red Glaze, 1810s, 5¾ In.
$688

Eldred's

Redware, Jug, Handle, Mottled Rust, Moss Green Glaze, Signed, 1810s, 8¾ In.
$406

Eldred's

Redware, Jug, Molded, Bearded Man, Leaves, Portrait Medallion, Bartmann, Bellarmine, 1700s, 10 In.
$1,080

Garth's Auctioneers & Appraisers

Redware, Pie Plate, Coggled Rim, Brown, Green Slip, 1800s, 8 In.
$1,586

Pook & Pook

R

433

REDWARE

Redware, Pie Plate, Coggled Rim, Swirled Yellow Slip Design, Mid 1800s, 11 ½ In.
$600

Garth's Auctioneers & Appraisers

Redware, Vase, Manganese & Lead Glaze, Neck Ring, Handles, Round Hill Pottery, c.1930, 9 ¾ In.
$761

Jeffrey S. Evans & Associates

Ridgway, Platter, Blue & White, India Temple, Mark, John & William Ridgway, 1800s, 21 x 18 ½ In.
$406

Bruneau & Co. Auctioneers

Jug, Molded, Bearded Man, Leaves, Portrait Medallion, Bartmann, Bellarmine, 1700s, 10 In. *illus*	1080
Jug, Oval, Black Glaze, Strap Handle, Late 1700s, 6 ¾ In., Pair	118
Jug, Oval, Bulbous Body, Applied Handle, Manganese, 1800s, 13 ½ In.	1098
Lamp Stand, Flat Top, Beaded Edge, Flared Base, Glazed, 1800s, 3 x 4 ¼ In.	163
Pie Plate, Coggled Rim, 3-Line Slip Trailed Exterior, 9 In.	288
Pie Plate, Coggled Rim, Brown, Green Slip, 1800s, 8 In. *illus*	1586
Pie Plate, Coggled Rim, Swirled Yellow Slip Design, Mid 1800s, 11 ½ In. *illus*	600
Pie Plate, Wavy Yellow Slip Line Decoration, 1800s, 11 In.	225
Pitcher, Mottled Brown & Green Glaze, Squat, Rolled Rim, Shenandoah Valley, 5 In.	730
Pitcher, Squat, Shaped Lip, Applied Handle, Mottled Greenish Glaze, 1850s, 8 ½ In.	230
Pitcher, Yellow Slip Exterior, Green, Brown Flower Scrolls, C-Scroll Handle, 6 x 5 In.	46
Plate, Bold Yellow Slip, Waves, Coggled Rim, c.1840, Pa., 12 ⅛ In.	4063
Plate, Coggled Rim, 3-Line Twisted Bar, Paired 3 Dots, 12 In.	489
Plate, Yellow Slip Design, Coggled Rim, Lead Glaze, Smith Pottery, Norwalk, 1830s, 10 In.	380
Plate, Yellow Slip, Apple Pie, Coggled Rim, Lead Glazed Interior, 1850s, 11 In.	4388
Plate, Yellow Slip, Coggled Rim, Initials SL, New England, 1800s, 8 ⅜ In.	150
Porringer, Slip Cable, Flaring Top, Loop Fingerhold, Turned Foot, 1800s, 2 ¾ x 4 ¼ In.	190
Puzzle Jug, Yellow 2-Line Slip, Reticulated, 3 Spouts, C-Scroll Handle, Early 1800s, 7 x 4 In.	288
Shaving Mug, Divided Interior, Manganese Splotch, Glaze, Applied Strap Handle, 1800s, 5 In.	650
Sugar, Yellow & Green Slip Dotted Decoration, Tapered Lid, Moravian	4636
Umbrella Stand, Tree Trunk Shape, Faux Bois, Flower, Leaves, Faux Bois, c.1900, 20 In.	336
Vase, Black Ground, Molded Handle, Curved Neck, Footed, Marked, Bird, 8 In.	59
Vase, Manganese & Lead Glaze, Neck Ring, Handles, Round Hill Pottery, c.1930, 9 ¾ In. *illus*	761

RIDGWAY

Ridgway pottery has been made in the Staffordshire district in England since 1792 by a series of companies with the name Ridgway. The company began making bone china in 1808. Ridgway became part of Royal Doulton in the 1960s. The transfer-design dinner sets are the most widely known product. Other pieces of Ridgway may be listed under Flow Blue.

Coupe, English Garden, Pattern On Interior, Scalloped Rim, 6 ⅛ In.	16
Garniture, Vase, Beaker Shape, Corey Hill, Blue, Red & Peach Paint, Marked, c.1800, 12 In., 3 Piece	313
Pitcher, Indus, Water Birds, Flowering Plants, Building In Background, Angled Handle, 11 In.	62
Plate, Bread & Butter, Chiswick, Flow Blue, Raised Scrolled Edge, 5 ¾ In.	18
Plate, Center Flowers, Cobalt Blue & Gilt Rim, 4 Flowers In Oval Cartouches, c.1825, 8 ½ In., Pair	160
Platter, Blue & White, India Temple, Mark, John & William Ridgway, 1800s, 21 x 18 ½ In. *illus*	406
Platter, Coaching Days, Oval, Scalloped Rim, Multicolor Transfer, 15 ¾ In.	80
Toilet Set, Indus, Water Birds, Flower Trim, Toothbrush Holder, 5 ¾ In., Shaving Mug 3 ½ In.	50

RIFLES *that are firearms made after 1900 are not listed in this book. BB guns and air rifles are listed in the Toy category.*

RIVIERA

Riviera dinnerware was made by the Homer Laughlin Co. of Newell, West Virginia, from 1938 to 1950. The pattern was similar in coloring to Fiesta and Harlequin. The Riviera plates and cup handles were square. For more prices, go to kovels.com.

Maroon, Butter, Cover, ½ Lb.	105
Turquoise, Butter, Cover, ½ Lb.	62
Yellow, Salt & Pepper	18

ROCKINGHAM

Rockingham, in the United States, is a pottery with a brown glaze that resembles tortoiseshell. It was made from 1840 to 1900 by many American potteries. Mottled brown Rockingham wares were first made in England at the Rockingham factory. Other types of ceramics were also made by the English firm.

R

Related pieces may be listed in the Bennington category.

Bank, Figural, Pig, Seated, Hooves Raised, Head Turned, Ears Lowered, Square Base, c.1880, 6 In.	90
Canister, Lid, Cylindrical, Horizontal Ridge, Yellowware, 6 x 8 In.	37
Chamber Pot, Round, Side Spout, 11 In.	18
Cuspidor, Round Base, Horizontal Ridge, Flared Neck, Oversized, Hotel, 10 x 8¾ In.	92
Figurine, Lion, Standing, Brown Glaze, Rectangular Stepped Base, c.1875, 10 x 12¾ In., Pair	300
Frame, Oval, Raised Flower Medallions, Toothed Inner Border, Stoneware, 1800s, 12 x 14 In. .. *illus*	313
Jardiniere, Pedestal, Ribbed, Geometric Trim, Light Brown Top & Base, 17½ In., Pair	344
Jug, Embossed, Hunt Scene, Fox Handle, Brown Glaze, 7½ In.	96

ROGERS, *see John Rogers category.*

ROOKWOOD

Rookwood pottery was made in Cincinnati, Ohio, beginning in 1880. All of this art pottery is marked, most with the famous flame mark. The *R* is reversed and placed back to back with the letter *P*. Flames surround the letters. After 1900, a Roman numeral was added to the mark to indicate the year. The company went bankrupt in 1941. It was bought and sold several times after that. For several years various owners tried to revive the pottery, but by 1967 it was out of business. The name and some of the molds were bought by a collector in Michigan in 1982. A few items were made beginning in 1983. In 2004, a group of Cincinnati investors bought the company and 3,700 original molds, the name, and trademark. Pottery was made in Cincinnati again beginning in 2006. Today the company makes architectural tile, art pottery, and special commissions. New items and a few old items with slight redesigns are made. Contemporary pieces are being made to complement the dinnerware line designed by John D. Wareham in 1921. Pieces are marked with the RP mark and a Roman numeral for the four-digit year date. Mold numbers on pieces made since 2006 begin with 10000.

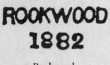

Rookwood
1882–1886

Rookwood
1886

Rookwood
1901

Ashtray, Figural, Bird, Perched, On Bowl, 1923, 4 In.	283
Bookends, Bird, Brown Glaze, Signed Margaret McDonald, 1956, 5 x 5 x 3 In., Pair	173
Bookends, Egyptian Woman, Kneeling Down, Matte Glaze, William McDonald, 5 In. .. *illus*	1512
Bookends, Flower Basket Shape, Multicolor Matte Glaze, 1927, 6 x 3 x 5 In., Pair	188
Bookends, Rook, Open Book Base, Flowers, Matte Glaze, 6½ x 6¼ x 6½ In.	1625
Bowl, Eggshell, Water Lily, White Glaze, Engraved, 1936, 2 In.	104
Bowl, Oval, 2 Nude Woman Handles, Sky Blue Interior, 1929, 7 In. *illus*	367
Bowl, Squat, Flowers, Bulbous Body, Vellum Glaze, Flame Mark, Ed Diers, 1915, 2¾ x 5 In.	250
Box, Lid, Hexagonal, Flowers, Green Matte, Elizabeth Lincoln, 1928, 2 x 5½ x 4 In.	240
Clock, Figural, Brass, Earthenware Glaze, Signed, 1950, 5½ In.	315
Ewer, Applied Handle, Flowers, Brown Glaze, Footed, 1892, 6½ In.	185
Ewer, Bats, Full Moon, Dull Finish, Yellow Clay, Maria Longworth Nichols, 1882, 12 In. *illus*	3751
Ewer, Iris, Trumpet Shape, Ruffled Rim, Anna M. Valentien, 1891, 8¼ In.	189
Figurine, Sailor On Horseback, White High Glaze, Marked, David Syler, 1938, 7½ In. . . *illus*	1815
Jug, Butterfly, Bulbous Body, Handle, Marked, 1883, 6¾ x 5 x 2½ In. *illus*	285
Lamp, Electric, Flowers, Glazed, Painted, 13 In.	207
Mug, Dog, Collie, Standard Glaze, Side Handle, E.T. Hurley, 1933, 4¾ In.	416
Mug, Indian Portrait, Standard Glaze, Grace Young, 1898, 4⅝ In. *illus*	2420
Paperweight, Bulldog, Reclining, White Glaze, 1934, 2¾ x 2 x 4½ In. *illus*	285
Paperweight, Carp, Blue, Tan Matte Glaze, Shirayamadani, c.1928, 2⅜ x 2 x 5 In. .... *illus*	469
Pencil Holder, Bird, Green Over Light Blue, Frogskin Effect, Pentagonal, 1925, 4¾ In.	787

Rockingham, Frame, Oval, Raised Flower Medallions, Toothed Inner Border, Stoneware, 1800s, 12 x 14 In. $313

Gray's Auctioneers, Inc.

Revised Rookwood Mark

The Rookwood Pottery went out of business in the 1960s; the molds and name were purchased in 1984. A new version of the RP flame mark is used. The Roman numerals for the entire year are used instead of just the last numerals: 1908 is VIII, 2008 is MMVIII.

Rookwood, Bookends, Egyptian Woman, Kneeling Down, Matte Glaze, William McDonald, 5 In. $1,512

Fontaine's Auction Gallery

Rookwood, Bowl, Oval, 2 Nude Woman Handles, Sky Blue Interior, 1929, 7 In. $367

R

Strawser Auction Group

ROOKWOOD

Rookwood, Ewer, Bats, Full Moon, Dull Finish, Yellow Clay, Maria Longworth Nichols, 1882, 12 In.
$3,751

Humler & Nolan

Rookwood, Figurine, Sailor On Horseback, White High Glaze, Marked, David Syler, 1938, 7 ½ In.
$1,815

Humler & Nolan

Rookwood, Jug, Butterfly, Bulbous Body, Handle, Marked, 1883, 6 ¾ x 5 x 2 ½ In.
$285

Treadway

Rookwood, Mug, Indian Portrait, Standard Glaze, Grace Young, 1898, 4 ⅝ In.
$2,420

Humler & Nolan

Rookwood, Paperweight, Bulldog, Reclining, White Glaze, 1934, 2 ¾ x 2 x 4 ½ In.
$285

Treadway

Rookwood, Paperweight, Carp, Blue, Tan Matte Glaze, Shirayamadani, c.1928, 2 ⅜ x 2 x 5 In.
$469

Toomey & Co. Auctioneers

Rookwood, Pitcher, Tan Matte Glaze, Gold Trim, Coral Leaves, White Flowers, Signed, HEW, 6 In.
$132

Garth's Auctioneers & Appraisers

Rookwood, Plaque, Sailboats, Venice Harbor, Vellum Glaze, Carl Schmidt, Frame, c.1916, 11 ¼ x 8 ⅜ In.
$6,655

Humler & Nolan

Rookwood, Scent Jar, Lid, White Flowers, Green Leaves & Vines, Artus Van Briggle, 1887, 6 In.
$378

Fontaine's Auction Gallery

Rookwood, Tray, Bird, Blue Rook, Signed, Margaret McDonald, 7 ½ In.
$649

Apple Tree Auction Center

Rookwood, Vase, Apple Blossoms, Matte Glaze, Oval, Flared Rim, Marked, H. McDonald, 13 In.
$1,089

Humler & Nolan

Rookwood, Vase, Dogwood Blossoms, White, Yellow, Sea Green Glaze, Constance Baker, 1903, 11 In.
$8,773

Humler & Nolan

Rookwood, Vase, Dragonflies, Tan Ground, Vellum Glaze, Marked, Sallie Toohey, 1904, 5 ¾ In.
$1,150

Humler & Nolan

Rookwood, Vase, Flowers, Blue, White, Signed, Margaret McDonald, 1920, 5 ½ In.
$266

Apple Tree Auction Center

Rookwood, Vase, Mushrooms, Iris Glaze, White & Brown Ground, Carl Schmidt, 1904, 6 ½ In.
$1,260

Fontaine's Auction Gallery

Rookwood, Vase, Portrait, Indian, Armstrong Arapaho, Sturgis Laurence, Marked, c.1900, 9 x 4 In.
$5,440

Morphy Auctions

Rookwood, Vase, Ships, Vellum Glaze, Flame Mark, Carl Schmidt, 1923, 11 x 4 In.
$1,500

Cowan's Auctions

Rookwood, Vase, White Blossoms, Blue Ground, Matte Glaze, Katherine Jones, 8 In.
$424

Humler & Nolan

Rookwood, Vase, Yellow Matte, Flowers, Carved, 1925, 8 ¼ In.
$135

Hartzell's Auction Gallery Inc.

Rorstrand, Jar, Potpourri, Openwork Lid, Animals, Landscape, Gunnar Nylund, Midcentury, 13 ½ x 10 In.
$163

New Haven Auctions

Rose Bowl, Art Glass, Red Ground, Multicolor Swirl Band, Signed, Kent Ipsen, 1975, 4 ⅞ In.
$293

Jeffrey S. Evans & Associates

Pitcher, Tan Matte Glaze, Gold Trim, Coral Leaves, White Flowers, Signed, HEW, 6 In. *illus*	132
Plaque, Landscape Scene, Vellum Glaze, Frame, Ed Diers, 1912, 20 x 14 ¾ In.	3654
Plaque, Sailboats, Venice Harbor, Vellum Glaze, Carl Schmidt, Frame, c.1916, 11 ¼ x 8 ⅜ In. .*illus*	6655
Plaque, Scenic, Birch Trees, Vellum Glaze, Marked, Ed Diers, Frame, 1896, 8 ½ x 6 ½ In.	3200
Plaque, Scenic, Near Lookout Mountain, Path, Trees, Vellum, E.T. Hurley, 1922, 9 x 12 In.	3375
Pot, Grape Clusters & Vine, Charles Todd, 1914, 5 ½ In.	480
Scent Jar, Lid, White Flowers, Green Leaves & Vines, Artus Van Briggle, 1887, 6 In. *illus*	378
Tray, Bird, Blue Rook, Signed, Margaret McDonald, 7 ½ In. *illus*	649
Vase, 2 Catfish, Glaze, Painted, 6 ½ x 7 ½ x 3 ¾ In.	1722
Vase, 3 Ducks, Spiky Flower Stalks, Blue, Anniversary Glaze, Jens Jensen, 1931, 5 ½ In.	910
Vase, Apple Blossoms, Matte Glaze, Oval, Flared Rim, Marked, H. McDonald, 13 In. *illus*	1089
Vase, Birds, Flowers, Vellum Matte Glaze, Lorinda Epply, 5 ¼ x 4 ½ In.	1125
Vase, Black Opal, Foxglove & Morning Glory, Glazed, Harriet Wilcox, 1927, 10 x 3 In.	1063
Vase, Blue, Fish, Swan, Marked, Jens Jensen, 1944, 10 In.	640
Vase, Bud, White, Marked, Loretta Holtkamp, 1951, 9 ⅞ In., Pair	288
Vase, Bulbous, Flowers, Lattice Bands, Green & White Glaze, Stand, 6 ¼ In.	266
Vase, Daisies, Brown Under Glaze, Molded Rim, Signed, I.B., 1902, 4 ½ In.	84
Vase, Dogwood Blossoms, White, Yellow, Sea Green Glaze, Constance Baker, 1903, 11 In. *illus*	8773
Vase, Dragonflies, Tan Ground, Vellum Glaze, Marked, Sallie Toohey, 1904, 5 ¾ In. *illus*	1150
Vase, Fish, Blue Vellum Glaze, Craquelure Ground, Artist Cipher, Etched, 1909, 4 ¾ x 5 In.	761
Vase, Flowers, Blue, White, Signed, Margaret McDonald, 1920, 5 ½ In. *illus*	266
Vase, Flowers, Glazed, Painted, Art Pottery, Josephine Ella Zettle, 1902, 7 In.	863
Vase, Flowers, Ruffled Rim, Silver Overlay, Kate Machette, 1892, 5 ½ x 3 ½ In.	1719
Vase, Flowers, Vellum Glaze, Lavender Neck, 2 Loop Handles, Shirayamadani, 1935, 6 In.	375
Vase, Landscape Scene, Trees, Placid Water, Multicolor, Vellum, Marked, c.1914, 5 ⅞ In.	556
Vase, Mushrooms, Iris Glaze, White & Brown Ground, Carl Schmidt, 1904, 6 ½ In. *illus*	1260
Vase, Nasturtium, Vellum Glaze, Molded Rim, Ed Diers, 1927, 8 x 4 ½ In.	878
Vase, Orange Tulip, Vellum Glaze, Impressed Marked, Shirayamadani, c.1945, 6 ¼ In.	308
Vase, Portrait, Indian, Armstrong Arapaho, Sturgis Laurence, Marked, c.1900, 9 x 4 In. *illus*	5440
Vase, Ships, Vellum Glaze, Flame Mark, Carl Schmidt, 1923, 11 x 4 In. *illus*	1500
Vase, White Blossoms, Blue Ground, Matte Glaze, Katherine Jones, 8 In. *illus*	424
Vase, Yellow Daffodils, Brown Ground, Swollen Neck, Marked, E. Lincoln, 1907, 8 In.	354
Vase, Yellow Matte, Flowers, Carved, 1925, 8 ¼ In. *illus*	135
Wall Pocket, Zigzag, Blue Matte Ground, Signed, 1926, 7 ½ x 2 ⅜ In.	144

RORSTRAND

Rörstrand

Rorstrand was established near Stockholm, Sweden, in 1726. By the nineteenth century Rorstrand was making English-style earthenware, bone china, porcelain, ironstone china, and majolica. The three-crown mark has been used since 1884. Rorstrand became part of the Hackman Group in 1991. Hackman was bought by Iittala Group in 2004. Fiskars Corporation bought Iittala in 2007 and Rorstrand is now a brand owned by Fiskars.

Bowl, Conical, Crystalline Glaze, Footed, Harry Stalhane, 7 x 3 In.	350
Figurine, Seagull, Wings Spread, Nest With Egg, 6 ¾ x 5 ¾ In.	90
Jar, Potpourri, Openwork Lid, Animals, Landscape, Gunnar Nylund, Midcentury, 13 ½ x 10 In. *illus*	163
Plate, Couple, Traditional Folk Costumes, 6 ¾ In.	38
Vase, 3-Sided, Blue Spike, Gunnar Nylund, 1950s, 8 In.	225

ROSALINE, *see Steuben category.*

ROSE BOWL

Rose bowls were popular during the 1880s. Rose petals were kept in the open bowl to add fragrance to a room, a popular idea in a time of limited personal hygiene. The glass bowls were made with crimped tops, which kept the petals inside. Many types of Victorian art glass were made into rose bowls.

Amber Glass, Multicolor Flowers, Crimped Rim, Polished Pontil Base, 2 ¾ x 3 ½ In.	60
Art Glass, Red Ground, Multicolor Swirl Band, Signed, Kent Ipsen, 1975, 4 ⅞ In. *illus*	293

R

Rose Bowl, Glass, Green Cut To Clear, Montrose, Dorflinger, 5 ¼ x 5 ¾ In. $1,920

Woody Auction

Rose Canton, Punch Bowl, Flowers, Butterflies, Key Borders, Medallion, Hardwood Stand, 1800s, 16 In. $2,750

Hindman

Rose Canton, Vase, Cylindrical, Cartouches, Birds, Flowering Branches, Flowers, Butterfly, 24 x 12 In. $50

Andrew Jones Auction

Rose Canton, Vase, Cylindrical, Cartouches, Flowers, Birds, Butterflies, Applied Gilt Dragon, 12 In. $384

Clars Auction Gallery

Rose Mandarin, Pitcher, Figures, Flowers, Butterflies, Handle, Spout, c.1850, 9 In. $344

Eldred's

Rose Mandarin, Punch Bowl, Gilt, Figures, Flowers, White Ground, Footed, c.1850, 10 ½ x 20 ½ In. $125

Eldred's

Rose Medallion, Punch Bowl, Multicolor, Butterflies, Figures, Birds, Flowers, Gilt, 1850s, 5 ⅜ x 13 ¼ In. $527

Jeffrey S. Evans & Associates

Rose Medallion, Vase, Mei Ping, Narrow Spout, Painted, Figural, Flowers, Leaves, Gilt Ground, 14 ½ In., Pair $295

Austin Auction Gallery

Rosenthal, Figurine, Dachshund Puppy, Brown Glaze, Art Deco, Theodor Karner, c.1935, 6 ½ x 7 In. $345

Lion and Unicorn

R

ROSE BOWL

Rosenthal, Figurine, Ice Bird, White Matte Glaze, Marked, Tapio Wirkkala, 5¾ In.
$153

Bunch Auctions

Roseville, Carnelian II, Vase, Beehive Shape, Turquoise Glaze, 13½ x 13 In.
$2,125

Toomey & Co. Auctioneers

TIP
Don't keep a house key in an obvious spot in the garage.

Roseville, Egypto, Vase, Hand Tooled Corn, Leathery Green Matte Glaze, Fluted Rim, 14 In.
$2,420

Humler & Nolan

Cut Glass, Diadem, Hobstars Alternating With Prisms, Meriden, 5¾ x 7 In.	480
Cut Glass, Nevada, Pairpoint, 5 x 6 In.	240
Glass, Green Cut To Clear, Montrose, Dorflinger, 5¼ x 5¾ In. .... *illus*	1920
Satin Glass, Blue, Enamel Scrolls & Flowers, Crimped Rim, Victorian, 4 In.	24
Satin Glass, Shaded Blue, Cased, Diamond Quilted, Crimped Rim, 5½ In.	36

ROSE CANTON

Rose Canton china is similar to Rose Mandarin and Rose Medallion, except that no people are pictured in the decoration. It was made in China during the nineteenth and twentieth centuries in greens, pinks, and other colors.

Platter, Oval, Flowers, Birds, Butterflies, 6 Medallions Around Edge, Gilt Trim, 18¾ x 15⅝ In. ..	558
Punch Bowl, Flowers, Butterflies, Key Borders, Medallion, Hardwood Stand, 1800s, 16 In. ..*illus*	2750
Vase, Cylindrical, Cartouches, Birds, Flowering Branches, Flowers, Butterfly, 24 x 12 In. .*illus*	50
Vase, Cylindrical, Cartouches, Flowers, Birds, Butterflies, Applied Gilt Dragon, 12 In. .... *illus*	384

ROSE MANDARIN

Rose Mandarin china is similar to Rose Canton and Rose Medallion. If the main design pictures only people in scenes, often in a garden, and is framed with a border of flowers, birds, insects, fruit, or fish, it is Rose Mandarin.

Mug, People In Top Panels, Birds & Flowers In Center Panels, Unmarked, 5¾ In.	279
Pitcher, Figures, Flowers, Butterflies, Handle, Spout, c.1850, 9 In. .... *illus*	344
Platter, Oval, Mandarin Scene, Flowers, Insect Border, Early 1800s, 10 x 13 In.	344
Punch Bowl, Gilt, Figures, Flowers, White Ground, Footed, c.1850, 10½ x 20½ In. .... *illus*	125

ROSE MEDALLION

Rose Medallion china was made in China during the nineteenth and twentieth centuries. It is a distinctive design with four or more panels of decoration around a central medallion that includes a bird or a peony. The panels show combinations of birds, people, flowers, fish, fruit, or insects. The panels have border designs of tree peonies and leaves. Pieces are colored in greens, pinks, and other colors. It is similar to Rose Canton and Rose Mandarin.

Bowl, Lid, Foo Dog Finial, People, Flowers, Parcel Gilt, Marked, 6½ In., Pair	148
Bowl, People, Flowers, Multicolor, White Ground, Rolled Rim, Mid 1800s, 6¾ In.	375
Dish, Entree, Lid, Oval, Figural Panel, Flowers, Butterfly, 1800s, 4 x 11 x 9 In., Pair	380
Fishbowl, Bands, Noble Figure, Outdoor Courtyards, Floral, Apocryphal Mark, 20 x 20½ In. .	148
Fishbowl, Flowers, Bulbous Body, Squat, Ornate, Gilt Rim, 16 x 19 In.	188
Garden Seat, Flowers, Figural Scenes, Porcelain, Chinese, 18 x 15 In.	125
Garden Seat, Porcelain, Flowers, Chinese, 19 In., Pair	531
Hat Stand, Birds, Leaves, Enamel, Iron Red Character, Marked, 12½ In., Pair	207
Jar, Birds & Flowers, People, Mounted, Gilt, Ring Handles, 1900s, 14 In.	113
Jar, Melon, Birds, Flowers, Parcel Gilt, 10 In., Pair	148
Jar, Temple, Lid, Birds, Floral, Parcel Gilt, Foo Dog Finial, Chinese, 16 In., Pair	1180
Platter, Famille Verte, Diamond Shape, Butterfly, 1700s, 15 x 10 x 9 In.	88
Punch Bowl, Bats, Shaped Vignettes, Birds, Flowers, Wide Rim, Multicolor, 1800s, 18 In.	885
Punch Bowl, Multicolor, Butterflies, Figures, Birds, Flowers, Gilt, 1850s, 5⅜ x 13¼ In. *illus*	527
Umbrella Stand, Parcel Gilt, Cylindrical, Flowers, Birds, Leaves, White Ground, Chinese, 24 In.	118
Vase, Birds, Flowers, Gilt Dragons, Foo Dogs, Flared Rim, 14½ In., Pair	266
Vase, Birds, Leaves, Flared Rim, Ruyi Shape Handles, 12½ In., Pair	207
Vase, Courtyard Scenes, Foo Dog Handles, Gilt Dragons, 1800s, 17½ In.	889
Vase, Encrusted Dragon, Birds, Flowers, Bronze Cap, Painted, Marked, 16 x 9 In.	1375
Vase, Flowers, Handles, Painted, 1800s, 10 In.	384
Vase, Gilt Dragon, Courting Scene, Flowers, Footed, 24¾ In., Pair	1792
Vase, Mei Ping, Narrow Spout, Painted, Figural, Flowers, Leaves, Gilt Ground, 14½ In., Pair *illus*	295
Vase, People, Bird, Flowers, Gilt, Dragon Shaped Handles, 1800s, 8 In.	125
Vase, Scenic, Tall Waisted Neck, Scalloped Rim, Dragon Faux Handles, 1800s, 14 In., Pair ...	1121

Warming Dish, Lid, Oval, Gilt Bud Shape Finial, Figural Panel, Flowers, 1800s, 7 x 18 x 13 In... 556

ROSE O'NEILL, *see Kewpie category.*

ROSENTHAL

Rosenthal porcelain was made at the factory established in Selb, Bavaria, in 1891. The factory is still making fine-quality tablewares and figurines. A series of Christmas plates was made from 1910. Other limited edition plates have been made since 1971. Rosenthal became part of the Arcturus Group in 2009.

Rosenthal China
1891–1904

Rosenthal China
1928

Rosenthal China
1948

Figurine, Cat, White, Seated, T. Karner, 4½ x 9 In.	125
Figurine, Dachshund Puppy, Brown Glaze, Art Deco, Theodor Karner, c.1935, 6½ x 7 In. *illus*	345
Figurine, Ice Bird, White Matte Glaze, Marked, Tapio Wirkkala, 5¾ In. *illus*	153
Plate, Garden Caprice, Spring Flowers, Gilt Leaves, Cream Ground, 10 In., 12 Piece	236
Vase, Birds, Flowers, Wiinblad, Studio Line, 9½ In.	47
Vase, Flowers Design, Black, Silver Overlay, 8¼ In.	94
Vase, Owl Shape, Blue Ground, Green, 7½ In.	177

ROSEVILLE

Roseville Pottery Company was organized in Roseville, Ohio, in 1890. Another plant was opened in Zanesville, Ohio, in 1898. Many types of pottery were made until 1954. Early wares include Sgraffito, Olympic, and Rozane. Later lines were often made with molded decorations, especially flowers and fruit. Most pieces are marked *Roseville*. Many reproductions made in China have been offered for sale since the 1980s.

Roseville Pottery Company
1914–1930

Roseville Pottery Company
1935–1954

Roseville Pottery Company
1939–1953

Aztec, Vase, Trumpet Shape, Gray Ground, Flowers, 11 In.	678
Baneda, Vase, Pink, 2 Side Handles, Footed, Red Crayon Mark, 6 In.	434
Bushberry, Umbrella Stand, Brown, Reticulated Handle, Marked, 20¼ In.	656
Carnelian II, Vase, Beehive Shape, Turquoise Glaze, 13½ x 13 In. *illus*	2125
Chloron, Jardiniere, Thick Curdled, Green Matte Glaze, 4 Handles, 11½ x 17 In.	406
Egypto, Vase, Green Ground, Molded Rim & Handle, Rozane, 16 In.	951
Egypto, Vase, Hand Tooled Corn, Leathery Green Matte Glaze, Fluted Rim, 14 In. *illus*	2420
Freesia, Pitcher, Ewer, Orange, Spout, Handle, Marked, 10½ x 6½ In., Pair	144
Futura, Basket, Hanging, Planter, Black, Pink, 23½ x 8 In.	150
Futura, Console, Sailboat, Flower Frog, 3½ x 12⅜ In. *illus*	363
Futura, Vase, Art Deco, Pink, Green, Square Vase, 7 x 3¾ In.	281
Futura, Vase, Ball Bottle Shape, Glazed, Underfoot, 8 In.	226
Imperial, Jardiniere, Brown & Green, 10 In.	94
Landscape, Jardiniere, Brown Glaze, 4 Handles, Harry Rhead, Signed, HR, 7⅜ x 10½ In.	938
Laurel, Vase, Green & Peach, Molded, Leaves, Applied Handle, 8½ In.	354
Mostique, Jardiniere, Tan, Leaves, Carved, 18 x 13 x 13 In.	400
Pauleo, Vase, Crystalis Glaze, Brown, Cylindrical, 24 x 14 In. *illus*	1875
Pine Cone, Basket, Brown, Branch Handle, Footed, Marked, 10¼ x 13 In.	393
Raymor, Vase, Blue, Glazed, Pottery, Aldo Londi, Italy, 1809, 7 x 5½ In.	156

Roseville, Futura, Console, Sailboat, Flower Frog, 3½ x 12⅜ In.
$363

Humler & Nolan

Roseville, Pauleo, Vase, Crystalis Glaze, Brown, Cylindrical, 24 x 14 In.
$1,875

Toomey & Co. Auctioneers

Roseville, Silhouette, Wall Pocket, Blue, Green Tones, Flowers, 8 In.
$90

Woody Auction

R

Roseville, Snowberry, Bookends, Green Tones, Open Book Shape, 5 ¼ x 5 ¼ In., Pair

$90

Woody Auction

Rowland & Marsellus, Plate, Biltmore House, Blue & White, Staffordshire, c.1890, 9 ¾ In.

$184

Richard D. Hatch & Associates

Roy Rogers, Tent, Yellow, Red Printed Logo, Front Flap, Store Display, Sample, 14 ½ x 24 In.

$125

Pook & Pook

Royal Bayreuth, Pitcher, Water, Devil & Cards, Figural Handle, 7 ½ In.

$350

Woody Auction

Raymor, Vase, Monumental, Honey Yellow, Glazed, Marked, Ben Seibel, 1950s, 21 In.	1125
Rozane, Jardiniere, Flowers, Leaves, Dimpled Green Ground, Squat, Marked, c.1920, 12 x 14 In.	70
Silhouette, Wall Pocket, Blue, Green Tones, Flowers, 8 In. .... *illus*	90
Snowberry, Basket, Hanging, Pink, White Blossoms, 2 Handles, 5 In.	70
Snowberry, Bookends, Green Tones, Open Book Shape, 5 ¼ x 5 ¼ In., Pair .... *illus*	90
Sunflower, Pot, Leaves, Green Ground, 2 Handles, 4 In.	283
Sunflower, Wall Pocket, Yellow, Green Leaves, Brown Ground, Molded Rim, 7 In.	472
Tulip, Pitcher, Blue, Crackle, Brown & Cream Ground, Pointed Spout, Handle, 7 ½ In.	37
Umbrella Stand, Peacock, Squeezebag, Blue Ground, Marked, F.H. Rhead, c.1908, 20 x 10 In.	21250
Windsor, Vase, Blue, Bulbous Body, 2 Handles, 9 ⅜ In.	1331
Wisteria, Vase, Embossed, Flowers & Leaves, Blue Ground, 5 In.	226
Wisteria, Vase, Pink, Green Leaves, Blue Drip Ground, 2 Angular Handles, 4 In.	81

ROWLAND & MARSELLUS

Rowland & Marsellus Company is part of a mark that appears on historical Staffordshire dating from the late nineteenth and early twentieth centuries. *Rowland & Marsellus* is the mark used by an American importing company in New York City. The company worked from 1893 to about 1937. Some of the pieces may have been made by the British Anchor Pottery Co. of Longton, England, for export to a New York firm. Many American views were made. Of special interest to collectors are the plates with rolled edges, usually blue and white.

Pitcher, Discovery Of America, Brown Transfer, Bulbous Neck, Angled Handle, 8 x 5 ½ In.	80
Plate, Biltmore House, Blue & White, Staffordshire, c.1890, 9 ¾ In. .... *illus*	184
Plate, Bunker Hill Monument, Blue Center, Multicolor Flowered Rim, 10 In.	15
Plate, Dinner, Souvenir Of Waterbury, Conn., Blue & White, 10 In.	40
Plate, Toronto, Canada, Blue Transfer, 10 In.	10

ROY ROGERS

Roy Rogers was born in 1911 in Cincinnati, Ohio. His birth name was Leonard Slye. In the 1930s, he made a living as a singer; in 1935, his group started work at a Los Angeles radio station. He appeared in his first movie in 1937. He began using the name Roy Rogers in 1938. From 1952 to 1957, he made 101 television shows. The other stars in the show were his wife, Dale Evans, his horse, Trigger, and his dog, Bullet. Rogers died in 1998. Roy Rogers memorabilia, including items from the Roy Rogers restaurants, are collected.

Book, Roy Rogers & The Gopher Creek Gunman, Hardcover, Whitman, 1945, 7 x 5 In.	33
Camera, Roy & Trigger, 620 Snapshot, Herbert George Co., 4 x 3 x 3 In.	75
Cap Pistol, Die Cast, Plated White Metal, Relief Signature, Geo. Schmidt Mfg., 1950s, 8 In.	175
Comic Book, Roy Buys Into Trouble, Vol. 1, No. 54, June 1952	20
Pitcher, Figural, Roy's Head, Hat, Kerchief, Plastic, F & F Mold & Die Co., 4 x 4 In.	44
Saddlebag, Brown, Roy Rogers King Of The Cowboys, 2 Compartments, Plastic, ULG, 12 In.	50
Tent, Yellow, Red Printed Logo, Front Flap, Store Display, Sample, 14 ½ x 24 In. .... *illus*	125
Toy, Trigger, Dodge Horse Trailer, Tin Lithograph, Red & Yellow, Blue Roof, Marx, c.1950, 15 In.	125

ROYAL BAYREUTH

Royal Bayreuth is the name of a factory that was founded in Tettau, Bavaria, in 1794. The factory closed in 2019. The marks have changed through the years. A stylized crest, the name Royal Bayreuth, and the word *Bavaria* appear in slightly different forms from 1870 to about 1919. Later dishes may include the words *U.S. Zone* (1945–1949), the year of the issue, or the word *Germany* instead of *Bavaria.* Related pieces may be found listed in the Rose Tapestry, Snow Babies, and Sunbonnet Babies categories.

R

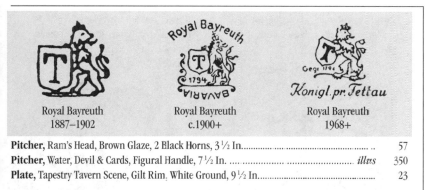

Royal Bayreuth 1887–1902	Royal Bayreuth c.1900+	Royal Bayreuth 1968+

Pitcher, Ram's Head, Brown Glaze, 2 Black Horns, 3½ In.	57
Pitcher, Water, Devil & Cards, Figural Handle, 7½ In. .... *illus*	350
Plate, Tapestry Tavern Scene, Gilt Rim, White Ground, 9½ In.	23

ROYAL BONN

Royal Bonn is the nineteenth- and twentieth-century trade name used by Franz Anton Mehlem, who had a pottery in Bonn, Germany, from 1836 to 1931. Porcelain and earthenware were made. Royal Bonn also made cases for Ansonia clocks. The factory was purchased by Villeroy & Boch in 1921 and closed in 1931. Many marks were used, most including the name *Bonn,* the initials *FAM,* and a crown.

Clock, Ansonia, Bracket, Gilt, Bronze, Porcelain Insert, Courting Scene, 18½ In. .... *illus*	369
Clock, Shelf, Flowers, Cobalt Blue Ground, Painted, 1800s, 12 x 14 In. .... *illus*	219
Clock, Shelf, La Savoie, Pink, Yellow Case, Flowers, Roman Numeral Dial, 11 x 9 In.	125
Ewer, Flowers, Gold Trim, Cream, White Ground, Applied Handle, 8½ In.	90
Jardiniere, Pedestal, Gilt, Flowers, Scrolled Handles, Multicolor, Late 1800s, 40 In.	504
Vase, Embossed Poppy, Green, Yellow & Brown Tones, Marked, 12 x 9 In. .... *illus*	300
Vase, Multicolor, Flowers, Green Ground, Pinched Neck, 8 In.	136
Vase, Portrait Of Young Woman, Leaves, Lavender Blossom, Signed, 7¼ In.	150
Vase, Portrait, Young Woman, Scenic, Fluted Rim, Round Base, Signed, 14 In. .... *illus*	300

ROYAL COPENHAGEN

Royal Copenhagen porcelain and pottery have been made in Denmark since 1775. The Christmas plate series started in 1908. The figurines with pale blue and gray glazes have remained popular in this century and are still being made. Many other old and new style porcelains are made today. In 2001 Royal Copenhagen became part of the Royal Scandinavia Group owned by the Danish company Axcel. Axcel sold Royal Copenhagen to the Finnish company Fiskars in December 2012.

Royal Copenhagen 1892	Royal Copenhagen 1894–1900	Royal Copenhagen 1935–present

Bowl, Console, Revolutionary War Scene, Silhouette Portrait, G. Washington, 1776, 6 x 13 In.	338
Bowl, Monteith, Flora Danica, 2 Handles, Scalloped Rim, 13 In.	5670
Figurine, Elephant, Standing, Glazed, 7½ In.	120
Figurine, Huntsman, Seated, Hound, Base Marked, 1900s, 8½ In.	128
Figurine, Lioness, Sitting, Gray, White, Blue Eyes, 6 x 12 In. ...	94
Figurine, Monkey, Stoneware, Knud Kyhn, 1951, 12¼ In. .... *illus*	305
Figurine, Wave & Rock, Marked, 18½ In.	406
Figurine, Woman, 2 Goats, Christian Thomsen, 1950, 9¼ In.	118
Figurine, Young Satyr, On Knees, Parrot, Gloss, Glazed, 7 x 5 In. .... *illus*	80
Group, Man Leading 2 Calves, Black Cap, Oval Base, 9 x 7 In.	70
Jar, Applied Lid, Stoneware, Incised Stripe, Bird Shape Finial, Thorkild Olsen, 1950s, 11 In...	380
Plate, Blue & White, Scalloped Rim, Reticulated Border, 10 In. .... *illus*	80
Plate, Salad, Flora Danica, Flowers, Marked, 7¾ In., 8 Piece	2560

Royal Bonn, Clock, Ansonia, Bracket, Gilt, Bronze, Porcelain Insert, Courting Scene, 18½ In.
$369

Rich Penn Auctions

Royal Bonn, Clock, Shelf, Flowers, Cobalt Blue Ground, Painted, 1800s, 12 x 14 In.
$219

Kamelot Auctions

Royal Bonn, Vase, Embossed Poppy, Green, Yellow & Brown Tones, Marked, 12 x 9 In.
$300

R

Woody Auction

Royal Bonn, Vase, Portrait, Young Woman, Scenic, Fluted Rim, Round Base, Signed, 14 In.
$300

Woody Auction

Royal Copenhagen, Figurine, Monkey, Stoneware, Knud Kyhn, 1951, 12¼ In.
$305

Neal Auction Company

Royal Copenhagen, Figurine, Young Satyr, On Knees, Parrot, Gloss, Glazed, 7 x 5 In.
$80

Woody Auction

Royal Copenhagen, Plate, Blue & White, Scalloped Rim, Reticulated Border, 10 In.
$80

Woody Auction

Royal Copenhagen, Vase, Pale Blue, Gray, Crackle Glaze, Gilt, Flared Rim, c.1950, 12¼ In.
$443

Leland Little Auctions

Royal Crown Derby, Bowl, Flowers, Leaves, White Ground, 10¼ In., Pair
$68

Strawser Auction Group

Royal Crown Derby, Plate, Round, Fish, Ferns, Weeds, Brown, Enamel, Thomas Tatlow, c.1815, 8½ In.
$1,008

Sotheby's

Royal Crown Derby, Tureen, Soup, Lid, Underplate, 2 Handles, Footed, Old Imari, 12½ In.
$500

Bruneau & Co. Auctioneers

Royal Crown Derby, Urn, Lid, Red Ground, Gold Flowers, 2 Handles, 5¼ x 5¼ In.
$225

Woody Auction

TIP
Some tea and coffee stains on dishes can be removed by rubbing them with damp baking soda.

Platter, Pierced Lid, Fish Shape Handle, Gilt Trim, Oval, 18 ¼ In. 2772
Vase, Clipper Ship At Sea, Lighthouse, Gray & Blue, Swollen Shoulder, 13 x 6 In. 250
Vase, Pale Blue, Gray, Crackle Glaze, Gilt, Flared Rim, c.1950, 12 ¼ In. .... *illus* 443

ROYAL CROWN DERBY

Royal Crown Derby Company, Ltd., is a name used on porcelain beginning in 1890. There is a complex family tree that includes the Derby, Crown Derby, and Royal Crown Derby porcelains. *Derby* has been marked on porcelain and bone china made in the city of Derby, England, since about 1750 when Andrew Planche and William Duesbury established the first china factory in Derby. In 1775, King George III honored the company by granting them a patent to use the royal crown in their backstamp and the company became known as *Crown Derby.* Pieces are marked with a crown and the letter *D* or the word *Derby.* When the original Derby factory closed in 1848, some of its former workers opened a smaller factory on King Street, Derby, and used Crown Derby's original molds and patterns. About 1876 the present company was formed when another factory opened under the name Derby Crown Porcelain Co. (1876–1890). Queen Victoria granted Derby Crown Porcelain a royal warrant in 1890 and the name became Royal Crown Derby Porcelain Co. Finally, in 1935 Royal Crown Derby bought the King Street factory, which brought Derby china under one company again. The Royal Crown Derby mark includes the name and a crown. The words *Made in England* were used after 1921. The company became part of Allied English Potteries Group in 1964 then merged into Royal Doulton Tableware. Royal Crown Derby Co. Ltd. was acquired by Steelite International in 2013. Kevin Oakes bought Royal Crown Derby in 2016. The company is still in business.

Royal Crown Derby
1877–1890

Royal Crown Derby
1890–1940

Royal Crown Derby
c.1976–2014

Bone Dish, Kidney Shape, Rust & Blue, Gold Rim, 1906, 7 ¾ In., 6 Piece........................... 266
Bowl, Flowers, Leaves, White Ground, 10 ¼ In., Pair .... *illus* 68
Breakfast Set, White, Ribbed, Blue & Gilt Band, Ring Finials, c.1790, 11 Piece 1650
Candlestick, Old Imari, Bone China, Gilt, Brass Fittings, 1930, 10 x 5 x 5 In., Pair 531
Charger, Golden Aves, Scalloped Border, Painted, Gilt, Birds, Flowers, 1973, 13 ⅜ In. 148
Plate, Gilt Rim, Cobalt Blue, White Center, Flowers, Tiffany & Co., 8 ½ In., 10 Piece.............. 780
Plate, Round, Fish, Ferns, Weeds, Brown, Enamel, Thomas Tatlow, c.1815, 8 ½ In. .... *illus* 1008
Tureen, Rectangular Lid, Flowers, Gilt, Loop Finial, White Ground, 1790, 7 In....................... 215
Tureen, Soup, Lid, Underplate, 2 Handles, Footed, Old Imari, 12 ½ In. .... *illus* 500
Urn, Lid, Red Ground, Gold Flowers, 2 Handles, 5 ¼ x 5 ¼ In. .... *illus* 225
Vase, Gilt, Multicolor, Flowers, Pinkish Ground, 5 In. 107
Vase, Lid, Gilt, Cobalt Blue, Flowers, 2 Handles, Marked, 12 ½ In. .... *illus* 633

ROYAL DOULTON

Royal Doulton is the name used on Doulton and Company pottery made from 1902 to the present. Doulton and Company of England was founded in 1853. Pieces made before 1902 are listed in this book under Doulton. Royal Doulton collectors pay high prices for the out-of-production figurines, character jugs, vases, and series wares. Some vases and animal figurines were made with a special red glaze called flambe. Sung and Chang glazed pieces are rare. The multicolored glaze is very thick and looks as if it were dropped on the clay. Bunnykins figurines were first made by Royal Doulton in 1939. In 2005 Royal Doulton was acquired by the Waterford Wedgwood Group. It was

Royal Crown Derby, Vase, Lid, Gilt, Cobalt Blue, Flowers, 2 Handles, Marked, 12 ½ In.
$633

Blackwell Auctions

Royal Doulton, Animal, Tiger, Stalking, Flambe, Glazed, HN 1082, 6 ¼ x 14 In.
$275

Woody Auction

Royal Doulton, Character Jug, Abraham Lincoln, D 6936, Presidential Series, Flag Handle, 1992, 6 ¾ x 7 In.
$259

Blackwell Auctions

R

Royal Doulton, Character Jug, Santa Claus, Doll & Drum Handle, D 6668, 1981, 7 ½ In.
$1,150

Lion and Unicorn

Royal Doulton, Figurine, Pussy, Black & White Dress, Brown Hair, HN 325, Signed, F.C. Stone, c.1918, 8 x 6 In.
$6,325

Lion and Unicorn

Royal Doulton, Pitcher, Charles Dickens, Keep My Memory Green, Faces, 10 ½ In.
$500

Woody Auction

bought by KPS Capital Partners of New York in 2009 and became part of WWRD Holdings. WWRD was bought by Fiskars Group in 2015. Beatrix Potter bunny figurines were made by Beswick and are listed in that category.

| Royal Doulton 1902–1922, 1927–1932 | Royal Doulton 1922–1956 | Royal Doulton c.2000–present |

Animal, Dog, Doberman, Black, Brown, Standing, Collar & Leash, Marked, RDA 8, 2003, 6 x 6 ½ In. ...	46
Animal, Monkey, Hand Raised To Ear, Sung, Flambe, Blue, Red Glaze, c.1912, 3 ½ x 3 ½ In.	3105
Animal, Tiger, Stalking, Flambe, Glazed, HN 1082, 6 ¼ x 14 In. .... *illus*	275
Bottle, Whiskey, Stoneware, Blue, Brown, Motto, Stopper, Marked, 1900s, 9 ¾ In..................	81
Bowl, Camels, Hieroglyphs, Isis, Palm Trees, Yellow Center, Handles, Footed, c.1920, 2 ½ x 8 In..	288
Bowl, Pottery, Chang Design, Cream, Amber, Purple, Red, Brown, Signed, 3 ¾ x 9 ¼ x 9 ¼ In.	240
Bowl, Royal Mail Steam Packet Co., Steamship, White, c.1915, 1 ½ x 2 ½ In.	12

Royal Doulton character jugs depict the head and shoulders of the subject. They are made in four sizes: large, 5 ¼ to 7 inches; small, 3 ¼ to 4 inches; miniature, 2 ¼ to 2 ½ inches; and tiny, 1 ¼ inches. Toby jugs portray a seated, full figure.

Character Jug, Abraham Lincoln, D 6936, Presidential Series, Flag Handle, 1992, 6 ¾ x 7 In. *illus*	259
Character Jug, King Arthur & Guinevere, D 6836, 2-Sided, Signed, Boothroyd, 1900s, 6 ½ In.	978
Character Jug, Queen Victoria, D 6816, Crown, Gold, Cream, Black, 7 In.	127
Character Jug, Santa Claus, D 6964, Bells Handle, Painted, Marked, Michael Abberley, 1996, 4 ½ In.	173
Character Jug, Santa Claus, Doll & Drum Handle, D 6668, 1981, 7 ½ In. .... *illus*	1150
Charger, Fox Hunt, Gilt Rim, Flow Blue, 14 In..	124
Cup & Saucer, Comic Strip, Pip, Squeak & Wilfred, Series Ware, Painted, 1900s, 5 ½ In.......	23
Cup & Saucer, White Ground, Multicolor, Butterfly, Figural Handle.................................	50
Decanter, Bagpiper, Whiskey, Dewars, Handle, Stopper, Signed, 9 In...............................	288
Decanter, Figural, Don Sandeman, Standing, Black, 10 ½ In..	35
Decanter, Seagers Dry Gin, Cobalt Blue, Ribbed Body, Hat Stopper, 1900s, 9 ¾ x 4 In.	23
Figurine, Bunnykins, Wicketkeeper, Glaze, Painted, Round Base, D. Andrews, DB 150, 3 ½ In....	35
Figurine, Cat, Flambe, Red, Seated, Pottery, HN 109, 5 x 3 In., Pair	94
Figurine, Dog, Poodle, White, HN 2631, 7 In., Pair	69
Figurine, Dragon, Flambe, Red Glaze, Orange, Black, HN 2085, 1973-96, 7 ½ In.	230
Figurine, Indian, Riding, Horse, Painted, HN 2376, Peggy Davies, 1967, 15 ¼ In..................	403
Figurine, Pussy, Black & White Dress, Brown Hair, HN 325, Signed, F.C. Stone, c.1918, 8 x 6 In. ..*illus*	6325
Figurine, Silks & Ribbons, Street Vendor Series, Old Woman, HN 2017, 1949-2001, 6 In.	58
Inkwell, Figural, Baby Suffragette, Head Tilts Back, Earthenware, c.1910, 3 ½ In...............	633
Liquor Container, William Grant, Oak Casks Handle, Painted, Backstamp, 1987, 7 In.............	58
Mug, Racing, Man, Horse, Orange, Cream, 1937, 5 ½ x 5 ½ In......................................	35
Mug, Stoneware, Twins Bowing, Glazed Rim, Signed, John Hassall, c.1906, 4 ½ x 3 ¾ In.......	58
Pitcher, Charles Dickens, Keep My Memory Green, Faces, 10 ½ In. .... *illus*	500
Pitcher, Geometric Designs, Bird Of Paradise, Titanian, Marked, 1900s, 7 x 6 In.	150
Platter, Geometric Designs, Bird Of Paradise, Titanian, Marked, c.1920s, 10 ½ In................	207
Sweetmeat, Slater, Cobalt Blue, White Flowers, Carved Bone Finial, Silver Plate Lid, 3 x 5 In..	60
Tankard, Battle Of Hastings, Bayeux Tapestry Series, Ceramic, c.1930, 5 ½ In.	35
Tobacco Jar, Lid, Fox Hunting, Glaze, Painted, Backstamped, D 5104, 4 ¾ In......................	92
Toothpick Holder, Fat Boy, Charles Dickens Series Ware, 1900s, 2 ¼ In.	115
Urn, Lid, Oval, Tunisian Scenes, Handle, Multicolor, Signed, H. Allen, England, 1900s, 7 ¾ In. ...	633
Vase, Camel & Desert Scene, Molded Rim, Flambe, 5 ½ In..	83
Vase, Cherry Blossoms, Multi Hued, Blue, Green, Profuse Gilt, Glazed, Titanian, c.1920, 6 x 5 In.	1150
Vase, Flowers, Gold Tapestry Ground, Flared Rim, Domed Base, 13 ½ In............................	62
Vase, Gourd Shape, Purple, Lavender, Glazed, 6 x 4 In.	374
Vase, Landscape, Cows In Field, Daisies, Flambe Glaze, Swollen Cylinder, 8 In...................	177

ROYAL DUX

Royal Dux is the more common name for the Duxer Porzellanmanufaktur, which was founded by E. Eichler in Dux, Bohemia (now Duchcov, Czech Republic), in 1860. By the turn of the twentieth century, the firm specialized in porcelain statuary and busts of Art Nouveau–style maidens, large porcelain figures, and ornate vases with three-dimensional figures climbing on the sides. The firm is still in business. It is now part of Czesky Porcelan (Czech Porcelain).

Candlestick, Woman, Green Dress, Arms On Lotus-Like Petal, Gilt Highlights, 1910s, 7 In., Pair ..*illus*		140
Centerpiece, Figural, Woman With Instrument, 2nd Woman Below, Marked, 18 x 14 In. ... *illus*		800
Figurine, Flapper, 2 Borzoi Dogs, Wood Brace, 15 In.		236
Figurine, Harlequin & Columbine, Dancing, Masked Ball, 19 In. .... *illus*		325
Figurine, Nude Running With Hound, Oval Base, 14¼ x 10 In.		70
Figurine, Shepherd Boy, Playing Pipes, Standing, Painted, Backstamp, 1900s, 12 In.		196
Figurine, Woman, Seated, Reading, Dress Falling Off Her Shoulders, 1900s, 18 In. ...... *illus*		330
Planter, Duck Shape, Multicolor, Glazed, Majolica, 7½ In.		622
Vase, Pink Flamingo, 2 Bamboo Sticks, Stone Shape Base, Majolica, 39 In.		1921

ROYAL FLEMISH

Royal Flemish glass was made during the late 1880s in New Bedford, Massachusetts, by the Mt. Washington Glass Works. It is a colored satin glass decorated with dark colors and raised gold designs. The glass was patented in 1894. It was supposed to resemble stained glass windows.

Biscuit Jar, 4 Coin Medallions, Quadruple Plate Mount, Mt. Washington, 1980s, 8 x 5 In. ..*illus*		873
Pickle Castor, Embossed, Star-Hobnail, Caladium Leaf, Mt. Washington, 1880s, 8 x 2 In.		293
Vase, Pillow Shape, Gold Trim, Dragon, Stars, Art Glass, 8¼ x 7¼ In. .... *illus*		748

ROYAL HAEGER, *see Haeger category.*

ROYAL HICKMAN

Royal Hickman designed pottery, glass, silver, aluminum, furniture, lamps, and other items. From 1938 to 1944 and again from the 1950s to 1969, he worked for Haeger Potteries. Mr. Hickman operated his own pottery in Tampa, Florida, during the 1940s. He moved to California and worked for Vernon Potteries. During the last years of his life he lived in Guadalajara, Mexico, and continued designing for Royal Haeger. He died in 1969. Pieces made in his pottery listed here are marked *Royal Hickman* or *Hickman*.

Figurine, Panther, Rock Ledge, Black, c.1950, 13 x 8 In.		142
Vase, 6 Palm Leaves Wrapped Around Berry Base, Teal Blue, 1940s, 13 x 17 x 2¾ In.		175

ROYAL NYMPHENBURG

Royal Nymphenburg is the modern name for the Nymphenburg porcelain factory, which was established at Neudeck ob der Au, Germany, in 1753 and moved to Nymphenburg in 1761. The company is still in existence. Marks include a checkered shield topped by a crown, a crowned *CT* with the year, and a contemporary shield mark on reproductions of eighteenth-century porcelain.

Plate, Cabinet, Reticulated, Floral, Gilt, c.1900s, 8¾ In., 4 Piece		177

ROYAL RUDOLSTADT, *see Rudolstadt category.*

ROYAL VIENNA, *see Beehive category.*

Royal Dux, Candlestick, Woman, Green Dress, Arms On Lotus-Like Petal, Gilt Highlights, 1910s, 7 In., Pair
$140

Jeffrey S. Evans & Associates

Royal Dux, Centerpiece, Figural, Woman With Instrument, 2nd Woman Below, Marked, 18 x 14 In.
$800

Morphy Auctions

Royal Dux, Figurine, Harlequin & Columbine, Dancing, Masked Ball, 19 In.
$325

Leland Little Auctions

R

Royal Dux, Figurine, Woman, Seated, Reading, Dress Falling Off Her Shoulders, 1900s, 18 In.
$330

Selkirk Auctioneers & Appraisers

Royal Flemish, Biscuit Jar, 4 Coin Medallions, Quadruple Plate Mount, Mt. Washington, 1980s, 8 x 5 In.
$878

Jeffrey S. Evans & Associates

Royal Flemish, Vase, Pillow Shape, Gold Trim, Dragon, Stars, Art Glass, 8 1/4 x 7 1/4 In.
$748

Richard D. Hatch & Associates

Royal Worcester, Candelabrum, 3-Light, Lotus, Frogs, Lizards, Bugs, 1800s, 17 3/4 In., Pair
$281

Eldred's

Royal Worcester, Figurine, Princess Elizabeth, Horse, Painted, Harry Davis, 1949, 5 1/4 x 15 1/4 In.
$3,910

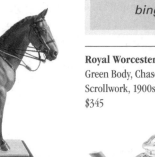

Lion and Unicorn

Royal Worcester, Group, Boy & Girl, Carrying Basket, Oval Cobblestone Base, Gilt Accent, Marked, c.1883, 8 1/8 In.
$468

Jeffrey S. Evans & Associates

> **TIP**
> *Remove stains from old ceramic vases by scrubbing with salt.*

Royal Worcester, Teapot, Cannonball, Oval Green Body, Chased Silver Overlay, Leafy Scrollwork, 1900s, 5 x 7 In.
$345

Lion and Unicorn

Royal Worcester, Vase, Gold Stencil, Figural Snake Handles, Marked, Davis Collamorre & Co., 5 In.
$275

Woody Auction

R

448

ROYAL WORCESTER

Royal Worcester is a name used by collectors. Worcester porcelains were made in Worcester, England, from about 1751. The firm went through many periods and name changes. It became the Worcester Royal Porcelain Company, Ltd., in 1862. Today collectors call the porcelains made after 1862 "Royal Worcester." In 1976, the firm merged with W.T. Copeland to become Royal Worcester Spode. The company was bought by the Portmeirion Group in 2009. Some early products of the factory are listed under Worcester. Related pieces may be listed under Copeland, Copeland Spode, and Spode.

Royal Worcester
1862–1875

Royal Worcester
1891

Royal Worcester
c.1959+

Candelabrum, 3-Light, Lotus, Frogs, Lizards, Bugs, 1800s, 17 3/4 In., Pair .... *illus*	281
Candlestick, Chamber, Blossom Mold, Scalloped Sides, Scroll Handle, Cream Ground, Gilt, 3 x 6 In..	70
Creamer, Greek Key Border, Elephant Head Handle, Tiffany & Co., New York, c.1879, 5 In.....	106
Ewer, Flowers, Cream Ground, Applied Dragon Handle, No. 1048, 4 1/4 In..............................	40
Figurine, Polo Player, Riding Horse, Rectangular Base, Doris Lindner, 7 x 8 In.....................	610
Figurine, Princess Elizabeth, Horse, Painted, Harry Davis, 1949, 5 1/4 x 15 1/4 In. .... *illus*	3910
Flask, Moon, Molded Angular Handles, Ivory Ground, Circular Medallions, c.1872, 10 In., Pair..	5292
Group, Boy & Girl, Carrying Basket, Oval Cobblestone Base, Gilt Accent, Marked, c.1883, 8 1/8 In. ..*illus*	468
Teapot, Cannonball, Oval Green Body, Chased Silver Overlay, Leafy Scrollwork, 1900s, 5 x 7 In. *illus*	345
Toothpick Holder, Egg & Mice, Leaves Base..	85
Vase, Flowers, Pink, Cream Ground, Pedestal Base, 2 Handles, No. 2256, 10 In.	150
Vase, Gold Stencil, Figural Snake Handles, Marked, Davis Collamorre & Co., 5 In. .... *illus*	275
Vase, Scenic, Reticulated, Double Well, Ivory Bone, White, Gold Trim, 1899, 3 1/4 In. .... *illus*	510

ROYCROFT

Roycroft products were made by the Roycrofter community of East Aurora, New York, from 1895 until 1938. The community was founded by Elbert Hubbard, famous philosopher, writer, and artist. The workshops owned by the community made furniture, metalware, leatherwork, embroidery, and jewelry. A print-shop produced many signs, books, and the magazines that promoted the sayings of Elbert Hubbard. Furniture by the Roycroft community is listed in the Furniture category.

Bookends, Copper, Hammered, Arts & Crafts Mission Style, 5 x 5 1/2 x 4 1/2 In...........................	92
Humidor, Lid, Cylindrical, Copper, Hammered, Flowers, Monogram, 6 1/2 In. .... *illus*	504
Lamp, Copper, Hammered, Helmet Shade, Ball Finial, Patina, 18 x 7 1/2 In......................... ...	2000
Lamp, Hammered, Copper, Orange, Steuben Shade, Rectangular Base, Early 1900s, 15 In. ..*illus*	2640
Letter Opener, Copper, Dagger Style, Tooled Handle, Hammered Blade, Impressed, c.1908, 11 In..	120
Tray, Copper, Hammered, Applied Handle, Circle, Stamped Orb & Cross, 1 1/2 x 15 1/2 x 18 In.	750
Vase, Copper, Hammered, Applied Nickel Silver, Stamped Orb & Cross, Dard Hunter, 6 x 3 In..	938
Vase, Copper, Hammered, Cylindrical, Walter Jennings, Marked, c.1918, 7 x 3 In. .... *illus*	2560

ROZANE, *see Roseville category.*

RRP

RRP, or RRP Roseville, is the mark used by the firm of Robinson-Ransbottom. It is not a mark of the more famous Roseville Pottery. The Ransbottom brothers started a pottery in 1900 in Ironspot, Ohio. In 1920, they merged with the Robinson Clay Product Company of Akron, Ohio, to become Robinson-Ransbottom. The factory closed in 2005.

Cookie Jar, Ball Shape, Footed, Apples, Leaves, Red, Green, Yellow, Brown, 8 1/2 x 9 In..........	48

Royal Worcester, Vase, Scenic, Reticulated, Double Well, Ivory Bone, White, Gold Trim, 1899, 3 1/4 In.
$510

Garth's Auctioneers & Appraisers

Roycroft, Humidor, Lid, Cylindrical, Copper, Hammered, Flowers, Monogram, 6 1/2 In.
$504

Fontaine's Auction Gallery

Roycroft, Lamp, Hammered, Copper, Orange, Steuben Shade, Rectangular Base, Early 1900s, 15 In.
$2,640

Cottone Auctions

R

Roycroft, Vase, Copper, Hammered, Cylindrical, Walter Jennings, Marked, c.1918, 7 x 3 In.
$2,560

Morphy Auctions

RS Poland, Box, Lid, Flowers, Molded, Green Tones, Pink Rose, 3 x 4 ¼ In.
$100

Woody Auction

RS Prussia, Cake Plate, Scenic, Swan & Columns, Satin Finish, 2 Handles, Marked, 11 ½ In.
$90

Woody Auction

Crock, Lid, Blue Spongeware, Tan Ground, Tab Handles, 8 ½ x 5 In.	38
Jardiniere, Dogwood, Brown To Green, 13 ¾ x 8 ½ In.	115
Jardiniere, Swirled, Light Green, Marked, 6 ½ x 7 ½ In.	24
Pitcher, Hobnailed, Peach, Ice Lip, Marked, c.1943, 8 ½ x 8 In.	48
Vase, Art Deco, Geometric, Pedestal, Pale Jade Green, Marked, 1930s, 5 x 7 In.	45

RS GERMANY

RS Germany is part of the wording in marks used by the Tillowitz, Germany, factory of Reinhold Schlegelmilch from 1914 until about 1945. The porcelain was sold decorated and undecorated. The Schlegelmilch families made porcelains marked in many ways. See also ES Germany, RS Poland, RS Prussia, RS Silesia, RS Suhl, and RS Tillowitz.

Cup & Saucer, Cream, Green & Brown Tones, Yellow Rose, Marked	18

RS POLAND

RS Poland (German) is a mark used by the Reinhold Schlegelmilch factory at Tillowitz from about 1946 to 1956. After 1956, the factory made porcelain marked *PT Poland*. This is one of many of the RS marks used. See also ES Germany, RS Germany, RS Prussia, RS Silesia, RS Suhl, and RS Tillowitz.

RS Poland
c.1945–1956

PT Tulowice
After 1945–1956

Box, Lid, Flowers, Molded, Green Tones, Pink Rose, 3 x 4 ¼ In.	*illus*	100

RS PRUSSIA

RS Prussia appears in several marks used on porcelain before 1917. Reinhold Schlegelmilch started his porcelain works in Suhl, Germany, in 1869. See also ES Germany, RS Germany, RS Poland, RS Silesia, RS Suhl, and RS Tillowitz.

RS Prussia
Late 1880s–1917

RS Prussia
c.1895–1917

Cake Plate, Scenic, Swan & Columns, Satin Finish, 2 Handles, Marked, 11 ½ In.	*illus*	90
Cup & Saucer, Green & White Tones, Pink Rose, Gold Trim, Footed, Marked, 2 ¼ x 4 ¼ In.		100
Cup, Swan & Gazebo Scene, Gilt Rim, Marked		60
Ferner, Flower Mold, White & Green Satin, Pink Rose, Gold Trim, Scalloped Base, 4 x 8 In.		100
Pitcher, Underplate, Lid, Syrup, Pink & White Satin, Flowers, Gilt Rim, 5 x 5 ¼ In.		200
Plate, Swan, River Scene, Trees, Multicolor, Marked, 6 ¼ In.		50
Teapot, Lid, Flower Shape Finial, Yellow & White Luster Finish, Pink Flowers, 5 ¼ In.		80
Vase, Green, Yellow Tones, Rose, Gold Trim, 2 Handles, Marked, 10 ¼ x 5 ¼ In.		175

RS SILESIA

RS Silesia appears on porcelain made at the Reinhold Schlegelmilch factory in Tillowitz, Germany, from the 1920s to the 1940s. The Schlegelmilch families made porcelains marked in many ways. See also ES Germany, RS Germany, RS Poland, RS Prussia, RS Suhl, and RS Tillowitz.

Dish, Nut, Flowers, Multicolor, Green Ground, Cut Out Handles, Marked, 9 x 5 In.	8

Sugar & Creamer, Roses, Pink, Gilt Handles, Arts & Crafts, c.1920	195
Tray, Daisies, Arts & Crafts, Open Gilt Handles, 16 x 5 In.	225

RS SUHL

RS Suhl is a mark used by the Reinhold Schlegelmilch factory in Suhl, Germany, between 1900 and 1917. The Schlegelmilch families made porcelains in many places. See also ES Germany, RS Germany, RS Poland, RS Prussia, RS Silesia, and RS Tillowitz.

Cup & Saucer, Bathing Beauties Scene, Green Ground, Brocade Gold Border	*illus*	250

RS TILLOWITZ

RS Tillowitz was marked on porcelain by the Reinhold Schlegelmilch factory at Tillowitz from the 1920s to the 1940s. Table services and ornamental pieces were made. See also ES Germany, RS Germany, RS Poland, RS Prussia, RS Silesia, and RS Suhl.

RS Tillowitz 1920s–1940s	RS Tillowitz 1932–1983

Cup & Saucer, White Ground, Pink & Lavender Luster, Flowers, Gold Enamel, Marked, 2¼ x 4 In.	70

RUBINA

Rubina is a glassware that shades from red to clear. It was first made by George Duncan and Sons of Pittsburgh, Pennsylvania, in about 1885. This coloring was used on many types of glassware.

Bowl, Hobnail, Hobbs & Brockunier, 4½ x 4½ In.	60
Celery Vase, Inverted Thumbprint, c.1900, 6 x 3¾ In.	95
Vase, Scalloped Rim, Shell Pattern Spiraling Down Stem, 8 In.	198
Wine Glass, Flowers, Globe Shape, Stem, Base, Moser, c.1880, 8 In., Pair	270

RUBINA VERDE

Rubina Verde is a Victorian glassware that was shaded from red to green. It was first made by Hobbs, Brockunier and Company of Wheeling, West Virginia, about 1890.

Cruet, Polka Dot, Globular, Vaseline Applied Handle, Hobbs, Brockunier & Co., c.1884, 6 In.	*illus*	211
Epergne, Satin Finish, Vaseline Rim, 3 Vases, Late 1800s, 24 x 13 In.		439
Vase, Swirled Neck, Flared Mouth, Raised Designs, c.1900, 5 In.		306

RUBY GLASS

Ruby glass is the dark red color of a ruby, the precious gemstone. It was a popular Victorian color that never went completely out of style. The glass was shaped by many different processes to make many different types of ruby glass. There was a revival of interest in the 1940s when modern-shaped ruby table glassware became fashionable. Sometimes the red color is added to clear glass by a process called flashing or staining. Flashed glass is clear glass dipped in colored glass, then pressed or cut. Stained glass has color painted on a clear glass. Then it is refired so the stain fuses with the glass. Pieces of glass colored in this way are indicated by the word *stained* in the description. Related items may be found in other categories, such as Cranberry Glass, Pressed Glass, and Souvenir.

Cocktail Shaker, American Fire Extinguisher, Chrome Trim, Text, 1930s, 12 In.	*illus*	9375
Pitcher, Red, Bulbous Shape, Clear Handle, 10½ In.		29

RS Suhl, Cup & Saucer, Bathing Beauties Scene, Green Ground, Brocade Gold Border
$250

Woody Auction

Rubina Verde, Cruet, Polka Dot, Globular, Vaseline Applied Handle, Hobbs, Brockunier & Co., c.1884, 6 In.
$211

Jeffrey S. Evans & Associates

Ruby Glass, Cocktail Shaker, American Fire Extinguisher, Chrome Trim, Text, 1930s, 12 In.
$9,375

Sotheby's

R

Rug, Afghan, Red Field, 5 Medallions, 6 Borders, Fringe, Afghanistan, 1900s, 5 Ft. 8 In. x 3 Ft. 5 In. $185

Brunk Auctions

Rug, Ardabil, Latch Hook Medallion, Panel, Geometric Guard Border, 1950s, 10 Ft. 10 In. x 6 Ft. 6 In. $360

Selkirk Auctioneers & Appraisers

Rug, Hereke, Prayer, Silk, Hand Knotted, Bird, Urn, Flowers, Multicolor, 2 Ft. 7 In. x 4 Ft. 6 In. $690

Blackwell Auctions

RUDOLSTADT

Rudolstadt was a faience factory in the Thuringia region of Germany from 1720 to about 1791. In 1854, Ernst Bohne began working in the area. From about 1887 to 1918, the New York and Rudolstadt Pottery made decorated porcelain marked with the RW and crown familiar to collectors. This porcelain was imported by Lewis Straus and Sons of New York, which later became Nathan Straus and Sons. The word *Royal* was included in their import mark. Collectors often call it "Royal Rudolstadt." Most pieces found today were made in the late nineteenth or early twentieth century. Additional pieces may be listed in the Kewpie category.

Group, 5 Girls, Holding Hands Around Well, Ernst Bohne Sohne, 6 5/8 In.	177
Vase, Painted, Flowers, Cream Ground, 2 Gilt Handles, Royal Rudolstadt, 11 In.	51
Vase, Roman Soldier, Chariot Scene, Cream Tones, Figural Handle, 11 1/2 x 8 In.	150

RUG

Rugs have been used in the American home since the seventeenth century. The oriental rug of that time was often used on a table, not on the floor. Rag rugs, hooked rugs, and braided rugs were made by housewives from scraps of material. American Indian rugs are listed in the Indian category.

Afghan, Red Field, 5 Medallions, 6 Borders, Fringe, Afghanistan, 1900s, 5 Ft. 8 In. x 3 Ft. 5 In. ..*illus*	185
Afghan, Red Field, Octagonal Medallions, 3 Rows, Diamond Border, Early 1900s, 9 Ft. 6 In. x 6 Ft.	832
Agra, India, Center Medallion, Animal, Multicolor, Red Field, 13 Ft. x 9 Ft. 6 In.	2880
Ardabil, Latch Hook Medallion, Panel, Geometric Guard Border, 1950s, 10 Ft. 10 In. x 6 Ft. 6 In. .*illus*	360
Art Deco, Wool, Flowers, Panels, Dragon, Clouds, Mountain, Chinese, 1920s, 4 Ft. 10 In. x 2 Ft. 6 In.	1275
Arts & Crafts, Rust Red Field, Repeating Motifs, Midnight Blue, Guard Border, 9 Ft. 2 In. x 11 Ft. 9 In.	413
Aubusson, Cream, Central Medallion, Pink, Olive, Gold, Green, Floral, 11 Ft. 2 In. x 26 Ft. 8 In.	2688
Aubusson, Dark Blue Center, Filigree, Wreath, Garland, Flowers, Border, 9 Ft. 10 In. x 7 Ft. 10 In.	189
Aubusson, Rectangular, Flowers, Multicolor, Louis Philippe, 16 Ft. x 10 Ft. 8 In.	438
Bagface, Silk, Shahsevan Kilim, Sumac, Red Field, Iran, c.1900, 1 Ft. 5 In x 1 Ft. 5 In.	100
Bakhtiari, Lozenge Shape Medallions, Blues, Rust Red, Blossoms, 7 Ft. 7 In. x 9 Ft.	240
Bakhtiari, Persian, Hand Knotted, 9 Panels, Wide Borders, Red & Blue, 6 Ft. 4 In. x 10 Ft. 2 In.	345
Bidjar, Herati Pattern, Navy Blue Field, Pink Border, Turtle Designs, c.1915, 3 Ft. 9 In. x 5 Ft. 6 In.	938
Bokhara, Red Field, 7 Rows Repeating Gul Motifs, 8 Ft. 3 In. x 11 Ft. 3 In.	443
Caucasian, Ivory, Red, Brown Field, Medallion, Blossoms, Branches, 1800s, 3 Ft. 6 In. x 4 Ft. 6 In.	813
Caucasian, Karabagh, Diamond Medallion, Tree Of Life, Early 1900s, 4 Ft. 10 In. x 3 Ft. 4 In.	1968
Chinese, Cloud & Bat, Red Ground, Blue Cloud, 4 Ft. 2 In. x 2 Ft. 1 In.	531
Daghestan, Red Ground, Blue Border, Dense Geometric Motif, Fringe, Wool, 5 Ft. 4 In. x 3 Ft. 2 In.	144
Dhurrie, Multicolor, Geometric Medallions, Celadon Green Field, Tan Border, 9 Ft. 3 In. x 11 Ft. 8 In.	344
Hamadan, Herati, Blue, Gold, Beige, Midnight Blue Field, Turtle Border, 15 Ft. x 5 Ft. 7 In.	1287
Hamadan, Herati, Floral, 3 Geometric Medallions, Red Ground, Blue Border, 9 Ft. 6 In.	375
Hamadan, Red & Blue Geometric Motifs, Repeating, 3 Minor Borders, Runner, 3 Ft. 4 In. x 16 Ft.	1298
Hamadan, Red Field, Dark Blue Medallion & Spandrels, Geometric Border, 4 Ft. 2 In. x 6 Ft. 8 In.	413
Herati, Blue Field, Floral, Diamond, Yellow & Red Borders, Kurdistan, Runner, 16 Ft. x 3 Ft. 7 In.	768
Hereke, Prayer, Silk, Hand Knotted, Bird, Urn, Flowers, Multicolor, 2 Ft. 7 In. x 4 Ft. 6 In. *illus*	690
Heriz, Gabled Central Medallion, Vines, Flowers, Leaves, Navy Blue Borders, 7 Ft. 10 In. x 10 Ft. 5 In.	1250
Heriz, Midnight Blue Rosette Medallion, Anchor Pendants, Leaf Border, 12 Ft. 8 In. x 8 Ft. 9 In.	2100
Heriz, Navy Blue, Gold Gabled Square Medallion, Navy Vine, Palmette Border, 7 Ft. 10 In. x 9 Ft. 9 In.	152
Heriz, Persian, Central Medallion, Geometric, Floral Pattern, c.1950, 12 Ft. 1 In. x 8 Ft. 10 In.	2011
Heriz, Serapi, Persian, Hand Knotted, Geometric, Blue, Red & Pink, Runner, 3 Ft. 10 In. x 9 Ft. 7 In.	20
Hooked, Album Quilt, 6 Square Panels, Flowers, Fruit, Birds, Black & Red Border, 1800s, 107 x 72 In.	68
Hooked, American Flag, Betsy Ross Style, 13 5-Pointed Stars, Late 1800s, 27 1/2 x 37 1/2 In.	64
Hooked, Birds In Tree, Green Ground, Multicolor Linear Border, 1895, 33 3/4 x 47 1/2 In.	937
Hooked, Boy Playing, Dog, Red Shirt, Blue Pants, Black Ground, 1950s, 32 x 29 In.	12
Hooked, Checkered Urns Of Flowers, Scrolls, Brown Border, Frame, c.1900, 36 x 71 In.	18
Hooked, Cow Pull Toy, Red Border, Mounted, Black Cotton Frame, 1900s, 16 x 27 1/2 In.	13
Hooked, Flowers, Bats, Sun, Black, Green, Yellow, Red, Round, Early 1900s, 56 In.	20
Hooked, Folk Art, Flower Vine, Diamond, Wool, On Linen Backed Stretcher, c.1870, 29 x 35 In.	30

Rug, Hooked, King Of Hearts, Rectangular, Multicolor, 1900s, 40 x 27 In.
$125

Bruneau & Co. Auctioneers

Rug, Hooked, Traditional Design, Squares, Black Border, Chevrons, Signed, CM, 39 x 60 In.
$163

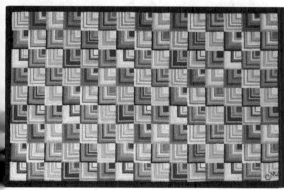

Eldred's

Rug, Indo-Persian, Pink-Red Field, Navy Blue, Floral Medallion, Guard Border, 4 Ft. 4 In. x 6 Ft.
$384

land Little Auctions

Rug, Isfahan, Navy Blue Field, Scrolls, Star Medallion, Apricot Guard Border, 4 Ft. 11 In. x 7 Ft. 10 In.
$2,596

Leland Little Auctions

Rug, Leopard Skin, On Black Felt, 6 Ft. 3 In. x 4 Ft. 1 In.
$944

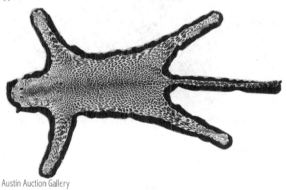

Austin Auction Gallery

TIP
Always keep a rug on a pad. It will wear out sooner on a bare floor.

Rug, Machine Woven, Blue Field, Golden Star Design, Brown Border, 12 Ft. 9 In. x 12 Ft. 10 In.
$649

Leland Little Auctions

R

RUG

Rug, Persian, Herati, Blue, Red, Faded Yellow Fields, Multiple Narrow Borders, 5 Ft. 10 In. x 7 Ft. 9 In.
$469

Eldred's

Rug, Sarouk, Farahan, Central Field, Flowers, Multicolor, 15 Ft. 8 In. x 12 Ft. 6 In.
$6,250

Neal Auction Company

Rug, Shirvan, 3 Diamond Medallions, Light Blue Ground, Camels, c.1900, 5 Ft. 4 In. x 3 Ft. 8 In.
$2,214

Brunk Auctions

Rug, Tabriz, Wool Carpet, Oriental, Scalloped Medallion, Blue, Flowers, 1900s, 12 Ft. 2 In. x 13 Ft.
$469

Bruneau & Co. Auctioneers

R

Hooked, Folk Art, Multidirectional, Flowers & Leaves, Sawtooth Border, Late 1800s, 44 x 35 In...	369
Hooked, King Of Hearts, Rectangular, Multicolor, 1900s, 40 x 27 In. .... *illus*	125
Hooked, Multicolor, Flowers, Baskets, Bird, Mounted, 25 ½ x 39 ½ In.	71
Hooked, Oval, Red Heart Hand Inside, Multicolor Ground, c.1920, 45 x 22 In...............	400
Hooked, Pictorial, Child, Feeding, Gray Horse, Apple Tree, Red Border, 37 x 48 In..........	625
Hooked, Sailboat, Flying American Flag, Wood Frame, Early 1900s, 32 x 45 In..............	250
Hooked, Traditional Design, Squares, Black Border, Chevrons, Signed, CM, 39 x 60 In. *illus*	163
Indo-Heriz, Navy Blue Field, 4 Medallions, Flowers, Leaves, Red Guard Border, 12 Ft. x 16 Ft. 4 In.	2596
Indo-Persian, Cream Field, Leaves, Flowers, Horizontal, Gold Medallion, 9 x 12 Ft.	384
Indo-Persian, Pictorial, Knotted Field, Hunting Vignettes, Navy Blue Border, 5 Ft. x 7 Ft. 4 In....	1770
Indo-Persian, Pink-Red Field, Navy Blue, Floral Medallion, Guard Border, 4 Ft. 4 In. x 6 Ft. *illus*	334
Indo-Persian, Red Field, Vines, Leaves & Palmette Motif, Dark Blue Border, 9 Ft. 11 In. x 8 Ft.	472
Indo-Persian, Round, Maroon Field, Scroll & Flowers, Fringe, 7 Ft. 1 In........................	502
Isfahan, Flowering Vines, Palmettes, Camel, Rose, White, Ivory, Blue Field, 5 Ft. 6 In. x 3 Ft. 6 In.	878
Isfahan, Navy Blue Field, Scrolls, Star Medallion, Apricot Guard Border, 4 Ft. 11 In. x 7 Ft. 10 In. *illus*	2596
Karabagh, Multicolor Cane Field, Indigo Medallions, Flower Border, Runner, 12 Ft. 3 In. x 4 Ft. 2 In.	3276
Karastan, Kirman, Flowering Vines, Palmettes, Ivory Field, Floral Border, 18 x 9 Ft.	1112
Kashan, Figural, Animal Design, Taupe Ground, Navy Border, Silk, 6 Ft. 6 In. x 4 Ft. 1 In....	840
Kashan, Midnight Blue, Beige Rosette Medallions, Vine, Palmette Border, 7 Ft. 6 In. x 4 Ft. 7 In.	5850
Kashan, Persian, Hand Knotted, Tassel, Flowers, Blue, Ivory, Green Border, 7 Ft. 9 In. x 10 Ft. 2 In..	316
Kashkuli, Multicolor Bands, Fringe, Signed, Runner, 2 Ft. 6 In. x 8 Ft.	1098
Kashmir, Embroidery, Multicolor, Arched Borders, Paisley Shawl, Wool, 1800s, 6 Ft. 9 In. x 6 Ft. 3 In.	344
Kazak, 3 Medallions, Red Ground, Salmon Pink, Olive Green, Blue Border, 6 Ft. 8 In. x 9 Ft.	1750
Kazak, Red Field, Quadrupeds, Ivory Geometric Border, Hooked Device, c.1900, 6 Ft. 1 In. x 4 Ft.	2772
Kilim, Red Field, 5 Medallions, Black Border, Fringe Ends, 5 Ft. 1 In. x 7 Ft.	295
Leopard Skin, On Black Felt, 6 Ft. 3 In. x 4 Ft. 1 In......................... *illus*	944
Lilihan, Dark Blue, Pale Pink, Green, Gabled Medallion, Flowers, Red Field, 6 Ft. 8 In. x 9 Ft. 4 In.	1000
Lilihan, Red Field, Flower Spray, Leaves Motif, Dark Blue Border, 7 Ft. 6 In. x 10 Ft. 2 In.	561
Machine Woven, Blue Field, Golden Star Design, Brown Border, 12 Ft. 9 In. x 12 Ft. 10 In. *illus*	649
Mahal, Cream Lobed Medallion, Crimson Field, Blue Spandrels, Red Border, 12 Ft. 2 In. x 8 Ft. 10 In.	4410
Mahal, Medallion, Red Field, Birds & Rabbits, Abrash Border, 1900s, 13 Ft. 1 In. x 9 Ft. 9 In.	875
Mashad, Persian, Hand Knotted, Flower Medallion, Red Ground, 12 Ft. 11 In. x 9 Ft. 7 In.....	708
Meshed, White Ground, Floral Tendril, Wide Main Border, 12 Ft. 1 In. x 9 Ft. 9 In..........	554
Mexican, Woven, Blue, Cream, Black, Diamond Center, 1930s, 6 Ft. x 4 Ft. 3 In...............	384
Needlepoint, Flower Medallion, Leaves Wreath, Red Field, Cream Border, 9 Ft. 6 In. x 17 Ft. 6 In.	177
Oriental, Hand Woven, Blue Ground, Stylized Flower Center, Red Border, 5 Ft. 6 In. x 3 Ft. 6 In..	173
Oushak, Pale Yellow Ground, Flowers, Pink, Olive & Blue, 14 Ft. 3 In. x 20 In...............	1536
Oushak, Red Field, Geometric, Blue, Green, Orange, Border, Early 1900s, 13 Ft. 1 In. x 11 Ft. 9 In.	1792
Persian, Central Medallion, Flowers, Red Ground, Fringe, Handmade, 6 Ft. 5 In. x 4 Ft. 3 In..	259
Persian, Herati, Blue, Red, Faded Yellow Fields, Multiple Narrow Borders, 5 Ft. 10 In. x 7 Ft. 9 In. *illus*	469
Persian, Kirman, Flowers, Multicolor, c.1960, 19 Ft. 7 In. x 10 Ft. 10 In.	875
Persian, Yilong, Hand Knotted, Cream Ground, Red, Light Blue, Short Tassel, 6 Ft. 1 In. x 8 Ft. 10 In.	115
Prayer, Silk, Hereke Style, Gold & Silver Thread, Calligraphy, Chinese, 4 Ft. 10 In. x 3 Ft. 3 In.	1534
Samarkand, Persian, Hand Knotted, Red, Yellow, Green, Burgundy, Pink, Tassels, 9 Ft. x 4 Ft. 5 In..	403
Sarouk, Farahan, Central Field, Flowers, Multicolor, 15 Ft. 8 In. x 12 Ft. 6 In. .... *illus*	6250
Sarouk, Pictorial, Blue Ground, Birds, Flowering Plants, Iran, c.1930, 7 Ft. x 4 Ft. 3 In........	1188
Senneh, Dark Blue Field, Flower Medallion, Red Spandrels, 3 Ft. 6 In. x 4 Ft. 10 In..............	384
Serapi, Hand Knotted, Oval, Maroon Ground, Flowers, Leaves, White Fringe, 4 Ft. x 4 Ft. 1 In........	177
Serapi, Peshawar, Multicolor, Brick, Medallion, 9 Ft. x 11 Ft. 9 In.	1375
Shirvan, 3 Diamond Medallions, Light Blue Ground, Camels, c.1900, 5 Ft. 4 In. x 3 Ft. 8 In. *illus*	2214
Sultanabad, Green Gray Field, Multicolor, Flowers, Palmettes, Gray Border, 1900s, 8 Ft. x 10 Ft. 4 In.	688
Sultanabad, Square, Flowers, Brown, Black, White, Agra, 11 Ft. 8 In. x 14 Ft. 9 In..........	2125
Tabriz, Persian, Oriental, Ivory Ground, Leaping Deer, Bird, Floral Borders, 1900s, 6 Ft. 5 In. x 5 Ft..	250
Tabriz, Persian, Silk, Hand Knotted, Medallion, Florets Border, Tassels, 3 Ft. 1 In. x 5 Ft. 5 In.....	345
Tabriz, Wool Carpet, Oriental, Scalloped Medallion, Blue, Flowers, 1900s, 12 Ft. 2 In. x 13 Ft. *illus*	469
Tibetan, Thangka, Central White Tara, Lotus Flower, Leafy Ground, 4 Ft. 11 In. x 3 Ft. 6 In. ...	156
Tibetan, Yellow Flowers, Ocher Ground, Light Green Border, 19 Ft. x 11 Ft. 11 In..................	370
Tribal, Caucasian, Oriental, Red, Blue, Geometric, Ivory Border, c.1910, 7 Ft. 4 In. x 5 Ft. 7 In.	219
Tribal, Hand Knotted Hertz, Low Pile, Geometric, Earth Tones, Tassel, 6 Ft. 6 In. x 3 Ft. 7 In..	288

Rug, Turkoman, Hand Knotted, Geometric Medallion, Red Field, Cream Fringe, 8 Ft. 5 In. x 6 Ft. 7 In.
$413

Austin Auction Gallery

Braided Rugs

The braided rug was first popular from the 1820s to the 1850s. It was made from braided strips of worn fabric that were sewn together, round and round, until a circular rug was made. This type of rug was back in style in the 1890s Colonial Revival rooms and is still popular today.

Russel Wright, Aluminum, Serving Set, Fork, Spoon, Wood Handle, 13 In.
$407

Palm Beach Modern Auctions

Russel Wright, Aluminum, Vase, Ball Shape, Spun, Raymor, 9 ¼ In.
$750

Palm Beach Modern Auctions

Russel Wright, Bowl, Amorphic, Speckled White, Dark Blue Interior, Stoneware, Bauer, 1945, 6 x 4 In. $100

Main Auction Galleries, Inc.

Russel Wright, Iroquois Casual, Carafe, Sugar, White Ground, Glazed, Stoneware, c.1955, 9¾ In. $1,000

Wright

Sabino, Figurine, Scottie, Opalescent, Rectangular Base, Signed, Mid 1900s, 3 In. $118

Leland Little Auctions

TIP
Be sure you have photographs and descriptions of your collections in case of a robbery. Keep them in a safe place away from your house.

Turkish, Orange, Gray Medallion, Red Field, Blue Spandrels, Gold Border, 3 Ft. 4 In. x 7 Ft. 3 In.		502
Turkish, Oriental, Flower Medallions, Red, Green, Gold, Ocher, Tan, Runner, 15 Ft. 7 In. x 2 Ft. 10 In.		375
Turkish, Prayer, Silk, Open Field, Flowers, Ivory & Celadon Border, Early 1900s, 4 Ft. 2 In. x 8 Ft. 8 In.		420
Turkoman, Hand Knotted, Geometric Medallion, Red Field, Cream Fringe, 8 Ft. 5 In. x 6 Ft. 7 In. *illus*		413
Zebra Hide, Black & White, Natural Shape, 6 Ft. 1 In. x 8 Ft. 10 In.		750
Zebra Hide, Natural Shape, Mounted On Felt, 1900s, 10 Ft. 5 In. x 6 Ft. 8 In.		850

RUSKIN

Ruskin is a British art pottery of the twentieth century. The Ruskin Pottery was started by William Howson Taylor, and his name was used as the mark until about 1899. The factory, at West Smethwick, Birmingham, England, stopped making new pieces in 1933 but continued to glaze and sell the remaining wares until 1935. The art pottery is noted for its exceptional glazes. They also made ceramic "stones" with the famous glaze to be used in jewelry.

Candlestick, Orange Luster, Impressed Mark, 1921, Pair		130
Vase, Mottled Yellow, Cylindrical, Flared Lip, 9 In.		110

RUSSEL WRIGHT

Russel Wright designed dinnerware in modern shapes for many companies. Iroquois China Company, Harker China Company, Sterling China Co., Steubenville Pottery, and Justin Tharaud and Sons made dishes marked *Russel Wright*. The Steubenville wares, first made in 1938, are the most common today. Wright was a designer of domestic and industrial wares, including furniture, aluminum, radios, interiors, and glassware. A new company, Bauer Pottery Company of Los Angeles, is making Russel Wright's American Modern dishes using molds made from original pieces. Pieces are marked *Russel Wright by Bauer Pottery California USA*. Russel Wright dinnerware and other original pieces by Wright are listed here. For more prices, go to kovels.com.

STERLING CHINA by *Russel Wright*	JUSTIN THARALD & SON *Russel Wright* MADE IN U.S.A.	*Russel Wright* FLAIR *by Paden* BOSTON 27
Russel Wright 1948–1950	Russel Wright 1948–1953	Russel Wright 1959–1960

Aluminum, Serving Set, Fork, Spoon, Wood Handle, 13 In. *illus*		407
Aluminum, Vase, Ball Shape, Spun, Raymor, 9¼ In. *illus*		750
American Modern, Celery Tray, Cedar Green, Rolled Edge, 12 x 3 In.		65
American Modern, Chop Plate, Gray, 13 x 13 In.		55
Bowl, Amorphic, Speckled White, Dark Blue Interior, Stoneware, Bauer, 1945, 6 x 4 In. *illus*		100
Casual Brown, Cup & Saucer		8
Casual Yellow, Salt & Pepper, Stacking		16
Iroquois Casual, Carafe, Sugar, White Ground, Glazed, Stoneware, c.1955, 9¾ In. *illus*		1000
Iroquois Casual, Cup & Saucer, Brown		24
Mid-Century, Coral Pink, Platter, Rounded Upturned Edges, 12 x 12 In.		25

SABINO

Sabino France

Sabino glass was made in the 1920s and 1930s in Paris, France. Founded by Marius-Ernest Sabino (1878–1961), the firm was noted for Art Deco lamps, vases, figurines, and animals in clear, colored, and opalescent glass. Production stopped during World War II but resumed in the 1960s with the manufacture of nude figurines and small opalescent glass animals. Pieces made in recent years are a slightly different color and can be recognized. Only vintage pieces are listed here.

Figurine, Scottie, Opalescent, Rectangular Base, Signed, Mid 1900s, 3 In. *illus*		118

R

Vase, Beehive, Blue Opalescent, Round, Honeycomb Ground, Raised Bees, Signed, 7 x 7 In.... 225

SALESMAN'S SAMPLE *may be listed in the Advertising or Stove category. Some are considered toys and are listed in the Toy category.*

SALT AND PEPPER SHAKERS

Salt and pepper shakers in matched sets were first used in the nineteenth century. Collectors are primarily interested in figural examples made after World War I. Huggers are pairs of shakers that appear to embrace each other. Many salt and pepper shakers are listed in other categories and can be located through the index at the back of this book.

Carrots, Orange, Green, Ceramic, Stamped Haoan, 6 In.		38
Daisies, Blue Coin Spot, Wilcox Silver Plate Frame, Victorian, 4¾ x 4¼ In. *illus*		200
Flowers, Butterfly, Yellow Trim, Tin, USA, 1950s, 3¾ In.		12
Skunks, Porcelain, Black, White Eyes, 2 x 2 In.		16
Turkey, Shannon Crystal, Czech Republic, 4 x 3½ x 2 In.		20
Vase Shape, Majolica, Coral, Pink Ground, Green Seaweed, Brown Shells, Etruscan, 4¼ In.		236

SAMPLER

ABCDE

Samplers were made in America from the early 1700s. The best examples were made from 1790 to 1840 on homemade fabrics. Long, narrow samplers are usually older than square ones. Early samplers just had stitching or alphabets. The later examples had numerals, borders, and pictorial decorations. Those with mottoes are mid-Victorian. A revival of interest in the 1930s produced simpler samplers, using machine-made textiles, usually with mottoes.

Adam & Eve, Alphabet, Hester Ann Brunner, 1835, Silk On Linen, Frame, 16 x 16 In.	1830
Adam & Eve, Verse, Animals, Floral Border, Elizabeth Turner, 1781, Frame, 23 x 16 In.	938
Alphabet, Birds, Dog, Angel, Red, Blue, Wool, Silk On Linen, Frame, 1800s, 18 x 26 In.	72
Alphabet, Birds, Victorine Bonnegent, Parish School Of Sewing, France, 1808, 12 x 13 In.	1065
Alphabet, Different Scripts, Verse, Strawberry Border, Mary Parker, Frame, 19½ x 19½ In.	1750
Alphabet, Elizabeth Lowden Langley, Silk, Giltwood Frame, Early 1800s, 16 x 11 In.	475
Alphabet, Floral Panels, Stylized Vine Border, Mary Parker, 1795, Silk On Gauze, 18 x 12 In.	1830
Alphabet, Flowers, 6-Point Star, 1844 & 1849, Black Wood Frame, 10 x 11¼ x 9¼ In.	293
Alphabet, Flowers, Margaret Bitter, Wood Frame, 1800s, 18 x 18 In.	188
Alphabet, Flowers, Susan P. Morehouse, Aged 13 Years, 1836, Frame, 16 x 17 In.	472
Alphabet, Flowers, Urns, Architectural, Martha Bradley, 1831, Cotton, Linen, Frame, 18 x 24 In. *illus*	277
Alphabet, Flowers, Verse, Go Forward, Rachel C. Pittenger, 1845, N.J., 18 In.	750
Alphabet, House, Family Initials, Cross In Center, 1876, Wool, 26 x 20½ In.	677
Alphabet, House, Floral, Margaret Gorman, Adams County, Age 15, 1867, Cotton, Linen, 10 x 8 In.	270
Alphabet, Numbers, Hearts, Flowers, Elizabeth R. French, Frame, 1800s, 19 x 20 In. *illus*	1063
Alphabet, Numbers, House, Martha Kirby, Sophia Melhuish, Aged 11, 1842, Linen, 16 x 13 In.	475
Alphabet, Numbers, Mary Robinson, 1788, Wool, Open Weave Ground, Maple Frame, 12 x 14 In.	266
Alphabet, Numbers, Verse, Horizontal Bands, Vine Border, Frame, Elizabeth Smith, 1834, 15 x 23 In.	644
Alphabet, Numbers, Vine Border, Elizabeth Daniels, Frame, c.1820, 13 x 17 In. *illus*	527
Alphabet, Upper & Lower Case, Jane Hamilton's, Wood Frame, 1840, 10 x 9 In.	147
Alphabet, Upper & Lowercase, Flowers, Geometric Border, Mary Black, Frame, 7 x 5 In.	5605
Alphabet, Vermont, Jane Wallace, Silk On Linen, Wood Frame, 1799, 16¾ x 10¼ In.	238
Alphabet, Verse, Flowers, Embroidered, Frame, c.1850, 21 In.	104
Alphabet, Verse, Peacocks, Jessie Sellar, 1848, Frame, 13¾ x 14¼ In.	202
Alphabet, Vine Border, Mariah Humphrey, Bird's-Eye Maple Frame, 1831, 11 x 12 In.	475
Basket Of Flowers, Silk On Linen, Gilt Molded Frame, c.1770, 16⅜ In.	688
Bible Verse, Floral Border, Jennet Low, 1809, On Linen, Wood Frame, 18 x 12 In.	207
Bird & Flowers, Trailing Vine Border, Elizabeth Gotwals, 1821, Silk On Linen, Frame, 10 x 8 In.	732
Family Record, Needlework, Flower Border, Harriet A. Ridgway, Frame, c.1827, 20 x 25 In. *illus*	468
Figures, Lion, Bird, Ostrich, Plants, Embroidery On Paper, Frame, c.1881, 19½ In.	52
Flowers, Geometric, Openwork, Silk On Linen Ground, Late 1600s, Frame, 14⅜ x 9⅞ In.	625

Salt & Pepper, Daisies, Blue Coin Spot, Wilcox Silver Plate Frame, Victorian, 4¾ x 4¼ In.
$200

Woody Auction

Sampler, Alphabet, Flowers, Urns, Architectural, Martha Bradley, 1831, Cotton, Linen, Frame, 18 x 24 In.
$277

Alderfer Auction Company

Sampler, Alphabet, Numbers, Hearts, Flowers, Elizabeth R. French, Frame, 1800s, 19 x 20 In.
$1,063

Eldred's

Sampler, Alphabet, Numbers, Vine Border, Elizabeth Daniels, Frame, c.1820, 13 x 17 In.
$527

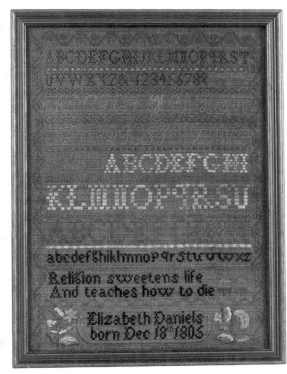

Jeffrey S. Evans & Associates

Sampler, Family Record, Needlework, Flower Border, Harriet A. Ridgway, Frame, c.1827, 20 x 25 In.
$468

Jeffrey S. Evans & Associates

Sampler, House, Sarah Ann Pinkerton, 1827, Silk On Linen, Wood Frame, 15 x 16 ½ In.
$413

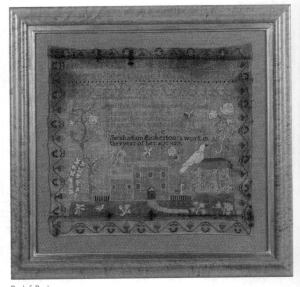

Pook & Pook

Sampler, Verse, Life Is Short & Miserable, Catherine Clopper, 1768, Wood Frame, 16 x 13 In.
$500

Eldred's

House, Sarah Ann Pinkerton, 1827, Silk On Linen, Wood Frame, 15 x 16½ In. .... *illus*	413
House, Urn, Flowers, Verse, Initials, Matilda Willits, 16th Year 1822, Silk On Linen, 15 In.	1375
Insects, Flowers, Baskets, Birds, Animals, Ann Bownals, 1818, Frame, 23 x 20 In.	375
Verse, Bold Crewelwork, Vase, Flowers, Ann Sink, 1814, Silk On Linen, Frame, 17½ x 17½ In.....	3416
Verse, Figures, Trees, Birds, What Conscience Dictates, R.I. School, 1800s, Frame, 19 x 15 In..	6875
Verse, Floral Border, Sabina Richardson, Aged 9 Years, 1845, Gilt Frame, 13 x 17 In....	118
Verse, Floral, Animals, Strawberry Border, Clarissa Jewitt II, 1838, Cotton, Wool, Frame, 25 x 21 In.	570
Verse, Flowers, Birds, Elizabeth Jane Pettit, 1827, Frame, 20 x 19 In.	527
Verse, Life Is Short & Miserable, Catherine Clopper, 1768, Wood Frame, 16 x 13 In. ...... *illus*	500
Verse, Swiftness Of Time, Flower Basket, Birds, Emma Leader, Aged 10, England, 1849, 18 x 13 In.	256

SAMSON

Samson and Company, a French firm specializing in the reproduction of collectible wares of many countries and periods, was founded in Paris in the early nineteenth century. Chelsea, Meissen, Famille Verte, and Chinese Export porcelain are some of the wares that have been reproduced by the company. The firm used fake marks similar to the real ones on the reproductions. It closed in 1969.

Pitcher, Chinese Export Style, Flowers, Pink, Purple, Orange, Raised Slip Decoration, 6 In..	110
Planter, Heart Shape, Blue Heart, Roses, Gold Leaves, Reticulated Edge, c.1959, 4¾ In.	42
Toothpick Holder, Armorial, Mask Handles, Footed, Gilt, 3 x 2 In.	29

SANDWICH GLASS

Sandwich glass is any of the myriad types of glass made by the Boston & Sandwich Glass Company of Sandwich, Massachusetts, between 1825 and 1888. It is often very difficult to be sure whether a piece was really made at the Sandwich factory because so many types were made there and similar pieces were made at other glass factories. Additional pieces may be listed under Pressed Glass and in other related categories.

Candlestick, Dark Cobalt Blue, Hexagonal, Stepped Base, c.1850, 9 In., Pair	344
Cologne Bottle, 9-Sided, Blown, Molded Horn, Flat Lip, Plain Base, 1850s, 6½ x 1¾ In.....	263
Compote, 3 Dolphins, 26 Petal Rim, Canary, Domed Circular Foot, 1850, 9 x 11 x 5 In. ....*illus*	2691
Goblet, Morning Glory, Lead, Soda Lime, Clear, Round Foot, 1860s, 6 x 3¼ x 3 In...............	211
Goblet, Vine, Stem, 2 Knops, Panel Top Foot, Table Ring, 1860s, 6⅜ x 3⅜ x 3 In.	152
Lamp, Whale Oil, Pewter Collars, Etched, Free-Blown, Pressed Base, 10½ In., Pair	313
Spoon Holder, Diamond Thumbprint, Petal Shape Rim, Canary, Circular Foot, 1850, 5¾ In. ... *illus*	1404
Tumbler, Worcester, Amber, Goblet Shape, Raised Circular Foot, 1845, 3 x 3 x 2 In. ...... *illus*	556

SARREGUEMINES

Sarreguemines is the name of a French town that is used as part of a china mark for Utzschneider and Company, a porcelain factory that made ceramics in Sarreguemines, Lorraine, France, from about 1775. Transfer-printed wares and majolica were made in the nineteenth century. The nineteenth-century pieces, most often found today, usually have colorful transfer-printed decorations showing peasants in local costumes.

Humidor, Monkey, Seated, Organ, Majolica, 9½ x 9 In.	185
Jug, Face, Woman, Wearing Crown, No. 3331, 8 In..	118
Server, Scallop Shell Shape, Coral Body, White & Yellow Edge, Black Handle, Brass Frame, 8 x 14 In..	130

SASCHA BRASTOFF

Sascha Brastoff made decorative accessories, ceramics, enamels on copper, and plastics of his own design. He headed a factory, Sascha Brastoff of California, Inc., in West Los Angeles, from 1953 until about 1973. He died in 1993. Pieces signed with the signature *Sascha Brastoff* were his work and are the most

Sandwich Glass, Compote, 3 Dolphins, 26 Petal Rim, Canary, Domed Circular Foot, 1850, 9 x 11 x 5 In.
$2,691

Jeffrey S. Evans & Associates

Sandwich Glass, Spoon Holder, Diamond Thumbprint, Petal Shape Rim, Canary, Circular Foot, 1850, 5¾ In.
$1,404

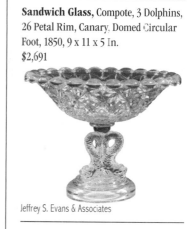

Jeffrey S. Evans & Associates

Sandwich Glass, Tumbler, Worcester, Amber, Goblet Shape, Raised Circular Foot, 1845, 3 x 3 x 2 In.
$556

Jeffrey S. Evans & Associates

This is an edited listing of current prices. Visit Kovels.com to check thousands of prices from previous years and sign up for free information on trends, tips, reproductions, marks, and more.

S

Satin Glass, Dish, Bird & Berry, Silver Plate Holder, Handle, Footed, Victorian, 5 ½ In.

$81

Richard D. Hatch & Associates

Satin Glass, Vase, Rainbow, Herringbone Design, Ruffled Top, 3 ¾ In.

$92

Richard D. Hatch & Associates

Satsuma, Bowl, Ribbed Body, Cobalt Blue Glaze, Painted Panels, Women, Hododa, 1800s, 10 ¾ In.

$1,380

Blackwell Auctions

expensive. Other pieces marked *Sascha B.* or with a stamped mark were made by others in his company.

Ashtray, Chi Bird, Tan, Brown, Yellow, c.1953, 8 x 6 In.	36
Ashtray, Red, Yellow, Cutout Cigarette Rests, Signed, 4 ½ In.	165
Dish, Lid, Cherries, Pear, Gold Swirls, Brown Ground, c.1947, 9 In.	48
Plate, Free-Form, Village, Houses, Gold Accents, 1950s, 10 x 9 In.	70
Tray, Genie, Trees, Tan, Mauve, Speckled Ground, c.1955, 17 x 9 In.	285

SATIN GLASS

Satin glass is a late-nineteenth-century art glass. It has a dull finish that is caused by hydrofluoric acid vapor treatment. Satin glass was made in many colors and sometimes has applied decorations. Satin glass is also listed by factory name, such as Webb, or in the Mother-of-Pearl category in this book.

Carafe, Beaded Drape, Green, Metal Collar, Fluted Rim, 7 ½ In.	30
Dish, Bird & Berry, Silver Plate Holder, Handle, Footed, Victorian, 5 ½ In. .... *illus*	81
Vase, Rainbow, Herringbone Design, Ruffled Top, 3 ¾ In. .... *illus*	92

SATSUMA

Satsuma is a Japanese pottery with a distinctive creamy beige crackled glaze. Most of the pieces were decorated with blue, red, green, orange, or gold. Almost all Satsuma found today was made after 1860, especially during the Meiji Period, 1868–1912. During World War I, Americans could not buy undecorated European porcelains. Women who liked to make hand-painted porcelains at home began to decorate white undecorated Satsuma. These pieces are known today as "American Satsuma."

Bowl, Crackled, Cream Ground, Multicolor, Figures, Wood Stand, Kinkozan, Late 1900s, 5 In.	413
Bowl, Dignitaries, Court Women, Landscape, Fish, Kinkozan, Signed, Late 1800s, 2 ⅝ In.	2520
Bowl, Elephant Design, Koi Fish, Porcelain, Marked, 15 ½ In.	47
Bowl, Painted, Enamel, Figure, Leaves, Birds, Japan, 4 ½ x 10 In., Pair	59
Bowl, Ribbed Body, Cobalt Blue Glaze, Painted Panels, Women, Hododa, 1800s, 10 ¾ In. ...*illus*	1380
Censer, Lid, Foo Dog Finial, 2 Dolphin Handles, Gilt, Footed, Japan, 20 In. .... *illus*	177
Charger, Immortal, 2 Yew Boughs, Landscape, Brocade Border, Late 1900s, 13 ⅝ In. .. *illus*	625
Charger, Painted, 36 Immortal Poets, Multicolor, Enamel, Gilt Ground, Porcelain, 1900s, 15 In.	295
Charger, Scalloped Rim, 20 Figures, Dragon, Hand Calligraphy, c.1850, 9 ¼ In.	94
Jardiniere, Gilt, Blue, Green & Red Intricate Design, Cream Ground, Signed, 8 ½ In.	469
Lamp, 2-Light, Bottle Shape, Painted, Moriage, Cream Ground, 1800s, 32 In.	59
Lamp, Electric, Flowers, Painted, Circular Base, 38 In., Pair	125
Urn, Lid, Foo Dog Finial, Scenic, Applied Handle, Tripod Feet, 14 In.	138
Vase, Band Of Scholar & Boy, Gilt Dot, Painted, Signed, 4 ¼ In.	1098
Vase, Bulbous, Group Of Women, Fan Shape Handle, Gold Trim, Late 1800s, 3 ⅝ In.	431
Vase, Dragon, Flying, Beast Handles, Art Deco, c.1920, 11 ½ In., Pair	219
Vase, Family Panels, Children, Multicolor, Bulbous, Painted, 19 x 8 In. .... *illus*	554
Vase, Geishas Grasping Parasols, Trees, Eva Powell, American Decorator, 9 ½ x 5 ¾ In. *illus*	666
Vase, Gold, Ruffled Rim, Figures, Elephant Shape Handles, 1800s, 9 ½ x 5 In.	63
Vase, Golden, Tan, Crackle Glaze, Wide Neck, White Chrysanthemums, Early 1900s, 18 In.	118
Vase, Japanese Figures, Flowers, Painted, Gold Highlights, Wood Stand, 8 ½ In.	819
Vase, Multicolor, Hand Painted Panels, Birds In Landscape, Wood Stand, Late 1800s, 14 x 7 In.	439
Vase, Painted, Birds, Cherry Blossom Trees, Blue Ground, Flared Rim, c.1900, 14 ½ In.	1140
Vase, Parcel Gilt, Dragon, Landscape, Purple Wisteria, 12 ¼ In.	472
Vase, Raised Chrysanthemums, Flat Rim, Miyagawa Kozan, 1800s, 13 ¼ x 7 In., Pair	2106
Vase, Scenes, Porcelain, Gilt, Painted, Marked, Hododa, 6 ¼ In.	500
Vase, Urn Shape, Warriors, Geishas, Cobalt Blue, Gilt, Japan, 7 ½ x 3 ½ In.	563

SATURDAY EVENING GIRLS, *see Paul Revere Pottery category.*

S

SCALES

Scales have been made to weigh everything from babies to gold. Collectors search for all types. Most popular are small gold dust scales, special grocery scales, and tall figural scales for people to use to check their weight.

Balance, Brass Pan, Iron, Wood Base, Patina, 36 x 44 x 13 In.		800
Balance, Brass, Cast Iron, Tabletop, Black Paint, Scoop, 19 In.		62
Balance, Cast Iron, Brass, Pan & Weights, Marked, Pa. Serial F, 10½ In.		31
Balance, Dodge Scale Co., Micrometer, Cast Metal Base, Marble, 15 x 24 x 11 In.		156
Balance, Fisher Scientific Co., Cast Iron, Black, Ruler, 16 In.		74
Balance, Henry Troemner, Phila., Brass, Copper, Lead Tag, County Inspector, 1800s, 30 In.		475
Balance, Librasco, Brass, Baluster Shape, 2 Pans, Wood Base, 7 Weights, Early 1900s, 20 x 18 In.		118
Balance, Sartorius Werke, Gottingen, Wood Case, Mid 1900s, 19 x 17 In.	*illus*	177
Balance, Wood Pans, Rope, 1800s, 35 In.		238
Balance, Wood, Marble, Ebonized, Glass Cover, 7¼ x 13¼ x 6 In.		125
Candy, National Stove Specialty Co., Cast Metal, Gold Painted Base, 14 x 19 x 7½ In.		219
Candy, Pennsylvania National Store Specialty Co., Cast Iron, Fan Shape, Green, 10 x 9 In.	*illus*	492
Candy, Toledo Springless, Style No. 12, Yellow Paint, Metal Scoop Tray, Label, c.1903, 19 x 19 In.		94
Computing, U.S. Slicing Machine Co., White Porcelain, Beveled Glass, 20 In.		55
Country Store, Dayton, Model No. 344, Enameled, Cast Iron, Countertop, 30 x 19 In.	*illus*	369
Jeweler's, Elmer & Amend, N.Y. City Approved, Metal, Brass, Wood, 6 In.		92
Meat, Johnys Grocery, 9th St., White, Red Letters, c.1940, 8¾ x 11 x 8 In.		283
Micrometer, Dodge Scale Co., Countertop, Nickel Plate, Marble Table, Early 1900s, 17 x 7 In.	*illus*	199
Parcel Post, Triner Peerless-Allsteel, Automatic, Metal, Green, Fan Shape Window, 28 x 25 In.		49
Postal, Kemper Thomas Co., Aluminum, Bakelite, c.1930, 3 In.		250
Precision, Christian Becker, Chainomatic Precision, Weights In Drawer, 16½ In.		94
Weighing, American Scale, Fortune, Character Readings, Your Future, 1900s, 51 In.		745
Weighing, Fairbanks, Cast Iron, Black Paint, Morse & Co., 13½ x 17 In.		62
Weighing, National, Coin-Operated, 1 Cent, Porcelain Dial, Top Sign, Silver, 69½ x 17½ x 13 In.		1968
Weighing, Peerless Weighing Machine Co., Porcelain, Lollipop Shape, Coin-Operated, 68 In.	*illus*	431
Weighing, Salter, Cast Iron, Brass, Enamel Dial, England, 10½ x 9 In.	*illus*	74
Weighing, Toledo, Cast Iron, Pink Paint, Stainless Scooper, 19 In.		98
Weighing, Toledo, Standing, Round, Square Pedestal, Brass, 77 In.		1140
Weighing, White, Painted, Iron, Scroll Work, 2 Brass Bowls, Arabic Script, Late 1800s, 7 x 16 In.	*illus*	561
Weight Set, Apothecary, Bronze, Squirrel Shape Hasp, Handle, 4 x 3 x 3½ In.		277

SCHAFER & VATER

Schafer & Vater, makers of small ceramic items, are best known for their amusing figurals. The factory was located in Volkstedt-Rudolstadt, Germany, from 1890 to 1962. Some pieces are marked with the crown and *R* mark, but many are unmarked.

Bottle, Baker, Holding Bottle, Proverb, Hat Stopper, 6¼ In.	75
Bottle, Man Holding Dog, Orange Scarf, Old Scotch & Little Scotch, 5½ In.	170
Figurine, Grinning Sailor, Red Curly Hair, We Don't Want To Fight, 7 In.	145
Jug, 3 Dutch Girl Faces, Wearing Bonnets, Blue Basketweave, c.1890, 4½ In.	95
Trinket Box, Man Seated, Woman At Table, Cat, Brown, Cream, 4½ In.	40

SCHEIER POTTERY

Scheier pottery was made by Edwin Scheier (1910–2008) and his wife, Mary (1908–2007). They met while they both worked for the WPA, and married in 1937. In 1939, they established their studio, Hillcrock Pottery, in Glade Spring, Virginia. Mary made the pottery and Edwin decorated it. From 1940 to 1968, Edwin taught at the University of New Hampshire and Mary was artist-in-residence. They moved to Oaxaca, Mexico, in 1968 to study the arts and crafts of the Zapotec Indians. When the Scheiers moved to Green Valley, Arizona, in 1978, Ed returned to pottery, making some of his biggest and best-known pieces.

Bowl, Carved, Fish, Blue, Glazed, Signed, New Hampshire, 5⅞ In.	*illus*	875

SCHEIER POTTERY

Satsuma, Censer, Lid, Foo Dog Finial, 2 Dolphin Handles, Gilt, Footed, Japan, 20 In.
$177

Austin Auction Gallery

Satsuma, Charger, Immortal, 2 Yew Boughs, Landscape, Brocade Border, Late 1900s, 13⅝ In.
$625

Charlton Hall Auctions

Satsuma, Vase, Family Panels, Children, Multicolor, Bulbous, Painted, 19 x 8 In.
$554

Alderfer Auction Company

S

Satsuma, Vase, Geishas Grasping Parasols, Trees, Eva Powell, American Decorator, 9 ½ x 5 ¾ In.
$666

Humler & Nolan

Scale, Balance, Sartorius Werke, Gottingen, Wood Case, Mid 1900s, 19 x 17 In.
$177

Leland Little Auctions

Scale, Candy, Pennsylvania National Store Specialty Co., Cast Iron, Fan Shape, Green, 10 x 9 In.
$492

Rich Penn Auctions

Scale, Country Store, Dayton, Model No. 344, Enameled, Cast Iron, Countertop, 30 x 19 In.
$369

Rich Penn Auctions

Scale, Micrometer, Dodge Scale Co., Countertop, Nickel Plate, Marble Table, Early 1900s, 17 x 7 In.
$199

Jeffrey S. Evans & Associates

Scale, Weighing, Peerless Weighing Machine Co., Porcelain, Lollipop Shape, Coin-Operated, 68 In.
$431

Rich Penn Auctions

Scale, Weighing, Salter, Cast Iron, Brass, Enamel Dial, England, 10 ½ x 9 In.
$74

Hartzell's Auction Gallery Inc.

Scale, Weighing, White, Painted, Iron, Scroll Work, 2 Brass Bowls, Arabic Script, Late 1800s, 7 x 16 In.
$561

Leland Little Auctions

> ### TIP
> *It pays to get to know dealers. If you discuss what you collect, the dealer will try to find something for you. Many dealers travel to the same shows every year and bring things for returning customers.*

Scheier, Bowl, Carved, Fish, Blue, Glazed, Signed, New Hampshire, 5 ⅞ In.
$875

Toomey & Co. Auctioneers

S

Bowl, Yellow Matte Glaze, Footed, Signed, 1950s, 2 ½ x 9 ¼ In.		120
Pitcher, Rooster, Black Ground, Glazed Earthenware, Handle, Signed, 11 ¾ x 6 x 7 ½ In.		688
Vase, Stoneware, Matte Glaze, Faces, Carved, Signed, 1993, 15 ½ In.		2750

SCHNEIDER GLASSWORKS

Schneider Glassworks was founded in 1917 at Epinay-sur-Seine, France, by Charles and Ernest Schneider. Art glass was made between 1918 and 1933. The company went bankrupt in 1939. Charles Schneider and his sons opened a new glassworks in 1949. Art glass was made until 1981, when the company closed. See also the Le Verre Francais category.

Bowl, Rose, Clear To Lavender Shading, Sea Anemone Shape, Pedestal, Signed, 6 x 6 In.		350
Lamp, Electric, Cone Shape Shade, Mottled Orange, Red, Blue Tones, Metal Base, 17 ¼ x 7 In.		450
Vase, Cameo, Nenuphar, Orange, Frosted, Dark Spatter Ground, Signed, Charder, 1928, 18 ¾ In. *illus*		1755
Vase, Jade, Orange & Yellow, Gold Grape, Dark Brown Leaves, Signed, 9 ½ x 4 x 4 In., Pair		861
Vase, Monumental, Molten Shade, Blue, Green, Orange, Etched, 27 In. *illus*		861
Vase, Red Mottled, Black, Applied Handle, Molded, 4 ½ In.		254
Vase, Swirl Body, Yellow To Clear, Blown, Brown Base, Signed, 7 In. *illus*		201
Vase, Yellow Ground, Tortoiseshell Overlay, Carved Scarab, Cameo, Marked, Charder, 13 x 8 In.		400

SCIENTIFIC INSTRUMENTS

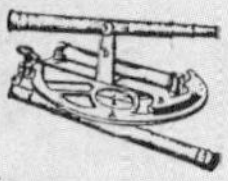

Scientific instruments of all kinds are included in this category. Other categories such as Barometer, Binoculars, Dental, Medical, Nautical, and Thermometer may also price scientific apparatus.

Calculator, Professor Fuller's, Spiral Slide Rule, Mahogany Case, 1800s, 4 x 4 x 17 In.		677
Compass & Sundial, F.L. West, Brass, Round, Roman Numerals, Marked, 2 ¾ In. *illus*		86
Compass, Desk, Hermes, Silver Plate, Chain, Glass Face, Signed, c.1975, 4 In.		2500
Compass, E.S. Ritchie & Sons, Black Paint, Glass, Directionals, 18 In.		277
Compass, Field, Benjamin Cole, George II, Mahogany, c.1750, Dial, 5 In.		305
Compass, Prismatic, Brass, Floating Dry Card, Hinged Prism, 2 Filters, c.1850, 3 In. *illus*		854
Compass, Sundial, Brass, Hinged Chapter, Engraved, Silver Dial, 1800s, 5 x 5 ½ In.		488
Compass, Surveyor's, Gedney King, Brass, Wood Case, Boston, 1800s, 3 x 13 In.		1000
Graphometer, Surveyor's, Brass, Rotating Alidade, Cabriole Legs, Slipper Feet, c.1850, 13 In. *illus*		549
Hourglass, De Beers & Louis Glick, Brass, Diamonds, Acrylic, Silicone Fluid, 1900s, 5 In. *illus*		8750
Hourglass, Turned Wood, Spindles, Circular Ends, Blown Glass, Early 1800s, 6 ¼ In.		813
Level, Surveyor's, Heller & Brightly, Brass, Black, Stand, Telescope, 64 In. *illus*		230
Machine, Elevator Flyball Cable, Wheel, Gears, Brake, Turning Mechanism, Iron, 28 x 24 In. *illus*		277
Magnifying Glass, Acid Etched, Acanthus Leaves, Sterling Silver Frame, J.F. Fradley & Co., 9 In. *illus*		106
Magnifying Glass, White Celluloid, Silver Plate Crown Fittings, Ornate Handle, 9 x 3 In.		90
Microscope, Smith & Beck, Binocular, No. 3544, Case, 19 In.		413
Planetarium, Trippensee, Movable Arms, Compass Dial, Stamped, 1960, 13 In. *illus*		644
Plotting Instrument, Henry Wadsworth, Circumcenter, Brass, 8 x 10 In.		240
Quadrant, John Gilbert II, Mahogany, T-Frame, Filters, Ivory Legs, London, c.1750, 5 x 18 In.		5625
Sextant, Hezzanith, Heath & Co., Mahogany, Hinged, Marked, Box, London, c.1936, 10 x 11 In.		313
Sighting Scope, Telescope, Black, No. 15629, Box, 9 In.		135
Telescope, Bardot & Sons, Brass, 3-Tube, Tripod, Wood Case, c.1870, 5 x 40 x 7 In.		644
Telescope, Brass, Interior Mirrors, Ball Swirl, Tripod Base, 1750s, 14 x 14 x 3 In.		1320
Telescope, Brass, Tripod Wooden Legs, Ball Feet, 19 x 18 In.		250
Telescope, Broadhurst Clarkson & Co., Brass Body, Shade, Brown Leather Case, 34 x 2 In.		150
Telescope, Gall & Lembke, New York, Wood Tripod, 72 In.		308
Telescope, Henri Gambey, Brass Wheel, Vernier Scales, Magnifier, Signed, c.1825, 15 In. *illus*		2500
Telescope, Iron & Brass, 2 Eyepieces, Wood Case, Tabletop, Late 1800s, 9 ¾ In.		236
Telescope, James Short London, Reflecting, Brass, Tripod Stand, Late 1900s, 21 ½ In. *illus*		531
Telescope, Mahogany, Brass, Tabletop, 3-Draw, Tripod Stand, 1800s, 4 x 21 In.		625
Telescope, Marine, Brass, Leather Grip, Rope Binding, Collapsible, Early 1800s, 45 x 2 In.		702
Telescope, Refractor, Brass, England, 1900s, 68 In.		128
Telescope, Reynolds & Branson, Brass, Focus Knob, Folding, Cabriole Legs, Slipper Feet, 14 In.		488
Transit, Surveyor's, Gurley, Black, Magnifier, Wood Box, Brass, 15 ½ In.		201

Schneider, Vase, Cameo, Nenuphar, Orange, Frosted, Dark Spatter Ground, Signed, Charder, 1928, 18 ¾ In

$1,755

Jeffrey S. Evans & Associates

Schneider, Vase, Monumental, Molten Shade, Blue, Green, Orange, Etched, 27 In.

$861

Brunk Auctions

Schneider, Vase, Swirl Body, Yellow To Clear, Blown, Brown Base, Signed, 7 In.

$201

Blackwell Auctions

S

463

Scientific Instrument, Compass & Sundial, F.L. West, Brass, Round, Roman Numerals, Marked, 2 ¾ In.
$86

Hartzell's Auction Gallery Inc.

Scientific Instrument, Compass, Prismatic, Brass, Floating Dry Card, Hinged Prism, 2 Filters, c.1850, 3 In.
$854

Neal Auction Company

Scientific Instrument, Graphometer, Surveyor's, Brass, Rotating Alidade, Cabriole Legs, Slipper Feet, c.1850, 13 In.
$549

Neal Auction Company

Scientific Instrument, Hourglass, De Beers & Louis Glick, Brass, Diamonds, Acrylic, Silicone Fluid, 1900s, 5 In.
$8,750

Wright

Scientific Instrument, Level, Surveyor's, Heller & Brightly, Brass, Black, Stand, Telescope, 64 In.
$230

Blackwell Auctions

Scientific Instrument, Machine, Elevator Flyball Cable, Wheel, Gears, Brake, Turning Mechanism, Iron, 28 x 24 In.
$277

Rich Penn Auctions

Scientific Instrument, Magnifying Glass, Acid Etched, Acanthus Leaves, Sterling Silver Frame, J.F. Fradley & Co., 9 In.
$106

Leland Little Auctions

Scientific Instrument, Planetarium, Trippensee, Movable Arms, Compass Dial, Stamped, 1960, 13 In.
$644

Jeffrey S. Evans & Associates

Scientific Instrument, Telescope, Henri Gambey, Brass Wheel, Vernier Scales, Magnifier, Signed, c.1825, 15 In.
$2,500

Eldred's

SCRIMSHAW

Scrimshaw is bone or ivory or whale's teeth carved by sailors and others for entertainment during the sailing-ship days. Some scrimshaw was carved as early as 1800. There are modern scrimshanders making pieces today on bone, ivory, or plastic. Other pieces may be found in the Ivory and Nautical categories. Collectors should be aware of the recent laws limiting the buying and selling of scrimshaw and elephant ivory.

Basket, Whalebone, Wood Lid, Swing Handle, Carved, Harbor Scene, 10 In.	*illus*	2268
Box, Cylindrical, Frog, Wood, Carved, Signed, Japan, Early 1900s, 6¾ In.	*illus*	431
Box, Removable Top, Applied Whalebone, Eagle, Black Interior, 1800s, 4 x 7 x 5 In.		600
Ditty Box, 2 Sailing Ships, Floral, Baleen, 1800s, 3 x 4¼ In.		113
Dresser Box, Whalebone, Geometric, Handles, Doors, Drawers, Late 1800s, 3 x 24 In.	*illus*	4688
Fid, Whalebone, Carved, Hand, Shaft, Spiral Ribbing, 1860s, 7¾ In.	*illus*	813
Fid, Whalebone, Narrow Turned Band, 1800s, 11¾ In.		500
Letter Opener, Whalebone, Handle, Inlay, Exotic Wood, c.1850, 9½ In.		200
Page Turner, Whalebone, Lady's Leg, Heart, Nail Heads, Baleen Blade, 10 In.	*illus*	531
Panel, Whalebone, Man, Woman, Geometric, Dolphins, Rococo, The Farewell, 1800s, 6 x 6 In.		6875
Pie Crimper, Whalebone, Carved, Handle, Fluted Wheel, Lady's Legs & Boots, c.1850, 7 In.	*illus*	1750
Pie Crimper, Whalebone, Snake Handle, Baleen Bands, 3 Tines, Sailor Made, c.1860, 5¾ In.	*illus*	18750
Pipe, Whalebone, Carved, Triangles, Diamonds, Crescents, Dots, 4 Stars, Whaleman, c.1850, 4 In.		1500
Rolling Pin, Whaleman, Handles, Baleen Banding, Hardwood Roller, 1800s, 15¾ In.	*illus*	813
Seal, Whalebone, Architectural Shape, Carved, 4 Column Shaft, c.1850, 3¾ In.		200
Seam Rubber, Whalebone, Shaped, Pique Inlay, Sailor Made, c.1850, 4½ In.	*illus*	375
Shoehorn, Figural Carved Finial, Skull, Crossbones, Mermaid, Couple, English Flag, 1800s, 9 In.		420
Tusk, Elephant, Village Scene, Carved, c.1950, 7 x 22½ x 3½ In.		1764
Tusk, Mammoth, Bald Eagle Catching Salmon, Petrified, Signed, B. Sutton, 1950s, 6 x 9 In.		204
Tusk, Walrus, Animals, Men, Structures, Ship, Marked, Alaska, c.1947, 20 In.	*illus*	441
Walrus Tusk, Inuit Life, Dogs, Reindeer, Polar Bear, 4 Men In Kayak, James Lee, c.1955, 21 In.		556
Whale's Tooth, Carved, Inuit Mask, U.S. Navy Sailor, American Flag, Initialed, JLP, 1800s, 4 In.		1755
Whale's Tooth, Eagle, Spread Wings, E Pluribus Unum, Ribbon, Signed, DM, 1950s, 4 In.		207
Whale's Tooth, Nautical & Patriotic, Sailing Ship, 1800s, 3¾ In.		443
Whale's Tooth, Ship On Choppy Seas, George Watson, 1850s, 6⅛ In.		1188
Whale's Tooth, Sovereign Of The Seas, Engraved, Clipper Ship, Signed, Linda, 1900s, 4¾ In.		313
Whale's Tooth, Sperm, 3-Masted Ship, Stepped Wood Stand, Late 1800s, 5¼ x 3⅜ x 2⅞ In.		936
Whale's Tooth, Thomas Jefferson, Flags, Eagle, Rendering Of Monticello, Early 1800s, 4 In.	*illus*	590
Whale's Tooth, Whaling Scene, Boats, Flags, Inscribed, Edw. Burdett, 8 In.	*illus*	118750
Whale's Tooth, Woman, Festooned Hat, Scarf, Flowers, William Sizer, c.1835, 7¼ In.	*illus*	3250
Yarn Swift, Whalebone, Ivory Clamp, Expanding Frame, 1800s, 7¾ In.		1750

SEG, *see Paul Revere Pottery category.*

SEVRES

Sevres porcelain has been made in Sevres, France, since 1769. Many copies of the famous ware have been made. The name originally referred to the works of the Royal Porcelain factory. The name now includes any of the wares made in the town of Sevres, France. The entwined lines with a center letter used as the mark is one of the most forged marks in antiques. Be very careful to identify Sevres by quality, not just by mark.

Bowl, Flowers, Leaf Shape Handles, Gilt, Pedestal, Late 1900s, 14 x 20 In.	295
Bowl, Parcel Gilt, Scrolled Handles, Porcelain, Bronze, Pedestal Base, 1900s, 15 x 22 In.	502
Box, Hinged Lid, Classic Scene, Cobalt Blue Border, Oval, Marked, 2¾ x 7½ In.	125
Cachepot, Turquoise, Flowers, Gilt, Handles, Painted, Marked, 1700s, 4 x 5½ In.	531
Compote, Cobalt Blue, Cadmium Red, Gilt, Porcelain, 11 x 6½ In., Pair	83
Creamer, Nude, Transfer Printed, Parcel, Gilt, Ball Finial, Handle, 1800s, 5⅜ In.	352
Cup & Saucer, Cobalt Blue Ground, Painted, 2 Riders & Horses, Chateau Tuileries *illus*	200
Dresser Box, Red Ground, Gilt, Courting Scene, Mallet, Porcelain, Late 1800s, 4 x 13 In.	500
Dresser Box, Round, Dark Blue Ground, Gilt, 5 x 7½ In.	480
Plate, Bourgogne, Portrait Of Woman In Veil, Pink Border, Flowers, Signed, Morin, 9½ In. *illus*	225

Scientific Instrument, Telescope, James Short London, Reflecting, Brass, Tripod Stand, Late 1900s, 21½ In. $531

Leland Little Auctions

Scrimshaw, Basket, Whalebone, Wood Lid, Swing Handle, Carved, Harbor Scene, 10 In. $2,268

Fontaine's Auction Gallery

Scrimshaw, Box, Cylindrical, Frog, Wood, Carved, Signed, Japan, Early 1900s, 6¾ In. $431

Blackwell Auctions

S

Scrimshaw, Dresser Box, Whalebone, Geometric, Handles, Doors, Drawers, Late 1800s, 3 x 24 In.
$4,688

Eldred's

Scrimshaw, Fid, Whalebone, Carved, Hand, Shaft, Spiral Ribbing, 1860s, 7¾ In.
$813

Eldred's

Scrimshaw, Page Turner, Whalebone, Lady's Leg, Heart, Nail Heads, Baleen Blade, 10 In.
$531

Eldred's

Scrimshaw, Pie Crimper, Whalebone, Carved, Handle, Fluted Wheel, Lady's Legs & Boots, c.1850, 7 In.
$1,750

Eldred's

Scrimshaw, Pie Crimper, Whalebone, Snake Handle, Baleen Bands, 3 Tines, Sailor Made, c.1860, 5¾ In.
$18,750

Eldred's

Scrimshaw, Rolling Pin, Whaleman, Handles, Baleen Banding, Hardwood Roller, 1800s, 15¾ In.
$813

Eldred's

Scrimshaw, Seam Rubber, Whalebone, Shaped, Pique Inlay, Sailor Made, c.1850, 4½ In.
$375

Eldred's

Scrimshaw, Tusk, Walrus, Animals, Men, Structures, Ship, Marked, Alaska, c.1947, 20 In.
$441

Fontaine's Auction Gallery

Scrimshaw, Whale's Tooth, Thomas Jefferson, Flags, Eagle, Rendering Of Monticello, Early 1800s, 4 In.
$590

Leland Little Auctions

S

Scrimshaw, Whale's Tooth, Whaling Scene, Boats, Flags, Inscribed, Edw. Burdett, 8 In.
$118,750

Eldred's

Scrimshaw, Whale's Tooth, Woman, Festooned Hat, Scarf, Flowers, William Sizer, c.1835, 7 ¼ In.
$3,250

Eldred's

Sevres, Cup & Saucer, Cobalt Blue Ground, Painted, 2 Riders & Horses, Chateau Tuileries
$200

Woody Auction

Sevres, Plate, Bourgogne, Portrait Of Woman In Veil, Pink Border, Flowers, Signed, Morin, 9 ½ In.
$225

Woody Auction

Sevres, Urn, Lid, Parcel Gilt, Blue Ground, Pineapple Finial, Painted, Pedestal Base, 1900s, 36 In.
$1,121

Austin Auction Gallery

Sevres, Urn, Monumental, Napoleonic, Cobalt Neck, Ormolu Handle, Signed, H. Desprez, 1850s, 34 In.
$4,500

Garth's Auctioneers & Appraisers

Sevres, Vase, Rose Pompadour, Woman, Bulbous, Pink, Gilt, France, 23 In.
$207

Austin Auction Gallery

Sevres, Vase, Yellow Ground, Painted Floral, Birds, Insects, 13 ⅜ In.
$325

Leland Little Auctions

S

Sewer Tile, Sculpture, Peafowl, Dark Brown Glaze, Stump Shape Base, 1900s, 22 ¼ In.
$813

Eldred's

Sewing, Box, Coromandel, Hinged Lid, Mother-Of-Pearl Inlays, Lower Writing Desk, 1800s, 7 x 12 In.
$354

Leland Little Auctions

Sewing, Box, Hinged Lid, Rosewood, Octagonal, c.1815, 5 x 11 In.
$295

Cottone Auctions

Sewing, Box, Landscape, Ivory, Carved, Handles, Compartments, Bun Feet, Chinese, 1800s, 3 x 11 In.
$8,750

Eldred's

Sewing, Clamp, Royal Woman, Crown, Epaulettes, Sash, Pincushion, Needle Holder, Early 1800s, 7 In.
$1,063

Eldred's

Sewing, Machine, New National, Painted Flowers, Hand Crank, 10 ½ x 17 ½ x 9 In.
$224

Morphy Auctions

Sewing, Needle Case, Butterfly Shape, Brass, A.W. Avery & Son, Redditch, Victorian, 5 In.
$1,046

Rich Penn Auctions

Shaker, Box, Pantry, Round, Blue, Wood, 1800s, 5 ¼ In.
$175

Eldred's

Shaker, Box, Sewing, 4-Finger, Copper Tacks, Swing Handle, 1900s, 9 ½ x 11 ¾ x 8 ½ In.
$410

Jeffrey S. Evans & Associates

Plate, Courting Scene, Gilt, Painted, Stand, Signed, Robert, Vincennes, 11 x 5 ½ In.	354
Plate, Cream Center, Blue Border, Portrait, Young Woman, 9 ½ In.	60
Plate, Napoleonic, Armorial, Gilt, White Ground, c.1870, 9 ¼ In.	207
Plate, Porte St. Honore & Porte D'Bernard, Blue Border, H. Desprez, 1800s, 10 In., Pair	148
Platter, Battle Of Pavia, Cobalt Blue Ground, Gilt, Underfoot, 16 x 11 In.	378
Urn, Lid, Gilt, Bronze, Finial, 2 Handles, Signed, Bertrand, Late 1800s, 16 ½ In.	1125
Urn, Lid, Parcel Gilt, Blue Ground, Pineapple Finial, Painted, Pedestal Base, 1900s, 36 In. illus	1121
Urn, Monumental, Napoleonic, Cobalt Neck, Ormolu Handle, Signed, H. Desprez, 1850s, 34 In. illus	4500
Vase, Rose Pompadour, Woman, Bulbous, Pink, Gilt, France, 23 In. illus	207
Vase, Yellow Ground, Painted, Floral, Birds, Insects, 13 ⅜ In. illus	325

SEWER TILE

Sewer tile figures were made by workers at the sewer tile and pipe factories in the Ohio area during the late nineteenth and early twentieth centuries. Figurines, small vases, and cemetery vases were favored. Often the finished vase was a piece of the original pipe with added decorations and markings. All types of sewer tile work are now considered folk art by collectors.

Bank, Pig, Brown Glaze, Ribbon, Early 1900s, 8 ¾ In.	94
Bookends, Owl, Brown, Carved, Early 1900s, 8 ¾ x 7 ¼ x 2 ¾ In., Pair	281
Figure, Lion, Reclining, Stepped Rectangular Base, Ohio, 9 ¾ x 5 x 7 In.	219
Figure, Lion, Seated, Scalloped Plinth, Rectangular Base, Signed, LE Wadsworth, Ohio, 6 In.	320
Figure, Rooster, Finely Molded, Bright Brown, Red Glaze, Late 1800s, 9 In.	1024
Sculpture, Peafowl, Dark Brown Glaze, Stump Shape Base, 1900s, 22 ¼ In. illus	813

SEWING

Sewing, knitting, and weaving equipment of all types is collected, from sewing birds that held the cloth to tape measures, needle books, and old wooden spools. Sewing machines are included here. Needlework pictures are listed in the Picture category.

Basket, Lid, Tassels & Beads, Woven, Chinese, Late 1800s, 4 ½ x 11 ½ In.	47
Basket, Woven, Splint, Painted, Low Stave Style, Wrapped Rim, White Oak, Late 1800s, 3 x 10 ¾ In.	410
Box, 3 Tiers, Walnut, Pine & Poplar, Turned Feet, Rockingham Co., 1910s, 14 ¼ In.	234
Box, Anglo-Indian, Hinged Lid, Ebonized, Wood Strapping, Bone Inlaid, Late 1800s, 5 x 12 In.	1121
Box, Carved, Ornate, Courting Couple, Hinged Lid, Continental, Late 1800s, 6 x 17 x 15 In.	236
Box, Chest Style, Wood, Mahogany, Drawers, Shapes, Inlay, Ball Feet, c.1850, 11 ½ In.	1250
Box, Coromandel, Hinged Lid, Mother-Of-Pearl Inlays, Lower Writing Desk, 1800s, 7 x 12 In. illus	354
Box, Hinged Lid, Papier-Mache, Black, Daisies, Butterfly, Painted, Late 1800s, 2 ½ x 11 x 9 In.	87
Box, Hinged Lid, Rosewood, Octagonal, c.1815, 5 x 11 In. illus	295
Box, Landscape, Ivory, Carved, Handles, Compartments, Bun Feet, Chinese, 1800s, 3 x 11 In. illus	8750
Box, Leaping Stag, Black Ground, Carved Drawer, Accoutrements Inside, 1800s, 9 x 12 ½ In.	732
Box, Lid, Mahogany, Maritime Scene, Compartments, Ball Feet, Trinity House, 1800s, 4 x 12 In.	1125
Box, Poplar, Bentwood, Stenciled, Flowers, Yellow Ground, 1800s, 5 x 5 ¼ In.	1037
Cabinet, Spool, Oak, 6 Drawers, Metal Pulls, 21 x 25 In.	226
Cabinet, Spool, see also the Advertising category under Cabinet, Spool.	
Clamp, C-Shape, Pincushion, Wrought Iron, 1800s, 6 In.	397
Clamp, Royal Woman, Crown, Epaulettes, Sash, Pincushion, Needle Holder, Early 1800s, 7 In. illus	1063
Etui, Scent Bottle, Stopper, 18K Gold, Contents, Pad, Pencil, Needle, Bobbin, France, 5 In.	6940
Machine, B. Eldredge Automatic, Black, Flowers, National Sewing Machine Co., 9 x 14 In.	103
Machine, Domestic, Cast Iron Base, Treadle, Flip Top, 40 x 27 In.	71
Machine, New National, Painted Flowers, Hand Crank, 10 ½ x 17 ½ x 9 In. illus	224
Needle Case, Butterfly Shape, Brass, A.W. Avery & Son, Redditch, Victorian, 5 In. illus	1046
Needle Case, Slide Lid, Walnut, Scrolled Handle, Chip Edges, 1800s, 2 ½ x 7 In.	163
Pincushion Dolls are listed in their own category.	
Pincushion, Cowhorn Shape, Cotton Velvet, Prisoner, Alferd Packer, Canon City, 10 In.	500
Pincushion, Heart Shape, Dove, Leaf, White, Red, Swirl Border, 1800s, 6 ½ x 6 In.	305
Pincushion, Iron Shape, Wood, Painted, Yellow & Red Leaves, Fabric Base, 1800s, 4 ⅝ x 6 ¾ x 3 In.	188
Scissors, Equestrian Handle, Silver, Stainless Steel, Hermes, c.1965, 8 ¼ In.	1875
Spool Cabinets are listed here or in the Advertising category under Cabinet, Spool.	

Shaker, Pantry Box, Lid, Bentwood, Oval, 4-Finger, Copper Tacks, 1850s, 4 ¼ x 10 ¼ In.
$660

Garth's Auctioneers & Appraisers

Scuttle Mug

A scuttle shaving mug is shaped like an old coal scuttle. There is an opening to hold the brush.

Shaving Mug, Occupational, Accountant, Gilt, Dean Rentfro, Blue Wrap, Elite Limoges, France, 3 In.
$369

Rich Penn Auctions

Shaving Mug, Occupational, Ambulance Driver, Gilt, Hospital Background, Chas. Mathews, 4 In.
$3,075

Rich Penn Auctions

S

Shearwater, Bowl, Round, Cream, Fruits, Stamped, 3 ½ In.
$590

Bunch Auctions

Shearwater, Vase, Sea, Earth, Sky Pattern, Bronze & White Glaze, Walter Inglis Anderson, 12 In.
$5,000

Neal Auction Company

Shirley Temple, Doll, Composition, Sleep Eyes, Open Mouth, Teeth, Flower Dress, 27 In.
$74

Apple Tree Auction Center

Tape Loom, Tabletop, Poplar Box, Oak Arch Top, Mid 1800s, 5 x 17 ¼ In.	263
Tape Loom, Wood, Cutout Crest, Chip Carved Bottom, Painted, Red, Green, 1800s, 7 x 6 In.	450
Tape Measure, Figural, Pig, Silvertone, Niagara Falls, 2 ¼ In.	13
Thimble, 14K Gold, Scent Bottle, Stopper, Engraved, 1 In.	1792
Yarn Winder, 7 Spools, Brass, Crack Operated, Cast Iron, Tabletop, 1800s, 16 x 22 ½ In.	222

SHAKER

Shaker items are characterized by simplicity, functionalism, and orderliness. There were many Shaker communities in America from the eighteenth century to the present day. The religious order made furniture, small wooden pieces, and packaged medicines, herbs, and jellies to sell to "outsiders." Other useful objects were made for use by members of the community. Shaker furniture is listed in this book in the Furniture category.

Basket, Woven Splint, 2 Swing Handles, Wrapped Rim, Light Brown, c.1880, 12 x 16 x 10 In.	406
Berry Bucket, Tin, Strap Bands, Bail Handle, Stave Construction, 1850s, 4 ½ x 5 ½ In.	660
Berry Bucket, Yellow Exterior, Oyster White Interior, Handle, c.1830, 6 x 4 x 6 In.	1375
Bonnet, Woven Straw, Black, White Cotton Bound Edge, Late 1800s, 6 ½ In.	100
Box, Dome Lid, Painted, American Flag, Drapery, Floral, 1800s, 12 ½ x 27 ½ x 14 In.	850
Box, Hinged Lid, Pine, Red Stain, Rounded Edge, Dovetailed, Ball Feet, Early 1800s, 6 x 14 In.	563
Box, Lift Top, Pine, Rounded Edge, Dovetailed, Red Stain, Ball Feet, Early 1800s, 6 x 14 x 8 In.	450
Box, Pantry, Round, Blue, Wood, 1800s, 5 ¼ In. .... *illus*	175
Box, Removable Lid, Oval, 4 Swallowtails On Base, 5 ½ x 13 ⅛ In.	344
Box, Sewing, 4-Finger, Copper Tacks, Swing Handle, 1900s, 9 ½ x 11 ¾ x 8 ½ In. .... *illus*	410
Box, Sewing, Bentwood, Swing Handle, 1900s, 4 ¼ In.	219
Brush, Turned Maple Handle, Blue Ribbon, Velvet Wrapped Horsehair Bristles, 9 ½ In.	275 to 344
Candle Box, Chamfered Sliding Lid, Dovetailed, Early 1800s, 4 ¾ x 11 In.	594
Carrier, Lid, 4-Finger, Oval, Swing Handle, Late 1800s, 8 ¼ x 10 ½ In.	469
Carrier, Oval, 2 Swallowtails, Swing Handle, Mt. Lebanon, N.Y., 3 x 14 ½ In.	469
Carrier, Sewing, Oval, Maroon Interior, 3 Swallowtails, Swing Handle, 2 ¼ x 7 In.	281
Pantry Box, Lid, 3-Finger, Oval, Nail Construction, Applied Label, c.1890, 1 ¼ x 3 ⅝ In.	625
Pantry Box, Lid, Bentwood, Oval, 4-Finger, Copper Tacks, 1850s, 4 ¼ x 10 ¼ In. .... *illus*	660
Pantry Box, Lid, Wood, Oval, Blue, Patina, 4 x 12 x 8 ½ In.	1356
Poster, Sewing Steps, Signed, John Kassay, Frame, 1971, 24 x 16 In.	200
Shelf, Wall, 2 Drawers, Knob Pulls, Beveled Edge, 4 ¼ x 23 In.	1625
Spice Box, Chamfered Sliding Lid, Pine & Poplar, Dovetailed, Eliza Brown, 1898, 2 ¾ x 6 In.	1000
Stove, Tin, Flat Top, Rounded Sides, Hinged Door, Front Vent, Late 1800s, 17 x 15 x 28 In.	1375
Washtub, Wood, Blue, Piggin Handle, Iron Bands, 1800s, 8 x 14 ½ x 10 ¼ In.	1076
Yarn Swift, Maple Post, Birch Slats, Turned Cup, Yellow Stain, 1800s, 27 In.	188

SHAVING MUG

Shaving mugs were popular from 1860 to 1900. Many types were made, including occupational mugs featuring pictures of men's jobs. There were scuttle mugs, silver-plated mugs, glass-lined mugs, and others.

Occupational, Accountant, Gilt, Dean Rentfro, Blue Wrap, Elite Limoges, France, 3 In. *illus*	369
Occupational, Ambulance Driver, Gilt, Hospital Background, Chas. Mathews, 4 In. .... *illus*	3075
Occupational, Fish Market, Gilt Inscription, A. Citarella, 1926, 4 ¾ x 4 In.	1280
Occupational, Tailor, Gold Gilt, Sash Parsons, 3 ¾ In.	86

Shawnee USA

SHAWNEE POTTERY

Shawnee Pottery was started in Zanesville, Ohio, in 1937. The company made vases, novelty ware, flowerpots, planters, lamps, and cookie jars. Three dinnerware lines were made: Corn, Lobster Ware, and Valencia (a solid color line). White Corn pattern utility pieces were made in 1945. Corn King was made from 1946 to 1954; Corn Queen, with darker green leaves and lighter colored corn, from 1954 to 1961. Shawnee produced pottery for George Rumrill during the late 1930s. The company closed in 1961.

Cookie Jar, Smiley Pig, Lid, Bank Head, Green Neckerchief, No. 60, 10 ½ In.	265

Pitcher, Bo Peep, Blue Bonnet, Blue Flower, 8½ In.	25
Pitcher, Smiley Pig, Blue & Red Flowers, Large, 1940s, 8 x 6 x 7¾ In.	31
Vase, 2 Handles, Quilted Diamond, Daisy Buttons, Round Base, Flared Neck, Yellow, No. 827, 7 x 6 In.	3

SHEARWATER POTTERY

Shearwater Pottery is a family business started in 1928 by Peter Anderson, with the help of his parents, Mr. and Mrs. G.W. Anderson Sr. The local Ocean Springs, Mississippi, clays were used to make the wares in the 1930s. The company was damaged by Hurricane Katrina in 2005 but was rebuilt and is still in business, now owned by Peter's four children.

Bowl, Round, Cream, Fruits, Stamped, 3½ In. .... *illus*	590
Figure, Duck, Green Glaze, c.1935, 8½ x 5½ In.	282
Vase, Purple Glaze, 2 Handles, Marked, 12 In.	610
Vase, Sea, Earth, Sky Pattern, Bronze & White Glaze, Walter Inglis Anderson, 12 In. .... *illus*	5000

SHEET MUSIC

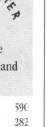

Sheet music from the past centuries is now collected. The favorites are examples with covers featuring artistic or historic pictures. Early sheet music covers were lithographed, but by the 1900s photographic reproductions were used. The early sheet music pages were larger than more recent sheets, and you must watch out for examples that were trimmed to fit in a twentieth-century piano bench and should be lower priced.

I'm Henry VIII, I Am, Herman's Hermits, On Tour, 1965.	10
In The Shadows, Piano, Herman Finck, Jack Drislane, Geo. W. Meyer, Jos. W. Stern & Co., 1910...	10
Making Sheep Eyes At Me, Barney McGee, 1908	15
New Englanders In California, Gold Rush, B.F. Foster, 1850, 13 x 10 In.	375
When I Have Sung My Songs, Ernest Charles, 1934	25

SHEFFIELD *items are listed in the Silver Plate and Silver-English categories.*

SHIRLEY TEMPLE

Shirley Temple, the famous movie star, was born in 1928. She made her first movie in 1932. She died in 2014. Thousands of items picturing Shirley have been and still are being made. Shirley Temple dolls were first made in 1934 by Ideal Toy Company. Millions of Shirley Temple cobalt blue glass dishes were made by Hazel Atlas Glass Company and U.S. Glass Company from 1934 to 1942. They were given away as premiums for Wheaties and Bisquick. A bowl, mug, and pitcher were made as a breakfast set. Some pieces were decorated with the picture of a very young Shirley, others used a picture of Shirley in her 1936 Captain January costume. Although collectors refer to a cobalt creamer, it is actually the 4½-inch-high milk pitcher from the breakfast set. Many of these items have been reproduced and are being sold today.

Dish Set, Glass, Cobalt Blue, Pitcher, 4½ In., Mug, 3⅝ In.	20
Doll Clothes, Sailor Costume, Bell Bottom Pants, Hat, Red Satin Ribbon, Fits 18-In. Doll	22
Doll, Composition, Blond Mohair Curls, Polka Dot Dress, Shoes, Ideal, 1930s, 13 In.	108
Doll, Composition, Hat, Ideal, Red, Yellow, Dress, Blond Hair, 27 In.	213
Doll, Composition, Mohair Wig, Open Mouth, Polka Dot Dress, Blue Ribbons, Ideal, 16 In. ...	336
Doll, Composition, Mohair Wig, Open Mouth, The World's Darling Pin, Ideal, 13 In.	110
Doll, Composition, Red & White Dress, 2 Birds On Yoke, White Shoes, Red Hat, Ideal, 27 In. .	213
Doll, Composition, Sleep Eyes, Mohair Wig, Braids, Heidi, Ideal, 18 In.	1250
Doll, Composition, Sleep Eyes, Open Mouth, 5-Piece Body, Plaid Dress, Ideal, 13 In.	106
Doll, Composition, Sleep Eyes, Open Mouth, Teeth, Flower Dress, 27 In. .... *illus*	74
Pin, The World's Darling, Genuine Shirley Temple Doll, Round, 1½ In.	15

Silver Flatware Sterling, Good Luck, Ice Cream Slice, Whiting, Late 1800s, 11 In.
$260

Leland Little Auctions

Silver Flatware Sterling, King Edward, Teaspoon, Gorham, 6 Piece
$144

Stevens Auction Co.

Silver Flatware Sterling, Versailles, Spoon, Marked, Gorham, 1900s, 6 In., 6 Piece
$185

Brunk Auctions

S

Silver Plate, Biscuit Box, Hinged Lid, Footed, Lee & Wigfall, Sheffield, 1900s, 9 In.
$256

Neal Auction Company

Silver Plate, Biscuit Box, Hinged Lid, Oval Cartouches, Floral, Ball Feet, Martin Hall & Co., 7½ In.
$319

Leland Little Auctions

Silver Plate, Biscuit Warmer, Hinged Lid, Shell Shape, Phoenix Mount Handle, England, Early 1900s, 10 In.
$125

Eldred's

Bad Company
Never put silverware and stainless-steel flatware in the dishwasher basket together. The stainless can damage the silver.

SILVER FLATWARE

Silver flatware includes many of the current and out-of-production sterling silver and silver-plated flatware patterns made in the past 125 years. Other silver is listed under Silver-American, Silver-English, etc. Most silver flatware sets that are missing a few pieces can be completed through the help of a silver matching service. Three U.S. silver company marks are shown here.

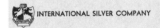

International Silver Co. 1928+

Reed & Barton c.1915+

Wallace Silversmiths, Inc. 1871–1956

SILVER FLATWARE PLATED
Albany, Asparagus Tongs, Wm. Hutton & Son, 1920, 9 In.	95
Brides Bouquet, Cream Soup Spoon, Alvin Silver, 1908, 5 In.	8
Caprice, Butter Spreader, Flat Handle, Oneida Silver, 6⅜ In.	7
Grosvenor, Relish Fork, Oneida, 1921, 6 In.	12
Meadowbrook, Sugar Tongs, Oneida, 1936, 3½ In.	15
Olive, Sauce Ladle, Rogers & Smith, 6 In.	18
Oxford, Butter Knife, Twist Handle, William Rogers & Son, 7½ In.	10

SILVER FLATWARE STERLING
Acanthus, Serving Spoon, Monogram, Engraved, Georg Jensen, Early 1900s, 8¾ In.	63
Blossom, Serving Spoon, Engraved, Signed, Georg Jensen, 8½ In.	295
Coffee Bean, Spoon, Bakelite, Cooper Brothers & Sons, England, c.1950, 3½ In., 6 Piece	42
Colonial, Spoon, Williamsburg, 8 In., 12 Piece	540
French Renaissance, Punch Ladle, Twist Handle, Reed & Barton, 15¾ In.	200
Good Luck, Ice Cream Slice, Whiting, Late 1800s, 11 In. ...... *illus*	260
Grande Imperiale, Ladle, Buccellati, 11⅛ In.	293
Hawthorn, Berry Spoon, Engraved Floral, Monogram, Gorham, Case, 11½ In.	50
Hizen, Sauce Ladle, Chrysanthemum & Crab On Handle, Gold Wash Bowl, Gorham, 1880s, 7 In. *illus*	344
Hound, Punch Ladle, Shaped Bowl, Hound On Handle, Gorham, 1865, 11¾ In.	1408
Imperial Chrysanthemum, Knife, Blunt Blade, Bolster, Gorham, 8½ In., 10 Piece	330
Imperial Chrysanthemum, Spoon, Gorham, Mermod & Jaccard, 7 In., 12 Piece	360
Iolas, Demitasse Spoon, Claude Lalanne, Signed, 1966, 4½ In., 6 Piece	4875
King Edward, Luncheon Fork, Gorham, 7 Piece	230
King Edward, Teaspoon, Gorham, 6 Piece ...... *illus*	144
Leaf & Berry, Bouillon Ladle, Leather Case, Knowles & Ladd, c.1855, 10 In.	469
Owl, Serving Fork, Engraved, Signed, Georg Jensen, 8 In.	531
Versailles, Spoon, Marked, Gorham, 1900s, 6 In., 6 Piece ...... *illus*	185

SILVER PLATE

Silver plate is not solid silver. It is a ware made of a metal, such as nickel or copper, that is covered with a thin coating of silver. The letters *EPNS* are often found on American and English silver-plated wares. *Sheffield* is a term with two meanings. Sometimes it refers to sterling silver made in the town of Sheffield, England. Sometimes it refers to an old form of plated silver made in England. Here are marks of three U.S. silver plate manufacturers.

Barbour Silver Co. 1892–1931

J.W. Tufts 1875–c.1915

Meriden Silver Plate Co. 1869–1898

Basket, Cut Style, Flower, Heron, Footed, Simpson, Hall & Miller, c.1890, 9 x 12 In. 46

Silver Plate, Centerpiece, Reticulated Bowl, Griffins, Glass Liner, Footed, 4 ½ In.
$1,408

Roland Auctioneers & Valuers

Silver Plate, Citrus Press, Curved Arm Support, Mounted, Black Marble Base, 11 ¾ In.
$305

Neal Auction Company

Silver Plate, Cocktail Shaker, Lighthouse Shape, Spurious Hallmarks, 13 ⅞ In.
$427

Neal Auction Company

Silver Plate, Condiment Holder, Revolving Ferris Wheel, Bird, Leaves, Simpson. Hall & Miller, 1880s, 15 In.
$556

Jeffrey S. Evans & Associates

Silver Plate, Cover, Meat, Dome Shape, Oak Handle, Shell & Gadroon Border, Early 1800s, 16 ¼ In.
$100

Eldred's

Silver Plate, Humidor, 2 Cherubs, Filigree Decor, Rectangular, Ball Feet, 1800s, 9 ½ x 11 ½ x 8 In.
$224

Fontaine's Auction Gallery

Silver Plate, Ice Bucket, Stitched Leather Handle, Signed, Hermes, c.1985, 14 ½ In.
$4,063

Wright

TIP
Do not display silver on unsealed wood, felt, wool, or velvet. They all contain sulfides that will tarnish the silver.

Silver Plate, Mirror, Lavender, Jasperware Plaque, Angel, Cherub, Continental, Early 1900s, 9 ½ In.
$70

Selkirk Auctioneers & Appraisers

S

SILVER PLATE

Silver Plate, Pitcher, Water, Set, Ornate, Victorian, Simpson, Hall, Miller & Co., 1880s, 23 x 17 x 10 In.
$878

Silver Plate, Samovar, 2 Deer Head Handles, Putto Finial, Cabriole Legs, Late 1800s, 21 x 11 x 12 In.
$284

Silver Plate, Tankard, Hinged Lid, Art Nouveau, Pierced Handle, WMF, Signed, A.K. & Cie, 14 In.
$441

Jeffrey S. Evans & Associates

Silver Plate, Pitcher, Wine, Mounted, Ornate, Etched Glass, WMF, Germany, Late 1800s, 14 ½ In.
$384

Fontaine's Auction Gallery

Fontaine's Auction Gallery

TIP
To prevent spots, always dry silver before putting it away.

Silver Plate, Server, Breakfast, Open Handle, Fluted Legs, Paw Feet, Atkin Brothers, Late 1800s, 9 x 9 x 15 In.
$154

Silver Plate, Tray, George III, Arms Of Sire Wauter De Cornewaille Center, Sheffield, c.1800, 17 In.
$1,375

Locati Auctions

Charlton Hall Auctions

Austin Auction Gallery

Silver Plate, Plateau, Mirror, Cast Frame, Rocky Rise, Leaves, Mahogany Backing, 1880s, 2 x 15 In.
$204

Silver Plate, Soup Ladle, Fluted, Ebony Handle, Late 1700s, 12 ½ In.
$50

Silver-American, Bowl, Flower Border, Marked, Mauser Mfg., New York, c.1887, 5 In.
$875

Garth's Auctioneers & Appraisers

Eldred's

Charlton Hall Auctions

Beaker, Thimble, Gold Wash, Engraved, Only A Thimble Full, 2 In. 150
Biscuit Box, Hinged Lid, Footed, Lee & Wigfall, Sheffield, 1900s, 9 In. *illus* 256
Biscuit Box, Hinged Lid, Oval Cartouches, Floral, Ball Feet, Martin Hall & Co., 7½ In. *illus* 319
Biscuit Box, Lid, Shaped Finial, Underplate, Gilt, Glass Jar, England, 1800s, 9¾ In., Pair 1250
Biscuit Warmer, Hinged Lid, Shell Shape, Phoenix Mount Handle, England, Early 1900s, 10 In. *illus* 125
Bottle Stand, Syphon, Pierced Body, 2 Handles, Maxfield & Sons, 7¼ In. 35
Bowl, Cabbage Head, Gem Eyed Squirrel, Pedal Shape Base, Ball Feet, Derby, 9 x 8 In. 115
Bowl, Candara, Smooth Organic Form, Marked, Lino Sabattini, Italy, 4½ x 9¾ In. 24
Bowl, Vegetable, Oval, Open, Reeded Border, Meriden Britannia, 10½ In., Pair 384
Bread Basket, Reticulated, Lion Heads, Gadrooned Border, Ring Handles, Early 1900s, 4 x 12 In. 531
Butter, Cover, Bird Finial, Handle, Footed, Simpson, Hall & Miller, c.1890, 13 In. 35
Cake Plate, Art Deco, Undulating Rim, Marked, George A. Henckel & Co., 8¾ In. 177
Carafe, Coffee, Silver Plate, Oval, Rosewood, Art Deco, Stamped, Pairpoint, c.1925, 18 x 9 In. 75
Centerpiece, Calla Lily Center, Rope Rim Border, Tripod Stem, Base, Victorian, 13 x 9 In. 70
Centerpiece, Reticulated Bowl, Griffins, Glass Liner, Footed, 4½ In. *illus* 1408
Chalice, Gold Cup, Engraved, Tapered Stem, Domed Base, 10 In. 472
Charger, Chippendale Style, Serpentine, Gadroon Border, 12¼ In., 10 Piece 1063
Citrus Press, Curved Arm Support, Mounted, Black Marble Base, 11¾ In. *illus* 305
Cocktail Shaker, Bell, 3 Sections, Marked, Mappin & Webb, London, 1930s, 12 In. 2375
Cocktail Shaker, Dumbbell, Fitted Strainer, England, 1940s, 12 In. 2125
Cocktail Shaker, Figural, Golf Bag, Derby, International Silver Co., c.1935, 13½ In. 1750
Cocktail Shaker, Lighthouse Shape, Spurious Hallmarks, 13⅞ In. *illus* 427
Cocktail Shaker, Lighthouse, International Silver Co., c.1927, 15 In. 17500
Cocktail Shaker, Tells You How, Rotating Band, Ingredients, Napier, c.1934 3250
Compote, Cherubs Design & Finial, Bronze, Late 1800s, 11 In. 120
Compote, Dome Lid, Reticulated Fruit, Vine, Leaves, Cobalt Blue, Blown Glass Liner, 8⅝ In. 157
Compote, Openwork Rim, Cornucopia Shape Pedestal, Marked SWS, 1800s, 7 x 8 In. 585
Condiment Holder, Revolving Ferris Wheel, Bird, Leaves, Simpson, Hall & Miller, 1880s, 15 In. *illus* 556
Cover, Meat, Dome Lid, Vegetables, Fruit, Leaves, Franco Lapini, 9½ x 11¾ In. 218
Cover, Meat, Dome Shape, Oak Handle, Shell & Gadroon Border, Early 1800s, 16¼ In. *illus* 100
Decanter Frame, Woman, Turban, Supports, Pattern Edge, Paw Feet, 1880s, 19 In. 120
Desk Stand, Stag's Head Pen Rest, 2 Inkwells, James Dixon & Sons, Late 1800s, 3 x 10 x 8 In. 277
Dish, Lid, Red Cabochon Finial, Beaded, Arts & Crafts, Early 1900s, 9½ In. 1063
Dish, Rectangular, Brown, Footed, Hammered, Marked, Gerita, 1966, 7¼ x 3 In. 188
Dish, Shell Shape, Ball & Claw Feet, John Sherwood & Sons, 1850s, 3¾ In., 3 Piece 5953
Epergne, 2 Bowls, Ruffled Rim, Footed, Painted, Victorian, 23 In. 374
Epergne, 6 Candleholders, Ornate, Engraved, To Henry Browning Esq., 1866, 28 x 16 In. 690
Figurine, Ganesha, Hindu Deity, Elephant, Seated, India, 16½ In. 142
Figurine, Pelican, Textured, Pierced, Onyx Eyes, Christofle France, 4⅜ x 4½ In. 118
Frame, Dachshund Shape, Articulated, 6 Compartments, Signed, Hermes, c.1955, 3 x 11 In. 6875
Humidor, 2 Cherubs, Filigree Decor, Rectangular, Ball Feet, 1800s, 9½ x 11½ x 8 In. *illus* 224
Humidor, Lid, Kate Greenaway, Little Bo Peep, 2-Sided, Embossed Birds, Meriden, 5 x 9 x 5 In. 250
Ice Bucket, Embossed Shield, Scrolls, 2 Lion Head Handles, Victorian, 8¾ x 7½ In. 201
Ice Bucket, Stitched Leather Handle, Signed, Hermes, c.1985, 14½ In. *illus* 4063
Mirror, 2 Flanking Peacocks, Scrolled Feet, Marked Isis, 12 x 13½ In. 441
Mirror, Art Nouveau Decor, Reclined, Woman Bottom, WMF, 20 x 12 In. 882
Mirror, Lavender, Jasperware Plaque, Angel, Cherub, Continental, Early 1900s, 9½ In. *illus* 70
Pantry Box, Lid, Shaker Style, Black, Gilt Flowers, Gorham, 1900s, 2¾ x 3¼ In. 250
Pitcher, Applied Stone Iguana Handle, Bulbous Body, Hand Hammered, Los Castillo, 9 In. 384
Pitcher, Hinged Lid, Cut Glass, Mounted, DRGM, 10½ In. 59
Pitcher, Water, Set, Ornate, Victorian, Simpson, Hall, Miller & Co., 1880s, 23 x 17 x 10 In. *illus* 878
Pitcher, Wine, Mounted, Ornate, Etched Glass, WMF, Germany, Late 1800s, 14½ In. *illus* 384
Plateau, Mirror, Cast Frame, Rocky Rise, Leaves, Mahogany Backing, 1880s, 2 x 15 In. *illus* 204
Plateau, Mirror, Circular, 4 Paw Feet, Ball Border, Early 1900s, 16 In. 256
Plateau, Mirror, Rockwork Surround, Old Backboards, Elkington & Co., 1857, 17 In. *illus* 610
Plateau, Mirror, Round, Beveled, Engraved, Claw Feet, Victorian, 4 In. 374
Plateau, Mirror, Round, Frame, 15¼ In. 100
Plateau, Mirror, Straight Gadroon Border, Lion Feet, Sheffield, c.1815, 2½ x 26 x 16 In. 3416
Punch Ladle, Cut Glass, Signed, Libbey, Star & Feather, Dipper, Marked, 13¼ In. 150
Salt & Pepper, Apple, Leaves, Stand, Victorian, Hartford, c.1890, 7½ In. 81

Silver-American, Bowl, Flower Shape, Peaked Petals, Tripart Base, Cartier, c.1950, 5¼ In.
$213

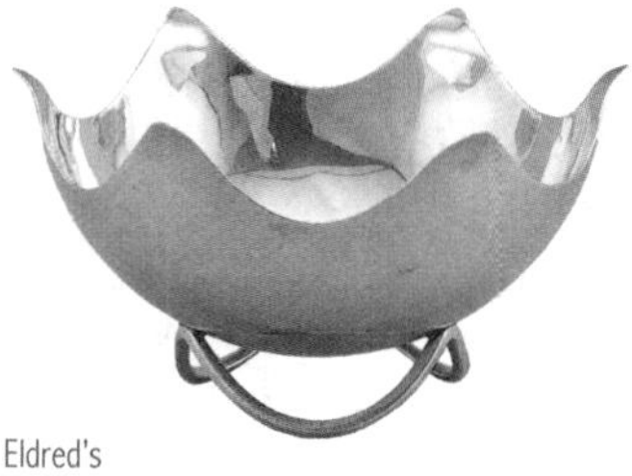

Eldred's

Invisible Mark?
A new technique called acoustical imaging can be used to make rubbed-out hallmarks on silver visible again. A special type of image similar to an ultrasound can show the slight compression of the metal where the silver was stamped with the hallmark. Sounds like a good tool for museums and the very, very serious collector.

Silver-American, Bowl, Footed, Roped Trim, Flowers, Marie Antoinette, Gorham, 4 x 12½ In.
$575

Pook & Pook

Silver-American, Bowl, Lid, Pomegranate Finial, Handles, Scrolled Feet, Monogram, Gorham, 1913, 8 In.
$679

Leland Little Auctions

S

Silver-American, Bowl, Shallow, Footed, Monogram, Marked, Frederick J. Gyllenberg, 2¾ In. $266

Bunch Auctions

Silver-American, Brandy Warmer, Bulbous, Spout, Turned Side Handle, Marked, John Hasselbring, 3¼ x 8 In. $125

Woody Auction

Silver-American, Centerpiece, Wide Scalloped Rim, Flowers, Repousse, Howard & Co., Late 1800s, 5 x 12 In. $1,404

Jeffrey S. Evans & Associates

Samovar, 2 Deer Head Handles, Putto Finial, Cabriole Legs, Late 1800s, 21 x 11 x 12 In. *illus*	284
Server, Breakfast, Open Handle, Fluted Legs, Paw Feet, Atkin Brothers, Late 1800s, 9 x 9 x 15 In. *illus*	154
Server, Dome Lid, Loop Handles, Neoclassical Design, Victorian, 9 x 10 In.	98
Server, Engraved, Handles, Footed, Mappin & Webb, 12¾ In.	100
Soup Ladle, Fluted, Ebony Handle, Late 1700s, 12½ In. *illus*	50
Spoon, Souvenir, see Souvenir category.	
Stand, Jewelry, 2 Cherubs, Swinging Box, Victorian, Marked, Reed & Barton, 14¾ In.	300
Tankard, Hinged Lid, Art Nouveau, Pierced Handle, WMF, Signed, A.K. & Cie, 14 In. ... *illus*	441
Tazza, Child, Standing, Dog, Aurora, Victorian, 6 In.	46
Teapot, Lid, Top Handle, Stand, Tray, Arts & Crafts, William R. Shirtcliffe & Son, Late 1800s, 11¾ In.	250
Tray, Footed, Ruffled Edge, Rectangular, Georgian, Marked, W.B., 14 In.	438
Tray, George III, Arms Of Sire Wauter De Cornewaille Center, Sheffield, c.1800, 17 In. . *illus*	1375
Tray, Grecian, Palmettes, Mahogany Stand, Meriden Britannia, Late 1800s, 20 x 34 In.	1534
Tray, Rectangular, Scalloped Edges, Marked, Sweden, 13½ x 18½ In.	813
Tray, Serving, Oval, Reeded Border, Paris, Christofle, 17 x 11¾ In.	123
Tray, Sheffield, Oval, Beaded Rim, George III, 2¾ x 23 In.	2360
Tray, Shell Pattern Edge, Monogram Center, Footed, Marked, Sheffield, 18¼ x 13 In.	62
Tray, Tea, Reeded Handles, Roped Edge, Feathered Scrolls, Pseudo Hallmarks, 20 x 31 In.	460
Tray, Warming, 2 Handles, Paw Feet, Rectangular, 15½ x 23½ In.	75
Tureen, Breakfast Warmer, Revolving, Hinged Dome Lid, Embossed, Egg Shape Dish, 11⅛ In.	94
Tureen, Lid, Engraved Armorial, Tray Insert, Shell Shape Handle, 1900s, 13 In.	125
Tureen, Lid, Greek Key, Egg & Dart Border, Beaded Handles, Monogram, Tiffany & Co., 12 x 16 In.	2772
Urn, Hot Water, Faucet, Shaped Handle, Mounted, Ball Feet, George III Style, 1800s, 23½ In.	358
Vase, Petal Type Flared Rim, Cloisonne, Gold Colored, Diaper Pattern Band, Late 1800s, 8 In.	1521
Warmer, Breakfast, Roll Top Dome, Solid & Pierced Inserts, Footed, Hukin & Heath, 14 In. .	83
Wine Cooler, Flared Rim, Pedestal Base, Scrollwork Design, Gorham, 10 In., Pair	354
Wine Cooler, Rococo Style Handles, Gadroon, Footed, 1800s, 10 In., Pair	338

SILVER-AMERICAN

American silver is listed here. Coin and sterling silver are included. Most of the sterling silver listed in this book is subdivided by country. There are also other pieces of silver and silver plate listed under special categories, such as Candelabrum, Napkin Ring, Silver Flatware, Silver Plate, Silver-Sterling, and Tiffany Silver. The meltdown price determines the value of solid silver items. Coin silver sells for less than sterling silver.

Gorham & Co. 1865+	International Silver Co. 1898–present	Reed & Barton Co. 1824–2015

Basket, 2 Handles, Bun Feet, Cut Glass, Engraved, 1891, 4½ x 6½ x 6¼ In.	219
Basket, Flowers, Flared Sides, Pierced Handle, Acanthus Scroll Feet, 19 x 11 x 9 In.	738
Basket, Fruit, Reticulated Body, Leafy Rim, Ferdinand Fuchs & Bros., c.1885, 12 In.	1250
Basket, Openwork Sides, Swing Handle, Beaded Edge, I.E. Caldwell & Co., 1850s, 9 x 7 In.	439
Basket, Oval, Handle, Engraved, Marked, Whiting, 1917, 7½ x 6¾ In.	188
Basket, Reticulated, Oval Bowl, Swing Handle, Marked, EB, GB, 1900s, 13½ x 7⅝ In.	375
Bowl, Art Nouveau, Shallow Lobed, Embossed Lilies, Flared Shaped Rim, 2 x 11 In.	427
Bowl, Chrysanthemum, Monogram, Marked, Duhme, 1900s, 3 x 14½ In.	512
Bowl, Engraved, Flower Drapery, Gilt, Dominick & Haff, 5 In.	472
Bowl, Flower Border, Marked, Mauser Mfg., New York, c.1887, 5 In. *illus*	875
Bowl, Flower Shape, Peaked Petals, Tripart Base, Cartier, c.1950, 5¼ In. *illus*	213
Bowl, Flower, Leaves, Scrolled Edge, Monogram, Marked, J.E. Caldwell, 14¼ In.	561
Bowl, Footed, Paul Revere Shape, International Silver Co., Mid 1900s, 6 In.	180
Bowl, Footed, Roped Trim, Flowers, Marie Antoinette, Gorham, 4 x 12½ In. *illus*	575
Bowl, Francis I, Oval, Leaf Bracket Feet, Reed & Barton, 1907, 3 x 15¼ x 11¾ In.	660
Bowl, Fruit, Fruits, Round, Orange Blossom, Wallace, 10 In.	260
Bowl, Grapevine, Footed, Monogram, Peter L. Krider & Co., 1800s, 6¼ In.	79

Bowl, Japonesque, Copper Cherries, Gilt, Gorham, 1881, 3 x 8½ x 8 In.	3520
Bowl, Jensen Style, Pedestal, Round Foot, Monogram, Genova Silver Co., 4½ In., Pair	570
Bowl, Lid, Pomegranate Finial, Handles, Scrolled Feet, Monogram, Gorham, 1913, 8 In. *illus*	679
Bowl, Lobed Body, Hand Wrought, Marked, 2¼ x 9½ In.	339
Bowl, Lobed Body, Molded Rim, Kalo Shop, 2⅛ x 6¼ In.	344
Bowl, Molded Rim, Gorham Mfg. Co., Early 1900s, 14 In.	715
Bowl, Paul Revere Style, Flared Rim, Pedestal Foot, National Silver Company, 4 x 8 In.	354
Bowl, Pedestal, Anthemion Border, Engraved Gothic, Gorham, 1878, 3¼ In.	366
Bowl, Repousse, Flowers, Engraved, Embossed, Stieff, 8¾ In.	295
Bowl, Repousse, Ornate Flowers, Stippled Ground, Pedestal, S. Kirk & Son, 1800s, 5 x 8 In.	1404
Bowl, Revere, Circular Foot, No. 227, Inscribed Fred H. Hill, Preisner, 7 In.	192
Bowl, Round, Footed, Reeded Border, Marked, Whiting, 4¼ x 9½ In.	563
Bowl, Scrolled Handles, Pedestal Base, Arts & Crafts, Theodore Hanford Pond, 4 In.	900
Bowl, Shallow, Footed, Monogram, Marked, Frederick J. Gyllenberg, 2¾ In. *illus*	266
Bowl, Shaped Rim, Applied Handles, Monogrammed, Ford & Tupper, c.1870, 6 x 12 In.	563
Bowl, Stepped Sides, Semi-Square, Monogram, Gorham, 1941, 2¼ x 9 x 9 In.	246
Bowl, Swag, Bell Flower, Marie Antoinette, Marked, Gorham, 1927, 3½ x 10¼ In.	512
Box, Lid, Carved Coral Rose Mount, Oval, Engraved, B.J.B., 1913, 1¼ x 1⅝ x 3⁹⁄₁₆ In.	1063
Brandy Warmer, Bulbous, Spout, Turned Side Handle, Marked, John Hasselbring, 3¼ x 8 In. *illus*	125
Bread Tray, Oval, Floral Pattern Rim & Handle, Marked, Webster Co., 1900s, 4 x 12 In.	132
Bread Tray, Reticulated, Molded Serpentine Rim, Monogram, Towle, 2⅜ x 10½ x 8 In.	192
Butter Knife, Master, Floral Engraved Blade, Medallion, Coin, Marked, WWH, 8 In.	104
Butter, Dome Cover, Oval, Handles, Engraved, 10 x 5 x 5 In.	2048
Cake Plate, Circular, Chased Border, Medallions, Engraved, Dominick & Haff, 12 In.	800
Candelabra are listed in the Candelabrum category.	
Candlesticks are listed in their own category.	
Card Case, Aesthetic Movement, Central Bird, Chain, Coin, c.1870, 3¾ x 2½ x ¼ In.	111
Centerpiece, Acorn Handle, Frederick W. Stark, International Silver Co., c.1937, 3½ In.	1820
Centerpiece, Charmont, Model No. 3143C, Flared Rim, Silver Plate Frog, International, 14 In.	974
Centerpiece, Crump & Low, Scrolling Leaves, Openwork Basket, Shreve, 1900s, 8 In.	780
Centerpiece, Elk Heads Handle, Flared Rim, Footed, Marked, Kidney & Johnson, 10½ In.	1888
Centerpiece, Wide Scalloped Rim, Flowers, Repousse, Howard & Co., Late 1800s, 5 x 12 In. *illus*	1404
Charger, Cast Grapevine Rim, Central Monogram, S. Kirk & Son Co., Early 1900s, 10¼ In.	344
Charger, Reticulated Rim, Marked, Graff, Washbourne & Dunn, c.1910, 1¾ x 18 x 19 In.	1188
Charger, Reticulated, Flowers, Leaves, Graff, Washbourne & Dunn, Early 1900s, 13½ In.	461
Cigarette Box, Lid, Mail Coach, Compartments, Gorham, 5¾ x 8½ x 4¾ In.	5120
Cocktail Shaker, Canted Sides, Curved Handle, S. Kirk & Son, 1950s, 9½ In.	450
Cocktail Shaker, Marked, Reed & Barton, Mid 1900s, 5½ In.	144
Cocktail Shaker, Trophy, Lake Forest Horse Show, R. Blackinton & Co., 1938, 11 In. *illus*	797
Coffeepot, Blossoms, Leaves, Eoff & Shephard, New York, c.1852-61, 11 x 9 x 6 In.	1169
Coffeepot, Dome Lid, Bird Finial, Pear Shape, Crest, Gooseneck, Coin, Wilson, c.1835, 11 In. *illus*	1000
Coffeepot, Engraved, Beaded, Hinged Lid, Finial, Wood & Hughes, c.1850, 12 In.	625
Compote, Classical Kylix Shape, Side Handles, Monogram, Gorham, Early 1900s, 4 x 9 In.	420
Compote, Lid, Repousse, Flowers, Engraved, J.E. Caldwell, 10¼ x 12 In.	2360
Compote, Ornate Body, Marked, Baldwin & Miller, 5 x 10 In.	406
Compote, Persian Pattern, Slender Stem, Tiered Base, International Silver, 1900s, 6½ In.	84
Compote, Ribbed Stem, Stepped Base, Towle, 6½ x 7¼ In., Pair	225
Compote, Step Base, Ribbed Stem, Fluted Rim, Reed & Barton, 1931, 3½ x 8⅛ In.	847
Creamer, Hinged Lid, Bull, Shreve & Co., 3⅜ x 5⅜ x 2 In.	738
Creamer, Shell Design, Engraved, Sproul, Coin, Marked, Bailey & Co., 1800s, 5¾ x 5¾ In.	224
Cup, Children, Marching, Instruments, Flag, Engraved, Early 1900s, 2¾ In.	125
Cup, Flowers, Angular Handle, Hollow Cast, Engraved, Coin, John A. Wiser, Gorham, c.1860, 3 In. *illus*	224
Dish, Octagonal Shape, Cut Corners, Marked, Alvin, 9½ In.	325
Dish, Octagonal, Repousse, Hand Wrought, Kalo Shop, 7 In. *illus*	500
Dish, Oval, Engraved, Flowers, Dominick & Haff, c.1881, 12¼ In.	438
Dish, Wedding Anniversary, Heart Shape, Ribbon Pattern, Footed, Gorham, c.1950, 3¾ In., Pair	48
Dresser Box, Hand Chased, Spider Webs, Stylized Flowers, Gorham, 5 x 16 x 7½ In. *illus*	3600
Ewer, Repousse, Floral, Footed, Applied Handle, Robert Rait, c.1840, 16 In.	1159
Ewer, Repousse, Grapevine Handle, Rim & Foot, Peter L. Krider & Co., 1800s, 15½ In., Pair *illus*	2806
Fish Server, Flower, Engraved, Embossed, Reed & Barton, Francis, 10½ In.	325

Silver-American, Cocktail Shaker, Trophy, Lake Forest Horse Show, R. Blackinton & Co., 1938, 11 In.
$797

Leland Little Auctions

Silver-American, Coffeepot, Dome Lid, Bird Finial, Pear Shape, Crest, Gooseneck, Coin, Wilson, c.1835, 11 In.
$1,000

New Orleans Auction Galleries

Silver-American, Cup, Flowers, Angular Handle, Hollow Cast, Engraved, Coin, John A. Wiser, Gorham, c.1860, 3 In.
$224

S

Neal Auction Company

Silver-American, Dish, Octagonal, Repousse, Hand Wrought, Kalo Shop, 7 In.
$500

Toomey & Co. Auctioneers

Silver-American, Dresser Box, Hand Chased, Spider Webs, Stylized Flowers, Gorham, 5 x 16 x 7 1/2 In.
$3,600

Cottone Auctions

Silver-American, Ewer, Repousse, Grapevine Handle, Rim & Foot, Peter L. Krider & Co., 1800s, 15 1/2 In., Pair
$2,806

Neal Auction Company

TIP
To loosen a silver saltshaker lid that is stuck to the glass shaker, immerse the top in white vinegar. Soak overnight.

Flagon, Hinged Lid, Cast Berries & Leaves, Flower Scrolls, Engraved, Gorham, 1886, 13 In...	5535
Goblet, Water, Flared Rim, Tapered Stem, Circular Foot, Whiting, c.1924, 6 1/2 In., 6 Piece	590
Goblet, Water, Francis I, Ernest Meyers, Reed & Barton, 1907, 6 In., 8 Piece	3750
Hip Flask, Hammered Finish, Engraved, Frank, Reed & Barton, 6 3/4 In...........................	266
Holder, Wine Bottle, Cagework Frame, Hinged Base, Gorham, Mark, 1904, 8 x 6 x 4 In., Pair	1845
Ice Tongs, Seesaw Rim, Brass, c.1935, 1/2 x 6 3/4 In.	313
Jar, Lid, Ball Finial, Repousse, Flowers, Leaves, Marked, Howard & Co., 3 3/4 In......................	236
Jar, Removable Lid, Glass, Ribbed, Floral Repousse, S. Kirk & Son, 1901, 6 x 5 In.	219
Jug, Pear Shape, Lid, Domed Base, Scroll Feet, Marked, S. Kirk, c.1880, 14 x 9 x 7 In.............	5228
Julep Cup, International, Lesley Willard Bissell, 3 1/4 In., 6 Piece........................	525
Julep Cup, Monogram, Banded Rim & Foot, S. Kirk & Son, 3 3/4 In., 10 Piece........................	2091
Julep Cup, Presidential, Richard Milhous Nixon, Beaded Rim, Mark J. Scearce, 3 3/4 x 3 In. ..	633
Ladle, Flowers & Leaves, J.E. Caldwell & Co., 11 1/2 In.	177
Loving Cup, 3 Handles, Presentation, Acid Etched, Church, Inscribed, Gorham, Late 1800s, 6 1/2 In..	625
Loving Cup, Gold Wash Interior, Figural Handle, Beaded Rim Border, Marked, Howard, 5 x 8 In.	175
Mug, Aesthetic Movement, Engraved Bird, Flowers, Whiting Mfg. Co., 3 1/4 x 3 x 4 1/4 In.	469
Mug, Blanche, Presentation, Coin, Landscape, Pedestal Base, George Lindner, c.1850, 5 In...*illus*	252
Mug, Embossed, Scroll Handle, Engraved Violet, Towle, 3 x 4 1/2 In.	70
Mug, Flowers, Engraved, Coin, John Wanamaker Duval, Child's, c.1850, 2 1/2 In.	130
Mug, Tyg, Presentation, Engraved, Curved Handle, Gorham, 1897, 6 5/8 In.............................	793
Napkin Rings are listed in their own category.	
Pepper Pot, Pierced Tops, Round Base, Coin, Monogram, N. Harding & Co., 1850s, 5 In., 2 Piece.	350
Pitcher Spoon, Hammered, Letter B, Marked, Kalo, 13 3/4 In.	219
Pitcher, Acanthus & Scroll Design, Engraved, Marked, Durgin, Detroit, 9 1/2 In. .... *illus*	812
Pitcher, Bead Rim, Embossed, Grapevine, Round Base, Jones, Shreve, Brown & Co., 1855, 11 In.	750
Pitcher, Flowers, Engraved, Marked, Lincoln & Foss, 9 3/4 x 8 1/2 In...........................	1063
Pitcher, Ornate, Engraved, Marked, J.E. Caldwell, Philadelphia, Early 1900s, 11 In. .... *illus*	688
Pitcher, Urn Shape, Grape, Vine, Wide Spout, Stepped Base, Marked, Gorham, Coin, 1850s, 9 In.	800
Pitcher, Water, Architectural, Engraved, S. Kirk & Son, 1896-1925, 15 x 8 x 6 In....................	3075
Pitcher, Water, Bulbous, Tapered Rim, Slanted Spout, Loop Handle, Gorham, 1956, 10 1/4 In. .*illus*	527
Pitcher, Water, Flowers & Wheat Repousse, Wide Spout, Footed, Coin, 1850s, 13 In.............	720
Pitcher, Water, Lilies Of The Valley, Monogram, Theodore B. Starr, N.Y., c.1900, 8 3/4 In. *illus*	688
Pitcher, Water, Pantheon Design, Monogram, Marked, J.S. Co., 9 1/2 In.	600
Pitcher, Water, Repousse, Grape Leaf, Scroll Handle, Coin, S.S. Cutler & Co., c.1850, 10 1/2 In..	3172
Pitcher, Water, Round Urn Shape, Scrolled Handle, Engraved, Hunt Silver Co., 42 1/2 In.	438
Pitcher, Water, Wide Spout, Colonial Line, Applied Handle, Marshall Field, 7 x 7 x 8 In. *illus*	813
Platter, Octagonal & Hexagonal Cartouche, Ridge & Scroll Design, Marked, Italy, 22 In.......	2124
Platter, Oval, Reeded Border, Wallace, 18 In..	488
Platter, Oval, Shaped Flange, Ribbon Style, Monogram, BCW, Reed & Barton, 16 x 11 In.	649
Punch Bowl, Grapevine, Stepped Panel Base, Reed & Barton, 8 x 12 1/2 In.	1098
Punch Bowl, Sons Of Liberty, Engraved, Massachusetts, Newbury Crafters, c.1950, 11 1/2 In.	1063
Punch Ladle, Fiddleback, Rattail Twist, Coin, Engraved, Marked, Duhme & Co., 12 In.........	345
Punch Set, Repousse Flowers, Footed, 12 Cups, S. Kirk & Son, Bowl, 7 x 14 In................	6150
Salad Servers, Fork & Spoon, Engraved, Reed & Barton, 9 In.	313
Salt & Pepper, Cylindrical, Allan Adler, c.1950, 2 1/4 In. .... *illus*	1000
Salt Cellar, Round, Flaring Base & Deep Well, Coin, Adrian Banker, 1750s, 1 1/4 x 3 In.	200
Sauceboat, Undertray, C-Scroll Handle, Marked, Whiting, 1900s, 5 In., Tray 6 In.	315
Serving Bowl, Flowers, Leafy Design, Beaded Rim, Watson Company, 10 In.	236
Serving Dish, Dome Lid, Flower Shape, Ring Finial, Monogram, Gorham, 5 x 10 In., Pair...	1062
Serving Spoon, Scalloped, Engraved, Embossed, 9 1/2 x 5 In.	161
Spoon, Apostle Handle, The Master, Engraved, Gorham, 1889, 7 5/8 In. .... *illus*	94
Spoon, Marriage, Engraved Leaves, Banding, Coin, Inscribed, OAS GED, 1740, 6 1/4 In.	75
Spoon, Reticulated, Engraved, Gorham, 9 1/4 x 5 5/8 In.	563
Sugar Tongs, Shell Pinchers, JNP In Cartouche, S. Drowne II, N.H., c.1790, 6 3/8 In..............	4690
Sugar, Lid, Swollen Top, Pineapple, J. & N. Richardson, Philadelphia, c.1795, 7 In...............	3660
Tazza, Engraved Initials, AMS, Marked, Gorham, 1941, 3 1/2 In., Pair........................	375
Tazza, Open Urn Shape, Bead Border, Handle, Shreve, Stanwood & Co., 1850s, 5 3/4 x 13 x 9 In....	896
Teapot, Baluster Shape, Handle, Spout, Finial, Kenilworth, International, 10 1/2 In...............	531
Teapot, Japanese Style, Circular Iron, Medallions, Spout, Stand, Marked, Gorham, 2 x 5 x 5 In..	3690
Toddy Ladle, Bifurcated Stem, Flaring Rim, Marked, J. Butler, Maine, c.1765, 14 In.	375
Tongs, Olive Branch Shape, Claw, Monogram, Gorham, 5 In..	34

Silver-American, Mug, Blanche, Presentation, Coin, Landscape, Pedestal Base, George Lindner, c.1850, 5 In.
$252

Brunk Auctions

Silver-American, Pitcher, Acanthus & Scroll Design, Engraved, Marked, Durgin, Detroit, 9½ In.
$812

Charlton Hall Auctions

Silver-American, Pitcher, Ornate, Engraved, Marked, J.E. Caldwell, Philadelphia, Early 1900s, 11 In.
$688

Charlton Hall Auctions

Silver-American, Pitcher, Water, Bulbous, Tapered Rim, Slanted Spout, Loop Handle, Gorham, 1956, 10¼ In.
$527

Jeffrey S. Evans & Associates

Silver-American, Pitcher, Water, Lilies Of The Valley, Monogram, Theodore B. Starr, N.Y., c.1900, 8¾ In.
$688

Eldred's

Silver-American, Pitcher, Water, Wide Spout, Colonial Line, Applied Handle, Marshall Field, 7 x 7 x 8 In.
$813

Toomey & Co. Auctioneers

Silver-American, Salt & Pepper, Cylindrical, Allan Adler, c.1950, 2¼ In.
$1,000

Wright

> **TIP**
> *Do not wrap silver in aluminum foil, news-paper, or plastic wrap. Never use rubber bands.*

Silver-American, Spoon, Apostle Handle, The Master, Engraved, Gorham, 1889, 7⅝ In.
$94

Leland Little Auctions

S

Silver-American, Tray, Oval, Cutout Handle, Reed & Barton, Stamped, 1 x 17 x 24½ In.
$1,750

Toomey & Co. Auctioneers

Silver-American, Tray, Oval, Shaped Edge, Scrolls, Leaves, Flowers, Dominick & Haff, 1902, 30½ In.
$3,690

Morphy Auctions

Silver-American, Vase, Applied Floral, Vine Handles, Ruffled Rim, George Shiebler & Co., 5¼ x 4 In.
$664

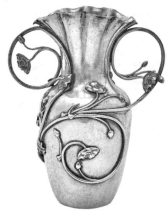

Treadway

Silver-American, Vase, Trumpet Shape, Weight Base, Sterling, Marked, Watson, 1900s, 10¼ In.
$123

Brunk Auctions

Tray, Chippendale Style Rim, Round, Engraved, M.L.W., Gorham, c.1962, 13¾ In.	878
Tray, Embossed, Scrolls & Flowers, Grape & Fruit Border, Gorham, 9¾ In.	236
Tray, Oval, Cutout Handle, Reed & Barton, Stamped, 1 x 17 x 24½ In. *illus*	1750
Tray, Oval, Repousse, Flowers, Engraved, Embossed, Stieff, 15 x 20½ In.	2478
Tray, Oval, Seafoam Border, Center Monogram, Marked, Whiting, 13¾ x 9½ In.	350
Tray, Oval, Shaped Edge, Scrolls, Leaves, Flowers, Dominick & Haff, 1902, 30½ In. *illus*	3690
Tray, Raised Rim, Oval, Webster Company, c.1950, 13½ In.	156
Tray, Repousse, Flowers, Leaves, Round, Marked, Charter & Co., 10½ In.	369
Tray, Reticulated, Aesthetic Fence, Bead Trim, Scroll Foot, Hoeker & Zoon, 1800s, 8 x 4 In.	142
Tray, Round, Engraved, Marked, Gorham, 9 In., Pair	201
Tray, Round, Molded Rim, Cartier, 1900s, 14 In.	688
Tray, Round, Piecrust Edge, Gedney Golf Club, Engraved, Poole Silver Co., 1951, 13½ In.	738
Tray, Round, Wrought, Lobe Sides, Monogram, KHR, Randahl, 10 In.	219
Tray, Serving, Castle Pattern, Repousse Rim, Monogram, Loring Andrews, Early 1900s, 27 x 19 In.	10880
Tray, Serving, Circular, Molded Edge, Marked, St. Louis Silversmith, Early 1900s, 21¼ In.	1560
Tray, Serving, NSDW & Co., 1910s, 20 x 14 In.	375
Tray, Serving, Oval, Whiting Manufacturing Co., c.1915, 9½ In.	384
Trophy, Cup, Scrolling Handles, Circular Foot, Marked, Mermod Jaccard & Co., c.1900, 7 In.	540
Trophy, Loving Cup, Hammered, Pedestal Base, 2 Handles, Muholland Brothers, 9 x 6 x 9 In.	374
Tureen, Lid, Oval, Flowers & Ferns, Loop Handle, Engraved, Jacobi & Jenkins, 12 x 15 x 9 In.	4725
Vase, Applied Floral, Vine Handles, Ruffled Rim, George Shiebler & Co., 5¼ x 4 In. *illus*	664
Vase, Landscape, Garden Scene, Architectural Elements, S. Kirk & Son, 13 x 5 x 5 In., Pair	2337
Vase, Trumpet Shape, Weight Base, Sterling, Marked, Watson, 1900s, 10¼ In. *illus*	123
Vase, Trumpet, Lid, Navarre Pattern, Watson Company, 17 In.	531

SILVER-ARABIAN

Ashtray, Coins, Maria Theresa Thaler Center, 3 Riyals Cigarette Rests, 3¾ In.	130

SILVER-ASIAN

Bowl, Hemispherical, Flowers, Peacocks, Scalloped Edge, Enamel, Bracket Feet, 5 x 9 x 9 In.	5535

SILVER-AUSTRIAN

Dish, Rococo Style, Floral Handle, Central Monogram, Marked VCD, Early 1900s, 14¼ In.	406
Ewer, Arabesque Spout, Vertical Panels, Lapis Lazuli, Hermann Boehm, Late 1800s, 7 In.	3750

SILVER-AUSTRO-HUNGARIAN

Bowl, Centerpiece, Lobed, Repousse, Flowers, 9½ In. *illus*	325
Sugar Box, Lid, Eagle Finial, Bulbous, Floral Cutwork, Pierced Feet, c.1872, 5½ x 5 In. *illus*	281
Vial, Perfume, Lid, Stopper, Chain, Cut Glass, 1800s, 2¾ In.	113

SILVER-BURMESE

Bowl, High Relief, Repousse, Tiger Attacking People & Animals, 2⅜ x 4 In.	144

SILVER-CHINESE

Bowl, Hand Chased, Banding Rim, Hallmark, 1800s, 2¾ In.	156
Box, Enamel, Gilt, Quail Shape, Filigree Feathers, 3¼ x 4¾ In., Pair	767
Box, Round, Engraved Dragons, Vermeil Interior, Tuck Chang, Late 1800s, 2 x 3 In.	60
Frame, Tabletop, Oval, Scrolling Flowers, 1900s, 9 x 10 In.	219
Ice Bucket, Repousse, 2 Handles, Octofoil Lobed Shape, Engraved, Embossed, Early 1900s, 7 In.	230
Mustard Pot, Hinged Lid, Barrel Shape, Dragons, Glass Insert, Early 1900s, 2¼ In. *illus*	188
Shot Glass, Cylindrical, Tapering Shape, Stippling Exterior, Hallmark, Late 1800s, 2 In.	36
Tray, Presentation, Ruffled Rim, Embossed Dragon Border, Zee Woo, Late 1800s, 6 In. *illus*	120
Vase, Owl & Birds, Perched, Blossom Branches, 2 Handles, Domed Base, Late 1800s, 31½ In.	1800

SILVER-CONTINENTAL

Beaker, 3 Coins, Mounted, Horizontal Bands, Bun Feet, Late 1800s, 4 In.	531
Bowl, Serving Pieces, Removable Lid, Loop Finial & Handle, Leaves, 8 In., Pair	8400
Charger, Repeated Shields, Crowned Lions Rim, Marked, 1900s, 16 In. *illus*	800
Punch Ladle, Turned, Ebonized Wood Handle, Shaped Bowl, Marked FW, 16 In.	81
Tankard, Central Medallion, Coat Of Arms, Coin Mounted, England, 1800s, 7½ In.	1188
Tray, Oval, Pierced Gallery, Handles, Scrolling Feet, Marked, 2 x 9¾ In.	500
Vase, Flowers, Painted, Gilt, White Ground, Guilloche Enamel, c.1900, 8½ In. *illus*	738
Vase, Hand Painted, Maiden & Cherub, Green Guilloche Ground, Enamel, 1800s, 12 x 4 In.	563

SILVER-DANISH

Georg Jensen is the most famous Danish silver company.

| Georg Jensen 1925–1932 | Georg Jensen 1933–1944 | Georg Jensen 1945–present |

Bowl, Georg Jensen, No. 414C, Flared Rim, Round Foot, c.1930, 8⅝ In.	938
Box, Hinged Lid, Circular, Georg Jensen, 4¼ In.	325
Coffeepot, Lid, Finial, Art Nouveau, Oval, Bone Handle, Georg Jensen, 7¾ x 8 x 5 In.	1287
Compote, Flared Bowl, Openwork Support, Stepped Foot, Georg Jensen, 1945, 5½ x 5¾ In.	976
Compote, Shell, Handle, Grapes, Leaves, Berries, Circular Base, Georg Jensen, 4 In.	2520
Pin, Grape Shape, Engraved, Embossed, Georg Jensen, Denmark, 1945, 1½ In.	125
Pitcher, Wood Handle, Beaded, Ropetwist Borders, Georg Jensen, Marked, 8 In.	3780
Salt & Pepper, Blossom, Spoon, Marked, Georg Jensen, 2½ In., Pair	438
Sauce Ladle, Curved Handle, Leafy, Georg Jensen, 1900s, 8 In. *illus*	138
Sauce Ladle, Hammered, Floral Handle, Marked, Grann & Laglye, 5⅛ In.	63
Serving Dish, Oval Lid, Grape Cluster Finial, Handle, Georg Jensen, 5¾ x 7 x 10⅝ In.	3125
Spoon, Pear Shape, Spiral Twist Stems, Openwork Handles, P. Hertsz, 11¼ In., Pair	94
Tazza, Shallow Bowl, Serrated Rim, Pedestal Foot, Georg Jensen, c.1940, 1⅜ x 3¾ In.	71
Tea & Coffee Set, Blossom Pattern, Georg Jensen, Kettle, Teapot, Spoons, 12 Piece	9150
Vase, Circular, Flaring Top, Stepped Foot, Georg Jensen, 1926-32, 8 x 5 x 5 In.	4095

SILVER-DUTCH

Box, Beaded Lid & Base, Round, Hendrik Nieuwenhuys, 1784, 3 x 5⅛ In. *illus*	850
Box, Hinged Lid, Repousse, Rectangular, 3½ x 14 x 5 In.	885
Tea Canister, Chased Figures, Playing Instrument, Paw Feet, Marked HH, c.1930, 5¼ In.	375
Tray, Round, Reticulated Gallery, Footed, Marked AHP, 1800s, 12¾ In.	938

SILVER-ENGLISH

English sterling silver is marked with a series of four or five small hallmarks. The standing lion mark is the most commonly seen sterling quality mark. The other marks indicate the city of origin, the maker, the year of manufacture, and the king or queen. These dates can be verified in many good books on silver. These prices are partially based on silver meltdown values.

| Standard quality mark | City mark – London | Date letter mark |

| Maker's mark |  | Sovereign's head mark |

Basket, George II, Pierced Trellis & Leaves, Shell & Scroll Border, E. Wakelin, 1751, 15 In.	4788
Basket, George III, Oval, Ribbed, Handle, Footed, Engraved, London, 1802, 4½ x 14 x 10 In.	563
Biscuit Box, Warmer, Ornate, Plated, 3-Sided, Handle, Late 1800s, 10 x 8¾ In. *illus*	316
Bowl, Engraved Coat Of Arms, Armorial, Openwork, Marked W, 1790s, 10⅜ In.	531
Bowl, Footed, Seashells, Scrolled Feet, Vermeil, Hunt & Roskell, 1901, 2½ x 4½ In. *illus*	420
Box, Rectangular, Street Scene, Hinged Lid, Foliage, Arts & Crafts, London, 1901, 3 x 5 x 3 In.	4613
Bread Tray, Incurved Sides, Footed, Ivory Handles, Charles Boyton, 1938, 14 In. *illus*	1197
Cake Basket, Engraved Coat Of Arms, Swing Handle, Samuel Herbert & Co., George II, 1754, 14 In.	2750
Cake Basket, Leafy, Engraved, Crichton Brothers, George V, 1917, 14 In. *illus*	1125
Candelabra are listed in the Candelabrum category.	
Candlesticks are listed in their own category.	
Card Case, Cathedral, Engine Turned, Edward Thomason, Victorian, 1848, 2½ x 3¾ In.	185

Silver-Austro-Hungarian, Bowl, Centerpiece, Lobed, Repousse, Flowers, 9½ In.
$325

Austin Auction Gallery

Silver-Austro-Hungarian, Sugar Box, Lid, Eagle Finial, Bulbous, Floral Cutwork, Pierced Feet, c.1872, 5½ x 5 In.
$281

Charlton Hall Auctions

Silver-Chinese, Mustard Pot, Hinged Lid, Barrel Shape, Dragons, Glass Insert, Early 1900s, 2¼ In.
$188

Selkirk Auctioneers & Appraisers

This is an edited listing of current prices. Visit Kovels.com to check thousands of prices from previous years and sign up for free information on trends, tips, reproductions, marks, and more.

Silver-Chinese, Tray, Presentation, Ruffled Rim, Embossed Dragon Border, Zee Woo, Late 1800s, 6 In.
$120

Garth's Auctioneers & Appraisers

Silver-Continental, Charger, Repeated Shields, Crowned Lions Rim, Marked, 1900s, 16 In.
$800

Locati Auctions

Silver-Continental, Vase, Flowers, Painted, Gilt, White Ground, Guilloche Enamel, c.1900, 8 ½ In.
$738

Leland Little Auctions

Silver-Danish, Sauce Ladle, Curved Handle, Leafy, Georg Jensen, 1900s, 8 In.
$138

Eldred's

> **TIP**
> Never drain silver
> on a rubber mat. It will
> tarnish faster.

Silver-Dutch, Box, Beaded Lid & Base, Round, Hendrik Nieuwenhuys, 1784, 3 x 5 ⅛ In.
$850

Pook & Pook

Silver-English, Biscuit Box, Warmer, Ornate, Plated, 3-Sided, Handle, Late 1800s, 10 x 8 ¾ In.
$316

Blackwell Auctions

Silver-English, Bowl, Footed, Seashells, Scrolled Feet, Vermeil, Hunt & Roskell, 1901, 2 ½ x 4 ½ In.
$420

Garth's Auctioneers & Appraisers

Silver-English, Bread Tray, Incurved Sides, Footed, Ivory Handles, Charles Boyton, 1938, 14 In.
$1,197

Morphy Auctions

> **TIP**
> Empty your silver
> saltshaker after every
> party to avoid corrosion.

Silver-English, Cake Basket, Leafy, Engraved, Crichton Brothers, George V, 1917, 14 In.
$1,125

Eldred's

S

Card Case, Sir Walter Scott Monument, Etched Scroll, Nathaniel Mills, 1843, 3 x 2 In...	923
Chalice, Gilt, Floral, Knopped Stem, Domed Base, George William Adams, Chawner & Co., 5 In. ..*illus*	944
Charger, Engraved Armorial Rim, Richard Garrard, 1840, 11 ½ In.	625
Chocolate Pot, Ornate Repousse, Chinese Woman Gathering Flowers, George III, 1795, 12 In. ..*illus*	1610
Cigarette Case, Envelope Shape, Pence Stamp, Engraved, N.C. Goodwin Jr, c.1880, 3 x 2 x 3 In..	468
Coffeepot, Baluster Body, Repousse, Ebony Handle, William Grundy, Georgian, c.1760, 11 In.	1100
Coffeepot, Chased Flowers, Armorial, Timothy Smith, Thomas Merryweather, George IV, 1824, 10 In.	688
Coffeepot, Lighthouse Shape, Baroque Heraldry, Wood Handle, Edward Feline, 1727, 7 In. ..*illus*	2375
Cover, Meat, Octagonal, Engraved Coat Of Arms, John Edwards III, 1801, 6 x 9 In., Pair........	1125
Creamer, Bright Cut, Engraved Leaves, Peter & William Bateman, c.1812, 3 ¾ In. .... *illus*	406
Cruet Set, 2 Cruets, Handles, Stand, Motto, Thomas Haming, George III, 1775, 9 x 11 In......	1585
Cup, Dome Lid, Baroque Style, Engraved, George Fox, London, 1902, 7 x 5 x 5 In.	3780
Demitasse Spoon, Fitted Case, Marked, Henry Clifford Davis, 1920, 4 ⅛ In......................	59
Desk Stand, 2 Glass Ink Pots, Candlestick, Gadroon Border, Bun Feet, Late 1800s, 8 x 12 In. .	207
Desk Stand, Oak, Plate, Bell, 2 Candleholders, 2 Ink Pots, Ball Feet, 1800s, 18 In.............	128
Desk Stand, Urn Center, Monogram, 2 Glass Bottles, Henry Wilkinson & Co., Sheffield, 1852, 7 In....	660
Dish, Meat, Oval Shape, Gadroon Rim, Engraved, Andrew Fogelberg, London, 1772, 16 x 21 In. .	2214
Dresser Box, Tortoiseshell Lid, 4 Applied Feet, Leather Bottom, Mappin & Webb, 3 In.	127
Ewer, Hinged Lid, Georgian, Gadroon, Spiral Knop, David Whyte, William Holmes, 1766, 11 In..	550
Fish Slice, Fiddle Handle, Pierced Blade, Albert Hernu, 1891, 11 ½ In................................	90
Frame, Picture, Elizabeth II, 1993, 5 ½ x 6 ⅝ In..	224
Goblet, Flowers, Chasing, Domed Foot, Monogram, London, 1807, 5 ½ In.........................	120
Hot Water Urn, Gadroon Shape Body, Pineapple Finial, Monogram, TAJ, George III, 1759, 20 In.	2304
Hot Water Urn, Reeded Legs, Lion Head & Ring Handle, Paul Storr, George III, 1804, 16 In.	5250
Hot Water Urn, Squat Urn, Stop Gadroon, 4 Terminals, Ball Feet, George III, 1798, 16 In. ..*illus*	3125
Humidor, Hinged Lid, Engraved Leaves, Mahogany Lining, 1907, 7 ½ x 9 ½ x 6 ¾ In............	390
Kettle, Hot Water, Dome Lid, Bulbous Shape, Ringed Handles, 16 In.	125
Kettle, Hot Water, Wood Handle, Tripod Base, Charles Stuart Harris, 1900s, 15 In. .... *illus*	2000
Kettle, Pear Shape, Engraved, Swing Handle, Shell Pad Feet, John Payne, 1767, 17 ¼ In.	2768
Kettle, Rococo Repousse, Scroll Legs, Stand, Walter & Charles Sissons, 1898, 14 x 7 x 10 In..	1169
Ladle, Engraved Crest, William Sumner, George III, 1794, 13 In...................................	115
Ladle, Onslow, Engraved Armorial, Arm Grasping Sword, Marked WC, George III, 1761, 6 In., Pair	238
Lamp, Circular, Dart Rim, Hinged Lid, Engraved, J.C. Edington, London, 1861, 8 x 3 x 3 In. .	1134
Marrow Spoon, Georgian, 8 ½ In..	175
Muffineer, Sugar Shaker, Pierced, Alstons & Hallam, 1939, 7 ½ In..................................	201
Mug, Acanthus Leaf, Cast Scroll Handle, Thomas Whipham, George III, 1765, 4 ¾ In.	344
Mug, Engraved, Arms & Crest, Marked, Gabriel Sleath, London, George I, 1725, 4 ¼ In.	1890
Mug, Repousse Design, Flowers, Handle, Footed, Engraved, George IV, London, 1819, 6 In. ...*illus*	375
Mustard Pot, Hinged Lid, Blue Glass Insert, Ball Feet, Barker Bros., Late 1900s, 2 ¼ In.	72
Napkin Rings are listed in their own category.	
Pitcher, Garland & Ribbon, Thomas Wallis & Jonathan Haynes, William IV, 1830, 12 In.	2500
Pitcher, Trophy, Bulbous, Hunting Scene, Marked, Elkington & Co., Birmingham, 1897, 13 ½ In.	4800
Pitcher, Water, Bulbous, Scroll Handle, Floral, Thomas Whitman & Charles Wright, 1764, 7 In..	512
Plate, Gadroon Border, Crested Cavetto, George III, London, 1808, 9 ¾ In. .... *illus*	427
Plate, Michelangelo's Pieta, Danbury & Yorkshire Mint, c.1974, 9 In.	266
Platter, Gadroon & Shell Cast Border, Paul Storr, 1810, 12 ⅛ x 15 ¼ In........................	2684
Porringer, Snakes, Ball Handle, Cast, Queen Elizabeth II, Maiden Voyage, 1966, 1 x 4 x 3 In. ....*illus*	84
Salt & Pepper, 4 Ball Feet, Edgar Finlay & Hugh Taylor, Birmingham, 1883, 2 ⅜ In.	165
Salt Cellar, Beaded Rim, Cast Feet, Engraved, George Fox, London, 1883, 2 x 3 x 3 In.	416
Salt, Open, Bright Cut, Engraved Sides, Bracket Feet, Marked TH, George III, 1792, 3 ¼ In.	150
Salt, Reeded Body, Gadroon, Shell Border, Round, Marked, 1807, 2 x 5 x 3 ¾ In., Pair	308
Salver, Engraved Arms, Rococo Cartouche, Footed, Dorothy Mills, George II, 1753, 23 In......	5292
Salver, Lobed, Beadwork Rim, Engraved, Footed, Martin, Hall & Co., c.1872, 10 In.	708
Salver, Oval, Flowers, Rococo, Beaded Rim, Engraved, William Laver, London, 1790, 19 x 14 x 1 In..	2091
Salver, Oval, Reeded Rim, Splayed Feet, Robert Hennell, George III, 1787, 6 ¾ In................	125
Salver, Piecrust Edge, Slipper Feet, Engraved Reserve, John Tuite, Georgian, 1737, 6 In........	375
Salver, Shallow, Gadroon, Shell Border, Heraldic Device, Marked, Paul Storr, 1808, 15 In.....	6150
Spoon, Apostle, Figural Terminal, Fig Shape, Marked RH, George II, 1750s, 7 ⅝ In..............	688
Stand, Teapot, Oval, Gadroon Border, 4 Scroll Feet, Edinburgh, 1806, 3 x 6 In.	256
Stirrup Cup, Fox Head, Engraved, C.T. & G, London, 1864, 4 ¾ In. ....*illus*	5228

Silver Numbers

Numbers such as 800 or 900 are used to indicate the quality of the silver in some European countries. Pieces marked 800 are considered solid silver and are usually German, Italian, or Russian. At least 925 parts out of 1,000 must be silver to be considered solid or sterling silver in the United States or England.

S

Silver-English, Coffeepot, Lighthouse Shape, Baroque Heraldry, Wood Handle, Edward Feline, 1727, 7 In.
$2,375

Charlton Hall Auctions

Silver-English, Creamer, Bright Cut, Engraved Leaves, Peter & William Bateman, c.1812, 3 ¾ In.
$406

Eldred's

Silver-English, Hot Water Urn, Squat Urn, Stop Gadroon, 4 Terminals, Ball Feet, George III, 1798, 16 In.
$3,125

Eldred's

Silver-English, Kettle, Hot Water, Wood Handle, Tripod Base, Charles Stuart Harris, 1900s, 15 In.
$2,000

Pook & Pook

Silver-English, Mug, Repousse Design, Flowers, Handle, Footed, Engraved, George IV, London, 1819, 6 In.
$375

Susanin's Auctioneers & Appraisers

Silver-English, Plate, Gadroon Border, Crested Cavetto, George III, London, 1808, 9 ¾ In.
$427

Neal Auction Company

Silver-English, Porringer, Snakes, Ball Handle, Cast, Queen Elizabeth II, Maiden Voyage, 1966, 1 x 4 x 3 In.
$84

Garth's Auctioneers & Appraisers

TIP
Use your silver often. It will tarnish less.

Silver-English, Stirrup Cup, Fox Head, Engraved, C.T. & G, London, 1864, 4 ¾ In.
$5,228

Morphy Auctions

S

Stuffing Spoon, Armorial, George William Adams, Chawner & Co., 1849, 12 In., Pair . *illus* 238
Sugar Castor, Lid, Square Foot, Tiffany & Company, Birmingham, c.1956, 8 ¼ x 2 ¾ In. ... *illus* 236
Sugar Castor, Lighthouse Shape, Dome Lid, Engraved, Mark, Thomas Rush, George III, 1734, 6 ¾ In. 150
Sugar Castor, Paneled Baluster Shape, Pedestal Foot, George III, 9 ⅛ In., Pair 732
Sugar Nips, Flower Branch, Bees, Beetles, Marked, John Hunt, London, 1837, 5 ⅝ In., Pair 504
Sugar Nips, Gilt, Shells, Leaves, Patricia Schuckmann, George I, c.1740, 5 In., Pair 378
Sugar Nips, Harlequin Shape, Snakes, Shell Bowls, William, Barrett, London, 1812, 4 In., Pair .. *illus* 882
Sugar Nips, Stork Shape, Applied Foot, Ely & Fearn, London, George II, 1808, 4 ¾ In., Pair.. 630
Taperstick, Flower Shape Mid Drip Pan, Footed, 1733, 2 ⅛ x 4 ¼ In., Pair 3904
Tazza, Gold Wash, Engraved, Cockatrice, Dragon, William Burwash, Georgian, 1813, 4 x 11 In.. 1150
Teapot, Coat Of Arms, Engraved, Chased Design, Robert Hennell, London, George III, 1700s, 5 ½ In. 600
Teapot, Engraved, Wood Handle, Finial, Ball Feet, Charles Fox, George III, 1813, 5 x 11 x 4 In. ... 468
Teapot, Hinged Lid, Finial, Lighthouse Shape, Ebony Handle, Solid, 8 ½ In. 300
Teapot, Hinged Lid, Wood Handle, Engraved John Langlands, Newcastle, 1795, 6 ¾ In. *illus* 575
Teapot, Lighthouse Shape, Engraved Armorial, Wood Handle, Gurney & Cook, 1731, 9 In. ... *illus* 2196
Teapot, Squat Oval, Rosette Finial, Gadroon Border, Ball Feet, Charles Price, 1817, 6 x 11 In.. 425
Teapot, Wood Handle, String Wrapped, Cymric, Liberty & Co., Impressed L&Co, 1900, 4 x 7 x 5 In. 504
Tray, Beaded Rim, Footed, Monogram, Sampson Mordan, A.M. Savory & Sons, 1864, 1 x 7 ¼ In. . *illus* 150
Tray, Gadroon Border, Scrolls, Leafy Handles, Atkin Brothers, Sheffield, Late 1800s, 27 In.... 148
Tray, Reticulated, Scrolled Handles, Ball Feet, Mappin & Webb, Sheffield, Late 1800s, 3 x 26 In. . 413
Tray, Scalloped Rim, Scrolls, Shell, Footed, William Barret II, George III, 1820, 14 In. 2106
Tray, Serving, Rectangular, Rounded Corner, Reeded Rim, James Dixon & Sons, 1922, 24 x 15 In.. 1989
Trinket Box, Lid, Guilloche, Lavender, Gold Inlay, Liberty & Co., 1910, 1 x 3 ½ In. 384
Trinket Box, Removable Lid, Inlaid, Gold Velvet, William Comyns & Sons, 1 ½ x 2 x 2 ¾ In. 165
Trophy Cup, Lid, Coursing, Neoclassical Style, Urn Shape, Engraved, Barnard Bros., London, 1864 1475
Trophy, Dome Lid, Campana Shape, Acanthus, 2 Handles, Gilt, 1817, 15 ½ x 8 ¼ In. 6765
Trophy, Urn Shape, Handles, Engraved, Gibson & Langman, London, 1888, 29 ½ x 14 In..... 4613
Urn, Georgian, Cobalt Blue Liner, Ball Feet, Monogram, Ellis Jacob Greenberg, 13 x 6 In., Pair... 2280
Urn, Lid, 2 Handles, Engraved, New York Racing Association, London, 1958, 8 ½ x 7 ½ In. ... 438
Urn, Lid, Angel Finial, Ribbed, Leafy, Lyre Lip Border, Snake Handles, 1921, 9 ½ In. 1020
Vinaigrette, Hinged Lid, Bloodstone Inset, Pierced Grill, Gilt, ⅝ x 1 ¾ x 1 ½ In. .... *illus* 183
Waiter, Ruffled Rim, Engraved, Cartouche, Ebenezer Coker, 1764-65, 10 x 10 x 1 In., Pair.... 923
Waste Bowl, Acanthus Leaf, Repousse, Gadroon Foot, 1797, 3 x 5 In. 338
Wick Trimmer, Scissors, Candle, Applied Snuffer, Pierced Handle, Benjamin May, 1783, 1 x 6 In. *illus* 250
Wine Coaster, Armorial, Scalloped Beaded Rim, Hester Bateman, George III, 1788, 4 ¾ In., Pair *illus* 2125
Wine Cooler, Campana Shape, Removable Insert, Floral Accented Rim, Twin Handles, 11 In., Pair 708
Wine Cooler, Removable Liner, Rococo Style, Molded Handles, Early 1800s, 10 x 12 x 8 In., Pair . 439

SILVER-FRENCH

Beaker, Flaring Rim, Gold Wash, Louis XVI, Mark, Paris, 1784, 2 ½ In. 163
Chalice, Clover Shape Base, Etched, Religious Scene, Panels & Quotes, Stones Inset, 10 In. .. 1875
Claret Jug, Cut Glass, Gilt, Handle, Finial, Marked, Louis Coignet, Paris, c.1890, 11 ¾ In...... 4788
Claret Jug, Dome Lid, Baluster Shape, Shields, Paris c.1880-1900, 15 In. 2460
Claret Jug, Dome Lid, Etched, Enamel, Baluster Shape Glass, Victor Saglier, c.1900, 9 In. *illus* 325
Creamer, Scrolled Handle & Feet, Charles-Alexandre Lavallee, Late 1800s, 4 ¾ In. 325
Demitasse Spoon, Les Phagocytes, Claude Lalanne, c.1991, 4 In., 8 Piece 4063
Fruit Knife, Hollow Handle, Neoclassical Design, 7 ⅞ In., 2 Piece 59
Pitcher, Globular, Roses, Engraved, Embossed, Mark, c.1890, 7 x 7 ½ x 6 ½ In., Pair 2460
Sauceboat, Leafy, Attached Undertray, Belle Epoque, 4 ¼ x 10 In. 427
Scoop, Pierced, Intricate Openwork, Reticulated Scoop, Minerva Mark, 1800s, 8 In. 81
Tureen, Dome Lid, Entwined Serpent Finial, Gadroon Rim, Ball Feet, 1800s, 9 ½ In. .. *illus* 1952
Tureen, Lid, Stylized Handles, Round Stepped Base, Weevil Mark, 1800s, 10 ½ In. 875
Tureen, Soup, Dome Lid, Egg & Dart Borders, Pierre-Marie Devilleclair, 1812, 12 x 17 x 9 In. 9150
Vase, Dome Lid, Pear Shape, Flat Chased Rim, Wood Scroll Handle, Splayed Feet, c.1790, 10 In. 5040
Vase, Presentation, Japanese Prince Takamatsu To Admiral Pratt, U.S.N. 1931, 10 x 5 In. 2691

SILVER-GERMAN

Basket, Bonbon, Scalloped Edge, Openwork Rim, Glass Insert, W.T. Binder, Early 1900s, 5 x 4 In. 38
Basket, Hanau Style, Rococo Floral & Garland Decor, Swing Handle, 10 x 5 ⅜ In. .... *illus* 236
Basket, Reticulated, 4 Putti, Flowers, Repousse, 2 ¾ x 12 In. 325
Beaker, Cherubs, Ornate, Flared Rim, Engraved, Keck & Schwarz, c.1900, 6 ⅜ In. .... *illus* 316

Silver-English, Stuffing Spoon, Armorial, George William Adams, Chawner & Co., 1849, 12 In., Pair
$238

Eldred's

Silver-English, Sugar Castor, Lid, Square Foot, Tiffany & Company, Birmingham, c.1956, 8 ¼ x 2 ¾ In.
$236

Austin Auction Gallery

Silver-English, Sugar Nips, Harlequin Shape, Snakes, Shell Bowls, William, Barrett, London, 1812, 4 In., Pair
$882

Sotheby's

S

Silver-English, Teapot, Hinged Lid, Wood Handle, Engraved John Langlands, Newcastle, 1795, 6¾ In.
$575

Pook & Pook

Silver-English, Teapot, Lighthouse Shape, Engraved Armorial, Wood Handle, Gurney & Cook, 1731, 9 In.
$2,196

Pook & Pook

Silver-English, Tray, Beaded Rim, Footed, Monogram, Sampson Mordan, A.M. Savory & Sons, 1864, 1 x 7¼ In.
$150

Woody Auction

TIP

If you have silver in an enclosed case, add a few mothballs to retard tarnishing.

Beaker, Lid, Parcel Gilt, 3 Busts, Tiberius, Julius Caesar, Vespanian, Marked BR, c.1710, 6 In...	5670
Bowl, 3-Footed Figural Base, 3 Swans, Upraised Wings, Marked, Knewitz, 5⅞ x 7¾ In.	403
Bowl, Beaded Rim & Base, Footed, Philipp Friedrich Bruglocher, Augsburg, 1900s, 3 In.......	300
Bowl, Openwork, Glass Liner, Flowers, Scrolled Feet, Storck & Sinsheimer, 1800s, 5¾ x 7 In. *illus*	380
Bowl, Round, Swirl Design, Footed, Engraved, 3 x 9½ In.	344
Chalice, Gilt, Leaves, Circular Base, 4 Portraits, Apostles, R. Bruun-Munster, 8 In.	2250
Cigarette Case, Rotating Medallion, St. George, Enamel Panel, Nude Woman, Gas, 1900s, 3 In.	500
Cocktail Shaker, Figural, Owl, Faux Beak Spout, Stopper, Ludwig Neresheimer Co., 8 In.	5250
Cocktail Shaker, Tavern Scenes, Rococo, Handles, Dolphins, Leaves, Gilt, c.1900, 11 In., Pair......	3024
Coffeepot, Hinged Lid, Long Spout, Loop Handle, Fluted Well, Marked, 1910s, 9⅝ In.	380
Cup, Wager, Male, Standing, Robes, Terrain Base, Marked, I Freeman & Son, 14 x 5 x 4 In. ..*illus*	2768
Figurine, Cherub & Wheelbarrow, Ornate, Engraved, 3 In.	201
Figurine, Knight On Horseback, Hardstone Accent, Marked, Hanau, 1900s, 12¼ x 7½ In...	5313
Salt & Pepper, Figural, Dutch Boy & Girl, Karl Sohnlein, Sohne Hanau, c.1900, 4 In. *illus*	473
Spoon, Peasant Woman, Bowl Repousse, Fruit, Engraved, Marked N & BM, Hanau, 8¾ In. ..	75
Tray, Serving, Oval, Scalloped Rim, Stamped, Handarbeit, Gayer & Krauss, 19½ In.............	708

SILVER-IRISH

Dish Ring, Potato, Pierced Repousse Figures, Animal, Monogram, Rocaille, 1899, 3 x 8 In. .*illus*	625
Dish Ring, Rocaille C-Scrolls, Cartouche, James Wakely & Frank Clark Wheeler, 1899, 7 In.	938
Goblet, 3 Handles, Hammered, Elkington & Co. Ltd., Edward VII, 1902, 6¾ In......	375

SILVER-ITALIAN

Box, Strawberry Shape, Lid, Leaves & Stem, Marked, Giulia Vischio, Venice, c.1940, 21 In.	8820
Centerpiece, 3 Dishes, Leaf Shape, Branch Handle, Marked, Gianmaria Buccellati, 1900s, 17 In.	5670
Centerpiece, Shell Shape, Hammered, Sea Star Feet, Marked, Buccellati, 1900s, 5 x 17 In. ....*illus*	5625
Dish, Shell Shape, Ruffled Rim, Scale Pattern, Gianmaria Buccellati, 1½ x 6 In.	313
Pitcher, Basket Weave Design, Scrolled Handle, Wide Spout, 7¾ In. .... *illus*	590
Salver, Shells, Scalloped Edge, 3 Scrolled Feet, Marked, Buccellati, 1 x 6¼ In.	407
Sculpture, Snail, Crawling, Shell Opens, Signed, M. Buccellati, ¾ x 2 x ¾ In. .... *illus*	691
Teapot, Lid, Cubist Shape, Wood Handle, Rossi & Arcandi, c.1987, 7 x 10½ x 4 In.	5040
Tureen, Lid, Pumpkin Shape, Embossed, Leaves, Stem Handle, Silva Giuseppe, Milan, 1950s, 12 In.	5040
Vase, Rectangular, Spreading Base, Lino Sabbatini, c.1970, 8¼ In. .... *illus*	248
Wine Cooler, Grapevine Handle, Enzo Cerfagli, Stamped, Late 1900s, 6¾ In.	425

SILVER-JAPANESE

Decanter, Mounted, Pierced, Flowers, Dragon, Imperial Hotel, Tokyo, 1949, 8¼ In.	228
Spoon, Court Woman, Holding Umbrella, 5½ In......	107
Trophy, Bowl, Engraved Chrysanthemums, 2 Leaf Shape Handles, Footed, Early 1900s, 9 In. .	4375

SILVER-MEXICAN

Silver objects have been made in Mexico since the days of the Aztecs. These marks are for three companies still making tableware and jewelry.

ChATO CASTiLLO STERLING MEXICO

Jorge "Chato" Castillo 1939+

Matl STERLING MEXICO 925

Matilde Eugenia Poulat 1934–1960

SANBORN'S STERLING H MADE IN MEXICO

Sanborn's 1931–present

Bowl, Flared, Rolled Rim, Cylindrical Foot, Bird On Rim, Mother-Of-Pearl Inlay, 3 x 7 In.....	5
Bowl, Lobed Lid & Body, Colonial Style, Leaf Finial, Pedestal Foot, 4½ In.	17
Bowl, Scalloped Rim, 3 Paw Feet, Hand Hammered, Marked 925, 1900s, 5¾ x 10¼ In.........	59
Box, Elephant Shape, Repousse, Floral, Blanket, Plata Villa Mexico, 1900s, 5 In.	23
Box, Swan Shape, Lid, Gold Washed Interior, Marked GR, 3½ x 4 x 2½ In...........................	15
Braserillo, Cinder Cup, Leaves, Baluster Form Pedestal, Scalloped Dish, 1900s, 3 In., Pair.....	17
Cocktail Shaker, Scrolled Handle, Tapered, Repousse, Floral Bands, Sanborn's, c.1950, 11 In. *illus*	64
Decanter, Monkey Shape, Hinged Head, Black Glass Eyes, Handle, Taxco, Mid 1900s, 11 In. *illus*	352
Figurine, Pheasant, Feathers, Marked, Maciel Sterling, 9½ x 18½ x 5 In., Pair....................	237

S

Silver-English, Vinaigrette, Hinged Lid, Bloodstone Inset, Pierced Grill, Gilt, ⁵⁄₈ x 1 ³⁄₄ x 1 ¹⁄₂ In.
$183

Neal Auction Company

Silver-English, Wick Trimmer, Scissors, Candle, Applied Snuffer, Pierced Handle, Benjamin May, 1783, 1 x 6 In.
$250

Woody Auction

Silver-English, Wine Coaster, Armorial, Scalloped Beaded Rim, Hester Bateman, George III, 1788, 4 ³⁄₄ In., Pair
$2,125

Eldred's

Silver-French, Claret Jug, Dome Lid, Etched, Enamel, Baluster Shape Glass, Victor Saglier, c.1900, 9 In.
$325

stin Auction Gallery

Silver-French, Tureen, Dome Lid, Entwined Serpent Finial, Gadroon Rim, Ball Feet, 1800s, 9 ¹⁄₂ In.
$1,952

Neal Auction Company

Silver-German, Basket, Hanau Style, Rococo Floral & Garland Decor, Swing Handle, 10 x 5 ³⁄₈ In.
$236

Leland Little Auctions

Silver-German, Beaker, Cherubs, Ornate, Flared Rim, Engraved, Keck & Schwarz, c.1900, 6 ³⁄₈ In.
$316

Blackwell Auctions

Silver-German, Bowl, Openwork, Glass Liner, Flowers, Scrolled Feet, Storck & Sinsheimer, 1800s, 5 ³⁄₄ x 7 In.
$380

Thomaston Place Auction Galleries

Silver-German, Cup, Wager, Male, Standing, Robes, Terrain Base, Marked, I Freeman & Son, 14 x 5 x 4 In.
$2,768

Morphy Auctions

S

Silver-German, Salt & Pepper, Figural, Dutch Boy & Girl, Karl Sohnlein, Sohne Hanau, c.1900, 4 In.
$473

Morphy Auctions

Silver-Irish, Dish Ring, Potato, Pierced Repousse Figures, Animal, Monogram, Rocaille, 1899, 3 x 8 In.
$625

Eldred's

Silver-Italian, Centerpiece, Shell Shape, Hammered, Sea Star Feet, Marked, Buccellati, 1900s, 5 x 17 In.
$5,625

Eldred's

Silver-Italian, Pitcher, Basket Weave Design, Scrolled Handle, Wide Spout, 7¾ In.
$590

Austin Auction Gallery

Silver-Italian, Sculpture, Snail, Crawling, Shell Opens, Signed, M. Buccellati, ¾ x 2 x¾ In.
$691

Treadway

Silver-Italian, Vase, Rectangular, Spreading Base, Lino Sabbatini, c.1970, 8¼ In.
$248

Leland Little Auctions

Silver-Mexican, Cocktail Shaker, Scrolled Handle, Tapered, Repousse, Floral Bands, Sanborn's, c.1950, 11 In.
$649

Austin Auction Gallery

Silver-Mexican, Decanter, Monkey Shape, Hinged Head, Black Glass Eyes, Handle, Taxco, Mid 1900s, 11 In.
$3,528

Sotheby's

Figurine, Pheasant, Stone Eyes, Gilt, Wood Base, Brown, Marked, 4¾ x 11 In., Pair...... 3125
Ice Bucket, Monkey Shape, Tail, Handle, Marked, Tane, Late 1900s, 5½ In......... 3780
Ice Bucket, Tapered, Faceted Shape, Loop Handles, Hammered, Sanborn's, 1950s, 4 x 7½ In.. 610
Pitcher, Milk, Wood Handle, Marked, Sanborn's, 4½ x 6 In......... 156
Plate, Petal Shape Rim, Sanborn's, Mid 1900s, 6 In., Pair...... 177
Punch Cup, Scrolled Handle, Domed, Circular Foot, Juvento Lopez Reyes, 1900s, 4 In., 11 Piece 1534
Spoon Warmer, Hinged Lid, Navette Shape Bowl, Leaves, Pedestal Foot, 6 In....... 148
Stirrup, Colonial, Side Slipper Shape, Repousse, Bird, Leaves, 6 x 9 In....... 443
Tray, Oval, Beaded Border, Loop Handle, Juventino Lopez Reyes, 22½ x 14 In....... 768
Tray, Rectangular, 2 Handles, Filigree Sides, Raised Border, 1¼ x 14 x 3½ In....... 156
Tray, Round, Lobed Border, Cast Rim, Handle, Marked, MRT, 1910s, 27¼ In. .... *illus* 1625
Tray, Serving, Rectangular, Shaped Rim, Sanborn's, c.1950, 18 x 12 In....... 1003
Tureen, Soup, Dome Lid, Handles, Footed, Conquistador, 10 x 16 In....... 2048
Vase, Bulbous, Flared Rim, Footed, Marked, Juventino Lopez Reyes, 6 In....... 31

SILVER-PERSIAN
Begging Bowl, Chased, Red Coral, Turquoise Stones, Hanging Chain, Late 1800s, 3 x 9 x 3 In.... 458
Bowl, Applied Beaded Edge, Hallmark, Early 1900s, 2½ x 8½ In. .... *illus* 578

SILVER-PERUVIAN
Font, Holy Water, Repousse, Leaves, 2-Headed Eagle, Shell Shape Basin & Feet, 7¾ x 13 In. 531
Pitcher, Bulbous Body, Wide Spout, Applied Handle, 1950s, 9¼ In....... 625
Pitcher, Water, Elongated Body, Fluted Round Base, Camusso, 1950s, 10⅝ In....... 406
Tray, Leaf Shape, Scalloped Rim, Welsch Plata, 15 In....... 207
Tray, Round, Scallop Edge, Crest Of Peru, Lacquer, Hook, 13 In....... 281

SILVER-PORTUGUESE
Tureen, Soup, Dome Lid, Coquille Finial, Dolphin & Acanthus Handles, Lisbon, Mid 1900s, 11 In....... 1708

SILVER-RUSSIAN

Russian silver is marked with the Cyrillic, or Russian, alphabet. The numbers 84, 88, or 91 indicate the silver content. Russian silver may be higher or lower than sterling standard. Other marks indicate maker, assayer, or city of manufacture. Many pieces of silver made in Russia are decorated with enamel. Faberge pieces are listed in their own category.

Silver–Russian Silver content numbers	Silver–Russian 1741–1900+	Silver–Russian 1896–1908

Bowl, Biscuit, Shallow, Handles, Moscow, 1879, 2½ x 12¾ x 8½ In. 5120
Cigarette Case, Hinged Lid, Pushbutton Clasp, Red Cabochon, Marked, MK, 1910s, 4 x 3 In. 410
Coffeepot, Shaped Rim, Curved Spout, Scrolled Handle, Quatrefoil Base, c.1855, 10 In. 644
Dish, Shallow Bowl, Raised Handle, 3 Scrolled Legs, Marked, PK, c.1880, 10¼ In....... 433
Goblet, Tapered, Bell Shaped Bowl, Engraved, Monogram, Nikifor Timofaev, c.1729, 5 In., Pair.. 1250
Kovsh, Enamel, Flowers, Petals, Leaves, Handle, Multicolor, Marked, HA, 3¾ x 2 x 1½ In.... 945
Spoon, Round Head, Scroll Handle, Enamel, Gustav Klingert, Late 1800s, 6½ In. 406
Sugar, 2 Handles, Finial, Lid, Pinched Feet, Mark, 17 In. 531
Trophy, Cup, Handle, Footed, Soviet Sportsmen, Engraved, 1946, 5¾ In. .... *illus* 144

SILVER-SCOTTISH
Cup, Presentation, Urn Shape, Masonic Lodge Of Scotland, Handles, Engraved, 1815, 8¾ In. .*illus* 594
Hot Water Urn, Acorn Finial, Ring Handles, Feet, W. & P. Cunningham, Edinburgh, 1700s, 19 In. *illus* 3538

SILVER-SPANISH
Bowl, Colonial Style, Saint Mary Finial, Praying, 8¼ x 8 In. 649
Bowl, Flat Rim, Raised Lobed Edge, Heart Shape Hinged Handle, Hammered, 1700s, 2 x 8 In. 2106
Bowl, Round, Applied, Acorn & Leaves, Footed, 5-Point Star, Barcelona, 9¼ In. 177
Braserillo, Ember Cup, 3 Scrolled Supports, Dog Head Terminals, Handles, 4 x 8 x 6¼ In... 472
Crown, Saint's, Cross Finial, Pierced Arches, Flowers, Colonial, 6 x 4⅛ In. .... *illus* 443

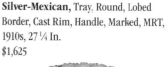

Silver-Mexican, Tray, Round, Lobed Border, Cast Rim, Handle, Marked, MRT, 1910s, 27¼ In.
$1,625

Eldred's

Silver-Persian, Bowl, Applied Beaded Edge, Hallmark, Early 1900s, 2½ x 8½ In.
$578

Lelanc Little Auctions

Silver-Russian, Trophy, Cup, Handle, Footed, Soviet Sportsmen, Engraved, 1946. 5¾ In.
$144

Blackwell Auctions

Silver-Scottish, Cup, Presentation, Urn Shape, Masonic Lodge Of Scotland, Handles, Engraved, 1815, 8¾ In.
$594

Charlton Hall Auctions

S

Silver-Scottish, Hot Water Urn, Acorn Finial, Ring Handles, Feet, W. & P. Cunningham, Edinburgh, 1700s, 19 In. **$3,538**

Neal Auction Company

Silver-Spanish, Crown, Saint's, Cross Finial, Pierced Arches, Flowers, Colonial, 6 x 4 1/8 In. **$443**

Austin Auction Gallery

Dish, Colonial Style, Circular, Ring Drop Handle, Leaves, 13 In.	354
Font, Holy Water, Colonial Style, Leaves, Cherub, Shell Shape Basin & Feet, 3 x 14 1/4 In. *illus*	561
Pitcher, Scrolled Handle, Scallop Pattern Spout, Flowers, J. Perez Fernandez, 1900s, 9 In.	413

SILVER-STERLING

Sterling silver is made with 925 parts silver out of 1,000 parts of metal. The word *sterling* is a quality guarantee used in the United States after about 1860. The word was used much earlier in England and Ireland. Other pieces of sterling quality silver are listed under Silver-American, Silver-English, etc.

Basket, Lily Design, Repousse, Swing Handle, Engraved, Embossed, Footed, R. Wallace, 10 In.	502
Basket, Reticulated, Whiting Manufacturing Co., New York, Late 1800s, 12 x 10 x 2 In.	236
Basket, Swing Handle, Round, Footed, 8 1/2 In.	295
Basket, Victorian Style, Beaded Edge, Openwork, William B. Meyers, 1 3/4 x 1 1/2 In.	115
Bowl, Lid, Leaf Decorated Rim, Pierced Inner Band, Footed, c.1950, 2 1/2 x 11 1/2 In.	329
Bowl, Oblong, Cherubs, Flowers, Engraved, Embossed, Signed, Fina, 14 x 9 x 2 In.	352
Box, Hand Wrought, Cedar Lining, Marked, Fries, 1 x 7 1/2 In.	531
Box, Repousse, Oval, Hinged Lid, Flower, Beading, Scrolls, Footed, 5 x 4 In.	375
Candelabra are listed in the Candelabrum category.	
Candlesticks are listed in their own category.	
Champagne Coupe, Viking Style, Shallow Bowl, Tapered Stem, Round Foot, c.1950, 3 1/2 In., 8 Piece.	443
Cigar Lighter, Fugh Dragon, Bear Tooth, Marked, 6 1/2 In.	945
Cigarette Case, Engraved, Bamboo Design, Hinged, 7 x 3 1/2 In.	295
Cigarette Case, Fleur-De-Lis, Engraved, Embossed, Hinged Top, c.1910, 2 x 3 In.	127
Compote, 3 Deer Supports, Standing, Scalloped Bowl & Base, Hallmark, 8 In. *illus*	567
Compote, Red Cased Glass, Footed, White Interior, Monogram, Marked, 6 In.	375
Decanter, Latticework, Holder, Cut Glass Insert, Monogram, 1800s, 10 1/4 In.	281
Dessert Spoon, Scrolled Leaves Handle, Marked, Box, 6 Piece	92
Dish, Classical Figures, Rectangular, Cobalt Blue Liner, Splayed Legs, 1800s, 4 1/2 x 6 1/4 In.	1080
Dish, Grape Bunches, Handles, Embossed, Footed, Dunham, 15 1/4 In.	500
Goblet, Cordial, Hammered, Shallow Bowl, Tapered Stem, Circular Foot, 4 1/4 In., 6 Piece	295
Grape Shears, Grape Leaf Shape Handles, Vining, Marked, 7 1/4 In. *illus*	71
Gravy Boat, Scalloped Cartouche, Handle, Engraved, Scallo, 6 1/2 In.	266
Jug, Grapevine, Engraved, Monogram, 14 1/2 x 6 x 5 1/2 In.	1890
Napkin Rings are listed in their own category.	
Necessaire, Woman, Picking Flowers, Enamel, Chain, 3 x 2 In.	115
Ornament, Table, Elephant, Standing, 4 Wheels, 6 x 10 x 5 In.	832
Perfume Bottle, Bird, Glass Eyes, Stopper, Alex Creighton, c.1875, 5 1/2 x 3 x 1 3/4 In.	2560
Pitcher, Cranberry, Glass, Grapevine, Handle, Round Base, Victorian, 9 x 4 1/2 In.	461
Pitcher, Water, Helmet Shape, Acanthus Scroll Handle, Wide Spout, Circular Foot, 10 1/2 In.	767
Plate, Shaped Rim, Marked, Lion Passant, Anchor, 6 5/8 In., 12 Piece	1320
Salt & Pepper, Gadroon, Stepped, Hoof Shape Feet, 5 1/4 In., 4 Piece	502
Salt, Victorian, Horse Hoof Shape, Gold Wash Interior, 1878, 1 1/2 In., 4 Piece	1875
Serving Spoon, Art Nouveau, Floral & Leaves Handle, 10 5/8 In. *illus*	213
Serving Spoon, Arts & Crafts, Monogram, K.V.R., William Waldo Dodge, 13 1/2 In.	230
Serving Spoon, Shape Handle, Marked, RW JW Exeter, 1800s, 13 In.	83
Spoon, Souvenir, see Souvenir category.	
Sprinkler, Twirled, Bulb Shaped Body, Ornate Base, 6 1/2 In.	207
Sugar Castor, Pineapple Finial, Swirl Handles, Square Base, Footed, 6 1/4 In.	266
Tazza, Georg Jensen Style, Circular Bowl, Spiral Stem, Domed Foot, c.1950, 6 1/2 In.	768
Teapot, Tilting, Gourd, Gadroon, Bone Fittings, Bun Feet, RW&S	649
Tray, 2 Handles, Embossed, Roses On Border, 29 1/2 x 18 1/2 In.	2599
Tray, II In Cartouche At Center, Oval, Reeded Rim, 4-Footed, Late 1700s, 7 In.	565
Tray, Oval, Ornate Rim Border, Flowers, 2 x 13 x 8 In.	489
Trophy, Motor Boat Race, Inscribed, Red Bank Gala Day, Tusk Handles, 1905, 8 1/2 In. *illus*	850
Trophy, Urn Shape, 2 Handles, Engraved, Domed Base, B. Foreman, 15 In.	708
Urn, Lid, Ornate Design, Gilt, Marked, Tane, 11 1/2 x 7 In., Pair	5938
Vase, Trumpet Shape, Flared Rim, Weighted Base, Monogram, 1800s, 14 3/4 In. *illus*	16
Vinaigrette, Hinged Lid, Rococo, Flowers, Scrolled, Bird Finial, 1700s, 1 x 1 1/2 x 3 1/4 In.	308

Silver-Sterling, Compote, 3 Deer Supports, Standing, Scalloped Bowl & Base, Hallmark, 8 In.
$567

Fontaine's Auction Gallery

Silver-Sterling, Grape Shears, Grape Leaf Shape Handles, Vining, Marked, 7¼ In.
$71

Bunch Auctions

TIP

Wash silver as soon as possible if it has touched salty foods, ketchup, mayonnaise, mustard, eggs, olives, salad dressings, or vinegar.

Silver-Sterling, Serving Spoon, Art Nouveau, Floral & Leaves Handle, 10⅝ In.
$213

ook & Pook

Silver-Sterling, Trophy, Motor Boat Race, Inscribed, Red Bank Gala Day, Tusk Handles, 1905, 8½ In.
$850

Pook & Pook

Silver-Sterling, Vase, Trumpet Shape, Flared Rim, Weighted Base, Monogram, 1800s, 14¾ In.
$163

Freeman's

Silver-Swedish, Cocktail Shaker, Bakelite, Folke Arstrom, c.1930, 8½ In.
$875

Wright

S

Sinclaire, Vase, Trumpet Shape, Stained Poppy Flowers, Frosted, Iridescent, Gilt, c.1915, 10 x 6 In. $322

Jeffrey S. Evans & Associates

Sleepy Eye, Pitcher, Indian Chief, Teepees, Blue, White, Embossed, 4 x 3 In. $165

AntiqueAdvertising.com

Sleepy Eye, Sugar, Indian Chief, Teepees, Blue, White, Embossed, 3⅜ In. $142

AntiqueAdvertising.com

SILVER-SWEDISH
Bowl, Crimped, Twist Edge Rim, Footed, c.1920, 2½ In. 153
Cocktail Shaker, Bakelite, Folke Arstrom, c.1930, 8½ In. .... *illus* 875
Tankard, Hinged Lid, Flowers, Medallion, 3 Ball Feet, C.G. Hallberg, 8 In. 1512
Vase, Raised Rim, Tapered Hexagonal Body, Karl Edvin, Signed, Wiwen Nilsson, 1950, 4 In.. 344

SILVER-SWISS
Bowl, Curling Handle, Openwork Stand, Marked, Bossard, Lucerne, 1900s, 8 x 6 x 3 In. 142
Cigarette Box, Silver, Enamel, Lid, Monogram, Art Deco, 3⅜ x 2⅛ In. 230

SILVER-TURKISH
Mirror, Wall, Hanging, Wedding, Sterling, Embossed, Scalloped Frame, Marked, 6½ In. 106

SINCLAIRE
Sinclaire cut glass was made by H.P. Sinclaire and Company of Corning, New York, between 1904 and 1929. He cut glass made at other factories until 1920. Pieces were made of clear glass as well as amber, blue, green, or ruby glass. Only a small percentage of Sinclaire glass is marked with the *S* in a wreath.

Candlestick, Amethyst, Amber Shoulder, Flared Rim, Round Saucer Foot, 10 In., 4 Piece..... 189
Tray, Clear Blank, 8-Sided, 17 Hobstars, Signed, 1¾ x 10½ In. 125
Vase, Trumpet Shape, Stained Poppy Flowers, Frosted, Iridescent, Gilt, c.1915, 10 x 6 In. *illus* 322

SLAG GLASS
Slag glass resembles a marble cake. It can be streaked with different colors. There were many types made from about 1880. Caramel slag is the incorrect name for chocolate glass made by Imperial Glass. Pink slag was an American product made by Harry Bastow and Thomas E.A. Dugan at Indiana, Pennsylvania, about 1900. Purple and blue slag were made in American and English factories in the 1880s. Red slag is a very late Victorian and twentieth-century glass. Other colors are known but are of less importance to the collector. New versions of chocolate glass and colored slag glass have been made.

Blue, Biscuit Jar, Lid, Drum Shape, Hat Shape Finial, 6½ x 5 In. 360
Green, Figurine, Owl, Sitting On Books, 3½ In. 49
Purple, Vase, Pedestal, Victorian Patterns, Flared, Scalloped Rim, 8½ In. 285
Red, Candy Dish, Footed, Scalloped Edge, Paneled, Lid. 18

SLEEPY EYE
Sleepy Eye collectors look for anything bearing the image of the nineteenth-century Indian chief with the drooping eyelid. The Sleepy Eye Milling Co., Sleepy Eye, Minnesota, used his portrait in advertising from 1883 to 1921. It offered many premiums, including stoneware and pottery steins, crocks, bowls, mugs, pitchers, and many advertising items, all decorated with the famous profile of the Indian. The popular pottery was made by Weir Pottery Co. from c.1899 to 1905. Weir merged with six other potteries and became Western Stoneware in 1906. Western Stoneware Co. made blue and white Sleepy Eye from 1906 until 1937, long after the flour mill went out of business in 1921. Reproductions of the pitchers are being made today. The original pitchers came in only five sizes: 4 inches, 5¼ inches, 6½ inches, 8 inches, and 9 inches. The Sleepy Eye image was also used by companies unrelated to the flour mill.

Pitcher, Indian Chief, Ironstone, Blue, White, Embossed Head, Landscape On Reverse, 8 In.. 5(
Pitcher, Indian Chief, Teepees, Blue, White, Embossed, 4 x 3 In. .... *illus* 16⁹
Stein, Indian Chief, Blue, Gray, Flemish, Stoneware, Figural Indian Head Handle, 7½ In..... 20(
Sugar, Indian Chief, Teepees, Blue, White, Embossed, 3⅜ In. .... *illus* 14⁷
Vase, Indian Chief, Cattails, Blue, Gray, Embossed, 8½ x 4¼ In. .... 8(

Snuffbox, Brass, Hinged Lid, Engraved, Comic Figure, Flowers, Initials EB, 1790s, 3 x 2 x 2 In.
$184

Forsythes' Auctions

Snuffbox, Brass, Hinged Lid, Geometric, Floral, Engraved, James Shew, c.1800, 1½ x 5 In.
$59

Leland Little Auctions

Snuffbox, Treen, Fish Shape, Hinged Lid, Ink Decor, Continental, 1800s, 2 x 6 In.
$263

Jeffrey S. Evans & Associates

Research Help
When doing research into the history of your antiques and collectibles, avoid depending on old books. Company materials, like original catalogs, are fine. New scientific methods, archaeological digs, and years of research have turned up many errors and myths found in early information.

SLOT MACHINES *are included in the Coin-Operated Machine category.*

SMITH BROTHERS

Smith Bros. Co.

Smith Brothers glass was made from 1874 to 1899. Alfred and Harry Smith had worked for the Mt. Washington Glass Company in New Bedford, Massachusetts, for seven years before going into their own shop. They made many pieces with enamel decoration.

Biscuit Jar, Green & Brown Ivy, Cream Ground, Silver Lid, Bail Handle, 7¼ In.	56
Bowl, Melon Ribbed, Pansy Blossoms, Pink, Yellow, Cream Ground, 5½ x 2 In.	147
Vase, Bulbous, Swirl, Purple Wisteria, c.1880, 7 x 4¼ In.	895

SNOW BABIES

Snow Babies, made from bisque and spattered with glitter sand, were first manufactured in 1864 by Hertwig and Company of Thuringia. Other German and Japanese companies copied the Hertwig designs. Originally, Snow Babies were made of candy and used as Christmas decorations. There are also Snow Babies tablewares made by Royal Bayreuth. Copies of the small Snow Babies figurines are being made today, and a line called "Snowbabies" was introduced by Department 56 in 1987. Don't confuse these with the original Snow Babies.

Figurine, Baby, On Tummy, Bow Mouth, Germany, 1½ In.	29

SNUFF BOTTLES *are listed in the Bottle category.*

SNUFFBOX

Snuffboxes held snuff. Taking snuff was popular long before cigarettes became available. The gentleman or lady would take a small pinch of the ground tobacco or snuff in the fingers, then sniff it and sneeze. Snuffboxes were made of many materials, including gold, silver, enameled metal, and wood. Most snuffboxes date from the late eighteenth or early nineteenth centuries.

Brass, Hinged Lid, Engraved, Comic Figure, Flowers, Initials EB, 1790s, 3 x 2 x 2 In.	*illus*	184
Brass, Hinged Lid, Geometric, Floral, Engraved, James Shew, c.1800, 1½ x 5 In.	*illus*	59
Silver, Enamel Lid, Central Ceramic Inset Plaque, Putti, Emile Langlois, 1900s, 2¾ In.		163
Silver, Hinged Lid, Inverted Egg Shape, Oval Foot, Bird Finial, 1700s, ¾ x 1 x 2 In.		338
Treen, Fish Shape, Hinged Lid, Ink Decor, Continental, 1800s, 2 x 6 In.	*illus*	263

SOAPSTONE

Soapstone is a mineral that was used for foot warmers or griddles because of its heat-retaining properties. Soapstone was carved into figurines and bowls in many countries in the nineteenth and twentieth centuries. Most of the soapstone collectibles seen today are from Asia. It is still being carved in the old styles.

Carving, Bear, Black, Stone Shape Base, Fran Jenkins, 9 x 16 In.	*illus*	688
Figurine, Eagle, Perched, Open Wings, Wood Base, 9 In.		74

SOFT PASTE

Soft paste is a name for a type of pottery. Although it looks very much like porcelain, it is a chemically different material. Most of the soft-paste wares were made in the early nineteenth century. Other pieces may be listed under Gaudy Dutch or Leeds.

Bowl, Scalloped Top, Blue, White, Footed, c.1800-20, 5⅛ In.	*illus*	420
Chocolate Pot, Shells & Butterflies, Octagonal Base, 9 In.		34

Soapstone, Carving, Bear, Black, Stone Shape Base, Fran Jenkins, 9 x 16 In. $688

Eldred's

Soft Paste, Bowl, Scalloped Top, Blue, White, Footed, c.1800-20, 5⅛ In. $420

Nadeau's Auction Gallery

Souvenir, Plate, U.S. Mint, Denver, Colo., Red Rose Border, Wheelock, Austria, c.1900, 7½ In. $188

Early American History Auctions

SOUVENIR

Souvenirs of a trip—what could be more fun? Our ancestors enjoyed the same thing and souvenirs were made for almost every location. Most of the souvenir pottery and porcelain pieces of the nineteenth century were made in England or Germany, even if the picture showed a North American scene. In the early twentieth century, the souvenir china business seems to have been dominated by the manufacturers in Japan, Taiwan, Hong Kong, England, and the United States. Souvenir china was also made in other countries after the 1960s. Another popular souvenir item is the souvenir spoon, made of sterling or silver plate. These are usually made in the country pictured on the spoon. Related pieces may be found in the Coronation, Olympics, and World's Fair categories.

Album, Wonderland 1906, Red Cover, Paper, Northern Pacific Railway, 9¾ x 6⅞ In.	154
Ashtray, Philco Radio, Ceramic, Brown Glaze, Cuba Havana Radio Convention, 1936, 2¾ x 4 x 4 In.	103
Book, Picturesque Yellowstone, 20 Photogravure Prints, Bloom Bros. Co., Early 1900s, 5 x 7 In..	185
Plate, Dempsey-Gibbons Fight, Scalloped Edge, Outdoor Scene In Center, Shelby, Mont., 1923, 9¼ In.	277
Plate, U.S. Mint, Denver, Colo., Red Rose Border, Wheelock, Austria, c.1900, 7½ In. .... *illus*	188
Spoon, Silver, Wilhelmina I, Twisted Handle, Coin, Dutch, 1940	9
Tambourine, Truck Off, Wood Handle, Marc Bolan & T-Rex On Tour, 1974, 9 In.	281
Thermometer, Embossed Silver, Owl, Serpent, Wood, P.O.P., Kansas City, 1911, 11 In.	90
Toothpick Holder, Cut Glass, The Famous Leadville, Colorado, U.S. Glass Company, 1890, 3¼ In.	18
Toothpick Holder, The Famous Leadville, Crisscross, Ruffled Rim, Colorado, 3¼ In.	15
Vase, Castle Craig Hubbard Park, Landscape, Tower, 3-Sided, Mt. Washington, 5 In.	48

SPANGLE GLASS

Spangle glass is multicolored glass made from odds and ends of colored glass rods. It includes metallic flakes of mica covered with gold, silver, nickel, or copper. Spangle glass is usually cased with a thin layer of clear glass over the multicolored layer. Similar glass is listed in the Vasa Murrhina category.

Jug, White Cased, Clear, Cream, Square Pinched Body, Reeded Neck, Hobbs, c.1883, 5 In. ... *illus*	819
Pitcher, Cobalt Blue, Square Pinched Body, Water, Beehive Neck, Hobbs, Brockunier, c.1883, 8 In.	2340

SPATTER GLASS

Spatter glass is a multicolored glass made from many small pieces of different colored glass. It is sometimes called End-of-Day glass. It is still being made.

Basket, Ruffled Top, C Thorn Looking Handle, Yellows & Pinks, 1880s, 5 x 5 x 5 In.	175
Cabinet Vase, Art Deco, 6-Sided, Base, Orange, White, Yellow, Blue, Czech, 5 In., Pair	150
Pitcher, Lobed Sides, Brown, Orange, Red, Yellow, Clear Handle, c.1880, 7 In.	145
Pitcher, Water, Frosted, Opal & Cranberry, Applied Handle, Northwood, 1880s, 8¾ In. .... *illus*	105
Rose Bowl, Blue, Silver Mica, 5 x 5½ In.	89
Sock Darner, White Ground, Yellow, Blue, Orange, 5½ x 2 In.	25

SPATTERWARE

Spatterware and spongeware are terms that have changed in meaning in recent years, causing much confusion for collectors. It is a type of ceramic. Some say that *spatterware* is the term used by Americans, *sponged ware* or *spongeware* by the English. The earliest pieces were made in the late eighteenth century, but most of the spatterware found today was made from about 1800 to 1850. Early spatterware was made in the Staffordshire district of England for sale in America. Collectors also use the word *spatterware* to refer to kitchen crockery with added spatter made in America during the late nineteenth and early twentieth centuries. Spongeware is very similar to spatterware in appearance. Designs were applied to ceramics by daubing the color on with a sponge or cloth. Many collectors do not differentiate between spongeware and spatterware and use the names interchangeably. Modern pottery is being made to resemble old spatterware and spongeware, but careful examination will show it is new.

Bowl, Rainbow, Alternating Bands, Black & Purple, 5 x 9¾ In.		1098
Mixing Bowl, Blue & Rust Over Yellowware, c.1890, 3 x 6 In.		15
Mug, Lid, Peafowl, On Branch, Blue, Green, Red, Tapered Loop Handle, 4⅜ In.		519
Plate, Festoon, 6 Demilune Arches, Red, Yellow, Green, England, 1800s, 8½ In.		7000
Plate, Rainbow, Sponged, Black, Yellow, Green, Red & Blue, Scalloped Rim, 1910s, 8¼ In.		4973
Plate, Tulip, Black & Purple, Rainbow, Green Leaves, 8½ In.		549
Platter, Cluster Of Buds, Allover Blue, Green Leaves, Paneled Border, 1800s, 12¼ In.		750
Platter, Meat, Trees, Blue, 8-Sided, White Ground, 15½ x 20 In.		2074
Sugar, Dome Lid, Floral Knop, Rainbow, Blue, Red, Green, England, 1800s, 4¾ In.		275
Sugar, Lid, Fort, White Ground, Flared Rim, Raised Molded Foot, 4½ In.		1464
Teapot, Lid, Dove, Perched On Leaves, Green, White Ground, Gooseneck Spout, 6¼ In.		1220
Teapot, Lid, Gooseneck Spout, Shaped Handle, Blue Design, Yellow Ground, 8½ In.		102
Teapot, Peafowl, Octagonal Shape, Concave Panels, Allover Red, England, 1800s, 7½ In.		350

SPELTER

Spelter is a synonym for a zinc alloy. Figurines, candlesticks, and other pieces were made of spelter and given a bronze or painted finish. The metal has been used since about the 1860s to make statues, tablewares, and lamps that resemble bronze. Spelter is soft and breaks easily. To test for spelter, scratch the base of the piece. Bronze is solid; spelter will show a silvery scratch.

Ewer, Sea Maiden Shape Handle, Clutching Nets, Sea Creatures, Late 1800s, 13 In. ..... *illus*		207
Sculpture, Elephant, Standing, Metal, Trunk, Driftwood Base, 21 x 23 In. .... *illus*		554
Sculpture, Man & Woman, Kissing, Sitting, Square Base, Marked, Auguste Rodin, 12½ In.		71
Sculpture, Noah's Ark, Waves, Animals, Gold & Silver, Marble Base, Meisler, Germany, 16 x 13 In		1875

SPINNING WHEEL

Spinning wheels in the corner have been symbols of earlier times for the past 150 years. Although spinning wheels date back to medieval days, the ones found today are rarely more than 150 years old. Because the style of the spinning wheel changed very little, it is often impossible to place an exact date on a wheel. There are different types for spinning flax or wool.

Ebony, Whalebone Accents, Sailor Made, Scalloped Base, Bulb Carvings, 1867, 36 x 17 x 12 In. ... *illus*		219
Mixed Wood, Flax, Warm Color, 1860s, 36½ In.	*illus*	47
Painted, Red & Black, Initials TMHS 1882, Stamped LL, c.1890, 39 In.		120
Upright, Hardwood, Turned Stretchers, Mid 1800s, 36½ In.		140

SPODE

Spode pottery, porcelain, and bone china were made by the Stoke-on-Trent factory of England founded by Josiah Spode about 1770. The firm became Copeland and Garrett from 1833 to 1847, then W.T. Copeland or W.T. Copeland and Sons until 1976. It then became Royal Worcester Spode Ltd. The company was bought by the Portmeirion Group in 2009. The word *Spode* appears on many pieces made by the factories. Most collectors include all the wares under the more familiar name of Spode. Porcelains are listed in this book by the name that appears on the piece. Related pieces may be listed under Copeland, Copeland Spode, and Royal Worcester.

SPODE	COPELAND & GARRETT LATE SPODE	ROYAL WORCESTER SPODE
Spode c.1770–1790	Copeland & Garrett c.1833–1847	Royal Worcester Spode Ltd. 1976– c.2009

Spangle Glass, Jug, White Cased, Clear, Cream, Square Pinched Body, Reeded Neck, Hobbs, c.1883, 5 In.
$819

Jeffrey S. Evans & Associates

Spatter Glass, Pitcher, Water, Frosted, Opal & Cranberry, Applied Handle, Northwood, 1880s, 8¾ In.
$105

Jeffrey S. Evans & Associates

Spelter, Ewer, Sea Maiden Shape Handle, Clutching Nets, Sea Creatures, Late 1800s, 13 In.
$207

Leland Little Auctions

Spelter, Sculpture, Elephant, Standing, Metal, Trunk, Driftwood Base, 21 x 23 In.
$554

Alderfer Auction Company

Spinning Wheel, Ebony, Whalebone Accents, Sailor Made, Scalloped Base, Bulb Carvings, 1867, 36 x 17 x 12 In.
$219

Bruneau & Co. Auctioneers

Spinning Wheel, Mixed Wood, Flax, Warm Color, 1860s, 36 ½ In.
$47

Jeffrey S. Evans & Associates

Cup & Saucer, Fleur-De-Lis, Gold & White, Scalloped Rim, Marked, 2 ¼ x 4 ¾ In.	30
Plate, Dinner, Cobalt Blue, Gilt Rim Edge, Marked, 10 ⅝ In., 11 Piece	207
Plate, Imperial Plate Of Persia, Collector, Lion, Shield, 10 ½ In. *illus*	300
Platter, Rural English Landscape, Dark Blue, Ruffled Rim, Marked, 12 x 15 In.	46
Tureen, Underplate, Flowers, Handle, Chinese Aesthetic Design, 7 x 11 ¼ In.	369
Vase, Spill, Mocha, Seaweed, White Flower Border, Footed, Early 1800s, 4 x 3 ½ In., Pair	492
Vase, Trumpet, Blue Ground, Flower Sprays, Blue, Pink, Gold Enamel, c.1823, 6 x 4 ½ In.	375

SPONGEWARE, *see Spatterware category.*

SPORTS, *Cards are listed in the Card category*

SPORTS

Sports equipment, sporting goods, brochures, and related items are listed here. Items are listed by sport. Other categories of interest are Bicycle, Card, Fishing, Sword, Toy, and Trap.

Baseball, Ball, Babe Ruth Autograph *illus*	183500
Baseball, Ball, Signed, Yankees Team, 27 Signatures, 1953 *illus*	1230
Baseball, Bat, Sterling Silver, 1975, 32 ¾ In.	5625
Baseball, Bat, Turned Northern Ash, Wall Display, Babe Ruth, Louisville Slugger, 1980, 48 In. *illus*	62
Baseball, Button, Mickey Mantle Fan Club, Portrait, Celluloid, Pinback, 1952, 1 ½ In. *illus*	23250
Baseball, Button, Ty Cobb, Artwork Portrait, Celluloid, Advertising Back Paper, 1 ¼ In. *illus*	17276
Basketball, Jersey, Red, Blue, Autographed, Chris Kaman, Frame, 48 x 33 In.	71
Exercise, Medicine Ball, Leather, 8 Strips, 2 Octagonal Patches, Early 1900s, 11 x 15 In.	443
Football, Ball, Washington Redskins, 40 Signatures, Wilson, 1979, 11 ¾ In. *illus*	192
Football, Helmet, NFL San Francisco, 49ers, Case, Signed, 11 ¾ x 14 ¾ In.	325
Football, Jersey, Florida Gators, Blue, Signed, Tim Tebow, Frame, 42 ¼ x 34 ¼ In.	207
Football, Razor Blade Bank, Slot In Helmet, Ceramic, 1940s-50s, 7 ½ In.	142
Football, Ring, Miami Dolphins 1971 AFC Champion, Diamond, 10K White Gold, Blue Ground, 8 In.	3375
Golf, Pin Flag, Masters, Yellow, Autographed, Jordan Spieth, 13 x 17 ⅜ In. *illus*	207
Horse Racing, Trophy, Belmont Driving Park, Engraved, Silver Plate, Wallace Bros., 1919, 16 ¾ In.	561
Horse Racing, Trophy, Bowl, Churchill Downs, Royal Strand, Handles, Silver Plate, 1997, 8 In.	427
Hunting, Game Rack, Molded, Mortised Frame, Black, Wrought Iron Hook, 1800s, 33 x 31 In.	187
Pool, Cue Rack, Quartersawn Oak, National Billiard Mfg. Co., Late 1700s, 58 x 35 x 4 In.	1476
Snowshoes, Northwoods, Bentwood, Leather Bindings, Wood Frame, Bob Maki, 10 x 36 In., Pair	148
Snowshoes, Paddle Shape, Pine & Rawhide, Handmade, 10 x 56 In., Pair	47

STAFFORDSHIRE

Staffordshire, England, has been a district making pottery and porcelain since the 1700s. Thousands of types of pottery and porcelain have been made in the many factories that worked in the area. Some of the most famous factories have been listed separately, such as Adams, Davenport, Ridgway, Rowland & Marsellus, Royal Doulton, Royal Worcester, Spode, Wedgwood, and others. Some Staffordshire pieces are listed under categories like Fairing, Flow Blue, Mulberry, Shaving Mug, etc.

Bowl, Allegheny Scenery, Black Transfer, 1800s, 10 ⅛ In.	288
Bowl, Historical, Blue Transfer, A Ship Of The Line In The Downs, 3 ⅜ x 9 In.	2074
Bowl, Vegetable, Dome Lid, Blue, Center Scene, 1830s, 6 ½ x 9 In.	480
Chamber Pot, Transferware, Comical Verses, 2 Handles, Underfoot, c.1850, 5 ¾ In.	366
Coffeepot, Historical, Blue Transfer, Wadsworth Tower, Paneled Body, 10 ½ In.	219
Cup & Saucer, White Ground, Cobalt Blue, Flowers, Gold Highlights, Marked	46
Cup, Texian Campaigne, Blue Transfer, Officer & Men, Campfire, James Beech, c.1850, 2 ½ In. *illus*	143
Figurine, Cat, Seated, Calico, Molded, Painted, Glazed, 13 ¼ In.	140
Figurine, Cat, Seated, Free-Standing Front Legs, Calico, Pink Ribbons, 1850s, 7 ½ In., Pair *illus*	45
Figurine, Cat, Seated, White & Black, Rectangular Base, c.1900, 7 In., Pair	24
Figurine, Dog, Seated, White Ground, Gray Dots On Coat, Multicolor, 13 x 4 x 9 ½ In.	13

Spode, Plate, Imperial Plate Of Persia, Collector, Lion, Shield, 10 ½ In.
$300

Woody Auction

Stitches Tell Baseball's Age
Baseball's National League used black and red stitches on baseballs until about 1934. American League balls had blue and red stitching.

Sports, Baseball, Ball, Babe Ruth Autograph
$183,500

Grey Flannel Auctions

Sports, Baseball, Ball, Signed, Yankees Team, 27 Signatures, 1953
$1,230

Brunk Auctions

Sports, Baseball, Bat, Turned Northern Ash, Wall Display, Babe Ruth, Louisville Slugger, 1980, 48 In.
$62

Brunk Auctions

TIP
If you're going to a sports card signing, bring along some extra items. Sometimes the signer will honor the extra requests.

Sports, Baseball, Button, Mickey Mantle Fan Club, Portrait, Celluloid, Pin Back, 1952, 1 ½ In.
$23,250

Hake's Auctions

Sports, Baseball, Button, Ty Cobb, Artwork Portrait, Celluloid, Advertising Back Paper, 1 ¼ In.
$17,276

Hake's Auctions

Sports, Football, Ball, Washington Redskins, 40 Signatures, Wilson, 1979, 11 ¾ In.
$192

Brunk Auctions

Sports, Golf, Pin Flag, Masters, Yellow, Autographed, Jordan Spieth, 13 x 17 ⅜ In.
$207

Austin Auction Gallery

S

STAFFORDSHIRE

Staffordshire, Cup, Texian Campaigne, Blue Transfer, Officer & Men, Campfire, James Beech, c.1850, 2 ½ In.
$148

Austin Auction Gallery

Staffordshire, Figurine, Cat, Seated, Free-Standing Front Legs, Calico, Pink Ribbons, 1850s, 7 ½ In., Pair
$450

Garth's Auctioneers & Appraisers

Staffordshire, Group, Vicar & Moses, Creamware, Painted, 10 In.
$240

Nadeau's Auction Gallery

Staffordshire, Plate, Texian Campaigne, Brown Transfer, Battle Of Palo Alto, James Beech, c.1850, 10 In.
$266

Austin Auction Gallery

Staffordshire, Teapot, Dome Lid, Agate, Pecton Shell, Scaly Dolphin Handle, Kylin Knop, c.1750, 5 In.
$4,410

Sotheby's

Staffordshire, Platter, Lake George, Blue Transfer, Seashell Border, Molded Rim, 1800s, 17 x 13 In.
$512

Brunk Auctions

Staffordshire, Stirrup Cup, Dog's Head, Black, White, Orange Nose, Glaze, 5 In.
$488

Nadeau's Auction Gallery

S

Figurine, Dog, Spaniel, Black & White, Seated, 7 In., Pair	316
Figurine, Dog, Spaniel, Seated, Gilt Details, Hand Painted, 1800s, 12 In., Pair	130
Figurine, Dog, Whippet, Sitting, Black Nose, Orange Glaze, 6½ In., Pair	1143
Figurine, Horse, Standing, Tree Trunk, Grassy Plinth, Mounted, Lamp Base, Late 1800s, 9 In.	561
Figurine, King, Standing, Wearing Crown, Maroon Cape, 6¼ In.	40
Figurine, Lion, Lying Down, Glass Eyes, Brown Glaze, Oval Base, Late 1800s, 9¾ In., Pair	354
Figurine, Rabbit, Black Splotched, White Ground, Green Lettuce, c.1850, 5¼ In., Pair	4680
Figurine, Shepherd, Standing, Carrying Lamb On His Back, Square Base, c.1800, 8 In.	295
Group, Vicar & Moses, Creamware, Painted, 10 In. .... illus	240
Jug, Cream, Lid, Green, Yellow Glaze, Molded Leaf, Crabstock Handle, 1760s, 5 In.	3375
Ladle, Sauce, Blue, Transfer Decorated, Flowers, England, c.1830, 6¼ In.	75
Lamp, Dog Shape, Spaniel, Seated, Wood Base, Brass Fittings, White, 1850s, 27 In., Pair	390
Mug, 3 Frogs Interior, White Ground, Flowers, Leaves, Shaped Rim & Base, Italy, 5 In.	158
Mug, Inscribed, To Washington The Patriot Of America, Red Transfer, Child's, c.1840, 2½ In.	299
Pitcher, Scalloped Rim, Wide Spout, Shaped Handle, Blue & White, Cauldon, Plymouth, 12 In.	45
Pitcher, Soft Paste, Gen. Washington, 13 Stars, Arrows, Olive Branch, Transfer, 1820s, 8 In.	1094
Plate, Entrance Of The Erie Canal Into The Hudson, Blue, Circular, Albany, 1800s, 10 In.	286
Plate, Texian Campaigne, Blue, Scalloped Edge, Marked, James Beech, c.1850, 9¼ In.	295
Plate, Texian Campaigne, Brown Transfer, Battle Of Palo Alto, James Beech, c.1850, 10 In. illus	266
Plate, William Henry Harrison, Portrait, Blue Transfer, Chickweed Border, 8 In.	500
Platter, Blind Boy & Mother In Garden, Blue Transfer, c.1850, 15 x 20 In.	250
Platter, Historical, Blue Transfer, View Of Dublin, Oval, 11¾ x 14¾ In.	2684
Platter, Lake George, Blue Transfer, Seashell Border, Molded Rim, 1800s, 17 x 13 In. .. illus	512
Platter, Landing Of General Lafayette, Hexagonal, Blue, New York, 1824, 15 x 11½ In.	360
Platter, Penn's Treaty, Blue Transfer, Geometric Border, Scalloped, 16 x 9½ In.	732
Platter, Transferware, Neoclassical, Shells, Birds & Figures Border, 1800s, 19 x 15 In.	266
Punch Bowl, Scratch Blue, Salt Glaze, Gilbot Tarleton & Debrow Tarleton, 1760, 4 x 9 In.	1500
Serving Bowl, Blue Transfer, Landing Of Lafayette, James & Ralph Clewes, c.1823, 5 x 9 In.	1063
Stirrup Cup, Dog's Head, Black, White, Orange Nose, Glaze, 5 In. .... illus	488
Teapot, 8-Sided, Soft Paste, Eagle & Shield Transfer, 13 Stars, Crossed Arrows, c.1845, 9 In.	375
Teapot, Dome Lid, Agate, Pecton Shell, Scaly Dolphin Handle, Kylin Knop, c.1750, 5 In. illus	4410
Toby Jugs are listed in their own category.	
Tureen, Lid, Blue Floral Transfer, Boat Shape, Leaf Bracket Finial, 1850s, 8 x 9 x 5 In.	192
Vase, Spill, Figural, 2 Figures, Hunter, Woman, Dead Game, Tree Trunk, 1800s, 6 In.	25
Wall Pocket, Tortoiseshell, Brown Glaze, Cornucopia Body, Molded Leaf, Vine, 1760s, 9¾ In.	594

STAINLESS STEEL

Stainless steel became available to artists and manufacturers about 1920. They used it to make flatware, tableware, and many decorative items.

Ashtray, Cylindrical, Revolving, Arne Jacobsen, Stelton, Denmark, 1964, 3¼ In. .... illus	125
Hair Comb, Georgian, 14 Tines, Openwork, Brass Cameo, c.1815, 4½ In.	650

STANGL POTTERY

Stangl Pottery traces its history back to the Fulper Pottery of New Jersey. In 1910, Johann Martin Stangl started working at Fulper. He left to work at Haeger Pottery from 1915 to 1920. Stangl returned to Fulper Pottery in 1920, became president in 1926, and changed the company name to Stangl Pottery in 1929. Stangl bought the firm in 1930. The pottery is known for dinnerware and a line of bird figurines. Martin Stangl died in 1972 and the pottery was sold to Frank Wheaton Jr. of Wheaton Industries. Production continued until 1978, when Pfaltzgraff Pottery purchased the right to the Stangl trademark and the remaining inventory was liquidated. A single bird figurine is identified by a number. Figurines made up of two birds are identified by a number followed by the letter *D* indicating Double.

Stainless Steel, Ashtray, Cylindrical, Revolving, Arne Jacobsen, Stelton, Denmark, 1964, 3¼ In.
$125

Wright

Stangl, Bird, Magpie Jay, No. 3758, Head Lowered, Green Leafy Base, 10¾ In.
$240

Woody Auction

Stangl, Golden Harvest, Tea Set, Golden Harvest, Teapot, Lid, Sugar & Creamer
$12

Woody Auction

Star Trek, Game, Pinball, Coin-Operated, 1 To 4 Players, Bally, 51 ½ x 22 x 69 ½ In. $462

Apple Tree Auction Center

Star Wars, Action Figure, Han Solo, Laser Pistol, Rebel Alliance Medal, Box, Kenner, 1977, 12 In. $810

Weiss Auctions

Star Wars, Mailbox, US Postal Service, Silver & Blue, Jedi Master Series, R2-D2, 49 ½ x 20 In. $523

Hartzell's Auction Gallery Inc.

	*Stangl*	*Stangl POTTERY TRENTON, N.J.*
Stangl 1926–1930	Stangl 1940s–1978	Stangl 1949–1953

Bank, Piggy, White Ground, Orange Tulips, Marked, 5 ½ In.	12
Bird, Double Bluebird, No. 3276D, Green Leafy Base, 8 x 6 ¾ In.	125
Bird, Double Orioles, No. 3402D, Black, Yellow, 6 In.	41
Bird, Magpie Jay, No. 3758, Head Lowered, Green Leafy Base, 10 ¾ In. ......*illus*	240
Bird, Paroquet Parakeet, No. 3449, Green & Yellow, c.1940, 5 ½ x 5 In.	68
Bird, Yellow Warbler, No. 3447, Blue Base, 5 In.	50
Plate, Green Rim, 3 Thistles In Center, Marked, 14 ¼ In.	4
Tea Set, Golden Harvest, Teapot, Lid, Sugar & Creamer ......*illus*	12

STAR TREK AND STAR WARS

Star Trek and Star Wars collectibles are included here. The original *Star Trek* television series ran from 1966 through 1969. The series spawned an animated TV series, three TV sequels, and a TV prequel. The first Star Trek movie was released in 1979 and eleven others followed, the most recent in 2016. The movie *Star Wars* opened in 1977. Sequels were released in 1980 and 1983; prequels in 1999, 2002, and 2005. *Star Wars: Episode VII* opened in 2015, which increased interest in Star Wars collectibles. *Star Wars: The Last Jedi* opened in 2017. *Star Wars: Episode IX* was released in 2019. Star Wars characters also appeared in *Rogue One: A Star Wars Story* (2016) and *Solo: A Star Wars Story* (2018). Other science fiction and fantasy collectibles can be found under Batman, Buck Rogers, Captain Marvel, Flash Gordon, Movie, Superman, and Toy.

STAR TREK

Action Figure, Guinam, Blue Dress, Playmates, 1995, 9 In.	18
Book, Promotional, Paramount 1992, 15 x 13 ½ In.	273
Book, The Enterprise Logs, Golden Press, Soft Cover, 224 Pages, 1976	20
Game, Pinball, Coin-Operated, 1 To 4 Players, Bally, 51 ½ x 22 x 69 ½ In. ......*illus*	462
Magazine, Star Trek The Motion Picture, A Marvel Super Special Magazine, No. 15, Signed	499
Prop, Borg Phaser, Gray, Painted, Cast Iron, Aluminum Tip, Velcro Straps, 1987-94, 5 x 2 In.	605
Stein, Original Cast, Ceramic, Metal Lid, 1994, 6 ½ x 4 ½ In.	124

STAR WARS

Action Figure, Han Solo, Laser Pistol, Rebel Alliance Medal, Box, Kenner, 1977, 12 In. *illus*	810
Action Figure, Lando Calrissian, Aluminum Coin, Power Of Force, 92-Back Card, Kenner, 1985, 4 In.	1298
Action Figure, Lando Calrissian, Blaster Pistol, Kenner, Unopened, 1997	24
Action Figure, Princess Leia Organa, Robe, Cape, Brush, No. 38070, Kenner, Box, 1977, 11 ½ In.	360
Bank, Talking, R2-D2, C3PO, Moves, Box, Think Way Toys, Light-Up, 1995	45
Bottle, Shampoo, Figural, Jabba The Hutt, Green, Omni Cosmetics, 1983, 4 x 3 x 3 ¾ In.	91
Clock, Alarm, Talking, Blue & White, C3PO & R2-D2 Figures, Battery, Box, Bradley, 8 x 6 ½ In.	90
Mailbox, US Postal Service, Silver & Blue, Jedi Master Series, R2-D2, 49 ½ x 20 In. ...... *illus*	523
Poster, Empire Strikes Back, Multicolor, Tom Jung, 1900s, 41 x 27 In.	125
Poster, Movie, Style B, Teaser, White Lettering, 20th Century Fox, 1977, 41 x 27 In. ...... *illus*	438
Tankard, Figural, Darth Vader, Ceramic, Jim Rumph, 1977, 7 In.	121
Toy, Model Kit, Darth Vader, Glow In Dark Light Saber, Box, MPC, 1979, 11 ½ In.	84
Trading Card, No. 225, Carrie Fisher, 1980	174

STEIN

Steins have been used by beer and ale drinkers for over 500 years. They have been made of ivory, porcelain, pottery, stoneware, faience, silver, pewter, wood, or glass in sizes up to nine gallons. Although some were made by

Mettlach, Meissen, Capo-di-Monte, and other famous factories, most were made by less important German potteries. The words *Geschutz* or *Musterschutz* on a stein are the German words for "patented" or "registered design," not company names. Steins are still being made in the old styles. Lithophane steins may be found in the Lithophane category.

Character, Frog, Playing Accordion, Pottery, ½ Liter...*illus*	420
Character, Pig, Pipe In Mouth, Seated On Music Box, Schierholz Porcelain, ½ Liter.......*illus*	570
Character, Skull Shape, Mounted, Book, Juvenes Dum Sumus & Gaudeamus Igitur, 6½ In ..*illus*	441
Faience, Musician, Playing Trombone, Porcelain, Proskau Factory, 1 Liter ....*illus*	2400
Glass, Beer, Green, Man, Slaying Dragon, Marked, Anno 662, 21¼ In...............................	403
Glass, Enamel Elk, Lime, Ribbed, Applied Handle, Pewter Flip Lid, 16 In.	70
Glass, Porcelain Wedding Plaque, Hand Painted, Pewter Lid, Dated, 1888, 7 x 6 In.............	38
Man, Standing Beside High Wheel Bicycle, Pottery, Merkelbach & Wick, ½ Liter .... *illus*	228
Mettlach steins are listed in the Mettlach category.	
Monkey, Skull Finial, Black, White, Handle, Germany, 8 x 5 In.	156
Occupational, Potter, Porcelain, Karl Baner, ½ Liter...*illus*	228
Porcelain, Capo-Di-Monte, Gold Highlights, Nymph Handle, Putti Finial, 1800s, 10 In........	360
Porcelain, Couple, Wine Cask, Rye, Hopfen U. Malz Gott Erhalt's, Germany, c.1900, 2 Liter, 16 In..	288
Regimental, 8 Chev. Regt. 2 Esk. Dillingen, 1908-11, 4-Sided Scenes, ½ Liter.................*illus*	480
Royal Vienna, Women, Seated, Enamel, Lid, c.1860, 1¾ In...	677
Stoneware, Creussen, Brown Pottery, Relief Molded Saints, Knob, Pewter Lid, 1600s, 7 In....	600

STEREO CARD

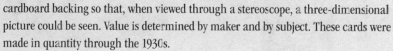

Stereo cards that were made for stereoscope viewers became popular after 1840. Two almost identical pictures were mounted on a stiff cardboard backing so that, when viewed through a stereoscope, a three-dimensional picture could be seen. Value is determined by maker and by subject. These cards were made in quantity through the 1930s.

Grand Canyon Rim, From Hance's Cove, Historical Information, H.C. White, 1906, 3½ x 7 In.	100
Rain In The Parlor, Boy Pouring Water On Girl, Universal Photo Art Co., 1904....................	5
Room For One More, 5 Boys On A Mule, E.W. Kelley, 1906	25
Ten Minutes For Refreshments, Mother & Baby, Kilburn Brothers, 1882	12

STEREOSCOPE

Stereoscopes were used for viewing stereo cards. The hand viewer was invented by Oliver Wendell Holmes, although more complicated table models were used before his was produced in 1859. Do not confuse the stereoscope with the stereopticon, a magic lantern that used glass slides.

Burl, Veneer, Revolving, Front Eye Apertures, Square Cabinet, Tabletop, 1800s, 21 In.	1046
Kawin & Co., Retractable Handle, Card Holder, Wood, Tin, 12 In.	125
Keystone View Co., Wood, Aluminum, 1905	159
Smith, Beck & Beck, Achromatic, Walnut, c.1860...	595
Stereo-Graphoscope, Viewer, Rosewood, Adjustable, Brass Rods, Folding Eyepiece, 1800s, 30 In. *illus*	369

STERLING SILVER, *see Silver-Sterling category.*

STEUBEN

Steuben glass was made at the Steuben Glass Works of Corning, New York. The factory, founded by Frederick Carder and T.G. Hawkes Sr., was purchased by the Corning Glass Company in 1918. Corning continued to make glass called Steuben. Many types of art glass were made at Steuben. Aurene is an iridescent glass. Schottenstein Stores Inc. bought 80 percent of the business in 2008. The factory closed in 2011. In 2014 the Corning Museum of Glass took over the factory and is

Star Wars, Poster, Movie, Style B, Teaser, White Lettering, 20th Century Fox, 1977, 41 x 27 In. $438

Selkirk Auctioneers & Appraisers

Missing Lids

Many beer steins seem to be missing their metal lids. In 1916, Germany needed metal for the war effort and citizens had to sell items made of gold, silver, brass, bronze, copper, and pewter to the government. The pewter steins and lids were melted for the war effort.

Stein, Character, Frog, Playing Accordion, Pottery, ½ Liter $420

Fox Auctions

S

Stein, Character, Pig, Pipe In Mouth, Seated On Music Box, Schierholz Porcelain, ½ Liter
$570

Stein, Character, Skull Shape, Mounted, Book, Juvenes Dum Sumus & Gaudeamus Igitur, 6 ½ In.
$441

Stein, Faience, Musician, Playing Trombone, Porcelain, Proskau Factory, 1 Liter
$2,400

Stein, Man, Standing Beside High Wheel Bicycle, Pottery, Merkelbach & Wick, ½ Liter
$228

Stein, Occupational, Potter, Porcelain, Karl Baner, ½ Liter
$228

Stein, Regimental, 8 Chev. Regt. 2 Esk. Dillingen, 1908-11, 4-Sided Scenes, ½ Liter
$480

Stereoscope, Stereo-Graphoscope, Viewer, Rosewood, Adjustable, Brass Rods, Folding Eyepiece, 1800s, 30 In.
$369

Steuben, Bowl, Calcite, Blue Aurene Interior, Frederick Carder, c.1920, 3 ½ x 12 In.
$305

Steuben, Bowl, Clear, Pedestal, Scrolled Foot, Blown Glass, George Thompson, 1940, 5 In.
$325

Steuben, Bowl, Gold Iridescent, Green Pulled Feather, Aurene, Signed, F. Carder, 2 ¼ x 4 ¾ In.
$200

S

reproducing some tableware, paperweights, and collectibles. Additional pieces may be found in the Cluthra and Perfume Bottle categories.

Bowl, Amethyst, Footed, Optic Rib, Fluted Rim, 2 ½ x 10 In.	150
Bowl, Blue, Silvered Rim, Mounted, Flowers, Footed, Aurene, 5 ½ In.	1560
Bowl, Calcite, Blue Aurene Interior, Frederick Carder, c.1920, 3 ½ x 12 In. *illus*	305
Bowl, Clear, 4 Scrolled Feet, John Dreves, 1940, 3 ¾ x 11 In.	207
Bowl, Clear, Oval, 2 Ribbed Handles, 4 ½ x 9 ½ In.	150
Bowl, Clear, Pedestal, Scrolled Foot, Blown Glass, George Thompson, 1940, 5 In. *illus*	325
Bowl, Clear, Scroll Foot, Signed, John Dreves, 1942, 4 In.	118
Bowl, Dome Lid, Clear, Pointed Finial, Donald Pollard, c.1956, 10 ½ In.	502
Bowl, Gold Iridescent, Green Pulled Feather, Aurene, Signed, F. Carder, 2 ¼ x 4 ¾ In. *illus*	200
Bowl, Red, Cameo Glass, Dragon, Cased, White Interior, Early 1900s, 2 ¾ x 6 ¼ In.	189
Bowl, Star Spangled, Footed, Etched Mark, George Thompson, 1961, 4 In., Pair	427
Bowl, Transportation, Clear, Signed, George Thompson & Sidney Waugh, 6 ½ x 7 ½ In. *illus*	3835
Candlestick, Green Jade, Waved Rim, Knopped Stem, Round Base, 5 x 4 ¾ In.	90
Christmas Tree, Cone Shape, Bubbles, Inclusions, Marked, David Dowler, c.1984, 8 x 4 In.	660
Compote, Amber, Flared Rim, Blue Ring Handles, Ribbed Stem, Circular Base, Signed, 5 In. *illus*	315
Compote, Clear, Applied Pink Threading, Spiral Stem, Prunts, 6 x 7 In.	250
Compote, Pedestal, Clear, Curled Feet, Circular Base, George Thompson, 1940, 5 In.	384
Compote, Pink, Molded, Clear Pedestal Foot, Flared Rim, 8 In.	23
Dish, Gold Calcite Interior, Pearl White Ground, Rolled Rim, 3 ¾ In.	125
Figurine, Eagle, Clear, Spread Wings, Perched On Ball, Blown, Wood Stand, Signed, 9 ¾ In.	173
Figurine, Kingfisher, Water Drop Shape, Leather Case, James Houston, 7 ½ In.	5400
Figurine, Trumpeting Elephant, Clear, Etched Mark, James Houston, 1964, 9 ¼ In.	488
Figurine, Unicorn Head, Clear, 18K Gold Horn, Signed, James Houston, c.1965, 17 In.	1121
Goblet, Clear, Air-Twist Stem, Engraved, George L. Thompson, 1950s, 12 In.	59
Goblet, Engraved, Floral Drapery, Air Trap Connector & Stem, Domed Foot, c.1925, 9 x 3 In.	410
Goblet, Water, Clear, Trumpet Shape, Art Glass, Circular Foot, 7 ¼ In., 12 Piece	325
Lamp Base, Yellow Jade, Blue, Acid Cut, Birds, Plants, Bronze Mounts, Aurene, 27 x 12 In. *illus*	2400
Lampshade, Domed, Brown Iridescent, Multicolor Banded, 6 x 10 In., Pair	2760
Lampshade, Domed, Iridescent, Wave Pattern, Green Ground, 4 ½ x 8 In. *illus*	1638
Lampshade, Gold, Curved, Ribbed, Aurene, 4 x 4 ¾ In., Pair	250
Lampshade, Iridescent, Cream Ground, Signed, Early 1900s, 5 ½ In., 3 Piece	590
Olive Dish, Snail Scroll Handle, Etched Mark, John Dreves, 1939, 3 ½ In., Pair	563
Paperweight, Blue Swirl Design, Round, Bubbles, 3 ¾ In. *illus*	378
Perfume Bottle, Blue Iridescent, Flame Stopper, Garlic Bulb Shape, Aurene, 8 In.	170
Perfume Bottle, Gold, Blue, Iridescent, Lobed Body, Stopper, Aurene, 5 ¾ In. *illus*	374
Perfume Bottle, Verre De Soie, Cylindrical, Fitted Stopper, 7 ¾ x 2 ¼ In.	250
Plate, Jade Green, 8 In., 6 Piece	189
Salt Dip, Gold Calcite Interior, Pearl White Ground, Ruffled Rim, 3 ¾ In.	100
Sculpture, American Flag, Block Shape, Raised Stripes, 50 Etched Stars, 3 ½ x 6 In.	484
Sculpture, Balloon Rally, Clear, Red Leather Case, Engraved, Bernard X, 1985, 10 In.	6240
Sculpture, Caterpillar, Clear, Crawling, 1900s, 12 In. *illus*	344
Sculpture, Fish, Clear Blown Glass, Air Trap Design, 18K Gold Lure, James Houston, 8 In.	3540
Sculpture, Mountains Of The Moon, Clear, George Thompson, c.1960, 4 ½ x 13 x 9 ⅝ In.	2057
Tumbler, Clear, Cylindrical, Dimple, Flat Base, 6 ½ In., 10 Piece	649
Vase, Aurene, Blue & Green Iridescence, Hearts, Vines, Art Glass, 7 ¼ In. *illus*	3840
Vase, Blue Iridescent, Grapevine, Etched, Aurene, 1900s, 10 ½ In. *illus*	1088
Vase, Blue Iridescent, Tree Stump, Aurene, Signed, 6 ¼ In.	86
Vase, Blue, Scalloped Opening, Aurene, Signed, 9 In., Pair	625
Vase, Bud, Gold, Aurene, Ruffled Rim, Signed, 6 x 2 ¾ x 2 ¾ In.	384
Vase, Bud, Jade Green, Mounted, Silver Crest, Round Base, 8 ¾ In.	200
Vase, Clear, Thick, Blown, Applied Scroll Handles, Late 1900s, 9 ½ In.	561
Vase, Green Optic Glass, Flared Rim, Polished Pontil, Fleur-De-Lis, Marked, c.1930, 13 In.	561
Vase, Ivory Ground, Mirror Black Handles, Signed, F. Carder, 9 ½ x 6 ¾ In. *illus*	500
Vase, Jade Green, Applied Alabaster Handles, Signed, 10 In. *illus*	504
Vase, Jade Green, Birds, Alabaster Foot, Shouldered, Etched, c.1928, 9 x 7 In. *illus*	644
Vase, Light Green, Tinted Fan Shape, Circular Base, c.1950, 8 ¾ In.	72
Vase, Mirror Black Over Alabaster, Acid Cut, Pussy Willow, 6 ½ x 6 In.	825

Steuben, Bowl, Transportation, Clear, Signed, George Thompson & Sidney Waugh, 6 ½ x 7 ½ In.
$3,835

Cottone Auctions

Steuben, Compote, Amber, Flared Rim, Blue Ring Handles, Ribbed Stem, Circular Base, Signed, 5 In.
$315

Fontaine's Auction Gallery

Steuben, Lamp Base, Yellow Jade, Blue, Acid Cut, Birds, Plants, Bronze Mounts, Aurene, 27 x 12 In.
$2,400

Cottone Auctions

S

STEUBEN

Steuben, Lampshade, Domed, Iridescent, Wave Pattern, Green Ground, 4 1/2 x 8 In.
$1,638

Fontaine's Auction Gallery

Steuben, Paperweight, Blue Swirl Design, Round, Bubbles, 3 3/4 In.
$378

Fontaine's Auction Gallery

Steuben, Perfume Bottle, Gold, Blue, Iridescent, Lobed Body, Stopper, Aurene, 5 3/4 In.
$374

Blackwell Auctions

Steuben, Sculpture, Caterpillar, Clear, Crawling, 1900s, 12 In.
$344

Bruneau & Co. Auctioneers

Steuben, Vase, Aurene, Blue & Green Iridescence, Hearts, Vines, Art Glass, 7 1/4 In.
$3,840

Morphy Auctions

Steuben, Vase, Blue Iridescent, Grapevine, Etched, Aurene, 1900s, 10 1/2 In.
$1,088

Brunk Auctions

Steuben, Vase, Ivory Ground, Mirror Black Handles, Signed, F. Carder, 9 1/2 x 6 3/4 In.
$500

Woody Auction

Steuben, Vase, Jade Green, Applied Alabaster Handles, Signed, 10 In.
$504

Fontaine's Auction Gallery

Steuben, Vase, Jade Green, Birds, Alabaster Foot, Shouldered, Etched, c.1928, 9 x 7 In.
$644

Jeffrey S. Evans & Associates

Steuben, Vase, Rouge Flambe, Opaque, Flared Rim, 5 In.
$6,615

Fontaine's Auction Gallery

S

504

Vase, Pedestal, Mirror Black, Optic Rib, Round Base, 6 1/4 x 8 1/2 In., Pair 400
Vase, Rouge Flambe, Opaque, Flared Rim, 5 In. .... *illus* 6615
Vase, Selenium Red, Flared Shape, Footed, Signed, Frederick Carder, 1920s, 12 x 4 In. . *illus* 1024
Vase, Strawberry Mansion, Trophy, Frederick Carder, c.1931, 11 5/8 x 9 1/2 In. 2124
Vase, Trumpet Shape, Deep Blue Iridescent, Disc Foot, Aurene, Signed, Early 1900s, 8 In. *illus* 472
Vase, Verre De Soie, Footed, Aquamarine Trim, Round Base, 7 x 5 1/4 In. 350
Wine, Selenium Red, Spiral Stem, Round Base, Signed, 6 3/4 In. 125

STEVENGRAPH

Stevengraphs are woven pictures made like fancy ribbons. They were manufactured by Thomas Stevens of Coventry, England, and became popular in 1862. Most are marked *Woven in silk by Thomas Stevens* or were mounted on a cardboard that tells the story of the Stevengraph. Other similar ribbon pictures have been made in England and Germany.

Bookmark, Morning Hymn, Light Blue Ground, Frame, 7 In. .... *illus* 38

STEVENS & WILLIAMS

Stevens & Williams of Stourbridge, England, made many types of glass, including layered, etched, cameo, cut, and art glass, between the 1830s and 1930s. Some pieces are signed *S & W.* Many pieces are decorated with flowers, leaves, and other designs based on nature.

Basket, Pink, Ruffled Rim, Clear Handle, Footed, 7 1/2 In. 40
Vase, Brilliant Cut, Pedestal, 12 Applied Tadpoles, Water Lilies, Signed, 14 x 6 In. 225
Vase, Bud, Pompeiian, Swirl, Blue, Cranberry, White Interior, Verre De Soie, c.1886, 7 In. *illus* 1170
Vase, Stick, Pompeiian Swirl, Bulbous, Cranberry Shading To Blue, 16 x 7 1/2 In. 500

STONE

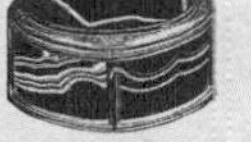

Stone includes those articles made of stones, coral, shells, and some other natural materials not listed elsewhere in this book. Micro mosaics (small decorative designs made by setting pieces of stone into a pattern), urns, vases, and other pieces made of natural stone are listed here. Stoneware is pottery and is listed in the Stoneware category. Alabaster, Jade, Malachite, Marble, and Soapstone are in their own categories.

Bust, Khmer Style, Mounted, Wood Base, 21 x 14 In. 472
Figure, Aztec, Onyx, Black, Malachite, Silver, Mother-Of-Pearl, Mexico, 1900s, 14 x 6 In. 443
Figure, Buddha, Carved, Seated, Bhumisparsha, Earlobes, Curled Hair, Multicolor, 17 x 10 In. ... 472
Figure, Buddha, Pink Quartz, Seated, Carved, Chinese, 6 1/2 In. .... *illus* 431
Figure, Chilong, Spinach Green, Hardstone, Carved, Hardwood Stand, Chinese, 5 5/8 In. 177
Figure, Dog, Dachshund, Chalcedony, Gold & Ruby Eyes, Carved, Russia, 2 1/4 In. .... *illus* 945
Figure, Dragon Fish, Purple Quartz, Mythical Creature, Carved, Chinese, 3 3/4 In. 144
Figure, Dragon Turtle, Pear Shape, 2 Bats, Orb, Pink & Gray, Chinese, 6 In. 71
Figure, Egyptian Relief Fragment, Sandstone, Face, Collar, Wig, Uraeus, 6 3/4 x 5 1/2 In. 1230
Figure, Gargoyle, Wings, Cast, 48 x 37 x 21 In., Pair 2250
Figure, Goldfish, Agate, Ruby Eyes, Carved, Swimming Shape, Russia, 1 x 2 In. 1071
Figure, Guanyin, Scepter, Hardstone, Pale Green, Carved, Hardwood Stand, Chinese, 10 x 3 1/4 In. . 118
Figure, Lion, Seated, Carved, Rectangular, Green Marble Base, Late 1800s, 2 x 3 1/2 In. 50
Figure, Persian Cat, Chalcedony, Carved, Pink, Cut Diamond Eyes, c.1920, 1 1/2 x 4 x 2 In. 3218
Figure, Polar Bear, Chalcedony, Carved, Cabochon Ruby Eyes, Wood Box, Marked, Russia, 2 x 3 In. .. 644
Geode, Sink Style, Amethyst, Crystal, Black Granite Base, 13 x 19 x 17 In. .... *illus* 502
Group, Woman & Attendant, Carved, Blue Hardstone, Wood Stand, Chinese, 6 1/4 In. 295
Head, Buddha, Sandstone, Carved, Khmer, Closed Eyes, Faint Smile, Stand, 11 1/4 In. 594
Libation Cup, Ram's Head, Chilong, Seated, Agate, Hardwood Stand, Chinese, 2 3/4 x 3 1/2 In. . 207
Pipe, Effigy, Bird Shape, Carved, 3 x 6 3/4 In. 98
Plaque, Man, Naked, Holding Arrow, Pietra-Dura, Green Ground, c.1950, 19 x 14 In. 660

Steuben, Vase, Selenium Red, Flared Shape, Footed, Signed, Frederick Carder, 1920s, 12 x 4 In.
$1,024

Neal Auction Company

Steuben, Vase, Trumpet Shape, Deep Blue Iridescent, Disc Foot, Aurene, Signed, Early 1900s, 8 In.
$472

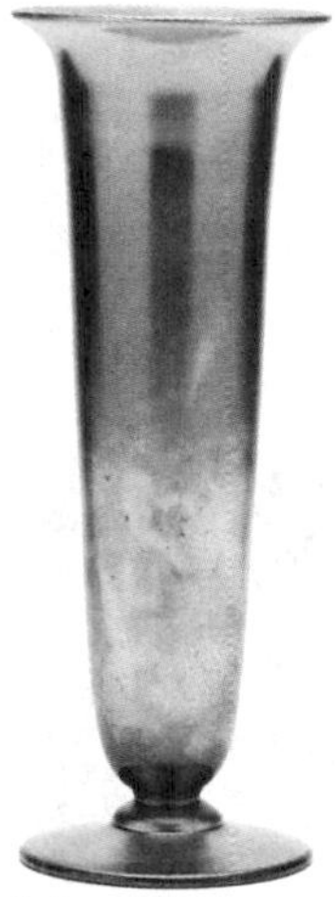

Leland Little Auctions

S

TIP
Remove dripped candle wax on a tabletop with a credit card. Scrape with the grain of the wood. When finished use furniture polish or wax to restore the top's luster.

Stevengraph, Bookmark, Morning Hymn, Light Blue Ground, Frame, 7 In. $38

Stevens & Williams, Vase, Bud, Pompeiian, Swirl, Blue, Cranberry, White Interior, Verre De Soie, c.1886, 7 In. $1,170

Stone, Figure, Buddha, Pink Quartz, Seated, Carved, Chinese, 6½ In. $431

Sculpture, Abstract, Lovers Embraced, Arms Outstretched, Granite, Carved, 36 In.	438
Sculpture, Dog, Sitting, Biting The Basket, Flowers, White, Square Base, 25 In.	148
Sculpture, Female Bust, Shona, Carved, Black Springstone, Chituwa Jemali, 25¼ In.	826
Sculpture, Standing Nude, Gray, Bauxite, Mixed Media, Dan Corbin, 1993, 53 In. *illus*	9375
Urn, Finial, Flaming, White, Carved, Square Base, Late 1800s, 22¾ In. *illus*	256
Vase, Hanging, Agate, Carved, Chilong Finial, Dragon, Koi, Chinese, 6½ x 3¾ In.	266
Vase, Rose Quartz, Teapot Shape, Lid, Carved, Dragon Finial, Chinese, 5⅜ x 6¼ In.	8540

STONEWARE

Stoneware is a coarse, glazed, and fired potter's ceramic that is used to make crocks, jugs, bowls, etc. It is often decorated with cobalt blue decorations. In the nineteenth and early twentieth centuries, potters often decorated crocks with blue numbers indicating the size of the container. A *2* meant 2 gallons. Stoneware is still being made. American stoneware is listed here.

Ashtray, Glazed, Signed, Leza McVey, c.1950, 1½ x 2 In.	344
Bank, Chicken Feed, Coin Slot, Billy Ray Hussey, North Carolina, Folk Art, 8 In.	295
Batter Jug, Brushed Cobalt Blue, Collared Rim, Arched & Loop Handle, Salt Glaze, 1890s, 7 In.	263
Batter Jug, Cobalt Blue Design, Wood Handle, F.H. Cowden, Harrisburg, 1800s, 8½ In. *illus*	388
Bottle, Oval, Groove Handles, Salt Glaze, Brown Iron Oxide Wash, 1910s, 6 Gal., 21 In.	468
Bowl, Bamboo, Brown, Tan, Glazed, Signed On Base, Chinese, 13 In.	115
Bowl, Glazed, White Circle, Leza McVey, c.1947, 8½ In. *illus*	1625
Bowl, Ribbed Body, Glaze, Blue, Cream, Signed, Makoto Yab, Massachusetts, 1900s, 4½ In. *illus*	625
Bust, Young Woman, Hair In Knot Atop Head, Earthtone, Glaze, 13½ In.	115
Butter, Cover, Figural, Rabbit, Lying Down, Blue Glazed Interior, 1900s, 3 x 8½ In.	163
Canner, Cobalt Blue Stencil, Rounded Rim, Albany Slip Interior, Salt Glaze, c.1875, 9½ In.	439
Churn, Brown Top, Removable Lid, Western Stoneware, 4 Gal.	400
Churn, Cobalt Blue Eagle, Lug Handle, Jas. Hamilton & Co., Greensboro, 1860s, 5 Gal., 18 In.	1750
Churn, Cobalt Blue Leaves, 2 Molded Handles, 1800s, 5 Gal., 18 In.	281
Churn, Cobalt Blue, Leaves, Marked, Western Stoneware Co., Monmouth, Ill., 2 Gal., 13 In.	74
Churn, Flared Mouth, 2 Incised Rings, Arched Handle, Strasburg, 1875, 16 x 9 In. *illus*	152
Churn, Lid, Albany Slip, 2 Applied Handles, Impressed 6, 1850s, 19 In.	158
Churn, Wire & Wood Bail Handles, Louisville Pottery, 2 Gal., 12 In.	136
Churn, Wood Lid, Bulbous Body, Applied Handles, Dasher, 1800s, 18¼ In.	138
Cream Jar, Cobalt Blue Freehand Lily, Blue Band, Tooled Neck, Western Pa., 1800s, 9 In.	375
Crock, Blue Spiral Flower, Round, Handle, F.T. Wright & Son, Taunton Mass., 1800s, 19 In.	110
Crock, Blue, Bee Sting Design, Brown, Molded, Rim & Handle, 12 In.	74
Crock, Brushed Cobalt Blue Flowers, 6, 2 Applied Handles, 1850s, 14 In.	132
Crock, Brushed Cobalt Blue Flying Bird, Applied Handles, 1850s, 8¾ x 10 In.	360
Crock, Cake, Cobalt Blue Tornado & Branch, Norton & Co., 1800s, 3 Gal., 6 x 13 In.	375
Crock, Cake, Squared Rim, Arched Handle, Cobalt Blue Dropped Flower, Pa., c.1875, 7 x 11 In. *illus*	410
Crock, Churn, Molded Rim & Handle, Brown Glazed, Pinched Neck, 5 Gal., 18 In.	58
Crock, Cobalt Blue Bird, Arched Handles, Salt Glaze, F.B. Norton & Co., 1868, 13½ In. *illus*	187
Crock, Cobalt Blue Bird, Molded Handle, Brady & Ryan, Ellenville, Pa, 7½ In.	254
Crock, Cobalt Blue Bowl Of Flowers, Footed, Applied Lug Handles, c.1880, 5 Gal., 12 In.	875
Crock, Cobalt Blue Butterfly, Molded Rim & Handle, Salt Glaze, 20 Gal.	1800
Crock, Cobalt Blue Chicken, Salt Glaze, Cylindrical, Arched Handles, c.1880, 3 Gal., 10 In.	702
Crock, Cobalt Blue Flower, Molded Rim, Ear Handle, 1800s, 10 In.	200
Crock, Cobalt Blue Flower, No. 2, Weave & Dot, Ear Handle, 1800s, 12½ In.	671
Crock, Cobalt Blue Flowers, Ear Handle, Molded Rim, 3 Gal., 14¼ In., 2 Piece	671
Crock, Cobalt Blue Flowers, Handles, Connolly & Palmer, New Brunswick, N.J., 3 Gal., 10 In. *illus*	138
Crock, Cobalt Blue Label, Converted To Lamp, Brushed, Hamilton & Jones, 1850s, 26 In.	202
Crock, Cobalt Blue Letters, Handles, Excelsior Works, Isaac Hewitt, Rices Landing, Pa., 1860s, 8 In.	3250
Crock, Cobalt Blue Stylized Flower, Nathaniel Hudson, Galway Village, 1860s, N.Y., 3 Gal.	1100
Crock, Cobalt Blue Tulip, Stripe, Tooled Rim, Midsection, 1850s, Gal., 9 In.	28
Crock, Cobalt Blue, Clasped Hands, Lug Handles, Salt Glaze, Synan Brothers, 7 x 8 In.	17
Crock, Cobalt Blue, Jar Shape, Molded Handle, Rim, Hamilton & Jones Greensboro, Pa., 5 Gal., 15 In.	42
Crock, Painted, Cobalt Blue Leaves, Applied Handles, Haxstun, Ottman & Co., 1800s, 10 In., 2 Gal.	11
Cuspidor, Cobalt Blue Feather, Flowers, Waisted, Drain Hole, Salt Glaze, c.1870, 4½ In.	38

Stone, Figure, Dog, Dachshund, Chalcedony, Gold & Ruby Eyes, Carved, Russia, 2 1/4 In.
$945

Fontaine's Auction Gallery

Stone, Geode, Sink Style, Amethyst, Crystal, Black Granite Base, 13 x 19 x 17 In.
$502

Austin Auction Gallery

Stone, Sculpture, Standing Nude, Gray, Bauxite, Mixed Media, Dan Corbin, 1993, 53 In.
$9,375

eal Auction Company

Stone, Urn, Finial, Flaming, White, Carved, Square Base, Late 1800s, 22 3/4 In.
$256

Hindman

Stoneware, Batter Jug, Cobalt Blue Design, Wood Handle, F.H. Cowden, Harrisburg, 1800s, 8 1/2 In.
$388

Pook & Pook

Stoneware, Bowl, Glazed, White Circle, Leza McVey, c.1947, 8 1/2 In.
$1,625

Wright

Stoneware, Bowl, Ribbed Body, Glaze, Blue, Cream, Signed, Makoto Yab, Massachusetts, 1900s, 4 1/2 In.
$625

Eldred's

Stoneware, Churn, Flared Mouth, 2 Incised Rings, Arched Handle, Strasburg, 1875, 16 x 9 In.
$152

Jeffrey S. Evans & Associates

Stoneware, Crock, Cake, Squared Rim, Arched Handle, Cobalt Blue Dropped Flower, Pa., c.1875, 7 x 11 In.
$410

Jeffrey S. Evans & Associates

S

507

Stoneware, Crock, Cobalt Blue Flowers, Handles, Connolly & Palmer, New Brunswick, N.J., 3 Gal., 10 In.
$138

Pook & Pook

Stoneware, Figurine, Bird, Kookaburra, Cobalt Blue, Green, Harry Simeon, England, c.1925, 5 ½ In.
$403

Lion and Unicorn

Stoneware, Figurine, Spaniel, Seated, Dark Brown Glaze, Albany Slip, Late 1800s, 9 ½ In.
$185

Brunk Auctions

Stoneware, Flask, Souter Johnny, Night Cap Spout, Salt Glaze, England, 1800s, 11 x 10 In.
$219

Lion and Unicorn

Stoneware, Flowerpot, Pinecones, Molded, D.G. Thompson, Morgantown, W. Va., c.1885, 8 x 11 In.
$8,400

Crocker Farm, Inc.

Stoneware Face Jugs
Face jugs are dark jugs with distorted faces, crooked teeth, and big eyes. Older face jugs, pieces with alkaline glaze, and jars with cobalt decorations—animals, plants, or people—sell for the highest prices.

Stoneware, Jar, Brushed Cobalt Blue Flowers, 2 Arched Handles, Salt Glaze, c.1850, 6 ⅞ In.
$2,106

Jeffrey S. Evans & Associates

Stoneware, Jar, Cobalt Blue Bird, Flower, Arched Handles, Salt Glaze, N.A. White & Son, c.1885, 15 In.
$702

Jeffrey S. Evans & Associates

Stoneware, Jug, Face, Applied Clay Features, Kaolin Eyes, Teeth, Olive Glaze, Miles Mill, S.C., c.1870, 5 In.
$31,200

Crocker Farm, Inc.

Stoneware, Jug, Snake, Frogskin Glaze, Thumbprint Handle, Fred Johnston, North Carolina, 15 x 9 In.
$443

Leland Little Auctions

S

Fat Lamp, Albany Slip Glaze, Strap Handle, Cone Shape Stem, Saucer Base, 1836, 6 In.	702
Feeder, Cobalt Blue Trim, Ear Handle, Finial, 1800s, 13 In.	336
Figurine, Bird, Kookaburra, Cobalt Blue, Green, Harry Simeon, England, c.1925, 5 ½ In. .... *illus*	403
Figurine, Lion, Reddish Curly Mane, Toothy Grin, Billy Ray Hussey, North Carolina, 19 In...	1121
Figurine, Spaniel, Seated, Dark Brown Glaze, Albany Slip, Late 1800s, 9 ½ In. .... *illus*	185
Flask, Souter Johnny, Night Cap Spout, Salt Glaze, England, 1800s, 11 x 10 In. .... *illus*	219
Flowerpot, Cobalt Blue Sgraffito, Molded Rim, Late 1800s, 5 ¾ x 6 ¾ In.	813
Flowerpot, Pinecones, Molded, D.G. Thompson, Morgantown, W. Va., c.1885, 8 x 11 In. *illus*	8400
Ginger Jar, Green, Monumental, Exotic Birds, Leafy Landscape, Stand, Chinese, 81 In.	79
Jar, Brushed Cobalt Blue Flower, Rockbridge, Tab Handles, Salt Glaze, c.1830, 12 ½ In.	1638
Jar, Brushed Cobalt Blue Flowers, 2 Arched Handles, Salt Glaze, c.1850, 6 ⅞ In. .... *illus*	2106
Jar, Bulbous Shape, Splashed Green Glaze, Chinese, 19 ⅛ In.	175
Jar, Cobalt Blue Bird On Branch, Cowden & Wilcox, Harrisburg, Pa., c.1865, 3 Gal. ...._	2880
Jar, Cobalt Blue Bird, Flower, Arched Handles, Salt Glaze, N.A. White & Son, c.1885, 15 In. . *illus*	702
Jar, Cobalt Blue Flowers, Lug Handles, Stamped Hamilton, Greensboro, Pa., 4 Gal., 15 In......	1875
Jar, Cobalt Blue Flowers, Molded Rim, Brown Interior, 1800s, 13 ¼ In.	238
Jar, Cobalt Blue Stencil, Bayless McCarthey & Co., Louisville, Ky., Salt Glaze, 8 ½ x 5 In.......	431
Jar, Ear Handle, Cream Ground, Mounted As Lamp, Norton & Son, 2 Gal., 14 In.	188
Jar, Oval, Flared Flat Top Rim, Applied Strap Handle, Georgia, 1850s, 5 Gal., 18 x 5 In.	199
Jar, Pinched Neck, Wm. Hare, Wilmington, Delaware, 1800s, 7 In.	100
Jug, Albany Slip Tulip, Handle, Wood Stopper, 1800s, 3 Gal., 15 ¾ In.	976
Jug, Brushed Cobalt Blue Flowers, Applied Handle, Mid 1800s, 14 ½ In.	330
Jug, Brushed Cobalt Blue Tulip, Yellow, Oval, Applied Handle, S. Risley, Norwich, 1910s, 15 In.	450
Jug, Cobalt Blue Bird On Branch, Molded Rim, Applied Handle, Impressed, 2, 1850s, 14 In....	274
Jug, Cobalt Blue Bird, Branch, Incised, Handle, D. Roberts & Co., Utica, c.1830, 15 In.....	1150
Jug, Cobalt Blue Bird, Handle, Cream Ground, 4 Gal., 17 ½ In.	283
Jug, Cobalt Blue Dancing Couple, Strap Handles, Alkaline Glaze, Chester Hewell, c.1985, 11 In.	761
Jug, Cobalt Blue Design, Bulbous, Rolled Rim, Applied Strap Handle, Late 1700s, 4 In...........	1500
Jug, Cobalt Blue Eagle Banner, Handle, Stamped, Riedinger & Caire, New York, 2 Gal., 13 ½ In. .	4270
Jug, Cobalt Blue Flower, 2 Curved Handles, Molded Rim, 1870, 14 In.	1180
Jug, Cobalt Blue Flower, Handle, Bulbous, 1800s, 2 Gal., 11 In.	90
Jug, Cobalt Blue Flower, Strap Handle, Salt Glaze, Oval, 1800s, 12 x 8 In.	339
Jug, Cobalt Blue Flowers, Oval Shape, Loop Handle, R.W. Russell, Pa., c.1850, 2 Gal., 13 ½ In. .	480
Jug, Cobalt Blue Label, Applied Handle, Stopper, John Harrison, 1850s, 10 In.	101
Jug, Cobalt Blue Leaves, Molded Handle, N. Clark Jr., 1800s, 14 In.	207
Jug, Cobalt Blue Squiggle, Red Paint, 3 Gal., 13 In.	111
Jug, Cobalt Blue Stencil, Strong, Cobb & Co., Cleveland, 2 Gal., 12 ½ In.	209
Jug, Cobalt Blue Tulip, Impressed, J. Young, Harrisburg, Pa., 1800s, 2 Gal., 15 In...............	1342
Jug, Cobalt Blue Tulip, Squat, Squared Mouth, Strap Handle, Frederick J. Caire, 1854, 9 ⅝ In.	234
Jug, Cobalt Blue Vertical Stripes, Tooled Rim, Western Pa., 1800s, ½ Gal., 9 ⅜ In.	1750
Jug, Cobalt Blue Wreath, Bulbous Body, Molded Rim, c.1861, 20 In.	1100
Jug, Ewer, Gray Earthenware, Wave Design, Handle, 1800s, 11 ¾ In..	594
Jug, Face, Applied Clay Features, Kaolin Eyes, Teeth, Olive Glaze, Miles Mill, S.C., c.1870, 5 In. *illus*	31200
Jug, Face, Green Alkaline Glaze, White Clay Eyes, Applied Strap Handle, Lanie Meaders, 10 In.....	1280
Jug, Snake, Coiled, Strap Handle, Salt Glaze, Signed, Marvin Bailey, 2007, 8 x 9 In............	219
Jug, Snake, Frogskin Glaze, Thumbprint Handle, Fred Johnston, North Carolina, 15 x 9 In. ..*illus*	443
Jug, Whiskey, Brown Glaze, Stencil, E.S. Pierce Co., Worcester, c.1910, 3 Gal., 16 In...............	190
Jug, Whiskey, Cream Ground, Phil Kelly, Virginia, c.1910, 3 Gal., 16 In. .... *illus*	236
Jug, Wide Band Collar, Cobalt Blue Cloud, Strap Handle, Thompson & Co., 1839, 14 ¼ In.	200
Lamp Base, Iron Slip, Pine Branch, Tooled Rim, Salt Glaze, M.L. Owen, 8 ¼ In.	92
Lamp Base, Lion Mask, Billy Ray Hussey, North Carolina, 10 ⅛ In....................................	118
Milk Pan, Cobalt Blue Brushed Leaves, Flat Top Rim, Pour Spout, Salt Glaze, c.1865, 4 In.	410
Milk Pan, Cobalt Blue Flowers, Feather, Squared Rim, Pour Spout, Salt Glaze, 1860s, 4 ⅜ In. ..	439
Mug, Black Letters, Father's Mug, Putty, Butterscotch, Black Band, England, c.1920, 9 In.	106
Pitcher, Batter, Blue, Bulbous, Handle, 2 Gal., 14 In.	360
Pitcher, Batter, Cream Ground, Wide Spout, Curved Handle, Gal.	85
Pitcher, Brushed Cobalt Blue Flowers & Leaves, Strap Handle, Zigler, c.1830, 8 ¾ In.	7605
Pitcher, Cobalt Blue Leaves, Brown Ground, Handle, 11 In.	215
Pitcher, Cobalt Blue Tulip, Molded Rim, Bulbous, 1800s, 11 In.	732
Pitcher, Commemorative, White, Eagle, Carved, Spurred Handle, Elmer Ellsworth, 8 ½ x 8 In...	406

Stoneware, Jug, Whiskey, Cream
Ground, Phil Kelly, Virginia, c.1910,
3 Gal., 16 In.
$236

Leland Little Auctions

Stoneware, Water Cooler, Cobalt Blue
Slip, Broadway, Street Scene, Oval, 1846,
7 Gal.
$480,000

Crocker Farm, Inc.

TIP
*Outdoor stonework
and statues, even if
made of granite, can
be damaged by acid
rain, frost, and plants
like ivy. Put garden
statues on stands to
keep the moisture
from the grass away
from the statue.
Wash with a hose
and a soft brush.*

S

Stoneware, Water Filter, Brown, Mounted As Lamp, Engraved, Embossed, London, 1800s, 38 In.
$154

Hindman

Store, Banana Crate, Painted, 2 Handles, Inland Trading Co., c.1920, 11½ x 35 In.
$207

Austin Auction Gallery

Store, Bin, Coffee, Hinged Sloped Lid, Japanned Tin, Red, c.1880, 19 In.
$308

Rich Penn Auctions

Pitcher, Molded, Indian Peace Sign, Blue, Pointed Spout, Handle, 8½ In.	62
Pitcher, Yellow Clay, Albany Slip, Presentation, Mrs. R. Pannabaker From Charles, 1891, 10 In.	6120
Planter, Bisque, Model F-507, Stained Pine Stand, John Follis & Rex Goode, c.1956, 14 In.	5000
Salt Box, Removable Lid, Clear Yellow Glaze, Molded, 5 x 6 In.	89
Sculpture, Bison, Walking, Glazed, Signed, Maliarik, 6 x 12 x 6 In.	750
Strainer, Cheese, Basket Shape, Pierced Holes, Brown Glaze, 12½ In.	188
Tankard, Hinged Lid, Portrait Cartouche, Pewter Mounted, Inscribed, DR 1681, 10⅞ In.	2125
Teapot, Painted, Spout, Bamboo Handle, Charles Spacey, 1900s, 9 x 3¼ In.	77
Urn, Campana, Flared Rim, Lion's Head Handles, Square Base, Speckle Glaze, 22 x 14 In., Pair.	2925
Vase, Bladder, Shark Tooth Design, Blue, Green Lines, Signed, Massachusetts, 1900s, 11 In.	563
Vase, Bulbous, Blue Glaze, Berndt Friberg, Sweden, 1965, 4¾ x 4¾ In.	375
Vase, Cizhou Type, Oval, Flattened Mouth, Engraved Flowers, White Ground, Chinese, 1800s, 10 In.	322
Vase, Cobalt Blue Grapevine, Alkaline, Feldspar & Flint Glaze, Joe Reinhardt, 9½ In.	89
Vase, Dancing Lions, Salt Glaze, Billy Ray Hussey, North Carolina, 12¾ In.	590
Vase, Gourd, Cobalt Blue Glaze, Molded Base, Otto & Vivika Heino, 1995, 7¼ In.	938
Water Cooler, Barrel Shape, Brushed Cobalt, Faux Hoops, New England, c.1870, 6 Gal., 14 In.	129
Water Cooler, Cobalt Blue Eagle, Salt Glaze, Molded Rim & Handle, 8 Gal.	425
Water Cooler, Cobalt Blue Slip, Broadway, Street Scene, Oval, 1846, 7 Gal. .... *illus*	480000
Water Cooler, Cobalt Blue Sponge, 6, Ice Water, Molded Rim, Western Stoneware, 6 Gal.	425
Water Filter, Brown, Mounted As Lamp, Engraved, Embossed, London, 1800s, 38 In. .. *illus*	154

STORE

Store fixtures, cases, cutters, and other items that have no company advertising as part of the decoration are listed here. Most items found in an old store are listed in the Advertising category in this book.

Banana Crate, Painted, 2 Handles, Inland Trading Co., c.1920, 11½ x 35 In. .... *illus*	207
Bin, Coffee, Hinged Sloped Lid, Japanned Tin, Red, c.1880, 19 In. .... *illus*	308
Bin, Slant Lid, Poplar, Painted, Red, 2 Greek Key Borders, A&P Logo, c.1900, 30½ In.	600
Cabinet, Display, Shopkeeper's, Oak, 4 Shelves, Metal Plaque, 1900s, 89 x 66 In.	1125
Cabinet, Hanging, 21 Drawers, Stamped Antiseptic Powder, 21 x 15¾ In.	200
Cabinet, White Pine, Beveled Overlapping Drawer Front, Turned Brass Knobs, 22 x 6 x 16 In.	207
Case, Collar Button, Oak, Curved Glass, Rotating Interior, Compartments, 7 x 15 x 8 In.	277
Case, Display, Molded Cornice, Glazed Door & Sides, Glass Shelves, Chinese, Late 1900s, 75 x 19 In.	325
Case, Display, Oak, Brass, Curved Glass, Mirrored Back, 31 x 18 In.	170
Case, Display, Oak, Plate Glass Panels, Sliding Doors, c.1900, 42 x 34 x 22 In.	360
Case, Display, Oak, Revolving Interior Shelves, Hinged Door, Cast Iron Handle, 29 x 19 In.	2460
Case, Display, Walnut, Shaped Upper Valances, Drawer, Glazed, Late 1800s, 16 x 14 x 9 In.	375
Cigar Cutter, Figural, Sterling Silver, Bear Head, Stag Antler Body, Donatus Soligen, 8 In.	441
Cigar Cutter, Sterling Silver Boar's Head, Red Gem-Set Eyes, Antler Handle, 8 x 2 x 1 In.	585
Coffee Grinders are listed in the Coffee Mill category.	
Cupboard, 2 Tiers, 3 Shelves & Cabinets, Oyster White, Painted, 1910s, 82½ In.	702
Dispenser, Paper, Iron, Wood Top & Base, Marked, Ace, 13 x 19½ In.	62
Display, Knife, Curved, Wavy Glass, Sliding Doors, Liner, 13 x 21 In.	259
Display, Knittel Show Case Co., Oak Frame, Rounded Front, c.1900, 12 x 60 x 23 In. .... *illus*	450
Display, Name Plate, Brass Tacked, Wood Frame, Salesman's Sample, c.1900, 12 x 10 In.	185
Holder, Ice Cream Cone, Rectangular, 12 Holes, Canted Sides, 2 Handholds, Wood, 4 x 17 In.	531
Rack, Baker's, Oak, Metal, 5 Shelves, Turned Supports, Combination Table Co., c.1890, 55 x 35 In.	861
Rack, Paper Bag, Fan Shape, Wood, Iron Stringholder, Late 1900s, 20 x 8 x 16 In.	338
Rack, Pine, Molded Top, Bullnose Side Molding, Yamanaka & Co., Early 1900s, 86 x 15 x 12 In.	1053
Shoe Stand, Nickel Plate, Brass, Scrolled Arms, Adjustable, Victorian, c.1900, 20 In.	123
Sign, Antiques, Arm Shape, Finger Pointing, Wood, White Letters on Black, 11 In. .... *illus*	375
Sign, Antiques, Wood, Painted White & Red, Pointed Detail, 2-Sided, 6 x 24 In.	120
Sign, Barber, Razor, Tin Blade, Black, Silver Wood Case, Late 1800s, 23½ In.	594
Sign, Blacksmith, Horseshoe Shape, Multicolor, Iron, 17 x 16 In.	688
Sign, Boot Trade, Black, Yellow, Cast Iron, Late 1800s, 26¼ In.	549
Sign, Deliver All Goods In Rear, Rectangular, Pressed Brass, 9¾ In.	338
Sign, Drugs & Stationery, Pine Board, Block Letters, White Ground, Late 1800s, 15 x 40 In.	475
Sign, Eyeglasses, Gold Metal Frame, Oval Green Lenses, 2-Sided, 29 In.	3172

S

Sign, Fresh Butter, Cow Shape, Wood, White, Black Spots, Metal Loops, 21 x 30 In.	384
Sign, Juicy Peach, Wood, Painted, 23 ½ x 5 ½ In. *illus*	106
Sign, Keep 2 Things, Painted, Wood, 1900s, 12 ½ x 41 In.	94
Sign, Prescriptions, Glass Panel, Rolling Light, Multicolor, 8 ¾ x 25 x 10 ½ In.	250
Sign, Wood, Black Font, Yellow, Boats & Motors For The Day, Frame, c.1930, 16 x 32 In. *illus*	594
Tobacco Cutter, Shield Shape Board, Wrought Iron Blade, Handle, Late 1800s, 5 x 17 In.	84

STOVE

Stoves have been used in America for heating since the eighteenth century and for cooking since the nineteenth century. Most types of wood, coal, gas, kerosene, and even some electric stoves are collected. Salesman's samples may be listed here or in Toy.

Cook, Favorite Stove & Range Co., Silver Trim & Feet, Iron, Salesman's Sample, c.1890, 27 In.	189
Cook, Quick Meal, Blue Speckled, Fire Box, Porcelain, 63 ¾ x 51 x 37 In.	923
Heater, Cast Iron, Engraved, Laundry, No. 40, SAM, 21 x 16 ½ In.	201
Ornamental Crest, For Parlor Stove, Rococo, Leaves, Openwork, Silver Plate, c.1870, 15 x 19 In.	98
Parlor, Cast Iron, Home Stove Co., No. 5, Black, Cox & Brothers, Philadelphia, 1852, 27 x 30 In	118
Stove Plate, Wedding Fable, 2 Angels Flying, Marlboro Furnace, Isaac Zane, 1768, 23 x 20 In.	3198

SUMIDA

Sumida is a Japanese pottery that was made from about 1895 to 1941. Pieces are usually everyday objects—vases, jardinieres, bowls, teapots, and decorative tiles. Most pieces have a very heavy orange-red, blue, brown, black, green, purple, or off-white glaze, with raised three-dimensional figures as decorations. The unglazed part is painted red, green, black, or orange. Sumida is sometimes mistakenly called Sumida gawa, but true Sumida gawa is a softer pottery made in the early 1800s.

Bowl, 9 Figures Around Rim, Red, Black Dripped Glaze, Signed, Inoue Ryosai, c.1900, 9 ½ In.	375
Teapot, Squat Oval Shape, Dragon, Red, Twig Bail Handle, Signed, 19th Century, 3 In. *illus*	344

SUNBONNET BABIES

Sunbonnet Babies were introduced in 1900 in the book *The Sunbonnet Babies.* The stories were by Eulalie Osgood Grover, illustrated by Bertha Corbett. The children's faces were completely hidden by the sunbonnets. The children had been pictured in black and white before this time, but the color pictures in the book were immediately successful. The Royal Bayreuth China Company made a full line of children's dishes decorated with the Sunbonnet Babies. Some Sunbonnet Babies plates have been reproduced, but they are clearly marked.

Mug, Friday, Sweeping, 2 ¾ In.	30
Nut Bowl, Sunday, Fishing, 3 Footed, Raised Gilt Rim, 4 x 2 ½ In.	89
Plate, Tuesday, Ironing, 7 ½ In.	45
Plate, Wednesday, Mending, 7 ½ In.	89
Sugar & Creamer, Monday Washing	75

SUNDERLAND LUSTER

Sunderland luster is a name given to a special type of pink luster made by Leeds, Newcastle, and other English firms during the nineteenth century. The luster broth glaze is metallic and glossy and appears to have bubbles in it. Other pieces of luster are listed in the Luster category.

Mug, Bridge Over River Wear, Black Transfer, Frog Interior, Pink Luster, 1910s, 5 ⅜ In. *illus*	263
Punch Bowl, Sailors, Poems, Pink Luster, Black Transfer Print, Footed, 1910s, 9 In.	222

Store, Display, Knittel Show Case Co., Oak Frame, Rounded Front, c.1900, 12 x 60 x 23 In.
$450

Garth's Auctioneers & Appraisers

TIP

If you are remodeling or redecorating, think about antiques and collectibles displayed in the work area. A workman will hammer on a wall without worrying about the shelves on the other side.

Store, Sign, Antiques, Arm Shape, Finger Pointing, Wood, White Letters On Black, 11 In.
$375

ANTIQUES

Eldred's

Store, Sign, Juicy Peach, Wood, Painted, 23 ½ x 5 ½ In.
$106

Copake Auction

S

Store, Sign, Wood, Black Font, Yellow, Boats & Motors For The Day, Frame, c.1930, 16 x 32 In.
$594

BOATS & MOTORS FOR THE DAY

Eldred's

Sumida, Teapot, Squat Oval Shape, Dragon, Red, Twig Bail Handle, Signed, 19th Century, 3 In.
$344

Eldred's

Sunderland, Mug, Bridge Over River Wear, Black Transfer, Frog Interior, Pink Luster, 1910s, 5⅝ In.
$263

Jeffrey S. Evans & Associates

Superman, Lunchbox, Fighting The Robot, Multicolor, Tin, Universal D.C., 1954
$1,875

Bruneau & Co. Auctioneers

TIP
A tennis ball can be used to rub out scuff marks on vintage linoleum tiles, the kind often used in houses before the 1960s.

SUPERMAN

Superman was created by two seventeen-year-olds in 1938. The first issue of Action Comics had the strip. Superman remains popular and became the hero of a radio show in 1940, cartoons in the 1940s, a television series, and several major movies.

Bank, Dime Register, Superman Breaking Chains, Tin, Square With Cut Corners	118
Comic Book, Action Comics, No. 158, The Kid From Krypton, July 1951, 12¾ x 8¼ In.	500
Lunch Box, Fighting The Robot, Multicolor, Tin, Universal D.C., 1954 .... *illus*	1875
Nutcracker, Painted, DC Comics, Taiwan, 1979, 10½ In., Pair	63
Poster, Amazing World Of Superman, Exhibition Center, Metropolis, Ill., 1973, 20 x 14 In.	50

SUSIE COOPER

Susie Cooper (1902–1995) began as a designer in 1925 working for the English firm A.E. Gray & Company. She left to work on her own as Susie Cooper Productions in 1929, decorating white ware bought from other potteries. In 1931 she formed Susie Cooper Pottery, Ltd. and moved her studio to Wood & Sons Crown Works. In 1950 it became Susie Cooper China, Ltd., and the company made china and earthenware. She bought Crown Works in 1959. It became part of the Wedgwood Group in 1966. Wedgwood closed Crown Works in 1979 and Cooper moved her studio to Adams & Sons. In 1986 she moved to the Isle of Man and worked as a free-lance designer. The name *Susie Cooper* appears with the company names on many pieces of ceramics.

A.E. Gray & Co. c.1925–1931	Susie Cooper 1932–1956	Susie Cooper 1932–1964

Charger, Wedding Band, Concentric Rings, Blue, Tan, c.1940, 16 In.	375
Coffeepot, Wedding Band Pattern, Kestrel Shape, Locking Lid, 1940s, 7 x 6 x 4 In.	275
Soup, Cream, Central Bouquet, Liner, Tab Handles	40

SWASTIKA KERAMOS

Swastika Keramos is a line of art pottery made from 1906 to 1908 by the Owen China Company of Minerva, Ohio. Many pieces were made with an iridescent glaze.

Ewer, Forest Scene, Multicolor, Iridescent Glazes, Marked, 10 In. .... *illus*	133
Vase, 2 Handles, Gold Iris, Maroon Iridescent Ground, 11 x 6¼ In.	48

SWORDS

Swords of all types that are of interest to collectors are listed here. The military dress sword with elaborate handle is probably the most wanted. A tsuba is a hand guard fitted to a Japanese sword between the handle and the blade. Be sure to display swords in a safe way, out of reach of children.

Artillery, Model 1832, 3 Fullers, Brass Fish Scale Handle, Ames Mfg. Co., 19 In.	750
Artillery, U.S. Army Model, Brass Handle, Eagle Pommel, Black Leather Scabbard, 1834, 25 In..	644
Backsword, Single Edged, Fuller, Spherical Pommel, Wood Grip, 1600s, 31½ In.	1375
Bayonet, Military, Wood, Brass Grip, Leather Case, France, 1874, 20½ In.	94
Cavalry, Saber, Gunmetal Gray, Wood Handle, Marked, Mansfield & Lamb, 1862, 35 In.	531
Cavalry, Saber, Officer's, Brass Guard, Shagreen Grip, Steel Scabbard, H.V. Allien & Co., N.Y., 34 In.	375
Cutlass, Curved, Cast Iron, Oval Knuckle Bore, Rolled Quillon, Marked, 27½ x 15 In.	469
Cutlass, Naval, Straight Blade, Punched Hilt, Leather Grip, Marked, Thomas Gill, 1804, 40 In....	1170
French, Lion's Head Pommel, Brass S, Wood Grip, Engraved, 29¾ x 5 In.	500

S

Hanger, Officer's, Single Fuller Blade, Brass Grip & Pommel, 1750, 30 In.	767
Hunting, Stag Handle, Half Fuller, Shell Guard, Leaves, Brass Pommel, Germany, c.1930, 22 In.	295
Infantry, Officer's, Spearpoint, Ivory Grip, Brass Finger Guard, Eagle Head Pommel, 32 In.	492
Iron, Serpent Shape Hilt, Wood Handle, Blacksmith, 1800s, 24 In. *illus*	2000
Military, 2 Back-To-Back Squirrels, Blade, Scabbard, Carl Eickhorn, 36 ½ In.	350
Naval, Etched Blade, Wire Rapped Shagreen Handle, A. Shuman & Co., 33 In. *illus*	441
Officer's, Artillery, Lion Design, Marked, Deutscher Officers Verein, Germany, 28 In.	135
Officer's, General & Staff, Fuller, Cupped Guard, Leather Scabbard, Sheets Of Silver, 31 In.	1250
Officer's, General, 2 Edge, Hearts In Guard, Marked, Charles Hebbert, 37 In.	1016
Officer's, Lion's Head Hilt, Jeweled Eyes, Scabbard, Alcoso, Germany, 40 In.	400
Persian, Gold & Silver, Curved, Damascus Blade, Leather Scabbard, Koftgari, 35 ¼ In.	1888
Rapier, Engraved Hand Guard, Wire Wrapped Grip, Germany, Late 1700s, 21 ½ x 9 ½ In.	1063
Saber, Ames, Model 1840, Cavalry, Silver Scabbard, 1846	567
Saber, Chassepot M-1866, Swirl Handle, Scabbard, France, 28 In.	60
Saber, Curved Blade, Ivory Grip, Chain Knuckle Bow, Gilt Scabbard, 14 ½ In.	861
Samurai, Katana, Cloth Handle, Gold Inlay, Tsuba, Lacquered Sheath, Japan, 39 In.	445
Samurai, Uchigatana Blade, Shagreen Grip, Japan, 1400s, 21 ¼ In.	518
Samurai, World War II, Silk Grip, Iron Tsuba, Leather Scabbard, Kai Gunto, 36 ¾ In.	1063
Samurai, Wrapped Handle, Curved Blade, Japan, 35 In.	504
Short, Stag Handle, Blade, Etched, Knight, Shield, Drum, Flag, Carl Eickhorn, c.1920, 19 In.	502
Staff Officer's, U.S., Spearpoint Blade, Shell Guard, W.A. Raymold, 5 x 30 In.	175

SYRACUSE

Syracuse is one of the trademarks used by the Onondaga Pottery of Syracuse, New York. They also used O.P. Co. The company was established in 1871. The name became the Syracuse China Company in 1966. Syracuse China closed in 2009. It was known for fine dinnerware and restaurant china.

IRONSTONE CHINA O.P. Co.	CHINA O.P. Co.	SYRACUSE China MADE IN U.S.A.
Syracuse China, Corp. 1871–1873	Syracuse China, Corp. 1892–1895	Syracuse China, Corp. 1966–1970

Airplane, Plate, Dinner, Airbrushed, Blue, Red, Marked, Onondaga Pottery, 3 Piece	65
Alpine, Cup & Saucer, Pink Flowers, Platinum Trim	12
Berkeley, Bowl, Fruit, Pink Flowers, Branches, 4 In.	8
Corabel, Bowl, Vegetable, Lid, Pink Flowers, Cream Ground, Platinum Trim	75
Palomino, Platter, Speckled Ground, Yellow, Orange & Brown Rings, 12 In.	15

TAPESTRY, *Porcelain, see Rose Tapestry category.*

TEA CADDY

Tea caddy is the name for a small box made to hold tea leaves. In the eighteenth century, tea was very expensive and it was stored under lock and key. The first tea caddies were made with locks. By the nineteenth century, tea was more plentiful and the tea caddy was larger. Often there were two sections, one for green tea, one for black tea.

Copper, Vase Shape, Flowers, Leaves, Silver Mounted, Gorham, 1882, 4 In.	1792
Copper, Vase Shape, Red, Applied Silver, Men In Boat, Fish, Crab, Gorham, 1882, 4 ¼ In.	2304
Fruitwood, Pear Shape, Wood Stem, Foil Lining, George III, England, 1700s, 7 x 3 ¾ In.	1989
Fruitwood, Removable Lid, Apple Shape, George III, Early 1800s, 5 ½ In. *illus*	875
Lacquer, Octagonal, 2 Engraved Compartments, Paw Feet, Chinese, 1850s, 5 x 9 x 6 In. *illus*	600
Mahogany, 3 Compartments, Brass Keyhole, Escutcheon, Bail Handle, 1800s, 5 ½ x 9 ¾ In.	295
Mahogany, Brass, Inlay, Handles, Paw Foot, 1800s, 13 x 7 x 8 ½ In.	118
Mahogany, Butterfly, Medallion, Octagonal Top, Inlay, 1800s, 4 ¾ x 6 ½ x 5 ¼ In.	196

Swastika Keramos, Ewer, Forest Scene, Multicolor, Iridescent Glazes, Marked, 10 In.
$133

Humler & Nolan

Sword, Iron, Serpent Shape Hilt, Wood Handle, Blacksmith, 1800s, 24 In.
$2,000

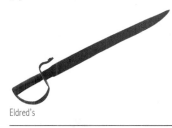

Eldred's

Sword, Naval, Etched Blade, Wire Rapped Shagreen Handle, A. Shuman & Co., 33 In.
$441

Fontaine's Auction Gallery

T

513

Tea Caddy, Fruitwood, Removable Lid, Apple Shape, George III, Early 1800s, 5 ½ In.
$875

Charlton Hall Auctions

Tea Caddy, Lacquer, Octagonal, 2 Engraved Compartments, Paw Feet, Chinese, 1850s, 5 x 9 x 6 In.
$600

Garth's Auctioneers & Appraisers

Tea Caddy, Mahogany, Hinged Lid, Carved, Inlaid Escutcheon, Melon Shape, Tin Lined, c.1860, 7 In.
$1,652

Leland Little Auctions

Tea Caddy, Mother-Of-Pearl Inlay, Hinged Lid, Flowers, Octagonal, 1880s, 4 x 7 x 4 In.
$585

Jeffrey S. Evans & Associates

Tea Caddy, Shell Veneer, Hinged Lid, Black, Gold, Rectangular, England, Early 1800s, 6 x 8 In.
$1,534

Cottone Auctions

Tea Caddy, Shell Veneer, Ivory Moldings, Cut Glass, Coffin Shape, Ball Feet, England, 1810s, 7 x 7 ¾ In.
$2,375

Eldred's

Tea Caddy, Tole, Lid, Leaves, Yellow, Red, Black Ground, 1800s, 7 ¾ In.
$549

Pook & Pook

T

Mahogany, Canted Corners, Shell & Vase Inlay, Lidded Boxes, George III, c.1810, 5 x 7 In...	1875
Mahogany, Dome Lid, Bracket Feet, Brass Bail Handle, Chippendale, 1780s, 6 x 10 x 5 In.....	202
Mahogany, Egg & Dart, Mother-Of-Pearl Inlay, Flat Ball Feet, 6 x 12 In.	224
Mahogany, Escutcheon, Lion Mask, Coffin Shape, Handles, Paw Feet, Early 1800s, 8 x 12 In..	384
Mahogany, Fitted Interior, Ring, Regency, Early 1800s, 5 3/8 x 8 3/4 In..............................	154
Mahogany, Hinged Lid, Bun Feet, Coffin Shape, English Regency, Early 1800s, 8 1/2 x 14 In.........	443
Mahogany, Hinged Lid, Carved, Inlaid Escutcheon, Melon Shape, Tin Lined, c.1860, 7 In. ...*illus*	1652
Mahogany, Hinged Lid, Compartment, Regency, 1800s, 5 7/8 x 11 7/8 x 5 7/8 In.....................	218
Mahogany, Hinged Lid, Divided & Lidded Compartments, Bun Feet, Georgian, 1800s, 6 x 12 In. ...	118
Mahogany, Hinged Lid, Inlaid Brass Escutcheons, Ring Handles, 3 Wells, 1850s, 7 x 12 x 7 In.	270
Mahogany, Hinged Lid, Veneer, Fruitwood Inlay, Fitted Interior, 1800s, 4 x 8 x 4 In.............	344
Mahogany, Inlaid Conch Shell, 2 Urns Of Flowers, Crossbanded Border, c.1790, 5 x 9 x 4 In.	300
Mahogany, Inlaid Panels, Fans, Canted Corner, Parquetry Edging, Early 1800s, 4 x 9 x 4 In. .	1872
Mahogany, Inlaid, Canted Corners, Shell & Vase Inlay, George III, Early 1800s, 5 x 7 In.	1875
Mahogany, Lift Lid, Canted Sides, Banded Inlay, Bentwood Swing Handle, 1800s, 6 x 6 x 5 In.	132
Mahogany, Satinwood, Parquetry, Inlay, Shells, 4 3/4 x 7 1/2 x 4 In...................................	156
Mahogany, Single Well, Inlaid, Bone Escutcheon, George III, c.1800, 4 1/2 In.	500
Mother-Of-Pearl Inlay, Hinged Lid, Flowers, Octagonal, 1880s, 4 x 7 x 4 In. ....*illus*	585
Mother-Of-Pearl, Brass Cartouche, Compartments, Escutcheon, England, 1800s, 5 x 8 1/4 In.	413
Mother-Of-Pearl, Tortoiseshell, Pagoda Shape, Concave Panel, Bun Feet, c.1825, 5 x 7 x 5 In.	1989
Porcelain, Pear Shape, Blue & White, Landscape, Japan, 8 x 5 1/2 In.	308
Rosewood, Hinged Lid, Applied Molding, Inlaid Brass, Coffin Shape, Bun Feet, 1850s, 7 x 12 x 6 In.	1440
Rosewood, Hinged Lid, Mother-Of-Pearl Inlay, Inset Handles, Velvet Interior, 7 x 15 In...	732
Satinwood, Lid, 3 Compartments, Oval Fan Inlaid Panels, 1850s, 6 x 9 x 5 In.	2340
Satinwood, Rosewood Band, 2 Interior Boxes, Ring Handles, George III, c.1810, 7 x 13 In.....	366
Satinwood, Rosewood, Banded, Brass, Lion Mask Ring Handles, Paw Feet, Early 1800s, 6 1/2 In.	366
Shell Veneer, Hinged Lid, Black, Gold, Rectangular, England, Early 1800s, 6 x 8 In. .. *illus*	1534
Shell Veneer, Ivory Moldings, Cut Glass, Coffin Shape, Ball Feet, England, 1810s, 7 x 7 3/4 In. *illus*	2375
Shell Veneer, Silver Inlay, Hinged Lid, Ball Feet, Georgian, 1800s, 4 1/2 x 5 In.................	531
Silver Filigree, Flowering Branches, Coral, Lobed, Enamel, Marked, Chinese, 7 1/4 In.	944
Silver, Chinoiserie, Engraved, Chinese Characters, George III, Thomas Nash, 1768, 4 In......	3528
Silver, Engraved Shell & Leaves, Fluted Lid, Urn Finial, Pierre Gillois, c.1768, 6 x 3 x 3 In.	523
Silver, Hinged Lid, Chamfered Corners, Starr & Marcus, U.S.A., c.1864, 4 1/2 x 6 1/2 In.............	1750
Silver, Hinged Lid, Flowers, Urn Finial, Engraved, Auguste Lesage, 1780, 4 3/4 x 4 3/4 In.	4636
Silver, Hinged Lid, Oblong Body, Ribbed Design, Thomas Johnson, London, 6 1/4 In...............	690
Silver, Repousse, Chased, Stag Finial, Armoire Shape, Turned Legs, 1890, 5 x 3 x 1 In.	439
Silver, Spinach Green, Cylindrical, Jade, Enamel, Hexagonal Base, Chinese, 6 1/4 x 4 3/4 In. ...	443
Stoneware, Molded Dot, Diaper, White Salt Glaze, Staffordshire, 1760s, 4 1/2 x 5 x 2 5/8 In... ...	938
Tole, Lid, Leaves, Yellow, Red, Black Ground, 1800s, 7 3/4 In. .... *illus*	549
Tortoiseshell, 2 Lidded Boxes, Pad Feet, George III, c.1810, 6 x 7 1/2 In.	3456
Tortoiseshell, Bombe, Coffin Shape, Pad Feet, George III, Early 1800s, 5 In. .... *illus*	2318
Tortoiseshell, Dome Lid, Serpentine Front, Silver Cartouche, Wood Feet, 1800s, 5 x 7 x 4 In..	2925
Tortoiseshell, Green, 2 Lidded Compartments, Pad Feet, George III, Early 1800s, 4 x 6 In. ....*illus*	4160
Tortoiseshell, Silver Mount, Coffin Shape, George III, c.1800, 5 3/4 x 7 x 4 1/2 In.............	6100
Walnut, Burl, 2 Tea Boxes, Square, Georgian, 1700s, 6 x 6 1/2 In.	115
Walnut, Dome Lid, Brass Mounted, Faux Grained, 2 Compartments, 1800s, 8 1/2 x 5 1/2 x 6 In.	148
Wood, Georgian Style, Fruit Shape, Bone Escutcheon, Silver Interior, 1900s, 6 In..................	295
Wood, Lid, Inlay, 6-Sided, Removable Interior, Leaves, 4 1/2 x 6 1/4 In.............................	400
Wood, Pear Shape Stem, Inlaid Bone Escutcheon, Lock, Lead Lining, c.1910, 7 In.................	590

TEA LEAF IRONSTONE

Tea leaf ironstone dishes are named for their decorations. There was a superstition that it was lucky if a whole tea leaf unfolded at the bottom of your teacup. This idea was translated into the pattern of dishes known as "tea leaf." By 1850 at least 12 English factories were making this pattern, and by the 1870s it was a popular pattern in many countries. The tea leaf was always a luster glaze in early wares, although now some pieces are made with a brown tea leaf. There are many variations of tea leaf designs, such as Teaberry, Pepper Leaf, and Gold Leaf. The

---

TEA LEAF IRONSTONE

Tea Caddy, Tortoiseshell, Bombe, Coffin Shape, Pad Feet, George III, Early 1800s, 5 In.
$2,318

Neal Auction Company

Tea Caddy, Tortoiseshell, Green, 2 Lidded Compartments, Pad Feet, George III, Early 1800s, 4 x 6 In.
$4,160

Neal Auction Company

Teco, Vase, Green Matte Glaze, 2 Handles, Impressed Mark, W.D. Gates, 3 3/4 x 3 1/8 In.
$938

Toomey & Co. Auctioneers

T

Teddy Bear, Alpha Farnell, Mohair, Turquoise, Curly Hair, Jointed, Hang Tag, 15 In.
$86

Apple Tree Auction Center

Teddy Bear, Steiff, Mohair, Apricot, Swivel Head, Hump, Shoebutton Eyes, Stitched Nose, c.1905, 24 In.
$21,600

Bertoia Auctions

Teddy Bear, Winnie The Pooh, Mohair, Golden, Red Sweater, Jointed, Growler, Steiff, 12 In.
$111

Apple Tree Auction Center

designs were used on many different white ironstone shapes, such as Bamboo, Lily of the Valley, Empress, and Cumbow.

Soup, Dish, Morning Glory, Richelieu Shape, Marked, James F. Wileman, c.1850, 9 In.	7
Teapot, Square Ridge Body, Squared Handle, Marked, H. Burgess, Burslem, England, 7 x 8¼ In.	29
Tureen, Soup, Scrolled Handles, Oval Foot, Anthony Shaw, 1800s, 9 x 8 x 14 In.	62

TECO

Teco is the mark used on the art pottery line made by the American Terra Cotta and Ceramic Company of Terra Cotta and Chicago, Illinois. The company was an offshoot of the firm founded by William D. Gates in 1881. The Teco line was first made in 1885 but was not sold commercially until 1902. It continued in production until 1922. Over 500 designs were made in a variety of colors, shapes, and glazes. The company closed in 1930.

Bowl, Salad, Green Matte Glaze, White Inside, 4 Buttresses, Marked, H. Smith, 12 x 6 In.	2625
Dish, Round, Green Frog Figure On Side, Stamped, 5 In.	438
Vase, Closed Handles, Angled, Flared Lip, Earthenware, Green Matte Glaze, W.D. Gates, 8½ x 4 In.	750
Vase, Green Matte Glaze, 2 Handles, Impressed Mark, W.D. Gates, 3¾ x 3⅛ In. .... *illus*	938
Vase, Green Matte Glaze, Cattails, Impressed, Fritz Albert, 22 x 7½ In.	10000
Vase, Long Neck, Pinched, 4 Lobes, Green Matte Glaze, Fritz Albert & W.D. Gates, Early 1900s, 15¾ In.	2080

TEDDY BEAR

Teddy bears were named for a president of the United States. The first teddy bear was a cuddly toy said to be inspired by a hunting trip made by President Theodore Roosevelt in 1902. He was praised because he saw a bear cub but did not shoot it. Morris and Rose Michtom started selling their stuffed bears as "teddy bears" and the name stayed. The Michtoms founded the Ideal Novelty and Toy Company. The German version of the teddy bear was made about the same time by the Steiff Company. There are many types of teddy bears and all are collected. The old ones are being reproduced. Other bears are listed in the Toy section.

Alpha Farnell, Mohair, Turquoise, Curly Hair, Jointed, Hang Tag, 15 In. .... *illus*	86
Mohair, Brown, Googly Eyes, Open Mouth, Jointed, Clifford Berryman, Steiff, 13 In.	62
Mohair, Golden, Googly Celluloid Eyes, Disc Jointed Neck, Stitched Nose, c.1900, 13 x 6 In.	424
Plush, Golden, Stitched Nose, Mouth, Jointed Head, Arms, Shoebutton Eyes, c.1920, 17¼ In.	367
Schuco, Mohair, Golden, Red Hat & Trousers, Shoebutton Eyes, Windup, 1900s, 5¼ In.	250
Steiff, Mohair, Apricot, Swivel Head, Hump, Shoebutton Eyes, Stitched Nose, c.1905, 24 In. *illus*	21600
Steiff, Mohair, Shoebutton Eyes, Felt Pads, c.1950, 8 In.	112
Winnie The Pooh, Mohair, Golden, Red Sweater, Jointed, Growler, Steiff, 12 In. .... *illus*	111

TELEPHONE

Telephones are wanted by collectors if the phones are old enough or unusual enough. The first telephone may have been made in Havana, Cuba, in 1849, but it was not patented. The first publicly demonstrated phone was used in Frankfurt, Germany, in 1860. The phone made by Alexander Graham Bell was shown at the Centennial Exhibition in Philadelphia in 1876, but it was not until 1877 that the first private phones were installed. Collectors today want all types of old phones, phone parts, and advertising. Even recent figural phones are popular.

Coin Box, Candlestick, 5 Cents, Painted, Metal, Courtesy Coin Box Co., 2½ x 5 In. ...... *illus*	12
Connecticut, Oak Case, Wall, 2 Bells, Engraved, Company Intercom, 11 x 6 In.	6
Jydsk Telefon Aktieselskab, Wall, Shelf, Oak, Black Handset, Scandinavia, 28 In. ..... *illus*	10
Kellogg Switchboard & Supply Co., Candlestick, Pay Station, Cash Drawer, 12½ x 12½ In. ...	108
Kellogg, Oak, 5-Bar Magneto, Wall Mount, c.1910, 19 In.	19
Phoneco, Highboy, Hand Crank, Rotary Dial, Black, 11½ x 8 x 5 In. .... *illus*	10

Telephone, Coin Box, Candlestick, 5 Cents, Painted, Metal, Courtesy Coin Box Co., 2 ½ x 5 In.
$123

Hartzell's Auction Gallery Inc.

Telephone, Jydsk Telefon Aktieselskab, Wall, Shelf, Oak, Black Handset, Scandinavia, 28 In.
$100

Selkirk Auctioneers & Appraisers

Telephone, Phoneco, Highboy, Hand Crank, Rotary Dial, Black, 11 ½ x 8 x 5 In.
$104

Blackwell Auctions

Telephone, Sign, Bell Telephone, Booth, Rectangular, Brass Placard, Black Ground, 18 x 3 In.
$123

Hartzell's Auction Gallery Inc.

Telephone, Wall, Oak, Mounted, Earpiece, Mouthpiece & Crank, 20 x 9 In.
$98

Hartzell's Auction Gallery Inc.

Telephone, Western Electric Co., Candlestick, Brass, Nickeled Surface, Stand, Marked, 11 ¾ In.
$135

Hartzell's Auction Gallery Inc.

Teplitz, Bust, Woman, Bare Breast, Ruffled Dress, Bonnet, Stellmacher, Amphora, 13 x 13 In.
$277

Morphy Auctions

Teplitz, Candlestick, Art Nouveau, Applied Figural Fairy, Mauve, Green Flecks, Ernst Wahliss, 10 x 7 In.
$2,176

Morphy Auctions

Teplitz, Candlestick, Iridized, Blue, Green, Red, Enamel, Long Handle, Amphora, RStK, 19 x 11 In.
$1,024

Morphy Auctions

Teplitz, Centerpiece, Young Woman, Lily Pad Leaves, Ernst Wahliss, Late 1800s, 9 x 9 In.
$384

Brunk Auctions

Teplitz, Figure, Venus, Draped, Shell Base, Riessner, Stellmacher & Kessel, 26 In.
$1,250

Charlton Hall Auctions

Teplitz, Vase, Art Deco, Leaf, Green, Blue, Brown Tones, 4 Handles, 14 x 7 ½ In.
$175

Woody Auction

Teplitz, Vase, Bulbous, Turquoise, Green Glaze, Handles, Amphora, 24 In.
$130

Bunch Auctions

Teplitz, Vase, Buttercup Flower, Long Stems, Matte & Enamel Glaze, Marked, Amphora, 21 x 10 In.
$3,075

Morphy Auctions

Teplitz, Vase, Cream Tones, Art Nouveau Woman, Green Trees, Amphora, 4 x 5 In.
$300

Woody Auction

T

Sign, Bell Telephone, Booth, Rectangular, Brass Placard, Black Ground, 18 x 3 In. ...... *illus* ... 123
Wall, Black, Bakelite Case, Crank, Beehive, Leich Electric, 10 ½ In. 74
Wall, Oak, Crank Model, Bakelite Mouthpiece, Receiver, c.1900, 24 x 9 ½ x 12 ½ In. 187
Wall, Oak, Mounted, Earpiece, Mouthpiece & Crank, 20 x 9 In. .... *illus* ... 98
Western Electric Co., Candlestick, Brass, Nickeled Surface, Stand, Marked, 11 ¾ In. .. *illus* ... 135
Western Electric Co., Wall, Oak, 2 Alarm Clocks, Rectangular, Crank, 23 In. 266

TELEVISION

Television sets are twentieth-century collectibles. Although the first television transmission took place in England in 1925, collectors find few sets that pre-date 1946. The first sets had only five channels, but by 1949 the additional UHF channels were included. The first color television set became available in 1951.

RCA, Blond Wood Cabinet, Splayed Feet With Metal Tips, 1960s 225

TEPLITZ

Teplitz refers to art pottery manufactured by a number of companies in the Teplitz-Turn area of Bohemia during the late nineteenth and early twentieth centuries. Two of these companies were the Alexandra Works founded by Ernst Wahliss, and the Amphora Porcelain Works, run by Riessner, Stellmacher, and Kessel.

Basket, Art Nouveau, Footed, Amphora, Late 1800s, 13 In. 316
Bowl, Figural, Young Woman's Head, Small Figures, E. Stellmacher, Amphora, 12 x 10 x 15 In... 677
Bust, Woman, Bare Breast, Ruffled Dress, Bonnet, Stellmacher, Amphora, 13 x 13 In. . *illus* ... 277
Candlestick, Art Nouveau, Applied Figural Fairy, Mauve, Green Flecks, Ernst Wahliss, 10 x 7 In. *illus* 2176
Candlestick, Iridized, Blue, Green, Red, Enamel, Long Handle, Amphora, RStK, 19 x 11 In. . *illus* 1024
Centerpiece, Young Woman, Lily Pad Leaves, Ernst Wahliss, Late 1800s, 9 x 9 In. ...... *illus* ... 384
Figure, Venus, Draped, Shell Base, Riessner, Stellmacher & Kessel, 26 In. .... *illus* 1250
Planter, Fruits, Grapes, Leaves, Green Ground, Amphora, 7 ½ x 12 In. 90
Vase, Art Deco, Leaf, Green, Blue, Brown Tones, 4 Handles, 14 x 7 ½ In. .... *illus* ... 175
Vase, Birds, Leaves, 2 Handles, Painted, Campina Series, Amphora, 21 ½ In. 94
Vase, Brown Ground, Bavaria, Ernst Wahliss, c.1899, 6 In. 158
Vase, Bulbous, Turquoise, Green Glaze, Handles, Amphora, 24 In. .... *illus* ... 130
Vase, Buttercup Flower, Long Stems, Matte & Enamel Glaze, Marked, Amphora, 21 x 10 In. *illus* 3075
Vase, Calla Lily, Applied Green Salamander, Brown, Marked, Stellmacher, 15 x 10 In............. 8610
Vase, Cream Tones, Art Nouveau Woman, Green Trees, Amphora, 4 x 5 In. .... *illus* ... 300
Vase, Cyclamen Blossoms, Blue, Gourd Shape, Embossed, Mark, 7 ½ x 7 ½ In. 313
Vase, Dandelions, Applied, Matte & Enamel Glazes, Amphora, 13 x 11 In. .... *illus* 3075
Vase, Earthtones, Drip Metallic Glaze, Elongated Handles, Amphora, Marked, Edda, 13 x 7 In......... 2460
Vase, Flower Panel, Iridized Glaze, Marked, Amphora, RStK, 13 x 7 In. .... *illus* 1230
Vase, Flowers, Cobalt Blue & Gold Trim, Art Nouveau, Amphora, Signed, Late 1800s, 6 In... . 127
Vase, Flowers, Handle, Art Pottery, Art Nouveau, Amphora, Late 1800s, 10 In., Pair.............. 161
Vase, Frog & Water Lily, Cream, Gold, Green, Applied Frog, Insect, Signed, Ed Stellmacher, 22 In. . *illus* 7995
Vase, Peacock Feather, Brown Ground, 2 Handles, Amphora, 13 In.......................... 254
Vase, Poppy, Gold Ground, Gourd, Amphora, c.1900, 7 ¾ In. .... *illus* ... 123
Vase, Portrait, Woman, Flowers, Enamel Glaze, Amphora, 18 x 10 In. .... *illus* 19680
Vase, Stylized Tree, Iridized, Enamel Glaze, Marked, Amphora, 19 x 11 In. .... *illus* 10455

TERRA-COTTA

Terra-cotta is a special type of pottery. It ranges from pale orange to dark reddish-brown in color. The color comes from the clay, which is fired but not always glazed in the finished piece.

Bust, Chinese Man, Chih Fan, Smiling, Marked, Jean Mich, France, 9 ¼ In............................ 184
Cigar & Match Holder, Striker, Man, Scarecrow, Stamped WS & S 80, 8 ¾ In. 100
Figurine, Cat, Faience Pottery, Blue Crackle Glaze, Flower Design, Italy, c.1950, 15 ½ In. *illus* 219
Figurine, Gnome, Standing, Wearing Black Hat, Stone Shape Base, c.1900, 23 In. 480
Figurine, Visage, Chrome Stand, Pablo Picasso, 1954, 2 ½ In. 2500

Teplitz, Vase, Dandelions, Applied, Matte & Enamel Glazes, Amphora, 13 x 11 In.
$3,075

Morphy Auctions

Teplitz, Vase, Flower Panel, Iridized Glaze, Marked, Amphora, RStK, 13 x 7 In.
$1,230

Morphy Auctions

Teplitz, Vase, Frog & Water Lily, Cream, Gold, Green, Applied Frog, Insect, Signed, Ed Stellmacher, 22 In.
$7,995

Morphy Auctions

T

Teplitz, Vase, Poppy, Gold Ground, Gourd, Amphora, c.1900, 7¾ In.
$123

Locati Auctions

Teplitz, Vase, Portrait, Woman, Flowers, Enamel Glaze, Amphora, 18 x 10 In.
$19,680

Morphy Auctions

Teplitz, Vase, Stylized Tree, Iridized, Enamel Glaze, Marked, Amphora, 19 x 11 In.
$10,455

Morphy Auctions

Group, 2 Cherubs, Flowers, Beaded, Gilt Base, Signed, 11 x 13 In. .... *illus*	240
Group, La Toilette, Josse-Francois-Joseph-Leriche, Signed, 1778, 28¼ In.	1764
Jar, Bulbous Shape, Loop Handles, Wrought Iron Stand, Early 1900s, 48 In...........	502
Olive Jar, Bulbous, Loop Handles, Continental, 1900s, 28 In.	561
Olive Jar, Bulbous, Yellow Glaze, Cartouche, Handle, Carved, Michelle Agresti, Italy, 14 In. ...*illus*	2345
Planter, Brown, Tan, Bulbous, Dragon Design, Embossed, 20 In.	165
Planter, Model F-112, Wrought Iron Stand, John Follis & Rex Goode, c.1960, 14½ In.	2500
Planter, Tapered, Raised Rim, Green Glaze, La Madeleine Anduze, Late 1900s, 37 In. . *illus*	354
Sculpture, 2 Cherubs, Tree Stump Draped, Rose Garlands, Signed, F. Foucher, 16½ In.	266
Sculpture, 2 Children, Flowers, Circular Base, Mandeville, Late 1800s, 20 In.........	354
Sculpture, Animalier, 2 Dogs, Attacking Wild Boar, Jules Moigniez, France, 11 x 17 x 12 In. ...	644
Sculpture, Head, Christ, Inset Glass Eyes, Painted, On Wood Base, 1800s, 14 x 7 x 6 In........	207
Sculpture, Indonesian Woman, Seated, Glazed, Mari Simmulson, 20 In.	413
Sculpture, Nude Woman, Seated, Black Marble, Stepped Plinth Base, Earline Heath King, 21 In.	236

TEXTILE

Textiles listed here include many types of printed fabrics and table and household linens. Some other textiles will be found under Clothing, Coverlet, Rug, Quilt, etc.

Flag, American, 13 Stars, Hand Sewn, c.1861, 51 In. .... *illus*	3375
Flag, American, 29 Stars, 13 Stripes, White Glazed Cotton, Frame, c.1847, 13 x 15 x 2 In........	4068
Flag, American, 34 Stars, Wool Bunting, Linen Hoist, Kansas Statehood, c.1861, 31 x 57 In...	6875
Flag, American, 38 Stars, Sewn, c.1880, 46 x 77 In..	2500
Flag, American, 39 Stars, Border Of International Flags, Pat. 1875, 16½ x 24 In.	256
Flag, American, 39 Stars, Parade, Woven Linen, Frame, 1889, 18⅛ x 25⅝ In........	345
Flag, American, 40 Stars, Parade, Cotton, c.1889, 14¾ x 22 In.........................	1216
Flag, American, 45 Stars, 13 Stripes, Printed Cloth, Frame, c.1900, 19 x 34 In.	738
Flag, American, 45 Stars, Silkscreen, Wood Frame, 1896, 17 x 26¾ In.	590
Flag, American, 48 Stars, Hoisting, 1940, 36 x 60 In.	1050
Flag, American, 48 Stars, Signed By Confederate Veterans, 1901, 19½ x 36 In.	1000
Flag, Communist Soviet Union, Naval, White, Red, Blue, Ensign, c.1950-92, 106½ x 69 In....	125
Fragment, Silk, Brocade Ecclesiastical, Gold Thread & Fringe, Flowers, Frame, 13 x 26 In...	100
Mat, Table, 9 Squares, 6 Hearts, Circular Pattern, Machine Stitched, 1910s, 24 x 23½ In......	140
Panel, Embroidery, Central Exotic Bird, Floral, Moth, Blue Ground, Chinese, 27 x 12 In.	150
Panel, Indian, Embroidery, 10 Figural, Silver Thread, Beads, Frame, 1900s, 81 x 46¼ In.....	128
Panel, Silk Embroidery, Gibbon, Brocade Mat, Painted Wood Frame, Late 1800s, 36 x 42 In.	590
Panel, Silk, Embroidered, Figures, Landscape, Dark Orange Ground, 1700s, 42 x 30 In........	590
Panel, Silk, Embroidered, Golden Tan Ground, Floral Blossoms, Black Frame, Chinese, 25 x 13 In.	118
Panel, Suzani, Millefiori Center, Floral, Silk Embroidery, Cotton Ground, 1800s, 93 x 73 In.	1599
Piano Shawl, Art Nouveau, Embroidered, Red & White, Fringe, Square, c.1900, 55 In...........	16-
Pillow, Brocade, Fringed, Red & Green, 1980, 24 x 24 In..	94
Pillow, Chicken, Nesting, Brown Wool, Red Linen Comb & Wattle, Button Eyes, 10 x 9 In.	2-
Pillow, Tapestry, Flowers, Red Ruffles, Multicolor, 18 x 21 In., Pair .... *illus*	46-
Sleeve Band, Embroidered, Figure, Trees, Floral, Wood Frame, 22½ x 5 In., Pair.................	39-
Tablecloth, Map, Canada, Scenes, Animals, Activities, Mountie, Maple Leaf Border, 1940s, 34 In.	4
Tablecloth, Silk, Panel Of Dragons Amid Clouds, Blue Ground, Chinese, 1800s, 42 x 51 In...	76
Tapestry, American Flag, 50 Stars, Printed, 68 x 51 In..	8
Tapestry, Aubusson, Beige Ground, Floral Medallion & Border, Wool, c.1950, 101 x 128 In....	30-
Tapestry, Classical Scene, Figures, Landscape, Leaves & Floral Border, Early 1900s, 53 x 79 In. ..	14
Tapestry, Flemish Style, Battle Of Pavia, Multicolor, Red Border, Early 1900s, 111 x 206 In. ...*illus*	472
Tapestry, Flemish, Hunt Scene, Wooded Landscape, Fortress, 1700s, 72 x 72 In.....................	364
Tapestry, Flowers, Butterflies, Heart, Wool, Era Industries, 55½ x 10½ In.	93
Tapestry, Jacquard, Rococo Style, Cotton, Couples Dancing, Hanging Bar, 1900s, 58 x 38 In. ..*illus*	1-
Tapestry, Medieval Style, Figures, Gilt Hanging Rod, Artis Flora, Late 1900s, 54 x 38 In. *illus*	14-
Tapestry, Needlepoint, Flower Bouquets, Grotesque Faces, Silk Back, 1800s, 64 x 50 In.........	8-
Tapestry, Unicorn Center, Brown Fence, Black, Floral Ground, Woven, 64 x 49 In. .... *illus*	52-
Thangka, Manjushri, Central Medallion, Buddha, Dragon, Yellow, Red Line Border, 45 x 32 In.	1-

TEXTILE

Terra-Cotta, Figurine, Cat, Faience Pottery, Blue Crackle Glaze, Flower Design, Italy, c.1950, 15 ½ In.
$219

Bruneau & Co. Auctioneers

Terra-Cotta, Group, 2 Cherubs, Flowers, Beaded, Gilt Base, Signed, 11 x 13 In.
$240

Cottone Auctions

Terra-Cotta, Olive Jar, Bulbous, Yellow Glaze, Cartouche, Handle, Carved, Michelle Agresti, Italy, 14 In.
$2,345

elkirk Auctioneers & Appraisers

Terra-Cotta, Planter, Tapered, Raised Rim, Green Glaze, La Madeleine Anduze, Late 1900s, 37 In.
$354

Leland Little Auctions

Textile, Flag, American, 13 Stars, Hand Sewn, c.1861, 51 In.
$3,375

Eldred's

Textile, Pillow, Tapestry, Flowers, Red Ruffles, Multicolor, 18 x 21 In., Pair
$469

Kamelot Auctions

Textile, Tapestry, Flemish Style, Battle Of Pavia, Multicolor, Red Border, Early 1900s, 111 x 206 In.
$4,720

Austin Auction Gallery

Textile, Tapestry, Jacquard, Rococo Style, Cotton, Couples Dancing, Hanging Bar, 1900s, 58 x 38 In.
$118

Austin Auction Gallery

521

Textile, Tapestry, Medieval Style, Figures, Gilt Hanging Rod, Artis Flora, Late 1900s, 54 x 38 In.
$148

Leland Little Auctions

Textile, Tapestry, Unicorn Center, Brown Fence, Black, Floral Ground, Woven, 64 x 49 In.
$523

Hartzell's Auction Gallery Inc.

Thermometer, Packard Motor Cars, Blue Ground, White Border, 38¼ In.
$213

Pook & Pook

THERMOMETER

Thermometer is a name that comes from the Greek word for heat. The thermometer was invented in 1731 to measure the temperature of either water or air. All kinds of thermometers are collected, but those with advertising messages are the most popular.

Black Forest, Carved, Oak Leaves, Deer, Wood, c.1890, 18 In.	330
Coca-Cola, Bottle Shape, Embossed, Heavy Tin Lithograph, 1950s, 29 In.	300
Figural, Man, Standing, Bronze, Stepped Base, 8 In.	177
Mail Pouch Tobacco, Painted, Black Ground, Tin, 39 In.	234
Packard Motor Cars, Blue Ground, White Border, 38¼ In. .... *illus*	213
We Recommend Ex-Lax For Constipation, Tin, Blue Ground, 39 x 8 In.	360

TIFFANY

Tiffany is a name that appears on items made by Louis Comfort Tiffany, the American glass designer who worked from about 1879 to 1933. His work included iridescent glass, Art Nouveau styles of design, and original contemporary styles. He was also noted for stained glass windows, unusual lamps, bronze work, pottery, and silver. Tiffany & Company, often called "Tiffany," is also listed in this section. The company was started by Charles Lewis Tiffany and John B. Young in 1837 in New York City. In 1853 the name was changed to Tiffany & Company. Louis Tiffany (1848–1933), Charles Tiffany's son, started his own business in 1879. It was named Louis Comfort Tiffany and Associated American Artists. In 1902 the name was changed to Tiffany Studios. Tiffany & Company is a store and is still working today. It is best known for silver and fine jewelry. Louis worked for his father's company as a decorator in 1900 but at the same time was working for his Tiffany Studios. Other types of Tiffany are listed under Tiffany Glass, Tiffany Gold, Tiffany Porcelain, Tiffany Pottery, or Tiffany Silver. The famous Tiffany lamps are listed in this section. Tiffany jewelry is listed in the Jewelry and Wristwatch categories. Some Tiffany Studio desk sets have matching clocks. They are listed here. Clocks made by Tiffany & Co. are listed in the Clock category. Reproductions of some types of Tiffany are being made.

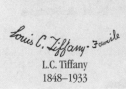

L.C. Tiffany	Tiffany Studios	Tiffany Studios
1848–1933	1902–1919	1902–1922+

Bookends, Bronze, Arch Shape, Engraved, Monogram, H.B.M, 5½ x 4½ In.	150
Bookends, Egyptian, Birds On Branch, Multicolor, Gilt Bronze, c.1920, 5 x 5 x 4 In., Pair	3024
Box, Storage, Rectangular, Inlaid Initials, CRS, Marked, 5½ x 12¾ x 8 In.	156
Calendar Frame, Dore Grape Leaf, Slag Glass, Brass, Marked, Tiffany Studios, 6 x 4½ In.	201
Calendar Frame, Zodiac Border, Bronze, Patina, Stamped Mark, 7¼ x 8¼ In. .... *illus*	1125
Candelabrum, 2-Light, Curved Arms, Snuffer, Top Handle, Fleur-De-Lis Base, 9 In. ......*illus*	2394
Candelabrum, 6-Light, Bronze, Green Glass, Candle Cups, Marked, 14½ x 21 x 4 In.	8610
Candle Lamp, Blown-Out Green Glass, 17 x 7 In. .... *illus*	15990
Candle Lamp, Gold, Ruffled Shade, Twisted, Base, Burner, Favrile, LCT, 12 In.	1020
Candle Lamp, Honeycomb Favrile Shade, Twist Stem, Inscribed, L.C.T., 13 x 8 In.	720
Candlestick, Art Glass Shade, Greenish Brown Patina Base, Tiffany Studios, 23 In., Pair ... *illus*	2880
Candlestick, Bronze, Cauldron Shape Top, Circular Base, Marked, Tiffany Studios, 17 In.	448
Candlestick, Bronze, Favrile Glass Balls, Pulled Feather Shade, Wirework Base, Marked, 21 In. ...*illus*	3720
Candlestick, Bronze, Leaves, Shade, Ruffled, Round Base, Favrile, Marked, 13½ x 5½ In.	453
Candlestick, Bronze, Puddle Design, Removable Bobeches, c.1900, 18 x 5 In., Pair	438
Candlestick, Cobra, Lily Pad Foot, Candle Cup, Greenish-Brown, Patina, Impressed, 7 In., Pair *illus*	180
Candlestick, Flower Form Candle Cup, Reeded Shaft, Turquoise, White, c.1910, 14¼ In., Pair	378
Candlestick, Flower Form, Bobeche Top, Thin Stem, Round Foot, Bronze, 20 x 5½ In. *illus*	693
Candlestick, Gilt, Bronze, Bulb Shape Holder, Slender Stem, Round Foot, c.1900, 19 In.	42

T

Tiffany, Calendar Frame, Zodiac Border, Bronze, Patina, Stamped Mark, 7 ¼ x 8 ¼ In.
$1,125

Toomey & Co. Auctioneers

Tiffany, Candelabrum, 2-Light, Curved Arms, Snuffer, Top Handle, Fleur-De-Lis Base, 9 In.
$2,394

Fontaine's Auction Gallery

Tiffany, Candle Lamp, Blown-Out Green Glass, 17 x 7 In.
$15,990

orphy Auctions

Tiffany, Candlestick, Art Glass Shade Greenish Brown Patina Base, Tiffany Studios, 23 In., Pair
$2,880

Cottone Auctions

Tiffany, Candlestick, Bronze, Favrile Glass Balls, Pulled Feather Shade, Wirework Base, Marked, 21 In.
$37,200

Cottone Auctions

Tiffany, Candlestick, Cobra, Lily Pad Foot, Candle Cup, Greenish-Brown, Patina, Impressed, 7 In., Pair
$1,800

Cottone Auctions

Tiffany, Candlestick, Flower Form, Bobeche Top, Thin Stem, Round Foot, Bronze, 20 x 5 ½ In.
$6,930

Fontaine's Auction Gallery

Tiffany, Clock, Alarm, Enameled, Roman Numerals, Quartz Movement, 4 x 4 In.
$98

Hartzell's Auction Gallery Inc.

Tiffany, Clock, Desk, Art Deco, Enameled Front, Key, Tiffany Furnaces, 3 x 4 In.
$13,530

Morphy Auctions

Tiffany, Frame, Grapevine, Bronze, Glass, 2 Panels, 9 ½ x 16 In.
$4,375

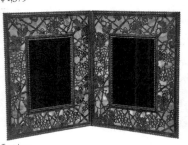

Treadway

Tiffany, Frame, Pine Needle, Brass, Caramel, White Glass Slag Panel, 1900s, 14 x 12 In.
$2,016

Brunk Auctions

Tiffany, Inkwell, Bronze, Green Blown Glass, Pumpkin Shape, Marked, New York, 4 ½ In.
$8,610

Morphy Auctions

> **TIP**
> *Hold glass shades carefully when you remove a light bulb from an old lamp. The Tiffany lily-shaped shade and others like it are held in place by the screwed-in bulb.*

Tiffany, Inkwell, Dome Lid, Blue Favrile, Gilt Brass Lid, Tiffany Studios, L.C.T., Early 1900s, 4 In.
$4,688

Eldred's

Tiffany, Lamp Shade, Jewel & Feather, Leaded Glass, Tiffany Studios, 16 In.
$4,425

Cottone Auctions

Tiffany, Lamp, Damascene Shade, Favrile Glass, Bronze Stand, Early 1900s, 51 ½ x 10 In.
$7,500

Cowan's Auctions

Tiffany, Lamp, Geometric Glass Shade, 3-Arm Spider, Bulbous, Bronze, Early 1900s, 16 x 12 In.
$5,535

Brunk Auctions

Tiffany, Lamp, Peony, Leaded Glass, Red, Pink, Green Leaves, Chased Pod Library Base, 31 In.
$104,550

Morphy Auctions

Tiffany, Lamp, Pomegranate Shade, Leaded Glass, Geometric Ground, Bronze Base, 22 In.
$13,440

Morphy Auctions

T

Tiffany, Paperweight, Bronze, Lion, Reclining, Stamped Marks, 1 ⅝ x 2 x 4 ⅞ In.
$1,000

Toomey & Co. Auctioneers

Tiffany, Trinket Box, Lid, Compass, Outlines Of Continents, Tiffany & Co., 3 x 4 ½ In.
$354

Leland Little Auctions

Tiffany, Vase, Agate, Gourd, Oval Shape, Swirl Design, Purple, Blue & Amber, Signed, 6 ⅝ In.
$10,080

Fontaine's Auction Gallery

Tiffany Glass, Bowl, Centerpiece, Dore Bronze Base, Favrile, Marked, 4 ¾ x 12 In.
$1,230

derfer Auction Company

Tiffany Glass, Bowl, Gold Iridescent, Ribbed, Scalloped Rim, Twisted Pinch Design, Favrile, 1900s, 8 x 3 In.
$438

Bruneau & Co. Auctioneers

Tiffany Glass, Bowl, Round, Wide Fluted Rim, Circular Foot, Iridescent, Favrile, 3 x 9 In.
$518

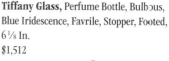

Blackwell Auctions

Tiffany Glass, Compote, Pastille, White & Pink Iridescent, Tapered Stem, Round Foot, L.C.T., c.1910, 6 In.
$590

Leland Little Auctions

Tiffany Glass, Perfume Bottle, Bulbous, Blue Iridescence, Favrile, Stopper, Footed, 6 ⅛ In.
$1,512

Fontaine's Auction Gallery

Tiffany Glass, Salt, Ruffled Rim, Iridescent, Favrile, Signed, L.C.T., 1 x 1 ½ In.
$369

Morphy Auctions

Tiffany Glass, Shade, Pulled Feather, Dome, Fitter Rim, Favrile, Signed, 4 ½ x 8 In.
$6,641

Treadway

T

Tiffany Glass, Sherbet, Gold Cup, Twisted Stem, Circular Dome Base, 6 In. $236

Cottone Auctions

Tiffany Glass, Vase, Carved, Green Heart Shape Leaf, Gold Iridescent, Signed, Louis C. Tiffany, 12 x 6 In. $2,250

Woody Auction

Candlestick, Scalloped Rim Shade, Gilt Bronze Base, Favrile, L.C.T., c.1910, 23 In., Pair	3024
Card Case, 4 Sapphires, Gold Wash Interior, 14K Yellow Gold, Marked, 3 1/2 x 3 In.	500
Chandelier, Bronze & Glass, Gold Iridescent, Chains, Favrile, Signed, 39 x 6 x 6 In.	7995
Clock, Alarm, Enameled, Roman Numerals, Quartz Movement, 4 x 4 In. *illus*	98
Clock, Ball, Numbers, Gold Dials, Marked, Swiss, 4 In.	575
Clock, Desk, Art Deco, Enameled Front, Key, Tiffany Furnaces, 3 x 4 In. *illus*	13530
Desk Tray, Dore Bronze, Stylized Border, Rectangular, 9/16 x 12 x 15 In.	313
Frame, Grapevine, Bronze, Favrile Glass, Patina, Tiffany Studios, 9 1/2 x 8 In.	1140
Frame, Grapevine, Bronze, Glass, 2 Panels, 9 1/2 x 16 In. *illus*	4375
Frame, Pine Needle, Brass, Caramel, White Glass Slag Panel, 1900s, 14 x 12 In. *illus*	2016
Frame, Pine Needle, Bronze, Purple, Green, Favrile Slag Glass, 10 x 8 In.	1500
Frame, Pine Needle, Bronze, Yellow & Green Glass, Beaded Edge, Patina, 7 1/2 x 6 In.	1610
Inkwell, Bronze, Green Blown Glass, Pumpkin Shape, Marked, New York, 4 1/2 In. *illus*	8610
Inkwell, Dome Lid, Blue Favrile, Gilt Brass Lid, Tiffany Studios, L.C.T., Early 1900s, 4 In. *illus*	4688
Inkwell, Green Slag Panels, Bronze Grapevine Frame, Marked, Tiffany Studios, 3 x 3 1/4 In.	500
Inkwell, Zodiac, Bronze, Hinged Lid, Impressed Marks, 3 1/2 x 6 1/2 In.	325
Inkwell, Zodiac, Bronze, Hinged Top, Milk Glass Ink Cup, Stamped, 6 In.	201
Lamp Shade, Jewel & Feather, Leaded Glass, Tiffany Studios, 16 In. *illus*	4425
Lamp, 3-Light, Lily, Iridescent Glass Shade, Candelabra Base Socket, c.1900, 13 1/2 In.	4063
Lamp, Counterbalance, Desk, Glass Shade, Bronze Base, Etched, L.C.T., c.1910, 38 x 10 x 7 In.	3218
Lamp, Damascene Shade, Favrile Glass, Bronze Stand, Early 1900s, 51 1/2 x 10 In. *illus*	7500
Lamp, Favrile Glass Shade, Bell Shape, Bronze Base, Engraved, L.C.T., c.1905, 18 x 10 x 6 In.	8820
Lamp, Favrile Shade, Brown Patina, Bronze Base, Signed, Tiffany Studios, 13 In.	5100
Lamp, Geometric Glass Shade, 3-Arm Spider, Bulbous, Bronze, Early 1900s, 16 x 12 In. *illus*	5535
Lamp, Geometric Shade, Leaded, Dichroic, Gilt Bronze Base, c.1910, 16 1/2 x 12 In.	9450
Lamp, Green Slag Glass, Domed Shade, Round Foot, Electric, Signed, 15 x 7 x 7 In.	8610
Lamp, Jewel & Feather, Leaded Glass Shade, Brownish-Gold Patina Base, 22 In.	9145
Lamp, Peony, Leaded Glass, Red, Pink, Green Leaves, Chased Pod Library Base, 31 In. *illus*	104550
Lamp, Pomegranate Shade, Leaded Glass, Geometric Ground, Bronze Base, 22 In. *illus*	13440
Magnifying Glass, Abalone, Dore Bronze, Stamped, 9 x 4 1/2 In.	688
Match Holder, Grapevine, Bronze, Gold Dore, Flared Rim, Impressed, 2 1/4 In.	485
Notepad Holder, Grapevine, Bronze, Glass, Green Slag, Hinged, Wood Base, 5 x 7 1/2 In.	403
Paperweight, Bronze, Lion, Reclining, Stamped Marks, 1 5/8 x 2 x 4 7/8 In. *illus*	1000
Paperweight, Bronze, Turtleback, Mounted, Tiffany Studios, 1 1/2 x 6 In.	1440
Paperweight, Bronze, Wave Design, Cypriote Glass, Reddish-Brown Patina, 3 5/8 x 3 In.	2520
Pitcher, Vase Shape, Greek Style, Warriors, Female Mask Finial, c.1854-71, 13 x 8 x 6 In.	5228
Postage Scale, Pine Needle, Bronze, Green Slag Inserts, Top Adjustment Screw, 3 In.	726
Sconce, Bronze, Paperweight Shade, Greenish-Brown, Patina, Signed 0949, 9 x 6 x 4 1/2 In.	5760
Sconce, Cast Bronze, Switch, Backplates, Favrile, Signed, L.C.T., 14 x 6 1/2 x 4 In., Pair	9225
Tray, Bronze Frame, Gilt, Mounted, Enamel Handles, Flowers, Tiffany Furnaces, 9 x 7 1/2 In.	1008
Tray, Bronze, Greenish Brown Patina, Green, Favrile, Tiffany Studios, 14 x 8 In.	1440
Trinket Box, Lid, Compass, Outlines Of Continents, Tiffany & Co., 3 x 4 1/2 In. *illus*	354
Vase, Agate, Gourd, Oval Shape, Swirl Design, Purple, Blue & Amber, Signed, 6 5/8 In. *illus*	10080
Vase, Skyscraper, White Glaze, Frank Lloyd Wright, Tiffany & Co., c.1980, 22 1/2 In.	3250

TIFFANY GLASS

Bookends, Lead Glass, Clear, Obelisk Shape, Truman Capote's, 3 3/4 In.	148
Bowl, Aqua Green, Iridescent, Flared Rim, Onionskin Textured Edge, Footed, 1844, 11 In.	527
Bowl, Centerpiece, Dore Bronze Base, Favrile, Marked, 4 3/4 x 12 In. *illus*	1230
Bowl, Flared Rim, Crisscrossed, Gold Iridescent, Favrile, Signed, 1900s, 6 3/4 In.	431
Bowl, Gold Iridescent, Favrile, c.1910, 3 3/4 In.	472
Bowl, Gold Iridescent, Flared, Footed, Favrile, Marked, 1848, 4 1/2 x 9 3/4 In.	440
Bowl, Gold Iridescent, Ribbed, Scalloped Rim, Twisted Pinch Design, Favrile, 1900s, 8 x 3 In. *illus*	438
Bowl, Leaf & Vine, Fluted Rim, Carved, Acid Etched, Engraved, 1925, 3 1/2 x 8 1/4 In.	214
Bowl, Morning Glory, Blue, Yellow Hued Flowers, Paperweight, Etched, Early 1900s, 3 x 9 In.	497
Bowl, Round, Wide Fluted Rim, Circular Foot, Iridescent, Favrile, 3 x 9 In. *illus*	51
Bowl, Wisteria, Favrile Pastel, Purple, Opalescent, Signed, c.1930, 7 5/8 In.	38
Compote, Iridescent, Fluted Rim, Round Footed, Favrile, Signed, c.1919, 3 x 7 1/2 x 5 3/4 In.	50
Compote, Pastille, White & Pink Iridescent, Tapered Stem, Round Foot, L.C.T., c.1910, 6 In. *illus*	59
Perfume Bottle, Bulbous, Blue Iridescence, Favrile, Stopper, Footed, 6 1/8 In. *illus*	151
Perfume Bottle, Pulled Feather, Stopper, Marked L.C. Tiffany-Favrile, Mid 1900s, 10 1/2 In.	20
Plate, Opalescent, Leaves Design, Clear Center, Pastel Blue Rim, Favrile, 10 1/2 In., Pair	126

T

Tiffany Glass, Vase, Cream Flowers, Green Leaves, Gold & Iridescent, Favrile, L.C. Tiffany, 9 x 6 In.
$3,150

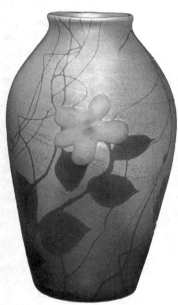

Morphy Auctions

Tiffany Glass, Vase, Flower Form, Iridescent, Leaves, Favrile, Signed, 11 ¾ x 4 ½ In.
$3,125

Treadway

Tiffany Glass, Vase, Iridescent White, Blue, Gold Interior, Marked, LCT, 1 ¾ x 3 ½ In.
$750

Woody Auction

Tiffany Glass, Vase, Paperweight, Flowers, Iridescent, Signed, 9 ¼ In.
$3,500

Susanin's Auctioneers & Appraisers

Tiffany Glass, Vase, Samian Red, Blue Favrile, Etched, 6 ¾ x 3 In.
$2,750

Toomey & Co. Auctioneers

Tiffany Glass, Vase, Trumpet Shape, Flower Form Holder, Ribbed Foot, Favrile, 16 ¾ In.
$630

Fontaine's Auction Gallery

Tiffany Glass, Wine, Gold Iridescent, Engraved, Cherry Branch, Signed, L.C.T. Favrile, 4 In.
$350

Woody Auction

T

Tiffany Silver, Asparagus Tongs, English King, Monogram, Engraved, Tiffany & Co., N.Y., 1892-1902, 7½ In. $500

Eldred's

TIP

Be sure to rinse a piece of silver until all of the polish is removed. If some remains in the crevices, it will continue to react and may lead to corrosion. A toothpick or toothbrush will help you get the polish out of crevices.

Tiffany Silver, Berry Spoon, Shell Shape, Gold Washed, Monogram, Olympian, Tiffany & Co., 1902-07, 8¾ In. $531

Eldred's

Tiffany Silver, Cigar Lighter, Leaves, Insects, Compartment, Gilt, Aesthetic Period, c.1875-91, 3 x 5 x 4 In. $1,536

Morphy Auctions

Salt Dip, Gold Favrile, Crimped Edge, Marked, LCT, 2¾ In.	125
Salt, Ruffled Rim, Iridescent, Favrile, Signed, L.C.T., 1 x 1½ In. ....*illus*	369
Shade, Pine Needle, Dome Shape, Leaded Green Slag Glass, Copper Filigree Overlay, 8 x 23 In.	1404
Shade, Pulled Feather, Dome, Fitter Rim, Favrile, Signed, 4½ x 8 In. ....*illus*	6641
Sherbet, Gold Cup, Twisted Stem, Circular Dome Base, 6 In. ....*illus*	236
Tumbler, Blown Gold Iridescent, Threaded Waist, Signed, L.C.T., c.1910, 3¾ In., 6 Piece	472
Tumbler, Engraved Berry & Vine, Gold Iridescent, Signed, L.C. Tiffany-Favrile, 4 In.	250
Tumbler, Gold Iridescent, Art, Bulbous, Flared Rim, L.C. Tiffany, 3¾ In.	181
Vase, Bottle Shape, Narrow Neck, Hooked Feather, Green Favrile, Miniature, Early 1900s, 5 In.	1408
Vase, Carved, Green Heart Shape Leaf, Gold Iridescent, Signed, Louis C. Tiffany, 12 x 6 In. ......*illus*	2250
Vase, Cream Flowers, Green Leaves, Gold & Iridescent, Favrile, L.C. Tiffany, 9 x 6 In. .. *illus*	3150
Vase, Flower Form, Iridescent, Leaves, Favrile, Signed, 11¾ x 4½ In. ....*illus*	3125
Vase, Flower Form, Ruffled Rim, Green Pull Feather, Gold Iridescent, Early 1900s, 4 x 5 In. .	761
Vase, Gold Favrile, Bulb Shape, Paneled Sides, Signed, Early 1900s, 3¾ In.	281
Vase, Gold Favrile, Flared Rim, Tiffany Studios, 7 In.	840
Vase, Gold Iridescent, Elongated Neck, Embossed, Bulbous, Favrile, 3¾ In.	203
Vase, Gold Iridescent, Favrile, Early 1900s, 8¼ In.	1625
Vase, Iridescent White, Blue, Gold Interior, Marked, LCT, 1¾ x 3½ In. ....*illus*	750
Vase, Leaf & Vine, Molded Rim, Carved, Acid Etched, L.C. Tiffany-Favrile, c.1914, 16 In.	6930
Vase, Paperweight, Flowers, Iridescent, Signed, 9¼ In. ....*illus*	3500
Vase, Pulled Feather, Trumpet Shape, Bronze Base, Signed, LCT, 14½ x 5½ In.	500
Vase, Samian Red, Blue Favrile, Etched, 6¾ x 3 In. ....*illus*	2750
Vase, Trumpet Shape, Flower Form Holder, Ribbed Foot, Favrile, 16¾ In. ....*illus*	630
Vase, Trumpet, Pulled Feather, Gold Iridescent, Bronze Base, L.C.T., 1810s, 14 x 5 In., Pair ...	1638
Wine, Gold Iridescent, Engraved, Cherry Branch, Signed, L.C.T. Favrile, 4 In. ....*illus*	350
Wine, Pastel Favrile, Twisted Reeded Stem, Striped Foot, Opalescent, Signed, c.1930, 7 In.	263
Wine, Pastel, Blue, Opalescence, Ribbed Stems, Saucer Foot, Favrile, 8 x 3 x 3 In., Pair	768

TIFFANY GOLD

Bookmark, Paper Clip Shape, 14k Gold, 2 In.	399
Pill Box, 14k Yellow Gold, Diamond Pattern, Slides In, 1940s, 2 x 1 In.	1051

TIFFANY PORCELAIN

Platter, Tiffany Blossom Pattern, Shouldered, Multicolor, 14 x 11 In.	195
Teapot, Yellow Basket Weave, Blackberries, Bamboo Style Handle, 6 x 8 In.	75

TIFFANY POTTERY

Vase, Poppies, High Relief, Bark Texture Ground, Bisque, Marked, 5⅞ In.	882
Vase, Trillium Shape, Yellow, Favrile, Marked, 7¼ x 6¾ In.	10000

TIFFANY SILVER

Asparagus Tongs, English King Pattern, Charles Grosjean, Pat. 1885, 7½ In.	490
Asparagus Tongs, English King, Monogram, Engraved, Tiffany & Co., N.Y., 1892-1902, 7½ In. *illus*	500
Berry Spoon, Shell Shape, Gold Washed, Monogram, Olympian, Tiffany & Co., 1902-07, 8¾ In. *illus*	531
Bottle Holder, Renaissance Revival, Chased, Flowers & Putti, 2¾ In., Pair	1020
Bowl, Paul Revere Design, Stepped Round Base, Marked, 1900s, 3½ x 7 In.	431
Bowl, Vegetable, Lid, Engraved, 3-Letter Script, Monogram, 5 x 10 x 7 In.	2125
Box, Hinged Lid, Engraved Gilt Presidential Seal, Lyndon B. Johnson, 4 x 3 x 1 In.	1875
Box, Painted, Porcelain Plaque, 4 Horses, Carriage, Rectangular, Tiffany & Co., 1⅝ x 9 In. .	1638
Cake Basket, Oblong, Slats, Floral Swags, Swing Handle, Footed, Engraved, c.1875-91, 12 x 9 x 6 In.	1280
Candleholder, Chrysanthemum Design, 3 Sockets, Footed, 9 x 11 In.	2880
Candlestick, Urn Socket, Paneled Post, 6-Sided Base, 1907, 8¾ In., Pair	344
Cigar Lighter, Leaves, Insects, Compartment, Gilt, Aesthetic Period, c.1875-91, 3 x 5 x 4 In. .*illus*	1536
Claret Jug, Dome Lid, Clear, Circular Cuts, Swirl Bottom, Engraved, 1875-91, 9 In., Pair	1968
Cocktail Shaker, Flowers Design, Strainer, Cap, Engraved, 1907-38, 8¼ x 16 In. ....*illus*	1638
Cocktail Shaker, Strainer & Cap, Wheat & Flower Design, 8¼ In.	3075
Coffeepot, Hinged Lid, Wood Handle, Monogram, Underfoot, Tiffany & Co., 9 In.	600
Compote, Flower, Narrow Stems, Footed Base, 1892-1902, 3½ In., Pair ....*illus*	685
Cup, Winged, Straight Handle, Ribbon, Tiffany & Co., 3⅛ x 5½ In.	225
Dish, Cabbage, Embossed, 1900s, 6 In., Pair	31
Dish, Round, Filigree Design, Footed, Monogram, EGB, 9½ In.	18
Dish, Scalloped Rim, Tiffany & Co., Early 1900s, 9¼ In.	58
Dresser Box, Lid, Engraved Flowers, Shell, Monogram, Early 1900s, 1 x 5 x 3 In.	38

T

Tiffany Silver, Cocktail Shaker, Flowers Design, Strainer, Cap, Engraved, 1907-38, 8¼ x 16 In.
$1,638

Morphy Auctions

Tiffany Silver, Compote, Flower, Narrow Stems, Footed Base, 1892-1902, 3½ In., Pair
$688

Eldred's

Tiffany Silver, Dresser Box, Rectangular, Woven Strips, Silver Gilt, Tiffany, 7¾ x 5 x 2 In.
$3,383

Morphy Auctions

Tiffany Silver, Goblet, Rowing Trophy, Bell Shape Bowl, Circular Base, Monogram, 1930, 6 In.
$431

Brunk Auctions

Tiffany Silver, Ladle, Ailanthus Design, Engraved Initials, AMS, Marked, New York, 1899, 11½ In.
$375

Charlton Hall Auctions

Tiffany Silver, Mug, Man, Mount Fuji, Engraved, Cast Rims, Child's, 1873-91, 3½ In.
$1,000

Eldred's

Tiffany Silver, Pot, Art Deco Style, Ball Finial, Circular Base, Tiffany & Co., c.1947, 8 In.
$390

Michaan's Auctions

T

Tiffany Silver, Serving Spoon, Chrysanthemum Handle, 1880, 9¾ In. $214

Neal Auction Company

Tiffany Silver, Shaker, Repousse, Rose & Leaves, Embossed, Marked, 4⅛ In., Pair $236

Bunch Auctions

Tiffany Silver, Spoon, English King,, Engraved, 1870, 5½ In. $230

Blackwell Auctions

Tile, Roof, Roosters, Molded, Sancai Palette, Green Ground, Chinese, 11¼ In., Pair $266

Austin Auction Gallery

Dresser Box, Rectangular, Woven Strips, Silver Gilt, Tiffany, 7¾ x 5 x 2 In.	*illus*	3383
Feeding Spoon, Baby, Padova, Box, Elsa Peretti, Tiffany & Co., 6⅛ In.		71
Goblet, Rowing Trophy, Bell Shape Bowl, Circular Base, Monogram, 1930, 6 In.	*illus*	431
Ladle, Ailanthus Design, Engraved Initials, AMS, Marked, New York, 1899, 11½ In.	*illus*	375
Ladle, Vine, Leaves, Engraved, Embossed, Monogram, ERG, 11 In.		590
Muddler, Gold Plated Knob, Bamboo, Marked, Tiffany & Co., 6¾ In.		250
Mug, Man, Mount Fuji, Engraved, Cast Rims, Child's, 1873-91, 3½ In.	*illus*	1000
Organizer, Desk, Rectangular, Gold Plated, c.1920, 1 x 6¾ In.		1000
Pill Box, Takeout Shape, Pagodas, Hinged, Marked, Favrile, 1¼ x 1 x ¾ In.		188
Pitcher, Flowers, Shells, Handle, Tiffany & Co., c.1878, 8¼ In.		2394
Pitcher, Spherical, Flower, Leaves, Concave Neck, Engraved, c.1854-70, 9½ x 7½ x 7 In.		2835
Pitcher, Water, Wave Edge, Laurel, Banded Repousse, Monogram, c.1900, 8 x 7¼ x 6 In.		1170
Pot, Art Deco Style, Ball Finial, Circular Base, Tiffany & Co., c.1947, 8 In.	*illus*	390
Punch Ladle, Wave Edge Pattern, Monogram, B, 1884, 12½ In.		250
Salver, Engraved, Round, Beaded Rim, Anthemion Feet, 1854-70, 10 In.		1230
Salver, Round, 2 Pierced Handles, Monogram, Tiffany & Co., Early 1900s, 11¼ In.		325
Serving Spoon, Chrysanthemum Handle, 1880, 9¾ In.	*illus*	214
Shaker, Repousse, Rose & Leaves, Embossed, Marked, 4⅛ In., Pair	*illus*	236
Soap Dish, Strap Handle, Tiffany, 1875-91, 2½ x 4½ x 3 In.		1230
Soup Spoon, Flemish, Tiffany & Co., 1911, 6⅞ In., 4 Piece		384
Spoon, English King, Engraved, 1870, 5½ In.	*illus*	230
Tazza, Reticulated Rim, Foot, Clover Leaves, Blooms, c.1920, 3½ x 7¾ In.		380
Tea Caddy, Dome Lid, Squat Vase Shape, Copper Line, 3⅜ In.		2091
Tea Caddy, Lid, Leaves, Hanging Flowers, Vase Shape, 1902-37, 4 x 3½ x 3½ In.		4305
Tray, Round, Scottish Heraldic Emblem, Laurel Garland Border, 1800s, 11 In.		570
Tray, Serving, Presentation, Square Shape, Chamfered Corners, Engraved, 1950s, 12 In.		702
Tray, Tea, Shaped Rim, Shells, Acanthus Leaves, Gadroon, Soldered, 1902, 24½ In.		200
Vase, Blossoms, Dangling Tendrils, Engraved, Curved Rim, c.1902-1907, 10 x 4 x 4 In.		3998
Vase, Trumpet Shape, Monogram, EDM, c.1907, 12 In.		649
Vase, Trumpet Shape, Strawberry Design, Engraved, Marked, c.1907, 10½ In.		1250
Wine Cooler, Lift-Up Lid, Knob Handle, Footed, Tiffany & Co., 1950s, 11½ In.		1625

TILE

Tiles have been used in most countries of the world as a sturdy building material for floors, roofs, fireplace surrounds, and surface toppings. The cuerda seca (dry cord) technique of decoration uses a greasy pigment to separate different glaze colors during firing. In cuenca (raised line) decorated tiles, the design is impressed, leaving ridges that separate the glaze colors. Many of the American tiles are listed in this book under the factory name.

Bird, Blue & Green, Cream Ground, Talavera, Mexico, 1900s, 4 x 4 In., 24 Piece		413
Bird, Rook, Perched, Black, White, Orange, 4½ In.		266
Fireplace, Ceramic, Green, Neoclassical, Figures, Birds, Carl Mueller, Late 1800s, 31 x 7 In.		1800
Retablo, Senora Del Rocio, Blue & White, Earthenware, 12 Tiles, Azulejo, 31¾ x 23¾ In.		826
Roof, Parrot, Perched, Green & Red Glaze, Chinese, 8¾ In., Pair		472
Roof, Roosters, Molded, Sancai Palette, Green Ground, Chinese, 11¼ In., Pair	*illus*	266
Stove, Baroque Style, 3 Sections, Slab Base, White Glaze, Ceramic, 1800s, 50 x 35 x 19 In.		322

TINWARE

Tinware containers for household use have been made in America since the seventeenth century. The first tin utensils were brought from Europe, but by 1798 tin plate was imported and local tinsmiths made the wares. Painted tin is called tole and is listed separately. Some tin kitchen items may be found listed under Kitchen. The lithographed tin containers used to hold food and tobacco are listed in the Advertising category under Tin.

Candlebox, Dome Lid, Hanging, Punched Star, Stag, 1800s, 13½ In.		24x
Canister, Dome Lid, Gray Smoke, Applied Handle, 34 In.		54x
Charger, Flowers, Leaves, Persian Style, Multicolor, Enamel, Glaze, Cantagalli, 1800s, 15 In.		162

T

Coffeepot, Potted Tulip & Daisy, Interlacing Bands, Gooseneck, M. Uebele, c.1840, 11 In......	1708
Coffeepot, Wrigglework, Gooseneck, Finial, Potted Floral, Stamped, Ketterer, 1800, 10¾ In. *illus*	2074
Foot Warmer, Punched Heart, Walnut, Wire Bail Handle, Pa., 1800s, 6 x 9 In.........................	175
Sconce, 3-Light, Crimped Arched Crest, Silver Mirror Plates, 1800s, 19 x 8½ In...................	1107
Sconce, Candle, Mirrored & Segmented Reflector Dish, Round, 1800s, 9 x 10 In., Pair	960
Tray, U.S. Frigate Constitution, Painted, Inscribed, Chas Newton, 1814, 22 x 30 In.............	1875

TOBACCO CUTTERS *are listed in the Store category.*

TOBACCO JAR

Tobacco jar collectors search for those made in odd shapes and colors. Because tobacco needs special conditions of humidity and air, it has been stored in humidors and other special containers since the eighteenth century. Some may be found in Advertising, Silver, or ceramic categories in this book.

Ceramic, De Rookende Amerikann, Native American Smoking, Ship, Harbor, Dutch, 1700s, 12 In.	1599
Humidor, Black Paint, Ebonized, Cigar, Modern, Square, 13 In..	154
Oak, The Jewett, Oak, Brass Label, Hardware, Humidor, Buffalo, 1890, 14 x 11 x 11 In..........	2880
Redware, Lid, Cylindrical Body, Flared Rim, Glaze, John Bell, c.1850, 7¼ In......................	469
Terra-Cotta, Figural, Man In Barrel, Stein In Hand, No. 3536 ....*illus*	72
Wood, Dog's Head, Glass Eyes, Wearing Hinged Hat, Carved, Black Forest, 6½ In. ....*illus*	882
Wood, Parquetry, Square, Inlay, Metal Liner, Humidor, 9¾ x 12 x 10 In................................	125

TOBY JUG

Toby jug is the name of a very special form of pitcher. It is shaped like the full figure of a man or woman. A pitcher that shows just the top half of a person is not correctly called a toby. It is often called a character jug. More examples of toby jugs can be found under Royal Doulton and other factory names. Some may be found in Advertising in this book.

Man, Hands In Pockets, Smiling, Blue Coat, Black Tricornered Hat, 10 In.	95
Man, On Stump, Pinch Of Snuff, Blue Jacket & Hat, Staffordshire, c.1880, 8¼ In........... ...	175
Man, Seated On Barrel, Salt Glaze, Brown Top & Base, Tan Body, Doulton, Late 1800s, 14 In. .	125
Martha Gunn, Seated, Wide Brim Hat, Feathers, Holding Flask & Glass, 11 In.	200
Mr. Punch, Hat Lid, Striped Coat, Majolica Glaze, Staffordshire, 12 In.	360
Napoleon, Black Hat, Yellow Vest, 5¾ In.	87

TOLE

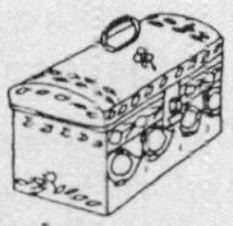

Tole is painted tin. It is sometimes called japanned ware, pontypool, or toleware. Most nineteenth-century tole is painted with an orange-red or black background and multicolored decorations. Many recent versions of toleware are made and sold. Related items may be listed in the Tinware category.

Box, Document, Dome Lid, Basswood & Pine, Green, Initials, EWH, c.1850, 8 x 18 x 10 In.....	240
Box, Document, Dome Lid, Hasp & Brass, Bail Handle, 1830s, 7 x 9½ In. ....*illus*	360
Box, Document, Hinged Lid, Flowers, Japanned Ground, Oval, c.1840, 9½ x 11 x 7 In.	115
Box, Document, Hinged Lid, Red Flowers, Green Leaves, Bail Handle, 1800s, 6½ x 3 In.	188
Box, Hinged Dome Lid, American Eagle, Spread Wing, Bail Handle, 1800s, 7¼ x 10 In........ ..	88
Bread Tray, Oval, Pierced Handles, Japanning, Fruit Design, White Band, 1830s, 3 x 12 In .	270
Cachepot, Louis Philippe, Landscape, Lion's Head Feet, Plinth Base, Early 1800s, 9¾ In., Pair	650
Cachepot, Parcel Gilt, Lion Mask, Ring Handles, Square Base, Late 1900s, 11 In., Pair	148
Canister, Lift-Up Lid, Wire Handle, Multicolor, Leaves, 3 x 4¼ In...	113
Coffeepot, Dome Lid, Lighthouse, Floral, Gooseneck Spout, Footed, c.1840, 10 x 8 x 6 In......	585
Coffeepot, Gooseneck Spout, Yellow, Green, Black Ground, Peach, Leaf, 1800s, 11 In.	750
Coffeepot, Japanned Ground, Yellow Swags, Floral Reserves, Blue Accents, 1830s, 9 In........	330
Coffeepot, Lighthouse Shape, Gooseneck Spout, Black Ground, Ear Handle, c.1900, 10½ In .	3904
Lamp, 2-Light, Black Figural Transfer, Rectangular Shade, Chrome Yellow, 19 x 10 x 5 In...	322
Lamp, 2-Light, Tea Canister, Green Painted, Landscape, Pleated Shade, 1800s, 26 In., Pair..	1062
Lamp, 3-Light, Eagle Finial, Dolphin Base, Brown Shade, Bronze, Painted, 25 x 13 In...........	125
Lamp, Regency Style, Brass, Black Shade, Domed Base, 1800s, 14 In., Pair...........................	195
Syrup, Lid, Red Ground, Peach, Grapes, Leaves, Strap Handle, Early 1900s, 5½ In..............	375

Tinware, Coffeepot, Wrigglework, Gooseneck, Finial, Potted Floral, Stamped, Ketterer, 1800, 10¾ In. $2,074

Pook & Pook

Tobacco Jar, Terra-Cotta, Figural, Man In Barrel, Stein In Hand, No. 3536 $72

Fox Auctions

Tobacco Jar, Wood, Dog's Head, Glass Eyes, Wearing Hinged Hat, Carved, Black Forest, 6½ In. $882

Fontaine's Auction Gallery

T

Tole, Box, Document, Dome Lid, Hasp &
Brass, Bail Handle, 1830s, 7 x 9 ½ In.
$360

Garth's Auctioneers & Appraisers

Tole, Teapot, Hinged Lid, Lighthouse
Shape, Flowers, Side Handle, Black
Ground, 1800s, 8 ½ In.
$854

Pook & Pook

Tole, Tray, Urn Of Flowers, Bird,
Reticulated Edge, Victorian, 1850s,
19 ½ x 27 In.
$480

Garth's Auctioneers & Appraisers

Tea Canister, Lid, Yellow Band, No. 7, Maroon Ground, 17 In.	96
Teapot, Hinged Lid, Lighthouse Shape, Flowers, Side Handle, Black Ground, 1800s, 8 ½ In. *illus*	854
Tray, Asphaltum Center, Black, Flowers, Octagonal, 1800s, 8 ¾ x 12 ½ In.	2074
Tray, Hitchcock Style, Wire Basket Of Fruit, Landscape, Rectangular, 1880s, 19 x 27 ¾ In.	468
Tray, Multicolor, Birds Of Paradise, Flowers, Gilt Trim, c.1870, 17 ½ x 24 In.	69
Tray, Serving, Eagle, Spread Wings, Scrollwork, Red Ribbon, Black Ground, 1800s, 19 x 26 In.	8125
Tray, Urn Of Flowers, Bird, Reticulated Edge, Victorian, 1850s, 19 ½ x 27 In. *illus*	480

TOM MIX

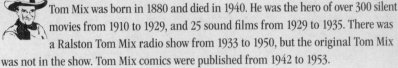

Tom Mix was born in 1880 and died in 1940. He was the hero of over 300 silent movies from 1910 to 1929, and 25 sound films from 1929 to 1935. There was a Ralston Tom Mix radio show from 1933 to 1950, but the original Tom Mix was not in the show. Tom Mix comics were published from 1942 to 1953.

Comic Book, Fawcett Publication, Issue No. 36, Volume 6, 1950	22
Hoard Of Montezuma, Big Little Book, 1937	12
Knife, Pocket, Tom, Gun, Horse, Plastic, Novelty Knife Co., 1990s, 3 In.	28
Toy, Horse, Rocking, Wood, White, Red Saddle, Logo, Yellow Rocker, Mengel Playthings, 39 In.	30

TOOL

Tools of all sorts are listed here, but most are related to industry. Other tools may be found listed under Iron, Kitchen, Tinware, and Wooden.

Anvil, Cast Iron, Pinched Hole, 6 Lb., 3 x 7 In. *illus*	86
Ax, Nessmuk Style, Steel Forged Head, Tiger Maple Handle, Leather Sheath, 15 In., Pair	1599
Bed Smoother, Maple, Blue, Painted, Horse Handle, Carved Hex Signs, 1800s, 5 ½ x 25 ¾ In. *illus*	527
Book Press, Oak, Tabletop, Side Hung Drawer, Screw Drive, 1800s, 43 x 22 ½ x 16 ½ In.	677
Box, Shoeshine, 2 Hinged Lids, Brass, Fitted Bottles, Turkey, c.1915, 17 x 32 In. *illus*	177
Caddy, Pine, Divided Interior, Shaped Handle, 1800s, 6 ¼ x 26 x 16 In.	125
Chest, Machinist, Oak, 7 Drawers, Schartow, 1920, 13 x 20 In.	266
Chest, Machinist, Oak, Drawers, Handle, 16 x 20 x 9 ½ In.	219
Chest, Oak, Scalloped Panel Case, Cast Iron Handle, Old White, Green, 1850s, 22 x 46 x 22 In.	240
Clamp, Goffering, Heart Design, Cutwork, 4 In.	523
Clock Jack, Iron & Wood Mechanism, Brass Frame, Spit Bar, England, 1700s, 9 ½ x 56 ¼ In.	4375
Comb, Weaving, Cherry, Relief, Carved, Geometric Design, Hand Loom, 1800s, 12 In. *illus*	188
Garden Seed Planter, American Standard, Tin, Wood, Iron, Painted, Stand, c.1880, 33 In.	77
Glove-Making Form, Birch, Mitten Shape, Gloversville, N.Y., c.1910, 14 In., 6 Piece	406
Grain Probe, Seedburo Equipment Co., Brass, 40 In., 2 Piece	154
Hay Rake, Horse Drawn, Spoke Wheels, Curved Tines, Salesman's Sample, 1859, 7 x 17 x 18 In.	1107
Hayfork, 4 Tines, Wood, 1800s, 65 In.	177
Hayfork, Split Hickory, 3 Tines, Wooden, Child's, Late 1800s, 35 ¼ In.	122
Holder, Watchmaker's, Clear Glass Dome Lid, Wood Base, Ball Feet, 1800s, 10 ½ In.	140
Ladder, Wood, Carved, African Dogon, Mali, 119 In.	354
Mallet, Baseball, Hammered Silver, Leather, Wood Handle, Harry Bertoia, c.1973, 14 In.	8750
Mallet, Circus, Laminated, Iron Bands, 33 x 9 ½ In.	118
Plane, Carpenter's, Maple, Carved Bird Handle, 1800s, 18 ¼ In. *illus*	549
Press, Cast Iron, Crank, Shapleigh Hardware, St. Louis, Early 1900s, 18 In.	79
Rake, Wood, Stick Shape Handle, Primitive, 1800s, 77 In.	138
Seeder, Iron Spike, Tipped Wheels, Walk Behind, Metal, 48 x 60 x 31 In.	313
Tractor Seat, Walter A. Wood, Iron, Embossed, Mounted On Wood Base, 21 In.	43
Workbench, Laminate Top, Oak Frame, Power Outlet, Late 1900s, 37 x 84 x 45 In. *illus*	531

TOOTHBRUSH HOLDER

Toothbrush holders were part of every bowl and pitcher set in the late nineteenth century. Most were oblong covered dishes. About 1920, manufacturers started to make children's toothbrush holders shaped like animals or cartoon characters. A few modern toothbrush holders are still being made.

Donkey, Cubist, Multicolor, Porcelain, Art Deco, c.1930, 4 ¼ x 1 ⅜ x 3 ¾ In.	32
Wall Mounted, Blue & White, Yellow & Blue Flowers, Gilt, Royal Saxe E.S. Germany, 7 x 4 In.	36

Tool, Anvil, Cast Iron, Pinched Hole, 6 Lb., 3 x 7 In.
$86

Hartzell's Auction Gallery Inc.

Tool, Bed Smoother, Maple, Blue, Painted, Horse Handle, Carved Hex Signs, 1800s, 5 ½ x 25 ¾ In.
$527

Jeffrey S. Evans & Associates

Early Construction Tools

Early construction tools include axes, adzes, saws, planes, chisels, drills, turning tools, hammers, vises, wrenches, screwdrivers, rules, and much more. Some nineteenth- and twentieth-century tools can be dated by the marks, usually the name of the company or person who made them.

Tool, Box, Shoeshine, 2 Hinged Lids, Brass, Fitted Bottles, Turkey, c.1915, 17 x 32 In.
$177

Leland Little Auctions

Tool, Comb, Weaving, Cherry, Relief, Carved, Geometric Design, Hand Loom, 1800s, 12 In.
$188

Eldred's

> ### TIP
> The best advice for a novice collector of tools is: If it looks like an unusual tool, save it. Try to identify it by consulting books, museums, the Internet, or old-timers. Don't paint it, wax it, refinish it, or otherwise change the condition.

Tool, Plane, Carpenter's, Maple, Carved Bird Handle, 1800s, 18 ¼ In.
$549

Pook & Pook

Tool, Workbench, Laminate Top, Oak Frame, Power Outlet, Late 1900s, 37 x 84 x 45 In.
$531

Austin Auction Gallery

T

Toothpick, Cased Glass, White, Rose, Ruffled Rim, Silver Plate Chick Pulling Cart, Tufts, c.1900, 5 In.
$234

Jeffrey S. Evans & Associates

Easy-Bake Is Easier
Easy-Bake Oven by Kenner was introduced in 1963. The lightbulb-heated miniature oven for children is still being made but with a less dangerous heat source. It was inducted into the National Toy Hall of Fame at The Strong National Museum of Play in 2006.

Toy, Airplane, Cast Iron, Nickel Props, Ribbed Wing, Embossed, TAT, Arrow, Kilgore, 1939, 11 x 13 In.
$2,460

Morphy Auctions

Toy, Airplane, Question Mark, Green, Silver, Nickel Plated Wheels, Cast Iron, Dent, 12-In. Wingspan
$1,220

Pook & Pook

TOOTHPICK HOLDER

Toothpick holders are sometimes called *toothpicks* by collectors. The variously shaped containers used to hold small wooden toothpicks are made of glass, china, or metal. Most of the toothpick holders are made of Victorian glass. Additional items may be found in other categories, such as Bisque, Silver Plate, Slag Glass, etc.

Cased Glass, White, Rose, Ruffled Rim, Silver Plate Chick Pulling Cart, Tufts, c.1900, 5 In. . *illus*	234
Egg, 2 Mice, Leafy Base, Porcelain, Royal Worcester	86
El Burrito, Donkey, Mixed Metal, 11 Toothpicks, Marked, Mexico, 20th Century, 3 x 5 In.	38
Glass, Gold Iridescent, Opalescent Rim, Ruby Glass Beads, 2 ½ In.	270
Glass, Iridescent Gold, Opalescent, Ruby Highlights, 2 ½ In.	225
Lettuce, Art Pottery, Hand Painted, Signed, Dodie Thayer, 3 x 2 In., Pair	512
Riding Boot, Sterling Silver, Hallmark, c.1940, 2 ¼ x 1 ½ x ½ In.	64

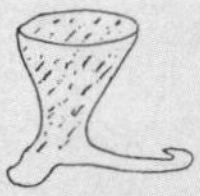

TORTOISESHELL GLASS

Tortoiseshell glass was made during the 1800s and after by the Sandwich Glass Works of Massachusetts and some firms in Germany. Tortoiseshell glass is, of course, named for its resemblance to real shell from a tortoise. It has been reproduced.

Egg, Rooster Finial, Metal, Green Eyes, Crowing, Round Metal Base, Scrolls, 4 ¼ In.	32
Powder Jar, Round, Squat, Silver Repousse Lid, c.1900, 2 ½ x 3 In.	80

TOTE, *see Purse category.*

TOY

Toy collectors have special clubs, magazines, and shows. Toys are designed to entice children, and today they have attracted new interest among adults who are still children at heart. All types of toys are collected. Tin toys, iron toys, battery-operated toys, and many others are collected by specialists. Penny toys are inexpensive tin toys made in Germany from the 1880s until about 1914. Some salesman's samples may be listed here. Dolls, Games, Teddy Bears, Bicycles, and other types of toys are listed in their own categories. Other toys may be found under company or celebrity names.

Airplane, Army Scout, Pressed Steel, Blue, Orange, Steelcraft, 17 ½ In.	150
Airplane, Bremen, Cast Ribbed Fuselage, 2 Seated Passengers, Iron, Hubley, 2 x 6 ½ x 7 In.	173
Airplane, Cargo, Jet Style, Tin Litho, Plastic, Pan American, Battery Operated, Marx, Box, 15 In. .	127
Airplane, Cast Iron, Green, Yellow, TAT, Kilgore, 1939, 3 ¼ x 11 In.	2460
Airplane, Cast Iron, Nickel Props, Ribbed Wing, Embossed, TAT, Arrow, Kilgore, 1939, 11 x 13 In. *illus*	2460
Airplane, Dagwood Solo Flight, Tin Lithograph, Yellow, Red, Windup, Marx, 11 ½ In.	425
Airplane, Fighter, Jet, Tin Lithograph, Crank, Machine Gun, Painted, Japan, 10 In.	92
Airplane, Fighter, Jet, U.S. Army, Tin Lithograph, Windup, Painted, Marx, 9 In.	92
Airplane, Ford, Trimotor, Gray, Red, 1417, Cast Iron, 11 ½ x 12 ½ In.	1680
Airplane, Jet, TWA, Tin Lithograph, Plastic, Engines Flash, Door, Battery Operated, Box, 14 In.	127
Airplane, Question Mark, Green, Silver, Nickel Plated Wheels, Cast Iron, Dent, 12-In. Wingspan .. *illus*	1220
Airplane, Right Plane, Propeller, Pilot, Passengers, Tin, 1900s, 29 ¾ In.	608
Airplane, Rookie Pilot, Tin Lithograph, Windup Mechanism, Louis Marx, 8 x 7 In. ..... *illus*	230
Airplane, Seaplane, Do-X, Blue, Red, Silver, Cast Iron, Nickel Plated Wheels, Hubley, 7 ½ In.	3416
Airplane, Seaplane, Friendship, Cast Iron, Yellow, Hubley, 4 ½ x 11 In.	6765
Airplane, Transport, Pressed Steel, Wing Span, Painted, 20 In.	109
Airplane, Turbo Prop, Green, White, Hand Commander, Tonka, 1982, 14 In.	37
Ambulance, U.S. Army, Rubber Tires, Painted, Keystone, 27 In.	575
Astronaut, Red Suit, Helmet, Holds Tool, Tin Litho, Battery Operated, Cragstan, Box, 1960s, 12 In.	1722
Bears are also listed in the Teddy Bear category.	
Bear, Painted, Cast Vinyl, Black, Stamped, Jun Takahashi, Kaws, 6 In. .... *illus*	1408
Bear, Standing, Shoebutton Eyes, Holding Stick, Rounded Base, Steiff, c.1906, 8 ¾ x 4 In.	2147
Bicycles that are large enough to ride are listed in the Bicycle category.	
Bird, Crow, Tin Lithograph, Plastic Feet, Windup, Kohler, 1950s, 3 ¼ x 7 ¼ In. .... *illus*	70
Boat, Ocean Liner, 2-Masted, 4 Lifeboats, Albert Ballin, Fleischmann, Marked, 11 x 20 x 6 In.	2400

SELECTED TOY MARKS WITH DATES USED

Gebruder Bing
1902–1934
Nuremburg, Germany

Gebruder Bing Co.
c.1923–1924
Nuremberg, Germany

F.A.O. Schwarz
1914
New York, N.Y.

Louis Marx & Co.
1920–1977
New York, N.Y.

Ernst Lehmann Co.
1881–c.1947, 1951–2006
Brandenburg, Germany; Nuremburg,
Germany

Ernst Lehmann Co.
1915
Brandenburg, Germany

Gebruder Marklin & Co.
1899+
Goppingen, Germany

Nomura Toy Industrial Co., Ltd.
1940s+
Tokyo, Japan

Meccano
1901+
Liverpool, England

Georges Carette & Co.
1905–1917
Nuremburg, Germany

Joseph Falk Co.
1895–1934
Nuremburg, Germany

H. Fischer & Co.
1908–1932
Nuremburg, Germany

Lineol
c. 1906–1963
Bradenburg, Germany

Blomer and Schüler
1919–1974
Nuremberg, Germany

Yonezawa Toys Co.
1950s–1970s
Tokyo, Japan

Toy, Airplane, Rookie Pilot, Tin Lithograph, Windup Mechanism, Louis Marx, 8 x 7 In.
$230

Blackwell Auctions

Toy, Bear, Painted, Cast Vinyl, Black, Stamped, Jun Takahashi, Kaws, 6 In.
$1,408

Neal Auction Company

Toy, Bird, Crow, Tin Lithograph, Plastic Feet, Windup, Kohler, 1950s, 3 ¼ x 7 ¼ In.
$70

Jeffrey S. Evans & Associates

> **TIP**
> *Rusted toys have very low value.*

Toy, Boat, Riverboat, Side Paddlewheels, Adirondack, Cast Iron, Wilkins, 5 ½ x 15 In.
$3,300

Morphy Auctions

Toy, Boy, Standing On 3-Wheel Platform, Sailor Outfit, Painted, Squeeze, Tin, 9 In.
$153

Pook & Pook

Toy, Bus, Double-Decker, Cast Iron, Green, Rubber Tires, 8 In.
$173

Blackwell Auctions

Toy, Bus, Double-Decker, Painted, Nickeled Figures, Kenton, 10 In.
$390

Bertoia Auctions

Toy, Bus, School, Die Cast, Enamel, Yellow, Redline, Hot Wheels, Mattel, 1970
$100

Matthew Bullock Auctioneers

Toy, Busy Miners, Cart On Track, Tin Lithograph, Windup, Louis Marx, Box, 16 In.
$171

Pook & Pook

Boat, Riverboat, Side Paddlewheels, Adirondack, Cast Iron, Wilkins, 5 ½ x 15 In. .... *illus*	3300
Bomber, Military, Tin Lithograph, Windup, Painted, Marx, 18 In...................................	104
Boy, Standing on 3-Wheel Platform, Sailor Outfit, Painted, Squeeze, Tin, 9 In. .... *illus*	153
Bulldozer, Yellow, Black, Metal & Plastic, Tonka, 12 In...	25
Bus, Double-Decker, Cast Iron, Green, Rubber Tires, 8 In. .... *illus*	173
Bus, Double-Decker, Painted, Nickeled Figures, Kenton, 10 In. .... *illus*	390
Bus, Fageol Safety Coach, Old Green Paint, Cast Wheels, Cast Iron, Arcade, Early 1900s, 3 x 12 In..	324
Bus, Greyhound, It's Such A Comfort To Take The Bus, Metal, Door Opens, Japan, 1950s, 11 In...	75
Bus, Nite Coach, Portholes, Embossed, Green & Orange, Cast Iron, Kenton, c.1915, 2 x 7 In...	420
Bus, School, Die Cast, Enamel, Yellow, Redline, Hot Wheels, Mattel, 1970 .... *illus*	100
Bus, Tin, 12 Windows, 4 Wheels, Blue, Cor-Cor, 1900s, 23 ¾ In.	375
Bus, Volkswagen, Aqua, Beach Bomb, Floral Stickers, Redline, Hot Wheels, Mattel, 1969	160
Busy Miners, Cart On Track, Tin Lithograph, Windup, Louis Marx, Box, 16 In. .... *illus*	171
Cabinet, Epicerie, Grocery, Washtub, Basket, Green Paint, France, 23 x 16 x 5 ¾ In. .... *illus*	74
Cannon, Solid Iron, Steel Wheels, Ebony Wood Base, Miniature, 5 ½ x 9 In.	150
Cap Gun, Colt .45, 6-Bullet, Cast Iron, Hubley, Red Box, 1958, 13 ½ In..........................	188
Cap Gun, Rifle, Western Scout, White Plastic Stock, Cast Iron, Hubley, Box, 32 In.	175
Car Set, Blue, Red, Green, Yellow, Rubber Wheels, Cast Iron, Marked, Hubley, Box, 4-In. Cars, 10 Piece	3960
Car, Alfa Romeo, Dooling Frog, Speed Racer, Gas Powered, Gray Paint, Rubber Tires, 4 In....	299
Car, Andy Gump, Driver, Cast Iron, Red, Nickel Wheels, Arcade, 6 x 7 In. .... *illus*	704
Car, Austin, A55 Cambridge, No. 29, Die Cast, Green, Matchbox, Lesney, England, Box	50
Car, Buick, Station Wagon, Metal, Red Body, Black Top, Friction, Marked, B, Japan, 8 ¼ In...	85
Car, Chevrolet, Classic Nomad, Off-White Interior, Redline, Hot Wheels, Mattel, 1969	100
Car, Chevrolet, Coupe, Black, Cast Iron, Rubber Tires, Arcade, 4 x 8 ¼ In.	660
Car, Classic Cord, Apple Green, Black Interior, Redline, Hot Wheels, Mattel, 1970................	300
Car, Corvette, Stingray, Silver, Buzz Ringer, Touch Tone Phone, Box, 12 ½ x 7 In.	40
Car, Dagwood, Crazy, Multicolor, Red Hat, Tin Lithograph, Windup, Marx, 8 In.	375
Car, Fire Rods, No. 16-83, Silverado, Die Cast, Annapolis Fire Rescue, Hot Wheels, Mattel......	450
Car, Ford, Classic 31 Woody, Copper, Off-White Interior, Redline, Hot Wheels, Mattel, 1968 *illus*	120
Car, Ford, Convertible, 1958, Metal, Blue, Lift Back, Battery Operated, TN, Japan, Repro Box, 10 In	95
Car, Ford, Cortina G.T., Superfast, No. 25, Die Cast, Brown, Matchbox, Lesney, Box	270
Car, Ford, Coupe, Cast Iron, Tom Sehloff, 1936, 10 ¾ In. .... *illus*	549
Car, Ford, Model T, Center Door, Cast Iron, Black, Arcade, 6 ½ In.	200
Car, Ford, Model T, Roadster, Female Driver, Orange Jacket, Tin, Windup, Bing, c.1920, 6 In. *illus*	234
Car, Ford, Model T, Sedan, Touring, Painted, Orange, Cast Iron, Arcade, c.1930, 6 ½ In........	80
Car, G-Man, Metal, Red Body, White Roof, Remote Control, Linemar, Japan, 8 ½ In............	95
Car, Jaguar, Blue, Die Cast, Steerable Wheels, Rubber Tires, Doepke, 18 In.	265
Car, Jaguar, No. 65, Die Cast, Blue, Matchbox, Lesney, England, Box................................	50
Car, Lamborghini Miura, P400, Superfast, No. 33, Gold, Matchbox, Lesney, Box .... *illus*	180
Car, Lotus Europa, Superfast, No. 5, Die Cast, Pink, Matchbox, Lesney, Box......................	45
Car, Mechanical Roadster, Tin Lithograph, Red Exterior, Windup, Distler, 3 ½ x 3 ⅝ x 9 ¾ In.	144
Car, Mercedes B-220, Automatic Jack, Metal, Black Paint, Hinged Trunk, Repro Box, 12 In...	175
Car, Mercedes-Benz 300, Prameta Kolner, Windup, Germany, 5 ¾ In.	55
Car, OHO, Driver, Tin Lithograph, Die Cast, Metal Wheels, Windup, Lehmann, 1930s, 4 x 4 In.	192
Car, Old Jalopy, Friction, Driver, Passenger, Painted, Marx, 7 In................................	104
Car, Police, Chevrolet, Remote Control, Metal, Green, Japan, Box.......................................	95
Car, Porsche, 917, Die Cast, Magenta, Redline, Hot Wheels, Mattel, 1969	140
Car, Porsche, Electromatic 7500, Rubber Tires, Battery Operated, Distler, 10 In................	183
Car, Python, Aqua, Black Roof, Brown Interior, Redline, Hot Wheels, Mattel, 1968 .... *illus*	75
Car, Racing, Alfa Romeo P2, Tin, Windup, Red, Shamrock On Hood, C.I.J., France, c.1924, 21 In.	2520
Car, Racing, Driver, 12 Pistons, Silver Spoke Wheels, Rubber Tires, Hubley, 3 x 10 x 3 In.	1200
Car, Racing, Driver, Yellow & Red, Green Roof, Tin, Windup, Marx, c.1920, 8 ½ In. ...... *illus*	200
Car, Racing, Duesenberg, Don Lewis, Stewart Spl., Cast Iron, 10 ½ In.	519
Car, Racing, NSU Record Racer, Tin Lithograph, Friction Power, Bandai, Japan, Box, 13 ¼ In.	519
Car, Racing, Piston, Driver, Cast Iron, Spoke Wheels, Green, Hubley, 10 ½ x 3 ½ In.............	1440
Car, Rolls-Royce, Tin, Robin's-Egg Blue Paint, Friction, Box, 8 In.	75
Car, Sight Seeing Auto No. 899, Driver, 4 Passengers, Cast Iron, Kenton, c.1910, 10 In........	2400
Car, Tether, Decal, Gilmore 5, Brushed Steel, Aluminum, Carved Wood, Rubber Wheels, c.1950, 18 In..	2250
Car, Watson Roadster, Carousel 1, 1958 Monza 500 Winner, Jim Rathmann, Die Cast, Red, Box .	120
Carousel, 2 Canopies, Hot Air Balloons, Tin, Airplanes, Dirigibles, Steam, Distler, 17 In........	1100

Toy, Cabinet, Epicerie, Grocery, Washtub, Basket, Green Paint, France, 23 x 16 x 5 ¾ In.
$74

Apple Tree Auction Center

Toy, Car, Andy Gump, Driver, Cast Iron, Red, Nickel Wheels, Arcade, 6 x 7 In.
$704

Morphy Auctions

Toy, Car, Ford, Classic 31 Woody, Copper, Off-White Interior, Redline, Hot Wheels, Mattel, 1968
$120

Matthew Bullock Auctioneers

TIP
Collectors pay higher prices for most plastic space-gun toys than for lithographed tin guns. The newer plastic toys have more futuristic designs.

T

Toy, Car, Ford, Coupe, Cast Iron, Tom Sehloff, 1936, 10¾ In.
$549

Pook & Pook

Toy, Car, Ford, Model T, Roadster, Female Driver, Orange Jacket, Tin, Windup, Bing, c.1920, 6 In.
$234

Jeffrey S. Evans & Associates

Toy, Car, Lamborghini Miura, P400, Superfast, No. 33, Gold, Matchbox, Lesney, Box
$180

Matthew Bullock Auctioneers

Toy, Car, Python, Aqua, Black Roof, Brown Interior, Redline, Hot Wheels, Mattel, 1968
$75

Matthew Bullock Auctioneers

Toy, Car, Racing, Driver, Yellow & Red, Green Roof, Tin, Windup, Marx, c.1920, 8½ In.
$200

Selkirk Auctioneers & Appraisers

Toy, Carousel, Musical, 4 Children On Rabbits, Bisque Heads, Silk Clothes, France, 18 x 14 In.
$1,353

Brunk Auctions

Toy, Cart, Dump, Pressed Steel, Cast Iron Driver, Clockwork, Kingsbury, Panama, 13 In.
$183

Pook & Pook

Toy, Cat, Black, Spots, Wire Whiskers, Wood, Wheels, Pull Toy, C.H. Nutting, 1900s, 14 x 20 x 6 In.
$207

Leland Little Auctions

Toy, Cat, Puss In Boots, Stuffed, Mohair, Jointed, Swivel Head, Steiff, 1910s, 12¼ In.
$556

Jeffrey S. Evans & Associates

T

Toy, Cat, Whimsical, Spring Tail, Painted, Penny Toy, Distler, 3 In.
$180

Bertoia Auctions

Toy, Clown, Playing Banjo, Celluloid Head,
Tin Painted Base, Marked, Germany,
9 x 5 1/2 x 5 In.
$1,020

Morphy Auctions

Toy, Cow, Holstein, Glass Eyes, Felt Udders,
Leather Collar, Steiff, c.1955, 21 x 33 In.
$1,521

ffrey S. Evans & Associates

Toy, Cupboard, Doll's, Wood, 4 Hinged Doors,
14 x 7 x 23 In.
$135

Apple Tree Auction Center

Toy, Ditcher, Buckeye, Crank, Chains On
Wheels, Red, Green, Kenton, 12 1/2 x 4 1/2 In.
$510

Morphy Auctions

Toy, Dog, Bulldog, Papier-Mache, Growler,
Wood Wheels, Pull Toy, c.1890, 14 In.
$1,159

Neal Auction Company

Toy, Dog, Poodle, White Mohair, Porcelain
Medallion, Squeaker, Club Edition, Steiff,
Box, 1931, 11 In.
$62

Apple Tree Auction Center

Toy, Dollhouse, 2 Rooms, Blue Roof, Glass
Windows, Hinged Front, Gottschalk,
14 1/2 x 9 3/4 In.
$615

Apple Tree Auction Center

T

Toy, Dollhouse, 4 Rooms, Porch, Balcony, Blue Roof, Elevator, Crank, Gottschalk, 23 x 10 x 8 In. $800

Apple Tree Auction Center

Toy, Dollhouse, 4 Story, 22-Room Mansion, Luxury, Multicolor, Lawbre Co., c.1986, 63 x 52 In. $6,000

Charlton Hall Auctions

Carousel, 3 Airplanes, Lithograph, Painted, Marked, Wilhelm Krauss, Germany, c.1925, 9 ½ In.	207
Carousel, Multicolor, Tin, Ring Winner, Lever Operated, 1900s, 12 ½ In.	192
Carousel, Musical, 4 Children On Rabbits, Bisque Heads, Silk Clothes, France, 18 x 14 In. .... *illus*	1353
Carriage, 3 Wheels, Driver, Umbrella Top, Open Car, Valet, Tin Litho, Lehmann, 1930s, 5 x 5 In.	324
Carriage, Doll's, Stroller, Green, Red Stripes, Wolf's Heads, Spoke Wheels, Hinged Bonnet, 41 In..	168
Cart, Dump, Pressed Steel, Cast Iron Driver, Clockwork, Kingsbury, Panama, 13 In. .... *illus*	183
Cart, Horse Drawn, Brutus Driver, Tin Lithograph, Windup, Louis Marx, Box, 7 ½ In.	366
Cart, Horse Drawn, Doctor's, Driver, Red, White Horse, Carpenter Toys, c.1880, 3 ¼ x 9 ½ In. .	246
Cart, Ox Drawn, Wheels, Black, Red, Welker & Crosby Co., c.1883, 11 x 4 ½ In.	720
Cat, Black, Spots, Wire Whiskers, Wood, Wheels, Pull Toy, C.H. Nutting, 1900s, 14 x 20 x 6 In. *illus*	207
Cat, Puss In Boots, Stuffed, Mohair, Jointed, Swivel Head, Steiff, 1910s, 12 ¼ In. .... *illus*	556
Cat, Whimsical, Spring Tail, Painted, Penny Toy, Distler, 3 In. .... *illus*	180
Chair, Doll's, Wood, 2 Slats, Painted Pink, Gilt Turnings, Decoupage Flowers, Joseph Lehn, 13 In. .	4148
Clown, Playing Banjo, Celluloid Head, Tin Painted Base, Marked, Germany, 9 x 5 ½ x 5 In. ...*illus*	1020
Cow, Holstein, Glass Eyes, Felt Udders, Leather Collar, Steiff, c.1955, 21 x 33 In. .... *illus*	1521
Cradle, Doll's, Pine, Hood, Applied Rocker, Painted, 1800s, 17 ½ In.	125
Crane, Red, Blue, Hand Crank, Structo Construction Co., 16 x 12 In.	59
Cupboard, Doll's, Wood, 4 Hinged Doors, 14 x 7 x 23 In. .... *illus*	135
Dancers, Tango, Painted, Tin, Clockwork, Gunthermann, 7 ½ In.	427
Delivery Wagon, City Delivery, 3 Horses, Driver, Painted, Harris Toy Co., c.1890, 7 x 15 ½ In.	2700
Derrick, Mobile Construction, Pressed & Painted Steel, Buddy L, c.1954, 24 x 8 In.	154
Diorama, Village, Mountain, Putz Style, Crank Mechanism, Showcase, 24 ¾ X 36 In.	671
Ditcher, Buckeye, Crank, Chains On Wheels, Red, Green, Kenton, 12 ½ x 4 ½ In. .... *illus*	510
Dog, Bulldog, Papier-Mache, Flocked, Glass Eyes, Wood Casters, Pull Toy, 21 In.	1037
Dog, Bulldog, Papier-Mache, Growler, Wood Wheels, Pull Toy, c.1890, 14 In. .... *illus*	1159
Dog, Poodle, White Mohair, Porcelain Medallion, Squeaker, Club Edition, Steiff, Box, 1931, 11 In. *illus*	62
Dog, Standing, White Body, Red Spots, Carved, Painted, 4 Spoke Wheels, Pull Toy, 10 In.	1845
Dolls are listed in the Doll category.	
Dollhouse, 2 Rooms, Blue Roof, Glass Windows, Hinged Front, Gottschalk, 14 ½ x 9 ¾ In. *illus*	615
Dollhouse, 2 Story, Paper On Wood, Front Stairs, Marked Germany, 17 x 9 x 9 ½ In.	480
Dollhouse, 3 Story, Wood, Electric Lighted Interior, 2 Chimneys, 1950s, 44 x 38 x 21 In.	351
Dollhouse, 4 Rooms, Porch, Balcony, Blue Roof, Elevator, Crank, Gottschalk, 23 x 10 x 8 In. ..*illus*	800
Dollhouse, 4 Story, 22-Room Mansion, Luxury, Multicolor, Lawbre Co., c.1986, 63 x 52 In. *illus*	6000
Dollhouse, Cafe, Table, Wine, Glass Dome, Signed, M. Simons, 2002, 12 ½ In.	35
Dollhouse, Cottage, Wood, Painted, Window Box, Flowers, Roof Lifts, Schoenhut, c.1920, 10 x 13 In.	1140
Dollhouse, Mixed Woods, Removable Hipped Roof, Red Chimney, 1910s, 18 x 16 x 26 In.	403
Donkey, Bucking, Clown, Tin Lithograph, Painted, Windup, 5 ½ In.	173
Drill, Grain, Green Lids, Old Style Decals, John Deere, Box, 1950, 7 In.	277
Duck, Pip-Squeak, Articulated Wings, Paper Label, V.S. Williams, Milford, 1800s, 3 ½ In.	519
Elephant, Gray Mohair, Beige Wool Tusks, Wood Eyes, On Wheels, Steiff, Box, 1903, 18 In. . *illus*	172
Elephant, Jumbo, Windup, Tin, Germany, 3 ½ In.	106
Ferris Wheel, 6 Double Carts, Figures, Chain, Spring Mechanism, Cast Iron, Hubley, 17 x 16 x 8 In..	1020
Ferris Wheel, Clown Face, 6 Cabins, Tin Lithograph, No. 172, J. Chein & Co., Box, 16 ¾ In. ..	213
Figure, Teddy Roosevelt, Safari, Helmet, Camera, Spear, Knife, Schoenhut, 8 In. .... *illus*	1220
Figure, Woman, Walker, Old Bavarian Woman, Basket, Holding Broom, Gunthermann, 7 In. ...*illus*	570
Fire Truck, Aerial, White Ladder, Paint Red, Pressed Steel, Tonka, 28 ¾ In.	49
Fire Truck, Driver, Ladders, Red, Cast Iron, Ahernz Fox, Hubley, 3 ¾ x 11 ¼ In.	1152
Fire Truck, Fire Dept., Red, Die Cast, Redline, Hot Wheels, Mattel, 1969	75
Fire Truck, Hose & Ladder, Pressed Steel, Red Paint, Buddy L, 25 ½ In. .... *illus*	546
Fire Truck, Knox, Pompier Style, 2 Ladders, Red & Black, Mechanical, c.1910, 29 In.	7930
Fire Truck, Mack, Ladder, Driver, Hose Reel, Rubber Tires, Red, Cast Iron, Arcade, 19 x 4 In..	390
Fire Truck, Painted, Red, Aerial Ladder, Pressed Steel, Keystone Mfg. Co., Early 1900s, 12 In. *illus*	378
Fire Truck, Pumper, Driver, Cast Iron, Rubber Tires, Spokes, Red, Hubley, 8 ½ x 13 In.	320
Fire Truck, Pumper, Metal Spokes, Nickeled Pumper, Rubber Tires, Cast Iron, Hubley, 8 x 13 x 4 In.	320
Fire Wagon, Horse Drawn, Hose Reel, 2 Men, Pink Wheels, Dent Hardware Co., c.1910, 7 ¼ x 22 In.	221
Fire Wagon, Horse Drawn, Red, Ladder, 6 Wheels, Cast Iron, Late 1800s, 8 ½ In.	54
Fire Wagon, Hose Reel, Yellow, Embossed Hose, Driver, Crank, Cast Iron, Kenton, 4 x 9 In. ..	42
Fire Wagon, Ladder, 2 Men, Horses, Nickel, Wheels, Dent Hardware Co., c.1910, 8 ¼ x 32 ¾ In.	330
Fire Wagon, Patrol, Horse Drawn, Driver, 6 Passengers, Black, Red, 5 ½ x 10 ½ In.	68
Fire Wagon, Pumper, Driver, Rubber Tires, Spokes, Red, Cast Iron, Hubley, 8 ½ x 13 ¼ In.	320

Toy, Elephant, Gray Mohair, Beige Wool Tusks, Wood Eyes, On Wheels, Steiff, Box, 1903, 18 In.
$172

Tree Auction Center   Apple

Toy, Figure, Teddy Roosevelt, Safari, Helmet, Camera, Spear, Knife, Schoenhut, 8 In.
$1,220

Pook & Pook

Toy, Figure, Woman, Walker, Old Bavarian Woman, Basket, Holding Broom, Gunthermann, 7 In.
$570

Bertoia Auctions

Toy, Fire Truck, Hose & Ladder, Pressed Steel, Red Paint, Buddy L, 25 ½ In.
$546

Blackwell Auctions

Toy, Fire Truck, Painted, Red, Aerial Ladder, Pressed Steel, Keystone Mfg. Co., Early 1900s, 12 In.
$378

Fontaine's Auction Gallery

Toy, Fire Wagon, Pumper, Horse Drawn, 2 Men, Pratt & Letchworth, c.1890, 9 x 25 In.
$3,000

Morphy Auctions

Toy, Flintstones, Fred, Driving Brontosaurus, Cloth Covered, Battery Operated, Marx, 23 x 11 In.
$144

Blackwell Auctions

Toy, Funny Face, Standing, Multicolor, Tin Litho, No. 535, Louis Marx, Box, c.1930, 10 ¾ In.
$315

Fontaine's Auction Gallery

T

Toy, Garage, Residential, Tin Lithograph, Red Shingled Roof, Marx, c.1950, 8 x 13 In. $125

Selkirk Auctioneers & Appraisers

Toy, Grasshopper, Daddy Long Legs, Cast Iron, Wire Antenna, Rubber Tires, Green, 4 x 14 In. $875

Morphy Auctions

Toy, Hoisting Tower, Pressed Steel, Green, Painted, Buddy L, c.1928, 29 In. $246

Rich Penn Auctions

Toy, Horse, Rocking, Carved, Horsehead, Button Eyes, Red Seat, Yellow, Footrest, 1800s, 19 x 12 In. $250

Eldred's

Toy, Horse, Rocking, Hide Covered, Saddle, Maple & Iron Base, Late 1800s, 37 In. $406

Eldred's

Lincoln Logs
Lincoln Logs were invented by John Lloyd Wright, son of the famous architect Frank Lloyd Wright.

Toy, Jester, Acrobat, Bisque Lower Arms, Satin Outfit, Chain, 13 In. $458

Pook & Pook

Toy, Joe Penner & Duck, Walker, Hat Pops Up, Tin Lithograph, Marx, 8 In. $300

Bertoia Auctions

Toy, Kangaroo, Joey In Pouch, Mohair, Jointed, Glass Eyes, Steiff, 22 In. $221

Apple Tree Auction Center

Toy, Monkey, Jocko, Brown Mohair, Jointed, Glass Eyes, Open Mouth, Beard, Steiff, 12 In. $62

Apple Tree Auction Center

Fire Wagon, Pumper, Horse Drawn, 2 Men, Pratt & Letchworth, c.1890, 9 x 25 In. ...... *illus*	3000
Firefighter, Climbing, Multicolor, Yellow Ladder, Windup, Louis Marx & Co.	125
Flintstones, Fred, Driving Brontosaurus, Cloth Covered, Battery Operated, Marx, 23 x 11 In *illus*	144
Fox, Aphrodite, Pink Viscose, White Belly & Chin, Jointed, Elena Abrosimova, 9 In.	185
Funny Face, Standing, Multicolor, Tin Litho, No. 535, Louis Marx, Box, c.1930, 10¾ In. *illus*	315
G.I. Joe, K-9 Pups, Tin, Windup, Walker, Unique Art	113
G.I. Joe, Soldier, Poseable, Green Jacket, Pants, Dog Tag, Hasbro, Box, 1964, 11 In.	520
Games are listed in the Game category.	
Garage, Residential, Tin Lithograph, Red Shingled Roof, Marx, c.1950, 8 x 13 In.........*illus*	125
Gas Pump, Texaco Fire-Chief, 2 Shelves, Tin, Bell, Red Ground, c.1960, 30 In.	105
Goat, Cream & Brown Fur, Lead Horns, Stick Legs, Platform, Pull Toy, Germany, 8 In...	549
Grader, Caterpillar, Die Cast, Red, No. 99, Mini Dinky Toy, Meccano, Box	45
Grasshopper, Daddy Long Legs, Cast Iron, Wire Antenna, Rubber Tires, Green, 4 x 14 In. *illus*	875
Gun, BB, Machine Gun, Pneumatic, Tripod Stand, Feltman, 1939, 26 x 37 x 18 In.	7680
Gun, Manmelter 3600 ZX, Sub-Atomic Disintegrator Pistol, Metal Case, 9½ x 12 x 3½ In...	610
Hansom Cab, Horse Drawn, Driver, Wheels, Painted, Pratt & Letchworth, c.1890, 13 x 4 In.	540
Happy Hooligan, Police Patrol, Wagon, 2 Horses, Kenton Hardware Co., c.1910, 17 x 4½ In	840
Hauler, Cast Iron, Trailer Winch, Heavy Duty Trailer, Red, Kilgore, 12½ x 3½ In.........	1845
Hoisting Tower, Pressed Steel, Green, Painted, Buddy L, c.1928, 29 In. .... *illus*	246
Horse & Cart, Brutus Driver, Tin Lithograph, Mechanical, Windup, Marx, Box, 7½ In.......	366
Horse & Wagon, Drag, Driver, Iron, Steel, Painted, Wilkins Toy Co., c.1910, 6½ x 21 In	256
Horse & Wagon, Phaeton, Woman Driver, Red, Black, Pratt & Letchworth, c.1890, 17½ x 5 In..	840
Horse & Wagon, Stakes, Driver, Green, Red, Brown, Pratt & Letchworth, c.1890, 6½ x 10 In.	510
Horse, Cream Fur, Brown Spots, Wrought Iron Base, 4 Wheels, Steiff, c.1950, 31 In.............	150
Horse, Mohair Hair Tail, Saddle, Standing, Platform, Painted, Pull Toy, 1800s, 16½ x 17 In.......	106
Horse, Rider, Cast Iron, Dowel, Push Toy, Wilkins, 5½ In.	305
Horse, Rocking, Carved Softwood, Beveled Seat, Ash Footrest, Early 1800s, 21 x 42 x 14 In. ..	1074
Horse, Rocking, Carved, Horsehead, Button Eyes, Red Seat, Yellow, Footrest, 1800s, 19 x 12 In. *illus*	250
Horse, Rocking, Detachable Base, Wheeled Platform, Vinyl Saddle, 1950s, 45 x 56 x 18 In......	585
Horse, Rocking, Fabric-Covered Body, Saddle, Push Pull, Red Base, Late 1800s, 30 x 42 In....	305
Horse, Rocking, Hide Covered, Saddle, Maple & Iron Base, Late 1800s, 37 In. .... *illus*	406
Horse, Rocking, Painted, Marked, Shoo Fly 1B, c.1940, 31½ x 13½ x 16 In.	59
Horse, Rocking, Wood Rocker, Painted, Steiff, 30 x 42 x 16 In....................................	172
Jazzbo Jim, Dancer On Roof, Holding Banjo, Tin Lithograph, Unique Art, c.1920, 9 In.	325
Jester, Acrobat, Bisque Lower Arms, Satin Outfit, Chain, 13 In. .... *illus*	458
Jetsons, Turnover Tank, Character Graphics, Tin Litho, Marx, Box, 1963, 4 x 3 In...............	523
Joe Penner & Duck, Walker, Hat Pops Up, Tin Lithograph, Marx, 8 In. .... *illus*	300
Jolly Jigger, Dancing, Plaid Suit, Top Hat, Holding Cane, Schoenhut, 17½ In.	397
Kangaroo, Joey In Pouch, Mohair, Jointed, Glass Eyes, Steiff, 22 In. .... *illus*	221
Komikal Kop, Policeman, Dog, Traffic B, Tin Lithograph, Windup, Marx, 7½ In..................	175
Landau, Horse Drawn, Coachman, Black, White, Yellow Wheels, Wilkins Toy Co., c.1890, 16 x 4 In.	984
Lincoln Tunnel, Cars, Policeman, Tin Lithograph, Windup, Unique Art Mfg., c.1930, 24 In.	100
Main Street Terminal, Tin Lithograph, Windup, Marx, c.1920, 24 In..........................	125
Martian Flying Saucer, Red Man In Space, Bubble Top, Tin Litho, Friction, TN, Japan, 6 x 6 In.	740
Merry-Go-Round, Playland, Children On Horses, Tin Lithograph, Windup, J. Chein, Box, 11 In..	270
Monkey, Jocko, Brown Mohair, Jointed, Glass Eyes, Open Mouth, Beard, Steiff, 12 In. .. *illus*	62
Motorcycle, 3 Wheels, Embossed, Traffic Car, Cast Iron, Rubber Tires, Hubley, 5 x 9 In.	480
Motorcycle, Crash Car, Police Driver, Brown Hat, Painted, Cast Iron, 11½ x 5 In. .... *illus*	1560
Motorcycle, Harley-Davidson, Dyna Wide Glide, Black & Silver, Hot Wheels, Box, 13 x 5 In...	25
Motorcycle, Harley-Davidson, Police, Policeman Rider, Green, Cast Iron, Hubley, 6½ In.	201
Motorcycle, Harley-Davidson, Sidecar, Cast Iron, Hubley, 6 In..............................	793
Motorcycle, Harley-Davidson, Sidecar, Police, Cast Iron, Rubber Tires, 9 x 5½ In. ...... *illus*	390
Motorcycle, Harley-Davidson, Softail, Purple, Silver & Black, Hot Wheels, Box, 13 x 5 In. *illus*	25
Motorcycle, Harley-Davidson, Tin Lithograph, Pistons Move, Friction, TN, Japan, 1959, 5 x 9 In. ...	400
Motorcycle, Indian, Embossed, Say It With Flowers, Iron, Don Lewis, c.1990, 11 x 5 x 5 In. ..	1792
Motorcycle, Indian, Police, Sidecar, Red & Black, Cast Iron, Hubley, 8¾ In........................	2440
Motorcycle, Indian, Sidecar, Man, Woman, Rubber Tires, Metal Spokes, Hubley, 4¾ x 10 In..	3000
Motorcycle, PDQ Delivery, Policeman Driver, Cast Iron, Vindex, Hubley, 9 x 6 In.	2040
Motorcycle, Police, Red, Electric Headlight, Cast Iron, Hubley, 6¼ In.......................	610
Motorcycle, Policeman, Cast Iron, Rubber Tires, Spoke Wheels, Henderson, 8½ x 3½ In...	1680
Motorcycle, Policeman, Tin Lithograph, Battery Operated, Modern Toys, Japan, c.1960, 7¾ In. *illus*	234

Toy, Motorcycle, Crash Car, Police
Driver, Brown Hat, Painted, Cast Iron,
11½ x 5 In.
$1,560

Morphy Auctions

Toy, Motorcycle, Harley-Davidson,
Sidecar, Police, Cast Iron, Rubber Tires,
9 x 5½ In.
$390

Morphy Auctions

Toy, Motorcycle, Harley-Davidson,
Softail, Purple, Silver & Black, Hot
Wheels, Box, 13 x 5 In.
$25

Matthew Bullock Auctioneers

Toy, Motorcycle, Policeman, Tin
Lithograph, Battery Operated, Modern
Toys, Japan, c.1960, 7¾ In.
$234

Jeffrey S. Evans & Associates

T

This is an edited listing of current
prices. Visit Kovels.com to check thousands of prices from previous years and
sign up for free information on trends,
tips, reproductions, marks, and more.

Toy, Motorcycle, Racing, Pea Shooter, No. 7, Silver & Blue, Cast Iron, Hubley, 5 ½ In.
$1,342

Pook & Pook

Toy, Musician, Bisque, Playing Cymbals, Painted Eyes, Closed Mouth, Pull Toy, 6 ¼ In.
$366

Pook & Pook

Toy, Pedal Car, Dump Truck, Mack, Metal, Red & Yellow, Steelcraft, Contemporary, 44 In.
$1,368

Bertoia Auctions

Toy, Pedal Car, Fire Chief, Metal, Bell, Boycraft, 38 In.
$4,320

Bertoia Auctions

Toy, Pedal Car, Fire Truck, Hook & Ladder, F.D. No. 1, Metal, Wood Ladders, AMF, 44 In.
$2,016

Bertoia Auctions

Toy, Pedal Car, Metal, Brown Patina, Rubber Wheels, c.1930
$320

Neal Auction Company

Toy, Pig, Folk Art, Carved, Painted, Leather Ears & Tail, Glass Eyes, Pull Toy, 1900s, 11 x 13 ½ In.
$1,586

Pook & Pook

Toy, Pool Player, Pool Table, Stick & Ball, Metal, Mechanical, Penny Toy, Early 1900s, 4 In.
$125

Selkirk Auctioneers & Appraisers

Toy, Puppet Stage, Punch & Judy, Papier-Mache, Crank Operated Curtain, Guignol, 58 x 26 In.
$1,159

Pook & Pook

Motorcycle, Racing, Pea Shooter, No. 7, Silver & Blue, Cast Iron, Hubley, 5 ½ In. .... *illus*	1342
Motorcycle, Rookie Cop, Tin Lithograph, Die Cast, Red, Yellow, Windup, Marx, c.1950, 5 x 8 In..	168
Motorcycle, Traffic Car, Red, Gray, Cast Iron, Rubber Tires, Spoke Wheels, Hubley, 5 x 9 In.	480
Motorcycle, U.S. Airmail, Policeman Driver, Cast Iron, Rubber Tires, Hubley, 9 x 6 In.	900
Musician, Bisque, Playing Cymbals, Painted Eyes, Closed Mouth, Pull Toy, 6 ¼ In. .... *illus*	366
Payloader, Shovel, No. 96, Die Cast, Light Yellow, Mini Dinky Toy, Meccano, Box	30
Pedal Car, Airplane, Metal, Gray, Red, Chrome Propeller, Stencil, Eagle, Airflow, 35 x 46 In.	750
Pedal Car, Dump Truck, Mack, Metal, Red & Yellow, Steelcraft, Contemporary, 44 In. . *illus*	1368
Pedal Car, Ferrari, F2 Racer, Red, Enamel, Steel, Chrome Accents, Late 1900s, 19 x 26 In. ...	502
Pedal Car, Fire Chief, Metal, Bell, Boycraft, 38 In. .... *illus*	4320
Pedal Car, Fire Truck, Hook & Ladder, F.D. No. 1, Metal, Wood Ladders, AMF, 44 In. .... *illus*	2016
Pedal Car, Metal, Brown Patina, Rubber Wheels, c.1930 .... *illus*	320
Pedal Car, Ride 'Em Steam Roller, Pressed Steel, Roof Seat, Steering Bar, Keystone, c.1928, 20 In..	800
Pedal Car, Tee Bird, Holiday, Ball Bearing, Painted, Murray, 1900s, 17 x 34 In.................	90
Pedal Car, Woody, Station Wagon, Garton, 1941, 21 x 47 x 16 In.	1722
Phaeton, Horse Drawn, Driver, Red, Black, Pratt & Letchworth, c.1890, 17 ½ x 5 In.	840
Pig, Folk Art, Carved, Painted, Leather Ears & Tail, Glass Eyes, Pull Toy, 1900s, 11 x 13 ½ In. *illus*	1586
Pool Player, Pool Table, Stick & Ball, Metal, Mechanical, Penny Toy, Early 1900s, 4 In. *illus*	125
Porter, Pushing Steamer Trunk On Cart, Yellow, Penny Toy, Early 1900s, 3 In.	100
Puppet Stage, Punch & Judy, Papier-Mache, Crank Operated Curtain, Guignol, 58 x 26 In. *illus*	1159
Quilt, Doll's, Rabbits, House, Flowers, Blue Ground, Rounded Corners, 29 x 20 In..............	60
Rabbit, Easter Bunny, Delivery, Riding, Painted, Wyandotte, 9 ½ In.	173
Rabbit, Riding Tricycle, Composition, Wire Frame Tricycle, Wood Wheels, Germany, 7 ¼ In.	671
Rhinoceros, Wood, Jointed, Schoenhut, 9 In. .... *illus*	330
Rifle, Atomic, Tom Corbett, Space Cadet, Silver, Plastic, Marx, Box..............................	519
Road Roller, Driver, Roller Wheels, Green, Cast Iron, Embossed Huber, Hubley, 5 ⅜ x 15 In.	800
Robot, Mr. Atom, Battery Operated, Advance Doll & Toy Co., Conn., Box, 1960s, 18 ½ In.	554
Robot, Revolves, Flashes, Chest Door Opens, Tin Litho, Battery, Alps, Japan, Box, 10 x 6 In...	1845
Robot, Rosco Astronaut, Blue, Tin Litho, Battery Operated, TN, Nomura, Japan, Box, 14 In..	1355
Roller Coaster, 2 Coaster Cars, Tin Lithograph, No. 275, J. Chein & Co., Box, 9 x 19 In.	188
Room Box, Bakery, Plywood, Checkerboard Design, Painted, 10 ½ x 20 x 10 ¾ In. ....*illus*	308
Room Box, Bathroom, Navy Blue, Faux Tile Walls, Marked, Castelltort Y Denia, 6 x 14 x 6 In.	74
Room Box, General Store, Drawers, Shelves, Counters, Marked, Gottschalk, 12 ¼ x 28 x 12 In. ..*illus*	111
Room Box, Kitchen, Ivory & Blue Paint, Wallpaper, 14 ½ x 28 x 14 In..........................	74
Room Box, Shop, Flowered Wallpaper Floor, Cabinets & Drawers, Mint Green, 15 x 22 x 15 In. ...	277
Rooster, Dressed, Walker, Nodding Head, Composition, Lead Feet, Germany, 10 In. ..... *illus*	390
Sand Loader, Pressed Steel, Decals, Painted, Metal Wheels, Buddy L, 20 In.	230
Schoolhouse, Red, Blue Roof, Paper Windows, Painted, Box, Late 1800s, 6 ½ x 4 x 6 ¾ In. ...	281
Scraper, No. 428, Caterpillar, Yellow, Scale Model, Eska, Box, 14 In.	483
Seal, Plush, Ride On, Metal Base, 4 Spoke Wheels, Cast Iron Hoop Handle, Steiff, 15 x 31 In.	118
Seesaw, Bell Ringers, Man & Woman, Rocking Action, Tin, Cast Iron, Pull Toy, 7 ½ In. *illus*	420
Seesaw, Papier-Mache, Iron, Painted, Arte Felguerez, 11 x 16 In...............................	118
Sewing Machine, Cast Iron, Tabletop, Willcox & Bibbs Sewing Machine Co., 10 x 8 In.	145
Sheep, Cream, Wooly Fur, Iron Wheels, Pull Toy, 6 In. .... *illus*	366
Skier, Rolf, Blue Suit, White Cap, Skis, Poles, Clockwork, Tin Lithograph, Lehmann, 7 ½ In. ..*illus*	2400
Sled, American Eagle, Inscribed, Willard, Painted, Late 1800s, 31 ½ In.	976
Sled, Antelope, Heart Cutout, Wood, Worn Blue Paint, Wood Runners, c.1900, 46 ½ In.	463
Sled, Black Deck, Red, White, Blue, Gold Swirls, Painted, Maine, Late 1800s, 30 In.	469
Sled, Wood Deck, Iron, Upturned Rails, Flowers, Pinstripes, Victorian, 1800s, 4 x 15 x 5 In...	1695
Sled, Wood, Hiawatha, Metal Runners With Steep Curve, Red Paint, Yellow Letters, 1800s, 28 In.	210
Soldier Set, Cavalry Service Dress, Black & Red Horses, Painted, Britains, Box, Soldier 3 ½ In...	50
Spaceship, Tin Lithograph, Blue, Yellow, Red, Windup, Marx, 12 In................................	188
Spaceship, Tom Corbett, Sparkling, Tin Litho, Space Graphics, Windup, Marx, Box, 1950s, 12 In.	984
Sparkler, Amos 'N' Andy, Andy, Glass Eyes, Tin Litho, Embossed, Germany, 1930s, 7 x 3 ½ In. ..*illus*	283
Sparkler, Cat, Felix, Short Ear Version, Nifty, Germany, 4 ½ In. .... *illus*	360
Steam Engine, 2 Parts, Factory Unit, Mounted, Cast Iron Base, Doll Toy, Early 1900s, 14 x 15 In.	125
Steam Engine, Model, Horizontal Boiler, Wood Base, Doll Et Cie, Germany, 11 x 15 x 6 In.....	1003
Steam Shovel, Metal, Orange Paint, Structo, 1940s, 16 In..	75
Steam Shovel, P&H, Cast Iron, Crank, Vindex, 17 x 6 In.	3900
Steam Shovel, Pressed Steel, Red & Black Paint, Keystone, 17 In.	69

Toy, Rhinoceros, Wood, Jointed, Schoenhut, 9 In.
$330

Bertoia Auctions

Toy, Room Box, Bakery, Plywood, Checkerboard Design, Painted, 10 ½ x 20 x 10 ¾ In.
$308

Apple Tree Auction Center

Toy, Room Box, General Store, Drawers, Shelves, Counters, Marked, Gottschalk, 12 ¼ x 28 x 12 In.
$111

Apple Tree Auction Center

TIP

To determine the age of a Tootsietoy vehicle, look at the wheels. From 1909 to 1932, the wheels were metal and painted black or gold. In the 1933 Tootsietoy catalog, vehicles had either metal wheels or wheels with metal hubs and white rubber tires. Plastic wheels were introduced in the 1950s.

T

Toy, Rooster, Dressed, Walker, Nodding Head, Composition, Lead Feet, Germany, 10 In.
$390

Bertoia Auctions

Toy, Seesaw, Bell Ringers, Man & Woman, Rocking Action, Tin, Cast Iron, Pull Toy, 7½ In.
$420

Bertoia Auctions

Toy, Sheep, Cream, Wooly Fur, Iron Wheels, Pull Toy, 6 In.
$366

Pook & Pook

Restoration, Good or Bad?

Restoration adds value to pressed steel toys like Buddy L according to one collector. But the question of restoration has plagued collectors in many fields and sometimes the rules change. Carousel horses have been stripped and repainted for years and it has added to the value. Now the "park paint" horses are starting to sell for more than restored examples.

Toy, Skier, Rolf, Blue Suit, White Cap, Skis, Poles, Clockwork, Tin Lithograph, Lehmann, 7½ In.
$2,400

Bertoia Auctions

Toy, Sparkler, Amos 'N' Andy, Andy, Glass Eyes, Tin Litho, Embossed, Germany, 1930s, 7 x 3½ In.
$283

AntiqueAdvertising.com

Toy, Sparkler, Cat, Felix, Short Ear Version, Nifty, Germany, 4½ In.
$360

Bertoia Auctions

Toy, Stove, Kenton, Star, 6 Burner Covers, Baffle, Salesman's Sample, Late 1800s, 20½ In.
$468

Jeffrey S. Evans & Associates

T

Stove, Kenton, Star, 6 Burner Covers, Baffle, Salesman's Sample, Late 1800s, 20½ In. . *illus*	468
Stove, Little May, Cast Iron, Sunburst On Doors, Kettle, Salesman's Sample, c.1890, 8 x 10 In.	280
Stove, Orr Painter & Co., 5 Burners, Pot, Pan, Cast Iron, Pa., 14 x 11 In. ..... *illus*	128
Stove, Rival, Nickel Plate, Bronze, Embossed, J. & E. Stevens, Salesman's Sample, 14 x 18 In. *illus*	369
Street Sweeper, Driver, Embossed, The Elgin, Cast Iron, Rubber Hose & Tires, 4⅜ x 8¾ In. .	2160
Surrey, Horse Drawn, 2 Seats, Driver, Wheels, Pratt & Letchworth, c.1890, 5¼ x 15½ In.....	608
Sweeping Mammy, Red & Yellow, Box, Lindstrom, 8 In.	677
Table, Doll's, Drop Leaf, Walnut, Spool Turned Legs, Late 1800s, 12 x 16 x 9 In.	84
Tango Dancers, Painted, Tin, Clockwork, Gunthermann, 7½ In.	427
Tank, A.M.X., Military, No. 817, Die Cast, Dinky Toys, Meccano, Box.....	50
Tank, Centurion, Military, No. 651, Die Cast, Dinky Super Toys, Meccano, Box.....	45
Taxi, Amos 'N' Andy, Fresh Air, Tin Lithograph, Marx, Box, c.1930, 8 In.	325
Taxi, Brown & White Cab, Copper Flashed Driver, Cast Iron, Hubley, 8¼	519
Taxi, Orange & Black Paint, Metal Bottom Plate, Hubley, 6 In., Pair	104
Taxi, Yell-O-Taxi, Tin, Windup, Orange & Black, Strauss, 8 In. ..... *illus*	275
Taxi, Yellow Cab, Black Trim, Driver, Cast Iron, Rubber Tires, 8 x 3½ In.	832
Teddy Bears are also listed in the Teddy Bear category.	
Teeter-Totter, 2 Rabbits, Tin Lithograph, Painted, 7½ In.....	69
Threshing Machine, Blue, Cast Iron, McCormick Deering, Arcade, Box, 3 x 4 In.	1536
Toy Chest, Circus, Elephant, Wood, Painted, 30 x 15½ x 20 In.....	148
Toy Chest, Federal, Walnut, 4 Drawers, Fluted Stiles, Salesman's Sample, 1820s, 9 x 10 In.....	563
Tractor, Backhoe, Yellow, Black, Die Cast, Trax, Dozer, Boom Arm, Tonka, 23½ In.	31
Tractor, Combine, Painted, Green & Yellow, John Deere, Box, 13 In.	185
Tractor, Fordson, Driver, Hand Crank, Nickel Scoop, Cast Iron, Hubley, 9 In. ..... *illus*	1342
Tractor, Green, Yellow, Black, Die Cast, Metal, Hot Wheels, 10 In.....	31
Tractor, McCormick Deering Farmall, Cast Iron, Rubber Tires, Arcade, 4½ x 6½ In.....	1968
Train Accessory, Railroad Station, Schoenhut, Wood, Painted, Sign, Window, c.1920, 9 x 11 In.	204
Train Accessory, Union Station, Tin Lithograph, Painted, Automatic Toy, Box, 20 In.	92
Train Car, Buddy L, Railroad Pile Driver, Painted, Pressed Steel, T Reproductions, 13 x 22 In.	308
Train Car, Ives, Locomotive, Whistler, Tin, Black & Red Paint, Bell, Clockwork, 8½ x 10 In.	1845
Train Car, Jehu Garlick, Locomotive & Tender, Live Steam, 1891, 6 In.....	2318
Train Car, Lehmann, Locomotive, Articulated, Black Ground, 19 In.....	236
Train Car, Locomotive, Birmingham & Gloster, Brass & Iron, Wood Boiler, Early 1800s, 8 In.	1037
Train Car, Passenger, Lever-Operated Doors, Pressed Steel, Lights, c.1930, 7 x 20 In.	152
Train Car, Passenger, Pennsylvania Express Limited, Metal, Silver, Friction, Box, 8 In.	65
Train Car, Steam Locomotive, Coal Tender, Boxcar, Red, Moline Pressed Steel, 1930, 9 x 26 x 16 In..	1560
Train Car, Wattman, Iron, Wood, Peacock, Painted, Philadelphia Zoo, Canada, 65 x 60 In. ...*illus*	688
Train Set, Marx, Bedrock Express, Flintstone, Stone Graphics, Tin, Zigzag Action, Bell, Box, 12 In..	416
Train Set, Twin Train, Tin Litho, Track, City Graphics, Windup, Technofix, Bim Bam, Box, 24 In. .	240
Train, Bullet, Metal, White, Blue Windows & Trim, Friction, Japan, 15½ In.....	95
Train, Flying Hamburger Train, Triebwagon Gauge, Die Cast Metal, Marklin, 1933, 30 In	688
Trolley, Brill, Old Time, Convertible Trolley, Brass, Window Panels, Operating Poles, Box, 20 In....	1006
Trolley, Horse Drawn, Transfer, Red, Black Horse, c.1890, 3¼ x 6½ In.	390
Truck, Arctic Ice Cream, Polar Brand, White, Black, Iron, Larry Seiber, Motorcade, 7½ In. .	125
Truck, Army Transport, Metal, Khaki Green, White Star, Flatbed, Cannon, Marx, Box, 13 In..	95
Truck, Army, Pressed Steel, Painted, Structo, 18 In.	529
Truck, Black Paint, 4 Wheels, Metal, Buddy L, 1900s, 12¼ In.	594
Truck, Cement Mixer, Jaeger, Scoop, Orange, Green, Cast Iron, Spoke Wheels, Kenton, 10 x 4½ In..	192
Truck, Cement Mixer, Pressed Steel, Painted, Buddy L, 24 In.	403
Truck, Cement Mixer, Pressed Steel, Red & Black Paint, Junior Series, Buddy L, 1920s, 10 x 25 In.	540
Truck, Cement Mixer, Spoke Wheels, Scoop, Mixer, Embossed Jaeger, Cast Iron, Kenton, 10 x 4 x 9 In..	192
Truck, Cheese Delivery, Kraft, GMC, Yellow, Smitty, 13¾ In.	144
Truck, Coal, Cast Iron, Driver, Spoke Wheels, Yellow, Green, 4⅜ x 10 In.	570
Truck, Coleccion, Camioncete, Mira Juguetes, Die Cast, Box, 4¾ x 3¾ In.....	50
Truck, Delivery, Railway Express, Pressed Steel, Buddy L, 25 In.	1220
Truck, Dump, American National, Pressed Steel, Painted, Red & White, c.1920, 12 x 9 In. ....*illus*	615
Truck, Dump, Cast Iron, Red, Green, 6 In. ..... *illus*	144
Truck, Dump, Foden, K-5, Yellow, Matchbox, Lesney, England, Box, King Size	60
Truck, Dump, Mack, Green, Red, Driver, Cast Iron, Rubber Tires, Hubley, 5 x 10¾ In.	625
Truck, Dump, Orange, Red, Blue & Green, Tin, Windup, Marx, c.1930, 10 In.	100
Truck, Dump, Packard, Pressed Steel, Crank, Decals, Keystone, c.1925, 28 In. .....*illus*	439

Toy, Stove, Orr Painter & Co., 5 Burners, Pot, Pan, Cast Iron, Pa., 14 x 11 In.
$128
Morphy Auctions

Toy, Stove, Rival, Nickel Plate, Bronze, Embossed, J. & E. Stevens, Salesman's Sample, 14 x 18 In.
$369

Rich Penn Auctions

Toy, Taxi, Yell-O-Taxi, Tin, Windup, Orange & Black, Strauss, 8 In.
$275

Pook & Pook

Toy, Tractor, Fordson, Driver, Hand Crank, Nickel Scoop, Cast Iron, Hubley, 9 In.
$1,342
Pook & Pook

Toy, Train Car, Wattman, Iron, Wood, Peacock, Painted, Philadelphia Zoo, Canada, 65 x 60 In.
$688

Kamelot Auctions

Toy, Truck, Dump, American National, Pressed Steel, Painted, Red & White, c.1920, 12 x 9 In.
$615

Rich Penn Auctions

Toy, Truck, Dump, Cast Iron, Red, Green, 6 In.
$144

Blackwell Auctions

Toy, Truck, Dump, Packard, Pressed Steel, Crank, Decals, Keystone, c.1925, 28 In.
$439

Jeffrey S. Evans & Associates

Truck, Dump, Red, Green, Tonka, 1956, 13 In.	161
Truck, Euclid, R-40, Die Cast, Yellow, No. 97, Mini Dinky Toy, Meccano, Box	35
Truck, Fageol Safety Coach, Cast Iron, Red Paint, White Rubber Tires, Arcade, c.1925, 12 ¼ In.	495
Truck, Ford, Bronco, 4x4 Mudster, Motorcycle, Die Cast, Hot Wheels, 1980, 3 In.	20
Truck, Hauler, Trailer Winch, Heavy Duty, Red, Cast Iron, Kilgore, 12 ½ x 3 ½ In.	1845
Truck, Ice, Mack, Cast Iron, Tongs, Blue, Arcade, 4 ¾ x 11 In.	2040
Truck, International Harvester, Red, Pressed Steel, Buddy L, 24 ½ In. *illus*	671
Truck, Lumber, Timber Toter, Pressed Steel & Die Cast, American Toy Co., 38 In.	366
Truck, Michigan Scraper, Die Cast, Yellow, No. 98, Mini Dinky Toy, Meccano, Box	35
Truck, Milk, Borden's, White, Red Letters, Cast Iron, Spoke Wheels, Hubley, 4 x 8 In. *illus*	2768
Truck, Parcel Delivery, Yellow Cab, Black & Orange, Cast Iron, Ironman, 8 In.	250
Truck, Police Patrol, Driver, 3 Passengers, Cast Iron, Rubber Tires, Kenton, 3 ¼ x 9 ¼ In.	800
Truck, Railway Express Agency, Van Body, Pressed Steel, Painted, Buddy L	175
Truck, Semi-Trailer, First Gear, Navajo, Die Cast, Blue, 53 Kenworth, Bull Nose, Box	60
Truck, Semi-Trailer, Mack, McLean Trucking Co., Die Cast, Smith-Miller, Smitty Toys, 32 In.	732
Truck, Steam Shovel Rear, Mack, Embossed Panama, Cast Iron, Rubber Tires, Hubley, 13 x 5 In.	780
Truck, Steam Shovel, General, Integral Driver, Cast Iron, Hubley, 8 ¼ In. *illus*	580
Truck, Tanker, American Oil Co., Red, Yellow Spokes, Driver, Cast Iron, 15 ½ x 4 In.	1968
Truck, Tanker, Doorless Cab, Operable Steering, Painted, Buddy L, 1926, 25 ½ In. *illus*	518
Truck, Tanker, Gasoline, Mack, Driver, Spoke Wheels, Green, Cast Iron, Arcade, 13 x 4 ½ In.	938
Truck, Tanker, GMC, Pressed Steel, Tank Cap, Steelcraft, 26 ½ In.	1342
Truck, Tanker, Shell, Wood, Decals, Painted, Rubber Tires, Buddy L, 28 In.	376
Truck, Tanker, Water, Army, Die Cast, No. 643, Dinky Toys, Meccano, Box *illus*	50
Truck, Tow Service, Red & Yellow, Die Cast, Redline, Hot Wheels, Mattel, 1969 *illus*	70
Truck, Tow, Blue, White, 24-Hour Service, Die Cast, Tonka, 14 In.	37
Truck, Tow, Industrial, Pressed Steel, Black & Red, Kiddies Metal Toys Inc., Box, 21 In.	750
Truck, Wood, Molded Cab, Yellow & Red Paint, Noma, 25 In., Pair	109
Truck, Wrecker, Driver, Red, Green, Mack, Cast Iron, Arcade, 11 x 3 ¾ In. *illus*	840
Typewriter, Black, Wood Base, Louis Marx & Co., c.1950, 6 x 11 ½ x 6 In. *illus*	76
Van, Dry Goods, First Gear International, Campbell, 66 Express, Die Cast, Yellow, Box	75
Wagon, Circus, Calliope, Driver, Musician, Horses, Painted, Royal Circus, Hubley, c.1906 *illus*	1020
Wagon, Circus, Horse Drawn, Giraffes, Driver, Royal Circus, Hubley, c.1906, 7 x 9 ¼ In.	2160
Wagon, Circus, Horse Drawn, Rhinos, Driver, Royal Circus, Hubley, c.1906, 15 ½ x 4 ½ In.	570
Wagon, Circus, Horse Drawn, Royal Circus, Driver, Tiger, Bear, Hubley, c.1906, 8 x 15 In.	720
Wagon, Circus, Royal Circus, Farmer Van, Driver, 2 Horses, Hubley, c.1906, 9 x 8 ½ In.	1107
Wagon, City Delivery, Horse Drawn, 3 Horses, Driver, Painted, Harris Toy Co., c.1890, 7 x 15 ½ In.	2700
Wagon, Dray, 2 Black Horses, Driver, Cast Iron, Green, Red, Pratt & Letchworth, 1890s, 17 In.	2400
Wagon, Dray, Horse Drawn, Driver, Iron, Steel, Painted, Wilkins Toy Co., c.1910, 6 ½ x 21 In.	256
Wagon, Farm, John Deere, 2 Horses, Seat, Green, Black, Red, Vindex, c.1929, 4 x 15 In.	1560
Wagon, Ice, 2 Horses, Driver, Hygeia, Ives Blakeslee & Co., c.1890, 7 ½ x 8 ¾ In.	1920
Wagon, Sheet Iron, Spoke Wheels, Wood Handle, Marathon, Child's, 1890, 22 x 10 x 21 In.	283
Wagon, Stake, Horse Drawn, Driver, Green, Red, Brown, Pratt & Letchworth, c.1890, 6 ½ x 10 In.	510
Wagon, Wood, Green, Yellow Font, Red Seat, 4 Wheels, Plate, 1850s, 26 ¼ In.	688
Wagon, Wood, Spoke Wheels, Painted, Stenciled, Paris Coaster, 18 x 40 x 18 In.	406
Washing Machine, Wood, Inscribed, Child's Delight, Splayed Legs, Late 1800s, 9 x 14 In. *illus*	915
Wheelbarrow, Mixed Woods, 8-Spoke Wood Wheel, Painted, Running Horse, c.1890, 14 x 40 x 16 In.	316
Wheelbarrow, Shaved Spokes, Iron Rim, Child's, S.A. Smith Toy Co., c.1920, 11 x 12 x 39 In.	176
Wheelbarrow, Wood, Painted, 2 Handles, Child's, Initial, Hide, 1900s, 11 ½ x 43 ½ In.	14
Xylophone, Push Pull, Wood, Plastic, 8 Multicolor Metal Bars, Mallet, Fisher Price, 1978, 14 In.	4
Zeppelin, Graff, Silver Body, Multicolor Decal, Pull Toy, Steelcraft, c.1930, 24 ½ In. *illus*	29
Zeppelin, Pressed Tin, Mammoth, Louis Marx & Co., c.1930, 7 x 27 ½ In.	31

TRAMP ART

Tramp art is a form of folk art made since the Civil War. It is usually made from chip-carved cigar boxes. Examples range from small boxes and picture frames t full-sized pieces of furniture. Collectors in the United States started collecting it about 1970, an examples from other countries, especially Germany, were imported and sold by antiques dealers

Box, Hinged Top, Brass Bail Handle, Cutout, Geometric, Carved, Walnut, 1880s, 8 x 16 x 10 In.	12
Box, Removable Lid, Geometric, 1800, 10 x 12 In.	30

Toy, Truck, International Harvester, Red, Pressed Steel, Buddy L, 24 ½ In.
$671

Pook & Pook

Toy, Truck, Milk, Borden's, White, Red Letters, Cast Iron, Spoke Wheels, Hubley, 4 x 8 In.
$2,768

Morphy Auctions

Toy, Truck, Steam Shovel, General, Integral Driver, Cast Iron, Hubley, 8 ¼ In.
$580

Pook & Pook

Toy, Truck, Tanker, Doorless Cab, Operable Steering, Painted, Buddy L, 1926, 25 ½ In.
$518

Blackwell Auctions

Toy, Truck, Tanker, Water, Army, Die Cast, No. 643, Dinky Toys, Meccano, Box
$50

Matthew Bullock Auctioneers

Toy, Truck, Tow Service, Red & Yellow, Die Cast, Redline, Hot Wheels, Mattel, 1969
$70

Matthew Bullock Auctioneers

Toy, Truck, Wrecker, Driver, Red, Green, Mack, Cast Iron, Arcade, 11 x 3 ¾ In.
$840

Morphy Auctions

Toy, Typewriter, Black, Wood Base, Louis Marx & Co., c.1950, 6 x 11 ½ x 6 In.
$76

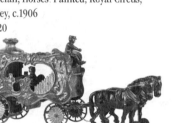

Fontaine's Auction Gallery

Toy, Wagon, Circus, Calliope, Driver, Musician, Horses, Painted, Royal Circus, Hubley, c.1906
$1,020

Morphy Auctions

Toy, Washing Machine, Wood, Inscribed, Child's Delight, Splayed Legs, Late 1800s, 9 x 14 In.
$915

Pook & Pook

T

Toy, Zeppelin, Graff, Silver Body, Multicolor Decal, Pull Toy, Steelcraft, c.1930, 24 ½ In.
$293

Jeffrey S. Evans & Associates

Tramp Art, Cabinet, Hanging, Seated Articulated Minstrel Figure, 4 Shelves, Late 1800s, 16 x 8 ¼ In.
$2,684

Pook & Pook

Tramp Art, Frame, Picture, Chip Carved, 13 Religious Images, Chromolithograph, c.1890, 26 x 18 In.
$295

Leland Little Auctions

Tramp Art, Wall Pocket, Crisscrossed, Wheel, Painted, c.1900, 39 ½ x 29 In.
$458

Pook & Pook

Trap, Bear, Kodiak, Hudson Bay, Cast Iron & Steel, Herter's, 11 x 43 In.
$923

Rich Penn Auctions

Trench Art, Ashtray, Figural, Man Smoking Pipe, Wood, Carved, Painted, Artillery Shell Base, 1944, 8 In.
$84

Milestone Auctions

Box, Spice, Cigar Box Shape, Glass Bead Pulls, c.1890, 11 x 6 In.	89
Box, Valuables, Hinged Lid, Fabric Panels, Bail Handle, Footed, c.1900, 6 x 13 In.	236
Cabinet, Hanging, Seated Articulated Minstrel Figure, 4 Shelves, Late 1800s, 16 x 8¼ In. *illus*	2684
Frame, Mixed Woods, Rectangular, Geometric, Carved, c.1900, 21 x 38 In.	826
Frame, Picture, Chip Carved, 13 Religious Images, Chromolithograph, c.1890, 26 x 18 In. *illus*	295
Mirror, Frame, Heart, Cross & Fouled Anchor, Black, Painted, Late 1800s, 14½ x 10½ In.	840
Mirror, Heart & Diamond Design, Octagonal, 1800s, 17¼ x 15¾ In.	275
Mirror, Molded Pediment, Sectioned Mirrors, Gilt, Late 1800s, 16¼ x 23¼ In.	188
Shelf, Cross Corners, 2 Shelves, Painted Yellow, c.1915, 28 x 33 x 4 In.	144
Wall Pocket, Crisscrossed, Wheel, Painted, c.1900, 39½ x 29 In. *illus*	458

TRAP

Traps for animals may be handmade. One of the most unusual is the mousetrap made so that when the mouse entered the trap, it was hit on the head with a mallet. Other traps were commercially manufactured and often are marked with the name of the manufacturer. Many traps were designed to be as humane as possible, and they would trap the live animal so it could be released in the woods.

Bear, Chain, Hand Forged, Triumph Trap Company, 6½ In.	316
Bear, Kodiak, Hudson Bay, Cast Iron & Steel, Herter's, 11 x 43 In. *illus*	923
Fly, Dome Lid, Glass, Blue Base, 3-Footed, Embossed, Pat. Oct. 28, 1890, 6¾ x 6 x 5¼ In.	322
Lobster, Rectangular, Wood, 12 x 34½ In.	58

TREEN, *see Wooden category.*

TRENCH ART

Trench art is a form of folk art made by soldiers. Metal casings from bullets and mortar shells were cut and decorated to form useful objects, such as vases. Coins and other things were used to make jewelry.

Artillery Shell, White Projectile, Embossed Rooster, S. Mihiel, Dated, 1917, 14 x 3½ In.	158
Ashtray, 4 Holders, Bullet In Center, Artillery Shell Base, Marked, 1944, 6 In.	37
Ashtray, Figural, Man Smoking Pipe, Wood, Carved, Painted, Artillery Shell Base, 1944, 8 In. *illus*	84
Canteen, Copper, Couple, Hugging, G. Lebargy Camp De Friedrichsfeld, Russia, c.1914, 5 x 6 In.	221
Cap, Officer's, Brass, Artillery Shells, 75mm, U.S. Seal, 3½ x 4 x 2¼ In. *illus*	158
Lamp Base, Electric, Shell Casing Center, 4 Large & 4 Small Caliber Rounds, 10mm, 12 x 4¾ In.	42
Mug, Artillery Shell, Brass, Large Caliber Round, Handle, 2 British Regimental Badges, WW II, 6 In.	62
Shell Casing, Large Caliber, Brass, Painted Wood Projectile, Silver, 3 Women, Eagle, 42 x 5½ In.	384
Vase, Artillery Shell, Brass, Embossed, 1917, Verdun, 1918, Flowering Vine, 12 x 3¾ In., Pair	1245
Vase, Artillery Shell, Pinched Waist, Argonne, A.E.F., To Mother From Son, 1919, 13½ x 3 In.	98
Vase, Artillery Shell, Repousse, Oak Branches & Pansies, World War I Era, 13½ In., Pair *illus*	177
Vase, Artillery Shells, Engraved, Ottoman Star, Signed, Neveu, 1914, 13¾ In., Pair	200
Vase, Brass, Embossed Design, Scalloped Rim, Marked, Verdun, 1918, 12¾ In.	98
Vase, Brass, Patina, Hammered Leaves, World War I, 13¾ In., Pair	148
Vase, Brass, Shell, Pointed Rim, Repousse Flowers, Textured Ground, World War I, 11 In., Pair	266
Vase, Shell Casing, Brass, Seated Man, Palm Tree On Reverse, Footed, Flared Rim, 1913, 11 In.	50
Watch, Airman's Union Hologere Dial, Cuff Band, Inscribed, Guadalcanal 1944, 2½ x 2 x 1¼ In.	425

TRIVET

Trivets are now used to hold hot dishes. Most trivets of the late nineteenth and early twentieth centuries were made to hold hot pressing irons. Iron or brass reproductions are being made of many of the old styles.

Brass, Downhearth, Rope Style Handles, Cabriole Front Legs, Early 1800s, 12 x 16½ In. *illus*	138
Brass, Heart Shape, Cutwork Design, 6 In.	135
Cast Iron, Hearts, Star, Bellows Shape, 3-Footed, Stamped Emic, 1940s, 9 x 4 In.	20
Iron, Copper Finish, Poinsettia, Round, Taiwan, 7 In.	20
Tile, Cast Iron Frame, Handle, Farmer Couple, Kissin' Don't Last, Japan, 6¾ In.	15

Trench Art, Cap, Officer's, Brass, Artillery Shells, 75mm, U.S. Seal, 3½ x 4 x 2¼ In.
$158

Matthew Bullock Auctioneers

Trench Art, Vase, Artillery Shell, Repousse, Oak Branches & Pansies, World War I Era, 13½ In., Pair
$177

Austin Auction Gallery

Trivet, Brass, Downhearth, Rope Style Handles, Cabriole Front Legs, Early 1800s, 12 x 16½ In.
$138

Eldred's

T

Trivet, Wrought Iron, Warmer, Rotating, Painted, Black, 1800s, 12 In. $88

Pook & Pook

Trunk, Dome Top, Leather Clad, Compartment, Handles, Portugal, 1800s, 25 ½ x 33 ½ In. $443

Austin Auction Gallery

Trunk, Gucci, Train Case, GG Diamante Canvas, Leather, Tan & Brown, FLG Emblem, 1960-80s, 9 ½ In. $288

Hindman

Louis Vuitton

Watch for luggage by Louis Vuitton. The company has been in business since 1854, and its trunks sell for hundreds and even thousands of dollars. Vuitton made the first flat, stackable trunks. They were made of canvas. The name *Louis Vuitton* is on clasps and locks and the trademark *LV* monogram, introduced in 1896, is on the canvas. Watch for fakes, especially pieces with LV fabric.

Wrought Iron, Hearth, Heart Shape, Curls, 3-Footed, 1800s, 5¾ x 13¾ In.		585
Wrought Iron, Warmer, Rotating, Painted, Black, 1800s, 12 In. .... *illus*		88

TRUNK

Trunks of many types were made. The nineteenth-century sea chest was often handmade of unpainted wood. Brass-fitted camphorwood chests were brought back from the Orient. Leather-covered trunks were popular from the late eighteenth to mid-nineteenth centuries. By 1895, trunks were covered with canvas or decorated sheet metal. Embossed metal coverings were used from 1870 to 1910. By 1925, trunks were covered with vulcanized fiber or undecorated metal. Suitcases are listed here.

Blanket, Lid, Iron Strap Hinges, Escutcheon, Bracket Feet, 1800s, 28¾ x 45½ In.		443
Campaign Chest, Fall Front, Teak, Brass Plaque, Initials, H.O.H., 1880s, 19¾ x 39 x 20 In.		468
Camphorwood, Brassbound & Handles, Mounted, Square Legs, Chinese, c.1850, 38 x 40 In.		875
Camphorwood, Brassbound, Straps, Side Handles, Lock Escutcheon, 1800s, 8 x 24 x 12 In.		556
Camphorwood, Lift Lid, Lion Head Drop Ring, Side Handles, Brassbound, 1800s, 16 x 35 x 18 In.		644
Dome Top, Decoupage Fish, Painted, Gray Ground, Late 1800s, 13 x 19 In.		148
Dome Top, Hinged Lid, Burlwood, Brass Mounts, Welled Interior, Brass Keyhole, 1800s, 12 In.		813
Dome Top, Hinged Lid, Oak, Strap Hinges, Iron Side Handles, 1700s, 29 x 49 x 25 In.		293
Dome Top, Hinged Lid, Pine Dovetailed Box, Red, New England, Early 1800s, 5¾ x 15 x 7 In.		438
Dome Top, Leather Clad, Compartment, Handles, Portugal, 1800s, 25½ x 33½ In. .... *illus*		443
Dome Top, Pine, Painted, Maritime Theme, Bail Handle, 1800s, 20½ x 37 In.		575
Gucci, Train Case, GG Diamante Canvas, Leather, Tan & Brown, FLG Emblem, 1960-80s, 9½ In. *illus*		288
Lacquered, Hinged Top, Figural, Landscapes, Red Ground, Iron, Chinese Export, 27 x 19 In.		88
Leather, Nailhead, Brass Mount, Continental, Late 1800s, 13 x 33 In.		128
Louis Vuitton, Duffle Bag, Canvas, Keepall 60, Bandouliere, Monogram Coated, 12 x 10 x 23 In.		708
Louis Vuitton, Logo, Canvas, Removable Basket, Squat Wheels, Early 1900s, 22 x 24 x 19 In. *illus*		8960
Louis Vuitton, Papillon, Leather, Straps, Brass Hardware, Zipper, Monogram, 6 x 12 In.		832
Louis Vuitton, Portable Bar, Epi Leather, Glass, Silver, Gold Plated Brass, c.1985, 8 x 16 In.		10000
Louis Vuitton, Porte Documents, Damier Ebene Canvas, Leather, Shoulder Strap, 2012, 10½ In.		875
Louis Vuitton, Shoe, Monogram, Brass Corners & Latches, Leather Handle, 8 x 24 x 21 In.		630
Louis Vuitton, Suitcase, Canvas, Hard Shell, Brown & Tan, BLK On Handle, 1970-80, 21 In.		576
Louis Vuitton, Suitcase, Hat Box, Canvas, Monogram, Strap, Linen Lined, 1989, 50 In.		1875
Louis Vuitton, Suitcase, Leather, 3 Pockets, Handle, Zipper, France, 25 x 21 In.		413
Louis Vuitton, Suitcase, Monogram, Tray, Leather Handle, Lock, Marked, 1950s, 18 x 28 In. *illus*		1188
Louis Vuitton, Train Case, Boite Bouteilles, Bottle Box, Leather, 1980-2000s, 8 In.		2304
Louis Vuitton, Travel Bag, Brown, Canvas, Gold Colored, Handles, Monogram, 1980-90s, 15½ In.		768
Maitland-Smith, Wood, Brass Accents, Nail Head Trim, Brown, 21½ x 36 x 18½ In.		594
Pine, Dome Lid, Leather Clad, Brass Tacks, Iron Handles, 1800s, 17 x 25 In.		236
Steamer, Metal Bound, Leather Handles, Brass Lock, Monogram, E.W.M.		24
Steamer, Oak Banding, Brass Fitting Interior, 4 Drawers, 2 Compartments, c.1900, 69 x 28 x 23 In.		360
Steamer, Studded Wood, Metal Strapwork, 3 Handles, Blocked Base, 22 x 33⅞ x 21⅝ In. .. *illus*		488
Storage, Brassbound, Lockplate, Handles, Hinged Top, Block Feet, Portugal, 1900s, 22 x 44 In.		472
Storage, Carved, Iron Strap, Handles, Bracket Feet, Painted, Indonesia, 14¼ x 25¼ In.		41
Storage, Hinged Lid, 3 Small Drawers, Side Handles, Brass, Copper Clad, 1900s, 14 x 20 x 13 In.		50
Storage, Hinged Lid, Oak, Lunette Edge, Carved, Block Feet, Continental, 1700s, 24 x 33 In.		38
Storage, Lift Lid, Sarreid Ltd. Style, Brass Clad, Copper Nails, Wood Lined, 13 x 9 In.		14
Storage, Renaissance Revival, Drop Front Panel, Carved, Bun Feet, Late 1800s, 24 x 44 In.		82
Storage, Rosewood, Rectangular, Brass Hinges, Cartouche, Handles, 1900s, 22½ x 43½ In.		64
Storage, Rustic Pine, Hinged Top, Paneled Sides, Plinth Base, 1900s, 29 x 54¾ x 31 In.		20
Suitcase, Brown Calf Leather, 2 Belt Straps, Brass Buckles, Escutcheon, Stand, 7 x 13 x 28 In.		6
Suitcase, Train, Leather, Brass, Bound Trunk Style, Marked, E.E.A., Early 1900s, 20 In.		2
Suitcase, Wood, Brass Handle & Lock, Leather Case, c.1940, 7 x 24 x 16 In.		27
Wood, Asian Style, Metal Hardware, 41 x 20 x 20 In.		10
Wood, Diminutive, Hump Top, Bentwood, Strap Handles, c.1900, 17 x 29 In.		8
Wood, Rustic, Hinged Top, Iron Bound, Carrying Handles, Dovetailed, 1800s, 11 x 26 x 16 In.		20

T

TUTHILL

Tuthill Cut Glass Company of Middletown, New York, worked from 1902 to 1923. Of special interest are the finely cut pieces of stemware and tableware.

Cheese & Cracker Server, Hobstar, Nailhead Diamond, Vesica, Zipper & Fan, Signed, 2¾ x 9 In...	125
Cologne Bottle, Pear & Apple, Ray Cut Base, 6¾ In.	250
Plate, Wheel Pattern, Quality Blank, Signed, 7 In.	500
Tray, Round, Intaglio Four Fruit, Deep Engraving, Signed, 12½ In.	750
Vase, Hobstar, Strawberry Diamond, Zipper & Fan, Scalloped Rim, Signed, 10 x 4¼ In.	70

TYPEWRITER

Typewriter collectors divide typewriters into two main classifications: the index machine, which has a pointer and a dial for letter selection, and the keyboard machine, most commonly seen today. The first successful typewriter was made by Sholes and Glidden in 1874.

Blickensderfer, No. 6, Aluminum Body, Metal Tag, Signed, 1800s, 6 x 13 x 9 In.	378
Hammond, Multiplex, Oak, Iron Stand, Caster Feet, Early 1900s, 34 x 23½ In. *illus*	315
Mignon, Index, Slant Front, Oak Case, Germany, c.1920, 9 x 14 In. *illus*	215
National, Upstroke Mechanism, 3 Rows, Curved Keyboard, Metal, 1800s, 7½ x 13 x 10 In.	2375
Odell's, No. 2, Nickel Plated, Metal Tag, Signed, Late 1800s, 6½ x 10½ x 12 In.	630
Olivetti, Valentine, Plastic, Enamel Steel, Red, Ettore Sottsass, Italy, 1969, 4 x 15 In. *illus*	563
Royal, Black, Round Metal Keys, Case, 12 x 11 x 5½ In.	86
Triumph, Matura Super, Pristine, Dust Cover, Germany, c.1950, 9¾ In.	113

TYPEWRITER RIBBON TIN

Typewriter ribbon tins are now being collected. The lithographed tin containers have been used since the 1870s. Most popular with collectors are tins with pictorial graphics.

Allied, Sea Gull On Wave, Art Deco, Black, Gray, White, 2½ In.	16
Bellaire, Burroughs Corp., White Slip, Black & Gold Graphics, 2⅝ In.	8
Keelox, Silkee Lox, There Is Nothing Finer, Blue, Yellow, 2½ In.	12

UMBRELLA

Umbrella collectors like rain or shine. The first known umbrella was owned by King Louis XIII of France in 1637. The earliest umbrellas were sunshades, not designed to be used in the rain. The umbrella was embellished and redesigned many times. In 1852, the fluted steel rib style was developed and it has remained the most useful style.

Bamboo Handle, Peacock, Blue, Green, Pink, Dome, Rice Paper, 1970s, 32 In.	40
Lucite Handle, Black, Red, Silver, Taffeta, Silvertone Wrist Chain, c.1950, 38 In.	55
Lucite Handle, J-Shape, Multicolor Stripes, c.1950, 32 In.	23
Parasol, Maple Handle, Blue Marble Hand Clasp, Silk, Lace Trim, c.1890, 15½ In.	189
Parasol, Patriotic, Bamboo Shaft, Printed Linen, Stars & Stripes, Child's, 1900s, 26½ In. *illus*	410

UNION PORCELAIN WORKS

Union Porcelain Works was originally William Boch & Brothers, located in Greenpoint, New York. Thomas C. Smith bought the company in 1861 and renamed it Union Porcelain Works. The company went through a series of ownership changes and finally closed about 1922. The company made a fine quality white porcelain that was often decorated in clear, bright colors. Don't confuse this company with its competitor, Charles Cartlidge and Company, also in Greenpoint.

Bowl, Flower Sprig, Green Banded Rim, Shaker, Mt. Lebanon, Late 1800s, 2⅜ x 10 In.	2125
Oyster Plate, 4 Wells, Shell Shape, Sea Life, Crab, Seaweed, White Ground, 8½ In.	113

Trunk, Louis Vuitton, Logo, Canvas, Removable Basket, Squat Wheels, Early 1900s, 22 x 24 x 19 In.
$8,960

Neal Auction Company

TIP
Double-hung windows can easily be fixed so they will not open wide enough for someone to crawl inside. The special lock for this can be removed from the inside.

Trunk, Louis Vuitton, Suitcase, Monogram, Tray, Leather Handle, Lock, Marked, 1950s, 18 x 28 In.
$1,188

Eldred's

Trunk, Steamer, Studded Wood, Metal Strapwork, 3 Handles, Blocked Base, 22 x 33⅞ x 21⅝ In.
$488

Neal Auction Company

U
V

Typewriter, Hammond, Multiplex, Oak, Iron Stand, Caster Feet, Early 1900s, 34 x 23 ½ In.
$315

Fontaine's Auction Gallery

Typewriter, Mignon, Index, Slant Front, Oak Case, Germany, c.1920, 9 x 14 In.
$215

Rich Penn Auctions

Typewriter, Olivetti, Valentine, Plastic, Enamel Steel, Red, Ettore Sottsass, Italy, 1969, 4 x 15 In.
$563

Wright

Umbrella, Parasol, Patriotic, Bamboo Shaft, Printed Linen, Stars & Stripes, Child's, 1900s, 26 ½ In.
$410

Jeffrey S. Evans & Associates

University City, Vase, Celadon & Ivory Crystalline Glaze, Gourd Form, Taxile Doat, 1914, 10 x 3 ½ In.
$81,250

Rago Arts and Auction Center

University City, Vase, Ivory & Peach Crystalline Glaze, E.G. Lewis, c.1912, 5 x 4 ½ In.
$6,250

Rago Arts and Auction Center

UNIVERSITY CITY POTTERY

University City Pottery, of University City, Missouri, worked from 1909 to 1915. Well-known artists, including Taxile Doat, Adelaide Alsop Robineau, and Frederick Hurten Rhead, worked there.

Vase, Celadon & Ivory Crystalline Glaze, Gourd Form, Taxile Doat, 1914, 10 x 3 ½ In. .. *illus*	81250
Vase, Ivory & Peach Crystalline Glaze, E.G. Lewis, c.1912, 5 x 4 ½ In. .... *illus*	6250

UNIVERSITY OF NORTH DAKOTA, *see North Dakota School of Mines category.*

VAL ST. LAMBERT

Val St Lambert

Val St. Lambert Cristalleries of Belgium was founded by Messieurs Kemlin and Lelievre in 1825. The company is still in operation. All types of table glassware and decorative glassware have been made. Pieces are often decorated with cut designs.

Decanter Set, Berncastel, Cranberry Cut To Clear, c.1960, Decanter 15 In., 7 Piece	344
Vase, Cut Overlay, Trumpet, Green, Clear, Rayed Diamond, Fan, Footed, 1910s, 12 x 4 x 5 In.	222
Vase, Engraved Flowers, Clear, Wavy Rim, Signed, 11 ½ x 5 ½ In.	550
Vase, Sommerso, Purple Hue, Etched & Gilded Crest, Mural Crown, c.1950, 11 In., Pair *illus*	472

VAN BRIGGLE POTTERY

Van Briggle Pottery was started by Artus Van Briggle in Colorado Springs, Colorado, after 1901. Van Briggle had been a decorator at Rookwood Pottery of Cincinnati, Ohio. He died in 1904 and his wife took over managing the pottery. One of the employees, Kenneth Stevenson, took over the company in 1969. He died in 1990 and his wife, Bertha, and son, Craig, ran the pottery. She died in 2010. The pottery closed in 2012. The wares usually have modeled relief decorations and a soft, matte glaze.

Lamp, Bird, On Branch, Cylindrical Shade, Butterflies, Gray Ground............................... ...	102
Vase, Bulbous, Matte Glaze, Signed, Colorado, 1901, 13 x 9 ½ In.................................... ...	1375
Vase, Despondency, Nude, Maroon, Blue Matte Glaze, c.1920, 13 x 6 ½ In. .... *illus*	1375
Vase, Despondency, Nude, Peach Ground, Artus Van Briggle, Late 1900s, 16 ½ In. .... *illus*	413
Vase, Gourd, Leaves Border, Black & Brown Ground, 4 ½ In.	96
Vase, Molded Poppy Seed Heads, Wide Mouth, Rose Matte Glaze, Early 1900s, 6 ½ In.............	1375
Vase, Mottled Green Glaze, Leaves Form Arches, Tapered, Marked, 1905, 8 x 3 In................. ..	1430
Vase, Ornamental Shoulder, Glazed, Early 1900s, 4 In.	95
Vase, Spear Leaves, Moss Green Over Walnut Brown Matte Glaze, c.1906, 4 ½ In. .... *illus*	908
Vase, Stylized Flower, Fluted Rim, Round Base, Glazed, Marked, 1907, 10 x 4 ¾ In.	1056
Vase, Thistles, Green Matte Glaze, Incised Mark, 1906, 9 x 7 ¼ In..	1000

VASELINE GLASS

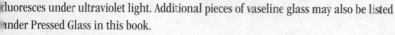

Vaseline glass is a greenish-yellow glassware resembling petroleum jelly. Pressed glass of the 1870s was often made of vaseline-colored glass. Some vaseline glass is still being made in old and new styles. The glass fluoresces under ultraviolet light. Additional pieces of vaseline glass may also be listed under Pressed Glass in this book.

Jar, Lid, Log Cabin Shape, Chimney Finial, Central Glass Co., c.1884, 7 x 2 ⅜ x 3 In. ..... *illus*	1287
Paperweight, Lion, Lying Down, Oval Base, John Derbyshire, Late 1800s, 5 x 7 ½ x 4 ½ In., Pair.	277
Vase, Opalescent, Raised, Gilt, Flowers, Nash, Early 1900s, 10 In..	207

VENETIAN GLASS, *see Glass-Venetian category.*

VENINI GLASS, *see Glass-Venetian category.*

Val St. Lambert, Vase, Sommerso, Purple Hue, Etched & Gilded Crest, Mural Crown, c.1950, 11 In., Pair
$472

Austin Auction Gallery

Van Briggle, Vase, Despondency, Nude, Maroon, Blue Matte Glaze, c.1920, 13 x 6 ½ In.
$1,375

Toomey & Co. Auctioneers

Van Briggle, Vase, Despondency, Nude, Peach Ground, Artus Van Briggle, Late 1900s, 16 ½ In.
$413

Austin Auction Gallery

U

V

Van Briggle, Vase, Spear Leaves, Moss Green Over Walnut Brown Matte Glaze, c.1906, 4½ In.

$908

Humler & Nolan

Vaseline Glass, Jar, Lid, Log Cabin Shape, Chimney Finial, Central Glass Co., c.1884, 7 x 2⅝ x 3 In.

$1,287

Jeffrey S. Evans & Associates

Verlys, Vase, Alpine Thistle, Art Glass, Frosted, Clear, Polished Rim, c.1935, 9 x 5¾ In.

$211

Jeffrey S. Evans & Associates

U
V

VERLYS

Verlys glass was made in Rouen, France, by the Societe Holophane Français, a company that started in 1920. It was made in Newark, Ohio, from 1935 to 1951. The art glass is either blown or molded. The American glass is signed with a diamond-point-scratched name, but the French pieces are marked with a molded signature. The designs resemble those used by Lalique.

Bowl, Blue, Round, 10 Elongated Teardrop Prunts On Base, Marked, 5½ x 8½ In.	57
Charger, Lotus Flower, Frosted, Water Lilies, France, 1900s, 13¾ In.	39
Vase, Alpine Thistle, Art Glass, Frosted, Clear, Polished Rim, c.1935, 9 x 5¾ In. ....*illus*	211
Vase, Frosted & Clear, Asian Figure, Landscape, 9⅜ In.	59

VERNON KILNS

Vernon Kilns was the name used by Vernon Potteries, Ltd. The company, which started in 1912 in Vernon, California, was originally called Poxon China. In 1931 the company was sold and renamed Vernon Kilns. It made dinnerware and figurines. It went out of business in 1953. The molds were bought by Metlox, which continued to make some patterns. Collectors search for the brightly colored dinnerware and the pieces designed by Rockwell Kent, Walt Disney, and Don Blanding. For more prices, go to kovels.com.

Arcadia, Chop Plate, 12¼ In.	20
Della Robbia, Plate, Bread & Butter, 6½ In.	6
Fruitdale, Salt & Pepper	25
Pink Lady, Gravy Boat, Underplate	38
Souvenir, Plate, State Of Iowa, c.1950, 10½ In.	16
Vineyard, Cup, Footed	6

VERRE DE SOIE

Verre de soie glass was first made by Frederick Carder at the Steuben Glass Works from about 1905 to 1930. It is an iridescent glass of soft white or very, very pale green. The name means "glass of silk," and it does resemble silk. Other factories have made verre de soie, and some of the English examples were made of different colors. Verre de soie is an art glass and is not related to the iridescent, pressed, white carnival glass mistakenly called by its name. Related pieces may be found in the Steuben category.

Compote, Fluted Rim, Aquamarine Trim, Round Base, Steuben, 3½ x 8 In.	125
Cruet, Iridescent, Hawkes Engraved, Pontil Mark, Art Glass, Footed, Steuben, c.1915, 8 x 6 In.	187

VIENNA, *see Beehive category.*

VIENNA ART

Vienna Art plates are round lithographed metal serving trays produced at the turn of the century. The designs, copied from Royal Vienna porcelain plates, usually featured a portrait of a woman encircled by a wide, ornate border. Many were used as advertising or promotional items and were produced in Coshocton, Ohio, by J. F. Meeks Tuscarora Advertising Co. and H.D. Beach's Standard Advertising Co. Some are listed in Advertising in this book.

Plate, Woman, Blond Bouffant Hair, Red Rim, Gilt Leaves, Square Giltwood Frame, 15 In.	125
Plate, Woman, Brown Hair, Gold Cap, Hoop Earrings, Red Dress, Shadowbox, Gilt Frame, 16 In.	61?
Plate, Woman, Long Brown Hair, Anheuser-Busch, Pat. 1905, Pair	18?
Plate, Woman, Long Brown Hair, Red Cap, Multicolor Rim, C. Pariseau & Co. Manchester, N.H., 10 In.	13?

VILLEROY & BOCH POTTERY

Villeroy & Boch Pottery of Mettlach was founded in 1836 when two competing potteries merged. Francois Boch and his sons began making pottery in France in 1748. They moved to Mettlach in 1809 and merged with competitor Nicolas Villeroy in 1836. The firm made many types of wares, including the famous Mettlach steins. Collectors can be confused because although Villeroy & Boch made most of its pieces in the city of Mettlach, Germany, the company also had factories in other locations. The dating code impressed on the bottom of most pieces makes it possible to determine the age of the piece. Additional items, including steins and earthenware pieces marked with the famous castle mark or the word *Mettlach*, may be found in the Mettlach category.

Plate, Cathedral Of Trier, c.1891, 10 In.	299
Punch Bowl, Lid, Underplate, Man, Woman, Drinking, Cartouche, Mettlach, 1800s, 16 x 16 In. *illus*	384
Trivet, Tile, Blue, Grape Clusters, Vines, Leaves, Footed, 6 x 6 In.	75
Tureen, Soup, Lid, Jasperware, Blue Green, Relief Dogs, Underplate, Mettlach, 15 x 14 In.	1534
Vase, Blue & White, River & Tree Scenes, Footed, Flat Rim, 6 ½ In.	49
Vase, Blue Green Ground, Etched Iris, Orange Glaze, Mettlach, 12 In.	708
Vase, Putty, Salt Glaze, Parian Figures, Silver Accents, c.1860, 10 In.	400

VOLKMAR POTTERY

VOLKMAR Corona N.Y

Volkmar Pottery was made by Charles Volkmar of New York from 1879 to about 1911. He was associated with several firms, including the Volkmar Ceramic Company, Volkmar and Cory, and Charles Volkmar and Son. He was hired by Durant Kilns of Bedford Village, New York, in 1910 to oversee production. Volkmar bought the business and after 1930 only the Volkmar name was used as a mark. Volkmar had been a painter, and his designs often look like oil paintings drawn on pottery.

Charger, Blue & White, Fort Scene, Flowering Vine Border, 11 ½ In.	23
Plate, Washington's Home, Mt. Vernon, Va., Blue & White, Marked, c.1900, 11 ½ In.	123
Tankard, Geese, Pond, Green, 7 In.	140
Vase, Squat, Green Flambe Glaze, Red Brown Highlights, Leon Volkmar, c.1920, 4 x 6 In.	93

VOLKSTEDT

Volkstedt was a soft-paste porcelain factory started in 1760 by Georg Heinrich Macheleid at Volkstedt, Thuringia. Volkstedt-Rudolstadt was a porcelain factory started at Volkstedt-Rudolstadt by Beyer and Bock in 1890. Most pieces seen in shops today are from the later factory.

Cachepot, Figural, Man With Scythe, Woman With Ladder, Flower Baskets, Multicolor, 23 In., Pair	240
Figurine, 2 Pheasants, Multicolor, No. 6857, Karl Ens, 8 ½ x 11 In. *illus*	125
Figurine, Lovers, Piano, Painted, Gilt, Flowers, Footed, 14 In. *illus*	649
Figurine, Parrot, Crested, Yellow, Pink, Blue, White Perch Base, Karl Ens, Early 1900s, 13 ¾ In.	180

WADE

WADE figures c.1936+

Wade pottery is made by the Wade Group of Potteries started in 1810 near Burslem, England. Several potteries merged to become George Wade & Son, Ltd., early in the twentieth century, and other potteries have been added through the years. The best-known Wade pieces are the small figurines called Whimsies. They were first were made in 1954. Special Whimsies were given away with Red Rose Tea beginning in 1967. The Disney figures are listed in this book in the Disneyana category.

Candleholder, Hippo, Gray, 2 In.	4
Figurine, Circus Clown, Holding Bucket, Green	3
Figurine, Circus Poodle, Standing On Barrel, 3 In.	7
Figurine, Circus Strong Man, Barbells, 2 In.	4
Mug, Piccadilly Circus, London, 4 In.	20
Mug, Tower Bridge, London, 4 In.	22

Villeroy & Boch, Punch Bowl, Lid, Underplate, Man, Woman, Drinking, Cartouche, Mettlach, 1800s, 16 x 16 In. $384

Bunch Auctions

Volkstedt, Figurine, 2 Pheasants, Multicolor, No. 6857, Karl Ens, 8 ½ x 11 In. $125

Woody Auction

Volkstedt, Figurine, Lovers, Piano, Painted, Gilt, Flowers, Footed, 14 In. $649

Bunch Auctions

TIP
Don't store ceramic dishes or figurines for long periods of time in old newspaper wrappings. The ink can make indelible stains on china.

W

Wall Pocket, Cornucopia Shape, Grapevine Panel, Bacchus, Ravens, Salt Glaze, England, c.1740, 9¾ In. $793

Pook & Pook

Walrath, Bowl, Applied Center, Kneeling Woman, Green, Brown Matte Glaze, 6 x 7¼ In. $406

Toomey & Co. Auctioneers

Watch, Elgin National Watch Co., Octagonal, 14K Gold, Numbers, 1½ In., Pocket $461

Hartzell's Auction Gallery Inc.

W

WALL POCKET

Wall pockets were popular in the 1930s. They were made by many American and European factories. Glass, pottery, porcelain, majolica, chalkware, and metal wall pockets can be found in many fanciful shapes.

Cornucopia Shape, Grapevine Panel, Bacchus, Ravens, Salt Glaze, England, c.1740, 9¾ In. *illus*	793
Cornucopia Shape, Molded, Multicolor Bird, Floral, Tin Glaze, 1750s, 8 In., Pair	2313
Cross, Anchor & Boat, Shaped Plaque, Mahogany, 1800s, 10½ x 14½ In.	600
Embroidered, Anchor, Mermaid, Roses, Hearts, 3 Openings, Maine, Frame, Early 1800s, 9 x 3 In.	1250
Flowers, Rococo Style, Gilt Metal, Late 1800s, 16¼ x 6 x 2¾ In., Pair	512

WALLACE NUTTING *photographs are listed under Print, Nutting.*

WALRATH

Walrath *Pottery*

Walrath was a potter who worked in New York City; Rochester, New York; and at the Newcomb Pottery in New Orleans, Louisiana. Frederick Walrath died in 1920. Pieces listed here are from his Rochester period.

Bowl, Applied Center, Kneeling Woman, Green, Brown Matte Glaze, 6 x 7¼ In. *illus*	406

WALT DISNEY, *see Disneyana category.*

WALTER, *see A. Walter category.*

WARWICK

IOGA

Warwick china was made in Wheeling, West Virginia, in a pottery working from 1887 to 1951. Many pieces were made with hand painted or decal decorations. The most familiar Warwick has a shaded brown background. The name *Warwick* is part of the mark and sometimes the mysterious word *IOGA* is also included.

Pitcher, Poppies, Squat Shape, Footed, c.1900, 8 In.	105
Pitcher, Red & Orange Flowers, Stems, Scroll Handle, 9½ x 6½ In.	74
Vase, Handle, Hibiscus, Brown Tone, c.1905, 7½ In.	50

WATCH

Watches small enough to fit in a man's pocket were important in Victorian times. It wasn't until World War I that the wristwatch was used. All types of watches are collected: silver, gold, or plated. Watches are listed here by company name or by style. Wristwatches are a separate category in this book.

Albin Bourquin, Hunting Case, Chaux De Fonds, 14K Rose Gold, Black Enamel, Swiss, Pocket	325
Aurora, Hunting Case, 14K Gold, Porcelain Face, Marked, J. Boss, c.1890, 2 In., Pocket	144
Bulova, Open Face, Accutron, Gold, Green Leather, Battery, 1960s, 1¼ In.	406
Ch. Meylan, Open Face, 18K Yellow Gold, Seconds Dial, Repeater, 31 Jewel, 2 In., Pocket	3510
Dudley, Masonic Symbols, Silver Dial, 9 Jewel, Chain, c.1924, 1¾ In., Pocket	4313
E. Howard, Hunting Case, 18K Yellow Gold, Key Wind, White Dial, Roman Numerals, 2¼ In.	3803
Elgin National Watch Co., Octagonal, 14K Gold, Numbers, 1½ In., Pocket *illus*	461
Elgin, Gold, 7 Jewel, Butterfly, Flower, Roman Numerals, Engraved, 1½ In., Pocket	69
Elgin, Hunting Case, Model 2, 14K Yellow Gold, Ornate, White Dial, 1904, 1⅜ In.	863
Elgin, Open Face, 10K Gold Case, Enamel, France, 1½ In.	207
Elgin, Square Case, 14K Gold, Fob Chain, National Watch Co., c.1919, Pocket	649
Golay Leresche, Open Face, 18K Gold, Quarter Hour Repeater, Roman Numerals, 2 In.	234
Gruen, Art Deco, White Porcelain, Roman Numerals, 14K Gold, Gruen, Swiss, ½ In.	12
Haas Neveux & Cie, Open Face, 18K Gold, Gold Case, Minute Repeater, c.1900, Pocket *illus*	702
Hamilton, Railroad, Ball, Open Face, Ornate Goldtone Case, Floral, c.1906, 2¼ In., Pocket	97
Hermes, World Time, Travel, Gold Plated, Brass, France, c.1975, 2 In., Pocket	140
Hunting Case, 14K Gold, Bouquet, Roman Numerals, Tricolor, Late 1800s, 1 In., Pocket *illus*	100
Hunting Case, 14K Gold, Ornate, Roman Numerals, Monogram, 1¾ In., Pocket *illus*	69
Kendall Guilloche, Enamel, Faberge Style, Purple, Egg Shape Case, Round Clock Face, 2 In.	42

Watch, Haas Neveux & Cie, Open Face, 18K Gold, Gold Case, Minute Repeater, c.1900, Pocket
$7,020

Jeffrey S. Evans & Associates

Watch, Hunting Case, 14K Gold, Bouquet, Roman Numerals, Tricolor, Late 1800s, 1 In., Pocket
$1,000

Eldred's

Watch, Hunting Case, 14K Gold, Ornate, Roman Numerals, Monogram, 1¾ In., Pocket
$690

Blackwell Auctions

Watch, Tiffany & Co., 18K Gold, Enamel, White Dial, Engraved, Marked, Pocket
$2,625

Charlton Hall Auctions

Watch, Waltham, 14K Yellow Gold, White Dial, Arabic Numerals, Fob Chain, 1902, 1 In., Pocket
$472

Austin Auction Gallery

W

Waterford, Chandelier, 5-Light, Hanging Teardrops, Cut Glass Prism, Signed, 21 In.

$978

Blackwell Auctions

Waterford, Ice Bucket, Millennium, Footed, 10 ½ In.

$438

Neal Auction Company

Waterford, Lamp, Electric, Cut Glass, Diamond Design, Fabric Shade, Metal Base, 28 x 17 ½ In.

$325

Austin Auction Gallery

Longines, Open Face, 14K Yellow Gold Case, Jewel Movement, c.1915, 1 ¹¹⁄₁₆ In.	374
M.S. Smith & Co., 18K Gold, Roman Numerals, Enamel, Engraved, Signed, 1 ¾ In., Pocket	1107
Seth Thomas, Open Face, 2-Tone Movement, White Dial, Minute Marker, c.1893, 2 ⅛ In.	201
Tiffany & Co., 18K Gold, Enamel, White Dial, Engraved, Marked, Pocket .... *illus*	2625
Vacheron & Constantine, 14K Gold Case, White Face, Minute Dial, Signed, Geneva, 2 In.	1560
Waltham, 14K Gold, Hunting Case, Engraved, Shield, Flowers, Marked, Roy, c.1909, Pocket..	575
Waltham, 14K Yellow Gold, White Dial, Arabic Numerals, Fob Chain, 1902, 1 In., Pocket ..... *illus*	472
Waltham, Rose Gold Plated, Porcelain Dial, Woman's, Late 1800s, Pocket	75

WATCH FOB

Watch fobs were worn on watch chains. They were popular during Victorian times and after. Many styles, especially advertising designs, are still made today.

Lady's Leg, Bone, Gold Trim, Mesh Chain, 8 In.	671
Porcelain, 3 Linked Hearts, Hand Painted Flowers, Goldtone Chain, 3 x 1 In.	115

WATERFORD

Waterford type glass resembles the famous glass made from 1783 to 1851 in the Waterford Glass Works in Ireland. It is a clear glass that was often decorated by cutting. Modern glass is being made again in Waterford, Ireland, and is marketed under the name Waterford. Waterford merged with Wedgwood in 1986 to form the Waterford Wedgwood Group. Most Waterford Wedgwood assets were bought by KPS Capital Partners of New York in 2009 and became part of WWRD Holdings. WWRD was bought by Fiskars in 2015 and Waterford is now a brand owned by Fiskars.

Bowl, Coin Cross, Celtic Braid Cuts, Circular Foot, Book Of Kells, Ireland, 6 ⅝ In.	118
Bowl, Colleen, Fluted Rim, Round Foot, 8 x 10 ¾ In.	344
Candlestick, Hanging Prisms, Scalloped Rim, Domed Base, 9 ½ In., Pair	266
Chandelier, 5-Light, Hanging Teardrops, Cut Glass Prism, Signed, 21 In. .... *illus*	978
Chandelier, 6-Light, Crystal, Scrolled Arms, Hanging Prisms, 25 In.	885
Chandelier, Lismore, Baluster Shape, Crystal Vase Style, Bulbous, Marked, 21 x 12 x 12 In. .	633
Decanter, Colleen, Brandy, Acorn Shape Finial, Crosshatch Design, Cut Glass, 12 In.	71
Decanter, Lismore, Ball Stopper, 10 ⅝ In., Pair	106
Goblet, Water, Lismore, Disc Foot, Marked, 6 ⅞ In., 9 Piece	472
Ice Bucket, Millennium, Footed, 10 ½ In. ...... *illus*	438
Lamp, Crystal, White Shade, Brass Base, Late 1900s, 29 In.	207
Lamp, Electric, Cut Glass, Diamond Design, Fabric Shade, Metal Base, 28 x 17 ½ In. ... *illus*	325
Lamp, Electric, Cut Glass, Diamond Design, Signed, 14 In.	316
Sherbet, Lismore, Disc Foot, 4 ⅛ In., 12 Piece	153
Tumbler, Iced Tea, Lismore, Disc Foot, 6 ½ In., 9 Piece	472
Wine, Lismore, Disc Foot, 7 ¾ In., 8 Piece	354

WATT

Watt family members bought the Globe pottery of Crooksville, Ohio, in 1922. They made pottery mixing bowls and tableware of the type made by Globe. In 1935 they changed the production and made the pieces with the freehand decorations that are popular with collectors today. Apple, Starflower, Rooster, Tulip, and Autumn Foliage are the best-known patterns. Pansy, also called Rio Rose, was the earliest pattern. Apple, the most popular pattern, can be dated from the leaves. Originally, the apples had three leaves; after 1958 two leaves were used. The plant closed in 1965. Reproductions of Apple, Dutch Tulip, Rooster, and Tulip have been made. For more prices, go to kovels.com.

Apple, Baker, Lid, 3-Leaf	9
Apple, Mixing Bowl, 2-Leaf, 7 ½ In.	6
Dutch Tulip, Casserole, Dome Lid, French Handle, Oven Ware, No. 18, 5 In., Pair	5

WAVE CREST

Wave Crest glass is an opaque white glassware manufactured by the **WAVE CREST WARE** Pairpoint Manufacturing Company of New Bedford, Massachusetts, and some French factories. It was decorated by the C.F. Monroe Company of Meriden, Connecticut. The glass was painted in pastel colors and decorated with flowers. The name Wave Crest was used starting in 1892.

Biscuit Jar, Lid, Blossom, Tree Branch, Silver Plate Collar, White, Light Blue Tones, 8 In.	40
Biscuit Jar, Lid, Silver Plate, Flowers, Handle, Engraved, 7¼ In.	118
Biscuit Jar, Metal Lid, Egg Crate Mold, Painted, Flowers, Gilt, Enamel Tracery, 7¾ In.	123
Box, Collars And Cuffs, Hinged Lid, Blue, White Tones, Flowers, Gilt Metal Feet, 7 x 7 In. *illus*	350
Dresser Box, Hinged Lid, Enamel, Pink Flowers, Green Ground, Kelva, 3¼ x 6 In. *illus*	338
Dresser Box, Hinged Lid, Round, White, Blue Enamel Flowers, 3 x 3¾ In.	60
Dresser Box, Hinged Lid, Swirl Mold, Pale Green, White, Pink Rose, Gilt Metal Feet, 6 x 7 In.	200
Ewer, Griffin Handles, Sunbonnet Girl, Flowers, White Ground, Bronze, 15¾ In., Pair	123
Ferner, Leaves, White, Engraved, Art Glass, Pairpoint Manufacturing Company, Signed, 7 In.	92
Jar, Gilt Metal Lid, Pink Flowers, Green, White Tones, Inset Jewels, Stamp Mark, 4 x 5 In.	200
Plaque, American Indian Portrait, Feather Headdress, Transfer, Paint, Gilt Frame, 12 In.	6457
Powder Box, Embossed Scroll Mold, Yellowish Tint, Enamel Flowers, 3½ x 5½ In.	175
Vase, Pink Poppy, Gilt Metal Feet, Handles, Banner Mark, 8¼ In.	175

WEAPON

Weapons listed here include instruments of combat other than guns, knives, rifles, or swords and clothing worn in combat. Firearms made after 1900 are not listed in this book. Knives and Swords are listed in their own categories.

Armor, Jousting, Maximillian Style, Full Suit, Wooden Base, c.1520, 64 In.	6600
Ax, Iron Blade, Raised Side Edges, Punched Holes, Wood Handle, Congo, c.1900, 16 x 5 In. *illus*	351
Ax, Wood, Wrapped Handle, Blade, Engraved, Africa, 28 x 8¾ In.	156
Caltrop, 4 Spikes, Iron, Handmade, c.1775, 3 In.	500
Helmet, Cabasset, Military, Steel, Narrow Brim, Attached Woven Liner, 1700s, 7 x 9 x 8 In.	649
Helmet, Pickelhaube, Metal Front Plate, Prussian Coat Of Arms, Visor, 1915, 11 x 11 x 8 In.	826
Helmet, U.S. Army, Infantry, American Eagle, Shield Plate, Leather Band, 1881, Size 6⅞ *illus*	236
Suit Of Armor, Chain Mail, Center Waist, Circular, Wood Base, Spain, 76 In. *illus*	1770
Truncheon, Police, Red & Gold, Black Background, Turned Ribbed Handle, Late 1800s, 16 In.	384
War Club, Indian, Round Stone Head, Wrapped Wood Handle, Sinew, Leather, 30 In.	350

WEATHER VANE

Weather vanes were used in seventeenth-century Boston. The direction of the wind was an indication of coming weather, important to the seafaring and farming communities. By the mid-nineteenth century, commercial weather vanes were made of metal. Many were shaped like animals. Ethan Allen, Dexter, and St. Julian are famous horses that were depicted. Today's collectors often consider weather vanes to be examples of folk art, even though they may not have been handmade.

American Indian, Crouching, Headdress, Bow, Arrow, Sheet Iron, Zinc, Late 1800s, 22 x 32 In.	2142
Banner, Arrow, Tin, Iron, Black Wooden Base, Late 1800s, 39 x 46 In.	344
Banner, Pointing Hand, Sheet Copper, Gilt, Ball Finial, Custom Stand, Late 1800s, 25 In.	3000
Bear, Full Body, Copper, Patina, Directionals, Chrome Balls, Mounted Plates, 1900s, 35 In.	295
Beaver, Zinc, Maple Leaf, Embossed Letters, Lightning Rod, Shinn, 1905, 8 x 29 x 1 In.	7345
Biplane, Copper, Verdigris Patina, Rectangular Base, 22½ In. *illus*	443
Buffalo, Standing, Cut Sheet Metal, Gilt Patina, Wood Stand, 18 x 26 In.	2596
Bull, Full Body, 2 Iron Sheets Riveted, Mounted, Stand, Late 1800s, 15 x 17½ In.	861
Car, Full Body, Zinc, Iron Directional, Gilt, Embossed, W.C.S., 7 x 28¾ x 1½ In.	3164
Cat, Jumping, Copper Bar, Original Paint, 1800s, 24 x 24 In.	8540
Cockerel, Full Body, Bronze, Gold Gilding, Wall Mount, Iron Bracket, 24 x 24½ In.	1638

Wave Crest, Box, Collars And Cuffs, Hinged Lid, Blue, White Tones, Flowers, Gilt Metal Feet, 7 x 7 In.
$350

Woody Auction

Wave Crest, Dresser Box, Hinged Lid, Enamel, Pink Flowers, Green Ground, Kelva, 3¼ x 6 In.
$338

Rich Penn Auctions

Weapon, Ax, Iron Blade, Raised Side Edges, Punched Holes, Wood Handle, Congo, c.1900, 16 x 5 In.
$351

Jeffrey S. Evans & Associates

W

This is an edited listing of current prices. Visit Kovels.com to check thousands of prices from previous years and sign up for free information on trends, tips, reproductions, marks, and more.

Weapon, Helmet, U.S. Army, Infantry, American Eagle, Shield Plate, Leather Band, 1881, Size 6⅞
$236

Leland Little Auctions

Weapon, Suit Of Armor, Chain Mail, Center Waist, Circular, Wood Base, Spain, 76 In.
$1,770

Austin Auction Gallery

Weather Vane, Biplane, Copper, Verdigris Patina, Rectangular Base, 22½ In.
$443

Copake Auction

Weather Vane, Eagle, Flat Full Body, Copper, Sphere, Cast Zinc Head, A.L. Jewel, c.1885, 19 x 24 In.
$9,000

Garth's Auctioneers & Appraisers

Think Before You Refinish
The original finish on an antique is considered part of the history of the piece and should be kept. If the original finish is removed, it can't be replaced and the value of the piece is lowered.

Weather Vane, Fisherman, Standing, Rowing, Striped Bass, Copper, Marked, John Garrett, 1900s, 12½ In.
$2,125

Eldred's

Weather Vane, Horse & Sulky, Copper, Wood Plinth Base, Harris & Co., 1800s, 18 x 21 In.
$625

Charlton Hall Auctions

Weather Vane, Horse, Running, Copper, Verdigris, Late 1800s, 17½ In.
$938

Eldred's

Weather Vane, Horse, Running, Flat, Copper, Molded, Zinc, A.S. Jewell & Co., 1800s, 17 x 23 In.
$1,845

Brunk Auctions

W

Cockerel, Standing, Sheet Copper, Verdigris, Rectangular Stand, c.1950, 25 In.	677
Codfish, Copper, Textured Scales, Gold Patina, Stand, 10 x 21 ½ In.	708
Cow, Full Body, Black, Zinc, Early 1900s, 9 x 15 In.	590
Cow, Full Body, Sheet Copper, Molded Face, Custom Stand, Cushing & Sons, c.1880, 15 x 25 In.	3625
Cow, Full Body, Sheet Copper, Molded, Zinc Head, Custom Stand, Late 1800s, 14 x 26 In.	5000
Cow, Full Body, Standing, Verdigris, Stand, Rectangular Base, 24 x 16 In.	2360
Cow, Standing, Full Body, Copper, Zinc Head & Horns, Red Finish, 29 In.	7625
Cow, Swell Body, Copper, Cast Iron Directionals, Early 1900s, 34 In.	519
Deer, Steel, Directional, Fleur-De-Lis Fletch, Sphere, Gilded, 1950s, 33 x 66 x 7 In.	702
Dog, Full Body, Sheet Copper, Molded, Gilt, Cushing & White, Late 1800s, 17 x 32 In.	5625
Dog, Running, Wood, Stand, Directionals, Painted, Square Base, 34 x 12 ½ In.	531
Dog's Profile, Setter, Pointing, Copper, Patina, Relief, Hollow, c.1900, 33 In.	1040
Eagle, Cast Head, Spread Wings, Hollow Body, Perched On Ball, Copper, Gilt, 1800s, 21 In.	3510
Eagle, Flat Full Body, Copper, Sphere, Cast Zinc Head, A.L. Jewel, c.1885, 19 x 24 In. .... illus	9000
Eagle, Full Body, Spread Wings, Ball, Arrow, Copper, Gilt, 39 ½ In.	2074
Eagle, On Ball, Copper, Directional, Painted, Wood Base, 18 x 15 In.	172
Eagle, Sheet Copper, Molded, Cast Zinc Head, Flat Full Body, Perched On Ball, 1850s, 27 In.	2500
Eagle, Spread Wings, Copper & Zinc, On Sphere, Parcel Gilt, Molded, c.1880, 14 In.	938
Eagle, Spread Wings, Copper, Verdigris, Ball, Mounted, Wooden Base, Late 1800s, 20 In.	375
Eagle, Spread Wings, Directionals, Copper, Steel Compass, Patina, Wood Mount, 39 x 23 x 18 In.	413
Eagle, Spread Wings, Gilt, Perched, Ball & Arrow, 4 Directionals, 1800s, 59 In.	1890
Fish, Cod, Full Body, Copper, Directionals, Wood Stand, Early 1900s, 31 In.	438
Fish, Copper, Mounted, Rectangular Base, 21 x 14 In.	590
Fish, Full Body, Copper, Gilt, Verdigris, Metal Stand, 26 In.	1586
Fish, Open Mouth, Fin, Scales, Stand, Rectangular Base, 24 x 6 ½ In.	1888
Fish, Sheet Copper, Molded, Gilt, Scale Details, Verdigris, Late 1800s, 26 ½ In.	4000
Fisherman, Standing, Rowing, Striped Bass, Copper, Marked, John Garrett, 1900s, 12 ½ In. .illus	2125
Galleon, Copper, Verdigris, Museum Style Stand, Late 1800s, 71 In.	3750
Goose, Spread Wings, Copper, Molded, Directionals, 52 x 29 In.	688
Grasshopper, Sheet Copper, Molded, Body Details, Applied Legs, Late 1800s, 42 In.	4063
Heron, Flight Position, Copper, Verdigris Patina, 15 ½ In.	590
Horse & Rider, Sheet Iron, Arrow Directional, Red, 1800s, 22 ½ In.	238
Horse & Rider, Trotting, Copper, Swell Body, 1800s, 24 ½ x 30 In.	13420
Horse & Sulky, Copper, Wood Plinth Base, Harris & Co., 1800s, 18 x 21 In. .... illus	625
Horse & Sulky, Rider, Whip, Swell Body, Copper, Mounted On Wood Base, Early 1900s, 31 In.	2928
Horse, Blackhawk, Flat Full Body, Sheet Copper, Molded, Cast Zinc Ears, 1880s, 28 In.	2500
Horse, Dappled, Full Body, Sheet Iron, Gray, White Mane & Tail, 1900s, 20 x 29 In.	125
Horse, Full Body, Copper, Molded, Partial Gilt Finish, 26 x 34 In.	3438
Horse, Full Body, Lightning Rod, Ear Of Corn, Directional, Zinc, 13 x 25 x 1 ¼ In.	6780
Horse, Galloping, Windmill Weight, Arrow, Cast Iron, 1900s, 27 ⅜ In.	438
Horse, On Stand, Standing, Patina, Tin, 27 ½ In.	305
Horse, Running, Copper, Verdigris, Late 1800s, 17 ½ In. .... illus	938
Horse, Running, Flat, Copper, Molded, Zinc, A.S. Jewell & Co., 1800s, 17 x 23 In. .... illus	1845
Horse, Running, Full Body, Copper & Zinc, Gilt, Rectangular Base, 1800s, 20 x 26 In. illus	2016
Horse, Running, Full Body, Copper, Cast Head, Early 1900s, 21 x 33 In.	1098
Horse, Running, Full Body, Copper, Cast Iron Directions, 66 In.	1200
Horse, Running, Full Body, Copper, Verdigris, Rectangular Base, 1800s, 40 In.	1875
Indian Chief, Copper, Standing, Holding Tomahawk, Bow, Strap Scrollwork, 70 x 50 In.	1170
Indian, Bow, Tomahawk, Zinc, Painted, Wood Base, 1950s, 71 In.	854
Indian, Hunter, Arrow, Full Body, Copper, Late 1900s, 36 x 29 In. .... illus	720
Locomotive, Sheet Metal, Articulated, Painted, Black, Late 1800s, 12 x 26 In. .... illus	500
Pig, Full Body, Sheet Copper, Molded, Gilt, Custom Stand, E.G. Washburn Co., c.1890, 15 x 29 In.	4063
Quill Pen, Copper, Verdigris, Wall Mount, Late 1800s, 16 In.	1125
Quill, Arrow, Copper, Green Patina, Mounted, Wood Base, 1800s, 18 x 37 In.	1187
Rabbit, Running, Cut Sheet Metal, Gilt Patina, Stand, 16 x 30 In.	1298
Raccoon, Moon, Star, Sun, Copper, Painted, 77 x 60 In.	1298
Ram, Copper, Attached Horns, Gilt, 1880, 28 x 30 In.	10800
Rooster With Chick, Feathered Arrow Directional, Iron, Rusty Finish, 31 x 21 In.	325
Rooster, Cast Iron, Tin, Feather Design, Metal Stand, Rochester, 1800s, 32 In. .... illus	2625
Rooster, Copper, Directionals, Arrow, Ball, Wood Stand, 54 In.	369
Rooster, Copper, Verdigris Patina, Directional, Pole, 71 In.	403

Weather Vane, Horse, Running, Full Body, Copper & Zinc, Gilt, Rectangular Base, 1800s, 20 x 26 In.
$2,016

Fontaine's Auction Gallery

Weather Vane, Indian, Hunter, Arrow, Full Body, Copper, Late 1900s, 36 x 29 In.
$720

Garth's Auctioneers & Appraisers

Weather Vane, Locomotive, Sheet Metal, Articulated, Painted, Black, Late 1800s, 12 x 26 In.
$500

Eldred's

W

563

Weather Vane, Rooster, Cast Iron, Tin, Feather Design, Metal Stand, Rochester, 1800s, 32 In.
$2,625

Eldred's

Weather Vane, Rooster, Full Body, Standing On Ball, Copper, Molded, Cast Iron Base, 1900s, 37 In.
$439

Jeffrey S. Evans & Associates

TIP
Pictures look best if hung on a light-colored wall.

Weather Vane, Sperm Whale, Cast Iron, Sheet Metal, Black, Harpoon Shape, Wind Vane, 15 In.
$469

Eldred's

W

Rooster, Flat Body, Copper, Arrow Directional, Cushing & Co., Late 1800s, 27 x 25 In.	1287
Rooster, Full Body, Sheet Metal, Crowing, Arrow, Painted, 25 x 20 ½ In.	106
Rooster, Full Body, Standing On Ball, Copper, Molded, Cast Iron Base, 1900s, 37 In. ... *illus*	439
Rooster, Silhouette, Sheet Metal, Lightning Rod, Wire Directional, c.1900, 14 x 32 x 2 In.	7345
Sailboat, Copper, Directionals, Ball, Wood Stand, 55 In.	246
Sailboat, Wood, Carved, Copper, Cast Directionals, Stand, 1900s, 18 x 21 ½ x 2 ½ In.	281
Sheep, Flat Full Body, Copper, Verdigris, L.W. Cushing & Sons, Late 1800s, 16 x 21 In.	1920
Silhouette, Cannon, Sheet Copper, Verdigris, 1800s, 10 ½ In.	1125
Sperm Whale, Cast Iron, Sheet Metal, Black, Harpoon Shape, Wind Vane, 15 In. .... *illus*	469
Sperm Whale, Copper, Verdigris, Patina, Mounted, Turned, Wood Post, White, Late 1900s, 48 In..	1375
Stag, Leaping, Copper, Cast Zinc Head & Antlers, Verdigris Patina, Late 1800s, 24 x 30 In.	9600
Whale, Copper, Sphere, Applied Verdigris Surface, Scroll Foot, Iron Base, c.1950, 73 x 24 In.	390
Whale, Tail Up, Cut Copper, Weathered Gold Patina, Red Glass Eye, Stand, 6 x 17 In.	610

Webb WEBB

Webb glass was made by Thomas Webb & Sons of Ambelcot, England. Many types of art and cameo glass were made by them during the Victorian era. Production ceased by 1991 and the factory was demolished in 1995. Webb Burmese and Webb Peachblow are special colored glasswares of the Victorian era. They are listed at the end of this section. Glassware that is not Burmese or Peachblow is included here.

Bowl, Diamond Quilted, Ruffled Rim, Pink Ground, 5 x 11 ½ In. .... *illus*	115
Jar, Lid, Honey Brown, White Overlay, Flowerheads, Leaves, Cameo, 1890-1900, 5 In.	1230
Perfume Bottle, Morning Glories, Violet, Turquoise, Silver Stopper, Cameo, 2 x 1 ¾ In. *illus*	1320
Syrup, Cranberry Glass, Blossom Flowers, c.1890, 7 ½ x 5 ¼ x 5 In.	180
Vase, Alexandrite, Flared Mushroom Rim, Round Base, 2 ¼ x 4 ¼ In. .... *illus*	525
Vase, Clematis Blossom, Butterflies, Blue Ground, Cameo, 7 x 7 In. .... *illus*	608
Vase, Cranberry Overlay, Flowers, Fluted Rim, Footed, Cameo, 9 ¾ x 6 ¼ In.	500
Vase, Hibiscus Flowers, Butterflies, White, Topaz, Cameo, 1880s, 7 ¾ In. .... *illus*	1404
Vase, Satin Glass, Brown, Enamel Blossom & Insect, Bulbous, 6 ¼ In.	150

WEBB BURMESE

Webb Burmese is a shaded Victorian glass made by Thomas Webb & Sons of Stourbridge, England, from 1886. Pieces are shades of pink to yellow.

Epergne, Fairy Lamp Shade, Brass Connector, 5 Flower Holders, Ruffled Edge, 1880s, 11 x 8 In. ..*illus*	2340
Fairy Lamp, Ribbed Embossed Candle Cup, Scalloped Rim, Hobnail, Marked, 1880s, 19 x 12 In..	1053

WEBB PEACHBLOW

Webb Peachblow is a shaded Victorian glass made by Thomas Webb & Sons of Stourbridge, England, from 1885.

Bowl, Red, Bluebird, White Enamel Flower, Leaves, England, 1804-1969, 9 x 2 In.	219
Vase, Flowers, Coralene Bird, Branch, Clear Applied Ribbed Handle, 10 x 7 ¾ In. .... *illus*	225

WEDGWOOD

Wedgwood, one of the world's most successful potteries, was founded by Josiah Wedgwood, who was considered a cripple by his brother and was forbidden to work at the family business. The pottery was established in England in 1759. The company used a variety of marks, including Wedgwood, Wedgwood & Bentley, Wedgwood & Sons, and Wedgwood's Stone China. A large variety of wares has been made, including the well-known jasperware, basalt, creamware, and even a limited amount of porcelain. There are two kinds of jasperware. One is made from two colors of clay; the other is made from one color of clay with a color dip to create the contrast in design. In 1986 Wedgwood and Waterford Crystal merged to form the Waterford Wedgwood Group. Most Waterford Wedgwood assets were bought by KPS Capital Partners of New York in 2009 and became part of WWRD Holdings. A small amount of Wedgwood is still made in England at the workshop

Webb, Bowl, Diamond Quilted, Ruffled Rim, Pink Ground, 5 x 11 ½ In.
$115

Blackwell Auctions

Webb, Perfume Bottle, Morning Glories, Violet, Turquoise, Silver Stopper, Cameo, 2 x 1 ¾ In.
$1,320

Morphy Auctions

Webb, Vase, Alexandrite, Flared Mushroom Rim, Round Base, 2 ¼ x 4 ¼ In.
$525

Woody Auction

Webb, Vase, Clematis Blossom, Butterflies, Blue Ground, Cameo, 7 x 7 In.
$608

Morphy Auctions

Webb, Vase, Hibiscus Flowers, Butterflies, White, Topaz, Cameo, 1880s, 7 ¾ In.
$1,404

Jeffrey S. Evans & Associates

Webb Burmese, Epergne, Fairy Lamp Shade, Brass Connector, 5 Flower Holders, Ruffled Edge, 1880s, 11 x 8 In.
$2,340

Jeffrey S. Evans & Associates

Webb Peachblow, Vase, Flowers, Coralene Bird, Branch, Clear Applied Ribbed Handle, 10 x 7 ¾ In.
$225

Woody Auction

Wedgwood, Bowl, Fairyland Luster, Magical Creatures Leaping, Star-Filled Sky, c.1920, 2 x 4 In.
$556

Jeffrey S. Evans & Associates

Wedgwood
The real Wedgwood company run by Josiah Wedgwood is spelled WEDGWOOD. Another English company took advantage of the name by using the mark WEDGEWOOD.

Wedgwood, Bowl, Fairyland Luster, Profuse Gilt, Glazed, Daisy Makeig Jones, c.1920, 4 x 9 In.
$4,830

Lion and Unicorn

W

Wedgwood, Jardiniere, Jasperware, Classic Scene, Blue Ground, White, Leaves Border, Marked, 7 x 8 In.
$125

Woody Auction

Wedgwood, Jardiniere, Majolica, Woman Medallions, 2 Handles, Black Ground, Flared Rim, 6 ½ In.
$565

Strawser Auction Group

Wedgwood, Plate, Peacock Center, Ruffled Edge, Red Rim, Earthenware, 9 ⅛ In.
$64

Hindman

TIP

It is said creativity comes from a messy, cluttered environment. It inspires ideas. Remember that the next time you rearrange your collectibles.

in Barlaston. Most is made in Asia. Wedgwood has been part of Fiskars Group since 2015. Other Wedgwood pieces may be listed under Flow Blue, Majolica, Tea Leaf Ironstone, or in other porcelain categories.

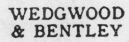

WEDGWOOD & BENTLEY	**WEDGWOOD** MADE IN ENGLAND	**W WEDGWOOD** ENGLAND 1759
Wedgwood & Bentley 1769–1780	Wedgwood 1940	Wedgwood 1998–present

Barber Bottle, Jasperware, Green, Medallions, Classical Design, Marked, 10 ½ In. ... 949
Biscuit Jar, Lid, Jasper Dip, White, Blue, Green, Plated Handle, Marked, 6 ½ In. ... 437
Bough Pot, Lid, Caneware, Rectangular, Classical Figures, 4 Wells, Turner, c.1800, 8 In. ... 688
Bowl, Black & Copper Dip, Roman Greek Designs, Carved, 1800s, 4 ½ In., Pair ... 345
Bowl, Butterfly Luster, Imperial, Mother-Of-Pearl Exterior, Multicolor, Enamel, c.1920, 8 In... 438
Bowl, Fairyland Luster, Blue, Footed, Daisy Makejg Jones, c.1920, 2 ½ x 5 ½ In. ... 920
Bowl, Fairyland Luster, Magical Creatures Leaping, Star-Filled Sky, c.1920, 2 x 4 In. ... *illus* 556
Bowl, Fairyland Luster, Profuse Gilt, Glazed, Daisy Makeig Jones, c.1920, 4 x 9 In. ... *illus* 4830
Bowl, Fairyland Luster, White Mice, Gilt Rim, Blue Ground, 5 ½ In. ... 283
Bust, Cato, Black Basalt, Mounted Atop, Waisted Circular Socle, Bentley, 1775, 19 In. ... 3750
Bust, Homer, Black Basalt, Mounted On Socle, England, 1800s, 13 In. ... 2706
Bust, Shakespeare, Black Basalt, Mounted, Shaped Socle, Bentley, c.1775, 13 ¼ In. ... 938
Cake Plate, Turquoise, Vines, Winged Dragon, Florentine, England, Early 1900s, 11 In. ... 31
Candlestick, Black Basalt, Dolphin, Shell Border, Rectangular Base, 1800, 8 ½ In., Pair ... 1500
Candlestick, Black Basalt, Griffin, Rectangular Base, 11 In. ... 863
Candlestick, Black Basalt, Triton, Holding Cornucopia Shape Sconce, Rocky Base, 1974, 10 In., Pair. 1063
Canopic Jar, Lid, Primrose, Jasperware, Terra-Cotta Ornaments, Marked, 9 ¼ x 4 ½ In. ... 1725
Clock, Jasperware, Wall, Bowl, Pale Green, Numbers, Marked, 6 In. ... 288
Compote, Dome Lid, Flower Frog, Jasperware, Blue, White, Cornucopias, Stars, Flowers, Marked, 7 In. 920
Crocus Pot, Black Basalt, Hedgehog, Holes, Mark, 1800s, 9 ¾ In. ... 690
Cup & Saucer, Jasperware, Green, Classic White Scenic Relief, Marked, 2 ½ x 4 ¼ In. ... 25
Ewer, Black Basalt, Bacchanalian Boys, Bulbous, Leafy Molded Handle, Bentley, c.1780, 10 In. 3250
Figure, Poor Maria, Carrara, Woman Seated, Dog, Impressed Mark, E. Keys, c.1855, 12 ½ In.. 563
Figurine, Black Basalt, Carved, Cupid, Holding Bow, Seated, 8 ½ In. ... 805
Fixture, Ceiling Light, Jasper Dip, Black, 5 Angels, Embossed, 13 In. ... 805
Humidor, Dragon Kenlock Ware, Black, Marked, England, 7 In. ... 322
Jar, Blackware, Geometric Design, Signed, Marie & Julian, 4 ¼ x 5 In. ... 313
Jardiniere, Crimson, Red, Lion Mask, Grapevine, Classical Design, 1800s, 8 In., Pair ... 2128
Jardiniere, Jasperware, Classic Scene, Blue Ground, White, Leaves Border, Marked, 7 x 8 In. *illus* 125
Jardiniere, Majolica, Woman Medallions, 2 Handles, Black Ground, Flared Rim, 6 ½ In. *illus* 565
Jug, Jasper Dip, Etruscan, Applied White Classical Figures, Crimson, Early 1900s, 5 ⅛ In. ... 438
Kettle, Lid, Black Basalt, Cupids, Sybil Finial, Trefoil Bail Handle, Early 1800s, 10 In. ... 1500
Lamp, Figural, Elephant Heads Tripod Base, Flowers, Chocolate, Turquoise, 1850s, 10 ½ In. 360
Pastille Burner, Lid, Jasper Dip, Tricolor, Black, 3 Dolphins, Holder, Mark, 5 In. ... 920
Plaque, Mark Antony, Jasperware, Oval, Brass Frame, Bentley, c.1775, 4 ¾ x 6 In. ... 1250
Plaque, White Jasper, Oval, Triumph Of Bacchus Relief, Wood Frame, Bentley, 1775, 9 In. ... 2000
Plate, Peacock Center, Ruffled Edge, Red Rim, Earthenware, 9 ⅛ In. ... *illus* 64
Platter, Majolica, Cream Ground, Black Rim, Flowers, Argenta, 11 ¾ In. ... 136
Platter, Rose & Jessamine, White Ground, Flow Blue, 19 x 15 In. ... 96
Shelf, Wall, Majolica, Putti Center, Shaped Top, Light Blue Curtain, 9 In. ... *illus* 537
Sweetmeat Set, Transfer Print, Central Dish, Mahogany Tray, Earthenware, Early 1800s, 21 In. 813
Tankard, Black Basalt, Cylindrical, Oak Leaf Band, Silver Mounted Rim, c.1800, 6 In. ... 313
Tazza, Majolica, Shallow Bowl, Relief, Frolicking Monkeys, Late 1800s, 8 x 11 In. ... 561
Tray, Grapes, Leaves & Stem, Cream Ground, Green, Scalloped Rim, 12 ½ In. ... 96
Tureen, Lid, Underplate, Chelsea House, Griffin Handles, Gilt, 11 ¾ In. ... 148
Urn, Black Basalt, Neoclassical Scenes, Flower Festoons, Lamp, Wood Base, 28 In. ... 188
Urn, Jasperware, Sage Green, White Lobed Handles, Mounted As Lamp, 27 ½ In., Pair ... 594
Urn, Lid, Jasper Dip, Lilac, Green, White, Bolted, Handles, Square Base, 12 In. ... 1495
Vase, Jasper Dip, Red, White Figures, Handles, Portland Design, 6 ½ In., Pair ... 2875
Vase, Jasperware, Black, Mythological, 2 Handles, Stand, Tiffany & Co., 1800s, 10 x 7 In. ... 3500

Vase, Jasperware, Blue, Flowers, Torches, Doves, 6 Circular Holes, 7 ½ In.	805
Vase, Lid, Black Basalt, Scrolled Leaf-Molded Handles, Boys Playing, Bentley, 1775, 14 In.	2625
Vase, Orange, Red, Green, Cobalt Blue, Daisy Makeig Jones, c.1920, 12 x 6 In.	4830
Vase, Prophyry, Lid, Terra-Cotta Widow Finials, Black Basalt Base, Bentley, c.1780, 9 In., Pair	1188
Vase, Square, Blue Luster, Celestial Dragon, Gilt, Backstamp, c.1920, 5 ½ x 7 ¾ In.	259
Vase, Trumpet, Pixies, Dragonflies, Red Luster, Gilt, Daisy Makeig Jones, c.1925, 6 In.	2300

WELLER

Weller pottery was first made in 1872 in Fultonham, Ohio. The firm moved to Zanesville, Ohio, in 1882. Artwares were introduced in 1893. Hundreds of lines of pottery were produced, including Louwelsa, Eocean, Dickens Ware, and Sicardo, before the pottery closed in 1948.

LONHUDA
Weller Pottery
1895–1896

LOUWELSA WELLER
Weller Pottery
1895–1918

WELLER POTTERY
Weller Pottery
1920s

Aurelian, Vase, Multicolor, Hydrangea, Fluted Rim, Signed, CJ Dibowski, 24 ¾ In. *illus*	1452
Baldin, Vase, Apple, Leaves, Red & Green, Underfoot, Marked, 6 In.	86
Coppertone, Bowl, Frog, Fish, Scalloped Rim, Green Matte Glaze, Stamped, 6 x 7 x 10 ½ In. *illus*	1875
Coppertone, Vase, Fluted Rim, Leaves, Flower, Frog, Round Base, 11 ½ x 5 ½ In.	529
Coppertone, Vase, Frog & Water Lily, Yellow, Green Ground, 4 In.	147
Dickens Ware, Lamp, Brown Shade, Glass Chimney, 3 Handles, Pad Feet, 21 In.	85
Dickens Ware, Tankard, Chief Black Heart Portrait, Side Handle, Anna Daugherty, 11 ⅞ In. *illus*	605
Eocean, Vase, Crackle, Grape Design, Molded Rim, Glaze, 8 ½ In.	295
Eocean, Vase, Flowers, Molded Rim, Pinched Neck, Glazed, 10 In.	136
Eocean, Vase, Rose, Nasturtium, Pale Green Leaves, Soft Mauve, Signed, Claude Leffler, 15 In.	484
Glendale, Vase, Bird, Standing Next To Nest, Cylindrical, 8 x 3 In.	150
Hudson, Vase, Irises, Blue, Fluted Rim, Made For Kappa Gamma, Hester Pillsbury, 15 In. *illus*	1815
Hudson, Vase, White & Yellow Flowers, Blue Ground, 2 Handles, 6 ¾ In.	158
Lasa, Vase, Sunrise Behind Mountains, Serene Water, Iridescent, Metallic Glaze, c.1920, 6 In. *illus*	222
Lasa, Vase, Tropical Landscape, Metallic Glaze, Signed, 7 ½ x 3 ½ In.	375
Louwelsa, Ewer, Flowers, Scalloped Rim, Dark Brown Glaze, 6 ½ In., Pair	113
Louwelsa, Tankard, 7 Barn Swallows In Flight, Impressed, R.G. Turner, 13 ¾ In.	787
Louwelsa, Vase, Flared Rim, Yellow Iris, Levi J. Burgess, Early 1900s, 10 ½ x 5 ½ In. *illus*	322
Louwelsa, Vase, Hand Painted, Red Roses, Black Interior, 10 ½ x 4 ¼ In.	38
Louwelsa, Vase, Pansies, Flared Rim, Signed, M. Lybarger, 18 In.	590
Louwelsa, Vase, Violets, Blue Ground, Glazed, Impressed Mark, 6 ½ x 3 ⅜ In.	313
Orris, Wall Pocket, Green, Flowers, Scalloped Rim, 8 In.	102
Sicardo, Vase, Blue Iridescent, Glazed, Leaves, Fruit, Early 1900s, 12 ½ In. *illus*	826
Sicardo, Vase, Iridescent, Scalloped Rim & Handle, 6 In.	1808
Sicardo, Vase, Lobed, Beetles, Scarabs, Stags, Rice Shades, Red, Blue, Green, 11 In. *illus*	4356
Sicardo, Vase, Molded Rim, Pear Shape, 4 ½ In.	649
Sicardo, Vase, Vibrant Iridescence, Arabesque Design, 15 In.	1386
Vase, Pinched Waist, Flowers, Brown, Green Tones, 11 ¼ In., Pair	175
Woodcraft, Wall Pocket, 2 Squirrels, Tree Branches, Earth Tones, Green Leaves, 8 x 13 In.	910
Zona, Jardiniere, Pedestal, Kingfisher, Cattails, Scenic Landscape, Earthtones, 31 x 13 In. *illus*	3075

WEMYSS

Wemyss ware was first made in 1882 by Robert Heron & Son, later called Fife Pottery, in Scotland. Large colorful flowers, hearts, and other symbols were hand painted on figurines, inkstands, jardinieres, candlesticks, buttons, pots, and other items. Fife Pottery closed in 1932. The molds and designs were used by a series of potteries until 1957. In 1985 the Wemyss name and designs were obtained by Griselda Hill. The Wemyss Ware trademark was registered in 1994. Modern Wemyss Ware in old styles is still being made.

Wedgwood, Shelf, Wall, Majolica, Putti Center, Shaped Top, Light Blue Curtain, 9 In.
$537

Strawser Auction Group

Weller, Aurelian, Vase, Multicolor, Hydrangea, Fluted Rim, Signed, CJ Dibowski, 24 ¾ In.
$1,452

Humler & Nolan

Weller, Coppertone, Bowl, Frog, Fish, Scalloped Rim, Green Matte Glaze, Stamped, 6 x 7 x 10 ½ In.
$1,875

Toomey & Co. Auctioneers

W

Weller, Dickens Ware, Tankard, Chief Black Heart Portrait, Side Handle, Anna Daugherty, 11 7/8 In.
$605

Humler & Nolan

Weller, Hudson, Vase, Irises, Blue, Fluted Rim, Made For Kappa Gamma, Hester Pillsbury, 15 In.
$1,815

Humler & Nolan

Weller, Lasa, Vase, Sunrise Behind Mountains, Serene Water, Iridescent, Metallic Glaze, c.1920, 6 In.
$222

Jeffrey S. Evans & Associates

Weller, Louwelsa, Vase, Flared Rim, Yellow Iris, Levi J. Burgess, Early 1900s, 10 1/2 x 5 1/2 In.
$322

Thomaston Place Auction Galleries

Weller, Sicardo, Vase, Blue Iridescent, Glazed, Leaves, Fruit, Early 1900s, 12 1/2 In.
$826

Cottone Auctions

Weller, Sicardo, Vase, Lobed, Beetles, Scarabs, Stags, Rice Shades, Red, Blue, Green, 11 In.
$4,356

Humler & Nolan

Weller, Zona, Jardiniere, Pedestal, Kingfisher, Cattails, Scenic Landscape, Earthtones, 31 x 13 In.
$3,075

Morphy Auctions

Wheatley, Tile, 2 Blue Winged Geese Standing, Wildly Flowering Vase, Matte Glaze, 12 1/2 x 6 3/8 In.
$363

Humler & Nolan

Willets, Vase, Peacock, Gilt Rim, Underfoot, Signed, C. Cass, Belleek, Late 1900s, 19 In.
$567

Fontaine's Auction Gallery

W

Bowl, Cherry Pattern, Green Rim, c.1890, 6 ½ x 3 In. 300
Plate, Pink Roses, Leaves, Green Rim, c.1900, 5 In. 120

WESTMORELAND GLASS

Westmoreland glass was made by the Westmoreland Glass Company of Grapeville, Pennsylvania, from 1889 to 1984. The company made clear and colored glass of many varieties, such as milk glass, pressed glass, and slag glass.

Westmoreland Glass
c.1910–c.1929, 1970s

Westmoreland Glass
Late 1940s–1981

Westmoreland Glass
1982–1984

Beaded Swirl & Ball, Cruet, 5 ¼ In. 35
Lily Of The Valley, Vase, Scalloped, Flared Rim, Footed, 7 In. 17
Old Quilt, Milk Glass, Compote, Square, 4 In. 12
Paneled Grape, Pitcher, Milk Glass, Footed, Pint 21

WHEATLEY POTTERY

Wheatley Pottery was founded by Thomas J. Wheatley in Cincinnati, Ohio. He had worked with the founders of the art pottery movement, including M. Louise McLaughlin of the Rookwood Pottery. He started T.J. Wheatley & Co. in 1880. That company was closed by 1884. Thomas Wheatley worked for Weller Pottery in Zanesville, Ohio, from 1897 to 1900. In 1903 he founded Wheatley Pottery Company in Cincinnati. Wheatley Pottery was purchased by the Cambridge Tile Manufacturing Company in 1927. Cambridge Tile closed in 1985.

Tile, 2 Blue Winged Geese Standing, Wildly Flowering Vase, Matte Glaze, 12 ½ x 6 ⅜ In. *illus* 363
Tile, Vase, Leaf, Flowers, Cream Ground, Art Pottery, Oak Frame, 11 ½ In. 330

WILLETS MANUFACTURING COMPANY

Willets Manufacturing Company of Trenton, New Jersey, began work in 1879. The company made belleek in the late 1880s and 1890s in shapes similar to those used by the Irish Belleek factory. It stopped working about 1912. A variety of marks were used, most including the name *Willets*.

Bowl, Ruffled Rim, Golden Handle, Flowers, Blackberry, Belleek, D. Merkle, c.1900, 4 ½ In. 72
Vase, Flowers, Cylindrical, Molded Rim, Multicolor, Franz Bischoff, Belleek, 16 In. 150
Vase, Peacock, Gilt Rim, Underfoot, Signed, C. Cass, Belleek, Late 1900s, 19 In. .... *illus* 567

WILLOW

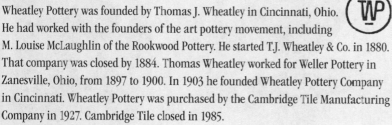

Willow pattern has been made in England since 1780. The pattern has been copied by factories in many countries, including Germany, Japan, and the United States. It is still being made. Willow was named for a pattern that pictures a bridge, birds, willow trees, and a Chinese landscape. Most pieces are blue and white. Some made after 1900 are pink and white.

Cup & Saucer, Pink & White, Japan 48
Dish, Pickle, Leaf Shape, Diaper Border, 19th Century, England, 5 ½ x 5 In. 55
Ladle, Blue & White, Round Bowl, Bent Handle, Victorian, c.1880, 12 In. 245
Plate, Landscape, Bridge, Birds, Willows, Blue & White, Buffalo China, 10 In., 4 Piece 83
Platter, Blue & White, Staffordshire, 19 x 15 In. 110

Window, Beveled, Multicolor, Flowers, Leaves & Stem, Geometric Border, 19 ½ In., Pair
$1,890

Fontaine's Auction Gallery

Window, Fruit, Leaves, Faceted Jewels, Amber Field, Amethyst Border, Frame, c.1890, 26 x 52 In.
$554

Rich Penn Auctions

Window, Leaded, Beveled, Zipper Cut, Diamond & Central Design, Oak Frame, 37 x 16 In., Pair
$630

Fontaine's Auction Gallery

W

Window, Leaded, Fleur-De-Lis, Central Torch, Multicolor, Frame, 1900s, 33 ½ x 35 In.
$176

Jeffrey S. Evans & Associates

Window, Portrait, Woman, Playing Harp, Povey Bros., Oak Frame, 1900s, 66 x 25 In.
$3,218

Thomaston Place Auction Galleries

Window, Stained, Arched Top, Flowers, Leaves, Birds, Wood Frame, 1900s, 60 x 23 In.
$1,003

Austin Auction Gallery

Window, Transom, Leaded, Jeweled, Ribbon, Fleur-De-Lis, White Ground, Wood Frame, 25 x 44 In.
$567

Fontaine's Auction Gallery

Wood Carving, Ashanti, Fertility Figure, Beaded Necklace, Mounted, Wood Stand, Akua'ba, Late 1800s, 11 In.
$702

Jeffrey S. Evans & Associates

Wood Carving, Bird, Teakwood, Stylized, Wire Legs, Jacob Hermann, Denmark, Late 1950s, 8 ½ In.
$1,121

Austin Auction Gallery

Wood Carving, Birds, Perched On Tree Branch, Mahogany, Painted, 1910s, 8 ¾ x 9 ¼ In.
$2,928

Pook & Pook

Wood Carving, Boar's Head, Glass Eyes, Open Mouth, Black Forest, Late 1800s, 14 x 9 In.
$1,260

Fontaine's Auction Gallery

Wood Carving, Buddha, Head, Tight Curl, Knot Of Wisdom Top, Long Earlobes, Serene Look, 23 In.
$472

Leland Little Auctions

WINDOW

Window glass that was stained and beveled was popular for houses during the late nineteenth and early twentieth centuries. Some was set in patterns like leaded glass. The old windows became popular with collectors in the 1970s; today, old and new examples are seen.

Beveled, Multicolor, Flowers, Leaves & Stem, Geometric Border, 19½ In., Pair .... *illus*	1890
Flowers, Multicolor, Wood Frame, 27 x 21 In., Pair..................................	288
Fruit, Leaves, Faceted Jewels, Amber Field, Amethyst Border, Frame, c.1890, 26 x 52 In. *illus*	554
Gothic Style, Leaded Glass, Multicolor, 36 x 30½ In..........................	325
Gothic Style, Rectangular Frame, 2 Arches, Stone, 46 x 33 In., Pair	3540
Leaded, Angel, Playing Trumpets, Leaves, Flowers, Shell, Scrollwork, 48½ x 24 In.	1512
Leaded, Beveled, Zipper Cut, Diamond & Central Design, Oak Frame, 37 x 16 In., Pair *illus*	630
Leaded, Clear Glass, Squares Pattern, Shapes, Side Panel, 26 x 27 In....................	118
Leaded, Fleur-De-Lis, Central Torch, Multicolor, Frame, 1900s, 33½ x 35 In. .... *illus*	176
Leaded, Jewels, Middle Eastern Maiden Medallion, 1800s, 46 x 31 In.	3360
Leaded, Mosaic, Jeweled, Flowers, Crescent Moons, Crackle Glass, Round, Early 1900s, 61 In.	3276
Leaded, Stained, 3 Biplanes, Wood Frame, 20 x 23½ In..........................	504
Leaded, Stained, Flowers, Scrolling Corner, Birds, Perched, On Branch, 24 In., 3 Piece	2898
Multicolor, Arch, Green Border, 1800s, 44 x 41½ In................................	443
Multicolor, Laurel, Wreath Plaque, Fleur-De-Lis, Pine Frame, c.1900, 19 x 48 In............	266
Multicolor, Milk Glass Cabochons, Cream Ground, Frame, 58 x 49 In....................	384
Painted, Musician, Medieval Style Dress, Playing Harp, 22 x 29 In.....................	177
Portrait, Woman, Playing Harp, Povey Bros., Oak Frame, 1900s, 66 x 25 In. .... *illus*	3218
Saloon, Red, Green, Brown, Slag Glass, Frame, c.1950, 23 x 52¾ In....................	55
Stained, Arched Top, Flowers, Leaves, Birds, Wood Frame, 1900s, 60 x 23 In. .... *illus*	1003
Telegraph Office, Glass, Black Frame, Baltimore & Ohio R.R., 29½ x 23 In.	295
Transom, Amethyst Tiles, Opal Slag Glass Columns, Ruby Jewels, Oak Frame, c.1915, 39 x 45 In.	185
Transom, Leaded, Jeweled, Ribbon, Fleur-De-Lis, White Ground, Wood Frame, 25 x 44 In. .. *illus*	567

WOOD CARVING

Wood carvings and wooden pieces are listed separately in this book. There are also wooden pieces found in other categories, such as Folk Art, Kitchen, and Tool.

2 Dolphins, Swimming, Reef, 37 In.	63
Altar Figure, Madonna & Child, Multicolor, Gilt, Metal Halo, Cloud Base, Early 1800s, 39 In.	5015
Altar Figure, Saint, Woman, Softwood, Floral Robes, Glass Eyes, Multicolor, 22 x 8 x 6 In.....	936
Altar, Tin, Vining Floral Relief, Pierced, Multicolor, 1900s, 30 x 18½ x 10¼ In.	316
American Kestrel, Paint, Glass Eyes, Driftwood, Round Base, Signed, Tom Ahern, 1982, 12 x 11 In.	431
Antelope, Lying Flat, Ebonized, Painted, Africa, 1900s, 38 In........................	48
Ashanti, Fertility Figure, Beaded Necklace, Mounted, Wood Stand, Akua'ba, Late 1800s, 11 In. .. *illus*	702
Asian Woman, Holding Basket, Lotus Flowers, 17 In................................	126
Bald Eagle, Rocky Perch, Snake Under Talons, Painted, Late 1900s, 20½ x 34½ In.	360
Bear, Standing, Glass Eyes, Black Forest, c.1910, 36 x 19 In.........................	2040
Beaver, Gnawing On Branch, George Servance, Thomasville, N.C., 10 x 14 In......................	443
Bird, Teakwood, Stylized, Wire Legs, Jacob Hermann, Denmark, Late 1950s, 8½ In. ... *illus*	1121
Bird, Walnut, Standing, Carved, Manzanita Burl, Signed, B. Neely, 1900s, 4 In.	77
Bird, Yellow, Brown, White Wings, Wire Legs, Branch Base, Joseph Moyer, Late 1800s, 6 In. ..	4688
Birds, Perched On Tree Branch, Mahogany, Painted, 1910s, 8¾ x 9¼ In. .... *illus*	2928
Blue Jay, Tree Trunk Base, Painted, Signed, W.T. Miller, Early 1900s, 5¾ x 7¾ In.	671
Boar's Head, Glass Eyes, Open Mouth, Black Forest, Late 1800s, 14 x 9 In. .... *illus*	1260
Brook Trout, Mounted, Oval Wood Backboard, Signed, F. Adamo, Late 1900s, 12½ In.	250
Buddha, Head, Tight Curl, Knot Of Wisdom Top, Long Earlobes, Serene Look, 23 In. ... *illus*	472
Buddha, Seated, Dhyanasana, Robes, Lacquered, Chinese, 27 In.	1020
Buddha, Seated, Gilt, Square Base, Gold Paint, Thailand, 25½ In.	201
Buddha, Seated, Painted, Metal Trim, Edo Period, Japan, 27 In.	443
Bulto, Santo Nino Perdido, Lost Child, Jose Rafael Aragon, New Mexico, 14 x 7 x 4 In. *illus*	7200
Busk, Beech, Face, Heart, Zigzag Borders, 1770, 12¾ In.	732
Bust, Benjamin Franklin, Mahogany, Shaped Base, 1800s, 13½ In........................	976

Wood Carving, Bulto, Santo Nino Perdido, Lost Child, Jose Rafael Aragon, New Mexico, 14 x 7 x 4 In.
$7,200

Cottone Auctions

Wood Carving, Carolina Wren, On Branch Stub, Signed, c.1973, 4¼ x 9 In.
$213

Eldred's

Wood Carving, Cherub, 2 Heads, Painted, Gilt, Late 1800s, 13½ In.
$567

Fontaine's Auction Gallery

W

Wood Carving, Crest, Ornamental, Crossed Sword, Quill Pen, Laurel Wreath, Gilt, 1900s, 11 x 17 In. $38

Selkirk Auctioneers & Appraisers

Wood Carving, Crucifix, Multicolor, Painted, Ebonized Cross, Spanish Colonial, 1800s, 33 In. $1,121

Austin Auction Gallery

Wood Carving, Deer Head, Wall Mount, Brown Antlers, Painted, Argentina, Late 1900s, 33 x 23 In. $708

Leland Little Auctions

Bust, Sir Walter Raleigh, Oak, Gathered Ruff, England, 18 In.	2625
Bust, Woman, Neoclassical, Oak, Floral Headpiece, Draped Gown, Continental, 23 ½ In.	1062
Bust, Woman, Wearing Hat, Hexagonal Base, Mark, Morelli, 1895, 12 In.	102
Canada Goose, Brown, Black, Spread Wings, Flying, Leaves, Wood Base, 14 x 11 x 12 ½ In.	71
Carnival Head, Mutton Chops, Red Lips, White Eyes, Black, Folk Art, 1910s, 13 ½ In.	644
Carolina Wren, On Branch Stub, Signed, c.1973, 4 ¼ x 9 In. .... *illus*	213
Cherub, 2 Heads, Painted, Gilt, Late 1800s, 13 ½ In. .... *illus*	567
Cherubim, Spread Wings, Multicolor, Gilt, Late 1800s, 29 x 27 In.	207
Christ Child Of The World, Standing, Gesso, Mounted, 1800s, 15 In.	168
Cigar Holder, Bear, Black Forest, Circular Base, c.1900, 7 In.	219
Codfish, Fins & Scales, Gilt, 2 Eyehooks Top, 1800s, 10 x 32 In.	4062
Cowboy On Horseback, Signed, Ervin Curt Teichman, Brazil, 22 x 19 x 3 In.	225
Crest, Ornamental, Crossed Sword, Quill Pen, Laurel Wreath, Gilt, 1900s, 11 x 17 In. .. *illus*	38
Cross, Spanish Colonial, Altar, Painted, Straw Decor, Stepped Base, 1800s, 25 In.	2242
Crow, Black, Glass Eyes, Circular Plinth Base, 11 In.	172
Crucifix, Fleur-De-Lis, Fruit Cluster, Flowers, 1800s, 13 Ft. 6 In.	6300
Crucifix, Multicolor, Painted, Ebonized Cross, Spanish Colonial, 1800s, 33 In. .... *illus*	1121
Crucifix, Relief Face, Hands, Feet, Painted, Glass Pane, Square Base, Mexico, 1800s, 17 ¼ In.	649
Deer Head, Wall Mount, Brown Antlers, Painted, Argentina, Late 1900s, 33 x 23 In. .... *illus*	708
Deer, Lying Down, Teak, Blue & Black, Removable Antlers, Southeast Asia, 1900s, 22 x 20 In., Pair	443
Deer, Reclining, Teak, Pink & Green, Removable Antler, Southeast Asia, 22 x 19 In., Pair	531
Deer, Standing, Glass Eyes, Rock Shape Base, Black Forest, 21 In., Pair .... *illus*	4725
Diorama, Mahogany, Cityscape, Tall Buildings, Charles Butler, 1950s, 9 x 24 x 2 In.	1375
Dog, Lying Down, Painted, Multicolor, Removable Ears, Late 1900s, 20 x 35 In.	266
Dog, Seated, Teak, Whitewash Finish, Late 1900s, 30 In. .... *illus*	472
Dolphin, Bottlenose, Painted, Black & White, Clark G. Voorhees Jr., 18 In.	3000
Drapery, Pine, Carved, American, 1800s, 42 In., Pair .... *illus*	732
Duck, Standing, Glass Eyes, Painted, Vergle Hodge & Charles Moore, 14 In.	55
Eagle, American Flag, 35 Stars, Shield, Painted, Gilt, George Stapf, Pennsylvania, 23 x 30 In. *illus*	4688
Eagle, Banner, Shield, Painted, Live & Let Live, Artistic Carving Co., 1900s, 17 x 45 ½ In. ... *illus*	2000
Eagle, Schimmel Style, Spread Wings, Painted, 6 x 12 ½ In. .... *illus*	675
Eagle, Spread Wings, Gilt, Multicolor, Shield, Artistic Carving Co., Boston, 6 x 26 In.	875
Eagle, Spread Wings, Pilothouse, Gilt, Signed, Claw, 21 ½ x 49 In.	263
Eagle, Spread Wings, Shield, Coat Of Arms, 3 Feathers, Oak, c.1880, 15 In.	540
Eagle, Spread Wings, Wall Mount, Perched, Gilt & Gesso, Chain, 2 Balls, Late 1800s, 10 In. .. *illus*	531
Element, Architectural, Bhairava Shiva, Teak, 21 In.	148
Elk, Barking, Standing, Natural Shape Ground, Branches & Leaves, Black Forest, 21 ½ In.	756
Fish, Pickerel, Mounted, Chain, Backboard, Frank Adamo, Late 1900s, 16 In. .... *illus*	138
Fish, Striped Bass, Rocks, Seagrass Base, Contemporary, 18 x 7 In.	1063
Foo Dog, Seated, Open Mouth, Chinese, 1800s, 15 In.	396
Fox, Female, 2 Young, Oval Rosewood Base, Anri, Gunther Granget, 1950s, 4 x 13 x 6 In.	374
God Of Longevity, Shoulao, Seated On Deer, Holds Peach, Character Marks, Early 1900s, 6 In.	148
Gondola, Flowers, Leaves, Back Design, Scalloped Top, 1800s, 19 x 48 In. .... *illus*	594
Great Horned Owl, Glass Eyes, Standing, Painted, Signed, Warfield, 1973, 13 In.	288
Great Horned Owl, Perched On Branch, Painted, Early 1900s, 10 ½ In. .... *illus*	250
Griffin, Seated, Oak, Rectangular Plinth Base, 1910s, 21 x 18 In., Pair	502
Guanyin, Intricately Carved, Standing, Wearing Robe, Square Base, Chinese, 13 ¾ In.	153
Guanyin, Standing, Holding, Lotus Blossom, Prayer Beads, Parcel Gilt, Plinth Base, 50 In. .. *illus*	531
Guanyin, Standing, Pours Water, Huanghuali, Chinese, 1930s, 14 In.	90
Horse, Stained Pine, Galloping Stride, Tiered Pedestal Base, Late 1900s, 22 x 27 In.	35
Horse, Tang Style, Multicolor, Painted, Glass Case, Chinese, 25 ½ In. .... *illus*	2950
Kingfisher, Standing, Mounted, Mushroom, Driftwood Base, Signed, F. Adamo, Late 1800s, 8 In.	62
Least Tern, White, Brown Beak, On Circular Wood Base, Stamped, Byron E. Bruffee, 7 x 9 In.	200
Leopard, Stretching, Fish Scale Pattern, Rectangular Plinth, Signed, Aberk 82, 9 In.	11
Luohan, Robes, Bald, Holding, Prayer Beads, Black, Chinese, 8 In. .... *illus*	53
Madonna & Child, Standing, Gilt, Painted, Octagonal Base, 41 ½ In. .... *illus*	43
Madonna, Silvertone Halo, Painted, Standing, Globe, Glass Cloche, Continental, 23 ½ In.	35
Madonna, Standing, Crossed Hands, Oak, Draped Robes, Continental, 1800s, 32 In. .. *illus*	20

Wood Carving, Deer, Standing, Glass Eyes, Rock, Shape Base, Black Forest, 21 In., Pair
$4,725

Fontaine's Auction Gallery

Wood Carving, Dog, Seated, Teak, Whitewash Finish, Late 1900s, 30 In.
$472

Leland Little Auctions

Wood Carving, Drapery, Pine, Carved, American, 1800s, 42 In., Pair
$732

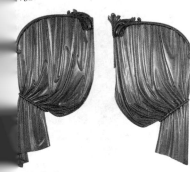

...eal Auction Company

Wood Carving, Eagle, American Flag, 35 Stars, Shield, Painted, Gilt, George Stapf, Pennsylvania, 23 x 30 In.
$4,688

Eldred's

Wood Carving, Eagle, Banner, Shield, Painted, Live & Let Live, Artistic Carving Co., 1900s, 17 x 45 ½ In.
$2,000

Eldred's

Wood Carving, Eagle, Schimmel Style, Spread Wings, Painted, 6 x 12 ½ In.
$675

Wood Carving, Eagle, Spread Wings, Wall Mount, Perched, Gilt & Gesso, Chain, 2 Balls, Late 1800s, 10 In.
$531

Leland Little Auctions

Wood Carving, Fish, Pickerel, Mounted, Chain, Backboard, Frank Adamo, Late 1900s, 16 In.
$138

Eldred's

Wood Carving, Gondola, Flowers, Leaves, Back Design, Scalloped Top, 1800s, 19 x 48 In.
$594

Charlton Hall Auctions

Pook & Pook

W

WOOD CARVING

Wood Carving, Great Horned Owl, Perched On Branch, Painted, Early 1900s, 10 ½ In.
$250

Eldred's

Wood Carving, Guanyin, Standing, Holding, Lotus Blossom, Prayer Beads, Parcel Gilt, Plinth Base, 50 In.
$531

Austin Auction Gallery

Wood Carving, Horse, Tang Style, Multicolor, Painted, Glass Case, Chinese, 25 ½ In.
$2,950

Austin Auction Gallery

Wood Carving, Luohan, Robes, Bald, Holding, Prayer Beads, Black, Chinese, 8 In.
$531

Leland Little Auctions

Wood Carving, Madonna & Child, Standing, Gilt, Painted, Octagonal Base, 41 ½ In.
$438

Susanin's Auctioneers & Appraisers

Wood Carving, Madonna, Standing, Crossed Hands, Oak, Draped Robes, Continental, 1800s, 32 In.
$207

Austin Auction Gallery

Wood Carving, Mask, Antelope, Elongated Nose, Tapered Chin, 6 Vertical Spikes, Africa, 31 x 10 In.
$266

Austin Auction Gallery

Wood Carving, Mask, Rangda, Queen Of The Demons, Bulging Eyes, Protruding Tongue, Multicolor, 45 In.
$295

Austin Auction Gallery

Wood Carving, Panel, Figural Scene, Pierced Lattice, Metal Screening, On Stand, 1700-1800s, 73 x 56 In.
$625

Charlton Hall Auctions

Wood Carving, Panel, Wall, Jacaranda Abstract, 39 x 18¾ In.
$488

Neal Auction Company

Wood Carving, Plaque, Deer Head, Antlers, Glass Eyes, 2 Rifles, Hunters Bag, Black Forest, c.1870, 31 x 18 In.
$4,500

Cottone Auctions

Wood Carving, Plaque, Eagle, Spread Wings, Banner, E Pluribus Unum, Shield, Multicolor, Early 1900s, 18 In.
$2,750

Eldred's

Wood Carving, Plaque, Fish, Multicolor, Painted, Rectangular, Frame, 12 x 48 In.
$406

Kamelot Auctions

Wood Carving, Saint Peter, Blue Robe, White Cape, Metal Halo, Late 1800s, 50 x 8 x 16 In.
$748

Forsythes' Auctions

Wood Carving, Santo, Saint Dominic, Multicolor, Mounted, Ebonized Plinth, 1800s, 13¾ In.
$413

Leland Little Auctions

575

W

Wood Carving, Santo, Virgin Mary, Crowned, Satin Dress, Multicolor, Spanish Colonial, 1800s, 23 In. $767

Austin Auction Gallery

Wood Carving, Seal, Outstretched Flippers, Glass Eyes, Life Size, 38 In. $1,125

Eldred's

Wood Carving, Uncle Sam, Holding Box, Flat Full Body, Mounted, Pine, Painted, 1910s, 73 In. $488

Pook & Pook

Mariner, Standing, Anchor, Painted, Square Base, 1910s, 34 In.	313
Mask, Antelope Headdress, Wrought Iron Straps, Steel Disc Eyes, Bambara, 1800s, 16 x 31 In.	2340
Mask, Antelope, Elongated Nose, Tapered Chin, 6 Vertical Spikes, Africa, 31 x 10 In. .... *illus*	266
Mask, Festival, Kuba Mukanga, Zaire, Elephant, Beadwork & Cowrie Shells, 1900s, 21 x 26 In...	413
Mask, Rangda, Queen Of The Demons, Bulging Eyes, Protruding Tongue, Multicolor, 45 In. *illus*	295
Mask, Senufo, Fire Spitter, Animal, Tusks, Shells, Africa, 39 ½ In.	325
Mask, Water Buffalo Head, Hollow, Copper Wire Eyes, Beaded, Africa, 26 x 18 x 11 In.	295
Panel, Figural Scene, Pierced Lattice, Metal Screening, On Stand, 1700-1800s, 73 x 56 In. *illus*	625
Panel, Oak, Fruit, Splines At Top, Grinning Gibbons, England, 25 ¼ x 17 ½ In.	468
Panel, Palace Battle Scene, Warriors, Horse, Gilt, Chinese, 8 x 16 ½ In.	115
Panel, Wall, Jacaranda Abstract, 39 x 18 ¾ In. *illus*	488
Panel, Wall, Oak, Eagle, Marked, Era Industries Inc., Evelyn & Jerome Ackerman, 12 x 9 In.	281
Panel, Woman, Long Hair, Touching Her Mouth, Signed, C. Zerepak, 20 x 12 ½ In.	24
Plaque, American Eagle, Spread Wings, Flag, Gilt, Paul White, 48 In.	1000
Plaque, Cape Cod, Fishing Shacks, Sailboat, Lighthouse, Ropework Frame, Late 1900s, 33 x 73 In.	625
Plaque, Codfish, Mahogany, Brown Stain, 1900s, 23 In.	938
Plaque, Deer Head, Antlers, Glass Eyes, 2 Rifles, Hunters Bag, Black Forest, c.1870, 31 x 18 In. ..*illus*	4500
Plaque, Eagle, American Shield & Banner, Distressed Paint, c.1950, 48 x 16 In.	900
Plaque, Eagle, Bellamy Style, Painted, Gilt, Red, White, Blue Shield, Early 1900s, 5 x 26 In. .	1063
Plaque, Eagle, Spread Wings, Banner, E Pluribus Unum, Shield, Multicolor, Early 1900s, 18 In. . *illus*	2750
Plaque, Eagle, Spread Wings, Clutching Union Shield, c.1975, 12 ½ x 44 In.	761
Plaque, Eagle, Spread Wings, God Bless America, Flag, 3 Stars, Painted, 33 x 18 In.	148
Plaque, Eagle, Spread Wings, Hollow, Water Gilt, Hanging, Early 1800s, 21 x 26 ½ x 8 In.	1287
Plaque, Eagle, Spread Wings, Shield, Arrow, Multicolor, 1900s, 15 x 44 ½ In.	768
Plaque, Eagle, Spread Wings, Signed, H.C. Myers, Pa., 1950s, 26 ½ In.	163
Plaque, Fish, Multicolor, Painted, Rectangular, Frame, 12 x 48 In. *illus*	406
Plaque, Rectangular, Eel Trap, Lobster, Sea Motifs, Frame, 24 x 42 ½ In.	250
Plaque, Songbirds, Perched, Tree, Leaves, Vernon B. Smith, 16 In.	1125
Rooster, Black, Red & Orange Paint, Standing, Circular Base, 1996, 19 ½ In.	46
Ruffed Grouse, Painted Plumage, Rectangular Base, Frank Finney, Late 1900s, 9 In.	2400
Saint Francis Of Assisi, Saint's Head, Tonsure, Split Beard, Glass Eyes, Italy, 12 ¼ In.	1989
Saint John The Baptist, Rectangular Plinth, Multicolor, Continental, 1700s, 24 ⅝ In.	1188
Saint Peter, Blue Robe, White Cape, Metal Halo, Late 1800s, 50 x 8 x 16 In. *illus*	748
Santo, Christ, Seated, Glass Eyes, Tin Halo, Black Glass Bead Rosary, 1900s, 18 x 8 x 6 In.	374
Santo, Franciscan Friar, Painted, Multicolor, Standing, Pedestal Base, 41 In.	413
Santo, Saint Dominic, Multicolor, Mounted, Ebonized Plinth, 1800s, 13 ¾ In. *illus*	413
Santo, Saint George Slaying The Dragon, Multicolor, Continental, 29 ½ In.	640
Santo, Virgin Mary, Crowned, Satin Dress, Multicolor, Spanish Colonial, 1800s, 23 In. *illus*	767
Sarcophagus, King Tutankhamen's, Miniature, Paint, Gold Ground, S. Marquez, 1900s, 38 In.	1625
Seal, Outstretched Flippers, Glass Eyes, Life Size, 38 In. *illus*	1125
Senufo, Bird, Painted, Burkina Faso, West Africa, 94 In.	2478
Sperm Whale, Painted, Black, White Teeth, Clark G. Voorhees Jr., 17 ¾ In.	1625
Spirit House, Teak, Stepped Stairs, Painted, Lacquered, Beaded, Thailand, 11 x 14 In.	213
Statue, Jesus Of Prague, Metal Crown, Inset Glass Eyes, Holding, Globus Cruciger, 1950s, 14 In..	502
Triptych, 3 Panels, Folding, Crucifixion, Cherub Crest, Painted, 21 ½ x 26 In.	295
Uncle Sam, Holding Box, Flat Full Body, Mounted, Pine, Painted, 1910s, 73 In. *illus*	488
Village People Playing Panpipe, Musical Instrument, 1900s, 41 x 36 x 11 In.	384
Virgin Mary, Crowned, Serpent Coiled Around Base, Multicolor, 1800s, 15 In.	120
Vishnu & Garuda, Canopy Of Feathers, Tortoise & Nagas, Bali, 41 In.	295
Wall Pocket, Dog, Hunting, Leaves, Pine, Painted, c.1900, 14 x 11 ¼ In.	2318
Wall Sculpture, Race Horse, Multicolor, Acrylic Resin, Custom Cut Panels, Contemporary, 29 x 13 In.	118
Whale, Black, Mounted, Driftwood Base, Signed, Adamo, Massachusetts, 1900s, 9 ¼ In.	125
Whale, Copper Fins, Mounted, Block Base, 24 In.	40
Winged Angel, Holding Grapes, Outstretched Hand, Canada, 1800s, 9 x 29 In. *illus*	562
Woman, Effigy, Standing, Rectangular Base, Africa, Early 1900s, 16 ¼ In.	12
Woman, Holding Shell Basin, Flower Garlands, Gray, Pedestal Base, 43 x 14 In.	5
Woman, Nude, Concrete Base, Thomas H. Williams, Georgia, c.1980, 58 In.	40
Woman, Nude, Lying Down, Oval Slate, 23 x 6 x 8 In.	5
Woman, Saint, Kneeling, Nativity Figure, Gilt, Painted, Spain, 1800s, 11 x 9 In. *illus*	50

WOODEN

Wooden wares were used in all parts of the home. Wood was used for many containers and tools. Small wooden pieces are called *treenware* in England, but the term *woodenware* is more common in the United States. Additional pieces may be found in the Advertising, Kitchen, and Tool categories.

Barrel, Primitive, Single Hollow Trunk, Applied Base, Early 1900s, 31 x 19 In.	443
Basket, Trug, Garden, Bentwood Top Handle, Painted, F.P., France, 13 x 17 x 11½ In. . *illus*	118
Berry Bucket, Shaker Style, Iron Straps, Bail Handle, 1800s, 3½ x 4½ In.	367
Bookrack, Whimsical, 2 Gnomes, Owl, Oak Trees, Leaves, Acorns, 13 In.	630
Bowl, Ash Burl, 1800s, 19¼ In.	1125
Bowl, Burl, Asymmetrical, Organic Shape, Red, Painted, Treenware, Late 1700s, 13 In. *illus*	1287
Bowl, Burl, Outer Rim Band, Grooved Foot, Treenware, Late 1700s, 3⅜ x 14¾ x 14½ In.	702
Bowl, Burl, Thin Walled, 2-Ring, Low Turned Foot, 1800s, 6¼ x 16½ In.	1875
Bowl, Burl, Turned Ash, Old Refinishing, Scrubbed Surface, 1800s, 2½ x 9¼ In.	480
Bowl, Burl, Turned, Molded Rim, New England, 1800s, 5 x 15½ In.	1098
Bowl, Burl, Turned, Mushroom Shape Finial, Underfoot, 1800s, 6 x 7½ In. *illus*	1440
Bowl, Burl, Warm Coffee, Shaped Rim & Foot, Carved, 1700s, 6½ x 17½ In.	1989
Bowl, Chopping, Carved Maple, Oval Cut, Early 1800s, 7 x 32 x 16½ In.	300
Bowl, Ebony, Carved, Alexandre Noll, France, c.1950, 1¾ In.	4063
Bowl, Grapevine, Forward Arrow, Mark, Biltmore Industries, Asheville, 3½ In.	633
Bowl, Maple, Burl, Handle, American Indians, Early 1800s, 3½ In.	375
Bowl, Maple, Turned, Blue, Gray, Raised Edge, Wafer Foot, New England, Late 1700s, 22 In.	1375
Bowl, Maple, Turned, Scrubbed Interior Finish, Blue, 3 x 12¾ x 11¾ In.	138
Bowl, Teak, Round, Footed, Henning Koppel, Denmark, c.1965, 4 In.	563
Bracket, Wall, Eagle, Perched, Raised Wings, Shaped Shelf, Gilt, 1900s, 12 x 10 In., Pair	885
Brushpot, Zitan Wood, Tapered, Cylindrical, Chinese, 7 x 6¼ In.	644
Bucket, Circular Hoop, Stave, Iron Bail Handle, Yellow, Black, 1800s, 5½ x 9 In.	594
Bucket, Green Paint, Swing Handle, Pine Staves, Hardwood Bands, Inset Base, Early 1800s, 9 In.	625
Bucket, Mahogany, Brass, 3 Bands, Bail Handle, Georgian Style, Early 1900s, 13 In.	148
Bucket, Pine, Tongue & Groove, 2 Metal Bands, Bail Handle, Late 1800s, 9 x 11¾ In.	439
Bucket, Red Paint, Metal Mount, Handle, 14 In. *illus*	37
Bucket, Shaker Style, Tin Strap Bands, Bail Handle, Painted, Mustard, 1850s, 6 x 7¼ In.	2040
Bucket, Slats, Brass Liner, Bail Handle, 13 In. *illus*	443
Bucket, Stave Construction, Green Ground, Lift-Up Lid, Applied Handle, 1800s, 10 In.	175
Bucket, Storage, Treen, Bentwood, Cylindrical, 3 Lapped Hoops, 1850s, 11½ In.	164
Bucket, Sugar, Lid, Bent Hickory, Maple, Swing Wood Handle, Stamped, 7 x 11¼ In.	518
Butler's Tray, Bellhop, Standing, Painted, Diamond Shape Base, c.1930, 32 In., Pair .. *illus*	207
Butler's Tray, Mahogany, Carved, Dovetailed, Leaves, Scrolled Handles, 1880s, 4 x 23 x 15 In. *illus*	1521
Canister, Lid, Peaseware, Turned Body, Bail Handle, Finial, 1800s, 11 x 14 In.	3660
Canister, Lid, Treenware, Barrel Shape, Angled Rim, Finial, 1850s, 14½ x 10 In. *illus*	129
Carrier, Dog, Dome Top, Handles, Casters, Absalom Backus, Jr., c.1902, 28 x 19 In. *illus*	1125
Chest, Hinged Lid, Decals, Flowers, Maroon Ground, Turned Feet, Lehnware, Miniature	1280
Child Minder, Twins, 2-Sided, Brown, Square Foot, Chinese, 23 x 30 x 26½ In.	125
Coaster, Wine, Silver Mount, Strapwork Rims, Omar Ramsden, London, 1935, 6¾ In., Pair.	3780
Compote, Beaded Rim, Carved Bears, Glass Eyes, Black Forest, c.1885, 9 In. *illus*	1560
Compote, Oak, Treenware, Thick Walled, Original Painted Flowers Band, Late 1800s, 6 x 11 In.	132
Container, Bulbous Shape, Circular Lid, Bail Handle, Peaseware, 11 In.	406
Container, Lid, Mustard Ground, Treenware, c.1850, 10 In.	3120
Cup, Flared Rim, Peach Ground, Flowers, Turned Foot, Lehnware, Joseph Long Lehn, 4 In.	438
Cup, Lid, Saffron, Poplar, Turned, Finial, Joseph Lehn, 5 In.	1830
Firkin, Finger Lapped Bands, Stave, Iron Tacks, Bentwood Bail Handle, 1800s, 14 x 15 x 15 In.	791
Firkin, Lid, Iron, Swing Handle, Painted, Red, 1800s, 7¾ In.	75
Firkin, Lid, Painted, Swing Handle, 7¼ In.	107
Firkin, Lid, Pine, Copper Tacks, Bentwood Handle, 9¾ In.	123
Firkin, Lid, Pine, Tongue & Groove Staves, Green, 1800s, 8¾ x 9 In.	200
Firkin, Lid, Swing Handle, Marked, C. Wilder & Son, Massachusetts, 1800s, 15 In.	128
Grain Bin, Lift Lid, Canted Lower Front, Double Well Interior, Painted, 1900, 44 x 48 x 25 In. . *illus*	570
Humidor, Cigar, Carved, Eagle, Glass Eyes, Deer Heads, Ram & Goat, Black Forest, 23 In.	3000
Humidor, Cigar, Mahogany, Brass, Mounted, Monogram, GCW, Early 1900s, 9 x 16 In.	118

WOODEN

Wood Carving, Winged Angel, Holding Grapes, Outstretched Hand, Canada, 1800s, 9 x 29 In.
$5,625

Eldred's

Wood Carving, Woman, Saint, Kneeling, Nativity Figure, Gilt, Painted, Spain, 1800s, 11 x 9 In.
$502

Austin Auction Gallery

Wooden, Basket, Trug, Garden, Bentwood Top Handle, Painted, F.P., France, 13 x 17 x 11½ In.
$118

Austin Auction Gallery

Wooden, Bowl, Burl, Asymmetrical, Organic Shape, Red, Painted, Treenware, Late 1700s, 13 In.
$1,287

Jeffrey S. Evans & Associates

W

Wooden, Bowl, Burl, Turned, Mushroom Shape Finial, Underfoot, 1800s, 6 x 7 ½ In.
$1,440

Garth's Auctioneers & Appraisers

Wooden, Bucket, Red Paint, Metal Mount, Handle, 14 In.
$37

Apple Tree Auction Center

Wooden, Bucket, Slats, Brass Liner, Bail Handle, 13 In.
$443

Leland Little Auctions

Wooden, Butler's Tray, Bellhop, Standing, Painted, Diamond Shape Base, c.1930, 32 In., Pair
$207

Leland Little Auctions

Wooden, Butler's Tray, Mahogany, Carved, Dovetailed, Leaves, Scrolled Handles, 1880s, 4 x 23 x 15 In.
$1,521

Jeffrey S. Evans & Associates

Wooden, Canister, Lid, Treenware, Barrel Shape, Angled Rim, Finial, 1850s, 14 ½ x 10 In.
$129

Jeffrey S. Evans & Associates

Wooden, Carrier, Dog, Dome Top, Handles, Casters, Absalom Backus, Jr., c.1902, 28 x 19 In.
$1,125

Eldred's

Wooden, Compote, Beaded Rim, Carved Bears, Glass Eyes, Black Forest, c.1885, 9 In.
$1,560

Cottone Auctions

Wooden, Grain Bin, Lift Lid, Canted Lower Front, Double Well Interior, Painted, 1900, 44 x 48 x 25 In.
$570

Garth's Auctioneers & Appraisers

W

Wooden, Ice Bucket, Teak, Pegged Top Handle, Red Liner, Signed, Dansk, 15 In.
$81

Richard D. Hatch & Associates

Wooden, Jardiniere, Napoleon III, Burl, Gilt Metal, Tole Liner, Late 1800s, 7 x 16 x 10 In.
$640

Hindman

Wooden, Jewelry Box, Dome Top, Spanish Galleon, 3 Drawers, Handles, Leather Clad, 11 x 14 x 8 In.
$767

Austin Auction Gallery

Wooden, Mannequin, Arm, Hand, Carved, Ebonized Base, Belgium, c.1940, 18 In.
$325

Leland Little Auctions

Wooden, Mannequin, Jointed, Carved Base, 78 x 30 ¾ x 25 In.
$563

Kamelot Auctions

Wooden, Model, J. Peterman Co., Metal, Working Gears, Marked, Paolo Bucciareli, 8 x 19 In.
$118

Leland Little Auctions

Wooden, Paddle, Burl, Clamshell Shape, Pierced Handle, 1700s, 5 ¼ In.
$4,500

Garth's Auctioneers & Appraisers

Wooden, Propeller, Airplane, Metal Edge, Sensenich Bros., Lititz, Pennsylvania, 70 In.
$563

Pook & Pook

Wooden, Tray, Apple, Pine, Canted Sides, Red, Yellow Sponge, John Boyer, 1800s, 4¾ x 9 x 9¼ In.
$3,660

Pook & Pook

Wooden, Tray, Dogwood Blossoms, Bees, Metal Tack Feet, Artisans Shop, Early 1900s, 18 x 10 In.
$1,046

Brunk Auctions

W

Wooden, Tray, Rosewood, Dragon, Chinese Silver Inlay, Rectangular, 14½ x 22 In.
$825

Pook & Pook

Wooden, Trolley Seat, Iron Stem, Base, Chicago Hdwr. & Foundry Co., c.1920, 30 x 10 In., 6 Piece
$677

Rich Penn Auctions

Wooden, Vase, Composite, Metal Interior, R & Y Augousti, 21¼ In.
$156

Susanin's Auctioneers & Appraisers

W

Ice Bucket, Teak, Pegged Top Handle, Red Liner, Signed, Dansk, 15 In. *illus*	81
Jar, Maple, Turned, Fitted Dome Lid, Bulbous, 4 x 7 In.	546
Jardiniere, Napoleon III, Burl, Gilt Metal, Tole Liner, Late 1800s, 7 x 16 x 10 In. *illus*	640
Jewelry Box, Dome Top, Spanish Galleon, 3 Drawers, Handles, Leather Clad, 11 x 14 x 8 In. *illus*	767
Mannequin, Arm, Hand, Carved, Ebonized Base, Belgium, c.1940, 18 In. *illus*	325
Mannequin, Artist's, Articulated, Carved, Lacquered, France, c.1920, 10½ In.	1500
Mannequin, Jointed, Carved Base, 78 x 30¾ x 25 In. *illus*	563
Model, J. Peterman Co., Metal, Working Gears, Marked, Paolo Bucciarelli, 8 x 19 In. *illus*	118
Model, Lighthouse, Carved, Light Socket, Removable Dome, Painted, 19 In.	148
Model, Wagon, Mahogany, Slatted Canopy, Sides, Metal Rim, Wheels, 1800s, 19 x 36 x 13 In.	556
Mold, Candle, Carved Tubes, Stamped, L. Bezemer & Zn. Helmond, Holland, Late 1800s, 22 In.	38
Mold, Cigar, 20 Cigars, Marked, Otto Boenicke, Berlin, 22 In., 2 Piece	43
Mortar & Pestle, Primitive, Worn, Domed Foot, Turned Pestle, 1800s	125
Paddle, Burl, Clamshell Shape, Pierced Handle, 1700s, 5¼ In. *illus*	4500
Pail, Good Girl, Cream Paint, Stars, Dog, Lion, Bail Handle, 1800s, 3¾ x 4¾ In.	848
Pail, Red, Yellow Bands, Wire Handle, Child, Murdock & Co., Late 1800s, 3¾ In.	213
Propeller, Airplane, Laminated Wood, Metal Edge, Sensenich, 72 In.	800
Propeller, Airplane, Metal Edge, Sensenich Bros., Lititz, Pennsylvania, 70 In. *illus*	563
Propeller, Airplane, Metal Hub, 105 x 12 x 9½ In.	2214
Stand, Bible, Hinged, Hand Cut, Foot & Shelf, Painted, 17 In.	71
Sugar Bucket, Lid, Painted, Salmon Swirls, Decorated Iron Bands, Joseph Lehn, c.1870, 9 In.	5124
Tray, Apple, Pine, Canted Sides, Red, Yellow Sponge, John Boyer, 1800s, 4¾ x 9 x 9¼ In. *illus*	3660
Tray, Black Lacquer, Rounded Corners, White Forearm Picture, Piero Fornasetti, 23 x 10 In.	720
Tray, Dogwood Blossoms, Bees, Metal Tack Feet, Artisans Shop, Early 1900s, 18 x 10 In. *illus*	1046
Tray, Gallery, Mahogany, Marquetry, Floral, Brass Handles, Late 1800s, 2 x 22 In.	384
Tray, Rosewood, Dragon, Chinese Silver Inlay, Rectangular, 14½ x 22 In. *illus*	825
Trolley Seat, Iron Stem, Base, Chicago Hdwr. & Foundry Co., c.1920, 30 x 10 In., 6 Piece *illus*	677
Tub, Burl, Turned, 4 Standing Ribs, Friction Fitted Cut Lid, Patina, 5⅝ x 4½ In.	259
Urn, Affixed Lid, Oak, 2 Putti Finial, Scrolling Leaves, Pedestal Foot, Late 1800s, 20 In.	944
Urn, Lid, Turned Mahogany, Finial, Footed, 1800s, 9¼ In.	100
Vase, Composite, Metal Interior, R & Y Augousti, 21¼ In. *illus*	156
Vase, Tulipwood, Turned, Doughnut Shape, Inscribed, Ed Moulthrop, 4¼ x 6¼ In.	1053
Watch Hutch, Curly, Bird's-Eye Maple, Molded Base, 4 Steeples, Shelf, 1830s, 14 x 9 x 7 In.	900
Watch Hutch, Walnut, Broken Arched Crest, Line, Circle Inlays, c.1800, 8¼ x 5 In. *illus*	9760

WORCESTER

Worcester porcelains were made in Worcester, England, from 1751. The firm went through many name changes and eventually, in 1862, became The Royal Worcester Porcelain Company Ltd. Collectors often refer to Dr. Wall, Barr, Flight, and other names that indicate time periods or artists at the factory. It became part of Royal Worcester Spode Ltd. in 1976. The company was bought by the Portmeirion Group in 2009. Related pieces may be found in the Royal Worcester category.

Bowl, Reticulated, Scalloped Rim, Blue Flowers, White Ground, Dr. Wall, 2½ x 9½ In.	207
Mug, Blue Scale Ground, Multicolor, Bird, 1800s, 4⅛ In., Pair	325
Mug, White, Blue Flowers, Fruit, Leaves, c.1770, 4 In. *illus*	128
Plate, Blue Scale, Exotic Birds, Dr. Wall, c.1770-80, 7⅝ In. *illus*	192
Plate, Round, Lion, Pink Roses, Gilt, Enamel, Auspicio Regis Et Senatus Anglin, c.1816, 9 In.	1638
Platter, Oval, Painted, Monochrome, Hope Service, Ship, Gilt Stars, 14⅜ In.	6048
Saucer, Round, Shells, Gold Rim, Flight & Barr, c.1820, 6 In., Pair *illus*	16
Sugar, Gilt Imari Palette, Barr, Flight & Barr, c.1805, 4¾ x 7⅛ In.	57

WORLD WAR

World War I and World War II souvenirs are collected today. Be careful not to store anything that includes live ammunition. Your local police will tell you how to dispose of the explosives. See also Sword and Trench Art.

WORLD WAR I

Box, Hinged Lid, Oak, Marquetry, Molded Edge, Allied Flags, Monogram, 4½ x 8½ x 6 In. 23

Wooden, Watch Hutch, Walnut, Broken Arched Crest, Line, Circle Inlays, c.1800, 8¼ x 5 In.
$9,760

Pook & Pook

Worcester, Mug, White, Blue Flowers, Fruit, Leaves, c.1770, 4 In.
$128

Hindman

Worcester, Plate, Blue Scale, Exotic Birds, Dr. Wall, c.1770-80, 7⅝ In.
$192

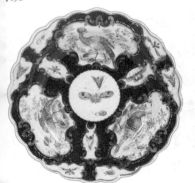

Ideal Auction Company

Worcester, Saucer, Round, Shells, Gold Rim, Flight & Barr, c.1820, 6 In., Pair
$166

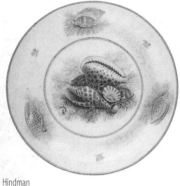

Hindman

World War I, Helmet, Pickelhaube, Leather & Brass, Painted, Eagle, c.1910, 8½ x 7 In.
$300

Michaan's Auctions

World War I, Poster, Keep 'Em Going!, U.S. Railroad Administration Anti-German, c.1918, 19¾ x 29½ In.
$594

Cowan's Auctions

World War I, Poster, Keep Him Free, Buy War Saving Stamps, Charles Livingston Bull, Lucite Frame, c.1918
$594

Charlton Hall Auctions

World War I, Poster, Victory Liberty Loan, Lithograph, Woman, Holding Flag, Frame, 1917, 44 x 31 In
$156

Garth's Auctioneers & Appraisers

World War I, Visor Cap, U.S. Marine, Sweat Band Interior, Leather Chin Strip, Brass, Size 7
$502

Leland Little Auctions

W

World War II, Badge, Navigator, U.S. Army Air Corps, Wing, Engraved, J.R. Gaunt, 3¼ x ¼ In.

$50

Cowan's Auctions

World War II, Bolo, Wood Handle, U.S. Marine Corps., Collins & Co., 16½ In.

$177

Austin Auction Gallery

World War II, Dagger, Brown Handle, Nazi Eagle, Scabbard, Hartkopf & Co., Germany, 14¼ In.

$384

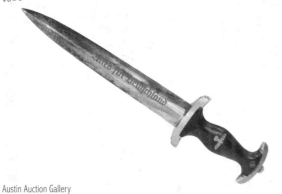

Austin Auction Gallery

World War II, Grenade, Ceramic, Fragmentation, Brown Glaze, Japan, 3¼ In.

$81

Blackwell Auctions

World War II, Medal, Order Of Saint Stanislaus, Cross, Gold, Burgundy Red, Porcelain Plaque, 2 In.

$2,858

Nadeau's Auction Gallery

World War II, Flag, Wool, 48 Machine Sewn Stars, 4 Iron Grommets, Invasion Of Okinawa, 28 x 52 In.

$3,500

Cowan's Auctions

Box, Military, Iron Safe, Side Handles, Initials Q.M.C., U.S.A., c.1917, 15 ½ x 27 x 15 In.	443
Helmet, Black Leather, Saxon Starburst, Applied Finial, Germany, c.1915, 7 In.	322
Helmet, Brass, Black, Kingdom Of Saxony, Gilt Toned, Germany, 8 x 7 In.	688
Helmet, Pickelhaube, Leather & Brass, Painted, Eagle, c.1910, 8 ½ x 7 In. .... *illus*	300
Poster, Civilians, Jewish Welfare Board, Black Frame, 32 x 21 ½ In..........................	83
Poster, Journee De Paris, 14 Juillet 1915, Black & White, Frame, 51 x 33 ½ In.	95
Poster, Keep 'Em Going!, U.S. Railroad Administration Anti-German, c.1918, 19 ¾ x 29 ½ In. *illus*	594
Poster, Keep Him Free, Buy War Saving Stamps, Charles Livingston Bull, Lucite Frame, c.1918 .*illus*	594
Poster, Man, Eagles, Fight World Famine, The Boys Working Reserve, Frame, 27 x 18 In.......	207
Poster, U.S. Fuel Administration, Order Your Coal Now, Black & Yellow, Litho, Frame, 28 x 20 In.	157
Poster, Uncle Sam, I Want You For The U.S. Army, Signed, J.M. Flagg, 1917, 40 x 30 In...........	3125
Poster, Victory Liberty Loan, Lithograph, Woman, Holding Flag, Frame, 1917, 44 x 31 In. *illus*	156
Sign, Victory, Orange Text, Carved, Painted, Wood Frame, c.1918, 14 x 64 ¼ In....................	2520
Stereoscope Slides, Classeur Verascopique, Battlefield Scenes, Fitted Slat Case, Early 1900s, 49 Slides	113
Visor Cap, U.S. Marine, Sweat Band Interior, Leather Chin Strip, Brass, Size 7 .... *illus*	502

WORLD WAR II

Badge, Navigator, U.S. Army Air Corps, Wing, Engraved, J.R. Gaunt, 3 ¼ x ¼ In. .... *illus*	50
Bolo, Wood Handle, U.S. Marine Corps., Collins & Co., 16 ½ In. .... *illus*	177
Camp Flag, 48 Stars, Inscribed 442 Inf. 100 Batl Nisei Proud USA, Fringe, 1946, 32 x 54 In..	2000
Dagger, Brown Handle, Nazi Eagle, Scabbard, Hartkopf & Co., Germany, 14 ¼ In. .... *illus*	384
Flag, Wool, 48 Machine Sewn Stars, 4 Iron Grommets, Invasion Of Okinawa, 28 x 52 In. *illus*	3500
Flight Jacket, U.S. Army Air Corps, A2, Leather, Insignias, Patches, c.1942	2340
Grenade, Ceramic, Fragmentation, Brown Glaze, Japan, 3 ¼ In. .... *illus*	81
Jacket, Bomber, 8th Air Force Patch, Leather, Paint, Airplanes, Madame Shoo, Size 40	4720
Jacket, U.S. Navy, Dark Brown, Buttons, Zipper, Pockets, 24 In.	236
Medal, Military, Silver Maltese Cross, Pale Blue Enamel, Crown, Russia, 1803, 1 ⅝ In..........	293
Medal, Order Of Saint Stanislaus, Cross, Gold, Burgundy Red, Porcelain Plaque, 2 In. *illus*	2858
Military Sword, Ray Skin Grip, Fabric Wrap, Plain Tsuba, Wooden Saya, Nakago, Japan, 38 In..	295
Parachute, Air Force, In Backpack, Canvas & Leather Straps, Reliance Mfg. Co., 1943	704
Poster, American Red Cross, For Their Sake Join Now, Walter Beach Humphrey, c.1940, 19 x 12 In.	75
Poster, Join The Lee Navy Volunteers, Lithographic, Frame, c.1942, 29 ¾ x 23 ½ In. ... *illus*	649
Stein, Hitler, Swastika, Pewter, Germany, 1934, 6 In..	85
Sword, Cavalry, Type 32, Metal Scabbard, Japan, 36 ½ In..	400
Sword, Military, Steel Blade, Wood Handle, Silk Wrapping, Japan, 27 In...........................	649
Sword, Wrapped Sharkskin, Kane Zane, Seki Arsenal, Japan, 25 x 1 ³⁄₁₆ In.....................	863
Telescope, Alidade, U.S. Navy, Oak Case, Brass Plate, Kollmorgan Optical, 1942, 6 x 15 In....	266

WORLD'S FAIR

World's Fair souvenirs from all of the fairs are collected. The first fair was the Great Exhibition of 1851 in London. Some other important exhibitions and fairs include Philadelphia, 1876 (Centennial); Chicago, 1893 (World's Columbian); Buffalo, 1901 (Pan-American); St. Louis, 1904 (Louisiana Purchase); Portland, 1905 (Lewis & Clark Centennial Exposition); Seattle, 1909 (Alaska-Yukon-Pacific Exposition); San Francisco, 1915 (Panama-Pacific); Paris (International Exposition of Modern Decorative and Industrial Arts), 1925; Philadelphia, 1926 (Sesqui-centennial); Chicago, 1933 (Century of Progress); Cleveland, 1936 (Great Lakes); San Francisco, 1939 (Golden Gate International); New York, 1939 (World of Tomorrow); Seattle, 1962 (Century 21); New York, 1964; Montreal, 1967; Knoxville (Energy Turns the World) 1982; New Orleans, 1984; Tsukuba, Japan, 1985; Vancouver, Canada, 1986; Brisbane, Australia, 1988; Seville, Spain, 1992; Genoa, Italy, 1992; Seoul, South Korea, 1993; Lisbon, Portugal, 1998; Hanover, Germany, 2000; Shanghai, China, 2010; and Milan, Italy, 2015. Memorabilia of fairs include directories, pictures, fabrics, ceramics, etc. Memorabilia from other similar celebrations may be listed in the Souvenir category.

Bank, 1893, Chicago, Columbus, Seated, Indian Pops Out, J. & E. Stevens, c.1893, 8 x 3 x 6 ½ In. .*illus*	390
Cigarette Case, 1933, Chicago, Patinated Brass, Woodgrain Finish, Money Clip, 3 ⅜ x 2 ⅞ In.	55

World War II, Poster, Join The Lee Navy Volunteers, Lithographic, Frame, c.1942, 29 ¾ x 23 ½ In.
$649

Leland Little Auctions

World's Fair, Bank, 1893, Chicago, Columbus, Seated, Indian Pops Out, J. & E. Stevens, c.1893, 8 x 3 x 6 ½ In.
$390

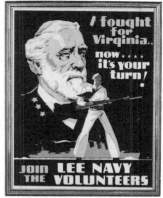

Morphy Auctions

Wristwatch, Blancpain, 18K Yellow Gold, Roman Numerals, 3-Date Calendar, Leather, Swiss, c.1980
$2,560

Morphy Auctions

W

This is an edited listing of current prices. Visit **Kovels.com** to check thousands of prices from previous years and sign up for free information on trends, tips, reproductions, marks, and more.

Wristwatch, Cartier, 18K Yellow Gold, Automatic, Sapphire Crystals, White Guilloche, 7 ¼ In.
$8,820

Morphy Auctions

Wristwatch, Ebel, Round, 14K Gold, Diamonds Edge, Marked, Swiss, Woman's, 1900s, ½ In.
$1,063

Bruneau & Co. Auctioneers

Wristwatch, Gucci, Chiodo, 18K Yellow Gold Case, Diamond Set Bezel, Mother-Of-Pearl Dial, 6 ½ In.
$3,480

Cottone Auctions

Wristwatch, LeCoultre, Futurematic, Port Hole, 14K Gold Face, 18K Gold Band, 17 Jewel
$3,304

Cottone Auctions

Wristwatch, Movado, 14K White Gold, Mother-Of-Pearl Dial, 36 Round Diamonds, Woman's, 1900s, 7 ½ In.
$1,287

Jeffrey S. Evans & Associates

Wristwatch, Patek Philippe, 18K Gold, Black, Leather, Roman Numerals, Calatrava, 1 ¼ In.
$8,750

Eldred's

Wristwatch, Patek Philippe, 18K Yellow Gold, Leather, 18 Jewel, Marked, Switzerland, c.1960s, 1 1/50 In.
$2,394

Morphy Auctions

> **TIP**
> *Wind your watch clock-wise. Don't wind it while it is on your wrist.*

Wristwatch, Rolex, Presidential, Oyster Perpetual Datejust, 18K Yellow Gold, Diamond, Woman's, 1 1/32 In.
$8,050

Blackwell Auctions

Wristwatch, Rolex, Steel, Oyster Perpetual, Arabic Numeral, Engraved, F.P. Bender, 1 ¼ In.
$885

Austin Auction Gallery

Compact, 1939, New York, Enamel, Trylon & Perisphere, Black Border, Mirror, Powder Puff	75
Cup, 1915, San Francisco, Thirteenth Labor Of Hercules, Ceramic Art Co., 6 1/8 x 3 1/2 In.........	1815
Fan, 1876, Philadelphia, Centennial, Flag, Eagle, 2-Sided, Shadowbox, 15 1/2 x 26 In.............	288
Paint Set, 1964, New York, 24 Paints, Brush, Hasbro, Box	100
Pillow Cover, 1909, Seattle, Alaska Yukon Pacific Expo, Linen, 17 1/2 x 30 In.	180
Plate, 1915, San Francisco, Panama-Pacific, Buildings, Blue & White, 1915, 10 In.	75
Plate, 1939, New York, Potter At Wheel, Signed Ellen..................................	107
Ribbon, 1893, Chicago, 400th Anniversary, Discovery Of America, White, Frame, 7 1/4 x 2 1/2 In.	225
Rose Bowl, 1893, Chicago, Peachblow, Ribbed Body, Mt. Washington, 2 3/4 x 3 In.	150
Toy, Bus, 1933, Chicago, Century Of Progress, Metal, Open Windows, Black Cab, 13 In..........	975

WPA

WPA is the abbreviation for Works Progress Administration, a program created by executive order in 1935 to provide jobs for millions of unemployed Americans. Artists were hired to create murals, paintings, drawings, and sculptures for public buildings. Pieces are marked *WPA* and may have the artist's name on them.

Charger, Matador, Ceramic, Signed, Fletcher Martin, c.1940, 12 1/2 In...............................	266
Sketch, Pencil, Railroad Workers, Signed, T.S., 1930s, 15 x 12 In.	625
Woodblock Print, Old Wharf, Wharf, Ladder, Shack, Donald Witherstine, c.1935, 18 x 15 In.	120

WRISTWATCH

Wristwatches came into use during World War I. Wristwatches are listed here by manufacturer or as advertising or character watches. Wristwatches may also be listed in other categories. Pocket watches are listed in the Watch category.

Blancpain, 18K Yellow Gold, Roman Numerals, 3-Date Calendar, Leather, Swiss, c.1980 *illus*	2560
Breitling Chronomat, Stainless Steel Case, Chocolate Brown Dial, Leather Band, 1 37/64 In..	1625
Cartier, 18K Yellow Gold, Automatic, Sapphire Crystals, White Guilloche, 7 1/4 In. .... *illus*	8820
Cartier, Stainless Steel, Mechanical, Automatic Winding, Steel Crown Cap, Woman's, 1 3/8 In.	938
Cartier, Tank, 18K Gold Plated, Roman Numeral, Leather Band, Woman's, Swiss, 7 1/2 x 53/16 In. ..	863
Cartier, Tank, Vermeil, Rectangular Dial, Leather Band, Swiss, Woman's, 1 x 7/8 In.	610
Chronograph, Joe Rodeo, Diamond, Roman Numeral, Stainless Steel Case, 1 27/32 x 35/64 In .	633
Corum Trapeze, Stainless Steel, Trapezoidal Case, Black Dial, Silvered Markers, Leather ...	720
Ebel, Round, 14K Gold, Diamonds Edge, Marked, Swiss, Woman's, 1900s, 1/2 In. .... *illus*	1063
Franck Muller, 18K Pink Gold, Number, Automatic, Leather, Switzerland, c.1995, 1 1/2 In.....	5040
Gucci, Chiodo, 18K Yellow Gold Case, Diamond Set Bezel, Mother-Of-Pearl Dial, 6 1/2 In. *illus*	3480
Hamilton, Platinum, Diamond, 14K White Gold Bracelet, Hinged Clasp, 6 3/4 In.	1534
Hamilton, Wadsworth, 14K Gold Cased, 19 Jewel, Lizard Bracelet, c.1947, 8 1/2 In.............	263
Hermes, Red, Leather, Goldtone, Roman Numerals, Marked, Bag, 1989, 7 In...................	375
Horizon, Marc Newson, 18K Rose Gold Case, Rubber Band, Ikepod, 2006, 44 mm Dial	6250
Invicta, 18K Yellow Gold, Numbers, Leather, Signed, Box, 1 3/4 x 2 In...........................	2432
LeCoultre, Futurematic, Port Hole, 14K Gold Face, 18K Gold Band, 17 Jewel .... *illus*	3304
Longines, 14K Gold, Square Face, Black Band, 1 x 1 1/2 In..	325
Longines, 14K Yellow Gold, 17 Jewel, Bracelet, c.1950, 6 1/4 x 1 In.	1521
Lucien Piccard, Seashark, 14K Yellow Gold, Tapered Hands, Leather Band, 1 11/32 x 3/4 In..... .	633
Movado, 14K White Gold, Mother-Of-Pearl Dial, 36 Round Diamonds, Woman's, 1900s, 7 1/2 In. *illus*	1287
Omega Speedmaster Schumacher, Chronograph, Stainless Steel, Yellow, 1996, 8 In.	1342
Omega, Art Deco Style, Diamonds, 14K White Gold Bracelet, Platinum Case, Woman's........	2124
Omega, Constellation, 18K Gold, Round Bezel, Leather Band, Woman's, Mid 1900s, 9 In...... .	1250
Omega, Stainless Steel, Sapphire Crystal, Chronometer, Seamaster Automatic, 11 3/4 In	2176
Patek Philippe, 18K Gold, Black, Leather, Roman Numerals, Calatrava, 1 1/4 In. .... *illus*	8750
Patek Philippe, 18K Yellow Gold, Leather, 18 Jewel, Marked, Switzerland, c.1960s, 1 In. ..... *illus*	2394
Patek Philippe, Platinum, 18 Jewel, 4 Diamonds, Painted Dial, Enamel Frame, Woman's, 1920, 1 In .	2300
Piaget, 14K White Gold, Diamond Hour Markers, Tapered Bracelet, Woman's, c.2005, 15/16 In..	4063
Rolex, 9K Yellow Gold, 17 Jewel, Speidel Bracelet, Swiss, Woman's, 1910s, 6 3/4 In.	410
Rolex, 18K Yellow Gold, Oyster Perpetual, Chronometer, Datejust, Diamonds, Woman's, 5 3/4 In..	5175
Rolex, Cellini, 18K White Gold, Gray, 3 Diamonds, Montres Rolex S.A., c.1976, 1 1/4 In.	3465
Rolex, Oyster Perpetual Date Just, Diamond Bezel, Stainless Bracelet	5605

WRISTWATCH

Wristwatch, Tiffany & Co., 18K Yellow Gold, Basket Weave Band, Hard Shell Case, Woman's, 1900s, 6 7/8 In.
$1,638

Jeffrey S. Evans & Associates

Wristwatch, Timex, 14K Gold, Turquoise, 2 Stones, Numbers, Boyd Tsosie, 1 x 4 3/4 In.
$2,360

Austin Auction Gallery

Wristwatch, Tissot, T-Classic, Stainless Steel, Date Indicator, Leather Band, 1853, 1 1/2 In.
$94

Austin Auction Gallery

W

Yellowware, Bowl, 3 Brown Band,
14 In.
$59

Copake Auction

Zanesville, Vase, La Moro, Molded
Leaves, Wild Roses, Matte Glaze,
W.F. Hall, 6 ¼ In.
$363

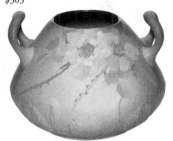

Humler & Nolan

Zsolnay, Bowl, Footed, Blue, Silver,
Green, Marbleized, Marked,
3 ¼ x 7 ¾ In.
$400

Woody Auction

Zsolnay, Vase, Black Ground, Flared
Rim, Iridescent, Flowers, Painted,
16 ½ In.
$590

Cottone Auctions

Rolex, Presidential, Oyster Perpetual Datejust, 18K Yellow Gold, Diamond, Woman's, 1 ¹/₃₂ In. ..*illus*	8050
Rolex, Steel, Oyster Perpetual, Arabic Numeral, Engraved, F.P. Bender, 1 ¼ In. .... *illus*	885
Tag Heuer, Automatic, Square, Leather, Black, Stainless Steel, 1 ½ In................................	2432
Tag Heuer, Chronograph, Calibre 36, Stainless Steel Case, Automatic, 1 ²¹/₃₂ In.	875
Tiffany & Co., 18K Yellow Gold, Basket Weave Band, Hard Shell Case, Woman's, 1900s, 6 ⅞ In. ..*illus*	1638
Timex, 14K Gold, Turquoise, 2 Stones, Numbers, Boyd Tsosie, 1 x 4 ¾ In. .... *illus*	2360
Tissot, T-Classic, Stainless Steel, Date Indicator, Leather Band, 1853, 1 ½ In. .... *illus*	94
Universal Geneve, 18K Yellow Gold, Engraved, Marian J Adam, Woman's, 6 ¾ In.................	2124

YELLOWWARE

Yellowware is a heavy earthenware made of a yellowish clay. It varies
in color from light yellow to orange-yellow. Many nineteenth- and
twentieth-century kitchen bowls and jugs were made of yellowware.
It was made in England and in the United States. Another form of pottery that is
sometimes classed as yellowware is listed in this book in the Mocha category.

Bank, Apple Shape, Brown, Yellow, 4 x 10 In..	185
Batter Bowl, Pour Spout, Embossed Hearts, 14 ½ x 5 In..	225
Bowl, 3 Brown Band, 14 In. .... *illus*	59
Bowl, Brown Spongeware, 8 ¼ x 5 ¼ In.	52
Bowl, Red & White Banded, 10 ½ x 5 In.	55
Mold, Sheaf Of Wheat, Octagonal Rim, Raised Foot, 7 x 5 x 3 In..	125

LA MORO ## ZANESVILLE

Zanesville Art Pottery was founded in 1900 by David Schmidt in
Zanesville, Ohio. The firm made faience umbrella stands, jardinieres, and pedestals.
The company closed in 1920 and Weller bought the factory. Many pieces are marked
with just the words *La Moro*.

Pitcher, Tankard, Brown Ground, Friar Portrait, Standard Glaze, La Moro, 15 In.	184
Vase, La Moro, Molded Leaves, Wild Roses, Matte Glaze, W.F. Hall, 6 ¼ In. .... *illus*	363

ZSOLNAY

Zsolnay pottery was made in Hungary after 1853 and was characterized by Persian, Art
Nouveau, or Hungarian motifs. A series of new Zsolnay figurines with green-gold luster
finish is available in many shops today. Early Zsolnay was not marked, but by 1878 the
tower trademark was used.

Zsolnay Porcelanmanufaktura   Zsolnay Porcelanmanufaktura   Zsolnay Porcelanmanufaktura
1878   1899–1920   1900+

Bowl, Footed, Blue, Silver, Green, Marbleized, Marked, 3 ¼ x 7 ¾ In. .... *illus*	400
Figurine, Water Carrier, Robed Woman, Rectangular Plinth, Laszlo Beszedes, c.1900, 15 ½ In..	1000
Figurine, Woman, Nude, Kneeling, Arms Behind Her Neck, Green Iridescent, 9 ½ In.	125
Jardiniere, Pierced Neck, Lobed Body, Flowers, Pecs Iridescent, Ruby Luster, c.1900, 6 ¾ In.	313
Planter, Ruffled Rim & Base, Shaped Handle, Flowers, Gilt, Green Ground, 8 x 10 In.	158
Vase, Black Ground, Flared Rim, Iridescent, Flowers, Painted, 16 ½ In. .... *illus*	590
Vase, Bulbous Body, Luster, Glazed Flowers, Pecs, Stamped, 3939, c.1900, 10 x 6 ¼ In.	936
Vase, Oxblood, Lavender Iridescent Glaze, Alternating Stripes & Flowers, 4 In........................	4063
Vase, Pecs Green Luster, Eosin Glaze, Scalloped Rim, Lobed Body, Late 1800s, 7 ½ In............	250
Vase, Persian Style, Reddish Brown, Flowers, White Ground, Late 1800s, 5 ¼ In.	130
Vase, Reticulated Rim & Base, Flowers, Gilt, Glazed, 7 ½ In..	113

W

INDEX

This index is computer-generated, making it as complete and accurate as possible. References in upper-case type are category listings. Those in lowercase letters refer to additional pages where pieces can be found. There is also an internal cross-referencing system used in the main part of the book, so if you look for a Kewpie doll in the Doll category, you will be told it is in its own category. There is additional information at the end of many paragraphs about where to find prices of pieces similar to yours.

PHOTO CREDITS

We have included the name of the auction house or photographer with each pictured object. This is a list of the addresses of those who have contributed photographs and information for this book. Every dealer or auction has to buy antiques to have items to sell. Call or email a dealer or auction house if you want to discuss buying or selling. If you need an appraisal or advice, remember that appraising is part of their business and fees may be charged.

21st Century Auctions
28015 Caraway Ln.
Saugus, CA 91350
21stcenturyauctions.com
661-422-6057

A.B. Levy's Auctions
5200 South Dixie Hwy.
West Palm Beach, FL 33405
ablevys.com
561-835-9139

Abington Auction Gallery
3263 North Dixie Hwy.
Fort Lauderdale, FL 33334
abingtonauctions.com
954-900-4869

Ahlers & Ogletree Auction Gallery
700 Miami Circle NE, Suite 210
Atlanta, GA 30324
aandoauctions.com
404-869-2478

Alderfer Auction Company
501 Fairgrounds Rd.
Hatfield, PA 19440
alderferauction.com
215-393-3000

Alex Cooper Auctioneers
908 York Rd.
Towson, MD 21204
alexcooper.com
410-828-4838

Amazon.com

Amero Auctions
1502 N. Lime Ave.
Sarasota, FL 34237
ameroauctions.com
941-330-1577

Andrew Jones Auctions
2221 S. Main St.
Los Angeles, CA 90007
andrewjonesauctions.com
213-748-8008

AntiqueAdvertising.com
P.O. Box 247
Cazenovia, NY 13035
antiqueadvertising.com
315-662-7625

Apple Tree Auction Center
1625 W. Church St.
Newark, OH 43055
appletreeauction.com
704-344-4282

Artcurial
7 Rond-Point des Champs-Élysées Marcel-Dassault
75008 Paris, France
artcurial.com
+33 1 42 99 20 20

Auctions at Showplace
40 West 25th St.
New York, NY 10010
nyshowplace.com
212-633-6063

Austin Auction Gallery
8414 Anderson Mill Rd.
Austin, TX 78729-4702
austinauction.com
512-258-5479

Bertoia Auctions
2141 DeMarco Dr.
Vineland, NJ 08360
bertoiaauctions.com
856-692-1881

Bill and Jill Insulators
103 Canterbury Ct.
Carlisle, MA 01741
billandjillinsulators.com
781-999-3048

Blackwell Auctions
10900 US Hwy. 19 N, Suite B
Clearwater, FL 33764
blackwellauctions.com
727-546-0200

Bonhams
101 New Bond St.
London W1S 1SR
UK
bonhams.com
+44 20 7447 7447

Bruneau & Co. Auctioneers
63 4th Ave.
Cranston, RI 02910
bruneauandco.com
401-533-9980

Brunk Auctions
P.O. Box 2135
Asheville, NC 28802
brunkauctions.com
825-254-6846

Bunch Auctions
1 Hillman Dr.
Chadds Ford, PA 19317
bunchauctions.com
610-558-1800

California Historical Design
1901 Broadway
Alameda, CA 94501
acstickley.com
510-647-3621

Charleston Estate Auctions
918 Lansing Dr., Suite E
Mt. Pleasant, SC 29464
charlestonestateauctions.com
843-696-3335

Charlton Hall Auctions
7 Lexington Dr.
West Columbia, SC 29170
charltonhallauctions.com
803-779-5678

Christie's
20 Rockefeller Plaza
New York, NY 10020
christies.com
212-636-2000

Chupp Auctions & Real Estate, LLC
890 S. Van Buren St.
Shipshewana, IN 46565
auctionzip.com/IN-Auctioneers/40698.html
260-768-7616

Clars Auction Gallery
5644 Telegraph Ave.
Oakland, CA 94609
clars.com
510-428-0100

ComicConnect.com
36 West 37th St., FL 6
New York, NY 10018
comicconnect.com
888-779-7377

Conestoga Auction Company,
a division of Hess Auction Group
768 Graystone Rd.
Manheim, PA 17545
hessauctiongroup.com
717-664-5238

Copake Auction
266 East Main St.
Copake, NY 12516
copakeauction.com
518-329-1142

Copley Fine Art Auctions
65 Sharp St.
Hingham, MA 02043
copleyart.com
617-536-0030

Cordier Auctions
1500 Paxton St.
Harrisburg, PA 17104
cordierauction.com
717-731-8662

Cottone Auctions
120 Court St.
Geneseo, NY 14454
cottoneauctions.com
585-243-1000

Cowan's Auctions
6270 Este Ave.
Cincinnati, OH 45232
cowanauctions.com
513-871-8670

Crescent City Auction Gallery
1330 St. Charles Ave.
New Orleans, LA 70130
crescentcityauctiongallery.com
504-529-5057

CRN Auctions
57 Bay State Rd.
Cambridge, MA 02138
crnauctions.com
617-661-9582

Crocker Farm, Inc.
15900 York Rd.
Sparks, MD 21152
crockerfarm.com
410-472-2016

Donley Auctions
8512 S. Union Rd.
Union, IL 60180
donleyauctions.com
815-923-7000

DuMouchelles
409 E. Jefferson Ave.
Detroit, MI 48226
dumoart.com
313-963-6255

Early American History Auctions
P.O. Box 3507
Rancho Santa Fe, CA 92067
earlyamerican.com
858-759-3290

eBay
ebay.com

Eldred's
P.O. Box 796
1483 Route 6A
East Dennis, MA 02641
eldreds.com
508-385-3116

Fairfield Auction
707 Main St. (Route 25)
Monroe, CT 06468
fairfieldauction.com
203-880-5200

Fontaine's Auction Gallery
1485 W. Housatonic St.
Pittsfield, MA 01201
fontainesauction.com
413-448-8922

Forsythes' Auctions
206 W. Main St.
Russellville, OH 45168
forsythesauctions.com
937-377-3700

Fox Auctions
P.O. Box 693
Rodeo, CA 94572
631-553-3841

Freeman's
1808 Chestnut St.
Philadelphia, PA 19103
freemansauction.com
215-563-9275

Garth's Auctioneers & Appraisers
P.O. Box 758
Columbus, OH 43216
garths.com
740-362-4771

Glass Works Auctions
102 Jefferson St.
East Greenville, PA 18041
glswrk-auction.com
215-679-5849

Goldin Auctions
160 E. Ninth Ave., Suite A
Runnemede, NJ 08078
goldinauctions.com
856-767-8550

Graham Lancaster Auctions
3 Railway St.
Toowoomba QLD 4350
Australia
gdlauctions.com.au

Gray's Auctioneers, Inc.
10717 Detroit Ave.
Cleveland, OH 44102
graysauctioneers.com
216-226-3300

Greenwich Auction
83 Harvard Ave.
Stamford, CT 06902
greenwichauction.net
203-355-9335

Grey Flannel Auctions
16411 N. 90th St., Suite 107
Scottsdale, AZ 85260
greyflannelauctions.com
631-288-7800

Grogan & Company
20 Charles St.
Boston, MA 02114
groganco.com
617-720-2020

Hake's Auctions
P.O. Box 12001
York, PA 17402
hakes.com
717-434-1600

Hampton Estate Auction
25 Peddlers Village
Lahaska, PA 18931
hamptonauction.com
855-226-4496

Hansons Auctioneers and Valuers Ltd.
Heage Lane
Etwall, Derbyshire DE65 6LS
UK
hansonsauctioneers.co.uk
+44 1283 733 988

Hartzell's Auction Gallery Inc.
521 Richmond Rd.
Bangor, PA 18013
hartzellsauction.com
610-588-5831

Heritage Auctions
2801 W. Airport Hwy.
Dallas, TX 75261-4127
ha.com
214-528-3500

Hindman
1338 W. Lake St.
Chicago, IL 60607
hindmanauctions.com
312-280-1212

Homestead Auctions
4217 S. Cleveland Massillon Rd.
Norton, OH 44203
homesteadauction.net
330-706-9950

Humler & Nolan
225 E. Sixth St., 4th Floor
Cincinnati, OH 45202
humlernolan.com
513-381-2041

Jaremos
6101 Long Prairie Rd., Suite 744-169
Flower Mound, TX 75028
jaremos.com
630-248-7785

Jeffrey S. Evans & Associates
P.O. Box 2638
Harrisonburg, VA 22801
jeffreysevans.com
540-434-3939

John McInnis Auctioneers
76 Main St.
Amesbury, MA 01913
mcinnisauctions.com
978-388-0400

John Moran Auctioneers
145 E. Walnut Ave.
Monrovia, CA 91016
johnmoran.com
626-793-1833

Julien's Auctions
8630 Hayden Place
Culver City, CA 90232
juliensauctions.com
310-836-1818

Kamelot Auctions
2220 E. Allegheny Ave.
Philadelphia, PA 19134
kamelotauctions.com
215-438-6990

Kaminski Auctions
117 Elliott St.
Beverly, MA 01915
kaminskiauctions.com
978-927-2223

Keystone Auctions LLC
218 E. Market St.
York, PA 17403
auctionsbykeystone.com
717-755-8954

Kodner Galleries, Inc.
45 S. Federal Hwy.
Dania Beach, FL 33004
kodner.com
954-925-2550

Leland Little Auctions
620 Cornerstone Ct.
Hillsborough, NC 27278
lelandlittle.com
919-644-1243

Lelands
435 State Route 34, Suite H
Matawan, NJ 07747
lelands.com
732-290-8000

Lion and Unicorn
485 S. Federal Hwy.
Dania Beach, FL 33004
whitleysauctioneers.com
954-866-8044

Locati Auctions
1425 Welsh Rd.
Maple Glen, PA 19002
locatillc.com
215-619-2873

Main Auction Galleries, Inc.
137 W. 4th St.
Cincinnati, OH 45202
mainauctiongalleries.com
513-621-1280

Martin Auction Co.
P.O. Box 2
100 Lick Creek Rd.
Anna, IL 62906
martinauctionco.com
618-833-3589

Matthew Bullock Auctioneers
421 E. Stevenson Rd.
Ottawa, IL 61350
bullockauctioneers.com
815-220-5005

Merrill's Auctions
P.O. Box 558
Williston, VT 05495
merrillsauction.com
802-878-2625

Michaan's Auctions
2751 Todd St.
Alameda, CA 94501
michaans.com
800-380-9822

Mid-Hudson Auction Galleries
179 Temple Hill Rd., Suite 100B
New Windsor, NY 12553
midhudsongalleries.com
914-882-7356

Mile High Card Company
858 W. Happy Canyon Rd., Suite 240
Castle Rock, CO 80108
milehighcardco.com
303-840-2784

Milestone Auctions
38198 Willoughby Pkwy.
Willoughby, OH 44094
milestoneauctions.com
440-527-8060

Morphy Auctions
2000 N. Reading Rd.
Denver, PA 17517
morphyauctions.com
877-968-8880

Nadeau's Auction Gallery
25 Meadow Rd.
Windsor, CT 06095
nadeausauction.com
860-249-2444

Neal Auction Company
4038 Magazine St.
New Orleans, LA 70115
nealauction.com
800-467-5329

Neue Auctions
23533 Mercantile Rd., Suite 119
Beachwood, OH 44122
neueauctions.com
216-245-6707

New Haven Auctions
14 Business Park Dr., Suite 5
Branford, CT 06405
475-234-5120
newhavenauctions.com

New Orleans Auction Galleries
333 St. Joseph St.
New Orleans, LA 70130
neworleansauction.com
504-566-1849

North American Auction Co.
34156 Frontage Rd.
Bozeman, MT 59715
northamericanauctioncompany.com
406-600-4418

Nye & Company
20 Beach St.
Bloomfield, NJ 07003
nyeandcompany.com
973-984-6900

Palm Beach Modern Auctions
417 Bunker Rd.
West Palm Beach, FL 33405
modernauctions.com
561-586-5500

PBA Galleries
605 Addison St.
Berkeley, CA 94710
pbagalleries.com
415-989-2665

Perfume Bottles Auction
1050 2nd Ave., #47
New York, NY 10022
perfumebottlesauction.com
917-881-8747

Phillips
450 Park Ave.
New York, NY 10022
phillips.com
212-940-1200

Pook & Pook
463 E. Lancaster Ave.
Downingtown, PA 19335
pookandpook.com
610-269-4040

Potter & Potter Auctions
3001 W. Belmont Ave.
Chicago, IL 60641
potterauctions.com
773-472-1442

Profiles in History
26662 Agoura Rd.
Calabasas, CA 91302
profilesinhistory.com
310-859-7701

PWCC Marketplace
7560 S.W. Durham Rd.
Tigard, OR 97224
pwccmarketplace.com

Rachel Davis Fine Arts
1304 W. 79th St.
Cleveland, OH 44102
216-9391190

Rachel Davis Fine Arts
1301 W. 79th St.
Cleveland, OH 44102
racheldavisfinearts.com
216-939-1190

Rafael Osona Nantucket Auctions
21 Washington St.
Nantucket, MA 02554
rafaelosonaauction.com
508-228-3942

Rago Arts and Auction Center
333 N. Main St.
Lambertville, NJ 08530
ragoarts.com
609-397-9374

Richard D. Hatch & Associates
913 Upward Rd.
Flat Rock, NC 28731
richardhatchauctions.com
828-696-3440

Richard Opfer Auctioneering, Inc.
1919 Greenspring Dr.
Timonium, MD 21093
forgegallery.com/opferauction
410-252-5035

Rich Penn Auctions
P.O. Box 1355
Waterloo, IA 50704
richpennauctions.com
319-291-6688

Ripley Auctions
2764 E. 55th Pl.
Indianapolis, IN 46220
ripleyauctions.com
317-251-5635

Roland Auctioneers & Valuers
150 School St.
Glen Cove, NY 11542
rolandsantiques.com
212-260-2000

Ron Rhoads Auctioneers
20 Bonnie Brae Rd.
Spring City, PA 19475
ronrhoads-auction.com
610-385-4818

RR Auction
1 State Route 101A, Suite 3
Amherst, NH 03031
rrauction.com
603-732-4280

Ruby Lane
381 Bush St., Suite 400
San Francisco, CA 94104
rubylane.com
415-362-7611

Santa Fe Art Auction
932 Railfan Rd
Santa Fe, NM 87505
santafeartauction.com
505-954-5858

Seeck Auctions
P.O. Box 377
Mason City, IA 50402
seeckauction.com
641-424-1116

Selkirk Auctioneers & Appraisers
555 Washington Ave., Suite 129
St. Louis, MO 63101
selkirkauctions.com
314-696-9041

Sotheby's
1334 York Ave.
New York, NY 10021
sothebys.com
212-606-7000

Soulis Auctions
P.O. Box 17
Lone Jack, MO 64070
dirksoulisauctions.com
816-566-2368

Stair Galleries
549 Warren St.
Hudson, NY 12534
stairgalleries.com
518-751-1000

Stephenson's Auction
1005 Industrial Blvd.
Southampton, PA 18966
stephensonsauction.com
215-322-6182

Stevens Auction Co.
P.O. Box 58
Aberdeen, MS 39730-0058
stevensauction.com
662-369-2200

Stony Ridge Auction
4230 Fremont Pike
P.O. Box 389
Lemoyne, OH 43441
stonyridgeauction.com
419-297-9045

Strawser Auction Group
200 N. Main St.
P.O. Box 332
Wolcottville, IN 46795
strawserauctions.com
260-854-2859

Susanin's Auctioneers & Appraisers
900 S. Clinton St.
Chicago, IL 60607
susanins.com
312-832-9800

Swann Auction Galleries
104 East 25th St.
New York, NY 10010
swanngalleries.com
212-254-4710

Theriault's
P.O. Box 151
Annapolis, MD 21404
theriaults.com
800-638-0422

Thomaston Place Auction Galleries
51 Atlantic Hwy.
Thomaston, ME 04861
thomastonauction.com
207-354-8141

Toomey & Co. Auctioneers
818 North Blvd.
Oak Park, IL 60301
toomeyco.com
708-383-5234

Treadway
2029 Madison Rd.
Cincinnati, OH 45208
treadwaygallery.com
513-321-6742

Treasureseeker Auctions
123 W. Bellevue Dr., Suite 2
Pasadena, CA 91105
treasureseekerauction.com
626-529-5775

Turner Auctions + Appraisals
461 Littlefield Ave.
South San Francisco, CA 94080
turnerauctionsonline.com
415-964-5250

Weiss Auctions
74 Merrick Rd.
Lynbrook, NY 11563
weissauctions.com
516-594-0731

White's Auctions
19 Jackson St.
Middleborough, MA 02346
whitesauctions.com
508-947-9281

Wiederseim Associates
1041 W. Bridge St.
Phoenixville, PA 19460
wiederseim.com
610-827-1910

Woody Auction
P.O. Box 618
317 S. Forrest St.
Douglass, KS 67039
woodyauction.com
316-747-2694

Wright
1440 W. Hubbard St.
Chicago, IL 60642
wright20.com
312-563-0020

ZenPlus
Itachibori 1-3-11, Daitai Bldg. 2F
Osaka Prefecture,
Osaka City, Nishi District, 550-0012
Japan
zenplus.jp
+ 06-4560-4070